Whole Foods Companion

Whole Foods Companion

A Guide for Adventurous Cooks, Curious Shoppers & Lovers of Natural Foods

Dianne Onstad

Chelsea Green Publishing Company
White River Junction, Vermont

Designed by Molly Cook Field, Optima Design

Printed in the United States of America.
99 98 97 96   1 2 3 4 5

This book has been written and published solely for informational and educational purposes. Please be advised that it is not our intention to provide medical advice or to substitute for the role of a physician in treating illness. While every care has been taken to ensure the accuracy of the contents herein, the author and publisher cannot accept legal responsibility for any problem arising out of experimentation with the substances described.

Library of Congress Cataloging-in-Publication Data

Onstad, Dianne, 1962–
Whole foods companion: a guide for adventurous chefs, curious shoppers, and lovers of natural foods / Dianne Onstad.
p. cm.
Includes bibliographical references and index.
ISBN 0-930031-83-0 (alk. paper)
1. Natural foods. 2. Cookery (Natural foods). I. Title.
TX369.054 1996   96-33441
641.5'63--dc20   CIP

Chelsea Green Publishing Company
Post Office Box 428
White River Junction, VT 05001

This book is dedicated with love to Kevin,
my companion in life's many adventures.

ACKNOWLEDGMENTS

First and foremost I want to express loving gratitude to my husband for providing unflagging encouragement during the research and writing of this book. Secondly, for graciously giving of their time and energy to provide valuable and often technical information, I wish to extend my appreciation to ethno-botanist Lorenz Schaller at the KUSA Seed Research Foundation for his extensive knowledge of cereal grains, and to Brigitte Mars, herbalist and reviewer extraordinarire. Thanks also to the Price-Pottenger Nutrition Foundation for the use of their comprehensive research library; to Trish Nungary Kerr for painstakingly reading an early draft and providing many valuable comments; to Dorothy Knight, Pat Connolly, John Curry, and the many other friends and family for their enthusiastic support and encouragement; and, of course, to Trevor, who daily reminded me that I needed time to play. Lastly, many thanks to Jim Schley, editor-in-chief at Chelsea Green Publishing Company for his willingness and foresight to take on this project and turn it into an outstanding and beautiful book.

KUSA Seed Research Foundation
P.O. Box 761
Ojai, CA 93024

Price-Pottenger Nutrition Foundation
P.O. Box 2614
La Mesa, CA 91943

CONTENTS

INTRODUCTION

"No man can be wise on an empty stomach."
— George Eliot

FOOD IS NECESSARY FOR LIFE TO EXIST. Much of our time on this planet is devoted to either thinking about food, hunting and gathering it (now called shopping), or preparing and consuming it. Trade routes, agriculture, and spices have occasioned war and conquest, and many fortunes have been made and lost because of food. The time is ripe to celebrate food for the central role it plays in our lives. It is a magical, precious gift from nature, one not to be taken lightly. This book provides a starting point for an exploration into the fascinating world of food, and will provide a wealth of information both historical and practical: where our foods originated, how they received their botanical and common names, the stories associated with them throughout their travels, how they are used for culinary purposes, and their many nutritional benefits.

There is a growing demand for wholesome and flavorful foods, a demand that will influence the way food is grown, packaged, and shipped in the future. Sales of organic produce are increasing as the public becomes aware of the dangers of food additives, chemical fertilizers, and insecticides. The term "organically grown" refers to a method of growing fruits and vegetables the way they were raised before the advent of industrial farming—without synthetic fertilizers, pesticides, or herbicides. Researchers at Rutgers University recently tested produce to find out just how much tastier and more nutritious organic produce really is. Their conclusion: organic produce has as much as a 75 percent higher mineral content than non-organic produce. Freshly-picked and unprocessed food can supply over two thousand different enzymes; these enzymes are destroyed by heat greater than 105 degrees Fahrenheit and by pasteurization, and their beneficial effects are greatly inhibited by chemical substances added either to the soil or during processing.

The foods profiled in this book are organized by category, for instance fruits or vegetables, and then organized alphabetically within each category. Some foods are placed by botanists in one category while popular use places them in another. For example, tomatoes and eggplants are botanically fruits, but are used as vegetables. For the purposes of this book, popular use will prevail. Products made from whole foods (such as apple juice or peanut butter) do not have separate entries but are covered along with their parent whole food. If you are unsure where to find any particular food, please check the index. Dairy products and eggs were omitted in order to concentrate solely on plant-based foods. Like the animals from which they come, these foods may carry large amounts of toxic chemicals including antibiotics, hormones, and pesticides, which are dangerous to health. Margarine, though not derived from animal sources, was also excluded because it is neither a whole nor a healthful food. A brief discussion of butter and margarine can be found in the introduction to the Nuts, Seeds, and Oils section.

This book is intended to be used as a reference, although I hope it will also be entertaining. Each entry contains information on the plant's botanical name, and the food's history, folklore, culinary use, and nutritional data. Although entries vary, according to how much information was available, there should be enough information in each case to identify an unfamiliar item at the market, then prepare and serve it successfully. The nutritional composition tables presented in this book, which compile all available information from a number of sources, provide only an estimate of the amounts of fat, carbohydrate, protein, vitamins, and minerals present, because nutrient value may vary up to 100 percent depending upon the quality of the soil in which the plants grew, the stage at which they were picked for shipment, and even weather conditions; methods and duration of storage and preparation also cause wide variations. Measurements are given in the standard gram (g), milligram (mg), microgram (mcg), and IU (International Unit) increments.

A note on botanical names: The botanical name of a plant consists of two parts. Of these, the first word indicates the genus or family, while the second identifies the species within the genus. These botanical names change from time to time, sometimes at a speed that must be disconcerting even for botanists. Some of the names given here may already be scheduled for replacement, but fortunately, obsolete names have a sort of afterlife and continue to enjoy some currency for a decade or more after they have been replaced.

The idea for this book grew out of my combined interests in organic gardening, cooking, and holistic health. After an initial study of food and its relation to health, I decided to research and compile the information I had found on natural foods into one comprehensive volume. This book is the culmination of my effort to discover the relationship between the foods we eat, the health of our bodies, and the clarity of our minds. It was not my intention to promote one manner of eating over another, and thus there is no recommendation for any particular "diet." There are many excellent books already written on that subject, quite a few of which are mentioned in the bibliography. Bon appetit!

"It is an obvious truth, all too often forgotten, that food is not only inseparable from the history of the human race, but basic to it. Without food there would be no human race, and no history."

— Reay Tannahill, *Food in History*

Fruits

"Every fruit has its secret."

—D.H. Lawrence

FRUITS

Fruits

THE ENGLISH WORD FRUIT derives from the Latin verb *frui*, meaning to enjoy or take pleasure in. Most people do enjoy these utterly irresistible delicacies of nature, and fruits generally have the edge over vegetables (for young and old alike) because they appeal to the voracious sweet tooth in us all. Fruit forms an increasingly significant proportion of the American diet: total consumption in the mid–1980s was over 200 pounds per person annually, compared to around 140 pounds at the turn of the century. However, most of this growth has been in the form of processed fruit, especially orange juice. Starting in the late 1950s, Americans began consuming more processed fruit than fresh, an unhealthful trend that continues even today. Rather than having your fruit sliced, diced, canned, juiced, jarred, jellied, frozen, sweetened, or concentrated, eat it fresh to enjoy its full flavor and nutritional properties.

When most people think of fruit, they think of such sweet, soft, succulent, refreshing, and delicious fruits like apples, oranges, berries, and melons. However, by strict definition, a fruit is the ripened ovary of a female flower. This scientific definition thus covers what we commonly call fruit, as well as nuts and some vegetables, including squash, pumpkins, and tomatoes. In 1893 the U.S. Supreme Court dealt with this confusion and ruled that a vegetable refers to a plant grown for an edible part that is generally eaten as part of the main course, while a fruit refers to a plant part generally eaten as an appetizer, dessert, or out of hand.

The following section on fruit deals only with those natural foods commonly used as fruits; the "vegetable fruits," as well as nuts, will be found in their respective sections. Botanically, fruits fall into four categories: **aggregate** fruits, which grow in clusters, like bananas and dates; **berries**, such as strawberries and raspberries, which have many seeds throughout; **drupes**, such as peaches and plums, which contain a single stone or pit; and **pomes**, such as apples or pears, which contain cores and small seeds. All fresh fruits contain the natural acids (malic, citric, and tartaric among others), necessary for the proper and prompt elimination of toxins, poisonous acids, and other impurities produced partly as natural byproducts of digestion and metabolism, and partly from external sources (air, water, pesticides, etc). These natural fruit acids are highly alkaline after they have been reduced in the body, and besides being strong cleansers, provide excellent protection against germs and disease. The human digestive tract is believed to have evolved around a diet of fruits and their close relatives, nuts and seeds. Fresh raw fruits and nuts contain all the vitamins, minerals, natural sugars, and amino acids required for human nutrition, and a diet consisting solely of fruit will quite rapidly disinfect the stomach and alimentary canal, with fresh fruits being far more effective for this purpose than stewed or canned fruits. Regular fruit consumption, like regular vegetable consumption, has been shown to offer significant protection against many chronic degenerative diseases, including cancer, heart disease, cataracts, and strokes.

CANNED AND FROZEN FRUIT

Canning is the most common way to preserve fruit to make it available out of season. Canned fruits lose varying amounts of vitamin C and beta carotene during processing (along with smaller quantities of other vitamins and minerals), and the processing turns their alkaline properties acidic, and therefore detrimental to the body. Fruit packed in heavy syrup can be highly caloric, due to the addition of excess quantities of sweeteners. In 1920 only 3 percent of the fruits and vegetables sold were canned; the vast majority were fresh from home gardens or nearby farms. Today canned goods are almost as popular as fresh produce: 40 percent of the fruits and vegetables sold in 1990 were fresh, while 27 percent were canned. Freezing fresh fruit has the effect of prolonging its life; the majority of frozen fruits are flash-frozen without having been heated, so there is very little nutrient loss, and most have no added sugar.

DRIED FRUIT

Another way to preserve fruit is by drying, either in the sun or with heated air, to reduce the water content to between 15 to 25 percent. Only a few nutrients are lost in the drying process; the main nutrient lost is vitamin C. Dried fruits provide quick energy and are a compact source of dietary fiber. There is no more fruit sugar in dried fruit than in raw; however, dried fruit has been concentrated and thus tastes sweeter. Fruits dried early in the season may undergo certain natural changes over subsequent months, the most obvious one being “sugaring,” in which tiny white crystals appear on the skin. This is just the crystallization of the natural sugars in the fruit collecting on the surface, and not a mold growth of some kind, as some people mistakenly think. Most people tend to eat more dried fruit than they would fresh fruit at one sitting; consuming more sugar than if the whole undried fruit were eaten. Buy unsulphured, unsweetened dried fruit (which is usually darker). To reconstitute dried fruit, cover with warm to hot water and let stand for several hours. The reconstituted fruit can be refrigerated in its soaking water for several weeks. Apricots, peaches, figs, and prunes in particular all taste much better when soaked, and the resulting liquid makes a delicious drink.

SULPHURED FRUIT

Dried fruits are frequently dipped in a sulphur solution or subjected to the fumes of burning sulphur. This is done for two reasons: 1) Bleaching the fruit gives it a more appealing color and appearance, so that those who buy foods by appearance buy such foods in greater quantity; 2) Sulphuring dried fruits enables the producers to put them on the market with a much higher water content—as high as thirty percent—so that proportionally less fruit is sold for the same price.

The main proponents for sulphuring claim that the process kills insects and prevents them from getting into the stored fruit. True, no self-respecting insect will eat sulphured fruit, but this is also an excellent reason for you to avoid it. Sulphur dioxide is a poison and the body treats it as such, combining the sulphurous acids with alkalies before being eliminated. This process robs the body of necessary alkaline bases. As well, sulphur compounds destroy B vitamins and can cause allergic reactions in sensitive individuals. Experiments conducted by Dr. H.W. Wiley, former chief chemist of the United States Department of Agriculture, demonstrated that the use of sulphurous acid in food is always harmful. It degenerates the kidneys, retards the formation of red corpuscles, and destroys vitamins.

Akee *(Blighia sapida)*

Blighia *was given in honor of the notorious Captain Bligh, who brought the plant to the West Indies.* Sapida *means savory or pleasant-tasting.*

General Information This tropical tree is native to the Ivory and Gold Coasts of West Africa, and was brought by Captain Bligh to the West Indies along with the breadfruit tree in the late eighteenth century. It was readily adopted there, and the akee became a familiar sight in dooryards and along roadsides. The fruit is leathery, pear-shaped, and yellow, flushed with a scarlet, three-lobed capsule. When fully mature, the three-inch-long fruits split open, exposing their large black seeds, which are encased in a fluffy yellow or cream-colored pulp resembling scrambled eggs. The akee must be allowed to open (preferably fully) before being detached from the tree. This allows the toxic properties of the arils to be largely dispelled by light as the fruit splits.

Akee

Nutritional Value Per 100 g Edible Portion

	Raw Arils
Protein	5.75 g
Fat	18.78 g
Fiber	3.45 g
Calcium	83 mg
Iron	5.52 mg
Phosphorus	98 mg
Thiamine (B_1)	0.10 mg
Riboflavin (B_2)	0.18 mg
Niacin (B_3)	3.74 mg
Ascorbic Acid (C)	65 mg

Buying Tips Select only firm, unbruised, fully open fruit.

Culinary Uses The yellow pulp (arils) is the only edible part. Although it can be eaten raw, the pulp is usually parboiled in salted water or milk and then lightly fried in butter, at which time it is said to be delicious. The pink tissue and seeds are extremely poisonous, as are underripe fruits which have not yet opened. The fruit is popular in Jamaica, and the canned arils are exported to the United Kingdom, where they are welcomed by Jamaican immigrants. Although technically a fruit, akee is usually served with meat or fish like a vegetable. Importation to the United States has been banned by the Food and Drug Administration due to the health hazards associated with the fruit.

Ambarella *(Spondias dulcis, S. cytherea)*

Also Known As: Otaheite Apple, Tahitian Quince, Polynesian Plum.

Spondias *was the name used by Theophrastus for this family of plants.* Dulcis *means sweet to the taste, or mild. The common name* ambarella *is a Sinhalese name for the fruit.*

General Information The ambarella is native from Melanesia through Polynesia, but has spread into tropical areas of both the Old and New World. It was introduced into Jamaica both in 1782 and 1792, the second time by Captain Bligh. The grayish-orange, plum-like fruits are produced in pendant clusters of twelve or more, each hanging from a long stalk. Oval and somewhat irregular or knobby, the fruits have a thin but tough skin which is often russetted. While still green and hard, the fruits fall to the ground over a period of several weeks; as they ripen, the skin and flesh turn a beautiful golden-yellow. Each fruit is about the size of an egg, and contains several seeds surrounded by a yellowish pulp. The ambarella has suffered for decades by comparison with the mango. At the proper stage, however, the fruit is relished by many and yields a delicious juice for beverages.

Ambarella

Nutritional Value Per 100 g Edible Portion

	Raw
Calories	157.3
Protein	0.50-0.80%
Fat	0.28-1.79%
Fiber	0.85-3.60%
Ascorbic Acid (C)	42 mg

Culinary Uses Still-firm fruits have flesh which is crisp, juicy, subacid, and a flavor and fragrance somewhat like pineapple. If allowed to soften, the aroma and flavor become musky and the flesh difficult to slice because of conspicuous and tough fibers. The unripe fruits are usually made into relishes, pickles, or sauce. Stewed with a little water and sugar, and then strained through a sieve, the ambarella makes a product comparable to applesauce, but with a richer flavor; it can be cooked down to make a preserve similar to apple butter. Young ambarella leaves are appealingly acid and are consumed raw in southeast Asia. In Indonesia, they are steamed and eaten as a vegetable with salted fish and rice, and also used as seasoning for various dishes.

Apple *(Malus sylvestris, M. pumila)*

> Malus *is the classical Greek name for a round fruit, from the Greek* malon *or* melon*;* sylvestris *means of woods and forests, and* pumila *means dwarf. The English word* apple *comes from the province of Italy called Abela, where the modern apple is thought to have first appeared.*

General Information Apple trees are members of the large Rose family. They are probably native to the Caucasus Mountains of western Asia, and perhaps to Anatolia, the Asian part of Turkey, where carbonized apples dating to 6500 B.C. have been found. Apples came to Britain with the Roman conquest, quite possibly with Julius Caesar himself, who took a keen interest in botany. Apple orchards were planted by Roman officers within their walled gardens, but they also sprang up about the native villages, evidence of a plundered orchard here and there. The apple was introduced into Massachusetts as early as 1623 by William Blackstone, minister to the settlers at Plymouth. So important were these trees to the early colonists that by 1646 Massachusetts had passed its first law stipulating "proper punishment" for anyone robbing an apple orchard. Almost every farm had an orchard of apples, grown for fermenting into hard cider. Visitors were offered not coffee, tea, or water, but cider: it was the common drink. The spread of apple cultivation in America was encouraged by a notably eccentric personality known as Johnny Appleseed. This itinerant preacher and accomplished nurseryman was christened John Chapman in the town of Leominster, Massachusetts in 1775. The barefoot Chapman wore an inverted mush pan hat, an old burlap bag shirt, and ragged trousers. The apple tree stock that he sold, gave away, and planted throughout the midwest helped future generations of pioneers. At the time of his death in March 1845, he had pushed as far west as Indiana, where he died at Fort Wayne.

The most popular temperate zone fruit, apples are grown in almost every state. Washington State, however, produces more than one-quarter of the whole United States apple crop. That state's orchards supposedly began from seeds of an apple given to Captain Aemilius Simpson of the Hudson Bay Company by a young woman from London at a farewell party. To please her, he had kept the seeds and planted them at Fort Vancouver, Washington in 1824. Only one of the seeds sprouted, and the tree in its first producing year bore only one apple, but in following years bore many more. Just eight varieties account for 80 percent of domestic apple production: Golden Delicious, Granny Smith, Jonathan, McIntosh, Red Delicious, Rome Beauty, Stayman, and York. American consumption of apples (and their processed products) is about 120 apples, or roughly 40 pounds annually per capita. The average person in France consumes five times as many apples, mostly in the form of fermented cider.

Lore and Legend

The apple seems to have had the widest and most mystical history in the popular tales of all countries. Aphrodite bears it in her hand, as does Eve. The serpent guards it, and the dragon watches it. It is the healing fruit of the Arabian tribes, and it bestows immortality on the Turks. Greek mythology relates that the origin of the Trojan War was attributed to the Apple of Discord, a golden apple thrown down in front of an assembly of the gods by the goddess of hate, Eris. Inscribed "For the Fairest," the apple was claimed by the three most eminent goddesses—Hera, Athena, and Aphrodite. Appointed to choose the most beautiful of the three, Paris was offered power and riches by Hera, wisdom and fame by Athena, or the most beautiful woman in the world by Aphrodite. Yielding to passion, Paris chose Aphrodite. He got what he desired, but in the process started the lengthy Trojan War, since the beautiful Helen just happened to be somebody else's wife. Another myth involves Hercules' obtaining the golden apples from the Gardens of the Hesperides, faithfully guarded by a sleepless dragon. One of the Norse myths tells of the goddess Idun, who supplied magic apples to all the gods so that they could stay eternally young. The fairy tales of the Brothers Grimm, which are all taken from old folktales and myths, have at least four stories involving apples, including the famous story of Snow White.

Buying Tips Purchase firm, well-colored fruit with intact stems and few or no blemishes. Organic apples are more prone to have blemishes than non-organic, but the taste is far superior. Elspeth Huxley, in her 1965 book *Brave New Victuals*, writes: "You cannot sell a blemished apple in the supermarket, but you can sell a tasteless one provided it is shiny, smooth, even, uniform and bright." For eating out of hand or grating into salads, choose a dessert variety; for pureeing, stewing or baking, use one of the larger cooking varieties.

Culinary Uses Apples are one of the most versatile of all fruits. They make an appearance in every manner of dish, from main courses, to salads and desserts, but are especially popular for apple pie! When you do cook apples, do so over low heat so that the delicate pectin, vitamins, and minerals will be preserved as much as possible. Sliced apples can be kept from turning brown by dipping them into an acidic solution such as lemon juice and water. Apple seeds are best discarded, as they contain moderate levels of cyanide. Seventy-five percent of the insecticide spray that is used on apples also ends up in the core and seeds. The small number of seeds in the typical core poses little risk of serious poisoning, since it takes an estimated half cup of seeds to kill the average adult. It is best, however, to remove the seeds before giving apples to children.

Health Benefits Astringent, tonic. In medicine the disinfectant and therapeutic qualities of the apple are highly valued. Naturally antitoxic, apples can modify the intestinal environment by reactivating the beneficial bacteria that normally flourish there. A highly digestible alkaline food, they have a high water content (around 85 percent) which quenches both immediate and cellular level thirst. Fibrous, juicy, and non-sticky, they help clean the teeth and exercise the gums when eaten raw. Apples contain both malic and tartaric acids, which help to remove impurities in the liver and inhibit the growth of ferments and disease-producing bacteria in the digestive tract. They also contain pectin, a gel-forming fiber which supplies galacturonic acid to prevent the putrefaction of protein. Pectin content also helps make apples an excellent intestinal broom, working as a bulking agent to gently push through the digestive tract and cleanse it along the way. This effect is particularly noticeable when impactions are present. Pectins are also powerful in protecting against the toxic effects of certain chemicals in the diet such as cyclamates. Studies indicate that eating apples daily will help reduce skin diseases, arthritis, and various lung and asthma problems; European research shows that apple pectin binds with radioactive residues and removes them from the body, along with lead, mercury, and other toxic heavy metals. Although the apple itself is not particularly high in iron, it contains an element that improves the assimilation of iron in companion foods. Apple leaves contain an antibiotic which, when crushed, can temporarily substitute for a bandage.

Varieties

THERE ARE OVER 7,500 VARIETIES, both cooking and dessert apples, all descended from the very tart and scarcely edible wild crab apple (*Pyrus baccata*) and the ancient apple of the Near East (*Pyrus malus*). Dessert apples are delicious out of hand, as the name implies, and most are also delicious cooked. Cooking apples may or may not be delicious raw, but when cooked become succulent and sweet.

Api Named for Appius, the Etruscan horticulturist who developed it, the Api remained in high esteem through many centuries. Grown in the royal French gardens, it was one of only seven varieties of apples deemed worthy to be served to Louis XIV. In France it can still be purchased under its original name, the *pomme d'Api*; in the United States it is generally known as the **Lady Apple**. It is a winter apple, small, somewhat flattened, and ranging in color from creamy yellow to deep crimson according to its exposure to the sun. The flesh is delicately perfumed and juicy, and because the skin is particularly flavorful it should not be peeled.

Baldwin First called Pecker or Woodpecker, this apple was later named Baldwin in honor of the Colonel who propagated it in Massachusetts in 1740. Readily available in the Northeast, Baldwins are a medium red apple, dull crimson on the side that faced the sun, with some yellow flecks and streaks underneath. An excellent eating and all-purpose apple, they have a sweet and slightly tangy flavor with a unique aftertaste that is pleasing and inviting. They sweeten during cooking but still retain their unique Baldwin flavor. Picked late in the season after the first frost, they retain their crispness and whiteness well into late November or early December.

Blenheim Orange One of the best apples of the Pippin family, the Blenheim Orange was popular in England for a century after its introduction around 1818. It is large, dull yellow and red, has crisp flesh and a flavor of unusual acidity, and is the classic Christmas apple, ripening in midwinter.

Braeburn This is a slightly tart, firm apple, excellent for fresh consumption as well as cooking and baking.

Bramley's Seedling or **Bramley** The most widely sold cooking apple in Britain, it has a very long keeping season, from early autumn right through to the following summer. Usually very large and irregular in shape, it is harvested commercially as a green apple, or green with faint red stripes, but will turn yellow if left on the tree. There are also crimson varieties.

Citerion The Citerion is a tart, crisp apple, very good for all uses: fresh, baking, juicing, sauce. It is not widely available.

Cortland A modern American variety, the Cortland was bred from the Ben Davis and McIntosh in New York in 1898. Grown in New England, Cortlands are medium sized, dark red or purplish-red all-purpose apples with lots of flavor. They have very white meat, good juice, and a semi-sweet flavor. Cortlands are exceptional as cooking or eating apples because they do not darken quickly when cut and exposed to oxygen. Cooking sweetens the flavor considerably, making for a rich, thick applesauce, as well as great traditional high-crust pies, because the pieces do not melt and cause the crust to collapse. Cortlands are crisper earlier in the season, but store well. They are available in late autumn.

Apple

Nutritional Value per 100 g Edible Portion

	Raw w/Skin	Raw w/o Skin	Processed Juice	Sweetened Applesauce	Dried Sulphured
Calories	59	57	47	76	275
Protein	0.19 g	0.15 g	0.06 g	0.18 g	1.00 g
Fat	0.36 g	0.31 g	0.11 g	0.18 g	1.60 g
Fiber	0.77 g	0.54 g	0.21 g	0.46 g	3.10 g
Calcium	7 mg	4 mg	7 mg	4 mg	31 mg
Iron	0.18 mg	0.07 mg	0.37 mg	0.35 mg	1.60 mg
Magnesium	5 mg	3 mg	3 mg	3 mg	n/a
Phosphorus	7 mg	7 mg	7 mg	7 mg	52 mg
Potassium	115 mg	113 mg	119 mg	61 mg	569 mg
Sodium	0 mg	0 mg	3 mg	3 mg	5 mg
Zinc	0.040 mg	0.040 mg	0.030 mg	0.040 mg	n/a
Copper	0.031 mg	0.041 mg	0.022 mg	0.043 mg	n/a
Manganese	0.023 mg	0.045 mg	0.113 mg	0.075 mg	n/a
Beta Carotene (A)	53 IU	44 IU	1 IU	11 IU	n/a
Thiamine (B_1)	0.017 mg	0.017 mg	0.021 mg	0.013 mg	0.060 mg
Riboflavin (B_2)	0.014 mg	0.010 mg	0.017 mg	0.028 mg	0.120 mg
Niacin (B_3)	0.077 mg	0.091 mg	0.100 mg	0.188 mg	0.500 mg
Pantothenic Acid (B_5)	0.061 mg	0.057 mg	n/a	0.052 mg	n/a
Pyridoxine (B_6)	0.048 mg	0.046 mg	0.030 mg	0.026 mg	n/a
Folic Acid (B_9)	2.8 mcg	0.400 mg	0.10 mcg	0.60 mcg	n/a
Ascorbic Acid (C)	5.70 mg	4.00 mg	0.90 mg	1.70 mg	10.00 mg
Tocopherol (E)	0.590 mg	0.270 mg	0.010 mg	n/a	n/a

Cox's Orange Pippin Developed in 1830 by a retired brewer named Richard Cox, the British boast that this is the finest dessert apple in the world. One of the best of the large family of Pippins, since its introduction in the first half of the nineteenth century it has become the most popular British apple. It is a medium-sized, round apple, dull brownish green with faint red stripes and a red flush on one side. It usually has a matte brown russeted area around the stem. The texture is crisp, the flavor solidly acid but balanced by sweetness. The seeds are loose and you can hear them when you shake the fruit. This apple is not widely available in North America; it is much more common in Britain and New Zealand.

Crab (American sweet; Garland; Prairie crab apple) A wild species, crab apples are small, acidic apples that can be either deeply red or yellow; they have a high pectin content and thus their main use is in making jellies and preserves. They are briefly available in autumn.

Crispin (Mutsu) A large green apple developed from crossing a Golden Delicious with a Japanese apple variety called Indo. Grown extensively in New York State, it is an all-purpose variety, with a firm texture and sweet flavor. The Crispin looks like a large Granny Smith, and has its crispness, but possesses the flavor and sweetness of a Golden Delicious. It is available year-round.

Discovery One of the first British apples to appear each season, it is named because it was a chance discovery by an amateur grower. It was first marketed on a large scale in the 1970s. The apple is bright green and crimson like a brighter version of a Worcester Pearmain, and the flesh often has a pink tinge on the sunny side. At first light and crisp, it softens quickly and must be eaten at once. The flavor is unique, with a hint of raspberries.

Empire The Empire is a relatively new variety from New York State, the result of crossing the McIntosh with a Red Delicious. The deep red skin is rather thick, but the crisp texture and sweet-tart taste make it ideal for eating fresh. The juicy yet crisp combination contributes to its growing popularity. Good but not great for pies and sauce. The Empire is available September through spring.

Fuji The Fuji is a Ralls Janet and Red Delicious cross that originated in Japan. Pale green and pink striped or blushed, it has a sweet-tart juicy taste and is ultra crisp like an Asian pear. An excellent eating apple, and works widely in all uses. Will keep for months if refrigerated.

Gala A new apple that exalts the qualities of its parent varieties: Gold Delicious/Orange Cox, Pippin/Red Delicious. This striking apple has a peach-like appearance, with its pinkish yellow skin striped or blushed with red. Sweet, flavorful, with a wonderfully crisp texture, it is excellent for fresh consumption and also makes a delicious pie.

Golden Yellow Delicious (or simply **Golden Delicious**) An American apple which appeared as a chance seedling on Anderson H. Mullin's West Virginia farm in 1890. Now the most widely grown apple in many countries, it is second in popularity in the United States only to the Red Delicious. Golden Delicious apples are somewhat smaller than their red cousins and are actually a hybrid development from a totally different source. They appear earlier than the red variety and keep longer, have a smooth shiny skin with a slight green tinge in early season, and become a deep, dark yellow by March. Firm and crisp when the skin is greenish, or less crisp but sweeter when completely golden. A versatile apple good for eating as well as cooking and juice. They are always sweet, make perfect dried apple slices, delicious unsweetened applesauce, and excellent cheese and wine companions. When the apple is grown in a cool climate, so that a reasonable amount of acid is formed, it can be very good; in warmer regions it can be insipid. The variety is popular with growers because the tree crops heavily.

Granny Smith These are the leading apples in Australia. The original tree, from the seed of an apple thrown out into the yard of Mrs. Thomas Smith of Eastwood near Sydney, was bearing by 1868. The Granny Smith is a medium to large-sized apple, oval to round in shape, with a very green, very bright white-dotted skin. The fruit is superhard, white and juicy, with a delightfully tart taste in early season and a somewhat sweeter flavor later on. The most popular of all the "green" apples, they are a worldwide choice both for cooking and eating (although they take longer than many to soften during cooking). Today Granny Smiths are grown primarily in Australia, New Zealand, and South Africa. Commercial imported fruit are often sprayed with an oil formula that, along with its natural tough skin, makes the peel difficult to digest. Yellow Grannys are overage or under-refrigerated or both and are unacceptable.

Gravenstein The Gravenstein originated in northern Germany or Denmark before 1800, and was imported to the U.S. in 1824. Scions (cuttings for grafting) were taken to California, and it soon became a popular American variety, especially for cooking. It is also eaten by those who like rather acidic apples. It is large, roundish, and slightly lopsided, yellow with bright red and orange stripes. Its main use is for applesauce, but it is also good eaten on its own or in desserts.

Idared An American apple bred in Idaho in the 1930s and 40s from the better known Jonathan and Wagener. A medium-sized, round red and yellow apple with a sweet, moderately acid flavor, it keeps and cooks well.

Jonathan (originally called the "Rick" after its discoverer) Jonathan apples were first found on the farm of Philip Rick in Woodstock, New York in 1880. This old favorite is a deep-yellow apple with both bright and dull red stripes. It is very round, with creamy-white meat that is semi-sweet in early season and sweeter later on. Considered one of the best eating apples, it has a highly aromatic, spicy taste that makes it very good for pies or applesauce. An excellent keeper, the Jonathan is not a very hard apple when fresh-picked, but neither does it soften much during storage.

Jonagold The Jonagold is a Jonathan/Golden cross. Thin-skinned, it is a wonderfully sweet and crisp apple, but does not store well. Buy only a few of these apples at a time, for quick and enjoyable consumption. It is an excellent eating apple, as well as being very good for other purposes.

Laxton A large and important group, these owe their name to Thomas Laxton (1830–90), who worked mainly on peas and strawberries but whose sons began in 1893 to experiment systematically in crossing apples. They produced thousands of cross-bred apples, from which many of the best British dessert apples are derived. A high proportion of them retain the name Laxton. They bear a general resemblance to Coxes, although they can usually be distinguished by their brighter color. The texture is crisp and the flavor light. The best known are **Laxton's Pearmain, Laxton's Superb, Laxton's Advance, Laxton's Leader,** and **Laxton's Fortune.**

Macoun Macouns first appeared in 1926, when a McIntosh was crossed with a Jersey Black. Today's Macouns have a light gray-maroon to deep vermilion shading with some striping and both white and very dark flecks. The meat is very white, crisp, juicy, and sweet, with no bitter taste to the peel. Macoun apples are considered the finest of all dessert apples. They are a small to large-sized apple, but the medium size eats best. Fresh-picked Macouns are as good as any apple anywhere and are considered the premium eating apple of the northeastern U.S., where they are mostly grown. However, they keep poorly.

McIntosh A popular North American variety named in 1811 for John McIntosh of Ontario, Canada, who discovered the chance seedling. A pioneer, John McIntosh settled at what is now Dundela, Ontario. In 1796, while clearing a forest along the Saint Lawrence River, he came across some small wild seedling apple trees. These he planted near his house. One of the trees bore especially delicious apples, and it was given the name of McIntosh Red. This tree lived and bore fruit for one hundred and twelve years, dying in 1908 after being injured by a fire. Paid for by popular subscription, a monument was later erected to mark the site of the original tree of one of the finest American apples. This all-purpose apple has also been excellent for cross-breeding; it has in turn given us such varieties as the Cortland, Spartan, Melba, Macoun, Niagara, Puritan, and others. In New York State, the world's largest producer of McIntosh apples, they are first picked on September 15 and show mostly green with a red blush. These early apples are excellent for an apple pie mix, because they tend to be slightly tart and very crisp. By October the McIntosh is three-quarters red and has sweetened considerably. By November the color is almost all red, the taste is very sweet, and the crispness and crunch seem to soften more than just a little. The late McIntosh makes a thick applesauce that requires little sweetener. This round, squat, shiny red/green apple has a fine high flavor, a spicy-sweet taste with an ever-so-slight tartness. Texture is tender but crisp. Does bruise easily and can get mushy if not kept consistently cold.

Newton This is a tart, crisp apple that is very good to eat and excellent for cooking; it also has an excellent keeping quality.

Newtown Pippin (Yellow Newtown) The original tree was found growing in Newtown, New York, site of present-day Flushing soon after 1700. It produced a heavy crop of yellowish-green apples that were crisp but juicy, acid but sweet, and had exceptional keeping qualities. The variety, spread by cuttings taken from the tree (which perished in 1805 as a result of excessive cutting) was soon grown over most of the settled parts of North America. The tree is awkwardly sensitive to soil and climate, so it lost popularity among growers towards the end of the nineteenth century. This green to yellow apple (sometimes with an attractive blush, but often simply with a green-yellow skin) has a moderately tart or even winelike taste, similar to Granny Smith. Excellent to eat as is due to its sweet, semi-juicy flavor and fairly crisp texture, it is also used in pies and for drying but most often for juice.

Northern Spy The origin of this appleis somewhat obscure but some say that the name may derive from the fact that Bloomfield, New York, where it originated in about 1800, was a site of activity for the Underground Railroad, a secret escape route by which southern slaves were brought to the North to freedom. This apple was long considered the perfect specimen and became something of a legend. Brightly striped with red-green skin, firm yellow flesh, and a tart, slightly acid flavor, it is suitable for pies or snacking. Not widely available.

Pippin Originally meaning any apple grown from a pip (seed), pippin is a name derived from the French *pepin*, meaning both pip and apple. By the sixteenth century the term had come to denote a hard, late-ripening, long-keeping apple of acid flavor. **Golden Pippin, Ribston Pippin, Cox's Orange Pippin,** and **Sturmer Pippin** are common varieties.

Red Astrachan This Russian apple was introduced into the United States in 1835. Grown in California, this green and red to entirely green apple has uses in cooking or eating. An early apple with a fruity, acid taste and plenty of character, it is apt to fall off the tree before it is fully ripe.

Red Delicious (or simply, **Delicious**) The Red Delicious began as a chance seedling on the farm of Hesse Hiatt of Peru, Iowa, in the late 1860s. Because it was self-planted, the tree was cut down in 1870, when it had become big enough to become an obstacle. New shoots appeared from the stump the following year, so it was allowed to grow. When the first apples appeared, Hiatt found them so superior in taste that he entered them in a contest held by a canning company. The judges agreed to award it a prize, but discovered that the basket in which the apples had arrived had lost its identifying label. Fortunately, Hiatt resubmitted the fruit the following year, and its career began. First marketed as Hiatt's Hawkeye, the Stark Brothers, a large fruit-growing concern, bought out Hiatt and renamed the variety Delicious. Since the 1940s it has been the leading American apple; however, it has been developed to a high state of color and uniformity, and thus its taste is greatly diminished. For most of the selling season it remains crisp and juicy, but by March it starts to soften and becomes mealy. The Red Delicious is triangular or heart-shaped, with the tapered bottom closing with the recognizable five points, or sheep nose, at the blossom end. It is sweet but insipid, lacking in acid, very juicy in its early stage, and wrapped in a thick peel. The size varies, but most are medium to very large, with the largest available around Christmas. Not necessarily the most flavorful or juicy, they are good for eating but only fair in cooking or juice making.

Rhode Island Greening This variety was developed in Rhode Island in approximately 1740 by a tavern keeper named "Green" at Green's End, Rhode Island. Rarely seen in commercial markets, this is a pale yellow-green apple that is often larger on one side. The skin is very tough and thick, often slightly bronzed, and with a touch of roughness. Picked after the frost, they are hard and crunchy with a crisp, sharp, refreshing, brisk acid taste, and make an excellent companion for wine and cheese. An excellent pie apple due to their juice, which thickens well in baking, they are used commercially for applesauce and frozen pies.

Rome Beauty An American apple that is named for Rome, Ohio, near where it was discovered in 1832 by the farmer Joel Gillett. One of his grafted trees had shot from below the graft. The stray branch began to produce large, red-striped apples of handsome appearance and rock-like solidity. The variety became popular, especially among growers, for it was easy to manage and the attractive fruit sold well. Hybrids like the Gallia Beauty, Monroe, and Ruby come from this variety. The Rome Beauty is a medium to large, roundish, deep red, shiny apple with crisply firm, very juicy and full flavored flesh. This is America's most popular cooking apple, but it is also good for eating out of hand. Early Rome apples (picked in September or October) are very hard, with a tart winey taste. They are excellent as part of an apple pie mix, since the pieces hold their shape and become sweeter in the baking. Later Rome apples, either picked ripe or allowed to ripen off the tree, are the true baking apples. They soften evenly without saucing up. The skin holds the fruit together, and the large size makes them a generous and attractive serving.

Shamrock A new variety, this green apple is much like a McIntosh: tart and tender.

Spartan A McIntosh/Pippin cross grown primarily in Canada. The Danes developed this firm apple with a custardlike taste that is popular for eating and cooking. Fairly tart, tender yet very flavorful and crisp, this variety cooks well and holds its firmness. Excellent all-purpose apple and a good keeper.

Starking Also called **Starking Delicious**, this variety from France is a crisp dessert apple with red-streaked skin and very white, sweet flesh. It is delicious with cheese or made into fritters.

Stayman (**Stayman's Winesap**) Derived from a Winesap seedling discovered in 1866 by Dr. Stayman, in Kansas, this medium red to purplish-red apple has a mildly tart taste, which makes it good for eating and some desserts. Picked after the first frost, it is hard and juicy, with white meat and a definite wine flavor. For the wine, cheese, and apple lover, the Stayman is the first choice. Winesaps make excellent apple pies either on their own or mixed with other varieties, and cook up into a light textured and distinctively flavored sauce. They are excellent cider apples, producing progressively sweeter juice as the season lengthens.

Wealthy The Wealthy arose in approximately 1860 from an unusually intent search by Peter Gideon of Minnesota for the perfect apple. Of all the seeds that he planted, the best fruit came from the cold-tolerant tree we know today; Wealthy was the given Christian name of his wife. The Wealthy reached the height of its commercial success in the 1910s and 1920s, but is commercially unimportant today. This medium red apple has a mildly acid taste, and is good for desserts or eating. The pinkish flesh softens quickly, so it lasts poorly, and should be eaten soon after purchase. It is available in mid-autumn.

White Astrachan Introduced to the United States in approximately 1820 from Russia. This is a greenish white apple that is good for cooking, now grown primarily in California.

White Pearmain The pearmains are the oldest English apple name, recorded in a Norfolk document of 1204. Although the place and date of its origin are unknown, the name is derived from the old French apple name *parmain* or *permain*, referring perhaps to a group of apples rather than a single variety. This yellow apple is grown primarily in California and is good for baking.

White Transparent An early ripening apple of Scandinavian or Russian origin, it was introduced to Britain and the United States in the mid-nineteenth century. As its name suggests, it is very pale with a transparent skin. The taste is mild but agreeable and the fruit should be used quickly, while still crisp, for cooking rather than dessert. It is available in late summer.

Winesap The winesap is one of the oldest American varieties, dating back to the colonial period. It was so named because it was often used as a cider apple. The winesap apple is a rugged country apple of dull rusty-red color with a touch of yellow in its ripe stage. Picked after the first frost, this apple has a hard, juicy texture, white meat, and a definite wine flavor. For the wine, cheese, and apple lover the Winesap is the first choice. Winesap apples make excellent apple pies either as part of an apple mix or by themselves since they cook up into a light-textured sauce with that distinctive Winesap flavor. They are also excellent cider apples, producing sweeter and sweeter juice as the apple season lengthens. It has a good keeping time and was very popular for this reason until controlled atmosphere storage made other varieties more available.

York Imperial This variety was developed in Pennsylvania, in approximately 1830. A red-skinned apple with a lopsided shape, its pinkish red skin is often dotted with pale spots, which don't affect the quality of the fruit. The flesh is yellow and moderately juicy, neither too tart nor too sweet. Yorks are good baking apples, holding their shape and flavor when cooked, and are now mostly a processing apple.

Byproducts

Apple cider is freshly pressed juice that has not been pasteurized or sweetened. This is the best-tasting form of apple juice, full of vitamins and free of all processed interference. Compared to store-bought apple juice, it is more flavorful but less sweet. Unlike clear, pasteurized apple juice, cider looks cloudy and sediment often collects at the bottom of the bottle. Because it is highly perishable, it must be kept under constant refrigeration, and even then may only last from ten to fourteen days. Freshly-squeezed apple cider is excellent for the body, and is especially beneficial for cleansing or reducing diets. Beneficial for the liver and gallbladder, it tends to speed up bowel action, but will produce flatulence if the bowels are not moving well.

Apple juice is fresh cider that has been pasteurized to guarantee that it will not turn into hard cider or vinegar. During this process most of its vitality is lost and the sugar content is dramatically increased by the heat process or by additional sweetening. All canned and bottled fruit juices are pasteurized, but need refrigeration after opening to prevent them from souring. Like most other processed foods, it is best avoided.

Hard cider has been left to ferment naturally. It can be dry or sweet, depending on the apple varieties used and whether fresh cider was added back after fermentation. The alcohol content ranges from 3 to 7 percent. European cider is usually naturally sparkling, bottled before fermentation is complete, or perhaps with carbonation added afterward.

Apricot *(Prunus armeniaca)*

Botanists have characterized this fruit as part of the large plum family, thus the Prunus *genus.* Armeniaca *signifies that the ancients believed that this tree originated in Armenia, a region in southwest Asia. The English word* apricot *came from the Latin* praecoquum, *which means precocious or early ripening.*

General Information The apricot is believed to be native to China, and to have been introduced by Alexander the Great to the Greco-Roman world around the fourth century B.C. A member of the large rose family, the apricot is a drupe, like its cousins the peach, plum, cherry, and almond. The oval orange-colored fruit resembles the related peach in shape, and the plum in flavor. Its cleft pit protects a kernel that tastes remarkably like the almond and is often used in brandies, preserves, marzipan, amaretti, and other confections. In bitter varieties, however, this kernel contains a strong compound that can be poisonous if eaten raw in large quantities over a period of time—an unlikely possibility. The Franciscan friars brought apricots to California in the late 1700s, and this state now produces almost all our fresh apricots. Apricots have been sun-dried in the Far and Middle East since ancient times. It

Lore and Legend

For those familiar with the rich sensuous smell of ripe apricots, it is perfectly clear why nectar (a beverage of fruit juice and pulp generally made from apricots) was the preferred drink of the Greek and Roman Gods. In eastern countries the apricot is known by the beautiful name of "Moon of the Faithful."

Apricot

Nutritional Value Per 100 g Edible Portion

	Fresh	Dried
Calories	48	260
Protein	1.40 g	5.00 g
Fat	0.39 g	0.50 g
Fiber	0.60 g	3.00 g
Calcium	14 mg	67 mg
Iron	0.54 mg	5.50 mg
Magnesium	8 mg	n/a
Phosphorus	19 mg	108 mg
Potassium	296 mg	979 mg
Sodium	1 mg	26 mg
Zinc	0.260 mg	n/a
Copper	0.089 mg	n/a
Manganese	0.079 mg	n/a
Beta Carotene (A)	2,612 IU	10,900 IU
Thiamine (B_1)	0.030 mg	0.010 mg
Riboflavin (B_2)	0.040 mg	0.160 mg
Niacin (B_3)	0.600 mg	3.300 mg
Pantothenic Acid (B_5)	0.240 mg	n/a
Pyridoxine (B_6)	0.054 mg	n/a
Folic Acid (B_9)	8.60 mcg	n/a
Ascorbic Acid (C)	10 mg	12 mg

requires six pounds of fresh fruit to result in one pound of dried, but the fruit loses nothing but water, and the nutrients are concentrated. Try to find apricots that have been dried naturally, without sulphur dioxide, which is harmful to the body and imparts a bitter taste.

Buying Tips A truly ripe apricot is golden-orange all over with no traces of green. They are best when deep orange with a red blush, and slightly soft to the touch. Avoid those that are overly soft, have bruises, or are wilted and shriveled. Most dried apricots contain sulphur dioxide, a noxious gas used to prevent discoloration. Look for the darker, non-sulphured variety instead.

Culinary Uses Many varieties of apricots are available, all of which are delectable. Tree-ripened apricots have the best flavor, but the fruit is so delicate that tree-ripened fruit is rarely available in stores. Immature apricots are greenish-yellow, and never attain the right sweetness or flavor; their flesh is firm and their taste sour. Once fully ripened, refrigerate promptly, as these delicate gems spoil rapidly. They are a natural partner to almonds in baked goods since they are closely related, as their almond-shaped pits attest. The kernels are not considered edible because of their amygdalin or laetrile content, which is considered poisonous by the FDA. Dried apricots, because they travel well and keep through the seasons, are used extensively in savory as well as sweet dishes. Their sharp sweetness complements meats, quick breads, and desserts; they are also excellent and convenient snacks for children, picnickers, and hikers.

Health Benefits Laxative. Like other bright orange fruits or vegetables, apricots contain highly concentrated amounts of beta carotene, or provitamin A, which is successful in thwarting certain cancers, especially those of the lung and skin. Dried apricots have an even higher concentration of beta carotene than the raw fruit. Tree-ripened apricots are one of the finest sources of copper, cobalt, and the organic iron necessary for building red corpuscles in the blood. This mineral richness makes them beneficial in cases of blood-related disorders such as anemia, acne, toxemia, and tuberculosis.

Atemoya *(Annona squamosa* x *A. cherimola)*

Annona *means year's harvest, suggested by the Haitian name* anon, *which is applied to one of the species.* Squamosa *means having scale-like leaves, or full of scales;* cherimola *derives from* chirimuyu, *the native name (see* ***Cherimoya****). The English name atemoya is a combination of ate (an old Mexican name for the sugar apple) and* moya *(from cherimoya).*

General Information Native to tropical America and the West Indies, the atemoya is one of a family of pudding-like creamy fruits whose arrival is fairly recent. As its name implies, it is a cross between a cherimoya and a sugar apple. This tough-skinned, grayish-green fruit resembles in size and shape a distorted, slightly melted, Stone Age artichoke. The rind has more prominent and angular areoles than those of the sugar apple, with tips that are rounded or slightly upturned. Although it was supposedly "invented" in 1908 by P.J. Wester, an employee of the U.S. Department of Agriculture, it turned out nature had already come up with the same cross in 1850 in Australia, and did so again in Israel in 1930.

Buying Tips Choose pale green atemoyas that are unblemished and have not cracked open. Those that are relatively thin-skinned and somewhat tender have the best flavor.

Culinary Uses This West Indian delicacy has a creamy, ivory-colored, virtually acid-free flesh studded with dark, slippery, watermelon-like seeds. At its best, the rich flesh tastes astonishingly like cooked vanilla custard with a hint of mango. When less than perfect, it can be rather starchy, like winter squash blended with pear. Atemoyas tend to be rather messy to eat; the best way is to cut them in half and eat the flesh a spoonful at a time, daintily spitting out the inedible seeds. The fruit can also be used in fruit salads, or pureed and served as a fruit sauce. Blended with orange juice, lime juice, and cream, it makes a delicious ice cream.

Atemoya

Nutritional Value Per 100 g Edible Portion

	Raw
Calories	94
Protein	1.07-1.4 g
Fat	0.4-0.6 g
Fiber	0.05-2.5 g
Calcium	17 mg
Iron	0.3 mg
Magnesium	32 mg
Potassium	250 mg
Sodium	4-5 mg
Zinc	0.2 mg
Beta Carotene (A)	10 mcg
Thiamine (B_1)	0.05 mg
Riboflavin (B_2)	0.07 mg
Niacin (B_3)	0.80 mg
Ascorbic Acid (C)	50 mg

Bael *(Aegle marmelos)*

Also Known As: Bengal Quince, Indian Quince, Stone Apple.

Aegle *comes from the Latin* Aegle, *one of the Hesperides.* Marmelos *is a Portuguese name for the fruit.*

General Information Belonging to the citrus family, this tree grows wild in much of central and southern India and southeast Asia. It is cultivated throughout India, mainly in temple gardens, due to its status as a sacred tree. The fruits look something like grayish-yellow oranges, and may have a thin hard shell, or a less hard but thick skin.

Lore and Legend

Hindus hold the tree sacred to Shiva and use its leaves in his worship. It is sacrilegious to cut down a bael tree, but to die under one assures immediate salvation.

Culinary Uses The segmented pulp inside is yellow, gummy, and full of seeds, but has an aromatic, refreshing flavor. It can be eaten plain, served with jaggery (palm sugar), or made into a marmalade, jelly, or drink. One popular Indian drink is made by beating the seeded pulp together with milk and sugar. Both the central core and seeds are inedible. Mature but still unripe fruits are made into jam with the addition of citric acid.

Health Benefits The fresh ripe pulp of the higher quality cultivars, and the "sherbet" made from it, are

Bael

Nutritional Value Per 100 g Edible Portion

	Raw
Protein	1.8-2.62 g
Fat	0.2-0.39 g
Beta Carotene (A)	55 mg
Thiamine (B_1)	0.13 mg
Riboflavin (B_2)	1.19 mg
Niacin (B_3)	1.10 mg
Ascorbic Acid (C)	8-60 mg

taken for their mild laxative, tonic, and digestive effects. It has been surmised that the psoralen in the pulp increases tolerance of sunlight and aids in maintaining normal skin color. Marmelosin, derived from the pulp, is given as a laxative and diuretic; in larger doses it lowers the rate of respiration, depresses heart action, and causes sleepiness.

Bakuri (*Platonia insignis*)

Platonia *derives from a personal name.* Insignis *means remarkable or distinguished.*

Bakuri

Nutritional Value Per 100 g Edible Portion

	Raw
Calories	105
Protein	1.9 g
Fiber	7.4 g
Calcium	20.0 mg
Iron	2.2 mg
Phosphorus	36.0 mg
Thiamine (B1)	0.04 mg
Riboflavin (B2)	0.04 mg
Niacin (B3)	0.50 mg
Ascorbic Acid (C)	33.0 mg

General Information The bakuri tree was first reported in European literature in 1614. The tree commonly grows wild in the Amazon region of northern Brazil and is especially abundant in the State of Para. Its native territory extends across the border into Colombia and northeast to the humid forests of Guyana. Seldom cultivated, the tree is always left standing for the sake of its fruits when land is cleared for planting or pastures. The roundish fruits, 3 to 5 inches wide, are yellow when ripe. Each has a hard rind and may weigh up to 32 ounces.

Culinary Uses Bakuri pulp is white, pithy, with a pleasant odor and subacid flavor, and contains up to four inedible seeds. Infertile seed compartments filled with pulp (called "filho") are the parts preferred by the natives. Although the fruit is eaten raw, it is more commonly used to make sherbet, ice cream,marmalade, or jelly.

Health Benefits The seeds contain 6 to 11 percent of an oil that is mixed with sweet almond oil and used to treat eczema and herpes.

Banana (*Musa acuminata*)

The banana plant was named Musa *in honor of Antonius Musa, the personal physician to Octavius Augustus, first emperor of Rome from 63–14* B.C. *Euphorbus Musa, the brother of Antonius, discovered the banana while in Africa as physician to the king of Numidia, an ally of Rome. He sent samples to Antonius, urging the banana's cultivation and use, and Antonius promoted it so successfully that it has carried the family name ever since.* Acuminata *means long-pointed or tapering, and usually refers to the flower petals. The classical writer Theophrastus recounted from Alexander the Great's reports of India that wise men were said to sit in the shade of the banana tree and eat its fruit—hence the earlier term* sapientum, *meaning of the wise men. The first European contact with the fruit came not long after 1402, when Portuguese sailors encountered it in West Africa; this is why the English name* banana *comes from a West African word, the Guinean* banema *or* banana.

General Information The origin of the banana is thought to be in East Asia and Oceania, but the tree and its long slender fruit (the red and green cooking varieties) have been known and used since ancient times, even before the cultivation of rice. During the first millenium A.D. the banana reached Africa, probably taken directly from the Malay region to

Madagascar. In 1482 the seafaring Portuguese found the banana on the Guinean coast and carried it with them to the Canary Islands. The Spanish missionary Friar Tomas de Berlanga took banana roots from the Canaries to Santo Domingo in the West Indies in 1516; later, when he was made Bishop of Panama, the fruit reached the American mainland with him. The new plant spread so quickly and became so well established that some early travelers thought it an indigenous American plant. Only in 1836 did the yellow banana appear, a mutant from the original red and green cooking banana. A Jamaican named Jean Francois Poujot observed one morning that the bananas on one of his plantation trees were uniquely yellow. Tasting the strange new fruit, he found it edible uncooked—ripe, sweet, and delicious—and recognizing their potential, soon planted acres of sweet yellow bananas. The international banana trade was started by two American entrepreneurs, Captain Lorenzo D. Baker in 1870 and Minor C. Keith in 1872, who independently of each other began to ship bananas from the Caribbean to New Orleans, Boston, and New York. They were offered as an exotic imported delicacy, and eaten with a knife and fork. At the 1876 Philadelphia Centennial Exposition, yellow bananas were sold as a "Curiosity of the Indies" for ten cents each and proved highly popular. By 1899 these two men had merged their interests to form the United Fruit Company, which still has great influence in Central America and the Islands. The flourishing banana industry is now one of the most profitable agricultural resources of many tropical countries.

Lore and Legend

There is an old Islamic myth, probably of Indian origin, that the banana was the forbidden fruit of the Tree of Knowledge of Good and Evil, which grew in the Garden of Eden. Furthermore, after the Fall, Adam and Eve covered their nakedness with banana leaves rather than those of the fig. This may account for the common West Indian practice of calling the banana fruit a fig.

The banana plant, contrary to popular notion, is not actually a tree but a giant perennial herb. Probably the largest plant without a woody stem, the trunk consists of a cylinder of tightly wrapped leaf-petiole sheaths. Pushing up through the center is the true stem, which emerges at the top as a flower spike or bud. Blossoms held in spirals on the tip grow into upturned "fingers," as many as twenty in a "hand," as many as fifteen hands in a bunch. After each harvest the pseudostem is either manually removed or allowed to die down naturally, but sideshoots or suckers from the same underground corm continue to grow, and these stems will produce bunches of bananas in the following season. Some plants have been known to remain in production for up to one hundred years. In a sense the plant is immortal, although in practice most banana plantations are started anew every five to twenty years. The long slender banana fruit is sterile; the tiny partial seeds will not regenerate, but serve only to release the hormone (ethylene gas and carbon dioxide) that turns green bananas ripe and yellow. Most bananas are cut while still quite green, even for local use in the tropics, where they are allowed to ripen in a shady place near the house. Fruit intended for export is shipped green and ripened using ethylene gas under carefully controlled conditions. Bananas are one of the most popular fresh fruits in the United States, with an average twenty-five pounds consumed per capita annually.

Buying Tips When selecting bananas, those which are full and plump will generally be found to have more flavor and delicacy. Slightly green bananas will quickly ripen at room temperature.

Culinary Uses A ripe banana has no trace of green on the skin; in fact, only when the skin becomes generously speckled with brown is the fruit perfectly ripe. If its skin will not break readily at the stem end for peeling, the banana is not ripe enough; if the skin adheres to the flesh, the banana is still too starchy to eat. Unripe bananas are mostly starch and hard to digest, while fully ripe fruits have converted most of their starch content into

Banana

Nutritional Value Per 100 g Edible Portion

	Raw	Dried
Calories	65.5-111.0	298
Protein	1.10-1.87 g	2.80-3.50 g
Fat	0.16-0.40 g	0.80-1.10 g
Fiber	0.33-1.07 g	2.10-3.00 g
Calcium	3.2-13.8 mg	n/a
Iron	0.4-1.5 mg	n/a
Magnesium	29 mg	n/a
Phosphorus	16.3-50.4 mg	n/a
Potassium	396 mg	n/a
Sodium	1 mg	n/a
Zinc	0.160 mg	n/a
Copper	0.104 mg	n/a
Manganese	0.152 mg	n/a
Beta Carotene(A)	81 mg	n/a
Thiamine (B_1)	0.040-0.540 mg	n/a
Riboflavin (B_2)	0.050-0.067 mg	n/a
Niacin (B_3)	0.600-1.050 mg	n/a
Pantothenic Acid (B_5)	0.260 mg	n/a
Pyridoxine (B_6)	0.578 mg	n/a
Folic Acid (B_9)	19.1 mcg	n/a
Ascorbic Acid (C)	5.60-36.40 mg	n/a
Tocopherol (E)	0.270 mg	n/a

sugar and the tannin element (which makes fresh fruit taste bitter and puckery) is greatly reduced. Bananas can be eaten raw straight out of their jackets, peeled and used in fruit salads, baked, fried, flambeed with liqueurs, or added to pies, desserts, ice creams, cakes, and bread. Where appearance is important they should be used immediately, or sprinkled with lemon juice to prevent discoloration. Refrigeration will stop the ripening process but turns the banana skins brown. The fruit itself is not harmed.

Although more than 90 percent of the bananas grown are used directly for food, several products are made from the remainder. A banana flour or powder is sometimes produced (but rarely exported) by spray-drying or drum-drying the mashed fruits. Candies and various confections are made by splitting and drying the bananas. Banana chips of commercial origin are made from bananas that are picked green, before the starch base turns to sugars, then sugar-sweetened and deep-fried like potato chips. Unsweetened chips are a dull product with an oily texture (from frying) and no banana flavor that few people would purchase twice. Make your own banana chips in a dehydrator; they will be more chewy than crunchy, with a rich dense banana flavor, and are quite definitely healthier. Dehydrated banana flakes are also available in some markets in vacuum-sealed cans, and are used on cereals, in baked goods, desserts, sauces, and other products.

Health Benefits The banana is not only one of the neatest and most conveniently packaged food items, but is also a powerhouse of nutritional energy. Fully ripe bananas are composed of 76 percent water, 20 percent sugar, 12 percent starch, a large contingent of vitamins and minerals, and a great deal of fiber. Green bananas contain anti-nutrients, proteins that inhibit the actions of amylase, an enzyme that permits digestion of starch and other complex carbohydrates. Wait until they are fully ripe before eating. Antifungal and antibiotic principles are found in both the peel and pulp of fully ripened bananas. Bananas feed the natural acidophilus bacteria of the bowel; their high vitamin and mineral content (especially potassium) benefits the muscular and nervous systems; their sugars are readily assimilated for use as fuel; and their pectin content helps heal ulcers and lower blood cholesterol. They are also rich in the amino acid tryptophan, which is known to promote sleep, and contain enzymes that assist in the manufacture of sexual hormones. For those striving to gain weight or build muscle bulk, bananas are a wonderful food (along with appropriate exercise). They are especially good for young children and infants, as they are easily digested and can be pureed with water to form a type of milk. Make sure to use only ripe bananas. Unripe bananas will tend to be constipating, while ripe ones are more laxative.

Varieties

THERE ARE THREE MAJOR KINDS OF BANANAS (but over 300 varieties): yellow, red, and Chicadita.

Lady Fingers, also called **Chicaditas**, are small dull-yellow bananas that are incredibly sweet. Their small size makes them perfect finger food for children (or adults).

Red bananas, or **Clarets**, are shorter and fatter than yellow bananas, and have thick red skins, dark creamy flesh, and a higher oil content. The taste of a red banana compared to a yellow banana is analogous to that of cream to milk; the red bananas are richer, more aromatic, smoother, and sweeter. To be fully ripe, a red banana must be swollen, slightly soft with perhaps a split skin, and the color turned from red to orange. **Apple bananas** have a more acid flavor than a regular yellow banana, and taste something like a mellow apple. These also must be very ripe before eating, or their consistency will be starchy.

Yellow bananas were introduced to North America by the United Fruit Company, now called United Brands. It is largely because of the effort of this unusual and controversial company that we enjoy a constant supply of this tropical fruit. By far the most common variety in the past was Manque or Gros Michel (Big Mike). The varieties known as Valery and Cavendish, which are more resistant to disease, are now the major varieties. These produce a large, straight, compact bunch, which makes them easy to ship.

Barberry *(Berberis vulgaris, Mahonia aquifolium)*

Berberis *derives from the Arabic for Barbary (North Africa).* Mahonia *was named in honor of Bernard M'Mahon, a prominent American horticulturist (1775–1816).* Vulgaris *means common, while* aquifolium *means having pointed leaves, or spiny-leaved. The English name* barberry *is a corruption of the Arabic name.*

General Information The Barberry *(B. vulgaris)*, a native of Europe and Asia, has been thoroughly naturalized in the eastern and middle United States, especially in New England. Formerly planted for its edible fruits as well as for ornamentation, today it has to compete with many other species and hybrids. *Berberis* berries are generally red, varying from coral to deep crimson, and tart. American barberries (*Mahonia*) are usually blue, either pale or dark-colored. *M. aquifolium*, the mountain grape or Oregon grape, which is the floral emblem of the State of Oregon, has blue-gray berries.

Culinary Uses Barberries are pleasantly acid and make a fine jelly or jam, and excellent juices and wines. In India some species are sun-dried to make "raisins," which are eaten as a dessert. The fruits ripen in September.

Health Benefits The root and stem bark of the plant contain tannin and a substance known as berberine, which may account for the plant's effectiveness in treating diarrhea. Berberine salts, derived from barberry and other plants, are used in eyedrops and eyewashes. In ancient Egypt a syrup made of common barberry mixed with fennel seed was used against plagues; this concoction was probably effective because modern research indicates that the plant has anti-bacterial properties that would help ward off infectious diseases. Barberry jelly provides relief for catarrhal infections, and the plain juice with a little sugar is a healing throat gargle.

Bignay (*Antidesma bunius*)

Also Known As: Chinese Laurel, Currant Tree, Salamander Tree.

> Antidesma *derives from a Greek term for banding, meaning the bark was used for cordage. The English name* bignay *derives from the Philippine name* bignai.

Bignay	
Nutritional Value Per 100 g Edible Portion	
	Raw
Protein	0.75 g
Calcium	0.12 mg
Iron	0.001 mg
Phosphorus	0.040 mg
Thiamine (B_1)	0.031 mg
Riboflavin (B_2)	0.072 mg
Niacin (B_3)	0.530 mg

General Information The bignay tree is native to India, Ceylon, and southeast Asia. It is grown in every village in Indonesia, where the clusters of fruit are common in the marketplaces. Quite a few trees were planted in southern Florida and the fruits utilized for jelly, but they are rarely used today. The round or ovoid fruits are borne in grapelike, pendant clusters that are extremely showy. Since the berries ripen unevenly, there are pale yellowish-green, white, bright-red, and nearly black stages all present at the same time. The thick skin is tough and leaves a bright purple stain on fabrics.

Culinary Uses Whole bignay fruits are very acid when unripe, much like cranberries; ripe fruits are subacid and slightly sweet. For some there is an unpleasant "aftertaste;" to others it is unnoticeable. Each fruit contains a single inedible stone. The fruits are popular with Malayan children. Elsewhere the fruits are made into preserves, and the richly-colored jelly was actually produced on a small commercial scale in southern Florida for a number of years. Juice from the fruit makes an excellent syrup and has been fermented into wine and brandy.

Bilimbi (*Averrhoa bilimbi*)

> *The* Averrhoa *genus was named in honor of* Averrhoes, *a twelfth century Arabic physician and philosopher.* Bilimbi *is the common name in India.*

General Information Probably a native of the Moluccas, the bilimbing asam is cultivated throughout much of Indonesia, the Philippines, Ceylon, and Burma. Introduced into Queensland, Australia about 1896, the tree was readily adopted and is now quite common. The fruit is ellipsoid or nearly cylindrical, and 1 1/2 to 4 inches long. Crisp when unripe, it turns from bright green to yellowish-green or nearly white when ripe.

Bilimbi	
Nutritional Value Per 100 g Edible Portion	
	Raw
Protein	0.61 g
Fiber	0.6 g
Calcium	3.4 mg
Iron	1.01 mg
Phosphorus	11.1 mg
Beta Carotene (A)	0.035 mg
Thiamine (B_1)	0.010 mg
Riboflavin (B_2)	0.026 mg
Niacin (B_3)	0.302 mg
Ascorbic Acid (C)	15.5 mg

Culinary Uses The outer skin is glossy, very thin, soft and tender, and the flesh green, jelly-like, juicy and extremely acid. There may be perhaps six or seven flattened, disc-like brown seeds about a quarter-inch wide. Generally regarded as too acidic to eat raw, the fruit is frequently used for making pickles, flavoring curries, and stewing as a vegetable.

Health Benefits In Java, the fruits are combined with pepper and eaten to cause sweating when people are feeling "under the weather." A paste of pickled bilimbis is smeared all over the body to hasten recovery after a fever. A conserve made from the fruit is administered as a treatment for coughs, beri-beri, and biliousness. Syrup prepared from the fruit is taken as a cure for fever and inflammation and to stop rectal bleeding and alleviate internal hemorrhoids. Very acid bilimbis are employed to clean the blade of a *kris* (dagger), and they serve as mordants in the preparation of an orange dye for silk fabrics. The juice, because of its oxalic acid content, is useful for bleaching stains from the hands, rust marks from white cloth, and tarnish from brass.

Biriba *(Rollinia mucosa)*

Also Known As: Wild Sugar Apple.

The Rollinia *genus was named in honor of the French historian Charles Rollin.* Mucosa *means slimy.* Biriba *is the popular Brazilian name.*

General Information The biriba is the fruit which many people find the best of the large Annonaceae family (which includes cherimoyas, atemoyas, and others). Native to Brazil, it is the favorite fruit in western Amazonia. In Rio de Janeiro, the biriba is so esteemed as to be called "the Countess's fruit." Seeds were first introduced into the United States by O.W. Barrett in 1908, and seedlings later distributed to pioneers in southern Florida, but only a few trees exist there today. Biriba fruits are 3 to 4 inches long, conical to heart-shaped, and have a creamy-yellow skin when fully ripe. Handling causes the wart-like protuberances on the ripe fruit to turn brown or near-black.

Biriba

Nutritional Value Per 100 g Edible Portion

	Raw
Calories	80
Protein	2.8 g
Fiber	1.3 g
Calcium	24 mg
Iron	1.2 mg
Phosphorus	26 mg
Thiamine (B_1)	0.04 mg
Riboflavin (B_2)	0.04 mg
Niacin (B_3)	0.50 mg
Ascorbic Acid (C)	33.0 mg

Culinary Uses The white or cream-colored flesh is sweet, juicy, and of a good flavor. It has a slender, opaque-white core and numerous dark-brown seeds, which are inedible. The fruit is eaten fresh or is fermented to make wine.

Health Benefits In its native lands, the biriba is regarded as a refrigerant and antiscorbutic.

Blackberry *(Rubus laciniatus, R. procerus, R. villosus)*

Rubus *comes from the Latin* ruber, *meaning red.* Laciniatus *means torn;* procerus *means tall;* villosus, *means villous or soft-hairy. The English name* blackberry *is a very good description, since the berries are a deep rich black color when fully ripe.*

General Information Blackberries are a relative of the rose, and like roses grow on thorny brambles or canes. The bushes are so vigorous and invasive that they quickly become a thick, scratchy, impenetrable mass, that is hard to eradicate. Since they grow wild in such abundance throughout the country, cultivation has been slow. Just the mere

Blackberry

Nutritional Value Per 100 g Edible Portion	Raw
Calories	52
Protein	0.72 g
Fat	0.39 g
Fiber	4.10 g
Calcium	32 mg
Iron	0.57 mg
Magnesium	20 mg
Phosphorus	21 mg
Potassium	196 mg
Sodium	0 mg
Zinc	0.270 mg
Copper	0.140 mg
Manganese	1.291 mg
Beta Carotene (A)	165 IU
Thiamine (B_1)	0.030 mg
Riboflavin (B_2)	0.040 mg
Niacin (B_3)	0.400 mg
Pantothenic Acid (B_5)	0.240 mg
Pyridoxine (B_6)	0.058 mg
Folic Acid (B_9)	n/a
Ascorbic Acid (C)	21 mg
Tocopherol (E)	0.600 mg

mention of blackberries will bring to mind for many people the annual excursions to gather this delicious fruit. They are well worth the cuts, scratches, and stains of picking. The berry itself has a distinct shape: a single berry is actually a group of "drupelets," tiny fruits clustered together around a core, with each drupelet containing one seed; this core does not separate from the fruit like the raspberry's does. **Dewberries** (*Rubus procumbens, R. canadensis*) are a more delicately flavored type of blackberry grown on trailing rather than upright plants, and are regarded as one of the tastiest of the entire *Rubus* species. **Boysenberries, Loganberries, Ollalieberries, Tayberries,** and **Youngberries** are hybrids of blackberries and either dewberries or red raspberries.

Buying Tips Look for bright, clean berries with uniform dark coloring. Check the bottom of the container to make sure it has not been stained from crushed or moldy fruit.

Culinary Uses Plump, sweet blackberries are larger, juicier, and grainier than raspberries, with a more assertive flavor. They deteriorate faster than most fruits and should be used the day they are gathered or purchased. When fully ripe, each drupelet turns a shiny purple-black, and the whole berry is soft and lush. Blackberries can be used in a multitude of ways. Straight off the bush is best, but they are also good mixed with cream, or cooked into cobblers, jams, pies, and other baked goods.

Health Benefits Astringent, tonic. Blackberries are valuable as a general tonic and blood cleanser. They are highly esteemed in relieving diarrhea due to their astringent and tonic effects, and for contracting tissues and reducing secretions. Overindulgence may cause constipation.

Blueberry (*Vaccinium corymbosum, V. ashei, V. angustifolium, V. myrtillus*)

Also Known As: Whortleberry, Bilberry, Hurtleberry.

Vaccinium *is the ancient Latin name for the blueberry bush, derived from* vacca, *meaning cow, and given because cows like the plants.* Corymbosum *means corymbose, or having a flat-topped inflorescence;* angustifolium *means narrow-leaved;* myrtillus *refers to its myrtle-like leaves. The English name* blueberry *is a good description of this blue-fruited plant;* bilberry *derives from the Danish* bolle, *meaning ball, referring to the berry's round, smooth appearance.*

General Information A relative of azaleas and rhododendrons, blueberries grow in the same climates. Low-bush blueberries (*V. angustifolium*), which flourish at ankle height, grow wild in the rocky uplands and sandy pine barrens of the upper northeastern United States and Canada, and locally provide berries that are very small but superbly flavorful. Rabbit-eye blueberry bushes (*V. ashei*), which are more abundant in the southern United States, grow to towering heights of thirty feet and produce medium-sized berries that are generally processed rather than marketed fresh. The variety of blueberry found in most grocery stores comes from the high-bush blueberry plant (*V. corymbosum*), which produces large, firm, light blueberries. In the early 1900s, Elizabeth White of New Jersey encouraged the cultivation of blue berries by offering prizes for outstanding bush specimens, and today nearly all commercially cultivated blueberry varieties sold in the United States are the result of her work. Some varieties of blueberry are mistakenly called huckleberries: the red huckleberry *(Vaccinium parvifolium)* of the northwest United States; the squaw huckleberry *(V. stamineum)* of the north, and the California huckleberry *(V. ovatum)*.

Buying Tips Ripe blueberries should be plump, clean and dry, full of color, and have a powdery "bloom" on the skins. Overripe berries are dull in appearance, soft and watery, or moldy. Watch out for stained or leaking containers, which indicate crushed or moldy berries within.

Culinary Uses Highly perishable, the berries will last only about seven days after picking. The use of blueberries as a fresh or stewed fruit, and in such dishes as blueberry pie and blueberry muffins, is well known. Combined with other fruits that provide additional tartness and pectin, they make an excellent jelly.

Blueberry

Nutritional Value Per 100 g Edible Portion

	Raw
Calories	56
Protein	0.67 g
Fat	0.38 g
Fiber	1.30 g
Calcium	6 mg
Iron	0.17 mg
Magnesium	5 mg
Phosphorus	10 mg
Potassium	89 mg
Sodium	6 mg
Zinc	0.110 mg
Copper	0.061 mg
Manganese	0.282 mg
Beta Carotene (A)	100 IU
Thiamine (B_1)	0.048 mg
Riboflavin (B_2)	0.050 mg
Niacin (B_3)	0.359 mg
Pantothenic Acid (B_5)	0.093 mg
Pyridoxine (B_6)	0.036 mg
Folic Acid (B_9)	6.4 mcg
Ascorbic Acid (C)	13 mg

Health Benefits Laxative. Blueberries are well known for their laxative effect, but they also make excellent blood cleansers, improve sluggish circulation, and benefit the eyesight (particularly nocturnal vision). During World War II, British Royal Air Force pilots consumed bilberry (a variety of blueberry) preserves before their night missions to improve their ability to see at night. After the war, numerous studies demonstrated that blueberry extracts do in fact improve nighttime visual acuity and lead to quicker adjustment to darkness and faster restoration of visual acuity after exposure to glare. Additional research suggests that blueberries may protect against the development of cataracts and glaucoma, and may be quite therapeutic in the treatment of varicose veins, hemorrhoids, and peptic ulcers. Fresh berries have a healing effect on any infection of the mouth, rejuvenate the pancreas, and their antiseptic value helps in relieving dysentery. Of the fresh temperate region fruits, the blueberry is one of the highest in iron.

Boysenberry *(Rubus ursinus,* var. *loganobaccus,* cv. *'Boysen')*

Rubus is from the Latin *ruber*, meaning red. The English name *boysenberry* was given in honor of its creator, Rudolf Boysen, who experimentally crossed the black raspberry and loganberry in 1923.

General Information Boysenberries are a slightly larger and more acidic blackberry that looks exactly like the black parent it came from. California plant breeders had said it was genetically impossible to cross black, logan, and raspberry varieties, but Rudolph Boysen

Boysenberry

Nutritional Value Per 100 g Edible Portion

	Raw
Calories	50
Protein	1.10 g
Fat	0.26 g
Fiber	2.70 g
Calcium	27 mg
Iron	0.85 mg
Magnesium	16 mg
Phosphorus	27 mg
Potassium	139 mg
Sodium	1 mg
Zinc	0.220 mg
Copper	0.080 mg
Manganese	0.547 mg
Beta Carotene (A)	67 IU
Thiamine (B_1)	0.053 mg
Riboflavin (B_2)	0.037 mg
Niacin (B_3)	0.767 mg
Pantothenic Acid (B_5)	0.250 mg
Pyridoxine (B_6)	0.056 mg
Folic Acid (B_9)	63.3 mcg
Ascorbic Acid (C)	3.10 mg

managed to do it. Mr. Boysen never cashed in on his discovery and the plants were largely forgotten for many years. In 1933, boysenberries were rediscovered and a southern California grower named Walter Knott started planting them extensively on his family's farm in Anaheim, California (Knott's Berry Farm), where they soon became the keystone of his family's fortune. Grown primarily for canning, the large, long, dark reddish-black berries are fully ripe only when each drupelet turns deep purple; just one light-colored drupelet will make the whole berry bitter.

Culinary Uses and **Health Benefits** Same as blackberries.

Breadfruit (*Artocarpus altilis*)

Artocarpus comes from the Greek words artos, meaning bread, and carpos, meaning fruit. The term altilis refers to the tallness of the tree. Its English name breadfruit comes from the fact that when the fruit is roasted whole between hot stones, the pulp achieves the consistency and taste of freshly baked bread.

General Information The breadfruit tree is a handsome tree believed native to a vast area extending from New Guinea through the Indo-Malayan Archipelago to Western Micronesia. A member of the mulberry family, the breadfruit is a valuable crop from southern Florida to Brazil, and during its eight month season provides the natives around the Gulf of Mexico and the Caribbean Sea with an important fruit, often the mainstay of their diet. The greenish-yellow fruit, with its reticulated pattern of small protrusions, sometimes reaches a foot in diameter and weighs up to ten pounds. It is similar to a pineapple in that the fruit is actually multiple fruits that have developed from the ovaries of a tight cluster of flowers rather than from a single flower. Both seedless and seeded forms of breadfruit are known. All seedless varieties must be cooked. The seeded type is grown primarily for its seeds, called breadnuts, which when cooked and eaten are said to taste like chestnuts. If ever your fate is that of Robinson Crusoe, remember that you can eat raw any breadfruit that has seeds.

Buying Tips If you don't plan to use breadfruit for a few days, select a specimen that is all green, evenly colored, hard, and with large scales. It should feel dense and heavy for its size, not spongy. If you want to use it immediately, choose one as your recipe calls for (immature through mature). All breadfruit store poorly, ripening very quickly.

Culinary Uses No one tasting breadfruit for the first time is likely to dispute that it is an acquired taste (and texture). When green and immature, raw breadfruit is hard and starchy like a raw potato, and equally unappealing. At this stage, the pulp is generally sliced and roasted, or baked whole in its thick skin between hot stones so that it nearly achieves the consistency and taste of freshly baked whole-wheat bread. As it gradually ripens and turns yellowish-green, the pulp when cooked acquires the flavor of a yam, and a texture that might be likened to that of an extremely starchy potato mixed with plantain, but much stickier than either. At this stage it is also frequently cored, stuffed with a rich filling of meat or cheese, and baked. Fully ripened, it becomes a dessert fruit, since its flesh becomes rather sweet and tacky with a slightly musky, fruity flavor, which at the same time is very bland. In countries that cultivate them, the breadfruit is cooked in all the ways that Europeans and North Americans prepare both white and sweet potatoes: boiled, baked, roasted, fried, steamed, mashed, creamed, pureed and turned into smooth soups, puddings, cakes, and pies. The pulp from ripe breadfruits is combined with coconut milk, salt, and sugar, and baked to make a pudding. Dried fruit is ground into flour, and when it is added to wheat flour the combination is more nutritious than wheat flour alone. The seeds from seeded breadfruit are edible. Usually boiled, roasted, or fried before being eaten, they are said to be so close to chestnuts in flavor and texture that they may be freely substituted in any chestnut recipe. See also reference for Breadnuts under "Nuts and Seeds."

Breadfruit

Nutritional Value Per 100 g Edible Portion

	Underripe, Raw	Ripe, Cooked
Calories	105-109	n/a
Protein	1.30-2.24 g	1.34 g
Fat	0.10-0.86 g	0.31 g
Fiber	1.08-2.10 g	1.50 g
Calcium	0.05-17.0 mg	0.022 mg
Iron	0.61-2.40 mg	n/a
Magnesium	25 mg	n/a
Phosphorus	0.04-30.0 mg	0.062 mg
Potassium	490 mg	n/a
Sodium	2 mg	n/a
Zinc	0.120 mg	n/a
Copper	0.084 mg	n/a
Manganese	0.060 mg	n/a
Beta Carotene (A)	35-40 IU	n/a
Thiamine (B_1)	0.080-0.085 mg	n/a
Riboflavin (B_2)	0.033-0.070 mg	n/a
Niacin (B_3)	0.506-0.920 mg	n/a
Pantothenic Acid (B_5)	0.457 mg	n/a
Ascorbic Acid (C)	15-33 mg	n/a

Lore and Legend

The breadfruit was regarded as a romantic symbol of abundance and easy living by early inhabitants of the Pacific Islands. Captain James Cook, the English navigator who explored the Pacific in 1770–1780, saw the tree during his voyages and reported in such glowing terms about the value of the breadfruit that the British government decided to transplant young breadfruit trees for use in its thriving slave colonies in the Jamaican West Indies. Captain William Bligh, who had sailed with Cook, was duly commissioned; thus began the infamous voyage of the HMS Bounty in 1786. The ship left Tahiti with more than a thousand young trees, but as a result of the mutiny led by Fletcher Christian, neither trees nor crew ever reached their destination. Bligh remade the journey in 1792, and in January of 1793 successfully landed a quantity of plants at the island of St. Vincent. The unfortunate breadfruit never became an important food plant in the West Indies, however, as the natives much preferred the already familiar bananas, plantains, and other native foods. Captain Bligh has been honored by having another fruit tree named after him, *Blighia sapida*, the akee; its fruit is edible, but only barely—eaten either unripe or overly ripe the fruit is highly poisonous and can cause death.

Calamondin *(Citrofortunella mitis)*

Also Known As: Calamansi, Calamondin Orange, Panama Orange, Golden or Scarlet Lime.

Citrofortunella *is a hybrid of Citrus and Fortunella (see kumquat).* Mitis *means mild, gentle, ripe, without thorns. The English name* calamondin *derives from the Tagalong name* kalamunding.

Calamondin

Nutritional Value Per 100 g Edible Portion	Raw
Calories	173/lb
Protein	0.86 %
Fat	2.41 %
Calcium	0.14 %
Iron	0.003 %
Phosphorus	0.07 %
Ascorbic Acid (C)	88.4-111.3 mg

General Information It is believed that this small citrus fruit is native to China and was taken early to the Philippines. Widely grown in India and throughout southern Asia and Malaysia, it is a common ornamental dooryard tree in Hawaii, the Bahamas, and parts of Central America. Dr. David Fairchild introduced the tree into Florida from Panama in 1899, and it quickly became popular in Florida and Texas. The round, orange-red, very aromatic and showy fruits are 1$^{3}/4$ inches wide, and contain only a few seeds.

Culinary Uses Looking like a small mandarin orange, the peeled fruit contains pulp which is orange, very juicy, highly acidic, and usually seedless. Halves or quarters may be served like orange slices, or pressed for the juice, which is primarily valued for making acid beverages, although it is often employed like lime or lemon juice to make salads, desserts, and custard pies. An excellent marmalade is made by using equal quantities calamondins and kumquats or papaya.

Health Benefits Rubbing calamondin juice on insect bites eliminates itching. Slightly diluted and drunk warm, it serves as a laxative. Combined with pepper, calamondin juice is prescribed in Malaya to expel phlegm.

Canistel *(Pouteria campechiana)*

Pouteria *is a native name for the plant, as is* canistel *for the fruit.*

Canistel

Nutritional Value Per 100 g Edible Portion	Raw
Calories	138.8
Protein	1.68 g
Fat	0.13 g
Fiber	0.10 g
Calcium	26.5 mg
Iron	0.92 mg
Phosphorus	37.3 mg
Beta Carotene (A)	0.32 mg
Thiamine (B_1)	0.170 mg
Riboflavin (B_2)	0.010 mg
Niacin (B_3)	3.720 mg
Ascorbic Acid (C)	58.1 mg

General Information Sometimes called egg-fruit, or yellow sapote because of its orange flesh, the canistel occurs wild in parts of southern Mexico, Belize, Guatemala, and El Salvador. The tree was introduced at low and medium elevations in the Philippines before 1924; it reached Hawaii about the same time. During World War II when RAF pilots and crewmen were under training in the Bahamas, they showed great fondness for the canistel and bought all they could find in the Nassau market. The fruit, widely variable in form and size, may be nearly round or somewhat oval, and is often bulged on one side. When unripe the fruit is green-skinned, hard, and gummy internally. Upon ripening, the skin turns lemon-yellow or pale orange-yellow, and is very smooth and glossy.

Culinary Uses The yellow flesh is relatively firm and mealy with a few fine fibers, and toward the center the fruit is softer and more pasty; it has often been likened in texture to the yolk of a hard-boiled egg. Fruits should not be allowed to become too soft and mushy before eating. The flavor is sweet, more or less musky, and somewhat like that of a baked sweet potato. There may be up to four hard, inedible freestone seeds. Some people enjoy the fruit with salt, pepper, and lime or lemon juice, either fresh or lightly baked. The pureed flesh may be used in custards or added to ice cream mix just before freezing. A rich milkshake, or "egg-fruit nog," is made by combining ripe canistel pulp, milk, sugar, vanilla, and nutmeg or other seasonings in an electric blender.

Cape Gooseberry (*Physalis peruviana*)

Also Known As: Poha.

> Physalis *is Greek for bladder, given to this plant because its thin calyx enlarges and encloses the fruit;* peruviana *means of Peruvian origin. The Cape in Cape Gooseberry refers to the Cape of Good Hope, where the plant was grown by early settlers before 1807. It is called "gooseberry": because its taste reminded the settlers of that fruit.*

General Information Although the fruit is thought to be native to Peru and Chile, it has been introduced into many other countries and is now widely cultivated. The plant seems to be successful wherever tomatoes can be grown. The yellow-green or orange fruit is about the size of a cherry. The small fruit enjoyed an early popularity in the Cape Province of South Africa, and when it traveled from there to New South Wales in Australia, where it was one of the few fresh fruits of the early settlers, it became widely known as the Cape Gooseberry. Throughout Australia and New Zealand the plant has become abundantly naturalized. It is surprising that this useful little fruit has received so little attention in the United States.

Cape Gooseberry

Nutritional Value Per 100 g Edible Portion

	Raw
Protein	0.054 g
Fat	0.16 g
Fiber	4.9 g
Calcium	8 mg
Iron	1.23 mg
Phosphorus	55.3 mg
Beta Carotene (A)	1.613 mg
Thiamine (B_1)	0.101 mg
Riboflavin (B_2)	0.032 mg
Niacin (B_3)	1.73 mg
Ascorbic Acid (C)	43 mg

Buying Tips Avoid greenish ones, and choose those that are yellow or orangey. A bit of dinginess on the balloony husks will not hurt the fruit. The fresh fruits can be stored in a sealed container and kept in a dry atmosphere for several months.

Culinary Uses Within the thin waxy skin is a juicy pulp and many small seeds, all with a distinctive flavor and grapelike tang. Cape gooseberries can be eaten raw, used in desserts like strawberries, canned whole, or used to make a good jam when combined with a fruit high in pectin. They add an intriguing flavor, texture, and color to apple pies. The husk is bitter and inedible. Unripe fruits are poisonous.

Capulin (*Prunus salicifolia*)

Also Known As: Wild Cherry, Black Cherry.

> *The large plum family was given the genus* Prunus, *a name derived from the ancient Greek name* proumne. Salicifolia *means having leaves like the willow,* Salix. Capulin *is a colloquial name for the fruit.*

General Information The capulin is a true cherry, and native throughout the Valley of Mexico from Sonora to Chiapas and Veracruz. It has been cultivated since early times and

Capulin

Nutritional Value Per 100 g Edible Portion

	Raw
Protein	0.105-0.185 g
Fat	0.26-0.37 g
Fiber	0.1-0.7 g
Calcium	17.2-25.1 mg
Iron	0.65-0.84 mg
Phosphorus	16.9-24.4 mg
Beta Carotene (A)	0.005-0.162 mg
Thiamine (B_1)	0.016-0.031 mg
Riboflavin (B_2)	0.018-0.028 mg
Niacin (B_3)	0.640-1.140 mg
Ascorbic Acid (C)	22.2-32.8 mg

is an important food in those areas. The aromatic fruit is round, three-eighths to three-quarters of an inch wide, with red or nearly black smooth, tender skin.

Culinary Uses The pale-green juicy pulp has an agreeably acid but slightly astringent flavor. Ripe fruits are eaten raw (minus the single stone), stewed, or made into jam. With skin and seeds removed, they are mixed with milk and served with vanilla and cinnamon as a dessert. They may also be fermented to make an alcoholic beverage.

Carambola (*Averrhoa carambola*)

Also Known As: Star Fruit, Chinese Star Fruit, Belimbing.

The carambola tree was given its Latin name in honor of Averrhoes, a twelfth century Arabic physician and philosopher; carambola *is an Indian name for the fruit, from the Sanskrit* karmara, *meaning food appetizer.*

Carambola

Nutritional Value Per 100 g Edible Portion

	Raw
Calories	35.7
Protein	0.38 g
Fat	0.08 g
Fiber	0.80-0.90 g
Calcium	4.4-6.0 mg
Iron	0.32-1.65 mg
Magnesium	9 mg
Phosphorus	15.5-21.0 mg
Potassium	163 mg
Sodium	2 mg
Zinc	0.110 mg
Copper	0.120 mg
Manganese	0.082 mg
Beta Carotene (A)	0.003-0.552 mg
Thiamine (B_1)	0.030-0.038 mg
Riboflavin (B_2)	0.019-0.030 mg
Niacin (B_3)	0.294-0.380 mg
Ascorbic Acid (C)	26-53 mg

General Information A tree melon that originated in Ceylon and the Moluccas, the carambola is now grown throughout Asia and Florida. The fruit is 2 1/2 to 6 inches long, with a waxy skin that ranges in color from orange-yellow to pale yellow, and has crisp, yellow, juicy flesh when ripe. Hanging on the tree, the fruit resembles yellow Chinese lanterns. There may be up to twelve flat, thin, brown seeds, or none at all. With its five or six prominent ridges, similar to an acorn squash, the fruit when sliced provides perfectly shaped stars that delight the eye and lighten the spirit. Of the two principal sorts of carambola, one is small and acidly sour, while the other is larger with a mild, almost bland, but sweeter flavor. Most tart varieties have very narrow ribs, while the sweet yellow varieties have thick, fleshy ones. The two white varieties marketed commercially are sweet.

Buying Tips Look for full, firm fruits from two to five inches long, with juicy-looking ribs. If green-ribbed fruit is purchased, be sure to let it fully ripen until it has a full floral-fruity aroma and the skin has turned yellow. Avoid those with brown, shriveled ribs.

Culinary Uses The carambola when green is very astringent like green gooseberries or sorrel, but when ripe is pleasantly acid-sweet and refreshing. The Chinese and Hindus eat the carambola when green as a vegetable, and when ripe as a fruit. Fully ripened sweet carambolas have a flavor that combines the flowery best of plums, McIntosh apples, pineapple, and Concord grapes with a citric edge. When sour, the flesh is

brightly sharp, as clean as a lemon, but less harsh and more fruity. Use fresh carambola as you would melons. Eat it plain, use it in salads, as a garnish on avocado or seafood, or float it in punch bowls. For the winter solstice, Christmas, Hanukkah, or New Year's Eve, a golden star on anything makes a festive and glamorous garnish. The fruits are also cooked into puddings, tarts, stews, and curries. Dried star fruit is available in some natural food stores.

Health Benefits In India, ripe fruits are administered to halt hemorrhages and to relieve bleeding hemorrhoids. A conserve of the fruit is said to allay biliousness and diarrhea, and to relieve hangovers from excessive alcohol consumption.

Carissa and Karanda *(Carissa macrocarpa, C. grandiflora, C. congesta)*

Also Known As: Natal Plum.

> Carissa *is an aboriginal name for the fruit.* Macrocarpa *means bearing large fruits or seed pods;* congesta *means congested or brought together. The fruit received its alternate name of Natal Plum because it was from the Natal Province of South Africa.*

General Information Two closely related fruits, the carissa is indigenous to the coastal region of Natal, South Africa, and the karanda to India, Burma, and Malacca. First introduced into the United States in 1886 by the horticulturist Theodore L. Meade, the carissa was introduced into Hawaii in 1905 and extensively distributed throughout the islands over the next few years. The fruit looks like a small scarlet plum with dark red seams. About $2\frac{1}{2}$ inches long and up to $1\frac{1}{2}$ inches wide, the fruit is green and rich in latex when unripe. As it ripens, the tender, smooth skin turns to a bright magenta red coated with a thin, whitish bloom, and finally dark-crimson. The flesh is soft and juicy, strawberry-red, flecked with white, and contains about a dozen thin brown seeds. The karanda was widely cultivated in India, and the fruit was popular with British residents because it reminded them of the gooseberry. Planted in the Philippines, the tree first fruited in 1915, and was described by P.J. Wester as "one of the best small fruits introduced into the Philippines within recent years." It has been cultivated in a limited manner in Florida and California. The small one-half inch to one-inch fruits turn dark-purple or nearly black when ripe.

Carissa and Karanda

Nutritional Value Per 100 g Edible Portion

	Raw Carissa	Raw Karanda
Calories	62	338-342/lb
Protein	0.50 g	0.39-0.66 %
Fat	1.30 g	2.57-4.63 %
Fiber	0.90 g	0.62-1.81 %
Calcium	11 mg	n/a
Iron	1.31 mg	n/a
Magnesium	16 mg	n/a
Phosphorus	7 mg	n/a
Potassium	260 mg	n/a
Sodium	3 mg	n/a
Copper	0.210 mg	n/a
Beta Carotene (A)	40 IU	n/a
Thiamine (B_1)	0.040 mg	n/a
Riboflavin (B_2)	0.060 mg	n/a
Niacin (B_3)	0.200 mg	n/a
Ascorbic Acid (C)	38 mg	9-11 mg

Culinary Uses The carissa must be fully ripe, dark red and slightly soft to the touch to be eaten raw. It can be eaten out of hand, without peeling or removing the seeds; the texture is slightly granular, the flavor mildly sharp and strawberry-flavored. Halved or quartered and seeded it is suitable for fruit salads, adding to gelatins, and as a topping for cakes, puddings, and ice cream. Ripe fruits make a filling for pies. In the semi-ripe stage the fruits are used for making jellies and jams. Ripe karandas have very acid to fairly sweet, juicy, red or pink pulp, which exudes flecks of latex. There may be two to eight small brown seeds. The sweeter types of karanda may be eaten raw out of hand, but the more acid ones are best stewed with plenty of sugar. Even so, the skin may be found to be tough and slightly bitter. The cooked syrup has been successfully utilized on a small scale by at least one soda-fountain operator in Florida. In Asia, the ripe fruits are utilized in curries, tarts, puddings, and chutneys. Green, sour fruits are turned into pickles.

Health Benefits Unripe fruits are used medicinally as an astringent, while ripe fruits are taken as an antiscorbutic and remedy for biliousness. The fruits have also been employed as agents in tanning and dyeing.

Cashew Apple (*Anacardium occidentale*)

The genus name Anacardium *means heart-shaped;* occidentale *means Western. The English word* cashew *is derived from the Brazilian Tupi-Indian word* acaju.

Cashew Apple

Nutritional Value Per 100 g Edible Portion

	Raw
Protein	0.101-0.162 g
Fat	0.05-0.50 g
Fiber	0.4-1.0 g
Calcium	0.9-5.4 mg
Iron	0.19-0.71 mg
Phosphorus	6.1-21.4 mg
Beta Carotene (A)	0.030-0.742 mg
Thiamine (B_1)	0.023-0.030 mg
Riboflavin (B_2)	0.130-0.400 mg
Niacin (B_3)	0.130-0.539 mg
Ascorbic Acid (C)	146.6-372.0 mg

General Information The tropical evergreen cashew shrub, whose relatives include the mango and pistachio, is native to northeast Brazil. In the sixteenth century, Portuguese traders introduced the tree into Mozambique and coastal India, but only as a soil retainer to stop coastal erosion. The cashew flourished, and soon extensive forests were formed in these locations and on nearby islands. The true fruit of the tree is the cashew nut, which resembles a miniature boxing glove. The nut hangs like an appendage from the base of the pseudofruit, the penduncle (stalk), which fills out, becoming fleshy and pear-shaped with yellow or red skin. An interesting feature is that the nut develops before the cashew "apple" or peduncle. In some countries, the apple has been highly utilized and the nut simply thrown away. Since the cashew apple spoils within twenty-four hours of harvest, it is almost never exported, and the fortunate few who have tried this fruit, either ripe or in preserves, say it is even tastier than the cashew nut.

Culinary Uses The fruit has pulp that is spongy, fibrous, very juicy, astringent, and acid to subacid. Locally, the fruits are chewed for their refreshing juice and the fibrous residue is discarded. The apples are also preserved in syrup on a small commercial scale.

Health Benefits Fresh cashew apple juice, without removal of tannin, is prescribed as a remedy for sore throat and chronic dysentery in Cuba and Brazil; fresh or distilled, the juice is a potent diuretic and said to possess sudorific properties.

Cassabanana *(Sicana odorifera)*

Also Known As: Sikana, Musk Cucumber.

Sicana *is a Peruvian name for the plant.* Odorifera *means fragrant or scented.*

General Information This fruit is probably native to Brazil, where the plant is grown as an ornamental vine. It was first mentioned by European writers in 1658 as cultivated and popular in Peru. People like to keep the fruit around the house, and especially in linen and clothes-closets, because of its long-lasting fragrance and the belief that it repels moths. It is also placed on church altars during Holy Week. Trial plantings in the United States have generally failed. Renowned for its strong, sweet, agreeable, melon-like odor, the striking fruit is ellipsoid or nearly cylindrical, 12 to 24 inches long, 3 to 5 inches wide, with an orange-red to dark purple or jet-black hard shell.

Cassabanana

Nutritional Value Per 100 g Edible Portion (without peel, seeds, central pulp)

	Raw
Protein	0.145 g
Fat	0.02 g
Fiber	1.1 g
Calcium	21.1 mg
Iron	0.33 mg
Phosphorus	24.5 mg
Beta Carotene (A)	0.11 mg
Thiamine (B_1)	0.058 mg
Riboflavin (B_2)	0.035 mg
Niacin (B_3)	0.767 mg
Ascorbic Acid (C)	13.9 mg

Culinary Uses The juicy orange or yellow flesh is firm, cantaloupe-like in texture, and highly aromatic. In the central cavity there is softer pulp, a soft, fleshy core, and numerous rows of flat, oval seeds. Unripe fruits can be used in soups and stews as a vegetable. Ripe ones are refreshing if eaten raw, but more often end up as jam.

Health Benefits In Puerto Rico, the flesh is cut up and steeped in water with added sugar, usually left overnight at room temperature so that it will slightly ferment. The resultant liquor is sipped frequently, and strips of the flesh are eaten to relieve sore throat.

Cherimoya *(Annona cherimola)*

Also Known As: Sherbet Fruit, Custard Fruit.

Annona *means year's harvest, suggested by the Haitian name* anon, *which is applied to one of the species. The English name* cherimoya *comes from* chirimuya, *a Quichuan word (from Incan Peru) meaning cold seeds, presumably an allusion to the wet freshness of the fruit and the large seeds.*

Cherimoya

Nutritional Value Per 100 g Edible Portion

	Raw
Calories	94
Protein	1.3-1.9 g
Fat	0.1-0.4 g
Fiber	2.0-2.2 g
Calcium	21.7-32.0 mg
Iron	0.5-0.8 mg
Phosphorus	30-40 mg
Beta Carotene (A)	10 IU
Thiamine (B_1)	0.100-0.117 mg
Riboflavin (B_2)	0.110-0.140 mg
Niacin (B_3)	0.900-1.300 mg
Ascorbic Acid (C)	5-16 mg

General Information Cherimoya trees began their history in the uplands of Colombia, Bolivia, and Ecuador as a wild tree taken into cultivation by the Incas. The nineteenth-century German naturalist and traveler Friedrich W.K. Humboldt, who left his scientific imprint throughout South America and Mexico, declared that this delicious fruit was well worth the hazardous trip across the Atlantic. Generally heart-shaped and ranging in size from a large apple to a small cantaloupe, cherimoyas look rather like leathery fat green pine cones or light green armadillos, as their skins are patterned with shingles or scales.

Buying Tips Select cherimoyas of any size with smooth and slightly yellow-green skin and that are firm or with a little give if you want to eat it within a day or so. Avoid fruits that are dark or splotched with many dark areas, as they may have been subjected to cold in transit and will not ripen properly. Handle them gently, as the skins are not as tough as they appear to be.

Culinary Uses When ripe, the fruit will give to pressure all around like a papaya or plum; do not cut until it is uniformly quite soft. The sweet, low-acid flesh is silky smooth and juicy, white or cream-colored, with a slight granular finish like a custard of fine pears. The ambrosial flavor is very sweet and fruity, touching on mango, pineapple, strawberry, papaya, or vanilla custard in varying proportions. Scattered at random throughout are quite a few watermelon-like black seeds, which are inedible. The easiest way to eat a cherimoya is to cut it in half lengthwise and take a spoon to it, daintily spitting out the seeds as you go, or else it can be peeled and either diced or pureed with other fruits to make drinks and sherbets.

Cherry, Acerola *(Malphigia punicifolia)*

Also Known As: Barbados Cherry, West Indian Cherry.

The botanical name Malphigia *was given in honor of Marcello Malpighi (1694), an Italian anatomist.* Punicifolia *means having leaves of reddish purple. The English word* cherry *can be traced back to the Assyrian* karsu *and Greek* kerasos. *The term* acerola *was adopted by the sixteenth-century colonizers of Puerto Rico, who thought the fruit resembled the fruit of a well-known but not closely related tree, the acerolo.*

Cherry, Acerola

Nutritional Value Per 100 g Edible Portion

	Raw Fruit	Raw Juice
Calories	32	21
Protein	0.40 g	0.40 g
Fat	0.30 g	0.30 g
Fiber	0.40 g	0.30 g
Calcium	12 mg	10 mg
Iron	0.20 mg	0.50 mg
Magnesium	18 mg	12 mg
Phosphorus	11 mg	9 mg
Potassium	146 mg	97 mg
Sodium	7 mg	3 mg
Beta Carotene (A)	767 IU	509 IU
Thiamine (B_1)	0.020 mg	0.020 mg
Riboflavin (B_2)	0.060 mg	0.060 mg
Niacin (B_3)	0.400 mg	0.400 mg
Pantothenic Acid (B_5)	0.309 mg	0.205 mg
Pyridoxine (B_6)	0.009 mg	0.004 mg
Ascorbic Acid (C)	1,677.60 mg	1,600.00 mg

General Information Acerola cherries are native to the Lesser Antilles and South America. Although they resemble the common American cherry, they are not botanically related. The fruits are borne singly or in twos or threes, and are oblate to round in shape but more or less obviously three-lobed. Each one-half to one-inch bright-red fruit contains orange-colored, very juicy but rather acidic pulp and three small seeds. In 1945 there was enormous interest in the acerola cherry due to its high ascorbic acid content, and numerous groves were planted. It was soon realized that synthetic sources of ascorbic acid were much cheaper to produce, and the acerola cherry could not compete economically.

Culinary Uses Unless fully ripe, the acerola cherry is very acidic, but when mature has a pleasant flavor. The flesh is juicy and moderately acid, more like a raspberry than a cherry in flavor. When cooked, it tastes like a tart apple. In its native West Indies, the fruit is eaten fresh or made into pies and preserves. The seeds are inedible.

Health Benefits This cherry is higher than any other known food source in natural vitamin

C, and as such is frequently combined with other high ascorbic acid foods, such as rose hips, in vitamin C pills and liquid drops.

Cherry, Common (*Prunus avium, P. cerasus*)

> Prunus *derives from the ancient Greek name* proumne*, their name for the plum tree family, of which the cherry is a member.* Avium *means of or for the birds, due to the birds' delight in this fruit; the term* cerasus *is from a region in Pontus (northeast Asia Minor). The English word* cherry *can be traced back to the Assyrian* karsu *and Greek* kerasos.

General Information The cherry tree is native to the temperate climates of eastern Europe and western Asia, where it has been cultivated since at least 600 B.C. Although cherries were being grown in Italy already by this time, the Roman general and gourmet Lucullus probably introduced a more popular variety around 69 B.C. and thus his name has become synonymous with the arrival of the fruit into Italy from Cerasus. The Egyptians, Greeks, and Romans all cherished and cultivated this tree, both for its beautiful blossoms and its fruit. In America, cherries were present early enough to have developed distinct species by the time the first colonists arrived; the colonists, however, brought the European variety with them. The European cherry was one of the plants that crossed the ocean to America soon after Columbus' discovery, increasing the already large number of Euro-Asiatic plants that arrived here during that period. The fruits, soft and small with thin skins surrounding juicy flesh and a large seed (pit), are borne on long, thin stems.

Buying Tips Select firm cherries that are bright, glossy, and plump, with fresh green stems, as dry brittle stems are a sign of over-ripeness and age. Avoid those that are soft, leaking, or too dark in color.

Culinary Uses Cherries when tree-ripened are sweet, lush, juicy, and incomparably superb. There are two basic varieties of cherries: sweet and sour. Sweet cherries (both red and yellow) should be plump and hard rather than soft to the touch, with the deepest

Cherry, Common

Nutritional Value Per 100 g Edible Portion

	Raw Sweet	Raw Sour	Maraschino w/liquid
Calories	72	50	116
Protein	1.20 g	1.0 g	0.20 g
Fat	0.96 g	0.30 g	0.20 g
Fiber	0.40 g	0.20 g	0.30 g
Calcium	15 mg	16 mg	n/a
Iron	0.39 mg	0.32 mg	n/a
Magnesium	11 mg	9 mg	n/a
Phosphorus	19 mg	15 mg	n/a
Potassium	224 mg	173 mg	n/a
Sodium	0 mg	3 mg	n/a
Zinc	0.060 mg	0.100 mg	n/a
Copper	0.095 mg	0.104 mg	n/a
Manganese	0.092 mg	0.112 mg	n/a
Beta Carotene (A)	214 IU	1,283 IU	n/a
Thiamine (B_1)	0.050 mg	0.030 mg	n/a
Riboflavin (B_2)	0.060 mg	0.040 mg	n/a
Niacin (B_3)	0.400 mg	0.400 mg	n/a
Pantothenic Acid (B_5)	0.127 mg	0.143 mg	n/a
Pyridoxine (B_6)	0.036 mg	0.044 mg	n/a
Folic Acid (B_9)	4.2 mcg	7.5 mcg	n/a
Ascorbic Acid (C)	7 mg	10 mg	n/a
Tocopherol (E)	n/a	0.130 mg	n/a

Lore and Legend

There is a Japanese story about a warrior who had for many of his youthful years played at Iyo beneath the branches of a cherry tree. Upon attaining a great age, and outliving all his family and friends, the only object that linked him to his past was his beloved cherry tree. One summer the tree died; this the old warrior took for a sign and was not consoled when a young sapling was planted nearby. During that winter, he spoke to the dead tree and pleaded with it to bear blossoms just once more. If it did, he promised, he would give up his life. Having given his promise, he spread a white sheet upon the ground and committed hara-kiri. As his blood soaked into the roots of the tree and his spirit into its sap, the dead tree burst into bloom; every year on his death day, though the ground is hard and all other trees lie dormant for the winter, this tree at Iyo blossoms.

colored ones being the sweetest. Highly perishable, they must be stored in the refrigerator until eaten (which usually does not take very long!). Sweet cherries can be eaten fresh or cooked. They also freeze and can well. As for pitting fresh cherries, find the method which suits you and watch out for the juice, which stains. Europeans often leave the pits in pastries as part of the sport (and to add more flavor), a practice Americans are unaccustomed to and generally dislike. Dried sweet cherries are becoming widely available, but are still comparatively expensive. Sour cherries can be made into excellent jams and jellies, canned, frozen, dried, or used to make wine. Of fresh fruits, commercial cherries and grapes often contain the most toxic chemical residues; favor organic cherries whenever possible, and wash the commercial ones well. Black cherry juice is wonderful for flavoring teas so that sugar can be avoided. Wine brings out the rich flavor of cherries, and many liqueurs are made from them.

Health Benefits Detoxifying, laxative, stimulant. Cherries are a good "spring cleaner" to stimulate and cleanse the digestive system, the darker ones being all the more valuable to the system as they contain a greater quantity of magnesium, iron, and silicon. A well-known remedy for gout, arthritis, and rheumatism, part of their action in rheumatic disorders occurs from their ability to eliminate excess body acids. Their potent anti-phlogistic and anti-putrid properties make them an excellent adjunct in combating the harmful effects of animal protein, and their high iron content makes them beneficial for the liver, blood, and gallbladder. One teaspoonful of concentrated cherry juice in a glass of water taken several times a day brings miraculous results in stopping constant urination, and can also help relieve painful urinary infections.

Varieties

Sweet cherries are generally dark and heart-shaped, with a sweet, rich flavor. The more popular varieties are Bing, Lambert, Chapman, Tartarian, and Royal Ann (Napoleon). The heaviest demand is for the Bing (named after Ah Bing, a Chinese gardener in the United States): it is an extra large, deep maroon to black fruit that is firm, highly flavored, and stands up well for shipping. The Royal Ann is the leading light-colored cherry, being light amber to yellow with a red blush, and having a delightful fresh flavor. The majority of each season's Royal Ann crop are dyed and bottled as maraschino cherries.

Sour or Pie cherries are smaller in size and lighter colored than sweet cherries. Since only a few types are actually sweet enough to eat from the tree, most sour cherries are marketed frozen or canned for sauce and pie filling rather than fresh. If and when you find them in the market, they will be as soft and juicy as dead-ripe plums. It is impossible to find them unbruised, so don't bother to try. Almost every familiar dessert that calls for cherries would do better with sour ones; many of these recipes were invented for the sour cherry. Their soft skins and pulp become creamy tender when subjected to heat, and the flavor blooms, delightfully fresh and acid. The only change in the recipe might be the need for additional sugar. Less common types of sour cherries are: **Choke-cherries**, a small, red, very tart cherry often eaten by birds before any fruit can be harvested for human consumption; **Sand cherries**, small, dark red fruits growing wild in the Rocky Mountains; **Ground cherries**, related to tomatoes, these grow on short, sprawling plants; and the **Black cherry**, a wild native American tree that yields small, edible cherries that can be used in pies.

Cherry, Cornelian (*Cornus mas*)

Cornus *is derived from the Latin word for horn, alluding to the hardness of the wood;* mas *means masculine or bold, referring to young trees, which produce only male flowers (they produce both male and female flowers plus fruit as they mature). The English name* cornelian *refers to the similarity of the fruit's coloring to that of the cornelian (or carnelian) quartz, which has a waxy luster and a deep reddish color.*

Lore and Legend

The famous and unsolvable Gordian knot was believed to have been formed from a thong of the Cornelian cherry's leathery bark. (Alexander the Great, acquainted with the problem, drew his sword and severed the knot, then went on to fulfill the prophecy that whoever could unfasten it would conquer the world.) In an old Turkish legend, it seems that when the Devil first saw the Cornelian cherry tree (called *kizilcik* in Turkish) covered with blossoms when no other fruit showed even a bud, he smiled to himself and said: "Aha! This tree will produce fruit first of all. I must be first there to secure it." So he made preparations, gathered up his basket, and took up his position under the tree. He waited and waited patiently, yet all the other fruit trees came into bloom and formed fruit, but still the *kizilcik* was not ready and ripe for eating. To his great surprise and chagrin he discovered that this was one of the very last fruits to ripen at the end of summer. Ever since then the Turks have called the tree "*Seytan alditan agaci*"—the tree that deceived Satan.

General Information The Cornelian cherry is native to regions of eastern Europe and western Asia. Botanically, the tree is a species of dogwood, unrelated to the common cherry. It was well known to the ancient Greeks and Romans, and references to the plant abound in their literature. The plant was grown in monastery gardens of Europe through the Middle Ages, and introduced to Britain in about the sixteenth century. By the eighteenth century, the plant was common in English gardens, where it was grown for its fruits, which were sometimes called cornel plums; the fruit was even familiar enough to be found in European markets up to the end of the nineteenth century. Over most of Europe and North America today, the cornelian cherry is admired solely as an ornamental plant, but the bright fruits do not go completely unnoticed. The fruits are generally oval in shape and sometimes as large as a small plum. They are fire-engine red, with a single, elongated stone and a flavor, akin to a tart cherry, which develops sweetness and aroma with full ripeness.

Culinary Uses This cherry has a tart flavor and some varieties can be slightly bitter. Western Europeans rarely ate this fruit out of hand (it was more bitter than current varieties), but made it into a thickened, sweet syrup and highly esteemed tarts. The juice also added a bright flavor to cider and perry (pear cider). Unripe fruits were pickled as a substitute for olives. In the Ukraine, cornelian cherries are a frequent ingredient in bottled soft drinks, conserves, wines, and liqueurs.

Health Benefits In folk medicine, the fruit is used to combat gout, anemia, skin diseases, painful joints, and disrupted metabolism. Fruit, leaves, or bark have been employed for gastrointestinal disorders and tuberculosis. Russian scientists have reported that the fruit contains components that leach radio-activity from the body. Sugar content ranges from 4 to 12 percent, and the acidity ranges from 1 to 4 percent. The vitamin C concentration commonly averages twice that of oranges.

Cherry, Jamaican *(Muntingia calabura)*

Cherry, Jamaican	
Nutritional Value Per 100 g Edible Portion	
	Raw
Protein	0.324 g
Fat	1.56 g
Fiber	4.6 g
Calcium	124.6 mg
Iron	1.18 mg
Phosphorus	84.0 mg
Beta Carotene (A)	0.019 mg
Thiamine (B_1)	0.065 mg
Riboflavin (B_2)	0.037 mg
Niacin (B_3)	0.554 mg
Ascorbic Acid (C)	80.5 mg

General Information Indigenous to southern Mexico, Central America, tropical South America, the Greater Antilles, St. Vincent and Trinidad, the Jamaican cherry tree is an abundant producer. The trees have a reputation for thriving with no care in poor soils, and grow wild on denuded mountainsides and on cliffs. They are presently being evaluated for reforestation in the Philippines where other trees have failed to grow, and also for wildlife sanctuaries since birds and bats are partial to the fruits. The fruits are round, with red or sometimes yellow smooth, thin, tender skins and light brown, soft, juicy pulp.

Culinary Uses The flesh has a very sweet, musky, somewhat fig-like flavor, and is filled with exceedingly minute yellowish seeds too fine to be noticed in eating. Usually eaten out of hand, it is also often cooked into tarts or made into jam.

Health Benefits The flowers are said to possess antiseptic properties. An infusion of the flowers is valued as an antispasmodic, and is taken to relieve headaches and the first symptoms of a cold.

Cherry, Nanking *(Prunus tomentosa)*

Also Known As: Downy Cherry, Mongolian Cherry, Manchu Cherry.

> Prunus *derives from the ancient Greek name* proumne*, their name for the plum tree family, of which the cherry is a member.* Tomentosa *means thickly matted with hairs. The alternate name of* downy cherry *derives from the downy hair that covers the plant in summer—the leaves, the new shoots, and even the fruits.*

General Information The Nanking cherry is native to central Asia, but has become naturalized from Japan and Korea west across China and Russia to Turkestan and the Himalayas. Generally grown in cold, semi-arid regions, the plant is the most common garden fruit plant in the Russian Far East. A beautifully colored spreading shrub or small tree, it is usually wider than its nine- to fifteen-foot height. Late spring brings the fruits, borne in profusion and ornamental in their own right. The plant was introduced into North America in 1882, and met with great enthusiasm. By the late twentieth century, however, enthusiasm has died down and the plant is relatively anonymous. The cherries ripen in early summer. Ripe fruits are generally brilliant red, although there are also pink and white varieties, and are about a half inch in diameter.

Culinary Uses These cherries have a sprightly, true cherry flavor (including the single pit), and a meaty texture. Due to their softness, they are rarely seen in commercial quantities. The best way to enjoy these gems is to stroll out into the garden and pop the ripe fruits straight into your mouth. Or, perhaps pick a few to use for a dessert. These cherries make a refreshing summer drink or, for those who wish to preserve them, beautiful, clear jelly.

Cherry, Surinam *(Eugenia uniflora)*

Also Known As: Brazilian Cherry, Cayenne Cherry, Pitanga.

The Eugenia *genus was named in honor of Prince Eugene of Savoy.* Uniflora *means one-flowered. The English name* Surinam cherry *is due to the fact that it is native to Surinam and the fruit is cherry-sized.*

Cherry, Surinam	
Nutritional Value Per 100 g Edible Portion	
	Raw
Calories	43-51
Protein	0.84-1.01 g
Fat	0.40-0.88 g
Fiber	0.34-0.60 g
Calcium	9 mg
Iron	0.2 mg
Phosphorus	11 mg
Beta Carotene (A)	1,200-2,000 IU
Thiamine (B_1)	0.030 mg
Riboflavin (B_2)	0.040 mg
Niacin (B_3)	0.030 mg
Ascorbic Acid (C)	20-30 mg

General Information The Surinam cherry is native from Surinam, Guyana, and French Guiana to southern Brazil and Uruguay. It was first described botanically from a plant growing in a garden in Pisa, Italy; it was believed to have been introduced from Goa, India. Portuguese voyagers are said to have carried the seed from Brazil to India, as they did the cashew. It was long ago planted on the Mediterranean coast of Africa and the European Riviera. The first Surinam cherry was introduced into coastal Israel in 1922 and aroused considerable interest because it produced fruit in May when other fruits are scarce. In Florida, the tree is one of the most common hedge plants throughout the central and southern parts of the state and the Florida Keys, but the fruits are mostly eaten by children. There are two distinct types: one bears the common bright-red fruit, while the other bears the rarer dark-crimson to nearly black fruit, which tends to be sweeter and less resinous. Each fruit is from 3/4 to 1 1/2 inches wide, oblate with seven or eight ribs. When mature, they are bright red to deep scarlet or dark, purplish maroon.

Culinary Uses Surinam cherries have thin skins and orange-red flesh that is melting and very juicy, acid to sweet, with a touch of resin and slight bitterness. There may be one fairly large, round seed or perhaps two or three smaller seeds, which are extremely resinous and inedible. Children enjoy the ripe fruit out of hand. For table use, they are best slit vertically along one side, then spread open to release the seed(s), and kept chilled for two or three hours to dispel most of their resinous character. If seeded and sprinkled with sugar before being refrigerated, they will become very mild and sweet, and exude a quantity of juice. These then can be served instead of strawberries on shortcake and topped with whipped cream. Surinam cherries are an excellent addition to fruit cups, salads, and custard puddings; they also add a delicious flavor to ice cream and sauces.

Chupa-Chupa	
Nutritional Value Per 100 g Edible Portion	
	Raw
Protein	0.129 g
Fat	0.10 g
Fiber	0.5 g
Calcium	18.4 mg
Iron	0.44 mg
Phosphorus	28.5 mg
Beta Carotene (A)	1.056 mg
Thiamine (B_1)	0.031 mg
Riboflavin (B_2)	0.023 mg
Niacin (B_3)	0.330 mg
Ascorbic Acid (C)	9.7 mg

Chupa-Chupa *(Quararibea cordata)*

Cordata *means heart-shaped or cordate.* Chupa-Chupa *is the colloquial name in Colombia and Peru, and descriptive of the manner in which the flesh is chewed from the large seeds.*

General Information The chupa-chupa tree grows wild in lowland rainforests of Peru, Ecuador, and adjacent areas of Brazil, especially around the mouth of the Javari River. The fruit is round, ovoid, or elliptic, with a prominent, rounded knob at the apex, and is capped with a leathery calyx at the base. About 5 inches long, and weighing up to 28 ounces, the fruit has a rind that is thick, leathery, greenish-brown, and downy.

Culinary Uses The flesh is orange-yellow, soft, juicy, sweet, and of agreeable flavor, tasting something like a cross between an apricot and mango. There are usually two to five seeds, and long fibers extend throughout the flesh, making it difficult to eat. Most commonly eaten out of hand, only those with the least fibrous flesh may be suitably utilized for juice or other processing.

Citron *(Citrus medica)*

Moses had specified the cedar cone, kadar *(*kedron *in Greek), to be used during the Feast of Tabernacles. When it fell into disfavor, the cedar cone was replaced by the citron, the Palestine Greeks calling the latter* kedromelon *(cedar apple).* Kedros *was Latinized as* cedrus*, and this evolved into* citrus *and subsequently into* citron*. The Latin term* medica *means coming from Media (a name for Persia); it also means healing.*

General Information The citron's place of origin is unknown but seeds have been found in Mesopotamian excavations dating back to 4000 B.C. It was long used in India as a medicine and fragrance, and the armies of Alexander the Great, upon their return from India to Macedonia, brought stories and seeds of the citron back to Europe in 325 B.C. Soon afterward the Greek writer Theophrastus commented that "the Median or Persian apple is not eaten, but is very fragrant," and added that it would protect clothes against moths. The Jews cultivated the citron intensely, with only the best fruits and used during the Feast of Tabernacles. A Jewish coin struck in 136 B.C. bore a representation of the citron on one side. In A.D. 300, a Chinese writer documented the gift of "40 Chinese bushels of citrons from Ta-ch'in" in A.D. 284, Ta-ch'in being understood to mean the Roman Empire, where the citron was a staple commercial food item.

Culinary Uses The citron looks like a huge, rough lemon, with most of its bulk being its thick dense skin. The flesh inside is dryish, either sour or sweet, with a weak lemon flavor. The peel, which has a unique resinous fragrance, is the most useful part. It is cut into small pieces, preserved in brine or sea water, then cooked, and finally candied. It may be crystallized to be eaten for its own sake, like other candied fruits, or the firm pulp may be used to make jellies or preserves. Candied fruit is used in fruit cakes and plum pudding. The peel may also be pressed to obtain an oil which is quite fragrant and which is used in the manufacture of medicines, liqueurs, and perfumes.

Lore and Legend

In modern Orthodox Jewish ritual, a special type of citron (in Hebrew, *etrog*) is used during the Feast of the Tabernacles as a symbol of God's bounty. It is ungrafted, nonedible, and must have its calyx intact. The original command for the Jewish practice is given in the Bible in the Book of Leviticus, composed at a time when the Jews could not yet have known the citron. Scholars believe that the cedar cone was meant, and that the Jews substituted the citron later because they were unhappy about the use of the cedar cone in rituals of other religions. The citron came to represent wealth in India, perhaps because of its splendid size. Thus the God of wealth, Kuvera, is always represented as holding a citron in one hand and a mongoose spewing jewels in the other. After the plant reached China in the fourth century A.D., a freak form (variant *sarcodactyla*) developed in which the fruit separated into five lobes like the fingers of a hand. This type, called Buddha's hand, was considered a symbol of happiness. For this reason and because of its especially fine scent, it was placed on household altars.

Health Benefits In ancient times and during the Middle Ages, the citron was employed as a remedy for seasickness, pulmonary troubles, intestinal ailments, and other disorders. Citron juice with wine was considered an effective purgative to rid the system of poison. The candied peel is sold in China as a stomachic, stimulant, expectorant, and tonic.

Citron

Nutritional Value Per 100 g Edible Portion

	Raw	Candied
Calories	n/a	314
Protein	0.081 g	0.20 g
Fat	0.04 g	0.30 g
Fiber	1.1 g	1.4 g
Calcium	36.5 mg	83 mg
Iron	0.55 mg	0.80 mg
Phosphorus	16.0 mg	24 mg
Potassium	n/a	120 mg
Sodium	n/a	290 mg
Beta Carotene (A)	0.009 mg	n/a
Thiamine (B_1)	0.052 mg	n/a
Riboflavin (B_2)	0.029 mg	n/a
Niacin (B_3)	0.125 mg	n/a
Ascorbic Acid (C)	368 mg	n/a

Cocona (*Solanum sessiliflorum*)

Solanum *comes from the Latin* solamen, *meaning solace or quieting.* Sessiliflorum *means with stalkless flowers.*

General Information The spineless cocona is apparently unknown in the wild, having been observed by botanists only in cultivation from Peru and Colombia to Venezuela and Brazil. In 1760 a Spanish surveyor, Apolinar Diez de la Fuente, found the cocona with maize and beans in an Indian garden between Guaharibos Falls and the juncture of the Casiquiare and Orinoco rivers. Borne singly or in compact clusters, the fruit may be round, oblong or conical. The thin, tough skin is coated with a slightly prickly, peach-like fuzz until the fruit is fully ripe, then it is smooth, golden to orange-yellow, red, or deep purple. Within is a one-quarter to three-eighths-inch layer of cream-colored firm flesh enclosing the yellow, jelly-like central pulp.

Cocona

Nutritional Value Per 100 g Edible Portion

	Raw
Protein	0.6 g
Fiber	0.4 g
Calcium	12 mg
Iron	0.6 mg
Phosphorus	14 mg
Beta Carotene (A)	140 mcg
Thiamine (B_1)	25 mcg
Niacin (B_3)	500 mcg

Culinary Uses The cut-open fruit has a faint, tomato-like aroma. The flesh has a mild flavor faintly suggestive of tomato, while the pulp has a pleasant, lime-like acidity. Abundant throughout the central pulp are thin cream-colored seeds which are edible. The ripe fruit is peeled and eaten out of hand, used in salads, or cooked with fish and meat stews. Sweetened, it is used to make sauce and pie filling. It is often processed as a nectar or juice, which when sweetened with sugar, is a popular cold beverage.

Cranberry *(Vaccinium oxycoccos, V. macrocarpon)*

Vaccinium *is the ancient Latin name for plants of the blueberry family, derived from* vacca, *meaning cow, and given because cows like the plant.* Oxycoccos *refers to its sharp leaves;* macrocarpon *means that it bears large fruits or seed pods. The English name* cranberry *is a shortened form of the earlier craneberry, given because the plant's blossoms grow downward and look like the head and neck of a crane; cranes also like to eat cranberries, which often grow in sandy peat bogs, one of their favorite habitats.*

General Information The cranberry is a small evergreen shrub related to the blueberry. The plants, with their slender creeping vines, are native to open bogs and swampy marshes from Alaska to Tennessee, preferring poor acidic soil. The oblong or nearly round berries are green at first, but turn red in September or October. When well protected by snow, they often will remain on the vine all winter. The American Indians, who paid homage to the cranberry in their legends, taught the settlers to make pemmican, a dried buffalo, venison, or bear meat preserve, pounded with animal fat and berries, that they took on hunting trips as a high-energy convenience food. The benzoic acid in the berry acted as a preservative and kept the mixture from turning rancid.

Buying Tips Look for firm, bright colored and plump cranberries. Avoid those that are soft, crushed, shriveled, or soft and sticky. In early days berries were selected by being rolled down a short flight of stairs. Good ones bounced like little rubber balls, soft ones stayed on the steps. Today's grading machines work on the same principle, with each berry being given seven chances to bounce over 4-inch high barriers as it passes along a conveyor belt. If the fruit does not pass the high-jump test it is discarded.

Cranberry
Nutritional Value Per 100 g Edible Portion

	Raw	Canned, Sweetened Sauce	Bottled, Sweetened Juice
Calories	49	146	65
Protein	0.39 g	0.10 g	0.10 g
Fat	0.20 g	0.20 g	0.10 g
Fiber	1.20 g	0.20 g	trace
Calcium	7 mg	6 mg	5 mg
Iron	0.20 mg	0.20 mg	0.30 mg
Magnesium	5 mg	n/a	3 mg
Phosphorus	9 mg	4 mg	3 mg
Potassium	71 mg	30 mg	10 mg
Sodium	1 mg	1 mg	1mg
Zinc	0.130 mg	n/a	0.020 mg
Copper	0.058 mg	n/a	0.013 mg
Manganese	0.157 mg	n/a	0.157 mg
Beta Carotene (A)	46 IU	20 IU	4 IU
Thiamine (B_1)	0.030 mg	0.010 mg	0.010 mg
Riboflavin (B_2)	0.020 mg	0.010 mg	0.010 mg
Niacin (B_3)	0.100 mg	trace	0.039 mg
Pantothenic Acid (B_5)	0.219 mg	n/a	0.067 mg
Pyridoxine (B_6)	0.065 mg	n/a	n/a
Folic Acid (B_9)	1.7 mcg	n/a	0.4 mcg
Ascorbic Acid (C)	13.5 mg	2.0 mg	2-40 mg

Culinary Uses Due to their very tart taste, few people eat cranberries in their fresh raw state. Cranberries are excellent used in cranberry nut bread, and pair well with nuts, wild rice, and whole grains. Compatible with other fall fruits such as apples and pears, its red color can magically enhance an otherwise mundane dish. Cranberries are generally made into sauces and jellies with a great deal of sugar syrup, at which point they are highly acidic and distinctly harmful to the body and best used either sparingly or avoided altogether. Dried cranberries can be used like raisins. Cranberry juice is always sweetened and diluted with water to make it palatable.

Health Benefits Cranberries are excellent curative and preventive therapy for the entire breathing apparatus as they contain one of nature's most potent vasodilators, which open up congested bronchial tubes. They also contain large amounts of benzoic acid, a natural preservative, which accounts for the Native American practice of adding the dried fruits to pemmican (a dried, preserved meat product). Long touted for their powers against bacterial infections and viruses of the bladder, kidneys, and urinary tract, cranberries are very high in tannic and oxalic acids, which create a distinctly acidic reaction within the body. Recent studies have shown that components in cranberry juice reduce the ability of *E. coli* bacteria to adhere to the lining of the bladder and urethra, thus greatly reducing the likelihood of infection.

Lore and Legend

It is believed that the Pilgrims learned how to prepare cranberries from the Indians. The berries kept so long without decay and were prized so highly by the colonists that ten barrels of them were shipped across the ocean as a gift to King Charles II, a long journey in slow-moving sailing vessels. The Pilgrims supposedly dined on cranberry dishes at the first Thanksgiving celebration in 1621, but cranberry sauce did not become a national tradition until after the Civil War, when General Ulysses S. Grant considered cranberry sauce such an essential part of Thanksgiving that he ordered it served to Union troops during the siege of Petersburg in 1864.

Currant *(Ribes rubrum, R. nigrum, R. americanum, R. odoratum)*

Currant

Nutritional Value Per 100 g Edible Portion

	Raw Black	Raw Red/White
Calories	63	56
Protein	1.40 g	1.40 g
Fat	0.41 g	0.20 g
Fiber	2.40 g	3.40 g
Calcium	55 mg	33 mg
Iron	1.54 mg	1.00 mg
Magnesium	24 mg	13 mg
Phosphorus	59 mg	44 mg
Potassium	322 mg	275 mg
Sodium	2 mg	1 mg
Zinc	0.270 mg	0.230 mg
Copper	0.086 mg	0.107 mg
Manganese	0.256 mg	0.186 mg
Beta Carotene (A)	230 IU	120 IU
Thiamine (B_1)	0.050 mg	0.040 mg
Riboflavin (B_2)	0.050 mg	0.050 mg
Niacin (B_3)	0.300 mg	0.100 mg
Pantothenic Acid (B_5)	0.398 mg	0.064 mg
Pyridoxine (B_6)	0.066 mg	0.070 mg
Ascorbic Acid (C)	181 mg	41 mg
Tocopherol (E)	1.0 mg	0.10 mg

Ribes *is believed to be derived from* ribas, *the Arabic name for Rheum Ribes; it is thought by some to be the Latinized form of* riebs, *which is an old German word for currant. The term* rubrum *signifies the red berries, while* nigrum *specifies the black variety;* americanum *means native to America, while* odoratum *means fragrantly scented. The English word* currant *is said to be derived from the resemblance of the fruit to the Corinth grapes or raisins.*

General Information Currants are a type of berry that should not be confused with the dried Zante currant, a small raisin made from dried Corinth grapes. Popular in northern European countries such as Great Britain, Germany, Scandinavia, and Russia, the currant has never caught on in southerly regions. The **European black currant** (*R. nigrum*) is a cold-climate plant native to northern Europe and north and central Asia. It is closer to the gooseberry than to the red currant, with fruit that is neither as sweet nor as flavorful as the red currant. Fruits are borne in strings, or chains, each fruit averaging three-eighths of an inch in diameter. **Red currants** (*R. rubrum*) are native to northeastern Europe as far as the Arctic Sea, and the steppes of northern Asia as far as Siberia and eastern Manchuria. The plant produces small, red, semi-transparent berries with a pleasantly sour taste. The white currant is botanically a red currant that has lost its pigmentation and some of its acidity. The **American black currant** (*R. americanum*) is native from New Mexico to Virginia, and north into Canada. Fruits, leaves, and shoots have the same pungent aroma as the European currant. The **Clove currant** (*R. odoratum*) is native to the American

Midwest as far north as Minnesota and as far south as Texas. Every spring, when the plant flowers, the profusion of red-tinged yellow trumpets puts on quite a show, and the whole plant has a heavy fragrance of clove and vanilla. The fruits are borne singly or in small clusters, and range in size from one-quarter to three-quarters of an inch in diameter. Usually the fruits are smooth, shiny, and blue-black, though some plants bear yellow or orange fruits.

Buying Tips Currants should be quite firm and translucent, with a deep rich color for the most flavor and a good acid balance.

Culinary Uses Red currants, when sufficiently dosed with sugar, can be eaten fresh, but their principal use has been in jellies, preserves, sauces, Scandinavian fruit soups, and desserts. Try substituting them in recipes for raspberries or cranberries and adjusting the sweetener as deemed necessary. White currants show up well when they are combined with more colorful fruits, and are usually less acidic than the red. The black currant lacks the brilliant flavor of the red current, especially when the fruit is raw. A few of them make a welcome addition to mixed fruit salads. The flavor of clove currants is intense, somewhat resinous, but fruity. In Finland, peasants make a currant-strawberry drink to carry them through the long dark winter. In England, the berry is essential to summer pudding, usually made with raspberries that also ripen in midsummer.

Health Benefits Fresh currant berries or their juice promote the appetite and can also be taken for an upset stomach. Long recommended for colds and as a laxative, when the berries are eaten whole the indigestible seeds provide bulk to help regulate activity of the bowels. Currant juice has a cleansing antiseptic effect on the system, helping to purify the blood and counteract anemia, and is beneficial for kidney and nervous system problems. When cooked with sugar, the berries tend to lose much of their beneficial medicinal value and become acid-forming.

Custard Apple

Nutritional Value Per 100 g Edible Portion

	Raw
Calories	80-101
Protein	1.17-2.47 g
Fat	0.5-0.6 g
Fiber	0.9-6.6 g
Calcium	17.6-27.0 mg
Iron	0.42-1.14 mg
Magnesium	18 mg
Phosphorus	14.7-32.1 mg
Potassium	382 mg
Sodium	4 mg
Beta Carotene (A)	0.007-0.018 mg
Thiamine (B_1)	0.075-0.119 mg
Riboflavin (B_2)	0.086-0.175 mg
Niacin (B_3)	0.528-1.190 mg
Pantothenic Acid (B_5)	0.135 mg
Pyridoxine (B_6)	0.221 mg
Ascorbic Acid (C)	15.0-44.4 mg

Custard Apple *(Annona reticulata)*

Also Known As: Bullock's Heart.

Annona *means year's harvest, suggested by the Haitian name* anon, *which is applied to one of the species.* Reticulata *means reticulated or netted. The English name* Custard Apple *is due to its custard-like texture and apple shape. The coloration of the fruit (reddish or brownish on the sunny side, dull yellow on the other) and its shape show enough resemblance to the heart of a bullock or other large mammal to justify the West Indian name of* Bullock's Heart.

General Information This tree is believed native to the West Indies, and thrives in coastal and lowland regions. Generally rated as the mediocre variety or "ugly duckling" of the genus, the tree is not especially attractive, has ill-smelling leaves, and flowers that never fully open. The heart-shaped or lopsided fruit varies from three to six inches in diameter and may weigh over two pounds. The skin, which is yellow or brownish when ripe with a blush, may be either faintly or distinctly "netted."

Culinary Uses The flesh of the custard apple is yellowish-white and has the typical custard-like granular texture of the Annona family, along with its many inedible seeds and a fibrous, central, pointed core that extends more than halfway through the fruit. Although the flavor is sweet and agreeable, it lacks the distinct character of the cherimoya, sugar apple, or atemoya. Most often it is used as a dessert fruit, or pureed, strained, and added to confections such as ice cream and milk shakes. The yellow-skinned varieties usually are superior to the brownish ones, with thicker and juicier flesh.

Health Benefits The unripe fruit is rich in tannin; dried and pulverized, it is employed against diarrhea and dysentery. The seeds, leaves, and young fruits are insecticidal. The leaves have been employed in tanning and yield a blue or black dye. Crushed leaves or a paste of the flesh may be poulticed on boils, abscesses, and ulcers. The seeds are so hard that they may be swallowed whole with no ill effects, but the kernels if chewed are very toxic.

Date (*Phoenix dactylifera*)

Theophrastus gave the name Phoenix *to the date palm, perhaps thinking of Phoenicia, where it was first encountered by the Greeks, or perhaps thinking of the fabled phoenix of Egypt. For like the mythological phoenix that rises from the ashes, the date tree has its feet in water and its head in the fires of heaven (oases or irrigation providing the former, desert sun the latter). The term* dactylifera *means finger-bearing, in reference to the dates, which hang fingerlike from the trees. The English word* date *derives (with a few convolutions) from the Greek* dactylos, *meaning finger.*

Date

Nutritional Value Per 100 g Edible Portion

	Fresh	Dried
Calories	142	274-293
Protein	0.9-2.6 g	1.7-3.9 g
Fat	0.6-1.5 g	0.1-1.2 g
Fiber	2.6-4.5 g	2.0-8.5 g
Calcium	34 mg	59-103 mg
Iron	6 mg	3.0-13.7 mg
Magnesium	n/a	35 mg
Phosphorus	350 mg	63-105 mg
Potassium	520 mg	648 mg
Sodium	n/a	3 mg
Zinc	n/a	0.290 mg
Copper	n/a	0.288 mg
Manganese	n/a	0.298 mg
Beta Carotene (A)	20-259 IU	50 IU
Thiamine (B_1)	0.070 mg	0.030-0.090 mg
Riboflavin (B_2)	0.080 mg	0.100-0.160 mg
Niacin (B_3)	4.4-6.9 mg	1.4-2.2 mg
Pantothenic Acid (B_5)	n/a	0.780 mg
Pyridoxine (B_6)	n/a	0.192 mg
Folic Acid (B_9)	n/a l	2.6 mcg
Ascorbic Acid (C)	30 mg	0 mg

General Information Date palms are believed to have originated in the Persian Gulf region and in ancient times were especially abundant between the Nile and Euphrates rivers. Nomads carried dates as sustenance on their travels and planted great quantities of pits at desert oases. In the Sahara Desert every oasis is a beautiful garden of date palms. As far back as 50,000 B.C. the date palm flourished on favorable lands, and developing man must have always found it valuable; even now it is said to have a different use for every day of the year, and many more besides. The stems and leaves are used for building huts, while the fibers of the leaves are used to manufacture baskets, ropes, hats, mats, and many other everyday objects. The wood of the tree is fairly combustible, and in some areas is the only wood product available to make fires. The palm itself made other contributions to the diet, the crown being tapped for its sugary sap, which could be fermented to make palm toddy. During the useful life of the tree the tapping was done with moderation, but when it had passed its peak a good deal more was drawn off, and ultimately, the tree was drained completely. Extremely long-lived, the palm produces a new section of leaves each and every year, often growing to one hundred feet in height; after one hundred years or so it is usually so tall that it falls over. Date palms start bearing in their fourth year and have their greatest production

Lore and Legend

The Arabs believe that, when creating the world, Allah formed the date palm not from common clay but out of material left over from the making of Adam. One of the most ancient symbolic forms of the Tree of Life in the subtropical desert regions of the Near East, the date palm is almost worshiped by the local nomadic inhabitants, for whom the tree is a symbol of fertility, and because its fruit is the main food supply for both man and beast. Among the Egyptians it is the symbolic Tree of the Year, because it produces one new set of branches every year. The palm leaf was the sacred emblem of Judea after the Exodus from Egypt, but the Roman legions in 53 B.C. took over the leaf as the emblem of their triumph and victory over Judea, and as a symbol of their plunder and destruction of Jerusalem. The Christians in 29 A.D. believed the palm leaf was symbolic of the triumphant entry of Christ into Jerusalem, when his path was strewn with palm leaves in defiance of the Roman rulers. The leaves of the palm are still used today as religious symbols by Christians on Palm Sunday and by Jews on Passover.

when they are about eighty years of age, producing on average one hundred pounds of fruit annually. The large bunches of fruit weigh over twenty pounds and contain as many as one thousand dates. So productive are these trees that dates are among the cheapest of staple foods (and often the only abundantly available food) for many African and Middle Eastern populations. During the eighteenth century Franciscan and Jesuit missionaries introduced the date palm into California, where it now thrives. The California date industry began only in the twentieth century, in 1902 according to some authorities, but now California produces over 99 percent of all dates sold in the United States.

Buying Tips Fresh, undried dates should be plump with shiny skins. Most varieties have smooth skins, but the large Medjools are usually wrinkled, sometimes with a thin white film of invert sugar on the surface that is quite normal. Excessive shriveling, a dry flaky appearance, or a fermented aroma indicates dates that are old or have been improperly stored. Soft dates should be refrigerated or frozen; dried dates store indefinitely at room temperature.

Culinary Uses Referred to as "candy that grows on trees," dates are sweet and chewy fruits that are delicious when eaten fresh. Most packaged dates, especially domestic ones, are dried and pasteurized to prevent molding, and corn syrup is often added to keep them from further drying out. Fresh dates keep extremely well under refrigeration for long periods of time, so there is no need to buy the poorer quality commercial dried fruits. Before using, slit them open and remove the stone. Dates also freeze well and so may be kept for an extended period. Dry or fresh dates can be eaten out of hand, may be seeded and stuffed, or can be added to many dishes such as fruit salads, cereals, puddings, and baked goods, often substituting for raisins or currants. Pitted dates, stuffed with either nuts or nut butters and rolled in coconut, are a delight to adult and child alike. Chopped dates on cereal make a wonderfully healthy sweetener, while crystallized dates (date sugar) can be used to replace other sweeteners in baked goods with excellent results. Date sugar is made solely from pitted, dehydrated, and pulverized dates. It is not technically considered a sugar but a food, since the whole fruit is used. This sweetener contains about 65 percent fructose and sucrose. Date sugar tastes sweet and mildly date-flavored, and has the same sweetening power as white sugar. When used in baked goods, its only drawback is that the granules do not dissolve when added to liquids.

Health Benefits In early medicine, dates were one of the four fruits renowned for curing throat and chest ailments (the other three were the fig, raisin, and jujube). Because of their tannin content, dates have been used medicinally as an astringent for intestinal troubles. Dates are heat-producing due to their high natural sugar content, and give energy to people who engage in physical exercise and hard work. This natural sugar is much better for a person than highly refined white sugar. The fiber or cellulose of the date is very soft and will not irritate a sensitive bowel or stomach, but does have a slight constipating tendency.

Varieties

DATES ARE CLASSIFIED AS SOFT, SEMIDRY, OR DRY/HARD, depending upon the softness of the ripe fruit. The soft or semidry varieties contain a considerable amount of moisture, and are more perishable than dry dates unless dried by either natural or artificial means. Dry dates, also called hard or camel dates, are not dates that have been deliberately dehydrated, but which simply contain relatively little moisture when ripe. Dry and fibrous even when fresh, they become extremely hard and sweet when further dried, and will keep for years; these are the staple food dates of the Arab world, particularly for nomads. Another classification is according to the kind of sugar contained in the ripe fruit. Invert-sugar dates contain dextrose and glucose; cane-sugar dates contain mostly cane sugar (sucrose). Most of the soft varieties are invert-sugar dates, while drier varieties are generally cane-sugar dates.

Barhi dates are a very soft, very sweet fruit when fully ripe. Traditionally eaten in the Middle East and Indian subcontinent at a stage when they are immature, starchy, rather astringent, and low in sugar, those of us in the West prefer them riper and sweeter. They are nearly cylindrical, with thick and richly flavored light amber to dark-brown flesh.

Deglet Noor dates are native to Algeria, where the name means "fingers of light." This variety is the leading commercial variety in the United States, constituting 85 percent of all date production. The fruits are medium to large in size, oblong, coral red ripening to amber, and curing to a deep rich brown. Very sweet and soft, they have a chewy caramel flavor, with the highest sugar content of any date. **Bread dates** are Deglet Noors that have been dried to a lower moisture content and are hard, dry, and chewy but not sticky.

Halawi dates are light amber in color, and look much like smaller versions of Deglet Noors. This date of Iraqi origin and name (meaning "sweet") is drier and chewier than the Medjool, with more of a distinctly sweet brown sugar taste.

Khadrawi dates are early ripening, dark-skinned, soft, sticky, chewy dates that contain invert sugar. Khadrawis can crystallize or become sugary, but this will not affect the eating quality. Important in Saudi Arabia and Iraq (where the name means "green"), the khadrawi is the cultivar most favored by Arabs, but is too dark in color to be popular on the American market.

Medjool dates are the most commonly available fresh date. Sweet, soft, and meaty, medjools are known for their remarkable size, often growing four to five times larger than the Deglet Noor, and larger than a prune. They are the main Moroccan variety.

Zahidi dates are the oldest known cultivar of dates. They are not quite as sweet as other dates and are generally smaller in size. Zahidis are cylindrical, light golden-brown, and semi-dry but harvested and sold in three stages: soft, medium-hard, and hard. Very popular for culinary purposes, they keep well for months.

Duku and Langsat *(Lansium domesticum)*

The genus name Lansium *derives from the Malayan name* lansa *or* lanseh. Domesticum *means domesticated.*

General Information Native to West Malaysia, these trees take about fifteen years to reach maturity, but the long wait is worthwhile since they then bear clusters of fruit twice a year. Langsats are typically the wild variety and dukus are slightly more domesticated, although both are widely cultivated. In the Philippines the tree is being utilized in reforestation of hilly areas. Langsat trees produce about twenty fruits in a cluster, each oval and just under one and one-half inches long, with a thin, pale fawn skin. Dukus have only about ten fruits to a cluster. They are round and larger than the langsat, about two inches in diameter, with thicker skins.

Lore and Legend

According to Philippine folklore, the fruits used to be so sour as to be quite inedible, and indeed were even toxic. But it happened one day that a beautiful woman with a child, traveling through the countryside, could find nothing else to eat but *lanzones* (their Philippine name). She accordingly picked one and gave it to the child. From then on the fruit acquired its present desirable characteristics, for the woman was none other than the Virgin Mary. However, the transformation that she wrought was not complete, since some lanzones still turn out to be very sour.

Langsat

Nutritional Value Per 100 g Edible Portion	Raw
Protein	0.8 g
Fiber	2.3 g
Calcium	20 mg
Phosphorus	30 mg
Beta Carotene (A)	13 IU
Thiamine (B_1)	89 mcg
Riboflavin (B_2)	124 mcg
Ascorbic Acid (C)	1 mg

Culinary Uses The flesh of both fruits is usually white (in some cultivated varieties of duku it is pink), juicy and refreshing, with a taste ranging from sour to sweet. Each fruit is composed of five segments, some of which may contain bitter, inedible seeds. They can be eaten raw (once the inedible peel is removed) or preserved with sugar, and the seedless ones bottled in syrup.

Health Benefits The dried peel is burned in Java, the aromatic smoke serving as a mosquito repellant and incense. An arrow poison has been made from the fruit peel and the tree bark, both of which possess a toxic property, lansium acid, which upon injection arrests heartbeat in frogs.

Durian *(Durio zibethinus)*

Duri *is the Malay word for spike, and the tree takes both its botanical and common name from the hard, spiky shell of the fruit.* Zibethinus *means foul-smelling, or smelling like a civet cat.*

General Information The durian is one of the longest-established inhabitants of the rain forests of southeast Asia, especially Borneo and other islands of the Malay Archipelago. A full-grown fruit may be anywhere from grapefruit to volleyball-sized, round or ovoid, weigh five pounds or more, and is covered with stout, sharply pointed spines. When ripe, it ranges

Lore and Legend

From southeast Asia to the Philippines everyone knows the durian, and whether it is loved or not, this most controversial of tropical fruits is always talked about. The fruit is widely believed to be an aphrodisiac in Malaya, Thailand, Indonesia, and the Philippines. An old Malay saying has it that "when the durians fall, the sarongs rise." The fruit is so well regarded by oriental lovers that the ownership of just one tree can make a man as well-off as if he owned a small business. It's a rough life, though, for owners often have to sleep under their trees to guard them. In the late 1920s, Durian Fruit Products of New York City launched a product named "Dur-India" as a "health-food accessory." The bottles sold for $9 a dozen, about a three-month supply. The tablets reputedly contained durian and a species of *Allium* from India, as well as a considerable amount of vitamin E; the company claimed the supplement provided "more concentrated healthful energy in food form than any other product the world affords," to keep the body vigorous and tireless, the mind alert with faculties undimmed, and the spirit youthful. The product never sold well and soon disappeared.

in color from brown to a dull yellow. Death by durian is not uncommon, since the tree may grow as high as one hundred feet, and the fruit is not fully ripe until it drops to the ground. It is wise to take care when walking near such trees during the durian season, keeping an eye out not only above but below as well, since the fruit has a strange appeal for tigers. The best of the many varieties is said to be grown in Thailand, and the Thai government has plans to can and export the fruit. There is a cultivar that has no smell, but almost all durians have a distinctive odor. The subject of striking comparisons, the smell has been compared to the civet cat, sewage, stale vomit, or (more mildly) onions and overripe cheese. Even Indonesians acknowledge that prolonged exposure to the smell may have negative effects, and the carriage of durians on public transport is forbidden. The fruits must be eaten shortly after harvest because they quickly turn rancid and sour.

Culinary Uses Most people find that while the smell of durian repels them, they are no longer aware of it once they start eating; it somehow combines with non-smelly but tasty substances to produce a characteristic rich, aromatic flavor. Alfred Russel Wallace, a widely traveled British naturalist, described the smell this way in 1872:

> A rich custard highly flavored with almonds gives the best idea of it, but there are occasional wafts of flavour that call to mind cream cheese, onion-sauce, sherry wine and other incongruous dishes. Then there is a rich glutinous smoothness in the pulp which nothing else possesses, but which adds to its delicacy. It is neither acid, nor sweet, nor juicy; yet it wants none of these qualities, for it is in itself perfect. It produces no nausea or other bad effect, and the more you eat of it the less you feel inclined to stop. (*The Treasury of Botany*, Vol. I, p. 435)

To eat the fruit, the common procedure is to split open the shell, which reveals five cells enveloped in a firm, cream-colored, sticky pulp, each containing up to four large chestnut-sized seeds. Well-chilled durian has a better flavor than room temperature. Durian is sometimes cooked and made into a sausage-shaped cake that retains some of its proper flavor but very little smell. The flesh has been canned in syrup for export, as well as dried for local use and export. Blocks of durian paste are frequently sold in native markets. Javanese prepare the flesh as a sauce to be served with rice; they also combine the minced flesh with minced onion, salt, and diluted vinegar as a kind of relish. The large seeds can be roasted like chestnuts and are said to taste like them.

Health Benefits Durian flesh is believed to serve as a vermifuge. Eating the fruit is alleged to restore the health of ailing humans and animals, as well as acting as an aphrodisiac.

Durian

Nutritional Value Per 100 g Edible Portion

	Raw
Calories	144
Protein	2.5-2.8 g
Fat	3.1-3.9 g
Fiber	1.7 g
Calcium	7.6-9.0 mg
Iron	0.73-1.0 mg
Phosphorus	37.8-44.0 mg
Beta Carotene (A)	20-30 IU
Thiamine (B_1)	0.240-0.352 mg
Riboflavin (B_2)	0.200 mg
Niacin (B_3)	0.683-0.700 mg
Ascorbic Acid (C)	23.9-25.0 mg
Tocopherol (E)	"High"

Elderberry *(Sambucus nigra, S. canadensis, S. mexicana)*

Elderberry

Nutritional Value Per 100 g Edible Portion	Raw
Calories	73
Protein	0.66 g
Fat	0.50 g
Fiber	7.00 g
Calcium	38 mg
Iron	1.60 mg
Phosphorus	39 mg
Potassium	280 mg
Beta Carotene (A)	600 IU
Thiamine (B_1)	0.070 mg
Riboflavin (B_2)	0.060 mg
Niacin (B_3)	0.500 mg
Pantothenic Acid (B_5)	0.140 mg
Pyridoxine (B_6)	0.230 mg
Ascorbic Acid (C)	36 mg

The genus Sambucus *is named after the* sambuca, *an ancient reed-like musical instrument.* Nigra *means black;* canadensis *means from Canada;* mexicana *means Mexican. The English word* elder *is from the Anglo-Saxon* aeld *meaning fire, due to the ancient practice of removing the pith from young branches to use as blowing tubes to kindle fires. These tubes were also made into shepherds' pipes, and thus another common name for the elder is the Pipe Tree.*

General Information Elderberry bushes are found almost everywhere in Europe, western Asia, and North America, wherever there is low damp ground. The trees bear white flower clusters and abundant deep purple or nearly black berries, both of which are edible when cooked. There are also red and blue-berried elder bushes, but the red variety are generally considered poisonous. Familiar to children of all ages, the straight-growing tough branches, from which the pith may be easily extracted, have been used through the years as simple pea-shooters, whistles, and as blow-pipes for kindling fires. An ancient musical instrument, the sambuca, which is trombone-like in tone, was fashioned from many such reed-like sticks. Elder wood once served to make shoemakers' pegs, butchers' skewers, and as needles for weaving nets.

Culinary Uses When raw, elderberries contain small amounts of a poisonous alkaloid, and have a sickly smell and taste. Cooking destroys the alkaloid and transforms the taste. In cooking, elderberries are often added to other fruits, especially apples. They yield an excellent wine and, combined with crab apples, produce a pretty jelly. The dried berries are used to make a fruity, flavorful tea much sought after by herb tea aficionados. Elderflowers are sometimes mixed with batter and baked into cakes, or used to flavor cooked fruit and jam by stirring the panful with a spray of flowers until the flavor is judged strong enough. Elderberry cordial, an unfermented and non-alcoholic concentrate, makes a delicious summer drink and can also be used as a topping for ice cream.

Health Benefits Elderberry tea is an old folk remedy for such conditions as colds, coughs, and influenza. A heavy syrup from the berry juice used as a hot drink was a remedy for coughs, and cold sufferers comforted themselves with hot toddies of mulled elderberry wine. Elderberry juice can relieve spasms of the face (known as tic douloureux or trigeminal neuralgia) and instigate cures of sciatica; adding 20 percent port wine speeds the healing. Elderflower water has been used to keep skin soft, wrinkles and freckles at bay, and to alleviate weariness. In recent years, science has discovered that elderberries contain viburnic acid, a substance that induces perspiration, and which is useful in cases of bronchitis and similar ailments. The flowers contain a glucoside, eldrin, which is identical to rutin.

Lore and Legend

Some claim that the elder is surrounded by a healing "aura." Ancient trees were believed to have a mysterious and supernatural history; carrying an elder twig close to the flesh was said to be a priceless charm for good luck and good health. Spirits were believed to reside in the shrub, and thus some people refused to cut it down or burn it. Legend also relates that the cross Christ was crucified upon was made of elder wood, and thus the bush cannot be struck by lightning.

Emblic *(Phyllanthus emblica)*

Also Known As: Malacca Tree.

The botanical name Phyllanthus *means leaf-flower, referring to the curious manner in which flowers grow along the edges of the leaf-like branches.*

Emblic

Nutritional Value Per 100 g Edible Portion

	Raw
Protein	0.07 g
Fat	0.2 g
Fiber	1.9 g
Calcium	12.5 mg
Iron	0.48 mg
Phosphorus	26.0 mg
Beta Carotene (A)	0.01 mg
Thiamine (B_1)	0.030 mg
Riboflavin (B_2)	0.050 mg
Niacin (B_3)	0.180 mg
Ascorbic Acid (C)	625-1561 mg

General Information Prized for its fruit in tropical Asia, the emblic tree is native to tropical southeastern Asia. It is regarded as sacred by Hindus, whose religion prescribes that the fruits be included in the diet for forty days after a fast, in order to restore vitality. It is a common practice in Indian homes to cook the fruits whole with sugar and saffron and to give one or two to a child every morning. In 1945 the fruits aroused enthusiasm when analyses found that they contained a rich natural source of vitamin C. However, interest quickly switched to the Acerola cherry, which was found to be as rich or richer in the vitamin than the emblic. The fruit is slightly ridged, round, hard to the touch, and almost stemless. Light green when underripe, they ripen to a whitish or dull yellowish-green, occasionally red.

Culinary Uses The skin of the emblic is thin and translucent, the flesh crisp and juicy but extremely acidic and astringent. Tightly embedded in the center of the flesh is a stone containing six small seeds. The fruit can be stewed with sugar, made into jams and relishes, baked into tarts, candied, added to other foods as seasoning during cooking, or the juice used to flavor vinegar.

Health Benefits Antiscorbutic, diuretic, laxative. Because of their high vitamin C content, emblic powder, tablets and candies were issued to Indian troops during WW II as part of daily rations. Of great importance in Asiatic medicine, the emblic is used in the treatment of a great number of ailments, especially those associated with the digestive organs. For most uses, the fruit juice is fermented or prepared in the form of a sherbet.

Feijoa *(Feijoa sellowiana)*

Also Known As: Pineapple Guava.

The feijoa is named after a botanist and former director of the National History Museum in San Sebastian, Spain, Senor Don da Silva Feijo; the sellowiana was given in honor of Herr F. Sellow, a German explorer who collected plant specimens in the province of Rio Grande do Sul in southern Brazil.

General Information The small evergreen feijoa tree with its gray-green leaves is native to extreme southern Brazil, northern Argentina, western Paraguay, and Uruguay. It can be grown in many warm temperate zones of the world, and was probably brought to southern Europe by the Spaniards. This fragrant tropical fruit has a slightly bumpy thin skin, with the color ranging from lime-green to olive. Resembling a fuzzless kiwi fruit, the egg-shaped, egg-sized green fruit is commercially grown today in New Zealand and California.

Feijoa

Nutritional Value Per 100 g Edible Portion	Raw
Calories	49
Protein	1.24 g
Fat	0.78 g
Calcium	4-17mg
Iron	0.05-0.08 mg
Magnesium	8-9 mg
Phosphorus	10-20 mg
Potassium	155-166 mg
Sodium	3-5 mg
Zinc	0.040 mg
Copper	0.055 mg
Manganese	0.085 mg
Beta Carotene (A)	0 IU
Thiamine (B_1)	0.008 mg
Riboflavin (B_2)	0.032 mg
Niacin (B_3)	0.289 mg
Pantothenic Acid (B_5)	0.228 mg
Pyridoxine (B_6)	0.050 mg
Folic Acid (B_9)	38 mcg
Ascorbic Acid (C)	28-35 mg

Buying Tips Select a feijoa with a full aroma, as immature feijoas can be quite bitter. If they are not as tender as a firmish plum or soft pear, leave to ripen for a few days until they are. Fully ripened fruit should have a pronounced bouquet of floral fruitiness.

Culinary Uses The thin green skin of the feijoa encloses a cream-to-tan, granular, medium soft flesh surrounding a jellyish central cavity filled with tiny edible seeds. The scent and taste is tart and perfumy, suggestive of pineapple, quince, spruce, and Concord grapes, with a dash of lemon and menthol; all this with a texture gritty like a dense Bosc pear. A slightly underripe fruit is not unpleasant, but it does not have the full, rich flavor that develops with maturity. To prepare the fruit, peel and serve in the desired manner. When served raw, feijoas are usually cut in half like miniature melons, with the flesh spooned out of the shell. Or the fruits can be peeled and sliced as an exotic addition to a fruit salad or compote. Feijoas may be used in any preparation calling for apples, but be aware that their distinctive flavor may dominate more subtly flavored dishes.

Health Benefits The fruit is rich in water-soluble iodine compounds. The percentage varies with locality and from year to year but the usual range is 1.65 to 3.90 milligrams per kilogram of fresh fruit.

Fig (*Ficus carica*)

The term Ficus *is the old Roman name for this fruit. Of the many different varieties, the best was considered to be that flourishing in Caria in Asia Minor, hence the modern botanical classification* Ficus carica. *The English name* fig *derives from the Latin* ficus.

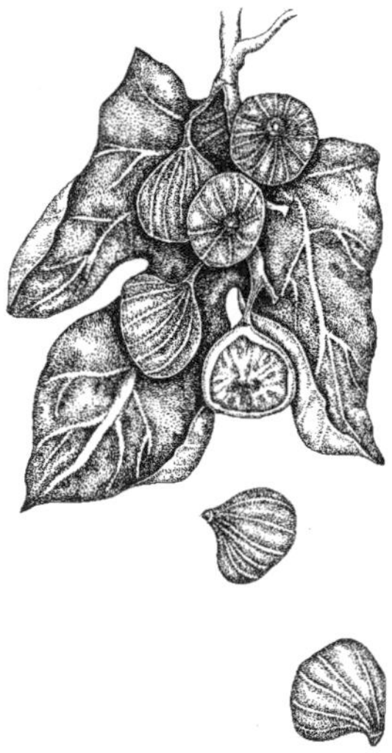

General Information The fig is a native of western Asia and can be found over a vast uninterrupted area stretching from eastern Iran through the Mediterranean countries to the Canary Isles, and is now grown in southwestern areas of the United States. The genus *Ficus* is unique in that no flowers ever form on the trees; instead, it bears its flowers inside a nearly closed receptacle that ripens into the fleshy, pear-shaped fruit, of which only the female fruits are edible. With over 750 species in the *Ficus* genus, there are figs which ripen underground, while others grow high in the air on plants dangling from other trees. Some figs are parasites that strangle and kill their hosts; others grow on low trailing shrubs in the desert or on tall trees in tropical forests. There are large figs and small figs, round figs and ovoid figs, spring figs, summer figs, and winter figs, and figs colored black, brown, red, purple, violet, green, yellow-green, yellow, and white.

The cultivation of figs goes back to the very earliest times. Drawings of figs dating back several centuries before Christ were found in the Gizeh pyramid, fig trees were grown in King Nebuchadnezzar's famous Hanging Gardens of Babylon, and are mentioned frequently throughout the Bible and even in Homer's Odyssey. While it may not have had the eight hundred uses of the date palm (although its leaves were a more convenient size and shape for the specialized requirements of the Garden of Eden), the fig sometimes fruited well where the date did not, most notably in Greece, where it found a place in the diet of rich and poor alike. The Greeks are said to have received the fig from Caria in Asia Minor, and they in turn introduced the plant to neighboring countries, although at one point in Greek history figs were in such high demand that their exportation was forbidden by law. In the mid-eighteenth century, the Spanish fathers introduced this fruit to California and planted figs at the first Catholic mission in San Diego, California. This black Mission fig is still an important variety in that state, which grows nearly 100 percent of the entire United States fig crop.

Lore and Legend

The fig tree is revered nearly everywhere as the Tree of Life and Knowledge, from Central Africa — where the natives believe their ancestral spirits live in fig trees — to the Far East — where Siddha Gautama found wisdom and divine illumination under the Bo tree (*Ficus religiosa*) and became the Buddha. The most revered fig tree in the world grows in the ruined city of Anuradhapura (now in Ceylon), said to have come from a cutting of the very Bo tree under which the Buddha sat, meditating his way to perfect knowledge. It was sent to Ceylon in 288 B.C., a present from the Indian emperor Asoka. Even the Moslems held the fig tree sacred, calling it the Tree of Heaven, as it was considered to be the most intelligent of all trees. Early Greek and Roman mythology claimed that the sacred fig was a gift to the people from the Greek god of wine and agriculture, Dionysus, and his Roman counterpart, Bacchus. When Cato the Elder advocated to the Roman Senate the conquest of Carthage, he used as his crowning argument the advantage of acquiring fruits as glorious as North African figs, specimens of which he pulled from his toga as exhibits. The fig's reputation spread far beyond the lands in which they grew. In the third century B.C., Bindusara, king of the Maurya dominions in India, wrote to Greece asking for some grape syrup, some figs and a philosopher. Grape syrup and figs, he was told with cool courtesy, would be sent to him with pleasure, but it was "against the law in Greece to trade in philosophers."

In Egypt, baskets of figs were included among the tomb furnishings of dynastic times, but they were not always there for gastronomic enjoyment. The Egyptians as a people were preoccupied by their digestion, believing that more illnesses had their source in the alimentary canal than any other bodily place, and they bombarded that system with every remedy in their less than prepossessing pharmacopoeia. The fig, with its mild laxative properties, must have qualified as that rare substance, a food that not only tasted good, but was beneficial. It was undoubtedly more palatable than the senna and castor oil that, then as now, were the main alternatives.

Buying Tips Ripe figs vary in color from greenish-yellow to purple, depending on the variety. Fresh fruits should be plump and teardrop shaped, evenly colored, and yield under gentle pressure; occasionally they are slightly wrinkled or cracked. Softness, moistness, and oozing nectar all indicate perfect ripeness, but figs are highly perishable at this stage and will not last long, even in the refrigerator. Avoid any that smell sour. Unripe figs, which exude a milky liquid from the stem, should be left at room temperature to mature.

Culinary Uses Cultivated for centuries as one of the most prized and nutritious of fruits, figs are highly cherished for their rich, sweet, alluring taste, which is nearly addictive (they have one of the highest sugar contents of cultivated fruits). Ripe figs are delicious; peeled or unpeeled, the fruits may be merely eaten on their own, cooked into pies, puddings, cakes, bread or other bakery products, or added to ice cream mixes. Hard, unripe figs are best stewed, then used in cakes, jams, or pickles, but lack the robust flavor of those that are fully ripe. Dried figs can be substituted in recipes that call for apricots, dates, or other dried fruits, and are especially good in baked goods; also try adding chopped dried figs to baked sweet potatoes or winter squash for a delicious new sensation. Over 85 percent of the fig crop is dried for market. Fig Newtons, that ubiquitous fig cookie, were first advertised in 1892 and named after the town of Newton in Massachusetts.

Health Benefits Laxative, restorative. The medicinal use of figs is almost as ancient as the plant itself, and the fruit has been used to treat nearly every known disease. Pliny, the Roman naturalist (A.D. 23/24–79), wrote: "Figs are restorative, and the best food that can be taken by those who are brought low by long sickness. . . professed wrestlers and champions were in times past fed with figs." Containing more mineral matter and more alkaline than most fruits, figs are great producers of energy and vitality. Either fresh or sun-dried, they work as an excellent natural laxative for sluggish bowels; the high mucin content and tiny seeds help gather toxic wastes and mucus in the colon and drag them out. Studies show that figs also help kill pernicious bacteria while promoting the buildup of friendly acidophilus bacteria in the bowel. Those who do not drink milk may want to add figs to their regular diet since the fig is one of the highest sources of readily assimilable calcium in the plant world. Although fresh raw figs are best, dried figs also give nourishment and energy to the body, especially during the winter months. Dried figs are typically preserved with potassium sorbate to help keep them moist without spoiling. Milk from the unripe fruit applied twice daily to warts helps remove them.

Varieties

Adriatic fig trees are prolific bearers, producing light green or yellowish-green fruits with pale pink or dark red flesh, very similar in appearance to Calimyrna but smaller and not as sweet. While good fresh, this variety is also frequently sold dried and is the principle variety used in making fig bars and fig paste.

Black mission figs are black or dark purple with pink flesh and are of medium to large size. They have a moist, chewy texture and distinctive sweet flavor. Spanish missionaries established a Franciscan mission in San Diego in 1769 and began to grow a Spanish black common fig which, under the names Mission, Black Mission, or Franciscana, is still one of the leading varieties. The dried version is smaller, drier, with an intense, dark, almost burnt flavor.

Calimyrna, or **California Smyrna**, is a large greenish-yellow fig that is less moist and not quite as sweet in its fresh state as the Black Mission. Considered to have a more traditional fig flavor and texture, this is the most popular dried variety. Often referred to as a caprifig, the Calimyrna is not self-pollinating and relies on an unusual method of pollination to produce mature edible fruit. Early growers of the Calimyrna (which started from the Turkish Smyrna) were puzzled because the fruit would drop off the tree before maturing. Finally, a researcher discovered that Calimyrna figs would remain on the trees if they received the pollen from an inedible fig called the caprifig. Each caprifig has a colony of small fig wasps, called Blastophaga, living inside. When the wasp larvae mature, they go in search of another fig to serve as a nest in order to reproduce. Calimyrna growers intervene just prior to this point and place baskets of caprifigs in their orchards. Female wasps then work their way into the Calimyrna figs, carrying a few grains of caprifig pollen on their wings and bodies. Once inside, the wasps discover that the structure of the Calimyrna fig is not suitable for laying eggs and depart, leaving the pollen behind. Thick-skinned Calimyrna figs are usually peeled when used fresh.

Kadota is a small "white" thick-skinned fig that is generally canned or sold fresh. Actually greenish-yellow in color with a violet-tinted flesh, it has only a few small "seeds."

Fig

Nutritional Value Per 100 g Edible Portion

	Raw	Dried
Calories	80	274
Protein	1.2-1.3 g	4.3 g
Fat	0.14-0.30 g	1.3 g
Fiber	1.2-2.2 g	5.6 g
Calcium	35.0-78.2 mg	126 mg
Iron	0.60-4.09 mg	3 mg
Magnesium	17 mg	59 mg
Phosphorus	22.0-32.9 mg	77 mg
Potassium	194-232 mg	640 mg
Sodium	1-2 mg	11-34 mg
Zinc	0.150 mg	0.510 mg
Copper	0.070 mg	0.313 mg
Manganese	0.128 mg	0.388 mg
Beta Carotene (A)	20-270 IU	80-133 IU
Thiamine (B_1)	0.034-0.060 mg	0.071 mg
Riboflavin (B_2)	0.053-0.079 mg	0.088 mg
Niacin (B_3)	0.320-0.412 mg	0.694 mg
Pantothenic Acid (B_5)	0.300 mg	0.435 mg
Pyridoxine (B_6)	0.113 mg	0.224 mg
Folic Acid (B_9)	n/a	7.5 mcg
Ascorbic Acid (C)	12.2-17.6 mg	0.8 mg

Gandaria *(Bouea gandaria)*

General Information Native to Malaya and Sumatra, the gandaria are the best known of the small mango-like fruits borne by this genus of trees. The fruit is oval or round, with thin, smooth, edible skin, yellow or apricot-colored when ripe. These "miniature mangoes" vary greatly in edibility, but the best are well worth eating.

Culinary Uses The yellow or orange pulp is juicy, varies from acid to sweet, and adheres to the leathery, whiskered stone. Most fruits are eaten in the same manner as mangos, but they may also be made into jam and chutney, pickles, or used in curries. When still immature, they are pickled in brine and used in curries. In Indonesia, the young leaves are marketed and eaten raw with rice.

Gandaria

Nutritional Value Per 100 g Edible Portion

	Raw
Protein	0.112 g
Fat	0.04 g
Fiber	0.6 g
Calcium	6 mg
Iron	0.31 mg
Phosphorus	10.8 mg
Beta Carotene (A)	0.043 mg
Thiamine (B_1)	0.031 mg
Riboflavin (B_2)	0.025 mg
Niacin (B_3)	0.286 mg
Ascorbic Acid (C)	75 mg

Gooseberry *(Ribes uva-crispa, R. hirtellum, R. grossularia)*

Ribes *probably derived from* ribas, *the Arabic name for Rheum Ribes, although some believe it to be the Latinized form of* riebs, *which is an old German word for currant.* Uva-crispa *means curved berry;* hirtellum *means somewhat hairy. The English name* gooseberry *is not a corruption of gorse-berry, as is often suggested, but comes from the Flemish* kruys, *meaning a cross, referring to the triple spines at the nodes. The word may also be related to the German* krauselbeere, *meaning crisp berry, which became* groseille *in French, hence* grossularia, *the specific name.*

General Information Gooseberries are derived mostly from two species: the European gooseberry (*Ribes uva-crispa*), native to the Caucasus Mountains and North Africa; and the American gooseberry (*R. hirtellum*), native to northeastern and north central United States and Canada. Popularity of the berry soared in eighteenth century England, when gardeners began vying to see who could grow the largest fruits. European gooseberries were brought to North America by early settlers, but most cultivars quickly succumbed, and only later when the European and American species were hybridized did cultivation succeed in North America. The gooseberry's promising career was quickly brought to a halt when the plant was restricted by federal law for being a carrier of white pine blister

Gooseberry

Nutritional Value Per 100 g Edible Portion

	Raw
Calories	44
Protein	0.88 g
Fat	0.58 g
Fiber	1.90 g
Calcium	25 mg
Iron	0.31 mg
Magnesium	10 mg
Phosphorus	27 mg
Potassium	198 mg
Sodium	1 mg
Zinc	0.120 mg
Copper	0.070 mg
Manganese	0.144 mg
Beta Carotene (A)	290 IU
Thiamine (B_1)	0.040 mg
Riboflavin (B_2)	0.030 mg
Niacin (B_3)	0.300 mg
Pantothenic Acid (B_5)	0.286 mg
Pyridoxine (B_6)	0.080 mg
Ascorbic Acid (C)	27.7 mg
Tocopherol (E)	0.370 mg

Lore and Legend

In one tale, a wart will vanish if pricked by a gooseberry spine that has passed through a wedding ring.

rust. The berries themselves vary enormously, running from fuzzy-prickly to downy or satin-smooth, from translucent to opaque, from white through shades of green to deep purple, from the size of a blueberry to that of a cherry tomato, and from mouth-puckering to lightly sweet. The white gooseberry has a veined, smooth, transparent skin, while the red gooseberry has a hairy surface. Most common in American markets are the small to medium-sized, celery-green summer berry and the very large, striated, yellow-green to purplish winter berry. This is one berry that is becoming less common in the markets due to its loss in popularity.

Buying Tips Choose hard, dry berries with a rich sheen. Those found in supermarkets, most often from New Zealand, are smooth, like large glass marbles. Avoid mushy berries or those with skins marred by splits or blemishes. The pink or purplish berries tend to be less tart.

Culinary Uses Gooseberries have a flavor all their own, and range over a wide spectrum. At one end are fruits with sour pulp and tough skin, while at the other are those whose tender skins envelop an aromatic, sweet pulp. Generally those found in the supermarket are the underripe, tart, sour kinds. Unless they are going to be pureed, top and tail them (taking off the spiny axis from top and bottom with scissors or knife) so as not to spike your guests. For cooking, date sugar is best for sweetening, or honey can be added after cooking. In Scandinavia, Hungary, and Russia, a chilled or hot soup of gooseberries and chicken stock, thickened with potato flour or cornstarch, and topped with whipped or sour cream, is a favorite first course. England's gooseberry fool is a classic dish. Gooseberries may also be made into conserves, jams, jellies, or pies and pastries when combined perhaps with apples.

Health Benefits Gooseberries have a beneficial effect on constipation, liver ailments, poor complexion, arthritis, and dyspepsia.

Gooseberry, Otaheite *(Phyllanthus acidus)*

The botanical name Phyllanthus *means "leaf-flower," referring to the curious manner in which flowers grow along the edges of the leaf-like branches; since the flowers develop into fruits, the fruits also occupy this odd position.* Acidus *means acidic. The Otaheite part of its name seems to indicate a connection with Tahiti, while their tart flavor recalls that of gooseberries.*

Gooseberry, Otaheite

Nutritional Value Per 100 g Edible Portion

	Raw
Protein	0.155 g
Fat	0.52 g
Fiber	0.8 g
Calcium	5.4 mg
Iron	3.25 mg
Phosphorus	17.9 mg
Beta Carotene (A)	0.019 mg
Thiamine (B_1)	0.025 mg
Riboflavin (B_2)	0.013 mg
Niacin (B_3)	0.292 mg
Ascorbic Acid (C)	4.6 mg

General Information The Otaheite gooseberry tree has been cultivated for centuries in southern India and parts of southeast Asia, and is an astonishingly abundant bearer, often providing two crops a year. The fruits are ribbed, grape-sized, and green at first, but ripen to a light yellow. Tightly embedded in the center is a hard, ribbed stone containing four to six seeds.

Culinary Uses The tart flavor recalls the flavor of the gooseberry, but there is no other connection. The flesh must be sliced from the stone, or the fruits cooked and then pressed through a sieve to separate the stones. They can be made into pickles and preserves, added to dishes or drinks as a flavoring, or cooked with sugar to provide a compote or pie filling. If cooked long enough with plenty of sugar, the fruit and juice turn ruby-red and yield a tasty jelly.

Health Benefits In India, the fruits are taken as a liver tonic and to enrich the blood, while the syrup is prescribed as a stomachic.

Grape and Raisin (*Vitis vinifera, V. labrusca, V. rotundita*)

Vitis *is the classical Latin name for the plant, and also has the general meaning of vine or branch. The term* vinifera *means wine-bearing.* Labrusca *signifies the wild vine, while* rotundita *means small and round. The English word* grape *comes from the Germanic word* krapfo, *meaning to hook. The English word* raisin *is derived from the Latin* racemus, *meaning a bunch of grapes or berries.*

General Information Grapes go so far back in time that the vine is thought to have been already established throughout the world even before the coming of man. Unquestionably, it was man's universal interest in the production of stimulating drinks that led to the vast amount of effort he put into viticulture (grape cultivation) from late prehistoric times onward. The beginnings of viticulture originate somewhere around the Caspian Sea, an area also considered the place of origin of *Vitis vinifera*, our most common grape. By the first century B.C., viticulture was a major source of revenue for the Romans (and thus encouraged by the government) and wine was popular throughout their empire. A precious trade item in the ancient Near East and also highly valued in ancient Rome, at one time two jars of raisins could be exchanged for a slave. Europeans encountering raisins on the Crusades recognized their keeping qualities as well as the intensely sweet, tangy richness lacking in their fresh counterpart. Returning home, they incorporated dried fruit and spices into their otherwise bland cooking. Until medieval times, raisins with their high sugar content were used as a sweetener second only to honey. As new colonization and widespread advance of peoples occurred, grapes were carried along; today they are cultivated on all continents and islands that are suitable in climate. There are between six thousand and eight thousand varieties of grapes (only forty to fifty are important commercially), nearly half of which are native to North America; in fact, when Leif Eriksson and the Vikings landed in the eleventh century, they named the land Vinland after the wild grapes that were so abundant. The new land remained Vinland until Amerigo Vespucci arrived and named it after himself. Martha's Vineyard, an island off the coast of Massachusetts, was also named for the abundant grapes growing on it (by Gosnold, an Englishman, in 1603).

Lore and Legend

Grapes figure prominently in the ancient literature and art of both the Western and Eastern hemispheres. Saturn gave the grape to Crete, Dionysos to Greece, Bacchus to Rome, Osiris to Egypt, and Geryon to Spain. Adam and Eve, as well as Noah, planted grapevines. The grape is certainly the fruit most associated with frivolity, as those who worshipped the gods of grapes and wine were notoriously addicted to wine, wild dances, and hedonistic excesses. The Greek poet Euripides praised the grape in eloquent terms, and the ancients gave clusters to newlyweds in the belief that their many seeds would bless the couple with many children. Clusters of grapes were frequently used on ancient coins (as well as some recent Italian and Israeli ones), and grapes and grapevines often appear as motifs on buildings and in illuminated manuscripts. After the fall of the Roman empire, during the ensuing Dark Ages when Christianity became a dominant religion, wine became associated with the church. Considered symbolic of the blood of Christ, wine became part of the communion ritual, and (in moderation) was believed one of the good things in life. Most monasteries soon had their own vineyards, tended by monks who slowly refined the process of winemaking, developing regional wines and techniques of fermentation still in use today.

Buying Tips When buying fresh grapes, choose plump ones firmly attached to their stems. Any remaining

Grape

Nutritional Value Per 100 g Edible Portion

	Raw (American) Concord	Raw (European) Muscat/Tokay	Processed Juice
Calories	63	71	61
Protein	0.63 g	0.66 g	0.56 g
Fat	0.35 g	0.58 g	0.08 g
Fiber	0.76 g	0.45 g	n/a
Calcium	14 mg	11 mg	9 mg
Iron	0.29 mg	0.26 mg	0.24 mg
Magnesium	5 mg	6 mg	10 mg
Phosphorus	10 mg	13 mg	11 mg
Potassium	191 mg	185 mg	132 mg
Sodium	2 mg	2 mg	3 mg
Zinc	0.040 mg	0.050 mg	0.050 mg
Copper	0.040 mg	0.090 mg	0.028 mg
Manganese	0.718 mg	0.058 mg	0.360 mg
Beta Carotene (A)	100 IU	73 IU	8 IU
Thiamine (B_1)	0.092 mg	0.092 mg	0.026 mg
Riboflavin (B_2)	0.057 mg	0.057 mg	0.037 mg
Niacin (B_3)	0.300 mg	0.300 mg	0.262 mg
Pantothenic Acid (B_5)	0.024 mg	0.024 mg	0.041 mg
Pyridoxine (B_6)	0.110 mg	0.110 mg	0.065 mg
Folic Acid (B_9)	3.9 mcg	3.9 mcg	2.6 mcg
Ascorbic Acid (C)	4 mg	10.8 mg	0.10 mg

bloom shows minimal handling. Darker varieties should be free from any green tinge, while the greenish-white grapes will show a slight amber color when ripe. The stems should be green; if they are dry, brown, or black, grapes will lack flavor, or if there is any puckering at the stem it indicates that the grapes are old.

Culinary Uses Grapes come in many colors and sizes, of which the tiny seedless grapes are said to be the finest. This fruit constitutes the largest fruit industry on the globe; they are sold fresh, dried into raisins, crushed for juice and wine, and preserved or canned for jelly and fruit cocktail. Grapes are used in fruit salads, desserts, and pies. Young, tender grape leaves are eminently edible. Used as a wrapper for rice and other fillings in Greek and Middle-Eastern cooking, they are also used to wrap some French cheeses. Bottled or canned grape leaves are sold in Greek and Middle-Eastern groceries, but if you have grapes growing on your property, you can use your own leaves as long as they are unsprayed. Fresh leaves should be blanched or steamed to soften them; canned leaves, usually packed in brine, should be rinsed to reduce their sodium content. Grapeseed oil is a pale, delicate oil extracted from grape seeds. When refrigerated, it will not cloud, and has a very high smoke point. Raisins are one of the all-time classic snack foods. Soft, sweet, and bite-size, they can be eaten alone, added to granola and trail mix, or combined with all manner of different dishes. They add color and sweetness to garden salads, custard pies, and rice pudding, and are frequent additions to candy, hot cereals, cookies, and breads. Raisin paste, made by grinding raisins in a food grinder until crushed and sticky, is a fine substitute or replacement for other sweeteners in baked goods and candies. Try mixing it with sesame tahini, sunflower seeds, and a bit of honey, and rolling into bite-sized balls.

Health Benefits Grapes are called "the queen of fruits" because of their excellent cleansing properties, and rank among the most potent of all medicinal foods. Among their most effective therapeutic applications is to cure constipation, gastritis, and chronic acidosis, which are common complaints for those who live on Western diets. The black variety of grapes are by far the most potent, being excellent detoxifiers of the whole body, but especially good for the digestive tract, liver, kidneys, and blood. Those following a diet solely of grapes for several days or weeks (known as the grape cure or ampelotherapy) will feel their powerful detoxifying and alkalinizing properties. Since eating grapes in quantity acts freely on the kidneys, this promotes the expulsion of poisons from the system. The simple sugars contained in raw grapes are precisely those used in cellular metabolism, and are easily and immediately absorbed into the bloodstream, ready for metabolic use. The best grapes are those that have seeds, for the outside of the seed contains tartaric acid (cream of tartar) which helps cut the mucus and catarrh of the body so they can be eliminated. Their high water content adds to the fluids necessary to eliminate hardened deposits that may have settled in the body, they are good blood builders due to their high iron content, and their

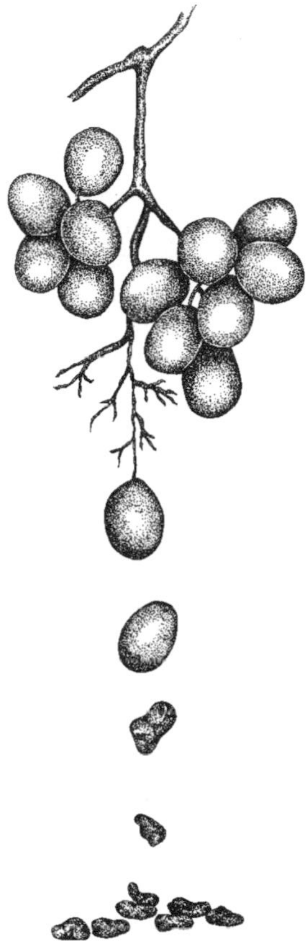

magnesium promotes peristalsis, although the skins and seeds can sometimes be irritating to those with colitis or ulcers. Recently, scientists have discovered that the ellagic acid found in grapes scavenges carcinogens as it moves through the body.

Raw grape juice is easily assimilated and called the "nectar of the gods" and "vegetarian milk" owing to its ability to sustain nursing infants deprived of mother's milk, and is a far superior option to pasteurized cow's milk. Combining grape juice equally with a nut milk quickly furnishes the system with new blood of the purest kind and is an excellent remedy for anemia.

Raisins have less acid than grapes since the acid has been dried out of them, but they are very high in sugar, so should be used in moderation. They have almost as much iron by weight as cooked dried beans or ground beef. Most raisins have been dried naturally in the sun, but some have been treated with sulphur or other preservatives to retain their color and moistness.

Varieties

There are four major classes of grapes grown in the United States: the American grape (*V. labrusca*), the European grape (*V. vinifera*), the muscadine (*V. rotundifolia*), and hybrids of the three. American grapes—sometimes referred to as Fox or Concord grapes—are native to the Northeast and grow in bunches, have skins that slip off easily, and are generally eaten fresh or made into jelly, juice, and occasionally wine. The American or *labrusca* grapes are the ones that Viking explorer Leif Eriksson found growing so abundantly on the east coast of North America, and of which Concord is the most familiar. The European grapes have tight skins and a typically winey flavor. They separate into three main categories: those used for wine, the dessert grapes, and the raisin grapes. Tokay is the prototype of *vinifera*, and these types grow only in California in a rather limited area. Among the "white" *vinifera* are Olivetta, with oval berries, and Thompson Seedless. Ribier heads the "black" *vinifera*, which are actually a very deep blue. Muscadine grapes, best characterized by the Scuppernong, are native to the Southeast. They grow in loose clusters, have a slightly spicy and musky flavor, and are eaten fresh or made into jelly and occasionally into a fruity wine. From the *muscadines* come the seedless packaged raisins. Only three varieties of grapes in this country are widely used in the production of raisins: Thompson Seedless, Muscat, and Black Corinth. Nearly all the commercially grown raisins in the United States (and about one-half of the total world supply) now come from the San Joaquin valley of California, where the raisin industry began booming in the 1870s after a heat wave dried the grape crop on the vine.

Black Beauty (**Beauty Seedless**) are the only seedless black grapes. They are spicy and sweet, resembling Concords in flavor. Their season runs from late May to early July.

Calmeria are pale green oval fruits with a mildly sweet flavor, comparatively thick skin, and a few small seeds. They are sometimes called **Lady Finger grapes** due to their elongated shape. Their season is only January and February.

Cardinal are a cross between the Flame Tokay and the Ribier. These large, dark red grapes have a pearly gray finish, a full fruity flavor, and few seeds. Their season runs mid-May through mid-August.

Raisin

Nutritional Value Per 100 g Edible Portion	Raw Brown Seedless	Raw Golden Seedless	Raw Currants
Calories	300	302	283
Protein	3.22 g	3.39 g	4.08 g
Fat	0.46 g	0.46 g	0.27 g
Fiber	1.28 g	1.43 g	1.57 g
Calcium	49 mg	53 mg	86 mg
Iron	2.08 mg	1.79 mg	3.26 mg
Magnesium	33 mg	35 mg	41 mg
Phosphorus	97 mg	115 mg	125 mg
Potassium	751 mg	746 mg	892 mg
Sodium	12 mg	12 mg	8 mg
Zinc	0.270 mg	0.320 mg	0.660 mg
Copper	0.309 mg	0.363 mg	0.468 mg
Manganese	0.308 mg	0.308 mg	0.469 mg
Beta Carotene (A)	8 IU	44 IU	73 IU
Thiamine (B_1)	0.156 mg	0.008 mg	0.160 mg
Riboflavin (B_2)	0.088 mg	0.191 mg	0.142 mg
Niacin (B_3)	0.818 mg	1.142 mg	1.615 mg
Pantothenic Acid (B_5)	0.045 mg	0.140 mg	0.045 mg
Pyridoxine (B_6)	0.249 mg	0.323 mg	0.296 mg
Folic Acid (B_9)	3.3 mcg	3.3 mcg	10.2 mcg
Ascorbic Acid (C)	3.3 mg	3.2 mg	4.7 mg

Champagne (**Black Corinth**) are tiny, purple, seedless fruits with a deliciously winey sweetness. Their season is September and October. Zante currants are Black Corinth grapes that have been dried primarily for the confectionery market. About one-quarter the size of regular raisins, these tiny fruits are incorrectly called "currants" because of their resemblance to currant berries and the mispronounced name (Corinth sounds like currant). They are also sometimes labeled Zante Currants, referring to the Greek island where this type of grape first grew. Substitute them in any recipe that calls for raisins; their small size does not interfere with the slicing of bread and cutting of cookies the way large raisins sometimes do. Their delicate flavor lends itself well to exotic recipes, such as spiced rice or stuffed mussels and grape leaves.

Concord are a medium-sized seeded dark blue-black or purple tough-skinned grape with a powdery bloom. This variety is native to North America, and originated in the 1840s near the Massachusetts town whose name it bears. They are very flavorful, with a sweet-tart tang and perfumy fragrance. Savored as table grapes, the Concord is the principal juice grape, and highly favored for jelly and wine. Their season is September and October.

Emperor are a European seeded variety with a mild cherrylike flavor that becomes quite sugary as it softens. The clusters are large, long, and well-filled. The fruit is a uniform elongated obovoid, light red or reddish-purple to deep purple in color, with a tough skin. Second only to Thompson Seedless in quantity grown, Emperors are heavily cultivated in Latin America and Mexico. California Emperors are an early fall arrival and last until mid-winter. A Thanksgiving and Christmas favorite, their season starts in October and runs well into March.

Flame Tokay is one of the prettiest of all the grape varieties. It is a long, elegant, bright red grape, with a definite velvety coat and large seeds. With its firm texture, abundant juice and sweetness, the Tokay has the most grape flavor of all the American grapes which, although they are sweet, are not sugary. Their season runs from late fall through January. Flame seedless raisins are extra-large and have a generously sweet, rich grape flavor.

Monukka are made into raisins that are nearly twice as large as Thompson Seedless and have a rich, robust grape flavor. A favorite among raisin connoisseurs, they are produced in limited quantities. Look for them at specialty shops and health food stores.

Muscats are very large, very round, slightly bronzed, dusty green or green-yellow grapes. They have a distinct musky wine flavor that conjures up monastic stone wine cellars full of oak kegs brooding in flickering candlelight. At their peak they are an excellent fruity table grape with a unique and enjoyable flavor; they are especially good with cheese and bread, but are also pressed for muscatel wine. Sometimes their aroma precedes their flavor, and the combination is heady. It is very difficult to find bad Muscat grapes since their season is so short, running only from early October through Thanksgiving. Raisins made from the Muscat grape are large, brown, and particularly fruity-tasting. Since this variety contains seeds, the raisins are either seeded mechanically, or sold with seeds. Muscat raisins are considered a specialty item used mostly for holiday baking, especially fruitcakes, and thus are usually sold just in the autumn and winter months.

Red Flame were created by grafting and hybridizing the Flame Tokay grape, which has seeds, with a round seedless variety like the Perlette. They are a plump, round, deep red, seedless grape which is best when hard as a marble. At their peak these grapes are crisp, sweet, meaty, and have the touch of wine flavor that characterizes their Tokay parent. Their season runs May through October.

Ribier are a very large, very dark purple-black, mildly sweet grape. They may not be seedless, but they are so sweet and juicy that nobody cares. There is another round black variety, called the **Exotica**, which are just like Ribiers, only bigger, harder, and blacker. Most stores sell Exoticas under the Ribier name. Their season is July through February.

Sultana are a large, pale yellow-green grape originally from Smyrna and grown for the Turkish sultans. The raisins from Sultana grapes are more popular in Europe than in the United States. These are particularly flavorful and soft, and can sometimes be purchased in gourmet shops and health food stores.

Thompson Seedless were first grown in California near Yuba City by Mr. William Thompson, and are now the most common variety, making up half of the California grape acreage. Fresh Thompson seedless clusters are large, long, and well-filled, with grapes that are light green, medium-sized and ellipsoidal. When fully ripe they are firm yet tender, with a flavor that is a tasty blend of sweet juicy meat and tart skin. Their season runs from late June into November. Natural seedless raisins are sun-dried Thompson Seedless grapes. They account for 95 percent of California raisins. The green grapes naturally develop a dark brown color as they dry in the sun, a process that takes from two to three weeks. Golden raisins are Thompson Seedless grapes that have been oven-dried to avoid the darkening effect of sunlight. They may also have been treated with sulphur dioxide, which destroys most of the nutrients, to preserve their light color. Check the labels well or use another variety of raisin.

Grapefruit *(Citrus* x. *paradisi)*

The term Citrus *derives from the Greek term for the citron,* kedromelon. Paradisi *means coming from paradise. The English name was coined in 1814 in the West Indies by Jamaican farmers.*

General Information The grapefruit is a relative newcomer to the citrus clan, an accidental hybrid between the pummelo and the orange. First described in 1750 by Griffith Hughes who called it the "forbidden fruit" of Barbados, seeds were brought to Florida by the French Count Odette Phillippe in 1823, but at first the trees were grown only as a novelty and the fruit little utilized. Several attempts have been made to change the name of the fruit to something "more appropriate," but the name grapefruit has prevailed except in Spanish-speaking areas, where it is called *toronja*. Florida started sending small shipments of the fruit to New York and Philadelphia between 1880 and 1885, thus setting in motion the colossal Florida citrus industry. For many years the grapefruit was not extremely popular because of

Lore and Legend

Following the United States stock market crash in 1929, citrus fruits could be had free for orange-colored food stamps (the color and name of the chief citrus fruit were only coincidental). This brought the grapefruit into families that had previously been so ignorant of it that welfare boards received the same complaint numerous times: that the fruit had been boiled for hours and still remained tough.

Grapefruit

Nutritional Value Per 100 g Edible Portion

	Fresh Fruit	Fresh Juice	Sweetened Canned Juice
Calories	34.4-46.4	37-42	46
Protein	0.5-1.0 g	0.4-0.5 g	0.58 g
Fat	0.06-0.20 g	0.1 g	0.09 g
Fiber	0.14-0.77 g	trace	0 g
Calcium	9.2-32.0 mg	9.0 mg	8 mg
Iron	0.24-0.70 mg	0.20 mg	0.36 mg
Magnesium	8 mg	12 mg	10 mg
Phosphorus	15.0-47.9 mg	15.0 mg	11 mg
Potassium	135-139 mg	162 mg	162 mg
Sodium	1.0 mg	1.0 mg	2 mg
Zinc	0.070 mg	0.050 mg	0.060 mg
Copper	0.047 mg	0.033 mg	0.048 mg
Manganese	0.012 mg	0.020 mg	0.020 mg
Beta Carotene (A)	10-440 IU	10-440 IU	0 IU
Thiamine (B_1)	0.040-0.057 mg	0.040 mg	0.040 mg
Riboflavin (B_2)	0.010-0.020 mg	0.020 mg	0.023 mg
Niacin (B_3)	0.157-0.290 mg	0.200 mg	0.319 mg
Pantothenic Acid (B_5)	0.283 mg	n/a	0.130 mg
Pyridoxine (B_6)	0.042 mg	n/a	0.020 mg
Folic Acid (B_9)	10.2 mcg	n/a	10.4 mcg
Ascorbic Acid (C)	36.0-49.8 mg	36-40 mg	26.9 mg
Tocopherol (E)	0.250 mg	n/a	n/a

its slightly bitter taste, but varieties have been bred which are sweeter. Red grapefruit were first spotted in the Rio Grande valley of Texas during the 1920s, and have since been transplanted to other parts of the world; the red grapefruit is now designated the state fruit of Texas. The thin-skinned, shiny, heavy Florida grapefruit is considered by many to be the juiciest, sweetest, most nutritious variety available.

Buying Tips Grapefruit of good quality should be heavy, well-shaped, even-colored, and have a smooth, thin, shiny skin that is firm but springy to the touch. The heavier fruits are usually thinner-skinned and contain more juice than those with coarse, puffy, or spongy skins.

Culinary Uses There are several varieties: white, which is best for juicing; pink, which is sweet enough to be eaten like an orange; and red, which is sweeter still. Generally considered a breakfast fruit, grapefruit is also used to make juice and marmalades, is added to fruit salads, ices, cakes, and desserts, and can be baked or grilled. It is best to eat grapefruit alone or with other acid fruits, and not in combination with sweet fruits or starches. The habit of sweetening them (with sugar or other sweetener) causes a fermentation of the sweetener in the system, which will then produce an acidic reaction in the body. Served before the main meal, grapefruit will stimulate the appetite and aid in digestion. Once grapefruit or its juice has been canned or in any way preserved, the value of the organic elements is lost and are of little value to the body.

Health Benefits Fresh grapefruit, due to its content of salicylic acid, has proved to be one of the most valuable fruits as an aid in the removal or dissolving of inorganic calcium that may have formed deposits in the joints (as in arthritis) as a result of excessive consumption of devitalized white flour and pasteurized milk products. Naringin, a flavonoid isolated from grapefruit, has been shown to promote the elimination of old red blood cells from the body, and normalizes hematocrit levels (percentage of red blood cells per volume of blood). This fruit is also excellent for the cardiovascular system, helping to lower blood cholesterol, and may even promote plaque removal from the arteries, protecting them from disease. Used externally, it is a natural antiseptic for wounds, and is valuable as a drug or poison eliminator. One word of caution though, avoid the extensive overuse of all citric acid fruits, as they are powerful dissolvers of the catarrhal accumulations in the body, and the elimination of too much toxic material all at once may cause boils, irritated nerves, diarrhea, and other problems. **Citrus seed extract**, usually derived primarily from grapefruit seeds, is available as a major ingredient in liquid extracts, capsules, and ointments. Among its common internal uses are: for diarrhea (especially "traveler's diarrhea"), allergies, candida, parasites, flu, strep throat, and staph infections. Externally it is applied in various dilutions for warts, athlete's foot, dandruff, and poison oak.

Ground Cherry (*Physalis pruinosa, P. alkekangi, P. pubescens*)

Also Known As: Chinese Lantern, Husk Cherry, Husk Tomato, Strawberry Tomato.

Physalis *is Greek for bladder, so named because of its thin calyx, which enlarges and encloses the fruit at maturity.* Pruinosa *means with a hoary bloom,* alkekangi *comes from the Persian name* kakunaj, *while* pubescens *means pubescent or downy. The fruit does not ripen until it falls to the ground, hence its English name* ground cherry.

General Information Native to the Americas, these small fruits of the nightshade family grow in open fields and along roads throughout the United States. In size and shape most ground cherries resemble a small, fanciful cherry tomato enclosed within a red Chinese paper lantern. Inside the paper husk there is a thin, waxy skin that surrounds a very juicy, dense pulp of the same brilliant color, whorled with soft, tiny, edible seeds. The berries drop to the ground before they are ready to eat, but in a week or two the husk dries and the fruit within turns a golden yellow. The ground cherry most commonly grown as an edible garden vegetable is *P. pruinosa*, which bears a canary-yellow fruit encased in a brownish husk.

Ground Cherry

Nutritional Value Per 100 g Edible Portion

	Raw
Calories	53
Protein	1.9 g
Fat	0.7 g
Fiber	2.8 g
Calcium	9 mg
Iron	1.0 mg
Phosphorus	40 mg
Beta Carotene (A)	720 IU
Thiamine (B_1)	0.11 mg
Riboflavin (B_2)	0.04 mg
Niacin (B_3)	2.8 mg
Ascorbic Acid (C)	11 mg

Culinary Uses Its unusual taste is part tomato, part strawberry, part gooseberry, and part grape, yet all its own: sweet and pleasantly acid, with a lightly bitter aftertaste. It has traditionally been used as a dessert fruit either in pies and preserves, or dried in sugar and eaten like raisins. Prepare it as you would a tomato, either raw or cooked, but remember to remove the husk prior to eating, as it is inedible and slightly toxic.

Grumichama (*Eugenia brasiliensis*)

The genus Eugenia *was named in honor of Prince Eugene of Savoy.* Brasiliensis *means native to Brazil.*

Grumichama

Nutritional Value Per 100 g Edible Portion

	Raw
Protein	0.102 g
Fiber	0.6 g
Calcium	39.5 mg
Iron	0.45 mg
Phosphorus	13.6 mg
Beta Carotene (A)	0.039 mg
Thiamine (B_1)	0.044 mg
Riboflavin (B_2)	0.031 mg
Niacin (B_3)	0.336 mg
Ascorbic Acid (C)	18.8 mg

General Information Native to southern Brazil and Peru, this tree bears a long-stalked crimson fruit between one-half and three-quarters inch in diameter, with soft flesh and mild flavor. The skin is thin, firm, and exudes dark-red juice. The grumichama tree is cultivated in and around Rio de Janeiro, and also in Paraguay. Over the years there have been efforts to encourage interest in the virtues of the grumichama in Florida, mainly because of the beauty and hardiness of the tree and the pleasant flavor of the fruits, but the sepals are a nuisance and there is too little flesh in proportion to seed for the fruit to be taken seriously.

Culinary Uses The red or white pulp is juicy and tastes much like a true cherry except for a touch of aromatic resin. It exists in several varieties, distinguished by the color of the flesh (dark red, vermilion, or white), all of equal merit. There are usually two or three hard inedible seeds. Fully ripe grumichamas are pleasant to nibble out of hand. In Hawaii, half-ripe fruits are made into pie, jam, or jelly.

Guava (*Psidium guajava, P. cattleianum, P. littorale* var. *longipes*)

The genus name Psidium *comes from the Greek psidion meaning pomegranate, so named due to the fact that the many small hard seeds recall the pomegranate.* Guajava *is a derivative of the Haitian native name* guayavu, *and our English name also derives from it.* Cattleianum *means similar to the* Cattleyas *of the orchid family, which are named after William Cattley, an early English horticulturist and naturalist.*

Guava

Nutritional Value Per 100 g Edible Portion

	Raw
Calories	36-50
Protein	0.9-1.0 g
Fat	0.1-0.5 g
Fiber	2.8-5.5 g
Calcium	9.1-17 mg
Iron	0.30-0.70 mg
Magnesium	10-25 mg
Phosphorus	17.8-30 mg
Potassium	284 mg
Sodium	3 mg
Zinc	0.230 mg
Copper	0.103 mg
Manganese	0.144 mg
Beta Carotene (A)	200-792 IU
Thiamine (B_1)	0.046 mg
Riboflavin (B_2)	0.03-0.04 mg
Niacin (B_3)	0.6-1.068 mg
Pantothenic Acid (B_5)	0.150 mg
Pyridoxine (B_6)	0.143 mg
Ascorbic Acid (C)	100-500 mg

General Information The guava is a small, fragrant, tropical tree of the myrrh family, originally from Peru and Brazil. Europeans first encountered and enjoyed the fruit when they arrived in Haiti, where the local name for it was *guayavu*; Spanish and Portuguese mariners soon spread the tree and its name to other regions. It apparently did not arrive in Hawaii until the early 1800s, but now occurs throughout the Pacific Islands either wild, as a home fruit tree, or planted in small commercial groves. This "apple of the tropics" is a prolific tree and grows freely, springing up from seeds dropped by birds. The fruit has an outer and inner zone, the last with many small gritty seeds, but there are seedless varieties. The **Strawberry** or **Cattley guava** (*P. cattleianum*) originated in Brazil, and is round and about an $1^1/2$ in diameter. It is dark crimson in color, has soft, spicy, strawberry-flavored flesh, and many hard inedible seeds.

Buying Tips Guavas vary in size, shape, and color, ranging from the size of an apple to that of a plum, and may be round or pear-shaped, rough or smooth-skinned, and greenish-white, yellow, or red in color. Large, pear-shaped, white ones are considered the best. The skin will give to gentle pressure when the fruit is ripe, and the whole fruit will have a pleasant floral scent.

Culinary Uses Inside this very aromatic fruit is a white, yellow, pink, or red flesh with a strangely exotic juicy flavor, acid yet sweet, along with a few sharp-edged seeds. Unripe guavas are astringent, but if picked when nearly ripe are soon ready to eat. Available fresh or canned, they are delicious in fruit salads, ices, cool drinks, desserts, and cakes, and their sharp taste makes them useful for stewing and making custards, tarts, and preserves. To eat fresh guavas, cut into quarters, remove the seeds and peel, and eat the flesh and pips. Canned guavas bear only a faint resemblance to the flavor of the fresh fruit. Bars of thick, rich guava paste and guava cheese are staple sweets in some countries, and guava jelly is almost universally marketed.

Health Benefits The guava is beneficial for the skeletal and lymphatic systems.

Huckleberry *(Gaylussacia baccata)*

Also Known As: Bilberry, Whortleberry, Hurtleberry.

The botanical name Gaylussacia *was given in honor of Joseph L. Gay-Lussac (1850), a French chemist and physicist;* baccata *means berry-producing. The English name* huckleberry *is believed a corruption of* hurtleberry.

Lore and Legend

Because huckleberries grew wild everywhere in cold-weather climates, they readily became associated by the 1700s with anything rural, tranquil, untouched. From there it was hardly a stretch to transform the meaning in the 1800s to "simple," "small," or "insignificant." Mark Twain used the word huckleberry in that sense in *A Connecticut Yankee in King Arthur's Court,* referring to some sharpie as "no huckleberry." His Huckleberry Finn, of course, represented the simple joys of bucolic childhood.

General Information Huckleberries, a member of the Heath family, are believed to have been used for human consumption since prehistoric times, even perhaps twenty-five to thirty centuries before Christ; this plant is reputedly one of the oldest living plants on earth. A single plant found in western Pennsylvania covers several square miles and is estimated by botanists to be over thirteen thousand years old (older than the oldest California redwood); it is one of the last surviving examples of the box huckleberry. Although the huckleberry resembles the blueberry and the two plants grow in the same regions, they are not actually related. The dark blue to black fruit of the true huckleberry is distinguished by the ten bony nutlets (or seeds), while the seeds of blueberries are so small as to be scarcely noticeable. The red "huckleberry" of the Pacific Coast is more likely the red whortleberry (*Vaccinium parvifolium*), related to both cranberries and blueberries. All huckleberries are edible, but some species are not very tasty. The garden huckleberry, which was developed by Luther Burbank, is closely related to the tomato.

Buying Tips Look for bright, clean berries with good uniform color. Check the bottom of the container to make sure it has not been stained from mushy or moldy fruit.

Culinary Uses This round, shiny fruit is sweet and pleasantly flavored, but more "seedy" than blueberries. Huckleberries are most often used in the preparation of sweets, preserves, and confectionery (they make an excellent pie), and can be used interchangeably with blueberries in many recipes.

Health Benefits Eating fresh huckleberries has been observed to regulate bowel action, stimulate appetite, end intestinal putrefaction, and expel ascarids. The fresh berries may require some individual experimentation, since they tend to produce diarrhea in some people while stopping it in others. Huckleberries are especially helpful in aiding the pancreas in digesting sugars and starches; they have the advantage of passing through the stomach without affecting it, then beginning to work in the small intestine. The dried berries have been found to be valuable in cases of edema. They are low in fat, and high in fiber, potassium, iron, phosphorus, sodium, calcium, vitamin B complex and vitamin C.

Ilama (*Annona diversifolia*)

Annona *means year's harvest, suggested by the Haitian name* anon, *which is applied to one of the species;* diversifolia *means having leaves of two or more forms. The name* ilama *is derived, via Spanish, from the native Mexican name* illamatzapotl *(which translates as* zapote de las viejas, *or old woman's sapote).*

Ilama

Nutritional Value Per 100 g Edible Portion

	Raw
Protein	0.447 g
Fat	0.16 g
Fiber	1.3 g
Calcium	31.6 mg
Iron	0.70 mg
Phosphorus	51.7 mg
Beta Carotene (A)	0.011 mg
Thiamine (B_1)	0.235 mg
Riboflavin (B_2)	0.297 mg
Niacin (B_3)	2.177 mg
Ascorbic Acid (C)	13.6 mg

General Information Native to Mexico, the ilama grows wild in foothills from the southwest coast of Mexico to the Pacific coast of Guatemala and El Salvador. The earliest known record of the fruit (1570) was made by Francisco Hernandez, who was sent by King Philip II of Spain to note any possible useful products of Mexico. For many years the tree was confused with either the soursop or the custard apple, and only in 1911 was it fully investigated and described by W.E. Safford of the United States Department of Agriculture's Bureau of Plant Industry and given its current botanical name. Like other members of its family, the fruit is conical, heart-shaped, or ovoid, with a rough skin that may be anything from green to magenta pink with a white bloom. Generally it is studded with protuberances, although some may be quite smooth.

Culinary Uses In green varieties, the flesh is white and sweet. Pink varieties usually have pink-tinged flesh near the rind and around the seeds and are somewhat tarter in flavor. The flesh of both is somewhat fibrous but smooth and custardy, with a quantity of hard, smooth, inedible seeds. Always consumed raw, the flesh is served either in the half-shell, or scooped out, chilled, and served with cream and sugar to intensify the flavor.

Jaboticaba (*Myrciaria cauliflora*)

The genus name Myrciaria *is probably related to* Myrtus, *the Myrtle family.* Cauliflora *refers to the fact that the tree develops flowers* (flora) *directly on the stem* (caulis). *The word* jaboticaba *is said to have been derived from the Tupi term* jabotim, *for turtle, and means "like turtle fat," presumably referring to the fruit pulp.*

General Information Native to and widely cultivated in the region of Rio de Janeiro, Brazil, this tree bears its fruits directly on the trunk, main limbs, and branches. Introduced into California at Santa Barbara about 1904, a few of the trees were still living in 1912, but all had died by 1939. Those introduced into Florida have done much better, and some still grow there today. The fruits are round and about one inch in diameter, bright green to maroon or purple in color, and not unlike a grape, but with a thicker skin.

Culinary Uses The white or pinkish pulp is translucent, and has an overall subacid to sweet, grapelike flavor that is sometimes quite astringent and spicy. There may be one to five light-brown seeds, which cling tenaciously to the pulp. The fruit is generally eaten fresh, without the skin and seeds. By squeezing the fruit between the thumb and forefinger, one can cause the skin to split and the pulp to slip into the mouth. Children in Brazil spend hours searching out and devouring the ripe fruit and eating the seeds with the pulp, but properly, the seeds should be discarded. Jaboticabas are often used for making jelly and marmalade, with the addition of pectin (and the removal of the skins from at least half the fruit to avoid a strong tannin flavor). Once harvested, the fruit ferments quickly at ordinary temperatures.

Health Benefits Regular quantities of the skins should not be consumed due to their high tannin content.

Jaboticaba

Nutritional Value Per 100 g Edible Portion

	Raw
Calories	45.7
Protein	0.11 g
Fat	0.01 g
Fiber	0.08 g
Calcium	6.3 mg
Iron	0.49 mg
Phosphorus	9.2 mg
Thiamine (B_1)	0.020 mg
Riboflavin (B_2)	0.020 mg
Niacin (B_3)	0.210 mg
Ascorbic Acid (C)	22.7-30.7 mg

Jackfruit (*Artocarpus heterophyllus*)

Artocarpus *comes from the Greek words* artos, *meaning bread, and* carpos, *meaning fruit;* heterophyllus *means having leaves of more than one form. The English name* jack *was given to this fruit by the Portuguese in the sixteenth century since it sounded like* tsjaka, *the Malayan name for the plant.*

General Information This tropical evergreen tree is believed to be indigenous to the rain forests of India and the Malayan Peninsula. The fruits grow sporadically on the trunk and large branches, a somewhat unusual habit called cauliflory, which also occurs in the cacao tree. Under normal conditions, a single tree may bear one hundred and fifty to two hundred and fifty huge fruits per year. Among the largest fruits of any tropical plant, the elongated green jackfruits, with their fissured hexagonal patterning and large spikes, frequently measure up to 3 feet in length, 18 inches in width, and weigh 40 to 50 pounds, with some weighing in at over 100 pounds. Like the pineapple, the jackfruit is a composite fruit, but not nearly so tidy, since the sections are clustered in irregular clumps. The interior is complex, consisting of large bulbs of yellow flesh enclosing a smooth oval seed, massed among narrow ribbons of tougher tissue and surrounding a central pithy core.

Culinary Uses The jackfruit is ripe when its skin is stretched out, the spikes stand clear of each other, and it starts to give off an aroma. Very fragrant jackfruit are overly ripe. The smell of a ripe fruit before it is opened is disagreeable to most (resembling decayed onions), but the thick, sweet, firm interior flesh has a sweet aroma and flavor reminiscent of pineapple and banana. Most often eaten fresh, the golden pulp may also be cooked with coconuts and spices, mixed in curries as a vegetable, included in fruit salads, boiled and dried for storage, or preserved in syrups. Westerners generally find the jackfruit most acceptable in the full-grown but unripe stage, at which time it is simply cut into chunks for cooking, boiled in lightly salted water until tender, and the flesh (and now edible seeds) cut from the rind and served as a vegetable. There may be up to five hundred large, starchy, kidney-shaped, edible seeds of medium size contained with the flesh. The raw seeds or "nuts" are indigestible due to the presence of a

Jackfruit

Nutritional Value Per 100 g Edible Portion

	Raw
Calories	98
Protein	1.3-1.9 g
Fat	0.1-0.3 g
Fiber	1.0-1.1 g
Calcium	22-34 mg
Iron	0.5 mg
Magnesium	37 mg
Phosphorus	38 mg
Potassium	407 mg
Sodium	2 mg
Zinc	0.42 mg
Copper	0.187 mg
Manganese	0.197 mg
Beta Carotene (A)	297-540 IU
Thiamine (B_1)	0.030 mg
Niacin (B_3)	0.400 mg
Pyridoxine (B_6)	0.108 mg
Ascorbic Acid (C)	8-10 mg

powerful trypsin inhibitor, and have a slightly unpleasant flavor that is removed by boiling or roasting, after which they taste much like European chestnuts. Once cooked, the seeds can be added to soups, stewed with meat, or made into a starchy flour.

Health Benefits The Chinese consider jackfruit pulp and seeds to be tonic, cooling, nutritious, and useful in overcoming the influence of alcohol on the system. The ripe fruit is somewhat laxative, and if eaten in excess will cause diarrhea.

Jambolan *(Syzygium cumini)*

Also Known As: Java Plum, Black Plum.

Syzygium *derives from the Greek word meaning united, and refers to the calyptrate petals. The name* cumini *is of Semitic origin, but unknown meaning.*

General Information The jambolan is native to India, Burma, Ceylon, and the Andaman Islands. By 1870 it had become established in Hawaii and occurs in a semiwild state on all the Hawaiian islands. In southern Florida, the tree was once commonly planted and fruits heavily, but only a small amount of the crop is utilized. The fruit grows in clusters, is round or oblong and often curved, one-half to two inches long. Starting green, it ripens to light magenta, then dark purple or nearly black.

Lore and Legend

In southern Asia, the tree is venerated by Buddhists, and it is commonly planted near Hindu temples because it is considered sacred to Krishna. The leaves and fruits are employed in worshiping the elephant-headed god, Ganesha or Vinaijaka.

Culinary Uses This fruit's juicy flesh is either white or purple, depending on the variety, and encloses at least one seed. The white-fleshed kind is generally sweeter than the other, but the taste is always astringent. Jambolans of good size and quality are eaten raw or may be made into tarts, sauces, and jam. Less desirable fruit is generously rubbed with salt before eating, or makes a good basis for cool drinks. All but decidedly inferior fruits have been utilized for their juice, which is much like grape juice. Jambolan vinegar, made throughout India, is an attractive clear purple, with a pleasant aroma and mild flavor.

Health Benefits The fruit is stated to be astringent, stomachic, carminative, antiscorbutic, and diuretic. Cooked to a thick jam, it is eaten to allay acute diarrhea. Juice from ripe fruits or jambolan vinegar may be administered in India in cases of enlargement of the spleen, chronic diarrhea, and urine retention. Water-diluted juice is used as a gargle for sore throats and as a lotion for ringworm of the scalp. The seeds contain an alkaloid, jambosine, and a glycoside, jambolin or antimellin, which halts the diastatic conversion of starch into sugar. The leaves, stems, flower buds, opened blossoms, and bark have some antibiotic properties.

Jambolan

Nutritional Value Per 100 g Edible Portion

	Raw
Calories	60
Protein	0.70-1.29 g
Fat	0.15-0.30 g
Fiber	0.3-0.9 g
Calcium	8.3-15 mg
Iron	1.20-1.62 mg
Magnesium	15-35 mg
Phosphorus	15.0-16.2 mg
Potassium	55-79 mg
Sodium	14.0-26.2 mg
Copper	0.230 mg
Beta Carotene (A)	10-80 IU
Thiamine (B_1)	0.008-0.030 mg
Riboflavin (B_2)	0.009-0.010 mg
Niacin (B_3)	0.200-0.290 mg
Pyridoxine (B_6)	0.038 mg
Folic Acid (B_9)	3 mcg
Ascorbic Acid (C)	5.7-18 mg

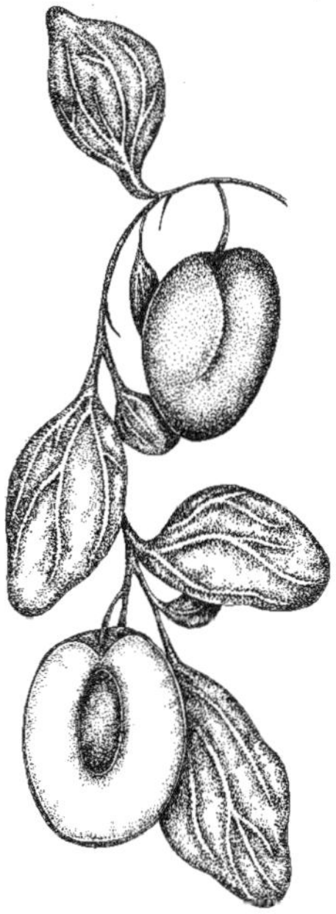

Jujube (*Zizyphus jujuba, Z. mauritiana*)

Also Known As: Chinese Jujube, Chinese Date.

> Zizyphus *derives from* zizouf, *the Arabian name.* Mauritiana *means coming from the Mauritius Island in the Indian Ocean. The English name* jujube *is a convoluted derivation of the Latin name.*

General Information The **Chinese jujube** *(Z. jujuba)* is the fruit of a small spiny tree that originated in China and which grows in mild-temperate, dry, and sub-tropical regions of both hemispheres. In China, this fruit has been grown and eaten for more than four thousand years, and even now China has more jujube trees than any other type of fruit tree (persimmons are second). The Roman scholar Pliny recorded that jujubes were brought to Rome from Syria sometime near the end of Augustus's reign, and from there spread throughout southern Europe and northern Africa. They reached America in 1837, and aroused some interest among horticulturists as an ornamental, but the fruit itself never caught on. Ranging in size from that of a cherry to a plum, the jujube is oblong or spherical in form, with a thin, reddish-brown skin and a whitish flesh of mealy texture and sweet flavor. The **Indian jujube** (*Z. mauritiana*) is native from the Province of Yunnan in southern China to Afghanistan, Malaysia, and Queensland, Australia. It is cultivated to some extent throughout its natural range, but mostly in India, where it is grown commercially; its flavor is generally considered less desirable.

Lore and Legend

When the Greek hero Ulysses reached the Land of the Lotus Eaters (now identified with the Tunisian island of Djerba), Homer tells us that his companions abandoned themselves to the local diet, forgetting home and families and desiring nothing except to remain in the country of the lotus, in perpetual idleness, forever. The Lotophagoi, according to ancient writers, lived on the lotus exclusively and also made an intoxicating drink from it. The lotus of Homer was most likely not the lotus of Buddha or of the Nile, but the Chinese date or jujube.

Culinary Uses Slightly underripe fruits have flesh that is juicy, acid or subacid to sweet, somewhat astringent, much like that of a crab apple. When just ripe, the fruit is mahogany colored and as shiny and smooth as if buffed with a cloth. At this stage, the flesh is crisp and sweet, reminiscent of an apple. If left to ripen a bit longer, the skin begins to wrinkle as the fruit loses water, and the flesh changes from light green to beige and becomes soft, musky, more datelike. In China, jujubes are eaten fresh, dried, smoked, pickled, candied, and as a butter. In candied form they are even more reminiscent of dates, with their long pointed (inedible) seeds and caramel-like texture. The fruit can also be boiled with rice or baked with breads, much like raisin bread.

Jujube

Nutritional Value Per 100 g Edible Portion

	Chinese Raw	Chinese Dried	Indian Raw	Indian Dried
Calories	79-105	287	n/a	473/lb
Protein	1.2 g	3.7 g	0.8 g	1.44 g
Fat	0.2 g	1.1 g	0.07 g	0.21 g
Fiber	1.4 g	3.0 g	0.60 g	1.28 g
Calcium	21 mg	79 mg	25.6 mg	n/a
Iron	0.48 mg	1.8 mg	0.76-1.8 mg	n/a
Magnesium	10 mg	37 mg	n/a	n/a
Phosphorus	23 mg	100 mg	26.8 mg	n/a
Potassium	250 mg	531 mg	n/a	n/a
Sodium	3 mg	9 mg	n/a	n/a
Zinc	0.050 mg	0.190 mg	n/a	n/a
Copper	0.073 mg	0.265 mg	n/a	n/a
Manganese	0.084 mg	0.305 mg	n/a	n/a
Beta Carotene (A)	40 IU	n/a	0.021 mg	n/a
Thiamine (B_1)	0.020 mg	0.210 mg	0.020-0.024 mg	n/a
Riboflavin (B_2)	0.040 mg	0.360 mg	0.020-0.038 mg	n/a
Niacin (B_3)	0.900 mg	0.500 mg	0.700-0.873 mg	n/a
Pyridoxine (B_6)	0.081 mg	n/a	n/a	n/a
Ascorbic Acid (C)	69 mg	13 mg	65.8-76.0 mg	n/a

Health Benefits The jujube has a high concentration of sugar, about 22 percent. Dried ripe fruit is a mild laxative, while fresh fruits are applied to cuts and ulcers or, when mixed with salt and chili peppers, are given for indigestion and biliousness.

Juneberry *(Amelanchier alnifolia, A. canadensis, A. laevis, A. oreophila, A. spicata)*

Also Known As: Serviceberry, Shadbush.

> Amelanchier *is from* amelancier, *the French Provençal name of* A. ovalis *and* A. vulgaris. Alnifolia *refers to the fact that the leaves are similar to alder* (alnus) *leaves.* Canadensis *refers to a Canadian origin;* laevis *means smooth, free from hairs or roughness;* oreophila *means mountain-loving;* spicata *means having spikes. The English name* juneberry *refers to the berries' season of ripening. The plant received its alternate name* serviceberry *due to its resemblance to the service tree, an ignored English fruit* (Sorbus domestica)*; the name* shadbush *refers to the fact the bush blossoms just when the shad appear in the rivers.*

General Information There are at least twenty-four different species of juneberry, and the plant grows wild throughout every province of Canada and every state in the continental United States. The American Indians pounded the berries with the meat and fat of game animals to make pemmican, and the berries were a staple of early white settlers on the northern plains. The various species include scrubby plants that hug the ground, trees fifty feet tall, and all sizes of trees and shrubs in between. Not a true berry botanically, the juneberry is a pome fruit akin to the apple and pear. Large quantities of the dark blue or purplish-black berries develop each summer, blueberry-sized or larger.

Culinary Uses The round fruit has a sweet and pleasant odor, and an equally sweet flavor. The berries are delicious any way you want to serve them. Dry them for the winter, cook them into sauces, or make jams, jellies, pies, puddings, muffins, even wine. The few small seeds are edible, and impart a slight almond taste.

Kiwano *(Cucumis metuliferus)*

Also Known As: Horned Melon, Horned Cucumber.

> Cucumis *is the old Latin name for the cucumber family.*

General Information This emigrant from Africa definitely wins prizes for its strange appearance. A brilliant golden-orange oval about five inches long, it has small protuberances all over its skin. Its appearance is at once startling and droll, like a comic-book creature either from the deep sea or outer space.

Culinary Uses and **Health Benefits** The rich green flesh, gelatinous and juicy, holds lots of white seeds like those of other melons. Its flavor is very subtle, many would say bland. The kiwano keeps at room temperature for up to six months.

Kiwi *(Actinidia chinensis)*

Also Known As: Chinese Gooseberry, due to the flavor and color of the flesh.

> *The genus name* Actinidia *comes from the Greek* aktin, *meaning ray or motion, and refers to the lighter colored rays in the crosswise-sliced fruit. The term* chinensis *denotes its Chinese origin. New Zealand growers in 1962 began calling this strange little fruit "kiwifruit" to give it more market appeal, and this name has become widely accepted. The term was commercially adopted as the trade name in 1974. The translation of the French term for kiwi* (souris vegetales) *is* vegetable mouse, *which is more descriptive than any of its other names, but might make some squeamish.*

General Information The kiwi plant, a vigorous climber, is native to the Yangtze Valley in northern China and the Zhejiang Province in eastern China, but the Chinese have never been overly fond of the fruit, regarding it primarily as a tonic for growing children and for women after childbirth. Kiwi fruits start out with rough green skins, which turn brown and fuzzy when ripe. E.H. ("Chinese") Wilson, the well-known plant explorer, shipped the first seed lots from Asia to England, France, and the United States around 1900. Most introductions emphasized the ornamental qualities of the vines; not so in New Zealand, where the fruits were recognized for their commercial potential. From a single seed lot planted in 1906, the "Chinese Gooseberry" quickly flourished. Years later, with increasing foreign demand and anti-communist sentiments running high, enterprising New Zealanders renamed the fruit after their national treasure, the kiwi bird. An appropriate choice, since these brown, fuzzy, egg-shaped fruits are as strange looking as their namesake bird.

Buying Tips When buying, look for undamaged fruit that yields evenly to gentle pressure, much like a not-quite-tender nectarine. Those that are still overly firm will soften and sweeten in a week at room temperature. If the fruit is refrigerated (and humidity maintained at 95 percent in a small plastic bag with a few holes) it will keep for nine months.

Kiwi

Nutritional Value Per 100 g Edible Portion

	Raw
Calories	66
Protein	0.79 g
Fat	0.07-0.44 g
Fiber	1.10 g
Calcium	16-26 mg
Iron	0.51 mg
Magnesium	30 mg
Phosphorus	40-64 mg
Potassium	332 mg
Sodium	5 mg
Beta Carotene (A)	175 IU
Thiamine (B_1)	0.02 mg
Riboflavin (B_2)	0.05 mg
Niacin (B_3)	0.50 mg
Ascorbic Acid (C)	75-105 mg

Culinary Uses Kiwi fruit has a sparkling emerald green interior flesh with a distinct bright center starburst and a cluster of very small dark purple or black edible seeds. Reminding some people of a cross between strawberries and bananas, the flesh is tart-sweet and slightly crisp-textured. Their hairy skin is inedible and must be removed before eating. Kiwis can be eaten on their own, sliced and added to salads, desserts, cakes, and jams, or used as an attractive garnish to salads. Like pineapple and papaya, kiwi contains an enzyme that tenderizes meat. It also curdles milk (but not heavy cream) and interferes with the action of gelatin. If you want to add kiwi fruit to gelatin, you should first briefly cook the fruit, which deactivates the actinidin enzyme. Similarly, it must be cooked before it is added to foods containing dairy products such as ice cream or yogurt, to which it will impart an off-flavor.

Health Benefits Kiwi fruit helps remove excess sodium buildup in the body, and contains enzymes similar to those in papaya and pineapple that help in correcting digestive problems.

Kumquat *(Fortunella margarita)*

This fruit was named in honor of Robert Fortune, an English traveler and collector of plants for the Royal Horticultural Society in London, who introduced the kumquat into Europe in 1846. Margarita *means pearl, probably due to its small size. The English name* kumquat *comes from the Chinese word* kam kwat, *which means golden orange, a fitting description of this brilliant fruit.*

Kumquat

Nutritional Value Per 100 g Edible Portion

	Raw
Calories	274
Protein	3.8 g
Fat	0.4 g
Fiber	3.7 g
Sodium	30 mg
Calcium	266 mg
Iron	1.7 mg
Magnesium	13 mg
Phosphorus	97 mg
Potassium	995 mg
Zinc	0.080 mg
Copper	0.107 mg
Manganese	0.086 mg
Beta Carotene (A)	2530 IU
Thiamine (B_1)	0.350 mg
Riboflavin (B_2)	0.400 mg
Ascorbic Acid (C)	151 mg

General Information Said to be a native of southeast China, this diminutive citrus-like fruit is not a true citrus, but is closely related. It was included in the Citrus genus until about 1915, when Dr. Walter Swingle set it apart in the genus *Fortunella*. Kumquat trees were known to exist at least by the seventeenth century, when their name entered the English language in the form of "cam-quit," but the fruit was not introduced into Europe until 1846. In Western countries, kumquat plants used to be placed on the table at fashionable dinners so that guests could pick the small tasty fruit at will. Kumquat fruits are small (one to two inches in length), oblong or roundish, bright orange in color, and with the same kind of peel texture as that of citrus fruits.

Buying Tips When buying, check to make sure the kumquats are plump, golden, firm and not soft-wet; if they come with foliage, you can gauge their freshness by the leaves. Because of their thin skins, they keep less well than oranges and other citrus fruits.

Culinary Uses Kumquats have an aromatic, sweet skin and a tartly sour and spicy interior flecked with little green seeds. The most popular way of treating kumquats in China has been to preserve them in honey. In the West, they are generally eaten whole, rind and all; they should be squeezed first to break and blend the juicy pulp. They can also be simmered in sugar, brandied, pickled, preserved, made into a sauce, or used whole as companions to fowl. They make a beautiful garnish, especially with dark chocolate desserts. Canned kumquats are exported from Taiwan and frequently served as dessert in Chinese restaurants. **Limequats,** a pale yellow Mexican lime-kumquat hybrid produced by Dr. Swingle in 1909, are a useful lime substitute that are eaten whole like the kumquat either with or without the pit.

Lemon *(Citrus limon)*

The term Citrus *derives from the Greek term for the citron,* kedromelon. *The species name* limon *is derived from the Arabic* laymun, *which also provided the English name.*

General Information The lemon tree is native to the tropical regions of northern India, with fruit that is a bright yellow ovoid berry, about three inches long, smooth, nipple-shaped at the end, with an acid, pale yellow pulp. Lemons were being cultivated in Greece and Rome in the fourth century A.D., but were always rare and expensive. It is the Moors who are credited with establishing the lemon orchards of Andalusia, and introducing the fruit into

Lore and Legend

In the third century A.D., the Romans believed that lemons were an antidote for all poisons, as illustrated by the tale of two criminals thrown to venomous snakes; the one who had eaten a lemon beforehand survived snakebite, while the other died. So great was the lemon's reputation that it became an accompaniment for fish meals in the belief that if a fishbone got stuck in the throat, the lemon juice would dissolve it. In Ceylon, there is a story that all the ogres dwelling in Ceylon live in a single lemon and if one can but find that lemon and cut it into pieces, they will all perish. The British Navy used lemon and lime juice extensively to combat the scurvy plaguing their seamen (see also **Limes**). During the California Gold Rush, scurvy was so rampant and fresh produce so scarce that miners were willing to pay a dollar apiece for lemons. The world's largest lemon weighed in at a whopping 5 pounds 13 ounces and was grown by Violet Philips of Queensland, Australia, in 1975.

Sicily. Northern Europe most likely did not receive lemons until between A.D. 1000–1200, when the Crusaders were returning from the Near East. Columbus introduced the lemon into the Western hemisphere, when he stopped at one of the Canary Islands in October of 1493 and gathered seeds of citrus fruits as well as other plants. Once the lemon reached the New World, it spread rapidly. Lemons were planted in St. Augustine, Florida, in 1565 when the Spanish settled there. Two centuries later, seeds were taken to California by the Franciscan Fathers when they moved from Mexico. Since 1950, California has produced more lemons than all of Europe combined. A single tree has been known to produce three thousand lemons a year, because lemon trees will bloom and ripen fruit in every month of the year. Commercial lemons are not permitted to grow until fully ripe, for they lose their desirable acidulous properties when allowed to mature and sometimes grow to enormous sizes. The main varieties of lemon sold in the United States are Eureka and Lisbon. The small, sweet, thin-skinned Meyer is rarely shipped to markets.

Buying Tips When purchased, lemons should be semisoft with a bright golden yellow color. Those tinged with green have not been properly "cured" and will be more acidic. Thick-skinned lemons will have less juice than thinner-skinned varieties.

Culinary Uses Lemons have long been considered the most versatile of the citrus family, except that the tart pulp is too sour for most people to eat raw. An important acidifying and flavoring agent, the lemon has a primary role in the taste of many dishes. It is a common accompaniment to fish or meat, and iced or hot tea. Lemon zest and/or juice will add a wonderful tang to soups, desserts, cakes, jams, and pickles; the juice can substitute perfectly for vinegar and is not irritating to the stomach lining; and slices of lemon make pretty garnishes for a wide range of sweet and savory dishes. One of the most common uses of lemons is for lemonade. The ascorbic acid in lemon juice will also prevent fruits like avocados and apples from oxidizing or turning brown when exposed to air after being cut. Another good use for lemon juice is to bleach linen or muslin: just moisten the cloth in lemon juice and then spread to dry in the sun. As well, the juice removes ink stains, iron rust, and fruit stains from fabrics. Rub the stain well with lemon juice, cover with salt, and put in the sun; repeat if necessary.

Health Benefits Astringent, antiseptic, refrigerant. Lemon juice has long been heralded as a tonic throughout the world; it is used as a gargle for sore throats, a lotion for sunburn, a cure for hiccups, and a popular home remedy for numerous ailments, particularly colds, coughs, and sore throats. Hot lemonade is noted as a diaphoretic, increasing perspiration and the production of fluids in the body, and thus is good to take prior to going to bed with a cold. Lemons, along with the rest of the citrus family, work as strong solvents in the body, stimulating the liver and gall bladder, and stirring up any inactive acids and latent toxic settlements that cannot be eliminated any other way. They contain a substance known as limonene, which is used to dissolve gallstones and which shows extreme promise as an anticancer agent. The highest content of limonene is found in the white spongy inner parts of the fruit. Lemons are wonderful for fevers, because a feverish body responds to citric

Lemon

Nutritional Value Per 100 g Edible Portion

	Raw Fruit w/o peel	Fresh Juice	Unsweetened Processed Juice	Undiluted Frozen Lemonade
Calories	29	25	23	195
Protein	1.1 g	0.38 g	0.4 g	0.2 g
Fat	0.3 g	0 g	0.1 g	0.1 g
Fiber	0.4 g	trace	trace	0.1 g
Sodium	2 mg	1 mg	1 mg	0.2 mg
Calcium	26 mg	7 mg	7 mg	4 mg
Iron	0.6 mg	0.03 mg	0.2 mg	0.2 mg
Magnesium	n/a	6 mg	n/a	n/a
Phosphorus	16 mg	6 mg	10 mg	6 mg
Potassium	138 mg	124 mg	141 mg	70 mg
Zinc	0.060 mg	0.050 mg	n/a	n/a
Copper	0.037 mg	0.029 mg	n/a	n/a
Manganese	n/a	0.008 mg	n/a	n/a
Beta Carotene (A)	29 IU	20 IU	20 IU	20 IU
Thiamine (B_1)	0.040 mg	0.030 mg	0.030 mg	0.020 mg
Riboflavin (B_2)	0.020 mg	0.010 mg	0.010 mg	0.030 mg
Niacin (B_3)	0.100 mg	0.100 mg	0.100 mg	0.300 mg
Pantothenic Acid (B_5)	0.190 mg	0.103 mg	n/a	n/a
Pyridoxine (B_6)	0.080 mg	0.051 mg	n/a	n/a
Folic Acid (B_9)	10.6 mcg	12.9 mcg	n/a	n/a
Ascorbic Acid (C)	53 mg	46 mg	42 mg	30 mg

acid fruits better than to any other food. Although acidic to the taste, citrus fruits have a strong alkaline reaction on the body provided that no sugar is added. They destroy putrefactive bacteria in both the intestines and mouth, and alleviate flatulence and indigestion in general. Their potassium content nourishes the brain and nerve cells, and their calcium strengthens the body structures and makes for healthy teeth. Lemons are an outstanding source of vitamin C, but much of this valuable vitamin is lost if the juice is left exposed to air or stored for very long. Externally, lemon juice can be used on sunburn, warts, and corns, and is currently enjoying a revival of interest as a hair rinse and facial astringent. It is a strong natural antiseptic; the juice destroys harmful bacteria found in cuts and other areas of infection. For skin problems, lemon juice can be applied directly to the skin and allowed to dry. Fresh lemon or lemon juice applied to the inflammation of poison ivy will bring immediate relief (an orange also works well).

Lime *(Citrus hystrix, C. aurantifolius, C. latifolia)*

The term Citrus *derives from the Greek term for the citron,* kedromelon. Hystrix *means porcupine-like;* aurantifolia *means golden-leaved;* latifolia *means broad-leaved. The English name* lime *is derived from the Arabic* lim.

General Information Of the two sour varieties of lime, the **Mexican lime**, also known as the **West Indian** or **Key lime**, is the variety longest known and most widely cultivated, and often referred to simply as "lime." The Mexican Lime is native to the Indo-Malayan region, and the tree has been cultivated for thousands of years both for its fruit and for its decorative foliage. It is assumed to have been carried to North Africa and the Near East by Arabs and taken by Crusaders from Palestine to Mediterranean Europe. It was taken by Columbus to Hispaniola (now Haiti), and Spanish settlers soon established it in Florida. There it acquired its modern name of Key Lime from the southerly chain of islands. They became a commercial crop in the Keys after 1906, when the combination of a severe hurricane and soil depletion forced the locals to abandon pineapple culture. Production peaked in 1923, but the hurricane of 1926 dealt a death blow to the Florida lime groves and they were never restored. During the 1950s an education campaign was introduced in the Florida Keys to arouse interest in the lime so that its cultivation would not disappear, but today there are no regular commercial sources of Key limes in the Florida Keys. Most now come from Mexico.

The origin of the **Tahiti lime** (or Persian Lime) is unknown, but it is presumed to be a hybrid of the Mexican lime and citron, or less likely, the lemon. It is believed that the tree was introduced into the Mediterranean region by way of Iran (formerly Persia); Portuguese traders later carried it to Brazil, and it only reached California between 1850 and 1880. Florida produces 90 percent of the national crop, for making fresh juice and for canned or frozen juice and concentrate. The Tahiti lime is bigger and lends itself more easily to large-scale agriculture than the Key lime because it keeps better, has no thorns, and grows a thick skin that withstands handling and long shipping. The fruit is very similar in size and coloring to the lemon, being oval or oblong, occasionally ribbed, or with a short neck, and between 1$^1/_2$ to 2$^1/_2$ inches wide and 2 to 3 inches long. The peel is vivid green until ripe, at which time it turns a pale yellow.

Lime

Nutritional Value Per 100 g Edible Portion

	Raw Fruit	Fresh Juice
Calories	30	27
Protein	0.07-0.112 g	0.44 g
Fat	0.04-0.17 g	0.10 g
Fiber	0.1-0.5 g	trace
Calcium	4.5-33.3 mg	9 mg
Iron	0.19-0.33 mg	0.03 mg
Magnesium	n/a	6 mg
Phosphorus	9.3-21.0 mg	7 mg
Potassium	102 mg	109 mg
Sodium	2 mg	1 mg
Zinc	0.110 mg	0.060 mg
Copper	0.065 mg	0.030 mg
Manganese	n/a	0.008 mg
Beta Carotene (A)	10 IU	10 IU
Thiamine (B_1)	0.019-0.068 mg	0.020 mg
Riboflavin (B_2)	0.011-0.023 mg	0.010 mg
Niacin (B_3)	0.140-0.250 mg	0.100 mg
Pantothenic Acid (B_5)	0.217 mg	0.138 mg
Pyridoxine (B_6)	n/a	0.043 mg
Folic Acid (B_9)	8.2 mcg	n/a
Ascorbic Acid (C)	30.0-48.7 mg	29.3 mg

Lore and Legend

Sir James Lind, the Scottish naval surgeon, observed the dramatic effect of eating oranges and lemons on sailors during long voyages. At the end of the eighteenth century it was accepted, by the British Navy at least, that the juice of citrus fruits was the only medicine that could conquer the scurvy (caused by lack of vitamin C) that was killing more seamen than enemy action. The Admiralty stood by this decision to the tune of 1.6 million gallons of lemon or lime juice in the period between 1795 and 1815. The mortality rate during this period showed a gratifyingly steep decline. British sailors acquired the nickname limeys from their daily ration of lime juice, which they drank along with their ration of rum. Limes could be imported cheaply and without risk from the English colony, Jamaica, while lemons had to be bought from Mediterranean countries with whom Britain was often at war.

The **Kaffir lime** (*Citrus hystix*) is knobby and bitter, but highly aromatic. The fruit is sometimes used for its acid juice, but the leaves and rind are a more common ingredient and appear frequently in Southeast Asian dishes.

Buying Tips Look for firm fruits with a good weight for their size. Avoid any that look shriveled or soft, or that have decayed spots or skin punctures.

Culinary Uses The small Mexican limes are nearly spherical, thin skinned, and usually contain several seeds. The green fruits are actually the immature fruits; these are the most desirable commercially because of their extreme acidity. The fully ripe, yellow lime does not have as high an acid content as the immature fruit and may be prepared and used in the same way the lemon is used, although they are sweeter. Because of its special bouquet and unique flavor, the Mexican lime is ideal for serving as a garnish and flavoring for fish and meats, for adding zest to cold drinks, and for making limeade. The juice is made into syrups, sauces, preserves, and pies similar to lemon pie. Key Lime Pie is internationally famous, but today is largely made from the frozen concentrate of the Tahiti lime. The Tahiti Lime usually has a seedless, light greenish-yellow pulp that is tender and acid, but without the distinctive bouquet of the Mexican lime. The flesh may be utilized for the same purposes as the Mexican lime—as a flavoring, alternative to vinegar, and limeade. Other uses for lime juice include cleaning the interiors of coffee pots or dissolving calcium deposits in tea kettles.

Health Benefits Astringent, antiseptic, refrigerant. Limes have all the same benefits to the body as lemons. Lime juice has been applied to relieve the effects of stinging corals with good results.

Lingonberry (*Vaccinium vitis idaea*)

Vaccinium *is the ancient Latin name for plants of the blueberry family, derived from* vacca, *meaning cow, and given because cows like the plant.* Vitis *means vine or branch;* idaea *means coming from either Mount Ida in Turkey or Mount Ida in Crete. The English name* lingonberry *derives from the Swedish* lingon, *meaning mountain cranberry.*

General Information This plant bears oval red berries similar to cranberries with a piquant flavor. The lingonberry is greatly esteemed in the Nordic countries; in Finland it is the most popular berry because of its pleasant flavor and good keeping quality.

Culinary Uses Crushed with sugar or made into a sauce, it is often served with meat; roast veal with cream sauce and lingonberry jam is one of the classic dishes of Finland.

Loganberry (*Rubus ursinus loganobaccus*)

Rubus *refers to the redness of the berry, while* ursinus *means pertaining to bears, and* loganobaccus *melds the name of Judge Logan, in whose garden they originated, with that of the Greek god Bacchus, the god of agriculture and wine.*

General Information Loganberries originated in the Santa Cruz, California garden of Judge James H. Logan. A natural hybrid of raspberries and dewberries, loganberries are dark red, more acidic, and very long in comparison to either blackberries or raspberries. Grown mostly for wine making, they have a sharp flavor and can be eaten in the same ways as blackberries and raspberries. One offspring of the loganberry is the **olallieberry**, a bright black, firm, sweet berry that was the result of a cross between the loganberry and youngberry.

Culinary Uses and **Health Benefits**. Same as blackberries.

Loganberry

Nutritional Value Per 100 g Edible Portion

	Raw
Calories	55
Protein	1.52 g
Fat	0.31 g
Fiber	3.0 g
Calcium	26 mg
Iron	0.64 mg
Magnesium	21 mg
Phosphorus	26 mg
Potassium	145 mg
Sodium	1 mg
Zinc	0.340 mg
Copper	0.117 mg
Manganese	1.247 mg
Beta Carotene (A)	35 IU
Thiamine (B_1)	0.050 mg
Riboflavin (B_2)	0.034 mg
Niacin (B_3)	0.840 mg
Pantothenic Acid (B_5)	0.244 mg
Pyridoxine (B_6)	0.065 mg
Folic Acid (B_9)	25.7 mcg
Ascorbic Acid (C)	15.3 mg

Longan *(Dimocarpus longan)*

Also Known As: Dragon's Eyes.

The genus name Dimocarpus *is believed to derive from the Greek words* di *(two),* morph *(form) and* carpos *(fruit), thus meaning a two-formed fruit. The species and English name* longan *is derived from the Chinese* bung yen *or* long yan, *which literally means dragon's eye.*

General Information Native to southern China and southeast Asia, the longan fruit ripens later than its relative the lychee, and withstands lower temperatures, thus making it a more commercially viable prospect. Introduced into Florida from southern China by the United States Department of Agriculture in 1903, the tree flourished in a few locations but never became widely popular. The fruits range from the size of an olive to a baby plum, from spherical to ovoid in shape, and are covered with a thin, rough-to-prickly brown shell (pericarp). They are sometimes called "dragon's eyes" because once the brown shell is peeled, the transparent, jelly-like fruit contains a large, dark seed in its center, which looks much like a large eye.

Longan

Nutritional Value Per 100 g Edible Portion

	Raw	Dried
Calories	60	286
Protein	1.31 g	4.90 g
Fat	0.10 g	0.40 g
Fiber	0.40 g	2.00 g
Calcium	1 mg	45 mg
Iron	0.13 mg	5.4 mg
Magnesium	10 mg	46 mg
Phosphorus	21 mg	196 mg
Potassium	266 mg	658 mg
Sodium	0 mg	48 mg
Zinc	0.050 mg	0.220 mg
Copper	0.169 mg	0.807 mg
Manganese	0.052 mg	0.248 mg
Thiamine (B_1)	0.031 mg	0.040 mg
Riboflavin (B_2)	0.140 mg	n/a
Niacin (B_3)	0.300 mg	n/a
Ascorbic Acid (C)	84 mg	28 mg

Buying Tips Look for heavy, uncracked longans. They will last several weeks if refrigerated.

Culinary Uses Once the outer shell is removed, which is rather like peeling a hard-boiled egg, the juicy, translucent, gray-white pulp is revealed. This clings to a large, smooth, ebony-colored seed that makes any kind of consumption other than pulling with your teeth rather tricky. The soft meat feels like a peeled grape to the tongue, and has a sweet taste with hints of gardenia, spruce, and musk. The stone itself is not edible. Longans are most commonly eaten raw, but they can also be poached in syrup or dried.

Health Benefits The flesh of the fruit is administered as a stomachic, febrifuge, and vermifuge, and is regarded as an antidote for poison. A decoction of the dried flesh is taken as a tonic and treatment for insomnia and neurasthenic neurosis. In both North and South Vietnam, the "eye" of the longan seed is pressed against a snake bite in the belief that it will absorb the venom.

Loquat *(Eriobotrya japonica)*

Also Known As: Japanese or Chinese Medlar

The name Eriobotrya *is a Greek word meaning woolly cluster, and* japonica *relates its Japanese heritage. The English name was adapted from the Cantonese* lu-kwyit, *meaning rush-orange.*

Loquat

Nutritional Value Per 100 g Edible Portion	Raw
Calories	47
Protein	0.43 g
Fat	0.20 g
Fiber	0.50 g
Calcium	16 mg
Iron	0.28 mg
Magnesium	13 mg
Phosphorus	27 mg
Potassium	266 mg
Sodium	1 mg
Zinc	0.050 mg
Copper	0.040 mg
Manganese	0.148 mg
Beta Carotene (A)	1528 IU
Thiamine (B_1)	0.019 mg
Riboflavin (B_2)	0.024 mg
Niacin (B_3)	0.180 mg
Ascorbic Acid (C)	1 mg

General Information The loquat is native to tropical regions of China and southern Japan, though it may have been introduced into Japan very early. It is closely related to the apple and pear of the temperate zones, and those who find other tropical fruits too sweet and rich will enjoy the loquat. The fruits grow in clusters of four to thirty, are oval, rounded, or pear-shaped, and 1 to 2 inches long. A little bit larger than the kumquat, and looking slightly like the medlar, the two are often confused, with the loquat sometimes called Japanese medlar in English. The spread of this species is mostly due to the fact that its fruits ripen extraordinarily early in the springtime, close to the beginning of the year. This is why the loquat became so popular, despite the fact that it is not one of the tastiest of fruits. Today there is nothing unusual in having fresh fruit available year round, but in the past it was considered exceptional and somewhat luxurious to have early fruits in the middle of winter.

Buying Tips Select large fruits that are tender and sweetly scented. Refrigerate only if on the verge of spoiling.

Culinary Uses This golden-skinned fruit resembles a small apricot in size and color, turning from green to yellow or orange when ripe. Its delicate yet firm, sweet-tart flesh can be orange, yellow, or white, and tastes randomly like plums, grapes, or cherries. It should be picked when perfectly ripe, so that the sugar content and juicy, refreshing pulp are at their best. If you take just one bite, the fruit might have a bitter taste; put the whole thing in your mouth and start chewing and it will be very sweet. Their skins are edible, but the large brown seed is not. If you live in a tropical or semitropical climate, just throw the seeds into your garden, as they sprout easily into trees. Although best when eaten straight from the tree, the fruit may also be added to fruit salads, blended with other fruits to make a delicious drink, made into preserves, stewed, or added to confectionery. When cooked, they have a flavor similar to poached plums.

Health Benefits The fruit is said to act as a sedative and is eaten to halt vomiting and thirst.

Lychee *(Litchi chinensis)*

Litchi *is the Chinese name for this fruit, while* lychee *is the anglicized version;* chinensis *specifies that it is of Chinese origin.*

General Information The lychee is native to lower elevations of the Kwangtung and Fukien provinces in southern China, where it flourishes along rivers and near the seacoast. Part of the soapberry family, lychee trees prefer a subtropical climate and will not flourish if

Lore and Legend

According to legend, lychees once caused a war in ancient China. In the Emperor's court there was a beautiful girl who liked fresh and dried lychees better than any other food. Eager to please his lovely subject, the Emperor sent soldiers to a distant province where lychees grew; after battling victoriously, the troops harvested the fruit and uprooted the trees to take them back to the Emperor's court. Traditionally the favorite fruit of southern China, during the first century A.D. the lychee was considered the finest of southern delicacies and a special courier service with swift horses was set up to bring fresh fruit from Canton north to the Imperial Court. When the Sung dynasty poet Su Tung-po was exiled to Hainan Island in the eleventh century, he declared that he could reconcile himself to banishment anywhere if he could but have three hundred lychees to eat every day.

conditions are not exactly right. Once rooted, however, they often live for a thousand years. The trees are beautiful, with branches that curve down like an open umbrella from heights of thirty to forty feet, and are prolific bearers, often producing heavily for two centuries. A comparative latecomer to North America, the first lychee crops ripened in Florida in 1916, and California now produces a moderate amount. The fruit is the size of a plumply round walnut or small plum, and is bright-red or brown with a hard scaly outer covering. The edible portion is the delicate whitish pulp between the outer covering and large brown interior seed.

Buying Tips Ripe lychees should be plump, with a tight skin, semi-firm to the touch, and a sweet flowery fragrance. Avoid those that are cracked, leaking, or giving off a fermented aroma. The shells may be mottled with brown, which does not affect the fruit's flavor.

Culinary Uses Once stripped of their shells, the fruits look like and have the consistency of large white grapes, with their juicy, translucent-looking flesh containing a large glossy brown pit in the middle. The taste and aroma are reminiscent of muscat grapes and roses, but sweeter, and have been compared by some to jellied incense. To eat the fresh lychee, a piece of the rind is broken off at one end and the pulp and seed are forced into the mouth by pressing with the fingers. The inedible seed is then discarded. Fresh lychees are best, but the fruits must be picked without delay when ripe because they lose their flavor and color after a few days. They may be kept a year or more in frozen storage if the temperature is continuously held near zero degrees Fahrenheit. In China, the traditional method of preserving the fruit is to hang them in clusters to dry in the sun; sun-dried fruits are considered to have a more delectable flavor than kiln-dried.

Lychee "nuts" are made by drying the fruit, which then becomes firm, sweet, and very dark in color. Like a nut with a raisin-like center, the flavor is often compared to a combination of nuts and Muscat grapes. Canned lychees, with rind and seed removed, retain some but not all of the hauntingly aromatic flavor of the fresh fruit. Lychees are frequently used as ingredients of sauces and jams, or made into wine.

Health Benefits Ingested in moderate amounts, the lychee is believed to relieve coughing and to have a beneficial effect on tumors and enlargements of the glands. The Chinese believe that excessive consumption of the raw fruit causes fever and nosebleed.

Lychee

Nutritional Value Per 100 g Edible Portion

	Raw	Dried
Calories	63-64	277
Protein	0.68-1.0 g	2.9-3.8 g
Fat	0.3-0.58 g	0.20-1.2 g
Fiber	0.23-0.4 g	1.4 g
Calcium	8-10 mg	33 mg
Iron	0.4 mg	1.7 mg
Magnesium	10 mg	42 mg
Phosphorus	30-42 mg	181 mg
Potassium	170 mg	1110 mg
Sodium	1-3 mg	3 mg
Zinc	0.070 mg	0.280 mg
Copper	0.148 mg	0.631 mg
Manganese	0.055 mg	0.234 mg
Thiamine (B_1)	0.011 mg	0.010 mg
Riboflavin (B_2)	0.065 mg	0.570 mg
Nicotinic Acid (B_3)	0.603 mg	3.100 mg
Ascorbic Acid (C)	24-60 mg	42-183 mg

Mamey *(Mammea americana)*

Also Known As: Mammee, Mammee Apple, St. Domingo Apricot, South American Apricot.

Mammea *derives from* mamey, *an aboriginal West Indian name for the fruit.* Americana *means native to the Americas.*

Mamey

Nutritional Value Per 100 g Edible Portion	Raw
Calories	44.5-45.3
Protein	0.088-0.470 g
Fat	0.15-0.99 g
Fiber	0.80-1.07 g
Calcium	4.0-19.5 mg
Iron	0.15-2.51 mg
Phosphorus	7.8-14.5 mg
Potassium	47 mg
Sodium	15 mg
Beta Carotene (A)	230 IU
Thiamine (B_1)	0.017-0.030 mg
Riboflavin (B_2)	0.025-0.068 mg
Niacin (B_3)	0.160-0.738 mg
Pantothenic Acid (B_5)	0.103 mg
Ascorbic Acid (C)	10.2-22.0 mg

General Information Native to the West Indies and northern South America, the mamey fruit is the size of an orange or larger, round with slight points at the top and bottom. The tough skin, yellowish-russet in color, is bitter, as is the covering of the three seeds.

Culinary Uses The fragrant golden-yellow or orange pulp between the skin and seeds varies from firm and crisp to tender, melting, and juicy. The fruit is appealingly fragrant, and pleasantly subacid in the best varieties, resembling the apricot or red raspberry in flavor. Fruits of poor quality may be too sour or mawkishly sweet. To facilitate peeling, the skin is scored from top to bottom and removed in strips. The whitish membrane beneath, which must also be removed, is usually scraped off, and the flesh is then cut off in slices, leaving any part that may adhere to the seed and trimming off any particles of seed-covering. Tender varieties are delicious raw, either plain in fruit salads, or served with cream and sugar or wine. Sliced flesh may also be cooked into pies or tarts, and is widely made into preserves such as spiced marmalade and pastes. Slightly underripe fruits, rich in pectin, are made into jelly.

Health Benefits An antibiotic principle was reported by the Agricultural Experiment Station, Rio Piedras, Puerto Rico, in 1951. In some persons, the fruit produces discomfort in the digestive system, so those trying it for the first time should eat only a small portion.

Mamoncillo *(Melicoccus bijugatus)*

Also Known As: Genip, Honeyberry.

Melicoccus *derives from a Greek term meaning honey berry, referring to the sweet taste of the fruit.* Bijugatus *means two yoked together, or having two pairs joined.*

Mamoncillo

Nutritional Value Per 100 g Edible Portion	Raw
Calories	58.11-73
Protein	0.50-1.0 g
Fat	0.08-0.2 g
Fiber	0.07-2.60 g
Calcium	3.4-15 mg
Iron	0.47-1.19 mg
Phosphorus	9.8-23.9 mg
Beta Carotene (A)	70 IU
Thiamine (B_1)	0.030-0.210 mg
Riboflavin (B_2)	0.010-0.200 mg
Niacin (B_3)	0.150-0.900 mg
Ascorbic Acid (C)	0.8-10.0 mg

General Information The mamoncillo fruit is borne on a large tree native to Colombia, Venezuela, and the island of Margarita. The small cherry-sized green fruit looks like a small lime, with its smooth leathery skin. The pulp is salmon-colored or yellowish, translucent, and juicy, but scant and somewhat fibrous.

Culinary Uses When fully ripe, the pulp is pleasantly acid-sweet and reminiscent of grapes, but if unripe, acidity predominates. In most fruits there is a single large hard-shelled seed. For eating out of hand, the rind is merely torn open at the stem end and the pulp-coated seed squeezed into the mouth and the juice sucked from the pulp until there is nothing left of it but the fiber. More commonly, the peeled fruits are boiled and the resulting juice is prized for cold drinks. The seeds are eaten after roasting.

Health Benefits In Venezuela, the astringent roasted seed kernels are pulverized, mixed with honey, and given to halt diarrhea. A dye has been made experimentally from the juice of the raw fruit, which leaves an indelible stain.

Lore and Legend

The sixteenth century Mogul Emperor Akbar, who ruled Northern India from 1556 to 1605, was so taken with the taste and fragrance of mangoes that he ordered an orchard of one hundred thousand trees to be planted at Darbhanga in Bihar. A Hindu legend relates that the beautiful daughter of the sun once escaped from a wicked sorceress by jumping into a lake and transforming herself into a golden lotus. The king of the land fell so in love with the lotus that the evil sorceress burned it to ashes. From the ashes grew a tree, the tree flowered, and the king then fell in love with this second flower. The flower became a fruit, a glorious mango, and the king fell in love with the mango. When the mango was ripe, it fell to the ground and split open; out stepped the daughter of the sun in all her resplendent glory, and the king recognized her as the wife whom he had lost long ago.

In India, there is a story that during one incarnation the Buddha was a merchant and trader. One day he stopped a traveling caravan at the edge of a forest to warn them that poisonous trees grew in the forest and that before tasting any unfamiliar fruit they should consult him. Having thus promised, the traders proceeded into the forest. Within the forest was a village, and within the village a what-fruit tree grew; the what-fruit tree looks exactly like a mango tree and the fruit tastes exactly like a mango, but are poisonous and cause immediate death. Some of the caravan's greedier members immediately hurried up to the tree and ate its luscious-looking fruit, while the others consulted the merchant, who told them not to touch it. As for the foolish members who were by now deathly ill, the merchant kindly treated them. Caravans on many other occasions had stopped by this tree, rashly eaten its fruit and died, at which time the villagers would fall upon and loot the caravan. On this particular day, they came expecting the usual spoils and found everyone alive and well. Surprised, they questioned the merchant as to how he knew that the tree was poisonous and not a mango. He said, "When near a village grows a tree/ Not hard to climb, 'tis plain to me/ Nor need I further proof to know/ No wholesome fruit thereon can grow!"

Mango *(Mangifera indica)*

*The Latin name for this plant is very descriptive: it means simply mango-bearing (*mangifera*) plant from India (*indica*). The English word* mango *is the native name for one species of the plant.*

General Information This favorite fruit of the Orient, one of the finest of the tropics, is a native of southeast Asia and India. Cultivated for over six thousand years, the enormous mango tree is a member of the sumac family and is related to the cashew. Creating an oasis wherever they stand with their thick, shiny green leaves, mango trees bear their fruit like giant upside-down lollipops hanging from long stems. Of the fifty species that grow naturally in the region from India eastward to the Philippines and Papua New Guinea, the Indian mango is indisputably supreme, being as one Indian poet so elegantly described, "sealed jars of paradisical honey." Baskets of mangoes there are considered a warm gesture of friendship. The fruit comes in varying shapes, sizes, and colors: pear, peach, heart, or kidney shapes are the most common, but some are long, thin, and S-shaped. Their size ranges from that of a plum to a large apple, and although they are usually orange, they may cover the full spectrum from green to yellow or red. Mangoes are one of the leading fruit crops in the world. In fact, more mangoes are consumed on a regular basis by more people in the world than are apples.

Buying Tips Choose firm heavy fruit that yield evenly to pressure, are almost as tender as an avocado, and are without blemishes. They should have a sweet, aromatic fragrance; when overripe, they are soft and the aroma is heady and slightly fermented. Green skins indicate the fruit will not fully ripen, while black-spotted skins indicate overripe fruit.

Culinary Uses Mangos have a unique-tasting orange flesh that is quite unlike any other fruit. When chilled, they have been described as a delicate blend between sweet and sour, as good as any peach-pineapple-apricot mousse you can concoct, rich and sweet but

Mango

Nutritional Value Per 100 g Edible Portion	Raw
Calories	62.1-63.7
Protein	0.36-0.40 g
Fat	0.30-0.53 g
Fiber	0.85-1.06 g
Calcium	6.1-12.8 mg
Iron	0.20-0.63 mg
Magnesium	9 mg
Phosphorus	5.5-17.9 mg
Potassium	156 mg
Sodium	2 mg
Zinc	0.040 mg
Copper	0.110 mg
Manganese	0.027 mg
Beta Carotene (A)	3894 IU
Thiamine (B_1)	0.020-0.073 mg
Riboflavin (B_2)	0.025-0.068 mg
Niacin (B_3)	0.025-0.707 mg
Pantothenic Acid (B_5)	0.160 mg
Pyridoxine (B_6)	0.134 mg
Ascorbic Acid (C)	7.8-172.0 mg
Tocopherol (E)	1.12 mg

never cloying. If unchilled, they sometimes have the faintest trace of turpentine flavor. These are some of the most awkward fruits to handle, as the flesh is very soft. The best way is to cut a thick slice lengthwise down either side of the stone, as near to it as possible, then scoop out the flesh. The skin is edible but chewy, and is generally peeled off; the large stone is inedible. Overly fibrous fruits are massaged, the stem-end cut off, and the juice squeezed directly into the mouth. Mangoes can be eaten on their own or used in fruit salads, cakes, drinks, jams, and chutneys. They go with all tropical fruits and flavorings, taking well to ginger, chiles, and coconut. They can be bought fresh or canned and are also available dried.

Health Benefits Mangoes are beneficial for the kidneys, combat acidity and poor digestion, are wonderful disinfectants in the body, relieve clogged pores of the skin, and reduce cysts. Many people claim the mango is a great blood cleanser, and that the juice will help reduce excessive body heat as well as fevers.

Mangosteen (*Garcinia mangostana*)

The genus Garcinia *was named after Laurence Garcin, who lived and collected plants in eighteenth-century India.* Mangostana *and the English name* mangosteen *derive from the Malay term* mangustan.

General Information The mangosteen is the fruit of a small tropical tree that is believed native to Malaysia and Indonesia. Requiring a hot and humid climate, the mangosteen is a slow-growing tree that may not begin to bear fruit until it is between ten and fifteen years old. The fruit is about the size of a mandarin orange, round and slightly flattened at each end, with a smooth thick rind and rich red-purple color.

Buying Tips To select the best fruits, choose those with the highest number of stigma lobes at the apex, for these always have the highest number of fleshy segments and the fewest seeds.

Culinary Uses The thick interior pulp (uneaten) encloses the nearly translucent white segments lying loose in the cup. The texture of each segment resembles that of a well-ripened plum, but is so delicate that it melts in the mouth like ice cream, with a flavor that is sweet, subacid, yet indescribably delicious. The mangosteen has often been described as the "Queen of Fruits," or at least as one of the world's best-flavored fruits. Jacobus Bontius compared it to nectar and ambrosia, said that it surpassed the golden apples of the Hesperides, and that it was "of all the fruits of the Indies by far the most delicious." The fruit is usually eaten fresh as a dessert. Holding the stem-end downward, cut around the middle completely through the rind, and lift off the top half. This leaves the fleshy segments exposed in the colorful "cup," or bottom half of the rind, which can be lifted out with a fork. More acidic fruits are best for preserving.

Health Benefits Dried fruits are shipped to Calcutta and China for medicinal use. The sliced and dried rind is powdered and administered to overcome dysentery. Made into an ointment, it is applied to eczema and other skin disorders.

Mangosteen

Nutritional Value Per 100 g Edible Portion

	Raw
Calories	60-63
Protein	0.50-0.60 g
Fat	0.1-0.6 g
Fiber	5.0-5.1 g
Calcium	0.01-8.0 mg
Iron	0.20-0.80 mg
Phosphorus	0.02-12.0 mg
Thiamine (B1)	0.03 mg
Ascorbic Acid (C)	1-2 mg

May Apple *(Podophyllum peltatum)*

Podophyllum *derives from Tournefort's* anapodophyllum, *or duck's foot leaf, from a fancied resemblance in the foliage.* Peltatum *means stalked from the surface rather than the edge, or peltate. The English name* May apple *is due to the plant's habit of blooming in April and fruiting in May.*

General Information The May apple is a beautiful but ill-smelling plant of the Barberry family that grows in dense patches along fences, roadsides, and in open woods. Native to eastern and midwestern North America, the edible fruit, which ripens in July or August, is about two inches long, egg-shaped, and yellow when ripe, with a many-seeded pulp within a rather tough skin.

Culinary Uses The fruits are best for eating when the plants are dying and falling to the ground. Then they are fully ripe, almost a golden yellow, and have the flavor of a strawberry. Many who know the fruit prefer to eat it raw, scooping the flesh from the skin with a spoon. The raw May apple may also be squeezed for juice or spread on bread as a raw jam. Do not eat the fruit when green, or any other part of the plant, because the roots, leaves, and stems contain a bitter resinous substance that is poisonous.

Health Benefits The highly toxic roots of the plant were used by Native Americans as an emetic, purgative and vermifuge. May apple roots also contain a resin called podophyllin, which was used by natives to cure veneral warts; this resin was "rediscovered" by the German physician Dr. Schopf in 1787. May apple was listed in the first edition of the *Pharmacopoeia* of the Massachusetts Medical Society in 1808, and gained entry into the *United States Pharmacopoeia* in 1820, where it remains as the standard treatment for venereal warts today. Studies show that the constituents of the podophyllotoxin obtained from the rhizomes actually suppress lymph cells while boosting the immune system.

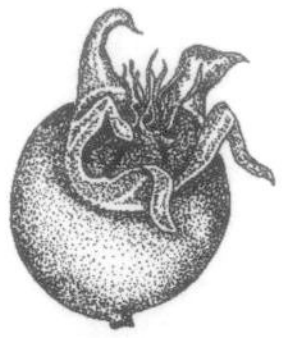

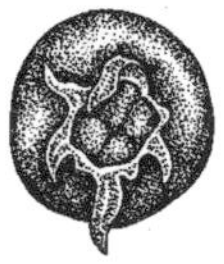

Medlar *(Mespilus germanica)*

Mespilus *is from an old Greek substantive name,* mespilon. Germanica *means native to Germanic regions (which it is not, but is where the taxonomists first encountered it). The English name* medlar *derives from the Latin name.*

General Information This unusual apple-like fruit, with its five seed vessels visible through the open bottom end, is most likely native to the west coast of the Caspian Sea, although remnants have also been found in East Germany. It may have been cultivated as far back as thirty centuries ago, but because the name medlar was also applied to the Cornelian cherry, stone fruits (*Prunus* family), and especially the hawthorn and cotoneaster, it is difficult to know for sure whether this is the fruit written about. Reaching its peak of popularity during the Middle Ages, medlars were familiar components of walled monastery gardens, and were a common market fruit as late as the nineteenth century. Today the plant is rarely cultivated in Europe or elsewhere. The fruits resemble small green russeted apples, tinged dull yellow or red. They must be fully matured on the tree before harvest, through the entire growing season and including perhaps the first few frosts, or else they will shrivel in storage and never attain a good flavor. Although the fruits do fully ripen in Italy, they rarely do so in cooler climates. The usual process in England, France, and central Europe is to pick the still-hard fruits, spread them out on shelves or straw, and give them two or three weeks to become well softened. This process is called "bletting," and the end result is that the hard, cream-colored interior turns brown and soft. Once bletted, medlars will keep for several weeks.

Culinary Uses Properly aged medlars have a flesh soft as a baked apple, with a brisk flavor incorporating apples, wine, and cinnamon. Embedded in the pulp are five large inedible seeds. Once popular in Victorian Britain, these "wineskins of morbidity," as D.H. Lawrence so elegantly described them, were served with sugar and cream, or made into jelly and cheese (mixed with eggs and butter like the more familiar lemon curd). The easiest way to eat a medlar is to suck the fruit empty, leaving skin and seeds behind. Or the pulp can be scooped out and folded into cream for a tasty dessert. The fruit is well suited to baking whole, stewing with butter, or for jams, jellies, tarts, and syrups.

Melon *(Cucumis melo)*

Cucumis *is simply the old Latin name for this family of plants. The term* melo *is short for* melopepon, *and comes from the Greek* melon, *which was a term applied to almost any kind of round fruit, and* pepon *meaning an edible gourd.*

General Information Melons, which belong to the same family as the cucumber, originated in the Near East and perhaps the northwest of India, and from there spread throughout Europe. It was during the Roman Empire that melons were introduced into Europe; they were not well known in northern Europe until the fifteenth century, when they became hugely popular at the French royal court. Melon seeds were carried to Haiti by Columbus, where they thrived and spread. The despair of gardeners and taxonomists alike, all melons belong to the same species and interbreed and overlap so readily that seed growers must plant different varieties at least a quarter mile apart to prevent cross-pollination from producing results very different than those desired.

Buying Tips Selecting a perfect melon is nearly impossible. For the best results, look for symmetry in shape, even coloring, and a warm, flowery aroma. For cantaloupe there are three major signs of ripeness: (1) no stem, but a smooth, shallow basin where the stem was once attached; (2) thick, coarse, and corky netting or veining over the surface; and (3) a yellowish-buff skin color under the netting. Overripeness is characterized by pronounced yellowing of the skin and a soft, watery, and insipid flesh.

Culinary Uses Melons are much prized for their sweet, delicate flavor. Usually eaten alone, they are also delicious in salads, preserves, ice creams, sorbets, and desserts. Ginger in any form seems to go uncommonly well with the fruit. Remove the seeds before serving. Given the sweetness of a perfectly ripe melon, it seems surprising that its sugar content accounts for only 5 percent of its weight, only half as much as for an apple or pear; yet since a melon is 94 percent water, this still gives sugar a five-to-one advantage over all the other taste-producing elements.

Health Benefits Melons are excellent cleansers and rehydrators of the body, being over 90 percent water, and this makes them very desirable during the hot summer months. They rejuvenate and alkalinize the body with their highly mineralized distilled water, as well as aiding in elimination. Their silicon content is high, especially when eaten right down to the rind. Cantaloupe has been shown to contain the compound adenosine, which is currently being used in patients with heart disease to keep the blood thin and to relieve angina attacks. All melons are such a perfect food for humans that they require no digestion whatsoever in the stomach; instead, they pass quickly through the stomach and into the small intestines for digestion and assimilation. This can happen, however, only when the stomach is empty and melons are eaten alone. If consumed with or after other foods that require complex digestion, melons cannot pass into the small intestines until the digestion of other foods is complete and thus they sit and stagnate, quickly fermenting and causing gastric distress.

Melon

Nutritional Value Per 100 g Edible Portion

	Raw Cantaloupe	Raw Honey Dew	Raw Casaba
Calories	35	35	26
Protein	0.88 g	0.46 g	0.90 g
Fat	0.28 g	0.10 g	0.10 g
Fiber	0.36 g	0.60 g	0.50 g
Calcium	11 mg	6 mg	5 mg
Iron	0.21 mg	0.07 mg	0.40 mg
Magnesium	11 mg	7 mg	8 mg
Phosphorus	17 mg	10 mg	7 mg
Potassium	309 mg	271 mg	210 mg
Sodium	9 mg	10 mg	12 mg
Zinc	0.160 mg	n/a	n/a
Copper	0.042 mg	0.041 mg	n/a
Manganese	0.047 mg	0.018 mg	n/a
Beta Carotene (A)	3224 IU	40 IU	30 IU
Thiamine (B_1)	0.036 mg	0.077 mg	0.060 mg
Riboflavin (B_2)	0.021 mg	0.018 mg	0.020 mg
Niacin (B_3)	0.574 mg	0.600 mg	0.400 mg
Pantothenic Acid (B_5)	0.128 mg	0.207 mg	n/a
Pyridoxine (B_6)	0.115 mg	0.059 mg	n/a
Folic Acid (B_9)	17.0 mcg	n/a	n/a
Ascorbic Acid (C)	42.2 mg	24.8 mg	16 mg
Tocopherol (E)	0.14 mg	n/a	n/a

Varieties

THERE ARE MANY DIFFERENT VARIETIES OF MELON, of which the most common are cantaloupe, honeydew, and watermelon. Most are available year-round, except for watermelon, which is in season only during the summer and early autumn.

Cantaloupes, botanically muskmelons, are native to India and Guinea, and have been cultivated for more than two thousand years. Their name comes from the town of Cantalupo ("wolf howl") in Italy, site of a palatial papal vacation home outside Rome, where the melons were reputedly first cultivated during the sixteenth century. For a ripe cantaloupe, pick one that is heavy for its size, with a pleasant aroma, the most pronounced, coarse, cream or golden netting, and an

Lore and Legend

One story recounted by Waverley Root tells of a melon half that was pitched by a heckler at Demosthenes during the course of a political debate in Greece. Demosthenes, never at a loss for words, is said to have promptly clapped the melon on his head and thanked the thrower for finding him a helmet to wear while fighting Philip of Macedonia. In one of the stories in the *Arabian Nights*, a child buys a melon to quench his thirst. Upon cutting it open he sees a tiny city, so he enters this microcosm, filled with buildings, people, and animals. On Mount Carmel there is a field of stones supposedly transformed from melons when a man named Elias ate too many, became ill, and cursed the whole lot. When the library of the town of Cavaillon in the South of France asked the great and prolific French author Alexandre Dumas for a complete set of his works, he told them that they were asking for over four hundred books, but that he would do his best to comply if they would send him every year a consignment of Cavaillon melons. They did, and he reciprocated; a highly satisfactory exchange for both parties.

even, dull color. The stem should be completely gone, with that end being smooth, slightly depressed, and yielding to slight pressure. Available late May through September; most abundant in June and July.

Casabas are a Turkish native, coming from Kasaba, where this melon was apparently first identified. It is a large, pumpkin-shaped fruit with light yellow or light green skin, and a rind with deep wrinkles that gather at the stem end. When it is fully ripe, the skin becomes slightly sticky, and you can tell it is ready. The fruit will not have any fragrance unless it is a great vine-ripened specimen, which will give off a very light floral scent. The flesh is pale, soft, sweet, and juicy, with a tinge of yellow around the seed bed. The casaba can give you the farthest extremes of the melon taste spectrum. When it is good, it is very, very good; but when it is bad. . . Casabas appear during melon-mania season, July through December.

Crenshaws are a hybrid between the Casaba and Persian melons that can weigh up to a hefty ten pounds. Considered the kings of melons, Crenshaws have rough, thick, salmon-orange or dark green skins that will bronze when ripe, and the fruit should feel soft to pressure all over, especially at the enlarged end. Those with a noticeably sweet, thick, rose-pepper aroma are fully ripe. The dense salmon-colored flesh is both sweet and spicy. Their season is July through October, peaking August through September.

Honeydews, both orange-fleshed and green-fleshed, originated in Asia, and it is believed that as early as 2400 B.C. this distinct type of muskmelon was growing in Egypt. The varieties that we eat today were developed around the turn of the century from a French strain called the White Antibes melon. Green honeydews should have a pale creamy yellowish-green skin, not a harsh greenish-white; orange honeydews should have a golden orange cast to their skin and a musky aroma when ripe. A slight "bloom," faint netting or freckles, a gentle "give," and a slightly sticky feeling all indicate a ripe melon. Both kinds should be heavy for their size, but avoid those that feel like billiard balls, as they were picked too soon. The cool lime-green flesh, bursting with juicy flavor and cradled in its thin porcelain shell, is the height of fruit delight. Available year-round, but peak is June through October.

Persian melons could be the ancestor of all melons; historians place their origin somewhere in the Middle East, most likely Persia. If Crenshaws are the king of melons, then Persians are the sultan. Slightly larger than a honeydew with a greener rind and finer netting than a cantaloupe, they are ripe when they are soft overall, the netting lightens and stands out, and the gray-green skin color turns to gray-gold. At its best the Persian exudes a perfume that is highly aromatic and unforgettable. Inside, the flesh is a deep orange, thick, firm, juicy, and full-flavored. Persian melons may not be as plentiful as the cantaloupe, but they are equally delicious and widely esteemed as having the thickest and richest-tasting flesh. Eating a Persian melon is an exotic and sensual experience; they make you sit up and take notice. Their season runs June through November, peaking in August and September.

Santa Claus melons are also called **Christmas melons** because they are widely available at Christmas time. They are oval, light green melons that resemble a small green- and gold-striped watermelon. About a foot long, they have mild, crisp flesh that is not as sweet as other melons. Their season is September through December.

Spanish melons are large melons with a dark green corrugated skin. They are difficult to select, as their skin remains green and hard even at maturity, but they will have a slight aroma and lose their slick surface, producing a subtle glow and stickiness. The yellow, juicy, firm flesh has a taste very similar to the crenshaw.

Watermelon See separate reference.

Mombin (*Spondias purpurea, S. mombin*)

Also Known As: Spanish Plum, Hog Plum.

> Spondias *derives from a Greek word used by Theophrastus for this family of plants.* Purpurea *means purple-colored.*

Mombin

Nutritional Value Per 100 g Edible Portion

	Raw Purple	Raw Yellow
Calories	n/a	21.8-48.1
Protein	0.096-0.261 g	1.28-1.38 g
Fat	0.03-0.17 g	0.10-0.56 g
Fiber	0.2-0.6 g	1.16-1.18 g
Calcium	6.1-23.9 mg	31.4 mg
Iron	0.09-1.22 mg	2.8 mg
Phosphorus	31.5-55.7 mg	n/a
Beta Carotene (A)	0.004-0.089 mg	71 IU
Thiamine (B_1)	0.033-0.103 mg	95 mcg
Riboflavin (B_2)	0.014-0.049 mg	50 mcg
Niacin (B_3)	0.540-1.770 mg	n/a
Ascorbic Acid (C)	26.4-73.0 mg	46.4 mg

General Information The **Red (purple) mombin** (*S. purpurea*) is a native of tropical America, from southern Mexico through northern Peru and Brazil. Spanish explorers carried the tree to the Philippines, where it has been widely adopted. Varying greatly in size, form, and palatability, the fruits are commonly oval or roundish, from one to two inches long, and range from deep red to yellow in color. The **Yellow mombin** (*S. mombin*) is native to Brazil and Costa Rica, with golden-yellow fruits that are aromatic and 1 to 1 1/2 inches in diameter.

Culinary Uses Good fruits have rich, juicy flesh with a fairly acid, spicy flavor, not unlike that of the cashew fruit but less pronounced. They may be eaten fresh, preferably ice-cold, stewed with sugar, or boiled and dried. The large, hard core at the center may be cracked and eaten like a nut. The fruits of the yellow mombin have flesh that is scant, fibrous, mildly acidic, juicy, and generally considered inferior to those of the red mombin. They are appreciated by children, or the juice used to prepare ice cream, beverages, and preserves.

Health Benefits Juice from the mombin is drunk as a diuretic and febrifuge.

Monstera (*Monstera deliciosa*)

Also Known As: Ceriman, Swiss-Cheese Plant, False Breadfruit.

> Monstera *derives from the Latin* monstrum, *meaning monster, and refers to its unnaturally marvelous shape, size, and deviation from normal form.* Deliciosa *means delicious.*

General Information The monstera is definitely a fruit for those who have a bent for the exotic. More people are familiar with the plant than the fruit. A creeping vine of the arum

Monstera

Nutritional Value Per Edible Portion	Raw
Calories	335/lb
Protein	1.81%
Fat	0.20%
Fiber	0.57%

lily family, the monstera is the familiar split-leaf philodendron, grown as a house plant for the sake of its unusual leaves. Native to wet forests of southern Mexico and Guatemala, in its natural habitat the plant grows to a great size and bears fruits that somewhat resemble long green corn cobs. The cream-colored spadix is at first sheltered by a waxy, white, calla-lily-like spathe, but soon develops into a green compound fruit eight to twelve inches or more in length and two to three and one-half inches thick. Made up of hexagonal plates or "scales," the thick, hard rind covers individual segments of ivory-colored juicy, fragrant pulp. Generally there are no seeds, but occasionally hard seeds the size of large pale green peas may occur in a few of the segments. Oxalic acid in the unripe fruit, the thin, black particles between segments (floral remnants) on the spadix, and even the ripe fruit itself, may cause irritation for some people. It is best to eat sparingly on the first occasion to make sure there are no undesirable reactions.

Culinary Uses The fruit should be cut from the plant with at least an inch of stem when the tile-like sections of rind separate slightly at the base, making it appear somewhat bulged. If kept at room temperature, the monstera will ripen progressively toward the apex over a period of five or six days. Wrapping the fruit in plastic or aluminum foil will often help it ripen in a more uniform way. As it ripens, the rind loosens along the whole length of the fruit, and when fully ripe the hexagonal plates on its surface split apart, exposing a creamy, tart-sweet fruit that looks something like a banana, with a pineapple-banana flavor. The flesh should be eaten only from fully-ripened portions. The ripe pulp, once pulled away from the inedible core, can be incorporated into fruit salads or served with ice cream. In the unlikely event of having an excess of fruit, it can be preserved by stewing segments with sugar and lime juice, then putting it up in jars.

Mulberry (*Morus alba, M. nigra, M. rubra*)

Morus *and* morarius *were the classical Latin names for the mulberry and come from the Latin verb* morari *meaning to delay, after the tree's habit of delaying spring bud formation until the cold weather has passed. The terms* alba *(white),* nigra *(black), and* rubra *(red) distinguish the three varieties. The English name* mulberry *is derived from the Latin.*

General Information The mulberry tree is a beautiful tree, growing in a weeping willow style, with the thin hanging branches forming an umbrella reaching almost to the ground. The white mulberry originated in the central and eastern mountainous regions of China, where it is thought to have been cultivated for at least five thousand years for feeding silkworms. Since the berries are almost pure sugar and virtually tasteless, and since silkworms seem to prefer the white mulberry leaves, this tree is used exclusively for the production of silk. White mulberry trees were introduced into the United States two hundred years ago in attempts at silk culture, but the experiment proved a failure. The black mulberry appears to have originated either in the southern part of the Caucasus or in the mountains of Nepal, and grows almost exclusively in Europe. This variety, having a better fruit, was spread and cultivated for human use

Lore and Legend

The mulberry tree was referred to as the "wisest" of trees by Pliny, for it refrained from budding until all danger of frost was over, at which time it burst into full flower overnight, making a great noise as it did so. Because it was wise, the tree was dedicated by the Greeks to Minerva, one of their goddesses of wisdom. In classical legend the red berries of the mulberry tree acquired their color only after two young, ill-fated Babylonian lovers, Pyramus and Thisbe, bled and died under a white mulberry tree. This legend is the source of the much-loved Shakespearean story of Romeo and Juliet.

while the other species were used almost exclusively for silkworm culture. The comparatively large black berries are sweet and pleasant. The red mulberry tree is native to the eastern United States from New York west to Nebraska, and down to the Gulf coast. The red berries are very sweet and flavorful but do not keep well. Although a mulberry fruit superficially resembles a blackberry, it is actually a cluster of small berries, each with an individually lobed surface and each formed from one of a cluster of flowers. The fruit must be allowed to ripen fully before being gathered; then, rather than being picked, it is allowed to fall off the tree. Their propensity for staining clothes and fingers is well known in the areas where mulberries grow.

Mulberry

Nutritional Value Per 100 g Edible Portion

	Raw
Calories	43
Protein	1.44 g
Fat	0.39 g
Fiber	0.96 g
Calcium	39 mg
Iron	1.85 mg
Magnesium	18 mg
Phosphorus	38 mg
Potassium	194 mg
Sodium	10 mg
Beta Carotene (A)	25 IU
Thiamine (B_1)	0.029 mg
Riboflavin (B_2)	0.101 mg
Niacin (B_3)	0.620 mg
Ascorbic Acid (C)	36.4 mg

Culinary Uses Mulberries are unusual berries both in taste and in the quality of their juice. They are delicious when fully ripe and fresh from the tree. Eat them by themselves or with cream, or use them to make pies or jams, a mildly astringent syrup, or mulberry wine. In medieval England, mulberries were made into murrey, a blue-black puree added to spiced meats or used as a pudding. Dried mulberries are a winter staple for some peoples living in the high foothills of the Himalayas.

Health Benefits Nutritionally, this fruit has the same kind of high mineral content as figs and other berries. If you find them (probably in their natural state, since few if any are commercially cultivated), you will enjoy a refreshing, delightful fruit with rather high amounts of important minerals and better-than-average fruit protein. At one time, mulberries were highly regarded as a general tonic for the whole system. Mulberries are excellent for stomach ulcers, help strengthen the blood, and are soothing to the nervous system due to their high phosphorus content. Mulberry juice is especially good for the digestive system.

Nance

Nutritional Value Per 100 g Edible Portion

	Raw
Protein	0.109-0.124 g
Fat	0.21-1.83 g
Fiber	2.5-5.8 g
Calcium	23.0-36.8 mg
Iron	0.62-1.01 mg
Phosphorus	12.6-15.7 mg
Beta Carotene (A)	0.002-0.060 mg
Thiamine (B_1)	0.009-0.014 mg
Riboflavin (B_2)	0.015-0.039 mg
Niacin (B_3)	0.266-0.327 mg
Ascorbic Acid (C)	90-192 mg

Nance *(Byrsonima crassifolia)*

The genus name Byrsonima *refers to the use of some species in the tanning process in Brazil.* Crassifolia *means thick-leaved.*

General Information The nance is a slow-growing shrub native to southern Mexico through the Pacific side of Central America to Peru and Brazil. Throughout its natural range, the fruit is consumed mainly by children, birds, and animals; some trees are under cultivation in Mexico and Central America. The orange-yellow fruit is particularly odorous, round, and from one-half to three-quarters of an inch wide with a thick skin. They fall to the ground when fully ripe and are very perishable; however, they can be stored for several months merely by being submerged in water.

Culinary Uses The white, juicy, oily pulp of the nance varies in flavor from insipid to sweet, acidic, or cheeselike. There is a single stone which contains from one to three seeds. Most fruits are eaten raw, but they may also be cooked into desserts, and used in soups or stuffings. Carbonated and fermented beverages can also be made from the fruit.

Naranjilla (*Solanum quitoense*)

Solanum *comes from the Latin* solamen, *meaning solace or quieting. The plant was given its scientific name of* quitoense *in 1793 by Jean-Baptiste Pierre Antoine de Monet de Lamarck, who is better known for his theory of evolution and zoological work than for his many botanical contributions. Lamarck was aware that the naranjilla came from Quito, which at that time referred not only to the city but also to the country that later became Ecuador. When the Spanish came to the New World, they called the fruit* naranjilla, *"little orange," because at maturity the white hairs rub off the fruits, and they resemble small oranges.*

Naranjilla

Nutritional Value Per 100 g Edible Portion

	Raw
Calories	23
Protein	0.107-0.60 g
Fat	0.10-0.24 g
Fiber	0.3-4.6 g
Calcium	5.9-12.4 mg
Iron	0.34-0.64 mg
Phosphorus	12.0-43.7 mg
Beta Carotene (A)	600 IU
Thiamine (B_1)	0.040-0.094 mg
Riboflavin (B_2)	0.030-0.047 mg
Niacin (B_3)	1.190-1.760 mg
Ascorbic Acid (C)	31.2-83.7 mg

General Information The usually spineless naranjilla is believed to be indigenous and most abundant in Peru, Ecuador, and southern Colombia. Many introductions of the plant were made into the United States, but the resulting plantings in California, Florida, and northern greenhouses flourished only briefly and eventually all died. The exhibition of fruits and fifteen hundred gallons of freshly made juice of Ecuadorian naranjillas at the New York World's Fair in 1939 aroused a great deal of interest. For a short while, the pulp was shipped to the States, blended with apple or pineapple juice, but the experiment failed due to improper processing and a resultant metallic taste. A most striking plant, its huge, dark green leaves and orange fruits are all rather densely pubescent, or fuzzy. Unaffected by season, fruit is produced throughout the year. The fruit can grow up to three inches across, is covered with a brown hairy coat which rubs off easily, and splits into four sections divided by membranes.

Culinary Uses Its acidulous, yellowish-green pulp encloses many tiny flat edible seeds, and tastes somewhat like a cross between a pineapple and either a strawberry or a lemon. Ripe naranjillas, freed of hairs, may be casually consumed out of hand by cutting in half and squeezing the contents of each half into the mouth and then discarding the empty shells. The flesh also is good added to ice cream mixes, made into sauces for native dishes, or utilized in making pies and various other desserts. The shells may be stuffed with a mixture of banana and other ingredients and baked. The most popular use of the naranjilla is to make juice, which is sweetened and served with ice cubes as a cool, foamy drink. Fully ripe naranjillas soften and ferment very quickly.

Nectarine (*Prunus persica,* var. *nucipersica, P. persica* var. *nectarina*)

Nectarine

Nutritional Value Per 100 g Edible Portion

	Raw
Calories	49
Protein	0.94 g
Fat	0.46 g
Fiber	0.40 g
Calcium	5 mg
Iron	0.15 mg
Magnesium	8 mg
Phosphorus	16 mg
Potassium	212 mg
Sodium	0 mg
Zinc	0.090 mg
Copper	0.073 mg
Manganese	0.044 mg
Beta Carotene (A)	736 IU
Thiamine (B_1)	0.017 mg
Riboflavin (B_2)	0.041 mg
Niacin (B_3)	0.990 mg
Pantothenic Acid (B_5)	0.158 mg
Pyridoxine (B_6)	0.025 mg
Folic Acid (B_9)	3.7 mcg
Ascorbic Acid (C)	5.4 mg

The nectarine is part of the large plum (Prunus) *genus, and was believed to have come from Persia (thus the* persica*). In the sixteenth and seventeenth centuries the nectarine was called* nucipersica *(persian nut) because it resembled the walnut in smoothness and color of the outer skin as well as in size and shape. The English word* nectarine *is believed to be derived from the Greek word* nektar, *which was the drink of the gods in Greek and Roman mythology, and to which this fruit was compared because of its superb flavor.*

General Information The origin of the nectarine, first described by a European writer in 1587, is a mystery. Nectarines are a true peach, not a cross between a peach and a plum as some suppose. Experiments show that peach trees can produce nectarines by bud variation, and nectarine trees also produce peaches; peach and nectarine trees may each produce a fruit that is half peach and half nectarine. Generally smaller than peaches, with a smooth fuzzless skin, nectarines have a slightly firmer flesh and tangier flavor. There are more than 150 nectarine varieties (both clingstone and freestone) that differ slightly in size, shape, taste, texture, and skin coloring. Of the two color variations, red and yellow, the red varieties are larger than the yellow, but both are usually deeply cleft. The yellow are more oval than round, golden in color, with a pink center near the stone.

Buying Tips Nectarines should be firm but not hard, slightly soft along their seam, golden with a red blush, and with a sweet fragrant aroma. Tree-ripened nectarines, locally available in season at farmer's markets, are incomparably superior to commercial nectarines.

Culinary Uses Nectarines may be used in any of the ways peaches or apricots are used: fresh as a table fruit, in fruit salads, stewed, baked, or made into preserves, jams, and ice cream. They can also be canned or dried.

Health Benefits Nectarines make an excellent digestive aid and body cleanser when eaten raw.

Orange (*Citrus sinensis, C. aurantium, C. reticulata*)

The term Citrus *derives from the Greek term for the citron,* kedromelon. Sinensis *means of Chinese origin;* aurantium *is a color designation meaning orange-red;* reticulata *means reticulated or netted. According to some authorities the English word* orange *derives from the Arabic* narandj, *which is derived from the Sanskrit* nagarunga, *meaning "fruit favored by the elephants;" others claim it derives from the Persian* narang, *meaning golden or orange.*

General Information Oranges are native to China and the Far East, and are a special kind of berry called a hesperidium. The earliest mention of citrus trees occurs in the

Shu-King, popularly known as the *Book of History;* this collection of documents is believed to have been edited by Confucius around 500 B.C. Throughout antiquity, the golden color of oranges marked them for the court and the temple, and made them generally coveted. Originally very small, bitter, and full of seeds, through constant efforts in cross-fertilization and selection over two hundred varieties of this delicious fruit are now cultivated, with a tremendous improvement in quality. Arab traders brought the bitter orange from the east and propagated it around the Mediterranean. The Moors introduced it to Spain, where it established itself and became known as the Seville orange. This sour orange (*Citrus aurantium*), appreciated for the scent of its flowers and peel and for the sourness of its juice in cooking, was followed in the fifteenth century by the introduction of the sweet orange, also from China, by the Portuguese. The sour orange is now more widely used as a propagation rootstock than for its fruit. The much more popular sweet variety was probably a mutant of the bitter orange, which appeared in China at least by the beginning of our era and probably before. Columbus and other European explorers brought bitter and sweet orange seeds and seedlings with them to the New World with the hopes of starting profitable orange plantations. Florida's groves were planted by Spanish missionaries, the most famous being perhaps the groves of Saint Augustine, which were laid out in 1565. When Father Junipero Serra and his Franciscan monks began establishing a chain of missions in southern California in 1769, they also brought and planted orange seeds.

Buying Tips Oranges should be weighty and firm, with smooth, thin, shiny skins, and give off a sweet fragrant aroma. Colors range from green-flecked yellow for the smaller juice oranges to deep orange for navels and mandarins. Avoid lightweight or thick-skinned oranges, as they are liable to have less juice. Also avoid those with soft or puffy spots.

Culinary Uses Because they oxidize so rapidly, oranges should be used within fifteen minutes of the time they are cut or peeled. Buy tree- and sun-ripened fruit whenever possible, as the acids from green or immature fruit may cause adverse reactions in the body. Sweeter

Orange

Nutritional Value Per 100 g Edible Portion

	Raw Fruit	Fresh Juice	Processed Juice	Frozen Concentrate	Raw Tangerine	Tangerine Juice
Calories	47-51	40-48	42	158	46	43
Protein	0.7-1.3 g	0.5-1.0 g	0.59 g	2.3 g	0.8 g	0.5 g
Fat	0.1-0.3 g	0.1-0.3 g	0.14 g	0.2 g	0.2 g	0.2 g
Fiber	0.5 g	0.1 g	0.1 g	0.2 g	0.5 g	0.1 g
Calcium	40-43 mg	10-11 mg	8 mg	33 mg	40 mg	18 mg
Iron	0.2-0.8 mg	0.2-0.3 mg	0.44 mg	0.4 mg	0.4 mg	0.20 mg
Magnesium	10 mg	11 mg	11 mg	n/a	12 mg	8 mg
Phosphorus	17-22 mg	15-19 mg	14 mg	55 mg	18 mg	14 mg
Potassium	190-200 mg	190-208 mg	175 mg	657 mg	126 mg	178 mg
Sodium	1 mg	1 mg	2 mg	2 mg	2 mg	1 mg
Zinc	0.070 mg	0.050 mg	0.070 mg	n/a	n/a	0.030 mg
Copper	0.045 mg	0.044 mg	0.057 mg	n/a	0.028 mg	0.025 mg
Manganese	0.025 mg	0.014 mg	0.014 mg	n/a	0.032 mg	0.037 mg
Beta Carotene (A)	200 IU	200 IU	175 IU	710 IU	420 IU	420 mg
Thiamine (B_1)	0.100 mg	0.090 mg	0.060 mg	0.300 mg	0.105 mg	0.060 mg
Riboflavin (B_2)	0.040 mg	0.030 mg	0.028 mg	0.050 mg	0.022 mg	0.020 mg
Niacin (B_3)	0.400 mg	0.400 mg	0.314 mg	1.200 mg	0.160 mg	0.100 mg
Pantothenic Acid (B_5)	0.250 mg	0.190 mg	0.150 mg	n/a	0.200 mg	n/a
Pyridoxine (B_6)	0.060 mg	0.040 mg	0.088 mg	n/a	0.067 mg	n/a
Folic Acid (B_9)	30.3 mcg	n/a	n/a	n/a	20.4 mcg	n/a
Ascorbic Acid (C)	45-61 mg	37-61 mg	34.4 mg	158 mg	31 mg	31 mg
Tocopherol (E)	0.24 mg	0.04 mg	n/a	n/a	n/a	n/a

fruits also have greater food value. Most citrus fruits are heavily treated with chemical dips and fumigants. Tree-ripened organic oranges are well worth searching for.

Health Benefits Carminative, stimulant, stomachic, tonic. The daily use of an orange will aid in toning up and purifying the entire system, acting as an internal antiseptic, tonic stimulant, and supportive agent. The natural acid and sugar in the orange aid digestion and stimulate the activity of the glands in the stomach. Freshly-squeezed oranges are predigested food in a delicious and attractive form, ready for immediate absorption and utilization; rich in lime and alkaline salts that counteract the tendency to acidosis, orange juice also has a general stimulating effect on the peristaltic activity of the colon. The amount of food value contained in the juice of a single large orange is about equal to that found in a slice of bread, but orange juice needs no digestion, whereas bread must undergo digestive processing for several hours before it can be used for energizing and strengthening the body. Although oranges are an excellent source of water-soluble vitamin C, this vitamin is the least stable of all the vitamins. Storage of orange juice at low temperatures destroys the vitamin to some extent, while sterilization (pasteurization) may destroy it completely. Eat the whole orange, excluding the very outer skin, to get the full benefits from the fruit.

Varieties

Bergamot (*Citrus bergamia*) is a variety of bitter orange (see also Seville) used mainly for perfumery and essential oils.

Blood oranges may be uniformly orange, a spotted blend of orange and red, or totally colored a flamboyant red, garnet, or purple. The original mutation that produced the color probably happened in seventeenth-century Sicily, and is due to a pigment (anthocyanin) not usually present in citrus fruits but common in other red fruits and flowers. Used primarily for eating, blood oranges are exceptionally sweet and juicy, literally bursting with rich, zesty, full-bodied citrus flavor, and have a deep raspberry aftertaste. The seedless pulp is juicy but firm, less acidic than common oranges, and the membranes separating the segments are downy and soft unless stored too long. Their season begins in December and runs through June.

Mandarins (*C. reticulata*) are also known as **Tangerines.** Although the names mandarin and tangerine are frequently used interchangeably in the United States, a tangerine is technically a subgroup of the mandarin orange. The name *mandarin* was originally no more than a nickname given to this small, loose-skinned, orange-like fruit, brought to England from China by Sir Abraham Hume in 1805. Derived from the title of high officials in the Chinese Empire, they are named mandarin by analogy either from the sense of superiority implied in the title or from the color of a Mandarin's robes. The name *tangerine* comes from Tangiers, a Moroccan seaport from which they were shipped. Between the years 1840 and 1850, the Italian Consul brought the mandarin orange to Louisiana, planting it on the consulate grounds at New Orleans. Always smaller and less acidic than oranges, mandarins have a loose, pebbly, dark orange or reddish-orange skin that separates easily from the flesh. Most are quite seedy and may be slightly tart, but very juicy. Quality mandarins should be heavy for their size, which indicates ample juice content. Of the many varieties, probably the best known are the Satsumas, which were developed in Japan during the sixteenth century. They are seedless and bright orange, with loose dullish skin; smaller ones are usually the sweetest. Mandarins are predominantly eaten out of hand, or the

Lore and Legend

Oranges are a favorite fruit in mythology, having been identified as the Golden Apples that grew in the mythological garden of the Hesperides, which in actual fact were probably the Canary Islands. Legend has it that the golden apple presented by Gaea, the ancient Greek goddess of the earth and fertility, as a wedding gift to Hera on the day she married Zeus, was in fact an orange, and that the seeds were planted in the Garden of the Hesperides. When the Moors invaded Spain in the tenth century, they brought oranges with them, but as a sacred fruit, to be used only in religious rites, for medicinal purposes, or as an exquisite flavoring in food and drink. Grown only within walled gardens, the fruits were guarded so jealously that any Christian who ate or even touched an orange did so on pain of death. Five hundred years later, when the Moors were driven out of Spain, these orange groves were perhaps their most valuable legacy. Long a symbol of love, orange blossoms were used by courtesans to sprinkle over their bedsheets and throughout their rooms. Ancient lovers bathed together in orange blossom water, and the fruit itself was given to newlyweds in the belief that its prolific number of seeds would ensure fertility and bless them with many offspring. The custom of using orange blossoms in wedding ceremonies dates back to Saracen brides, who wore orange blossoms on their wedding day; the blossoms were regarded as a symbol of prosperity and fecundity due to the fact that the orange tree bears ripe fruit and blossoms at the same time, and wearing the blossoms represented an appeal to the spirit of the orange tree that the bride should not be barren. The orange, as a traditional Chinese symbol of good luck and prosperity, is still used today in Chinese New Year's celebrations.

sections utilized in fruit salads, gelatins, puddings, or on cakes. Very small types are canned in syrup. Their season runs November through May, peaking in December and January.

Navel oranges are a native of Bahia, Brazil, and are named for the belly button-like spot at their blossom end. Washington navels were introduced to the United States in 1870 to fill the need for a good early variety of orange; since they were sponsored by the U.S. Department of Agriculture in Washington, D.C., they came to be called Washington navels. Their skins are quite bumpy, an indication that they will have thick skins. These seem to be the preferred orange for eating out of hand; their thick rinds are easy to peel and the flesh is sweet and moist, usually seedless. Juice pressed from navels turns bitter with exposure to air. Their season begins in November, with the peak from March through May.

Ortaniques are a cross between an orange and a tangerine. Flattened in shape, with a medium skin, this hybrid is very juicy and makes a good substitute for either of its parent fruits. Ortaniques can be eaten on their own, in salads, ice creams, desserts, and cakes.

Sevilles (*C. aurantium*), also known as **Bitter** or **Sour oranges**, are native to southeastern Asia and are reported to have been brought from the east by the Moors, who cultivated plantations of the trees around Seville, from which they derived their name. For five hundred years they were the only orange in Europe, and they were the first orange to reach the New World. Usually imported from Spain, they are considered too sour to be enjoyed out of hand and so are used for candied peel, marmalade, and liqueur. To approximate the tangy juice, combine three tablespoons each of orange and grapefruit juice with two tablespoons of lemon juice and one teaspoon of grated grapefruit zest to make one-half cup. The leaves and flowers, since they are more aromatic than the sweet orange, are used in cosmetics for fragrance.

Tangors are a cross between the mandarin and sweet orange. The two tangors generally available are the **Murcott** (or honey tangerine) and the **Temple**, which is seedy and thin-skinned, with sweet, tangy juice.

Tangelos are deliberate or accidental hybrids of a mandarin orange and either the grapefruit or pummelo. They look rather like large unsymmetrical oranges, with skin a deep orange shaded with bronze. The most popular variety, **Minneola**, has a very distinct knob-like projection on the stem end. Look for hard shiny specimens that feel heavy in your hand. Their colorful orange flesh is juicy but not seedless, with a taste like a blend of orange and tangerine that can be either very tart or very sweet. Peel and prepare like oranges, or squeeze for a wonderfully refreshing juice. Their season runs October through April, peaking November through February.

Temple oranges, sometimes called **Royal Mandarins**, are a cross between a tangerine and an orange. They resemble overgrown tangerines with a flattish skin, which may be heavily bronzed and slightly rough. Often they have a slight protrusion or cap at the blossom end, and the skin emits a distinctive oil fragrance. Their soft skin is easy to peel, and their red-orange flesh is very sweet and juicy, with a pleasant flavor similar to that of a tangy orange. Their seasons runs from December through March.

Valencia oranges are the most widely grown orange, accounting for about half the domestic crop produced each year. They range in size from small to nearly grapefruit size, with a smooth thin skin and slightly oval shape. Their sweet, juicy pulp may have numerous seeds, but is well worth eating, and makes an outstanding juice as well. Both the California and Florida varieties produce for about eight or nine months a year. Florida oranges reach their low point in late fall, California ones in late spring. Their season runs March through December.

Papaya (*Carica papaya*)

Also Known As: Mando (Brazil), Lichasa (Puerto Rico), Paw Paw (Caribbean), Melon Zapote (Mexico). In Cuba the term "papaya" is slang for "the female fruit" or sexual organs, and thus polite Cubans call it Fruta Bomba, or bomb fruit.

> *The genus* Carica *refers to the ancient region called Karia in Asia Minor.*
> *The English name* papaya *is a corruption of the Carib name* ababai.

General Information The papaya originated in the lowlands of eastern Central America and is second only to the banana in importance to South and Central America. Spanish and Portuguese invaders took to the fruit and quickly spread it to their other settlements in the West and East Indies; it was also taken to the Pacific Islands, and by 1800 was being grown in all tropical regions. An extraordinarily generous bearer, the papaya plant is not really a tree, but rather a large shrub, similar in appearance to a palm, which puts forth a branchless trunk. This "trunk" grows to about twenty feet, but does not harden to bark. Atop this shaft rests a radiating crest of giant leaves under which cluster the ponderous fruits, giving the whole the look of a coconut palm. The large oval or pear-shaped fruit (sometimes called the "melon that grows on trees") can range in size from one to twenty pounds, maturing in eighteen months from the time the seed is planted.

Buying Tips Choose fruit that feels heavy for its size, is slightly soft to the touch, and which is at least half-yellow or yellow-orange rather than green. Avoid overly soft or bruised fruit, or any with soft or hard spots.

Culinary Uses Hawaiian papayas are the size of an average hand, and are rich and sweetly flavored. Mexican papayas can be as large as a small watermelon, but they tend to have a thin, gamey flavor that is less attractive. Varying widely in size and color, the most common varieties are yellow- or orange-skinned and are shaped something like an

Papaya

Nutritional Value Per 100 g Edible Portion	Raw
Calories	23.1-25.8
Protein	0.081-0.34 g
Fat	0.05-0.96 g
Fiber	0.5-1.3 g
Calcium	12.9-40.8 mg
Iron	0.25-0.78 mg
Magnesium	10 mg
Phosphorus	5.3-22.0 mg
Potassium	257 mg
Sodium	3 mg
Zinc	0.07 mg
Copper	0.016 mg
Manganese	0.011 mg
Beta Carotene (A)	2014 IU
Thiamine (B_1)	0.021-0.036 mg
Riboflavin (B_2)	0.024-0.058 mg
Niacin (B_3)	0.227-0.555 mg
Pantothenic Acid (B_5)	0.218 mg
Pyridoxine (B_6)	0.019 mg
Ascorbic Acid (C)	35.5-71.3 mg

elongated melon or pear. Papaya's lush pink to orange flesh has a fairly sweet flavor similar to apricots and ginger, but sometimes with a peppery bite. In the central cavity lie shiny, gray to black peppercorn-size seeds that are edible, although most people dislike and discard them. To use, slice open and scoop out the seeds. Papaya combines wonderfully with sliced kiwifruit for breakfast. Peeled chunks can be used raw in salads, or baked, sautéed, poached, or otherwise used in desserts and preserves. Cooked papaya does not turn mushy, but remains firm and pliant. The black seeds are crunchy, and have a peppery taste like mustard and cress. They can be used as a garnish, as a substitute for capers, eaten raw, or crushed for a mildly spicy condiment.

Dried papaya, if it has any flavor at all, has been sugar-sweetened. Honey-sweetened papaya is a dishonest term, the fruit having been soaked in a sugar solution with only a small amount of honey added.

Health Benefits Digestive, stomachic, vermifuge, vulnerary. Papaya is probably best known for its ability to aid digestion and tenderize meat. This is due to its papain content, a proteinase enzyme similar to pepsin (produced by the gastric juices of the stomach). The enzyme is found only in the fresh milky juice of the unripe fruit or the brownish powder to which it dries, and very little if any is found in the fully ripe fruit. Papaya also contains carpaine, a compound providing anti-tumor activity. Papaya juice has been used externally to remove freckles; internally it is easily digestible and cleanses the digestive tract, eliminating gastric indigestion, reducing gas, soothing irritation and inflammation, cleansing and detoxifying the entire body, and acting as an effective vermifuge. Papaya as an important part of the diet will greatly improve the skin, nails, and hair, as well as keep your eyes clear and bright.

Passion Fruit *(Passiflora edulis, P. ligularis, P. quadrangularis, P. molissima)*

Also Known As: Granadilla.

> *The flower was named by the Jesuit Fathers* Flos Passionis, *Passionflower, or* Flor de las cinco llagas, *Flower of the Five Wounds. The term* edulis *means edible;* ligularis *means ligulate or strap-shaped;* quadrangularis *means quadrangular or four-angled;* molissima *means softest or mildest. The English name* passion fruit *is from an interesting interpretation of the fruit's flowers, which are said to represent elements of the Passion (crucifixion) of Christ.*

General Information Several types of passion fruit are grown: purple, sweet, giant, and banana. The **Purple passion fruit** (*P. edulis*) is a climbing perennial native from southern Brazil through Paraguay to northern Argentina, and widely cultivated in tropical regions. Nearly perfectly round, the three- to six-inch fruit has a tough rind ranging in hue from dark purple to light yellow or pumpkin color, and within the rind a cavity containing an aromatic mass of membranous sacs filled with orange-colored, pulpy juice and hundreds of small, hard seeds. **Sweet passion fruit** or granadillas (*P. ligularis*) are native to Central and South America. The fruits are orange-yellow when ripe, and have a sprightly, aromatic flavor. The **Giant passion fruit** (*P. quadrangularis*), often called giant granadilla, is native to the hotter regions of tropical America and is the largest of the passion fruits. Up to eight inches long, the

Passion Fruit

Nutritional Value Per 100 g Edible Portion

	Raw Purple	Raw Sweet	Raw Giant	Raw Banana
Calories	97	n/a	n/a	25
Protein	2.2 g	0.340-0.474 g	0.112-0.299 g	0.6 g
Fat	0.7 g	1.50-3.18 g	0.15-1.29 g	0.1 g
Fiber	10.95 g	3.2-5.6 g	0.7-3.6 g	0.3 g
Calcium	12 mg	5.6-13.7 mg	9.2-13.8 mg	4 mg
Iron	1.6 mg	0.58-1.56 mg	0.80-2.93 mg	0.4 mg
Magnesium	29 mg	n/a	n/a	n/a
Phosphorus	68 mg	44.0-78.0 mg	17.1-39.3 mg	20 mg
Potassium	348 mg	n/a	n/a	n/a
Sodium	28 mg	n/a	n/a	n/a
Beta Carotene (A)	700 IU	to 0.035 mg	0.004-0.019 mg	n/a
Thiamine (B_1)	n/a	to 0.002 mg	to 0.003 mg	n/a
Riboflavin (B_2)	0.130 mg	0.063-0.125 mg	0.033-0.120 mg	0.030 mg
Niacin (B_3)	1.500 mg	1.420-1.813 mg	0.378-15.300 mg	2.500 mg
Ascorbic Acid (C)	30 mg	10.8-28.1 mg	14.3 mg	70 mg

delicate skin is a pale greenish or yellow color, often blushing with pink and shading to brown when ripe. The fruit gives off a pleasing aroma but is often bland in flavor, and is best combined with other fruits that have more flavor. **Banana passion fruit** (*P. molissima*) are oval and long, more banana-like in shape, with pulp that is not quite as sweet as the purple variety.

Buying Tips Ripe fruit should be firm and heavy with wrinkled skins, and have a little "give," much like a pear. If the skin is not deeply wrinkled, but only shriveled and unappealing, keep the fruit at room temperature until it is.

Culinary Uses Passion fruit is egg-shaped, with a strange knobby skin of brownish-yellow or rich purple color. Despite its strange outside appearance, inside is a sweetly sensuous, golden flesh full of small black edible seeds. The flavor is strong, tangy, almost punchy, combining pineapple, lemon, and guava. Passion fruit may be eaten straight from the skin like a melon, added to fruit salads, made into juice, pureed and used as a sauce to decorate and flavor desserts, or made into jam. The pulp of the banana passion fruit is not quite as juicy and sweet as that of the purple passion fruit, but still tasty.

Lore and Legend

In the sixteenth century, when the Jesuit missionaries arrived with the conquistadores in South America, they found a blooming vine which they believed to be the same flower that, according to Christian legend, was seen growing upon the cross in one of the many visions of St. Francis of Assisi (1182–1226). In this vine, whose various parts are said to represent certain aspects of the Passion (crucifixion) of Christ, the Jesuit missionaries fancied they had discovered not only a marvelous symbol, but that they had received an assurance of the ultimate triumph of Christianity. The ten white petals represented the ten faithful apostles. Two are absent, representing Peter, who deceived and denied his Lord, and Judas, who betrayed him. The corona symbolized the crown of thorns or halo that surrounded Jesus' head, and the five bright red stamens the five wounds. The ovary signified the hammer, and the three styles, with their rounded heads, the three nails. The tendrils are suggestive of the cords or whips with which he was beaten, while the small seed vessel is the sponge filled with vinegar that was offered to quench Jesus' thirst. When the flower is not entirely opened, it resembles a star, the Star of the East as seen by the three wise men.

South American natives, who had been cultivating these vines since time immemorial, feasted upon its yellow egglike fruits, and the Jesuit Fathers interpreted this too as a heavenly sign, that the Indians were hungering for Christianity. Throwing themselves with great religious zeal into converting these yearning heathens to Christianity, the Fathers succeeded in a remarkably short time.

Pawpaw (*Asimina triloba*)

Asimina *is from Asiminier, a French and Indian name.* Triloba *means three-lobed. The English name* pawpaw *(sometimes spelled papaw) is derived from the American Indian name for the fruit.*

Pawpaw

Nutritional Value Per 100 g Edible Portion	Raw
Calories	85
Protein	5.2 g
Fat	0.9 g

General Information This small native North American tree is generally found growing in thickets along river banks as far north on the East Coast as New York State, and as far west as Nebraska. In 1916 a prize of one hundred dollars was offered by the American Genetic Association—fifty dollars for the largest tree, and fifty dollars for the best fruit specimen. Since then, however, little has been done to spread and improve the tree. The pawpaw tree has the appearance of being an escapee from the tropics, and is in fact a member of the tropical and subtropical custard apple family. The fruits when mature resemble stubby bananas with obtuse ends, often 4 or 5 inches long, and more than an 1 1/2 thick. When ripe, they are greenish-yellow, turning speckled and streaked with brown a few days after they are pulled from the tree. The smooth skin, without the knobs or reticulations characteristic of its tropical relatives, encloses pulp that is creamy yellow, soft and smooth, and surrounds two rows of large inedible brown seeds. A few pawpaw trees yield fruit with orange pulp, and these are considered the finest.

Buying Tips Pawpaws should not be picked until after the first heavy frost. Choose greenish-yellow fruit that is slightly soft.

Culinary Uses Pawpaws have a rich, sweet, creamy flavor evocative of bananas, but with the additional hints of vanilla custard, pineapple, and mango. All this is overlaid with a heavy fragrance that some may find cloying. Fully ripe fruit does not store very well, but will last several months if picked firm-ripe and refrigerated. The best way to eat a fresh pawpaw is to halve it and scoop the flesh out with a spoon; another way is by removing the skin like a banana, but the two do not separate quite as easily. Pawpaw is usually eaten raw. It does not take kindly to cooking, as its flavor is easily driven away by heat, but it can be baked with care or made into various desserts.

Peach (*Prunus persica vulgaris*)

This tree is part of the large plum family, thus the Prunus *genus.* Persica *is simply an epithet meaning Persian, partly because it flourished so well in Persia that it came to be regarded as a native Persian fruit, and partly because one of its many nicknames was the Persian plum.* Vulgaris *means it was a commonly grown plant. The English name* peach *derives ultimately from the Latin* persica.

General Information The peach tree is a low spreading tree cultivated in both China and Persia since ancient times, and probably Chinese in origin, being found in Chinese writings as far back as the tenth century B.C. It began its long westward journey in caravans that carried it to India and on to Persia, where it became naturalized and where invading Roman legions encountered it, calling it *malus Persicus*, or Persian apple. The Roman Emperor Claudius is credited with establishing it in Greece, and soon Greek legend and myth were filled with

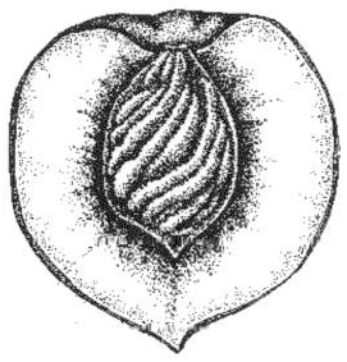

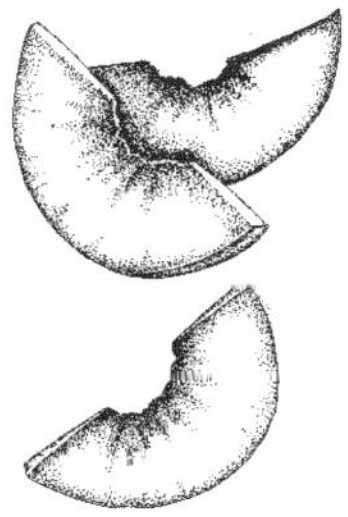

stories of the Persian apple, the golden fruit of the gods. Peaches were among the first trees the Spaniards planted in Mexico, Brazil, the West Indies, and the California missions. Early explorers and settlers planted peaches up and down the eastern seaboard of North America, while the Indians carried the fruit westward, planting peach stones about their campsites and along trails from Florida to the Great Lakes. By the mid-1700s, the fruit was so firmly established that some botanists assumed that the peach was native to America. Today the peach is one of the most widely cultivated fruit trees throughout the world, wherever the soil and climate are suitable. They are the third most popular fruit grown in the United States, coming in right behind apples and oranges, and are among the most popular fruits for eating out of hand.

Buying Tips Ripe peaches should be firm and free from blemishes, yielding to gentle pressure. They should have a warm, fragrant aroma and a fresh, softly colorful appearance of either whitish or yellowish color, combined with a red color or blush depending on the variety. Those tinged with green were picked immature and will not ripen satisfactorily; they will develop only a pale weak color, little or no flavor, and tough rubbery flesh. Fuzzy peaches are less likely to have been heavily sprayed with pesticides, since fuzz indicates they have escaped the commercial "bathhouse."

Culinary Uses The flavor of peaches should be warm, syrupy, and sensuous, the very epitome of summer. Peaches do not gain in sugar content after being picked, as there is no reserve of starch to draw from. They are best eaten straight from the tree, edible fuzzy skin and all, but can be added to fruit salads, baked in desserts, or made into jams and jellies. Peaches go beautifully with other fruit, especially raspberries and other drupes or stone fruits—apricots, cherries, plums, and almonds—that ripen at the same time. Peaches and cream are natural companions. When sugar is added, the reaction in the body becomes acidic; when cooked or canned, their vital elements are lost.

Health Benefits Diuretic, expectorant, laxative, sedative. Peaches are easily digested, have a strong alkaline reaction on the body, stimulate the secretion of the digestive juices, help improve the health of the skin, and add color to the complexion. They have both laxative and diuretic qualities and are an aid in cleansing the system whenever there is kidney and bladder trouble. With fewer calories and a higher water content than apples or pears, peaches are an excellent fruit for hot summer days. For a "peaches and cream" complexion, apply a poultice of blended fresh peach on the face, let dry, then rinse and pat dry. Peach leaf taken as a tea destroys worms.

Peach

Nutritional Value Per 100 g Edible Portion

	Raw	Dried, Sulphured
Calories	43	262
Protein	0.70 g	3.1 g
Fat	0.09 g	0.7 g
Fiber	0.64 g	3.1 g
Calcium	5 mg	48 mg
Iron	0.11 mg	6.00 mg
Magnesium	7 mg	n/a
Phosphorus	12 mg	117 mg
Potassium	197 mg	950 mg
Sodium	0 mg	16 mg
Zinc	0.140 mg	n/a
Copper	0.068 mg	n/a
Manganese	0.047 mg	n/a
Beta Carotene (A)	535 IU	3,900 IU
Thiamine (B_1)	0.017 mg	0.010 mg
Riboflavin (B_2)	0.041 mg	0.190 mg
Niacin (B_3)	0.990 mg	5.300 mg
Pantothenic Acid (B_5)	0.170 mg	n/a
Pyridoxine (B_6)	0.018 mg	n/a
Folic Acid (B_9)	3.4 mcg	n/a
Ascorbic Acid (C)	6.6 mg	18.0 mg

Varieties

There are hundreds of varieties of peaches, but two basic categories—clingstone and freestone—which denote whether the flesh adheres to or breaks free of the pit. Both categories include both red and yellow peaches. White peaches, with their delicate perfume and exquisite juiciness, are worth seeking out. They are more fragile and expensive, but peach perfectionists prize them.

Lore and Legend

The peach tree in China is called the Tree of the Fairy Fruit. It is the symbol of immortality because the Peach Tree of the Gods, which grew in the mythical gardens of Hsi Wang My, the Royal Lady of the West, bloomed only once every three thousand years, to yield the ripened Fruits of Eternal Life. Those who eat of these fruits have health, virility, and the gift of immortality conferred upon them. The sacred food of the Eight Taoist Immortals, and the most important sacred plant in the Chinese Taoist religion, the peach was considered a symbol of immortality and of the Tao, the way of attaining this immortality. Even today the Chinese consider the peach a symbol of longevity, and plates and bowls used for birthday celebrations are often decorated with peaches and their blossoms.

In Japan there is a popular folktale that goes as follows: one day, while washing her clothes at the river, an old woman saw a large, round, pink object splashing and rolling about in the water. Carefully fishing it out, she found it was a peach so large that it would feed her husband and herself for several days. When they broke it open, a tiny child was found inside the stone. Bringing him up with great love and devotion, they gave him everything they could afford. When he was grown, he invaded the Island of the Devils, where he defeated the demons and seized their treasure, laying it at the feet of his beloved foster parents.

Clingstone peaches arrive first in the season, appearing in June and lasting until August. Most have skins that are either all yellow or yellow with a large red area, and flesh that is red around a stone that cannot be removed easily. They tend to be juicier, sweeter, and softer-textured than freestones, making excellent dessert peaches by themselves or blended into fruit shakes and ice cream. Less convenient to prepare because of the stones, these are the type most commonly used for canning and jam.

Freestone varieties tend to be later, arriving in July and lasting into September. These are the most popular variety for eating fresh since they can be split in half by hand and the stone easily removed. Freestones are larger than clingstones, are less juicy, and have a firmer texture, but they are nevertheless very fragrant and sweet tasting, and are excellent for canning and baking into pies. Freestone peaches range from the red-skinned Havens and Harknesses to the longish, golden-yellow skinned Elberta peach.

Pear (*Pyrus communis*)

Pyrus *is the classical Latin name for the pear tree, while* communis *means common, general, or gregarious. The English word* pear *derives from the Latin term.*

General Information The pear tree seems to have originated in western Asia around the Caspian Sea. More than five thousand varieties can now be listed, some spread throughout the world, others found in only one country, or even limited to a small locality. In 1850, pears were so popular in France that it was the fashion among the elite to see who could raise the best specimen, and the fruit was celebrated in song and verse. In the United States, the pear is almost as much a national favorite as the apple, to which it is related—both are members of the rose family and pome fruits (those with a distinct seeded core). Pear trees were brought to North America by early colonists, who used cuttings from European stock, and the fruit was introduced into California by Franciscan monks who planted them in mission gardens. Unlike most tree fruits, pears are best ripened off the tree; when tree-ripened, they develop little grit cells, or stones, in the flesh. Separated from the tree, this process cannot take place, and they ripen evenly and smoothly with a creamy texture.

Buying Tips Select firm, unblemished fruit. They are fully ripe when they give to gentle pressure. Since pears ripen from the core outward, be careful not to let them soften too much, as they will turn to mush. Avoid those that are bruised, have rough scaly areas, or soft flesh near the stem.

Culinary Uses Pears are elegantly seductive. Sweet, juicy, wonderfully textured, and highly nutritious, they have the most subtle taste of all orchard fruit, and leave the palate delightfully fresh and clean. They are probably the easiest fruit to identify by their shape: the small stem end gradually broadens to a plump blossom end like a bell. Properly ripened, pears are so tender they were once called the "butter fruit." They can be used in all the same ways as apples, including for cider (called perry). Fresh pears make wonderful companions for wine, bread, and a mixture of sharp cheeses. Hollowed pear halves make attractive boats for various fillings. Cooked pears are inclined to blandness.

Health Benefits Pears are extremely rich in alkaline elements, have a strong diuretic action, are helpful for constipation and poor digestion, and are valuable as general cleansers of the system. Their iodine content helps to keep the thyroid functioning properly and the metabolism balanced. Pears are an excellent source of water-soluble fibers, including pectin. In fact, pears are actually higher in pectin than apples. The regular consumption of pears is believed to result in a pure complexion and shiny hair. Dried pears are a good energy producer in the wintertime as well as a delicious snack year-round. When cooked, canned or processed, their greatest value is lost, the organic elements having been converted into inorganic matter.

Pear

Nutritional Value Per 100 g Edible Portion

	Raw
Calories	59
Protein	0.39 g
Fat	0.40 g
Fiber	1.40 g
Calcium	11 mg
Iron	0.25 mg
Magnesium	6 mg
Phosphorus	11 mg
Potassium	125 mg
Sodium	0 mg
Zinc	0.120 mg
Copper	0.113 mg
Manganese	0.076 mg
Beta Carotene (A)	20 IU
Thiamine (B_1)	0.020 mg
Riboflavin (B_2)	0.040 mg
Niacin (B_3)	0.100 mg
Pantothenic Acid (B_5)	0.070 mg
Pyridoxine (B_6)	0.018 mg
Folic Acid (B_9)	7.3 mcg
Ascorbic Acid (C)	4 mg
Tocopherol (E)	0.50 mg

Varieties

Anjou (Beurre d'Anjou) are the most abundant winter variety of pear. Originating in France or Belgium in the nineteenth century, they are a round, yellowish-green pear that tapers bluntly to the stem end, with a thick, barely noticeable neck and no waistline. Belonging to the bergamot group of pears, their skin remains green but develops a definite glow when ripe, and they should be eaten only when they yield to gentle pressure. Although the skin is not tough, it is not as sweet as the meat and has a slightly grainy texture. The flesh is spicy-sweet and juicy with a firm texture. Anjous are a wonderful dessert pear; their firm texture makes them the best pear for cooking and baking, since they never seem to lose their shape. Available from October through May.

Bartletts were first raised in 1770 in Berkshire, England, by a schoolmaster named John Stair. Arriving in London, this variety of pear was called Williams after Mr. Williams of Middlesex, who distributed them. In 1798 or 1799, it was brought to the United States and planted in Dorchester, Massachusetts under the name of Williams' Bon Chretien. Enoch Bartlett acquired the estate in 1817 and, not knowing the true name of the pear, distributed it under his own name. In other parts of the world it is still known as Williams or Williams' Bon-Chretien. The Bartlett is a pyriform pear, with a definite waistline and a long stem; they are large, golden yellow summer pears, bell-shaped, with smooth, clear skin that is often blushed with red. It has white, finely grained flesh, and is juicy and delicious. The yellow variety ripens very quickly once picked, and bruises easily (even loud noises are said to hurt them); they are best eaten while still flecked with green. The most common variety grown today, Bartletts comprise more than 65 percent of commercial production. They are excellent canners and dessert fruit but are too fragile for lunch bags, picnic baskets, and carrying around in your pocket. Available July through December.

Red Bartletts are a development of Northwestern pear growers and are fast becoming increasingly available. The red skin is heavier than the yellow variety, the pigment resists disease better, and the ripening process is not quite so quick. Three-quarters red, solid at the cone end and striped below the waist, they are ripe when the yellow area shows slight green and the striped area is still red, not russet or brown.

Bosc (Beurre Bosc) are a member of the conical pear family, and are long,tapered, and waistless. They are generally medium-sized, dark yellow, with rough brown skins and long, narrow necks. When properly ripened, they become a dark russet color and respond to gentle pressure. The meat is firm and almost crunchy, cream-colored, very juicy, and smooth-textured. The larger ones usually have the best flavor and sweetness. An excellent pear for eating out of hand and that holds up well in lunch pails, picnic baskets, and fruit bowls, they are also wonderful baked, broiled, poached, or preserved. Available from October through May.

Clapp pears are hardly ever shipped, but are frequently available at many road-side stands and farmer's markets. The green Clapp pear has a thinner skin than most, while the red Clapp has a heavier skin and a slightly firmer texture. Of med-ium size, they have very white flesh, a high sugar content, and plenty of juice.

Comice (**Doyenne du Comice**—meaning "best of the show") pears have the reputation of being the sweetest and most flavorful, and are considered by many to be the best. These pears have a definite pyriform shape, with a short, wide stem end, a waistline, and a very wide blossom end. Somewhat squattish and irregularly formed, they are heavily perfumed, with a heady, musky fragrance. Their color during peak ripeness is a soft green that glows with a golden aura, and is sometimes slightly bronzed or flecked. Similar in size to the Anjou, they are distinguished from their cousin by a red blush. Their skin is so thin and the flesh so wet that anything more than a gentle stroke leaves a mark; their creamy smooth texture literally melts in the mouth. Best when eaten fresh, they are also delectable baked into desserts. Available from October through January.

Packhams (Packham's Triumph) are mostly imported, although some are grown in California. Coming in primarily medium and large premium sizes, this pear has a definite pear shape, but the wide bottom is irregular, with a deep blossom end. They also have a perfume that adds to their exotic flavor. Very, very juicy and sweet, a Packham pear at its peak (just turning soft gold all over) begs to be taken home. Available from late June to September.

Seckels are a true American pear, having been discovered as a mutant sometime around the time of the Revolution. They take their name from the man who acquired the land in Delaware where the original tree was discovered. They have hard green skin that turns slightly golden and develops a light red blush when ripe, a spicy aroma, and crisp but sweet flesh. Always very small and frequently only bite-sized, these are a fun fruit for all, but make an especially good children's fruit as they seem to be just the right size for a child. Served fresh, poached, or pickled whole, these eye-catchers are sure to please with their sweet flesh. Available from September through January.

Winter Nelis are a fooler: these pears are ripe when the skins are green, with light brown russet spots. They are a late winter and early spring pear with a squat shape, dull green skin, and firm, crisp flesh that has a spicy rich flavor. These pears are excellent for baking and are used mostly for dessert.

Pear, Asian *(Pyrus ussuriensis, P. pyrifolia)*

Also Known As: Sand Pears.

Pyrus is the classical Latin name for the pear tree, while ussuriensis means coming from Ussuri (in East Asia); pyrifolia means having foliage like the common pear. The English name Asian Pear was given because these members of the pear family are Asian in heritage.

Pear, Asian

Nutritional Value Per 100 g Edible Portion

	Raw
Calories	42
Protein	0.50 g
Fat	0.23 g
Fiber	n/a
Calcium	4 mg
Iron	n/a
Magnesium	8 mg
Phosphorus	11 mg
Potassium	121 mg
Sodium	0 mg
Zinc	0.02 mg
Copper	0.050 mg
Manganese	0.060 mg
Beta Carotene (A)	0 IU
Thiamine (B_1)	0.009 mg
Riboflavin (B_2)	0.010 mg
Niacin (B_3)	0.219 mg
Pantothenic Acid (B_5)	0.070 mg
Pyridoxine (B_6)	0.022 mg
Folic Acid (B_9)	8 mcg
Ascorbic Acid (C)	1.2 mg-3.8 g

General Information The Sand or Asian Pear developed in Asia. The Chinese have been growing and eating Asian pears for the past 2,500 to 3,000 years. By the time of the Han dynasty (first century B.C.), there were large orchards planted along the Huai and Yellow rivers. There are currently over three thousand cultivars grown in China, but only twenty-five varieties or so are known in the United States. Asian pears were introduced to North America during the Gold Rush by Chinese miners who grew the trees along streams of the Sierra Nevada. Distinguished from the European "butter fruit" pear with its soft, melting flesh, sand pears have hard flesh with numerous "sand" or grit cells. Since there are numerous Far Eastern pear varieties marketed under the same name, you will find a wide range of seemingly disparate fruits: they can be petite and chartreuse, mammoth and reddish-brown, smooth-skinned and lacquer-like, or sprinkled with a confetti of russeting.

Buying Tips Choose the most fragrant Asian pears. They are hard when ripe, but should be stored in the refrigerator.

Culinary Uses Asian pears are all crunch and juice, so crisp-firm they can be cut paper thin, their sweet nectar welling up and pouring off each slice. Ready to eat when you buy them, they can be stored for a long period if refrigerated. Looking like and eaten like apples, their flavor ranges from sweet with just a hint of perfume to sweet with a strong floral aroma. They have a mellower flavor and more juice than either apples or European pears, but are granular in texture. Cooked, they resemble the European pears in flavor, but the flesh remains slightly firm and meaty. Allow a much longer cooking time than you would for other pears.

Pejibaye *(Bactris gasipaes)*

Also Known As: Peach Palm.

Bactris *derives from the Greek* bactron, *meaning cane, as the young stems were used for walking sticks.*

General Information The pejibaye is indigenous to the Amazonian areas of Colombia, Ecuador, Peru, and Brazil and is little known outside of tropical Central America. Yellow to orange or scarlet, turning purple when fully ripe, the two- to six-centimeter fruit is ovoid, oblate, cylindrical, or conical. The skin is thin, the flesh yellow to light orange, sweet yet occasionally with a trace of bitterness, and dry and mealy. Some fruits are seedless, but normally there is a single conical seed. Borne in bunches of up to three hundred

Pejibaye	
Nutritional Value Per 100 g Edible Portion	
	Raw
Protein	0.340-0.633 g
Fat	3.10-8.17 g
Fiber	0.8-1.4 g
Calcium	8.9-40.4 mg
Iron	0.85-2.25 mg
Phosphorus	33.5-55.2 mg
Beta Carotene (A)	0.290-2.760 mg
Thiamine (B_1)	0.037-0.070 mg
Riboflavin (B_2)	0.099-0.154 mg
Niacin (B_3)	0.667-1.945 mg
Ascorbic Acid (C)	14.8-41.4 mg

fruits, there may be as many as thirteen bunches on a single trunk, and under ideal conditions two crops are harvested per year.

Culinary Uses Because the fruit is caustic in its natural state, it is commonly prepared by boiling in salted water for three hours, or by roasting. Once boiled or roasted, the flesh and inedible skin separate easily from the seed. The white seed kernel is sometimes cooked and eaten, and is said to have a flavor like coconut. However, the seeds are considered to be difficult to digest. Young flowers may be chopped and added to omelettes, while palm hearts are served in salads or prepared with eggs and vegetables in a casserole.

Health Benefits Pejibaye fruit can provide more carbohydrate and protein per hectare (2.47 acres) than corn. This protein contains seven of the eight essential amino acids (excluding only tryptophan), along with ten other non-essential amino acids.

Pepino (*Solanum muricatum*)

Also Known As: Melon Pear, Mellowfruit.

> Solanum *comes from the Latin* solamen, *meaning solace or quieting.* Muricatum *means muricate, roughed by means of hard points. The English word* pepino *means cucumber in Spanish, in reference to their shape.*

General Information The pepino is a member of the nightshade family, like potatoes, peppers, and tomatoes. This small bush is native to temperate Andean areas of Peru and Chile, and cultivated elsewhere in Central and South America. Efforts to promote the pepino as a commercial crop in California during the 1920s were unsuccessful, but it has since been brought into cultivation in Australia and New Zealand. The shape of the fruit is evocative of a large acorn, a skewed heart, or a giant teardrop, while its skin is yellow-gold and frequently streaked with lavender. The thin skin is very smooth, like that of its relative the eggplant. One variety (**Rio Barba**) is vine-like and its fruits resemble small cucumbers, thus justifying the name pepino. A typical fruit is about three inches in diameter near the stem end, and five inches long.

Buying Tips Choose aromatic fruits (the size does not affect the flavor) that give to gentle pressure like a partly ripe plum, avoiding those with dents or bruises. The fruit should smell lightly sweet, almost honeysuckle-like. The undercolor of the skin should be golden to pinky-apricot when fully ripe, not greenish or mustardy.

Culinary Uses Pepinos range from plum- to cantaloupe-sized, are slightly heart-shaped, and have fragrant yellow-gold flesh surrounding a central pocket of seeds, like a melon. The mild pulp compares to the finest textured and juiciest melon, although less sweet, while its aroma suggests a perfumed Bartlett pear blended with vanilla and honey. Serve pepino like melon, or use it in fruit salads. Both seeds and skins are edible, but the skins tend to be tough and unpalatable, so are best pulled off once the fruit is sliced.

Health Benefits Low in fat, high in fiber and vitamin C.

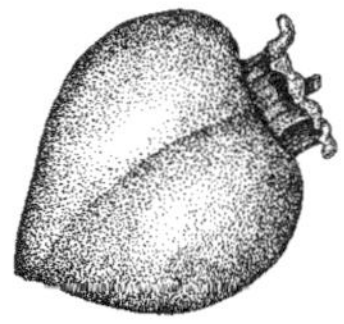

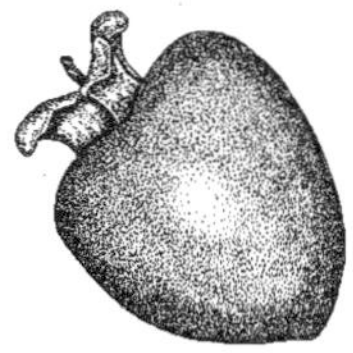

Persimmon *(Diospyros virginiana, D. kaki)*

Diospyrus *comes from the Greek words* dios, *meaning god (in this case Jupiter or Jove), and* pyros, *meaning grain; thus Jove's grain, alluding to its succulent edible fruits. One of the European species of* Diospyros *is said to have caused oblivion, transporting the eater to heaven, the land of Jove. The term* virginiana *means that this variety was first encountered in that state (Virginia);* kaki *is the Japanese name for the fruit. The English name* persimmon *comes from the Algonquin Indian* putchamin *or* pessemin, *meaning dried fruit, since well into the colonial era dried persimmons were stored and eaten like figs.*

General Information The persimmon that is native to the United States (*D. virginiana*), grows wild from Connecticut to Florida, and from Texas to Kansas. This persimmon is much smaller than the Oriental variety, about the size of a walnut or cherry tomato, but resembles the larger heart-shaped oriental persimmon in both its bright coloring and the gooey texture of the inner flesh. They have a stronger fragrance and flavor, sweet and luscious, approaching the richness of dates. Sufficient quantities grow to satisfy local demand, but few outside the region have tasted the fruit since little or no shipping is done. Native Americans recognized the honeyed sweetness of the ripe fruit hanging like small orange balls from the bare branches of the tree in late fall. They dried persimmons to eat during the long winters, or baked them into breads and puddings. The oriental persimmon *(D. kaki)* is probably native to China, and is widely cultivated in both China and Japan. The Japanese consider it their national fruit, but it is more properly called the Oriental rather than Japanese persimmon. Commodore Perry's expedition, which opened Japan to world commerce in 1852, is credited with the introduction of this fruit to the United States. Contrary to popular folklore, persimmons do not need a frost to fully ripen; those fruits with a dark orange color can be picked while still solid and ripened fully off the tree. You can wait for them to become so ripe that they fall off the tree by themselves, or by shaking it you can bring down a shower of fruit. In Israel, a form of persimmon known as a Sharon fruit is grown without the high tannic acid content.

Buying Tips Good quality fruit is well-shaped, plump, smooth, and highly colored, with an unbroken skin and an attached stem cap. They are very fragile when fully ripe, so handle with care.

Lore and Legend

In Japan, every child knows the origins of the persimmon tree from one of the miraculous tales about the childhood of the great Samurai leader of the twelfth century, Yoshitsune. Yoshitsune and the great giant Benkei met in a confrontation one day, and the giant was knocked over by a blow from Yoshitsune, who was no bigger than a boot, but braver than a tiger. The noise of the fall was so tremendous that the earth shook and split open; out of the crack came a tree covered with beautiful orange-red fruit that were full of juice for the two thirsty fighters. From then on the two warriors were inseparable, and Benkei became Yoshitsune's champion fighter.

Persimmon

Nutritional Value Per 100 g Edible Portion

	Raw Japanese	Raw American
Calories	70	127
Protein	0.58 g	0.8 g
Fat	0.19 g	0.4 g
Fiber	1.48 g	1.5 g
Calcium	8 mg	27 mg
Iron	0.15 mg	2.5 mg
Magnesium	9 mg	n/a
Phosphorus	17 mg	26 mg
Potassium	161 mg	310 mg
Sodium	1 mg	1 mg
Zinc	0.11 mg	n/a
Copper	0.113 mg	n/a
Manganese	0.355 mg	n/a
Beta Carotene (A)	2167 IU	n/a
Thiamine (B_1)	0.030 mg	n/a
Riboflavin (B_2)	0.020 mg	n/a
Niacin (B_3)	0.100 mg	n/a
Folic Acid (B_9)	7.5 mcg	n/a
Ascorbic Acid (C)	7.5 mg	66 mg

Too-firm persimmons will ripen in a few days on their own, or faster if enclosed in a bag with a banana or apple, whose natural ethylene gas will help them ripen.

Culinary Uses Persimmons look rather like bright orange plastic tomatoes. Allow them to ripen at room temperature until soft and rather mushy, much like a soft ripe plum. Underripe fruits can be very unpleasantly astringent due to their tannin content, but this tannin disappears as the fruit ripens and sweetens. In general, persimmons that have dark-colored flesh are sweeter and less astringent, and may be eaten before they become too soft. Varieties with light-colored flesh, with the exception of the Fuyu variety, are astringent until they soften. To eat, remove the stem cap, cut in half, and scoop out the soft, brilliantly colored, sensuous flesh. Their texture and flavor is rich, soft, sweet, and spicy, with the texture of a very ripe warm mango, the taste of apricot-papaya custard, and the sweetness of a tree sap like maple syrup. Persimmons are best enjoyed on their own or in fruit salads, but can be added to puddings and cakes or made into jams and chutneys. They take to many of the same simple flavorings as do mango and papaya, so that a touch of citrus or ginger sets them off nicely. In eastern Asia, the custom has been to dry them for winter use. In this process the flesh turns blackish, and a fine coating of sugar develops on the surface. These sweet dried fruits are a particular favorite in China for the New Year celebration in February. Surplus persimmons may be converted into molasses, cider, beer, and wine. Roasted seeds have been used as a coffee substitute.

Health Benefits Persimmons soothe sore throats and irritated intestinal tracts, are noted for their mild laxative qualities, and contain enzymes that break down damaged cells and foreign microbes.

Varieties

Hachiya persimmons are the largest and most handsome oriental variety grown in this country. As a rule, California produces a seedless variety, while the Hachiya grown in Florida has one or more seeds. They are the size of a nectarine or large plum, slightly teardrop-shaped, and the skin is a glossy deep red-orange. To be ripe, this large showy fruit with its deep yellow or pink flesh must be very soft, with almost a pudding-like consistency.

Fuyus are the yellow-orange, tomato-shaped variety of persimmon most commonly grown and enjoyed in Israel and Japan. Hard and eaten crisp like an apple, they can be eaten out of hand, or peeled and cut in slices across the fruit to reveal the beautiful flower formation in the center.

Pineapple (*Ananas comosus*)

Ananas *was the Carib name for this plant which, despite the sound, has nothing to do with bananas but comes from a Guarani word meaning excellent fruit.* Comosus *means with long hair. It is neither a pine nor an apple, and its English name,* pineapple, *is only an illustrative term for its form, which resembles a pine cone.*

General Information The unusual-looking pineapple plant is native to southern Brazil and Paraguay, and was carried by Indians throughout South and Central America to Mexico and the West Indies long before the arrival of Europeans. The sailors of the Columbus expedition of 1493 encountered the pineapple on the island of Guadeloupe, and were both astonished and delighted by its qualities. The native Indians believed that the pineapple had been brought to Guadeloupe from the Amazon many generations before by the warlike and ferocious Caribs, whose custom it was to bring home seeds, roots, and plants from the places they invaded. The plant consists of a rosette of stiff, sharp-pointed, thorn-edged leaves, with a stem rising from the center that reaches a height of three or four feet. Near the summit of the stem, it swells into a fruit. Resembling a pine cone, the pineapple is not even a fruit in the ordinary sense of the word, but a sorosis, a multiple organ that forms when the fruits of a hundred or more separate flowers on a spike coalesce to form a pulpy mass. There are no records of just when or how the pineapple arrived in Hawaii, although the most generally accepted theory is that they either floated in from a wrecked Spanish or Portuguese ship, or were brought ashore by sailors and discarded. The first white settlers found it growing wild beside the sugar cane, and it did not take many years for them to realize its possible commercial value, with the first commercial plantings being set out about 1840. In 1898, the young J.D. Dole arrived in Hawaii, along with hundreds of settlers who had been granted Hawaiian homesteads. He persuaded the homesteaders to plant their land to pineapples, and soon the pineapple industry was born. For many years, Hawaii supplied 70 percent of the world's canned pineapple and 85 percent of the canned pineapple juice, but labor costs have shifted a large segment of the industry from Hawaii to the Philippines.

Lore and Legend

Europeans were completely infatuated with pineapples, even though their climate was unsuited to growing them. Eating them took some getting used to, however. Charles V, King of Spain and Holy Roman Emperor, refused to taste a specimen for fear of being poisoned, while Louis XIV of France rashly bit into the strange fruit before it could be peeled, and thus cut his mouth on the scaly skin. In 1700 a Leyden merchant named La Cour devised a glass house in which a pineapple that was sweet and fragrant was grown to good-sized maturity. The event caused great excitement, and greenhouses soon became an extremely popular hobby and status symbol. The pineapples thus grown became a popular dessert among the privileged, but many of the fruits were considered too valuable to simply eat, and were first rented out for table decorations. Native West Indians hung pineapples or pineapple crowns on village gates and dwelling entrances as signs of abundance and hospitality within (but they planted thick hedges of pineapple plants around their villages to keep strangers out—effective protective barriers, for the sharp, spiky edges of pineapple leaves can inflict nasty cuts). The association of pineapples with hospitality and abundance was copied by the Spanish; pineapples were carved on doorways and gateposts, and cabinetmakers decorated bedposts, desk finials, chests, and chairs with them. A century later, the pineapple motif had found its way back to America and was used especially in the southern colonies.

Buying Tips Pineapples, unlike most other fruits, do not ripen or sweeten after picking. Since they have no reserve of starch to be converted into sugar, they start to deteriorate instead. Look for large, plump, heavy fruit with fresh, deep green plumage. Skin coloring may be green or yellow-gold depending on the variety. The base should be slightly soft, and there is generally a sweet, but not fermented, aroma. Avoid fruit that is old-looking, dry, or that is starting to decay at the base. To ensure a uniformly sweet fruit, remove the leaves and stand the pineapple upside-down at room temperature so the sweet juice concentrated at the base can run throughout.

Culinary Uses One of the most popular tropical fruits due to its high sugar content and lush flavor, it is not a fruit to make a whole meal out of. Pineapples contain a large amount of bromelin, a protein-digesting enzyme, which is so powerful that plantation and cannery workers have to wear rubber gloves to avoid having their hands literally eaten away. Recognizing this quality, early Hawaiians cooked and baked their meat overlaid with chunks of pineapple; this had a tenderizing effect on the toughest animal meat and was the culinary forerunner of ham decorated with pineapple slices. Bromelin is also responsible for the fact that a gelatin dessert made with fresh pineapple will not set unless an additional gelling agent

Pineapple

Nutritional Value Per 100 g Edible Portion

	Raw
Calories	49
Protein	0.39 g
Fat	0.43 g
Fiber	0.3-0.6 g
Calcium	6.2-37.2 mg
Iron	0.27-.05 mg
Magnesium	14 mg
Phosphorus	6.6-11.9 mg
Potassium	113 mg
Sodium	1.0-1.4 mg
Zinc	0.080 mg
Copper	0.110 mg
Manganese	1.649 mg
Beta Carotene (A)	23 IU
Thiamine (B_1)	0.048-0.138 mg
Riboflavin (B_2)	0.011-0.040 mg
Niacin (B_3)	0.130-0.267 mg
Pantothenic Acid (B_5)	0.160 mg
Pyridoxine (B_6)	0.090 mg
Folic Acid (B_9)	10.6 mcg
Ascorbic Acid (C)	27.0-65.2 mg
Tocopherol (E)	0.10 mg

such as agar-agar is added. Cooked or canned pineapple and juice no longer contain bromelin, since the enzyme is quickly destroyed by heating. To prepare fresh pineapple, slice off the crown and bottom, then cut downward along the skin with a heavy, sharp knife. Remove the "eyes" with a knife tip. The central core is tough and fibrous, so it is usually cut out. Fresh pineapple is best eaten with other acidic or sub-acid fruits. America's second most popular sherbet flavor, after orange, is pineapple, and pineapple is its third most popular canned fruit, after applesauce and peaches.

Dried pineapple is almost always "honey-dipped" or, more precisely, immersed in a sugar water solution that may or may not have a small amount of honey added. The end product is up to 80 percent sugar. Unsweetened dried pineapple, which is dipped in pineapple juice concentrate, is dark in color and harder to find.

Health Benefits Detoxicant, diuretic. The pineapple early on became an important medicinal plant. Its fermented juice was made into an alcoholic drink, used for fevers and to relieve body heat in hot weather; externally pineapple juice was used for dissolving painful corns and to cure skin ailments. Pineapples contain a fair amount of acids—notably citric, malic, and tartaric—which in their organic form exert a diuretic action, aid digestion and elimination, and help clear mucous waste from bronchial tissues. They are very rich in bromelin, a proteolytic (protein-digesting) enzyme; bromelin literally "digests" dead or diseased cells and foreign microbes in the throat. The greatest value of pineapple juice lies in its digestive power, which closely resembles that of human gastric juices.

Plum and Prune *(Prunus domestica, P. americana, P. salicina)*

The large plum tree family was given the genus Prunus, *a name derived from the ancient Greek name* proumne. *The term* domestica *refers to the domesticated variety as opposed to the wild one;* americana *signifies the American variety, while* salicina *means willow-like. The interchangeable use of the terms* plum *and* prune *dates back several centuries. The English word* plum *is originally Anglo-Saxon, while* prune *is French; at one time they were probably synonymous. It is uncertain just when the word prune was first used to designate a dried plum or a plum suitable for drying.*

General Information Plums are the second most cultivated fruit in the world after apples, and have thousands of varieties, of which only twenty are grown commercially. Technically a drupe—a pitted fruit—related to the nectarine, peach, and apricot, the plum is far more diverse than its relatives, and comes in a wider range of shapes, sizes, and colors: it can be red, maroon, black, pink, green, or yellow. Its flavor also may vary from extremely sweet to quite tart. All plums have skins that are shiny when unripe and that change to a dull matte color as they ripen and sweeten; plums left to ripen on the tree until they soften develop dark brown areas that taste bitter. The early colonists found plums growing wild along the entire Eastern coast; these native plums today have little commercial value, and the European plum (*P. domestica*) has replaced them. The European variety is believed indigenous to western Asia

Lore and Legend

The founder of Taoism, the Asian philosophy that urges one to follow nature and not interfere with the natural goodness of the human heart, was Lao-tse, supposedly born white-haired under a plum tree in 604 B.C. Lao-tse's family name (Li) also means "plum tree." Although many other trees play significant roles in Chinese mythology, the plum tree is singularly associated with great age and therefore wisdom. Plum blossoms carved on jade symbolize resurrection.

in the region south of the Caucasus Mountains, and to have been introduced to the Mediterranean regions by Alexander the Great. These are smaller, denser, and less juicy than their Japanese counterparts; their skin color is always blue or purple, and their pits are usually freestone. The Japanese variety (*P. salicina*) are the non-prune plums. Originally from China, these plums were introduced into Japan some three hundred years ago, and the Japanese were so diligent about cultivating and improving them that they have made them their own. In the late nineteenth century, dozens of varieties from Europe and Asia were assiduously cultivated in America, primarily in California. One of the most influential plum breeders (alone developing sixty varieties) was the famed horticulturist Luther Burbank, who in 1907 developed a variety called Santa Rosa, which now accounts for about one-third of the total domestic crop.

Prunes can be either fresh or dried. Compared to plums, prunes have a firmer, meatier flesh, higher sugar content, often a higher acid content, and are adaptable to drying. Ripe, fresh prunes are never wrinkled and are always blue or purple; the flesh is greenish but browns up slightly at the stone, which is always freestone and easily removed. The present dried prune industry is based on the French prune, Prune d'Agen, named after a town in Aquitaine in the southwest of France. This variety was taken to California in 1856 by Louis Pellier, a young apprentice seaman who jumped ship in San Francisco Bay in 1849. He never struck it rich panning for gold, but he and his brothers fared well with their prune orchard. California production is now so great that it dominates the commerce in prunes and provides a high proportion of those sold in France itself. Commercial dried prunes are made by drying prune plums, which are dipped in a mild alkaline solution so that tiny cracks will form in their skins, allowing moisture to escape evenly as they dry. They are not usually treated with sulphur dioxide, but may have undergone other processes to tenderize them or soften the skins, and may be coated with mineral oil.

Plum and Prune

Nutritional Value Per 100 g Edible Portion

	Raw Damson	Raw Japanese	Raw Prune-Type	Raw Dried Prune
Calories	66	48	75	239
Protein	0.5 g	0.5 g	0.8 g	2.61 g
Fat	trace	0.2 g	0.2 g	0.52 g
Fiber	0.4 g	0.6 g	0.4 g	2.04 g
Calcium	18 mg	12 mg	12 mg	51 mg
Iron	0.50 mg	0.5 mg	0.5 mg	2.48 mg
Phosphorus	17 mg	18 mg	18 mg	79 mg
Potassium	299 mg	170 mg	170 mg	745 mg
Sodium	2 mg	1 mg	1 mg	4 mg
Beta Carotene (A)	300 IU	250 IU	300-1340 IU	1987 IU
Thiamine (B_1)	0.08 mg	0.03 mg	0.03 mg	0.081 mg
Riboflavin (B_2)	0.03 mg	0.03 mg	0.03 mg	0.162 mg
Niacin (B_3)	0.50 mg	0.50 mg	0.50 mg	1.961 mg
Pyridoxine (B_6)	0.05 mg	0.05 mg	0.03 mg	0.264 mg
Ascorbic Acid (C)	n/a	6 mg	4 mg	3.3 mg

Buying Tips Plums of good quality are plump, clean, of fresh appearance, full colored for the particular variety, and soft enough to yield to slight pressure. Avoid shriveled, split, or hard fruit. Mature but not fully ripened plums will come to full fragrance and softness in a few days at room temperature.

Culinary Uses Plums fall into two basic categories, dessert and cooking, though there are many varieties of each. Although both dessert and cooking plums can be cooked, only dessert plums are sweet enough to be eaten raw. Plums can be eaten in pies, puddings, cakes, jams, and desserts. Chopped plums add sweetness to muffins, quick bread, or coffee cake, while sliced plums bring new color and texture to a variety of salads. Prunes, both fresh and dried, are excellent for snacking or baking, and make a tasty addition to many dishes.

Health Benefits Laxative, stimulant. The plum is a dynamic fruit, energy-giving and stimulating to the nerves. It contains several fruit acids, some of which have a tendency to irritate the kidneys. Plums and prunes contain oxalic acid, which in its natural state is excellent for both constipation and an inactive liver; when cooked, this oxalic acid becomes inorganic and is harmful to the body. It is best to eat this fruit either raw or dried, and not cooked into any sort of sauces or pastries. Prunes are known for their strong laxative action. When dried they contain a high phosphorus content, and their content of other salts is valuable as food for the blood, brain, and nerves.

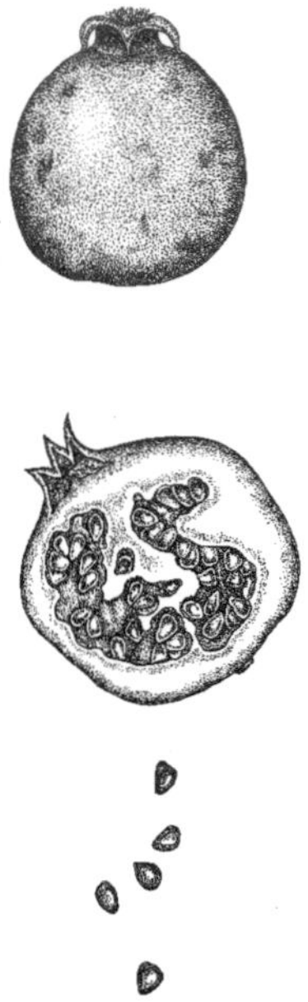

Pomegranate *(Punica granatum)*

The Romans called the pomegranate Malus punica *or* Punicum malum, *the Punic apple, which indicates its transmission to Italy via Carthage (Punicus), where the best pomegranates grew. Its English name* pomegranate *was derived from the Latin* pomum, *meaning apple, and* granatum, *meaning with seeds, bestowed on account of its many seeds.*

General Information A Persian and south Asian native, the unusual pomegranate is one of the oldest fruits known to man. It has vied for leadership in popularity and importance with the fig and the grape since the earliest times. Long considered a native of China, it was brought to that country from Kabul, Afghanistan under the Han dynasty in 126 B.C. When the Moors conquered Spain about 800 A.D., they introduced the pomegranate into the Iberian peninsula and the fruit became the emblem of Granada, whose name was derived from it. When an explosive shell that strewed metal particles over a wide area was invented, the French military, mindful of the seed-scattering characteristics of the pomegranate, called the explosive a *grenade*, and the special regiments founded in 1791 who launched these new weapons were called *grenadiers*. The Spanish conquistadors brought the pomegranate to America, where it quickly escaped from cultivation, no doubt because of the plenitude of its seeds.

Pomegranate

Nutritional Value Per 100 g Edible Portion

	Raw
Calories	63-78
Protein	0.05-1.6 g
Fat	0.3-0.9 g
Fiber	3.4-5.0 g
Calcium	3-12 mg
Iron	0.3-1.2 mg
Phosphorus	8-37 mg
Potassium	259 mg
Sodium	3 mg
Beta Carotene (A)	trace
Thiamine (B_1)	0.003-0.030 mg
Riboflavin (B_2)	0.012-0.030 mg
Niacin (B_3)	0.180-0.300 mg
Pantothenic Acid (B_5)	0.596 mg
Pyridoxine (B_6)	0.105 mg
Ascorbic Acid (C)	4.0-4.2 mg

Buying Tips A pomegranate of good quality should be fresh looking, plump, and heavy for its size, with a hard reddish-brown rind. Favor larger fruits over smaller ones, and heavier over lighter, as these promise more juice.

Culinary Uses This "seedy apple" is unique in that its thin, rough rind contains a multitude of seeds, each surrounded by bright red or crimson juicy pulp, and sectioned by a bitter spongy membrane. Cut in half, the fruit is so decorative that a favorite fabric of Renaissance Italy carried the design of the opened fruit. Each section contains a considerable number of long, angular seeds embedded in the pink-to-crimson pulp so inextricably as to oblige the eater either to develop skill in sucking the pulp away from the seeds or to swallow seeds and all. One way to obtain its refreshing juice easily is to bruise the fruit by rolling it on a hard surface until entirely soft, then puncture the end of it, insert a straw, and drink the piquantly sweet juice. Or cut a thin slice off the stem end, cut the fruit into sections, and peel back the skin to free the pips; to release the juice, press the seeds in a sieve over a bowl. The juice can be used as a flavoring in fruit juices, jelled desserts, and sauces. The seeds are edible, and some people readily enjoy their crunch and color, adding them as a garnish to salads, soups, sauces, and desserts.

Lore and Legend

The pomegranate, with its mystic origin and early sacred associations, has been a central character in the myths and legends of many peoples. It was long revered by the Persians and Jews, an old tradition having identified it as the forbidden fruit given by Eve to Adam. The ripe and half-open pomegranate, displaying its many seeds, was the symbol of fecundity, abundance, and eternal life in Semitic antiquity; along with wheat and grapes, the pomegranate was regarded as one of the prime attributes of Ibritz, the Hittite god of agriculture. It also became the Chinese symbol for numerous male offspring who rise to fame and glory and behave in a virtuous and filial manner. At weddings the sugared seeds were offered to the guests and, when the newlyweds entered their bedchamber, pomegranates were thrown to the floor so that the bursting fruits strewed their seeds all over the room, signifying that the marriage should be happy and blessed with many children.

However, actually eating the fruit is a different story altogether. When Adam and Eve ate this fruit of the forbidden tree, they exchanged Paradise for nine-to-five, mortgage and car payments, and atomic bombs. Persephone (the Greek goddess of spring and fruit and the daughter of Demeter, goddess of agriculture), while held captive by Hades in the underworld, vowed not to eat until her release but she soon succumbed and ate a pomegranate, spitting out all the seeds except six, which she swallowed. Thus was created the yearly cycle of six months of growth and abundance and six months of winter. (The story varies geographically: Californians say she ate only one or two seeds, while Eskimos say she ate the whole thing.) Mohammed advised his followers to eat pomegranates, for he believed they purged the system of hatred and envy.

Health Benefits Anthelmintic, astringent. Pomegranate juice is cleansing and cooling to the system, is excellent for bladder disorders, and has a slight purgative effect. The rind and partitions of the pomegranate are not generally eaten due to their high tannic acid content. The astringent quality of the rind does, however, make for an excellent skin wash.

Prickly Pear

Nutritional Value Per 100 g Edible Portion

	Raw
Calories	41
Protein	0.73 g
Fat	0.51 g
Fiber	1.81 g
Calcium	56 mg
Iron	0.30 mg
Magnesium	85 mg
Phosphorus	24 mg
Potassium	220 mg
Sodium	5 mg
Beta Carotene (A)	51 IU
Thiamine (B_1)	0.014 mg
Riboflavin (B_2)	0.060 mg
Niacin (B_3)	0.460 mg
Ascorbic Acid (C)	14 mg

Prickly Pear *(Opuntia ficus-indica, O. megacantha)*

Also Known As: Barbary Pear, Cactus Pear, Indian Pear, Indian Fig.

Opuntia *was an old Latin name used by Pliny for this plant, probably derived from Opus, a town in Greece.* Ficus-indica *means Indian fig;* megacantha *is a term meaning of great angle. The English name* prickly pear *is an apt description.*

General Information Neither a pear nor a fig, this fruit comes from any of numerous cacti of the genus *Opuntia,* which are native to the drier regions between Central America and the great deserts of the United States. Soon after the discovery of the Americas, the plant was exported to Spain, and found a hospitable climate in Sicily and other dry regions of the Mediterranean. Both fruits and "leaves" are enjoyed there as delicacies. Technically a berry, the cactus "pear" is the size of a small pear or large egg. Hostile and thorny, the fruit grows on a cactus with many sharp thorns. Fruit skins range from medium green to dark magenta, while the interior may be a brilliant red-violet or ruby color. All domestic prickly pears are gently processed to remove the glasslike thorns that dot the surface of the fruit, but be careful, since there are usually a few hidden ones left. The "leaves" are most commonly used as a vegetable, and are discussed in the **Vegetables** section under **Nopal Cactus**.

Buying Tips Choose prickly pears that are tender but not squishy, full and deep-colored, not faded. The darker-colored fruits tend to be sweeter and tastier. Beware of moldy spots, which warn of interior mush. If the fruit is very firm, let soften a few days at room temperature.

Culinary Uses This prickly fruit does not even remotely look like it wants to be eaten. The inedible spiny skin encloses a brilliantly colored pulp, which may be red, purple, deep orange, or rose pink. Soft and spongy, juicy, tartly sweet yet refreshing, it has an aroma very similar to watermelon. To eat this daunting fruit, it is easiest to use a knife and fork, cutting lengthwise and slicing the pulp away from the skin. Watch out for the multiple small hard bony seeds which, though some say they are edible, are a nuisance. Some people may desire to add a bit of sweetener to offset the taste, which can be tart. Prickly pears are eaten by themselves, used in fruit salads, pureed and added to fruit drinks or iced beverages, or can even be made into jelly and candy. In the Middle East, fruit vendors sell them from trays of shaved ice, and they make a pleasant, cool treat on a hot day.

Pulasan (*Nephelium mutabile*)

Pulasan

Nutritional Value Per 100 g Edible Portion

	Raw
Protein	0.82 g
Fat	0.55 g
Fiber	0.14 g
Calcium	0.01–0.05 mg
Iron	0.002 mg

Nephelium *is an ancient name transferred from the burdock, because of some similarity in the rough fruits.* Mutabile *means changeable, mutable.*

General Information Closely related to the rambutan and sometimes confused with it, the pulasan is native to western Malaysia and Thailand. It is little known elsewhere in the New World except in Costa Rica, where it is occasionally grown and the fruits sometimes appear in the marketplaces. The ovoid fruit is two or three inches long, red or yellow, with a thick leathery rind.

Culinary Uses The glistening white or yellowish-white flesh clings to the seed, but has a flavor generally much sweeter than the rambutan. The fruits are eaten raw or made into preserves. Boiled or roasted seeds are used to prepare a cocoa-like beverage.

Pummelo (*Citrus grandis, C. maxima*)

Also Known As: Pomelo, Shaddock

The term Citrus *derives from the Greek term for the citron,* kedromelon; maxima *means largest. The origin of the name* pummelo *derives from the Dutch* pompelmous, pomp- *from the beginning of the name for pumpkin, and* -limoes, *meaning a citron; in other words, a large pumpkin-sized citron. The alternative name* shaddock *was given this fruit to honor Captain Shaddock, the seventeenth century (1696) English ship commander who introduced the fruit to Europe via the West Indies.*

General Information A strange fruit with an interesting past, the pummelo originated in southeastern Asia and Malaysia, and is the world's largest citrus fruit. A beneficial attribute of the pummelo is its relatively high tolerance to saline conditions, such that it can easily be grown around river deltas and brackish marsh areas. Said to be the grandparent of the grapefruit, this sour pulpy fruit can weigh up to twenty-two pounds, and ranges in size from a baby cantaloupe to nearly that of a basketball. It is slightly pear-shaped or round, greenish to yellow or pinkish, with an enormously thick, rather soft pith and rind that begs to be conserved. Its spread westward was in the wake of other, more prized citrus fruits. Arabs took it to Spain, where it is still cultivated on a small scale.

Pummelo

Nutritional Value Per 100 g Edible Portion

	Raw
Calories	25-58
Protein	0.5-0.74 g
Fat	0.20-0.56 g
Fiber	0.30-0.82 g
Calcium	21-30 mg
Iron	0.3-0.5 mg
Magnesium	6 mg
Phosphorus	20-27 mg
Potassium	216 mg
Sodium	1 mg
Zinc	0.08 mg
Copper	0.048 mg
Manganese	0.017 mg
Beta Carotene (A)	20 IU
Thiamine (B_1)	0.040-0.070 mg
Riboflavin (B_2)	0.027 mg
Niacin (B_3)	0.300 mg
Pyridoxine (B_6)	0.036 mg
Ascorbic Acid (C)	30-43 mg

Buying Tips If you have a choice of pummelos, look for what you would in a grapefruit: heaviness, filled-out skin, and a rich aroma. Avoid those with soft or pitted patches.

Culinary Uses The quality of the pale yellow to pink fruit differs dramatically from one variety to another: from pleasantly juicy to dryish, from slightly acid to very sweet, from enormously seedy to seedless, from insipid to spectacular. It is usually eaten on its own like grapefruit; make sure to remove the entire thick layer of inedible white pith. For the best flavor, each segment must also be skinned. This strange fruit is eaten with salt in southeast Asia, and a delicious paradisical dessert or salad is made in China with pieces of pummelo combined with oranges, dates, nuts, and mayonnaise.

Health Benefits In the Philippines and southeast Asia, decoctions of the leaves, flowers, and rind are given for their sedative effect in cases of epilepsy and convulsive coughing. The fruit juice is taken as a febrifuge.

Quince (*Cydonia oblonga, C. cydonia*)

The Greeks first obtained the quince from Cydonia in Crete (now Canea), from which place the fruit derived its name of Cydonia, *and of which the English name* quince *is a corruption.* Oblonga *is simply a descriptive term meaning oblong.*

General Information Quinces grew wild in Kashmir long before recorded history. In the warm Persian climate, quinces were able to develop sweetness and succulence, so its cultivation spread to other parts of the Mediterranean even before the apple. The Greeks encountered them in Cydonia on the island of Crete; when they were carried back to Athens, they assumed the name of the port from which they came—*Malus cydonia*, or "apples of Cydonia." Romans held the fruit in high regard, and quinces were preserved in honey (called *melimelum* or honey apple), used as a flavoring, and made into wine. There are many varieties of this hard and acid Asiatic fruit of the rose family which, although one of the earliest known fruits and cultivated for some four millennia, is not one that has a wide contemporary appeal. Quinces were once thought to be a type of pear, and in fact

Quince

Nutritional Value Per 100 g Edible Portion	Raw
Calories	57
Protein	0.4 g
Fat	0.1 g
Fiber	1.7 g
Calcium	11 mg
Iron	0.7 mg
Magnesium	8 mg
Phosphorus	17 mg
Potassium	197 mg
Sodium	4 mg
Copper	0.130 mg
Beta Carotene (A)	40 IU
Thiamine (B_1)	0.020 mg
Riboflavin (B_2)	0.030 mg
Niacin (B_3)	0.200 mg
Pantothenic Acid (B_5)	0.081 mg
Pyridoxine (B_6)	0.040 mg
Ascorbic Acid (C)	15 mg

pears are now often grown on quince rootstock, but the two fruits simply cannot be hybridized. In medieval times most Europeans ate them fresh as well as cooking and preserving them. When first picked, quinces wear a downy coat of fuzz like a peach, but mechanical rubbing usually eliminates this. They are generally a sour, astringent fruit, resembling a hard-fleshed, sandy-textured yellow apple, and in the past were sometimes referred to as "golden apples." Quince preserves were carried as an antiscorbutic, particularly for tropical expeditions, on Portuguese and Spanish ships. In the Middle Ages, the best quinces were held to be those from Portugal. This is why the term "marmalade" comes from *marmelo*, the Portuguese word for quince, the fruit originally used to make marmalade.

Buying Tips Choose large, aromatic, smooth fruits, which are easier to peel and less wasteful than small, knotty ones. They are best when tree-ripened in a warm climate, at which time the natural fruit sugars have matured. Although they never soften, they do bruise easily.

Culinary Uses Quince have a musky, penetrating aroma reminiscent of pineapple, guava, pear, or apple depending on the variety you have in hand, but their flavor is rather bland and acidic. This green to golden-colored pome is unusual among fruits in that it is almost always eaten cooked. Its yellow flesh tends to be acidic, hard, and rather unpalatable (although on rare occasions one finds a fully tree-ripened one), but when cooked becomes tender, scented, tasty, and turns a delightful shade of pink. The fruit maintains its shape beautifully even with long cooking, and so it affords grandiose experimentation. Stewing, baking, poaching, or braising brings out the unique quince flavor, which complements meat, savory, or sweet dishes. Stewed, they make an excellent dessert, a breakfast dish with cream, or a side dish. Or add a small proportion of cooked fruit to pear and apple dishes (including pies and applesauce) for a surprising amplification of flavor. Most often, though, the fruit is simply made into preserves, either alone or mixed with other fruits such as apples and pears. It has even more pectin (the thickening agent of preserves) than apples, and thus is well suited to this purpose. Although the peel cooks to an edible texture, it is best removed, as it tends to add an undesirable bitterness.

Lore and Legend

The Greeks and Romans held the quince sacred to Venus, who is often depicted with a quince in her right hand as the gift she received from Paris. Being the sacred fruit of the goddess of love, the quince was regarded as the symbol of love, happiness, and fertility. In Athens, quinces were tossed into the bridal chariot in which the groom was conducting his bride to their new home, where she would be offered a piece of wedding cake flavored with sesame, honey, and, as a charm for fruitfulness,either a date or a quince. Quinces were also thought to be the forbidden fruit of the Garden of Eden. In Roman times, as described by Plutarch, the quince was picked green, submerged in honey, and left to ripen in time to serve at Roman wedding feasts as a perfect symbolic dessert. The custom of a newly married pair sharing a quince as a token of love was handed down, and throughout the Middle Ages quinces were used at every wedding feast. The "golden apples" of Virgil are believed to be quinces, as they were the only "golden" fruit known in his time, oranges having only been introduced later at the time of the Crusades. Quinces were also reputed to protect against the Evil Eye, and were painted on the walls and eaves of Roman houses for that purpose.

Health Benefits The fruit has an acid taste, is slightly astringent, makes a good sedative, and is a good stomach medicine, allaying gas and vomiting. When used in its fully ripened state without the addition of sugar, quince is beneficial for the liver, counteracts constipation, and helps alkalinize the system. Underripe fruits are extremely acid-forming. The juice makes an excellent gargle.

Rambutan *(Nephelium lappaceum)*

Nephelium *is an ancient name transferred from the burdock because of some similarity in the rough fruit.* Lappaceum *means having small burrs. The English name* rambutan *derives from the Malayan word for hair,* rambut, *due to the long "hairs" on the outside of the fruit.*

General Information Native to the western lowlands of Malaysia, the rambutan is closely related to the lychee. The fruits vary in quality and type, and there are crimson, greenish, yellow, and orange-skinned varieties. They are ovoid or ellipsoid in shape, one to three inches long or about the size of a plum, with a leathery rind covered with soft spines. The somewhat hairy covering is responsible for the common name of the fruit.

Rambutan

Nutritional Value Per 100 g Edible Portion

	Raw
Protein	0.46 g
Fiber	0.24 g
Calcium	10.6 mg
Phosphorus	12.9 mg
Ascorbic Acid (C)	30 mg

Culinary Uses The flesh is highly aromatic, white or rose-tinted, translucent, juicy, and adhering somewhat to the seed within. The inner part of the fruit is smaller than a lychee, but the outside looks larger because of the long "hairs." The flavor is usually more acid than the lychee. Most often eaten out of hand after tearing the rind open, the peeled fruits are also occasionally stewed as a dessert or preserved in syrup. The seeds, which are reputedly poisonous when raw, are sometimes roasted and eaten, and it is said they have an almond-like flavor.

Health Benefits The fruit acts as a vermifuge and febrifuge, and is taken to relieve diarrhea and dysentery.

Raspberry *(Rubus idaeus, R. strigosus)*

Rubus *is from the Latin* ruber, *meaning red. The term* idaeus *relates the raspberry to Mt. Ida in Asia Minor (Turkey), where it grows in abundance;* strigosus *means that the plant is strigose (having bristles or scales that lay flat). The English name* raspberry *comes from the Old English* raspis, *of obscure origin but probably connected with the slightly hairy "rasping" surface of the fruit.*

General Information Raspberries are members of the rose family, and attest to this by their thorny canes. The European raspberry, *R. idaeus*, sometimes called by its French name of *framboise*, grows almost everywhere throughout Europe, as far north as Scandinavia, and extends through northern Asia into the Orient. The American red raspberry is *R. strigosus*, first heard of in 1607 when the French lawyer, traveler, and writer Marc Lescarbot accom-

Raspberry

Nutritional Value Per 100 g Edible Portion

	Raw Fruit	Leaves, Dried
Calories	49	275
Protein	0.91 g	11.30 g
Fat	0.55 g	1.70 g
Fiber	3.00 g	8.20 g
Calcium	22 mg	1,210 mg
Iron	0.57 mg	101.0 mg
Magnesium	18 mg	319 mg
Phosphorus	12 mg	234 mg
Potassium	152 mg	1,340 mg
Sodium	0 mg	7.7 mg
Zinc	0.46 mg	trace
Copper	0.074 mg	n/a
Manganese	1.013 mg	146.000 mg
Beta Carotene (A)	130 IU	18,963 IU
Thiamine (B_1)	0.030 mg	0.340 mg
Riboflavin (B_2)	0.090 mg	trace
Niacin (B_3)	0.900 mg	38.200 mg
Pantothenic Acid (B_5)	0.240 mg	n/a
Pyridoxine (B_6)	0.057 mg	n/a
Folic Acid (B_9)	n/a	n/a
Ascorbic Acid (C)	25 mg	367 mg
Tocopherol (E)	0.30 mg	n/a

panied an expedition to Canada and reported that his fellow explorers "amused themselves by gathering raspberries." A shrub with prickly stems and pale green leaves, the plant is divided by the color of its fruit into two basic types: red and black. The black tends to be smaller and seedier than the red, but distinctly aromatic. Yellow raspberries, often found growing wild in many areas, particularly in Maryland, are considered a variant of red. Purple raspberries are considered a hybrid between the red and black species, and are a little more tart than either. The marketed berry is usually the cultivated red variety. The main difference between blackberries and raspberries is that the blackberry stem core stays with the berries, whereas ripe raspberries detach from the core.

Buying Tips Look for bright, clean berries with uniform coloring. Check the bottom of the container to make sure it has not been stained from crushed or moldy fruit. Handle them as little as possible, since they are so perishable. Wash only if absolutely necessary, as this rinses off their heady perfume.

Culinary Uses The raspberry suggests its probable Asian heritage, being rich, exotic, spice-laden with just a hint of musk. Extremely fragile, it turns to pulp if simply held in the hand too long. This renders fresh raspberries an expensive and rare summer fruit. Most cultivated raspberries are red, but there are also varieties in yellow, apricot, amber, and purple, all similar in flavor and texture. A sprinkling of fresh raspberries makes an artful garnish for desserts and fruit dishes. Their considerable vitamin properties are mostly lost during cooking, so that although raspberry jellies, jams, and preserves may taste good, they have only a fraction of their original natural vitamins. The addition of sugar renders them acidic and detrimental to the body.

Health Benefits Antiemetic, astringent, laxative. Raspberries lead all the berries nutritionally, and all fresh foods in fully digestible elements, being almost totally assimilated by the body during digestion. They are considered a good cleanser for mucus, for catarrhal conditions, and for toxins in the body. Very beneficial for all female organs and problems, they help relieve menstrual cramps, and will decrease the menstrual flow if necessary without stopping it altogether. Raspberry leaf tea is queen among pregnancy herbs, frequently taken by pregnant women to prevent miscarriages, allay nausea and vomiting, increase milk flow, and reduce labor pains. For those who are not pregnant, the tea nourishes the reproductive organs, relieves menstrual cramps, and works as an effective antidiarrheal agent. Raspberry leaves possess the classic properties of astringent herbs, especially the tannins and fruit acids (citric and malic). The nutritional profile shows a manganese content (146 milligrams per 100 grams in the dried leaves) twice as high as any other herb, making it one of the richest sources of this mineral.

Rhubarb *(Rheum rhabarbarum, R. rhaponticum, R. hybridum)*

The technical name of the genus is said to be derived from Rha, *the ancient name of the Volga River, on whose banks the plants grow; other authorities derive the name from the Greek* rheo, *meaning to flow, in allusion to its purgative properties.* Rhaponticum *refers to the region of the Rha that flows into the Pontus (at the southern end of the Black Sea);* hybridum *means of mixed parentage, a hybrid. The English name* rhubarb *is a derivative of the Latin phrase* rha barbarum, *meaning the region of the Rha River inhabited by the barbarians (any non-Roman).*

Rhubarb

Nutritional Value Per 100 g Edible Portion

	Raw	Cooked w/Sugar
Calories	21	116
Protein	0.90 g	0.39 g
Fat	0.20 g	0.05 g
Fiber	0.70 g	0.80 g
Calcium	86 mg	145 mg
Iron	0.22 mg	0.21 mg
Magnesium	12 mg	12 mg
Phosphorus	14 mg	8 mg
Potassium	288 mg	96 mg
Sodium	4 mg	1 mg
Zinc	0.100 mg	0.080 mg
Copper	0.021 mg	0.027 mg
Manganese	0.196 mg	0.073 mg
Beta Carotene (A)	100 IU	69 IU
Thiamine (B_1)	0.020 mg	0.018 mg
Riboflavin (B_2)	0.030 mg	0.023 mg
Niacin (B_3)	0.300 mg	0.200 mg
Pantothenic Acid (B_5)	0.085 mg	0.050 mg
Pyridoxine (B_6)	0.024 mg	0.020 mg
Folic Acid (B_9)	7.1 mcg	5.3 mcg
Ascorbic Acid (C)	8 mg	3.3 mg

General Information Rhubarb is botanically a vegetable, but the U.S. Customs Court at Buffalo, New York, ruled in 1947 that it should be classed as a fruit, since that is how it is normally used. Part of the buckwheat family, the most popular type of rhubarb comes from a species that originated in Siberia or Mongolia. In 1608, an Italian botanist named Prosper Alpinus decided to introduce Siberian rhubarb into Europe as a possible substitute for the exorbitantly costly Chinese rhubarb, the root of which was used only medicinally. Edible rhubarb remained a curiosity until the early 1800s, when people began using the stalks for pies and puddings. Introduced into what is now Alaska by early seventeenth century Russian trappers and traders to counteract the problems of scurvy, rhubarb came into its own in 1880 when gold seekers rushed to Juneau. By the mid-nineteenth century it was popular, particularly in the New England states, as a pie and pastry filling, or pressed into homemade wine. Chinese rhubarb, which is entirely different from our garden variety, has been used medicinally since about 2700 B.C.

Buying Tips Look for moderately thin pink or red stalks. The greener, thicker stalks are stringier, sourer, and coarser. The leaves are poisonous and should be discarded.

Culinary Uses Rhubarb comes in two main varieties: hothouse-grown (pink or light red stalks, with yellow leaves) and field-grown (dark red stalks, with green leaves). The hothouse variety has a somewhat milder flavor and is less stringy. Never eaten raw, the stalks are very tart and need quite a bit of sweetening to be palatable. Their main use is in sauces and pies. To prepare, trim both ends and cut the stalks into 1-inch chunks and stew (or bake) with plenty of sugar. Rhubarb cooks very quickly, fiber and sugar dissolving into a puddle of syrup; cook it no longer than necessary. Use the stems only—the leaves and roots are highly poisonous.

Health Benefits The purgative principle in rhubarb is a group of substances allied to chrysophanic acid and is present mainly in the root. The stalks contain a substantial amount of oxalic acid, which is harmful if eaten to excess. Few if any other plants have such a high concentration of this acid. The stalks, though edible, contain amounts that can interfere with calcium absorption. Cooking converts the oxalic acid into an inorganic crystalline form which is then deposited in vast quantities throughout the body. The only benefit rhubarb may have is its immediate laxative effect.

Rose Apple *(Syzygium jambos, S. malaccense, S. samarangense, S. aqueum)*

Syzygium *derives from the Greek word meaning united, and refers to the calyptrate petals.* Jambos *is a Malaysian name;* aqueum *means aqueus or watery.*

General Information This group of fruits might be better called by the Indian/Malay name *jambu*. Indigenous to southeast Asia or the Indian subcontinent, they bear a superficial resemblance to apples, but are quite different to eat. The true **Rose apple** or **Malabar plum** (*S. jambos*) tree produces fruit that may reach the size of a small apple, is round or slightly pear-shaped, two inches long, with smooth, thin, pale yellow or pinkish waxy skin, and capped with a prominent green calyx. The yellowish flesh is crisp, mealy, dry to juicy, slightly rose-scented, but rather tasteless. In the center are several brown seeds that rattle when the fruit is shaken. The **Malay rose apple** *(S. malaccense)* spread throughout the Pacific Islands in very early times, for it is featured in Fijian mythology, and the wood was used by ancient Hawaiians to make idols. The flowers are considered sacred to Pele, the fiery volcano goddess. It has been recorded that before the arrival of missionaries in Hawaii there were no fruits except bananas, coconuts, and the Malay apple. The tree bears fruit that are roundish but slightly oblong and narrowed at the stalk end. These fruits have waxy skins, are rosy with faint white markings when ripe, and have flesh that is scented, juicy, and slightly sweet. The **Java rose apple** or **Samarang rose apple** (*S. samarangense*) bears fruit that are nearly round or bell-shaped. They are commonly pale green or whitish, but sometimes pink. The pink fruits are juicier and more flavorful. The skin is very thin, the flesh white, spongy, dry to juicy, subacid, and very bland in flavor. There may be one or two seeds. The **Watery rose apple** or **Water apple** (*S. aqueum*) has an uneven shape, wider at the apex than at the base. Color varies from white to bright pink, with flesh that is white or pink, crisp and watery, and sweetly scented. There may be several small seeds.

Rose Apple

Nutritional Value Per 100 g Edible Portion

	Raw True Rose	Raw Malay Rose	Raw Java Rose
Calories	56	n/a	n/a
Protein	0.5-0.7 g	0.5-0.7 g	0.50 g
Fat	0.2-0.3 g	0.1-0.2 g	n/a
Fiber	1.1-1.9 g	0.6-0.8 g	n/a
Calcium	29.0-45.2 mg	5.6-5.9 mg	0.01 g
Iron	0.45-1.20 mg	0.20-0.82 mg	0.001 g
Magnesium	4 mg	n/a	n/a
Phosphorus	11.7-30.0 mg	11.6-17.9 mg	0.03 g
Potassium	50 mg	n/a	n/a
Sodium	34.1 mg	n/a	n/a
Beta Carotene (A)	123-235 IU	3-10 IU	n/a
Thiamine (B_1)	0.010-0.190 mg	15-39 mcg	n/a
Riboflavin (B_2)	0.028-0.050 mg	20-39 mcg	n/a
Niacin (B_3)	0.521-0.800 mg	0.210-0.400 mg	n/a
Ascorbic Acid (C)	3-37 mg	6.5-17.0 mg	n/a

Culinary Uses The ripe fruit of all the rose apples is eaten raw, though many people consider it insipid. Most often, the fruit is eaten by children for its thirst-quenching abilities. The fruit is best stewed with cloves or other flavoring and served with cream as a dessert. The slightly unripe fruits are sometimes used for making jelly and pickles, and are often cooked with acid fruits to the benefit of both, and made into sauce or preserves. In Puerto Rico, both red and white table wines are made from the Malay apple.

Health Benefits In India, the fruit is regarded as a tonic for the brain and liver. An infusion of the fruit acts as a diuretic. The seeds are employed against diarrhea, dysentery, and catarrh. In Nicaragua, it has been claimed that an infusion of roasted, powdered seeds is beneficial to diabetics, while in Colombia the seeds are believed to have an anesthetic property.

Roselle *(Hibiscus sabdariffa)*

Also Known As: Red Sorrel, Jamaica Sorrel, Florida Cranberry.

> Hibiscus *is an old Greek name for the mallow.* Sabdariffa *comes from a West Indian name. The English name* roselle *is a diminutive term meaning little rose.*

General Information Roselle, even though it is frequently called Jamaica sorrel, did not reach Jamaica until the beginning of the eighteenth century, and is not a close relation of sorrel Native from India to Malaysia, the plant is unusual in that its main edible part is not the fruit but the calyx of the fruit, what is familiar as the little green star on top of a tomato or strawberry. In this instance it is red, large, and fleshy, and enwraps a small, useless fruit. Roselle jam was popular for some time at the turn of the century. In 1892 there were two factories producing roselle jam in Queensland, Australia, which exported considerable quantities to Europe. Later, in 1909, there were no more than four acres left of roselle plantings in Queensland. Currently the plant is attracting the attention of food and beverage manufacturers as well as pharmaceutical concerns, who feel it may have possibilities as a natural food product and as a colorant to replace some synthetic dyes.

Roselle

Nutritional Value Per 100 g Edible Portion	Raw
Calories	49
Protein	1.145 g
Fat	2.61 g
Fiber	12.0 g
Calcium	1263 mg
Iron	8.98 mg
Phosphorus	273.2 mg
Beta Carotene (A)	287 IU
Thiamine (B_1)	0.117 mg
Riboflavin (B_2)	0.277 mg
Niacin (B_3)	3.765 mg
Ascorbic Acid (C)	6.7 mg

Culinary Uses Roselle is best prepared for use by washing, then making an incision around the tough base of the calyx below the bracts to free and remove it with the seed capsule attached. The calyces are then ready for immediate use, and may be merely chopped and added to fruit salads, cooked as a side dish, or stewed to make a cranberry-flavored sauce or filling for tarts or pies. They are made into a refreshing sour "sorrel" drink (or "ade") in the West Indies, and a Jamaican traditional Christmas drink is prepared by putting roselle into an earthenware jug with a little grated ginger and sugar as desired, pouring boiling water over the mixture, and letting it stand overnight. This liquid is then drained off and served with ice (and a dash of rum). The calyces are marketed dried (usually under the name Flor de Jamaica) as well as fresh, and are the source of a red food coloring. Young leaves and tender stems of roselle are eaten raw in salads, cooked as greens, or added to curries as seasoning.

Health Benefits In India, Africa, and Mexico, all above-ground parts of the roselle plant are valued in native medicine. Infusions of the leaves or calyces are regarded as diuretic, cholerectic, febrifugal, and hypotensive, decreasing the viscosity of the blood and stimulating intestinal peristalsis. Pharmacognosists in Senegal recommend roselle extract for lowering blood pressure, while in Guatemala roselle "ade" is a favorite remedy for the aftereffects of alcohol overindulgence.

Rowan and Sorb *(Sorbus aucuparia, S. torminalis)*

Sorbus *is the ancient Latin name for this family of plants.* Aucuparia *means bird-catching, due to bird-catchers in Germany and elsewhere who would trap small birds in hair nooses baited with rowan berries;* torminalis *means useful against colic. The English name* Rowan *is of Scandinavian origin, akin to Old Norse* reynir, *meaning rowan, and to Old English* read, *meaning red.* Sorb *derives from the French word* sorbe, *meaning fruit of the service tree, and ultimately from the Latin* sorbum.

General Information The rowan bush grows wild in Europe and parts of Asia, especially in mountainous regions. Related to the large rose family, some sixty-seven species are found in North America alone. The bright scarlet berries are pretty, but have limited use. North American Indians ate them fresh, dried some to grind the seeds into a mealy flour, cooked the berries into jams and jellies, or made wine. The sorb tends to grow further south in Europe and bear larger fruits than the rowan. Its fruits are called sorb apples because they are recognizably like small apples or pears in shape and color. The tree is a magnificent sight, conspicuous across the open fields. The hard, fine-grained wood of the sorb tree was once much in demand for screws and by wood engravers. In October or late September, the fruit turns beautifully yellow and red among the long oval leaves, but should be left until after the first frosts. Only after the fruit has fallen and turned soft and brown (a process called "bletting")will the astringency be gone, and the fruit palatable for eating. The fruit can also be picked off the tree and brought into the house to gradually soften.

Lore and Legend

The Scots believed that if you nailed a rowan branch above the doorway of either the house or barn, no ghosts or evil spirits of any kind could enter therein. Young lambs were forced to jump through a rowan-branch hoop to deter witches from stealing them.

Culinary Uses Much too sour and astringent to be eaten raw, rowan fruits are best suited to making rowan jelly, which has a fine clear red color; its pleasing tartness makes it a good accompaniment for wild game or fowl. Scandinavians make a rowan liqueur of a curious orange color. Sorb fruits are sour and astringent, although less so after exposure to the mellowing effect of frost. Bletting makes them palatable, but not exciting. Earlier in the century, the French made a kind of cider from the sorb, but now make a form of liqueur that is supposed to be quite good.

Health Benefits To early western European doctors, the sorb was good for the digestion, for fevers accompanied by diarrhea and for hemorrhages.

Rumberry *(Myrciaria floribunda)*

The genus name Myrciaria *probably is related to Myrtus, the myrtle family.* Floribunda *means abounding in flowers, or freely flowering. The English name* rumberry *is most likely due to the fact that the berry was used to flavor rums and other liqueurs.*

General Information Native to much of Central and South America (where it is also known as **Guavaberry**), the rumberry is a tiny fruit that was once in fair demand. It has occasionally been cultivated in Bermuda but rarely elsewhere. Throughout its natural range, when land is cleared for pastures, the tree is left standing for the sake of its fruits. The fruit is round or oblate, 1/4 to 1/2 in diameter, yellow-orange or so dark red as to be nearly black, and highly aromatic.

Culinary Uses The flavor is bittersweet, balsam-like, with one globular seed. In Cuba, the fruits are relished out of hand and are made into jam. People on the island of St. John, where the fruits are said to be "unusually good," use the preserved fruits in tarts. The local guavaberry liqueur is made from the fruits with pure grain alcohol, rum, raw sugar, and spices and is a special treat at Christmastime. Large quantities of fermented juice, strong wine and heavy liqueur were at one time made and exported, primarily to Denmark.

Health Benefits The fruits are sold by herbalists in Camaguey for the purpose of making a depurative syrup; the decoction is taken as a treatment for liver complaints.

Santol (*Sandoricum koetjape*)

Santol

Nutritional Value Per 100 g Edible Portion

	Raw Yellow	Raw Red
Protein	0.118 g	0.89%
Fat	0.10 g	1.43%
Fiber	0.10 g	2.30%
Calcium	4.3 mg	0.01%
Iron	0.42 mg	0.002%
Phosphorus	17.4 mg	0.03%
Beta Carotene (A)	0.003 mg	n/a
Thiamine (B_1)	0.045 mg	0.037 mg
Niacin (B_3)	0.741 mg	0.016 mg
Ascorbic Acid (C)	86 mg	0.78 mg

General Information Native to Malaya and parts of former Indochina, the medium-sized santol tree occurs in two main forms, one with sweet fruit and leaves, which wither yellow, the other with sour fruit and leaves, which turn to red. The fruit is globose or oblate, with wrinkles extending a short distance from the base, one and one-half to three inches wide, and yellowish to golden, sometimes blushed with pink.

Culinary Uses The downy rind may be thin or thick and contains a thin, milky juice. It is edible, as is the white, translucent, juicy pulp surrounding the three to five brown, inedible seeds. Sometimes having an aroma of peach, these fruits are eaten fresh, dried, candied, or pickled. Santol marmalade is sometimes imported into the United States from the Philippines.

Health Benefits Preserved pulp is employed medicinally as an astringent, as is the quince in Europe.

Sapodilla (*Manilkara zapota*)

Manilkara *is the Malaysian name for the fruit;* zapota *comes from the Latin American* tzapotl*, which apparently means soft. The English word* sapodilla *is a diminutive form of* sapota*, the anglicized form of* zapota.

General Information The sapodilla is the fruit of the sapota tree, a stately evergreen native to Yucatan and possibly other nearby parts of southern Mexico, as well as northern Belize and northeastern Guatemala. The tree bark contains a milky substance known commercially as chicle, which is used in the production of chewing gum. The fruit is a small round or oval berry between two and four inches in diameter, with a brown fuzz over its yellow skin. The flesh is yellow-brown, sometimes pinkish, with a soft, translucent, meltingly juicy pulp containing several inedible flat black seeds in a central

Sapodilla

Nutritional Value Per 100 g Edible Portion	Raw
Calories	83
Protein	0.44 g
Fat	1.10 g
Fiber	1.40 g
Calcium	21 mg
Iron	0.80 mg
Phosphorus	12 mg
Potassium	193 mg
Sodium	12 mg
Beta Carotene (A)	60 IU
Thiamine (B_1)	n/a
Riboflavin (B_2)	0.020 mg
Niacin (B_3)	0.200 mg
Pantothenic Acid (B_5)	0.252 mg
Pyridoxine (B_6)	0.037 mg
Ascorbic Acid (C)	14.7 mg

cavity. The aspect of the interior resembles that of a pear, except that the seeds are larger.

Buying Tips Select fruit that is somewhat soft and smooth—too hard can indicate an unpleasant gritty interior. Until fully ripened, the fruit is too astringent to be edible. Left at room temperature, hard fruit will soften to good taste and texture.

Culinary Uses Described as having "the sweet perfumes of honey, jasmine, and lily of the valley," the flavor of the sapodilla has been compared to that of brown sugar or maple syrup. The yellowish pulp may be smooth or granular, but when of good quality is always fragrant and melting like bananas or apricots. It is usually chilled, cut in half, and eaten from the inedible half-shell, although in the West Indies the fruit may be boiled down to make a sweet syrup. If the pulp is too soft to slice, mash it for use in puddings, custards, quick breads, or ice creams. Care must be taken not to swallow the seeds, as their protruding hook might cause lodging in the throat. Ingestion of more than six seeds causes abdominal pain and vomiting.

Health Benefits Because of their tannin content, young immature fruits are boiled and the decoction taken to stop diarrhea. An infusion of young fruits and flowers is drunk to relieve pulmonary complaints.

Sapote, White *(Casimiroa edulis)*

The genus Casimiroa *was named in honor of Cardinal Casimiro Gomez de Ortega, a Spanish botanist of the eighteenth century.* Edulis *means edible. The English word* sapote *derives from the Mexican name* tzapotl, *a general term applied to all soft, sweet fruits.*

Sapote, White

Nutritional Value Per 100 g Edible Portion	Raw
Calories	125
Protein	0.143 g
Fat	0.03 g
Fiber	0.9 g
Calcium	9.9 mg
Iron	0.33 mg
Phosphorus	20.4 mg
Beta Carotene (A)	410 IU
Thiamine (B_1)	0.042 mg
Riboflavin (B_2)	0.043 mg
Niacin (B_3)	0.472 mg
Ascorbic Acid (C)	30.3 mg

General Information The semitropical white sapote grows wild in Central America and is cultivated in some Latin American countries. Looking like a green pippin apple, sapotes are orange-sized with a thin green to yellow skin containing a nearly seedless, coreless white flesh that is mild and creamy-textured. With its ambrosial aroma and soft, juicy texture, it is one of the many new and exotic fruits that is destined to gain in popularity. It has been grown in California since the nineteenth century and also grows in Florida, but is still scarce in northern markets. The rarely seen black sapote is a rather leathery green-skinned member of the *Diospyrus* clan that has flesh the color and texture of chocolate pudding when fully ripe. The green and yellow varieties of sapote are not commonly exported, but are reputed to be of better flavor than the white.

Buying Tips Choose firm fruits of orange or grapefruit size that are free of bruises and that are green or yellowish-green in color. When the fruit has softened so that it has a give like a ripe avocado, it is ripe.

Culinary Uses This fruit has a very sweet, mild flavor that may hint of peaches, lemons, mango, coconut, caramel, or vanilla, depending upon the variety. The skin is inedible; the seeds, which are embedded at random, may be flat and chip-like or the size and shape of orange seeds, and are toxic if eaten. The fruits are easiest to eat when cut in half so that the delicate custardy flesh can be scooped out with a spoon, but they can also be used in preserves or fruit sauces. One recommendation is to cut the flesh into sections and serve with cream and sugar.

Health Benefits. Chemists, verifying comments on the fruit made as long ago as the sixteenth century, have found soporific substances in it. Its skin is inedible, and the seed is said to be fatally toxic if eaten by humans or animals.

Soursop (*Annona muricata*)

Also Known As: Guanabana, Prickly Custard Apple.

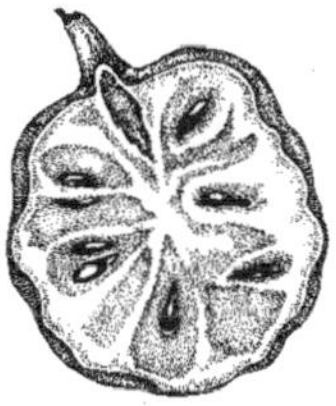

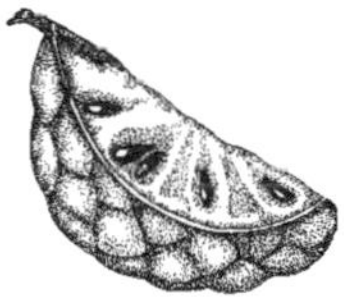

> Annona *means year's harvest, suggested by the Haitian name* anon, *which is applied to one of the species.* Muricata *means roughened on the surface with sharp, hard points.*

General Information This tropical fruit is native to and common in tropical South America and the West Indies. One of the first fruit trees taken from America to the tropical regions of the Old World, the soursop became widely distributed from southeast China to Australia and the lowlands of East and West Africa. The small tree bears its fruits indiscriminately on twigs, branches, or trunk, flowering and bearing fruit more or less continuously, though there usually is a principal ripening season. The fruits range from four to twelve inches in length and weigh up to a maximum of nearly eleven pounds. They are ellipsoid or irregularly ovoid, one side growing faster than the other. The skin has a leathery appearance, but is thin and surprisingly tender; dark green to begin with, the skin later turns yellowish-green and yellow when over-ripe. Because of the soft spines on the skin, the soursop is sometimes called the prickly custard apple.

Culinary Uses The white flesh consists of numerous segments, mostly seedless (just as well, since the seeds contain toxins and are to be avoided), and varies from poor to very good. At its best, it is soft and juicy with a rich, musky, rather acid and almost fermented quality, and has a pleasant aroma reminiscent of pineapple. The soursop is more acid than its relations, but the acidity varies, and some fruits are suitable for eating raw. Others have to be dressed with sugar to make them palatable. Seeded soursop has for years been canned in Mexico and served in Mexican restaurants in New York and other northern cities. Since the fruits are often so juicy that it would be more appropriate to speak of drinking rather than eating them, they are good

Soursop

Nutritional Value Per 100 g Edible Portion

	Raw
Calories	53.1-61.3
Protein	1.0 g
Fat	0.97 g
Fiber	0.79 g
Calcium	10.3 mg
Iron	0.64 mg
Magnesium	21 mg
Phosphorus	27.7 mg
Potassium	278 mg
Sodium	14 mg
Beta Carotene (A)	2 IU
Thiamine (B_1)	0.110 mg
Riboflavin (B_2)	0.050 mg
Niacin (B_3)	1.280 mg
Pantothenic Acid (B_5)	0.253 mg
Pyridoxine (B_6)	0.059 mg
Ascorbic Acid (C)	29.6 mg

candidates for use in beverages or sherbets, and for jellies and preserves. In the tropics, various drinks made from seeded and sweetened pulp beaten with milk or water.

Health Benefits The juice of the ripe fruit is said to be diuretic and a remedy for hematuria and urethritis. Taken when fasting, it is believed to relieve liver ailments and leprosy. Pulverized immature fruits, which are very astringent, are decocted as a dysentery remedy.

Star Apple *(Chrysophyllum cainito)*

Chrysophyllum *means golden-leaved.* Cainito *is the West Indian name for the star apple. The English name* star apple *is due to the fact that when the fruit is cut transversely, the seed cells are seen to radiate from the central core like an asterisk or many-pointed star.*

General Information This member of the Sapodilla family was long believed to be indigenous to Central America, but the botanists Paul Standley and Louis Williams have declared that it is not native to that area, no Nahuatl name has been found, and the tree may properly belong to the West Indies. In Haiti, the star apple was the favorite fruit of King Christophe, who held court under the shade of a very large specimen at Milot. The tree is grown occasionally in southern Florida and Hawaii, where it was introduced before 1901. The tree has always been prized for its ornamental value as well as for its fruits. The fruit is the size of a small apple, either white-green or dark purple, with a soft pulp containing a central "star" of six to eleven flat, brown seeds set in translucent jelly. The glossy, leathery skin adheres tightly to the inner rind.

Star Apple

Nutritional Value Per 100 g Edible Portion

	Raw
Calories	67.2
Protein	0.72-2.33 g
Fiber	0.55-3.30 g
Calcium	7.4-17.3 mg
Iron	0.30-0.68 mg
Phosphorus	15.9-22.0 mg
Beta Carotene (A)	0.004-0.039 mg
Thiamine (B_1)	0.018-0.080 mg
Riboflavin (B_2)	0.013-0.040 mg
Niacin (B_3)	0.935-1.340 mg
Ascorbic Acid (C)	3.0-15.2 mg

Culinary Uses Star apple pulp is soft, white, and milky. The flavor is sweet and characteristic of the sapodilla family, but to be good the fruit must be fully ripened on the tree. It is usually eaten fresh and chilled, the flesh spooned out from around the seed cells and core, but can be made into preserves. A combination of the chopped flesh mixed with mango, citrus, pineapple, and coconut water is frozen and served as Jamaica Fruit Salad Ice. Fruits must not be bitten into, as the skin and rind are inedible. When opening a star apple, one should not allow any of the bitter latex of the skin to contact the edible flesh.

Health Benefits The ripe fruit, because of its mucilaginous character, is eaten to soothe inflammation in laryngitis and pneumonia. It is given as a treatment for diabetes mellitus, and as a decoction is gargled to relieve angina. In Venezuela, the slightly unripe fruits are eaten to overcome intestinal disturbances; however, in excess, they cause constipation.

Strawberry *(Fragaria virginiana, F. vesca, F. moschata)*

> Fraga *was the ancient Latin name, and refers to the fruit's wonderfully enticing fragrance. The term* virginiana *means from Virginia;* vesca *means weak or thin;* moschata *means having a musky scent. The etymology of the English name* strawberry *is often disputed: one group claims that it was because straw was used between the rows to keep the berries clean and to protect them in wintertime; another explanation is that in Europe ripe berries were threaded on straws to be carried to market; a third contingent claims that the name was originally strewberry because the berries appear to be strewn or scattered among the leaves of the plant.*

General Information Strawberries are probably the most popular of all the berries, and indigenous to both the Old and New Worlds. There are approximately seventy-five varieties of wild strawberries found in the United States alone, all of them edible. The commercial fruits we know today are the result of an 1835 cross between one of the small, wild strawberries native to Europe and North America and a walnut-sized strawberry of Chile. A French spy on a mission to Chile smuggled the large Chilean strawberry home to France, and in King Louis XV's garden at Versailles the plant was crossed with another strawberry, *F. virginiana*, which Virginian colonists had sent back to England. Although the cross produced a berry of good size and flavor, wild strawberries have a flavor that is unequaled by any commercial berry. The alpine strawberry (*F. vesca*) is a form of wood strawberry, the wild strawberry of antiquity. It was discovered about three hundred years ago east of Grenoble in the low Alps, and since the fruit was larger and the plant bore continuously throughout the growing season, it soon surpassed other wood strawberries in popularity. Some strains of alpine strawberry produce fruits colored creamy white or yellow, slightly larger than the red, and with just a hint of pineapple flavor. The musk strawberry (*F. moschata*) is larger than the alpine strawberry and grows wild to a limited extent in the shaded forests of central Europe, north into Scandinavia, and east into Russia. The strawberry itself is an unusual fruit in that its seeds are embedded in its surface rather than protected within. The sweetest and most nutritious strawberries are those that have been sun-ripened on the plant, due to the fact that the amount of vitamin C increases the longer the berries remain unpicked in the sun.

Strawberry

Nutritional Value Per 100 g Edible Portion

	Raw
Calories	30
Protein	0.61 g
Fat	0.37 g
Fiber	0.53 g
Calcium	14 mg
Iron	0.38 mg
Magnesium	10 mg
Phosphorus	19 mg
Potassium	166 mg
Sodium	1 mg
Zinc	0.130 mg
Copper	0.049 mg
Manganese	0.290 mg
Beta Carotene (A)	27 IU
Thiamine (B_1)	0.020 mg
Riboflavin (B_2)	0.066 mg
Niacin (B_3)	0.230 mg
Pantothenic Acid (B_5)	0.340 mg
Pyridoxine (B_6)	0.059 mg
Folic Acid (B_9)	17.7 mcg
Ascorbic Acid (C)	56.7 mg
Tocopherol (E)	0.12 mg

Buying Tips All berries should be unblemished, fully and deeply colored without any runny or bleeding spots, slightly soft, fragrant, and have their stems intact. Avoid those with green or white tips as well as overly large varieties, since

Lore and Legend

The early Greeks had a taboo against eating any red foods, including wild strawberries, and this added mystery to the fruit, leading many to believe that it possessed great powers. Strawberries are often associated with fairy folk, and in Bavaria, a basket of the fruit is sometimes tied between a cow's horns to please the elves so that they bless the cow with abundant milk. During the Middle Ages, pregnant women avoided the berries because they believed their children would be born with ugly red birthmarks if they ate them. In art and literature the strawberry is usually a symbol of sensuality and earthly desire.

they have not had enough sun to ripen thoroughly and develop their full sweetness. Both alpine and musk strawberries are flavorless until becoming dead ripe, at which time they become extremely soft and aromatic (plus hard to ship).

Culinary Uses At their best, strawberries have a musky aroma and are sweet but acid, almost pineapple-like, in flavor. Fruits of the alpine strawberry have an intense, wild strawberry flavor, while the musk strawberry tastes like a combination of strawberry, raspberry, and pineapple. Wash them just before using, if at all, and remove the stems and hulls. An American favorite is strawberry shortcake, but the berries also appear on Belgian waffles, in jams and jellies, and as an adornment for various dishes. A natural complement to strawberries is cream in various forms, whether whipped into clouds, slightly soured, clotted as in Devonshire cream, or enriched with egg into a custard; a low-fat substitute such as yogurt is also good.

Health Benefits Strawberries are highly rated as a skin-cleansing food, even though skin eruptions may increase at first as they rid the blood of harmful toxins. Hives or other allergic reactions to the berries are most likely due to eating them in their unripe state, or when they have not been fully vine-ripened. Strawberries are recommended as essential for cardiac health and offer good nutritional energy that is easy to digest and process. All berries, but especially strawberries, are good sources of the anti-cancer compound ellagic acid. They are among the highest organic sodium fruits, and thus are eliminative and good for the intestinal tract; however, the seeds can be irritating where there is colitis or inflammation of the bowel. Their considerable vitamin properties are mostly lost during cooking, so that although strawberry jelly, jams, and preserves may taste good, they have only a fraction of their original natural vitamins. The addition of sugar renders them acidic and detrimental to the body. Strawberry leaf tea has many of the same properties as raspberry leaf tea, and may be used to ease diarrhea, increase the flow of milk after birth, and restore strength. A cut strawberry rubbed over the face after washing will whiten the skin and remove a slight sunburn.

Strawberry Pear (*Hylocereus undatus*)

Also Known As: Pitaya, Night Blooming Cereus.

Hylocereus *derives from a Greek term for wood.* Undatus *means wavy, not flat, undulate.*

General Information The cacti bearing these fruits are indigenous to Central America. The species reached Hawaii in 1830 among a shipment of plants loaded at a Mexican port en route from Boston to Canton China. Most of the other plants died and were being discarded during a stopover Hawaii, but the strawberry pear was still partly alive, so cuttings were planted. The cuttings flourished and the cactus became a common ornamental throughout the islands, where it blooms spectacularly but rarely sets fruit. The fruit is oval to oblong, up to four inches long, and may be bright red, peach-colored, or yellow.

Strawberry Pear

Nutritional Value Per 100 g Edible Portion

	Raw
Protein	0.159-0.229 g
Fat	0.21-0.61 g
Fiber	0.7-0.9 g
Calcium	6.3-8.8 mg
Iron	0.55-0.65 mg
Phosphorus	30.2-36.1 mg
Beta Carotene (A)	0.005-0.012 mg
Thiamine (B_1)	0.028-0.043 mg
Riboflavin (B_2)	0.043-0.045 mg
Niacin (B_3)	0.297-0.430 mg
Ascorbic Acid (C)	8.0-9.0 mg

Culinary Uses Pitaya flesh is sweet, white, juicy, and contains numerous tiny black seeds. Most often the fruit is chilled and cut in half so that the flesh can be eaten with a spoon. The juice makes a refreshing beverage. A syrup made of the whole fruit is used to color pastries and candy, while the unopened flower bud can be cooked and eaten as a vegetable.

Sugar Apple (*Annona squamosa*)

Also Known As: Sweetsop (in contrast to the Soursop), and Scaly custard apple in reference to its scales, which cover the greenish-yellow skin under a whitish bloom.

Annona *means year's harvest, suggested by the Haitian name* anon, *which is applied to one of the species.* Squamosa *means having scale-like leaves or full of scales.*

General Information Sugar apple is the English name used in the West Indies and Americas for the fruit of a small tree commonly cultivated in tropical South America. Its original home is unknown, but the Spaniards probably carried seeds from the New World to the Philippines, and the Portuguese are believed to have introduced the fruit to southern India before 1590. For those living in the interior of Brazil, the sugar apple is one of the most important fruits. The compound fruits, which ripen constantly over a period of six to seven months, are nearly round, ovoid, or conical, two and one-third to four inches long, and their thick rinds, composed of knobby segments, are pale green, gray-green, or bluish-green. The fruit is of delicate construction and is liable to come apart when ripe unless carefully handled.

Culinary Uses The pulp is either yellow or white, tender, delicate, and delicious, uniting an agreeable sweetness with the delightful fragrance of rose water. Many of the segments enclose a single oblong, black or dark-brown inedible seed about one-half inch long. There

Sugar Apple

Nutritional Value Per 100 g Edible Portion

	Raw
Calories	88.9-95.7
Protein	1.53-2.38 g
Fat	0.26-1.10 g
Fiber	1.14-2.50 g
Calcium	19.4-44.7 mg
Iron	0.28-1.34 mg
Magnesium	21 mg
Phosphorus	23.6-55.3 mg
Potassium	247 mg
Sodium	9 mg
Beta Carotene (A)	5-7 IU
Thiamine (B_1)	0.100-0.130 mg
Riboflavin (B_2)	0.113-0.167 mg
Niacin (B_3)	0.654-0.931 mg
Pantothenic Acid (B_5)	0.226 mg
Pyridoxine (B_6)	0.200 mg
Ascorbic Acid (C)	34.7-42.2 mg

may be as many as thirty-eight seeds per fruit, although some trees bear seedless fruit. The sugar apple is usually eaten as a dessert; the fruit is broken open and the flesh segments spooned out and enjoyed while the inedible seeds are spat out. It may also be used to make sherbets and to flavor ice creams, but is never cooked.

Health Benefits The green fruit, which is very astringent, is employed against diarrhea in El Salvador. In India, the crushed ripe fruit, mixed with salt, is applied to tumors. The seeds are acrid and poisonous.

Tamarillo *(Cyphomandra betacea)*

Also Known As: Tree Tomato.

Cyphomandra *is a Greek term referring to the hump-shaped anthers.* Betacea *means beet-like. The New Zealanders, who are the major commercial growers of this fruit, decided to market what was formerly known as the* tree tomato *as the* tamarillo, *and the name stuck.*

General Information Indigenous to Peru, the tamarillo is a tropical fruit related to the tomato. It must have been carried at an early date to East Africa, Asia, and the East Indies, as it is well established in those regions. It was introduced into New Zealand in 1891, where commercial growing on a small scale began about 1920. Flushed by their success in bestowing the name "kiwi" on the Chinese gooseberry, New Zealanders decided that the tree tomato should be called the tamarillo, and it now widely goes by that name. Shortages of tropical fruits in World War II justified an increased level of production. In nursery catalogs in the United States, the plant is frequently advertised and sold for growing indoors in pots as a curiosity. The size and shape of an egg, the tamarillo fruit looks rather like an elongated plum with its reddish-yellow or crimson skin.

Tamarillo

Nutritional Value Per 100 g Edible Portion

	Raw
Protein	1.5 g
Fat	0.06-1.28 g
Fiber	1.4-4.2 g
Calcium	3.9-11.3 mg
Iron	0.66-0.94 mg
Phosphorus	52.5-65.5 mg
Beta Carotene (A)	540 IU
Thiamine (B_1)	0.038-0.137 mg
Riboflavin (B_2)	0.035-0.048 mg
Niacin (B_3)	1.100-1.380 mg
Ascorbic Acid (C)	23.3-33.9 mg

Buying Tips Look for firm, heavy fruits that yield slightly to pressure. The more predominant the yellow tones, the sweeter and milder the fruit. Hard fruit will ripen at room temperature.

Culinary Uses This stunning and aromatic fruit is reddish-yellow or purple when ripe, with the yellower fruit often milder and sweeter than the darker. Inside, the yellow or deep coppery-orange flesh has two purple whorls of black seeds which are edible, and a plum-like texture that is pleasantly rich, sweet, and slightly astringent. Smelling vaguely of sun-ripened tomatoes, this pleasantly bitter, almost meaty fruit may be eaten raw but is well suited for cooking. Its taste has the sour notes of tomatoes, the subtlety of cooked carrots, and the slight punch of wintergreen. Baked, broiled, or stewed, used in savory dishes, sauces, or preserves, its sweet-spicy flavor will mysteriously deepen and enhance any other fruits when used in moderation. Because of its dense texture and assertive flavor, it holds its own in highly seasoned preparations such as chutneys, salsas, relishes, and other sauces. The fruit should not be cut on a wooden or other permeable surface, as the juice will make an indelible stain. The peel is not edible, so must be removed.

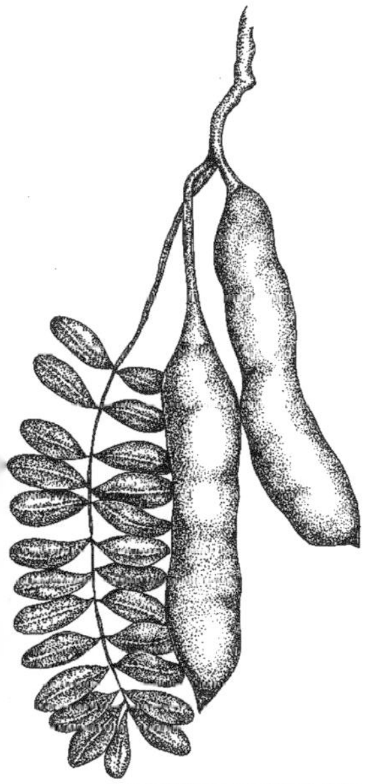

Tamarind (*Tamarindus indica*)

Also Known As: Indian Date.

> Tamarindus *comes from the Arabic* tamr-hindi, *meaning Indian date.*
> Indica *means native to or introduced from India.*

General Information The tamarind tree is a massive, slow-growing, ornamental leguminous tree native to tropical East Africa. Known as "Indian dates" because of their sticky, fibrous appearance, the fruits are flattish and beanlike. The irregularly curved cinnamon-colored pods range from three to eight inches long. At first the pods are tender-skinned with green, highly acidic flesh and soft, whitish seeds; as the fruit matures, the pods fills out, the pulp turns brown or reddish-brown, and the skin becomes brittle and easily cracked. It is a peculiarity of the fruit that it contains both more acid and more sugar than any other fruit. Although often referred to as "tamarind seed," it is in fact the pulp around the seeds which is used.

Lore and Legend

There is a superstition that it is harmful to sleep under or to tie a horse to a tamarind tree, probably due to the corrosive effect that fallen leaves have on fabrics in damp weather, and to the fact that few plants survive beneath the tree. Many Burmese believe that the tree represents the dwelling-place of the rain god, and that the tree raises the temperature in its immediate vicinity. In Malaya, small pieces of tamarind along with coconut milk are placed in the mouth of an infant at birth, and the bark and fruit are given to elephants to make them wise.

Culinary Uses Tender, immature, very sour pods are cooked as seasoning with rice, fish, and meats in India. The fully-grown but still unripe fruits are roasted in coals until the skins burst; the skins are then peeled back and the pulp dipped in wood ashes and eaten. Fully ripe, fresh fruit has a spicy date-apricot flavor and is enjoyed out of hand by children and adults alike. The pulp is an important ingredient in chutneys, curries, and sauces, including some brands of Worcestershire and barbecue sauce. When purchased dried, the fruit is first soaked in water and the soaking liquid and pulp used (the seeds are discarded). In one sweet preparation, powdered sugar is added to the fresh pulp until it no longer sticks to the fingers, at which time the concoction is shaped into balls and coated with more powdered sugar. Dehydrated tamarinds are also used to prepare confections, and the resulting sweetmeats are commonly found in Jamaica, Cuba, and the Dominican Republic. The fruit may be made into a variety of refreshing beverages, syrups, or sherbet. Combined with guava, papaya, or banana, the pulp makes a delicious preserve.

Tamarind

Nutritional Value Per 100 g Edible Portion

	Raw
Calories	115-230
Protein	3.10 g
Fat	0.1 g
Fiber	5.6 g
Calcium	35-170 mg
Iron	1.3-10.9 mg
Magnesium	92 mg
Phosphorus	54-110 mg
Potassium	375-628 mg
Sodium	24 mg
Beta Carotene (A)	15-30 IU
Thiamine (B_1)	0.160-0.428 mg
Riboflavin (B_2)	0.070-0.152 mg
Niacin (B_3)	0.600-1.938 mg
Pantothenic Acid (B_5)	0.143 mg
Pyridoxine (B_6)	0.066 mg
Ascorbic Acid (C)	0.7-3.0 mg

In India, young leaves and very young seedlings and flowers are cooked and eaten as greens; in Zimbabwe, the leaves are added to soup and the flowers are a common ingredient in salads.

Health Benefits Anthelmintic, carminative, laxative, refrigerant. The principal use of the ripe, sweet-sour, stringy pulp throughout the Americas and Caribbean is as a mild laxative. The pulp of the fruit contains citric, tartaric, and malic acids, which give it cooling properties; therefore, it is a useful drink for those ill with fever, as well as a popular cooling beverage in hot countries. Alone, or in combination with lime juice, honey, dates, milk, or spices, the pulp is considered effective as a digestive, as a remedy for biliousness, and as an antiscorbutic. In native practices, the pulp is applied on inflammations, used in a gargle for sore throats, and administered to alleviate sunstroke and alcoholic intoxication. Lotions and extracts made from the leaves and flowers are used in treating conjunctivitis, dysentery, jaundice, hemorrhoids, and many other ailments.

Tomatillo *(Physalis ixocarpa)*

Also Known As: Mexican Green Tomato, Mexican Husk Tomato, Tomato Verde, Chinese Lantern Plants.

> Physalis *comes from the Greek* physa *for bladder, and was given this plant because the fruit is enclosed within a thin calyx.* Ixocarpa *means sticky or glutinous-fruited.* Tomatillo *is a Spanish word that means little tomato.*

General Information A prominent staple in Aztec and Mayan economies, the tomatillo plant abounds in Mexico and the highlands of Guatemala. This strange-looking member of the nightshade family has the usual *Physalis* structure, the calyx enlarging with the fruit and becoming straw-colored and papery, often splitting. It resembles a green cherry tomato, ranging in size from an inch in diameter to plum-sized, but is more lustrous and firm. The skin color may be anywhere from yellow-green to purplish, but the fruit is most commonly used in its unripe green state.

Buying Tips Choose fruits that are firm, hard, and dry, with clean, close-fitting husks that show no blackness or mold. The unhusked fresh fruits can be stored in single layers in a cool, dry atmosphere for several months.

Culinary Uses The flesh is pale yellow, crisp or soft, acid to sweet or insipid, and contains many tiny seeds. In texture and flavor it is reminiscent of a green plum with a sweet-sour taste, not as sour as a lemon, and with a delightful aroma of freshly-mown hay. The tangy tomatillo is most frequently featured in Southwestern and Mexican cuisine in the form of a sauce, *salsa verde*. They are almost always cooked to develop their lemony-herbal flavor and to soften their rather solid hides, but they can be used raw for a sharper flavor. Like red tomatoes, tomatillo's gelatinous texture makes for great sauce potential. The husk is inedible and must be removed before use.

Health Benefits It is said in Mexico that a decoction of the calyces will cure diabetes.

Tomatillo

Nutritional Value Per 100 g Edible Portion	Raw
Calories	32
Protein	0.17-0.70 g
Fat	0.6 g
Fiber	0.6-1.7 g
Calcium	6.3-10.9 mg
Iron	0.57-1.4 mg
Magnesium	23 mg
Phosphorus	21.9-40.0 mg
Potassium	243 mg
Sodium	0.4 mg
Zinc	0.220 mg
Copper	0.079 mg
Manganese	0.153 mg
Beta Carotene (A)	80 IU
Thiamine (B_1)	0.054-0.106 mg
Riboflavin (B_2)	0.023-0.057 mg
Niacin (B_3)	2.100-2.700 mg
Pantothenic Acid (B5)	0.150 mg
Pyridoxine (B_6)	0.056 mg
Folic Acid (B_9)	7.0 mcg
Ascorbic Acid (C)	2.0-4.8 mg

Ugli Fruit (*Citrus*)

The term Citrus *derives from the Greek term for the citron,* kedromelon*. The English name* Ugli Fruit *is copyrighted by the Jamaican exporter G.G.R. Sharp, the name having originated in response to the fruit's appearance.*

General Information A citrus hybrid, the ugli is a cross between the grapefruit and either a tangerine or orange that originated in Jamaica. A chance seedling, it was propagated by F.G. Sharp at Trout Hall, then exported in 1934 to England by his son. Popular in the English markets, where it was generally called the "ugly," it soon made its appearance in other countries. Looking rather like a large, lumpy grapefruit, it has a puffy, thick, knobby, slightly loose-fitting skin which may range from lime green to light orange in color. This skin often forms a furrowed collar or neck on the rounded or slightly pear-shaped fruit. Not altogether an unsightly fruit, it is simply not as sleek and regularly colored as the more common citrus fruits.

Buying Tips Look for fruits that are heavy for their size, with a preference for smaller fruits with their sweeter flavor, with no sign of drying at the stem end. Any amount of mottling, bronzing, surface scarring, or uneven coloring is perfectly normal. The fruit should have a little bit of give, like a grapefruit.

Culinary Uses The ugli fruit's loosely adhering coat is a cinch to peel, and the pinkish or yellowy-orange flesh is sweeter than its grapefruit parent and nearly seedless. Once cut, the fruit fairly overflows with sweet juice from its atypically large, tender juice sacs. The acid-sweet flesh is unusually soft and succulent, with a full, zesty flavor. It can be cut and eaten like a grapefruit, peeled and eaten like an orange, or cooked into preserves.

Health Benefits Low fat, high in fiber and vitamin C.

Umeboshi *(Prunus salicina)*

Also Known As: Salt Plum, Japanese Plum.

This plum is part of the Prunus *family, thus the genus name, while* salicina *means willow-like or resembling the willow tree,* salix.

General Information The ume or Japanese plum is a sour green fruit resembling an unripe apricot. The tree was introduced to Japan at least thirteen hundred years ago from the Chinese mainland and quickly adapted. The fruit was soon popular among the Japanese, more so than it had been among the Chinese. The hard green plums are picked in the early spring, washed, then packed into vats with crude sea salt for about a month. The salt draws the juice out of the plums by osmosis, so that they are soon covered by a liquid conventionally called "plum vinegar." The plums are then sun dried while mineral-rich purple shiso leaves (*Iresine herbistii,* also known as perilla or beefsteak) are added to the brine, imparting to it a beautiful deep red color, sweet taste, and fragrant bouquet. The shiso leaves also provide a natural preservative, which is known to possess over one thousand times the preserving ability of synthetic preservatives. Next, the plums are returned to the brine for additional pickling; they are soaked overnight and dried daily in the sun for seven days. The plums are then removed and aged for an additional four months to develop subtle qualities of flavor, taste, and appearance. Quality umeboshi contains only ume, salt, and shiso leaves.

Culinary Uses **Whole umeboshi** plums generally come complete with pit and shiso leaf. The whole plums can be boiled with rice or sliced into stir-fried vegetables. The leaf can also be added while cooking to add flavor and color. **Ume extract/concentrate** is made by reducing 1 kilogram (2.2 pounds) of fresh plums to 20 grams (less than an ounce) of thick, dark syrup. The concentrate contains no salt, unlike the plums or paste. It is generally made into a drink to relieve acidic conditions, but also is an excellent aid for travelers because of its digestive soothing properties. **Umeboshi paste** is the pureed umeboshi minus pits and shiso. Less expensive than whole umeboshi and more convenient to use, the paste can replace salt in salad dressings, spreads, seasonings, and sauces, or be cooked with grains, beans, and vegetables. In paste form or whole, umeboshi keeps for several years at room temperature. **Umeboshi vinegar** is the pink brine drawn from kegs of mature umeboshi. This liquid has a deep cherry aroma and fruity sour flavor. Technically not a vinegar because it contains salt, it may be substituted for vinegar and salt in any recipe, where it imparts a light, refreshing citrus-like flavor. It especially enhances salad dressings and steamed vegetables.

Health Benefits Umeboshi has remarkable healing properties, alkalinizing the digestive system, helping to strengthen blood quality, and relieving indigestion due to overeating, overindulgence in alcohol, or morning sickness. Its high citric acid content eliminates from the body lactic acid, a major contributor to fatigue, colds, flu, viruses, diseases, and chronic illnesses. Low in fat, high in iron and vitamin C.

Wampee (*Clausena lansium*)

> Clausena *is from a personal name of unknown origin. The English name* wampee *is derived from the Chinese* huang-p'i-kuo.

General Information The wampee is native to southern China and the northern part of former French Indochina. It is cultivated to a limited extent in Queensland, Australia, and Hawaii. Brought to Florida in 1908, a few specimens have been growing for years, but the fruit is generally unknown to most residents. The fruits hang in showy, loose clusters of several strands, being round or conical, up to one inch long with five faint, pale ridges extending a short distance down from the apex. The thin, pliable, but tough rind is a light brownish-yellow, minutely hairy, and dotted with tiny raised brown oil glands.

Culinary Uses The flesh is yellowish-white or colorless, grapelike, mucilaginous, juicy, pleasantly sweet, subacid, or sour, and may contain up to five bright green seeds. A fully ripe, peeled wampee is agreeable to eat out of hand, discarding the large seed(s). The seeded pulp can be added to fruit cups, gelatins or other desserts, or made into pie or jam. In southeast Asia, a bottled carbonated beverage resembling champagne is made by fermenting the fruit with sugar and straining off the juice.

Health Benefits The fruit is said to have stomachic and cooling effects and to act as a vermifuge. The Chinese believe that if one has eaten too many lychees, eating the wampee will counteract the bad effects. Lychees should be eaten when one is hungry, and wampees only on a full stomach. Florida-grown fruits have shown 28.8 to 29.2 milligrams of ascorbic acid per 100 grams of flesh.

Watermelon (*Citrullus lanatus, C. vulgaris*)

> Citrullus *is the diminutive form of citrus, said to be an allusion to the shape of the fruits and the color of the flesh, which resemble those characteristics in the fruits of the orange and/or citron. The term* lanatus *means woolly, while* vulgaris *means an ordinary fruit, commonly grown. The English name* watermelon *is appropriate since its juicy flesh is over 90 percent water.*

General Information Watermelon originated in desert areas of tropical and sub-tropical Africa, and is botanically different from the rest of the melon group. Eaten and cultivated in Egypt and India well before 2500 B.C., the one great advantage of this fruit, which encouraged its spread to lands around the Mediterranean and eastward into Asia, was its 90 percent water content. This made watermelon a valuable source of drinking water in desert areas and an especially useful source of potable liquid where water supplies were polluted. In 1857 the Scottish missionary and explorer David Livingstone described the abundance of watermelons in the vast dry plateaus of the Kalahari Desert of the Bechuanaland in central South Africa. He noted that the fruits were variable in taste—some bitter and others sweet—and that the natives and all the animals of the region ate them ravenously. There are more than fifty varieties, of various shapes, colors, and sizes, which are generally divided into "picnic" and "icebox" varieties. Picnic types are larger, usually weighing fifteen to fifty pounds; icebox varieties—designed to fit into a refrigerator—weigh between five and fifteen pounds. Watermelons do grow larger under the right conditions, however: the 1991 *Guinness Book of World Records* gives the prize to a 279-pound specimen grown in 1988 by Bill Rogerson of Robertsville, North Carolina. Most watermelons have the familiar red flesh, but there are also orange- and yellow- fleshed varieties, as well as some that are seedless. There is little taste difference among the different varieties. Watermelon consumption in the United States peaked in 1960 at 17.2 pounds per person, but dropped steadily after that, reaching rock bottom two decades later when Americans ate only 10.6 pounds per person. Lately, however, they are making a comeback.

Buying Tips Few people can agree on just how to pick a ripe watermelon. Some say that it should have a skin that is dull and slightly waxy, with ends that are not pointy but rounded and well filled out (evidently the non-pointy ones are female and sweeter), heavy for its size, with a bottom that is a pale creamy yellow and not white. Others swear by the thumping method, looking for a deep hollow sound rather than a dull thud. Another method is to look for one with a dry brown stem and then scrape the rind with a fingernail; when the green skin comes off easily, the melon is deemed ready to eat. When the melons are cut, your job is much easier. The best ones have bright red flesh with dark brown or black seeds. Avoid melons with white streaks, or that have deeply colored "mealy" areas around the seeds.

Watermelon

Nutritional Value Per 100 g Edible Portion

	Raw
Calories	32
Protein	0.62 g
Fat	0.43 g
Fiber	0.30 g
Calcium	8 mg
Iron	0.17 mg
Magnesium	11 mg
Phosphorus	9 mg
Potassium	116 mg
Sodium	2 mg
Zinc	0.07 mg
Copper	0.032 mg
Manganese	0.037 mg
Beta Carotene (A)	366 IU
Thiamine (B_1)	0.080 mg
Riboflavin (B_2)	0.020 mg
Niacin (B_3)	0.200 mg
Pantothenic Acid (B_5)	0.212 mg
Pyridoxine (B_6)	0.144 mg
Folic Acid (B_9)	2.2 mcg
Ascorbic Acid (C)	9.6 mg

Culinary Uses Watermelon is something most everyone loves because it is refreshingly sweet. On a hot summer day nothing beats a freshly cut slice. To serve, either slice or cut into chunks. Italians like to make watermelon puddings, particularly the *gelu u muluni* of Sicily, made with ground almonds, chocolate, and cinnamon. Americans prefer simpler watermelon desserts, such as fruit cups, melon balls, or ices. The rind makes a tasty old-fashioned pickle. Fully ripe seeds are edible, and are considered quite tasty by many cultures. See reference under **Nuts, Seeds, and Oils**.

Health Benefits Watermelon is used as a cooling food in hot weather, for treatment of thirst, and to relieve mental depression. As it contains a whopping 92 percent water, it is popular with dieters. Its high quality water content is an excellent cleanser and detoxifier for the whole body, and has the greatest dissolving power of inorganic minerals in the body out of all the fruits and vegetables. Surprisingly, it has only half the sugar (5 percent) of an apple, but tastes much sweeter because sugar is its main taste-producing element. One of nature's safest and most dependable diuretics, watermelon has a remarkable ability to quickly and completely wash out the bladder. The white rind of the watermelon is one of the highest organic sodium foods in nature, and the outside peel one of the best sources of chlorophyll. The rind can be juiced and drunk, or small amounts can be eaten.

Wood Apple *(Feronia limonia)*

Also Known As: Elephant Apple, because both the tree and its fruit formerly had the botanical name F. elephantum, because it is a favorite of elephants.

The genus Feronia *is named after Feronia, the Roman goddess of forests.* Limonia *perhaps means lemon-like or lemon-scented.*

General Information The small wood apple tree is found in most parts of the Indian sub-continent and eastward to the China Sea. Traditionally a "poor man's food" until processing techniques were developed in the mid-1950s, the tree is now cultivated along roads and occasionally in orchards. Fruit is tested for maturity by dropping samples onto a hard surface from a height of one foot. Immature fruits bounce, while mature fruits do not. After harvesting, the fruits are kept in the sun for two weeks to fully ripen, and the hard rinds must be cracked open with a hammer to eat.

Wood Apple

Nutritional Value Per 100 g Edible Portion	
Protein	8.00%
Fat	1.45%
Calcium	0.17%
Iron	0.07%
Phosphorus	0.08%

Culinary Uses The round, apple-size, gray fruits have hard shells and contain an odorous brown, sticky, mealy pulp, which is used to make sherbets, jellies, and chutneys in India. The pulp is also eaten raw with sugar or seasoning, but is inconveniently full of small seeds. A bottled nectar is made by diluting the pulp with water, passing it through a pulper to remove seeds and fiber, further diluting, straining, and pasteurizing.

Health Benefits The fruit is much used in India as a liver and cardiac tonic, and when unripe, as an astringent means of halting diarrhea and dysentery. The pulp is poulticed onto bites and stings of venomous insects, as is the powdered rind.

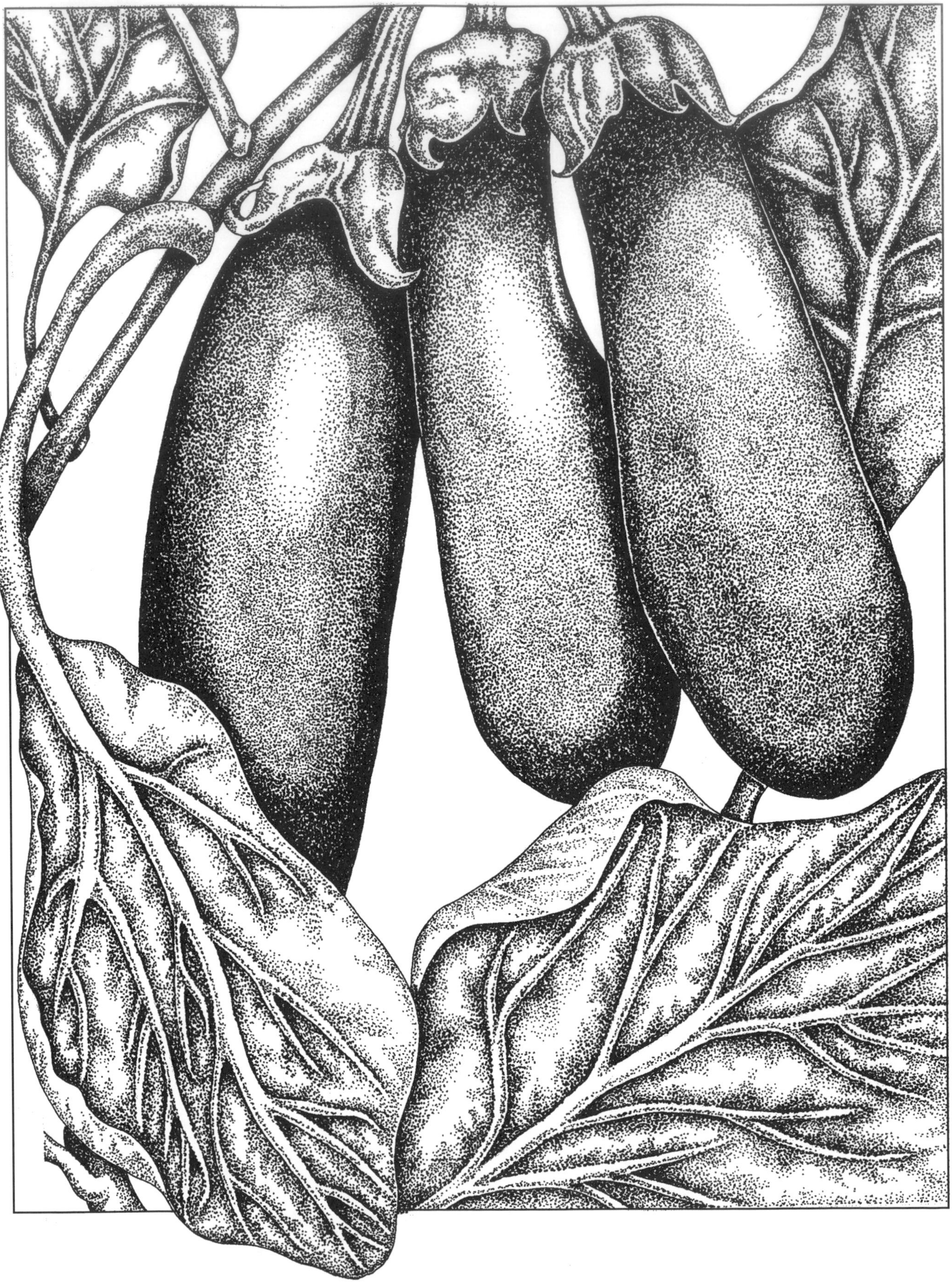

Vegetables

"Ho! 'tis the time of salads."

—Laurence Sterne, *Tristram Shandy*

VEGETABLES

Vegetables

WHAT IS THE DIFFERENCE BETWEEN A VEGETABLE AND A FRUIT? In 1893, this question came before the U.S. Supreme Court, which ruled that a vegetable refers to those edible parts of plants generally eaten as part of the main course, while a fruit refers to a plant part generally eaten as an appetizer, dessert, or out of hand. Typical parts of plants used as vegetables include bulbs (garlic and onion), flowers (broccoli and cauliflower), fruits (pumpkins and tomatoes), leaves (spinach and lettuce), roots (carrots and beets), seeds (legumes, peas, and corn), stalks (celery), stems (asparagus), and tubers (potatoes and yams).

There are hundreds of types and thousands of varieties of vegetables from which to choose. Preference should always be given toward those which are freshest and in season; the tastiest and most nutritious vegetables are those that are consumed immediately after picking or harvesting. Generally speaking, the longer vegetables are exposed to air, heat, and water, the less nutritious they will be. "Fresh" vegetables shipped from long distances and displayed for several days in a store may actually be less nutritious than those which are flash-frozen shortly after harvesting. Canned vegetables (both home canned and commercially canned) are heated to high temperatures, which destroys some of the vitamin content, including up to 50 percent of the vitamin C. If the canning liquid is not utilized (many people drain the liquid off because of its possible high sodium content), even more nutrients are lost. Canned vegetables, which lack the flavor and texture of produce that is fresh or frozen, should be considered a viable alternative only if no fresh or frozen produce is available. Dehydrated and powdered vegetables are even lower in nutrients than canned, because of their lengthy exposure to air or heat.

The English word *vegetable* derives from the Latin *vegetus*, meaning active or lively, and both Roman slave and patrician thought all food from the fertile earth was a boon to amatory pursuits. In later cultures vegetables would be spurned by the nobility; our word *garbage*, interestingly enough, comes from the Latin *gerbe*, meaning green stuff.

Arracacha *(Arracacia xanthorrhiza)*

Also Known As: Peruvian Carrot.

The genus name Arracacia, *as well as the English name, come from the Spanish name for the plant, while* xanthorrhiza *means yellow-rooted.*

General Information Native to the Andean highlands from Venezuela to Bolivia, arracacha is an herbaceous perennial that produces large, thick, edible, carrot-shaped, starchy roots with a color suggesting parsnip. Secondary tubers (offshoots of the main tuber) are an important carbohydrate foodstuff and are boiled or fried as a table vegetable, or used as an ingredient in stews.

Arracacha

Nutritional Value Per 100 g Edible Portion	
Calories	104
Protein	0.80 g
Fat	0.20 g
Calcium	29 mg
Iron	1.20 mg
Phosphorus	58 mg
Beta Carotene (A)	60 IU
Thiamine (B_1)	0.060 mg
Riboflavin (B_2)	0.040 mg
Niacin (B_3)	3.400 mg
Ascorbic Acid (C)	28 mg

Culinary Uses Arracacha has a delicate flavor, a crisp texture, and either white, creamy-yellow, or purple flesh. The small, young roots may be baked, fried, or used in soups and stews like potatoes. A flour from the roots is used to make breads and pancakes. The older, coarse main rootstocks and mature leaves are used to feed livestock, and the young stems are used for salads or a table vegetable. Harvesting cannot be delayed, because roots left in the ground become fibrous and tough and develop a strong, unpleasant flavor.

Health Benefits The tubers are reported to have a starch content ranging from about 10 to 25 percent, and to be similar in many respects to that of cassava; the starch is easily digested and can be used in infant and invalid foods.

Artichoke, Chinese *(Stachys sieboldii, S. affinis)*

Stachys *is from an old Greek name meaning spike, applied by Dioscorides to this and another group of plants;* sieboldii *is in honor of Philipp Franz von Siebold (1796–1866). The English name* Chinese artichoke *refers to the fact that they resemble Jerusalem artichokes.*

General Information Chinese artichokes are the tubers of an erect, hairy, herbaceous Chinese perennial that resembles the Jerusalem artichoke but which are more slender and knotty. These little tubers also go by the name of "crosnes" in Europe; the name comes from the small French town of that name where they were first introduced in 1882, and from where they are exported. There is no reason why this vegetable should not be sold on a wider scale and relatively cheaply, for they grow easily and abundantly.

Buying Tips Select tubers that are firm and pearly white, indicating that they are absolutely fresh, or a yellowish beige, which means they are a few days older but still perfectly good to eat.

Culinary Uses In taste, Chinese artichokes have an exquisite flavor, somewhere between Jerusalem artichokes and salsify, and can be used in the same way. To cook, trim the ends and rinse thoroughly. Simmer in just enough salted water to cover, or steam them. A dash of lemon juice will heighten their flavor. Cook until tender rather than *al dente*, but not until mushy and collapsing. They are delicious served as they are, with a large pat of butter and a sprinkling of chopped parsley, chervil, chives, or tarragon. They can also be grated into vegetable salads, or used as a side vegetable dish. Their peel, which is hard to remove, is edible and can be left on.

Artichoke, Globe (*Cynara cardunculus scolymus, C. scolymus*)

The artichoke's botanical name Cynara, *from the Latin* canina, *meaning canine, is derived from the similarity of the involucral spines to a dog's tooth;* cardunculus *means little thistle;* scolymus *is from the Greek* skolymos, *meaning thistle. The English name* artichoke *is derived from the Arabic* al-khurshuf, *also meaning thistle; the term* globe *because of its globular shape.*

General Information Globe artichokes are an edible variety of thistle in the sunflower family that originated in the Mediterranean. Raised for their fleshy immature flower buds, the plant will produce a beautiful cluster of violet-blue flowers, colorful enough to grace any garden, if not cut down to be used as a vegetable. The edible flower bud is enclosed by green leaflike scales, or bracts. Both the bracts and the base of the flower or "heart" are edible. Nearly all of the globe artichokes grown in the United States are from Castroville in Monterey County, California, south of San Francisco, the "artichoke capital of the world."

Artichoke, Globe

Nutritional Value Per 100 g Edible Portion

	Raw	Cooked
Calories	47	50
Protein	3.27 g	3.48 g
Fat	0.15 g	0.16 g
Fiber	1.17 g	1.25 g
Calcium	44 mg	45 mg
Iron	1.28 mg	1.29 mg
Magnesium	60 mg	60 mg
Phosphorus	90 mg	86 mg
Potassium	370 mg	354 mg
Sodium	94 mg	95 mg
Zinc	0.490 mg	0.490 mg
Copper	0.231 mg	0.233 mg
Manganese	0.256 mg	0.259 mg
Beta Carotene (A)	185 IU	177 IU
Thiamine (B_1)	0.072 mg	0.065 mg
Riboflavin (B_2)	0.066 mg	0.066 mg
Niacin (B_3)	1.046 mg	1.001 mg
Pantothenic Acid (B_5)	0.338 mg	0.342 mg
Pyridoxine (B_6)	0.116 mg	0.111 mg
Folic Acid (B_9)	68 mcg	51 mcg
Ascorbic Acid (C)	11.7 mg	10.0 mg

Buying Tips Choose artichokes that are heavy for their size, compact and firm in the winter and spring, somewhat flared and conical in the summer and fall. Overmature artichokes are lighter in color, have tannish leaves that are open or spreading, the tips and scales of the leaves are hard, and the center is fuzzy and dark pink or purple. If you are not sure about the freshness of an artichoke, squeeze it: you will hear a squeaky sound if the leaves are still plump and crisp. The absolutely best artichokes are those lightly touched by frost, with their outer leaves colored bronze to brown.

Culinary Uses Globe artichokes have a daunting appearance, but are not as difficult to cook as they appear and their nut-like flavor is worth the attempt. One of the easiest ways to prepare them is by boiling, tops down, in water with the aid of a steamer. They are done when a fork can easily penetrate the base. Once baked, boiled or stuffed, pull off the leaves one by one, and dip the fleshy ends into melted butter or another favorite sauce, pulling the ends through your teeth to extract the tasty pulp. Inside the bud is the "choke," a tuft of slender hay-colored fibers resembling cornsilk. Beneath the choke is the artichoke bottom, sometimes called the heart, although artichoke hearts more correctly refer to younger globes with small or insignificant chokes. Dense and velvety, the entire bottom can be cut into quarters, dipped and eaten. The artichoke is the one vegetable that appears to be larger after you finish eating it, so compact are its petals.

Lore and Legend

The artichoke, said to have been created when a beautiful woman was turned into a thistle, was popular in Elizabethan England. They became quite fashionable among monarchs and courtiers, and Catherine de Medici—who may have brought them to France from her native Italy—is said to have eaten so many at one sixteenth-century feast that she "nearly burst." Rumored to be a potent aphrodisiac, artichokes were prescribed by doctors for their male patients who sought to increase bedroom performance.

Health Benefits Diuretic, digestive. Fresh artichokes are low in calories because most of the carbohydrate is in the form of inulin, a polysaccharide or starch that is not utilized by the body for energy metabolism, but which does provide nutrition to health-promoting bacteria in the intestinal tract. It has also been shown to improve blood-sugar control in diabetics. Stored for any length of time, however, this inulin is broken down into other sugars. Recent research indicates that the globe artichoke may neutralize the effect of certain toxic substances, as well as benefit heart activity and the gastrointestinal tract. Their active ingredients are caffeylquinic acids (such as cynarin), found in highest concentrations in the leaves, but also in the bracts and heart. Artichoke leaf extracts (with their glycosides, flavonoids, and tannins) have demonstrated significant liver-protecting and regenerating effects, promoting the flow of bile and fat to and from the liver. They lower the level of cholesterol in the blood and prevent excessive fatty deposits in liver tissue and the blood, thereby warding off arteriosclerosis.

Artichoke, Jerusalem *(Helianthus tuberosus)*

Helianthus *is from the Greek words* helios *(sun) and* anthos *(flower); together they signify that the plant is a member of the sunflower genus;* tuberosus *applies to the roots, which are tuberous. Its English name* Jerusalem artichoke *does not imply that the plant is native to Palestine, as it might seem. One theory is that Jerusalem is a corruption of the Italian* girasola, *meaning turning to the sun; another theory is that it comes from the English alteration of* Ter Neusen, *the Netherlands location from which the plant was introduced into England.* Artichoke *is derived from the Arabic* al-khurshuf, *meaning thistle.*

Artichoke, Jerusalem

Nutritional Value Per 100 g Edible Portion

	Raw
Calories	76
Protein	2.00 g
Fat	0.01 g
Fiber	0.80 g
Calcium	14 mg
Iron	3.40 mg
Magnesium	17 mg
Phosphorus	78 mg
Manganese	0.060 mg
Beta Carotene (A)	20 IU
Thiamine (B_1)	0.200 mg
Riboflavin (B_2)	0.060 mg
Niacin (B_3)	1.300 mg
Ascorbic Acid (C)	4.0 mg

General Information Jerusalem artichokes are native to North America, the tubers of a perennial sunflower that produces brilliant yellow flowers. "Discovered" by Sir Walter Raleigh's 1585 expedition to the Virginia region, where the Indians were found growing them, a better name for these knobby gnarled little roots might be sunflower artichokes or sunchokes. The Jerusalem artichoke plant has numerous creeping roots, which produce tubers like the common potato. These tubers are of a longish, slightly flattened shape and are generally gathered in the spring or fall. In Europe, most notably France, the vegetable was improved and cultivated, and today there are over two hundred varieties.

Buying Tips Choose the smoothest, firmest tubers with the fewest protrusions. Avoid any with wrinkled skins or green blotched areas.

Culinary Uses Knobby and gnarled, resembling a small nubby potato or a piece of gingerroot, these little roots offer no clue to the flavor of their firm white flesh, which is delicate, nut-like, and slightly sweet. Jerusalem artichokes can vary in color from beige to brownish-red. Grated or sliced raw chokes add crunch and flavor to either raw or cooked vegetable salads, or can be

Lore and Legend

A Huron Indian legend explains the origin of the Jerusalem artichoke as follows: A Feast of Dreams was held so that the chief's son could choose his life power force. After feasting on roast dog, the boy became very sick; in his delirium he called upon the thunder god, who was so pleased that he began to roll his thunder drums, alarming the tribe. The tribe chanted and prayed that another image would reveal itself to the child. Finally the boy's eyes opened and he noticed that sunflowers had grown up all around him. These became his symbol. But the thunder god became angry, and sent hailstones down to destroy the flowers. This act brought the sun into battle, pushing the thunder god aside, and causing the hailstones to sink into the earth and become edible tubers. These tubers were Jerusalem artichokes, which would provide food and medicine for the boy's people for many years to come.

snacked on with a creamy dip. The little tubers do not need to be peeled before cooking as the peels are edible (just clean them as well as possible). Cooked and used in the same manner as potatoes, they can be boiled, steamed, or fried, and are excellent mashed to a creamy purée and dotted with butter. The vegetable's sweetness invites onion, cream, and dashes of clove, cinnamon, or nutmeg. Combined with a bit of flour and egg, grated sunchokes make hearty pancakes. Flour made from ground dried Jerusalem artichokes makes a nutritious addition to baked goods or pasta.

Health Benefits Jerusalem artichokes make a good potato substitute for diabetics and others who cannot eat potatoes, since the artichokes store their carbohydrates in the form of inulin rather than sugar. Inulin is a polysaccharide or starch that is not utilized by the body for energy metabolism, but does provide nutrition to health -promoting bacteria in the intestinal tract. It has also been shown to improve blood-sugar control in diabetics. The inulin in sunchokes can sometimes cause flatulence; if you have never sampled sunchokes, first try them in small amounts. They are an incomparable source of iron, almost on a par with meats, yet with minimal fat content.

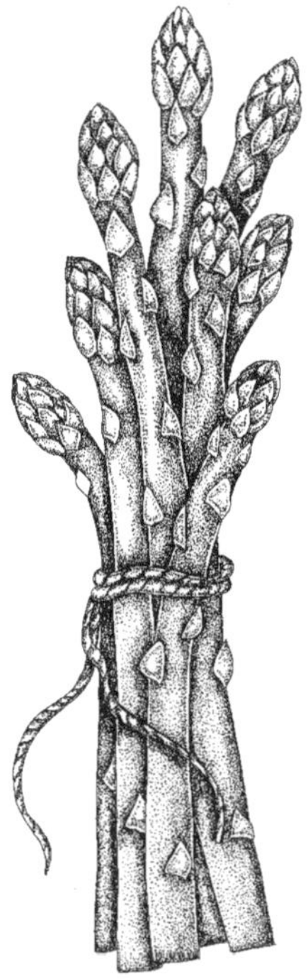

Asparagus *(Asparagus officinalis)*

The botanical name is derived from asparag, *the Persian word for all kinds of tender shoots picked and eaten while very young.* Officinalis *means of the workshop, alluding to apothecaries' shops, and signifies that the plant was once part of the official pharmacopeia of Rome.*

General Information Asparagus originated in the desert regions of eastern North Africa, where the Arabs ate it long before their recorded history. The ancient Phoenicians introduced asparagus to the Greeks and Romans, who cultivated it as early as 200 B.C. Some stalks grown at Ravenna are recorded as weighing three to a pound, while others in the Getulia plains of Africa were actually twelve feet tall. Cultivated asparagus has been a luxury item throughout its history, but it escapes cultivation so easily that it is found wild, free for the gathering, in whatever regions it is cultivated. Many people find the wild variety tastier and prefer it over the cultivated. One intuitively knows that asparagus is a primitive plant when one sees its broad point poking up through the ground, looking alien compared to other garden denizens. It bears no true leaves, but the small scales appearing on the edible stalk perform the function of leaves. One of spring's first vegetables, asparagus is related to onions, garlic, and other plants in the lily family. There are three main types: green, white, and (more rarely) purple, each of which comprise many varieties.

Lore and Legend

The ancient Egyptians cultivated asparagus and considered it a worthy offering for their gods. Given its blatantly phallic shape, it is inevitable that asparagus has long been considered an aphrodisiac.

Asparagus

Nutritional Value Per 100 g Edible Portion	Raw	Cooked
Calories	23	24
Protein	2.28 g	2.59 g
Fat	0.20 g	0.31 g
Fiber	n/a	0.83 g
Calcium	21 mg	20 mg
Iron	0.87 mg	0.73 mg
Magnesium	18 mg	10 mg
Phosphorus	56 mg	54 mg
Potassium	273 mg	160 mg
Sodium	2 mg	11 mg
Zinc	0.460 mg	0.420 mg
Copper	0.176 mg	0.112 mg
Manganese	0.262 mg	0.152 mg
Beta Carotene (A)	583 IU	539 IU
Thiamine (B_1)	0.140 mg	0.123 mg
Riboflavin (B_2)	0.128 mg	0.126 mg
Niacin (B_3)	1.170 mg	1.082 mg
Pyridoxine (B_6)	0.131 mg	0.122 mg
Folic Acid (B_9)	128 mcg	146 mcg
Ascorbic Acid (C)	13.2 mg	10.8 mg
Tocopherol (E)	1.98 mg	n/a

Buying Tips Only the young green shoots or spears of asparagus are eaten. The spears should be bright green, perfectly straight, firm and brittle, with tips that are tight, compact, and pointed. Avoid any that are very thin or very thick, as these will tend to be tough and stringy, and any with open, wilted, shriveled, or yellowing tips. Unless you plan to eat it immediately, asparagus is best stored in a cool place below 41 degrees, or the coldest part of the refrigerator with the stems wrapped in a damp paper towel.

Culinary Uses Fresh asparagus tastes best when cooked only briefly, a fact obviously appreciated by the ancient Roman Emperor Augustus, who is said to have described a task quickly done as taking "less time than to cook asparagus." Before steaming, boiling, or grilling, snap off the tough lower stem-end by holding a spear in both hands and bending it; it will break where the tender and tough parts meet. Asparagus can be served as a hot vegetable, as a cold addition to salads, in soups, or as a sandwich filling. Canned asparagus has lost all of its wholesome qualities and is best avoided.

Health Benefits Aperient, diaphoretic, diuretic, laxative. Asparagus was used medicinally long before it was eaten as a vegetable. The Greeks and Romans used it for relieving the pain of toothaches and for preventing bee stings. The actual medicinal property is a substance called asparagine, nature's most effective kidney diuretic, which breaks up the oxalic and uric acid crystals in the kidneys and muscles and eliminates them through the urine. (Occasionally this will produce a strong odor in the urine, which is only temporary.) Asparagus also contains substantial amounts of aspartic acid, an amino acid that neutralizes the excess amounts of ammonia that linger in our bodies and make us tired, and a substance called rutin, a factor in preventing small blood vessels from rupturing. Its high water content and roughage encourage evacuation of the bowels by increasing fecal bulk with undigested fiber; it is also a good blood builder due to its chlorophyll content, and contains many of the elements that build the liver, kidneys, skin, ligaments, and bones.

Avocado *(Persea americana)*

Also Known As: Alligator Pear.

Persea *is an ancient Greek name for an Egyptian tree with sweet fruit; the term* americana *means coming from the Americas. The English word* avocado *is a corruption of the Nahuatlan Mexican* ahuacatl, *itself an Aztec shortening of* ahuacacuahatl, *which means testicle tree. The Aztecs explained that their* ahuacatl *was given the name not only because the fruit resembled a testicle and grew in pairs, but because it greatly excited sexual passion. It received its pseudonym* Alligator Pear *due to its rough leathery skin.*

General Information The avocado is originally from southern Mexico and Central America. The first written account of the avocado is contained in the 1526 report of Gonzalo Hernandez de Oviedo, who saw the tree in Colombia near the Isthmus of Panama. Technically a fruit but generally regarded as a vegetable, avocados are the green,usually pear-shaped fruits of a subtropical tree in the laurel family. They become mature on the tree but will not ripen or soften until picked. About five hundred varieties, with great variation in size, shape, and texture, are grown in tropical climates from South America to Australia; only fifty to seventy varieties are grown in the United States. Florida avocados are larger and rounder than their California counterparts, and can often be identified by their bright green, smooth-skinned peels; ounce for ounce, these Florida varieties have about half the fat content of the California varieties, and thus are not as rich or creamy. Of all the varieties, the most common is the Hass, which is a dark green to purple-black, rough-skinned avocado that has a higher oil content than most other varieties. About the size and shape of a pear, they are a light greenish-yellow inside, with a custardy-smooth texture and rich buttery flavor.

Buying Tips Avocados are best purchased firm and allowed to sit out and soften until they yield to gentle pressure. Once ripe, they need to be kept refrigerated or they will over-ripen and turn rancid.

Avocado

Nutritional Value Per 100 g Edible Portion

	California	Florida
Calories	177	112
Protein	2.11 g	1.59 g
Fat	17.33 g	8.87 g
Fiber	2.11 g	2.11 g
Calcium	11 mg	11 mg
Iron	1.18 mg	0.53 mg
Magnesium	41 mg	34 mg
Phosphorus	42 mg	39 mg
Potassium	634 mg	488 mg
Sodium	12 mg	5 mg
Zinc	0.420 mg	0.420 mg
Copper	0.266 mg	0.251 mg
Manganese	0.244 mg	0.170 mg
Beta Carotene (A)	612 IU	612 IU
Thiamine (B_1)	0.108 mg	0.108 mg
Riboflavin (B_2)	0.122 mg	0.122 mg
Niacin (B_3)	1.921 mg	1.921 mg
Pantothenic Acid (B_5)	0.971 mg	0.971 mg
Pyridoxine (B_6)	0.280 mg	0.280 mg
Folic Acid (B_9)	65.5 mcg	53.3 mcg
Ascorbic Acid (C)	7.9 mg	7.9 mg
Tocopherol (E)	1.34 mg	n/a

Culinary Uses Unlike most tree fruits, which are sweet and juicy, avocados are creamy, almost buttery, and have a mild nutty flavor. Generally used as a vegetable, avocados blend well with almost any flavor and mix well with either vegetables or fruit, making them an excellent addition to salads, sandwiches, guacamole, and other dishes. Avocados produce a bland-flavored oil suitable for everything from salad dressings to sautéing, since it has a very high smoke point of 520°F.

Health Benefits The avocado is one of the world's most perfect foods. At their peak, they contain a high amount of fruit oil, a relatively rare element that gives the avocado its smooth mellow taste, nut-like flavor, and high food energy value. They have a perfectly balanced pH, being neither acid nor alkaline, are easily digested, and are very rich in mineral elements that regulate body functions and stimulate growth. Especially noteworthy are its iron and copper contents, which aid in red blood regeneration and the prevention of nutritional anemia. One of the most valuable sources of organic fat and protein, avocados as a regular part of your daily diet will improve hair and skin quality as well as soothe the digestive tract; however, those with liver problems will find it hard to digest due to its fat content. It takes ten avocados to make one teaspoon of pure avocado oil, which can harm the liver, whereas ten avocados in their natural state do no harm to the body. Avocado oil is 11.56 percent saturated, 70.55 percent monounsaturated, and 13.49 percent polyunsaturated.

Bamboo Shoots *(Bambusa, Arundinaria, Dendrocalamus, Phyllostachys)*

The genus name and the English term bamboo *comes from the Malayan word* bambu. Arundinaria *is derived from the Latin term* arundo, *meaning reed-like;* Dendrocalamus *derives from the Greek terms* dendron, *meaning tree, and* calamus, *meaning reed;* Phyllostachys *means spike-leaved.*

Bamboo Shoots

Nutritional Value Per 100 g Edible Portion

	Raw	Cooked
Calories	27	12
Protein	2.60 g	1.53 g
Fat	0.30 g	0.22 g
Fiber	0.70 g	0.65 g
Calcium	13 mg	12 mg
Iron	0.50 mg	0.24 mg
Magnesium	3 mg	3 mg
Phosphorus	59 mg	20 mg
Potassium	533 mg	533 mg
Sodium	4 mg	4 mg
Beta Carotene (A)	20 IU	0 IU
Thiamine (B_1)	0.150 mg	0.020 mg
Riboflavin (B_2)	0.070 mg	0.050 mg
Niacin (B_3)	0.600 mg	0.300 mg
Ascorbic Acid (C)	4 mg	0 mg

General Information Bamboo shoots are literally the shoots—the young, sprouting stems—of a bamboo plant, a type of grass rather than a tree. These new shoots can grow up to a foot in twenty-four hours. Usually cut shortly after they first appear, most bamboo shoots are cone-shaped, six inches to a foot tall, and three inches in diameter. The shoots may also be "hilled"; they are piled with soil as they grow, which prevents the development of the green pigment chlorophyll. Once the tough overlapping sheath is stripped off, the white shoot is ready for eating either raw or cooked.

Culinary Uses The young shoots taste something like sweet, young corn. Fresh whole bamboo shoots should have the outer layer peeled to expose the white flesh. Cut small-diameter shoots into rings one node at a time; cut large shoots into slices. If the shoots are sweet, they are edible raw in salads or with dips as an appetizer. However, most shoots are bitter until parboiled for fifteen to twenty minutes. Change the water after the first ten minutes, and drain shoots when done boiling. The raw shoots deteriorate very quickly, so process or serve them on the day they are harvested. Use as you would any boiled vegetable. Serve along with butter, salt, and pepper, use in stir-fries, or add to casseroles. Their texture and sweetness make them an exotic addition to soups and stews. Be extra careful in preparing fresh shoots, as some varieties are covered with fine sharp hairs that can perforate the intestines if not removed before eating. The canned form are precooked and need only to be heated through after rinsing; however the flavor does not compare in succulence with the fresh variety.

Lore and Legend

The bamboo plant is symbolic of many attributes, including long life, strength and grace, and serves a multitude of functions for the peoples of Asia.

Basella *(Basella alba, B. rubra)*

Also Known As: Ceylon Spinach, Malabar Spinach, Pasali, Pu-tin-choi.

Basella *is the native Malabar name for the plant.* Alba *means white;* rubra *means red. The red variety has leaves, stems, and flowers that are slightly tinged with red or purple.*

General Information Native to India and the tropical regions of the Far East, basella does not withstand frosts and grows poorly, if at all, in cold weather. In tropical regions, the plant is cultivated as both an ornamental and vegetable perennial, while in temperate regions it can be grown as an annual, warm-weather substitute for spinach. This little-known plant shares many of the same characteristics of the beet and spinach family. The more common dark-green variety has round or oval, very thick leaves on vines that grow up to four feet in length. If given climbing supports, the plants will produce clean, grit-free leaves all summer. To harvest, simply cut the tips of the vines, about three to five inches in length.

Culinary Uses Basella's thick, succulent leaves have a flavor much milder than that of chard or turnip tops. Being smooth, they are easy to clean and prepare. Flowers, unless very young, are tough; very old leaves are also undesirable. Asian cooks prepare both leaves and stems as a pot herb, steaming or stir-frying them. The vegetable can also be added to light soups, or mixed with other vegetables. Try it as a substitute in your favorite spinach recipes. Although the odor of the cooking leaves is rather strong, the leaves themselves have a mild, delicate flavor. Take care not to overcook them, or the stems will become somewhat gelatinous.

Health Benefits The leaves are rich in vitamins A and C, and are a good source of calcium and iron.

Bean, Broad/Fava *(Vicia faba)*

Vicia *is a classical name for the vetch (a variety of legume);* faba *comes from the Greek word* phago, *meaning to eat. As its English name suggests, the broad bean is substantial in size.*

General Information The broad bean is considered native to the Mediterranean basin, and is probably the only bean native to the Old World. Seeds have been found in Egypt dating back to between 2400 and 2200 B.C.; a brown Egyptian variety provides the staple named *ful.* A large bean resembling a lima in size and shape, the broad bean is about one and one-quarter inches long, light brown in color, with a dark line running down the ridge where it is split. As a vegetable the broad bean retained its popularity in Europe not only because it could be dried and stored, but because for many centuries it was the only bean readily available. The broad bean was so important that, together with other pulses, from the early Middle Ages onward there was a death sentence for theft from open fields of beans, peas, and lentils. It has remained a favorite throughout the major continents with the exception of North America, where it is just now becoming more available.

Bean, Broad/Fava

Nutritional Value Per 100 g Edible Portion

	Fresh Raw	Fresh Cooked
Calories	72	56
Protein	5.60 g	4.80 g
Fat	0.60 g	0.50 g
Fiber	2.20 g	1.90 g
Calcium	22 mg	18 mg
Iron	1.90 mg	1.50 mg
Magnesium	38 mg	31 mg
Phosphorus	95 mg	73 mg
Potassium	250 mg	193 mg
Sodium	50 mg	41 mg
Beta Carotene (A)	350 IU	270 IU
Thiamine (B_1)	0.170 mg	0.128 mg
Riboflavin (B_2)	0.110 mg	0.090 mg
Niacin (B_3)	1.500 mg	1.200 mg
Ascorbic Acid (C)	33.0 mg	19.8 mg

Buying Tips Look for the smallest, crispest, most evenly green pods, with some discoloration to be expected.

Culinary Uses Young fresh broad beans are usually shelled, but the young pods can sometimes be eaten if tender enough. Young beans can be eaten raw, while older ones are best cooked and added to salads or used as a side vegetable. Try gently stewing them in a little butter, lightly touched with savory, thyme, or sage. Cook large heavy beans longer, then crush to make a purée, adding cream, butter, and a little lemon juice. Unless the beans are very young, they benefit from having their bitter outer layers removed.

Health Benefits See reference under **Legumes.**

Drumstick Bean

Nutritional Value Per 100 g Edible Portion

	Leafy Tips Raw	Leafy Tips Cooked	Pods Raw	Pods Cooked
Calories	64	60	37	36
Protein	9.40 g	5.27 g	2.10 g	2.09 g
Fat	1.40 g	0.93 g	0.20 g	0.19 g
Fiber	1.50 g	1.72 g	1.30 g	1.84 g
Calcium	n/a	n/a	30 mg	20 mg
Iron	4.00 mg	2.32 mg	0.36 mg	0.45 mg
Magnesium	147 mg	151 mg	45 mg	42 mg
Phosphorus	112 mg	67 mg	50 mg	49 mg
Potassium	337 mg	344 mg	461 mg	457 mg
Sodium	9 mg	9 mg	42 mg	43 mg
Beta Carotene (A)	7564 IU	7013 IU	74 IU	70 IU
Thiamine (B_1)	0.257 mg	0.222 mg	0.053 mg	0.046 mg
Riboflavin (B_2)	0.660 mg	0.509 mg	0.074 mg	0.068 mg
Niacin (B_3)	2.220 mg	1.995 mg	0.620 mg	0.590 mg
Pyridoxine (B_6)	1.200 mg	n/a	0.120 mg	n/a
Ascorbic Acid (C)	51.7 mg	31.0 mg	n/a	n/a

Bean, Drumstick

(Moringa oleifera, M. pterygosperma)

Moringa probably derives from the Malayan name murinna. Oleifera *means oil-bearing. The English name* drumstick bean *is due to its drumstick-like shape.*

General Information Native to India, the drumstick bean grows on a small tree in warm, humid climates. The nine-ribbed pods are often 1 1/2 inches long, and contain minute three-angled winged seeds.

Culinary Uses The grated root has a peppery flavor similar to horseradish. The young shoots are succulent, but when purchased outside of their native country tend to be rather tough.

Bean, Green/Snap *(Phaseolus)*

The scientific name Phaseolus *was bestowed in 39* B.C. *by Calumella, who observed that the seeds look like a "small boat."*

General Information Green beans, or snap beans as they are more properly called, are said to be native to Central or South America, and were introduced into Europe in the sixteenth century. Among the most common vegetables grown and eaten in North America, these edible-podded legumes are grown for their pods, which are picked while young and the seeds still small and tender. There are over 150 varieties of green beans in cultivation today, including thick runner beans, the more slender French beans, and the yellow wax bean.

Buying Tips Green beans should be crisp, firm, long, slender, feel velvety, and look fresh and bright-colored. To be at their best, beans should break with a crisp snap and the insides should be fresh and juicy.

Bean, Green/Snap

Nutritional Value Per 100 g Edible Portion

	Raw	Cooked
Calories	31	35
Protein	1.82 g	1.89 g
Fat	0.12 g	0.28 g
Fiber	1.10 g	1.43 g
Calcium	37 mg	46 mg
Iron	1.04 mg	1.28 mg
Magnesium	25 mg	25 mg
Phosphorus	38 mg	39 mg
Potassium	209 mg	299 mg
Sodium	6 mg	3 mg
Zinc	0.240 mg	0.360 mg
Copper	0.069 mg	0.103 mg
Manganese	0.214 mg	0.294 mg
Beta Carotene (A)	668 IU	666 IU
Thiamine (B_1)	0.084 mg	0.074 mg
Riboflavin (B_2)	0.105 mg	0.097 mg
Niacin (B_3)	0.752 mg	0.614 mg
Pantothenic Acid (B_5)	0.094 mg	0.074 mg
Pyridoxine (B_6)	0.074 mg	0.056 mg
Folic Acid (B_9)	36.5 mcg	33.3 mcg
Ascorbic Acid (C)	16.3 mg	9.7 mg
Tocopherol (E)	0.020 mg	n/a

Lore and Legend

Up until the nineteenth century, snap beans had strings along their pods, just as other members of the bean family do. In the varieties grown specifically for their seeds (Great Northern and Navy beans, for example), this tough line of fiber was useful because it acted as a seam that split and released the plump, edible beans inside. However, in the kinds of beans eaten pod and all, the strings served no useful purpose and detracted from the vegetables' appeal. In the late 1800s, American plant scientists became interested in the "stringiness" problem and set to work to build a better green bean. One pioneer researcher of the period succeeded in producing nine different types, all tasty and "stringless." Over time, other experts followed up with improvements of their own, and today all snap beans are stringless at the harvesting stage.

Culinary Uses Boiled, steamed, stir-fried, or sautéed, green beans can be eaten cold in salads, as a vegetable in their own right, or added to savory dishes and quiches. The heirloom varieties of beans have strings that need to be removed prior to cooking; this is a time-consuming process, but the heirloom varieties are generally more flavorful.

Health Benefits Beans, with their abundance of potassium, supply the alkaline needs of the pancreas and salivary glands. The yellow or wax bean is considered inferior to the green bean in nutritional value.

Bean, Winged *(Psophocarpus tetragonolobus)*

Also Known As: Asparagus Pea, Goa Bean.

Winged beans were given the botanical name Psophocarpus *from the Greek words for noise and fruit, referring to the fact that the pods, when gathered and laid in the sun, inflate and explode with a loud noise. The term* tetragonolobus *means it has a four-angled pod. The English term* winged *refers to the bean's winged flares.*

General Information Grown almost exclusively in tropical southeast Asia, New Guinea, the Philippines, and Ghana, the winged bean is a tropical climbing plant that has had a long use as a staple legume in those countries and was virtually unknown in the rest of the world until 1975. A twining vine, it grows to over three meters when supported, and continuously bears pods once mature. The pods have four longitudinal jagged "wings," and contain up to twenty seeds weighing about 3 grams each. The smooth, shiny seeds may be white, brown, black, or mottled. The winged bean is cultivated largely for its decorative young, tender pods, which are picked when no more than one or two inches long, and then sliced and cooked like green beans.

Buying Tips Choose the smallest pods for the best flavor, those in which seeds have not yet developed, and then cook immediately, for they wilt and collapse within a few days.

Culinary Uses The whole plant is edible—seeds, tubers, leaves, and flowers. Young leaves and shoots are said to taste like spinach; the flowers are sweetened by nectar and resemble mushrooms in flavor when lightly sautéed. The immature seeds within the young pods taste like a cross between garden peas and asparagus; when mature, the seeds must be cooked before eating and are usually roasted and eaten like peanuts. Cooked beans have a flavor between that of a string bean and a shell bean: meatier, blander, and starchier-tasting than string beans, but crunchier and greener-flavored than a shell bean. Winged beans can be used in any manner you would string beans—they do well in soups or stir-fries, are good boiled as a side dish, or pickled. The seeds can also be ground into flour for

Bean, Winged

Nutritional Value Per 100 g Edible Portion

	Beans Fresh, Raw	Beans Fresh, Cooked	Beans Dried, Raw	Beans Dried, Cooked	Leaves Raw	Tuber Raw
Calories	49	38	409	147	74	159
Protein	6.95 g	5.31 g	29.65 g	10.62 g	5.85 g	11.60 g
Fat	0.87 g	0.66 g	16.32 g	5.84 g	1.10 g	0.90 g
Fiber	2.57 g	1.38 g	6.85 g	2.45 g	2.50 g	7.40 g
Calcium	84 mg	61 mg	440 mg	142 mg	224 mg	30 mg
Iron	1.50 mg	1.09 mg	13.44 mg	4.33 mg	4.00 mg	2.00 mg
Magnesium	34 mg	30 mg	179 mg	54 mg	8 mg	n/a
Phosphorus	37 mg	25 mg	451 mg	153 mg	63 mg	45 mg
Potassium	223 mg	274 mg	977 mg	280 mg	176 mg	n/a
Sodium	4 mg	4 mg	38 mg	13 mg	n/a	n/a
Beta Carotene (A)	128 IU	88 IU	0 IU	0 IU	n/a	n/a
Thiamine (B_1)	0.140 mg	0.086 mg	1.030 mg	0.295 mg	n/a	n/a
Riboflavin (B_2)	0.100 mg	0.072 mg	0.450 mg	0.129 mg	n/a	n/a
Niacin (B_3)	0.900 mg	0.652 mg	3.090 mg	0.830 mg	n/a	n/a
Pyridoxine (B_6)	0.113 mg	0.082 mg	0.175 mg	0.047 mg	n/a	n/a
Folic Acid (B_9)	n/a	n/a	44.6 mcg	10.4 mcg	n/a	n/a
Ascorbic Acid (C)	n/a	9.8 mg	0 mg	0 mg	n/a	n/a

bread, pressed to yield an edible oil, or sprouted and turned into bean curd. The protein-rich roots are not wasted either, with the immature tuberous roots eaten like potatoes.

Health Benefits Winged beans have an exceedingly high nutritional value very similar to that of soybeans. The seeds are rich in tocopherol, an antioxidant that increases vitamin A use in the human body.

Bean, Yard-Long *(Vigna unguiculata sesquipedalis)*

Also Known As: Asparagus Bean, Chinese Long Bean, Pea Bean, Dow Gok.

> *This genus was named* Vigna *in honor of Dominic Vigni, a Paduan commentator on Theophrastus in the seventeenth century. The term* unguiculata *means clawed or claw-like, while* sesquipedalis *means a foot and a half in length, its normal length when picked for cooking. The English name* yard-long bean *comes from its pod, which on occasions will reach up to a yard in length.*

General Information A native of Asia and other semitropical regions, the climbing herbaceous yard-long bean is a close relative of the black-eyed pea. Of the several varieties, the two most common contain black or red beans. With stalks that reach up to twelve feet in height, the plants produce very long, pliable, stringbean-like pods. The beans are generally sold in their immature stage, when they are between eighteen and twenty-four inches in length. Several varieties of long bean are eaten in Asia, as are the leaves and the mature beans.

Buying Tips Purchase pods that are pencil-thin and firm, in which the peas have not matured. They will be comparatively flexible, but should not appear dry or overly limp.

Bean, Yard-Long

Nutritional Value Per 100 g Edible Portion

	Fresh Raw	Fresh Cooked	Dried Raw	Dried Cooked
Calories	47	47	347	118
Protein	2.80 g	2.53 g	24.33 g	8.29 g
Fat	0.40 g	0.10 g	1.31 g	0.45 g
Fiber	n/a	1.51 g	4.77 g	1.62 g
Calcium	50 mg	44 mg	138 mg	42 mg
Iron	0.47 mg	0.98 mg	8.61 mg	2.64 mg
Magnesium	44 mg	42 mg	338 mg	98 mg
Phosphorus	59 mg	57 mg	559 mg	181 mg
Potassium	240 mg	290 mg	1157 mg	315 mg
Sodium	4 mg	4 mg	17 mg	5 mg
Zinc	n/a	n/a	3.500 mg	1.080 mg
Copper	n/a	n/a	0.879 mg	0.225 mg
Manganese	n/a	n/a	1.590 mg	0.487 mg
Beta Carotene (A)	865 IU	450 IU	52 IU	16 IU
Thiamine (B_1)	0.107 mg	0.085 mg	0.887 mg	0.212 mg
Riboflavin (B_2)	0.110 mg	0.099 mg	0.235 mg	0.064 mg
Niacin (B_3)	0.410 mg	0.630 mg	2.158 mg	0.551 mg
Pantothenic Acid (B_5)	n/a	n/a	1.556 mg	0.398 mg
Pyridoxine (B_6)	n/a	n/a	0.371 mg	0.095 mg
Folic Acid (B_9)	n/a	n/a	657.9 mcg	145.7 mcg
Ascorbic Acid (C)	18.8 mg	16.2 mg	1.6 mg	0.4 mg

Culinary Uses Yard-long beans are not crisp and sweet like fresh common green beans, but have a crunch that is solid but not juicy, and a flavor that is leguminous, reminiscent of asparagus combined with peas. The paler variety cooks up to become somewhat sweeter and meatier than the deeper-colored, which tends to be more fibrous and less delicate. When treated as a green bean—steamed or boiled—the taste is pleasant, though not spectacular. However, the bean is perfect for sautés and stir-frying, which brings out the best of its texture and flavor, especially when combined with the rich flavors and textures of ginger, nuts, fermented black beans, garlic, assertive herbs, or chili peppers.

Beet *(Beta vulgaris)*

The beet is said to get its botanical name Beta *from the Greek letter* beta, *because the swollen root was thought to more or less resemble it. The term* vulgaris *means common or vulgar. The English word* beet *derives from the French word* bete, *meaning beast, because the vegetable reminded early cooks of a bleeding animal when it was cut open.*

General Information The beet is descended from a wild slender-rooted plant that grew abundantly in southern Europe, especially in sandy soil near seacoasts. A member of the ubiquitous goosefoot family, beets are related to chard, spinach, sugar beets, and quinoa.

There are actually four types of beets: the garden beet; the "leaf" beet (also called chard); the sugarbeet, which is processed into refined sugar; and the mangold beet, grown mostly in Europe for cattle feed. Beets with rounded roots, like those we eat today, are a comparatively recent variety, propagated in northerm Europe in about the sixteenth century. Red beet and white chard were both known to the ancients, but only the leaves were used for culinary purposes, while the root was employed medicinally.

Buying Tips Fresh, first-quality beets should have a good globular shape, with smooth, firm flesh and a deep red color. Size or shape do not matter in selection, but avoid those

Beet

Nutritional Value Per 100 g Edible Portion

	Beet Raw	Beet Cooked	Greens Raw	Greens Cooked
Calories	44	31	19	27
Protein	1.48 g	1.06 g	1.82 g	2.57 g
Fat	0.14 g	0.05 g	0.06 g	0.20 g
Fiber	0.80 g	0.85 g	1.30 g	1.05 g
Calcium	16 mg	11 mg	119 mg	114 mg
Iron	0.91 mg	0.62 mg	3.30 mg	1.90 mg
Magnesium	21 mg	37 mg	72 mg	68 mg
Phosphorus	48 mg	31 mg	40 mg	41 mg
Potassium	324 mg	312 mg	547 mg	909 mg
Sodium	72 mg	49 mg	201 mg	241 mg
Zinc	0.370 mg	0.250 mg	0.380 mg	0.500 mg
Copper	0.083 mg	0.057 mg	0.191 mg	0.251 mg
Manganese	0.352 mg	0.240 mg	n/a	n/a
Beta Carotene (A)	20 IU	13 IU	6100 IU	5100 IU
Thiamine (B_1)	0.050 mg	0.031 mg	0.100 mg	0.117 mg
Riboflavin (B_2)	0.020 mg	0.014 mg	0.220 mg	0.289 mg
Niacin (B_3)	0.400 mg	0.273 mg	0.400 mg	0.499 mg
Pantothenic Acid (B_5)	0.150 mg	0.097 mg	0.250 mg	0.329 mg
Pyridoxine (B_6)	0.046 mg	0.031 mg	0.106 mg	0.132 mg
Folic Acid (B_9)	92.6 mcg	53.2 mcg	n/a	n/a
Ascorbic Acid (C)	11.0 mg	5.5 mg	30.0 mg	24.9 mg
Tocopherol (E)	n/a	n/a	1.50 mg	n/a

that can be identified by a short neck, deep scars, or several circles of leaf scars around the top of the beet, as they have remained in the ground too long and are liable to be tough and woody.

Culinary Uses Beets, with their distinctive ruby-red coloring and sweet earthy flavor, complement many foods. Freshly cooked beets have a flavor much superior to that of canned beets, with which most people are all too familiar; try them freshly prepared at home and see if perhaps you like beets after all. Beets can be shredded raw into salads, pickled, boiled, baked, or added to soups such as the popular Russian borscht. The leaves are also edible and make a great side dish either sautéed or steamed, or they can be shredded and added to fresh garden salads.

Health Benefits One of nature's best bodily cleansers, beets will help dissolve and eliminate acid crystals from the kidneys, eliminate blood toxemia, which causes varicose veins, build strong blood by enriching the red corpuscles, detoxify the liver and gallbladder, and eliminate pocket acid material in the bowel. Since beets lubricate the intestines, they are recommended for constipation. For most people, beets also have the propensity to turn bodily waste products bright pink or red, as the group of pigments known as betacyanin are not easily metabolized. Beet greens are higher in nutritional value than beet roots, but the cooked greens have a high content of oxalic acid, and so moderation is advised.

Bitter Melon *(Momordica charantia)*

Also Known As: Carilla Fruit, Kareli, Balsam Pear, Bitter Cucumber.

> Momordica *comes from the Latin* momordi *and* mordeo *meaning to bite, since the seeds appear to have been bitten;* charantia *is a pre-Linnaean name. The English name* bitter melon *is appropriate, since this fruit is distinctly bitter.*

General Information This warty-skinned melon is not a true melon, but rather an immature summer squash shaped like an Anaheim pepper. Native to tropical Asia and Africa, this climbing plant produces fruits up to eight inches in length with lumpy, ridged skin the color of pale jade and which turns yellow or orange when ripe. Its flesh is the same tone, only lighter, and contains brown seeds. Generally it is eaten in its unripe state. This classic Chinese and East Indian vegetable is rarely seen in grocery stores, but can be grown easily in most home gardens and yards.

Bitter Melon

Nutritional Value Per 100 g Edible Portion

	Leafy Tips Raw	Leafy Tips Cooked	Pods Raw	Pods Cooked
Calories	30	35	17	19
Protein	5.30 g	3.60 g	1.00 g	0.84 g
Fat	0.69 g	0.20 g	0.17 g	0.18 g
Fiber	2.28 g	1.87 g	1.40 g	1.05 g
Calcium	84 mg	42 mg	19 mg	9 mg
Iron	2.04 mg	1.02 mg	0.43 mg	0.38 mg
Magnesium	85 mg	94 mg	17 mg	16 mg
Phosphorus	99 mg	77 mg	31 mg	36 mg
Potassium	608 mg	602 mg	296 mg	319 mg
Sodium	11 mg	13 mg	5 mg	6 mg
Beta Carotene (A)	1734 IU	1733 IU	380 IU	113 IU
Thiamine (B_1)	0.181 mg	0.147 mg	0.040 mg	0.051 mg
Riboflavin (B_2)	0.362 mg	0.282 mg	0.040 mg	0.053 mg
Niacin (B_3)	1.110 mg	0.995 mg	0.400 mg	0.280 mg
Folic Acid (B_9)	n/a	87.6 mcg	72.0 mcg	n/a
Ascorbic Acid (C)	88.0 mg	55.6 mg	84.0 mg	33.0 mg

Buying Tips Choose small melons that are firm and not shriveled, free from blemishes or damage. The younger the melon the less bitter it is; the least bitter are between three and four inches in length. Most people consider the fruits inedible once they start to turn yellow.

Culinary Uses Although the bitter melon is a popular ingredient in Indian and Asian cookery, it is a novelty food for most Americans. As its name implies, the bitter melon is indeed bitter; in fact, it is advisable to first soak it in salted water, boil it lightly, and then discard the water before continuing to cook it further. The flesh is soft when cooked, somewhat like that of summer squash, and has a definite bitter taste due to the presence of quinine. If you like quinine water or strong beer, you will probably like bitter melon. It goes well in stir-fries, soups, or baked vegetable dishes. Pieces of bitter melon are a common ingredient in Indian pickles and are sometimes used in curries. The tender shoots and leaves can be cooked as a kind of spinach.

Health Benefits Bitter melon was originally an Asian medicine believed to purify the blood, and the leaves were used to treat sore-eyed elephants. It contains a compound known as charantin that is more potent than the drug tolbutamide, which is often used in the treatment of diabetes to lower blood-sugar levels. Bitter melon also contains an insulin-like compound referred to as polypeptide-P or vegetable insulin. Since polypeptide-P and bitter melon appear to have fewer side effects than insulin, they have been suggested as replacements for insulin in some patients. The ripe fruit has been shown to exhibit some rather profound anticancer effects, especially in leukemia. The ripe seeds are reputedly a purgative.

Bottle Gourd (*Lagenaria siceraria*)

Also Known As: Doodhi, Calabash Gourd.

> Lagenaria *comes from the Latin* lagena, *meaning large flask. This vegetable is called the* bottle gourd *because when dried it is scooped out and used as a container.*

General Information Native to tropical regions, the bottle gourd now grows in temperate zones, either wild or grown commercially. It is a climbing annual vine reaching up to forty feet in length, clinging to whatever will support it. The gourds are of various shapes and interesting colors, giving rise to the ornamental uses for which many people acquire them. The narrow necks of gourds have made excellent tobacco pipes, while the rounded

Bottle Gourd

Nutritional Value Per 100 g Edible Portion

	Raw	Cooked
Calories	14	15
Protein	0.62 g	0.60 g
Fat	0.02 g	0.02 g
Fiber	0.56 g	0.63 g
Calcium	26 mg	24 mg
Iron	0.20 mg	0.25 mg
Magnesium	11 mg	11 mg
Phosphorus	13 mg	13 mg
Potassium	150 mg	170 mg
Sodium	2 mg	2 mg
Zinc	0.70 mg	n/a
Beta Carotene (A)	0 IU	0 IU
Thiamine (B_1)	0.029 mg	0.029 mg
Riboflavin (B_2)	0.022 mg	0.022 mg
Niacin (B_3)	0.320 mg	0.390 mg
Pyridoxine (B_6)	0.040 mg	n/a
Folic Acid (B_9)	5.9 mcg	n/a
Ascorbic Acid (C)	10.1 mg	8.5 mg

bodies have been used for dippers, cups, pitchers, or any other kind of cooking utensil. Various Indian tribes used mature gourds as rattles for dances and ceremonies, since the seeds in mature gourds rattle. The bottle gourd usually resembles a large pale-green cucumber, and has been cultivated for so long that its exact origins are unknown. Because it dries out so well, it can be preserved indefinitely, and remains of it have been found in Mexico dating from 7000 B.C., and in Egypt dating from 4000 B.C.

Buying Tips Choose gourds that are free from blemishes and not withered.

Culinary Uses Only the young fruits with their comparatively soft shells are eaten. The bottle gourd has a bland flavor and is a useful vegetable for adding to stews and curries. To cook, peel and remove any large seeds. It is available summer through autumn.

Broccoli (*Brassica oleracea, Italica* group)

The Latin name Brassica *derives from the Celtic* bresic*, and although the Romans are usually credited with introducing it into Europe, it is possible that the Celts preceded them. The term* oleracea *refers to a vegetable garden herb that is used in cooking;* italica *means Italian or coming from Italy. The English name* broccoli *derives from the Italian plural diminutive of* brocco*, which means arm, branch, or shoot (and which itself derives from the Latin* braccium*).*

General Information Broccoli was developed from cabbage ancestry by the Etruscans, wizards of edible horticulture. Closely related to cauliflower, broccoli has thick stems that branch into clusters of flower buds. Although commercially grown in France and Italy in the sixteenth century, broccoli was not well known in the United States until 1923, when the D'Arrigo Brothers Company made a trial planting of Italian sprouting broccoli in California. A few crates were sent to Boston, and by 1925 the market was well established. Sprouting broccoli is the most familiar variety, but others such as Calabrese, Chinese, and heading are also available.

Buying Tips Look for fresh green color in the heads, leaves, and stems. Stalks should be tender and firm, with compact buds. Overly mature broccoli will give itself away by yellow "flowers" showing inside the buds.

Culinary Uses Florets, stalks, and leaves are all edible and have an excellent yet cabbage-related taste that is all their own. Fresh broccoli does not keep very long, so use immediately. If the lower portion of the stalk is tough and woody, and if the bud clusters

Broccoli

Nutritional Value Per 100 g Edible Portion

	Raw	Cooked
Calories	28	28
Protein	2.98 g	2.98 g
Fat	0.35 g	0.35 g
Fiber	1.11 g	1.11 g
Calcium	48 mg	46 mg
Iron	0.88 mg	0.84 mg
Magnesium	25 mg	24 mg
Phosphorus	66 mg	59 mg
Potassium	325 mg	292 mg
Sodium	27 mg	26 mg
Zinc	0.400 mg	0.380 mg
Copper	0.045 mg	0.043 mg
Manganese	0.229 mg	0.218 mg
Beta Carotene (A)	3,000 IU	1,388 IU
Thiamine (B_1)	0.065 mg	0.055 mg
Riboflavin (B_2)	0.119 mg	0.113 mg
Niacin (B_3)	0.638 mg	0.574 mg
Pantothenic Acid (B_5)	0.535 mg	0.508 mg
Pyridoxine (B_6)	0.159 mg	0.143 mg
Folic Acid (B_9)	71.0 mcg	50.0 mcg
Ascorbic Acid (C)	93.2 mg	74.6 mg
Tocopherol (E)	0.46 mg	n/a

are open and yellow, the broccoli is overmature and will be tough. Raw broccoli florets are excellent added to salads or used for vegetable dip platters; steamed broccoli goes well with most any dish; stalks can be peeled and cut or shredded for sautéed vegetable dishes, soups, or casseroles. The leaves may be prepared like other greens such as chard or spinach.

Health Benefits Raw broccoli contains almost as much calcium as whole milk, and is linked to lowering the risk of cancer. It is best if undercooked; the more green that is left in broccoli, the more chlorophyll will be left to counteract the sulphur compounds that form gas. Broccoli contains abundant pantothenic acid (B_5) and vitamin A, which benefit rough skin. All *Brassica*-genus vegetables contain dithiolthiones, a group of compounds that have anti-cancer, antioxidant properties; indoles, substances that protect against breast and colon cancer; sulphur, which has antibiotic and antiviral characteristics; and lutein and zeaxanthin, pigments that protect plants (and thus indirectly humans) from the harmful effects of photo-oxidation by filtering out visible blue light. This family of vegetables also mildly stimulates the liver and other tissues out of stagnancy.

Broccoli Raab *(Brassica oleracea rapa, B. rapa parachinensis, B. campestris)*

Also Known As: Rape, Rapini, Cima di Rapa, Choy Sum, Turnip Tops.

The Latin name Brassica *derives from the Celtic* bresic, *and although the Romans are usually credited with introducing it into Europe, it is possible that the Celts preceded them. The term* oleracea *refers to a vegetable garden herb that is used in cooking,* rapa *is from the Latin for turnip,* parachinensis *means coming from near China, and* campestris *means of the fields or plains. The English name* broccoli *derives from the Italian plural diminutive of* brocco, *which means arm, branch, or shoot.*

General Information Resembling thin, leafy, sparsely budded broccoli stalks, broccoli raab is the tender shoot of the wintered-over turnip. A hardy biennial, the turnip produces a well-developed root and/or luxuriant leaves the first year; then the leaves die back, and the root gradually gets less succulent and more woody. Come spring, the plant sends up a pulpy and juicy stem with a seedpod at its tip. This sprout grows to twelve inches or so before flowering, its tip resembling a miniature head of broccoli. The dark, bluish-green stems with their flat bright green leaves and small tassel of little yellow flowers taste best when six to eight inches long, since the longer, older shoots will be thick and tough at the base.

Buying Tips Broccoli raab should be dark forest green, succulent looking, not wilted, and the stalks should not be overly fat or they will be tough. There may be some flowering buds, but most should be closed.

Culinary Uses As it varies between slightly bitter and ferociously acerbic, one would never call broccoli raab mild. Very pungent, it has hints of spinach,broccoli, collards, and mustard greens, with pleasantly sour or tart notes. Stalk, leaf, and flowers can all be used in the same manner as cabbage and kale, adding zest to bland dishes and holding its own with stronger-flavored ones. The leaves, when properly cooked, are delightfully tender and leave a fresh, brisk taste on the palate. When steamed, broccoli raab should be cooked slowly and until just tender, and then served with a drizzle of olive oil, a squirt of lemon juice, and fresh ground pepper.

Health Benefits Broccoli raab is beneficial to the heart, lungs, and intestines. All *Brassica*-genus vegetables contain dithiolthiones, a group of compounds that have anti-cancer, antioxidant properties; indoles, substances that protect against breast and colon cancer; and sulphur, which has antibiotic and antiviral characteristics. This family of vegetables also mildly stimulates the liver and other tissues out of stagnancy. Low in fat, and high in fiber, potassium, calcium, and vitamins A and C.

Brussels Sprouts (*Brassica oleracea, Gemmifera* group)

Its Latin name Brassica *derives from the Celtic* bresic. *The term* oleracea *refers to a vegetable garden herb which is used in cooking; the term* gemmifera, *meaning diamond maker, comes from their reputed ability to enhance mental prowess. These little cabbages carry the name* Brussels *because they were first grown in Brussels, Belgium.*

General Information A relative newcomer to the cabbage family, Brussels sprouts are generally believed to have evolved from a variety of Savoy cabbage during the seventeenth or eighteenth century. One of the few vegetables to have originated in northern Europe, this vegetable is one of the weirdest looking plants in a garden: twenty to forty "baby cabbages" grow in spiral fashion on a tall-stemmed stalk which instead of a single large head at the end of the stalk, sprouts numerous small heads along its stem. Simply plucked off the stem as they mature, these pale green nubbins are prized for their miniature shape and mild cabbage flavor.

Buying Tips The smaller the sprout, the better the flavor, with the best size being no greater than 1 1/2 inches in diameter, compact, and bright green; old or overly large Brussels sprouts have a disagreeable and bitter flavor. Good sprouts are firm, fresh-looking, and of good green color. Puffy, soft sprouts are usually inferior in quality and flavor, and leaves that are wilted or yellow indicate aging.

Brussels Sprouts

Nutritional Value Per 100 g Edible Portion

	Raw	Cooked
Calories	43	39
Protein	3.38 g	2.55 g
Fat	0.30 g	0.51 g
Fiber	1.51 g	1.37 g
Calcium	42 mg	36 mg
Iron	1.40 mg	1.20 mg
Magnesium	23 mg	20 mg
Phosphorus	69 mg	56 mg
Potassium	389 mg	317 mg
Sodium	25 mg	21 mg
Zinc	0.420 mg	0.330 mg
Copper	0.070 mg	0.083 mg
Manganese	0.337 mg	0.227 mg
Beta Carotene (A)	883 IU	719 IU
Thiamine (B_1)	0.139 mg	0.107 mg
Riboflavin (B_2)	0.090 mg	0.080 mg
Niacin (B_3)	0.745 mg	0.607 mg
Pantothenic Acid (B_5)	0.309 mg	0.252 mg
Pyridoxine (B_6)	0.219 mg	0.178 mg
Folic Acid (B_9)	61.1 mcg	60.0 mcg
Ascorbic Acid (C)	85.0 mg	62.0 mg
Tocopherol (E)	0.88 mg	0.85 mg

Culinary Uses The flavor of Brussels sprouts is hearty and nutlike. Their flavor actually improves with a frost, so they are a favored fall and winter food. Young, tender sprouts can be eaten raw; lengthwise slices, which reveal an attractive cross section, are suitable for salads or for dipping. They can also be steamed as a side vegetable, but their flavor will easily overshadow very mild or delicate foods. They are best paired with flavorful foods such as sharp cheese or assertive seasonings.

Health Benefits Brussels sprouts are rich in alkalizing elements, with specific affinity for the pancreas, and help reduce the risk of cancer, especially colon cancer. All *Brassica*-genus vegetables contain dithiolthiones, a group of compounds that have anti-cancer, antioxidant properties; indoles, substances that protect against breast and colon cancer; and sulphur, which has antibiotic and antiviral characteristics. This family of vegetables also mildly stimulates the liver and other tissues out of stagnancy.

Burdock Root (*Arctium lappa*)

Also Known As: Gobo, Great Burdock, Beggar's Button.

> Arctium *is derived from the Greek* arktos, *meaning a bear, an allusion to the roughness of the burrs;* lappa *comes either from a word meaning to seize, or from the Celtic* llap, *meaning a hand, on account of its prehensile properties. The English name* burdock *is a combination of* bur*—from the Latin* burra, *meaning a lock of wool, such as is often found entangled with it when sheep have passed by—and* dock, *Old English for plant.*

General Information This Siberian native is cultivated primarily in Japan under the name of gobo, but thrives throughout many parts of the world as a common weed. The long, thin taproot is unbelievably difficult to dig, as it penetrates deep into the soil and clings tenaciously. The skin of the root is brown, while its somewhat fibrous flesh is white.

Buying Tips Choose soil-covered specimens that are firm and relatively crisp, like a fresh carrot, not limp and bendable like an old one. Store for a few days at most, wrapped in a damp cloth or paper towel in the refrigerator.

Culinary Uses Burdock has the rich, heady aroma of freshly dug earth, while its delicious, earthy flavor is very similar to that of artichoke hearts or salsify. Never used raw, the rather fibrous root is first peeled, and then slivered or cut into chips and added to delicate soups, stews, vegetables, and bean or grain dishes, where it adds a pleasantly chewy texture and subtly sweet taste. It may also be cooked in the same manner as carrots, but allow a longer cooking time. This plant is also used as an herb (see reference under Herbs, Spices, and Other Foods).

Health Benefits Burdock is esteemed for its blood-purifying qualities and for strengthening the kidneys and sexual organs.

Burdock Root

Nutritional Value Per 100 g Edible Portion

	Raw	Cooked
Calories	72	88
Protein	1.53 g	2.09 g
Fat	0.15 g	0.14 g
Fiber	1.94 g	1.83 g
Calcium	41 mg	49 mg
Iron	0.80 mg	0.77 mg
Magnesium	38 mg	39 mg
Phosphorus	51 mg	93 mg
Potassium	308 mg	360 mg
Sodium	5 mg	4 mg
Beta Carotene (A)	0 IU	0 IU
Thiamine (B_1)	0.010 mg	0.039 mg
Riboflavin (B_2)	0.030 mg	0.058 mg
Niacin (B_3)	0.300 mg	0.320 mg
Ascorbic Acid (C)	3.0 mg	n/a

Cabbage *(Brassica oleracea capitata)*

The Latin name Brassica *derives from the Celtic* bresic. *The term* oleracea *refers to a vegetable garden herb that is used in cooking;* capitata *means headed or capitate. The origin of the English name* cabbage *comes from the Latin* caput *meaning head, because of its head-shaped form.*

General Information Cabbage is one of the most ancient vegetables; there is evidence that it has been in cultivation for more than 4,000 years, and has been domesticated for at least 2,500 years. The modern-day cabbage developed from a wild variety brought to Europe from Asia by roving bands of Celtic people around 600 B.C. Cabbage spread as a food crop throughout northern Europe because it was well adapted to growing in cooler climates, had high yields per acre, and could be stored over the winter in cold cellars. It became immensely popular among the ancient Greeks and Romans, although the cabbage eaten then seems to have been a non-heading variety with loose leaves. During the Middle Ages, farmers in northern Europe developed compact-headed varieties with overlapping leaves that were capable of thriving in cold climates, and people who had little else to eat came to rely upon this sturdy vegetable to survive the harsh winters. Brought to the Americas by the French navigator Jacques Cartier in 1536, cabbage has been cultivated here ever since in many varieties. Centuries of cultivation have produced other forms of the cabbage family, including kale, kohlrabi, cauliflower, broccoli, and Brussels sprouts.

Lore and Legend

The Romans claimed that their prized cabbages originated either from the sweat of Jupiter, shed while nervously attempting to explain away the rival pronouncements of a pair of opposing oracles, or from the tears of Lycurgus, King of the Edonians, unluckily apprehended by the god Dionysus in the shortsighted act of tearing up the sacred grapevines. While trussed and awaiting his unspeakable punishment, Lycurgus wept profusely, and with good reason. Dionysus, not known as "the raging god" for nothing, first blinded Lycurgus and then tore him limb from limb. Meanwhile, Lycurgus's tears, which had fallen to the ground, sprang up as cabbages. As revered in Greece and Rome as the onion in Egypt, and so sacred that one swore oaths on it, cabbages were considered a panacea for all ills. The Roman consul Cato the Elder, in the second century B.C., attributed such mystical powers to cabbages that he believed men could live solely on them as a diet. He remained convinced even after his wife and son died, his cabbages unable to cure their illnesses. The Emperor Claudius (a glutton and drunkard, but no gourmet) once convoked the Senate to vote on the question of whether any dish surpassed corned beef and cabbage; the Senate dutifully responded that none did. The pharaohs of Egypt considered cabbage an aid to drinking and ate large quantities of cooked cabbage before their drinking bouts on the premise that this would enable them to imbibe more beer and wine without succumbing. The world's largest cabbage was grown by William Collingwood of County Durham, England, in 1865, and weighed in at 123 pounds.

Buying Tips When selecting, look for heads that are compact and of reasonable size, with leaves that are tender, not withered or puffy, and not damaged by shipping or insects.

Culinary Uses The economical cabbage has a crisp texture and strong flavor. Raw cabbage can be cut into wedges for an appetizer, or shredded for salads, with leafy types torn like lettuce rather than shredded. Cabbage can also be steamed, boiled, stir-fried, or made into the infamous German sauerkraut or Russian cabbage soup. Red cabbage reacts like litmus paper when cooked—it turns blue in the presence of an alkali (i.e., the lime in tap water), so if you want to preserve the color, some type of acid (i.e., vinegar) needs to be added.

Health Benefits Cabbage, both red and green, is one of the least expensive of the vitamin-protective foods, and one of the most healthful. Raw cabbage detoxifies the stomach and upper bowels of putrefactive wastes, thereby improving digestive efficiency and facilitating rapid elimination. It also works to alkalinize the body, stimulate the immune system, kill harmful bacteria and

Cabbage

Nutritional Value Per 100 g Edible Portion

	Green Raw	Green Cooked	Red Raw	Red Cooked	Savoy Raw	Savoy Cooked
Calories	24	21	27	21	27	24
Protein	1.21 g	0.96 g	1.39 g	1.05 g	2.00 g	1.80 g
Fat	0.18 g	0.25 g	0.26 g	0.20 g	0.10 g	0.09 g
Fiber	0.80 g	0.60 g	1.00 g	0.76 g	0.80 g	0.70 g
Calcium	47 mg	33 mg	51 mg	37 mg	35 mg	30 mg
Iron	0.56 mg	0.39 mg	0.49 mg	0.35 mg	0.40 mg	0.38 mg
Magnesium	15 mg	15 mg	15 mg	11 mg	28 mg	24 mg
Phosphorus	23 mg	25 mg	42 mg	29 mg	42 mg	33 mg
Potassium	246 mg	205 mg	206 mg	140 mg	230 mg	184 mg
Sodium	18 mg	19 mg	11 mg	8 mg	28 mg	24 mg
Zinc	0.180 mg	0.160 mg	0.210 mg	0.150 mg	n/a	n/a
Copper	0.023 mg	0.028 mg	0.097 mg	0.069 mg	n/a	n/a
Manganese	0.159 mg	0.129 mg	0.180 mg	0.129 mg	n/a	n/a
Beta Carotene (A)	126 IU	86 IU	40 IU	27 IU	1,000 IU	889 IU
Thiamine (B_1)	0.050 mg	0.057 mg	0.050 mg	0.034 mg	0.070 mg	0.051 mg
Riboflavin (B_2)	0.030 mg	0.055 mg	0.030 mg	0.020 mg	0.030 mg	0.020 mg
Niacin (B_3)	0.300 mg	0.230 mg	0.300 mg	0.200 mg	0.300 mg	0.024 mg
Pantothenic Acid (B_5)	0.140 mg	0.063 mg	0.324 mg	0.220 mg	n/a	n/a
Pyridoxine (B_6)	0.095 mg	0.064 mg	0.210 mg	0.140 mg	0.190 mg	0.152 mg
Folic Acid (B_9)	56.7 mcg	20.3 mcg	20.7 mcg	12.6 mcg	n/a	n/a
Ascorbic Acid (C)	47.3 mg	24.3 mg	57.0 mg	34.4 mg	31.0 mg	17.0 mg
Tocopherol (E)	1.67 mg	n/a	n/a	n/a	n/a	n/a

viruses, soothe and heal ulcers, help prevent cancer, and clear up the complexion. Raw, saltless sauerkraut is excellent for cleansing and rejuvenating the digestive tract, and promotes better nutrient absorption as well as the growth of healthful (acidophilus) intestinal flora. For those lacking body heat, cabbage's sulphur and iron content will improve circulation. Cabbage contains iodine and is a rich source of vitamin C; the outer leaves are concentrated in vitamin E and contain at least a third more calcium than the inner leaves. All *Brassica*-genus vegetables contain dithiolthiones, a group of compounds that have anti-cancer, antioxidant properties; indoles, substances that protect against breast and colon cancer; and sulphur, which has antibiotic and antiviral characteristics. This family of vegetables also mildly stimulates the liver and other tissues out of stagnancy.

Varieties

MOST CABBAGE IS GREEN, but there are also red, white, and purple varieties. Heads can vary in size from round to oval or conical and be firm or loose, with some even having curly, crinkled leaves. The most common are the smooth-leaved green varieties that have a compact round head with many thick, overlapping leaves.

Danish, also called **Hollander**, is a late season type with round, oval, or slightly flattened heads and smooth, tightly compacted leaves that will keep longer than other types.

Domestic types form slightly looser, round, or flattened heads, with curled leaves that are more brittle than any of the Danish types. Pale green in color, and considered an early season cabbage, the domestic type is often used to make sauerkraut and does not store well.

Red or **Purple** is similar to domestic cabbage, although it has reddish-purple and white-streaked leaves. Red cabbage takes longer to mature than green varieties and thus frequently has tougher leaves. Usually cooked with vinegar to preserve its color, red cabbage is frequently pickled.

Savoy is a type of green cabbage, probably of Italian origin. Yellowish-green with loose, crinkly leaves that form its head, the savoy is the most tender and sweet of the cabbages. Its wrinkly leaves, which make a decorative alternative to the plain ones of the green cabbage, are used in recipes for stuffed cabbage leaves.

Cardoon (*Cynara cardunculus altilis, Scolymus cardunculus*)

The botanical name Cynara, *from the Latin* canina *or* canine, *is derived from the similarity of the involucral spines to the dog's tooth.* Cardunculus *means little thistle, and* altilis *means rather tall.* Scolymus *is from the Greek* skolymos, *meaning thistle. The English name* cardoon *is derived from the Latin* carduus, *also meaning thistle.*

Cardoon

Nutritional Value Per 100 g Edible Portion

	Raw	Cooked
Calories	20	22
Protein	0.70 g	0.76 g
Fat	0.10 g	0.11 g
Fiber	n/a	n/a
Calcium	70 mg	72 mg
Iron	0.70 mg	0.73 mg
Magnesium	42 mg	43 mg
Phosphorus	23 mg	23 mg
Potassium	400 mg	392 mg
Sodium	170 mg	176 mg
Beta Carotene (A)	120 IU	118 IU
Thiamine (B_1)	0.020 mg	0.018 mg
Riboflavin (B_2)	0.030 mg	0.031 mg
Niacin (B_3)	0.300 mg	0.294 mg
Ascorbic Acid (C)	2.0 mg	1.7 mg

General Information This member of the thistle family, native to the Mediterranean region, is relatively unknown in North America but is quite common in Italian and French cuisine. The Romans relished the cardoon's huge leaf stalks so much that they imported them from Libya and Spain in massive quantities. Growing to heights of four feet, the cardoon looks very much like a globe artichoke plant, but its leaves are spinier, its flower heads are spiny-tipped, and it has a less appetizing appearance. The silver-gray stalks grow in bunches like celery, but are flatter, longer, and wider, with slightly notched sides and a brushed suede finish. The tender stalks and root are eaten rather than the fruiting head. Cardoons brought a high price in Rome in the second century, and in Spain an extract for curdling milk to produce cheese was made from the dried flowers.

Buying Tips Choose smallish, comparatively firm stalks with little browning or wilting. A short shank indicates a young, tender plant. Leaves should be very dark green.

Culinary Uses The cardoon's flavor is complex, bitter, and sweet, with hints of artichoke heart, celery, and salsify. Some say the juicy stalks possess mushroom and asparagus sweetness laced with escarole bitterness. Stalks can be used like celery in casseroles, soups, and vegetable dishes, where their soft meatiness will impart a subtle, mysterious flavor. Try them prepared like French fries for a conversation starter. The roots and leaves are also edible, the roots being used as a cooked vegetable, or either of them in soups, salads, and casseroles.

Carrot *(Daucus carota sativa)*

> Daucus *is the old Greek name for the wild ancestor of the carrot, still to be found in the hedgerows of Europe, which has long been of service as food and medicine.* Carota *is the Latin name for the same plant, perhaps deriving from a Greek verb meaning to burn, in reference to the flaming color of the vegetable;* sativa *indicates the fact this plant has long been cultivated.*

General Information Most probably native to the region of Afghanistan, where there still exists the greatest diversity, the carrot has not always been orange nor so very sweet. Purple was the color of the first carrot, colored by anthocyanins. During the ninth and tenth centuries, the carrot spread throughout the Islamic world, and reached Holland by the fourteenth century. The carrot's horticultural changes are credited to the Hollanders, who introduced it to England during the Elizabethan period. Over decades of breeding, they changed the coloring from purple to pale white, and then increasingly to bright orange. Orange won out over purple because the orange color doesn't bleed in cooking. The carrot's orange pigment (carotene) is the most durable, especially compared to chlorophyll's green, which turns olive drab with cooking. Two particular varieties of carrot, the Long Orange and the Horn, are the source of almost all our finest eating carrots today. The popular Nantes variety is a descendent of the Horn, developed in the French city of Nantes. Americans were late in embracing the carrot, and only after the first World War did there develop true enthusiasm. One of the most valuable root crops grown for human consumption, the carrot comes in an amazing variety of colors—including orange, yellow, red, white, and purple—and shapes, including long, short, slender, stubby, pointed, blunt, and even bulbous. However, the only carrots widely grown in North America are the slender, pointed, orange ones.

Carrot

Nutritional Value Per 100 g Edible Portion

	Raw	Cooked
Calories	43	45
Protein	1.03 g	1.09 g
Fat	0.19 g	0.18 g
Fiber	1.04 g	1.47 g
Calcium	27 mg	31 mg
Iron	0.50 mg	0.62 mg
Magnesium	15 mg	13 mg
Phosphorus	44 mg	30 mg
Potassium	323 mg	227 mg
Sodium	35 mg	66 mg
Zinc	0.200 mg	0.300 mg
Copper	0.047 mg	0.134 mg
Manganese	0.142 mg	0.752 mg
Beta Carotene (A)	28,129 IU	24,554 IU
Thiamine (B_1)	0.097 mg	0.034 mg
Riboflavin (B_2)	0.059 mg	0.056 mg
Niacin (B_3)	0.928 mg	0.506 mg
Pantothenic Acid (B_5)	0.197 mg	0.304 mg
Pyridoxine (B_6)	0.147 mg	0.246 mg
Folic Acid (B_9)	14.0 mcg	13.9 mcg
Ascorbic Acid (C)	9.3 mg	2.3 mg
Tocopherol (E)	0.44 mg	0.42 mg

Buying Tips When purchasing carrots, look for firm, smooth, well-shaped ones of good color and fresh appearance, with fresh green tops. If newly picked carrots with their lacy green fronds are available, these are the freshest and tastiest. Cellophane packages of carrots have frequently been stored for months, and have lost some of their flavor and nutrients. Smaller carrots also tend to be more flavorful than large ones, since large ones will tend to get fibrous and woody. Avoid dry, rubbery carrots. Strong orange color is directly related to nutrition; the more color a carrot has, the more carotene, which the body turns into vitamin A, it contains.

Culinary Uses Carrots are so sweet-tasting, brightly colored, and versatile as to be considered an important part of appetizers, main dishes, and desserts. They contain more sugar than any other vegetable except beets, which makes them quite popular. The tastiest and most nutritious way to eat them is pulled fresh from the garden and washed, but if you do not have that luxury, then either cut into sticks or shredded for salads will have to do. It is preferable not to peel carrots, as many of the nutrients are in or just under the peels; simply scrub well to remove any dirt and remove the ends. Their bright color makes them appealing and appetizing (cooked or raw) to serve with

Lore and Legend

The ancient Greek word for carrot, *philon*, comes from their word for love, as this root was considered a potent aphrodisiac. The Emperor Caligula, who had a fun-loving streak, once fed the entire Roman Senate a feast of carrots in hopes of watching them run sexually amok. Fashionable ladies in the English court once thought carrot foliage and flowers so attractive that they used them to adorn their hair and hats.

dinner, in salads, with other hot or cold vegetables, or with apples and nuts. There isn't much that has not been done to the carrot: whether sautéed, boiled, puréed, gratinéed, made into soufflés, cooked in cream, glazed in butter, or added to stocks and casseroles, they are always delicious. Don't ignore the carrot greens (tops); because of their high phosphorus content these should also be eaten raw in salads or cooked in soups.

Health Benefits Anthelmintic, carminative, diuretic, stimulant. Carrots and their juice are one of the best detoxifiers when consumed in quantity, alkalinizing, cleansing, nourishing, and stimulating almost every system in the body. Carrots deliver abundant supplies of readily assimilable vitamins, minerals, and enzymes to cells, giving them the fuel they require to slough off morbid wastes and rebuild healthy cells. One of the best foods for the liver and digestive tract, they help kidney function, help prevent and treat cancer, balance the endocrine and adrenal systems, depress blood cholesterol, and increase bulk elimination from the colon. Quality carrots are very rich in the antioxidant beta carotene, the precursor to vitamin A that makes them so beneficial for the eyes and vision (carrots actually were used during wars to help aviators overcome night blindness). They contain large amounts of silicon, which strengthens the connective tissues and aids calcium metabolism; as well, they contain an essential oil that kills parasites and unhealthy intestinal bacteria. Potassium salts in carrots account for the diuretic action, while at the same time carrot soup makes an effective remedy for diarrhea and is easily digestible for those suffering from stomach and intestinal problems.

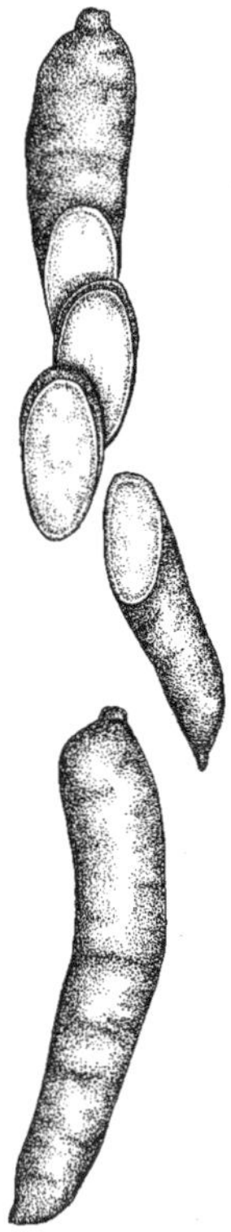

Cassava (*Manihot utilissima, M. esculenta*)

Also Known As: Manioc, Brazilian Arrowroot, Yuca, Tapioca.

> Manihot *is the plant's native Brazilian name. The term* utilissima *designates a plant that is very useful, while* esculenta *means esculent or edible. The English word* cassava *is from a Taino word* cac abi, *while* tapioca *comes from the Tupi (Brazilian) word* typyoca.

General Information A native of equatorial America and Florida, the cassava plant is little known to most people in the temperate zones except in the form of tapioca, although it is one of the important food plants of the tropics. Cassava belongs to the Euphorbiaceae, or spurge family, which includes the Para rubber tree, our best source of natural rubber, and the poinsettia, a well-known Christmas ornamental. The edible part of the rather tall and shrubby plant is the long, starchy, tuberous root, which somewhat resembles a sweet potato but is usually much larger, some growing to a yard in length and weighing several pounds. There are two broad groups, the sweet maniocs and the bitter. The tubers of the sweet varieties are eaten as cooked vegetables, as they contain negligible traces of toxic compounds. Bitter varieties contain far higher concentrations of poisonous hydrocyanide compounds, and require special preparation to make them safe to eat. The native technique was either to boil the dark brown roots very thoroughly and then mash them, or to peel and grate the roots, and then squeeze out the juices under heavy pressure. These juices, boiled hard, were used to make cassareep sauce and also threw a starchy sediment that became granular when dried: tapioca. The pulp was shaped into flat cakes, slowly cooked on a griddle, and eaten as well.

Cassava

Nutritional Value Per 100 g Edible Portion	Dry Raw	Pearl Tapioca
Calories	120	341
Protein	3.10 g	0.19 g
Fat	0.39 g	0.02 g
Fiber	2.49 g	n/a
Calcium	91 mg	20 mg
Iron	3.60 mg	1.58 mg
Magnesium	66 mg	1 mg
Phosphorus	70 mg	7 mg
Potassium	764 mg	11 mg
Sodium	8 mg	1 mg
Beta Carotene (A)	10 IU	n/a
Thiamine (B_1)	0.225 mg	0.004 mg
Riboflavin (B_2)	0.101 mg	0 mg
Niacin (B_3)	1.400 mg	0 mg
Ascorbic Acid (C)	48.2 mg	0 mg

Buying Tips Look for cassava that is as completely bark-covered as possible, although the bark is always patchy. There should be no sliminess, mold, or hairline cracks, and it should smell clean and fresh. Do not buy tubers that show any grayish-blue fibers or even the slightest darkening near the skin.

Culinary Uses The swollen roots are shaped like long, narrow sweet potatoes and covered with what looks like bark. Beneath the rough brown coat, through which may be visible rosy or tan patches, is flesh that is as hard, dense, and white as coconut. The softly fibrous, starchy flesh becomes almost translucent when cooked, with a sweetness, butteriness, and glutinous chewiness that is much appreciated by many, but not all. At its simplest, it is boiled or baked, and almost always sauced. In stews, it both thickens and absorbs juices. At one time cassava was in great demand in the United States in the form of tapioca, but this popular pudding has now largely been replaced by gelatins and instant puddings.

Health Benefits Cooked into pudding, tapioca makes a light, nutritious, and easily digested food for invalids.

Cauliflower (*Brassica oleracea, Botrytis* group)

The Latin name Brassica *derives from the Celtic* bresic. *The term* oleracea *refers to a vegetable garden herb that is used in cooking, while* botrytis *is a Greek word meaning cluster-like or grape-like. The English word* cauliflower *comes from the Latin words* caulis, *meaning stem or cabbage, and* flos, *flower.*

Lore and Legend

In Queen Anne's time the term cauliflower was a comical phrase for a clerical wig, later referring to anyone who wore powder on his head.

General Information Cauliflower, like its cousin broccoli, is a member of the cabbage family, and one that took centuries of cultivation to produce a tight head of clustered flower buds in place of the compact leaves of the cabbage head. Thousands of tiny white flower buds are closely packed into even larger buds, forming florets that make up the single large round head or "flower." Cauliflower was introduced into medieval Europe by the Arabs during their occupation of Spain, and by the twelfth century, Spaniards were eating as many as three varieties of the vegetable. In sixteenth-century England, cauliflower was called "Cyprus coleworts," probably because it was first imported from the island of Cyprus. A new green variety has been developed commercially that is a cross between conventional cauliflower and broccoli. The head resembles cauliflower, but the color is chartreuse, rather than the dark green of broccoli.

Buying Tips Quality cauliflower is creamy or snowy white, clean, heavy, firm, and compact, with outer leaves that are fresh and green. Avoid any that has the appearance of being rice-like or granular, speckled, or spotted, or that has yellowing leaves. The size of the vegetable has little to do with its quality.

Cauliflower

Nutritional Value Per 100 g Edible Portion	Raw	Cooked
Calories	24	24
Protein	1.99 g	1.87 g
Fat	0.18 g	0.17 g
Fiber	0.85 g	0.82 g
Calcium	29 mg	27 mg
Iron	0.58 mg	0.42 mg
Magnesium	14 mg	11 mg
Phosphorus	46 mg	35 mg
Potassium	355 mg	323 mg
Sodium	15 mg	6 mg
Zinc	0.180 mg	0.240 mg
Copper	0.032 mg	0.091 mg
Manganese	0.203 mg	0.178 mg
Beta Carotene (A)	16 IU	14 IU
Thiamine (B_1)	0.076 mg	0.063 mg
Riboflavin (B_2)	0.057 mg	0.052 mg
Niacin (B_3)	0.633 mg	0.552 mg
Pantothenic Acid (B_5)	0.141 mg	0.122 mg
Pyridoxine (B_6)	0.231 mg	0.202 mg
Folic Acid (B_9)	66.1 mcg	51.2 mcg
Ascorbic Acid (C)	71.5 mg	55.4 mg
Tocopherol (E)	0.03 mg	n/a

Culinary Uses Cauliflower can be served raw in salads and vegetable dip platters, or cooked and served as a vegetable either on its own or combined with other vegetables. If cauliflower is cooked too long, it will bring about the decomposition of its sulphur compounds and form an offensive odor. Green cauliflower has a pleasant taste, cooks more quickly than the white variety, and is less apt to give off the usual cabbage-like odor while cooking. Since cauliflower is a type of cabbage, the leaves, flower stalk, and midveins of the big leaves make excellent eating.

Health Benefits Cauliflower is not as nutrient-dense as many of the other cabbage family vegetables. Its white color is a sign that it contains far less of the beneficial carotenes and chlorophyll, but it is a good source of boron because cauliflower does not grow well in boron-deficient soils. Cauliflower helps purify the blood, aids bleeding gums if eaten raw, and is helpful in cases of asthma, kidney and bladder disorders, high blood pressure, and constipation. Because its high sulphur content may cause indigestion and hinder the assimilation of food, cauliflower should be used in moderation and not combined with other sulphur-rich foods. All *Brassica*-genus vegetables contain dithiolthiones, a group of compounds that have anti-cancer, antioxidant properties; indoles, substances that protect against breast and colon cancer; and sulphur, which has antibiotic and antiviral characteristics. This family of vegetables also mildly stimulates the liver and other tissues out of stagnancy.

Cee Gwa (*Luffa acutangula*)

Also Known As: Chinese Okra, Angled Luffa.

Luffa *is the Arabic name for this family of plants;* acutangula *means acutely or sharply angled.*

General Information This close relative of the luffa sponge is presumed native to India. Distinguished by its ten sharp ridges and dull green skin, the long, narrow cee gwa squash rather resembles large okra pods in that it is tapered and grows wider away from the stem. The fruit on the market, which may be three feet long, is actually immature; fully mature fruits reach nine feet in length. They are best when only six inches long. The fruits need to be harvested young, as old ones become fibrous; old fruits are actually used as scrubbers.

Culinary Uses and **Health Benefits** Cee gwa can be eaten raw in salads, but most often is used cooked, when it has a pleasant earthy flavor and a texture reminiscent of zucchini. To prepare, slice off the ridges and both ends, and scrape the skin lightly. In China, this strange vegetable is frequently deep-fried or used in soups. One early-nineteenth-century English botanical writer, William Roxburgh, said that cee gwa was almost as good as green peas when boiled, dressed with butter, and seasoned with salt and pepper. The juice from mature fruits is valued medicinally as a purgative.

Celeriac

Nutritional Value Per 100 g Edible Portion

	Raw	Cooked
Calories	39	25
Protein	1.50 g	0.96 g
Fat	0.30 g	0.19 g
Fiber	1.30 g	0.83 g
Calcium	43 mg	26 mg
Iron	0.70 mg	0.43 mg
Magnesium	20 mg	12 mg
Phosphorus	115 mg	66 mg
Potassium	300 mg	173 mg
Sodium	100 mg	61 mg
Beta Carotene (A)	0 IU	0 IU
Thiamine (B_1)	0.050 mg	0.027 mg
Riboflavin (B_2)	0.060 mg	0.037 mg
Niacin (B_3)	0.700 mg	0.427 mg
Pyridoxine (B_6)	0.165 mg	0.101 mg
Ascorbic Acid (C)	8.0 mg	3.6 mg

Celeriac *(Apium graveolens* var. *rapaceum)*

Also Known As: Celery Root, Knob Celery.

Apium *derives either from the Latin* apis, *meaning bee, because bees go dotty over its tiny white flowers, or from a prehistoric Indo-European word for water, which would be appropriate, since celeriac prefers wet soils and salt marshes. The term* graveolens *means heavy-scented;* rapaceum *means pertaining to turnips, or turnip-like. The English name* celeriac *derives from the Latin* celer, *meaning quick-acting or swift, in reference to its remedial reputation.*

General Information Swiss botanists gave the first description of celeriac in about 1600. Not a true root, celeriac is a special variety of celery that is cultivated for its swollen stem base rather than its upper branches. Looking like an irregular, brown turnip, with many small roots extending from its base, the swollen form would be at home in tales by the brothers Grimm. Between an apple and a cantaloupe in size, the two- to four-inch lopsided sphere is embossed and channeled, decorated with whorls, crevices, and disorderly rootlets, and is often scruffy and muddy. It became popular in Europe in the eighteenth century, but has never been very popular in England or the United States.

Buying Tips In choosing, favor smaller roots over the larger, as the latter tend to be pithy, and buy only those that are firm, pressing the tops of the roots to check for internal rot.

Culinary Uses Celeriac tastes much like a combination of celery and parsley, only stronger and with a smoky flavor. It is one of the few vegetables that must be peeled before using, and the innermost woody section may be too fibrous to use. You can do anything with celeriac that you can with turnips, and more. Once peeled, it can be eaten raw in salads, or blanched, steamed, boiled, puréed, and stir-fried. Cut into matchsticks, its chewy crunch and assertive flavor are easy crowd pleasers. Cooked celeriac mixed with an equal quantity of potato makes a delicately flavored purée. The stalks and leaves are not eaten.

Health Benefits As a celery-related plant, celeriac has been known for its diuretic qualities, and is useful to those with kidney stones and arthritic conditions. Celeriac is beneficial to the lymphatic, nervous, and urinary systems.

Celery *(Apium graveolens)*

Apium *derives either from the Latin* apis, *meaning bee, because bees go dotty over its tiny white flowers, or from a prehistoric Indo-European word for water, which would be appropriate, since celery prefers wet soils and salt marshes. The term* graveolens *means heavy-scented. The English name* celery *derives from the Latin* celer, *meaning quick-acting or swift, in reference to its remedial reputation.*

General Information Originally a wild plant that grew along the muddy Mediterranean wetlands where sea and land waters mingled, wild celery has a bitter flavor and pungent

Celery

Nutritional Value Per 100 g Edible Portion

	Raw	Cooked
Calories	16	18
Protein	0.75 g	0.83 g
Fat	0.14 g	0.16 g
Fiber	0.80 g	0.88 g
Calcium	40 mg	42 mg
Iron	0.40 mg	0.42 mg
Magnesium	11 mg	12 mg
Phosphorus	25 mg	25 mg
Potassium	287 mg	284 mg
Sodium	87 mg	91 mg
Zinc	0.130 mg	0.140 mg
Copper	0.034 mg	0.036 mg
Manganese	0.102 mg	0.106 mg
Beta Carotene (A)	134 IU	132 IU
Thiamine (B_1)	0.046 mg	0.043 mg
Riboflavin (B_2)	0.045 mg	0.047 mg
Niacin (B_3)	0.323 mg	0.319 mg
Pantothenic Acid (B_5)	0.186 mg	0.195 mg
Pyridoxine (B_6)	0.087 mg	0.086 mg
Folic Acid (B_9)	28.0 mcg	22.0 mcg
Ascorbic Acid (C)	7.0 mg	6.1 mg
Tocopherol (E)	0.36 mg	n/a

odor. Celery as we know it today was developed during the seventeenth century by the Italians and French to produce a less woody, sweeter variety. It belongs to the same plant family (Umbellifer) as carrots, parsley, and fennel, all of which get their characteristic flavor from the volatile oils found in the stems, leaves, and seeds. Celery is typically harvested after its first year of growth, when the stalks are thick and leafy. Some plants, however, are allowed to grow a second year, which results in the formation of seeds. The seeds, as well as the dried leaves, called celery flakes, are popular as seasonings. There are two main varieties: green-ribbed with large green leaves (also called Pascal celery), and golden celery, either blanched with ethylene gas or grown in darkness to change the typical green color to light white or golden with yellow-green leaves.

Buying Tips When buying, choose crisp stalks of medium length, thickness, and solidity, brittle enough to snap easily. Whole heads should have plenty of small inner stalks and "heart."

Culinary Uses The flavor of celery is distinctively sharp and tangy, the small, deep green leafy types being sharper than the larger white varieties. Of the most benefit when eaten raw either alone or as part of sandwiches and dips, celery is also flavorful when cooked with tomatoes or green peppers. Celery leaves, because they are so tough and strongly flavored, should be chopped, liquefied, and added to other vegetables to lessen their strong taste.

Health Benefits Diuretic. Celery contains compounds known as coumarins that appear to be useful in cancer prevention and which enhance the activity of certain white blood cells; these compounds also tone the vascular system, lower blood pressure, and may be useful in cases of migraines.

A favorite reducing food because of its few calories, celery's high water content makes it especially good to eat with foods that are more concentrated, particularly heavy starches. Strongly alkaline, it counteracts acidosis, halts digestive fermentation of foods, purifies the bloodstream, aids digestion, and can help clear up skin problems. If there is stiffness, creaking, or cracking in the joints, our bodies are lacking in organic sodium (the "youth" element that helps keep muscles limber and pliable) and have built up inorganic calcium deposits. Celery's rich organic sodium content dislodges these calcium deposits from joints and holds them in solution until they can be eliminated through the kidneys; it also provides organic calcium and silicon for the repair of damaged ligaments and bones. Celery may also promote the onset of menstruation; use it only in moderate amounts during pregnancy.

Lore and Legend

Although at times it has been associated with funerals and thought an omen of ill luck, the ancient Greeks valued celery highly, and awarded it as a prize to winners in many of their sporting contests. Legend has it that medieval magicians tucked celery seeds into their shoes in order to fly.

Chaya (*Cnidoscolus chayamansa*)

General Information This fast-growing ornamental and shade shrub is a source of nutritious green leaves and shoots. The plants vary from smooth to hairy, and the hairy plants sting like nettles, so that harvesters must wear gloves. The stinging disappears with cooking. Cultivated plants are almost free of stinging hairs.

Culinary Uses and **Health Benefits** Chaya must be cooked before eating: the fresh leaves contain toxic hydrocyanic glycosides, but cooking deactivates them. The young shoots and tender leaves are cooked and eaten like spinach. They are probably suitable for canning or freezing for local and export markets, but this has not yet been attempted. Reportedly they are high in protein, calcium, iron, carotene, thiamine, riboflavin, niacin, and ascorbic acid.

Chinese Cabbage (*Brassica chinensis, B. rapa, Perkinensis* group)

The Latin name Brassica *derives from the Celtic* bresic; chinensis *designates Chinese or coming from China.*

General Information Long appreciated for its delicate flavor and crisp texture, Chinese cabbage has been cultivated since before the Christian era. The two most popular varieties are Bok choy and Pe-tsai.

Chinese Cabbage

Nutritional Value Per 100 g Edible Portion

	Bok Choy Raw	Bok Choy Cooked	Pe-tsai Raw	Pe-tsai Cooked
Calories	13	12	16	14
Protein	1.50 g	1.56 g	1.20 g	1.50 g
Fat	0.20 g	0.16 g	0.20 g	0.17 g
Fiber	0.60 g	0.60 g	0.60 g	0.50 g
Calcium	105 mg	93 mg	77 mg	32 mg
Iron	0.80 mg	1.04 mg	0.31 mg	0.30 mg
Magnesium	19 mg	11 mg	13 mg	10 mg
Phosphorus	37 mg	29 mg	29 mg	39 mg
Potassium	252 mg	371 mg	238 mg	225 mg
Sodium	65 mg	34 mg	9 mg	9 mg
Zinc	n/a	n/a	0.23 mg	0.18 mg
Beta Carotene (A)	3,000 IU	2,568 IU	1,200 IU	967 IU
Thiamine (B_1)	0.040 mg	0.032 mg	0.040 mg	0.044 mg
Riboflavin (B_2)	0.070 mg	0.063 mg	0.050 mg	0.044 mg
Niacin (B_3)	0.500 mg	0.428 mg	0.400 mg	0.500 mg
Pantothenic Acid (B_5)	n/a	n/a	0.105 mg	0.080 mg
Pyridoxine (B_6)	n/a	n/a	0.232 mg	0.177 mg
Folic Acid (B_9)	n/a	n/a	78.7 mcg	53.4 mcg
Ascorbic Acid (C)	45.0 mg	26.0 mg	27.0 mg	15.8 mg
Tocopherol (E)	n/a	n/a	0.12 mg	n/a

Health Benefits Chinese cabbage contains just 20 percent of the sulphur of round-head cabbage. It also moistens the intestines and treats constipation. According to Oriental medicine, stalk vegetables raise energy and are expansive and cooling foods. All *Brassica*-genus vegetables contain dithiolthiones, a group of compounds that have anti-cancer, anti-oxidant properties; indoles, substances that protect against breast and colon cancer; and sulphur, which has antibiotic and antiviral characteristics. This family of vegetables also mildly stimulates the liver and other tissues out of stagnancy.

Varieties

Bok choy (also called **Chinese chard** and **Chinese mustard**) originates from southeastern China. The cluster of thick, greenish-white stalks are ten to twenty inches long with broad, dark green leaves. Select fresh, crisp, firm heads with leaves that do not look wilted. One advantage that bok choy shares with many members of the leafy green cabbage family is an excellent shelf life. The crunchy stalks have a delicately mild, juicy sweetness that suggests romaine lettuce, while the leaves are soft, somewhat peppery and cabbagey. Often cut into pieces and stir-fried, bok choy stalks can also be served raw in salads or added to soups. The leaves withstand cooking better than spinach and do not become gooey, but should always be steamed—never boiled.

Pe-tsai (also called **Chinese cabbage**, **Celery cabbage**, or **Napa**) belongs to the Napa cabbage family. It looks very much like romaine lettuce, with its fairly compact, conical head, but the crinkled leaves are pale green. Pe-tsai's delicate mild flavor has been described as a cabbage that even cabbage-haters love. Favored for stir-fried vegetable dishes, the leaves are tender, crisp, and juicy; the white heart of the head is a real delicacy.

Collards *(Brassica oleracea, Acephala group)*

The botanical name Brassica *derives from the Celtic* bresic; oleracea *refers to a vegetable garden herb that is used in cooking;* acephala, *meaning without a head, refers to its loose-leafed, nonheading shape. The English name is a corruption of the Anglo-Saxon* coleworts *or* colewyrts, *meaning literally "cabbage plants."*

Collards

Nutritional Value Per 100 g Edible Portion

	Raw	Cooked
Calories	31	27
Protein	1.57 g	1.35 g
Fat	0.22 g	0.19 g
Fiber	0.57 g	0.49 g
Calcium	29 mg	23 mg
Iron	0.19 mg	0.16 mg
Magnesium	9 mg	7 mg
Phosphorus	10 mg	8 mg
Potassium	169 mg	131 mg
Sodium	20 mg	16 mg
Zinc	0.130 mg	0.110 mg
Copper	0.039 mg	0.032 mg
Manganese	0.276 mg	0.226 mg
Beta Carotene (A)	3,330 IU	2,727 IU
Thiamine (B_1)	0.029 mg	0.021 mg
Riboflavin (B_2)	0.064 mg	0.052 mg
Niacin (B_3)	0.374 mg	0.290 mg
Pantothenic Acid (B_5)	0.064 mg	0.052 mg
Pyridoxine (B_6)	0.067 mg	0.052 mg
Folic Acid (B_9)	12.0 mcg	6.0 mcg
Ascorbic Acid (C)	23.3 mg	12.1 mg

General Information Collards are native to the eastern Mediterranean countries or to Asia Minor, and are one of the oldest members of the cabbage family. They made their way to the New World in the seventeenth century with the slave trade. Extremely hardy and adaptable to both hot and cold climates, collards are unfussy growers and abundant producers of "greens," or leaves. The deep bluish-green leaves, each on a fairly long, heavy stalk (too tough to eat) resemble cabbage, but are oval, fairly flat, and paddlelike, not round and curved like heading cabbage. Despite their long history and nutritional benefits, collards have never gained wide acceptance except in the southeastern United States.

Buying Tips Choose relatively small, firm, springy leaves that show no yellowing or insect holes.

Culinary Uses Collard greens are more tender than kale and less pungent than mustard greens, with an assertively earthy flavor. Young greens can be eaten raw, chopped into a mixed green salad. Older leaves need to be cooked, in the manner of spinach. Substantial enough to replace meat, this traditional southern favorite is commonly cooked with bacon or salt pork.

Health Benefits All *Brassica*-genus vegetables contain dithiolthiones, a group of compounds that have anti-cancer, antioxidant properties; indoles, substances that protect against breast and colon cancer; and sulphur, which has antibiotic and antiviral characteristics. This family of vegetables also mildly stimulates the liver and other tissues out of stagnancy.

Corn *(Zea mays saccharata)*

Also Known As: Sweetcorn, Maize.

In 1737, Linnaeus christened the species Zea mays, *from the Greek* zeia, *for grain or cereal, and the Taino Indian* mahiz. *The term* saccharata *means containing sugar or sweet. The English word* corn *comes from the Old Norse word* korn, *which means a grain-sized lump of something. The term has historically meant any sort of kernel or grain, whatever the dominant grain of the country happened to be. In England, for example, corn refers to wheat, and in Scotland or Ireland the term refers to oats.*

General Information The only cereal that is native to North America, corn is actually a type of grass; its proper name is maize, a word of Indian origin. Sweet corn was being grown by the Indians at least by the beginning of the seventeenth century on the eastern side of the Appalachians, where the Iroquois were raising it along the headwaters of the Susquehanna River in central New York. It was "discovered" there in 1799 and planted along the coast, but it evoked no particular interest among the colonists, and only began to be widely cultivated after the Civil War. Today, canned sweet corn is America's favorite preserved vegetable, and has been outselling all others since World War I. Harvested at an immature stage so that the kernels are tender and juicy, at its peak of flavor sweet corn contains 5 to 6 percent sugar by weight.

Corn

Nutritional Value Per 100 g Edible Portion

	Raw	Cooked	Frozen & Cooked
Calories	86	108	81
Protein	3.22 g	3.32 g	3.02 g
Fat	1.18 g	1.28 g	0.07 g
Fiber	0.70 g	0.60 g	0.48 g
Calcium	2 mg	2 mg	2 mg
Iron	0.52 mg	0.61 mg	0.30 mg
Magnesium	37 mg	32 mg	18 mg
Phosphorus	89 mg	103 mg	47 mg
Potassium	270 mg	249 mg	139 mg
Sodium	15.2 mg	17 mg	5 mg
Zinc	0.450 mg	0.480 mg	0.350 mg
Copper	0.054 mg	0.053 mg	0.033 mg
Manganese	0.161 mg	0.194 mg	0.180 mg
Beta Carotene (A)	281 IU	217 IU	248 IU
Thiamine (B_1)	0.200 mg	0.215 mg	0.069 mg
Riboflavin (B_2)	0.060 mg	0.072 mg	0.073 mg
Niacin (B_3)	1.700 mg	1.614 mg	1.283 mg
Pantothenic Acid (B_5)	0.760 mg	0.878 mg	0.217 mg
Pyridoxine (B_6)	0.055 mg	0.060 mg	0.100 mg
Folic Acid (B_9)	45.8 mcg	46.4 mcg	22.8 mcg
Ascorbic Acid (C)	6.8 mg	6.2 mg	2.6 mg

Buying Tips When buying fresh sweetcorn, look for creamy-colored cobs/ears surrounded by green leaves. If possible, pull back the husk and puncture a kernel with your fingernail. If the corn is fresh, the kernel will exude a milky liquid; if not ripe, it will exude water; and if past its prime, the kernels will be tough and the milk will be doughy.

Culinary Uses Many varieties of sweetcorn are introduced each year, and nowadays, fresh and frozen corn on the cob is available year-round. Once picked, sweet corn should be eaten as soon as possible, for the sugar begins to turn to starch immediately after it is separated from the stalk. Usually boiled and eaten off the cob, the kernels can be scraped off after cooking and eaten separately, or added to baked goods.

Health Benefits Fresh corn on the cob has properties similar to dried corn but contains more enzymes, more of certain vitamins, and is better suited to the warmer seasons. Corn is very high in fiber, is one of the best balanced starches (along with brown rice and barley), and its carbohydrate is the easiest of all the grains to digest. Yellow corn is helpful in building bone and muscle, and is excellent food for the brain and nervous system. Corn is said to help prevent cancer and lower the risk of heart disease and cavities.

Cucumber *(Cucumis sativus, C. melo)*

Cucumis *is the old Latin name for this plant, derived from the Latin word for gourd.* Sativus *refers to the fact that this plant has long been cultivated;* melo *means melon.*

General Information The ordinary cucumber, a member of the gourd and squash family and a native of India and Egypt, was cultivated very early in Asia and Europe, and was a popular vegetable with the Greeks and Romans. Centuries before thermos jugs, travelers in desert caravans carried cucumbers because the green skins effectively protected the cool fresh liquid within, which could assuage thirst, and the flesh provided a refreshing food. The cucumber was introduced into Europe by Alexander the Great. Centuries later, Julius Caesar exalted it in Rome after his Eastern campaigns. Cucumbers came to the western hemisphere with Columbus, who planted them in his experimental gardens in 1493. There are three basic types of cucumbers: the long, thin, smooth variety known as the Oriental (or European), hot-house or greenhouse cucumber; the shorter, thicker, slicing cucumber; and the small round varieties known as pickling cucumbers. Oriental (or European) cucumbers are smooth-skinned, about a foot in length, and are generally sweeter and more tender than their field grown cousins. In contrast to the other varieties, they are always cultivated in greenhouses. The slicing cucumbers most often seen are six to nine inches long and have glossy, dark green skin and tapering ends. Pickling varieties are smaller and squatter, and have bumpy, light green skins.

Lore and Legend

In biblical times, eating cucumbers was thought to offer protection against deadly insects and snakes. There is some mention of the cucumber as an emblem of fertility; one Buddhist legend tells of Sagara's wife, who had sixty-thousand offspring, the first of which was a cucumber that climbed to heaven on its own vine. The Roman Emperor Tiberius is reputed to have been so fond of cucumbers that he ate them daily, ten a day. They were even grown in special moveable frames so that his supply would never be interrupted when he traveled. It was customary to pick cucumbers at the full of the moon, in hopes of getting the very biggest, which were also considered the very best. One medieval gardener advised draping the plants in comforting "thin coverlets" in the event of violently inclement weather, as they were said to be frightened of thunderstorms.

Cucumber

Nutritional Value Per 100 g Edible Portion

	Raw
Calories	13
Protein	0.54 g
Fat	0.13 g
Fiber	0.60 g
Calcium	14 mg
Iron	0.28 mg
Magnesium	11 mg
Phosphorus	17 mg
Potassium	149 mg
Sodium	2 mg
Zinc	0.230 mg
Copper	0.040 mg
Manganese	0.061 mg
Beta Carotene (A)	45 IU
Thiamine (B_1)	0.030 mg
Riboflavin (B_2)	0.020 mg
Niacin (B_3)	0.300 mg
Pantothenic Acid (B_5)	0.250 mg
Pyridoxine (B_6)	0.052 mg
Folic Acid (B_9)	13.9 mcg
Ascorbic Acid (C)	4.7 mg
Tocopherol (E)	0.15 mg

Buying Tips Cucumbers should be firm, fresh, bright, well-shaped, of medium or dark green color, with small immature seeds. Withered or shriveled specimens should be avoided.

Culinary Uses Cucumbers often come to market waxed to slow the rate of spoilage, and should be peeled. Generally eaten raw as part of a salad, they may also be served thinly sliced for a delightful summer dish. Some might prefer them lightly cooked, as they are served in the East. Over 70 percent of the U.S. cucumber crop is used to make pickles.

Health Benefits Diuretic, laxative. Cucumbers are an alkaline, nonstarchy, cooling vegetable, rich in minerals that neutralize blood acidosis. It has been said that the lowly cucumber is the best natural diuretic known, facilitating excretion of wastes through the kidneys, so that they need not be purged through the skin, and helping dissolve uric acid accumulations such as kidney and bladder stones. Among other enzymes, the cucumber contains erepsin, an enzyme that helps to digest proteins, and thus it is beneficial as a digestive aid; this property also enables cucumbers to destroy worms, especially tapeworms. Its potassium content makes the cucumber highly useful for conditions of both high and low blood pressure. Cucumber skins are rich in silicon, chlorophyll, and although slightly bitter, are well worth eating for their nutritional properties.

Eggplant (*Solanum melongena,* var. *esculentum*)

Also Known As: Aubergine, Guinea Squash.

The name Solanum melongena, *which means soothing mad apple, is due to the eggplant's unwarranted reputation for inducing instant insanity in the unwary eater. According to available records, the early types of eggplant had small ovoid white fruits resembling eggs, which accounts for its English name.*

General Information Botanists believe the original eggplant blossomed somewhere in south central Asia—possibly India—where its peculiar-looking fruits, bitter taste, and nasty thorns did little to recommend it. Nonetheless, some hardy soul eventually domesticated it, and by the third century A.D. the Chinese were gingerly debating its dietary potential. Reaching Europe in the twelfth century by way of Arab merchant caravans, the eggplant was eventually introduced to the United States by Thomas Jefferson, who experimented with the seeds and cuttings of many foreign plants. Until the twentieth century, Americans valued the eggplant more as an ornament or table decoration than as a flavorful, versatile food. This was due in part to its reputation in Europe, where eating eggplant was suspected to cause madness, not to mention leprosy, cancer, and bad breath. The large berries vary in shape from round to oblong, and in color from white to purple, with some even striped. The most common eggplant variety sold in the United States is large and purple with a shiny, patent-leather-like skin, developed because it showed bruise marks less and grew to a larger size. Increasingly, you will find other varieties, including miniature eggplants, that come in a range of shapes and colors. These small eggplants are generally sweeter and more tender than their larger counterparts; they also have thinner skins and contain fewer seeds.

Buying Tips When buying, look for a well-rounded, symmetrical eggplant with a satin-smooth, uniformly colored skin; tan patches, scars, or bruises on the skin indicate decay, which will appear as discolorations in the flesh beneath. Any with wrinkled or flabby-looking skin will probably be bitter. Those that are light for their size have fewer seeds. A mature eggplant may be as long as twelve

Eggplant

Nutritional Value Per 100 g Edible Portion

	Raw	Cooked
Calories	26	28
Protein	1.10 g	0.83 g
Fat	0.10 g	0.23 g
Fiber	1.00 g	0.97 g
Calcium	36 mg	6 mg
Iron	0.55 mg	0.35 mg
Magnesium	11 mg	13 mg
Phosphorus	33 mg	22 mg
Potassium	219 mg	248 mg
Sodium	4 mg	3 mg
Zinc	0.150 mg	0.150 mg
Copper	0.112 mg	0.108 mg
Manganese	0.140 mg	0.136 mg
Beta Carotene (A)	70 IU	64 IU
Thiamine (B_1)	0.090 mg	0.076 mg
Riboflavin (B_2)	0.020 mg	0.020 mg
Niacin (B_3)	0.600 mg	0.600 mg
Pantothenic Acid (B_5)	0.081 mg	0.075 mg
Pyridoxine (B_6)	0.094 mg	0.086 mg
Folic Acid (B_9)	17.6 mcg	14.4 mcg
Ascorbic Acid (C)	1.6 mg	1.3 mg
Tocopherol (E)	0.03 mg	n/a

Lore and Legend

At about the same time that Gerard was lamenting the eggplant's aphrodisiac effect in England, the concubine Rada-Hera was concocting the most famous of aphrodisiac eggplant dishes for her husband, the legendary Turkish Bey Mustaph Mehere—the same who weighed 400 pounds and took 170 wives and innumerable concubines over his 123-year life span (1488–1611). Rada-Hera (his second wife) made the dish so well that she was the only wife he never discarded, mainly because she kept the recipe secret and Mustaph believed that the purée was the key to his virility and longevity. So while all Mustaph's other wives were discarded when they turned twenty, Rada-Hera had free run of the palace until she died a natural death in 1571.

inches or as small as two inches; medium-sized specimens, three to six inches in diameter, are likely to be young, sweet, and tender, while oversized specimens may be tough, seedy, and bitter.

Culinary Uses Eggplants have such a pleasing color and shape that they are almost as enjoyable just to look at as they are to eat. Astonishingly adaptable, they can be fried, boiled, baked, stuffed, or sautéed; they are excellent served individually as a main dish, appetizer, or as part of a larger cast of ingredients. The beautiful skin is edible and does not need to be removed. A traditional substitute for meat in Middle Eastern cooking, they are quite spongy and soak up whatever oils or juices they are cooked in. Eggplant is used for a number of national dishes, including Turkey's *imam biyaldi*, eggplant simmered in olive oil for several hours; France's *ratatouille*, a stew of onions, garlic, zucchini, spices, and chopped eggplant; and Italy's *caponata*, pickled eggplant.

Health Benefits Since eggplant is more than 90 percent water, it is low in calories. It helps clear stagnant blood by dissolving the congealed blood and accumulations such as tumors, and has a hemostatic action (reduces bleeding). Eggplant is a rich source of bioflavonoids, which renew arteries and prevent strokes and other hemorrhages. As it has a soothing and stabilizing effect on the nervous system, a protective action on arteries damaged by cholesterol, and even helps to prevent certain cancers, eggplant has a strong future.

Fennel *(Foeniculum vulgaris)*

Also Known As: Finocchio.

> Foeniculum *is the diminutive of the Latin word for hay, due in part to its smell;* vulgare *means common or vulgar. The English word* fennel *is derived from its Latin name.*

General Information Fennel is apparently a native of southern Europe, but has been naturalized in many places around the world. A member of the parsley family prized for its mild licorice flavor, and particularly valued by the Italians and French, fennel is slowly gaining a wider appreciation in the United States. There are three kinds of edible fennel: one is an herb, and two are vegetables. **Common fennel** (*F. vulgaris*) is grown for its seeds and leaves, which are used to flavor soups and fish sauces (see reference in the **Herb** section); **Sicilian fennel** (*F. vulgaris azoricum*) is grown in southern Italy for its tender young stems, which are eaten like celery or asparagus; **Florence fennel** or **Finocchio** (*F. vulgaris dulce*) is cultivated for its very thick, basal leaf stalks. The plant resembles a plump celery plant, except that its leaves are finer and more feathery, like dill; its three swollen leaf bases overlap to form a sort of false bulb.

Buying Tips Choose Florence fennel bulbs that are 2 1/2 to 3 inches in diameter; beyond that they become tough and stringy. Bulbs should be firm and clean, the stalks straight and firm,

Fennel

Nutritional Value Per 100 g Edible Portion	Raw Bulb
Calories	31
Protein	1.24 g
Fat	0.20 g
Fiber	n/a
Calcium	49 mg
Iron	n/a
Magnesium	17 mg
Phosphorus	50 mg
Potassium	414 mg
Sodium	52 mg
Zinc	0.200 mg
Copper	0.066 mg
Manganese	0.191 mg
Beta Carotene (A)	n/a
Thiamine (B_1)	0.010 mg
Riboflavin (B_2)	0.032 mg
Niacin (B_3)	0.640 mg
Pantothenic Acid (B_5)	0.232 mg
Pyridoxine (B_6)	0.047 mg
Folic Acid (B_9)	27.0 mcg
Ascorbic Acid (C)	12.0 mg

and the leaves fresh and green; if any flowers are present on the stalks, the bulb is overmature. Avoid any bulbs that show brown spots or signs of splitting.

Culinary Uses Fennel has a mild sweet flavor akin to licorice or anise. All parts of it are edible, from the overlapping layers of bulb all the way to the stems and leaves. The stalks and bulb can be used raw, chopped into salads, or cooked. Sautéing in butter with a simple fresh herb highlights its pleasant taste, and steamed fennel with cream sauce is also excellent. English cooks in centuries past made a cold fennel soup with the sliced stalks, some wine, sugar, ginger, and almonds. The leaves are used as an herb. When juicing fennel, mix it with carrots, apples, pears, or celery to cut down on its licorice-like intensity.

Health Benefits Among herbalists, fennel is viewed in several ways: as an intestinal antispasmodic, for relieving intestinal spasms or cramps; as a carminative, for relieving or expelling gas; as a stomachic, for toning and strengthening the stomach; and as an anodyne, for relieving or soothing pain. Fennel also contains substances known as phytoestrogens, which make it useful in treating many female complaints, especially menopause. Fennel is even higher in coumarin compounds than celery or carrots.

Flower Blossoms and Other Edible Blossoms

General Information Flower and other edible blossoms invite the eye and delight the heart. The culinary use of flowers dates back thousands of years; the first recorded mention was 140 years before the Christian Era. When choosing flowers, there are several important guidelines that should be followed. First, be sure to use only edible blossoms. Ensure that the flowers selected have been grown without the use of pesticides or other chemical sprays. Flowers from the florist are quite often treated, so those from a reliable source, such as an untreated home garden, are best. If gathering flowers from the garden, they should be picked early in the day and in dry weather. Rinse quickly under gently running cool water. Do not gather more than one day in advance, as the blossoms wilt quickly. Before using in any preparation, remove the pistils, stamens, and the white part at the base of the petals; this "heel" will impart a bitter flavor to the finished dish.

Culinary Uses With their delicate flavors and wild colors, flowers add poetry to any meal. Some, like squash or zucchini blossoms, are large enough to be stuffed and cooked, while others simply add their sweet scent and piquant coloring to salads, festive desserts, or platters. Use a salad dressing that is light in vinegar or lemon juice, as a highly acidic dressing will both discolor the petals and overwhelm their subtle flavor. For centuries in Europe, flowers flavored salads, puddings, tarts, custards, liqueurs, and candies. They were eaten raw, pulped, fried, and used in stuffing fowl. The Chinese make tea from many flowers, including jasmine, rose, lotus, peony, narcissus, and marigold. Not all flowers are edible, though, and those that are must be acquired from safe sources so as to avoid pesticides, herbicides, and other toxic chemicals.

Varieties

Flower blossoms that are edible include: borage, calendula, chrysanthemum, daisy, day lily, geranium, hollyhock, honeysuckle, lavender, lobelia, marigold, nasturtium, pansy, rose, Scotch broom, sweet pea, and violet. Nasturtium buds or young seed pods are often pickled and used as a substitute for capers, and their tender, young leaves add a peppery flavor to salad. Only the flowers are edible on sweet peas; the pods are poisonous. Avoid flowers from bulbs, as some may be toxic (such as daffodils and tulips).

Fruit blossoms are almost too precious to eat, but if there is an abundance, then indulge in some. All edible fruits have edible blossoms; apple, peach, plum, orange, and lemon are all fragrant and delicately flavored. Cherry and strawberry blossoms are a special delicacy.

Herb blossoms include: borage, chive, dill, garlic, marjoram, oregano, rosemary, savory, tarragon, and thyme.

Vegetable blossoms for the table include: arugula, bean, chicory, cucumber, pea, and squash. Blossoms can be picked from any squash, winter or summer variety, but zucchini plants produce particularly luxuriant blooms.

Lore and Legend

With their wild beauty and connection with the mysteries of reproduction, flowers were often associated with magic, sorcery, and witchcraft. One popular brew of flowers in the Middle Ages was said to enable one to see fairies.

Glasswort *(Salicornia europea, S. herbacea)*

Also Known As: Marsh Samphire, Saltwort.

Salicornia *is from the Latin words for salt and horn, since these are saline plants with horn-like branches.* Europea *means European, while* herbacea *means herbaceous, or not woody.*

General Information Jointed like green coral polished smooth and shiny by the sea, glasswort is a mild seashore succulent that grows profusely on mudflats below the high tide line. Resembling baby aloe, glasswort is sold by fish-mongers from spring through early summer, and is at its prime in May, when the shoots are large enough to have some substance but before the central core begins to get woody.

Buying Tips When you choose, select plants that are firm and bright, not flabby or slimy. No soft or discolored spots should be evident.

Culinary Uses Glasswort is very crunchy and salty, like brined baby string beans. When young, it is crisp, pleasantly deep-sea tasting, an unusual summer pleasure that grows in abundance along the Atlantic and Pacific coasts. Toss it into salads, fresh, for a saline crunch. Slightly older plants need to be steamed or boiled briefly for only a few minutes. To prepare, rinse thoroughly and trim off any damaged parts and the woody base. Eat like asparagus with melted butter, or chill to combine with vegetables, seafood, or meat in a composed salad. Glasswort has a natural affinity with fish, and does well when prepared jointly. It can also be pickled.

Good King Henry *(Chenopodium bonus-henricus)*

Also Known As: Wild Spinach, Lincolnshire Asparagus, Fat Hen.

> Chenopodium *is a Greek word meaning goosefoot and alludes to the shape of the leaves;* bonus-henricus *simply means good Henry. The English name* Good King Henry *refers to the much-loved king Henry VII of England.*

General Information Once widely cultivated in European and American gardens, this British native is now rarely seen. A member of the goosefoot family, it is a coarse, many-branched plant that grows to a height of about two feet, and whose leaves are smooth, arrowhead-shaped, and dark green with purplish centers.

Culinary Uses Cut the young stalks as they appear in early spring; they need no further preparation other than cleaning before they are cooked in whatever manner is preferred. Older stalks should be peeled to remove the tough outer skin before cooking. The stalks are said to resemble asparagus in flavor. Young leaves can be harvested and steamed like spinach or other greens, while the shoots and flower heads are prepared like asparagus. Older leaves tend to be very bitter.

Health Benefits The plant's medicinal properties were held in high regard during times past, and it was widely known as Mercury goosefoot and wild Mercury, in honor of the ancient Roman god of medicine.

Heart of Palm *(Euterpe edulis)*

> *The genus* Euterpe *is named after the Muse of music and lyric poetry from Greek mythology;* edulis *means edible.*

General Information A tropical delicacy, palm hearts are the growing tips of palm trees, the cylindrical bundle of leaf bases that may be several inches in diameter and several feet long. Unfortunately, cutting out the heart also completely destroys the tree. Hearts of palm are an important vegetable in Brazil, have spread northward to Florida, and are now becoming popular in the fashionable cuisines of the United States and Europe.

Culinary Uses Slender, ivory-colored, and delicately flavored, hearts of palm resemble white asparagus, sans tips, and taste something like an artichoke. It is rare to find them fresh outside Brazil, but the canned, marinated varieties are also excellent used as a vegetable or added to salads and appetizers. They consist of several layers of skin, like leeks, but have the delicate flavor of asparagus.

Hops *(Humulus lupulus)*

> Humulus *is a Latin name of unknown origin;* lupulus *means small wolf, after their habit of climbing over other plants (wolfing them).*

General Information Hops will grow anywhere except in desert areas, growing vertically and rampantly. The bracts (modified leaves) and flowers of the female hop plants are used to flavor beer, whether it be commercial or home brew. The edible flowers are small, papery green cones that are harvested in fall.

Culinary Uses The conelike flowers are used as a seasoning. Young spring shoots, which look like thin branched asparagus, are a delicious spring favorite in France. To prepare them for eating, snap off the top six inches of the shoot. The whole tender tip is eaten. Cook and serve as you would asparagus. They are particularly good with a cream sauce.

Horseradish *(Armoracia lapathifolia, A. rusticana)*

> Armoracia *was the Roman name for a wild radish that cannot be identified with certainty as horseradish. The term* rusticana *means rustic, or pertaining to the country. It received its English name* horseradish *due to its large size, and to distinguish it from the common radish.*

General Information Horseradish is a member of the mustard family, believed native to Hungary or Russia. Its characteristic hot flavor is produced by mustard oil, which dissipates rapidly after cutting or grating and is thoroughly destroyed by heat. Each root has quite a different shape, but they are generally from six inches to a foot long, and from one to three inches in diameter, with several rounded protuberances at one end. Beauty is definitely not this root's strong point; the skin is the color and texture of a scruffy, wrinkled, gnarled parsnip root, and may or may not have green tops.

Buying Tips Horseradish is available as a whole fresh root, as a dried powder, or in commercial preparations. Look for roots that are exceptionally hard and free of spongy or soft spots; avoid sprouting, greenish-tinged ones, which may have a bitter layer that requires deep paring. The whole root stays fresh in the refrigerator for months; once grated, however, horseradish spoils rapidly.

Culinary Uses The flavor of horseradish is hot and biting, but with a pungency that is somehow refreshing and cooling. By far the strongest flavored of cultivated vegetables, horseradish roots are best when raw and freshly grated, as the pungent taste is completely destroyed by cooking. Like good-quality pepper, it should be grated directly onto the food soon before eating, or its volatile flavor dissipates. Add horseradish to vegetables, soups, meats, dressings, anything you want to spice up. Most familiar to Westerners in condiment form, horseradish sauce is made by peeling and grinding the roots, then mixing them with vinegar.

Health Benefits Antiscorbutic, antiseptic, diuretic, rubefacient, stimulant Horseradish has long been famed for its medicinal qualities. It is an excellent solvent of excess mucus in the system, stimulates the appetite, and aids in the secretion of digestive juices, but if taken in excess may be irritating to the kidneys and bladder. Applied as a poultice, the mustard oil (allylisothiocyanate) in horseradish irritates the skin and causes the small blood vessels just under the surface to dilate, increasing the flow of blood and making the skin feel warm. An infusion of horseradish in milk makes an excellent cosmetic for the skin and helps restore freshness and color to the cheeks; horseradish juice, mixed with white vinegar and applied externally, is reputed to remove freckles. Low in fat, high in fiber, sulphur, fluorine, potassium, and vitamin C.

Jicama *(Pachyrhizus erosus, P. tuberosus)*

> Pachyrhizus *comes from two Greek words meaning thick root;* erosus *means erose or jagged, as if gnawed;* tuberosus *means tuberous. The English name* jicama *is derived from the Nahuatlan Indian* xicama, *meaning edible storage root.*

General Information Native to Mexico and the headwater region of the Amazon in South America, jicama is the fleshy underground tuber of a leguminous plant. Above ground, this plant is a high-climbing vine with showy flowers and inedible pea pods; below ground, the large tuber is top-shaped, with a rough brown skin.

Buying Tips Always choose jicamas that look firm and unblemished.

Culinary Uses The jicama's juicy snowy-white interior is crunchy and sweetly bland, tasting like a cross between an apple and pear. Specimens that are heavy-skinned and dryish may be fibrous and starchy instead of sweet—as dull as a raw potato; these are best used in a cooked dish. Jicama could not be easier to prepare, requiring only the peeling of its thinnish, sandy-tan, matte skin. Do not peel jicama until just before it is to be served or eaten, because this vegetable tends to dry out and become hard and fibrous once cut. Its relatively bland taste makes it suitable for most every dish, from salads and fruit medleys to stir-fries. It is delicious when served raw in salads or when added to soups or stews for an extra crispy texture. The Chinese use jicama as they use water chestnuts in stir-fried dishes, because of its similar taste and texture. Jicama can even be baked like a potato or grated and used as a pie filling.

Health Benefits Low in fat, high in fiber, potassium, iron, calcium, and vitamins A, B complex, and C.

Jinengo *(Dioscorea pentaphylla)*

Also Known As: Mountain Yam, Wild Yam.

> *This family of plants was given the genus name* Dioscorea *in honor of Dioscorides, a Greek naturalist of the first or second century* A.D. Pentaphylla *means five-leaved.*

General Information This buff-colored tuber is slightly hairy and grows to lengths of three feet. Native Americans and Asians value this wild mountain yam both as a food and for its medicinal properties.

Jinengo

Nutritional Value Per 100 g Edible Portion

	Raw	Cooked
Calories	67	82
Protein	1.34 g	1.73 g
Fat	0.10 g	0.08 g
Fiber	0.45 g	0.56 g
Calcium	26 mg	8 mg
Iron	0.44 mg	0.43 mg
Magnesium	12 mg	10 mg
Phosphorus	34 mg	40 mg
Potassium	418 mg	495 mg
Sodium	13 mg	12 mg
Beta Carotene (A)	0 IU	0 IU
Thiamine (B_1)	0.102 mg	0.086 mg
Riboflavin (B_2)	0.019 mg	0.014 mg
Niacin (B_3)	0.481 mg	0.130 mg
Ascorbic Acid (C)	2.6 mg	0 mg

Culinary Uses Jinengo may be cooked like potato chips or potato patties. Grated raw jinengo is one of the most gooey substances imaginable; because of this mucilaginous quality, it is often used as a binder to hold other ingredients together, but loses this quality when cooked.

Health Benefits Add tamari to grated raw jinengo and you have a digestive aid highly esteemed in Japanese and macrobiotic cuisines, containing even more of the starch-digesting enzyme diastase than does daikon. Jinengo also contains allantoin, which is beneficial for stomach ulcers and asthma.

Kale (*Brassica oleracea* var. *acephala*)

The Latin name Brassica *derives from the Celtic* bresic*;* oleracea *refers to a vegetable garden herb that is used in cooking. The distinctive part of kale's scientific name is* acephala, *meaning headless, which separates it (and collards, a non-curly sibling) from the rest of the cabbage brood. The Latin word* caulis, *meaning stem or cabbage, is the root of the English name* kale.

Kale

Nutritional Value Per 100 g Edible Portion

	Blue Raw	Blue Cooked	Scotch Raw	Scotch Cooked
Calories	50	32	42	28
Protein	3.30 g	1.90 g	2.80 g	1.90 g
Fat	0.70 g	0.40 g	0.60 g	0.41 g
Fiber	1.50 g	0.80 g	1.23 g	0.85 g
Calcium	135 mg	72 mg	205 mg	132 mg
Iron	1.70 mg	0.90 mg	3.00 mg	1.93 mg
Magnesium	34 mg	18 mg	88 mg	57 mg
Phosphorus	56 mg	28 mg	62 mg	38 mg
Potassium	447 mg	228 mg	450 mg	274 mg
Sodium	43 mg	23 mg	70 mg	45 mg
Zinc	0.440 mg	0.240 mg	0.370 mg	0.240 mg
Copper	0.290 mg	0.156 mg	0.243 mg	0.156 mg
Manganese	0.774 mg	0.416 mg	0.648 mg	0.417 mg
Beta Carotene (A)	8900 IU	7400 IU	3100 IU	1994 IU
Thiamine (B_1)	0.110 mg	0.053 mg	0.070 mg	0.040 mg
Riboflavin (B_2)	0.130 mg	0.070 mg	0.060 mg	0.039 mg
Niacin (B_3)	1.000 mg	0.500 mg	1.300 mg	0.792 mg
Pantothenic Acid (B_5)	0.091 mg	0.049 mg	0.076 mg	0.048 mg
Pyridoxine (B_6)	0.271 mg	0.138 mg	0.227 mg	0.139 mg
Folic Acid (B_9)	29.3 mcg	13.3 mcg	n/a	13.3 mcg
Ascorbic Acid (C)	120.0 mg	41.0 mg	130.0 mg	52.8 mg

General Information Kale is native either to the eastern Mediterranean region or to Asia Minor. A botanically primitive, "headless" member of the cabbage family, kale appears in today's gardens in much the same form as it did several thousand years ago. Perhaps kale has changed so little over time simply because horticultural fiddling seemed unnecessary. In addition to being among the most vigorous, prolific, and easy-to-grow vegetables, this uncomplicated plant is resistant to cold, is simple to harvest, store, and prepare, and is rich in vitamins and minerals. There are two common varieties: Scotch kale has curly, bright green to greenish-yellow leaves; blue kale has deep green to bluish leaves that are plume-like with frilled edges. The flowering variety is also edible, but is not generally as tender, and serves better in an ornamental role. Kale supplies fresh greens throughout the year, and frost only heightens the flavor by releasing its high sugar content.

Buying Tips Select small deep-colored bunches with clean, slightly moist leaves. The more crinkled the leaves, the better the taste, with the younger plants being the most tender.

Culinary Uses Kale has a cabbagelike flavor, with a sharpness that some people dislike. During the winter months, the leaves are at their most flavorful and tender. As versatile as cabbage or spinach, baby kale can be part of a green salad (in moderation, as it is strong-tasting and chewy). It can also be cooked: steamed for a few minutes, the leaves whole or cut into strips; stir-fried with ginger and garlic; or sautéed with butter and oil, adding garlic, onion, caraway, or fennel to your liking. In the spring, the young shoots may be gathered; they have a more delicate flavor than the leaves, with a taste that suggests hazelnuts.

Health Benefits Kale is valuable as an internal body cleanser, but has a tendency to generate flatulence when the body is overly acidic. It is also beneficial for the digestive and nervous systems, builds up the calcium content of the body, and is one of the cancer preventative foods. All *Brassica*-genus vegetables contain dithiolthiones, a group of compounds that have anti-cancer, antioxidant properties; indoles, substances that protect against breast and colon cancer; and sulphur, which has antibiotic and antiviral characteristics. This family of vegetables also mildly stimulates the liver and other tissues out of stagnancy.

Kohlrabi *(Brassica oleracea gongylodes caulorapa)*

The Latin name Brassica *derives from the Celtic* bresic; oleracea *refers to a vegetable garden herb that is used in cooking. The term* gongylodes *means roundish or swollen, while* caulorapa *means stem-turnip. The English name* kohlrabi *is derived from the Latin words* caulis, *meaning stem, and* rapa, *meaning turnip.*

Kohlrabi

Nutritional Value Per 100 g Edible Portion

	Raw	Cooked
Calories	27	29
Protein	1.70 g	1.80 g
Fat	0.10 g	0.11 g
Fiber	1.00 g	1.10 g
Calcium	24 mg	25 mg
Iron	0.40 mg	0.40 mg
Magnesium	19 mg	19 mg
Phosphorus	46 mg	45 mg
Potassium	350 mg	340 mg
Sodium	20 mg	21 mg
Beta Carotene (A)	36 IU	35 IU
Thiamine (B_1)	0.050 mg	0.040 mg
Riboflavin (B_2)	0.020 mg	0.020 mg
Niacin (B_3)	0.400 mg	0.390 mg
Pantothenic Acid (B_5)	0.165 mg	n/a
Pyridoxine (B_6)	0.150 mg	n/a
Ascorbic Acid (C)	62.0 mg	54.0 mg

General Information The odd-looking kohlrabi is native to northern Europe, another member of the large cabbage family. Instead of a head of closely packed leaves, this cabbage mutant has a globular swelling of the stem just above the ground, either green or purple, some three or four inches in diameter.

Buying Tips The condition of the tops is a good indication of quality; tops should be young and green, and the thickened stem firm and crisp, with the smaller ones milder and sweeter.

Culinary Uses Kohlrabi has a crisp texture and tangy turnip-like taste, but is sweeter, juicier, crisper, and more delicate than any turnip. Kohlrabi can be grated and eaten raw in salads, where it provides a taste reminiscent of radishes. Cooked in any manner—blanched, steamed, boiled, braised, or sautéed—it tastes more like turnips or mild cabbage.

Health Benefits Kohlrabi is an excellent blood and kidney cleanser, helping to clear poor complexions resulting from toxemia, and is also good for the skeletal, digestive, and lymphatic systems. All *Brassica*-genus vegetables contain dithiolthiones, a group of compounds that have anti-cancer, antioxidant properties; indoles, substances that protect against breast and colon cancer; and sulphur, which has antibiotic and antiviral characteristics. This family of vegetables also mildly stimulates the liver and other tissues out of stagnancy.

Lettuce and Other Salad Greens *(Lactuca sativa)*

The botanical name Lactuca *is derived from the Latin word* lac, *meaning milk, and refers to the plant's milky, mildly soporific juice.* Sativa *refers to the fact that this plant has long been cultivated. The English name* lettuce *is a derivative of the Latin.*

General Information Wild lettuce originated along the Mediterranean littoral, and was known as an edible green throughout antiquity. Belonging to the plant family that includes daisies and thistles, the primitive forms of lettuce had long stems and large leaves. It appeared in Greek and Roman gardens 500 years before the start of the Christian Era, but was considered a luxury and reserved for feast days and the tables of the wealthy. Brought into common favor by Antonius Musa, physician to the Emperor Augustus, lettuce was prescribed as a health-giving food; before that, lettuce was usually eaten as a dessert. Emperor Domitian invented salad dressing, and lettuce quickly became an hors d'oeuvre. Horace later relates that no proper patrician feast began without a salad of lettuce and radishes to stimulate the appetite and "to relax the alimentary canal," preparing the body for a surfeit of food. Columbus brought lettuce to America in 1493; a quick crop, it was favored by greens-hungry early explorers. Sometime during the sixteenth century, close-packed heads of lettuce were developed, with loose-headed ones appearing about a century later. Under the domineering aegis of Louis XIV, who liked his lettuce seasoned with tarragon, pimpernel, basil, and violets, the seventeenth-century French

Lettuce & Salad Greens

Nutritional Value Per 100 g Edible Portion

	Arugula	Belgian Endive	Bibb and Boston	Celtuce	Curly Leaf Endive
Calories	25	15	13	22	17
Protein	2.58 g	1.00 g	1.29 g	0.85 g	1.25 g
Fat	0.66 g	0.10 g	0.22 g	0.30 g	0.20 g
Fiber	n/a	n/a	n/a	0.40 g	0.90 g
Calcium	160 mg	n/a	n/a	39 mg	52 mg
Iron	n/a	0.50 mg	0.30 mg	0.55 mg	0.83 mg
Magnesium	47 mg	13 mg	n/a	28 mg	15 mg
Phosphorus	52 mg	21 mg	n/a	39 mg	28 mg
Potassium	369 mg	182 mg	257 mg	330 mg	314 mg
Sodium	27 mg	7 mg	5 mg	11 mg	22 mg
Zinc	0.470 mg	n/a	0.170 mg	n/a	0.790 mg
Copper	0.076 mg	n/a	0.023 mg	n/a	0.099 mg
Manganese	0.321 mg	n/a	0.133 mg	n/a	0.420 mg
Beta Carotene (A)	2,373 IU	0 IU	970 IU	3,500 IU	2,050 IU
Thiamine (B_1)	0.044 mg	0.070 mg	0.060 mg	0.055 mg	0.080 mg
Riboflavin (B_2)	0.086 mg	0.140 mg	0.060 mg	0.070 mg	0.075 mg
Niacin (B_3)	0.305 mg	0.500 mg	0.300 mg	0.550 mg	0.400 mg
Pantothenic Acid (B_5)	0.437 mg	n/a	n/a	n/a	0.900 mg
Pyridoxine (B_6)	0.073 mg	0.045 mg	n/a	n/a	0.020 mg
Folic Acid (B_9)	97 mcg	n/a	73.3 mcg	n/a	142.0 mcg
Ascorbic Acid (C)	n/a	10.0 mg	8.0 mg	19.5 mg	6.5 mg
Tocopherol (E)	n/a	n/a	n/a	n/a	n/a

popularized the lettuce salad. There are five general types of common lettuce: **crisphead (iceberg), butterhead (Boston, Bibb), Cos (Romaine), leaf (bunching),** and **stem.**

Buying Tips Make sure all salad greens are fresh, crisp, not wilted, and if a headed variety, the head should be fairly firm to hard. Rust-colored spots, though not aesthetically pleasing, are harmless. They are caused by wide fluctuations in temperature during the growing process. Loose outer leaves are called "wrapper leaves," and are usually the most nutritious. Unless damaged, they should not be trimmed off.

Lore and Legend

Because the "milk" in lettuce was believed to possess aphrodisiac qualities, the Egyptian fertility god Min had lettuce offered to him. Early Greek fertility festivals (seventh century B.C.) were known as Adonis festivals, and quick-growing lettuce was planted in pots and carried to symbolize the transitory quality of life. These potted plants, called the Gardens of Adonis, were possibly the beginnings of the custom of raising plants in pots around the house. In central Europe, lettuce was looked upon as the zealously guarded property of the devil, but his demons lurked in the lettuce-beds only during the day; at night, when the demons were off on their nefarious business, however, witches were likely to be abroad. Only from dawn to sunrise were the beds left unguarded, and the peasants were very careful to gather the lettuce at that time and no other.

Culinary Uses The flavor of lettuce ranges from mild and watery to sharply pungent. Its most common use is that of a salad ingredient. For extra crispness and crunchiness, place your completed salad in the freezer for a few minutes before serving. Lettuce is compatible with all fruits and vegetables and has only about 70 calories per head, so don't be shy when building your salads.

Health Benefits Anodyne, antispasmodic, expectorant, sedative. Lettuce of every variety is among humankind's most valuable healing foods because of its large organic water content, ranging from 92 to 95 percent. Nearly all the necessary vitamins are found in lettuce, with the outer leaves being the most valuable. A good rule of thumb is that the greener and darker the leaf, the more nutritious it is. Lettuce contains the most silicon of common vegetables, a nutrient that helps renew joints, bones, arteries, and all connective tissues. The plant is at its medicinal best when it has bolted to seed; at that point it contains a milky juice whose sedative, narcotic, and anesthetic qualities are well recognized. Lettuce helps cure insomnia and nightmares, and can allay excessive physical desire. An old name for it is "the herb of eunuchs," yet in one of those paradoxes of nature, lettuce is also the plant of fertility, since it is exceptionally rich in vitamin E, a key element in the reproductive process.

Varieties

Arugula (*Eruca vesicaria sativa*), also known as **Rucola** and **Rocket**, is a Mediterranean-region type of lettuce that grows so plentifully in the wild that it was not cultivated until recently. The serrated leaves are attractive, between oak-leaf lettuce and dandelion in shape, and have an appealing but sharp flavor and aroma that is both earthy, peppery, and mustard-like. Like watercress, it is more than a leafy green, less than a strong herb. Favored as a salad herb in Italy, Greece, and France, it is best used when the leaves are no more than three inches long and then only as a seasoning herb.

Belgian or **French endive** *(Cichonum endiva)*, a member of the chicory family, is really Witloof (meaning whiteleaf) chicory. The first Belgian endives were grown by accident in the nineteenth century when some chicory roots that had been left in a dark spot began to sprout. A Brussels horticulturist then set to work developing the vegetable in earnest. Later, when a shipment of cultivated endives sent to Paris became a hit, the Belgian endive industry was launched. Looking like small, tightly wrapped, white-husked ears of corn, or perhaps a fat cigar, these little plants have a distinctive, pleasantly bitter taste. The fresh leaves are smooth and wax-like and add an appealing pungency and crispness to salads. Cooked whole, Belgian endives have a tenderness and succulence all their own. While they have even fewer vitamins and minerals than iceberg lettuce, they do have more flavor. The supply and quality are best between September through April.

Bibb and **Boston lettuce** are two of the more common types of butterhead lettuce. Bibb lettuce is a small cup-shaped lettuce, similar to the petals of a rose, and was named after Major John Bibb, its developer. The tender leaves are a deep rich green, blending to a whitish green toward the core. It has a distinct crispness and flavor, delicate, mild, and sweet. It is considered the choicest member of the lettuce family, and also the most expensive. Boston lettuce is a little larger than a softball, loosely headed, with leaves that have an oily feeling. Outer leaves are a deep dark green, while the inner leaves shade almost to white along the stalk. Not especially crisp, the leaves are sweet and soft, getting softer and sweeter as you reach the heart.

Celtuce, also known as **Asparagus lettuce** or **Stem lettuce**, is a native of China. In 1938 a missionary from western China, close to the Tibetan border, sent a few seeds of a vegetable eaten there to an American seed company. This plant, given the English name celtuce because it looks like a cross between celery and lettuce, is now grown in the United States to some extent. Celtuce produces light green leaves in the shape of a rosette; these are comparable in taste and texture to romaine or cos rather than to the more delicate kinds of leaf lettuce. Older leaves contain a milky sap that makes the leaves too bitter even for those who fancy bitter foods. As the plant bolts to a seedhead, the stalk that bears the leaves elongates and will reach heights of up to five feet. This celery-like stem remains tasty until the flower buds develop. For the tastiest dining, the stem should be harvested when about one inch in diameter at the base. Before eating, peel off the outer skin to get rid of the sap tubes that carry the bitter milky sap. What remains is a soft, cool green core that lies somewhere near cucumber or mild summer squash in flavor. The stalks can be

Lettuce & Salad Greens

Nutritional Value Per 100 g Edible Portion

	Escarole	Iceberg	Loose-Leaf	Mâche	Radicchio	Romaine
Calories	20	13	18	21	23	16
Protein	1.70 g	1.01 g	1.30 g	2.00 g	1.43 g	1.62 g
Fat	0.10 g	0.19 g	0.30 g	0.40 g	0.25 g	0.20 g
Fiber	0.90 g	0.53 g	0.70 g	0.80 g	n/a	0.70 g
Calcium	81 mg	19 mg	68 mg	n/a	19 mg	36 mg
Iron	1.70 mg	0.50 mg	1.40 mg	n/a	n/a	1.10 mg
Magnesium	n/a	9 mg	11 mg	n/a	13 mg	6 mg
Phosphorus	54 mg	20 mg	25 mg	n/a	40 mg	45 mg
Potassium	294 mg	158 mg	264 mg	n/a	302 mg	290 mg
Sodium	14 mg	9 mg	9 mg	n/a	22 mg	8 mg
Zinc	n/a	0.220 mg	n/a	n/a	0.620 mg	n/a
Copper	n/a	0.028 mg	n/a	n/a	0.341 mg	n/a
Manganese	n/a	0.151 mg	n/a	n/a	0.138 mg	n/a
Beta Carotene (A)	3,300 IU	330 IU	1,900 IU	n/a	27 IU	2,600 IU
Thiamine (B_1)	0.070 mg	0.046 mg	0.050 mg	n/a	0.016 mg	0.100 mg
Riboflavin (B_2)	0.140 mg	0.030 mg	0.080 mg	n/a	0.028 mg	0.100 mg
Niacin (B_3)	0.500 mg	0.187 mg	0.400 mg	n/a	0.255 mg	0.500 mg
Pantothenic Acid (B_5)	n/a	0.046 mg	0.200 mg	n/a	0.269 mg	n/a
Pyridoxine (B_6)	n/a	0.040 mg	0.055 mg	n/a	0.057 mg	n/a
Folic Acid (B_9)	n/a	56.0 mcg	n/a	n/a	60.0 mcg	135.7 mcg
Ascorbic Acid (C)	10.0 mg	3.9 mg	18.0 mg	n/a	8.0 mg	24.0 mg
Tocopherol (E)	n/a	0.40 mg	n/a	n/a	n/a	n/a

served raw as a finger food with a dip, or sliced into a salad. Their crispness also makes them a natural choice for stir-frying, or for serving au gratin. The young leaves and heart are eaten like lettuce.

Garden cress (*Lepidium sativum*) is also known as **Curled cress** and **Pepper grass**. This plant is thought to have originated in western Asia, and was a popular garden vegetable in ancient Greece. A cool weather plant, it flourishes in most temperate regions all over the world in clearings, fields, and alongside roads where the soil is somewhat dry. Sometimes crisped like parsley, garden cress leaves are small and green, varying greatly from species to species and from habitat to habitat. Growing upright anywhere from eight to twenty-four inches tall, and producing white or reddish flowers, the flowers are followed by tiny papery pouches containing hot seeds that add a special tang to soups and salad dressings. Garden cress is generally eaten at the seedling stage. It has a peppery taste and is used raw in salads and sandwiches. Available all year, it is easy to grow at home and is extremely nutritious, offering 9,300 IU (International Units) per 100 grams of vitamin A, and good amounts of vitamin C, iron, and calcium. **Winter cress** (*Barbarea verna, B. vulgaris, B. praecox*), also known as **American cress** and **Land cress**, is indigenous to America and Europe. This variety was named after St. Barbara in the belief that eating these greens on that saint's special day (December 4) would bring good luck. Often found growing wild along streams and roadside swamps, the hardy, low-growing winter cress has dark green leaves that form a rosette pattern and look rather like those of watercress, though somewhat thinner and less succulent. It will grow from eight to thirty inches long and sends forth small clusters of edible bright yellow flowers followed by pointed, 1 1/2 to 2 1/2 inch long seed pods that supply good bird seed. Winter cress greens taste like watercress when raw, but more like mustard greens when cooked.

Curly-leafed endive (*Cichorium endiva crispa*) is often called **Chicory** in other countries. Although closely related botanically, the word *endive* is used to designate plants with narrow, finely divided, curly leaves; *chicory* is a wild- looking green plant with narrow raggedy leaves and a bitter taste. Endive has a large, loose head with crisp, narrow white ribs. Slightly bitter in flavor, it can be served raw or lightly cooked like spinach. Endive is especially rich in minerals.

Escarole (*Cichorium endiva latifolium*), a variety of endive, is sometimes confused with curly-leafed endive. Broad, fleshy, ruffled green leaves that shade from deep green on the outside to butter yellow in the center make up the flat head of escarole. Sturdy and crisp, escarole adds a slightly sharp flavor to tossed salads and is particularly good in combination with sweeter leaves such as romaine. It may also be lightly cooked like spinach.

Iceberg, also known as **Crisphead lettuce**, is the most commonly used but least nutritious of all the varieties of lettuce. The name "iceberg" apparently resulted from the commercial practice in years past of shipping lettuce in ice-filled rail cars to maintain crispness; most iceberg lettuce is still grown in California and shipped elsewhere. A headed lettuce with large, crisp, pale green leaves, firm heads, and little flavor, commercial iceberg is one of the most chemically treated crops. Its one nutritional benefit is that it offers bulk to the intestinal tract.

Loose-leaf, Bunching, or **Leaf lettuce** is the type of lettuce most often grown in home gardens. A tasty bunch, they are a mixture of non-heading greens whose flat, frilled, or double-ruffled leaves in bright green, dark red, and bronze are ornamental as well as delectable in the salad bowl. Quite delicate, leaf lettuce does not store or ship well. Its semi-crisp texture and mild flavor make for soft gentle salads with a sweet flavor.

Mâche (*Valerianella olitoria, V. locusta*), also known as **Corn salad**, **Fetticus**, and **Lamb's lettuce**, is an attractive blue-green European salad herb. The leaves may be variably broad or narrow, dark or medium green, round or spoon-shaped, and sweetly nutty or simply green-flavored. The soft, young leaves are best. Slightly chewy and firm in texture, the leaves make beautiful arranged salads, and may also be used as an attractive and flavorful garnish for cream soup or delicate vegetable purées.

Radicchio (*Cichorium intybus*), also known as **Red chicory**, is another member of the chicory family, and hails from the Treviso area in northern Italy. Its brash striated magenta color and firm crisp leaves make it a dramatic addition to mixed salads and an excellent garnish; its arresting flavor, which borders on sweet, yet is slightly bitter and peppery, also endears it to many palates. Select small-headed radicchio that have a firm white core and that look garden fresh rather than travel-weary, since old radicchio is decidedly bitter. Mostly commonly thought of as a salad green, the sturdy leaves afford much wider use. It may be freely substituted in any chicory or endive recipe; briefly sautéed for a warm salad with mushrooms, cheese and olives; added to soups, or individual leaves may be used as salad cups or wrappers for tasty tidbits.

Romaine or **Cos lettuce** (*Lactuca sativa longifolia*), has heads that are loose, long, and cylindrical, and stiff broad leaves that shade from yellowish-white at the center to dark green at the tips. Individual leaves are elongated ovals, rather loaf-shaped, reminiscent of kitchen tasting spoons; although coarse in texture, the leaves have a semi-sweet taste, with the lighter inner leaves being particularly tender, flavorful, and considered by many salad lovers a necessity in tossed green salads. The common name *romaine* is a corruption of Roman; the even older name *cos* is taken from the Greek island of Kos, the birthplace of the famous physician Hippocrates, where the Romans originally obtained these mildly tangy leaves. One of the best lettuces nutritionally, romaine contains a substantial amount of iron and vitamin E.

Watercress (see separate reference).

Lotus Root

Nutritional Value Per 100 g Edible Portion

	Raw	Cooked
Calories	56	66
Protein	2.60 g	1.58 g
Fat	0.10 g	0.07 g
Fiber	0.80 g	0.85 g
Calcium	45 mg	26 mg
Iron	1.16 mg	0.90 mg
Magnesium	23 mg	22 mg
Phosphorus	100 mg	78 mg
Potassium	556 mg	363 mg
Sodium	40 mg	45 mg
Beta Carotene (A)	0 IU	0 IU
Thiamine (B_1)	0.160 mg	0.127 mg
Riboflavin (B_2)	0.220 mg	0.010 mg
Niacin (B_3)	0.400 mg	0.300 mg
Ascorbic Acid (C)	44.0 mg	27.4 mg

Lotus (*Nelumbo nuciferum*)

Nelumbo *comes from the name of the plant in Singhalese (Sri Lanka), and* nuciferum *means nut-bearing. The English word* lotus *is derived from the Hebraic* lot, *meaning myrrh.*

General Information The lotus plant grows in tropical paddies with its sausage-shaped roots submerged in the mud, and its beautiful leaves and blossoms floating on top of the water. The blossom, widely featured in Indian and Oriental art, is edible as well, as are its leaves, roots, and seeds (see reference for seeds under **Nuts and Seeds**)

Buying Tips The sausage-shaped lotus root varies between 5 and 12 inches in length, and from two to three inches in diameter. They may be clean or dirt-caked. The skin is thin but tough, a fawn to pinkish color.

Culinary Uses The flesh of the root varies from buff to rose or salmon-tinted, and each is pierced with ten air tunnels that, when sliced crosswise, look something like snowflakes, or strangely symmetrical rounds of Swiss

Lore and Legend

"In the beginning were the waters. Matter readied itself. The sun glowed. And a lotus slowly opened, holding the universe on its golden pericarp." The elegant, sweet-scented lotus has long been regarded with reverence by those in the East. The Egyptian lotus, dedicated to Horus, God of the sun, was the age-old solar symbol of reproductive power and fertility since it grew upon the life-giving Nile; Horus himself was represented in mythology as issuing from the cup of the lotus blossom, thus signifying immortality and eternal youth. The Hindu god Brahma was also born in the sacred bosom of the flower. The five petals of the flower symbolize the five stages in the Hindu wheel of life: birth, initiation, marriage, rest from labor, and death. Chinese Buddhists believe in the Western Heaven with its Sacred Lake of Lotuses, a place where souls of the deceased faithful sleep in lotus buds until the appointed time when they are admitted to Paradise.

cheese. The starchy yet crunchy flesh is slightly sweet and mild, tasting somewhat like water chestnuts. The crunchy texture does not dissipate with cooking. Thin, lacy slices make a nice garnish for salads, or the root may be sliced or grated for use in soups, stews, sautéed dishes, or stir-fries. It can be cooked like other starchy vegetables such as turnips, potatoes, jicama, or water chestnuts. Peel before use. Dried lotus root is also available in many specialty shops; reconstituted, it may be substituted for the fresh root in most dishes. Lotus root flour is made from the dried and powdered root; this gluten-free flour is used in Chinese and Japanese cooking as a thickener for sauces. Tender young lotus leaves are used either raw as part of a green salad or lightly cooked as a hot vegetable. The mature leaves are used as a wrapping and impart their aroma to what is inside. The seeds can be dried, roasted, or pickled (they cannot be eaten raw). Flower petals may be floated on a clear soup.

Health Benefits In Oriental medicine, lotus root is considered a warming food and prescribed for lung-related ailments, to increase energy, control blood pressure, neutralize toxins, and help digestion. The linking part between the two roots is considered the most medicinal.

Martynia *(Proboscidea louisianica, P. annua, P. parviflora)*

Also Known As: Unicorn Flower, Proboscis Plant, Devil's Claw, Ram's Horn.

The genus name Proboscidea *means proboscis-like, which this plant certainly qualifies for;* louisianica *means coming from Louisiana,* annua *means annual,* parviflora *means small-flowered. The plant was given its English name* martynia *in honor of John Martyn (1699–1768), a professor of botany at Cambridge.*

General Information Native to southwestern North America, martynia is a warm weather annual with heavy stems, coarse roots, and soft, crinkly foliage. Rather wide-spreading, its hairy stems tend to wander off in all directions. The showy flowers come in a variety of hues from purple, pink, and yellow. Following the flowers come the edible seedpods, soft and fuzzily green, which resemble curved okra pods. Seedpods left to mature and dry on the vine gradually harden, darken, and split until two dark horns form at the beaked end. The outer skin drops off and the black seeds fall, leaving a "devil's claw."

Culinary Uses Young seedpods can be pickled or used in soups.

Mushrooms, Truffles, and Other Fungi

The word mushroom *is derived from the Frankish word* mussiriones, *which referred to the meadow mushroom, and from the French* mousseron, *meaning they grow on moist moss.*

General Information Of all the world's foods, perhaps the strangest are mushrooms. For centuries these primitive plants have been linked with magic and myth. A fungi without roots, leaves, flowers, or seeds, mushrooms lack chlorophyll to photosynthesize nourishment from sunlight, and so must receive their nourishment instead from other organic matter, as do scavengers or parasites. Thousands of mushroom species grow in the wild, but many edible species have poisonous lookalikes. By the 1600s, the French had begun cultivating mushrooms to keep up with the local demand. Most of the farming took place in caves that had once been mined for building stone. In 1867, one cave in Mery was said to contain twenty-one miles of beds and produce three thousand pounds of mushrooms daily.

The part of the mushroom that we recognize is actually the fruit of the fungus, which remains underground. Colors range across the palette, from the glowing yellow of the chanterelle, to the shrouded black horn-of-plenty called *trompettes-des-mortes* (death's trumpets) by the French, and everything in between: violet, purple, pastels, and even bright enamel. These wonders of natural design often have stunning appearances, from the vaulted, arched ribs of the chanterelle, to the honeycombed morel, to the ostrich-egg-sized giant puffball. The mushroom is perhaps the most fertile plant in the world, each one producing not just billions of spores, but trillions. Mushroom spores are everywhere; they impregnate the earth, awaiting the opportunity to grow.

Mushrooms and Truffles

Nutritional Value Per 100 g Edible Portion

	Common Raw	Common Cooked	Enoki Raw	Shiitake Dried	Shiitake Cooked
Calories	25	27	35	296	55
Protein	2.09 g	2.17 g	1.54 g	9.58 g	1.56 g
Fat	0.42 g	0.47 g	0.39 g	0.99 g	0.22 g
Fiber	0.75 g	0.87 g	n/a	11.50 g	1.96 g
Calcium	5 mg	6 mg	1 mg	11 mg	3 mg
Iron	1.24 mg	1.74 mg	n/a	1.72 mg	0.44 mg
Magnesium	10 mg	12 mg	16 mg	132 mg	14 mg
Phosphorus	104 mg	87 mg	113 mg	294 mg	29 mg
Potassium	370 mg	356 mg	381 mg	1534 mg	117 mg
Sodium	4 mg	2 mg	3 mg	13 mg	4 mg
Zinc	0.73 mg	0.87 mg	0.57 mg	n/a	n/a
Copper	0.492 mg	0.504 mg	0.067 mg	n/a	n/a
Manganese	0.112 mg	0.115 mg	0.082 mg	n/a	n/a
Beta Carotene (A)	0 IU	0 IU	7 IU	0 IU	0 IU
Thiamine (B_1)	0.102 mg	0.073 mg	0.086 mg	0.300 mg	0.037 mg
Riboflavin (B_2)	0.449 mg	0.300 mg	0.105 mg	1.270 mg	0.170 mg
Niacin (B_3)	4.116 mg	4.460 mg	3.645 mg	14.100 mg	1.500 mg
Pantothenic Acid (B_5)	2.200 mg	2.160 mg	0.926 mg	n/a	n/a
Pyridoxine (B_6)	0.097 mg	0.095 mg	0.043 mg	n/a	n/a
Folic Acid (B_9)	21.1 mcg	18.2 mcg	30.0 mcg	n/a	n/a
Ascorbic Acid (C)	3.5 mg	4.0 mg	11.9 mg	3.5 mg	0.3 mg
Tocopherol (E)	0.08 mg	n/a	n/a	n/a	n/a

Culinary Uses Mushrooms are among the most costly, exotic, and delectable of foods. Like a sponge, they soak up the essence of whatever they are cooked in. Sautéed or as part of a sauce, they add a meatlike flavor and color. Mushrooms have no sugars (and are therefore a good food for diabetics), very little carbohydrate (mostly in the form of indigestible cellulose), many minerals and vitamins (varying with the species), and a good deal of protein (not all of it assimilable).

Health Benefits Asian mushrooms (shiitake, oyster, enoki, and mo-er, or black tree fungus) have been found to thin the blood, which lowers cholesterol and helps prevent strokes and heart attacks. They also stimulate the immune system, help prevent cancer, and possibly help conditions such as rheumatoid arthritis and multiple sclerosis. Studies at Budapest's Institute of Pathology and Experimental Cancer Research have shown that lentinan, a polysaccharide found in shiitakes, is a promising anti-cancer agent and immune-system stimulant. Mushrooms are among the few rich organic sources of germanium, which increases oxygen efficiency, counteracts the effects of pollutants, and increases resistance to disease. They are also rich in zinc, which is valuable in treating skin injuries, regulating prostate gland function, and helping the metabolism of animal and plant proteins. Mushrooms in general neutralize toxic residues in the body from the consumption of animal protein.

Varieties

Chanterelle (*Cantharellus cibarius*), also known as **Girolle** or **Egg mushrooms**, range from bright yellow to orange in color and are shaped like a curving trumpet. There is enormous variation in flavor and size among chanterelles from different locations: they can range from pleasantly mild and meaty to flowery, nutty, and softly cinnamony. Most smell faintly of apricots, and taste slightly peppery when cooked. The intensity of a raw chanterelle's aroma foretells the strength of its flavor when cooked. Available fresh from mid-June through February, they can also be found dried or canned. However, the dried version tends to be tough as rawhide, while the canned ones are too often insipid. For maximum enjoyment, lightly sauté in olive oil and add a dash of salt or tamari. Their firm flesh requires longer cooking than other fungi, and will remain chewy.

Cloud ears (*Auricularia polytricha*), also called **Black mushrooms**, **Black fungus**, **Wood ears**, **Tree ears**, **Judas' ear**, and **Jew's ear**, do actually resemble the ear with a small stretch of the imagination. Long a staple of Chinese cooking, they have been available dried but now are occasionally found fresh. When soaked and rehydrated, the charcoal-black matter blossoms back into its suspended glutinous chewy texture. Mild-tasting and chewy, cloud ears are used to add texture to stir-fries or cold vinaigrette salads. To rehydrate, cover with boiling water and allow to soak for thirty minutes.

Common or **Button mushrooms** (*Agaricus bisporus, A. campestris*) are relatives of the wild field mushroom bred for their shipping and keeping properties, not their taste. Generally plump and dome-like, they have a delicate flavor and can be snow white, tan, or brown in color. All three commercial strains have the same subtle, nutty-sweet taste, but lack the vitality, medicinal properties, and flavor of wild mushrooms. They are also one of the most chemically treated crops. Choose those with caps that are closed or just slightly open. Avoid those with wide-open caps and dark gills, those that are markedly pitted or discolored, and those with a spongy texture.

Enoki (*Flammulina velutipes*), also known as **Snow puffs** or **Golden needles**, are a long, slender, sprout-like mushroom with a diminutive round head and creamy white color. They have a crisp texture with a mild, slightly tangy and citrusy taste, and are

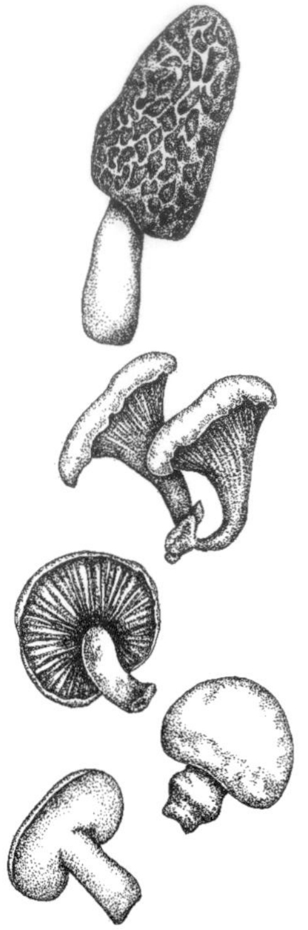

best served raw, as you would sprouts, in salads and sandwiches, or floated on top of soups. Cook only lightly, as they will toughen if cooked for very long. Supermarkets usually carry enokis with roots still attached in sealed plastic packages; they will stay fresh for several days in the refrigerator in these packages. Enokis stimulate the immune system, helping to fight off viruses and tumors.

Morels (*Morchella esculenta*) are easy to recognize with their brown, sponge-like caps pitted with hollows in which the spores are produced, and which gives rise to its other common name of **Sponge** mushroom. These long-capped mushrooms are black, ivory, or yellow, and tiny to fist-sized or larger. A favorite in French cuisine, morels offer an unusually intense earthy flavor that is hard to describe, but which may suggest warm autumn leaves, hazelnuts, or even nutmeg. Dried morels are richer, more intense, and smokier than the fresh; they should have a strong woodsy flavor. Soak the dried variety just a couple of minutes in warm water before use. Morels are excellent with pasta, noodles, or rice dishes. When they are available fresh during spring and early summer, select those that smell sweet and look fresh. This tasty mushroom tends to harbor grit and sometimes insects in its honeycombed cap, so it needs careful washing.

Oyster mushrooms (*Pleurotus ostreatus*), also known as **Tree oysters** or **Chilblains**, can be as tiny as peas or as broad as fried eggs, depending on the strain and its provenance. Pearl to grey in color, usually ruffled and fan-shaped, the smooth deep-gilled caps narrow at the base to a short stubby stem, which attaches them to their cluster of kin. Oyster mushrooms have a flavor that is delicate and mellow; they can be eaten raw, but their dense chewy texture becomes tender and oyster-flavored when cooked. It is best not to overpower them with other strong flavors; break or cut into bite-sized pieces and add to sautés, stir-fries, or soups near the end of cooking. Fresh oyster mushrooms are most abundant in spring and fall in the wild, but cultivated ones are available year-round.

Porcini mushrooms (*Boletus edulis*), also known as **Cepes** or **Boleti**, received the Italian name porcini due to their resemblance to little pigs, and with their coolie-style caps and bulging stems, they resemble Walt Disney's dancing mushrooms in *Fantasia*. The Greeks and Romans used the term *bolites* to describe the best edible mushrooms, but this term has since been applied only to the genus *Boletus*. These wild mushrooms are generally imported dried from Italy. They lose nothing in the transition, though, because they are cut and dried at their peak of ripeness; in fact, the flavor actually intensifies. Fresh porcini range in color from white to reddish-brown, and have a smooth, meaty texture and pungent, woodsy, earthy flavor. Caps can range from one to ten inches in diameter, and one fresh mushroom can weigh up to a pound. To choose good-quality porcini, look for caps that are fully opened (but not to gills), fleshy and whole, and with a stout stem. Porcini are traditionally used to flavor sauces, stews, and rice dishes, but are also good sautéed for a pasta topping or grilled with olive oil and herbs. The dried variety can be rehydrated by soaking in warm water for fifteen to thirty minutes, then rinsed to remove any remaining dirt or grit.

Portobello or **Brown mushrooms** are among the giants of the mushroom world, with their thick, flat, deep brown caps sometimes reaching ten or more inches in diameter. Both the caps and the sturdy stems are edible; just trim the gritty stem end and wipe the top with a damp cloth. Available year-round in many markets, their flavor and texture are almost steak-like when grilled, which is a favorite preparation. They are also excellent added to stews and soups.

Shiitake mushrooms (*Lentinus edodes*), also known as **Oak mushrooms** or **Oriental black mushrooms**, are large, umbrella-shaped mushrooms, dark brown to almost black in color. Shiitakes take their name from the shii tree *(Pasania)* on which they grow, although they will also grow on oak and hornbeam. Once sold only in dried form, shiitakes are now readily available fresh; they are succulent, meltingly tender, and high-priced mushrooms that enhance almost any dish. Try them in soups, stews, sauces, and stir-fries; fresh ones are also delicious baked or grilled. The stems and caps are both edible (although the stems tend to be tough and fibrous), and their rich, meaty flavor goes a long way. When purchasing fresh shiitakes, look for firm, fleshy specimens that are flat and dark, with more cap than stem, and still a little closed rather than open. The more aromatic, the more flavor they will have. Dried shiitake are readily available in most markets. To reconstitute dried mushrooms, submerge them in warm water for at least thirty minutes (one or two hours is preferable); discard the tough stems before use. Shiitakes contain numerous enzymes and vitamins not normally found in plants (including D, B_2, and B_{12}), which may explain the healing qualities traditionally associated with them that scientific studies are now corroborating.

Straw mushrooms look like storybook toadstools. These small conical mushrooms have pointed crowns that are dark brown at the tips and shade to taupe at the base. They have a delicate texture and distinct flavor.

Truffles (*Tuber melanosperm, T. magnatum*) are fungi, but they have taken on a value far beyond any type of mushroom. Reputed as the most delicious food known to man, the truffle has long been regarded as an aphrodisiac without peer. Truffles might very well act as a general stimulant to the system, for they contain a not inconsiderable dose of invigorating mineral salts—including iron. Prized for their flavor, these "diamonds of cookery" have proven nearly impossible to cultivate, and are difficult to harvest in the wild; consequently, they have always been treated as an expensive delicacy. They are never likely to descend to a price within reach of the average consumer, for every year the demand increases and the supply diminishes. The ancient Greeks believed that truffles were created by thunderbolts striking the earth during preautumnal storms, a legend based on the fact that heavy August rains tend to bring a good truffle crop. The plants grow underground, attached to the roots of host trees (usually oak or hazel), and must be sniffed out by pigs or dogs trained specifically to detect their scent. All truffles have a textured surface and dense flesh; their earthy, sometimes garlicky flavor is imparted to any food with which they are stored, cooked, or served. Because of their intense flavor and high price, truffles are used sparingly, either sliced or grated raw over hot foods. Two main types of truffles exist: the black Perigord (from France and southern Italy) and the white Piedmontese (from northern Italy). Black truffles are usually peeled before serving and the peelings are saved to flavor soups and stocks. They are also available canned and in a paste form, but the canned truffles do not have the aroma and flavor of fresh ones. White truffles are never cooked, but are sliced thin and sprinkled over whatever dish they are to adorn; if it is a hot dish, they are added at the last moment, after the cooking is over.

Lore and Legend

Mushrooms, the edible fungi that the ancients called "the plant without leaves," have captured the attention of many peoples. Most ancient cultures believed that the mushroom was magic fare, that it was created by bolts of lightning. Because ordinary citizens did not rate such magic food, in Egypt none but the pharaohs were permitted to partake of this "mysterious night-growing" vegetable. The Greeks and Romans likewise placed mushrooms in a class by themselves, considering them to be food of and for the gods, although that did not stop upper-class Romans from eating them. Julius Caesar even passed stringent laws specifying who could enjoy them and who could not. The Greek city Mycenae possibly takes its name from *mykes* or mushrooms, the legend being that Perseus, hot and thirsty, picked a mushroom and drank the water flowing from it, and then expressed his gratitude by naming the city in its honor. In Asian folklore, mushrooms are esteemed as a longevity tonic. In fact, the symbol for the Chinese god of longevity, Shoulau, is a walking stick capped by a mushroom ornament.

Mustard Greens *(Brassica juncea rugosa)*

The Latin name Brassica *derives from the Celtic* bresic; juncea *means Juneas- or rush-like;* rugosa *means rugose or wrinkled. The English name* mustard *is derived from the Latin* mustum ardens, *or burning must, referring to the early French practice of grinding the pungent seeds with grape must (the still-fermenting juice of wine grapes).*

General Information There are three varieties of mustard grown for greens: one has large, smooth, broad, oval leaves with thick, white ribs; another has wider, bright yellow-green leaves that are curly at the tips; the third has large, smooth leaves with narrow ribs. These greens vary in size and texture, but all have the same pleasantly pungent and bitter taste. The large-leafed pungent garden mustards grown in this country are generally the brown or Indian mustard.

Mustard Greens

Nutritional Value Per 100 g Edible Portion

	Raw	Cooked
Calories	26	15
Protein	2.70 g	2.26 g
Fat	0.20 g	0.24 g
Fiber	1.10 g	0.69 g
Calcium	103 mg	74 mg
Iron	1.46 mg	0.70 mg
Magnesium	32 mg	15 mg
Phosphorus	43 mg	41 mg
Potassium	354 mg	202 mg
Sodium	25 mg	16 mg
Beta Carotene (A)	5,300 IU	3,031 IU
Thiamine (B_1)	0.080 mg	0.041 mg
Riboflavin (B_2)	0.110 mg	0.063 mg
Niacin (B_3)	0.800 mg	0.433 mg
Pantothenic Acid (B_5)	0.210 mg	0.120 mg
Ascorbic Acid (C)	70.0 mg	25.3 mg
Tocopherol (E)	2.01 mg	n/a

Buying Tips Select the smaller leaves, as these will be more tender. They should be of good color, fresh, tender, and crisp. Poor quality is indicated by leaves that are dirty, discolored, wilted, or spotted. While some varieties are naturally yellow, avoid overly yellowed or brown leaves, and those that are very dry with fibrous stems.

Culinary Uses Mustard greens have a strong pungent flavor not appreciated by everyone. Young tender leaves can be used in salads, while the stronger-flavored older leaves are used as cooked greens like spinach. They are especially delicious lightly sautéed with garlic. Mixing them with other vegetables helps cut down on their strong, biting taste.

Health Benefits Because of their high water content, mustard greens are a good cleansing food, an excellent tonic, and are useful in ridding the system of poisonous substances. They are also used as a counter-irritant or as an ingredient of mustard plasters and stimulating liniments. All *Brassica*-genus vegetables contain dithiolthiones, a group of compounds that have anti-cancer, antioxidant properties; indoles, substances that protect against breast and colon cancer; and sulphur, which has antibiotic and antiviral characteristics. This family of vegetables also mildly stimulates the liver and other tissues out of stagnancy.

Nopal Cactus *(Opuntia ficus-indica, O. megacantha)*

Also Known As: Prickly Pear, Barbary Pear, Cactus Pear, Indian Pear, Indian Fig.

Opuntia *was an old Latin name used by Pliny for this plant, probably derived from Opus, a town in Greece.* Ficus-indica *means Indian fig;* megacantha *means large-fruited. The English name* nopal *comes from the Nahuatl* nopalli.

General Information Nopal cactus pads or "leaves" come from any of numerous cacti of the genus *Opuntia*, which are native to the drier regions between Central America and the great deserts of the United States. The Spanish imported this plant from Mexico to Europe soon after the discovery of America; it found a hospitable climate in Sicily and other Mediterranean regions, where it is cultivated and highly enjoyed. The fleshy spiked leaves take the form of flattish discs or pods stacked one on another, inspiring the American name beavertail cactus for the plants. The fruits are also eaten, and discussed under the name Prickly Pear in the **Fruit** section.

Buying Tips Pads should be small, bright green, about 8 inches long, resilient, and not limp or dry. They will likely be de-spined, or of a cultivated spineless variety, but you will still need to trim the "eyes" just in case there are any tiny prickers remaining.

Culinary Uses The flavor of nopal cactus pads or "leaves" is said to resemble artichoke hearts, string beans, or lima beans, with a texture similar to okra. Peeled and cooked, they exude a mucilaginous substance that does not appeal to some, but its soft crunchy texture and pleasant mild flavor make this vegetable worth experimenting with at least once. While some recommend steaming the pads (and then serving them with lemon juice), others use this strange vegetable in gumbo, vegetable soups, omelets, casseroles, chopped into salads, or served in long sticks like carrot sticks. Nopales, canned or bottled with additional spices and herbs, are a tolerable substitute for fresh and should be used in cooked dishes, bearing in mind the extra seasoning, usually chili-hot.

Health Benefits Nopal is marvelously rich in all minerals, vitamins, and protein. Low in fat, high in calcium, magnesium, phosphorus, iron, beta carotene, and vitamins A, B complex, and C.

Okra (*Hibiscus esculenta, Abelmoscus esculentus*)

Hibiscus *is an old Latin name of unknown meaning for this family of plants;* esculenta *means esculent or edible. The English name* okra *derives from* nkruman *or* nkrumun*, from the Twi language spoken on the Gold Coast of Africa. In other parts of the world where the vegetable is popular—the Caribbean, South America, the Middle East, India, and Africa—it is still referred to as* gumbo*, from the Umbundun* ochinggombo *or* ngombo.

General Information Okra originated in Africa, probably in the region of Ethiopia, where it still grows wild, and was brought to the European continent by the Moors. It is believed that the French introduced the plant into the United States early in the eighteenth century, because it is a popular ingredient in the famed French cuisine of New Orleans. A tall warm-weather plant related to hibiscus and cotton that is raised for its edible pods, okra grows on a showy, flowering bush, and the foliage in some types can reach a height of seven to ten feet. The finger-like edible pods, sometimes called "lady fingers," are actually immature seed pods that develop from the plant's pretty red-throated yellow blooms. If allowed to fully ripen, okra becomes fibrous and indigestible. In most varieties, the pods are slender, deep green, and ridged, growing up to seven inches long but picked for commercial use before reaching this length.

Okra

Nutritional Value Per 100 g Edible Portion

	Raw	Cooked
Calories	38	32
Protein	2.00 g	1.87 g
Fat	0.10 g	0.17 g
Fiber	0.94 g	0.90 g
Calcium	81 mg	63 mg
Iron	0.80 mg	0.45 mg
Magnesium	57 mg	57 mg
Phosphorus	63 mg	56 mg
Potassium	303 mg	322 mg
Sodium	8 mg	5 mg
Zinc	0.600 mg	0.550 mg
Copper	0.094 mg	0.086 mg
Manganese	0.990 mg	0.911 mg
Beta Carotene (A)	660 IU	575 IU
Thiamine (B_1)	0.200 mg	0.132 mg
Riboflavin (B_2)	0.060 mg	0.055 mg
Niacin (B_3)	1.000 mg	0.871 mg
Pantothenic Acid (B_5)	0.245 mg	0.213 mg
Pyridoxine (B_6)	0.215 mg	0.187 mg
Folic Acid (B_9)	87.8 mcg	45.7 mcg
Ascorbic Acid (C)	21.1 mg	16.3 mg

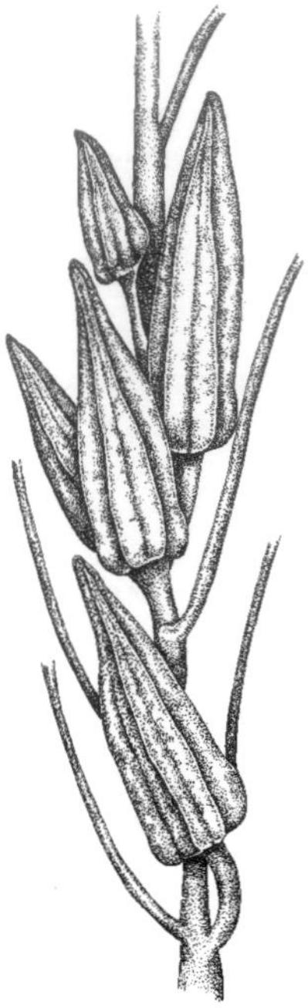

One miniature type, marketed as "Chinese okra," has plumper, more rounded pods that are two to three inches long.

Buying Tips When purchasing, choose small pods that are firm, springy, and resilient when pressed, richly green, and show no signs of surface discoloration. Those less than three inches long are preferable; large pods are often hard or tough, but these can be dried and ground into a protein-rich flour.

Culinary Uses A favorite vegetable throughout the southeastern United States, okra has a subtly tart yet clean flavor that falls between that of eggplant and asparagus (some say green beans and gooseberries). Wash them just before preparing and cut off the woody stem ends, but only at the last moment, or the pods will quickly start oozing. Inside the tapering, fuzzy green pod is a soft tissue that exudes a sticky juice when cooked. This stickiness is what makes okra a thickener, and also why many people turn up their noses at its mere mention. The trick to cooking okra is simply not to overcook it; prolonged cooking only promotes gooeyness. A main ingredient in gumbos and curries, okra will thicken any dish to which it is added. It can be boiled, baked, sautéed, stuffed, or fried with meat, onions, tomatoes, or other vegetables. When cooked in utensils made of copper, brass, iron, or tin, okra may discolor and turn an extremely unappetizing black. Okra flour is a nutritious addition to broths and soups.

Health Benefits Okra contains a vegetable mucin that is soothing to irritated membranes of the intestinal tract.

Onion *(Allium cepa)*

> Allium *is the ancient Latin name for the garlic family, possibly taken from the Celtic* all, *meaning pungent;* cepa *is an old Latin term for onion. Because the onion bulb is a single united entity rather than a conglomeration of separate cloves as found in garlic, it was referred to by the Roman Columella in* A.D. *42 as* unio *or* unionem, *meaning united, from which the common English name is derived.*

General Information The onion is considered to be of Central Asian origin, and propagated by the Indo-European tribes in their separate migrations. A member of the lily family along with asparagus, and one of the oldest vegetables known to man, its use goes back many millennia. The oldest known body of law, the Code of Hammurabi, stipulates that the needy shall receive a monthly ration of bread and onions. Evidently the onions were regarded as primarily a food for the poor, who ate it raw on bread, a combination which formed their staple diet. In America, Cortez saw onions on his way to Tenochtitlan, while farther north and a century later, Pere Marquette told of being saved from starvation by eating native wild American onions. This was in 1624, when his explorations took him from Green Bay to a point on the southern shore of Lake Michigan that still commemorates its abundance in onions by having taken for its name the Indian word for their odor: Chicago. This slightly less assertive cousin of garlic offers many varieties to choose from, with a wide range of shapes, sizes, colors, and pungency. An indispensable pantry staple and the most universally eaten vegetable, the onion is truly an all-season vegetable.

Onion Family

Nutritional Value Per 100 g Edible Portion

	Onion Raw	Onion Cooked	Onion Powder	Powder 1 tsp.
Calories	38	44	347	7
Protein	1.16 g	1.36 g	10.12 g	0.21 g
Fat	0.16 g	0.19 g	1.05 g	0.02 g
Fiber	0.59 g	0.69 g	5.69 g	0.12 g
Calcium	20 mg	22 mg	363 mg	8 mg
Iron	0.22 mg	0.24 mg	2.56 mg	0.05 mg
Magnesium	10 mg	11 mg	122 mg	3 mg
Phosphorus	33 mg	35 mg	340 mg	7 mg
Potassium	157 mg	166 mg	943 mg	20 mg
Sodium	3 mg	3 mg	54 mg	1 mg
Zinc	0.190 mg	0.210 mg	2.320 mg	0.050 mg
Copper	0.060 mg	0.067 mg	0.177 mg	n/a
Manganese	0.137 mg	0.153 mg	0.374 mg	n/a
Beta Carotene (A)	0 IU	0 IU	trace	n/a
Thiamine (B_1)	0.042 mg	0.042 mg	0.418 mg	0.009 mg
Riboflavin (B_2)	0.020 m	0.023 mg	0.056 mg	0.001 mg
Niacin (B_3)	0.148 mg	0.165 mg	0.647 mg	0.014 mg
Pantothenic Acid (B_5)	0.106 mg	0.113 mg	n/a	n/a
Pyridoxine (B_6)	0.116 mg	0.129 mg	n/a	n/a
Folic Acid (B_9)	19.0 mcg	15.0 mcg	n/a	n/a
Ascorbic Acid (C)	6.4 mg	5.2 mg	14.69 mg	0.31 mg
Tocopherol (E)	0.31 mg	n/a	n/a	n/a

Buying Tips Onions should be firm and well-shaped, with dry, paperlike skins. Avoid those that are sprouting or have a wet, soggy feeling at the neck. Size has nothing to do with quality. Scallions and chives should have fresh, green tops.

Culinary Uses The pungent flavor and aroma of the onion is familiar to everyone. Milder than garlic yet still pungent, all types of onions, from the small white onions to the large Spanish variety, are indispensable in the kitchen. The strongest and most pungently flavored are the white onions; yellow onions are milder and sweeter, and red varieties even more so. All varieties can be eaten raw in salads, or baked, boiled, steamed, fried, braised, or stuffed. During the cooking process, some of the pungent volatile oils are lost, and their flavor becomes sweeter and milder. Dehydrated or frozen onions have less flavor, so you will need to add more than when using regular onions. Holding an onion under cold water while peeling prevents the oil fumes from rising and causing tears. The fumes contain ammonia, an irritant to the eyes and nose.

Health Benefits Anthelmintic, antiseptic, antispasmodic, carminative, detoxicant, diuretic, expectorant, stimulant, stomachic, tonic. Folklore about the curative powers of this versatile vegetable is plentiful, including claims that you can soothe the pain of a toothache with a raw onion or stifle a cough with a sweetened brew of simmered onions. Onions are similar to their cousin garlic in medicinal factors; used as an infection fighter and antibiotic, a diuretic, blood pressure regulator, expectorant, heart tonic (reducing the heart rate), contraceptive, and aphrodisiac. Historically used for asthma, onions inhibit the production of compounds that cause the bronchial muscle to spasm, and also relax the bronchial muscle. Onions are rich sources of the potent anticancer bioflavinoid quercetin, which is not destroyed by cooking. The sulphur compounds in onions help to end putrefactive and fermentation processes in the gastrointestinal tract, help remove heavy metals and parasites, and will retard the retention of fluids and cleanse the system of urea and sodium. Eaten raw, they promote transpiration and cleanse the pores as effectively as a good sauna bath. Chewing raw onions for five minutes kills all the germs in your mouth, making it sterile; this could be beneficial the next time you get a cold. According to researchers in the United States and India, onions also kill the germs that cause tooth decay. Because their action is stimulating and hot if taken internally, onions are not recommended for those practicing celibacy.

Varieties

Bermuda or **Spanish onions** are medium to large, round or oval white onions with dry white shells and dark-green or gray stripes running vertically from the root to the

Onion Family

Nutritional Value Per 100 g Edible Portion

	Leek Raw	Leek Cooked	Shallot Raw	Spring Raw
Calories	61	31	72	32-34
Protein	1.50 g	0.81 g	2.50 g	1.83-1.90 g
Fat	0.30 g	0.20 g	0.10 g	0.19-0.40 g
Fiber	1.51 g	0.82 g	0.70 g	0.95-1.00 g
Calcium	59 mg	30 mg	37 mg	18-72 mg
Iron	2.10 mg	1.10 mg	1.20 mg	1.48 mg
Magnesium	28 mg	14 mg	n/a	20 mg
Phosphorus	35 mg	17 mg	60 mg	37-49 mg
Potassium	180 mg	87 mg	334 mg	276 mg
Sodium	20 mg	10 mg	12 mg	16 mg
Zinc	n/a	n/a	n/a	0.390 mg
Copper	n/a	n/a	n/a	0.083 mg
Manganese	n/a	n/a	n/a	0.160 mg
Beta Carotene (A)	95 IU	46 IU	n/a	385 IU
Thiamine (B_1)	0.060 mg	0.026 mg	0.060 mg	0.055 mg
Riboflavin (B_2)	0.030 mg	0.020 mg	0.020 mg	0.080 mg
Niacin (B_3)	0.400 mg	0.200 mg	0.200 mg	0.525 mg
Pantothenic Acid (B_5)	n/a	n/a	n/a	0.075 mg
Pyridoxine (B_6)	n/a	n/a	n/a	n/a
Folic Acid (B_9)	64.1 mcg	24.3 mcg	n/a	64.0 mcg
Ascorbic Acid (C)	12.0 mg	4.2 mg	8.0 mg	18.8-27.0 mg
Tocopherol (E)	0.92 mg	n/a	n/a	n/a

stem. Mild and sweet, these are the favorite for raw use, but they can also be used for cooking. It is my understanding that true Bermuda onions are no longer available in the United States; however, Americans call any white onion a Bermuda onion, although they are really "Bermuda-type" onions, a variety of the original. Mostly imported from Mexico, they are available from late summer through December.

Chives (see reference under **Herbs, Spices, and Other Foods.**

Globe onions, also called **Yellow** or **White**, are the best all-purpose onion and the ones most often seen in supermarket bins. These ubiquitous medium-sized onions encompass many different varieties, with subtle differences in taste or texture, the smaller ones generally being more pungent and the larger sweeter. These are available year-round and are the best keeping variety.

Leeks (*A. ampeloprasum, Porrum* group) are the most subtle and sweet-tasting members of the onion family, with a flavor described as less fine but more robust than asparagus. They look like overgrown green onions with broad, flat leaves eight to fifteen inches long that shade to dark green at the tips, and a white cylindrical base up to 2 inches in diameter. They can be substituted for onions in any dish. Raw leeks taste hot and bitter, but cooked they have a creamy, almost buttery, onion flavor, which makes them good in soups, casseroles, or dressings. To prepare, cut off the roots and tops, leaving 8 to 10 inches of bulb and lower leaf. Slice down the middle almost to the core, hold under running water or immerse in a basin of water, and gently pull each layer away from the bulb. Rinse well to remove any soil which the plant is prone to accumulate. There is a legend in Wales that when the Saxons invaded in the sixth century A.D., St. David, patron saint of Wales, directed the Britons to wear leeks on their caps to distinguish them from the enemy. In memory of the heroic resistance by the Britons, the leek became the national emblem of Wales. Even today in Wales and Ireland, house leeks often cover the cottage roofs, and in their midst a few garden leeks are planted, not to have them handy for picking, but as a protection against lightning and witches, for lightning greatly dislikes a leek and will go elsewhere, and no witch will come near this plant, which is sacred to St. David. Leeks share many of the same healthful qualities as onions and garlic, but are considerably less potent. Leeks are available from September through March.

Wild Leek, also called **Ramp**, is unusual for an onion. Its scallion-slim stalk, streaked with violet, puts out broad, tapering, graceful leaves resembling those of lily of the valley. The leaves emerge in early spring, then die back soon after. Wild leeks have a wild, woodsy aroma and ferocious onion-garlic flavor despite their ladylike appearance. In the southern Appalachians, its appearance is the cause of spring celebrations throughout the area, most notably the Ramp Romp in West Virginia. Choose wild leeks that are firm, springy, and bright green. The roots should always be intact and downright dirty; if trimmed or washed, they develop an unpleasant smell and lose their fresh flavor. To prepare, slip off the first layer of skin from the bulbs, trim the roots, and remove any yellowing or wilted leaves. Generally considered too pungent for raw consumption, they can be cooked in just about any manner that you would cultivated leeks, but with discretion, as they are quite a bit stronger.

Maui onions are grown, not surprisingly, in Maui, Hawaii, and are usually pearly-pale and flattened, but may also be yellowish and globose. The Hawiian soil and weather conditions produce an onion that is low in bite, high in sugar and moisture; the same onion grown elsewhere is more like a common yellow onion. This sweet, moist onion appears in markets from April through June,primarily on the West Coast.

Red Italian, Creole, or **Red-Purple onions** are always sweet unless they have been stored too long. These have a stronger flavor than Bermuda and Spanish onions, but are still mild enough to be eaten raw. Fresh-picked small ones can be eaten whole like a small apple with a minimum of damage to social conversation. Their purplish color makes them a good addition to salads and sandwiches, or they can be chopped and used as a garnish. They are best when they are hard, with deep maroon dry shells and shiny first layers. Avoid those that have been peeled to an inner layer, those with double bulbs (generally hotter), or any that are soft at the stem end. Larger ones are generally stronger than small ones, and round ones sweeter than flat. Available from early summer through fall.

Shallots (*A. cepa, Aggregatum* group) Knights returning to England and France from crusades brought shallots back from Syria during the twelfth century, and they acquired the French name *eschalot* from the erroneous belief that they came from Ashkalon in Palestine. A small mild variety of onion, shallots smell and taste like onions, but they look like dark garlic, with clusters of brown- or gray-skinned bulbs. When you want just a hint of onion and garlic flavor, especially in sauces, use shallots. They not only have a mild flavor, but they are also tender, so they cook quickly. Three to four medium shallot bulbs equals the flavor of one medium yellow onion. They are usually available from September through December.

Small white onions and **Pearl onions** are miniature white onions that are best peeled and cooked whole. Pearl onions, the smallest of all onions, are mild and tasty. So densely planted that they may attain a size of only an inch in diameter, they may have layered skins like miniature onions or a single flesh layer like a garlic clove. Available in various colors, they're great creamed or gratinéed, or in kebabs. Pickled pearl onions (used mostly in salads or as a garnish for cocktails) can be purchased in jars at the supermarket. The larger white onions look like a slightly larger version of pearls. Both are used whole in soups and stews or simmered with other vegetables, affording great eye appeal in fancy dishes. They are available from September through December.

Spring onions/Scallions (*A. fistulosum*), often referred to as **Green onions,** are a fast-growing type of onion that does not form bulbs. The term *scallion* comes from the Biblical Ashkelon, where the plants were called *ascalons*. Technically, scallions are harvested before there is any bulb formation, while green onions have developed small bulbs—about one to two inches in diameter. Both have dark green cylindrical stalks that are white at the root base. These mild-flavored onions are edible from their crisp tops down to their tender white bulbs. Not only do they add color and texture to salads, but their zippy bite affords a counterpoint to heavier soups and entrees. They are available year-round, peaking between April and November.

Lore and Legend

Praise of the onion has been sung throughout history, except perhaps in India, where onions and garlic were never truly regarded as quite respectable. There the vegetable is not considered fit to be eaten by Brahmins, a tradition that goes back at least to the Ordinances of Manu (about the sixth century B.C.) where it is written "garlic, onions also, leeks and mushrooms, are not to be eaten by the twice-born, as well as things arising from impurity." The Turks have a legend that places the onion and garlic right at the beginning of time; when the Devil was sent out of Paradise and first set foot on earth, on the spot where he placed his right foot there grew the onion and in the place of the left sprang up garlic. Early Egyptians esteemed the onion as a source of strength; the thousands of slaves who built the pyramids were fed a diet consisting largely of onions and garlic, which at the least would have given them remarkably strong breath. Part of the every-day diet of common Egyptians, onions were not eaten by the priests, but it appeared on the altars of gods and in religious rituals, even as a temple decoration as a representation of eternity. The lowly onion symbolized the universe, since in their cosmogony the various spheres of hell, earth, and heaven were concentric, like its layers. According to a Native American Indian legend, a group of seven young Indian wives were fond of eating onions, but their husbands, disliking the pungent smell, became angry and forbade the practice. The wives, having thought it over and discussed it among themselves, decided that they preferred their onions to their husbands, so they used magical ropes made of eagle down to float up into the sky, where they remain as the Pleiades, presumably eating onions to their hearts' content. The poet Carl Sandburg contended that "Life is like an onion. You peel it off one layer at a time; and sometimes you weep."

Vidalia onions are named after the town in Georgia where they grow. Said by many to be the most delicious variety of onion, they are coppery colored, elongated, and very hard. These juicy sweet onions (with more sugar than an apple) have unlimited uses, but are mostly eaten raw and in salads. Availability is limited, only in May and June, although occasionally in July.

Yellow onions (see **Globe**).

Walla Walla onions are grown in Washington state in and around the city whose name they bear. For the most part they are light gold-beige, quite round, and creamy, with very thick layers that make perfect onion rings. They range widely in size, from a mere 3 ounces to nearly 1 1/2 pounds. At their best raw or only lightly cooked, they quickly become mushy when subjected to heat. Walla Wallas make their appearance from July through October.

Orach (*Atriplex hortensis*)

Also Known As: Salt Bush, Musk Weed, Mountain or French Spinach.

> Atriplex *derives from a Greek name for the plant;* hortensis *means belonging to the* hortus *or garden.*

General Information Native to Europe and Siberia, garden orach has a long history as one of the oldest cultivated plants. Widely recognized among the ancient Greeks and Romans as a medicinal plant, orach became very popular in medieval Europe both for culinary and medicinal purposes. Early settlers brought orach to the New World where it became a fairly standard vegetable; during the nineteenth century, however, it fell out of favor and has widely been replaced by spinach. There are three main types: white orach, which has pale green leaves; red orach, which has dark reddish stems and leaves; and green orach. The white variety is generally considered the sweetest and most tender.

Culinary Uses Orach has a mild flavor and contains much less acid than most other varieties of spinach. The tender leaves that arise from the top of the plant are considered the best to eat. Older leaves are tough and unpleasant tasting. Young stems and stalks can be used in all the same manners that spinach or sorrel are used. Boiled and buttered, creamed, added to quiches, rolled up in crepes, tossed in salads, or added to soups, orach is delicious in its own right. The French and English use orach in various soups and stews or serve it steamed as a side dish, while the Italians add it to their pasta.

Health Benefits Early Greeks and Romans used orach to soothe sore throats, ease indigestion, and cure jaundice.

Parsley Root *(Petroselinum crispum tuberosum)*

Also Known As: Hamburg Parsley, Turnip-Rooted Parsley.

> *The ancient Greek Dioscorides named this plant* petroselinum *from the Greek words* petros, *meaning rock, and* selinon, *meaning celery, because it grew in rocky places.* Crispum *means curled;* tuberosum *means tuberous or root. The English word* parsley *is a corruption of the Latin.*

General Information Parsley is believed to be indigenous to Sardinia, Turkey, Algeria, and Lebanon, where it still grows wild. This variety of parsley is grown not for its leaves, but for its root. The small, irregularly shaped root looks like a small parsnip (often double rooted) attached to large, feathery parsley leaves (which are edible but bland).

Buying Tips Select roots that are firm and preferably have their greens intact.

Culinary Uses Parsley root tastes somewhere between celeriac and carrot; it is aromatic, slightly aggressive, and herbal-pungent. Most often used to flavor soups and stews, the root adds depth and aroma to hearty main course dishes, and combines well with other roots and tubers. It can also be used on its own—creamed, puréed, steamed, or boiled and buttered.

Health Benefits Low in fat, high in fiber, sodium, and vitamin C.

Parsnip *(Pastinaca sativum)*

> *The parsnip was once a major Roman foodstuff called* pastinacea, *after the Latin word* pastus *for food.* Sativum *refers to the fact that this plant has long been cultivated. The English name* parsnip *is a derivative of the Latin.*

General Information Parsnips grew wild (and still do) in parts of Europe and the Caucasus long before their cultivation. This member of the carrot family looks like a large, rather anemic white carrot, with a starchy root that is among the most nourishing in the whole carrot family. Since the Middle Ages, the potato has gradually replaced the parsnip as a filling high-starch vegetable, but there was a time when the sweet, nutty, aromatic flavor

Parsnip

Nutritional Value Per 100 g Edible Portion

	Raw	Cooked
Calories	75	81
Protein	1.20 g	1.32 g
Fat	0.30 g	0.30 g
Fiber	2.00 g	2.20 g
Calcium	36 mg	37 mg
Iron	0.59 mg	0.58 mg
Magnesium	29 mg	29 mg
Phosphorus	71 mg	69 mg
Potassium	375 mg	367 mg
Sodium	10 mg	10 mg
Zinc	0.590 mg	0.260 mg
Copper	0.120 mg	0.138 mg
Manganese	0.560 mg	0.294 mg
Beta Carotene (A)	0 IU	0 IU
Thiamine (B_1)	0.090 mg	0.083 mg
Riboflavin (B_2)	0.050 mg	0.051 mg
Niacin (B_3)	0.700 mg	0.724 mg
Pantothenic Acid (B_5)	0.600 mg	0.588 mg
Pyridoxine (B_6)	0.090 mg	0.093 mg
Folic Acid (B_9)	66.8 mcg	58.2 mcg
Ascorbic Acid (C)	17.0 mg	13.0 mg
Tocopherol (E)	1.0 mg	n/a

of parsnips was a popular table delight for emperors and peasants alike. In ancient Rome, parsnips were reserved for the aristocracy, who liked them drowned in honey or combined with fruit in little cakes. The Roman Emperor Tiberius was so fond of their sweet, nut-like flavor that he had them specially imported from Germany when they were out of season in Italy.

Buying Tips Smooth, firm, well-shaped parsnips of small to medium size are generally the best quality, but some grow up to twenty inches long and are still tender and sweet. Softness may indicate decay and discoloration may indicate freezing.

Culinary Uses Parsnips have a sweet nutty flavor that some actually complain is too sweet. They are best after being exposed to cold temperatures, so that their starch content is converted into sugar. If tender, parsnips can be eaten raw. Small pieces of raw parsnip add texture and a tingly taste to mixed green salads. If cooked, they should be steamed, not boiled, to obtain their full flavor, then peeled and served, preferably with salt, pepper, and butter. Because of their strong, dominating flavor, use parsnips with discretion in soups and stews.

Health Benefits Diuretic. Parsnips hold a specific affinity toward the kidneys, stomach, and spleen, and are helpful in conditions of bladder and kidney stones. Loaded with more food energy than most common vegetables, they help detoxify and cleanse the body, and improve bowel action.

Lore and Legend

Parsnips have carried some strange superstitions: carrying one was said to ward off snakebite, but if you forgot and got bitten, according to the Greeks you could crush a parsnip and mix it with the pork fat they used to grease their chariot wheels, spread the paste on the wound, and be cured. Many people thought parsnips were dangerous—especially old ones, which they believed would cause insanity.

Pea *(Pisum sativum)*

The word pease *is of Sanskrit origin, which became* pisum *in Latin and* pease *in early English. The final 'e' was dropped in the mistaken belief that it was a plural.* Sativum *refers to the fact that this plant has long been cultivated.*

General Information The pea is such an ancient food plant that its center of origin is uncertain, although it is usually attributed to a band of territory sweeping from the Near East into Central Asia. Part of the legume family, peas in their dried form have been used as a staple food since ancient times, being found even in Egyptian tombs. Hot pea soup was peddled in the streets of Athens, while fried peas were sold to spectators in lieu of popcorn at the Roman circus and in theaters. Upper-class Romans ate their peas with salted whale

Pea

Nutritional Value Per 100 g Edible Portion

	Raw	Cooked	Edible Pod Raw	Edible Pod Cooked	Sprouted Raw	Sprouted Cooked
Calories	81	84	42	42	128	118
Protein	5.42 g	5.36 g	2.80 g	3.27 g	8.80 g	7.05 g
Fat	0.40 g	0.22 g	0.20 g	0.23 g	0.68 g	0.51 g
Fiber	2.21 g	2.31 g	2.50 g	1.04 g	2.78 g	3.3 g
Calcium	25 mg	27 mg	43 mg	42 mg	36 mg	26 mg
Iron	1.47 mg	1.54 mg	2.08 mg	1.97 mg	2.26 mg	1.67 mg
Magnesium	33 mg	39 mg	24 mg	26 mg	56 mg	41 mg
Phosphorus	108 mg	117 mg	53 mg	55 mg	165 mg	24 mg
Potassium	244 mg	271 mg	200 mg	240 mg	381 mg	268 mg
Sodium	5 mg	3 mg	4 mg	4 mg	20 mg	3 mg
Zinc	1.240 mg	1.190 mg	n/a	0.370 mg	1.050 mg	0.780 mg
Copper	0.176 mg	0.173 mg	n/a	0.077 mg	0.272 mg	0.020 mg
Manganese	0.410 mg	0.525 mg	n/a	0.168 mg	0.438 mg	0.325 mg
Beta Carotene (A)	640 IU	597 IU	145 IU	131 IU	166 IU	107 IU
Thiamine (B_1)	0.266 mg	0.259 mg	0.150 mg	0.128 mg	0.225 mg	0.216 mg
Riboflavin (B_2)	0.132 mg	0.149 mg	0.080 mg	0.076 mg	0.155 mg	0.285 mg
Niacin (B_3)	2.090 mg	2.021 mg	0.600 mg	0.539 mg	3.088 mg	1.072 mg
Pantothenic Acid (B_5)	0.104 mg	0.153 mg	0.750 mg	0.673 mg	1.029 mg	0.683 mg
Pyridoxine (B_6)	0.169 mg	0.216 mg	0.160 mg	0.144 mg	0.265 mg	0.128 mg
Folic Acid (B_9)	65.0 mcg	63.3 mcg	n/a	n/a	144.0 mcg	36.3 mcg
Ascorbic Acid (C)	40.0 mg	14.2 mg	60.0 mg	47.9 mg	10.4 mg	6.6 mg
Tocopherol (E)	0.13 mg	n/a	n/a	n/a	n/a	n/a

meat, while the lower classes had to make do with porridge. A new sweet-tasting pea was introduced in the sixteenth century, and was tailor-made for the new custom of eating peas fresh. When Catherine de Medici married King Henry II of France, she introduced his countrymen to small, sweet, fresh *piselli novelli* (new peas), which she had brought from her home in Florence, Italy. These tender gems were adopted enthusiastically by the fashionable French, who dubbed them *petits pois*, the name still in use worldwide to describe a very tasty type of baby pea. The first peas in America were planted by Christopher Columbus in 1493 on Isabella Island, and the new vegetable was adopted enthusiastically by the Indians. The cultivated pea comprises two main varieties—the field pea, now used mostly for forage and for dried peas; and the garden pea, with its high sugar content, considered by some to be the aristocrat of the pea family.

Buying Tips Choose crisp, young, uniformly green, well-filled pods. A yellowish pod indicates overmaturity.

Culinary Uses Fresh garden peas have a delicate sweet flavor that is well worth the time-consuming effort of shelling them. Use as soon as possible after buying because their sugar quickly turns to starch and they lose flavor. The finest of all are those picked very young and called petits pois (tiny, sweet, very young, and tender), but other varieties are also delectable. Peas can be boiled or steamed, puréed, used in soups, salads, savory dishes, and casseroles, and are delicious served with fresh mint. Canned or frozen peas lack much of the flavor of fresh peas.

Health Benefits Fresh peas are of much greater value as an item of food when eaten raw in salads than when cooked, but it takes a strong digestive tract to properly digest raw peas. Slightly diuretic, peas help control blood sugar levels, and contain lectins, which dissolve clumps of red blood cells that are destined to become clots. Peas also contain anti-

Lore and Legend

Most peas in ancient times were consumed dried, the drying process being considered essential to cure the pea of its "noxious and stomach-destroying" qualities. Uncured peas were occasionally left on the vines by farmers with the intention of poisoning pestiferous rabbits, who may have gotten the better end of the deal. Abundant in folklore, peas were a favorite of Thor, the thunder god of Norse mythology, and are still eaten on Thor's day, or Thursday, in Germany. They were often connected with wooing, possibly as a fertility symbol, and were used for divination: to dream of a dry pea was a portent of a coming marriage. In parts of Europe, peas are still thrown in the lap of a bride on her wedding day to insure fertility. Then there's the Hans Christian Andersen story that everyone knows, of a princess so sensitive that she could feel a pea under all those mattresses.

fertility agents. In areas of Tibet where there are high consumptions of peas, the fertility rate is considerably suppressed, reduced by more than 50 percent.

Varieties

English peas have pods that are not edible. The large, bulging, grass green pods enclose peas that are typically round and sweet. Most are picked when they are still immature and their sugar content is highest. As they continue to ripen, some of the sugar turns to starch, and the amount of protein increases. Peas intended for drying are left to mature.

Snow peas have firm, crisp, flat, bright green edible pods that taper at both ends, and contain very small, underdeveloped peas. The classic snow pea must be picked before the inner peas begin to bulge out and stringiness develops; like other peas, they should be consumed as soon after picking as possible, since their high sugar content quickly turns to starch. For snow peas that are crisp, sweet, and colorful, steam, blanch, or stir-fry for no more than a brief minute or two.

Sugar snap peas, also known as **Mangetouts**, are a hybrid developed by breeder Calvin Lamborn of the Gallatin Valley Seed Company in Twin Falls, Idaho in the 1970s. Looking just like traditional English peas, the sugar snap pea is the result of a cross between a tough-podded mutant of a processing pea and a conventional snow pea, giving the best of both varieties. These peas have stubby, crunchy, sweet, edible pods enclosing fat, sweet peas. Uncooked, the peas and their pods are crisp and delicious. When ever-so-lightly steamed or blanched, their color turns a dazzling emerald green and their sweetness intensifies. They should be quickly sautéed or stir-fried for only about two minutes, as overcooking destroys their crisp texture. Older peas may need to be strung on both seams.

Peppers and Chilis *(Capsicum annuum, C. frutescens)*

The botanical term Capsicum *arrived on the scene in 1700 under the auspices of Joseph Pitton de Tournefort, early plant taxonomist and plant-hunter for the spectacular gardens of Louis XIV. The name is thought to come from either the Latin* capsa, *meaning box, for the hollow box-like shape of some varieties of the fruit, or from the Greek* kapto, *meaning to bite, for the pepper's acrid tongue-searing pungency. The term* annuum *signifies an annual or yearly plant;* frutescens *means shrubby or bushy. Columbus voyaged to the New World in search of India and its black pepper; unsuccessful but undaunted, he named the most pungent New World food "pepper" and the people who cultivated it "Indians." The English word* chili *is from the Nahuatl name* chilli, *the term applied to all members, and which also means red.*

General Information Native to the Americas, peppers and chilis are not related in any manner to black pepper. Along with corn, beans, and squash, the capsicums were among the first plants cultivated in the agriculturally revolutionized Americas. They vary in size and shape, and anyone who judges the spiciness or sweetness of a pepper by its color is bound to be misled. The hotness of a pepper is determined by a bitter substance called capsaicin that is located in the skins, seeds, and interior ribs. When the skins and seeds are removed, peppers are less spicy. Today there are over one hundred sweet pepper cultivars on the market and over half as many hot. Chili peppers refuse to be tamed, codified, classified, and otherwise put in their place. Adventurous and spirited, they mix and match, reproduce unpredictably and prolifically, and generally run their own show. Differentiated by their use, chili peppers are pungent and used as a spice, while sweet peppers are mild, sweet, and used as a vegetable. The heating effect of chilis is measured on an objective scale of 1 to 120. Since the jalapeño, which numbs the mouths of those unaccustomed to it, is rated at 15, it is difficult to imagine what might happen to the unwary consumer of a 120-proof chili.

Buying Tips Look for peppers that are firm and well-shaped. They should be thick-fleshed and either bright red or green. Avoid those that have punctured skins or look wilted and tired.

Culinary Uses Peppers have many uses and their popularity as a comestible—condiment, spice, and vegetable—is growing rapidly. Sweet varieties are served raw in salads and as finger foods, or can be stuffed, sautéed, or puréed. They are excellent combined with apples, cheese, nuts, and dried fruits. Hot chili peppers add zest to any number of dishes, and are an important ingredient in Mexican and Spanish style foods. For those not accustomed to their fire, they should be used sparingly. Fresh chili peppers should be minced as small as possible, so the eater does not get an overwhelmingly hot bite. Experiment with the different types of chilis to learn their pungency and to develop a taste or tolerance for them. Avoid rubbing your eyes, nose, or lips with your hands after you have handled chilis, as severe burning will result. In the United States, perhaps the best known use of capsicums is in chili, a dish named after its peppery prime ingredient.

Health Benefits Antibacterial, stimulant. The capsaicin in peppers is one of the best stimulants; when the body is properly stimulated, the healing and cleansing process starts, allowing the body to function normally. Capsaicin is a pungent, bitter resin that contains a phenolic chemical, and thus makes it an antibacterial agent. The volatile alkaloid capsaicine provides many of the stimulant properties, but has no narcotic effects. Peppers and chilis normalize blood pressure, improve the entire circulatory system, boost secretion of saliva and stomach acids, increase peristaltic movement, and feed the cell structure of the arteries, veins, and capillaries so they will regain elasticity. Peppers contain vitamin A, which makes bodily tissues more resistant, especially to colds, and promotes growth and the feeling of well-being; vitamin B, which aids in food absorption and normalizes the brain and nervous system by increasing metabolic processes; and vitamin C (up to six times as much as oranges), which is a wonderful health promoter as it wards off acidosis. We get the benefit of this vitamin C if we eat fresh, raw green peppers; they lose about 30 percent of this vitamin C when fully matured or cooked; the vitamin essentially vanishes altogether when dried. Fiery hot chili peppers are irritants and, if overeaten, can be overstimulating to the digestive tract, particularly the intestines, kidneys and bladder, but work wonders for clearing out the sinuses.

Varieties

Anaheim Also known as **California long green, New Mexico chili, Chile verde, Red chili, Chile Colorado,** these are the longest of the peppers (up to eight inches in length), and are narrow, slightly twisted, and usually a medium to light green,

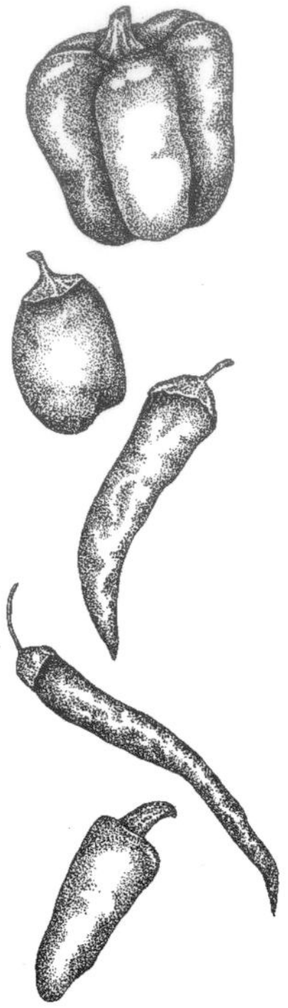

deepening to red at maturity. Legend has it that the original ancestor of the Anaheim was brought to New Mexico from Mexico in 1597 by Don Juan de Onate, the founder and first governor of Santa Fe. Some three hundred years later, a visiting Californian named Emilio Ortega acquired some descendants of Onate's peppers and with them established a highly successful chili cannery in 1900 at Anaheim, California, calling the peppers Anaheim after the location of the cannery. The most common chili pepper available in the United States, the mildly hot Anaheims are frequently stuffed for chiles relleños, and are the peppers that make up the ubiquitous red or green sauce that accompanies the food of New Mexico. Its flavor is one of the most neutral of the chilis, which makes it the favorite of less macho taste buds. This chili can easily be added to any dish in strips or chopped bits to wake up simple vegetable, meat, or egg dishes. Roasted and peeled, it becomes tender and succulent, with a pleasantly bittersweet, fresh taste. In its mature red stage, it is used in the preparation of chili powder and paprika. Dried maroon Anaheims are woven into the festive ropes or ristras you see in shops through the southwestern United States.

Banana Also known as **Hungarian yellow wax, Sweet banana,** and **Hot Hungarian wax,** these peppers are fairly long (five to six inches), tapering, and moderately narrow. They start pale, translucent, creamy yellow, and then ripen into orange and scarlet on the vine. Their size, shape, and color have caused them to be compared to bananas. The sweet form is generally called the Banana pepper, while the hot variety is the Hungarian wax. Both of them are scarlet when fully mature; however, one seldom sees the red stage because they are consumed before maturity is reached, and the Hungarian wax gets so hot it is almost inedible. Traditionally, these peppers are pickled, but they can be slivered fresh into salads, or added to bean and grain dishes where they add flavor and color—but test the pungency first. The hot variety is particularly good in salsas, salads, and pickled vegetables.

Peppers & Chilis

Nutritional Value Per 100 g Edible Portion

	Bell	Hot Chili	Canned Pimiento
Calories	27	40	23
Protein	0.89-1.00 g	2.00 g	1.10 g
Fat	0.19-0.21 g	0.20 g	0.30 g
Fiber	0.44 g	1.80 g	1.05 g
Calcium	9-11 mg	18 mg	6 mg
Iron	0.46 mg	1.20 mg	1.68 mg
Magnesium	10-12 mg	25 mg	6 mg
Phosphorus	19-24 mg	46 mg	17 mg
Potassium	177-212 mg	340 mg	158 mg
Sodium	2 mg	7 mg	14 mg
Zinc	0.120-0.170 mg	0.300 mg	0.190 mg
Copper	0.065-0.107 mg	0.174 mg	0.049 mg
Manganese	0.116-0.117 mg	0.237 mg	0.092 mg
Beta Carotene (A)*	238-5,700 IU	770-10,750 IU	2,655 IU
Thiamine (B_1)	0.028-0.066 mg	0.090 mg	0.017 mg
Riboflavin (B_2)	0.025-0.030 mg	0.090 mg	0.060 mg
Niacin (B_3)	0.509-0.890 mg	0.950 mg	0.615 mg
Pantothenic Acid (B_5)	0.080-0.168 mg	0.061 mg	n/a
Pyridoxine (B_6)	0.168-0.248 mg	0.278 mg	0.215 mg
Folic Acid (B_9)	22.0-26.0 mcg	23.4 mcg	6.0 mcg
Ascorbic Acid (C)	89.3-190.0 mg	242.5 mg	84.9 mg
Tocopherol (E)	0.68 mg	n/a	n/a

*Red varieties highest

Bell Also known as **Green** or **Sweet** peppers, these are usually box- or heart-shaped. The most common is the green bell pepper, which has thick green flesh, a minimum of seeds, and a heavy outer skin. Red peppers are actually green peppers that have been allowed to ripen on the plant; they are softer than green peppers and sweeter, since they are riper. There are also white, deep purple, and bright yellow varieties, which taste much like the red varieties but tend to be a little crisper. Purple varieties are eggplant-colored on the outside but green inside, with a fresh snappy taste; yellow varieties are extremely sweet-tasting. Cooking may render the purple variety an unpalatable gray, so it is most often enjoyed raw. Bell peppers are sautéed and served as a vegetable; chopped and added to flavor casserole dishes; used in ethnic dishes; or served raw in salads and as a garnish. Because of their unique shape, you can stuff them with any number of mixes—from cheese to rice or nut mixes.

Cascabel are small, round, moderately hot peppers with smooth skins. About $1\frac{1}{2}$ inches in diameter,

Lore and Legend

Chili peppers were cultivated by the Incas of Peru, and were among the gifts with which the Inca king attempted to bribe Pizarro. One variety among those given to Pizarro is known as Rocoto; although described as "murderous" and by latter-day Peruvians as "hot enough to kill a gringo," it evidently did not do the trick. Pizarro accepted his peppers, macaws, llamas, gold, and silver, and went on to destroy the Inca civilization anyway. Peppers were so highly valued in ancient Peru that the pods were employed as a medium of exchange. In fact, until the middle of the twentieth century, one could purchase items in the plaza of Cuzco with a handful of pepper pods, known as *rantii*. Peru's government has recently decreed that hot chili sauce has decidedly aphrodisiac qualities and ordered it not to be used in prison food, advising that the sauce is not "appropriate for men forced to live a limited life style."

cascabels in their fresh state may be either green or barn red. Their nutty flavor comes to the forefront with roasting. Dried, their skin turns a brownish, translucent red, and the seeds rattle around inside, from whence it received its name meaning "jingle bell" in Spanish.

Cayenne peppers received their name from Cayenne, French Guiana. These long, thin peppers are exceedingly hot, so fiery that removal of their veins and seeds is highly recommended. Whole fresh or dried cayennes, which vary in size from four to twelve inches, are the favored spice used by Creole and Cajun cooks to give their gumbos, shrimp creoles, and crayfish dishes special zest, and are highly favored for sauces. It has a flavor similar to the tabasco pepper, which is used primarily in bottled hot sauces. The prepared condiment cayenne pepper may or may not contain true cayenne peppers.

Chipotles are smoke-dried jalapeños. They can be either a two-tone brown or brick red, ranging in size between two to three inches long and about three-quarters of an inch wide. Their characteristic very hot to searing flavor comes from the smoke-drying process. Chipotles come from Mexico dried, *en escabeche* (pickled), and in tomato sauce. They add their fire and smoky spiciness to chili con carne and barbecue sauces, and are a bold chili flavoring for mild bean, rice, corn, or cheese dishes.

Fresno are medium-sized light green peppers that mature to cherry red, are pointed, and about the same size as the more familiar jalapeño. Named after the city of Fresno, California, these peppers are very hot and are best used as a seasoning rather than as a vegetable. Use while green, and mince sparingly into dips, salads, or guacamole.

Habaneros (*Capsicum chinense*) are small lantern-shaped peppers, measuring about two inches by two inches. Curvaceous and bright, habaneros come in orange, green, red, and yellow. They hold the distinction of being the most fiery of all domesticated peppers, with a burning heat and deep floral flavor; however, their heat can sneak up on you, so beware of taking a second bite if you think the first one was not hot enough (which is unlikely).

Jalapeños originated in Mexico and were named for the town of Xalapa in the state of Veracruz. Blunt-tipped, smooth-skinned and slightly tapered, they have unusually dense, rich flesh for their petite size. Usually deep green, they occasionally appear in the market in their mature red form, which is prone to show a slight cracking lengthwise. Their powerful bite has assured their place on nachos and in other bland melted-cheese combinations, while a small amount in spoonbreads, cornbreads, soufflés, sauces, or pasta dough makes a snappy difference. Roasting makes them more concentrated in flavor but less hot.

Pimientos are a small, roughly heart-shaped, richly sweet pepper reintroduced to this hemisphere from Spain in 1911. Pimiento is a Spanish term meaning pepper, and is the name adopted by the Associated Pimiento Canners of Georgia for the sweet, thick-fleshed, bright red Capsicum that is usually canned or stuffed into green olives. Very aromatic, attractive, and tasty, the pimiento is regrettably known to most people solely as the red bit inside a green olive. Fresh pimientos are mild yet flavorful, and their thick meaty flesh makes them delicious in salads, vegetable dishes, and excellent candidates for roasting.

Poblanos, also known as **Anchos** in their dried form, are named after the valley of Puebla, south of Mexico City, where these peppers were first cultivated. This glossy, richly green pepper, shiny as patent leather, resembles a slightly flattened green bell pepper, but is pointed at the tip and rather heart-shaped. They range in size from four to five inches long and from two to three inches wide. Usually very mild, with an occasional pungent aberration, this variety has a remarkably full, earthy, herbal, and fruity flavor and aroma; cooked and peeled, it develops even greater taste and tenderness. With thick flesh that makes it perfect for stuffing, this versatile pepper is a delicious addition to corn dishes, soups, vegetables, sauces, and salads. Dried anchos are flat, wrinkled, and heart-shaped, ranging in color from oxblood to almost black. Rehydrated, they become crimson again.

Santa Fe Grande, also called **Caloro, Caribe,** and **Goldspike**, is a tapered conical pepper that is generally marketed yellow, but can also be orange to red. Moderately hot to very hot, with a pleasant sweetness, it is primarily used for pickles, uncooked sauces, or relishes. They may also be roasted and peeled, then cut in tiny strips or minced for garnishing cooked vegetable salads, or to add to cornmeal mixes.

Serranos are searing, suitable for those people who enjoy breathing fire. It is believed that the serrano originated on the mountain ridges (*serranias*) north of Puebla and Hidalgo in Mexico, from which it acquired its name. This smooth, sleek, small, narrow green to orange chili pepper, one to two inches long and no more than one inch wide, looks innocuous, but is not. Packing a tremendous wallop, the burn is intense, immediate, and lasting. More widely used in Mexico and the southwestern United States than any of the other fresh chili peppers, it may be used raw or roasted, mixed with whatever one wishes to spice up, or made into an uncooked sauce.

Plantain (*Musa paradisiaca*)

The plant was given the genus designation Musa *to honor Antonio Musa, physician to Octavius Augustus, the first emperor of Rome 63–14* B.C. Paradisiaca *means of parks or gardens. The English name* plantain *derives from the Latin* platanus *and Greek* platys *meaning broad, referring to the large leaves.*

General Information Plantains are a type of banana that is only eaten cooked. Figuring prominently in Latin American and Asian cookery as a starchy substitute for bread or potatoes, plantains are slowly being introduced to the United States. The most common varieties of plantain look like a large, straight banana, and come in various colors, among them green, yellow, red, red-violet, and mottled black.

Buying Tips Avoid any that are cracked or overly soft, but do not be intimidated by a black or brown peel, for as plantains ripen they also darken. Fully ripe black plantains should give like firm bananas; if they are hard, they should be thrown out.

Culinary Uses Plantains have a mild, bland, almost squashlike flavor that begs for spices. When the peel is green or yellow, the flavor of the flesh is bland and its texture simply starchy. As the plantain ripens and the peel changes to brown or black, it plays the role of both fruit and

Plantain

Nutritional Value Per 100 g Edible Portion

	Raw	Cooked
Calories	122	116
Protein	1.30 g	0.79 g
Fat	0.37 g	0.18 g
Fiber	0.50 g	n/a
Calcium	3 mg	2 mg
Iron	0.60 mg	0.58 mg
Magnesium	37 mg	32 mg
Phosphorus	34 mg	28 mg
Potassium	499 mg	465 mg
Sodium	4 mg	5 mg
Zinc	0.140 mg	0.130 mg
Copper	0.081 mg	0.066 mg
Beta Carotene (A)	10-1,200 IU	909 IU
Thiamine (B_1)	0.052 mg	0.046 mg
Riboflavin (B_2)	0.054 mg	0.052 mg
Niacin (B_3)	0.686 mg	0.756 mg
Pantothenic Acid (B_5)	0.260 mg	0.233 mg
Pyridoxine (B_6)	0.299 mg	0.240 mg
Folic Acid (B_9)	22.0 mcg	26.0 mcg
Ascorbic Acid (C)	18.4 mg	10.9 mg

vegetable, having a sweetness and banana aroma, but keeping a firm shape when cooked. Never eaten raw, the salmon-colored pulp can be fried, boiled, mashed, sautéed, or baked. Cooked, chopped ripe plantains also make a more than acceptable component of soups, stews, and omelets.

Health Benefits Plantains have been employed in cases of dyspepsia and ulcers, since they strengthen the surface cells of the stomach lining. Unripe green plantains are the most potent against ulcers.

Potato (*Solanum tuberosum*)

> Solanum *comes from the Latin* solamen, *meaning solace or quieting;* tuberosum *means tuberous. The English name* potato, *derived from the West Indian name* batata *for the sweet potato, is a mistake that goes back to the time of its introduction into Europe.*

General Information Native to the bleak Andean highlands of South America, the potato is related to the eggplant, pepper, and tomato. One of the world's major food crops, potatoes are tubers, swollen stems that grow underground and are propagated by budding rather than by seeds. With over five thousand varieties, and new and improved hybrids being developed daily, try them all, and find your own favorite. Potatoes crossed the Atlantic to Europe before landing in North America in the early 1700s. Except in a few European countries where it became popular soon after its introduction, and a few other places like Ireland where its cultivation precisely met contemporary needs, the beloved potato was only reluctantly accepted as food, and it took well over two hundred years for the potato to become widely distributed. Although crop failures meant mass starvation, the peasants of Europe remained remarkably obdurate, and refused to eat the potato because they believed it caused diarrhea, poisoned the soil, and helped spread the dreaded Plague. In 1900, Americans ate 200 pounds of potatoes per person annually; by 1980, Americans ate only 120 pounds—75 pounds of fresh potatoes and 45 pounds of processed potatoes (they were all fresh in 1900).

Potato

Nutritional Value Per 100 g Edible Portion

	Raw Flesh	Raw Skin	Baked w/Skin	Boiled w/Skin	Flour
Calories	79	58	109	87	351
Protein	2.07 g	2.57 g	2.30 g	1.87 g	8.00 g
Fat	0.10 g	0.10 g	0.10 g	0.10 g	0.80 g
Fiber	0.44 g	1.79 g	0.66 g	0.32 g	1.60 g
Calcium	7 mg	30 mg	10 mg	5 mg	33 mg
Iron	0.76 mg	3.24 mg	1.36 mg	0.31 mg	17.20 mg
Magnesium	21 mg	23 mg	27 mg	22 mg	n/a
Phosphorus	46 mg	38 mg	57 mg	44 mg	178 mg
Potassium	543 mg	413 mg	418 mg	379 mg	1588 mg
Sodium	6 mg	10 mg	8 mg	4 mg	34 mg
Zinc	0.390 mg	0.350 mg	0.320 mg	0.300 mg	n/a
Copper	0.259 mg	0.423 mg	0.305 mg	0.188 mg	n/a
Manganese	0.263 mg	0.602 mg	0.229 mg	0.138 mg	n/a
Beta Carotene (A)	n/a	n/a	n/a	n/a	0 IU
Thiamine (B_1)	0.088 mg	0.021 mg	0.107 mg	0.106 mg	0.420 mg
Riboflavin (B_2)	0.035 mg	0.038 mg	0.033 mg	0.020 mg	0.140 mg
Niacin (B_3)	1.484 mg	1.033 mg	1.645 mg	1.439 mg	3.400 mg
Pantothenic Acid (B_5)	0.380 mg	n/a	0.555 mg	0.520 mg	n/a
Pyridoxine (B_6)	0.260 mg	0.239 mg	0.347 mg	0.299 mg	n/a
Folic Acid (B_9)	12.8 mcg	17.3 mcg	11.0 mcg	10.0 mcg	n/a
Ascorbic Acid (C)	19.7 mg	11.4 mg	12.9 mg	13.0 mg	19.0 mg
Tocopherol (E)	0.06 mg	n/a	n/a	0.04 mg	n/a

Lore and Legend

Francisco Pizarro, who stumbled upon the potato somewhere outside of Quito, Ecuador, must have had an imaginative palate, describing his vegetable find as "a tasty, mealy truffle." Under the name tartuffo, the potato was introduced to Spain in 1534. Hailed as a revitalizer for impotence, potatoes were sold on the strength of that belief for fantastic prices, in some instances as high as one thousand dollars a pound. From there, the potato meandered into Italy and France, where it was rejected by the general public on the grounds that the knobby, deep-eyed tubers resembled leprous hands and feet and were doubtless carriers of the disease. In 1565, Sir John Hawkins brought the potato plant to Ireland, and in 1585 Sir Francis Drake introduced it to England. A few of Drake's potatoes were given to Sir Walter Raleigh, who planted them on his estate near Cork, Ireland, and later gallantly made a gift of potato plants to Queen Elizabeth I. The local gentry were promptly invited to a royal banquet featuring potatoes at every course. Unfortunately, Queen Elizabeth's cooks, uneducated in the matter of potatoes, tossed out the lumpy-looking tubers and brought to the royal table a dish of boiled stems and leaves (quite poisonous), which promptly made all in attendance deathly ill. Understandably, potatoes were banned from court, and it was some centuries before they managed to live down their public image.

In the early part of the nineteenth century the potato had become the dominant food in Ireland. The overcrowded Irish could supply their food needs without difficulty when growing potatoes on small plots of land. In fact, it was almost the sole food of the peasantry, with a typical family (man, wife, and four children) said to consume up to 250 pounds of the tubers weekly, eked out with 40 pounds of oatmeal, a little milk, and an occasional salted herring. Two things are too serious to joke about, an old Irish saying goes: marriage and potatoes. The potato-dependent Irish referred to their tubers—seriously—as the Apples of Life. When blight struck in 1845 and 1846, wiping out nearly the entire crop, famine followed. An estimated one and a half million people died as a result, and another million emigrated, many of them to the Americas.

Perhaps the most creative use of the potato in history was that of master criminal John Dillinger, who carved a pistol out of a potato, stained it with iodine (iodine turns starch black), and used it to escape from jail.

Buying Tips Choose potatoes that are firm, without sprouts, green skins, or spots, indicating exposure to light during storage or growth.

Culinary Uses Potatoes are a starchy vegetable that everybody has a preferred method of preparing and eating. Both sprouts and green spots contain solanine and are potentially toxic, and so should be mercilessly excised before cooking and eating. Otherwise, the skins should be left on, as significant quantities of vitamins and minerals are either in or just beneath the skin; in peeling, these nutrients and fiber are lost and practically nothing is left except acid-forming starch. Although potatoes may be grated or sliced raw and used in salads, most people prefer to either bake, boil, fry, or mash theirs. The average American eats about 125 pounds of potatoes a year, about half of which are fresh, while the other half are processed—either frozen,dehydrated, French-fried, or chipped. Over five billion pounds of potatoes a year go to make French fries alone.

Health Benefits Potatoes are excellent fuel food, despite their reputation of being fattening. Raw potatoes contain a sugary carbohydrate that is readily digested and enters the bloodstream slowly to provide the constant energy we need. When potatoes are cooked in any manner except steaming, the value of the mineral elements and most of the vitamins are lost, and the sugars are converted into starchy carbohydrates, which leave an acid end product in the process of digestion. Steamed potatoes retain the most vitamins and minerals and are still strongly alkaline. Fried in fat, potatoes are not only indigestible but also have a tendency to create a disturbance of the liver and gall bladder. Potatoes and their juice are great rejuvenators, helping to cleanse the system and benefiting the liver, tissues, and muscles. Their rich potassium content is helpful for those who use too much salt and high-sodium food in their diets. The skin of the potato is reputed to contain an acidophilus culture beneficial in the renewal of intestinal flora. Fresh potato juice is considered to have antibiotic properties, and is a rich source of vitamin C, enzymes, and minerals.

Byproducts

Potato flour, also known as **Potato starch,** is made of the entire cooked, dried, and ground potato. A useful item around the kitchen, it can serve as a binder for meat and vegetable patties, can be used in baking to condition the dough (as well as add subtle flavor and nutrients), and is an ideal thickener for sauces, gravies, and soups, as it cooks quickly and smoothly and leaves no raw taste. To use as a thickener, substitute 1 tablespoon potato flour for 2 tablespoons all-purpose flour.

Pumpkin (*Cucurbita maxima, C. mixta, C. pepo*)

Cucurbita *is the old classical Latin name for a gourd;* mixta *means mixed, and* pepo *comes from the Greek word* pepon, *meaning sun-ripened or mellow. The English name* pumpkin *derives from the Greek word, to which was later added the diminutive "-kin" ending.*

Pumpkin

Nutritional Value Per 100 g Edible Portion

	Raw	Cooked
Calories	26	20
Protein	1.00 g	0.72 g
Fat	0.10 g	0.07 g
Fiber	1.10 g	0.83 g
Calcium	21 mg	15 mg
Iron	0.80 mg	0.57 mg
Magnesium	12 mg	9 mg
Phosphorus	44 mg	30 mg
Potassium	340 mg	230 mg
Sodium	1 mg	1 mg
Beta Carotene (A)	1,600 IU	1,082 IU
Thiamine (B_1)	0.050 mg	0.031 mg
Riboflavin (B_2)	0.110 mg	0.078 mg
Niacin (B_3)	0.600 mg	0.413 mg
Ascorbic Acid (C)	9.0 mg	4.7 mg
Tocopherol (E)	1.0 mg	n/a

General Information The pumpkin, along with other squashes, is native to the Americas. The first Pilgrims barely survived their first winter in 1620 with the help of the lowly pumpkin; they knew sweet and fragrant melons but had never seen these hardy cousins, which the Indians grew as staples between corn and beans. Ranging in size from less than a pound to more than one hundred pounds (*National Geographic World* reported an 816-pound monster grown in Nova Scotia in 1990), the pumpkin also comes in a variety of colors ranging from white and peach to even blue and aqua. Deep orange is the color most familiar to Americans. European pumpkins mature sooner than their American counterparts, but are generally pale yellow in color and the flesh is less firm than the American variety; Russian pumpkins have white flesh and pale green skins. First cultivated by American Indians, who dried and made them into a type of flour, most pumpkins now are used either for the traditional Halloween jack-o'-lantern or for pumpkin pie.

Buying Tips Pumpkins of quality should be heavy for their size and free of blemishes, with a hard rind; the variety generally considered best for cooking are the small variety called Sugar Pumpkins.

Culinary Uses Nobody can argue the popularity of pumpkin pie . . . or pumpkin bread, pumpkin butter, pumpkin bars, and pumpkin ice cream!

Lore and Legend

The best of the pumpkin tales is one of Aesop's fables, which tells of a man who lay beneath an oak tree, criticizing the Creator for hanging a tiny acorn on so huge a tree, but an enormous pumpkin on such a slender vine. Then, the story goes, an acorn fell and hit him on the nose. Jack-o'-lanterns are an essential part of Halloween, the day before All Saints' Day on November 1. Several Indian tribes carved the shells into ritual masks, a practice that continues, but shorn of its religious implications. Who Jack was is far from certain, but an Irish legend has it that there was a man named Jack who, forbidden to enter Heaven because of his stinginess and barred from Hell because of his practical jokes, was condemned to walk the earth with his lantern until Judgment Day. The pumpkin was a symbol of fruitfulness, rebirth, and health in early China, where it is still called the Emperor of the Garden. In 1988, Leonard Stellpflug of Rush, New York, trucked a 653 1/2 pound pumpkin to the annual World Pumpkin Confederation weigh-in in Collins, New York. It broke the old squash record by almost 50 pounds. When asked how he grew it, Stellpflug shrugged and said, "Well-rotted manure and twenty-two pounds of fertilizer per plant."

To prepare, scrape out all the interior seeds and membrane, saving the seeds if you plan to eat them later. Peel off the skin with a vegetable peeler or sharp knife. Generally thought of only as a cooked vegetable, pumpkin can be eaten raw and is delicious when very finely grated and served in combination with grated carrots and beets as a base for salads. It can also be baked or boiled like other winter squash, and used in soups, stews, and many baked goods (including cornbread) in addition to pies. In the Caribbean pumpkin is braised into spicy, fragrant stews with chilis, legumes, and sometimes meat. The French cook it into soup and serve it within its own tureen-like shell. The early male blossoms can be picked for salads, sautéing, or stuffing. The seeds are also edible, and are discussed under **Nuts, Seeds, and Oils**.

Health Benefits Diuretic, laxative. Pumpkin is alkaline in reaction and raises the blood pressure, thus helping the blood to carry nourishment to various parts of the body. Cooked pumpkin destroys intestinal worms, but not as effectively as pumpkin seeds. Cooking pumpkins converts them from a readily digested sugar to a starchy carbohydrate.

Radish *(Raphanus sativus)*

The botanical name Raphanus *is from the Greek expression* raphanos, *meaning easily raised.* Sativus *refers to the fact that this plant has long been cultivated. The common English name* radish *comes from the Latin* radix, *meaning root.*

General Information Radishes are native to China, and have been eaten in Egypt since the beginnings of civilization. Herodotus records an Egyptian inscription which stated that the builders of the Great Pyramid ate enormous quantities of a radish called *gurmaia* together with onion and garlic (*History* II.cxxv). The first cultivated radishes in Egypt were probably those grown for radish-seed oil, which was widely used before Egypt acquired the olive. Radish-seed oil was still so important in Pliny's time that he complained about farmers who ceased to grow grain in order to sow radishes because they produced great quantities of profitable high-priced oil. Radish plants are believed to have been under cultivation in Europe as early as Neolithic times. This member of the mustard family has been widely propagated and now has many different varieties—those we are familiar with in salads, some grown only for cooking, and even some grown solely for their green tops.

Buying Tips A good-quality radish is brightly colored, well-formed, smooth, firm, and crisp. Those that are soft, spongy, or wilted should be avoided. Fresh radishes with the greens attached can be stored for three to five days in the refrigerator, while radishes with the greens removed can be stored in the refrigerator for two to four weeks.

Culinary Uses The flavor of radishes can vary widely from mild to peppery, and you may see radishes that are white, pink, purple, or black, as well as ruby red; each size and color has its own degree of hotness. Best used when young, radishes become woody and difficult to digest when too old. Most often eaten raw, radishes make beautiful garnishes and are a good brightener for any green salad, with their crisp texture and fresh flavor. They can also be cooked, and briefly steaming them transforms their tangy bite into a delicate sweet flavor much like a sweet turnip. As with many other root vegetables, their green tops are edible and lend a peppery taste to salads and soups; however, the tops do not lend themselves to steaming or boiling.

Health Benefits Diuretic, stimulant. Radishes contain a volatile ether which has a particular affinity as a solvent for mucus or phlegm, cleansing and expelling gallstones from the bladder, and cleansing the kidneys. They are especially good for hoarseness, clearing the sinuses, and sore throats. Radishes have enzymes that are valuable in aiding the secretion of digestive juices, most beneficial when eating heavy starchy foods such as grains, pastas, and potatoes. Regular use will help prevent viral infections such as the common cold and influenza.

Radish

Nutritional Value Per 100 g Edible Portion

	Small Red Raw	Daikon Raw	Daikon Cooked	Daikon Dried	Icicle Raw	Seeds Sprouted
Calories	17	18	17	271	14	41
Protein	0.60 g	0.60 g	0.67 g	7.90 g	1.10 g	3.81 g
Fat	0.54 g	0.10 g	0.24 g	0.72 g	0.10 g	2.53 g
Fiber	0.54 g	0.64 g	0.49 g	8.37 g	0.70 g	n/a
Calcium	21 mg	27 mg	17 mg	629 mg	27 mg	51 mg
Iron	0.29 mg	0.40 mg	0.15 mg	6.73 mg	0.80 mg	0.86 mg
Magnesium	9 mg	16 mg	9 mg	170 mg	9 mg	44 mg
Phosphorus	18 mg	23 mg	24 mg	204 mg	28 mg	113 mg
Potassium	232 mg	227 mg	285 mg	3,494 mg	280 mg	86 mg
Sodium	24 mg	21 mg	13 mg	278 mg	16 mg	6 mg
Zinc	0.300 mg	n/a	n/a	n/a	n/a	0.560 mg
Copper	0.040 mg	n/a	n/a	n/a	n/a	0.120 mg
Manganese	0.070 mg	n/a	n/a	n/a	n/a	0.260 mg
Beta Carotene (A)	8 IU	0 IU	0 IU	0 IU	0 IU	391 IU
Thiamine (B_1)	0.005 mg	0.020 mg	0 mg	0.270 mg	0.030 mg	0.102 mg
Riboflavin (B_2)	0.045 mg	0.020 mg	0.023 mg	0.680 mg	0.020 mg	0.103 mg
Niacin (B_3)	0.300 mg	0.200 mg	0.150 mg	3.400 mg	0.300 mg	2.853 mg
Pantothenic Acid (B_5)	0.088 mg	n/a	n/a	n/a	0.184 mg	0.733 mg
Pyridoxine (B_6)	0.071 mg	n/a	n/a	n/a	0.075 mg	0.285 mg
Folic Acid (B_9)	27.0 mcg	n/a	n/a	n/a	14.0 mcg	94.7 mcg
Ascorbic Acid (C)	22.8 mg	22.0 mg	15.1 mg	0 mg	29.0 mg	28.9 mg

Lore and Legend

A Talmudic story relates that Judea was once widely renowned for producing enormous garden plants, and in fact one radish was so large that a fox was able to hollow it out and make it his home. After he left, curious onlookers weighed the vegetable and found it to be nearly a hundred pounds! A German botanist in the mid-sixteenth century did report seeing some radishes that weighed a hundred pounds, giving credence to the story. Oaxaca, Mexico celebrates the Night of the Radishes on December 23 by carving giant radishes into fantastic figures of animals and people.

Varieties

Black radishes are sturdy characters that look like sooty black or matte brown-black turnips. Select very firm, comparatively heavy dark globes that show no flabbiness, pitting, sponginess, or cracks. The firm, dry, creamy white flesh may be almost as pungent as horseradish, and can be either coarsely shredded (with or without skin) or sliced thin and added raw to salads and cheeses; their peppery bite works well in stir-fries, soups, and stews. Excellent keeping vegetables, black radishes store well for months in the refrigerator, but will mellow during storage. They are available primarily in winter and early spring.

Daikon or **Japanese radish,** is known in Japan as the "giant white radish." This sturdy winter radish is six inches to a foot long (weighing up to fifty pounds if the farmer permits), white, cylindrical, and tapered at the tip like a carrot. Look for those that have a satiny sheen and are firm, not spongy. The root should be heavy, solid, and unblemished, with the pungent smell of radish. Sweet and juicy, when grated it has a cleansing, mildly sharp flavor that provides a crisp counterpoint to salty food. Raw daikon can be slivered, grated, diced, or sliced to add its crunch and zip to relishes and salads. It can also be used in soups and stir-fries, or pickled whole. Fresh raw daikon is known to contain diuretics, decongestants, digestive enzymes, and a substance that inhibits the formation of carcinogens in the body. It is available year-round, peaking in July through November.

Icicle radishes are white both inside and out. They are usually several inches long, with a bite that may be either mild or hot.

Red radishes are the most common variety of radish in North America. The size and shape of a cherry, some markets now offer elongated red radishes that are more pungent than the small round ones.

Horseradish (See separate reference).

Rutabaga (*Brassica napus, Napobrassica* group)

Also Known As: Swedish Turnip.

> *The Latin name* Brassica *derives from the Celtic* bresic; napobrassica *means turnip-cabbage. The English word* rutabaga *comes from the Swedish* rotabagge, *which means round root.*

General Information The rutabaga was developed by the Swiss botanist Gaspard Bauhin from a series of judicious turnip-cabbage crosses; the result turned out to be tailor-made for the fields of the chilly north, since the plants are slow growers that prefer a cool climate, and will not thrive where summers are exceedingly hot. This member of the cabbage family has a large yellow-orange bulb that is either globular or elongated, and is both larger and sweeter than turnips. At their best during the winter, the large, blue-green tops are usually trimmed before being shipped to market, and their bulbs waxed to prevent loss of moisture.

Buying Tips The roots should be firm and fairly smooth, with few leaf scars around the crown or fibrous roots at the base. Avoid those that are light for their size, or soft and

Rutabaga

Nutritional Value Per 100 g Edible Portion

	Raw	Cooked
Calories	36	34
Protein	1.20 g	1.10 g
Fat	0.20 g	0.19 g
Fiber	1.10 g	1.04 g
Calcium	47 mg	42 mg
Iron	0.52 mg	0.47 mg
Magnesium	23 mg	21 mg
Phosphorus	58 mg	49 mg
Potassium	337 mg	287 mg
Sodium	20 mg	18 mg
Zinc	0.340 mg	0.300 mg
Copper	0.040 mg	0.036 mg
Manganese	0.170 mg	0.153 mg
Beta Carotene (A)	0 IU	0 IU
Thiamine (B_1)	0.090 mg	0.072 mg
Riboflavin (B_2)	0.040 mg	0.036 mg
Niacin (B_3)	0.700 mg	0.630 mg
Pantothenic Acid (B_5)	0.160 mg	0.137 mg
Pyridoxine (B_6)	0.100 mg	0.090 mg
Folic Acid (B_9)	20.5 mcg	15.5 mcg
Ascorbic Acid (C)	25.0 mg	21.9 mg
Tocopherol (E)	0.15 mg	0.15 mg

shriveled, as they are likely to be tough, woody, or hollow. It is common practice to encase the root in paraffin to extend its shelf life, so they need to be peeled.

Culinary Uses Rutabagas have a mild, sweet flavor and readily absorb other flavors. Use rutabagas raw in salads or for hors d'oeuvres by peeling and then cutting them into cubes, curls, sticks, or triangles. They can also be steamed, baked, roasted with meat, sliced and fried, boiled and mashed (delicious mixed with potatoes and carrots) or cubed, blanched, and added to stews and soups.

Health Benefits Rutabagas are sometimes recommended for cases of constipation, but are apt to cause flatulence due to their content of mustard oil, and should not be used by anyone who suffers from kidney troubles. All *Brassica*-genus vegetables contain dithiolthiones, a group of compounds that have anti-cancer, antioxidant properties; indoles, substances that protect against breast and colon cancer; and sulphur, which has antibiotic and antiviral characteristics. This family of vegetables also mildly stimulates the liver and other tissues out of stagnancy.

Salsify *(Tragopogon porrifolium)*

Also Known As: Oyster Plant, Vegetable Oyster, Goatsbeard.

Tragopogon *means goat's beard and refers to the milky white seed filaments (like dandelion fluff) that distinguish members of this genus.* Porrifolius *means leek-leaved and describes to a degree the grassy, flat greens. The English word* salsify *comes from the Italian* sassefrica, *meaning the plant which accompanies stones, after its predisposition for rocky land.*

General Information Salsify is a member of the chicory family believed to be native to the Mediterranean basin, possibly first on the African side. The English began growing salsify both as a vegetable and as an ornamental sometime after 1500, and it appeared on the American scene during the 1700s. Salsify produces fleshy roots the first year, then sets purple or rose-colored flowers the next. Generally imported to North American markets from Belgium, it is also a popular vegetable grown in many home gardens, and readily grows wild. The long, buff-skinned root looks like a hairy and under-nourished parsnip, and has white, mild-tasting flesh. In the United States it is often difficult to find salsify in the markets, while in Europe it is readily available during its season and turns up frequently in fritters, as a basis for cream soups, or even cooked like asparagus.

Buying Tips The root will be up to eight inches long and have many tiny protruding

Salsify

Nutritional Value Per 100 g Edible Portion	Raw	Cooked
Calories	82	68
Protein	3.30 g	2.73 g
Fat	0.20 g	0.17 g
Fiber	1.80 g	1.49 g
Calcium	60 mg	47 mg
Iron	0.70 mg	0.55 mg
Magnesium	23 mg	18 mg
Phosphorus	75 mg	56 mg
Potassium	380 mg	283 mg
Sodium	20 mg	16 mg
Beta Carotene (A)	0 IU	0 IU
Thiamine (B_1)	0.080 mg	0.056 mg
Riboflavin (B_2)	0.220 mg	0.173 mg
Niacin (B_3)	0.500 mg	0.392 mg
Ascorbic Acid (C)	8.0 mg	4.6 mg

rootlets. Select those that are firm and crisp rather than soft, and prefer smaller over larger ones, which may be pithy.

Culinary Uses The flavor of salsify combines a slightly sour-sweet taste with a mild, salty flavor similar to an oyster. Delicious steamed, boiled, sautéed, baked, deep fried, or chunked into soups and stews, this vegetable is something to look forward to in the fall, and especially after a frost, when their flavor improves. Salsify skin is edible, but needs a good scrubbing before cooking. The immature purple bud may be cooked and eaten, and is reminiscent of asparagus in flavor; the tender young leaves are a good salad ingredient. In the early spring, the young flower stalks can be eaten raw or cooked like asparagus.

Health Benefits Salsify contains a natural insulin that helps the pancreas digest starches. In some, salsify has been known to cause serious gastric grumbling, so test in moderation to find your tolerance.

Salsify, Black (*Scorzonera hispanica*)

Also Known As: Scorzonera.

Scorzonera *comes from either* scorzanera, *Italian for black bark, or from* escorco, *the Catalan word for viper, so named because the plant's juices were thought to provide an antidote to snakebite. The plant was introduced to European culture through Spanish seed, hence* hispanica. *The English word* salsify *comes from the Italian* sassefrica, *meaning the plant which accompanies stones, after its predisposition for rocky land.*

General Information Indigenous to central and southern Europe, black salsify was relatively unknown except to wild food gatherers until the sixteenth century. During the Middle Ages, it became one of the most important vegetables in Europe, being considered a potent tonic and a remedy for smallpox. The Spanish began to cultivate the plant during the eighteenth century, and its use spread to kitchens all over the English-speaking world. The vegetable fell out of flavor in the Victorian era, supposedly because fastidious cooks began peeling the "dirty" black skin from the root before cooking. This not only ruined the flavor, but also put an end to whatever tonic properties the root possessed. Not visually appealing, this delectable root resembles a muddy brown, non-tapering, petrified carrot. It is usually more regularly shaped, longer, and smoother than white salsify. Scorzonera is described by some as inferior to salsify, and by others as superior.

Culinary Uses Black salsify has a faint coconut or oyster flavor. Generally eaten steamed, baked, boiled, or fried, the roots should always be soaked well before using to remove the bitter taste. The skin only needs a light scrubbing rather than peeling, and offers interesting color relief and flavor to all manner of dishes. The southwest of France has a specialty of cooking unopened scorzonera buds in omelets; they are described as more exquisite than asparagus tips.

Health Benefits Like Jerusalem artichokes, black salsify roots contain inulin, and are thus valuable to diabetics, who can use them as a source of carbohydrate. The inulin is responsible for the sweet quality in the flavor. In some, salsify has been known to cause serious gastric grumbling, so test in moderation to find your tolerance. Low in fat, high in fiber, calcium, and iron.

Sea Kale *(Crambe maritima)*

Also Known As: Sea Colewort.

Maritima *means maritime, or of the sea.*

General Information Growing wild along the cliffs and beaches of the English, Continental, and Irish coasts, sea kale is quite a large plant with broad, toothed, bluish-green leaves and white flowers borne on a two-foot-long stalk. Once planted, sea kale will continue to yield for about ten years. The young shoots and leaves were early recognized as a delicate and choice food, but not until the late eighteenth century was the plant given a place in the garden. Harvested in the spring, the shoots must be blanched to be tender. In mid-summer the plants will produce attractive flowers.

Culinary Uses and **Health Benefits** Choose shoots that are six to nine inches long. These have a delicate, nutty, slightly bitter flavor, and are delicious when eaten raw with cheese, in salads, or prepared like asparagus. Traditionally, the leaf stalks are tied in bundles and cooked in salted water for about twenty minutes, then served hot with melted butter.

Sea Vegetables

General Information The use of seaweeds and sea vegetables as foods and medicine is not new, but was originally confined mostly to Asian cookery. These sea plants have no roots, as land plants do, nor do they have branches and stalks in the same sense, but cling by means of "holdfasts." Over 435 varieties have been discovered so far, and these are generally grouped into three kinds depending on color—the brown, the red, and the green. The particular color is related to the spectrum of light available to the plants for photosynthesis. Sea vegetables are now becoming more well known and accepted in the Western hemisphere.

Culinary Uses Seaweeds and sea vegetables are highly versatile foods that can easily be incorporated into numerous styles of cuisine, enhancing and complementing the flavors and textures. Most expand considerably when soaked, and since their flavor goes a long way, only a small amount is needed. Depending on the variety, they can be grilled, broiled, stir-fried, or chopped and added to soups, stews, salads, and many other dishes. All of us probably eat a large quantity of seaweed every day without knowing it—it appears as a binder and thickener in foods such as ice creams, candies, jams, soups, and sauces, not to mention its use in toothpaste, cosmetics, and certain medications.

Health Benefits The medicinal properties of sea vegetables are voluminous. Human blood contains all one hundred or so minerals and trace elements in the ocean; since

seaweeds contain these elements (up to ten to twenty times the value of land plants) in the most assimilable form because their minerals and elements are integrated into living plant tissue, they are an excellent source for food and medicine. Benefits include reducing blood cholesterol, and helping disorders of the genito-urinary and reproductive systems. Sea vegetables have antibiotic properties known to be effective against penicillin-resistant bacteria and are credited with anti-aging properties. They also hold considerable water when passing through the digestive tract, forming a gel which increases the bulk and speed of the stools. Kelp and other seaweeds are used by the Chinese to soften and reduce hardened masses in the body; they contain a full range of minerals, including trace minerals, often deficient in people with degenerative diseases.

Studies conducted at Canada's McGill University have shown that some seaweeds (including arame, hiziki, and kombu) can help remove radioactive strontium from the body by means of alginic acid, which binds with strontium in the blood and carries it out of the system. Seaweeds are one of the few good sources of organic fluorine, a nutrient that boosts the body's defenses and strengthens the teeth and bones. Since fluorine is lost with even minimal cooking, one must eat dried seaweeds raw (after soaking) to gain any fluorine benefit. The iodine content in seaweed prevents goiter and is indispensable to thyroid function; the thyroid influences digestive and metabolic efficiency, and a deficiency of iodine can result in a lack of energy, an inability to metabolize foods, and weight gain. Much of the vitamin B_{12} previously thought to be contained in seaweeds is actually an "analogue" that may counteract the effectiveness of any true B_{12}. Lastly, they have long been acclaimed as beauty aids, believed to help maintain beautiful healthy skin and lustrous hair.

Varieties

Alaria (*Alaria esculenta, A. marginata*) is biologically almost identical to wakame, but is harvested primarily in Maine. It has a wilder taste than wakame and requires longer cooking. Dried alaria can be added to soups or cooked as a vegetable with other vegetables or tofu. Baked, it can be crumbled and used as a garnish. Alaria is high in iodine, bromine, and all the B vitamins, including B_{12}.

Arame (*Eisenia arborea*) is a kelp closely related to wakame and kombu that is harvested in Japan, Peru, and the Pacific North American coast. The blades, which grow in wide leaves up to a foot in length, are sliced into long, stringlike strands, cooked, sun-dried, and packaged. With its mild, sweet taste, most Westerners enjoy this variety immediately. Arame is noted for treatment of the spleen, pancreas, female disorders, and high blood pressure. It is highly concentrated in iron and calcium, and one of the richest sources of iodine.

Dulse (*Rhodymenia palmata, Palmaria palmata*) is a red seaweed with flat, fan-shaped fronds that grows from the temperate to frigid zones of the Atlantic and Pacific. The use of dulse as a food dates back to the eighteenth century in the British Isles, where it was commonly eaten with fish, potatoes, and butter. Dried dulse can be eaten raw; chopped or crumbled for salads, soups, and vegetable dishes; or twisted on a tong and roasted. Because of its salty taste, it is frequently used as a salt substitute. Dubbed the "beef jerky of the sea" because of its chewy, stringy texture and salty taste, it is often an immediate favorite of those first tasting seaweed, which may not be true for other sea vegetables. This highly alkaline vegetable is an excellent source of iron, and also contains excellent quantities of iodine and manganese, which activate enzyme systems.

Hijiki (*Hizikia fusiforme*) has been used for hundreds of years in Japan, where it is known as the "bearer of wealth and beauty." It grows over the rocks and sea bottom like a carpet of stem-roots, or erect like a bush up to six feet high. The harvested plants are cut and sun-dried, boiled until soft, then dried again. The black dried hijiki should be soaked before use; the soaking process will cause it to quadruple in size, and the color to lighten to a deep brown. With a milder taste than dulse, kombu, or nori, hijiki blends well with many foods. Hijiki is very mineral rich; because of its calcium (1,300 milligrams per 100 grams) and iron contents, this sea vegetable is highly recommended during pregnancy. In the Far East, it is esteemed as a food that increases beauty, and strengthens and adds luster to the hair.

Irish moss (*Chondrus crispus*), also known as **Carrageen,** is found in great abundance off the Atlantic coasts of Europe and America. The name carrageen in fact comes from a coastal town in southeastern Ireland. During the potato famine of the mid-nineteenth century, thousands of Irish saved themselves from starvation by eating this flat, red, fernlike seaweed. Inedible when raw, Irish moss can be cut up and added to soups or stews. It is somewhat cartilaginous and flexible, but when dried becomes brittle. It bleaches to creamy-white when exposed to sunlight. Most Irish moss that is harvested is processed for its jelly-like extract, carrageenan, used as a thickening agent. Carrageenan is popular in desserts, puddings, yogurt, and other dairy products because it will jell in cool water. Boiled with milk and sugar, it makes a tasty white pudding with a high mucilage content—a soothing food for people with sore throats. Long noted for its medicinal properties, Irish moss is used in cough preparations, for digestive disorders and ulcers, kidney ailments, heart disease, and glandular irregularities, and as a bowel regulator. It contains calcium chloride, which acts as a heart tonic and glandular balancer, and is especially high in iodine and potassium.

Sea Vegetables

Nutritional Value Per 100 g Edible Portion

	Dulse, Dried	Irish Moss	Kombu	Nori	Wakame
Calories	n/a	49	43	35	45
Protein	13.30 g	1.51 g	1.68 g	5.81 g	3.03 g
Fat	n/a	0.16 g	0.56 g	0.28 g	0.64 g
Fiber	n/a	n/a	1.33 g	0.27 g	0.54 g
Calcium	632 mg	72 mg	168 mg	70 mg	150 mg
Iron	79.20 mg	8.90 mg	2.85 mg	1.80 mg	2.18 mg
Magnesium	593 mg	n/a	121 mg	2 mg	107 mg
Phosphorus	386 mg	157 mg	42 mg	58 mg	80 mg
Potassium	2,270 mg	63 mg	89 mg	356 mg	50 mg
Sodium	9,917 mg	67 mg	233 mg	48 mg	872 mg
Zinc	3.900 mg	1.950 mg	1.230 mg	1.050 mg	0.380 mg
Copper	n/a	0.149 mg	0.130 mg	0.264 mg	0.284 mg
Manganese	3.700 mg	0.370 mg	0.200 mg	0.988 mg	1.400 mg
Beta Carotene (A)	8,010 IU	n/a	116 IU	5,202 IU	360 IU
Thiamine (B_1)	0.160 mg	0.015 mg	0.050 mg	0.098 mg	0.060 mg
Riboflavin (B_2)	0.110 mg	0.466 mg	0.150 mg	0.446 mg	0.230 mg
Niacin (B_3)	3.200 mg	0.593 mg	0.470 mg	1.470 mg	1.600 mg
Pantothenic Acid (B_5)	n/a	0.176 mg	n/a	n/a	n/a
Pyridoxine (B_6)	n/a	n/a	n/a	0.159 mg	n/a
Folic Acid (B_9)	n/a	n/a	180.0 mcg	n/a	n/a
Ascorbic Acid (C)	12.0 mg	n/a	n/a	39.0 mg	3.0 mg
Tocopherol (E)	n/a	n/a	0.87 mg	n/a	n/a

Kelp (*Fucus* and *Laminaria*) is the fastest growing plant on land or in the sea, growing up to two feet a day and reaching lengths of over one thousand feet. The kelp family includes nearly nine hundred known varieties, including kombu, wakame, and arame; however, these sea vegetables are packaged under their own names. After harvesting and drying, kelp that is to be sold for human consumption is usually powdered for use in capsules or added to supplements and seasonings. Powdered kelp has a "sea" flavor that adds a subtle salty flavor to salads, soups, vegetables, baked goods, or beverages. Dried kelp can be diced and added to soups and stews. Kelp greatly increases the nutritional value of all food prepared with it, as it is considered the most completely mineralized food.

Kombu (*Laminaria longicruris, L. digitata*) is one of the better known and more versatile sea vegetables, also called **Tangle, Oarweed,** or **Sea cabbage.** A brown seaweed that has been eaten by people in Russia, Wales, and Iceland for several hundred years, its broad blackish-grey ribbons are dried, boiled, compressed, dried again, and finally shredded or powdered. Usually sold in five- to six-inch dried pieces, it is also sold as nalto kombu (shredded kombu that cooks quickly), tororo kombu (vinegared, shaved kombu that needs little or no cooking), shio-kombu (boiled, soy-sauce flavored kombu), kombu-zuke (lightly pickled kombu), and kombu-ko (powdered kombu that can be sprinkled on food or used in drinks). It can be eaten raw as a vegetable, used in stews or soup stock, as a food wrapper, or eaten on its own either deep-fried or baked. Added to a pot of beans, kombu helps them to cook faster and renders them more digestible because it balances the protein and oils as well as softens their tough fibers. Especially delicious with root vegetables, it should first be soaked for fifteen minutes, then cooked beneath the vegetables. More than any other sea vegetable, kombu takes preeminent place in Japan, where it is the foundation for the numerous broths and stocks (dashi) that flavor so many Japanese dishes. Kombu contains significant amounts of glutamic acid, the basis of monosodium glutamate (MSG), but acts as an antidote to excess sodium consumption, reduces blood cholesterol, and lowers hypertension. High in sugar, potassium, iodine, calcium, and vitamins A and C.

Nori (*Porphyra tenera*), also called **Laver,** is classified as a red seaweed, although it is bright lavender in the water. Dried, it turns a dark purple or black color, but then turns green when cooked or toasted. High-quality nori possesses a deep color and brilliant luster, while l esser-quality nori is dull and flat. Gaelic people of the British Isles have long made flat breads from flour and laver, known as laver bread. In south Wales, it is a traditional breakfast food, coated in oatmeal before being fried and served with bacon and eggs. In the Far East, nori is sometimes boiled to produce a gel in cooking, but most often it is simply wrapped around rice balls, used for sushi, or lightly toasted and cut into strips for garnishes. It can also be chopped or broken to be added to soups and salads. Nori has the highest protein content (48 percent of dry weight) and is the most easily digested of the seaweeds. It also contains an enzyme that helps break down cholesterol deposits. Nori is exceedingly high in vitamin A, B_1, and niacin (B_3).

Sea lettuce (*Ulva*) is a bright green, ribbed plant that resembles leaf lettuce. It has a mild flavor and is good as a fresh, finely chopped salad green when picked at an early stage. Older fronds may be dried and added to soups.

Wakame (*Undaria pinnatifida*) is a brown Japanese seaweed that grows in long, thin, ribbon-like strands and sporophylls—fingerlike protrusions—that reportedly taste like peanuts. This versatile and sweet-tasting seaweed can be toasted and crumbled for use as a condiment, in soups and salads, to flavor the Japanese stock *dashi*, and can also be soaked and cut into strips for wrapping up pieces of raw fish to make sushi. The best quality wakame has a thin rather than wide center stipe, but since it is impossible to determine the stipe size when the plant is dried, purchasing reputable brand names is the best way to obtain quality wakame. Once rehydrated, the stipe is generally cut out and reserved for soup stock. Dried wakame can be added to soups or cooked as a vegetable with other vegetables or tofu. Baked, it can be crumbled and used as a garnish. As with other sea vegetables, wakame contains alginic acid, a polysaccharide component that is released by gastric acids during digestion. When the alginic acid enters the intestines it can combine with sodium or heavy metals and eliminate them from the system. As a result, eating wakame will alleviate hypertension caused by excessive sodium consumption and reduce the heavy metal toxicity of the body.

Skirret (*Sium sisarum*)

Sium *comes from* sion, *the old Greek named used by Dioscorides;* sisarum *means like sisal. The English name* skirret *is derived from the Dutch* suikerwortel *meaning sugar root.*

General Information A member of the carrot and parsley family native to China and Japan, skirret is cultivated for the bunch of wrinkled greyish roots that form the crown. During the fifteenth century, skirret enjoyed a fairly wide acceptance in Europe and ranked as one of the major kitchen vegetables in English and American gardens during the seventeenth and eighteenth centuries. The seventeenth-century gardeners Parkinson and Evelyn praised skirret as one of the most acceptable and pleasant root vegetables, and provided recipes for boiled, stewed, and roasted skirret. In the end, however, skirret lost out to the carrot, salsify, and even to the parsnip.

Lore and Legend

The Emperor Tiberius is said to have been so fond of skirret roots that he sought tributes of them from the warring Germans.

Culinary Uses The roots have a sweet, tender white flesh which, when cooked like salsify or parsnips, is highly esteemed in Asian cuisine. To prepare, simply scrub the roots and cut them into suitable lengths for cooking; they can then be boiled with a bit of salt and served with butter, or stewed, braised, baked, batter-fried, or creamed. They are also delicious when mashed with potatoes. Raw skirret can be grated or chopped into salads, or dressed in a vinegar marinade for its own salad.

Spinach (*Spinacia oleracea*)

Spinacia *comes from the term* spina *meaning spine and alludes to its spiny fruit;* oleracea *refers to a vegetable garden herb which is used in cooking.*

General Information Spinach originated in or near Persia, cultivated there for the delectation of their exotic long-haired cats, and later reached Spain by way of the invading Moors around 1100–1200 A.D. This member of the goosefoot family was entirely unknown to the Greeks and Romans. Spinach was probably brought to the United States early in colonial days, but commercial cultivation did not start until about 1806, and the first curly-leafed variety was introduced in 1828. Popularized in comic strips by the Herculean feats of Popeye the sailor, spinach is not usually a favorite vegetable among children. There are three basic types of spinach. Savoy has crinkly, curly leaves with a dark green color; it is the type sold in fresh bunches at most markets. Flat or smooth-leaf spinach has un-wrinkled, spade-shaped leaves that are easier to clean than savoy; varieties of this type are generally used for canned and frozen spinach as well as soups, baby foods, and other processed foods. Increasingly popular are semi-savoy varieties, which have slightly crinkled leaves. These offer

Lore and Legend

Spinach has been regarded in folklore as a plant with remarkable abilities to restore energy, increase vitality, and improve the quality of the blood. The popular cartoon Popeye is a testament to this.

Spinach

Nutritional Value Per 100 g Edible Portion

	Raw	Cooked
Calories	22	23
Protein	2.86 g	2.97 g
Fat	0.35 g	0.26 g
Fiber	0.89 g	0.88 g
Calcium	99 mg	136 mg
Iron	2.71 mg	3.57 mg
Magnesium	79 mg	87 mg
Phosphorus	49 mg	56 mg
Potassium	558 mg	466 mg
Sodium	79 mg	70 mg
Zinc	0.530 mg	0.760 mg
Copper	0.130 mg	0.174 mg
Manganese	0.897 mg	0.935 mg
Beta Carotene (A)	6,715 IU	8,190 IU
Thiamine (B_1)	0.078 mg	0.095 mg
Riboflavin (B_2)	0.189 mg	0.236 mg
Niacin (B_3)	0.724 mg	0.490 mg
Pantothenic Acid (B_5)	0.065 mg	0.145 mg
Pyridoxine (B_6)	0.195 mg	0.242 mg
Folic Acid (B_9)	194.4 mcg	145.8 mcg
Ascorbic Acid (C)	28.1 mg	9.8 mg
Tocopherol (E)	1.88 mg	n/a

some of the texture of savoy, but are not as difficult to clean; they are cultivated for both the fresh market and for processing.

Buying Tips Leaves should be a dark green color, clean, and fresh-looking. Avoid bunches with yellow leaves or those that are wilted, bruised, or crushed.

Culinary Uses Raw spinach is an excellent salad green, light and tasty. Cooked spinach has a slightly acid aftertaste; many cooks enjoy this flavor, but if you are not one of them, try adding two pats of butter or a splash of milk or cream. The secret of cooking spinach is to cook it quickly in very little water; it reduces in size dramatically, so be sure to buy sufficient quantity. Spinach can also be used as a stuffing for pancakes, quiches, and other savory dishes.

Health Benefits Laxative. Raw spinach is one of nature's best antidotes for lower bowel stagnation, detoxifying the digestive tract, restoring the pH balance, soothing intestinal inflammation, promoting peristalsis, and providing the organic mineral salts required for repair and maintenance of the colon. Its rich iron and chlorophyll content helps build healthy blood, while its vitamin A content is valuable for the eyes. The oxalic acid found in spinach is in a natural and beneficial form when raw. Cooking converts this acid into an inorganic form which binds with calcium to form a compound that the body cannot absorb, and which is then deposited in the kidneys and helps to create a calcium deficiency within the body.

Spinach, New Zealand *(Tetragonia expansa, T. tetragonioides)*

Tetragonia *is a Greek word meaning four-angled and refers to its four-angled seed;* expansa *means expanded, and suggests its willingness to spread widely.*

General Information Native to New Zealand and Australia, the man who was chiefly responsible for the transfer of New Zealand spinach to Europe was Captain James Cook. On his first circumnavigation of the world he took along Sir Joseph Banks, a botanist who discovered the plant in New Zealand in 1770 and brought back samples of seeds. Planted in Kew Gardens in 1772, they were promptly forgotten; apparently, it did not occur to anybody that the plant might be edible. On Cook's second voyage, a botanist named Foster found the plant growing abundantly near Queen Charlotte's Straight, and was reminded by its thick, fleshy leaves of the spinach substitute orach. He took it aboard ship as a possible remedy for scurvy, which had been plaguing the crew, and discovered that it did indeed offer protection against that malady. Europeans were not very excited about the new plant, cultivating it almost exclusively as a curiosity in botanical gardens or, later, as a houseplant for its attractive, fleshy, triangular leaves. Even today, one would be hard put to find New Zealand Spinach in the markets; usually those who want to eat it have to grow it themselves. Chiefly used for furnishing greens during the hot summer months, when common spinach does not grow well, its endearing property to gardeners is its ability to withstand heat, actually thriving in the hot summer sun.

Spinach, New Zealand

Nutritional Value Per 100 g Edible Portion

	Raw	Cooked
Calories	14	12
Protein	1.50 g	1.30 g
Fat	0.20 g	0.17 g
Fiber	0.70 g	0.61 g
Calcium	58 mg	48 mg
Iron	0.80 mg	0.66 mg
Magnesium	39 mg	32 mg
Phosphorus	28 mg	22 mg
Potassium	130 mg	102 mg
Sodium	130 mg	107 mg
Beta Carotene (A)	4,400 IU	3,622 IU
Thiamine (B_1)	0.040 mg	0.030 mg
Riboflavin (B_2)	0.130 mg	0.107 mg
Niacin (B_3)	0.500 mg	0.390 mg
Pantothenic Acid (B_5)	0.312 mg	0.256 mg
Ascorbic Acid (C)	30.0 mg	16.0 mg

Culinary Uses New Zealand spinach tastes very similar to regular spinach, but is somewhat tougher. With leaves that are smaller and more porous, they have the same uses. Most experts agree that it has to be cooked in order to be considered palatable. Once cooked, it becomes a pulpy mass, more unctuous than spinach in consistency, which some think makes it more agreeable eating, while others think not. Young tender leaves are much superior to older ones, which tend to develop a taste too assertive to please everyone. One system for picking leaves is to take only the leafy tips of branches where new growth is developing.

Health Benefits New Zealand spinach contains much the same health-giving elements as true spinach, though with considerably less iron and more oxalic acid.

Sprouts

General Information Sprouts result when almost any bean, grain, or seed is soaked overnight and allowed to grow, releasing all of its stored nutrients in a burst of vitality as it attempts to become a full-sized plant. When you eat these tiny, easy-to-digest plants, you are literally getting the best of what the plant has to offer, since they are at their nutritional peak. During sprouting, vitamin and enzyme content increase dramatically, while starch is converted into simple sugars, protein is turned into amino acids and peptones, and crude fat is broken down into free fatty acids. Hence, the sprouting process predigests the nutrients, making them easier to assimilate and metabolize. Ancient manuscripts show that by 3000 B.C., the Chinese were eating bean sprouts on a regular basis. The Emperor of China at that time also recorded certain therapeutic uses of sprouts in a book about medicinal herbs.

Culinary Uses Sprouts have now gone mainstream, with alfalfa and mung bean sprouts showing up in almost every grocery store, but many more besides can be sprouted right in your own kitchen. Their crisp, crunchy texture makes them a great addition to salads and sandwiches, and you can use them fresh or cooked in a great many dishes, adding them whole for just the last brief minute. For those sprouting at home, use only seeds that are whole and preservative-free, and eat them soon after they are "ripened" (exposed to sunlight for chlorophyll) to get the full nutritional benefit. The rinse schedule will depend upon where you live, since the more humidity in the air, the less you should water, as excessive moisture will promote mold. This means you may have to rinse three or four times a day in Phoenix, Arizona but only once or twice a day in Miami, Florida. Sprouted wheat berries may be ground and added to bread dough, where they assist in the rising process and give it a special flavor. If adding a cup of sprouted wheat berries, subtract 1/2 cup of flour and 1/2 cup of water from the recipe; the berries may be left whole, but are better ground, as some hard ones may lurk in the crust.

Health Benefits Stimulant. In the late sixteenth century, Li Shih Chen's *Pen Ts'ao Kang Mu*, an exhaustive work on Chinese pharmaceuticals and herbs, which took over twenty-six years to complete, discussed the medicinal value of sprouts, suggesting their use in reducing inflammation, obtaining a laxative effect, remedying dropsy and rheumatism, and building and toning the body. The life energy and enzymes in fresh sprouts stimulate the body's inherent self-cleansing and self-healing abilities, and if no heavy cooked foods are taken as well, the overall metabolism is speeded up because it is not weighed down by hard-to-digest food. Their high water content helps flush toxic poisons from the system, thus slowing the aging clock; they are also rich in nitrilosides, substances that break down into chemicals (benzaldehydes) that selectively destroy only cancer cells. Sprouts even enhance the sex life, providing more and better quality vitamin E (known as a fertility vitamin) than wheat germ.

Varieties

Aduki sprouts are a fine grasslike sprout with a sweet nutty taste and texture. Their mild flavor and crunchy texture make them versatile in salads, Chinese-style marinated vegetables, green drinks, sprout loaves, and sandwiches.

Alfalfa is sprout queen and ubiquitous in every salad bar. These threadlike white sprouts, with tiny green tops and a mild nutty flavor, are a favorite in salads and sandwiches. One of the most nutritious foods you can eat, these require the shortest soaking time (only five hours), and provide large quantities—two tablespoons of seeds will yield one full quart of sprouts. People with autoimmune diseases, particularly rheumatoid arthritis and lupus, have noted aggravations of symptoms when eating alfalfa sprouts, but no problems have been noted using non-grain sprouts such as clover, sunflower, or buckwheat.

Almonds when sprouted have a crunchy texture and are easy to digest. They are an excellent source of protein, vitamins, and minerals.

Barley sprouts are particularly high in vitamin C and the B complex group, and contain several key amino acids. Like most other grain sprouts, it is recommended to eat them when less than one inch long, or else they will weave themselves into a thick thatch.

Buckwheat must have its outer hull intact for sprouting. Seven-day-old buckwheat sprouts has rich red stems and round, deep green leaves. More palatable than wheatgrass, buckwheat sprouts can be eaten on its own, used in salads, juices, and soups, and is delicious up to the flowering stage.

Clover sprouts are usually those of red clover, and look very similar to alfalfa sprouts. Tangy and crisp, these sprouts have a milder, sweeter taste than alfalfa, and are sprouted in the same manner.

Fenugreek sprouts have an aggressive flavor that are best combined with other sprouts. They provide a tangy seasoning in salads and vegetable dishes. One tablespoon will yield about a quart of sprouts, which are ready when one inch long. If you cook them, do not do so for more than three or four minutes, or else they will become bitter. Fenugreek sprouts are a powerful liver and kidney cleanser, and an excellent source of phosphorus and iron.

Lentil sprouts are peppery and crisp, and tastier if allowed to grow longer than the recommended one-half inch. Three-quarters of a cup yields one quart of sprouts, and they require only four hours of soaking.

Sprouts

Nutritional Value Per 100 g Edible Portion

	Alfalfa, Raw	Mung, Raw
Calories	29	30
Protein	3.99 g	3.04 g
Fat	0.69 g	0.18 g
Fiber	1.64 g	0.81 g
Calcium	32 mg	13 mg
Iron	0.96 mg	0.91 mg
Magnesium	27 mg	21 mg
Phosphorus	70 mg	54 mg
Potassium	79 mg	149 mg
Sodium	6 mg	6 mg
Zinc	0.92 mg	0.41 mg
Beta Carotene (A)	155 IU	21 IU
Thiamine (B_1)	0.076 mg	0.084 mg
Riboflavin (B_2)	0.126 mg	0.124 mg
Niacin (B_3)	0.481 mg	0.749 mg
Pantothenic Acid (B_5)	0.563 mg	0.380 mg
Pyridoxine (B_6)	0.034 mg	0.088 mg
Folic Acid (B_9)	36.0 mcg	60.8 mcg
Ascorbic Acid (C)	8.2 mg	13.2 mg

Mung bean sprouts are larger and crunchier than alfalfa sprouts, with a blander flavor. These popular "Chinese bean sprouts" are a staple in Asian dishes and are excellent in stir-fries, soups, and salads. One-half cup of mung beans will yield one quart of sprouts, ready to eat in about four days.

Pumpkin sprouts are a fast-growing nutritious sprout since the seeds are always hulled. Best when eaten after about twenty-four hours of sprouting, pumpkin sprouts contain high-quality proteins.

Radish sprouts have a zesty, tangy flavor that is delicious in salads. Ready to eat when they are an inch long, they are a powerful liver and kidney cleanser, and high in potassium.

Sesame sprouts are best grown from unhulled seeds, since these have not been treated with chemical solvents (to remove the hulls). These tiny seeds require only a short period of time for sprouting, usually one to three days, and are best when eaten small, as they get bitter quickly.

Soybean sprouts have a stronger flavor than mung sprouts and are best used cooked, since they are both hard to digest in their raw state and contain small amounts of toxins that could be harmful if consumed frequently in sizable quantities. Soak overnight, allow to sprout for three to five days, and use when the sprouts are under one inch in length.

Sunflower seed sprouts are mildly flavored like alfalfa, but much crunchier. These seeds are ready in the shortest amount of time, from two to three days, and develop a bitter taste if allowed to sprout over one-quarter of an inch. Two cups of seeds will produce one quart of sprouts.

Wheat sprouts are sweetest if the sprout does not exceed the length of the grain. Wheat sprouts are considered the most delicious of the sprouting grains by some sprout devotees. If you grow them longer, they quickly turn into wheatgrass.

Squash *(Cucurbita)*

Also Known As: Marrow, Gourd.

> Cucurbita *is the old classical Latin name for a gourd. The English name* squash *comes from the Narragansett Indian word* askutasquash, *which means green-raw-unripe, which was the way the Naragansetts ate it.*

General Information Marrows, squashes, and gourds are all part of a large family of edible gourds that grow on vines. The Europeans who encountered squashes and pumpkins in America had to compare them to melons or some other European vegetable or fruit, because they had never seen anything quite like them before and had no word for them. It is possible that squash was the very first food to be cultivated by American Indians; it seems at least to have been the first within what has been called the Indian triad—maize, beans, and squash. Archeological finds in Mexican caves, dated variously from 4000 to 9000 B.C., yielded squash seeds of cultivated varieties, while beans found with them were still from wild plants; maize did not appear at all until much later. There are as many different varieties of squash as there are shapes. **Summer squash,** with their fanciful shapes and bright colors, are a welcome summer vegetable. Their soft thin skins enclose small edible seeds, and their tender flesh is mild but charmingly flavorful when they are small and garden fresh; as their size or time past harvest increases, their flavor rapidly diminishes. These prolific plants produce offspring continuously throughout the growing season, moving from bud to table in just a matter of days. **Winter squash** are generally larger in size than summer squash with hard, inedible, shell-like skins and fully developed seeds. They are slower growing, months passing from the time they blossom until the time they are fully mature and ready to be harvested in the fall. Their dense sweet flesh reflects a whole summer of accumulating energy from sun and soil.

Culinary Uses Fresh young summer squash has soft moist flesh that cooks quickly. Served finely sliced in salads or as crudités, they are also popular steamed, baked, and as ingredients in stir-fries, casseroles, and soups. Overly mature summer squash, with their tough skin and dry flesh, are best suited to stuffing and baking. Winter squash is generally prepared by first removing the fibrous matter and seeds from the center and then steaming, broiling, or baking them (on the half-shell or with a stuffing mix); those with the deepest-colored flesh are usually the sweetest. Most winter squash varieties can be used interchangeably in recipes, where their sweet moist flesh adds sensational color and flavor to baked goods, custards, soufflés, soups, spreads, and of course pies. Spaghetti squash is often prepared as a substitute for spaghetti by baking or steaming until the rind softens; then it is cut in half lengthwise, and the spaghetti-like strands removed and flavored with a favorite seasoning (pasta sauce, etc.). For those with young children, puréed and strained squash makes an excellent baby food. The blossoms of all members of the squash family are edible. Picked just before they open, these yellow flowers are delicious sliced and tossed into salads, stuffed and baked, or batter coated and deep fried. The seeds are also edible and, once hulled, can be eaten in the same manner as pumpkin seeds.

Health Benefits Both summer and winter squash are highly alkaline foods and excellent remedies for acidosis of the liver and blood. Summer squash, with its light, bright flavor, is more suited for the hot summer months. Winter squash are apt fare for cold winter days, since they are a concentrated food and substantially filling.

Squash, Summer

Nutritional Value Per 100 g Edible Portion

	Chayote Raw	Chayote Cooked	Crookneck Raw	Crookneck Cooked	Pattypan Raw	Pattypan Cooked
Calories	24	24	19	20	18	16
Protein	0.90 g	0.62 g	0.94 g	0.91 g	1.20 g	1.03 g
Fat	0.30 g	0.48 g	0.24 g	0.31 g	0.20 g	0.17 g
Fiber	0.70 g	0.58 g	0.55 g	0.60 g	0.55 g	0.48 g
Calcium	19 mg	13 mg	21 mg	27 mg	19 mg	15 mg
Iron	0.40 mg	0.22 mg	0.48 mg	0.36 mg	0.40 mg	0.33 mg
Magnesium	14 mg	12 mg	21 mg	24 mg	23 mg	19 mg
Phosphorus	26 mg	29 mg	32 mg	39 mg	36 mg	28 mg
Potassium	150 mg	173 mg	212 mg	192 mg	182 mg	140 mg
Sodium	4 mg	1 mg	2 mg	1 mg	1 mg	1 mg
Zinc	n/a	n/a	0.290 mg	0.390 mg	0.290 mg	0.240 mg
Copper	n/a	n/a	0.102 mg	0.103 mg	0.102 mg	0.083 mg
Manganese	n/a	n/a	0.157 mg	0.213 mg	0.157 mg	0.128 mg
Beta Carotene (A)	56 IU	47 IU	338 IU	287 IU	110 IU	85 IU
Thiamine (B_1)	0.030 mg	0.026 mg	0.052 mg	0.049 mg	0.070 mg	0.051 mg
Riboflavin (B_2)	0.040 mg	0.040 mg	0.043 mg	0.049 mg	0.030 mg	0.025 mg
Niacin (B_3)	0.500 mg	0.420 mg	0.454 mg	0.513 mg	0.600 mg	0.464 mg
Pantothenic Acid (B_5)	0.483 mg	0.408 mg	0.102 mg	0.137 mg	0.102 mg	0.079 mg
Pyridoxine (B_6)	n/a	n/a	0.109 mg	0.094 mg	0.109 mg	0.085 mg
Folic Acid (B_9)	n/a	n/a	22.9 mcg	20.1 mcg	30.1 mcg	20.7 mcg
Ascorbic Acid (C)	11.0 mg	8.0 mg	8.4 mg	5.5 mg	18.0 mg	10.8 mg
Tocopherol (E)	n/a	n/a	n/a	n/a	n/a	n/a

Compared with summer squash, winter squash contains greater amounts of natural sugars, carbohydrates, and vitamin A. Nutritionally packed and one of the mildest and easiest vegetables to digest, squashes are low in calories and particularly high in vitamin A and potassium. According to Chinese medicine, squash helps to reduce inflammation, while consumption of the raw seeds expels roundworms and tapeworms.

Summer Squash Varieties

Chayote (*Sechium edule*) is a pear-shaped squash native to Mexico and Central America (its name is from the Aztec Nahuatl *chayotl*). Also known as **Mango squash, Pepinello,** and **Vegetable pear,** chayotes have soft pale skins that vary from creamy white to dark green. Female fruit is smooth skinned and lumpy with slight ridges. It is fleshier and preferred over the male fruit, which is covered with warty spines. Although they are furrowed and slightly pitted by nature, they should not look as though these indentations have been made by external forces, nor should they look shriveled, but should be completely firm to the touch. Choose smaller chayotes over larger, as the latter get insipid with size. Use as quickly as possible; if stored in the refrigerator for a week or more, they soon develop an unpleasant moldy flavor. The pale green flesh is crisp and finely textured, with a taste and consistency that blends cucumber, zucchini, and a bit of kohlrabi. Young chayote need not be peeled, while older ones are best peeled. The fruits, young shoots, leaves, and large fleshy roots are all used as culinary vegetables. Baked or fried, creamed for desserts or soups, chayote may be substituted in any recipe calling for summer squash. However, their bland flavor begs for big gutsy flavorings—chilis, spices, garlic, tomatoes, or cheese. Their mild, almost non-existent taste also means they can be, and often are, used in sweet dishes, simmered in a scented syrup like pears and served cold, or baked in slices with cinnamon, nutmeg, and sugar, or honey, lemon, and butter. The single large seed, which is edible once cooked, has a taste reminiscent of a lima bean and an almond. Its root, large and tuberous and up to twenty pounds in weight, looks and tastes like a yam.

Squash, Summer

Nutritional Value Per 100 g Edible Portion

	Spaghetti Raw	Spaghetti Cooked	Zucchini Raw	Zucchini Cooked
Calories	33	29	14	16
Protein	0.64 g	0.66 g	1.16 g	0.64 g
Fat	0.57 g	0.26 g	0.14 g	0.05 g
Fiber	1.40 g	1.40 g	0.45 g	0.50 g
Calcium	23 mg	21 mg	15 mg	13 mg
Iron	0.31 mg	0.34 mg	0.42 mg	0.35 mg
Magnesium	12 mg	11 mg	22 mg	22 mg
Phosphorus	12 mg	14 mg	32 mg	40 mg
Potassium	108 mg	117 mg	248 mg	253 mg
Sodium	17 mg	18 mg	3 mg	3 mg
Zinc	0.190 mg	0.200 mg	0.200 mg	0.180 mg
Copper	0.037 mg	0.035 mg	0.057 mg	0.086 mg
Manganese	n/a	n/a	0.127 mg	0.178 mg
Beta Carotene (A)	50 IU	110 IU	340 IU	240 IU
Thiamine (B_1)	0.037 mg	0.038 mg	0.070 mg	0.041 mg
Riboflavin (B_2)	0.018 mg	0.022 mg	0.030 mg	0.041 mg
Niacin (B_3)	0.950 mg	0.810 mg	0.400 mg	0.428 mg
Pantothenic Acid (B_5)	0.360 mg	0.355 mg	0.083 mg	0.114 mg
Pyridoxine (B_6)	0.101 mg	0.099 mg	0.089 mg	0.078 mg
Folic Acid (B_9)	12.0 mcg	8.0 mcg	22.1 mcg	16.8 mcg
Ascorbic Acid (C)	2.1 mg	3.5 mg	9.0 mg	4.6 mg
Tocopherol (E)	n/a	n/a	n/a	n/a

Crookneck and **Straightneck** (*Cucurbita moschata*) types range from four to six inches long, and have a bulbous blossom end and a long curved neck reminiscent of a goose. They have bumpy, bright yellow skins and creamy yellow flesh. The straightneck varieties have a straight neck, but same bumpy yellow skin.

Gooseneck squash (*Trichosanthes cucumeriana*), also known as **Snake squash,** is a curled, eye-catching squash native to south

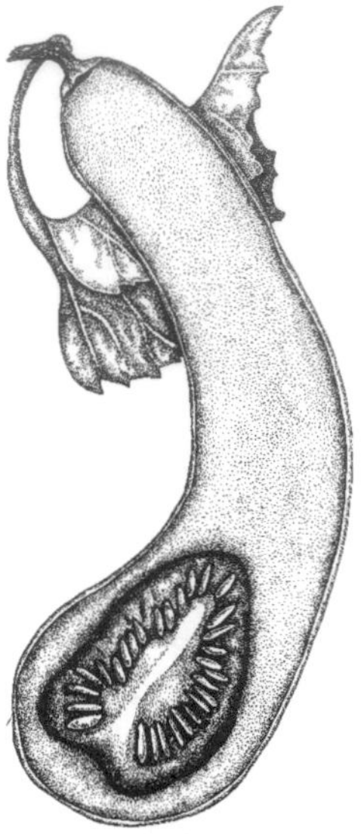

east Asia and Australia, but which can be grown in America and Europe. Eaten in the summer when immature and thin-skinned, it is usually sliced into rounds and steamed, or boiled and served with butter, salt, pepper, and herbs such as tarragon, dill, or marjoram.

Pattypan or **Scallop squash** look rather like thick round pin cushions with scalloped edges. They are at their best when they do not exceed four inches in diameter, and are pale green rather than their mature white or cream. Their flesh has a somewhat buttery taste, and the skin, flesh, and seeds are all edible.

Spaghetti squash (*Cucurbita pepo*) is a large oblong summer squash with smooth lemon-yellow skin. Once cooked, the creamy golden flesh separates into miles of swirly, crisp-tender, spaghetti-like strands. The taste is quite bland, lightly sweet and fresh, its light squash flavor making a perfect saucing medium. Look for very hard, smooth, evenly colored squash without ridges, spots, or bumps. Avoid greenish, honeydew-colored squash, which may be immature or have sprouting seeds. Larger spaghetti squash have better flavor and thicker strands.

Zucchini (*Cucurbita pepo*) is by far the most popular summer squash. Called a **Marrow** by the British, a **Courgette** by the French, and a zucchini by the Italians, this prolific shiny green squash ranges in size from four inches to baseball bat size, but is best when five to eight inches long. Longer zucchini tend to have seeds which are large, tough, and preferably removed before using. Unrivaled in versatility, zucchini may be eaten raw in salads, marinated, stir-fried, stuffed and baked, puréed for soups or sauces, or even made into pickles and marmalade. The blossoms are a special delicacy, either tossed into a salad or batter dipped and deep-fried. Or try the blossoms stuffed with a combination of cheese, meat, herbs, nuts, eggs, bread crumbs, rice, or potatoes. The world's longest zucchini was raised by Nick Balaci of Johnson City, New York, who grew a 69 1/2 inch Romanian zucchini in 1987.

Winter Squash Varieties

Acorn squash (*Cucurbita pepo*), sometimes called **Table Queen,** are shaped like a giant ribbed acorn with a definite pointed end. The slightly dry, orange-colored flesh of both green and golden varieties has a definite nut-like flavor, with the golden variety tending to be a little sweeter and the green moister. Their large seed cavities are perfect for stuffing, and they are best when baked. Unlike most winter squashes, acorns do not contain much beta carotene, but are still considered medicinal for the stomach and spleen.

Banana squash (*Cucurbita maxima*) are very large, long, cylindrical squashes that may weigh up to thirty pounds. Their thick, hard skins range in color from pale yellow to ivory, and their finely textured flesh is creamy orange or pink, sweet and dry. Often available cut into manageably-sized pieces, this squash is excellent combined with baked potatoes.

Butternut squash (*Caryoka nuciferum*) are reminiscent of a peanut in shape and color, with a large, round, fleshy bottom that encloses the seeds, and a cylindrical upper part that is solid flesh. Their smooth hard skins are a deep butterscotch color (avoid those with streaks of green), and their flesh is a deep orange, with a distinctive butterscotch flavor that most people find delicious. Very small butternuts are especially sweet, and because their skins are thinner than those of other winter squash, may be cooked and puréed with the skin intact. Steamed or baked like other squashes, they make excellent single servings when cut in half, cooked until soft, then served with a topping of butter and maple syrup.

Calabaza (*Cucurbita moschata*) are huge squashes whose mottled skin may be evergreen, sunset, or buff, speckled, or striated, but are always relatively smooth and hard-shelled when mature. Usually sold in chunks or slices, since few could tote the entire large vegetable, this versatile squash may be easily substituted for any other winter squash in dishes where it does not stand alone. The best calabazas are fine-grained, sweet, moist but not watery, and ravishingly orange.

Delicata (*Cucurbita pepo*) are elongated green and tan-striped squashes with tender yellow flesh. Also called **Bohemian** or **Sweet potato squash**, it first arrived on the scene as early as 1894, introduced by the now-defunct Peter Henderson Company of New York City. The size and shape of a large cucumber, the delicata has a moist, creamy yellow flesh that tastes and smells like a blend of corn, butternut squash, and sweet potato. Younger squashes may have skins tender enough to eat once cooked. They are best when steamed or baked, and are not recommended for soups or baking into desserts.

Golden nugget (*Cucurbita maxima*) are small round squashes that look like miniature fairytale pumpkins. Salmon-colored, with a finely ridged, very hard shell, this squash was developed at North Dakota State University in 1966, and is a close relative of the acorn squash. The moist, smooth, bright orange flesh has a mild squash flavor, which can range from delightfully sweet and buttery to not-so-sweet and dull-bland. Choose those that have a dull, matte look to the rind; a shiny finish indicates that the squash was picked immature and will be tasteless. Golden nuggets can be opened like pumpkins, scooped clean, brushed inside with butter and seasonings, and baked whole. They can also be split and baked like acorn squash.

Hubbards (*Cucurbita maxima*) are named after Elizabeth Hubbard of Massachusetts, and are an old extensive group of squashes that are usually plump and round in the middle,

Squash, Winter

Nutritional Value Per 100 g Edible Portion

	Acorn Raw	Acorn Cooked	Butternut Raw	Butternut Cooked	Hubbard Raw	Hubbard Cooked
Calories	40	56	45	40	40	50
Protein	0.80 g	1.12 g	1.00 g	0.90 g	2.00 g	2.48 g
Fat	0.10 g	0.14 g	0.10 g	0.09 g	0.50 g	0.62 g
Fiber	1.40 g	1.96 g	1.40 g	1.26 g	1.40 g	1.74 g
Calcium	33 mg	44 mg	48 mg	41 mg	14 mg	17 mg
Iron	0.70 mg	0.93 mg	0.70 mg	0.60 mg	0.40 mg	0.47 mg
Magnesium	32 mg	43 mg	34 mg	29 mg	19 mg	22 mg
Phosphorus	36 mg	45 mg	33 mg	27 mg	21 mg	23 mg
Potassium	347 mg	437 mg	352 mg	284 mg	320 mg	358 mg
Sodium	3 mg	4 mg	4 mg	4 mg	7 mg	8 mg
Zinc	0.130 mg	0.170 mg	0.150 mg	0.130 mg	0.130 mg	0.150 mg
Copper	0.065 mg	0.086 mg	0.072 mg	0.065 mg	0.064 mg	0.045 mg
Beta Carotene (A)	340 IU	428 IU	7,800 IU	7,001 IU	5,400 IU	6,035 IU
Thiamine (B_1)	0.140 mg	0.167 mg	0.100 mg	0.072 mg	0.070 mg	0.074 mg
Riboflavin (B_2)	0.010 mg	0.013 mg	0.020 mg	0.017 mg	0.040 mg	0.047 mg
Niacin (B_3)	0.700 mg	0.881 mg	1.200 mg	0.969 mg	0.500 mg	0.558 mg
Pantothenic Acid (B_5)	0.400 mg	0.504 mg	0.400 mg	0.359 mg	0.400 mg	0.447 mg
Pyridoxine (B_6)	0.154 mg	0.194 mg	0.154 mg	0.124 mg	0.154 mg	0.172 mg
Folic Acid (B_9)	16.7 mcg	18.7 mcg	26.7 mcg	19.2 mcg	16.4 mcg	16.2 mcg
Ascorbic Acid (C)	11.0 mg	10.8 mg	21.0 mg	15.1 mg	11.0 mg	9.5 mg
Tocopherol (E)	n/a	n/a	n/a	n/a	n/a	n/a

with tapered necks. Ranging from dark green to blue-gray and orange-red, and weighing from five to twenty pounds, these warty, thick-skinned squashes have sweet, dry, orange flesh. Excellent in pumpkin pie, they have a thicker, firmer texture than fresh pumpkin, "set up" easier, and require less sugar.

Kabocha is a generic grouping for many strains of Japanese pumpkin and winter squash of both *Cucurbita maxima* and *Cucurbita moschata* species. Resembling the buttercup or turban squashes, with their flattened drum or turban shape, they range from one to seven pounds, with rough, mottled rinds that are thick and deep green (sometimes orange), with paler uneven stripes and markings. The mustard-yellow flesh is sweet and rich-tasting, tender and floury dry, like a balance between sweet potato and pumpkin. Almost fiberless and with the highest sugar content of any squash, it is excellent baked with butter and served as a side dish, or stuffed with vegetables for a main course.

Pumpkin (see separate reference).

Turban (*Cucurbita maxima*), also called **Buttercup,** were developed in 1932 at North Dakota Agricultural College (now State University) by Dr. A.F. Yeager. Long esteemed by many growers as the ideal winter squash, this turban-shaped squash with its distinctive pale "beanie" is hard and thin-skinned, dark bluish-green with dramatic reddish-orange flecks and stripes, and ranges in size from three to five pounds. The bright orange flesh is tender, sweet, and custardy smooth when steamed; when baked it is denser and drier. It may be used in any manner you would butternut or acorn squash.

Sweet Potato (*Ipomoea batatas*)

Also Known As: Batata, Boniato.

> *The scientific name comes from the Greek* ips*, meaning worm or bindweed, and* homoios*, meaning like or similar to, since Carolus Linnaeus—the eighteenth-century Swedish botanist, famed for his system of plant classification—thought the twining vines looked unpleasantly like worms. The plants were called* batatas *in their native West Indies and southern United States.*

General Information Sweet potatoes are not related to potatoes or yams, but are a plump, smooth-skinned, tuberous member of the morning-glory family native to the West Indies and southern United States. Discovered by Columbus on his second trip to the New World, the sweet potato was sent back to Spain in 1494 along with many other new foods. The Chinese found the sweet potato in the Philippines in 1594, when a famine in the Fujian province prompted the governor to send an expedition there in search of food plants. Now growing in all warm moist areas of the world, the large, thick, sweet and mealy root almost entirely replaces the use of potatoes in some regions. There are literally hundreds of sweet potato varieties, most having yellow-brown or coppery colored skins with yellow, bright orange, or yellow-red flesh, and ranging in shape from long and slender to round. Varieties with yellowish, fawn-colored skins are relatively dry and mealy; these are most popular in the North. This type is sometimes called Jersey because it was once the main type grown in New Jersey. Sweeter, moister varieties with reddish skins and vivid orange flesh are more common in the southern United States. These softer-fleshed varieties are usually fatter or rounder than the firm-fleshed type, and are most often mistakenly referred to as yams.

Buying Tips Choose sweet potatoes that are firm and relatively unblemished, without soft or moldy ends. Buy organic whenever possible, because sweet potatoes tend to pick up a musty taste from soil that has been treated with pesticides. They should be kept in a cool dry

Sweet Potato

Nutritional Value Per 100 g Edible Portion

	Raw	Baked In Skin	Boiled No Skin	Candied
Calories	105	103	105	137
Protein	1.65 g	1.72 g	1.65 g	0.87 g
Fat	0.30 g	0.11 g	0.30 g	3.25 g
Fiber	0.85 g	0.80 g	0.85 g	0.39 g
Calcium	22 mg	28 mg	21 mg	26 mg
Iron	0.59 mg	0.45 mg	0.56 mg	1.13 mg
Magnesium	10 mg	20 mg	10 mg	11 mg
Phosphorus	28 mg	55 mg	27 mg	26 mg
Potassium	204 mg	348 mg	184 mg	189 mg
Sodium	13 mg	10 mg	13 mg	70 mg
Zinc	0.280 mg	0.290 mg	0.270 mg	0.150 mg
Copper	0.169 mg	0.208 mg	0.161 mg	0.102 mg
Manganese	0.355 mg	0.560 mg	0.337 mg	n/a
Beta Carotene (A)	20,063 IU	21,822 IU	17,054 IU	4,189 IU
Thiamine (B_1)	0.066 mg	0.073 mg	0.053 mg	0.018 mg
Riboflavin (B_2)	0.147 mg	0.127 mg	0.140 mg	0.042 mg
Niacin (B_3)	0.674 mg	0.604 mg	0.640 mg	0.394 mg
Pantothenic Acid (B_5)	0.591 mg	0.646 mg	0.532 mg	n/a
Pyridoxine (B_6)	0.257 mg	0.241 mg	0.244 mg	0.041 mg
Folic Acid (B_9)	13.8 mcg	22.6 mcg	11.1 mcg	11.4 mcg
Cobalamin (B_{12})	n/a	n/a	n/a	0.030 mg
Ascorbic Acid (C)	22.7 mg	24.6 mg	17.1 mg	6.7 mg
Tocopherol (E)	4.56 mg	n/a	n/a	n/a

place, where they will keep for a month or longer; at normal room temperatures they should be used within a week. Never store them in the refrigerator, where they are likely to develop a hard core and an "off" flavor.

Culinary Uses Sweet potatoes are probably best known for their role as a traditional accompaniment to Thanksgiving dinner, but should be enjoyed more frequently. Much like a regular potato, sweet potatoes can be roasted, boiled, steamed, baked in casseroles and sweet dishes, or baked in their jackets and eaten as a side vegetable. Whenever possible, they should be cooked in their edible skins to conserve the nutrients. Cooked and mashed sweet potatoes can replace up to one quarter of the wheat flour in breads, and are excellent in other baked goods such as cakes, cookies, muffins, or pies, where their flavor is enhanced by a sprinkling of sweet spice such as cinnamon, nutmeg, ground cloves, or allspice.

Health Benefits So nutritious that people can live on them (and have), the sweet potato is easily digestible and good for the eliminative system, ulcers, inflamed colons, and those with poor blood circulation. When raw, they are very alkaline for the system; cooking affects these tubers in the same way as regular potatoes, making them much more acidic. They are also beneficial for detoxifying the system, since they contain substances called phytochelatins that can bind heavy metals like cadmium, copper, mercury and lead, and thus participate in metal detoxification of body tissue. If a child accidentally swallows a metallic object such as a coin, feed him plenty of sweet potato; the sweet potato will stick to the object and allow it to pass through easier.

Swiss Chard *(Beta vulgaris cicla)*

Also Known As: Chard, Leaf Beet, Spinach Beet.

Beta *is believed to have come from the Greek letter* beta; vulgaris *means common or vulgar, and* cicla *is derived from* sicula, *which refers to Sicily, one of the places where chard first grew. The English word* chard *is derived from the Latin word for thistle,* carduus. *Although chard is not part of the thistle family, the word eventually came to mean the stalk or ribs of some vegetables, such as chard and cardoon. Sometimes called* Swiss chard, *this vegetable was so dubbed because of a Swiss botanist who, in the sixteenth century, described yellow chard.*

General Information Wild chard, like other wild beets, probably originated in the Mediterranean region, and can still be found there, as well as in Asia Minor and the Near East.

Swiss Chard

Nutritional Value Per 100 g Edible Portion

	Raw	Cooked
Calories	19	20
Protein	1.80 g	1.88 g
Fat	0.20 g	0.08 g
Fiber	0.80 g	0.94 g
Calcium	51 mg	58 mg
Iron	1.80 mg	2.26 mg
Magnesium	81 mg	86 mg
Phosphorus	46 mg	33 mg
Potassium	379 mg	549 mg
Sodium	213 mg	179 mg
Beta Carotene (A)	3,300 IU	3,139 IU
Thiamine (B_1)	0.040 mg	0.034 mg
Riboflavin (B_2)	0.090 mg	0.086 mg
Niacin (B_3)	0.400 mg	0.360 mg
Pantothenic Acid (B_5)	0.172 mg	0.163 mg
Ascorbic Acid (C)	30.0 mg	18.0 mg

This member of the beet family does not develop an enlarged fleshy root like the others, but is grown for its large crisp leaves and fleshy leaf stalks. Varying in color from yellowish to dark green or even red, the large glossy leaves have thickened midribs, and may be either smooth or crinkled. The stalks resemble thin, flattened celery and range from a pale celadon color to vivid scarlet. Red varieties are known as rhubarb chard.

Buying Tips Choose crisp bunches with firm, bright leaves. Very rarely will you find anything smaller than ten to twelve inches in the market; for smaller ones, you will have to grow your own.

Culinary Uses Swiss chard has a mild delicate flavor, earthy and sweet like a combination of beets and spinach. The green-leaved, cream-stemmed variety tastes closer to spinach. Young leaves and stalks can be chopped and added raw to salads, where it adds a pleasant and zesty beet-like flavor and spinachy texture. Those of medium size can be quickly sautéed, either just the leaves or with the stalks, for a pleasant side vegetable. Older leaves and stalks are best steamed, boiled, or added to soups. Any treatment that suits spinach will suit chard leaves, but chard must be cooked longer, although not too long, as the vitamin content decreases with cooking. Avoid cooking in aluminum or iron pans, as chard will tend to discolor.

Health Benefits Chard has a high oxalic acid content, beneficial in the uncooked state, but harmful when cooked because it becomes inorganic and is destructive of calcium. Swiss chard is beneficial to the digestive system.

Taro

Nutritional Value Per 100 g Edible Portion

	Raw	Cooked	Chips
Calories	40-107	44-142	477
Protein	1.50-2.79 g	0.52-4.16 g	2.04 g
Fat	0.20-0.97 g	0.11-0.68 g	25.47 g
Fiber	0.80-1.75 g	0.86-2.28 g	1.18 g
Calcium	43-129 mg	18-149 mg	45 mg
Iron	0.55-1.30 mg	0.72-1.56 mg	1.35 mg
Magnesium	33-47 mg	30-51 mg	84 mg
Phosphorus	45-84 mg	67-76 mg	131 mg
Potassium	591-606 mg	484-623 mg	824 mg
Sodium	11-50 mg	15-54 mg	369 mg
Beta Carotene (A)	0-2,045 IU	0-1,764 IU	0 IU
Thiamine (B_1)	0.062-0.095 mg	0.044-0.107 mg	0.053 mg
Riboflavin (B_2)	0.025-0.244 mg	0.028-0.198 mg	0.029 mg
Niacin (B_3)	0.600-0.995 mg	0.480-0.510 mg	0.040 mg
Ascorbic Acid (C)	4.5-96.0 mg	5.0-38.0 mg	n/a

Taro (*Colocasia esculenta, C. antiquorum*)

Also Known As: Eddo, Dasheen, Malanga, Tania, Elephant Ear.

Colocasia *is an old Greek name for this plant;* esculenta *means esculent or edible, and* antiquorum *means of or relating to the ancients. The common Jamaican name for the root,* dasheen, *derives from* de Chine *(from China), as the root was imported from southeast Asia to feed the slaves in the West Indies. The English word* taro *is the Polynesian name for the plant.*

General Information Of East Indian origin, the taro is a potato-like plant whose globose rhizome, of considerable weight and size, constitutes a staple food for populations living in the tropical areas of Africa and Asia. The plant produces two types of tubers. The most commonly seen are the large brown, shaggy, turnip-shaped corms (the swollen tip of an under-

Taro

Nutritional Value Per 100 g Edible Portion

	Leaves Raw	Leaves Cooked	Shoots Raw	Shoots Cooked
Calories	42	24	11	14
Protein	4.98 g	2.72 g	0.92 g	0.73 g
Fat	0.74 g	0.41 g	0.09 g	0.08 g
Fiber	2.02 g	0.54 g	0.58 g	0.54 g
Calcium	107 mg	86 mg	12 mg	14 mg
Iron	2.25 mg	1.18 mg	0.60 mg	0.41 mg
Magnesium	45 mg	20 mg	8 mg	8 mg
Phosphorus	60 mg	27 mg	28 mg	26 mg
Potassium	648 mg	460 mg	332 mg	344 mg
Sodium	3 mg	2 mg	1 mg	2 mg
Beta Carotene (A)	4,825 IU	4,238 IU	50 IU	n/a
Thiamine (B_1)	0.209 mg	0.139 mg	0.040 mg	n/a
Riboflavin (B_2)	0.456 mg	0.380 mg	0.050 mg	n/a
Niacin (B_3)	1.513 mg	1.267 mg	0.800 mg	n/a
Ascorbic Acid (C)	52.0 mg	35.5 mg	21.0 mg	n/a

ground stem that stores carbohydrates for the plant's growth). These are often cut to expose the smooth, very light flesh inside. The other type is small and elongated, about the size of a plump Brazil nut, and although smoother, is still quite hairy, and may sprout a pinkish bud at the tip. These little subsidiary tubers, called cormels, grow attached to the main corm by rootlets, six to twenty per corm. Reportedly, thousands of varieties are known, with the flesh color of the corms ranging from white to yellow and pink. The pink-fleshed variety, which is one of the favorites today, reputedly was reserved for royalty in early times in Hawaii.

Buying Tips Choose taro that is very firm and plump, with no sign of withering. Do not refrigerate, but use at or before the time it starts to become soft.

Culinary Uses The flavor of taro combines chestnuts and potatoes. Large corms are dry, nutty, and sweet, while the small cormels are moist and smooth, best for steaming or boiling whole. Although taro's most familiar use is probably Hawaiian *poi*, a sticky fermented paste that few visitors find palatable, the rhizomes can be eaten in many of the same ways as potatoes. Small or large corms can be steamed or boiled, and take well to soups and stews, absorbing rich and fatty juices without disintegrating. When baked, their delicate nutty flavor becomes intensified and meaty, but they dry out considerably and need to be basted with butter or another sauce. Pan-fried or deep-fried taro is excellent, with more texture and flavor than most fried starches, crisping while keeping its identity. Be aware that its light flesh turns a dappled gray or violet when cooked, and that it must be served piping hot, or it becomes unpleasantly dense and waxy.

NOTE: taro must be eaten cooked, never raw, as it contains a poisonous substance that must be deactivated by heat.

The large, green leaves of the taro plant, called **callaloo**, are also eaten. Good in soups and stir-fries, the leaves have a string attached to the stem that must be removed before cooking.

Health Benefits Easily digested, taro has been recommended for use in baby foods, and is used medicinally to prepare external plasters for the treatment of cysts, tumors, and boils. Occasionally the roots may contain high concentrations of calcium oxalate, which may cause temporary discomfort when eaten.

Tomato *(Lycopersicon esculentum)*

Lycopersicon is the Latinized nickname wolfpeach, given the tomato by the French botanist Tournefort during the mid-sixteenth century, when it was often mistaken for the wolf peach written about by Galen thirteen centuries before. Peach was for its luscious appearance, wolf for its presumptive poisonous qualities, in analogy to pieces of aconite-sprinkled meat thrown out as bait to destroy wolves. The term esculentum *means esculent or edible. The English word* tomato *is a Spanish rendering of the Nahuatl (Mexican Indian)* tomatl.

General Information The tomato is a member of the nightshade family that came originally from western South America, where small-fruited wild forms, described by botanists as weedy and aggressive, still proliferate. The invading Spaniards saw the *tomatl* growing in Montezuma's gardens in 1519 and described it recognizably, though in less than glowing terms: they found the sprawling vines scraggly and ugly. Still, Cortez brought tomato seeds back with him to Europe, along with the more spectacular plunder, and *tomatl* plants were soon growing as curiosities in the sunny gardens of Renaissance Spain. The earliest European record of the tomato is the description in 1544 by the Renaissance botanist Pier-andrea Mattioli of Siena, who did not even give the tomato a name until ten years later. At that time he called them *pomi d'oro*, golden apples, so presumably it was a yellow variety he knew. However, he also called them *mala insana*, unhealthy fruit, and for centuries there was much confusion about the tomato's goodness and healthfulness. There are thousands of known tomato varieties, which differ greatly in color and shape, with cultivars adapted to any number of climates. The most common shapes are the large, round varieties such as **Jersey** and **Beefsteak;** the small, pear-shaped **Plum** or **Italian Roma** tomatoes, which make such good sauces; and the small, round **Cherry** tomatoes. Yellow varieties tend to be the least acidic. By cultivation and use the tomato is a vegetable; botanically it is a fruit, and can be classified as a berry, since it is pulpy and contains one or more seeds that are not stones. As the result of a tariff dispute, when an importer contended that the tomato was a fruit and therefore not subject to vegetable import duties, the plant was officially proclaimed a vegetable in 1893 by the U.S. Supreme Court. They ruled it should be classified a vegetable because it was most frequently served in soup or with the main course of a meal as a vegetable would be. Joseph Campbell brought out his famous canned Tomato Soup in 1897, shortly after chemist John Dorrance, at a weekly salary of $7.59, worked out the formula for condensing it.

Tomato

Nutritional Value Per 100 g Edible Portion

	Raw	Cooked	Sun-Dried Dry	Sun-Dried Oil-Packed
Calories	21	27	258	213
Protein	0.85 g	1.07 g	14.11 g	5.06 g
Fat	0.33 g	0.41 g	2.97 g	14.08 g
Fiber	0.65 g	0.82 g	n/a	n/a
Calcium	5 mg	6 mg	110 mg	47 mg
Iron	0.45 mg	0.56 mg	n/a	n/a
Magnesium	11 mg	14 mg	194 mg	81 mg
Phosphorus	24 mg	31 mg	356 mg	139 mg
Potassium	222 mg	279 mg	3,427 mg	1,565 mg
Sodium	9 mg	11 mg	2,095 mg	266 mg
Zinc	0.090 mg	0.110 mg	1.990 mg	0.780 mg
Copper	0.074 mg	0.093 mg	1.423 mg	0.473 mg
Manganese	0.105 mg	0.132 mg	1.846 mg	0.466 mg
Beta Carotene (A)	623 IU	743 IU	874 IU	1,286 IU
Thiamine (B_1)	0.059 mg	0.070 mg	0.528 mg	0.193 mg
Riboflavin (B_2)	0.048 mg	0.057 mg	0.489 mg	0.383 mg
Niacin (B_3)	0.628 mg	0.749 mg	9.050 mg	3.630 mg
Pantothenic Acid (B_5)	0.247 mg	0.295 mg	2.087 mg	0.479 mg
Pyridoxine (B_6)	0.080 mg	0.095 mg	0.332 mg	0.319 mg
Folic Acid (B_9)	15.0 mcg	13.0 mcg	68.0 mcg	23.0 mcg
Ascorbic Acid (C)	19.1 mg	22.8 mg	39.2 mg	101.8 mg
Tocopherol (E)	0.34 mg	n/a	n/a	n/a

Lore and Legend

Although the early Aztecs of Mexico considered the tomato a "health" food and reverently offered it to their gods of healing, Europeans shunned it because of its association with known poisonous plants, and because its bright shiny colors—red, orange, yellow, and white—were highly suspicious. The turning point for the pro-tomato faction in America, according to time-honored legend, occurred on the steps of the Salem, New Jersey courthouse on September 26, 1820. That was the day when Colonel Robert Gibbon Johnson ate, in public and without ill effect, an entire basketful of tomatoes. Colonel Johnson, an enthusiastic gardener, had earlier introduced the tomato to the farmers of Salem after a trip abroad in 1808, and each year offered a prize for the largest fruit grown. A forceful individualist and notorious eccentric, the Colonel wanted his introduction to be regarded as more than an ornamental bush, so when he announced that he would in public eat not one, but a *whole basket* of "wolf peaches," a large crowd of some two thousand curious people from miles around gathered to watch him commit certain suicide. Dressed in his habitual black suit with impeccable white ruffles, a tricorn hat, black gloves, and gold-topped walking stick, the Colonel made an imposing figure as he ascended the courthouse steps at high noon to the accompaniment of a dirgelike tune played by the local firemen's band. Selecting a tomato from his basket, he held it aloft and launched into his spiel:

> The time will come when this luscious, golden apple, rich in nutritive value, a delight to the eye, a joy to the palate, whether fried, baked, broiled, or eaten raw, will form the foundation of a great garden industry, and will be recognized, eaten and enjoyed as an edible food . . . And to help speed that enlightened day, to help dispel the tall tales, the fantastic fables that you have been hearing about the thing, to show you that it is not poisonous, that it will not strike you dead, I am going to eat one right now! —Hendrickson, *Foods For Love,* pp. 188–189.

Colonel Johnson bit into the tomato, and the juicy bite could be heard through the silence, until he bit again, and again—at least one female spectator screaming and fainting with each succeeding bite. The crowd was amazed to see the courageous Colonel still on his feet as he devoured tomato after tomato. He soon converted most onlookers, but not until the entire basket was empty did the band strike up a victory march and the crowd begin to chant a cheer. The Colonel's personal physician, Dr. James Van Meeter, had taken a dim view of the proposed tomato-eating and had been quoted as saying, "The foolish colonel will foam and froth at the mouth and double over with appendicitis. All that oxalic acid! One dose and you're dead." Barring immediate effects, it was feared that the tomato skins would stick to the lining of the stomach and eventually cause cancer (tomatoes were generally held to induce cancer until nearly the end of the nineteenth century). Dr. Van Meeter stayed, black bag in hand, until the whole basketful of tomatoes had been devoured, and then quietly slunk away. The Colonel, undaunted, continued to live in undisputed health to the ripe old age of seventy-nine.

Ketchup started out at *ketsiap*, a sauce developed in the seventeenth century by the Chinese that would never have appealed to Westerners. It was a tangy potion of fish entrails, vinegar, and spices, and was used mainly on fish. Exported to Malaya, where it was called *kechap*, the strange purée was sold to English sailors in the early eighteenth century. Back in England it caught on quickly, but English cooks substituted mushrooms for the fish entrails. The first printed recipe, from Richard Brigg's 1792 cookbook *The New Art of Cookery*, called it catsup and included tomatoes as an ingredient (a rarity for the time, because tomatoes were still considered poisonous). Henry Heinz was the first to use the term ketchup when he started advertising the product in the early 1900s; he liked the unique spelling. Other competitors slowly followed suit, the last making the change in 1988. Ketchup is now consumed at the rate of seven 14-ounce bottles per person annually.

Buying Tips Choose firm, plump tomatoes with an aromatic tomato fragrance. Avoid soft, overripe tomatoes with blemishes, bruises, soft spots, or growth cracks.

Culinary Uses Fully vine-ripened tomatoes are sweet and juicy, with a slight tang. Because they are best when picked straight from the vine, even people who are not avid gardeners like to grow them. As they are extremely fragile when ripe, most commercial tomatoes are picked and shipped green, and then artificially ripened in ethylene gas chambers. They may need a little help to finish ripening—keep them upside down at room temperature, out of direct sunlight, until they turn richly red. Those tomatoes whose skins are red but whose seeds or internal parts are still green were picked too soon; the seeds inside should be brown when a tomato is fully ripe. Hydroponically grown tomatoes may be cosmetically perfect, but tend to lack flavor. Researchers at the USDA found that vine-ripened tomatoes grown outdoors in sunlight are twice as rich in vitamin C as their greenhouse counterparts. Tomatoes add flavor and color to a wide variety of both raw and cooked dishes, and are used in more spicy sauces, canned in more soups, drunk in more juices, are indispensable to more salads, and slopped on more pizzas, than any other vegetable. No other fruit or vegetable has such mass appeal. Cherry tomatoes, because of their small size, are perfect for tossing whole into salads. Sun-dried tomatoes have an explosive concentrated flavor that provides a tremendous flavor boost. One other very important application for the tomato (or tomato juice) is as a neutralizer for butyl mercaptan, the nose-shriveling prime ingredient in the defense spray of skunks.

Health Benefits Tomatoes contain over 93 percent water. A natural antiseptic, fresh raw tomatoes contain a great deal of citric acid, which has an alkaline reaction if digested when no starches or sugars are present. Their chlorine content increases the alkalinity of the blood and helps to stimulate the liver in its function as a filter for body and toxic wastes. Raw tomato (whole and juice form) is especially effective in reducing liver inflammation due to hepatitis and cirrhosis. Never eat raw green tomatoes, as they contain a toxin known as solanine, and the acids in the green tomato are very detrimental to the body. Cooked or canned tomatoes have most of their nutrients destroyed and the acids have changed to an inorganic form that is acid-forming. Tomatoes can potentially interfere with calcium metabolism, and thus large quantities should not be consumed on a regular basis.

Turnip *(Brassica rapa)*

> *The Latin name* Brassica *derives from the Celtic* bresic; rapa *was the Latin name for turnips. Our Engish word* turnip *derives from the Middle English name for the plant,* nepe *or* naep, *which when combined with the Anglo-Saxon word* turn, *meaning to make round, became* turnaep *and then* turnip.

General Information The turnip is reported to have come from Russia, Siberia, and the Scandinavian peninsula. Introduced into the New World by Jacques Cartier when he visited Canada in 1540, the vegetable flourished there and quickly spread southward. The Virginia colonists must have brought seeds with them, for turnips are said to have grown there in 1609. The Indians took to them at once, for they were superior to the wild roots they had been eating. Indian women baked or roasted them whole in their skins, a method which brought out their full flavor. In 1850 a turnip weighing one hundred pounds was grown in California. This member of the cabbage family has round or top-shaped roots, white skin with purplish or greenish crowns, and thin, green, hairy leaves. Since it flourishes in poor and

Lore and Legend

There is an old story about an ancient king who was exceedingly fond of a certain fish and requested it of his chef for dinner. The chef, being unable to find any of that particular kind of fish, instead bought a large white turnip, carved it into the shape of a fish, baked it, and then served it to the king on a fish platter. The king was delighted and exclaimed that it was the best fish he had ever eaten!

impoverished soils and keeps well, this rustic vegetable has endeared itself to the poor and given some cause to scorn it. Often confused with its cousin the rutabaga, turnips are smaller, more perishable, can be eaten raw, and are most frequently sold with their tops. The two do taste somewhat similar, however, and in many recipes are interchangeable.

Buying Tips Look for smooth, firm roots with their root end and stem base intact. If these parts are trimmed away and yellowed at the incision, the turnip will be lacking in flavor. Favor small or medium-small turnips, as large ones are often pithy and lack flavor.

Culinary Uses Raw turnips have a refreshing, tangy flavor similar to a mild radish, and when cooked are pleasantly sweet. Those grown during the hot summer months are decidedly pungent but mellow somewhat with cooking. When fresh and young, turnips can be used raw in salads. When cooked with other foods, they have the remarkable ability to absorb flavors, which makes them succulent and rich.

Turnip greens can be cooked in the same manner as spinach, slivered and stir-fried, or, as they have been for generations, stewed with pork. They do not make good salad greens, as they are much too bitter and tough. The tops are generally found separate from the familiar roots. Look for relatively small, tender leaves that are moist and well-cooled. The stems are not used. Do not cook in aluminum or iron pans, as these will discolor the root or leaves.

Health Benefits Raw grated turnip serves as a digestive aid and cleans the teeth. Because of its sulphur content, it warms and purifies the body, while its alkalizing nature helps detoxify the body. The mildly pungent qualities are easily destroyed through cooking; sliced raw turnip is superior to the cooked, but cooked turnips are also a warming food and said to energize the stomach and intestines. If you have a weak digestive system, turnips may cause flatulence. The greens help cleanse the blood of toxins, and are good for controlling calcium in the body, as are all other greens. Turnip juice is especially good for mucous and catarrhal conditions. All *Brassica*-genus vegetables contain dithiolthiones, a group of compounds that have anti-cancer, antioxidant properties; indoles, substances that protect against breast

Turnip

Nutritional Value Per 100 g Edible Portion

	Root, Raw	Root, Cooked	Greens, Raw	Greens, Cooked
Calories	27	18	27	20
Protein	0.90 g	0.71 g	1.50 g	1.14 g
Fat	0.10 g	0.08 g	0.30 g	0.23 g
Fiber	0.90 g	0.71 g	0.80 g	0.61 g
Calcium	30 mg	22 mg	190 mg	137 mg
Iron	0.30 mg	0.22 mg	1.10 mg	0.80 mg
Magnesium	11 mg	8 mg	31 mg	22 mg
Phosphorus	27 mg	19 mg	42 mg	29 mg
Potassium	191 mg	135 mg	296 mg	203 mg
Sodium	67 mg	50 mg	40 mg	29 mg
Zinc	n/a	n/a	0.190 mg	0.140 mg
Copper	n/a	n/a	0.350 mg	0.253 mg
Manganese	n/a	n/a	0.466 mg	0.337 mg
Beta Carotene (A)	0 IU	0 IU	7,600 IU	5,498 IU
Thiamine (B_1)	0.040 mg	0.027 mg	0.070 mg	0.045 mg
Riboflavin (B_2)	0.030 mg	0.023 mg	0.100 mg	0.072 mg
Niacin (B_3)	0.400 mg	0.299 mg	0.600 mg	0.411 mg
Pantothenic Acid (B_5)	0.200 mg	0.142 mg	0.380 mg	0.274 mg
Pyridoxine (B_6)	0.090 mg	0.067 mg	0.263 mg	0.180 mg
Folic Acid (B_9)	14.5 mcg	9.2 mcg	194.4 mcg	118.4 mcg
Ascorbic Acid (C)	21.0 mg	11.6 mg	60.0 mg	27.4 mg
Tocopherol (E)	n/a	n/a	2.24 mg	n/a

and colon cancer; and sulphur, which has antibiotic and antiviral characteristics. This family of vegetables also mildly stimulates the liver and other tissues out of stagnancy.

NOTE: Turnips and rutabagas contain especially high amounts of compounds (goitrogens) that interfere with thyroid function. Their use by individuals with low thyroid function should be limited, or else foods high in iodine, such as kelp, should also be consumed.

Wasabi *(Eutrema wasabi, Wasabia japonica)*

Also Known As: Japanese Horseradish.

> Japonica *means coming from Japan.*

General Information Wasabi is the green Japanese radish with the assertive flavor and sinus-clearing effect you may have enjoyed in sushi. Although not related to common horseradish, it is often called Japanese horseradish because its kick is nearly as potent. The more fragrant of the two, wasabi root is gnarled and warty on the outside, with pale, soft green flesh on the inside.

Buying Tips Look for a plump and fresh-looking root that is preferably not sprouting; avoid one that is withered.

Culinary Uses Used sparingly, wasabi adds a pungent "cleansing" bite to foods, and makes an interesting addition to soy sauce and other dipping sauces. Powdered wasabi, in convenient small tins or foil envelopes, is more frequently available. It should be greenish-gray, and not bright green. Mix it into a paste with water just before serving to preserve its flavor and digestive enzymes. Wasabi paste is often used to season sushi or its dipping sauce. In a pinch, it can also substitute for horseradish in recipes.

Health Benefits This aromatic root provides more than bite. Wasabi has an abundance of protein-digesting enzymes that make it a perfect condiment with raw fish dishes such as sashimi and sushi.

Water Chestnut *(Eleocharis dulcis, Trapa natans, T. bicornis)*

> Eleocharis *is a Greek word that means delighting in marshes; the term* dulcis *signifies sweet-tasting.* Trapa *is an abbreviation of the Old English* calcatrippe *or* caltrap, *an ancient instrument of war. The insidious iron ball with four sharp-pointed spikes was employed to impede and harass the enemy's cavalry. Since the dark brown, hard-shelled, woody fruit of the water chestnut has four woody horns or spine-like projections that resemble that dreaded military weapon, it was named after it;* natans *means floating or swimming. The English name* water chestnut *was given because it looks like a grubby chestnut in size and shape, and because it grows under water.*

General Information The name water chestnut alone usually refers to *Trapa natans*, the European water chestnut; the addition of "Chinese" to the name changes the reference to *Eleocharis dulcis*. The **European water chestnut** is the fruit of an annual herbaceous plant

Water Chestnut

Nutritional Value Per 100 g Edible Portion

	Chinese Raw	Canned w/Liquid
Calories	106	50
Protein	1.40 g	0.88 g
Fat	0.10 g	0.06 g
Fiber	0.80 g	0.58 g
Calcium	11 mg	4 mg
Iron	0.60 mg	0.87 mg
Magnesium	22 mg	5 mg
Phosphorus	63 mg	19 mg
Potassium	584 mg	118 mg
Sodium	14 mg	8 mg
Zinc	n/a	0.38 mg
Beta Carotene (A)	0 IU	4 IU
Thiamine (B_1)	0.140 mg	0.011 mg
Riboflavin (B_2)	0.200 mg	0.024 mg
Niacin (B_3)	1.000 mg	0.360 mg
Ascorbic Acid (C)	4.0 mg	1.3 mg

belonging to the evening primrose family. Native to tropical Africa, central Europe, and eastern Asia, the floating, annual aquatic plants, with their beautifully mottled foliage, grow luxuriantly in standing water, floating on the surface of ponds, pools, lakes, and irrigation tanks. The edible part is technically a corm—the swollen tip of an underground stem that stores carbohydrates for the plant's growth. The corms are two to three inches wide from tip to tip of their horns, and about one inch in depth. One large, white, starchy kernel is enclosed within each corm.

The **Chinese water chestnut** (*E. dulcis*) is the corm or tuber of an Asiatic sedge, a grasslike annual plant common to marshy environments. The corms, about one-and-a-half inches in diameter, are formed on rhizomes down to a depth of some ten inches. At harvest time, the corms have often formed a solid mass of edible material. Once harvested, they look rather like muddy little tulip bulbs, dressed in shabby brown-to-black coats decorated with frayed leaf scales.

Another variety of "water chestnut" sold in Asian markets is the **Water caltrops** (*Trapa bicornis*), related to the European water chestnut. These shiny black, rather nefarious-looking horned nuts grow on a floating water plant like their cousin, but have two horns instead of four. This variety must be boiled for an hour before use, to destroy possible parasites harmful to the digestive system. The Chinese eat them shelled and cooked in various vegetable and meat combinations, or preserved as sweetmeats.

Buying Tips Select fresh corms that are rock hard and free of withering or soft spots. Do not worry if they are very dirty, for they clean up well. Always buy more than you think you will need, as there is large waste in peeling, and there will usually be a few bad ones in the lot.

Culinary Uses Water chestnuts have a delicate and delicious flavor, reminiscent of sugar cane, sweet corn, and coconut. They look like gladiolus bulbs, with fibrous chestnut-brown skins enclosing the sweet firm flesh. The most memorable property of the water chestnut is its crunch. Although jicama and Asian pears come close to the refreshing crisp texture of this water vegetable, they do not match its refreshing delicacy or its juicy sweet flavor. Once the skins are removed, water chestnuts may be added raw to fresh fruit salads, hot or cold vegetables, rice, or noodles. It does not take many, as the texture and flavor are defined and satisfying. In China, the raw corms are eaten out of hand as a substitute for fresh fruit, or cooked alone as a winter vegetable. Cooking enhances the flavor and does not detract from its texture or crispness. Although readily available canned, the canned water chestnuts lose some sweetness but retain their crispness and color.

Health Benefits Originally valued as a medicinal plant, water chestnuts are considered *yin,* or cooling, and are thought to disperse excess heat, be beneficial for diabetes and jaundice, and sweeten the breath. A paste made from dried ground water chestnuts is fed to children who accidentally swallow coins.

Watercress

Nutritional Value Per 100 g Edible Portion

	Raw
Calories	11
Protein	2.30 g
Fat	0.10 g
Fiber	0.70 g
Calcium	120 mg
Iron	0.20 mg
Magnesium	21 mg
Phosphorus	60 mg
Potassium	330 mg
Sodium	41 mg
Beta Carotene (A)	4,700 IU
Thiamine (B_1)	0.090 mg
Riboflavin (B_2)	0.120 mg
Niacin (B_3)	0.200 mg
Pantothenic Acid (B_5)	0.310 mg
Pyridoxine (B_6)	0.129 mg
Ascorbic Acid (C)	43.0 mg
Tocopherol (E)	1.0 mg

Watercress (*Nasturtium officinale*)

Nasturtium is a contraction of the Latin phrase nasus tortus, a convulsed nose, on account of its pungency. Officinale means of the workshop, alluding to apothecaries' shops, and signifying that the plant was once part of the official pharmacopeia of Rome. The English name watercress comes from the fact that the plant is one of the water-loving members of the cress family.

General Information Watercress is Eurasian in origin, a succulent, leafy, vivid green aquatic plant of the mustard family. No wild edible plant has enjoyed a longer and more accepted spot in history, from the ancient Middle East to Old England. Watercress was probably introduced to America in the 1600s as a familiar and dependable plant that could be grown in the numerous fresh-water streams near the first settlements. It provided a salad green much of the year, or a boiled vegetable to serve with meat; more importantly, it was a powerful antiscorbutic. Weed-like in its hardiness, it has spread and now thrives in each of the fifty states. Watercress, with its small, round, pungent leaves, grows alongside gently flowing streams and ponds, but should be gathered only from those with clean clear water. Cultivated and wild watercress are the same variety, but the domesticated plant is generally larger—up to seven inches—and has a thicker stem.

Buying Tips Choose bunches that look fresh and have no yellowed leaves. Wilted, bruised, or yellowing leaves are signs of inferior quality and improper handling. Wash with extra care, as the leaves are prone to harbor aquatic insects.

Culinary Uses Just as delightful as chancing upon a pure stream boasting watercress is munching on this lively, peppery plant. Surprisingly, the bite and aroma are not fiery, but leave the palate cool and refreshed. As a salad green, watercress should be used as an accompaniment to lettuce or other mild-tasting leaves. Use it as a garnish, as an ingredient in soups, or in an avocado sandwich. It also tastes delicious in stuffings, omelets, mashed potatoes, or other cheese dishes. When steamed, it loses much of its bite and tastes quite unique. Add it to completed dishes and use daily if possible.

Health Benefits Antiscorbutic, diuretic, expectorant, purgative, stimulant, stomachic. Watercress has an ability to energize the internal organs, aids in breaking up kidney or bladder stones, and is one of the best foods for purifying the blood and taking care of catarrhal conditions. Watercress is excellent in vegetable juices or herb teas. Especially kind to the skin, if crushed and applied with a swab of cotton it relieves irritations and helps heal acne, eczema, and other skin irritations and infections. Watercress has an abundant iodine content.

Lore and Legend

One hot summer day while out hunting, King Louis IX of France was overcome by thirst and called for a drink. Since no liquid was within reach, he was instead handed a bunch of watercress. Louis crunched its peppery leaves and found himself so surprisingly refreshed that he decided on the spot to honor both the plant and the place that had provided it. The arms of the city of Vernon, now in the French department of Eure, to this day bear three fleurs-de-lis, the royal symbol, on one side, and three bunches of watercress on the other.

Wax Gourd *(Benincasa hispida)*

Also Known As: Chinese Winter Melon, Chinese Fuzzy Gourd, Doan Gwa.

The genus Benincasa *was named in honor of an Italian nobleman;* hispida *means hispid, or bristly.*

General Information Grown throughout the Asian tropics, the wax gourd is little known elsewhere. There are two main varieties: the smaller Fuzzy Melon and the large Winter Melon. Fuzzy melons come in two shapes: either narrow and cylindrical, like squash, or like a stubby pill capsule. Harvested young at around one pound, they are easy to spot because they are truly hairy. Winter melon is watermelon-green and grows to one hundred pounds. Its melon-like fruit has a thick flesh that is white, crisp, and juicy. An outstanding feature is its resistance to spoilage. Preserved from microorganisms by its waxy coating, the fruit can be stored without refrigeration for as long as a year. The plants are prolific, rapid growers, and three or four crops can be produced each year. The plant, an annual creeping vine, resembles a pumpkin vine. Most often sold cut, its pale green skin has a thick and waxy bloom that looks like frost.

Wax Gourd

Nutritional Value Per 100 g Edible Portion

	Raw	Cooked
Calories	13	13
Protein	0.40 g	0.40 g
Fat	0.20 g	0.20 g
Fiber	0.50 g	0.51 g
Calcium	19 mg	18 mg
Iron	0.40 mg	0.38 mg
Phosphorus	19 mg	17 mg
Potassium	6 mg	5 mg
Sodium	111 mg	107 mg
Beta Carotene (A)	0 IU	0 IU
Thiamine (B_1)	0.040 mg	0.034 mg
Riboflavin (B_2)	0.110 mg	0.001 mg
Niacin (B_3)	0.400 mg	0.384 mg
Ascorbic Acid (C)	13.0 mg	10.5 mg

Buying Tips Select one that is firm and unblemished.

Culinary Uses Young leaves, flower buds, and vine tips are boiled and eaten as greens. The fruit's sweetish white flesh can be consumed during various stages of maturity, but is not generally eaten raw. The subtly-flavored, easily digested mature flesh may be used as a cucumber substitute, a cooked vegetable, or food extender. It takes on the flavors of other foods it is cooked with, yet retains its pleasing crispness. Many compare its flavor to the chayote. It is a favorite soup ingredient in Oriental cuisine, while in India and Cuba a popular dessert is made by cooking the pulp in syrup. The melon is also found in savory concoctions, candies, and pickles. The pulp has many flat, oval, light-brown seeds up to 2.5 centimeters long, which can be fried and eaten like pumpkin seeds. The seeds also yield a pale oil.

Health Benefits Nutritionally and medicinally, the wax gourd is more similar to summer squash than winter.

Yam *(Dioscorea rotundata, D. cayenensis, D. composita)*

The genus name Dioscorea *was given in honor of Dioscorides, a Greek physician and naturalist of the first or second century* A.D. *The term* rotundata *means rotund or portly;* cayenensis *means coming from Cayenne, the island that is the capital of French Guiana;* composita *means composite. Its English name* yam *is of African origin, coming from the Guinean verb* nyami, *meaning to eat.*

General Information Yams are a large tuberous root largely confined to the tropics of West Africa and Asia. In the United States, yams can only be grown in the deep South.

Lore and Legend

It may well be that yams are worshiped because they can become awesomely huge. In the Pacific Island of Ponape, the size of yams is described as two-man, four-man, or six-man, designating the number of men needed to lift the tuber. Tubers up to six feet long and weighing six hundred pounds have been recorded. The Trobriand Islanders build intricately decorated wooden "yam houses" where the splendid tubers are ensconced to be viewed by neighbors. In Cuba, yams are considered festival food, to be saved for special occasions.

Instead of growing underground like potatoes, yams grow on plants and hang from plant stems. Their weight causes the stems to bend to the soil, and the yams become partially embedded like an exposed underground tuber. Not to be confused with the American yam, which is just another name for the moist-fleshed variety of sweet potato, true yams may grow to a remarkable size, up to six feet long and more than six hundred pounds. Their flesh may be yellow, red, or even purple. Of the more than six hundred species, those most commonly encountered are brown, black-brown, or rusty-tan, and all are shaggy-coated. Common types are **Elephant's foot** or **Suram**, **Taro** or **Dasheen**, and the **Cocoyam**, all of which look similar to enormous potatoes. The **Boniato** looks like a sweet potato with its ruddy pink skin but has white flesh. A bit tubbier than the American sweet potato, its interior white flesh is drier—more like that of a regular white potato.

In 1936, Japanese chemists formulated by partial synthesis steroidal sapogenins, primarily diosgenin, from the glycoside saponins richly found in the barbasco, a wild yam native to Mexico. Diosgenin was able to be converted into progesterone, an intermediary in cortisone production, by 1940. While progesterone can be derived from diosgenin, this can only be done by a chemist in the laboratory; humans cannot produce progesterone in their bodies from yams or their extracts. In 1956, Dr. Gregory Pincus announced that he had formulated a drug that would stop ovulation and hence prevent conception. Up to that time, steroids that prevented conception had to be taken by injection, whereas it now became possible to use oral administration. Although most birth-control pills are wholly synthetic today, *Dioscorea* still figures in their origin. Other steroid drugs derived from diosgenin include anti-inflammatory compounds such as topical hormones and systemic corticosteroids, androgens, estrogens, progestogens, and other sex hormone combinations.

Yam

Nutritional Value Per 100 g Edible Portion

	Raw	Cooked
Calories	118	116
Protein	1.53 g	1.49 g
Fat	0.17 g	0.14 g
Fiber	n/a	n/a
Calcium	17 mg	14 mg
Iron	0.54 mg	0.52 mg
Magnesium	21 mg	18 mg
Phosphorus	55 mg	49 mg
Potassium	816 mg	670 mg
Sodium	9 mg	8 mg
Zinc	0.240 mg	0.200 mg
Copper	0.178 mg	0.152 mg
Beta Carotene (A)	0 IU	0 IU
Thiamine (B_1)	0.112 mg	0.095 mg
Riboflavin (B_2)	0.032 mg	0.028 mg
Niacin (B_3)	0.758 mg	0.552 mg
Pantothenic Acid (B_5)	0.314 mg	0.311 mg
Pyridoxine (B_6)	0.293 mg	0.228 mg
Folic Acid (B_9)	23.0 mcg	16.0 mcg
Ascorbic Acid (C)	17.1 mg	12.1 mg

Buying Tips Choose yams that are regularly shaped and very hard, with no cracks or soft or shrunken spots. Although they are available in many sizes, those with the best flavor weigh less than two or three pounds. Store as you would potatoes—never in the refrigerator, but in the potato bin or any cool, dry, dark place.

Culinary Uses Yams have a flavor and texture much like a mealy potato—loose, coarse, dry, and rather bland. The raw flesh is crisp, slippery, mucilaginous, and either white, ivory, or yellow. As versatile as the potato, yams can be boiled, roasted, mashed, fried, or made into casseroles, and are a perfect foil for strong, spicy vegetable mixtures. They absorb other flavors well, but are enhanced by a sprinkling of sweet spice such as cinnamon, nutmeg, ground cloves, or allspice. The skin is not edible, so should be removed. Added to soups or stews, yam's delicate nutty flavor will sweeten the pot. Frequently it is used in place of sweet potatoes in stews, chilies, and soups. On the islands where the boniato is a common food, people are fond of turning it into chips, much as we do with the common potato.

Health Benefits Antiarthritic, antispasmodic, diuretic, emmenagogue. The yam is hailed as a medicinal tonic for many uses, working as an agent to prevent miscarriages, and to treat asthma. They also contain simple peptide substances called phytochelatins that can bind heavy metals like cadmium, copper, mercury, and lead, and thus participate in metal detoxification of body tissue. Those species of yam containing diosgenin are medicinally efficacious for fatigue, inflammation, spasms, stress, colitis, Irritable Bowel Syndrome, PMS, and menopausal complaints. The plant estrogen (phytoestrogen) seems to act as a key to unlock and potentiate existing estrogen in the body, thus eliminating or easing many of the symptoms of low estrogen.

Yautia *(Xanthosoma sagittifolium)*

Also Known As: Cocoyam, Dasheen, Malanga, Tannia.

> Xanthosoma *is Greek for yellow body, and refers to the stigma;* sagittifolium *means arrow-leaved. This vegetable is called* yautia *by Puerto Ricans, and* malanga *by Colombians.*

General Information The funny-looking, potato-like yautia originated in the Americas in both dry and swampy soils. The forty or so species of this vegetable, all native to the American tropics, include some of the oldest root crops in the world. Their close resemblance to a related tuber, *Colocasia esculenta* (most commonly known as taro), has produced a score of common names that overlap the two, blurring the distinguishing characteristics. Like the taro, the yautia is a thin-skinned shaggy cormel that surrounds a larger rootlike corm, but is larger than the taro and frequently club-shaped. Only the cormels are normally used for human consumption, while the corms are used for animal feed and for replanting. This plant is also grown for its long-stalked, arrow-shaped leaves; the leaves are often sold separately from the tubers, and can be boiled and eaten like swiss chard ribs.

Buying Tips Select relatively light-colored, very hard specimens with no soft, shriveled, or moldy areas. They should have a fresh smell.

Culinary Uses The yautia has a unique creamy texture and more pronounced flavor than most starchy tropical tubers—vaguely musty and earthy, and tending more towards nut than potatoes. The interior may be cream, yellow, or pinkish, and has an extremely crisp, slippery texture. Do not consume raw; once peeled, it can be boiled, baked, fried, or ground into flour. The smooth, melting quality that the crisp tuber develops when boiled is most surprising—somewhere between that of cooked dried pinto beans and waxy new potatoes. In a stew it flavors, thickens, and adds creaminess. Yautia makes an excellent bland foil for spicy side dishes or condiments.

Health Benefits Low in fat, high in thiamine, riboflavin, vitamin C, and iron.

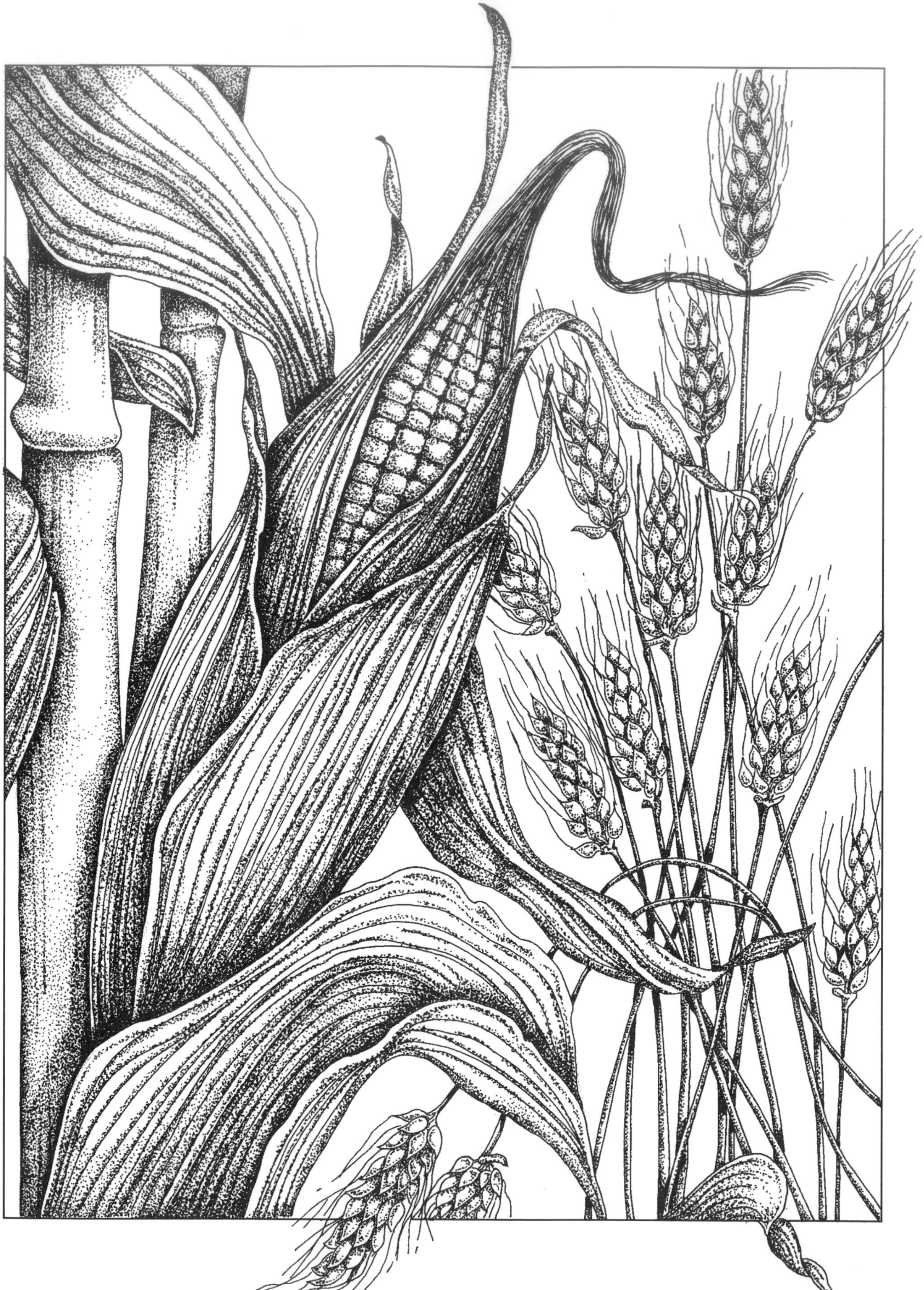

Grains

"The smallest grain of meal would suit my necessity better than this pearl."

—La Fontaine, *Fables*

GRAINS

Grains

GRAINS ARE THE SEEDS AND FRUITS OF CEREAL GRASSES that grow in a widevariety of climates and conditions; members of this cereal grass family are commonly referred to as "cereal" grains. The word *cereal* is derived from Ceres, the Roman goddess of agriculture. Archaeological evidence shows that wheat and barley were used over ten thousand years ago by people living in the "Fertile Crescent," a broad, crescent-shaped area that curved northward and eastward from what is now the eastern border of Egypt, to the Taurus Mountains of southern Turkey, across the Zagros Mountains of western Iran, and down to the Persian Gulf. By 4000 B.C., millet farming was well-established along the upper Yellow River in China. About the same time, rice was being cultivated in southeast Asia. Since dried grains store well, it is not surprising that their cultivation spread as people traveled to new lands.

Good quality grain is whole and contains few specimens that are broken, scratched, or deteriorated. It would seem that cosmetically beautiful grains of the same size and color would indicate quality, but these grains are actually hybridized seed, which is less vital than unhybridized varieties. Whole grains are perfect examples of the term "complex carbohydrates," because they contain the complete package with its bran layer, endosperm, and germ intact. Anatomy and structure is basically the same for all grains. The bran is composed of tissues between the outer seed coat and the thin aleurone layer of the endosperm. This bran layer contains fiber, minerals, and protein, adds bulk to the digestive system, and stabilizes blood sugar. Inside the bran layer is the endosperm, the storage compartment of the grain. This starchy interior section is meant to sustain the seedling until it grows leaves for manufacturing its own food. Life springs from the embryo, or germ, which is a rich source of valuable protein, minerals, and vitamins, particularly vitamin E. Vitamin E is an anti-oxidant nutrient that prevents the destruction of cells by compounds known as free radicals, and is also critical to reproductive function, circulation, and healthy skin. Whole grains are an important source of vegetable lignins, a group of compounds with anti-tumor and antioxidant properties. The rich fiber in grains produces short-chain fatty acids, including butyrate, acetate, and propionate, which inhibit candida yeast growth. Butyrate in particular has been shown to suppress the growth of cancer in the colon of humans, and cancer in general in animals.

Before a grain has fully turned to starch and is considered ripe, it can be eaten raw. This milky stage is when it is highest in grape sugar content (similar to that found in thoroughly ripe fruit); once ripened, the sugars in the grain have turned to starch, and before starch can be used by the body, the outer cellulose wall must be broken by grinding or cooking. All grains in their mature state have a tendency to cause acidosis because they contain mostly protein, carbohydrate, and phosphoric acid. Soaking grains overnight before cooking them starts the sprouting process, which helps to break down the starch and protein into compounds that are easier to digest, thus substantially increasing the protein, vitamin, and enzyme content available. The grain may be cooked in this water, as it is rich in nutrients.

For the fun of it, as well as for flavor and nutritional variations, there is a whole realm of different grain flours to play with. Each flour excels in its own way and can transform what might otherwise be a mundane dish into a culinary masterpiece. Any whole grain flour has a limited shelf life. It is ideal to grind your own flour eight to twelve hours prior to use; flour used sooner is "green" and performs erratically. During the few hours of aging, some of the enzymes that might otherwise have interfered with yeast activity have oxidized, taming the flour enough to give consistent results. Further aging, however, does not further improve the flour. To the contrary: each day after grinding, flour loses from 10 to 20 percent of its oxidizable enzymes and vitamins, depending on storage conditions. Traditionally, when bread was made, the dough was allowed to rest for a number of hours to allow time for certain enzymes to work on the phytin (an organic phosphorus compound that interferes with the utilization of nutrients); in the same time, the moistened bran had a chance to become softened and more easily digested.

The type of mill that grinds the grain has a surprising effect on a flour's performance, flavor, and nutrition. Stone-ground flour is a superior quality flour. Since the layers are flaked off the grains, the milling process does not overheat the flour and the nutrients are retained, rather than lost. Making flour with steel roller mills and hammer mills is a fast way of doing it, where the grain is not so much ground as it is splintered and crushed. There are both gross and subtle differences between steel-crushed and stone-ground flour. On the gross level, stone-ground flour comes out both cooler and coarser, resulting in higher food and fiber values. As well, there is a definite consensus, among people who have worked with both, that stone-ground flour tastes better, with a richer, fuller, nuttier flavor. A number of stone flour mills, either manual or electric, are available for home use, and for those who do a lot of baking these home mills are an excellent investment. Be aware, however, that certain flours cannot be made with stone mills. Oats have a high fat and moisture content and tend to clog stone mills readily unless the grain has been oven-dried in advance. Corn is also a problem, since the kernels are so hard they tend to pit the stones quickly. Much the same holds true for garbanzo beans, which are too large and hard for a stone mill to handle efficiently without damage.

FLOUR MILLING HISTORY

For centuries, grain was ground in small water- or wind-powered mills scattered throughout the countryside. These old mills pulverized the oily germ of the grain along with the starchy endosperm, with the germ giving the flour its characteristic yellow-brown color and also turning it rancid within a few weeks. According to the adjustment of the stones and the fineness of the sifter, different grades could be produced, but the quality was not consistent, and much of the grain ground in this manner was not very clean.

A new method of milling flour was introduced from Hungary in the 1840s, where iron rollers processed the grain more consistently than the old stone mills. These new roller mills, however, squeezed the grain in such a way that the endosperm popped out of its coating, leaving the germ behind to be sieved off with the bran. As a result, the new roller-milled flour was whiter than stone-ground and could be stored for months, even years, without deteriorating. This pleased not only the millers, bakers, and grocers, but their customers as well, and with the introduction in the 1870s of porcelain rollers—which had no problems of rusting and were easier to clean—this type of milling became the general practice. The discarded wheat germ and bran, unfortunately, contained most of the nutrients of the grain. Unlike the refining of gold, which removes impurities and makes the product much more valuable, the refining of cereal grains removes most of the valuable nutrients and makes the grain much less valuable from a nutritional standpoint.

The history of white bread indicates that the main reason for milling flour until it was white was political. White bread was less tasty and more expensive than whole-grain bread, and white flour took inordinately more time to produce. But because white bread was neither common, easily affordable, nor the same color as whole-grain bread, it became a status symbol that could separate the rich from the poor. White bread became associated with those in power, dark bread with the common man. By the thirteenth century, in the most lavish and extravagant Arabian courts, white bread, along with roast kid and wine, was considered a supreme mark of self-indulgence.

RANCIDITY AND STORAGE

Though they have a long shelf life compared to fruits and vegetables, whole grains are still subject to spoilage. Their natural oils will turn rancid, and they can also fall prey to insect infestation and mold. Grains tightly sealed in closed containers or plastic bags will keep for about three months in a cool, dry place (less in hot or humid weather), and storage in the refrigerator will hold them for at least six months. Frozen grain will keep almost indefinitely; the exceptions are oats and oat bran, which are higher in fat than other grains and so can turn rancid after being frozen only two or three months. Therefore, buy only as much as you will need in that period of time. Telltale signs of age and spoilage in grains are not as obvious as in fruits and vegetables. Of primary concern is mold, which is a sign of grain that is either old or that has been improperly stored and allowed to absorb too much moisture. If your wheat, barley, or rye has any green or partially green grains, they are not immature, but moldy. The exception to this rule is rice, where immature green grains are common and inconsequential.

When grains are cracked, rolled, or milled in any manner, their vitality is destroyed. Without their protective sheath, the contents are subject to oxidation, and the oil inherent in the grain begins to oxidize and turn rancid. Light and heat speed the process. Rancid foods are toxic to the body and are considered by many to be carcinogenic. If whole grain flour is over three months old and has not been kept in the freezer, it should be discarded.

HEALTH

Some people cannot tolerate gluten, a composition of two proteins (gliadin and glutenin) that are found in many grains but which are highest in wheat, followed at a distance by rye, oats, and barley. Gluten is what gives flour elasticity and strength, and allows breads to "rise." After kneading, gluten traps the carbon dioxide produced by yeast or a chemical leavening agent, resulting in the expansion or "rising" of the dough. This combination of proteins has been found to contribute to the cause of several serious diseases, including schizophrenia, celiac disease, and dermatitis herpetiformis. Celiac disease, also known as nontropical sprue, is an intestinal disorder caused by the inability to utilize gluten. It is characterized by diarrhea, malabsorption of nutrients, and an abnormally small intestinal structure that reverts back to normal when dietary gluten is removed and thereafter avoided. The elimination of gluten from the diet causes rapid improvement in the health of most people with celiac disease and dermatitis herpetiformis, and a few of those with schizophrenia. Oats are also often found on a list of foods for gluten-sensitive individuals to avoid. However, when fed to patients with celiac disease, they generally do not cause reactions. A one-pound loaf of bread contains about 40 grams of gluten. This amount of gluten, if eaten in a single day, can cause problems even for "healthy" people. The gluten causes changes in the intestinal lining that retard the absorption of nutrients.

Amaranth (*Amaranthus hypocondriacus, A. melancholicus, A. caudatus, A. cruentus*)

Amaranthus*, as well as the English* amaranth *comes from the Greek* amarantos*, meaning deathless or unfading, because this plant's flowers retain their color and appearance even when dried.* Hypocondriacus *means having a somber appearance;* melan-cholicus *means melancholy, hanging, or drooping;* caudatus *means caudate or tailed;* cruentus *means bloody, and refers to its often blood-red coloring.*

Amaranth

Nutritional Value Per 100 g Edible Portion

	Raw Whole Grain	Raw Leaves	Cooked Leaves
Calories	374	26	21
Protein	14.45 g	2.46 g	2.11 g
Fat	6.51 g	0.33 g	0.18 g
Fiber	3.77 g	0.98 g	1.31 g
Calcium	153 mg	215 mg	209 mg
Iron	7.59 mg	2.32 mg	2.26 mg
Magnesium	266 mg	55 mg	55 mg
Phosphorus	455 mg	50 mg	72 mg
Potassium	366 mg	611 mg	641 mg
Sodium	21 mg	20 mg	21 mg
Zinc	3.18 mg	0.90 mg	n/a
Copper	0.777 mg	0.162 mg	n/a
Manganese	2.260 mg	n/a	n/a
Beta Carotene (A)	n/a	2,917 IU	2,770 IU
Thiamine (B_1)	0.080 mg	0.027 mg	0.020 mg
Riboflavin (B_2)	0.208 mg	0.158 mg	0.134 mg
Niacin (B_3)	1.286 mg	0.658 mg	0.559 mg
Pantothenic Acid (B_5)	1.047 mg	n/a	n/a
Pyridoxine (B_6)	0.223 mg	n/a	n/a
Folic Acid (B_9)	49.0 mcg	85.3 mcg	n/a
Ascorbic Acid (C)	4.2 mg	43.3 mg	41.1 mg

General Information Amaranth is the seed of a broadleaf plant rather than a grass, and thus is not strictly speaking a grain, but the edible seed is classed by use as such. There are about five hundred species of amaranth, with types that thrive in environments ranging from the wet tropics to semi-arid lands and from sea level up to altitudes of ten thousand feet. Indigenous to India and the Americas, amaranth is so hardy that it grows vigorously under the most adverse conditions, tolerating very acid or highly alkaline soils, long equatorial days or short temperate ones, dry spells, heat, and mildly salty conditions. Each seed head resembles a bushy corn tassel, and yields hundreds of small round seeds the size of poppy seeds. A single plant, with its multiple seed heads, may produce up to fifty thousand seeds in colors of cream, gold, or pink. The leaves also vary in color, with stems and flowers of purple, orange, red, or gold. One variety grown for its leaves, frequently known as Chinese Spinach (*Amar-anthus gangeticus*), has dark green leaves that are tinged with red and slightly fuzzy. Like spinach, the whole plant can be eaten, but the leaves and tender stems are preferred. Plants grown for grain are pale-seeded since their appearance, flavor, and popping capability are considered best. The wild, dark-seeded varieties are generally used as potherbs and ornamentals; they are not as suitable for grain. Amaranth sustained the Aztec culture until 1521, when Cortez arrived and

Lore and Legend

The amaranth, both plant and grain, has frequently been connected with religious ceremonies throughout history. Montezuma collected a tribute of some two hundred thousand bushels of amaranth seed annually—almost the equal of the tribute in maize—from seventeen provinces of the Aztec Empire. The grain had a great religious significance for the Aztecs, who fashioned statues of their war and fire gods from the grain paste, mixing it either with honey or sacrificial blood. These statues were then carried in ceremonial processions, at the end of which they were broken and eaten by the Aztecs or fed to the slaves who were about to be sacrificed. To the Christian Cortez and his followers, this was nothing more than heathen idolatry, a pagan travesty of the Eucharist. Thus the fields of amaranth were burned and it was decreed that anyone in possession of the grain would have both hands cut off. Zuni legends relate that amaranth was one of the plants brought up from the underworld at the time of the Zunis' emergence, and it was a staple grain until the Corn Maiden brought them corn. To the Greeks, the unfading amaranth was a symbol of immortality, and they used the plant to embellish the images of their gods and tombs. The early Christian church also adopted the amaranth as symbolic of immortality. Whether in monastery gardens or on altars during the Middle Ages, their rich purples, royal reds, and golds blended perfectly with the exquisite colors of stained-glass windows, saints' robes, and altar hangings in church and shrine. In 1653, Queen Cristina of Sweden set up the Amaranter Order of Knighthood, obviously bearing in mind the plant's mystical associations.

banished the crop. Surviving in remote pockets in the wild, it was "rediscovered" in 1972 by a United States botanical research team.

Culinary Uses Amaranth is considered unusual because, like quinoa and unlike other grains, it is edible as both a vegetable and a grain. The greens, with their widely varied colors, add vibrant depth to salads and make a nutritious as well as tasty green vegetable. The leaves are described as being similar in taste to spinach but with a more assertive pepperiness, while the stems taste more like artichokes. Older stems may be tough, so the younger the better. Amaranth greens and stems can be used in every way you would use spinach and other greens—in quiches, omelets, casseroles, vegetable medleys, soups, or purées. They are particularly concentrated, with an abundance of nutrients.

The amaranth grain is one that, unless you have an inquisitive palate, may take some adjusting to. It has a strong but pleasantly nutty wild flavor and can be used whole, popped like corn, steamed and flattened into a flake, or ground into flour. The whole grain cooks easily and quickly to a cereal-like consistency, but it retains its shape and the hulls stay firm and chewy, never getting soft or mushy. Added in moderation, amaranth's distinctive peppery-spicy flavor can be used to enhance the mild taste of grains like rice, buckwheat, millet, or oats. It has marvelous versatility as an ingredient in a range of dishes: breads, salads, soups, candies, pancakes, pilafs, or breakfast cereals. Adding small quantities of the whole cooked grain to batters helps baked goods retain moisture and lightness.

Health Benefits Astringent. Nutritionally, amaranth is higher in protein than either corn or beans, higher in fiber than wheat, corn, rice or soybeans, rich in vitamins, and exceptionally rich in the essential amino acid lysine, absent or very low in most other cereal grains. It is also higher in calcium and the supporting calcium cofactors—magnesium and silicon—than milk, and has an iron content up to four times that of brown rice. As an herb, amaranth works as an astringent, having the effect of contracting tissues and limiting gland secretion; thus it is helpful for excessive menstrual bleeding or diarrhea.

Byproducts

Amaranth flour, because it has no gluten, is especially appreciated by those who have grain or gluten sensitivities. Added in small amounts to baked goods, the flour boosts both flavor and nutrition. Generally only a small portion is used in leavened products, while unleavened products such as flatbreads, crackers, and cookies may use a higher percentage. Some cultures commonly use the flour for gruel, pancakes, tortillas, breads, and other baked goods.

Popped amaranth, with its nutty flavor, can be eaten like popcorn or added to a range of recipes to add flavor and lighten the results. One cup of amaranth will yield three to four cups popped. Small amounts are easiest popped in a Japanese sesame seed toaster (available at most Japanese supply shops); larger amounts can be done in a wok or heavy skillet. Popped amaranth will not keep long and quickly turns rancid.

Barley (*Hordeum vulgare, H. distichon, H. hexastichon*)

Hordeum *is the ancient Latin name for barley.* Vulgare *means common or vulgar;* distichon *refers to the two-rowed variety;* hexastichon *is the six-rowed. The English word* barley *is a corruption of the Latin* far, *another name used for this grain.*

Lore and Legend

Barley was used as the basic unit of the Sumerian measuring system from 4000 to 2000 B.C. The Babylonian Code of Hammurabi (1750 B.C.) records that it was frequently used as a means of simple monetary exchange, and even among the Ethiopians, land rent or laborers could be paid in this manner. For the Hebrews, Greeks, and Romans (who represented their agricultural goddess Ceres with barley plaited into her crown) it was the chief bread flour crop and was heralded as a food for potency and vigor. The Greeks trained their athletes on barley-mush because it was considered the mildest of all cereals, while Roman gladiators, called *hordearii* (barley eaters), ate the grain to build up strength. Barley in ancient India was dedicated to the god Indra, known as "He who ripens barley"; Hindus still use the grains in their religious celebrations, at weddings, childbirths, funerals, and other rites. In the writings of ancient China, the seed-rich, heavily-bearded barley was considered a symbol of male potency, and the grain is mentioned as one of the five most sacred cultivated crops, the others being rice, millet, soybeans, and wheat.

General Information Barley is a hardy cereal grain believed to have originated from a wild form somewhere in western Asia or the Ethiopian highlands. It was used as a feedstuff for both man and beast in ancient Egypt between 6000 and 5000 B.C., and in China by 2800 B.C.; it was also one of the grain staples in early Europe until it was replaced by rye and wheat. When leavened bread became common, barley lost much of its importance for breadmaking because of its low gluten content. The several varieties are usually divided according to the number of grains along the ear: the two-rowed coffee or Peruvian barley (*H. distichon*); the four-rowed spring or common barley (*H. vulgare*); and the six-rowed variety (*H. hexastichon*), which was popular in ancient times. Probably the most ancient cultivated grain, barley is considered one of the five most important cereal crops in the world, its grains being used for human food, in malt brewing, and as livestock feed. In ancient times, barley was often used to make bread, but its use for the making of various alcoholic drinks is probably the main reason it is still grown. Brought to the New World by Dutch and British colonists primarily to make beer, over one-third of the current crop is still used for that purpose, with less than one-tenth being used for human consumption (the rest is used for animal feed). In fact, beer was even named after this grain, deriving from one of its older names, *bere*. Barley has two inedible outer hulls, which are typically removed by machine. The next inner layer is called the aleurone, which is rich in protein, B vitamins, and fiber. Most barley, however, is subjected to further processing (pearling) to remove this layer as well. Pearled barley is thus nutritionally inferior to hulled whole barley.

Culinary Uses Most barley found in stores is pearled, and it is this form that most people are familiar with. Its mild sweet flavor and chewy texture has made it a traditional favorite for thickening soups and stews. Cooked on its own it will make a pleasant alternative to potatoes, rice, or pasta, as well as an innovative salad and casserole ingredient.

Health Benefits Barley is highly regarded as a nutritious food, and excellent for underweight individuals. Soothing to the digestive tract and liver, it is said to help heal stomach ulcers, prevent tooth decay, and loss of hair, and to improve the condition of finger and toenails. Barley has blood-cholesterol lowering abilities, and in some areas of the world where barley is a staple both as a cereal and flour, heart disease rates are low. Whole barley, sometimes called "sproutable," is mildly laxative, and contains far more nutrition than the commonly used "pearled" variety. Roasting before cooking makes barley, considered the most acid-forming grain, more alkalinizing. Sprouted barley treats indigestion from starchy food stagnation, strengthens weak digestion, and tonifies the stomach. Dried sprouted barley contains 66,000 International Units Beta Carotene (A) per 100 grams. Processing removes many of its nutrients and health benefits, so the less processed, the better.

Byproducts

Barley flakes, or **Rolled barley**, are processed in exactly the same manner as oatmeal, which allows them to cook quicker than the whole grain form. The flakes can be used for a chewy breakfast porridge, eaten raw in muesli, or toasted and used as a thickening agent in soups, stews, and baked goods.

Barley flour is starchy, soft, and has a sweet, earthy taste. Whole grain barley flour yields a cakelike crumb (and sometimes a grayish color) and can be substituted for all or part of the wheat flour in recipes although some suggest that for bread baking, more of a blend is desirable since barley has a very low gluten content and will not rise much on its own; its maltose content, which enhances the growth of yeast cells in leavened breads, may make up for this. The flour can also be used as a thickening agent.

Barley grits are coarsely ground whole hulled barley grains that have been toasted. More similar to bulgur than to corn (hominy) grits, barley grits cook quickly and are excellent when cooked and served in place of rice, used as a breakfast cereal, or in baking.

Hulled barley, also known as **Groats**, and either **Pot** or **Scotch barley**, is the whole grain that has gone through two pearlings to remove the inedible spikelet (two outer husks). "Hull-less" barley is a special variety that has a softer, easily removable hull. Hulled barley is the most nutritious form of the grain because only the outer inedible hull is removed (not the bran), leaving it rich in dietary fiber, vitamins and minerals. These light brown grains require strenuous chewing in order to be fully digested, but have a pronounced appealing flavor. They can be used as a whole grain cereal, or added to soups and casseroles; their cooking time is longer than the pearled variety.

Malt powder/malt sugar is a buff-colored, crystalline powder made by evaporating the water out of malt syrup. Primarily used for brewing, malt sugar is becoming increasingly available in stores as a sugar replacement. Since malt powder absorbs moisture very easily (in the process becoming rock-hard), it needs to be stored in a well-sealed glass jar. Stored properly, malt powder has a lengthy shelf life.

Malt syrup is made from raw unhulled barley soaked in drums of temperature- and humidity-controlled water to allow it to sprout. Sprouting activates the enzymes in the grain that begin breaking down the starch into simple sugars (maltose). After two

Barley

Nutritional Value Per 100 g Edible Portion

	Raw Whole Grain	Raw Pearled	Cooked Pearled	Malt Syrup
Calories	354	352	123	318
Protein	12.48 g	9.91 g	2.26 g	6.2 g
Fat	2.30 g	1.16 g	0.44 g	0 g
Fiber	2.85 g	0.74 g	0.23 g	n/a
Calcium	33 mg	29 mg	11 mg	61 mg
Iron	3.60 mg	2.50 mg	1.33 mg	0.96 mg
Magnesium	133 mg	79 mg	22 mg	72 mg
Phosphorus	264 mg	221 mg	54 mg	236 mg
Potassium	452 mg	280 mg	93 mg	320 mg
Sodium	12 mg	9 mg	3 mg	35 mg
Zinc	2.770 mg	2.130 mg	0.820 mg	0.140 mg
Copper	0.498 mg	0.420 mg	0.105 mg	0.200 mg
Manganese	1.943 mg	1.322 mg	0.259 mg	0.100 mg
Beta Carotene (A)	n/a	22 IU	n/a	0 IU
Thiamine (B_1)	0.646 mg	0.191 mg	0.083 mg	n/a
Riboflavin (B_2)	0.285 mg	0.114 mg	0.062 mg	0.393 mg
Niacin (B_3)	n/a	4.604 mg	2.063 mg	8.120 mg
Pantothenic Acid (B_5)	n/a	0.282 mg	0.135 mg	0.171 mg
Pyridoxine (B_6)	0.318 mg	0.260 mg	0.115 mg	0.500 mg
Folic Acid (B_9)	19.0 mcg	23.0 mcg	16.0 mcg	12.0 mcg
Ascorbic Acid (C)	0 mg	0 mg	0 mg	0 mg
Tocopherol (E)	0.57 mg	0.02 mg	n/a	n/a

or three days, this sprouted grain is kiln dried, and the grain is ground, briefly dipped in an acid solution, and heated with water to form the mildly sweet, concentrated liquid we know as malt syrup. If this liquid is subjected to further heating and evaporating, it will become malt extract and maltose (malt sugar), a crystalline, colorless powder. Malt syrup is about 65 percent maltose, which tastes only 20 to 30 percent as sweet as sucrose (white sugar). It should be stored in a cool place, as warmth may cause it to ferment. Malt syrups are also made from wheat, rice, barley and rice, or barley and corn. Malt syrup is less concentrated in flavor than other sweeteners and adds a subtle and mild, rather than bold, sweetness to cooked or baked products. Traditionally used in beer making, hot and cold malted milk drinks, and in some breakfast cereals, malt syrup added to bread recipes not only promotes yeast activity, but also gives better body and texture while enhancing the flavor of other ingredients. It also adds a warm, rich color to breads. Because malt syrup is high in complex carbohydrates, it enters the bloodstream slowly, and can be considered a balanced sweetener that will not upset blood-sugar levels.

Pearl barley is the most common form in the United States. To produce these uniform ivory-colored granules, the barley grains are scoured six times during milling to completely remove their double outer husk (the spikelet) and the bran layers. The thorough milling, however, removes almost all of their fiber, along with over half the protein, fat, and mineral content. This is an inferior product, healthwise, to the whole hulled variety. However, it is used in times of illness when other foods cannot be tolerated, as it is the mildest and least irritating of the cereals. It has a very mild nut-like taste, cooks quickly, and readily absorbs the flavors of its companion ingredients in soups, salads, and side dishes. An instant form of pearl barley, called **quick barley**, cooks even faster because it is precooked by steaming.

Buckwheat (*Fagopyrum esculentum, F. tartaricum*)

The scientific name Fagopyrum *is derived from* fagus, *meaning beech tree, and* pyrum, *meaning cereal, because of the resemblance between the buckwheat fruits and those of the beech tree.* Esculentum *means esculent or edible;* tartaricum *means coming from Tartary (an indefinite historical region in Asia and Europe extending from the Sea of Japan to the Dnieper River in Russia). The English name* buckwheat *is a corruption of the Dutch* bockweit, *meaning beech wheat, reflecting its physical resemblance to beechnuts and its nutritional similarity to wheat.*

General Information Buckwheat is native to the regions of Manchuria and Siberia, an ancient hardy plant that grows rapidly even in poor, rocky soil and extreme climates. Instead of growing tall and straight, buckwheat is branching and weedlike, with heart-shaped leaves and fragrant white flowers that are attractive to bees. The three-cornered seed has an inedible black outer hull that must be removed, yielding a tan-colored interior kernel. First cultivated in China, it was introduced to Europe in the Middle Ages by the Crusaders, who brought it back to Venice from Asia Minor. During the sixteenth century the plant spread throughout Europe and achieved some importance due to its ability to thrive on poorer soils; at that time it was generally known as *Saracen wheat* or *corn, saracen* being a term given to most foreign things, but especially those introduced by the Moslems and Turks. Until the turn of the century, impoverished cultures from Eastern Europe to the United States' Deep South depended on buckwheat for porridge and as an extender for costly wheat flour. Its popularity declined rapidly in the early part of the twentieth century, but it is now making a strong comeback in health food circles. The Japanese especially make wide use of it for many types of noodles (called *soba*). Buckwheat, due to its extreme hardiness and resistance to disease, is one of the few commercially grown grains that is not routinely doused with insecticides.

Lore and Legend

Japanese goldsmiths have long used buckwheat dough to collect the gold dust in their shops, and the grain is therefore considered a potent charm for collecting riches. When a Japanese family moves to a new house, presents of buckwheat noodles (*soba*) are given to all the neighbors to express wishes for their good fortune and for long lasting friendships between them; these noodles are also eaten each New Year's Eve in the hopes of acquiring the luck for amassing money during the coming year.

Culinary Uses The buckwheat grown in Europe has a rather mild taste, distinctly different from the buckwheat grown in the United States, which can be quite strong and musky. After harvesting, the black, hard, inedible outer shell has to be removed in order to gain access to the inner kernel. This kernel is then split into pieces, called groats, which are either sold raw or roasted (known by the Russian name *kasha*). The unroasted groats are a greenish color, have a mellow flavor, and are frequently substituted for white or brown rice. Although the raw groats are nutritionally superior, roasting brings out the flavor and increases the availability of iron. The roasted variety usually works best for culinary purposes, unless used for cereal. Buckwheat can be eaten as a cereal, a side dish, or incorporated into a main dish, where it blends well with onions, dill, mushrooms, winter squash, and cabbage. It imparts a delicious flavor to stuffings, pilafs, soups, and stews. Most people are familiar with buckwheat only in the form of pancakes or crêpes.

Health Benefits Buckwheat is a power-packed grain, special in that it contains all eight essential amino acids as well as the glucoside rutin, a substance that is helpful in strengthening the capillaries, aiding in circulation, and protecting against the effects of radiation. More than any other known cereal grain, buckwheat is high in the essential amino acid lysine. It is an excellent food for cold weather months due to its warming and drying

Buckwheat

Nutritional Value Per 100 g Edible Portion

	Raw Whole Grain	Cooked Kasha	Whole Grain Dark Flour	Light Flour
Calories	343	92	335	347
Protein	13.25 g	3.38 g	12.62 g	6.4 g
Fat	3.40 g	0.62 g	3.10 g	1.2 g
Fiber	9.90 g	0.52 g	1.60 g	0.50 g
Calcium	18 mg	7 mg	41 mg	11 mg
Iron	2.20 mg	0.80 mg	4.06 mg	1.00 mg
Magnesium	231 mg	51 mg	251 mg	n/a
Phosphorus	347 mg	70 mg	337 mg	88 mg
Potassium	460 mg	88 mg	577 mg	320 mg
Sodium	1 mg	4 mg	n/a	n/a
Zinc	2.400 mg	0.610 mg	3.120 mg	n/a
Copper	1.100 mg	0.146 mg	0.515 mg	n/a
Manganese	1.300 mg	0.403 mg	2.030 mg	n/a
Thiamine (B_1)	0.101 mg	0.040 mg	0.417 mg	0.080 mg
Riboflavin (B_2)	0.425 mg	0.039 mg	0.190 mg	0.040 mg
Niacin (B_3)	7.020 mg	0.940 mg	6.150 mg	0.400 mg
Pantothenic Acid (B_5)	n/a	0.359 mg	0.440 mg	n/a
Pyridoxine (B_6)	0.210 mg	0.077 mg	0.582 mg	n/a
Folic Acid (B_9)	30.0 mcg	14.0 mcg	54.0 mcg	n/a
Ascorbic Acid (C)	0 mg	0 mg	0 mg	0 mg

effects on the body; however, because of this astringent action, it is not recommended for those with skin allergies or cancer as it may prevent cells from cleansing themselves. Buckwheat also has the reputation of being a good blood builder and neutralizer of toxic acidic wastes in the system, and can be eaten by many people who are allergic to other grains. Roasted buckwheat (*kasha*) is a rich source of fiber and silica, which forms butyrate, a short-chain fatty acid, thus detoxifying the intestines and suppressing the growth of cancers. The roasting process converts buckwheat into one of the few alkalinizing grains. Young buckwheat greens (from seeds with a hard inedible black covering that drops off after sprouting), are excellent sources of chlorophyll, enzymes, and vitamins.

Byproducts

Buckwheat flour is a beautiful gray and black speckled flour with an assertive, musky, slightly bitter flavor. Dark buckwheat flour is preferable to light buckwheat flour: it has had only 20 percent of the husk removed, whereas the lighter flour has had 50 percent removed. This beautifully light flour has been traditionally used for making pancakes and crêpes; their Russian counterparts, called *blinis*, are not limited solely to the breakfast table. Buckwheat flour will not rise on its own since it does not contain gluten, but combined with wheat flour it makes delicious bread with the density of a brick, but the tender moistness of pudding.

Buckwheat grits are groats that have been coarsely cracked. Sold as buckwheat cereal or cream of buckwheat, these finely ground, unroasted groats cook quickly and develop a soft, creamy texture. Because they have been broken, grits lack the vitality and freshness of the whole groat, but are easily digestible. Popular as a filler in many Polish sausages, they are also excellent in soufflés and desserts, as well as a breakfast cereal or a rice-pudding-style dessert.

Buckwheat groats are the seeds that have been hulled. Whole buckwheat with the inedible black hull intact is suitable only for sprouting. The groats are available either unroasted (white or lightly green) or roasted (brown, known as *kasha*). The white unroasted groats have a fairly mild flavor and can be substituted in dishes that call for white or brown rice. Roasted buckwheat has a more assertive flavor, which many people prefer.

Kasha is the brown roasted buckwheat groats, which come in four forms: fine grind, which cooks quickly and is less chewy than the other grinds; medium and coarse grinds, which are good for all-around use; and the whole roasted groat, which is uncracked and good for pilafs. Kasha is also ground to make a flour that can be used for pancakes, crisp thin cakes, and Japanese noodles called *soba*.

Corn/Maize (*Zea mays*)

The Indians called this grain mahiz. *In 1737 Linnaeus christened the species* Zea mays, *from the Greek* zeia *meaning grain or cereal, and* mays *being a spelling variant of the original Indian* mahiz. *The term* corn *comes from the Old Norse word* korn, *which means a grain-sized lump of something. The term has historically meant any sort of kernel or grain, whatever the dominant grain of the country happened to be. Be aware that if you ask for corn in Scotland or Ireland, the term refers to oats, while in Europe, you may be given wheat; if you request maize, it will be assumed that you mean to feed it to your pigs, for that is the destiny of most corn in Europe.*

General Information Corn, or maize, originated as a spiky little weed in Central and South America, where it is thought to have grown wild about nine thousand years ago. The Indians of that region had been using corn for so long that by the time Europeans arrived they had no record of where it had come from; the wild form had by that time disappeared and been replaced by a multitude of cultivated varieties. Corn was so plentiful that it was planted along the roadsides so that those in want might help themselves; nobody in Mexico could die of hunger at a time when Europeans could and frequently did. Geneticists group the world's corn into races, some three hundred at last count. The Incas of Peru hybridized corn and used vast irrigation systems for their fields; by the time of the Spanish conquest, they were in fact probably the most skilled cultivators of maize in America, and it is reasonable to assume that they had extensive knowledge and experience in selectively breeding only those varieties which they found of special value as food. By the time of Columbus's arrival, the Indians had already developed more than two hundred types of maize—one of the most remarkable plant breeding achievements in history. Of all the new foodstuffs Columbus encountered, maize was to be the most important in later history; yet because his search was for exotic

Corn

Nutritional Value Per 100 g Edible Portion

	Raw Whole Grain	Whole Grain Cornmeal	Degermed Enriched Cornmeal	Bran	Germ
Calories	365	362	366	224	490
Protein	9.42 g	8.12 g	8.48 g	8.36 g	17.0 g
Fat	4.74 g	3.59 g	1.65 g	0.92 g	25.00 g
Fiber	2.90 g	1.84 g	0.62 g	8.46 g	20.80 g
Calcium	7 mg	6 mg	5 mg	42 mg	0 mg
Iron	2.71 mg	3.45 mg	4.13 mg	2.79 mg	7.80 mg
Magnesium	127 mg	127 mg	40 mg	64 mg	672 mg
Phosphorus	210 mg	241 mg	84 mg	72 mg	1587 mg
Potassium	287 mg	287 mg	162 mg	44 mg	1420 mg
Sodium	35 mg	35 mg	3 mg	7 mg	31 mg
Zinc	2.210 mg	1.820 mg	0.720 mg	1.560 mg	10.600 mg
Copper	0.314 mg	0.193 mg	0.078 mg	0.248 mg	0.500 mg
Manganese	0.485 mg	0.498 mg	0.105 mg	0.140 mg	n/a
Beta Carotene (A)	n/a	469 IU	413 IU	71 IU	60 IU
Thiamine (B_1)	0.385 mg	0.385 mg	0.715 mg	0.010 mg	1.700 mg
Riboflavin (B_2)	0.201 mg	0.201 mg	0.407 mg	0.100 mg	0.750 mg
Niacin (B_3)	3.627 mg	3.632 mg	5.034 mg	2.735 mg	2.200 mg
Pantothenic Acid (B_5)	0.424 mg	0.425 mg	0.312 mg	0.636 mg	n/a
Pyridoxine (B_6)	0.622 mg	0.304 mg	0.257 mg	0.152 mg	1.410 mg
Folic Acid (B_9)	n/a	n/a	48.0 mcg	4.0 mcg	90.0 mcg
Ascorbic Acid (C)	0 mg	0 mg	0 mg	0 mg	4 mg
Tocopherol (E)	0.490 mg	n/a	0.150 mg	n/a	n/a

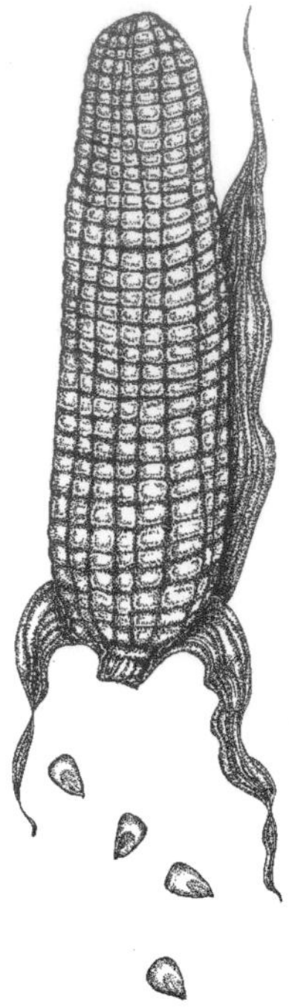

spices and elusive gold, he hardly took notice when the Indians gave him a gift of the grain. He evidently mistook corn for a plant native to Europe, and reported that the Indians ate the fruit of the wild sorghum. While yellow corn predominates today, the Native Americans prized corn with colorful kernels—blue, red, pink, and black—or with bands, spots, or stripes. The rainbow of coloring results primarily from concentrations of different pigments (such as carotenes and flavonoids) contained in the aleurone (the outer layer of the endosperm), and from centuries of breeding for traits such as size, flavor, and pest resistance. Corn has a unique cob structure such that the numerous kernels are firmly attached to a rigid axis, the cob, instead of being covered by floral glumes, and the entire ear is enclosed by modified leaf sheaths. This communal rather than individual protection has the great disadvantage of impeding grain dispersal, and the domestic form we know today is in fact dependent upon man's intervention for its continued survival.

Corn has remained a grain of the Americas, sustaining the diets and pocketbooks of many, and modern Americans would be hard-pressed to find a way to live without it. In a typical day one might wear cotton clothes that have had their fibers strengthened by cornstarch; have corn flakes for breakfast, or eggs laid by corn-fed chickens; drive to work in a car powered in part by ethanol, a fuel derived from corn; read a magazine that has had its paper fibers bound with cornstarch to keep them together as they race through high-speed presses; drink a cola sweetened with corn syrup; and eat possibly several varieties of meat from animals fattened on corn feed. Corn products show up in toothpaste, alcohol, dog food, trash bags, glue, canned goods, shoe polish, fireworks, lotions, crayons, ink, batteries, margarine, marshmallows, mustard, ice cream, aspirin, paint, cosmetics—the list keeps going on, ad infinitum.

Culinary Uses Throughout history, corn—or maize, as it is known in most places—has turned up in a hundred different forms and has provided the base grain for many thousands of dishes in cultures around the world. Available in a myriad of forms, there is one to suit any purpose or taste preference. The most common use is in baking, and all types of cornmeal and corn flour can be used, where they will provide a crumbly, somewhat gritty texture. Because cornmeal is unique in flavor and texture, there is no substitute for it.

Corn

Nutritional Value Per 100 g Edible Portion

	Whole Grain Corn Flour	Cornstarch	Plain Popcorn	Light Corn Syrup	High-Fructose Corn Syrup
Calories	361	381	386	282	281
Protein	6.93 g	0.26 g	12.7 g	0 g	0 g
Fat	3.86 g	0.05 g	5.0 g	0 g	0 g
Fiber	1.34 g	0.09 g	2.2 g	0 g	0 g
Calcium	7 mg	2 mg	11 mg	3 mg	0 mg
Iron	2.38 mg	0.47 mg	2.7 mg	0.05 mg	0.03 mg
Magnesium	93 mg	3 mg	n/a	2 mg	0 mg
Phosphorus	272 mg	13 mg	281 mg	2 mg	n/a
Potassium	315 mg	3 mg	n/a	4 mg	0 mg
Sodium	5 mg	9 mg	3 mg	121 mg	2 mg
Zinc	1.730 mg	0.060 mg	n/a	0.020 mg	0.020 mg
Copper	0.230 mg	0.050 mg	n/a	0.010 mg	0.029 mg
Manganese	0.460 mg	0.053 mg	n/a	0.088 mg	n/a
Beta Carotene (A)	n/a	n/a	n/a	0 IU	0 IU
Thiamine (B_1)	0.246 mg	n/a	n/a	0.011 mg	n/a
Riboflavin (B_2)	0.080 mg	n/a	0.120 mg	0.009 mg	0.019 mg
Niacin (B_3)	1.900 mg	n/a	2.200 mg	0.020 mg	0 mg
Pantothenic Acid (B_5)	0.658 mg	n/a	n/a	0.023 mg	0.011 mg
Pyridoxine (B_6)	n/a	n/a	n/a	0.009 mg	0 mg
Folic Acid (B_9)	25.0 mcg	n/a	n/a	0 mg	0 mg
Ascorbic Acid (C)	0 mg	0 mg	0 mg	0 mg	0 mg
Tocopherol (E)	n/a	0 mg	n/a	n/a	0 mg

Lore and Legend

The Incas of Peru, the Mayans of Central America, and the Aztecs of Mexico used maize not only as a food, but as currency, fuel, jewelry, and building material. Every maize-growing tribe had its corn gods, corn mothers or corn maidens—deities of maize, revered by special corn-sowing dances, rain ceremonies, prayer-rites for the sprouting seed, and festivals of thanks at harvest time. The Hopi Indians, who predominantly used blue corn, relate one corn myth: "Yaapa, the Mockingbird, placed many different kinds of corn before the tribes. The Navajo took yellow ears, Sioux picked the white, Havasupai wanted the red, Ute selected the flint, Apache chose the longest ears. My people picked up the last and smallest ear, the blue corn. This meant the Hopi would have a long-lasting but hard life." Another tale, much like that of the Greek Apollo and Daphne, tells of a brave who was so in love with a beautiful maiden that he slept outside her hut to offer her his protection. One night, he found her walking in her sleep and followed her. Although she ran fast, he finally caught her, but it was not a young woman whom he embraced. In her fear she had prayed that she might be transformed, and was changed into a tall cornstalk, her hair turning into silk and her hands into cobs. Perhaps the most beautiful symbolic fable is about White Earth, the only survivor in the world after all men were destroyed. She was told by her brother that she would be courted by five suitors, and to accept none until the fifth appeared. First came Usama: when he was rejected, he became tobacco. Next came Wapako, round and pudgy, who turned into a pumpkin. Third was Ashkossim, a melon, and fourth was Kokees, a bean. Then came a sound like music in the wind, and it was the fifth suitor, whom White Earth immediately chose as her husband. The rains came after the wedding and all the previous suitors grew and flourished, but the tallest and best was the corn, her husband, Mondahmin.

Health Benefits One of the best balanced starches, fresh raw (or lightly steamed) corn is easy to digest, but after the grain has been dried, corn and corn cereals are some of the most difficult of all the cereals to digest. Yellow corn is helpful in building bone and muscle, and is excellent food for the brain and nervous system. Corn is said to help prevent cancer and lower risk of heart disease and cavities. Corn oil is high in linoleic acid, and also has fair amounts of oleic, linolenic, and arachidonic acids. The whole grain oil has been found to correct the over-alkalinity of the bodily system, and some doctors recommend it (either taken by spoonful or applied directly to the skin) in cases of eczema-type skin disorders. Corn oil is 12.70 percent saturated, 24.20 percent monosaturated, and 58.70 percent polyunsaturated.

Varieties

There are five basic types of corn: dent corn, flint corn, flour corn, popcorn, and sweet corn. Each of these were once grown in varieties of four different colors: red, white, yellow, and blue, some of which are still available today.

Dent corn (*Z. mays indentata*) is the most widely grown corn in the United States. A hard variety whose seeds literally indent after drying, this is the variety commonly available in stores, and is the grain from which most yellow cornmeal is milled. Harder and starchier than sweet corn, 90 percent of dent corn is used for animal feed, and the rest is processed into breakfast foods, cornstarch, corn oils, and corn syrups.

Flint corn (*Z. mays indurata*), also known as **Indian corn**, is a hard-kerneled corn most often used as animal feed, with some of the colored varieties now gaining in popularity commercially. **Blue corn** is literally blue, and has a sweeter, more delicate flavor than the yellow variety, along with about 20 percent more protein and higher levels of minerals and the amino acid lysine. This open-pollinated flint corn has been grown by the Indians of the Southwest for centuries, and is now being used by corn

chip and tortilla manufacturers to make uniquely colored products with a rich corn flavor. Open-pollinated corn has a wider genetic base than hybridized varieties and produces a crop that resembles the previous generation; these varieties are available through specialized seed companies selling heirloom seeds. **Multi-colored** corn has stunning ears with colors ranging from yellow, black, blue, and violet to red, pink, and white. No two ears are alike in the pattern of their colors. If you have access to a flour mill, buy some to grind into a rich-tasting, sweet cornmeal, and use as you would other cornmeals.

Flour corn (*Z. mays amylacea*) has a thin outer layer and a soft inner endosperm that is easy to grind and chew. This is the variety that is most often ground into corn flour or cornstarch, and used as a thickening agent.

Popcorn (*Z. mays everta*) is a type of maize that looks similar to other types of corn, except that the ears and kernels are smaller. First cultivated by the Incas, it is grown specifically for its use as a snack food. The kernels have a hard outer hull and endosperm, which seal in its relatively high moisture content of 14 percent. When heated, this moisture turns to steam and since there is no place for it to escape, the kernel literally explodes, everting or turning inside out, to relieve the pressure. Two agronomists, Charles Bowman and Orville Redenbacher, started developing the modern varieties of popcorn in the 1940s, while seeking to develop large and fluffy popcorn with a low percentage of duds. They succeeded in 1952, and although the companies that sold popcorn were not interested because the new strain cost too much to produce and market, Orville was so convinced the public would buy his new popcorn that he packaged and distributed it himself. Only a few years later his popcorn became the nation's number one seller. Because of this "popcorn pioneer," there are now varieties that can be popped to forty times their original kernel size. Popcorn is harder to digest than other varieties of corn.

Sweet corn is used as a vegetable (see reference under **Vegetable** section).

Byproducts

Corn bran is the outer layer of the corn kernel and can be used in exactly the same way as wheat bran, oat bran, or rice bran to add soluble fiber to the diet.

Corn flakes are not to be confused with the cornflake of supermarket breakfast cereal notoriety. This is the crushed whole kernel of corn, with all its natural goodness intact. Unlike most whole flaked grains, which need only to be soaked before eating, corn flakes require light cooking.

Corn flour/cornstarch is a fine silken powder milled generally from only the inner endosperm layer of the grain (usually dent corn), although it can also be made from the whole kernel. Because corn has a high oil content, whole grain corn flour quickly turns rancid, while the degerminated corn flour, which has had the hull, germ, and nutrients refined out, has an indefinite shelf life, but is limp and bland in comparison. Usually used as a thickening agent for sauces, soups, or pudding, it can also be used to make tortillas and other flatbreads. Corn flour absorbs more water than other flours and will yield a drier, crumblier product with a sweet corn flavor and beautiful golden color. When mixed with water to a creamy consistency and boiled, it will form a clear jelly. Cornstarch mixed into a paste with castor oil provides an excellent poultice to relieve skin irritations. The dry starch is a good baby powder and frequently an ingredient in commercial baby talc products.

Corn germ is the heart of the corn and is nutritionally the richest part. Compared to wheat germ, corn germ has more vitamin E, more iron, more zinc and fiber, and is a complete protein rich in lysine. It has all the uses of wheat germ—in baking, sprinkled on cereals, soups, and salads—and one more: being a bit bigger and crunchier than wheat germ, it makes a delicious snack eaten right out of the container.

Corn grits are made by coarsely grinding whole dried kernels of yellow or white corn. Almost all the bran and germ are removed during processing. Therefore, grits provide less nutrition than does whole corn (fully one-half to two-thirds of the vitamins are lost). Grits are often artificially enriched with vitamins and minerals to replace those lost during processing. They make a savory, quick-cooking cereal, and can be used to make pancakes and souffles.

Cornmeal is the coarsely ground grain, which may or may not have been hulled and degerminated. The absolutely best cornmeal is stone-ground whole-grain corn, which retains not only the germ but has a full robust flavor and its full complement of vitamins and minerals. The commercial supermarket's degerminated, overmilled, overheated, synthetic, vitamin-enriched cornmeal contains less than half the nutrients as whole-grain cornmeal, and even less taste. Cornmeal can be made into a porridge known as corn pone, or used in cakes, breads, tamales, desserts, and pancakes. Since it has a low gluten content, it will not leaven bread, but can be used for sprinkling over the bread or baking surface before baking, thus adding a distinct flavor and texture. **Blue cornmeal** or **"Hopi corn"** is a favored ingredient in breads of the American Southwest. Slightly grainier and sweeter than yellow corn, it makes a purple-pink, blue-green, or lavender-tinged baked product depending on the type of ingredients it is combined with. A squeeze of lime juice into blue corn batter will change it to pink. It needs a bit more fat when used to make muffins, biscuits, and tortillas, and is available in a variety of grinds.

Corn oil is one of the most popular oils, and its domestic use dates back to the American Indians. Because of corn's low oil content, extremely high temperatures and toxic solvents are needed to extract what oil there is efficiently. Oil that has been pressed from the whole grain rather than just the germ will be dark gold or amber in color, have a rich, buttery corn flavor, and a heady popcorn-like aroma. Most commercial oil, however, is extracted from only the germ, a by-product of such products as breakfast cereals, cornstarch, and corn syrup. This pallid oil is then further filtered, deodorized, and bleached for commercial sale, giving consumers a bland, tasteless product. Half the corn oil produced is usually made into margarine, and the rest processed as salad or cooking oil, mayonnaise, salad dressings, or shortening. Corn oil is not suitable for deep-frying, since it foams easily.

Corn syrup was originally made by the Peruvians and Mexicans from the stalks of the corn plant rather than the kernels. Juice from the stalks was pressed out and then boiled down to a sweet syrup, similar to the process used for sorghum molasses. Commercial corn syrup production was started in the early 1900s and marketed under the name glucose (corn syrup is almost pure glucose), a name which evidently did not catch on because consumers thought the syrup was made from glue. To overcome this prejudice, the company renamed it "corn syrup," and the product then became popular. Made from chemically purified cornstarch (from the starchy endosperm), the starch is mixed with water and either hydrochloric or sulfuric acid, then steamed to convert it to "commercial glucose," a highly refined glucose. This dark and odd-smelling substance is deodorized and filtered to produce the odorless, clear, and virtually tasteless liquid called corn syrup. Oftentimes, the syrup is mixed with sugar to increase its sweetness. So-called dark corn syrup is often artificially caramel colored. Corn sugar—also called solid glucose, dextrose, or starch sugar—is made in the same manner as corn syrup, although more acid is used and the product is steamed for a longer period of time. You may be a big user of corn syrup and not know it, since it makes an appearance in almost all commercial candies and baked goods. The syrup is commonly added not only as a sweetener, but also to thicken foods (such as ketchup), to add body, to prevent crystallization in frozen foods and ice cream, and to retain moisture. Dried and powdered corn syrup solids are found in nondairy creamers, imitation fruit drinks, and pudding mixes, and are a primary ingredient in imitation maple syrup.

Dried corn is usually dent corn that has had most of the water removed in the drying process, although any of the varieties can be similarly dried. It can be used in its dry form by grinding it into meal or flour, or it can be reconstituted in water and then added to soups, casseroles, and other dishes.

Hominy is made by taking whole field corn and treating it with slaked (hydrated) lime or a combination of unslaked lime, calcium carbonate, lye, and wood ash. This acts to loosen the hulls and partially "cook" the kernels, while also puffing them up. The corn is then washed to remove the hulls, bleached (depending on use), dried, and used in dishes such as soups and stews. Very little nutritional value remains after processing in this manner.

Masa is made from whole kernel corn that is soaked or boiled in dilute alkalis (lime, calcium hydroxide), wood ashes (potassium hydroxide), or lye (sodium hydroxide) for 30 minutes. The kernels are then drained, washed, and ground into a paste or masa. This paste can then be shaped into balls, flattened, and cooked on a hot griddle like a pancake.

Parched corn, also called **Corn nuts** and **Corn nuggets**, is a snack food made from whole corn kernels. These crunchy morsels are made by soaking the corn in water or brine (salted water) until they swell. They are then deep-fat fried or baked until golden brown, and heavily salted. Although not very nutritious, they are tasty. Besides eating them as snacks, try them in cookies, casseroles, or breads as you would real nuts.

Polenta is simply cooked cornmeal (either whole or degerminated). Frequently, prepared polenta is made from the coarse meal left after the oil has been squeezed out of the kernels, with a fine granular texture more similar to semolina than cornmeal. Formerly used primarily by the poor, it has become a more sophisticated dish; either fried or grilled, it is frequently served with vegetables or as an accompaniment for sauces. In Italy the name polenta is also given to the dish made from it.

Posole is parched and dried white corn; it needs to be parched, or else dried corn is virtually impossible to cook whole. This traditional Mexican food has a delicately sweet flavor and is delicious on its own, cooked with other grains, or ground into meal.

Job's Tears *(Coix lacryma-jobi)*

Also Known As: Hato Mugi.

> Coix *comes from the Greek name* koix *for the doom palm.* Lacryma *are tears,* jobi *means of Job. Its name is derived from the fanciful resemblance between its gleaming pearl-white seeds and the appearance of teardrops (legend had it they were from Job) as they fall sparkling from the eye.*

General Information Job's tears, a relative newcomer to the health food scene, is a true cereal grain of the millet family native to India and the Philippines. This large pearled barley lookalike has long been respected in the Far East for its many virtues and light, refreshing

Lore and Legend

Christian legend relates that this plant grew from the tears of Job, whose proverbial sufferings and troubles did not make him lose faith in God. These beadlike seeds, staple food to the hill tribes of India and medicine to the Chinese, were used for rosaries in the Near East and for magic necklaces in ancient Persia.

taste. When its hard, dark, tear-shaped hull is intact, it is used as a decorative bead for necklaces and rosaries.

Culinary Uses Job's tears has a light and refreshing taste that is excellent either on its own or combined with other grains, being less sticky than either rice or barley. It is best to soak it prior to use, as this will reduce the lengthy cooking time. It can also be added to long-cooking soups for body and flavor.

Health Benefits This grain has soothing properties for the stomach and nervous system, helps purify the blood, and restores general health. Low in fat, high in calcium and iron.

Kamut *(Triticum durum)*

Linnaeus provided the genus name, choosing Triticum, *an old Latin name for cereal;* durum *means hard.* Kamut *is an ancient Egyptian word that is believed to refer to wheat. The organically grown, pure, uncrossed strain has received the registered trademark name* Kamut; *this trademark belongs to Montana Flour & Grains (the Quinn family).*

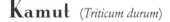

General Information Kamut is an ancient relative of modern durum wheat, a variety believed to have originated some six thousand years ago around Egypt and the Tigris/Euphrates river basin. Although later nearly completely replaced by other strains of wheat, kamut was nonetheless continuously grown until the mid-twentieth century by farmers who prized its rich flavor. Because kamut has not been hybridized and scientifically "improved," its self-pollinating kernels replicate those from ancient history grown thousands of years ago.

Culinary Uses Kamut is a truly versatile grain with a rich, almost buttery, delicious flavor. When cracked into a coarse meal and cooked, it makes one of the best-tasting cereals you will ever eat. Kamut pasta is as pleasing in texture and taste as the finest semolina (refined durum) pasta. Ground into a flour, it produces light-textured, delicious whole grain breads and other baked goods, and since it contains gluten, it can be used for yeasted breads. You can do almost anything with kamut that you can do with ordinary wheat, adding it to salads, pilafs, or stews. Consumer experience indicates that many with wheat allergies tolerate kamut products without negative effects.

Kamut

Nutritional Value Per 100 g Edible Portion

	Raw Whole Grain
Calories	359
Protein	17.3 g
Fat	2.6 g
Fiber	1.8 g
Calcium	31.0 mg
Iron	4.2 mg
Magnesium	153 mg
Phosphorus	411 mg
Potassium	446 mg
Sodium	3.8 mg
Zinc	4.3 mg
Thiamine (B_1)	0.450 mg
Riboflavin (B_2)	0.120 mg
Niacin (B_3)	5.540 mg
Pantothenic Acid (B_5)	0.230 mg
Pyridoxine (B_6)	0.080 mg
Folic Acid (B_9)	37.5 mcg
Tocopherol (E)	1.7 mg

Lore and Legend

In 1949, following World War II, a U.S. airman stationed in Portugal was given thirty-six kernels of a large and unique Egyptian grain; each kernel was two to three times the size of common wheat, and had a distinctive hump in the middle. Told that the oversized kernels had been found in King Tut's tomb (untrue, but it made for an intriguing story), he mailed the seeds to his father, a wheat farmer in Fort Benton, Montana. Thirty-two of the seeds germinated, and for a while the harvest of those few plants attracted some attention at local county fairs as "King Tut's Wheat." Then the novelty wore off and the grain was all but forgotten, the fields eventually going to cattle feed. In the 1970s, another wheat farmer from Montana, Bob Quinn, remembered seeing this grain in his childhood and sought out what he could find of the remaining seed. In 1977, he located a pint jar of the Egyptian grain, and the father and son team of Mack and Bob Quinn spent the next decade carefully selecting and propagating it on their ranch near Big Sandy, Montana. A sample of kamut was taken to the Natural Products Expo West '86 in Anaheim, California, where serious commercial interest started and has grown steadily ever since. It has since been introduced to the natural foods market, where it is gaining rapidly in popularity.

Health Benefits Kamut is a high-energy grain of greater nutritional value than regular wheat strains, easier to digest, and more compatible with human physiology. It does have less fiber, though, because the huge size of the grain gives a lower ratio of hull to volume. Although it contains gluten, most gluten-sensitive individuals find they are able to tolerate it in moderation.

Millet *(Panicum miliaceum, P. italica, Setaria italica)*

> Panicum *is an old Latin name for Italian millet;* miliaceum *is a term meaning pertaining to millet, while* italica *means coming from Italy. Its English name derives from the Latin* mille, *meaning a thousand, referring to the prolificacy of the seed.*

General Information Millet is a grain native to the East Indies and North Africa that has been cultivated in India, Africa, and the Middle East since time immemorial. In ancient Egypt, millet was used to make bread, and was a staple in China before rice was introduced. Botanically, this grass is more ancient than rice, barley, wheat, or rye. Particularly well suited to poor soil and adverse climates, millet manages to lie dormant through long periods of drought, then sprouts with the first rainfalls and is ready to harvest in just forty-five days. A surprisingly large variety of different plants fall under this genus, ranging from sorghum, t'ef, and Job's Tears, to the small pearl-like grains that we know and eat as "common" millet. In North America, where millet is grown primarily for bird seed, this delicious grain is only beginning to be appreciated; it is widely used in the Eastern Hemisphere and is renowned as a staple food of the long-living Hunzas of the Himalayas.

Culinary Uses Available in several forms, this tiny round yellowish seed (resembling a mustard seed) has a bland to slightly nutty flavor. The whole grain swells to a fluffy texture in cooking; toasting it in a little oil before cooking enhances the flavor and keeps the tiny grains from clumping together. It can be cooked into a tasty breakfast porridge eaten with nuts and dried fruit, or can be eaten raw when sprinkled over other foods. Millet also makes an excellent substitute for rice, or a tasty addition to stuffed vegetables, croquettes, stews, casseroles, pilafs, breads, and gravies.

Millet

Nutritional Value Per 100 g Edible Portion	Raw Whole Grain	Cooked Whole Grain
Calories	378	119
Protein	11.02 g	3.51 g
Fat	4.22 g	1.00 g
Fiber	1.03 g	0.36 g
Calcium	8 mg	3 mg
Iron	3.01 mg	0.63 mg
Magnesium	114 mg	44 mg
Phosphorus	285 mg	100 mg
Potassium	195 mg	62 mg
Sodium	5 mg	2 mg
Zinc	1.680 mg	0.910 mg
Copper	0.750 mg	0.161 mg
Manganese	1.632 mg	0.272 mg
Thiamine (B_1)	0.420 mg	0.106 mg
Riboflavin (B_2)	0.290 mg	0.082 mg
Niacin (B_3)	4.720 mg	1.330 mg
Pantothenic Acid (B_5)	0.848 mg	0.171 mg
Pyridoxine (B_6)	0.384 mg	0.108 mg
Tocopherol (E)	0.050 mg	n/a

Health Benefits Millet is a gluten-free, easily digestible grain that is one of the most outstanding alkaline foods in the world, as well as one of the least allergenic. Exceedingly nutritious, it contains an abundance of minerals and vitamins, and the most complete protein of any of the true cereal grains. Millet is rich in fiber and silica, which detoxify the intestines and form butyrate, a short-chain fatty acid that has been shown to suppress the growth of cancers. It is also anti-fungal, and is one of the best grains for those with *Candida* problems.

Byproducts

Cracked millet falls between whole millet and millet meal in size and can serve as a substitute for either. Finer in texture and quicker-cooking than the whole grain, it will add a slightly crunchy texture to breads or main dishes. Used as a cereal, it is excellent liberally laced with toasted sesame seeds and honey.

Millet flour has a distinctive sweet flavor and will give a dry, delicate, cakelike crumb and yellow color to baked goods. On its own it can be used interchangeably with t'ef flour and is often used to prepare injera flatbreads. To make a leavened product, though, it needs to be combined with other flours because it is low in gluten. Added to any product, it will add flavor and nutrition; use it as a thickener in soups and stews, for texture in baked goods, or myriad other uses.

Millet meal is a coarsely ground meal used for baked goods and cereal. It can be purchased pre-ground or it can be ground at home from whole millet, using a home mill or small electric spice (or coffee) grinder. It is best when freshly ground, or else the meal acquires a bitter taste. The ancient Romans made their bread of millet meal and wheat flour; try adding one-half cup meal to each five cups of wheat flour in your next batch of bread and enjoy the rich flavor.

Puffed millet is the whole grain that is puffed under pressure. Sold in specialty food stores or natural food outlets, it is an excellent snack food, makes a light and tasty addition to puddings and bread, and is a superior breakfast cereal.

Oats (*Avena sativa*)

Avena *is the old Latin name for the plant, while* sativa *means cultivated. The English name* oat *comes from the Old English* ate.

General Information Oats seem to be of western European origin, probably developed from two wild grasses, the common wild oat (*A. fatua*) and the wild red oat (*A. sterilis*), around 2500 B.C. Most likely they traveled to northern Europe along with the raiders, the merchant caravans, the invaders and the plunderers—along with their horses and the food carried to feed them. In cold northern climes such as the British Isles and Scandinavia where few other grains would grow, oats were of great importance and soon became a staple food. By the thirteenth century oats, then known as pilcorn, were a part of every Scot's daily fare. They were also a popular food among the poor, who could not grow wheat or afford wheaten flour. Oats arrived in the New World in 1602, and were planted on the Elizabeth Isles off the coast of Massachusetts, where they soon flourished. An annual grass that can grow to heights of two to five feet, only about five percent of the entire oat crop is consumed by humans, with the rest grown primarily as livestock feed. There are both winter and spring varieties, as with wheat. The grains, known as groats, are most often crushed to make oatmeal, oat flour, and oat flakes. Americans only consume about eleven pounds of oats per capita annually, mostly in the form of oatmeal for breakfast.

Culinary Uses For all of northern Europe, oats are a part of the culinary heritage, and for the Scots no celebration or cookbook would be complete without their appearance. While the whole groat (minus the inedible outer hull) may be cooked like brown rice, most oats are consumed in the form of oatmeal. Like wheat, oats are high in gluten and can be used for thickening and enriching soups, for extending meat loaves, for stuffings, pilafs, cakes, breads, muffins, pancakes, granola, and muesli.

Health Benefits Oats contain a higher proportion of fat and protein than most other grains, and rightly have a reputation for being a warming food appropriate for cold climates. Oats also contain an antioxidant that delays rancidity; thus the groats can be ground into flour that is longer-lasting than whole wheat flour. The rolled variety are easily and quickly digested, and take less time to cook than steel-cut oats. They are best eaten alone, as milk and sugar will cause them to ferment in the stomach, with all the possible benefits lost. Many people find that oats will act as a mild laxative due to their high fiber content, and they are reputedly beneficial for those with an under-functioning thyroid gland. Their rich silicon content helps renew the bones and all connective tissue. Externally, oats have an anti-inflammatory effect on certain skin problems such as contact eczema, and some physicians recommend oatmeal packs to treat psoriasis. Oat flour is an effective skin cleanser and can replace soap when necessary. Added to bath water it will soothe the itch of irritations such as eczema, poison ivy, and poison oak, or if made into a thick poultice it can be applied directly to the affected areas.

Oats

Nutritional Value Per 100 g Edible Portion

	Raw Whole Grain	Raw (Rolled) Oatmeal	Cooked Oatmeal	Raw Bran	Cooked Bran
Calories	389	384	62	246	40
Protein	16.89 g	16.0 g	2.6 g	17.3 g	3.21 g
Fat	6.90 g	6.3 g	1.0 g	7.03 g	0.86 g
Fiber	n/a	1.1 g	0.20 g	2.17 g	0.37 g
Calcium	54 mg	52 mg	8 mg	58 mg	10 mg
Iron	4.72 mg	4.21 mg	0.68 mg	5.41 mg	0.88 mg
Magnesium	177 mg	148 mg	24 mg	235 mg	40 mg
Phosphorus	523 mg	474 mg	76 mg	734 mg	119 mg
Potassium	429 mg	350 mg	56 mg	566 mg	92 mg
Sodium	2 mg	4 mg	1 mg	4 mg	1 mg
Zinc	3.970 mg	3.070 mg	0.490 mg	3.110 mg	0.530 mg
Copper	0.626 mg	0.343 mg	0.055 mg	0.403 mg	0.066 mg
Manganese	4.916 mg	3.630 mg	0.585 mg	5.630 mg	0.964 mg
Beta Carotene (A)	n/a	101 IU	16 IU	n/a	n/a
Thiamine (B_1)	0.763 mg	0.730 mg	0.110 mg	1.170 mg	0.160 mg
Riboflavin (B_2)	0.139 mg	0.140 mg	0.020 mg	0.220 mg	0.034 mg
Niacin (B_3)	0.961 mg	0.780 mg	0.130 mg	0.934 mg	0.144 mg
Pantothenic Acid (B_5)	1.349 mg	1.245 mg	0.200 mg	1.494 mg	0.217 mg
Pyridoxine (B_6)	0.119 mg	0.120 mg	0.020 mg	0.165 mg	0.025 mg
Folic Acid (B_9)	56.0 mcg	32.0 mcg	4.0 mcg	52.0 mcg	6.0 mcg
Ascorbic Acid (C)	0 mg	0 mg	0 mg	0 mg	0 mg
Tocopherol (E)	1.090 mg	1.510 mg	n/a	n/a	n/a

Lore and Legend

In ancient plant lore, an offering of oats showed an appreciation for someone's music; this evidently was an allusion to the shepherd's pipe, the popular "oaten straw" of pastorals. Tea made from oats achieved a curious reputation in the early part of the twentieth century as being able to "cure the opium habit," and reduce the craving for cigarettes.

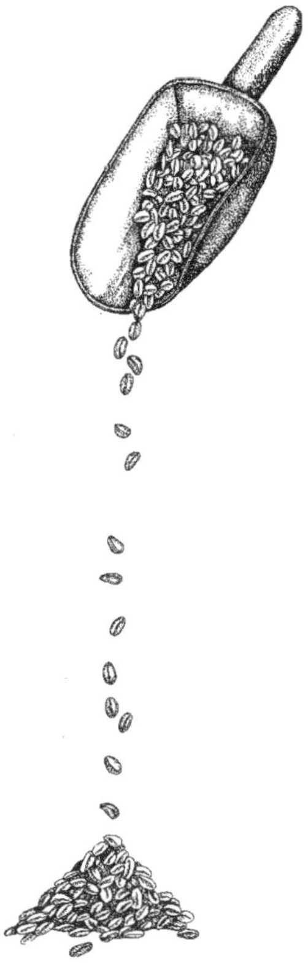

Byproducts

Oat bran is the outer covering of the hulled oat groat. Although not the universal panacea for health problems that was originally claimed, studies show that the consumption of oat bran does help lower blood cholesterol levels, as do rice, corn, and wheat brans, due to their fiber content. Oat bran is a delicious and nutritious addition to any baked product. Since it is the oil in the bran that contains the nutrients, all brans need to be stored in the refrigerator to prevent rancidity.

Oat flour, also known as **Flaked oats**, retains most of the nutrients present in whole oats, as the bran and germ remain intact in processing. It can be used interchangeably with whole-wheat pastry flour in some recipes, giving a moist delicate sweetness to breads, pancakes, biscuits, scones, and other pastry products. The addition of oat flour to baked goods gives the added benefit of a natural antioxidant, which enables baked products to retain their freshness longer. Oats have only a moderate gluten content, so they need to be combined with wheat flour or other high gluten-content flour when making leavened bread. Oat flour can also be used as a thickening agent in sauces, soups, and stews. If you can't find oat flour at a health food store, you can make your own by whirring rolled oats in an electric blender and then sifting to remove the coarser elements.

Oat groats are hulled, whole kernels that have been cleaned and dried. They are roasted slightly during the cleaning and hulling process, but have virtually the same nutrients as the whole grain; plus, the roasting process adds richness to the flavor. Softer than a wheat berry, oat groats can be pounded with a wooden mallet or rolled on a flat surface with a rolling pin, so they will cook quicker than in their original form. They are used in baking, as a cereal, or added to other grains for chewiness.

Rolled oats are made from groats that have been hulled, steamed, and rolled flat into flakes. **"Instant"** or **"Quick oats"** are groats that have been pre-cooked in water, dried, and rolled super-thin; although quicker cooking, they have less nutritional value due to their exposure to high heat during processing. Both varieties may be ground into a coarse meal suitable for bread making, or used whole in cereals, cookies, cakes, breads, and as toppings for fruit crisps. Rolled oats made from the whole grain are subject to rancidity within one to three months after milling; thus it is advisable to store any bulk quantities that will not be used within one month below 40°F.

Steel-cut oats, also known as **Scotch** or **Irish oats,** are natural, unrefined oat groats that have been processed with a minimal amount of heat by steel blades, cutting them into two or three small pieces. Available in coarse and fine grinds, the finer the slicing, the quicker the grain cooks. They still contain everything that is in the whole oat, retaining most of their B vitamins even through processing. With their fairly long cooking time they are best used for tasty, chewy cereals, but cooked steel-cut oats can be blended with various flours for baking.

Whole oats are unprocessed and retain the beneficial bran and germ. This whole form stores well without substantial deterioration; any of the processed forms will deteriorate rapidly. They can be used in baking (after being cooked), as a cereal, added to other grains for chewiness, or sprouted. Sprouting dramatically increases the supply of B vitamins and also releases other minerals for use.

Quinoa (*Chenopodium quinoa*)

Chenopodium *means goose-footed, and this plant genus characteristically has leaves shaped like a goose's foot.* Quinoa *means mother in Quechua Indian, one of two primary Andean languages of the South American altiplano.*

General Information Quinoa (pronounced keen-wah) was a principal grain of the Incas, given sacred status as a "mother grain," and thus targeted by Spanish colonization tactics. For four hundred years it survived only in remote, inaccessible areas of the Andean altiplano (high plains), but is now enjoying a resurgence in popularity. Botanically, quinoa is not a true grain since it belongs not to the grass family but the *Chenopodium* family, which also includes beets, spinach, lamb's quarters, chard, and sugar beet. Best grown at altitudes above 10,000 feet, this grain positively flourishes under extreme conditions, including poor soil, thin cold air, hot sun, frost, short growing days, minimal rainfall, and even drought. There are hundreds of varieties, with Peruvian and Bolivian seed banks alone having over eighteen hundred different ecotype samples. Growing three to nine feet in height, with its seeds in large clusters at the end of the stalk, quinoa comes in a dazzling array of colors: red, pink, orange, yellow, lavender, purple, green, black, and white. Store-bought seeds are usually a pale yellow color and look like a cross between sesame seed and millet. These small, disk-shaped seeds are slightly raised in the center, with a thin band running around their periphery; when the seeds are cooked, the band partially separates from the seed, but the curved form of the seed remains. Each seed is thickly covered with saponin, a resin-like substance with an extremely bitter soapy taste, which protects the grains from birds and insects. Seeds sold commercially have already been washed to remove this substance (although more washing wouldn't hurt), but any seed grown at home needs to be rinsed and drained five or ten times under cold running water; the more rinsing, the milder the flavor of the cooked grain.

Culinary Uses Quinoa is fast becoming a popular staple in North America due to its mild flavor and fluffy texture. Sometimes called "vegetarian caviar" because of its soft crunchy consistency, this tiny grain has a delicious nutty flavor reminiscent of couscous and peanuts, and most who try it for the first time immediately like it. Toasting it lightly before cooking will enhance its flavor even further. Ready to eat in less than fifteen minutes, it puffs up to four times its dry volume and becomes fairly translucent, looking rather like cooked couscous sprinkled with little crescent-moon spirals. The few small black or colored seeds are "wild quinoa," and with the exception of looking a bit different and not cooking fully, they are no problem and it is not necessary to spend time removing them. Quinoa makes a quick and tasty substitute for bulgur, rice, or couscous, or it can be added to soups, stews, casseroles, salads, or cookies.

The Aymara Indians on the altiplano of Bolivia still use the entire plant from top to bottom: the seeds are eaten whole in the manner of rice, or toasted, and ground into flour for tortillas. The leaves are eaten as a vegetable or used to feed farm animals; the stalks are burned as fuel; even the wash water from rinsing the seeds is frequently used as a shampoo.

Health Benefits Quinoa is valued in fitness circles as a high-energy food, and among the convalescing for its ease of digestion. It also appears to be gluten-free, which makes it valuable for those with wheat allergies. Quinoa offers a great amount of high-quality protein; its protein content is far

Quinoa

Nutritional Value Per 100 g Edible Portion

	Raw Whole Grain	Flour
Calories	374	354
Protein	13.10 g	10.40 g
Fat	5.80 g	4.00 g
Fiber	n/a	3.80 g
Calcium	60 mg	94 mg
Iron	9.25 mg	5.60 mg
Magnesium	210 mg	n/a
Phosphorus	410 mg	129 mg
Potassium	740 mg	n/a
Zinc	3.300 mg	n/a
Copper	0.820 mg	n/a
Thiamine (B_1)	0.198 mg	0.190 mg
Riboflavin (B_2)	0.396 mg	0.240 mg
Niacin (B_3)	2.930 mg	0.700 mg
Ascorbic Acid (C)	0 mg	0 mg

Lore and Legend

Inca legend says quinoa was the remains of a heavenly banquet, easy to believe once you have seen its multitude of vivid colors. In 1976, Dr. Stephen L. Gorad and his friend Don McKinley were told about quinoa by Oscar Icharo, the Bolivian religious leader who had mentioned quinoa in his teachings as "a very nutritious food which is good to eat when doing mystical work." When Gorad went to La Paz, Bolivia in 1978, he searched out the grain, found a sample, tried and liked it, and returned with fifty pounds. Availability problems stopped the two from marketing quinoa in the United States, because gathering grain by going from one remote Indian settlement to another was not economically feasible, and there was at that time no support for developing quinoa on a commercial basis. In 1982, while Dr. Gorad was living in Chile and teaching and writing about holistic health, he received a letter from Don McKinley asking for seed. The first crops were planted in the 8,000-foot-high San Luis Valley. These first crops were successful, and more fields have been planted in the high altiplano regions of Colorado and western Canada to help supply current demand.

higher than corn, barley, or rice, and only a few types of wheat even approximate the favorable variety and levels of amino acids it provides (including the critical lysine). Quinoa has more calcium than milk, and is higher in fat content than most other grain. The Peruvian Indians used this grain liberally, not only because it is rich in minerals, but also because of its benefit to nursing mothers in that it is a powerful stimulant to the flow of milk.

Byproducts

Quinoa flour happily combines the best features of whole-grain and white flours, imparting a light, delicate crumb full of flavor and nutrients. It is a preferred flour for fine pastries and increases the flavor range and depth of the finished product, but because it lacks gluten, it is best combined with wheat or other gluten-containing flour for leavened products. Add this versatile flour to pancakes, muffins, crackers, cookies, pastries, and breads. Because of its high oil content, quinoa flour should be refrigerated to prevent rancidity and used within three to six months. Quinoa flour is quick and easy to make at home in your blender. To make one cup of flour, place three-fourths cup quinoa in a blender or nut grinder and whiz for several minutes. Much softer than wheat or corn, quinoa pulverizes within a few minutes, yielding a slightly beady flour that is finer than cornmeal.

Rice (*Oryza sativa*)

The scientific name Oryza, *depending on the scholar, comes from either the Greek* oriza, *meaning Orient, the Arabic name* Eruz, *or an ancient Chinese name;* sativa *means widely cultivated. Its common name in all western tongues (*riso *in Italian,* reis *in German,* riz *in French,* arroz *in Spanish, and* rice *in English) is derived from the Greek* oriza.

General Information There are over seven thousand varieties of rice, each with its own distinct flavor, texture, aroma, color, length of grain, and degree of translucency. One of the principal Asian foods and a staple grain for over half the world's population, rice was developed from wild grasses found in Asia and Indochina. It is said that when Buddhism spread from the Indian subcontinent to the Far East it brought along the custom of eating rice. The Chinese word for rice means "good grain of life"; in many parts of the Far East, the word for rice is the same as that for life, food, or agriculture. Reaching Japan during the second century B.C., rice became so important in feudal times that a man's holdings were ranked not according to their acreage, but according to the amount of rice they produced, and samurai were paid in rice. Rice is now widely cultivated throughout the world in areas with warm climates and abundant water. It is difficult for Westerners, who eat less than twenty pounds of rice annually, to appreciate all the many subtleties of rice in Asia, where it plays a central rather than a supporting role in cuisine. Among the varieties present in Song dynasty China were: pink rice, white rice, yellow rice, mature rice, and winter rice, each with its own unique characteristics, and some with an almost flower-like fragrance. For many in the Far East, rice provides half the daily caloric intake, and up to four hundred pounds per person may be eaten annually.

Rice came to the United States in 1693, when a ship bound for England from Madagascar was blown off course by a severe storm, forcing it to dock at Charleston, South Carolina. To pay for repairs and emergency supplies, the captain of the ship gave the colony's governor several bags of seed rice. Henry Woodward, described as one of the founders of the Carolinas, planted it in his own garden in dry soil, where it died. Lord Ashley, a member of the London proprietary board for the Carolinas, later sent a hundred-pound bag of seed rice and perhaps some instructions for planting. By the year 1700, rice was Carolina's leading export. In 1784, seventeen years before he entered the White House, Thomas Jefferson served as American Minister to France, where his most urgent task was to establish an export market for American goods. French interest could be aroused in only one product—rice from the plantations of Carolina and Georgia. However, there was a small problem in that during the Revolution, the British occupying Charleston and Savannah had shipped all of America's rice, including seed stocks, to England; now, with no seed available, none could be produced for the French market. While wrestling with his dilemma, Jefferson learned of the existence of a new and improved Italian strain of rice; he also learned that to prevent its cultivation by competing nations Italy had prohibited its export, imposing harsh penalties for violators. Undaunted, he went to Italy, somehow obtained two sacks of the grain, and smuggled out his contraband successfully. Jefferson's illicit rice soon revitalized America's languishing rice plantations.

Rice is covered with an inedible husk that has to be removed before eating, a task presently done commercially with rubber rollers. Beneath the hull lays another layer,

Rice

Nutritional Value Per 100 g Edible Portion

	Raw Brown Long-Grain	Cooked Brown Long-Grain	Raw Brown Medium-Grain	Cooked Brown Medium-Grain
Calories	370	111	362	112
Protein	7.94 g	2.58 g	7.50 g	2.32 g
Fat	2.92 g	0.90 g	2.68 g	0.83 g
Fiber	1.32 g	0.34 g	0.95 g	0.29 g
Calcium	23 mg	10 mg	33 mg	10 mg
Iron	1.47 mg	0.42 mg	1.80 mg	0.53 mg
Magnesium	143 mg	43 mg	143 mg	44 mg
Phosphorus	333 mg	83 mg	264 mg	77 mg
Potassium	223 mg	43 mg	268 mg	79 mg
Sodium	7 mg	5 mg	4 mg	1 mg
Zinc	2.020 mg	0.630 mg	2.020 mg	0.620 mg
Copper	0.277 mg	0.100 mg	0.277 mg	0.081 mg
Manganese	3.743 mg	0.905 mg	3.743 mg	1.097 mg
Thiamine (B_1)	0.401 mg	0.096 mg	0.413 mg	0.102 mg
Riboflavin (B_2)	0.093 mg	0.025 mg	0.043 mg	0.012 mg
Niacin (B_3)	5.091 mg	1.528 mg	4.308 mg	1.330 mg
Pantothenic Acid (B_5)	1.493 mg	0.285 mg	1.493 mg	0.392 mg
Pyridoxine (B_6)	0.509 mg	0.145 mg	0.509 mg	0.149 mg
Folic Acid (B_9)	20 mcg	4 mcg	20 mcg	4 mcg
Tocopherol (E)	0.680 mg	n/a	0.680 mg	n/a

Lore and Legend

Since rice is such an important staple, it has always served as an emblem of happiness, nourishment, and fecundity. The Chinese considered it a gift direct from heaven, and in the annual ceremony of sowing five kinds of seeds (rice, wheat, barley, millet, and soybeans), instituted by the Emperor Shen-nung or Chin-nong in 2800 B.C., rice plays the principal part; the reigning emperor himself must sow it, whereas the four other species may be sown by the princes of his family. Being a symbol of fertility, it was used to pelt newlywed couples in order to bring them good luck and assure them many children; this custom still exists today in many countries. Upsetting a rice bowl was said to be an omen of great ill fortune, and to deliberately overturn someone else's bowl was the greatest insult to that person and his family. In Malayan tradition, rice has a soul similar to humans and is presided over by the great Rice Mother; flowering rice is therefore treated with the great consideration and respect accorded a pregnant woman, and no sudden or loud noises are allowed in its vicinity for fear that it should take fright and miscarry. In Japan there is a special deity, Inari the rice-bearer, whose shrines dot the rural landscape. The most popular folk festival, the Hatsuuma, is held before these shrines on the 12th of February, to pray for a good crop of rice.

similar to the bran in wheat, which contains 10 percent of the protein, 85 percent of the fat, 70 percent of the minerals, and a large amount of the B vitamins. This layer is left on for whole-grain (or brown) rice, while for processed (or white) rice it is removed; its removal helps the rice cook faster, but also results in the loss of important fiber, vitamins, and minerals. While brown rice is an excellent food, white processed rice is nothing but raw starch, an item already superfluous in the American diet.

Culinary Uses Rice dishes run the gamut from basic to elaborate. Plain steamed or simmered rice is, of course, a fine accompaniment to most any meal. Rice is so versatile that it should be experimented with—make risotto, pilaf, pudding, or eat it as a breakfast cereal. All cooked rice is an excellent addition to bread doughs. "A meal without rice," according to one Chinese saying, "is like a beautiful girl with only one eye." In the Philippines you can stuff your guests with food, but if there is no rice it is not considered that you have offered them a meal.

Health Benefits Rice is said to calm the nervous system, relieve mental depression, and strengthen the internal organs. Although lower in protein than many other cereal grains, its protein level is still good because it contains relatively high levels of the amino acid lysine.

Varieties

Long-grain rice accounts for 75 percent of the U.S. domestic crop. These slender grains are four to five times longer than they are wide. If properly cooked, they will be dry, light, and fluffy, with separate grains. This is the type most often used in Indian cooking. Long-grain rice is richer in the starch amylose, which helps render a dry, fluffy cooked product. **Medium-grain** rice is popular in Asian and Latin American cultures, and is the type most commonly processed to make cold cereals. About twice as long as it is wide, it cooks up moister and tenderer than long-grain varieties. **Short-grain** rice is a popular feature of Asian cuisine. This variety may be almost oval or round in shape, and upon cooking tends to have a stickier, softer texture than its counterparts. Of the three types of rice, short-grain has the highest percentage of amylopectin, the starch that makes rice sticky, or clump together when cooked. This makes it easy to eat with chopsticks, and ideal for dishes like sushi.

Arborio rice is a popular short-grain rice imported mainly from the Po Valley region of Italy. This favorite of Italian cuisine is a starchy, nearly round, white rice, with a translucent outer portion and opaque center. Arborio absorbs up to five times its weight in liquid as it cooks, yielding a firm, creamy product with an al dente consistency and lots of flavor. Traditionally used for cooking the Italian dish *risotto,* it also works well for paella and rice pudding.

Basmati is a long-grain rice named after the tropical basmati blossom of southeast Asia. This aromatic variety is also available in Calmati and Texmati varieties, grown respectively in California and Texas. Generally, basmati rice is aged for at least a year after harvest in order to fully develop its nutty flavor. Unlike other types of rice, the grains elongate more than they plump as they cook, and because it is lower in starch than other long-grain types, basmati turns out flaky and separate. Fluffy, light, with an aroma of buttered peanuts, and very popular in cooking, basmati comes in both brown and white versions.

Brown rice is the whole rice kernel from which only the outer hull has been removed, and is available in three sizes: short-, medium- and long-grain. It has a richer, chewier texture than white rice, and a sweet nutty flavor. Because it has not been highly processed, brown rice is the only form of the grain that contains vitamin E and retains most of its B vitamins. If the long cooking time is intimidating, there are also quick-cooking and instant forms sold. Brown rice is subject to rancidity within one to three months after milling. Storage is advised at under 40°F for any bulk quantities that will not be used within one month.

Glutinous white rice is a short-grained rice popular in Japan and other Asian countries. Very sticky, chewy, and resilient, this starchy grain turns translucent when cooked and can be formed into balls, without added ingredients, or used in the preparation of sushi. See also Sweet Brown Rice.

Golden Rose brown rice is a medium-grain brown rice with the nutty flavor of a short-grain and fluffy texture of a long-grain. It is very versatile and can be used interchangeably with other varieties.

Rice

Nutritional Value Per 100 g Edible Portion

	Raw White Enriched Medium-Grain	Cooked White Enriched Medium-Grain	Cooked White Enriched Short-Grain	Cooked White Glutinous
Calories	360	130	130	97
Protein	6.61 g	2.38 g	2.36 g	2.02 g
Fat	0.58 g	0.21 g	0.19 g	0.19 g
Fiber	0.26 g	0.09 g	0.10 g	0.07 g
Calcium	9 mg	3 mg	1 mg	2 mg
Iron	4.36 mg	1.49 mg	1.46 mg	0.14 mg
Magnesium	35 mg	13 mg	8 mg	5 mg
Phosphorus	108 mg	37 mg	33 mg	8 mg
Potassium	86 mg	29 mg	26 mg	10 mg
Sodium	1 mg	0 mg	0 mg	5 mg
Zinc	1.160 mg	0.420 mg	0.400 mg	0.410 mg
Copper	0.110 mg	0.038 mg	0.072 mg	0.049 mg
Manganese	1.100 mg	0.377 mg	0.357 mg	0.262 mg
Thiamine (B_1)	0.578 mg	0.167 mg	0.164 mg	0.020 mg
Riboflavin (B_2)	0.048 mg	0.016 mg	0.016 mg	0.013 mg
Niacin (B_3)	5.093 mg	1.835 mg	1.493 mg	0.290 mg
Pantothenic Acid (B_5)	1.342 mg	0.411 mg	0.397 mg	0.215 mg
Pyridoxine (B_6)	0.145 mg	0.050 mg	0.059 mg	0.026 mg
Folic Acid (B_9)	9 mcg	2 mcg	2 mcg	1 mcg

Instant white rice is a medium-grain white rice that has been milled and polished, fully cooked, and then dehydrated. Much less nutritious than brown rice, and lacking the satisfying texture of regular white rice, it takes about five minutes to prepare.

Japonica, or **Thai black rice,** is a deep purple long-grain rice from Thailand. Though grown in Thailand for centuries, it is among the newest novelty imports to become available. Unlike most varieties of long-grain rice, Japonica rice is quite sticky and shiny, with a grass-like flavor, and in Thailand is usually used for making desserts. Another unusual aspect is that its dark colored bran dissolves when cooked and imparts the dark color both to the water and the whole grain.

Jasmine rice is a long-grain white rice grown in the southern United States and Thailand. Popular in southeast Asian cuisine, this rice is soft and slightly sticky, very white, delicately flavored, and aromatic. Very similar in flavor to basmati, Jasmine rice can easily be substituted for both the domestic and imported varieties.

Parboiled (converted) rice is a medium-grain rice that is steamed (or boiled) and pressurized before milling. The steaming process forces about 70 percent of the nutrients from the hull, bran, and germ back into the starchy part of the grain; when milled into white rice, then, the biggest loss is that most of the fiber is forfeited. The term "parboiled" is slightly misleading; the rice is not pre-cooked, and is actually somewhat harder than regular rice. More nutritious than regular white rice, and taking longer to cook, the grains will be very fluffy and separate.

Pudding rice is a variety that can be either black or white. Used mainly in China and Japan, it becomes sticky and sweet when boiled, and is therefore used mainly in baking and confectionery.

Red rice or **Christmas rice** is a short-grain russet-brown rice similar in color to Wehani, and with an unusual wild mushroom-like flavor. This strain is now being grown domestically in California by the Lundberg family.

Sweet brown rice is a short-grain rice that is a favorite among children, and esteemed for its warming and strengthening properties. It has a sweet flavor, sticky texture, and is ideal for making sushi or the Japanese delicacy *mochi*. Roasted and ground, it makes an unusually tasty and easily digested hot breakfast cereal; ground into flour it is marvelous in baked goods, gravies, and pancakes.

Wehani rice is a plump, long-grain reddish-brown rice developed by the Lundberg brothers, California farmers who pioneered the cultivation of organic rice, and is named after its developers—Wendell, Eldon, Homer, Albert, and Harlan Lundberg. It has a chewy texture and earthy aroma (smelling distinctly like popping corn), and tastes very much like a slightly stronger flavored, sticky, short-grain brown rice. The water it is cooked in will turn mahogany from the color in the bran and stain the whole grain.

White rice is produced by stripping off the outer brown layer of bran, leaving a pure white starchy carbohydrate. Most of the vitamins, minerals, and fiber are lost during this process, and without its natural outer protective layer, the central core of carbohydrate is exposed to

Rice

Nutritional Value Per 100 g Edible Portion

	Raw White Unenriched Long-Grain	Cooked White Enriched Long-Grain	Parboiled Cooked White Enriched Long-Grain	Instant Cooked White Enriched Long-Grain
Calories	365	129	114	98
Protein	7.13 g	2.69 g	2.29 g	2.06 g
Fat	0.66 g	0.28 g	0.27 g	0.16 g
Fiber	0.30 g	0.10 g	0.17 g	0.10 g
Calcium	28 mg	11 mg	19 mg	8 mg
Iron	0.80 mg	1.10 mg	1.13 mg	0.63 mg
Magnesium	25 mg	13 mg	12 mg	5 mg
Phosphorus	115 mg	47 mg	42 mg	14 mg
Potassium	115 mg	39 mg	37 mg	4 mg
Sodium	5 mg	2 mg	3 mg	3 mg
Zinc	1.090 mg	0.460 mg	0.310 mg	0.240 mg
Copper	0.220 mg	0.063 mg	0.094 mg	0.065 mg
Manganese	1.088 mg	0.467 mg	0.260 mg	0.235 mg
Thiamine (B_1)	0.070 mg	0.163 mg	0.250 mg	0.075 mg
Riboflavin (B_2)	0.049 mg	0.013 mg	0.018 mg	0.046 mg
Niacin (B_3)	1.600 mg	1.476 mg	1.400 mg	0.880 mg
Pantothenic Acid (B_5)	1.014 mg	0.390 mg	0.324 mg	0.178 mg
Pyridoxine (B_6)	0.164 mg	0.093 mg	0.019 mg	0.010 mg
Folic Acid (B_9)	8 mcg	3 mcg	4 mcg	4 mcg
Tocopherol (E)	0.110 mg	n/a	n/a	n/a

molds, bacteria, and insects. To prevent loss from spoilage, some manufacturers coat the rice with an outer layer of talc and glucose (sugar). Talc is the amorphous form of the same substance that asbestos consists of, and talc used for coating rice is often contaminated with large numbers of actual asbestos fibers. When ingested, asbestos fibers are suspected of causing various cancers. Package recommendations to wash the rice before using are futile, because even after nine thorough washings some talc remains. Talc-coated rice is sold mostly in Hawaii, California, and Puerto Rico.

Wild pecan rice is a rather exotic sounding long-grain variety that was developed by Louisiana State University and that is grown only in the Acadian bayou country of southern Louisiana. A cross between a Louisiana long-grain rice and several species of Indochina aromatic rices, it is a rather sticky, dark brown rice that is gently milled to retain most of the bran, and that has a taste slightly evocative of the pecan nut.

Byproducts

Amasake is made by introducing koji enzymes (*Aspergillus oryzae*) from fermented rice into whole-grain cooked sweet rice, and then incubating the whole mixture. The enzymes convert the complex carbohydrates of the rice into simple sugars, mainly maltose and glucose, much like malting barley. Made for hundreds of years by the Japanese, in the summer this refreshingly sweet beverage was served cool, while in the winter it was served hot with grated ginger. Amasake is sold as either a plain or flavored beverage. Imported amasake is thicker and richer than the domestic varieties, more like rice pudding. It can be drunk as is, used as a dessert, a leavener in baking, as a natural sweetening agent, baby food, or salad dressing, and makes great kefir and smoothies. Frozen amasake makes excellent ice cream. Because amasake is a fermented food, it is readily digestible, and aids in the digestion of other foods.

Brown rice syrup is prepared by adding dried sprouted barley or barley enzymes to cooked whole-grain rice and fermenting the mixture until the malt enzymes convert some of the rice starch into glucose (about 3 percent) and maltose (about 45 percent). This liquid is then cooked until it thickens to a syrupy consistency. Syrups made from organic brown rice have a slight butterscotch flavor. It adds a subtle and mild, rather than bold, sweetness to cooked or baked products, and has only about two-thirds the sweetening power of white sugar, one-half that of maple syrup, and one-third that of honey. Because brown rice syrup is high in complex carbohydrates it enters the bloodstream slowly, and can

Rice

Nutritional Value Per 100 g Edible Portion

	Raw Rice Bran	Raw Rice Polish	Cooked Rice Cream	Brown Rice Flour	White Rice Flour
Calories	316	265	50	363	366
Protein	13.35 g	12.1 g	0.8 g	7.23 g	5.95 g
Fat	20.85 g	12.8 g	trace	2.78 g	1.42 g
Fiber	11.5 g	2.4 g	trace	1.29 g	0.80 g
Calcium	57 mg	69 mg	2 mg	11 mg	10 mg
Iron	18.54 mg	16.1 mg	0.7 mg	1.98 mg	0.35 mg
Magnesium	781 mg	n/a	n/a	112 mg	35 mg
Phosphorus	1677 mg	1106 mg	13 mg	337 mg	98 mg
Potassium	1485 mg	714 mg	trace	289 mg	76 mg
Sodium	5 mg	trace	176 mg	8 mg	0 mg
Zinc	6.040 mg	n/a	n/a	2.450 mg	0.800 mg
Copper	0.728 mg	n/a	n/a	0.230 mg	0.130 mg
Manganese	14.210 mg	n/a	n/a	4.013 mg	1.200 mg
Thiamine (B_1)	2.753 mg	1.840 mg	0.060 mg	0.443 mg	0.138 mg
Riboflavin (B_2)	0.284 mg	0.180 mg	0.010 mg	0.080 mg	0.021 mg
Niacin (B_3)	33.995 mg	28.200 mg	0.800 mg	6.340 mg	2.590 mg
Pantothenic Acid (B_5)	7.390 mg	n/a	n/a	1.591 mg	0.819 mg
Pyridoxine (B_6)	4.070 mg	n/a	n/a	0.736 mg	0.436 mg
Folic Acid (B_9)	63 mcg	n/a	n/a	16 mcg	4 mcg

be considered a balanced sweetener that will not upset blood-sugar levels. Very easy to digest, it is also hypoallergenic and contains no fructose or sucrose. Made from only slightly polished whole grain rice, it contains all the nutritional benefits of the rice. Rice syrup has a powdered counterpart, made by pulverizing crystals prepared from the liquid; these crystals will dissolve readily in liquid.

Puffed rice is made by puffing the rice under pressure, thus filling the grains with air. Puffed rice makes an excellent cold breakfast cereal, and can also be used for making cakes and candy.

Rice bran is made from the outer layer of the rice kernel that contains the bran and a small part of the germ. We owe its existence to the fact that the majority of people in North America eat refined white rice, the processing of which leaves a rich "waste" bran. Nearly twice as high in soluble dietary fiber as oat bran, it can be used the same way: sprinkled on cereal, or used in baking cookies, breads, or muffins.

Rice cream is a roasted brown rice flour that is generally used for making a cooked breakfast cereal, pudding, or thick broth. You can make your own by toasting brown rice in a heavy frying pan, then grinding it to a powder in a blender, and re-roasting it over medium heat.

Rice flakes are made either from brown and/or white rice that is heated and pressed flat under pressure, much the same way as rolled oats, but a bit thicker. These can be used to make a variety of mueslis, cooked breakfast cereals, or can be included in breads and other baked goods.

Rice flour is a gluten-free flour made from primarily brown rice; this sweet, slightly gummy flour has a crystalline appearance and contains a wide range of vitamins and minerals. It is most successfully used when combined in low ratios with other flours. Adding brown rice flour to baked goods usually results in a drier product, but imparts a lively, seedlike flavor. Excellent for pie crusts, breads, crackers, noodles, cakes, and biscuits, this flour is also used as a thickening agent, as well as for dusting bread dough, because it absorbs moisture slowly, drying the dough's surface without adhering to it.

Rice grits are coarsely ground brown rice grains that are good for quick hot cereals, puddings, or wherever the fluffy texture of whole rice is not required.

Rice polish is the inner bran layers, as well as small parts of the germ taken off the rice during the process of making white rice. With its high vitamin and mineral content, it gives a nutritional boost when added to other products. Use as you would rice bran or wheat germ.

Rizcous is a pre-cooked cracked rice that may be used interchangeably with bulgur wheat or couscous.

Rice, Wild *(Zizania aquatica)*

Zizania is an old Greek name for a weed, probably the darnel, that grows among wheat. Aquatica simply means aquatic.

General Information Wild rice is neither a rice nor a grain, but the seed of an aquatic grass native to the Great Lakes region that is cooked and used like a grain. This tall, tubular, reedy aquatic grass grows four to eight feet above the water line, in swamps and along

Rice, Wild

Nutritional Value Per 100 g Edible Portion

	Raw	Cooked
Calories	357	101
Protein	14.73 g	3.99 g
Fat	1.08 g	0.34 g
Fiber	1.44 g	0.33 g
Calcium	21 mg	3 mg
Iron	1.96 mg	0.60 mg
Magnesium	177 mg	32 mg
Phosphorus	433 mg	82 mg
Potassium	427 mg	101 mg
Sodium	7 mg	3 mg
Zinc	5.960 mg	1.340 mg
Copper	0.524 mg	0.121 mg
Manganese	1.329 mg	0.282 mg
Beta Carotene (A)	19 IU	0 IU
Thiamine (B_1)	0.115 mg	0.052 mg
Riboflavin (B_2)	0.262 mg	0.087 mg
Niacin (B_3)	6.733 mg	1.287 mg
Pantothenic Acid (B_5)	1.074 mg	0.154 mg
Pyridoxine (B_6)	0.391 mg	0.135 mg
Folic Acid (B_9)	95 mcg	26 mcg

the borders of streams in shallow water. The slender grains are nearly three-quarters of an inch long, round, and almost black, and fall soon after ripening. About 40 percent of the harvesting is still done by hand in the traditional manner by Native Americans in canoes. The rest is cultivated in man-made paddies and machine-harvested, with California being the largest producer. Hand-harvested rice is immediately parched over open fires, giving it a variety of distinct matte colors from a ruddy red-brown to a subtle gray-green. Paddy rice is left to cure (and slightly ferment) out in the weather for several weeks after harvesting, where it will develop the characteristic shiny, dark kernels and distinctive taste. It is then heated, which gelatinizes the starch and deepens the coloring. Labels usually note if the rice is hand-harvested or cultivated, but the color will tell you immediately how it was grown.

Lore and Legend

In the Chippewa region of the Great Lakes, wild rice is called *manomin* by the Native Americans, meaning "gift from the Creator."

Culinary Uses There are three grades of wild rice: 1) "Select," which contains short broken grains; 2) "Extra-fancy," which has uniform half-inch-long grains and is the most common variety available; and 3) "Giant," the most expensive, with grains that are uniformly one inch in length. All grades can be used interchangeably in recipes. Known as the "gourmet grain," it has actually been a staple in the Chippewa and Sioux Indian diets for centuries. Each brand of wild rice has its own particular taste, so if you have experienced some very strong or bitter types, experiment with other brands. If you find the chewy, nutty, smoky flavor of wild rice too strong on its own, use it in combination with other rices to mellow the strong woodsy flavor, or use the more delicately flavored hand-harvested varieties. Properly cooked wild rice will split and be fluffy. It is frequently used in pilafs or soups, salads and stuffings, or when precooked makes an excellent addition to yeast breads, muffins, and pancakes; even the addition of a small amount imparts its distinctive character to other ingredients. The hulled seeds can be eaten raw as a snack, but few people probably eat wild rice this way.

Byproducts

Wild rice flour is good in baked goods, pancakes, waffles, or muffins, where it adds its distinctive nutty flavor.

Rye *(Secale cereale)*

Secale *is an ancient Latin name, said to be derived from* seco, *meaning to cut;* cereale *means pertaining to Ceres (the Roman goddess of agriculture) or agriculture itself. The English word* rye *derives its origin from the Lithuanian* rugys.

General Information Rye is a large herbaceous annual plant whose stalks can grow to more than three feet in height, and seems to have developed from a wild species of northeastern European grain. A feisty, scrappy survivor that is able to sustain itself in severe climates, it was cultivated early on by inhabitants in the colder regions of western Asia and in the mountainous northern regions of Europe. For the rest of Europe and the Mediterranean, rye was a rather late bloomer; the Egyptians and Sumerians did not include it among their range of crops, and the ancient Greeks and Turks considered it only an intrusive and obnoxious weed. Rye was widely distributed throughout Europe during the Middle Ages and taken to Britain by the Saxons in 500 A.D. The basic bread of medieval Britain consisted of coarsely ground rye and pea flours, sometimes with a little barley flour mixed in. For poorer folk in much of Europe during the Middle Ages, this cereal grain was a staple, and is still consumed in much of eastern Europe and Russia. Rye gained favor in Russia because it was able to tolerate the severe climate better than other grains, and rye bread is still a common sight on tables throughout that region. It probably came to North America with the Dutch, German, and French settlers, the French first planting it in seventeenth-century Nova Scotia. The popularity of rye spread throughout the West as the frontier was pushed to the Pacific Ocean, not because the pioneers thought so highly of black bread, but because rye whiskey has always been one of the largest uses for this grain in America. Of the world's cereal crop, rye makes up only about 1 percent, and its popularity is only now starting to revive after a long decline.

Rye has from time to time made spectacular appearances on the stage of history because of its greatest weakness—its susceptibility to ergot, which rarely appears in any other cereal. Ergot is a parasitic fungus, *Claviceps purpurea,* that forms hornlike, purplish-black masses that are easily identified in the grain and, when found, are separated out before processing. The fungus is highly toxic to humans, and provokes uncontrollable muscular contractions. One of the principal poisons (out of a possible 20) of ergot is ergotamine. When ergotamine gets into flour, and the flour is made into dough and baked, the poison is transformed into lysergic acid diethylamide, or LSD. During the Middle Ages, ergot was responsible for frequent epidemics of what was called Holy Fire or Saint Anthony's Fire—a condition characterized by various effects, from violent manifestations that led to death, to milder reactions, which may not have been perceived as having been provoked by any external agent: deafness, dimming eyesight, or psychotic disorders, including hallucination. Frequently there was a loss of blood flow to the extremities, resulting in intense pain and eventually gangrene. Ergot also causes miscarriage, and medieval women used ergot to provoke abortions (it is still being used for this purpose in some areas today).

Culinary Uses Rye is slenderer than wheat, has blue-gray overtones, and a strong, full, robust and tangy flavor. Due to this hearty flavor, rye has been used mainly in breads such as rye bread, the well-known Scandinavian crispbread

Rye

Nutritional Value Per 100 g Edible Portion

	Whole Grain	Dark Flour	Medium Flour	Light Flour
Calories	335	324	354	367
Protein	14.76 g	14.03 g	9.39 g	8.39 g
Fat	2.5 g	2.69 g	1.77 g	1.36 g
Fiber	1.50 g	1.46 g	1.40 g	1.30 g
Calcium	33 mg	56 mg	24 mg	21 mg
Iron	2.67 mg	6.45 mg	2.12 mg	1.80 mg
Magnesium	121 mg	248 mg	75 mg	70 mg
Phosphorus	374 mg	632 mg	207 mg	194 mg
Potassium	264 mg	730 mg	340 mg	233 mg
Sodium	6 mg	1 mg	3 mg	2 mg
Zinc	3.730 mg	5.620 mg	1.990 mg	1.750 mg
Copper	0.450 mg	0.750 mg	0.287 mg	0.250 mg
Manganese	2.680 mg	6.730 mg	5.460 mg	1.970 mg
Thiamine (B_1)	n/a	0.316 mg	0.287 mg	0.331 mg
Riboflavin (B_2)	n/a	0.251 mg	0.114 mg	0.090 mg
Niacin (B_3)	n/a	4.270 mg	1.727 mg	0.800 mg
Pantothenic Acid (B_5)	n/a	1.456 mg	0.492 mg	0.665 mg
Pyridoxine (B_6)	0.294 mg	0.443 mg	0.268 mg	0.234 mg
Folic Acid (B_9)	n/a	60 mcg	19 mcg	22 mcg
Tocopherol (E)	1.280 mg	1.410 mg	0.790 mg	0.430 mg

and in drinks such as whisky in America, gin in Holland, and beer in Russia. Available in whole, cracked, flake, and flour forms, the grain is very versatile and has a wide range of uses: try simmering rye berries with either wheat berries or brown rice; combine cracked rye with cracked wheat; and cook rye flakes in combination with oatmeal. Or enjoy rye's distinctive flavor on its own, using the berries in wheat-berry recipes, cracked rye in cracked-wheat recipes, and rye flakes in oatmeal dishes. The flour is used to make the dark heavy "black bread" which, despite the fact that many people affect to dislike it, stays fresh longer than wheaten bread, has more taste, and is very filling. It is lower in gluten content than wheat, and thus is well suited to making pastries, in which the development of gluten would produce toughness. On the other hand, it is more difficult to work into a loaf that will rise nicely.

Health Benefits Rye is said to build muscles and promote energy and endurance. It also cleans and renews arteries; aids fingernail, hair, and bone formation; and benefits the liver. Rye possesses the power to reenergize anemic bodies and rebuild the entire digestive system through its high carbohydrate content and its richness in nitrogenous matter. Eaten in its raw, sprouted state or as soaked flakes rye provides fluorine, which increases tooth enamel strength. Rye fiber supplies a rich source of noncellulose polysaccharides, with a high water-binding capacity. By binding water in the intestinal tract, rye breads give the sensation of fullness. Of all the grains, rye has the highest percentage of the essential amino acid lysine. Rye breads are gently laxative, and help prevent arteriosclerosis.

Byproducts

Cracked rye or **Rye cereal** is made of whole rye berries that have been broken or ground into small pieces. It can be cooked for a hot breakfast cereal, combined with cracked wheat or rolled oats for variety, or added to soups.

Rye berries are the whole kernels with just the outer husks removed. Rye berries can be sprouted and used in soups, salads, or breads; unsprouted, they can be used for the same dishes, or cooked like rice.

Rye flakes are whole grains that have been heated until soft, then pressed and rolled between high-pressure rollers, and lightly toasted. The flakes look very similar to rolled oats, but are slightly thicker. Rye flakes can be cooked and eaten as a hearty breakfast cereal, are excellent added to breads and muffins, and are frequently used as a meat extender in meat loaves or as a thickener for soups.

Rye flour is sweet and tangy rather than sour. Whole-grain rye flour is best, then dark rye flour, and lastly light rye flour, the difference being how much bran is left in. The main ingredient in black bread, pumpernickel bread, and some crispbreads, rye flour also makes excellent pancakes. Since it has little gluten, rye flour has to be mixed with up to two-thirds wheat or other gluten-containing flour when used to make leavened breads. True pumpernickel bread is generally made from rye kernels coarsely ground into a meal, and the dough then flavored with caraway or dill seed.

Rye grits are the whole grain that has been cracked into six or eight separate pieces. It is often used as a cereal, as a main course replacement for rice or potatoes, or mixed with other grains or gluten flour for breads. They require slightly longer cooking than most other grain grits—about 45 minutes.

Rye meal is simply coarsely ground whole rye flour of the consistency of cornmeal that can be used in the same manner as regular flour. Rye meal will give the crunchy texture that is characteristic of some types of bread.

Sorghum *(Sorghum bicolor)*

The word sorghum *comes from the Latin* Syricum granum, *meaning Syrian grain.* Bicolor *means two-colored.*

General Information Grain sorghum is native to Africa and is believed by some to have been domesticated either in the savannah zone of eastern Africa, or in India. In the seventeenth and eighteen centuries, sorghum, then called guinea corn, was brought to the West Indies and the British colonies by slave ships traveling from Africa. Somewhat resembling maize in vegetative features and bearing its grain in a terminal cluster, this grain is more drought-tolerant than most cereals, and hence is of great importance in semiarid regions that will not support the growth of the major cereal plants. Widely used by people in Africa and Asia, where it is known by its Arabic name of *dourra*, only recently has grain sorghum became an important crop in the United States; grown in the southwest, it is used primarily for animal feed. The grain sorghums grown in the United States are classified into seven groups, the best of which are kafir, milo, and durra. The **kafirs** come from South Africa, and have thick, juicy stalks, large leaves, and cylindrical heads that bear white, pink, or red seeds. The **milos** are from east central Africa and have wavy leaves, less juicy stalks, and larger salmon, pink, or cream-colored seeds. The **durras,** from North Africa and the Near East, have bearded, fuzzy heads, large flat seeds, and dry stalks. Other important varieties of sorghum are the **Great** or **Turkish millet** (*S. durra, S. vulgare*), and **Sugar sorghum** (*S. saccharatum*), which is cultivated chiefly for the sugary syrup contained within the stems.

Sorghum

Nutritional Value Per 100 g Edible Portion

	Raw Whole Grain	Syrup
Calories	339	290
Protein	11.30 g	0 g
Fat	3.30 g	0 g
Fiber	2.40 g	0.10 g
Calcium	28 mg	150 mg
Iron	4.40 mg	3.80 mg
Phosphorus	287 mg	56 mg
Potassium	350 mg	1000 mg
Thiamine (B_1)	0.237 mg	0.100 mg
Riboflavin (B_2)	0.142 mg	0.155 mg
Niacin (B_3)	2.927 mg	0.100 mg

Culinary Uses The whole grains can be used much like rice, either boiled or ground into meal for bread or porridge. Sorghum flour is gluten-free, and so produces flattish bread on its own.

Spelt *(Triticum aestivum, Spelta* group)

Also Known As: Dinkel, Farro.

Linnaeus provided the genus name, choosing Triticum, *an old Latin name for cereal.* Aestivum *means summer. The English word* spelt *of is Germanic origin, possibly meaning split.*

Spelt

Nutritional Value Per 100 g Edible Portion

	Raw Whole Grain
Calories	293
Protein	12.7 g
Fat	1.98 g
Fiber	13.9 g
Calcium	6 mg
Iron	2.79 mg
Phosphorus	463 mg
Potassium	420 mg
Sodium	2 mg
Thiamine (B_1)	0.430 mg
Riboflavin (B_2)	0.110 mg
Niacin (B_3)	3.620 mg

General Information Spelt is believed to be among the most ancient of cultivated wheats. Its recorded use has been most prevalent in Europe, where its history goes back about nine thousand years. Because the plant tolerates poorly drained, low-fertility soils, it was and still is an excellent alternative to common wheat for many farmers. Throughout history, spelt remained a popular bread wheat until this century, when it was rejected by both Hitler and the "green revolution" of the 1960s, because of its bulky edible husks and because its yields were lower than modern high-yield varieties. Fortunately, it was still cultivated by enough visionary or stubbornly independent small farmers in out-of-the-way fields in Europe until its popularity

began to grow again. Part of its rise in popularity is attributed to new translations of the mystical writings of St. Hildegard of Bingen, a twelfth-century mystic who praised spelt as the grain best tolerated by the body. Widely recognized among many Europeans, this grain is now becoming familiar to American households.

Culinary Uses To the eye, spelt looks like a common grain of wheat, but in the mouth it immediately softens. Like kamut, spelt provides both the versatility and familiarity of common wheat, while delivering optimum flavor and nutrients along with a low allergenic profile. As a whole grain, it may be substituted for common wheat, and as a flour may be substituted for whole-wheat flour in cookies, sauces, and baked goods. It is an excellent bread wheat, making a satisfying and fine-textured bread.

Health Benefits Spelt's high water solubility equates with "bio-availability," meaning that the nutrients dissolve rapidly in liquid and become readily available to the body with only a minimum of digestive work. Because it is not a hybridized grain, it is generally higher in protein, vitamins, and minerals than common wheat. Although spelt contains gluten, those with gluten sensitivity can usually tolerate it.

T'ef/Teff (*Eragrostis tef, E. abyssinica*)

Eragrostis *comes either from the Greek* eros, *meaning love, or* er, *meaning spring, combined with* agrostis, *which means grass;* abyssinica *means coming from Abyssinia. The name* t'ef *literally translates from the Ethiopian Amharic word* teffa *as lost, due to the fact that much of the tiny seed disappears when handled and cannot be found if dropped.*

General Information T'ef originated at the source of the Blue Nile in the rugged, windswept African alps. As with many other grains, this grain was a foraged wild grass that eventually became cultivated. There are now more than two thousand individual strains of this important fine-bladed cereal grass, varying from short to tall and from compact to spreading in form. The historically fierce and proud Ethiopians attribute their prowess to this iron-rich and iron-colored grain; other grains, easier to cultivate and harvest, thrive in Abyssinia, but for millennia t'ef has been their premier crop. It is also cultivated for hay in Kenya and Australia, and the straw is still used to make adobe in Ethiopia. Only twice the size of the period at the end of this sentence, with 150 grains equal in weight to one single kernel of wheat, t'ef's miniscule size makes harvesting difficult. Like other heirloom plants, t'ef is not monochromatic—its seeds may be white, red-purple, or brown. It is a superb garden ornamental, with its silvery stalks and brightly colored heads.

T'ef

Nutritional Value Per 100 g Edible Portion

	Raw Whole Grain
Calories	328
Protein	9.6 g
Fat	2.6 g
Fiber	2.7 g
Calcium	172 mg
Iron	75.5 mg
Phosphorus	313 mg
Beta Carotene (A)	5 mg
Thiamine (B_1)	0.130 mg
Riboflavin (B_2)	0.120 mg
Niacin (B_3)	1.400 mg

Culinary Uses Because of its excellent nutrition and pleasing flavor, t'ef is no longer an ethnic secret. It is available in three colors—white, red, or brown—each with its own distinctly pleasant flavor. The mild white t'ef has an almost chestnut-like flavor, while the darker colors are more earthy, with a taste like hazelnuts. Whole-grain t'ef can be cooked into a tasty breakfast porridge, with the darker grains giving a rich rustic flavor and the white more of a delicate creamy cereal. It can also be added to soups or stews, where it will burst open and provide body and flavor if cooked for at least thirty minutes; it is not well suited to pilafs and salads, as it will give more of a gritty texture than desired. T'ef flour can be mixed in combination with any other grain to impart its light pleasing flavor (although it will add some grittiness). It is unique in that it has its own symbiotic yeast, similar to grapes, which remains through harvesting and milling. Because of this intrinsic yeast, t'ef is an ideal starter for naturally leavened bread; add pure water to t'ef flour, and within an hour it will start to bubble and ferment. For a naturally leavened bread, mix one cup of t'ef flour with one-and-a-half cups of water, cover, and allow to stand at room temperature for a day. This fermented mixture can then be substituted for sourdough starter in bread. By itself, t'ef flour is best suited for flatbreads, quick breads, and dessert breads.

Health Benefits The overall nutrition of this small grain is outstanding. The reason t'ef is packed with nutrients is because it is so tiny that it has proportionally more hull (pericarp) than other grains; this outer layer is nutritionally superior to the inner layer. Plus, its tiny size makes it impractical to hull or degerm, so the entire grain is milled, which leaves all the nutrients intact. T'ef is lower in manganese than other cereals, but more than compensates with its higher mineral content, which includes iron, calcium, copper, and zinc. The darker varieties are higher in iron than the white, while the white tends to be higher in protein. Also important is its low allergenic profile, with initial reports indicating that most people suffering from wheat and corn allergies may safely eat t'ef.

Lore and Legend

T'ef was introduced to the United States by an Idaho farmer, Wayne Carlson, who was in Ethiopia working on a medical research project. He developed a taste for the native staple, a spongy fermented flatbread called *injera*, and when he returned to Idaho found himself hungering for this unusual grain. Since none was available, he imported seed and today t'ef is grown commercially in the high desert volcanic fields of Idaho and distributed through natural foods stores.

Byproducts

T'ef flour is a granular rather than starchy flour that is highly versatile and lends itself well to numerous dishes. Because of its symbiotic yeast, it is unsuitable on its own for most leavened breads (combine it with wheat or other gluten-containing flour only up to 20 percent), although this property makes it excellent as a substitute for sourdough starters. T'ef flour may be substituted for wheat flour in many cookie, sauce, pancake, muffin, and quick bread recipes. The white variety is lighter and more suited to cakes and pastries than the darker varieties. T'ef flour is easily made at home in a grain, coffee, or nut mill.

Triticale (*Triticum secale*)

This grain started its life as a hybrid between wheat and rye, and the name reflects this: Triticum *being the Latin genus for wheat, while* secale *is the genus for rye. The English name* triticale *is a contraction of the two names.*

General Information Triticale is a cereal grain developed in 1875 by Swedish researchers by cross-breeding several different species of durum wheat, hard red winter wheat, and rye, to combine the high lysine content and ruggedness of rye with the overall high protein content of wheat. The few seeds produced from the first hybrid plant were sterile, but in 1937 a French researcher succeeded in producing a fertile cross, and triticale became the first human-engineered grain in history. Subsequent research during the 1950s led to significant improvements; triticale as we now know it is twice as large and heavy as wheat, and in some field tests the plant has yielded nearly twice as much grain. Considered by its

Triticale

Nutritional Value Per 100 g Edible Portion

	Raw, Whole Grain	Whole Grain Flour
Calories	336	338
Protein	13.05 g	13.18 g
Fat	2.09 g	1.81 g
Fiber	2.60 g	1.50 g
Calcium	37 mg	35 mg
Iron	2.57 mg	2.59 mg
Magnesium	130 mg	153 mg
Phosphorus	358 mg	321 mg
Potassium	332 mg	466 mg
Sodium	5 mg	2 mg
Zinc	3.450 mg	2.660 mg
Copper	0.457 mg	0.559 mg
Manganese	3.210 mg	4.185 mg
Thiamine (B_1)	0.416 mg	0.378 mg
Riboflavin (B_2)	0.134 mg	0.132 mg
Niacin (B_3)	1.430 mg	2.860 mg
Pantothenic Acid (B_5)	1.323 mg	2.167 mg
Pyridoxine (B_6)	0.138 mg	0.403 mg
Folic Acid (B_9)	73 mcg	74 mcg
Tocopherol (E)	0.900 mg	0.200 mg

developers to be "science's gift to the world," it gained some popularity during the 1970s but then waned, and is only now regaining some of its former appeal.

Culinary Uses Triticale's flavor is richer and more nutlike than that of wheat, without the assertiveness of rye. If available, buy the whole grain and sprout it, and then enjoy the chewy texture on its own as a snack, or add the sprouts (best when no longer than the grain itself) to salads, casseroles, brown rice dishes, or soups. The whole grains can also be cooked like rice, with a resultant flavor resembling whole wheat and pecans. The flour contains enough gluten to be used alone as a bread flour, or when used in combination with other flours adds its distinctive flavor.

Health Benefits Triticale is slightly higher in lysine than wheat, and depending on growing conditions its protein content ranges from 13 to 20 percent.

Byproducts

Cracked triticale is the coarsely ground whole kernel. Like any processed grain, it has a shorter cooking time than the whole grain. You can make your own cracked triticale by processing whole kernels in a blender until they are coarsely ground. Cracked triticale can be used in any manner as cracked wheat.

Triticale flakes are the berries that have been steamed and flattened, much like rolled oats. The flakes can be used in the same manner as oat flakes, but have a slightly longer cooking time.

Triticale flour is a nutritious, sweet-tasting flour that gives a pleasingly nutty and slightly ryelike flavor to bread. Although it has enough gluten to be used on its own, for the best texture and leavening abilities, it is best used in combination with wheat flours. Leavened triticale bread will only stand gentle kneading and one rising is sufficient. The flour can also be used in quick breads, cookies, and pancakes.

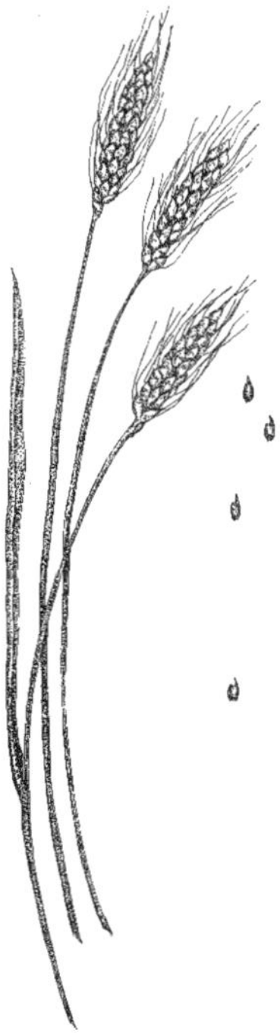

Wheat *(Triticum)*

Linnaeus provided the genus name, choosing Triticum*, an old Latin name for cereal. The English name* wheat *appears to have two derivatives, the Sanskrit* sveta *and the Old English* hwaete*, both meaning white, and thus distinguishing this grain from the other, darker cereals with which the Germanic races were familiar.*

General Information Wheat dates back thousands of years in Chinese and Egyptian records. There is evidence of wheat cultivation in the Middle East as early as ten thousand years ago. By 4000 B.C. it was growing in the Indus and Euphrates valleys, by 2500 B.C. in China, by 2000 B.C. in Europe west to England. Of paramount importance to Rome, it has been suggested that many of her initial overseas conquests were undertaken in order to obtain areas most favorable to the cultivation of wheat, in particular Sicily and Sardinia, Carthaginian Africa, and Egypt. The invasions of northern Germanic peoples into Europe largely displaced wheat and replaced it with their preferred rye. As Europe emerged from the Dark Ages, wheaten bread regained its popularity, but was largely restricted to the rich who could afford it; the poor had to make do with various mixtures of grains, leguminous plants, and nuts to make bread flour. Only during the nineteenth century did wheaten bread become commonly accessible for all.

There was no wheat in North America when the white man came, nor was there any rye, oats, barley, or millet. In 1493, Columbus planted wheat in the West Indies "to prove the soil." Spanish ships took the grain to Mexico, and by 1687 wheat was widely grown in the vice-royalty of New Spain. Almost all American colonists brought wheat with them from Europe. As the country expanded beyond the Appalachians, wheat went with the pioneers. By the mid-nineteenth century wheat was well established in what would later become America's grain belt. In 1898 the United States Department of Agriculture sent Mark Carleton to Russia to find a spring wheat to complement the sole crop of winter wheat. The result of his visit was the introduction to the United States of durum wheat, the hardest-kerneled of all wheat, which was rust-resistant and adapted to dry conditions. Due to our current preference for white bread, wheat is the world's most widely distributed and cultivated cereal grain, and is grown in nearly every country. For many cultures, wheat has replaced the more traditional (and often more nutritious) grains of corn, buckwheat, rye, barley, quinoa, t'ef, and millet as the staple grain. More wheat is produced in the United States than anywhere else in the world, but the greatest part of that is consumed in highly refined forms.

Culinary Uses For most of the ten thousand years that wheat has been cultivated, the grain has been used as it is harvested, or ground into various grades of flour, mixed with water, and cooked to produce one of the many kinds of bread that are staples the world over.

Health Benefits Wheat tends to stimulate the liver to cleanse itself of toxins. This cleansing may be experienced as an "allergy" if there is an abundance of toxins stored there; once the liver has regained its healthful state, wheat consumption does not generally produce any reaction. This relatively recent phenomenon of wheat allergy is due partly to its being consumed in so highly refined a form. Many people have found that it is the commercial highly-processed wheat they are allergic to, but not organically grown wheat used in its whole-grain form. Other heirloom varieties of wheat such as kamut and spelt also seem to cause fewer allergic reactions. As well, those with allergies to wheat or other cereals are almost never allergic to them in their grass or sprouted stage. Whole wheat is the most nutritious, since the nutritious bran and germ are left intact. Whole wheat also contains traces of barium and vanadium, both essential to the health of the heart. Refined wheat has been stripped of both bran and germ, losing as much as 80 percent of its vitamins and minerals and 93 percent of its fiber. So-called "enriched" white bread, which has had all of its original vitamins and minerals removed, has nothing left but raw starch of such little nutritive value that even most bacteria will not voluntarily eat it. Into this insipid starch synthetic chemicals are added, which form only part of the missing vitamin B complex, and are not properly ingestible by humans because they are not properly balanced. Naturally leavened breads are easier to digest, since they contain lactobacillus essential to the proper digestion of complex carbohydrates, and contain no phytic acid, which has been tied to anemia, rickets, and nervous disorders. They are also believed to be cancer inhibitors, whereas yeasted breads explode the starch cells of the bread, creating cell patterns and bioelectrical energy identical to cancer cells.

In India, where wheat has been a major part of the diet for many thousands of years, the ancient medical traditions have ascribed it special and unique properties. It is said to be particularly prone to produce growth, thus being especially suitable as a food for growing children. It is also prescribed for convalescents, but traditional Indian physicians are wary of its growth-producing tendency in adults and suspect it of aggravating the tendency to develop cysts and other benign growths and tumors in the body. Wheat is also especially good at helping put on extra pounds, even when they are not wanted.

This traditional "staff of life" is now consumed in such gluttonous amounts that most everybody overconsumes it. In many families wheat in some form is served three times a day at meals and then snacked on in between, culminating in a habit of eating bread with almost everything we eat. This excludes other important foods, and wheat becomes more of a poison than a benefit to the body. In excess, wheat robs calcium

Wheat

Nutritional Value Per 100 g Edible Portion

	Hard Red Spring Wheat	Hard Red Winter Wheat	Soft Red Winter Wheat
Calories	329	327	331
Protein	15.40 g	12.61 g	10.35 g
Fat	1.92 g	1.54 g	1.56 g
Fiber	2.28 g	2.29 g	1.72 g
Calcium	25 mg	29 mg	27 mg
Iron	3.60 mg	3.19 mg	3.21 mg
Magnesium	124 mg	126 mg	126 mg
Phosphorus	332 mg	288 mg	493 mg
Potassium	340 mg	363 mg	397 mg
Sodium	2 mg	2 mg	2 mg
Zinc	2.780 mg	2.650 mg	2.630 mg
Copper	0.410 mg	0.434 mg	0.450 mg
Manganese	4.055 mg	3.985 mg	4.391 mg
Thiamine (B_1)	0.504 mg	0.383 mg	0.394 mg
Riboflavin (B_2)	0.110 mg	0.115 mg	0.096 mg
Niacin (B_3)	5.710 mg	5.464 mg	4.800 mg
Pantothenic Acid (B_5)	0.935 mg	0.954 mg	0.850 mg
Pyridoxine (B_6)	0.336 mg	0.300 mg	0.272 mg
Folic Acid (B_9)	43 mcg	38 mcg	41 mcg
Ascorbic Acid (C)	0 mg	0 mg	0 mg
Tocopherol (E)	1.01 mg	1.01 mg	1.01 mg

Wheat

Nutritional Value Per 100 g Edible Portion

	Hard White Wheat	Soft White Wheat	Durum Wheat
Calories	342	340	339
Protein	11.31 g	10.69 g	13.68 g
Fat	1.71 g	1.99 g	2.47 g
Fiber	n/a	n/a	n/a
Calcium	32 mg	34 mg	34 mg
Iron	4.56 mg	5.37 mg	3.52 mg
Magnesium	93 mg	90 mg	144 mg
Phosphorus	355 mg	402 mg	508 mg
Potassium	432 mg	435 mg	431 mg
Sodium	n/a	n/a	2 mg
Zinc	3.330 mg	3.460 mg	4.160 mg
Copper	0.363 mg	0.426 mg	0.553 mg
Manganese	3.821 mg	3.406 mg	3.012 mg
Thiamine (B_1)	0.387 mg	0.410 mg	0.419 mg
Riboflavin (B_2)	0.108 mg	0.107 mg	0.121 mg
Niacin (B_3)	4.381 mg	4.766 mg	6.738 mg
Pantothenic Acid (B_5)	n/a	n/a	n/a
Pyridoxine (B_6)	0.368	0.378	0.419
Folic Acid (B_9)	n/a	n/a	n/a
Ascorbic Acid (C)	0 mg	0 mg	0 mg
Tocopherol (E)	1.01 mg	1.01 mg	1.01 mg

from the body. Wheat is also the most acid-forming of the cereals.

Varieties of Wheat

There are literally thousands of varieties of wheat grown around the world, with some agronomists counting as many as thirty thousand, but many of these varieties have declined in popularity and are restricted to cattle feed. The most common species grown and distributed are **Common wheat** (*T. vulgare*), **Winter** or **Lammas wheat** (*T. hybernum*), **Spring** or **Summer wheat** (*T. aestivum*), and **Durum wheat** (*T. durum*).

Common wheat is primarily milled into flour to be used in breads and cakes. Of the common wheat varieties, there are sub-species including **Hard wheat, Soft wheat, Red** or **White wheats, Spring** and **Winter wheats.**

Durum wheat (from the Latin *durus*, meaning hard or tough) is a hard spring wheat that was crossed with a wild cereal called oat grass thousands of years ago. Of desert ancestry, durum wheat is famous for its ability to thrive despite hardships, and has for millenia been the most important food crop produced in most Mediterranean countries. The most esteemed durums have jewel-like, near-transparent kernels that are a lustrous, beautiful, amber-yellow color. Durum wheat makes especially excellent pasta due to its hard starch granules, which stick together.

Hard wheat is a bronze-colored wheat with a high gluten content that is used for bread. It is the gluten (from the protein in the starchy center—the endosperm—of the grain) that imparts the elastic and tenacious consistency to dough and allows the leavening and rising process. Color and growing season also are indicative of gluten content: **Red wheats** tend to be higher in gluten than **White wheats,** and **Spring wheats** are generally higher in gluten than **Winter wheats.** Hard spring wheat is a fast-growing wheat cultivated where the winters are severe; it is sown in the spring and harvested in the fall, and is the wheat of choice for bread making. Hard winter wheat is cultivated where winters are mild; it is sown in the fall, at which time it germinates, but then lies dormant through the winter and starts growing again in the spring. Harvested in the late spring or early summer, winter wheat is normally higher in minerals because it has a longer growing season, and thus establishes a more extensive root system.

Soft wheat is a light golden color and is often called white wheat. With more starch and less gluten than hard wheat, it is less suited to bread making, the fluffier grains being better suited to cakes, pastries, desserts, and sauces. As with hard wheat, soft wheat may be either a winter or spring variety.

Byproducts

Bulgur, also known as **Wheat pilaf,** is made from wheat berries that have been pearled (the bran removed), steamed, dried, and then cracked into a variety of textures. This process yields a quicker-cooking, lighter-textured, and nuttier-flavored dish than does cracked or whole wheat. The difference between bulgur and cracked wheat is that cracked wheat is simply wheat that has been cracked but not yet cooked, while bulgur has been cooked; bulgur wheat will be uniform in color, while cracked wheat will have a lighter colored interior. Bulgur originated in the Middle East, where it is a dietary staple much like rice in Asia and kasha in Russia. Since conservation of fuel was and still is of great importance, large quantities of wheat berries were processed into bulgur, then cooked quickly in small batches for daily consumption. The original method was to roast it in open braziers, dry it in the sun, then crack it with a mortar and pestle. Today the methods have been mechanized, but the basic process remains similar. Dark bulgur has a slightly stronger taste and is made from hard red wheat, while white bulgur is made from soft white wheat and has a more delicate flavor. When cooked, bulgur swells to a fluffy texture similar in appearance to couscous, and the two can often be used interchangeably. It is the main ingredient in the Lebanese dish tabbouleh, and can be used in salads, pilafs, casseroles, stuffings, and bread doughs.

Couscous is the steamed, dried, and cracked grains of durum wheat, using only the inner starchy endosperm (although a whole wheat couscous is now available). More refined than bulgur, it has a pale creamy color, pleasant light texture, and pasta-like flavor when cooked. It is the main ingredient of the North African dish of the same name, but it is also delicious serve with vegetable stew, used in place of rice, mixed with vegetables or salad ingredients, or made into desserts and cakes. The nutri-

Wheat

Nutritional Value Per 100 g Edible Portion

	Raw Bran	Raw Germ	Toasted Germ	Sprouted
Calories	216	360	382	198
Protein	15.55 g	23.15 g	29.10 g	7.49 g
Fat	4.25 g	9.72 g	10.70 g	1.27 g
Fiber	7.19 g	2.82 g	2.30 g	n/a
Calcium	73 mg	39 mg	45 mg	28 mg
Iron	10.57 mg	6.26 mg	9.09 mg	2.14 mg
Magnesium	611 mg	239 mg	320 mg	82 mg
Phosphorus	1013 mg	842 mg	1146 mg	200 mg
Potassium	1182 mg	892 mg	947 mg	169 mg
Sodium	2 mg	12 mg	4 mg	16 mg
Zinc	7.270 mg	12.290 mg	16.670 mg	1.650 mg
Copper	0.998 mg	0.796 mg	0.620 mg	0.261 mg
Manganese	11.500 mg	13.301 mg	19.956 mg	1.858 mg
Beta Carotene (A)	n/a	n/a	n/a	66,000 IU*
Thiamine (B_1)	0.523 mg	1.882 mg	1.670 mg	0.225 mg
Riboflavin (B_2)	0.577 mg	0.499 mg	0.820 mg	0.155 mg
Niacin (B_3)	13.578 mg	6.813 mg	5.590 mg	3.087 mg
Pantothenic Acid (B_5)	2.181 mg	2.257 mg	1.387 mg	0.947 mg
Pyridoxine (B_6)	1.303 mg	1.300 mg	0.978 mg	0.265 mg
Folic Acid (B_9)	79 mcg	281 mcg	352 mcg	n/a
Ascorbic Acid (C)	0 mg	0 mg	6 mg	2.600 mg
Tocopherol (E)	1.490 mg	14.07 mg	n/a	n/a

* Dried grass

tional benefits of couscous are similar to any refined pasta product. The name is derived from an Arabic word meaning to pulverize or crush.

Cracked wheat consists of whole wheat berries that are machine-cracked into coarse or medium granulation. Not to be confused with bulgur, cracked wheat has a white interior, while bulgur (because it is cooked) has a uniform coloring. Cracked wheat has an agreeably wheaty flavor and can replace rice or other grains in most recipes; baked or boiled, it makes an excellent substitute for rice with its fairly sticky texture and slight crunchiness. It also makes a popular breakfast cereal, and is good added to casseroles, soups, breads, or substituted for bulgur in tabbouleh and other main dishes. For better flavor and greater nutritional value, purchase whole wheat and coarsely grind it yourself at home in a flour mill or blender, rather than purchasing the commercial variety.

Diastatic malt To make diastatic malt, sprout wheat berries until the sprouts are the same length as the grain, about two days. Drain well, spread in thin layers on large baking sheets, and dry in an oven at 150°F maximum for about eight hours. The dried sprouts can then be ground into a meal that keeps indefinitely in a tightly closed glass jar stored either in the refrigerator or freezer. The malt helps you bake loaves of bread without adding some sort of sweetener. The action of the malt enzymes on the yeast and flour improves the flavor and appearance of a loaf of bread, and in addition gives it a finer texture and helps it stay fresh longer. Use only one tablespoon for a batch of dough yielding three or four loaves of bread; too much will make bread overly sweet, dark, and sticky.

Farina is also known as **Cream of wheat,** and can be made from either the whole grain minus the hull, or from simply the inner starchy endosperm. Looking like minuscule white pellets, farina is generally used as a hot breakfast cereal, and can also be used for desserts and dumplings.

Gluten is the protein found principally in wheat. When made into a dough, this protein becomes glutenous (elastic) and traps gas bubbles released from the yeast; in fact, without gluten, yeast cannot perform its leavening function. Some people are allergic to gluten and so use the gluten-free grains, which are amaranth, corn, millet, quinoa, and rice. Most professional bakers and many home bakers add the pale yellow gluten flour to their bread dough. The addition of just 5 to 10 percent gluten flour significantly increases a dough's leavening power, which corresponds to a higher, lighter loaf. Unlike whole-grain flours, gluten has an indefinite shelf life because its germ has been refined away.

Green wheat berries are the kernels of wheat picked while still green and unripe, and then dried. They have a grassy flavor and are commonly used for casseroles, soups, stews, pilafs, and can also be ground into flour.

Seitan is made from whole-wheat flour that is mixed with water, kneaded, and rinsed to remove the starch and some bran until a glutenous dough is obtained. After boiling in water, this dough is called **kofu,** which can be further processed into many forms, just one of which is seitan; by simmering it in a stock of tamari soy sauce, water and kombu sea vegetable, the dough becomes seitan. Seitan typically comes in small tubs of margarine size. The thick brown paste can be used in sandwiches or as a meat substitute in cooked dishes. Seitan, monosodium glutamate (MSG), and other gluten products should be avoided by people who are sensitive to them.

Wheat berries are the whole grain, which can be cooked and eaten like rice, sprouted into wheat grass, or ground into flour. Available in either hard or soft wheat varieties, cooked whole wheat berries provide more jaw exercise than other grains, and are thus rarely eaten whole.

Wheat bran accounts for about 15 percent of the wheat kernel, and is composed of six fibrous protective outer layers of the grain. A by-product of white flour production, wheat bran is relatively rich in nutrients but less so than wheat germ. Typically added to provide bulk and fiber for the deficient American diet, it is used in breakfast cereals, casseroles, and baked goods. It is highly recommended as a natural cure for constipation. Better than just adding the bran, however, would be to remove refined products from the diet and substitute whole-grain versions.

Wheat flakes, also known as **Rolled wheat,** are wheat berries that have been heated and pressed in the same manner as rolled oats. The flakes are quick-cooking and can be used as a hot breakfast cereal, for muesli, or added to baked goods.

Wheat germ is the heart of the wheat, the embryo from which the new plant grows. Although it comprises only 2 to 3 percent of the whole wheat berry, it is nutritionally the richest part, being a rich source of protein, vitamin B complex and E, phosphorus, iron, and magnesium. Wheat germ is one of the very few places in nature in which the entire vitamin B complex is found. Widely available as a waste product from the milling of white flour, it comes either raw or toasted. Raw wheat germ goes rancid within 72 hours from the point of milling, even faster if it is not refrigerated. Rancidity occurs because most wheat germ is rolled into flakes, which breaks open the sac containing the wheat germ oil and exposes it to air. Since vitamin E is an antioxidant, there is a brief grace period. But you can be almost certain that if the wheat germ flakes were not vacuum packed within the day they were rolled, they will be rancid. Most people have not tasted fresh sweet raw wheat germ, since most of that sold in stores is not of highest quality. The best way to buy wheat germ is to buy it in the unrolled form, variously known as

Wheat

Nutritional Value Per 100 g Edible Portion

	Dry Whole-Grain Bulgur	Cooked Whole-Grain Bulgur	Dry Couscous	Cooked Couscous
Calories	342	83	376	112
Protein	12.29 g	3.08 g	12.76 g	3.79 g
Fat	1.33 g	0.24 g	0.64 g	0.16 g
Fiber	1.78 g	0.35 g	0.58 g	0.14 g
Calcium	35 mg	10 mg	24 mg	8 mg
Iron	2.46 mg	0.96 mg	1.08 mg	0.38 mg
Magnesium	164 mg	32 mg	44 mg	8 mg
Phosphorus	300 mg	40 mg	170 mg	22 mg
Potassium	410 mg	68 mg	166 mg	58 mg
Sodium	17 mg	5 mg	10 mg	5 mg
Zinc	1.930 mg	0.570 mg	0.830 mg	0.260 mg
Copper	0.335 mg	0.075 mg	0.247 mg	0.041 mg
Manganese	3.048 mg	0.609 mg	0.780 mg	0.084 mg
Thiamine (B_1)	0.232 mg	0.057 mg	0.163 mg	0.063 mg
Riboflavin (B_2)	0.115 mg	0.028 mg	0.078 mg	0.027 mg
Niacin (B_3)	5.114 mg	1.000 mg	3.490 mg	0.983 mg
Pantothenic Acid (B_5)	1.045 mg	0.344 mg	1.243 mg	0.371 mg
Pyridoxine (B_6)	0.342 mg	0.083 mg	0.110 mg	0.051 mg
Folic Acid (B_9)	27 mcg	18 mcg	20 mcg	15 mcg
Ascorbic Acid (C)	0 mg	0 mg	0 mg	0 mg
Tocopherol (E)	0.060 mg	n/a	n/a	n/a

"embryo," "chunk," or "unflaked" wheat germ, but this type is hard to find. Thus it is better to buy the lightly toasted kind which, although it may have slightly fewer nutrients, is still beneficial in the diet and has a pleasant nutty flavor. Wheat germ has traditionally been added to cereals, fruit, and in breads. The best way to get wheat germ, however, is to eat the whole grain itself, or whole grain products.

Wheat germ oil An extract of the heart of the wheat berry, wheat germ oil is generally consumed not as a cooking or salad oil but as a dietary supplement. Wheat germ oil goes rancid rapidly once the bottle is opened (within a week). Not only are all the beneficial vitamins, including the all-important vitamin E, destroyed when wheat germ oil turns rancid, but the harmful chemicals created in the oil by the process of oxidation can cause many serious health disorders on their own, including cancer. Perhaps the best way to consume wheat germ oil is by consuming the whole wheat kernel in its natural form. Quality wheat germ oil is rich in inositol, which enhances the metabolism of fats, thereby reducing the excretory burden on skin; it contains pyridoxine, which enhances peristalsis and improves digestion and assimilation of nutrients and elimination of wastes; contains octacosanol, which protects the heart and improves heart function; and is high in vitamin E content, offering twice as much if not more vitamin E than any other common vegetable oil. Consuming wheat germ oil between meals or when the stomach is empty will allow the nutrients to be better utilized and less affected by any rancid fats that may be present in the digestive tract. Wheat germ oil is 18.80 percent saturated, 15.10 percent monosaturated, and 61.70 percent polyunsaturated. It also contains significant amounts of zinc and vitamin E (3.80 mg and 149.40 mg per 100 grams of oil, respectively).

Wheat grass is wheat that has been sprouted to the point where it resembles grass. Young grass less than four days old may be finely cut and added to salads or blended with other foods. When adding to cooked foods, it should be added just before serving and not cooked with the food. Older grass can be chewed to extract the juice and the pulp spit out, or juiced in a special grinder. Wheat grass has been known for centuries for its healing qualities and as a blood detoxifier and purifier. It is a very active solvent that works directly on the liver to release old medicines, drugs, nicotine, chemicals from food, and other toxins, and stimulates the liver's rejuvenation abilities; it is very alkalinizing to the bowel and soothing to ulcers, cuts, and abrasions of all kinds, both inside and out. Wheat grass efficiently neutralizes the toxicity of sodium fluoride, which is used in the fluoridation of tap water (and as a rat poison). It may be taken internally, used as a wash for throat and eyes, or as a topical application (scalp tonic, cleanser). Chlorophyll makes up nearly 70 percent of the plant's solid content and is its most important nutrient; nearly identical to human blood, chlorophyll differs only in that it uses magnesium as a bond instead of iron. Wheat grass contains virtually a full selection of minerals, vitamins, enzymes, and protein. It can also contain trace amounts of vitamin B_{12}. If grown in rich soil, it can pick up more than ninety minerals out of the estimated possible 102. Cereal grasses offer unique digestive enzymes not available in such concentration in other foods, enzymes that help resolve indigestible and toxic substances in food. Also present are the antioxidant enzyme superoxide dismutase (SOD) and the special fraction P4D1, both of which slow cellular deterioration and mutation and are therefore useful in the treatment of degenerative disease and in the reversal of aging. P4D1 also has anti-inflammatory properties. People with allergies to wheat or other cereals are almost never allergic to them in their grass stage. Wheat grass is especially rich in selenium, potassium, calcium, magnesium, zinc, and vitamins A and E.

Wheat grass juice is an extract made from cut wheat grass, juiced in a special wheat grass press. The flavor has been described as so sweet that it borders on astringency, and is one that few people claim to enjoy. The juice can be mixed with other juices, or is also available in tablet form.

Varieties of Flour

FLOUR IS A SOFT, DRY POWDER THAT IS USUALLY GROUND FROM GRAIN, though it can also be made from vegetables, fruits, legumes, or nuts. Wheat flours are available in many forms, most of which are high in gluten and excellent for bread-making and general baking. The refining of flour can drastically change the content and proportion of vitamins, minerals, protein, and even in some cases, toxic contaminants. When whole wheat is milled into white flour, 83 percent of the nutrients are removed, leaving a product that is so useless as a food that it must be fortified with synthetic vitamins. While some people disdain whole-wheat flour products because they are denser, others prefer them because of their hearty, full-bodied flavor. White flour on its own has little or no flavor, and relies on other ingredients for flavor. A naturally leavened bread made of fresh, stone-ground whole-wheat flour, pure water, and sea salt is incomparable in texture and flavor to any other bread. It has multiple nuances of flavor and is fundamentally satisfying. Stone-ground flour is the highest quality available, since the oil in the germ is distributed evenly through-

Wheat Flour

Nutritional Value Per 100 g Edible Portion

	Whole Wheat	Enriched White Bread	Enriched White Cake	All-purpose Enriched White	Enriched Semolina
Calories	339	361	362	364	360
Protein	13.70 g	11.98 g	8.20 g	10.33 g	12.68 g
Fat	1.87 g	1.66 g	0.86 g	0.98 g	1.05 g
Fiber	2.10 g	n/a	n/a	0.25 g	n/a
Calcium	34 mg	15 mg	14 mg	15 mg	17 mg
Iron	3.88 mg	4.41 mg	7.32 mg	4.64 mg	4.36 mg
Magnesium	138 mg	25 mg	16 mg	22 mg	47 mg
Phosphorus	346 mg	97 mg	85 mg	108 mg	136 mg
Potassium	405 mg	100 mg	105 mg	107 mg	186 mg
Sodium	5 mg	2 mg	2 mg	2 mg	1 mg
Zinc	2.930 mg	0.850 mg	0.620 mg	0.700 mg	1.050 mg
Copper	0.382 mg	0.182 mg	0.139 mg	0.144 mg	0.189 mg
Manganese	3.799 mg	0.792 mg	0.634 mg	0.682 mg	0.619 mg
Thiamine (B_1)	0.447 mg	0.812 mg	0.892 mg	0.785 mg	0.811 mg
Riboflavin (B_2)	0.215 mg	0.512 mg	0.430 mg	0.494 mg	0.571 mg
Niacin (B_3)	6.365 mg	7.554 mg	6.790 mg	5.904 mg	5.990 mg
Pantothenic Acid (B_5)	1.008 mg	n/a	0.458 mg	0.438 mg	0.580 mg
Pyridoxine (B_6)	0.341 mg	0.037 mg	0.033 mg	0.044 mg	0.103 mg
Folic Acid (B_9)	44 mcg	29 mcg	19 mcg	26 mcg	72 mcg
Tocopherol (E)	n/a	0.030 mg	0.040 mg	n/a	0.260 mg

out the flour, and the flour is not overly heated during milling, which turns the oil rancid. High-speed mills heat the flour and do not distribute the oil evenly, thus creating masses of rancid oil that flavor the flour and spoil it.

Proper storage of flour is extremely important. White flour will not deteriorate for several years even if left out in an open container. Whole-wheat or unbleached flour, however, contains all its vital nutrients and thus will not only go rancid quickly but may also attract unwanted insects. Ideally, fresh ground flour should be used within five days of milling, but it will last approximately three months refrigerated and six months to a year frozen. If the flour does become infested, you can either use as is with the extra protein, sift out the insects and eggs and then either use or freeze for later use, or throw out the offending lot.

All-purpose/Enriched flour is the ultimate result of modern milling techniques, and the flour with which most people are familiar. It is consistently fine, soft, and pure white, blends well with other ingredients, and keeps indefinitely on the shelf. Milled from the starchy endosperms of a blend of hard and soft wheat, this flour does not contain the germ or bran, which are rich in minerals, vitamins, proteins, and fiber. The freshly milled flour is slightly yellow, so to whiten it manufacturers either let the flour age naturally or speed up the process by adding up to thirty chemicals (such as benzoyl peroxide or acetone peroxide) to make it whiter, fluffier, and to improve its workability as dough. This processing gives the flour more immediate gluten-producing potential. The manufacturer may also add a number of additives, such as emulsifiers, colorings, flavorings, preservatives, and antioxidants to prolong shelf life. With the addition of three synthetic B vitamins and iron, it can be called "enriched." All-purpose flour is used for general cooking and baking purposes, but does not perform as well as other flours.

Bolted wheat flour is produced through a refining technique developed by the Romans. The ground flour was sifted through bolts of finely woven silk fabric to remove hulls and up to 50 percent of the bran and germ. The light delicate loaves that could be prepared from such sifted flour were the prerogative of the privileged classes and were considered an enviable delicacy; in fact, to serve anything but white bread on a ceremonial occasion was considered an insult. Of limited availability today, bolted flour yields a bread with a higher volume than 100 percent whole-wheat flour, and more nutritional value than white flour.

Gluten flour is a mixture of wheat flour and gluten, the proteins of wheat that remain after the starch, bran, and germ are washed from the flour. Made to contain twice the gluten strength of regular bread flour, gluten flour is used as a strengthening agent with other flours that are low in gluten-producing potential, and is frequently found in commercial wheat bread and other baked goods.

Graham flour is named after its developer, Sylvester Graham, an American physician who in the early nineteenth century was already fighting for dietary reform. He spoke out against the atrocity of worthless white bread, saying thousands of people "eat the most miserable trash that can be imagined, in the form of bread, and never seem to think that they can possibly have anything better, nor even that it is an evil to eat such vile stuff as they do." Brown in color and coarse in texture, graham flour is the whole wheat flour from winter wheat which has had the endosperm very finely ground and the bran layers and germ returned; it makes delicious if somewhat densely-textured bread, which takes longer to rise than the white variety. Commercial graham flours will often have some of the germ removed to allow for a prolonged shelf life.

Lore and Legend

Wheat has long been the symbol of prosperity, fertility, abundance, and life. All ancient fertility gods and goddesses of harvest, from the Hittite Ibritz and the Egyptian Nepri and Isis to the Greek Demeter and Roman Ceres, took wheat as one of their symbols. For it was the fertility gods and goddesses who looked after the continuance of the race both from within itself, by begetting children, and from without, in assuring that there would always be sufficient food to eat. Following mother's milk, wheat was—in the fullest sense of the word—the principal food, the veritable staff of life for people of European and Mideastern ancestry. Wheat in a sheaf, as well as being the emblem of agriculture and fertility, stands for autumn, harvest, and death. This is consistent with fertility gods of ancient myth, who died (and were resurrected) yearly for the benefit of mankind. Bearded wheat stands for faithfulness, rejuvenating fire, and the vital (including sexual) urge.

The great religious significance of bread goes back to the proud days of ancient Rome, when bread was so important that a special goddess of the ovens, Fornax, was honored each year by placing flowers over all ovens. Bakers, usually freed slaves, were not permitted to change their vocations, and their sons had to follow in their fathers' floury footsteps. For Christians, bread symbolizes the body of Christ; bread in the form of wafers plays a central role in the fundamental Christian sacrament of Holy Communion, while Christ himself said, "I am the bread of life." In Italy, each and every loaf of bread is an extension of the church wafer. Bakers cross themselves to bless the bread before closing the oven door. Leave a knife in a loaf and you have put a knife into the heart of Jesus; be prepared for bad luck. Placing a loaf upside down on the table or dropping a slice on the floor brings more bad luck. Purgatory is the punishment for wasting bread. For Jews too, bread—in the form of matzoh, an unleavened bread—has major religious significance, for it is eaten during Passover to symbolize their escape from Egyptian bondage more than three thousand years ago.

Granary flour is a blend of whole-wheat and rye flours, malted grains, and caramel. As its constituents suggest, it has a slightly sweet, malted flavor and makes excellent bread and pastry.

Matzoh meal is made by grinding matzohs, Jewish unleavened crispbreads made of wheat flour and water, into meal consistency. Of medium or fine grind, matzoh meal is used for Jewish Passover cakes, to thicken soups, and in place of flour or bread crumbs.

Panocha is a flour ground from sprouted wheat, the sprouting process converting carbohydrates into easily digestible simple sugars. Subtle yet satisfyingly sweet, panocha is a popular ingredient in Mexican holiday baked goods, and can be found in the Southwest and Latin American markets.

Self-raising flour is all-purpose white flour (see above) with additional salt, a leavening agent such as baking soda or baking powder, and an acid-releasing substance. The strength of the leavening agent deteriorates within two months, so it needs to be used immediately after purchase, especially in damp climates. Due to delays in merchandising or storing, the leavens may have already lost their potency by the time it is purchased. This flour is not recommended, since it is neither nutritious nor suitable for making breads or any leavened product; used in pastry it gives a spongy rather than flaky texture.

Semolina is a refined flour produced from the starchy inner endosperm of durum wheat. Semolina flour is not the same as semolina meal, which is a coarse-ground cereal like farina that is used in a similar manner as cornmeal. Semolina flour is most often used to make pasta and couscous, because its chemical structure allows it to retain whatever shape it is made into, and it will not dissolve when boiled. It can also be used in gnocchi, desserts, or as a tasty addition to Italian-style breads.

Unbleached wheat flour is all-purpose flour that has been spared the bleaching process, and which may or may not have some of the bran and germ added back in. For those who find 100 percent whole-wheat products too heavy, the addition of some unbleached flour will yield a lighter product. A more nutritious alternative is to buy a good quality multi-grain flour, which also yields a lighter product.

Wheat germ flour is made by finely grinding raw wheat germ; this flour is very perishable and must be kept refrigerated or frozen. It can be added to breads, cakes, and cookies, and lends a finer texture to baked goods than adding the unground wheat germ.

White flour is made strictly from the starchy endosperm, with no additional bran or germ. Because the germ is the part that decomposes most readily, omitting it from the flour greatly increases the shelf life of the product. The bran, although it is not subject to spoilage, is also removed from the flour because it makes bread heavy and dark, and interferes with the springy texture that is often desired. This flour is then bleached and treated with a multitude of chemicals to form a lighter, fluffier product. One of the substances added during the bleaching process is alloxan, which destroys the beta cells of the insulin-prod-ucing pancreas. After bleaching, white flour often has dough conditioners added that reduce the need for kneading. White flour can remain in the grocery store at room temperature almost indefinitely without becoming rancid, a boon for retailers but not for consumers. This fake food, with little or negative nutritional value, is an integral part of more than 90 percent of the baked products sold.

Whole-wheat bread flour is the finely ground grains of hard wheat kernels, where the germ, bran, and endosperm are all used. Since hard wheat contains a higher amount of gluten than soft wheat, this flour is ideal for bread making. Once milled, the oil in the wheat germ starts to oxidize and go rancid; store any whole-wheat flour in a cool dark place (preferably the refrigerator or freezer) and use within a month of milling. Flour with a bitter taste is rancid and should be discarded. The highest quality flour is stone-ground, so that the oil released from the germ is distributed evenly throughout, and not heated to extremes so that it becomes rancid.

Whole-wheat pastry flour is made from soft wheat rather than hard wheat. Because soft wheat flour is lower in gluten, it is best suited for and the preferred flour for pastries, cakes, cookies, and other delicate baked goods, although it can be mixed with hard wheat flour to make bread. This flour requires the same care as whole-wheat bread flour.

Legumes

"Let me put my faith in the bean."

— Maxine Kumin, "Shelling Jacob's Cattle Beans"

LEGUMES

Legumes

A STAPLE FOOD THROUGHOUT THE WORLD FOR THOUSANDS OF YEARS, beans are so ancient that the word frequently referred to any seed, and the original root word was probably associated with the Sanskrit verb "to eat." The dried seeds of pod-bearing plants, which include all types of beans, peas and lentils, are also known as pulses, a word that is linked to the Latin word *puls*, meaning porridge, and the Greek *poltos*, meaning poultice. Legumes add color, variety, texture, taste, and protein to the diet, so do not avoid them because of their flatulent reputation. Keep a variety on hand, but only buy a pound or so at a time so that they do not get old and tough.

In ancient times beans and lentils were associated with men and women of immense strength, and were consumed when preparing for strenuous activities. The Greeks and Romans made much use of pulses in their diet; chickpea and lupine seeds were sold hot in the streets, providing a nourishing cheap meal for the poor, and Pliny, always ready to condemn the extravagant tastes of his time, highly recommended such economical fare. Roman literature contains many references to beans, though one is left with a feeling that they were considered a food more properly fit for the proletariat. Beans have also been the staple food of armies and navies from ancient Rome to the modern juggernauts, since they store easily and are not highly perishable. The Americas have their own heritage of beans, legumes being crucial to the survival of the ancient Indians of the Americas, both North and South; their dried beans frequently saw them through the harsh winters. The history of beans in the Massachusetts Colony of Boston dates as far back as the middle of the seventeenth century, when beans were used for elections each year—white beans for a "yes" vote, black beans for "nay" or an abstention.

The notorious flatulence caused by beans stems from the fact that they are one of the most difficult foods of the vegetable realm to digest, except for nuts and vegetable oils. Because the human digestive system cannot break down some of the complex sugars (stachyose and raffinose) found in legumes, they end up intact in the large intestine, where bacteria ferment them and produce carbon dioxide and hydrogen, the two main components of gastrointestinal gas. Fortunately, you can make your beans more user-friendly by following these tips: (1) Soak the beans overnight in an appropriate amount of water. This is best done in the refrigerator, to prevent fermentation. (2) Never cook beans in their soaking water, which contains large amounts of the indigestible natural sugars. Drain the soaked beans and add fresh liquid before thorough cooking. (3) Try adding a pinch of ginger, Mexican epazote (an herb with a flavor similar to cilantro), Indian asafetida (also known as hing), or summer savory to the beans during cooking. These spices cut down on production of gas as well as add flavoring. (4) Sprout them first. Sprouting increases the protein content, decreases the starch content, and shortens the cooking time. It also helps provide more bulk and nutrition without increased cost, and the sprouting process greatly reduces the aftereffects of stomach gas. (5) Keep your meals simple. A staple dinner of rice, beans, and vegetables is less likely to cause flatulence than one which also contains bread, fruit and dairy products.

Beans help reduce blood cholesterol, control insulin and blood sugar, lower blood pressure, regulate colon functions, and prevent constipation. Nearly all peas, beans, and lentils are recommended for cleansing arteries, partly because legumes are a good source of choline, a lipotrophic agent that controls fat metabolism; choline is also a primary component of lecithin.

Aduki/Adzuki Bean *(Phaseolus angularis)*

Also Known As: Azuki, Adsuki, Asuki.

The scientific name Phaseolus *was bestowed in 39 B.C. by Calumella, who observed that the seeds look like a "small boat";* angularis *means angular or angled. The English name* aduki *comes from the Japanese name* azuki, *which means good health.*

General Information Adukis have been cultivated for millennia in China and Japan, where they are known as the "king of beans." Brought to America from Japan in 1854 by Admiral Perry, this small dark bean, about a quarter-inch long and oval in shape, looks almost too good to eat, more like a polished stone to be treasured than a mere dried bean. They are usually dark red with a thin white line down the ridge, although straw-colored, brown, and even black aduki beans can be found. Aduki imported from Japan are lightly polished to a bright sheen and are the most costly. Domestic and Chinese adukis are not polished, and as a result, have a just-noticeable gritty texture.

Culinary Uses Aduki beans can be eaten pod and all if picked young and tender. Cook them as you would snap beans. Mature shelled beans have a creamy texture and a pleasant nutty flavor. Those who follow a macrobiotic regimen use them in an endless variety of ways—alone as a vegetable, mixed with rice or other grains to give them

Aduki/Adzuki Bean

Nutritional Value Per 100 g Edible Portion

	Dried Raw	Dried Cooked
Calories	329	128
Protein	19.87 g	7.52 g
Fat	0.53 g	0.10 g
Fiber	5.26 g	2.02 g
Calcium	66 mg	28 mg
Iron	4.98 mg	2.00 mg
Magnesium	127 mg	52 mg
Phosphorus	381 mg	168 mg
Potassium	1,254 mg	532 mg
Sodium	5 mg	8 mg
Zinc	5.040 mg	1.770 mg
Copper	1.094 mg	0.298 mg
Manganese	1.730 mg	0.573 mg
Beta Carotene (A)	17 IU	6 IU
Thiamine (B_1)	0.455 mg	0.115 mg
Riboflavin (B_2)	0.220 mg	0.064 mg
Niacin (B_3)	2.630 mg	0.717 mg
Ascorbic Acid (C)	0 mg	0 mg

Lore and Legend

Since the Han Dynasty in China (206 B.C. to A.D. 220), red beans have meant good fortune because of their color and are eaten without fail on festive occasions. This tradition was adopted by the Japanese, and a steamed glutinous rice and red bean dish is consumed at birthdays, weddings, and on New Year's—at which time the bean is also scattered about the house to keep bad spirits away.

a festive pink hue, in soups, and even as pie filling. In the Orient, aduki beans are eaten fresh, dried, sprouted, mashed into a sweet candied paste, and sometimes ground into flour. Sprouted, they taste very similar to mung beans, but when cooked they are a little chewier, and require from eight to ten minutes of cooking instead of the three or four typical for mung bean sprouts. Aduki beans are also available powdered or in a paste form, which consists of mashed red beans, shortening, and sugar.

Health Benefits Adukis are one of the most digestible beans, and are reputedly healers of the kidneys.

Black-Eyed Bean/Pea (*Vigna unguiculata, V. sinensis, Dolichos unguiculatus*)

Also Known As: Black-Eyed Suzies, Cow Peas, Southern Peas, Lobia Dal, Lady Peas, Cream Peas, Brown-Eyed Peas, Crowder Peas, China Peas.

The genus Vigna *were named in honor of Dominic Vigni, a Paduan commentator on Theophrastus in the seventeenth century.* Dolichos *comes from a Greek word meaning long or racecourse. The term* unguiculatus *means clawed or claw-like;* sinensis *means of Chinese origin. Their English name comes from the fact that they have a black area known as an eye on one side.*

Black-Eyed Bean/Pea

Nutritional Value Per 100 g Edible Portion

	Fresh Raw	Fresh Cooked	Dried Raw	Dried Cooked	Canned
Calories	90	97	336	116	77
Protein	2.95 g	3.17 g	23.52 g	7.73 g	4.74 g
Fat	0.35 g	0.38 g	1.26 g	0.53 g	0.55 g
Fiber	1.80 g	1.94 g	4.58 g	2.31 g	0.68 g
Calcium	126 mg	128 mg	110 mg	24 mg	20 mg
Iron	1.10 mg	1.12 mg	8.27 mg	2.51 mg	0.97 mg
Magnesium	51 mg	52 mg	184 mg	53 mg	28 mg
Phosphorus	53 mg	51 mg	424 mg	156 mg	70 mg
Potassium	431 mg	418 mg	1,112 mg	278 mg	172 mg
Sodium	4 mg	4 mg	16 mg	4 mg	299 mg
Zinc	1.010 mg	1.030 mg	3.370 mg	1.290 mg	0.700 mg
Copper	0.130 mg	0.133 mg	0.845 mg	0.268 mg	0.117 mg
Manganese	0.560 mg	0.572 mg	1.528 mg	0.475 mg	0.283 mg
Beta Carotene (A)	817 IU	791 IU	50 IU	15 IU	13 IU
Thiamine (B_1)	0.110 mg	0.101 mg	0.853 mg	0.202 mg	0.076 mg
Riboflavin (B_2)	0.145 mg	0.148 mg	0.226 mg	0.055 mg	0.074 mg
Niacin (B_3)	1.450 mg	1.403 mg	2.075 mg	0.495 mg	0.354 mg
Pantothenic Acid (B_5)	0.151 mg	0.154 mg	1.496 mg	0.411 mg	0.190 mg
Pyridoxine (B_6)	0.067 mg	0.065 mg	0.357 mg	0.100 mg	0.045 mg
Folic Acid (B_9)	168.0 mcg	127.0 mcg	632.6 mcg	207.9 mcg	51.2 mcg
Ascorbic Acid (C)	2.5 mg	2.2 mg	1.5 mg	0.4 mg	2.70 mg

General Information Since this bean is related to the mung bean and other Chinese legumes, it is thought to have originated in China. From there it probably traveled by sea to the Arabic countries and into Africa. It reached the West Indies before the mainland of North America, probably arriving in Jamaica about 1674. When it arrived in the southern United States, the bean became known as the black-eyed pea from the black spot on one end; it is also sometimes called the blackeye bean, or simply the blackeye. Black-eyed beans are similar to small haricot beans, medium in size (about one-half inch long), creamy-white in color, slightly kidney-shaped, and plump with an irregular dark purple or black circle along the ridge of the bean.

Black-Eyed Bean/Pea

Nutritional Value Per 100 g Edible Portion	Young Pods Raw	Young Pods Cooked
Calories	44	34
Protein	3.30 g	2.60 g
Fat	0.30 g	0.30 g
Fiber	1.70 g	1.70 g
Calcium	65 mg	55 mg
Iron	1.00 mg	0.70 mg
Phosphorus	65 mg	49 mg
Potassium	215 mg	196 mg
Sodium	4 mg	3 mg
Beta Carotene (A)	1,600 IU	1,400 IU
Thiamine (B_1)	0.150 mg	0.090 mg
Riboflavin (B_2)	0.140 mg	0.090 mg
Niacin (B_3)	1.200 mg	0.800 mg
Ascorbic Acid (C)	33.0 mg	17.0 mg

Culinary Uses Very young, unripe black-eyed beans in the pod are used the same way as green beans. The adult beans are savory and robust, with a subtle, earthy, yet sweet, nutty flavor and a smooth, buttery texture. Used fresh or dried, they are excellent in salads or combined with steamed greens. They are particularly useful because they cook in about forty minutes without soaking. Black-eyed peas are the basis for the famous dish Hoppin' John, which is a mixture of black-eyed peas and rice.

Lore and Legend

Black-eyed peas, traditionally eaten on New Year's Day, are supposed to bring luck for the following year.

Broad/Fava Bean (*Vicia faba, Faba vulgaris*)

Also Known As: Horse Beans, Daffa Beans, Windsor Beans, Grosse Bohnen.

Vicia *is a classical name for the vetch family (a type of legume), and is believed to come from the Latin* vincire, *meaning to bind or twist.* Faba *comes from the Greek* phago, *meaning to eat, as this plant yields edible seeds. The specific term* vulgaris *means common. As its English name suggests, the broad bean is substantial in size.*

General Information The broad bean is considered native to the Mediterranean basin, with seeds being found in Egypt dating back to between 2400 and 2200 B.C. A large bean resembling a lima in size, it is about one-and-a-quarter inches long, of light brown color and oval shape, with a dark line running down the ridge where it is split. As a vegetable the broad bean retained its popularity in Europe not only because it could be dried and saved for eating later, but because for many centuries it was the only readily available bean. So important was it that, together with other pulses, from the early Middle Ages onward there was a death sentence for theft from open fields of beans, peas, and lentils. It has remained a favorite throughout the major continents with the exception of North America, where it is just now becoming widely available. *Ful medames* are a small variety of broad bean widely eaten in the Middle East; its white counterpart is called *ful nabed*. These smaller variety have given their name to one of Egypt's national dishes, in which they are baked with eggs, cumin, and garlic.

Culinary Uses Fresh fava beans are large, flat, and oval, with a firm creamy texture and dainty nutty taste. Young beans are quite tender, but as they mature, the skin covering the bean becomes coarser and tougher. Older beans need this coarse outer skin removed or "slipped" before they are eaten. Dried favas look like large lima beans, and have a mealy, granular texture and assertive flavor; the dried beans need long, slow cooking and their thick skins peeled before eating. Favas can be eaten on their own, in casseroles, or in salads. Served hot with melted butter, seasoned with salt and freshly ground pepper, and sprinkled with chopped parsley or basil, they are delicious. In most recipes, favas can be substituted for limas.

Health Benefits Fava beans provide similar nutritional benefits to common beans.

NOTE: Favism is a painful blood condition brought on by eating fava beans or by inhaling the pollen from the flowering plant. Evidently this is an inborn error of metabolism, a genetic defect that causes the red blood cells to rupture after the individual comes in contact with them. There is no known way to remove or inactivate the responsible substances. Favism is thought to affect up to 35 percent of some Mediterranean populations and 10 percent of American Blacks. Symptoms of favism include dizziness, nausea, and vomiting, followed by severe anemia.

Broad/Fava Bean

Nutritional Value Per 100 g Edible Portion

	Dried Raw	Dried Cooked	Canned
Calories	341	110	71
Protein	26.12 g	7.60 g	5.47 g
Fat	1.53 g	0.40 g	0.22 g
Fiber	2.97 g	0.95 g	0.42 g
Calcium	103 mg	36 mg	26 mg
Iron	6.70 mg	1.50 mg	1.00 mg
Magnesium	192 mg	43 mg	32 mg
Phosphorus	421 mg	125 mg	79 mg
Potassium	1,062 mg	268 mg	242 mg
Sodium	13 mg	5 mg	453 mg
Zinc	3.140 mg	1.010 mg	0.620 mg
Copper	0.824 mg	0.259 mg	0.109 mg
Manganese	1.626 mg	0.421 mg	0.288 mg
Beta Carotene (A)	53 IU	15 IU	10 IU
Thiamine (B_1)	0.555 mg	0.097 mg	0.020 mg
Riboflavin (B_2)	0.333 mg	0.089 mg	0.050 mg
Niacin (B_3)	2.832 mg	0.711 mg	0.960 mg
Pantothenic Acid (B_5)	0.976 mg	0.157 mg	0.119 mg
Pyridoxine (B_6)	0.366 mg	0.072 mg	0.045 mg
Folic Acid (B_9)	422.9 mcg	104.1 mcg	32.7 mcg
Ascorbic Acid (C)	1.4 mg	0.3 mg	1.8 mg

Lore and Legend

In the Greek and Roman world the broad bean was highly regarded, although there have been some very curious beliefs regarding these beans. Herodotus (*History*, II.xxxvii) recounts that the Egyptian priests regarded broad beans with horror as unclean, and Pythagoras, who imported many Egyptian elements into his religion, similarly despised them. A tenet of his doctrine of metempsychosis is that souls may transmigrate into beans after death. This may have some connection with the fact that bean feasts traditionally ended funerals, and that they figured in rites to rid households of the evil effects occasioned by the nocturnal visits of lemurs, the wandering souls of the wicked (in England, several beans were placed in graves to keep ghosts away, and if you happened to see a ghost, you were to spit a bean at it). Yet broad beans were popular enough with the layfolk, to whom they were distributed by candidates for public office at election times. The politicians were not simply currying favor, since the beans were used as voting tokens during magisterial elections. This custom was later remarked upon by Plutarch, whose proverbial dictum *abstineto a fabis* (abstain from beans) passed into English. No one is sure now whether this was an injunction to refrain from politics and bribery, or from involvement in civil affairs (a continuing of the Pythagorean and priestly prejudice), or a warning against dabbling in the supernatural, since beans have been connected not only with

Continued on next page

Lore and Legend, continued from previous page

ghosts and death but also with supernatural spirits and witches. Scottish witches, it was once believed, rode the air not on a broomstick but on a beanstalk. Since the time of the Middle Ages (and earlier in Rome at the Saturnalian festivities, the holiday that became transformed into Twelfth Night), beans were the main ingredient in the Twelfth Night Cake, which also contained honey, flour, ginger, and pepper. This was a sacred cake: one portion was for God, one for the Holy Virgin, and three for the Magi. In Rome even now, a holiday cake is baked with one fava bean hidden inside and the one who gets the piece with the bean is crowned king (or queen) of the festivities.

Chickpea *(Cicer arietinum)*

Also Known As: Garbanzo, Ceci, Gram, Kali Chana, Kabuli Chana.

Cicer *is the ancient Latin name for the vetch plant.* Arietinum *translates as ramlike, since the ancient Romans thought the bean resembled a ram's head with curling horns. The curious name of* chickpea *that English has fastened to this Asiatic legume is merely a phonetic adaptation of the original Latin* cicer *and the French* pois chiche.

Chickpea

Nutritional Value Per 100 g Edible Portion

	Dried Raw	Dried Cooked	Canned
Calories	364	164	119
Protein	19.30 g	8.86 g	4.95 g
Fat	6.04 g	2.59 g	1.14 g
Fiber	4.09 g	2.50 g	1.36 g
Calcium	105 mg	49 mg	32 mg
Iron	6.24 mg	2.89 mg	1.35 mg
Magnesium	115 mg	48 mg	29 mg
Phosphorus	366 mg	168 mg	90 mg
Potassium	875 mg	291 mg	172 mg
Sodium	24 mg	7 mg	299 mg
Zinc	3.430 mg	1.530 mg	1.060 mg
Copper	0.847 mg	0.352 mg	0.174 mg
Manganese	2.204 mg	1.030 mg	0.604 mg
Beta Carotene (A)	67 IU	27 IU	24 IU
Thiamine (B_1)	0.477 mg	0.116 mg	0.029 mg
Riboflavin (B_2)	0.212 mg	0.063 mg	0.033 mg
Niacin (B_3)	1.541 mg	0.526 mg	0.138 mg
Pantothenic Acid (B_5)	1.588 mg	0.286 mg	0.299 mg
Pyridoxine (B_6)	0.535 mg	0.139 mg	0.473 mg
Folic Acid (B_9)	556.6 mcg	172.0 mcg	66.8 mcg
Ascorbic Acid (C)	4.0 mg	1.3 mg	3.8 mg

General Information Chickpeas are said to have been first cultivated about 5000 B.C. in ancient Mesopotamia; they then migrated to the eastern Mediterranean, India, and other parts of Asia. It was introduced into Europe through Spain, where they are called **Garbanzos**. Chickpeas do not resemble garden peas at all. The short, hairy pods contain only one or two seeds instead of the usual five or more seeds of other legumes. Roughly the size and shape of small hazelnuts, these medium-sized (3/8-inch) dried peas are usually tan-colored, but there are also other varieties—red, white, black, and a small, dark brown variety known as *channa dal* (used primarily in Middle Eastern cookery). The varieties called *kali chana* or *kabuli chana* are black on the outside and cream-colored on the inside.

Culinary Uses Chickpeas have a flavor that is full-bodied, nutty, and rich, reminiscent of chestnuts with a bit of crunch. A popular legume in many parts of the world, chickpeas are very hard and need to be soaked well before long, slow cooking. They are the most important of the pulse crops in India and are made into cakes, puddings, and savory dishes. In the Middle East, one of the two most popular pureed chickpea dishes is called *humous*, a savory spread made with sesame paste, garlic, and lemon; the other is *falafel*, a ball or patty made of ground chickpeas and spices that is fried as a fritter.

> ### Lore and Legend
>
> There is a legend that the chickpea plant was cursed by the Virgin Mary because it refused to hide the Holy Family. Since the plant grows to only eighteen inches in height, the Holy Family would have had to be dwarfs to be hidden at all.

Whole cooked chickpeas, which maintain their shape, can be used in salads, casseroles, and other dishes.

Byproducts

Chickpea flour, also known as **besan**, **gram**, or **garbanzo flour,** is made from ground chickpeas; in color it resembles corn flour, but it performs more like the flour ground from millet. This high-protein flour cooks dry and powdery, almost chalky, and lends a sweet, rich chickpea flavor. Since it is gluten-free, it is used only in small quantities for leavened breads. A good thickening agent for soups and stews, it needs to be stirred vigorously to eradicate all the lumps. In India, the flour mixed with water forms a batter that is used to coat foods for frying.

Jack Bean *(Canavalia ensiformis, C. gladiata)*

Canavalia *comes from an aboriginal name for the plant.* Ensiformis *and* gladiata *both mean sword-like or sword-shaped.*

General Information Jack beans are native to the tropics of both hemispheres, and were used in Mexico as early as 3000 B.C. A prostrate trailing or twining plant, they now grow wild in the tropics of Asia and Africa and are cultivated as vegetables in Australia. Although grown mainly as a green manure or fodder crop, the seedpods are quite edible. The pods reach a length of ten to fourteen inches, with the pod walls becoming very hard and dense when ripe. The large, white, turgid beans bear a prominent seed-scar, and are packed crosswise into the pod, imbedded in a very thin, white, papery lining.

Culinary Uses Pods of jack beans make passable snap beans when not more than four to six inches long. The beans, when roasted and ground, are also said to make a suitable coffee substitute.

Health Benefits Low fat, high in fiber.

Kidney Bean Family *(Phaseolus vulgaris)*

The scientific name Phaseolus *was bestowed in 39 B.C. by Calumella, who observed that the seeds look like a "small boat." The specific term* vulgaris *means common. The bean takes its English name* kidney *from the anatomically suggestive shape and color of the seeds.*

> ### Lore and Legend
>
> The Egyptians made the kidney bean an object of sacred worship due to its close resemblance to the male testicle, and forbade its use as food. In Italy, beans are distributed among the poor on the anniversary of a death.

General Information Kidney beans are an ancient cultivar of some seven thousand years ago from southwestern Mexico, where this common bean developed into hundreds of different varieties. Spanish explorers exported it to Europe in the sixteenth century, where it and its traveling companion the potato caused an entire revolution in eating habits. In both Europe and Asia, these two vegetables have led to a growing lack of interest in whole ranges of native vegetables. The bean takes its name from its distinct kidney shape and comes in two colors: a deep reddish-brown, almost purplish in color, and also a light red variety, more amber in hue.

Culinary Uses Red kidney beans have a robust full-bodied flavor and rich, creamy texture. The skins of these red beans contain toxins that must be removed after soaking by boiling fast for 10 minutes, and then replacing this first cooking water with fresh water. Best known for their use in spicy Mexican dishes, kidney beans are also used in soups, casseroles, and salads. In the West Indies they are cooked with coconut milk, hot chilis, and herbs.

Varieties

There are now some five hundred varieties and many more sub-varieties of kidney beans.

Anasazi bean The name *anasazi* comes from a Navaho word meaning ancient ones. Cultivated in past centuries by the cliff-dwelling Anasazi Indians of the American Southwest, these beans are still grown and treasured by inhabitants of

Kidney Beans

Nutritional Value Per 100 g Edible Portion

	All Types Sprouted Raw	All Types Sprouted Cooked	Black Bean Dried Raw	Black Bean Dried Cooked	Bolita Dried Raw	Bolita Dried Cooked
Calories	29	33	341	132	343	149
Protein	4.20 g	4.83 g	21.60 g	8.86 g	20.96 g	9.06 g
Fat	0.50 g	0.58 g	1.42 g	0.54 g	1.13 g	0.49 g
Fiber	n/a	n/a	5.28 g	2.03 g	2.90 g	1.60 g
Calcium	17 mg	19 mg	123 mg	27 mg	130 mg	52 mg
Iron	0.81 mg	0.89 mg	5.02 mg	2.10 mg	6.77 mg	2.30 mg
Magnesium	21 mg	23 mg	171 mg	70 mg	182 mg	65 mg
Phosphorus	37 mg	38 mg	352 mg	140 mg	415 mg	165 mg
Potassium	187 mg	194 mg	1,483 mg	355 mg	1,464 mg	508 mg
Sodium	n/a	n/a	5 mg	1 mg	8 mg	2 mg
Zinc	n/a	n/a	3.650 mg	1.120 mg	2.550 mg	0.960 mg
Copper	n/a	n/a	0.841 mg	0.209 mg	0.810 mg	0.271 mg
Manganese	n/a	n/a	1.060 mg	0.444 mg	1.376 mg	0.548 mg
Beta Carotene (A)	2 IU	2 IU	17 IU	6 IU	0 IU	0 IU
Thiamine (B_1)	0.370 mg	0.362 mg	0.900 mg	0.244 mg	0.772 mg	0.257 mg
Riboflavin (B_2)	0.250 mg	0.273 mg	0.193 mg	0.059 mg	0.192 mg	0.063 mg
Niacin (B_3)	2.920 mg	3.024 mg	1.955 mg	0.505 mg	1.892 mg	0.570 mg
Pantothenic Acid (B_5)	n/a	n/a	0.899 mg	0.242 mg	0.997 mg	0.299 mg
Pyridoxine (B_6)	n/a	n/a	0.286 mg	0.069 mg	0.527 mg	0.175 mg
Folic Acid (B_9)	n/a	n/a	444.3 mcg	148.8 mcg	463.2 mcg	168.3 mcg
Ascorbic Acid (C)	38.7 mg	35.6 mg	0 mg	0 mg	0 mg	0 mg

that region. Generally believed to be descendants of the Jacob's Cattle bean, which they closely resemble, the beautiful mottled purple and white anasazi beans are a bit smaller and plumper, but lack the distinguishing freckles. Their rich smoky flavor combines the best of both flavor and texture of pinto and kidney beans, and may be freely substituted for either. Compared to other beans, anasazi are easier to digest, because they contain only one-fifth the complex sugars that tend to cause flatulence.

Appaloosa beans are an old legume grown in the Palouse area of eastern Washington State and northern Idaho, famed for the speckled horse of the same name. These comparatively large (3/4-inch), thinly shaped beans are a beautiful creamy white with a distinguishing black diagonal splotch. Appaloosa beans have a tender texture with a rich, earthy, mushroom flavor. Wonderful in ethnic soups and stews, they are especially receptive to seasonings like jalapeños, fresh ginger, turmeric, and cilantro.

Black beans are small, oblong, matte black beans with creamy-white ivory flesh. Also known as **Turtle beans** and ***Frijoles Negros,*** they are a staple throughout much of Latin America. These pea-sized beans have a strong, slightly sweet, earthy flavor and a soft, creamy texture. Very versatile, they make terrific chilis, bean pancakes, soups, refried beans, or work well as part of a bean salad. They are the basis for *feijoada*, Brazil's once-

Kidney Beans

Nutritional Value Per 100 g Edible Portion

	Cranberry Dried Raw	Cranberry Dried Cooked	Great Northern Dried Raw	Great Northern Dried Cooked	Navy Sprouted Raw	Navy Sprouted Cooked
Calories	335	136	339	118	67	78
Protein	23.03 g	9.34 g	21.86 g	8.33 g	6.15 g	7.07 g
Fat	1.23 g	0.46 g	1.14 g	0.45 g	0.70 g	0.81 g
Fiber	2.49 g	1.00 g	6.74 g	2.98 g	2.50 g	2.88 g
Calcium	127 mg	50 mg	175 mg	68 mg	15 mg	16 mg
Iron	5.00 mg	2.09 mg	5.47 mg	2.13 mg	1.93 mg	2.11 mg
Magnesium	156 mg	50 mg	189 mg	50 mg	101 mg	111 mg
Phosphorus	372 mg	135 mg	447 mg	165 mg	100 mg	103 mg
Potassium	1332 mg	387 mg	1387 mg	391 mg	307 mg	317 mg
Sodium	6 mg	1 mg	14 mg	2 mg	n/a	n/a
Zinc	3.630 mg	1.140 mg	2.310 mg	0.880 mg	n/a	n/a
Copper	0.794 mg	0.231 mg	0.837 mg	0.247 mg	n/a	n/a
Manganese	0.920 mg	0.370 mg	1.423 mg	0.518 mg	n/a	n/a
Beta Carotene (A)	2 IU	0 IU	3 IU	1 IU	4 IU	4 IU
Thiamine (B_1)	0.747 mg	0.210 mg	0.653 mg	0.158 mg	0.390 mg	0.381 mg
Riboflavin (B_2)	0.213 mg	0.069 mg	0.237 mg	0.059 mg	0.215 mg	0.235 mg
Niacin (B_3)	1.455 mg	0.515 mg	1.955 mg	0.681 mg	1.220 mg	1.263 mg
Pantothenic Acid (B_5)	0.748 mg	0.240 mg	1.098 mg	0.266 mg	n/a	n/a
Pyridoxine (B_6)	0.309 mg	0.081 mg	0.447 mg	0.117 mg	n/a	n/a
Folic Acid (B_9)	604.1 mcg	206.8 mcg	482.0 mcg	102.2 mcg	n/a	n/a
Ascorbic Acid (C)	0 mg	0 mg	5.3 mg	1.3 mg	18.8 mg	17.3 mg

weekly traditional national dish, as well as Cuban black bean soup with rum, and *Moros y Cristianos* (Moors and Christians), a dish of white rice and black beans.

Bolita The name *bolita* is a Spanish term meaning little ball. Also known as **Pink beans**, bolitas are obviously a relative of the pinto bean, but are highly irregular in size, shape, and color, looking as diverse as a handful of pebbles in a creek. Predominantly pink, but ranging from buff to yellow, the bolita has a sweet, rich, meaty flavor with a slightly mealy texture, and may be used interchangeably in any pinto or kidney bean recipe. They are higher in calcium and sodium than most other beans.

Calypso The English name *calypso* comes from an island nymph in Greek mythology who detained Odysseus on his journey home from Troy. A plump, nearly round, kidney-shaped bean that has a dramatic appearance, calypsos are half white and half black, with the addition of one black polka dot for emphasis; this novel bean looks as though the ancient Chinese yin and yang symbol of harmony had been imprinted on its surface. Their smooth, silky texture makes them a terrific addition to soups and stews, and they are especially well suited to Indian and American Southwestern seasonings of tomatoes and cilantro.

Kidney Beans

Nutritional Value Per 100 g Edible Portion

	Navy Dried Raw	Navy Dried Cooked	Pinto Dried Raw	Pinto Dried Cooked	Red Dried Raw	Red Dried Cooked
Calories	335	142	340	137	337	127
Protein	22.33 g	8.70 g	20.88 g	8.21 g	22.53 g	8.67 g
Fat	1.28 g	0.57 g	1.13 g	0.52 g	1.06 g	0.50 g
Fiber	5.52 g	3.14 g	6.01 g	3.02 g	6.19 g	2.81 g
Calcium	155 mg	70 mg	121 mg	48 mg	83 mg	28 mg
Iron	6.44 mg	2.48 mg	5.88 mg	2.61 mg	6.69 mg	2.94 mg
Magnesium	173 mg	59 mg	159 mg	55 mg	138 mg	45 mg
Phosphorus	443 mg	157 mg	418 mg	160 mg	406 mg	142 mg
Potassium	1,140 mg	368 mg	1,328 mg	468 mg	1,359 mg	403 mg
Sodium	14 mg	1 mg	10 mg	2 mg	12 mg	2 mg
Zinc	2.540 mg	1.060 mg	2.540 mg	1.080 mg	2.790 mg	1.070 mg
Copper	0.879 mg	0.295 mg	0.774 mg	0.257 mg	0.699 mg	0.242 mg
Manganese	1.309 mg	0.556 mg	1.130 mg	0.556 mg	1.111 mg	0.477 mg
Beta Carotene (A)	4 IU	2 IU	5 IU	2 IU	8 IU	0 IU
Thiamine (B_1)	0.645 mg	0.202 mg	0.555 mg	0.186 mg	0.608 mg	0.160 mg
Riboflavin (B_2)	0.232 mg	0.061 mg	0.238 mg	0.091 mg	0.215 mg	0.058 mg
Niacin (B_3)	2.063 mg	0.531 mg	1.446 mg	0.400 mg	2.110 mg	0.578 mg
Pantothenic Acid (B_5)	0.680 mg	0.255 mg	0.763 mg	0.285 mg	0.780 mg	0.220 mg
Pyridoxine (B_6)	0.437 mg	0.164 mg	0.443 mg	0.155 mg	0.397 mg	0.120 mg
Folic Acid (B_9)	369.7 mcg	139.9 mcg	506.3 mcg	172.0 mcg	394.1 mcg	129.6 mcg
Ascorbic Acid (C)	3.0 mg	0.9 mg	7.3 mg	2.1 mg	4.5 mg	1.2 mg
Tocopherol (E)	0.34 mg	n/a	n/a	n/a	n/a	n/a

Cannellini are a white kidney bean originally cultivated in South America, but associated with and extremely popular in central Italy, Greece, and France. These large white beans are sold in canned form and often used in Italian dishes. Their smooth, nutty flavor makes them a top choice for minestrone soup and other Mediterranean dishes.

China yellow beans, also known as **Sulphur beans**, are not native to China but are a traditional bean from Maine. This sulphur-colored bean is small and oval, and possesses a silky soft texture and mellow flavor. They are delicious simmered into a smooth puree with ginger, turmeric, and corn oil, and are excellent as a gravy for grains, pasta, or vegetables.

Cranberry beans are a dark tan bean with a pink cast and wine-colored dappling, about the same size as pinto beans. Also known as **October beans**, **Romans**, ***Borlotti***, and **Shellouts**, the pods of these beans resemble the bean itself, with wine-colored stripes on a cream background. Cranberry beans have a mealier texture than pinto beans but a sweeter, more delicate flavor. They become tender very easily and absorb aromatic spices and herbs well, but in the process of cooking lose their markings and become a solid pink color. In New England the beans, either freshly shelled or dried, are used in succotash, but they can be used in any recipe calling for kidney or pinto beans, in bean patties, or with cooked pasta, in casseroles, chilis, and soups.

European soldier beans These beans received their name from the splash of color shaped in the silhouette of a soldier standing at attention. Chalk white, kidney-shaped beans that are grown in Maine and other cool regions of North America, they are easily distinguished by their colored pattern. European soldiers are excellent in vegetable soups such as garbure or minestrone.

Flageolet The name *flageolet* is a corruption of the Latin *phaseolus* strengthened by an imagined likeness to the flute-like musical instrument of that name. A dwarf variety of the haricot, these "Rolls Royce of beans" originated in the Americas but were commercially developed in France during the 1800s. Instead of being allowed to fully mature, the young beans are removed from their pods while still a soft pale green. Delicate in flavor, color, and texture, flageolets can be eaten fresh or dried, but are best fresh, when their soft, creamy texture and delicate taste make them especially good as a vegetable or in salads. Just boil and serve with butter and freshly ground black pepper.

Great Northern beans are larger than navy beans, flattish, slightly kidney-shaped, and bright white. They have a mild flavor and creamy texture that makes them ideal in any baked bean recipe or casserole, as well as in soups and stews.

Haricot/Navy beans The French used these beans as such an integral part of the traditional meat-and-vegetable stew known as *hericoq* that they eventually took over the name as their own. While in India, Alexander the Great encountered great fields of haricot beans. He ordered his cook to prepare them and was so pleased with the result that he brought a large quantity of the beans back to Europe, where they eventually became the fare of the lower classes. The term haricot usually refers to the large white haricot, or to its smaller counterpart, the ***pearl haricot***. Both have a slightly green undertone produced by pale veining. Haricots are probably best known for their use in commercial baked beans, but are also a traditional ingredient of the French cassoulet. **Navy beans** are a smaller member of the large haricot family, sometimes referred to as pea-beans because of their size. They received their name as a result of their universal (if

Kidney Beans

Nutritional Value Per 100 g Edible Portion

	Great Northern Canned	Kidney Canned	Navy Canned	Pinto Canned
Calories	114	85	113	78
Protein	7.37 g	5.25 g	7.53 g	4.56 g
Fat	0.39 g	0.34 g	0.43 g	0.32 g
Fiber	2.27 g	0.93 g	1.86 g	1.26 g
Calcium	53 mg	24 mg	47 mg	37 mg
Iron	1.57 mg	1.26 mg	1.85 mg	1.61 mg
Magnesium	51 mg	28 mg	47 mg	27 mg
Phosphorus	136 mg	94 mg	134 mg	92 mg
Potassium	351 mg	257 mg	288 mg	301 mg
Sodium	4 mg	341 mg	448 mg	416 mg
Zinc	0.650 mg	0.550 mg	0.770 mg	0.690 mg
Copper	0.160 mg	0.150 mg	0.208 mg	0.140 mg
Manganese	0.408 mg	0.242 mg	0.375 mg	0.229 mg
Beta Carotene (A)	1 IU	0 IU	1 IU	1 IU
Thiamine (B_1)	0.143 mg	0.105 mg	0.141 mg	0.101 mg
Riboflavin (B_2)	0.060 mg	0.088 mg	0.055 mg	0.063 mg
Niacin (B_3)	0.461 mg	0.456 mg	0.487 mg	0.292 mg
Pantothenic Acid (B_5)	0.278 mg	0.150 mg	0.172 mg	0.136 mg
Pyridoxine (B_6)	0.106 mg	0.022 mg	0.103 mg	0.074 mg
Folic Acid (B_9)	81.3 mcg	50.6 mcg	62.3 mcg	60.2 mcg
Ascorbic Acid (C)	1.3 mg	1.1 mg	0.7 mg	0.7 mg

not always acceptable) appearance aboard all ships at sea, including frigates, battleships, and submarines. Some packagers do not differentiate between navy beans, pea beans, or even Great Northern beans, and thus there may be several varieties in one package. French Navy beans have a delicious bacon-like flavor and a unique silken texture.

Jacob's cattle beans Also known as **Coach dogs**, **Dalmation beans**, and **Trout beans**, these beans were named for their resemblance to the animals of the Biblical Jacob. A relatively long (5/8-inch), slim, creamy white bean with a large, dark maroon-colored splotch and tiny satellite freckles of the same color, Jacob's cattle beans have been grown in New England since colonial days and are a favorite of that region. They can be used interchangeably with Anasazi or Pinto beans, and are excellent in bean salads.

Maine yellow eyes are small oval beans with a pale gold hue and creamy texture. These beans are likely the original ingredient in Boston baked beans. They are still used today instead of black-eyed peas for the southern dish Hoppin' John, and are delicious substituted for mung beans in the Indian stewed rice and bean dish, *kitcheree*.

Pinto beans are native to India, and are the most commonly grown bean in the United States after soybeans. This highly hybridized bean is identified by its squarish blunt shape and its buff-to-pink coloring, which is splotched like a pinto pony. Even the name means painted or spotted, having derived from the Spanish *pinctus*. Pinto beans have an earthy, full-bodied flavor and a mealy texture. They are the traditional bean used for tacos and refried beans, *frijoles refritos*, in Southwestern and Mexican cooking; they are also used in chilis, soups (especially minestrone), salads, and pates. A variety known as **Rattlesnake beans** are a new hybrid, the name of which is derived from the shape and markings on the pods as well as on the beans themselves.

Lentil (*Lens culinaris esculenta, Vicia lens*)

> Lens *is the ancient name for the lentil family, while* vicia *is the classical Latin name for the vetches believed to derive from the Latin* vincire, *meaning to bind or twist. The term* culinaris *refers to the kitchen or food;* esculenta *means esculent or edible. The English word* lentil *derived from a diminutive of the Latin* lens.

General Information The lentil is a small, pea-like plant of the vetch family that produces small pods containing two lentils apiece. The plant probably originated in the Near East or Mediterranean region and still has an important dietary place there. Because of their Asian origin, many lentils are often referred to by their Indian names as types of ***dal***. Lentils were known in Egypt and India around 2000 B.C., and were eaten by the ancient Jews, as in the story of Esau, who renounced his birthright for a dish of lentils (pottage). Considered one of the most delicious and nutritious of the legumes, lentils are eaten throughout the world as an inexpensive source of protein. Consistently cheap in comparison with most other available foods, this fact has earned them the contempt of the snobbish and pretentious, being called "poor man's meat," although they have simultaneously received praise from those capable of judging foods by other criteria than price. In Catholic countries, lentils were standard Lenten fare for those who could not afford fish. The country that consumes the greatest number of lentils is India, which grows more than fifty varieties.

Culinary Uses In recent years lentils have become one of the most popular legumes, and a wide variety are used in Europe, the Middle East, India, and Africa. In the United States, red, brown, and green lentils are the most common varieties. These small, disk-shaped beans cook quickly, need no presoaking, and have a distinctive, somewhat peppery flavor. The smaller yellow and orange lentils puree very easily, which makes them use-ful in

Lentil

Nutritional Value Per 100 g Edible Portion

	Dried Raw	Dried Cooked	Sprouted Raw	Sprouted Cooked
Calories	338	116	106	101
Protein	28.06 g	9.02 g	8.96 g	8.80 g
Fat	0.96 g	0.38 g	0.55 g	0.45 g
Fiber	5.20 g	2.76 g	3.05 g	1.10 g
Calcium	51 mg	19 mg	25 mg	14 mg
Iron	9.02 mg	3.33 mg	3.21 mg	3.10 mg
Magnesium	107 mg	36 mg	37 mg	35 mg
Phosphorus	454 mg	180 mg	173 mg	153 mg
Potassium	905 mg	369 mg	322 mg	284 mg
Sodium	10 mg	2 mg	11 mg	n/a
Zinc	3.610 mg	1.270 mg	1.510 mg	1.600 mg
Copper	0.852 mg	0.251 mg	0.352 mg	0.337 mg
Manganese	1.429 mg	0.494 mg	0.506 mg	0.502 mg
Beta Carotene (A)	39 IU	8 IU	45 IU	41 IU
Thiamine (B_1)	0.475 mg	0.169 mg	0.228 mg	0.220 mg
Riboflavin (B_2)	0.245 mg	0.073 mg	0.128 mg	0.090 mg
Niacin (B_3)	2.621 mg	1.060 mg	1.128 mg	1.200 mg
Pantothenic Acid (B_5)	1.849 mg	0.638 mg	0.578 mg	0.571 mg
Pyridoxine (B_6)	0.535 mg	0.178 mg	0.190 mg	n/a
Folic Acid (B_9)	432.8 mcg	180.8 mcg	99.9 mcg	n/a
Ascorbic Acid (C)	6.2 mg	1.5 mg	16.5 mg	12.6 mg

> ## Lore and Legend
>
> The Egyptians held lentils in the highest esteem; they were served liberally to children because it was believed that the beans enlightened their minds, opened their hearts, and made them cheerful. On the other hand, the Romans felt lentils slowed the mind, and one scholar went so far as to trace their name to the Latin word *lentus*, meaning slow and sluggish. Their famed shape inspired astronomers and physicists to name their disk-shaped double convex optic glass a "lens."

soups. The others retain their shape well after cooking and can be served as a vegetable, on their own, or in casseroles and salads. Lentils play a particularly important part in Indian curries and other dishes (where they are known as *dal*).

Health Benefits Lentils are very easily digested, neutralize muscle acids, help build glands and blood, and provide a rich supply of minerals for nearly every organ, gland, and tissue in the body. They are especially good for the heart, and when pureed are soothing for those suffering from stomach ulcers and colitis.

Varieties

Brown lentils are probably the most common in the United States. Smaller and plumper than the green variety, they have a more defined earthy taste, and remain whole when cooked.

French lentils are a "Persian" strain prized for their subtle yet distinctive flavor. These tiny, plump, olive-green and slate colored beans are so heavily mottled they are almost black. They cook up firmer than most other varieties and have a slightly peppery flavor.

Green lentils are an unusual "Persian" variety grown primarily in the Northwest that are about half the size of common lentils. Very flavorful and savory, they cook to a rich, earthy brown, are tender but retain their shape, and are among the heartiest and most full-flavored of the legumes.

Puy lentils are popular in France and considered by some to be the best-flavored lentil. They retain their shape when cooked.

Lima/Butter Bean (*Phaseolus limensis, P. lunatus*)

Also Known As: Madagascar, Burma, Rangoon, Habas Grandes (large varieties); Baby Limas, Sieva Beans, Butter Beans, Civet Beans, Dixie Speckled Butter Beans, Florida Speckled Pole Limas (small varieties).

> *The scientific name* Phaseolus *was bestowed in 39 B.C. by Calumella, who observed that the seeds look like a "small boat." The specific term* limensis *means coming from Lima, while* lunatus *means crescent- or moon-shaped. Lima beans are named after their city of approximate origin in Peru.*

General Information These beans, christened "lima" after the capital of Peru, are native to the Peruvian altiplano, with origins that can be traced back to about 1000 A.D. Known and used by the pre-Columbian Incas, this "aristocrat of the bean family" was introduced to Mauritius and Madagascar around the eighteenth century, where its cultivation became of great importance. Today this large creamy-white or pale-green bean is the main legume crop in tropical Africa. The large thick-seeded "potato" type

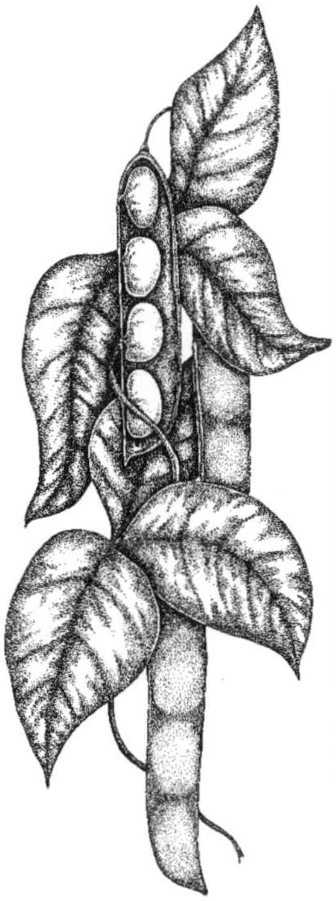

limas (also known as Fordhooks or Butter limas) have large pods and are fleshy, but are not likely to split at maturity. The baby lima bean is a smaller, milder-tasting variety; the pods are small and numerous, and will split open when mature. **Christmas limas** are an heirloom bean larger than the regular lima, about one to one-and-a-quarter inches long, and plumper, with a maroon batik-like pattern on a creamy background. Prized for their buttery chestnut-like flavor as well as their beauty, Christmas Limas are smoother than supermarket limas, and cook without soaking. They are delicious in bean side dishes and salads.

Culinary Uses Lima beans have a soft, floury texture and a smooth, creamy, savory, slightly starchy, distinctive flavor. When selecting lima beans, look for quality pods that are fresh, bright green in color, and well-filled. The beans themselves when shelled should be plump with tender green to greenish-white skins, that puncture easily when tested. Hard, tough skins mean the bean is overmature and will probably lack flavor. The beans are also available dried, canned, or frozen; frozen are the most flavorful, but they are salted. Lima beans are delicious in salads, soups, or with corn and other vegetables. Served hot with melted butter and chopped chives or dill, or with sauteed onions and mushrooms, they are delicious.

Health Benefits Unlike other beans, the lima bean contains enough of the potentially toxic cyanide compounds to require special cooking attention. Boil the beans in

Lima Bean

Nutritional Value Per 100 g Edible Portion

	Fresh Raw	Fresh Cooked	Dried Raw	Dried Cooked
Calories	113	123	335	126
Protein	6.84 g	6.81 g	20.62 g	8.04 g
Fat	0.86 g	0.32 g	0.93 g	0.38 g
Fiber	1.89 g	2.09 g	5.71 g	3.59 g
Calcium	34 mg	32 mg	81 mg	29 mg
Iron	3.14 mg	2.45 mg	6.19 mg	2.40 mg
Magnesium	58 mg	74 mg	188 mg	53 mg
Phosphorus	136 mg	130 mg	370 mg	127 mg
Potassium	467 mg	570 mg	1403 mg	401 mg
Sodium	8 mg	17 mg	13 mg	3 mg
Zinc	0.780 mg	0.790 mg	2.600 mg	1.030 mg
Copper	0.318 mg	0.305 mg	0.665 mg	0.215 mg
Manganese	1.215 mg	1.252 mg	1.686 mg	0.585 mg
Beta Carotene (A)	303 IU	370 IU	5 IU	0 IU
Thiamine (B_1)	0.217 mg	0.140 mg	0.574 mg	0.161 mg
Riboflavin (B_2)	0.103 mg	0.096 mg	0.218 mg	0.055 mg
Niacin (B_3)	1.474 mg	1.040 mg	1.712 mg	0.660 mg
Pantothenic Acid (B_5)	0.247 mg	0.257 mg	1.265 mg	0.472 mg
Pyridoxine (B_6)	0.204 mg	0.193 mg	0.327 mg	0.078 mg
Folic Acid (B_9)	n/a	n/a	400.2 mcg	149.9 mcg
Ascorbic Acid (C)	23.4 mg	10.1 mg	0 mg	0 mg

Lima Bean

Nutritional Value Per 100 g Edible Portion

	Large Dried Raw	Large Dried Cooked	Large Canned
Calories	338	115	79
Protein	21.46 g	7.80 g	4.93 g
Fat	0.69 g	0.38 g	0.17 g
Fiber	6.34 g	3.09 g	1.23 g
Calcium	81 mg	17 mg	21 mg
Iron	7.51 mg	2.39 mg	1.81 mg
Magnesium	224 mg	43 mg	39 mg
Phosphorus	385 mg	111 mg	74 mg
Potassium	1724 mg	508 mg	220 mg
Sodium	18 mg	2 mg	336 mg
Zinc	2.830 mg	0.950 mg	0.650 mg
Copper	0.740 mg	0.235 mg	0.180 mg
Manganese	1.672 mg	0.516 mg	0.363 mg
Beta Carotene (A)	0 IU	0 IU	0 IU
Thiamine (B_1)	0.507 mg	0.161 mg	0.055 mg
Riboflavin (B_2)	0.202 mg	0.055 mg	0.034 mg
Niacin (B_3)	1.537 mg	0.421 mg	0.261 mg
Pantothenic Acid (B_5)	1.355 mg	0.422 mg	0.259 mg
Pyridoxine (B_6)	0.512 mg	0.161 mg	0.091 mg
Folic Acid (B_9)	395.1 mcg	83.1 mcg	50.4 mcg
Ascorbic Acid (C)	0 mg	0 mg	0 mg

an uncovered pot so that the hydrogen cyanide gas will escape with the steam. It is advisable to prepare all lima beans—fresh, dried, or sprouted—in this manner. Fresh lima beans are a high protein alkaline food of great value to the muscular system. Dry limas are hard to digest, and the dry skin is irritating to an inflamed digestive system.

Lupine (*Lupinus sativus*)

The genus name Lupinus *comes from the Latin* lupus, *meaning wolf or destroyer, because it was thought that these plants depleted (wolfed) the fertility of the soil by their numbers and strong growth.* Sativus *refers to the fact that this plant has long been cultivated.*

General Information The lupine originated in the Mediterranean basin and can still be found growing wild in Sicily and other regions. Cultivated in Egypt two thousand years before Christ, this plant has been a staple food for the poor and used as animal forage. In ancient Rome cooked lupines were distributed free to the people on holy days and festivals. In recent years, the lupine has often been grown as green manure to enrich the soil because of the nitrogen-fixing bacteria nodules found on the roots.

Culinary Uses Although of high nutritive value, the lupine is of very little importance today as food; it is used more as a snack, like peanuts, salted almonds, and roasted pumpkin seeds. The tan beans are available in jars of brine or you can buy them dried. Looking like wide yellowish full moons, to eat them requires coordination and a little practice. Slipping the bean into your mouth, apply just enough pressure to pierce the tough seed coat and slip out the crunchy, chewy bean. Discard the translucent seed covering. The beans are very mild, requiring salt, pepper, and vinegar to add zip. They are best purchased pre-cooked, for cooking is a laborious process that takes several days.

Lupine

Nutritional Value Per 100 g Edible Portion

	Dried Raw	Dried Cooked
Calories	371	119
Protein	36.17 g	15.57 g
Fat	9.74 g	2.92 g
Fiber	13.77 g	0.67 g
Calcium	176 mg	51 mg
Iron	4.36 mg	1.20 mg
Magnesium	198 mg	54 mg
Phosphorus	440 mg	128 mg
Potassium	1,013 mg	245 mg
Sodium	15 mg	4 mg
Zinc	4.750 mg	1.380 mg
Copper	1.022 mg	0.231 mg
Beta Carotene (A)	n/a	n/a
Thiamine (B1)	0.640 mg	0.134 mg
Riboflavin (B2)	0.220 mg	0.053 mg
Niacin (B3)	2.190 mg	0.495 mg

Mung Bean *(Phaseolus aureus, Vigna radiata)*

Also Known As: Green Grams, Black Grams, Split Golden Grams, Sabat Moong (whole), Moong Dal (hulled).

> *The scientific name* Phaseolus *was bestowed in 39* B.C. *by Calumella, who observed that the seeds look like a "small boat." The specific term* aureus *means golden. The English name* mung *derives from the Sanskrit* mudga.

General Information The mung bean is native to India, where it was first cultivated about 1500 B.C. It later spread to China, becoming a favorite there. These humble, olive-green beans are best known to us as the slender, silvery bean sprout of Chinese cuisine.

Culinary Uses The sweet-flavored pods of the mung bean are eaten as a green vegetable when they are young and tender. The dried beans cook more quickly than most and become soft, rich, starchy, and sweet, similar to split peas. Although they are commonly used in stews, on their own, or in Indian curries, they are perhaps best known in their sprouted form as bean sprouts. Whole beans are available at natural food stores; split and skinless beans are sold as mung (moong) dal at Indian grocery stores. Mung bean flour, ground from the dried beans, is widely used in India.

Health Benefits One of the most important beans therapeutically, mung beans are particularly useful because of their capacity to cleanse the heart and vascular system, and reduce toxicity. Sprouted mung beans are very cooling and are used to detoxify the body.

Mung Bean

Nutritional Value Per 100 g Edible Portion

	Dried Raw	Dried Cooked	Sprouted Raw	Sprouted Cooked
Calories	347	105	30	21
Protein	23.86 g	7.02 g	3.04 g	2.03 g
Fat	1.15 g	0.38 g	0.18 g	0.09 g
Fiber	5.27 g	0.46 g	0.81 g	0.52 g
Calcium	132 mg	27 mg	13 mg	12 mg
Iron	6.74 mg	1.40 mg	0.91 mg	0.65 mg
Magnesium	189 mg	48 mg	21 mg	14 mg
Phosphorus	367 mg	99 mg	54 mg	28 mg
Potassium	1246 mg	266 mg	149 mg	101 mg
Sodium	15 mg	2 mg	6 mg	10 mg
Zinc	2.680 mg	0.840 mg	0.410 mg	0.470 mg
Copper	0.941 mg	0.156 mg	0.164 mg	0.122 mg
Manganese	1.035 mg	0.298 mg	0.188 mg	0.140 mg
Beta Carotene (A)	114 IU	24 IU	21 IU	14 IU
Thiamine (B_1)	0.621 mg	0.164 mg	0.084 mg	0.050 mg
Riboflavin (B_2)	0.233 mg	0.061 mg	0.124 mg	0.102 mg
Niacin (B_3)	2.251 mg	0.577 mg	0.749 mg	0.817 mg
Pantothenic Acid (B_5)	1.910 mg	0.410 mg	0.380 mg	0.243 mg
Pyridoxine (B_6)	0.382 mg	0.067 mg	0.088 mg	n/a
Folic Acid (B_9)	624.9 mcg	158.8 mcg	60.8 mcg	n/a
Ascorbic Acid (C)	4.8 mg	1.0 mg	13.2 mg	11.4 mg

Peas, Dried *(Pisum sativum)*

Pisum *is the old Greek and Latin name for the pea.* Sativum *refers to the fact that this plant has long been cultivated. The English word* pea *derives from the Greek* pison.

General Information The garden pea appears to have derived from the field pea (*Pisum arvense*) through centuries of cultivation and selection for certain desired characteristics. Dried peas hail from the Middle East and date back to about 6000 B.C. Their use spread throughout the Mediterranean, and they were eaten in this form by both the Greeks and Romans. Today, almost 80 percent of the world's crop is utilized as dried peas rather than as fresh peas. In the United States, however, this is reversed, with 90 percent of the peas being eaten as green peas. Dried peas are a useful part of the store cupboard, particularly as fresh ones have such a short season. Once these peas are dried and their skins removed, they split apart naturally. Whole green peas are those that have been shelled from the pod and dried. Green split peas have the outer seed coat removed and are then divided in half.

Culinary Uses Both split and whole peas are small and possess a soft, grainy texture marked with a certain distinctively sweet flavor. The whole dried peas are the "peas porridge" of our nursery rhymes—cooked to a puree and then mashed. Whole peas can also be used as a side vegetable, while the split varieties make excellent purees and yield a good flour that flavors and thickens beautifully. Green split peas are favored in the United States and Great Britain, while yellow split peas, which have a more pronounced nutlike flavor, are preferred in Scandinavian and other northern European countries.

Health Benefits Split peas are highly digestible, and help tone the stomach and liver.

Byproducts

Split pea flour Made from dried and ground yellow split peas, this cannot be used on its own as a flour in the conventional sense, but makes a good thickener for soups or stews.

Pea, Dried

Nutritional Value Per 100 g Edible Portion

	Dried Raw	Dried Cooked
Calories	341	118
Protein	24.55 g	8.34 g
Fat	1.16 g	0.39 g
Fiber	3.72 g	1.97 g
Calcium	55 mg	14 mg
Iron	4.43 mg	1.29 mg
Magnesium	115 mg	36 mg
Phosphorus	366 mg	99 mg
Potassium	981 mg	362 mg
Sodium	15 mg	2 mg
Zinc	3.010 mg	1.000 mg
Copper	0.866 mg	0.181 mg
Manganese	1.391 mg	0.396 mg
Beta Carotene (A)	149 IU	7 IU
Thiamine (B1)	0.726 mg	0.190 mg
Riboflavin (B2)	0.215 mg	0.056 mg
Niacin (B3)	2.889 mg	0.890 mg
Pantothenic Acid (B5)	1.758 mg	0.595 mg
Pyridoxine (B6)	0.174 mg	0.048 mg
Folic Acid (B9)	273.8 mcg	64.9 mcg
Ascorbic Acid (C)	1.8 mg	0.4 mg
Tocopherol (E)	0.09 mg	n/a

Pigeon Pea (*Vigna sinensis*)

Also Known As: Gunga Peas, Longo Peas, Toor Dal, Congo Peas, No-Eyed Peas, Catjang Beans.

This genus was named Vigna *in honor of Dominic Vigni, a Paduan commentator on Theophrastus in the seventeenth century. The specific term* sinensis *means Chinese, or coming from China.*

General Information Probably native to Africa, the pigeon pea had reached tropical Asia in prehistoric times. Cultivated in Egypt four thousand years ago, this very old bean was brought to the southern parts of the United States and the Caribbean by slaves brought from Africa. Widely grown in India, these peas in that country are known as "red grams" and are one of most important pulses after chickpeas; the split seeds are cooked to provide *dal*, the familiar pulse dish. Closely related to the cowpea, the pigeon pea grows in semi-arid tropical conditions, doing well in places like Florida. Its long, twisted, fuzzy pods enclose beans that are grayish-yellow in color, about one-quarter inch long, plump, in the shape of a pouch or purse with an elongated eye on the flattish cotyledon.

Pigeon Pea

Nutritional Value Per 100 g Edible Portion

	Fresh Raw	Fresh Cooked	Dried Raw	Dried Cooked
Calories	136	111	343	121
Protein	7.20 g	5.96 g	21.70 g	6.76 g
Fat	1.64 g	1.36 g	1.49 g	0.38 g
Fiber	2.67 g	2.90 g	3.12 g	1.10 g
Calcium	42 mg	35 mg	130 mg	43 mg
Iron	1.60 mg	1.32 mg	5.23 mg	1.11 mg
Magnesium	n/a	40 mg	183 mg	46 mg
Phosphorus	127 mg	105 mg	367 mg	119 mg
Potassium	552 mg	456 mg	1392 mg	384 mg
Sodium	5 mg	4 mg	17 mg	5 mg
Zinc	n/a	n/a	2.76 mg	0.90 mg
Beta Carotene (A)	140 IU	130 IU	28 IU	3 IU
Thiamine (B_1)	0.400 mg	0.350 mg	0.643 mg	0.146 mg
Riboflavin (B_2)	0.170 mg	0.166 mg	0.187 mg	0.059 mg
Niacin (B_3)	2.200 mg	2.153 mg	2.965 mg	0.781 mg
Pantothenic Acid (B_5)	0.680 mg	0.630 mg	1.266 mg	0.319 mg
Pyridoxine (B_6)	n/a	n/a	0.283 mg	0.050 mg
Folic Acid (B_9)	n/a	n/a	456.0 mcg	110.8 mcg
Ascorbic Acid (C)	39.0 mg	28.1 mg	0 mg	0 mg

Culinary Uses This pungently flavored bean is used in combination with rice in many dishes throughout Hispanic communities.

Scarlet Runner Bean

(*Phaseolus multiflorus, P. coccineus*)

Also Known As: Multiflora, Painted Lady Bean.

The scientific name Phaseolus *was bestowed in 39* B.C. *by Calumella, who observed that the seeds look like a "small boat." The specific term* multiflorus *means many-flowered;* coccineus *means scarlet. They received their English name from the vividly hued flowers that grow on their low growing runner vines.*

General Information From the mountainous slopes of South or Central America come Scarlet Runner beans, first cultivated for their large ornamental blossoms. These large, intensely scarlet, showy flowers are edible and taste very similar to the bean itself before they mature. In its native climate this bean is a perennial whose bulbous root lies dormant in the ground during the winter, sending up new shoots the following spring; in North America it must generally be treated as an annual. The plant was brought to the British Isles in the seventeenth century as an ornamental and decorative plant. Runner beans can be eaten as snap beans when the pods are young, in their immature form as green shell beans, or matured for dried shell beans. The green, eight- to nine-inch pods contain three or four large kidney-shaped seeds, between seven-eighths and one inch long, and are russet red with heavy black mottling near the eye of the bean. There is also a white runner bean grown in the Netherlands and preferred there to its scarlet cousin.

Culinary Uses The Scarlet Runner, like many other legumes, can be used either fresh or dried. The pods can be picked young and eaten whole like string beans, with some left on the plant to mature for drying. Slightly older pods produce beans with finer-textured flesh and a thinner, tenderer skin than the dried variety, which present a floury compact meat and tough skin. The fully mature fresh beans are prepared like fresh lima beans, and are quite tasty with herb butter, sauteed shallots, or cheese. These brightly colored, vibrantly flavored beans are excellent in chili and salads.

Health Benefits Low fat, high in fiber.

Soy/Soya Bean *(Glycine max, Soja max)*

Glycine comes from the Greek word glukos for sweet, while max means large. The English word soy derives from the Cantonese shi-yau.

General Information The soy bean or white gram is first mentioned in China about 2800 B.C. but had been cultivated for a considerable time before that. Just as wheat became respectable under the Han dynasty in China, so did the soy bean, formerly regarded as a coarse rustic food; the index of extreme poverty was having nothing but soy beans to chew and water to drink. The primary recommendation of the bean was that it produced a good crop even in bad years, but a few of its many other virtues seem to have been made manifest in the early days of the Han. Not until the sixth century did the soy bean find its way to nearby Japan, and Europe did not see it until the eighteenth century, when missionaries sent the bean back to Europe. They were introduced into the United States by Dr. Charles Fearn, an Englishman who discovered them on a trip to China. President Woodrow Wilson asked Dr. Fearn to assist the war effort during World War I, and the versatile soy bean with its many products was suggested as a nourishing substitute or extender for scarce foods. Its great advantages were cheapness, high protein content, and bland flavor, which was easily enhanced. In 1954, an invention by R.A. Boyer made possible a method of spinning soy protein into fibers, similar to the manufacture of rayon. The fibers were stretched and molded into forms resembling

Soy Bean

Nutritional Value Per 100 g Edible Portion

	Green Raw	Green Cooked	Sprouted Raw	Sprouted Cooked	Kernels Roasted w/salt
Calories	147	141	122	81	471
Protein	12.95 g	12.35 g	13.09 g	8.47 g	35.22 g
Fat	6.80 g	6.40 g	6.70 g	4.45 g	25.40 g
Fiber	2.05 g	1.85 g	2.30 g	1.95 g	4.60 g
Calcium	197 mg	145 mg	67 mg	59 mg	138 mg
Iron	3.55 mg	2.50 mg	2.10 mg	1.31 mg	3.90 mg
Magnesium	n/a	n/a	72 mg	60 mg	145 mg
Phosphorus	194 mg	158 mg	164 mg	135 mg	363 mg
Potassium	n/a	n/a	484 mg	355 mg	1470 mg
Sodium	n/a	n/a	14 mg	10 mg	163 mg
Zinc	n/a	n/a	1.170 mg	1.040 mg	3.140 mg
Copper	n/a	n/a	0.427 mg	0.330 mg	0.828 mg
Manganese	n/a	n/a	0.702 mg	0.710 mg	2.158 mg
Beta Carotene (A)	180 IU	156 IU	11 IU	11 IU	200 IU
Thiamine (B_1)	0.435 mg	0.260 mg	0.340 mg	0.205 mg	0.100 mg
Riboflavin (B_2)	0.175 mg	0.155 mg	0.118 mg	0.053 mg	0.145 mg
Niacin (B_3)	1.650 mg	1.250 mg	1.148 mg	1.092 mg	1.410 mg
Pantothenic Acid (B_5)	n/a	n/a	0.929 mg	0.743 mg	0.453 mg
Pyridoxine (B_6)	n/a	n/a	0.176 mg	n/a	0.208 mg
Folic Acid (B_9)	n/a	n/a	172.0 mcg	n/a	211.0 mcg
Ascorbic Acid (C)	29.0 mg	17.0 mg	15.3 mg	8.3 mg	2.2 mg

various meats (especially ham and chicken), and flavored appropriately to suggest the product they imitated. The products were tasty, nourishing, and cheap, but met with consumer resistance in many areas. Only now are many soy products finding widespread acceptance.

In the period between the two world wars, soy beans became an important crop. The United States is now the world's largest grower of soy beans, but over 90 percent of the crop still goes to feed animals rather than humans. Most of that used for human consumption is made into margarine, shortening, salad oil, and cooking oil. The rows of "vegetable oil" on supermarket shelves are primarily soy oil. The process of extracting oil from soy beans is particularly difficult, as the beans must be roasted and treated with high heat and chemical solvents (usually hexane) before they will yield any quantity of oil. Once extracted, the oil is bleached, "deodorized," and lightly hydrogenated to stabilize the flavor. The end product is a fully refined edible oil without much flavor.

Culinary Uses The preeminent legume crop in the world, the soy bean is a staple in Asian countries. Regarded as the "meat of the earth" in the Far East for thousands of years, there are over one thousand varieties including white, yellow, brown, black, and multicolored. Over the centuries the soy bean has become a complete food industry in itself, providing a milk substitute, curd (tofu), sauce, cheese, oil for cooking and making

Soy Bean

Nutritional Value Per 100 g Edible Portion

	Mature, Dry Raw	Mature, Dry Cooked	Miso	Okara	Shoyu
Calories	416	173	206	77	53
Protein	36.49 g	16.64 g	11.81 g	3.22 g	5.17 g
Fat	19.94 g	8.97 g	6.07 g	1.73 g	0.08 g
Fiber	4.96 g	2.03 g	2.47 g	4.12 g	0 g
Calcium	277 mg	102 mg	66 mg	80 mg	17 mg
Iron	15.70 mg	5.14 mg	2.74 mg	1.30 mg	2.02 mg
Magnesium	280 mg	86 mg	42 mg	26 mg	34 mg
Phosphorus	704 mg	245 mg	153 mg	60 mg	110 mg
Potassium	1797 mg	515 mg	164 mg	213 mg	180 mg
Sodium	2 mg	1 mg	3647 mg	9 mg	5715 mg
Zinc	4.890 mg	1.150 mg	3.320 mg	n/a	0.370 mg
Copper	1.658 mg	0.407 mg	0.437 mg	n/a	0.115 mg
Manganese	2.517 mg	0.824 mg	0.859 mg	n/a	n/a
Beta Carotene (A)	24 IU	9 IU	87 IU	0 IU	0 IU
Thiamine (B_1)	0.874 mg	0.155 mg	0.097 mg	0.020 mg	0.050 mg
Riboflavin (B_2)	0.870 mg	0.285 mg	0.250 mg	0.020 mg	0.130 mg
Niacin (B_3)	1.623 mg	0.399 mg	0.860 mg	0.100 mg	3.360 mg
Pantothenic Acid (B_5)	0.793 mg	0.179 mg	0.258 mg	n/a	0.320 mg
Pyridoxine (B_6)	0.377 mg	0.234 mg	0.215 mg	n/a	0.170 mg
Folic Acid (B_9)	375.1 mcg	53.8 mcg	33.0 mcg	n/a	15.5 mcg
Cobalamin (B_{12})	0 mcg	0 mcg	0.21 mcg	0 mcg	0 mcg
Ascorbic Acid (C)	6.0 mg	1.7 mg	0 mg	0 mg	0 mg
Tocopherol (E)	0.85 mg	n/a	n/a	n/a	n/a

margarine and salad dressings, flour to enrich pasta and breakfast cereals, and bean sprouts. Cooked on their own, soy beans have a rich deep flavor and are wonderfully palatable. The whole cooked bean does not soften like other beans and has a gelatinous, slippery texture that most Americans find unpleasant. Young soy sprouts are very tasty and make a fine dish by themselves or an excellent addition to a vegetable salad. Unless well-cooked, soy beans inhibit the digestive enzyme trypsin, making them difficult to digest. The fermentation process, such as that used in tempeh, tofu, miso, and soy sauce, eliminates this enzyme, and the resulting products are highly digestible. In natural food stores, you may be able to find a few expeller-pressed, unrefined soy oils. Dark in color, they have a strong "beany" odor and nut-like flavor. Because of its strong flavor, the oil may not be suitable for some dishes, although it is excellent for use in baking, since its high lecithin content gives preservative qualities to breads, cakes, and cookies. The oil can foam during frying, which may not be desirable in some dishes. Refined soy oil has one of the highest smoke points of all vegetable oils so it is frequently used as a cooking oil.

Lore and Legend

A Japanese myth relates that the god of the sea, Susano, angrily refused his watery realm and was disowned by the Creator. He wandered around, causing trouble, until he became hungry and visited the goddess of food. But he didn't like what she offered him, so he killed her and crushed her body into the ground. On the site sprang five plants: rice, millet, barley, large beans, and soy beans.

Health Benefits Soy beans contain large quantities of trypsin inhibitors, one of the substances that can interfere with digestion. This enzyme is inactivated by heat, sprouting, or by fermentation. Soy beans are unique among beans in containing the eight essential amino acids, and are concentrated in essential fatty acids (including Omega-3); they are also the primary commercial source of lecithin, an essential nutrient that helps control cholesterol. The beans also help regulate insulin and blood sugar levels, bowel functions, and help prevent certain cancers, most notably of the stomach. Soy beans, like peas and other legumes, are rich in isoflavones, also known as phytoestrogens (plant estrogens). These isoflavones actually bind to estrogen receptors and thus prevent the binding of the body's own estrogen to the receptor. This effect does not disrupt the normal reproductive functions of estrogen, but could conceivably inhibit fertility or help replace estrogen in postmenopausal women. Many tumors, especially breast cancers, are stimulated by human estrogen, thus these phytoestrogens may counteract some of the hormone's cancer-causing potential. Soy bean oil is 14.40 percent saturated, 23.30 percent monounsaturated, and 57.90 percent polyunsaturated. It also contains traces of calcium, iron, magnesium, phosphorus, and vitamin E.

Byproducts

Fresh green soy beans are the Japanese version of popcorn. Harvested immature in their green seedpods, the beans are steamed or boiled whole, then drained and set out in bowls for munching. Popped from their shells, the beans have a buttery taste and smooth nonstarchy texture that appeals as much to kids as it does to adults. You may be able to find raw green soy beans in the freezer case of an Asian market. Either steam or boil them (fresh or frozen) for ten to fifteen minutes, drain and serve.

Miso is a fermented food, made by adding an enzymatic culture (*Aspergillus oryzae*) to a base of cooked soy beans or a combination of soy beans and a variety of grain (usually wheat, barley, or rice). Salt and water are the only other ingredients of natural miso. The mixture is packed into earthenware or wooden vessels, sealed airtight, and fermented, slowly in cool weather and more quickly in warm weather. After aging, the enzymes have reduced the proteins, starches, and fats into amino acids, simple sugars, and fatty acids. The flavors marry and mellow, and the paste is now thick, dark, salty, and pungent. There are several types of miso: mugi (barley), hatcho (soy only), and kome (brown rice) are among the most common. **Mugi miso,** also called **red miso,** is dark colored and of medium flavor strength. It is the preferred miso for everyday use, and is particularly good for temperate weather. **Hatcho miso** is usually the thickest and strongest in flavor, and favored for cold weather. It is lower in salt and higher in protein than its grain-containing counterparts. This is the variety favored by famous warlords and the emperor of Japan. **Kome miso,** also called **light** or **white** miso, is yellow to amber in color, relatively sweet and mild, and used particularly in hot weather. Mass-produced "white" miso is made with white rice, aged no more than three months, is light in color and complete with chemical preservatives—this cannot be considered a natural food. In addition to being a soup base, miso is great for flavoring sauces, gravies, grains, dips, spreads, dressings, and marinades. An excellent spread can be made by mixing miso with roasted tahini (sesame butter), chopped scallions, and herbs. Always use unpasteurized miso, since this is a live food, and prolonged cooking kills the benefi-

Soy Bean

Nutritional Value Per 100 g Edible Portion

	Flour, Full-Fat Raw	Flour, Full-Fat Roasted	Flour Low-Fat Raw	Flour Defatted Raw	Isolate (prepared with sodium)
Calories	433-436	439-441	326-370	327-329	334-338
Protein	34.54-37.80 g	34.80-38.09 g	46.53-50.93 g	47.01-51.46 g	80.69-88.32 g
Fat	20.65 g	21.86 g	6.70 g	1.22 g	3.39 g
Fiber	4.72 g	2.23 g	4.23 g	4.27 g	0.26 g
Calcium	206 mg	188 mg	188 mg	241 mg	178 mg
Iron	6.37 mg	5.82 mg	5.99 mg	9.24 mg	14.50 mg
Magnesium	429 mg	369 mg	229 mg	290 mg	39 mg
Phosphorus	494 mg	476 mg	593 mg	674 mg	776 mg
Potassium	2515 mg	2041 mg	2570 mg	2384 mg	81 mg
Sodium	13 mg	12 mg	18 mg	20 mg	1005 mg
Zinc	3.920 mg	3.580 mg	1.180 mg	2.460 mg	4.030 g
Copper	2.920 mg	2.221 mg	5.080 mg	4.065 mg	1.599 mg
Manganese	2.275 mg	2.077 mg	3.080 mg	3.018 mg	1.493 mg
Beta Carotene (A)	120 IU	110 IU	40 IU	40 IU	0 IU
Thiamine (B_1)	0.581 mg	0.412 mg	0.380 mg	0.698 mg	0.176 mg
Riboflavin (B_2)	1.160 mg	0.941 mg	0.285 mg	0.253 mg	0.100 mg
Niacin (B_3)	4.320 mg	3.286 mg	2.160 mg	2.612 mg	1.438 mg
Pantothenic Acid (B_5)	1.590 mg	1.209 mg	1.820 mg	1.995 mg	0.060 mg
Pyridoxine (B_6)	0.461 mg	0.351 mg	0.522 mg	0.574 mg	n/a
Folic Acid (B_9)	345.0 mcg	227.4 mcg	410.0 mcg	305.4 mcg	176.1 mcg
Ascorbic Acid (C)	0 mg	0 mg	0 mg	0 mg	0 mg

cial microorganisms. Because it absorbs toxins from plastic containers, it should be transferred into glass, wood, or enamel for prolonged storage. Miso is a source of nutrients that can block our uptake of radioactive substances such as cobalt-60 and strontium-90; it also contains a binding agent called zybiocolin which is effective in detoxifying and eliminating radioactive elements from the body. Low in calories and fat, miso is a superb source of easily assimilated complete protein; it actually increases the protein quality of other foods with which it is combined. Rich in minerals and vitamins, including the elusive B_{12}, unpasteurized miso contains live microorganisms and enzymes that facilitate digestion and promote an alkaline environment in the body. According to traditional medicine, miso promotes long life and good health.

Okara is the pulp that remains after soy milk processing, when the "milk" is strained from the beans. It is highly perishable and must be used quickly or frozen for later use. When baked, okara develops a texture and flavor akin to coconut, and can be added to granola or cookies. If you want to experiment with okara without making soy milk, you can get some from a local tofu processor, or look for ready-made okara patties in the natural foods freezer case.

Shoyu is fermented from whole soy beans, wheat koji, salt, and water. After aging for a year or two, a superior shoyu has a full, round flavor and mellow aftertaste. Thinner and lighter in flavor than tamari, much of its sweet aroma and flavor is lost during long cooking, so it is best used as a seasoning and added just before serving. About 95 percent of the soy sauce consumed in Japan is shoyu and about 95 percent of the "tamari" imported to the West has actually been shoyu, mistakenly identified. Commercial shoyu is made from defatted soy meal, and the fermentation process is artificially accelerated by temperature control; it may also contain preservatives and other additives.

Soy cheese and **yogurt** Soy cheese was designed as a substitute for dairy cheese, but it simply does not taste like, feel like, or melt like real cheese. Moreover, some companies have added casein, a milk protein, so that their product will melt better. Soy yogurt is cultured from rich soy milk, using active bacteria cultures. It is available in many flavors and has the advantages of being lactose- and cholesterol-free.

Soy flour contributes to a tender, moist, and nicely browned finish in baked goods, and adds a good color and slightly nutty flavor to foods; it extends their keeping ability, inhibits fat absorption, and provides a nutritional boost. It can successfully replace up to 25 percent of wheat flour in baked goods, although less should be used in breads that require rising since soy flour contains no gluten. **Defatted soy flour** is from soy meal left after the chemical solvent method of extraction for soy oil and contains less than 1 percent fat and 50 percent protein. It is an incomplete food and thus not recommended. **Full-fat soy flour** is made from whole soybeans that have been hulled, cracked, and heat-treated to remove the beany flavor, as well as to increase the value of the protein and deactivate certain enzymes that cause deterioration during storage. The beans are then cooled and ground into a flour that contains about 20 percent fat and 35 percent protein. **Low-fat soy flour** is from soy meal left by the expeller method of extraction for oil. It has 6 percent fat and 45 percent protein. It is an incomplete food derived from a highly refined process, and thus not recommended.

Soy grits are made from raw or partially cooked soy beans that have been cracked into eight or ten pieces. The bland grits are a good texturizer and make a nutritious addition to cooked grains such as rice without altering the flavor. However, soy grits are not a whole food, and have not been processed to eliminate the enzymes that inhibit digestion.

Defatted soy grits are made from soy bean meal, the by-product of soy oil manufacture.

Soy milk is made either by boiling soy beans and pouring off the water, or by finely grinding soaked beans, mixing them with water, and straining off the "milk." The resulting liquid is a thick, heavy milk that is brought to a boil before it can be used; otherwise it tastes "green" and "beany" and contains an enzyme that prevents digestion. Soy milk has a slightly nutty flavor and works as a universal substitute for dairy milk in everything from breakfast cereal to cooked and baked products (but is not very successful in tea or coffee). Rich soy milk, made with proportionally more soybeans per volume of water, can be whipped like cream or made into homemade soy yogurt and ice cream. Fresh soy milk can be kept in the refrigerator for about four days; after that it tends to become sour and separate (clabber), at which time it can be used in place of buttermilk or yogurt in cooking and baking. A longer-lasting soy milk comes in aseptic cartons, which have an indefinite shelf life before opening, and last for several weeks in the refrigerator after opening.

Soy nuts are a tasty alternative to peanuts. Since they are not widely available commercially, try making them at home. Soak a quantity of soy beans for eight hours, drain, spread them on oiled cookie sheets, and roast in a 350° oven for about 30 minutes, stirring occasionally. When they are golden brown, remove them from the oven and season to taste with a sprinkle of plain or garlic salt; for a spicier version, add some cayenne pepper or Cajun seasoning mix. Store in an airtight container in a cool place. Coarsely ground soy nuts can be used in place of bacon bits in salads and sandwiches. Because they

Soy Bean

Nutritional Value Per 100 g Edible Portion

	Soy Meal Defatted, Raw	Soy Milk	Soy Sauce (imitation)	Sufu	Tamari
Calories	337-339	33	41	116	60
Protein	44.95-49.20 g	2.75 g	2.43 g	8.15 g	10.51 g
Fat	2.39 g	1.91 g	0.08 g	8.00 g	0.10 g
Fiber	5.79 g	1.10 g	0 g	0.31 g	0 g
Calcium	244 mg	4 mg	5 mg	46 mg	20 mg
Iron	13.70 mg	0.58 mg	1.49 mg	1.98 mg	2.38 mg
Magnesium	306 mg	19 mg	6 mg	52 mg	40 mg
Phosphorus	701 mg	49 mg	93 mg	73 mg	130 mg
Potassium	2,490 mg	141 mg	152 mg	75 mg	212 mg
Sodium	3 mg	12 mg	5,689 mg	2,873 mg	5,586 mg
Zinc	5.060 mg	0.230 mg	0.310 mg	n/a	0.430 mg
Copper	2.000 mg	0.120 mg	0.097 mg	n/a	0.135 mg
Manganese	3.800 mg	0.170 mg	n/a	n/a	n/a
Beta Carotene (A)	40 IU	32 IU	0 IU	n/a	0 IU
Thiamine (B_1)	0.691 mg	0.161 mg	0.042 mg	n/a	0.059 mg
Riboflavin (B_2)	0.251 mg	0.070 mg	0.109 mg	n/a	0.152 mg
Niacin (B_3)	2.587 mg	0.147 mg	2.828 mg	n/a	3.951 mg
Pantothenic Acid (B_5)	1.976 mg	0.048 mg	0.269 mg	n/a	0.376 mg
Pyridoxine (B_6)	0.569 mg	0.041 mg	0.143 mg	n/a	0.200 mg
Folic Acid (B_9)	302.6 mcg	1.5 mcg	13.0 mcg	n/a	18.2 mcg
Ascorbic Acid (C)	0 mg	0 mg	0 mg	n/a	0 mg

have not gone through the fermentation process, they are hard to digest, and once seasoned are high in sodium.

Soy oil In natural food stores, you may be able to find a few expeller-pressed, unrefined soy oils. Dark in color, they have a strong "beany" odor and nutlike flavor. Because of its strong flavor, the oil may not be suitable for some dishes, although it is excellent for use in baking, since its high lecithin content gives preservative qualities to breads, cakes, and cookies. The oil can foam during frying, which may not be desirable in some dishes. Refined soy oil has one of the highest smoke points of all vegetable oils so it is frequently used as a cooking oil.

Soy protein isolate is the meal remaining after the beans have been processed for oil, and this is then bathed in acid, base, and alcohol solutions to remove any carbohydrate remaining. The protein content is between 90 and 95 percent. These isolates are used in various products, including infant formulas, meal replacement formulas, meat products, dairy-type whipped toppings, frozen desserts, and milk alternatives. Wherever soy protein isolate is included in an ingredient listing, it is best to exclude that product from your diet.

Soy sauce is a generic term applied to three different but related products: tamari, shoyu, and common soy sauce. Each is a dark brown, richly flavored liquid made from a soy bean base. Soy sauce is a salty brown sauce made, like miso, by fermenting soy beans with *Aspergillus oryzae* and wheat. It originated in China over 2,500 years ago, and was introduced into Japan in the seventh century A.D. Unfortunately, much of the popular soy sauce sold today is literally made overnight. The soy beans are broken down chemically and mixed with caramel coloring, salt, corn syrup, water, and usually a preservative. Look for good-quality brands that brew it traditionally. High-quality soy sauce supplies good amounts of free amino acids, but its popularity is primarily due to the flavor that it imparts to other foods. An essential ingredient in Asian cooking, soy sauce is used to enhance virtually all dishes—among them sauces, rice, and soups. The average annual per capita consumption of soy sauce in Japan is about 3 gallons.

Sufu is inoculated and fermented tofu, pickled in rice wine and brine, which is eaten as a condiment.

Tamari is a natural by-product of making miso; it is the liquid that forms on the top of miso as it ferments. It has a rich, full-bodied flavor and is smoother and more complex than ordinary soy sauce. Not usually available commercially, much of what is labeled tamari is actually shoyu, or an inferior soy sauce made without wheat.

Tempeh is an ancient Indonesian staple made from cooked, split, fermented soy beans bound together with a white thread-like mycelium (*Rhizopus oligosporus*), which makes the soy easier to digest and provides many valuable vitamins. In addition to plain soy tempeh, you may find it in various combinations with grains, vegetables, or nuts. With its nutty aroma and dense chewy texture, it is frequently used as a meat substitute in dishes like stir-fries or sloppy joes. Because tempeh is a whole, fermented food, it is more beneficial than tofu. The *Rhizopus* mold produces a medicinal antibiotic to increase the body's resistance to infections and free it of chemical toxins. When tempeh was first introduced into America in the 1970s, it was generally produced by cottage industries, and B_{12} levels often were quite high (4 mcg/100g). But by the late 1980s, most tempeh contained no B_{12} whatsoever, as it was being produced in larger batches, and in machines and facilities designed to be more easily cleaned (B_{12}-rich bacteria thrive in less sanitary conditions).

Some companies have now taken the B_{12} listing off their containers, while others inoculate the tempeh with bacteria that produce the vitamin.

Tofu is made by first soaking, blending, and cooking soy beans, then filtering them through cloth to yield soy milk. A coagulant—generally a mineral salt such as calcium sulfate, calcium chloride, or magnesium chloride—is added to the soy milk to make it curdle. After the semi-solid curds separate from the liquid "whey," the curds are pressed and formed into compact blocks of ivory-colored tofu. Tofu comes in several varieties, from soft to extra-firm, depending upon the amount of liquid removed. Soft tofu is often used to make frostings for cakes and dips for chips and vegetables, while firmer styles which hold their shape are used in stir-fries and soups. Freezing and thawing tofu will change it dramatically, creating a chewy, meat-like texture that absorbs marinades and flavorings, and which is great for "American" dishes like chili and tacos. Tofu is also used as a substitute for eggs and other dairy products in baked goods, where it imparts a light moist texture yet does not alter the flavor. Tofu has a cooling nature and helps relieve inflammation of the stomach and neutralize toxins.

TVP, or **Textured vegetable protein**, is made from the soy bean meal left after the oil is processed out. This meal is then put through various acid, base, and alcohol solutions to remove virtually all the carbohydrate, leaving soy protein isolate. The isolate can then be "textured" by means of fiber-spinning or extrusion and processed into marketable foodstuffs. The extrusion process creates small chunks of soy protein that are firm and chewy like meat but lacking in flavor and color. With the addition of flavorings, seasonings, and sometimes wheat gluten or other grains, these products can simulate a wide variety of animal foods. Used commercially as a meat extender and appearing in many popular vegetarian convenience foods, these meat analogs were first developed and produced in response to the needs of Seventh-Day Adventists and World War II meat rationing. Although these highly processed products may be convenient, the finished product is comparable chemically to plastic.

Yuba is made from the skins formed on hot soy bean milk, layered and pressed into slabs or cakes, and eaten as a meat substitute. They must be soaked before use, and make an unusual addition to braised vegetables.

Soy Bean

Nutritional Value Per 100 g Edible Portion

	Tempeh	Tofu Raw, Firm	Tofu Raw, Regular	Tofu Dried-Frozen
Calories	199	145	76	480
Protein	18.95 g	15.78 g	8.08 g	47.94 g
Fat	7.68 g	8.72 g	4.78 g	30.34 g
Fiber	2.99 g	0.15 g	0.08 g	0.16 g
Calcium	93 mg	205 mg	105 mg	364 mg
Iron	2.26 mg	10.47 mg	5.36 mg	9.73 mg
Magnesium	70 mg	94 mg	103 mg	59 mg
Phosphorus	206 mg	190 mg	97 mg	483 mg
Potassium	367 mg	237 mg	121 mg	20 mg
Sodium	6 mg	14 mg	7 mg	6 mg
Zinc	1.810 mg	1.570 mg	0.800 mg	4.900 mg
Copper	0.670 mg	0.378 mg	0.193 mg	1.179 mg
Manganese	1.430 mg	1.181 mg	0.605 mg	3.689 mg
Beta Carotene (A)	686 IU	166 IU	85 IU	518 IU
Thiamine (B_1)	0.131 mg	0.158 mg	0.081 mg	0.494 mg
Riboflavin (B_2)	0.111 mg	0.102 mg	0.052 mg	0.317 mg
Niacin (B_3)	4.630 mg	0.381 mg	0.195 mg	1.189 mg
Pantothenic Acid (B_5)	0.355 mg	0.133 mg	0.068 mg	0.415 mg
Pyridoxine (B_6)	0.299 mg	0.092 mg	0.047 mg	0.286 mg
Folic Acid (B_9)	52.0 mcg	29.3 mcg	15.0 mcg	91.5 mcg
Cobalamin (B_{12})	0.84 mcg	0 mcg	0 mcg	0 mcg
Ascorbic Acid (C)	0 mg	0.2 mg	0.1 mg	0.7 mg

Tepary Bean (*Phaseolus acutifolius latifolius*)

The scientific name Phaseolus *was bestowed in 39* B.C. *by Calumella, who observed that the seeds look like a "small boat." The specific term* acutifolius *means acutely- or sharp-leaved;* latifolius *means wide-leaved. The English name* tepary *is of unknown origin.*

General Information Tepary beans were heavily cultivated by Mexican Indians near Tehuacan about five thousand years ago. In all probability the tepary formed one of the principal food crops of that ancient and unknown agricultural race, the ruins of whose cities and irrigating canals are now the only witnesses of their former presence and prosperity. The beans reached Europe as an archaeological specimen in 1888, part of an exhibit of materials excavated from the Los Muertos prehistoric site in Arizona. This drought-resistant bean is a rapid grower, ideally suited to the hot, dry climates of western Texas, Arizona, and New Mexico. The pods are about three inches long, two-fifths of an inch wide, and somewhat flattened; the beans themselves may be white, yellow, brown, or dotted, and are the size of navy beans.

Culinary Uses Resembling the Great northern or navy bean, with coloring ranging from white to brown, the tepary bean has generally been limited to regional dishes in the areas in which they grow. Well-cooked teparies are light and mealy and have a rich bean-like aroma.

Health Benefits The tepary bean is less gas-forming than many other beans. Medical studies in Australia have shown that the tepary bean has a significant effect on controlling blood-glucose responses while flattening blood-sugar levels, both important factors in controlling adult-onset diabetes. Low in fat, high in fiber.

Urd Bean

Nutritional Value Per 100 g Edible Portion

	Dried Raw	Dried Cooked
Calories	351	105
Protein	25.06 g	7.54 g
Fat	1.83 g	0.55 g
Fiber	4.43 g	1.33 g
Calcium	196 mg	53 mg
Iron	6.84 mg	1.75 mg
Magnesium	260 mg	63 mg
Phosphorus	575 mg	156 mg
Potassium	1025 mg	231 mg
Sodium	26 mg	7 mg
Zinc	3.080 mg	0.830 mg
Copper	0.659 mg	0.139 mg
Manganese	1.614 mg	0.412 mg
Beta Carotene (A)	114 IU	31 IU
Thiamine (B_1)	0.355 mg	0.150 mg
Riboflavin (B_2)	0.280 mg	0.075 mg
Niacin (B_3)	1.800 mg	1.500 mg
Pantothenic Acid (B_5)	1.920 mg	0.433 mg
Pyridoxine (B_6)	0.275 mg	0.058 mg
Folic Acid (B_9)	628.2 mcg	94.4 mcg
Ascorbic Acid (C)	4.8 mg	1.0 mg

Urd Bean (*Phaseolus mungo*)

Also Known As: Urd Dal, Black Gram.

The scientific name Phaseolus *was bestowed in 39* B.C. *by Calumella, who observed that the seeds look like a "small boat." The specific term* mungo *comes from the Indian name* moong *for this type of bean. The English name* urd *is from the Hindi name for the plant.*

General Information The urd bean is thought to be native to India and is widely grown both in India and the Far East. The long, hairy pods contain oblong, blackish seeds similar in size and shape to their cousin the mung bean.

Culinary Uses Urd beans look very similar to mung beans. They are available whole, split and skinless, and can be used whole as a side vegetable, or puréed and used in soups.

Nuts, Seeds, and Oils

"The hardy nut, in solid mail secure,
Impregnable to winter's frosts, repays
Its hoarder's care."

—Somerville, *Hobbinol*

"Though I do not believe that a plant will spring up where no seed has been, I have great faith in a seed. Convince me that you have a seed there, and I am prepared to expect wonders."

—Henry David Thoreau, *The Dispersion of Seeds*

NUTS, SEEDS, and OILS

Nuts, Seeds, and Oils

THE TERM *nut* COMES FROM THE OLD ENGLISH *hnutu* AND THE LATIN *nux*, or *nutriens*, meaning to nourish. Botanically, nuts are single-seeded, dry, hard-shelled fruits that must be cracked open, but the term is also used for any seed or fruit with an edible kernel in a hard or brittle shell (i.e., peanuts and coconuts). Nuts and seeds are compact packages of highly concentrated nutrients prepared by nature to supply all the requirements of a living plant, be it a flower, bush, or tree. They are hermetically sealed within their protective shells to guard against bacterial contamination, and are doubly protected by the skin covering the kernel. Nuts and seeds are marketed in a variety of forms: shelled or in the shell, raw or roasted, salted or spiced or unseasoned, prepackaged or in bulk. In general, the more processing and packaging they have been subjected to, the higher the price. Although considered by most Americans to be strictly snack food, nuts and seeds are a valuable source of vitamins, minerals, and protein, and can be used in cooking just like any other vegetable.

When buying nuts and seeds in the shell, look for clean ones with bright, well-shaped shells that are heavy for their size, as this indicates fresher, meatier kernels. The shell is a natural protector against free-radical damage caused by light and air. Make sure that the shells are free from splits, cracks, stains, holes, or other surface imperfections. When purchasing nuts already shelled, avoid limp, rubbery, dark, or shriveled nut meat, and do not eat or use moldy nuts or seeds, since these may not be safe. Whole nuts and seeds in the shell will remain freshest for the longest period of time, while those that have been further processed (chopped, ground, or roasted) are more prone to spoilage or rancidity, and should be refrigerated. Most packages of crushed, slivered, and broken nut pieces are already rancid when purchased, so if possible process your own. Almonds are less prone to rancidity, while walnuts and cashews are more so, due to their higher oil content. This rich oil content also concentrates pesticides, and so organic nuts and seeds should be sought out. All nuts and seeds should be stored in their shells in glass containers (oil-rich foods combine with plastic to form plasticides) in a cold dark place such as the refrigerator or freezer. Add these versatile foods ground to baked goods, chopped or ground slightly and mixed into casseroles or salads, browned and served with cooked or raw vegetables, pureed into smooth butters, or soaked then ground and strained to make nut and seed "milks."

Nuts and seeds are endowed with a nearly complete array of vitamins and minerals. They are rich in protein of high biological value, and a study of the relative protein content of nuts, milk, and meat shows that pound for pound most nuts contain as much as or more protein than meat and milk. Nuts are fairly rich in starches and sugars, are three to four times richer in mineral salts than flesh or milk, and contain far more vitamins, while nut protein is easily assimilated and does not form uric acid. They are also high in essential fatty acids, which facilitate oxygen transport, assist proteins in building body cells, aid glandular activity, convert carotene into vitamin A, and complement vitamin D and calcium. Because they are such a dense and concentrated food, it is important that nuts be properly chewed before swallowing for ease of digestion. Nuts and seeds, along with legumes, contain compounds known as phytosterols. These plant compounds are structurally similar to cholesterol and steroid hormones. Phytosterols function to inhibit the absorption of cholesterol by blocking absorption sites, and thus lower total cholesterol count. Phytosterols have also been shown to enhance immune functions, inhibit the Epstein-Barr virus, prevent chemically induced cancers in animals, and exhibit numerous anticancer effects.

Nuts and seeds have long been used as a source of oil for culinary, medicinal, and cosmetic purposes. Certain oils offer advantages over others for specific applications. For example, olive, sesame, soy, and canola oil are more stable than other vegetable oils, so they are preferred for use when exposing foods to heat. Highly polyunsaturated oils such as flax, safflower, and sunflower are not recommended for exposure to heat because the heat changes the chemical structures of the fatty acids and forms free radicals; instead, these are best suited for salad dressings. Other oils such as cottonseed, coconut, and palm oils are best avoided. Coconut and palm oils consist primarily of saturated fat (which is usually solid at room temperatures), while cottonseed oil may contain toxic residues because cotton plants are so heavily sprayed during cultivation and because the oil contains gossypol, a substance known to inhibit sperm function. In fact, gossypol is being investigated as the "male birth control pill."

Of the three types of fat (saturated, monounsaturated, and polyunsaturated), the saturated variety seems to be the most problematic. The first reason to avoid saturated fats is that they cause blood cholesterol levels to rise and this condition appears to be strongly associated with coronary heart and artery disease. Secondly, a diet high in saturated fat results in the production of large amounts of bile acid, which may be a cause of colon cancer. Lastly, saturated fat causes the red blood cells to clump together and line up much like a stack of poker chips. This slows blood circulation and decreases oxygen uptake by vital tissues for up to nine hours; the blood stream can be so overloaded that the brain is deprived of sufficient oxygen to carry on normal waking activities (cerebral anoxia).

In a modern oil-pressing facility, the starting material (whether seed, nut, grain, or legume) is first mechanically cleaned to prepare it for either chemical or mechanical extraction. With chemical extraction, the material is typically rolled into meal (for example, seed meal or cornmeal) and then mixed with a chemical solvent such as hexane. Once the solvent has separated the oil from the meal, the mixture is exposed to high heat to distill the solvent. Although most of the solvent is removed by this means, traces can still be found. The oil to be produced is then usually further processed (degummed, bleached, deodorized, and so on) to produce a "refined" oil. A refined oil is one that has had some or all of its "impurities"—vitamin E, lecithin, chlorophyll, carotenes, aromatic oils, and free fatty acids—removed. Many of these "impurities" have important health-promoting properties. In the process of refining, the oil is exposed not only to extremely high heat, but also to caustic substances such as phosphoric acid and sodium hydroxide. Because the refined oil has been stripped of most of its natural protection against damage, synthetic antioxidants like BHT are then added as stabilizers and preservatives.

The mechanical method usually differs only in how the oil is initially extracted. The starting material may or may not be cooked at high temperatures for up to two hours to liquefy the oil content and then mechanically pressed through an expeller. The pressure can be as high as several tons per square inch. This results in the generation of heat, usually around 200°F. The higher the heat, the better the oil yield. Oil pressed in this manner can be filtered and sold as "cold-pressed" (no external heat was added during the extraction); as natural, crude, or unrefined oil; it can be processed further to produce a refined oil. Even oil that has undergone refinement can still be labeled cold-pressed as long as no external heat was applied during the extraction.

Although far from ideal, the best oils commonly available in the United States are the cold-pressed unrefined oils. Do not expect these oils to taste as "clean" as the highly processed commercial varieties you may have grown accustomed to. Cold-pressed unrefined oils still retain much of their original flavor.

The rancidity process in oils starts immediately. Both heat and air will speed up its deterioration. All oil is best kept in a closed container at a temperature no more than 65°F, preferably lower (the refrigerator is best). The highly monounsaturated oils tend to solidify at very cool refrigerator temperatures, which does not present a problem. The effect of light on oil is far worse than air, rapidly altering the unsaturated fatty acids into free-radical chains. To counteract this, store all oil in dark or opaque containers. Also, oil readily combines with most types of plastic to form toxic plasticides. If sold in plastic, remove promptly and store in glass containers.

Although margarine is frequently believed to be more healthful, the truth is that butter and margarine have the same amount of calories and contain just as much fat; what's more, margarine will contribute to the very problems the commercials imply it will prevent, particularly heart disease. The hydrogenated fats in margarine cause extremely elevated cholesterol levels, and deaths from heart disease and cancer are highest among consumers of this type of fat. Most margarines made from soy and safflower oils and sold as "natural" are also hydrogenated and just as harmful as any other margarine. High-quality butter in moderate amounts can be handled by the body much more easily than margarine, which is a chemical compound. Butter is excellent fuel for the body's basic metabolic functions, and contains many nourishing substances, among the foremost of which is butyric acid, an easily digested short-chain fatty acid that has powerful antiviral, antifungal, and anti-cancer properties, and which raises the level of the antiviral chemical interferon in the body. Butyric acid also has characteristics found to be helpful in the prevention and treatment of Alzheimer's disease. Butter does contain cholesterol, but cholesterol is required for the proper functioning of bodily cells. The average North American diet is severely deficient in the vitamins, minerals, and fiber needed to metabolize cholesterol and fats. Good-quality butter in a diet rich in nutrients and fiber poses no health risk. The best-quality butter comes from organic farms, where no pesticides or antibiotics are used. **Ghee**, which is clarified butter or butter from which the water and milk solids have been removed, is an excellent appetizer, helps digestion because it stimulates the secretion of digestive juices, and enhances the flavor of foods. Like butter, ghee contains butyric acid. When used with various herbs, ghee carries their medicinal properties to the tissues. It does not increase cholesterol as many other oils do, but promotes the healing of wounds, relieves chronic fever, anemia, and blood disorders, is useful for detoxification, alleviates peptic ulcer and colitis, and is good generally for the eyes, nose, and skin. Indian lore also purports that ghee helps to enhance intelligence, understanding, and memory.

Acorn (*Quercus alba, Q. virens, Q. rubra*)

Quercus *is derived from the Celtic* quer, *meaning fine, and* cuez, *meaning tree. Ultimately, the word is believed to have been derived from the Sanskrit word for door, and many cultures believed trees in general to be doorways to other worlds and dimensions.* Alba *means white;* virens *means green. The English word* acorn *is derived from the Old English* aecern, *meaning oak fruit, or fruit of the tree.*

General Information The oak is indigenous to temperate regions of the Northern Hemisphere and to high altitudes in the tropics. A member of the beech family, oak trees are prolific producers, annually producing more nuts in North America than all of the region's other nut trees taken together, both wild and cultivated. Acorns are round to oblong in shape and fit into cups of rough bark; when the nuts are ripe, the cups separate

Lore and Legend

Of all the trees in prehistoric times, the oak was the most widely venerated because in many ancient mythologies it was the primordial first tree and the tree from which humanity sprang. Abraham received the angel of Jehovah under its branches; the Greeks dedicated it to Zeus because his oracle in Dodona was located in a grove of oaks; and the Romans held it sacred to Jupiter. Long associated with thunder gods in European culture, this may be due to the fact that oaks seem to attract more lightning than any other tree. Because the oak provided the life-giving acorn, the main food for many Nordic tribes, the tree became a symbol of fecundity and immortality, and was under the immediate protection of the Norse god Thor. It was considered an act of sacrilege to mutilate these trees in even a small degree. The oak tree was also the sacred tree of the pagan Dagda, the Good God and Creator of the ancient Irish Gaels. It was the celestial tree of the Celtic Druids, and no Druidic ceremony or rite took place without the aid of the oak tree and its satellite, the mistletoe; even their diet consisted mainly of acorns and berries. In fact, the name druid derived from the Greek word for tree (particularly oak), *drus;* a wood nymph was a *druas.* Aesop recounts the fable of the man who lay beneath an oak tree criticizing the Creator for placing so tiny an acorn on so huge a tree, while the mammoth pumpkin grows on so delicate a vine. But when an acorn fell and hit him on the nose, he decided that perhaps the Creator was right after all, for what if that acorn had been in proportion to the tree?

To Romans during Pliny's day the oak symbolized bravery, and a crown of oak leaves was a glorious reward for outstanding military valor, particularly for saving a citizen's life in battle. The northern European peoples also believed in the heroic and victorious symbolism of the oak leaf cluster, and this symbolism survives today in American military decorations, with the Oak Leaf Cluster bestowed as an additional honor on those already decorated for exceptional service.

and the nuts drop to the ground. Many Greek and Latin writers referred to acorns as wholesome fare. Early Athenians evidently ate them, and several classical writers say the same of the idyllic Arcadians in the "Golden Age" of innocence. With the rising abundance of cereal grains, the acorn lost its importance as a staple food, and was relegated to the role of poor man's fare and swine fodder. The drawback to most acorns is their bitter taste, which comes from tannic acid. Of the almost three hundred species of oaks, only a very few (particularly the white oak and evergreen oak) produce nuts that are sweet, naturally delicious, and edible when they drop ripe from the tree. Acorns represented an important source of food for American Indians, who removed the bitter substance by boiling the nuts until the kernels were palatable, or by grinding them and placing the resultant meal in water for a day to soak out the bitter substances.

Acorn

Nutritional Value Per 100 g Edible Portion

	Raw	Dried
Calories	369	509
Protein	6.15 g	8.10 g
Fat	23.86 g	31.41 g
Fiber	2.57 g	3.38 g
Calcium	41 mg	54 mg
Iron	0.79 mg	1.04 mg
Magnesium	62 mg	82 mg
Phosphorus	79 mg	103 mg
Potassium	539 mg	709 mg
Sodium	0 mg	0 mg
Zinc	0.510 mg	0.670 mg
Copper	0.621 mg	0.818 mg
Thiamine (B_1)	0.112 mg	0.149 mg
Riboflavin (B_2)	0.118 mg	0.154 mg
Niacin (B_3)	1.827 mg	2.406 mg
Ascorbic Acid (C)	0 mg	0 mg

Culinary Uses The flavor of acorns seems to be a matter of opinion. Some consider it to be rough and disagreeable, while others claim that fresh sweet acorns, roasted and salted, provide a good snack food, tasting like a cross between sunflower seeds and popcorn. Ground into meal, acorns can be used in the same manner as corn meal.

Alfalfa *(Medicago sativa)*

Also Known As: Chilean Clover, Buffalo Grass, Lucerne, Purple Medic.

> *The name* Medicago *is derived from the Media region in Persia, where this important plant was thought to have originated. The Greeks called it* medicai, *the Romans* medica *or* herba medica, *all meaning coming from Media.* Sativa *means cultivated. The Arabs named this herb* al-fac-facah, *meaning father of all foods, which the Spanish changed to* alfalfa.

General Information Alfalfa is a deep-rooting, bushy perennial resembling leggy clover that grows to three feet in height and produces the smallest, but most popular, seeds of the legume family. The plant was introduced into the Mediterranean Greek and Roman world about 470 B.C., during the time of the Persian Wars. The ancient Arabs fed it to their horses in the belief that it made their horses swift and strong, and the Romans (believing or at least hoping the same) started cultivating it as a forage crop starting in the first or second century A.D. Not until the seventeenth century did alfalfa arrive in western Europe, at which time it was given the name *lucerna,* meaning lamp, after the bright shiny appearance of the seeds. Ultimately, alfalfa reached North America with the Spanish Conquistadores, who planted it in Mexico and Chile. Gold prospectors carried it from South America into California. Although still highly prized by farmers as animal forage, the sprouted seeds have become so popular for human consumption in the last 30 years that they are now found in stores and restaurants everywhere.

Alfalfa

Nutritional Value Per 100 g Edible Portion

	Sprouted Raw	Dried
Calories	29	269
Protein	3.99 g	19.9 g
Fat	0.69 g	4.3 g
Fiber	1.64 g	21.0 g
Calcium	32 mg	899 mg
Iron	0.96 mg	26 mg
Magnesium	27 mg	230 mg
Phosphorus	70 mg	150 mg
Potassium	79 mg	1200 mg
Sodium	6 mg	17 mg
Zinc	0.920 mg	trace
Copper	0.157 mg	n/a
Manganese	0.188 mg	2.530 mg
Beta Carotene (A)	155 IU	24,800 IU
Thiamine (B_1)	0.076 mg	0.190 mg
Riboflavin (B_2)	0.126 mg	1.420 mg
Niacin (B_3)	0.481 mg	9.700 mg
Pantothenic Acid (B_5)	0.563 mg	n/a
Pyridoxine (B_6)	0.034 mg	n/a
Folic Acid (B_9)	36.0 mcg	n/a
Ascorbic Acid (C)	8.2 mg	147 mg

Culinary Uses The leaves, flowering tops, seeds and sprouts of alfalfa are all edible, but what is most often seen and eaten are the sprouts. Easily grown, alfalfa sprouts find their way into salads and sandwiches of every kind, where their delicate taste endears them to many hearts and palates. The light brown unsprouted seeds may also be sprinkled over salads, casseroles, breads, and pastries, adding a delicious nutty flavor.

Health Benefits Nutritive, stomachic, tonic. Alfalfa is one of the most complete and nutritionally rich of all foods tested. It is noteworthy for its exceptional amount of trace minerals, for having all eight essential amino acids, and for being so high in vitamins A and D, calcium, phosphorus, iron, and potassium. Medicinally, it has anti-inflammatory properties, is very effective in cleansing toxins from the large intestine and bloodstream, is a natural pain reliever, contains natural fluorine which prevents tooth decay and helps rebuild decayed teeth, and provides a boost to the immune system. Its high beta carotene (vitamin A) content acts to strengthen the epithelial cells of the mucous membranes of the stomach, while its high chlorophyll content works as a natural deodorizer, infection fighter, and to purify the blood. The combination of alfalfa and mint tea is regarded as a soothing beverage and an aid to digestion, probably due to the fact that alfalfa contains the digestive enzyme betaine. Alfalfa tea provides a nutrient boost, prevents exhaustion, and relieves bloating, arthritis, rheumatism, colitis, ulcers, and anemia.

NOTE: Alfalfa sprouts and seeds should be avoided by those with rheumatoid arthritis and systemic lupus, due to their rich content of the amino acid canavanine, which can ignite inflammations in these conditions. Alfalfa leaf, however, is not a source of this amino acid, and may be used by those with rheumatoid diseases.

Almond (*Prunus dulcis, P. amygdalus*)

The almond tree is part of the plum family, and thus the genus Prunus. Dulcis *means sweet, while* amygdalus *is the old Latin name for the almond. The English word* almond *came from the French* amande, *a derivative of* amygdalus.

General Information The graceful almond tree is native to North Africa, West Asia, and the Mediterranean. Botanically, almonds are a fruit—the ancient ancestor of later fruits that have large stones for seeds, like nectarines, peaches, plums, and apricots. The almond itself has a tough, greenish-gray hull that looks very much like a small, elongated peach. This hull splits open at maturity, revealing the familiar almond shell, which encases the edible nut. Two types of almonds are grown: sweet and bitter. The sweet is the only one used as a nut, mostly for desserts and confectionery items. Bitter almonds are cheaper and easier to grow, but contain prussic acid and are suitable for use only after the removal of this poison by heat. The bitter almond provides the main source of bitter almond oil, which is used both as a flavoring and as an ingredient in cosmetic skin preparations. Almonds were brought to California in 1843 by Spanish missionaries, and today this state produces the world's largest share of almonds. They remain a dominant nut in world trade and the most widely grown and eaten tree nut.

Culinary Uses For freshness, purchase whole almonds and then slice or chop them just prior to use. The thin brown skin of a shelled almond should be intact and unscratched, as it provides some protection from rancidity. Slice an almond kernel in half and examine its texture. A solid white nutmeat denotes freshness, while a honeycomb-textured kernel or yellow color indicates rancidity. Although the skin is edible, some authorities claim that it should be removed due to its astringent tendencies. Almonds are widely used in confectionery, are made into drinks and liqueurs, combine successfully with cheese and vegetables to make a good stuffing, and may be added raw to salads. Use almonds in tandem with almond oil for reinforced flavor in baking, or to give body to a salad dressing.

Health Benefits Demulcent, emollient. Almonds are traditionally regarded as having some special healing and protecting properties; some doctors even "prescribe" almonds daily for their patients. The most alkaline of all nuts (but still slightly acidic), almonds are particularly valuable as an essential "building food" for those who are underweight. Their high fat, carbohydrate, and protein content make them an ideal food for strengthening the body when there is no need to worry about the increase in the supply of fat. Almonds contain a small amount of amygdalin, better known as laetrile, which has resulted in their gaining a reputation as an anticancer food; however, unlike apricot kernels, almonds are safe to consume, even in large amounts. Best eaten raw, they are easy to digest when well masticated or ground fine.

Lore and Legend

Greek mythology relates that a beautiful Thracian princess named Phyllis was deserted on her wedding day by her lover, Demophon. After waiting many years for him to return, she eventually died of a broken heart. In sympathy and for eternal compensation, the gods transformed her into an almond tree (called *Phylla* by the Greeks), a symbol of hope. When Demophon finally returned it was too late, and when the leafless, flowerless, and forlorn tree was shown him as the memorial of Phyllis, he clasped it in his arms, whereupon it burst forth into bloom—an emblem of true love inextinguishable by death. In Greece almonds in uneven numbers of three, five, or seven are offered to guests for good fortune and happiness at christenings, weddings, and the ordination of priests. Shelled almonds and raisins, combined, were early symbols of good luck for Jews. The nuts and fruits, packaged together, are still popular in Eastern Europe.

Another beautiful legend comes from Portugal. A Moorish prince from the deep south of Portugal (Algarve) married a Scandinavian princess, who pined away in that snowless land for lack of winter and the sight of snow. Her prince relieved her homesickness by planting almond trees so thickly along the entire coast that when they bloomed, their white blossoms covered the land each spring with a snowy-white blanket.

NOTE: Since almonds have a high ratio of arginine to lysine, they should be avoided by individuals susceptible to cold sores or herpes infections; arginine promotes (and lysine prevents) the activation of the virus.

Byproducts

Almond butter is made from either raw or roasted almonds ground to a creamy consistency. This can be used on toast or in baked goods, wherever you would use peanut butter.

Almond

Nutritional Value Per 100 g Edible Portion	Dried, Unblanched
Calories	589
Protein	19.95 g
Fat	52.21 g
Fiber	2.71 g
Calcium	266 mg
Iron	3.66 mg
Magnesium	296 mg
Phosphorus	520 mg
Potassium	732 mg
Sodium	11 mg
Zinc	2.920 mg
Copper	0.942 mg
Manganese	2.273 mg
Beta Carotene (A)	0 mg
Thiamine (B_1)	0.211 mg
Riboflavin (B_2)	0.779 mg
Niacin (B_3)	3.361 mg
Pantothenic Acid (B_5)	0.471 mg
Pyridoxine (B_6)	0.113 mg
Folic Acid (B_9)	58.7 mcg
Ascorbic Acid (C)	0.600 mg
Tocopherol (E)	24.01 mg

Almond extract is made from the oil of the bitter almond, a cousin to the sweet almond. The oil is diluted with water and alcohol to make this common flavoring.

Almond milk is made from almonds that have been soaked, crushed, and strained. This delicately sweet and satisfying beverage is a wonderful dairy-free and soy-free milk that can be directly substituted for cow's milk. Although it is available commercially, almond milk produced at home is easily made, and tastes fresher and sweeter.

Almond oil is made by crushing whole raw almonds to extract the oil. Food-grade almonds are expensive nuts, making a quality almond oil expensive and very difficult to find in a truly cold-pressed form. Unrefined almond oil is sweet, pleasant tasting, and known for its high content of vitamins A and E. Therapeutically, the oil has been used for treating gastric ulcers, as a laxative, and as an antiseptic for the intestines, as well as to help stabilize the nervous system. It is also a time-honored balm for dry or sunburned skin, a skin beautifier, and a massage oil. Almond oil is 8.20 percent saturated, 69.90 percent monounsaturated, 17.40 percent polyunsaturated, and contains 39.2 mg/100g tocopherol (vitamin E).

Almond, Tropical *(Terminalia catappa)*

The scientific binomial is descriptive, for Terminalia *refers to the manner in which the leaves are borne in bunches on the branch ends; while* catappa *comes from a Malayan name for the tree.*

General Information Native to the sandy coasts of Malaysia and other regions of southeast Asia, the tropical almond tree was taken by Captain Bligh to St. Vincent in the West Indies in 1793, along with the breadfruit. The fruits are about the size of a plum and are slightly compressed on two sides. They have a tender skin and a thin layer of edible, juicy pulp surrounding a thick, spongy shell, which is very difficult to crack.

Culinary Uses The crisp, white nutmeat of the small, slender kernel has a delicious flavor reminiscent of the true almond, to which the tropical almond is not related. The nuts are edible raw or roasted, and are popular and highly regarded in the Far East, having been described by one writer as "beyond comparison the most delicious nut of any kind India affords." The kernels yield a sweet, colorless, nondrying, edible oil, "Indian almond oil," which resembles true almond oil in flavor and odor. Highly esteemed as a table oil in India and Malaysia, it does not readily become rancid.

Almondette (*Buchanania lanzan*)

Also Known As: Calumpang, Chironji.

The English name almondette *means little almond.*

General Information The almondette tree is native to southeast Asia, and grows best in the deciduous forests of hot dry regions. The tree bears black, single-seeded fruits measuring about one-half inch in diameter which enclose the pear-shaped kernels; often mottled, these kernels are no more than a quarter-inch in length. Virtually unknown in the United States, the almondette is an important article of commerce in central India, where it is known as *chironji*.

Culinary Uses The delicious flavor of almondettes may be compared to a combination of almond and pistachio. In India the nuts are eaten raw or roasted, as substitutes for almonds, and since early times they have been prized as a sweetmeat when cooked. One of the native Indian breads consists of pounding the dried fruits (with the kernel intact), and then drying and baking the resulting nutloaf. These nuts also yield a light yellow, wholesome oil, which has a pleasant aroma and makes a satisfactory substitute for either almond or olive oil.

Health Benefits Rich in oil and protein, almondette nuts are composed of over 50 percent oil, and 12 percent protein.

Beechnut (*Fagus grandifolia, F. sylvatica*)

Fagus *is from the Greek word* phagein, *meaning to eat, referring to the edible character of the nuts. The term* grandifolia *means large-leaved, while* sylvatica *means forest-loving. The common name of the beech tree, found in varying forms throughout the Teutonic dialects, means, with difference of gender, either "a book" or "a beech."*

Beechnut

Nutritional Value Per 100 g Edible Portion

	Dried
Calories	576
Protein	6.20 g
Fat	50.00 g
Fiber	3.70 g
Calcium	1 mg

Lore and Legend

The beech has been intimately associated with books and writing since antiquity, and thus has become the symbolic tree of the graphic arts. Early runic tablets were made from thin slabs of smooth beech bark, and as a monumental tree the beech has no rival: for many centuries its bark has served as a convenient place to register challenges to the enemy, post epitaphs, and carve the initials of loved ones.

General Information The stately beech tree with its smooth silvery-gray bark, blue-green leaves, and symmetrical round canopy, is one of the most beautiful trees found in North America and Europe. The nuts are larger and more numerous in more northerly climes. Like their relative the acorn, beechnuts are now used primarily as animal fodder, although some regions in Scandinavia still use them to make meal for bread.

Culinary Uses The beechnut is similar to the chestnut in flavor, but has a much higher fat content. One of the sweetest nuts from the northern forests, those gathered from the wild may be eaten fresh, dried, or roasted. Unless properly dried, fresh nuts will deteriorate within a few weeks. Flour or meal is prepared by mashing the nutmeats, allowing the resultant paste to dry out, then grinding it. This meal can then be used to make bread or biscuits, or combined with other flours in baked products.

Health Benefits Beechnuts, according to some authorities, contain small amounts of toxins and thus should either not be consumed in quantity or be avoided entirely.

Brazil Nut *(Bertholletia excelsa)*

Also Known As: Para Nut, Cream Nut.

> *This tree was given its Latin name* Bertholletia *in honor of Louis Claude Berthollet, a French chemist; the term* excelsa *means tall. Its English name indicates its place of origin, Brazil.*

General Information From the Amazon River forests come Brazil nuts, fruits of huge broad-leaf evergreen trees whose trunks may grow up to six feet in diameter and reach straight up to immense heights of 150 feet. These trees are not cultivated but grow wild, and all attempts thus far at cultivation have met with resounding failure. Each tree bears between two hundred and four hundred large fruits, which when ripe are dark brown, pear-shaped, about the size of a man's head, and weigh between two and four pounds; in total these fruits contain approximately five hundred pounds of unshelled Brazil nuts. Most are harvested by waiting for the fruit to ripen and fall to the ground—a potentially lethal event, since they fall from great heights. When the fruits are broken open, there is a coconut-like pod containing between twelve and twenty-four nuts all packed neatly together like orange segments. Each dark brown nut is up to two inches in length and triangular in shape. A quarter of the crop is shelled before export, chiefly from the city of Para. Although these trees are important to the Brazilian economy, the oily nuts are not part of the native diet since the climate is too hot for so oily a food. For the most part, Brazil nuts are enjoyed as a delicacy in foreign lands thousands of miles away from where they grow.

Brazil Nut

Nutritional Value Per 100 g Edible Portion

	Dried, Unblanched
Calories	656
Protein	14.34 g
Fat	66.22 g
Fiber	2.29 g
Calcium	176 mg
Iron	3.40 mg
Magnesium	225 mg
Phosphorus	600 mg
Potassium	600 mg
Sodium	2 mg
Zinc	4.590 mg
Copper	1.770 mg
Manganese	0.774 mg
Thiamine (B1)	1.000 mg
Riboflavin (B2)	0.122 mg
Niacin (B3)	1.622 mg
Pantothenic Acid (B5)	0.236 mg
Pyridoxine (B6)	0.251 mg
Folic Acid (B9)	4 mcg
Ascorbic Acid (C)	0.70 mg
Tocopherol (E)	7.60 mg

Culinary Uses Brazil nuts are sweet and flavorful, with a rich, creamy texture and delicate flavor. They are best purchased in the shell, since their high oil content predisposes them to turn rancid quickly; after purchasing, they should always be refrigerated and used within two or three months. Brazil nuts are excellent for eating raw in muesli and salads, as a stuffing for dates, or just as a snack on their own. They also can be added to vegetarian loaves and burgers, casseroles, stuffings, and soups. Try them as the "core" of baked apples.

Health Benefits The Brazil nut is among the most acid of nuts due to its high protein content, and has an oil content of nearly 70 percent. Brazil nuts are good sources of the amino acids methionine and cysteine, making them a good complementary protein source for vegetarians. For those doing hard physical work, both the nuts and the butter made from them are very nourishing.

Breadnut *(Artocarpus altilis, Brosimum alicastrum)*

Artocarpus *comes from the Greek words* artos, *meaning bread, and* carpos, *meaning fruit. The term* altilis *refers to the tallness of the tree.* Brosimum *derives from a Greek term meaning edible. Its English name* breadfruit *for the fruit comes from the fact that when it is roasted whole between hot stones, the pulp achieves the consistency and taste of freshly baked bread.*

General Information Two related trees produce nuts or seeds that are designated as breadnuts: the breadnut tree, and the seeded variety of the breadfruit. The evergreen breadnut (*Brosimum alicastrum*) is native to southern Mexico, Central America, and the Caribbean. Ripe breadnut fruits are yellow, about one inch in diameter, and contain a single seed or breadnut about the size of a small chestnut. The scanty pulp is edible. The breadfruit tree (*Artocarpus altilis*) is a handsome tree believed native to a vast area extending from New Guinea through the Indo-Malayan Archipelago to western Micronesia. A member of the mulberry family, the breadfruit is a valuable crop from southern Florida to Brazil, and during its eight-month season provides the natives around the Gulf of Mexico and the Caribbean Sea with an important fruit, often the mainstay of their diet. Both seedless and seeded forms of breadfruit are known. The seeded type is grown primarily for its seeds, called breadnuts, which when cooked and eaten are said to taste like chestnuts.

Lore and Legend

The seeded breadfruit, native of the hot, moist Pacific Islands, was regarded for years as a romantic symbol of abundance and easy living.

Culinary Uses When breadnut seeds are boiled, their flavor is somewhat like potatoes. Ground breadnut seeds may be added to cold milk and sugar to make a nutritious and tasty milkshake. Roasted seeds develop a nutty cocoa flavor, and a beverage somewhat similar to coffee can be prepared by grinding the roasted seeds and steeping them in boiling water. The seeds from seeded breadfruit are usually boiled, roasted, or fried before being eaten, when they are said to be so close to chestnuts in flavor and texture that they may be freely substituted in any chestnut recipe. See also **Breadfruit** reference under **Fruits.**

Breadnut

Nutritional Value Per 100 g Edible Portion

	Breadfruit Seeds Raw	Breadfruit Seeds, Boiled	Breadnut Seeds, Raw	Breadnut Seeds, Dried
Calories	191	168	217	367
Protein	7.40 g	5.30 g	5.97 g	8.62 g
Fat	5.59 g	2.30 g	0.99 g	1.68 g
Fiber	1.69 g	1.80 g	2.53 g	5.60 g
Calcium	36 mg	61 mg	98 mg	94 mg
Iron	3.67 mg	0.60 mg	2.09 mg	4.60 mg
Phosphorus	175 mg	124 mg	67 mg	178 mg
Beta Carotene (A)	256 IU	n/a	248 IU	216 IU
Thiamine (B_1)	0.482 mg	0.290 mg	0.055 mg	0.030 mg
Riboflavin (B_2)	0.301 mg	0.170 mg	0.055 mg	0.140 mg
Niacin (B_3)	0.438 mg	5.300 mg	0.880 mg	2.100 mg
Pantothenic Acid (B_5)	0.877 mg	n/a	n/a	n/a
Ascorbic Acid (C)	6.6 mg	n/a	27.4 mg	46.6 mg

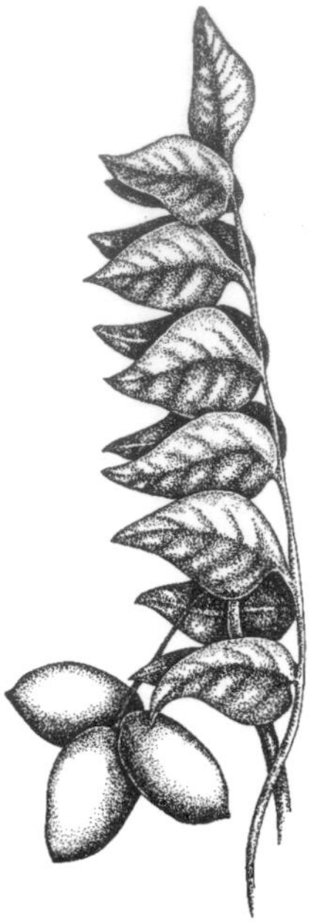

Butternut *(Juglans cinerea)*

Also Known As: Oilnut, White Walnut.

The generic term Juglans is a contraction of the Latin Jovis glans, nut of Jupiter or of "the Gods," after the ancient belief that the gods dined on walnuts. The term cinerea means ash-colored and refers to the color of the foliage. The English term butternut is due to the high oil content in the nut.

Butternut

Nutritional Value Per 100 g Edible Portion

	Dried
Calories	612
Protein	24.90 g
Fat	56.98 g
Fiber	1.87 g
Calcium	53 mg
Iron	4.02 mg
Magnesium	237 mg
Phosphorus	446 mg
Potassium	421 mg
Sodium	1 mg
Zinc	3.130 mg
Copper	0.450 mg
Manganese	6.560 mg

General Information The butternut is native to North America and grows over most of the eastern half of the United States. It differs from the black walnut in that the tree is usually smaller and has lighter-colored bark. The oblong or cylindrical fruits that enclose the nuts are about two-and-a-half inches in length, sharp-pointed at the apex, and have a rough, jagged surface. A thin husk with numerous sticky hairs and a pungent but not unpleasant odor covers the outside. The shell is hard, rough, and walnut-like. Since the shell is so hard and thick, it is generally difficult to crack the nuts without shattering the kernels.

Culinary Uses Butternuts have a deliciously sweet yet distinctive, slightly spicy flavor. Young tender butternuts, gathered in the summer while still green, can be pickled in the same manner as walnuts. Fully mature nuts are good eaten alone or in baked goods. The trees can also be tapped for their sweet sap, like sugar maples.

Candlenut *(Aleurites moluccana)*

Aleurites *is from a Greek term meaning farinose or floury;* moluccana *means coming from the Moluccas. The nut derives its English name from the fact that natives of Hawaii string the kernels on a stick and light them as we do candles. Due to the very oily nature of the nuts, they serve this purpose well.*

General Information This small evergreen tree is native to most warm countries of the East: India, southern Japan, Malaysia, and nearly all the islands of the Pacific Ocean.

Culinary Uses The nuts are round, one to two inches across, each containing either one or two waxy white kernels possessing a flavor similar to walnuts, and are widely consumed as a flavoring ingredient after suitable preparation. The usual practice is to roast the nuts until they can be cracked open, and then to sauté the kernels crushed with other ingredients such as shallots, garlic, and chili peppers, to produce an aromatic mixture for use in savory dishes.

Canola Oil

General Information Canola oil is made from the seeds of Rape (*Brassica rapa oleifera, B. campestris, B. napus*), a plant in the cabbage and turnip family that dates back to antiquity in eastern Europe and Asia. The small, round, usually black seeds grow in long slender pods similar to mustard, and have a nutty flavor like sesame seeds, but with a surprising sweetness and tang. With a name like rape seed, neither the seeds nor oil caught on in the United States, so currently they are under production using their Canadian name, canola (shorthand for Canadian oil/low-acid), both as a snack seed and for oil production.

Culinary Uses Unrefined canola oil has a fresh golden color and rich savory flavor, but most canola oil found in stores is highly processed and rather mild. It is best suited for dishes where you do not want a pronounced flavor, or it can be used directly on salads, raw vegetables, potatoes, and grains. Due to its Omega-3 fatty acid content, canola oil should not be used for cooking over 320°F.

Health Benefits Canola oil contains one of the lowest amounts of saturated fat, and is among the highest for monounsaturated fat content of any edible oil. Therapeutically, it has been used to protect artery walls and as protection against blood clots. Unfortunately, rape seeds contain erucic acid, which causes fatty degeneration of the heart, kidney, adrenals, and thyroid. Low-erucic canola oil (less than 30 percent) is 5.60 percent saturated, 62.40 percent monounsaturated, and 27.70 percent polyunsaturated. High-erucic canola oil (greater than 30 percent) is 5.40 percent saturated, 66.40 percent monounsaturated, and 23.80 percent polyunsaturated.

Cashew (*Anacardium occidentale*)

The generic name Anacardium *means heart-shaped;* occidentale *means western. The English word* cashew *is derived from the Brazilian Tupi-Indian word* acaju.

General Information The tropical evergreen cashew shrub, whose relatives include the mango and pistachio, is native to the West Indies, Brazil, and India. The nut is actually the seed of the fleshy, orange-colored, pear-shaped cashew apple; instead of being on the inside of the fruit, however, it hangs like an appendage from the base. Since the cashew apple spoils within twenty-four hours of harvest, it is almost never exported, and the fortunate few who have tried this fruit, either ripe or in preserves, say it is even tastier than the cashew nut. The kidney-shaped nuts have hard shells with two layers; between the layers is a black resinous liquid called cardol, which is caustic and can form blisters on the skin. During processing, this liquid is removed and used to make paints, varnishes, and insecticides.

Culinary Uses Cashew nuts are bean-shaped, eggshell white, and plump with a slightly sweet, bland flavor. They are never sold in the shell, and cannot be considered a raw nut since they are heated during processing. The cashew nut is very versatile, as it can be used in making nut milks and butters, cream soups, ice cream, breads, and stuffings, or just eaten plain. For a special main dish, try mushroom and cashew stroganoff.

Cashew

Nutritional Value Per 100 g Edible Portion	Dry Roasted
Calories	574
Protein	15.31 g
Fat	46.35 g
Fiber	0.70 g
Calcium	45 mg
Iron	6.00 mg
Magnesium	260 mg
Phosphorus	490 mg
Potassium	565 mg
Sodium	16 mg
Zinc	5.600 mg
Copper	2.220 mg
Beta Carotene (A)	0 mg
Thiamine (B_1)	0.200 mg
Riboflavin (B_2)	0.200 mg
Niacin (B_3)	1.400 mg
Pantothenic Acid (B_5)	1.217 mg
Pyridoxine (B_6)	0.256 mg
Folic Acid (B_9)	69.2 mcg
Ascorbic Acid (C)	0 mg
Tocopherol (E)	0.57 mg

Health Benefits Cashews are helpful for emaciation, problems with teeth and gums, and lack of vitality. They contain a high content of oleic acid (versus polyunsaturated oils). Cashews do not combine well with any form of starch, especially bread.

Byproducts

Cashew butter is made by grinding cashews in a blender or food grinder until the consistency of peanut butter. This spread can then be used on crackers and bread, or in sauces and soups as a thickener. Another type of cashew butter is made by melting regular butter, adding seasonings, and mixing in cashew pieces; use this as a sauce with vegetables.

Cashew milk made from soaked and ground cashews may be used to replace whole dairy milk in the same proportions for almost all recipes. Because the cashew nut is soft, it can be blended to a smooth white liquid with no residue.

Castor Oil *(Ricinus communis)*

Ricinus *is the name in classical languages applied to the castor bean seed;* communis *means common or widely known. The English name* castor *comes from the Greek term for beaver,* kastor, *and is related to the earlier Sanskrit term* kasturi, *meaning musk. Beaver musk* (castoreum) *was a valuable commodity, used not only as a perfume base but also as a cathartic in ancient medicine. Since the oil of the castor bean was similarly used as a cathartic, it was named after the beaver.*

General Information The castor oil plant, native to western Asia and Africa, often grows thirty or forty feet high. The mature seed capsules, each containing three bean-like seeds, explode and scatter their seeds as they dry. From the seeds a pale viscous oil has been pressed since antiquity. This oil, with its unpleasant, acrid taste, is one of the oldest medicinal prescriptions, and has been used throughout the ages as a purgative for many ills of the stomach, spleen, bowels, uterus, and as a cure for intestinal worms. The Egyptians used castor oil as lamp oil and as an unguent; they also purged their systems three times a month by drinking the oil mixed with beer. The Greeks and Romans—taking note, no doubt, that the beans are poisonous—used the oil only externally, and it was not until the late eighteenth century that the oil regained its ancient role as a laxative. All parts of the plant, but especially the seeds, are toxic to humans and animals, and should never be eaten. Eating a single castor bean can kill a child. The toxic action is due to ricin, a severe irritant that produces nausea, vomiting, gastric pain, diarrhea, thirst, and dimness of vision. Hulled and crushed at temperatures below 100°F, the beans yield a clear or yellowish poison-free oil rich in ricinolein, which irritates the intestines, causing them to expel their contents.

Health Benefits Laxative. Castor oil is a mild enough laxative to use even for small babies. For chronic constipation, one tablespoon of castor oil should be taken with a cup of ginger tea; this tonic will neutralize toxins and relieve gas and constipation. The oil may also be applied externally for itches, cutaneous complaints, or rubbed on the nipples of a nursing mother after each time the child has nursed in order to prevent soreness. Castor oil makes an excellent hair tonic as well as a massage oil. Used as an external poultice, it dissolves and draws out cysts, tumors, warts, growths, and other toxic accumulations. It also has an emollient effect and will help soften and remove scars. For these purposes, soak a wool flannel cloth with castor oil and apply one or more times daily to the affected area for one or two hours. For increased effectiveness, put a protective layer on the poultice and apply heat directly on top of it with a hot water bottle or heating pad. The tea of the castor root is used as an anti-inflammatory to treat many disorders such as arthritis, sciatica, chronic backache, and muscle spasms.

Chestnut *(Castanea sativa, C. dentata)*

Castanea is said to have been derived either from the city Kastanea in Pontus, Asia Minor, or from a town of the same name in Thessaly, Greece, from where chestnuts were first introduced into Europe. Sativa *refers to the fact that this nut has long been cultivated;* dentata *means toothed, usually with sharp, outward pointing teeth. The English word* chestnut *is derived from the Latin.*

General Information Most of the chestnut trees now found in the United States are a variety native to southern Europe. The native American chestnut grew abundantly in the United States until the early twentieth century, when some diseased trees imported from Asia and planted on Long Island in 1904 spread a fungus that nearly obliterated all the native trees. Only a few groves in California and the Pacific Northwest escaped the general destruction. New stocks have been planted, but most of the chestnuts sold for eating today are imported from Italy and Japan. Once considered a staple food, the mound-shaped, smooth, thin, brown-skinned nut grows two or three inside of a hard prickly burr. After the burrs fall to the ground, they are gathered and the chestnuts removed. Although the chestnut is called a nut, looks and feels like a nut, and has a shell like a nut, it is shown by analysis to be more closely related to the starchy grains. Furthermore, chestnuts are sweet and soft, without the characteristic crunchiness of nuts.

Lore and Legend

The Greek Xenophon's army supposedly lived on chestnuts during its retreat from Asia Minor in 401–399 B.C. In Tuscany the nuts have a sacred connotation: they are eaten on Saint Simon's Day, and on the Feast of Saint Martin are distributed to the poor.

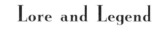

Chestnut

Nutritional Value Per 100 g Edible Portion

	Raw Unpeeled	Boiled Steamed	Roasted	Flour
Calories	213	131	245	362
Protein	2.42 g	2.00 g	3.17 g	6.10 g
Fat	2.26 g	1.38 g	2.20 g	3.70 g
Fiber	1.71 g	0.70 g	1.90 g	2.00 g
Calcium	27 mg	46 mg	29 mg	50 mg
Iron	1.01 mg	1.73 mg	0.91 mg	3.20 mg
Magnesium	32 mg	54 mg	33 mg	n/a
Phosphorus	93 mg	99 mg	107 mg	164 mg
Potassium	518 mg	715 mg	592 mg	847 mg
Sodium	3 mg	27 mg	2 mg	11 mg
Zinc	0.520 mg	0.250 mg	0.570 mg	n/a
Copper	0.447 mg	0.472 mg	0.507 mg	n/a
Manganese	0.952 mg	0.854 mg	1.180 mg	n/a
Beta Carotene (A)	28 IU	n/a	24 IU	n/a
Thiamine (B_1)	0.238 mg	n/a	0.243 mg	0.230 mg
Riboflavin (B_2)	0.168 mg	n/a	0.175 mg	0.370 mg
Niacin (B_3)	1.179 mg	n/a	1.342 mg	1.000 mg
Pantothenic Acid (B_5)	0.509 mg	n/a	0.554 mg	n/a
Pyridoxine (B_6)	0.376 mg	n/a	0.497 mg	n/a
Folic Acid (B_9)	62 mcg	n/a	70 mcg	n/a
Ascorbic Acid (C)	43 mg	n/a	26 mg	n/a

Culinary Uses Chestnuts have graced tables on several continents for centuries in the widest variety of forms, from the exalted *marrons glaces* to common porridge. Fresh chestnuts are quite starchy and not very sweet when first picked, but after a few days of curing, some of the starch turns to sugar and the large, soft nuts develop a gentle sweetness. Never eaten raw due to their tannic acid content, they are the only nut treated as a vegetable and must be boiled or roasted before eating. The cooked nuts can be used chopped in stuffings, sprinkled over vegetables, or pureed in soups. Because of their high starch content, Europeans often use them as a substitute for potatoes or noodles, and the combination of chestnuts and sweet potatoes is a favorite of many. Dried chestnuts are a useful time-saving standby and are considered sweeter than fresh chestnuts, although their texture is less floury than that of fresh chestnuts. They need to be soaked for about one hour and then cooked like legumes before use. In replacing fresh chestnuts with the dried variety, allow one part dried to three parts fresh. Canned whole chestnuts and chestnut purée (available either plain or sweetened) are used in soups, desserts, crêpes, and cakes. Whole chestnuts preserved in sugar or syrup as *marrons glaces* make a sweet treat or garnish.

Byproducts

Chestnut flour is a fragrant, sweet-tasting flour which forms a firm and unyielding paste. Generally available in specialty shops, it makes a tasty addition to pastries, cookies, and tarts. Rather heavy on its own, it is best combined with other flours.

Chia (*Salvia columbariae, S. hispanica*)

Salvia *is derived from the Latin* salvere*, which means to save, to be well or healthy;* columbariae *and* hispanica *mean Columbian and Hispanic (Mexican), referring to their places of origin. The English name* chia *comes from the Mayan* chiabaan*, meaning strong or strengthening.*

General Information The chia plant is native to the warm and temperate regions of the southwestern North American deserts and Central America. This small member of the sage family grows on the plains, hills, and valleys over much of California and northern Mexico, growing from an annual root with a slender branching stem terminated by several curious whorls containing the seeds. The seeds are flat, dark, round, and have a slippery feeling to the touch. *Columbariae's* seeds are a golden tan, while *hispanica's* are a grey-black (a few are white) and look rather like flattened, washed-out poppy seeds. Used as a staple food long before corn was developed, chia seeds were used by indigenous people as a highly nutritious and energy-generating food and medicine.

Culinary Uses Chia seeds by themselves taste much like wheat germ. Both varieties of chia seeds are hard and smooth as long as they are dry, but when placed in warm water, or any liquid for that matter, they rapidly begin to soften and swell, increasing their original size by four or five times. If plain water surrounds the seeds, it turns to a clear gelatin and the entire tapioca-like substance is pleasant to eat, especially if a little sweetener is added. Others prefer to grind the seeds in a blender and then sprinkle the meal directly on cereal. This meal can also be added to salads, soups, or baked products. The sprouted seeds taste much like watercress. As the seeds cannot be sprouted in the conventional manner because of their highly mucilaginous nature, there are earthenware containers (usually animal shaped) especially made for this purpose.

Chia

Nutritional Value Per 100 g Edible Portion

	Dried
Calories	472
Protein	16.62 g
Fat	26.25 g
Fiber	25.30 g
Calcium	529 mg
Iron	10.00 mg
Phosphorus	604 mg
Zinc	5.320 mg
Copper	1.660 mg
Beta Carotene (A)	36 IU
Thiamine (B_1)	0.869 mg
Riboflavin (B_2)	0.166 mg
Niacin (B_3)	5.817 mg

Health Benefits The energizing value of chia seeds was well known to the American Indians, who made use of the potent seeds to sustain them on long desert marches and runs. It is said that a handful of seeds, roasted and ground, will maintain a person throughout a day of hard exertion such as continuous running. Next to flax, chia seeds are the highest source of Omega-3 fatty acids. Chia seeds of the southwestern variety (*S. columbariae*) are more nutritious than the Mexican variety.

Chilean Wild Nut *(Gevuina avellana)*

> *This plant was named after Avella Vecchia, near Naples in southern Italy.* Gevuina *derives from the Chilean name.*

General Information Also known as the Chilean Hazel, this evergreen tree is a member of the macadamia family. The natural habitat of the tree is the cold region of southern Chile, extending from the snowline on the Pacific slopes of the Andes down to the seacoast. The fruits are fleshy drupes about the size of cherries that become coral-red when ripe and contain a single seed, somewhat smaller than the macadamia nut, which is enclosed within a hard woody shell.

Culinary Uses These nuts are pleasant tasting, similar in flavor to the European hazelnut—thus their common name in Chile of "avellano." The kernels may be eaten fresh, but they are usually roasted and sold in small paper bags like peanuts.

Coconut *(Cocos nucifera)*

> *The generic name* Cocos *and the English name* coconut *are derived from the Spanish/Portuguese word* coco *meaning monkey face. Sixteenth-century Spanish and Portuguese explorers gave the coconut this name because the three scars or markings on the base of the shell resemble a monkey's face: two of the germinating holes represent the eyes, the third the nose. The term* nucifera *means nut-bearing.*

General Information The coconut palm is believed to be native to Polynesia, Malaysia, and southern Asia. Considered the "king" of plants by the local inhabitants of tropical and subtropical regions, the plants are often the only cash crop, and may be the primary source of food as well. In Sanskrit the coconut palm is called *kalpa vriksha,* meaning "tree which gives all that is necessary for living." Practically all parts of the plant can be used in one manner or another: the trunk provides excellent wood, the leaves are used for basket weaving and roofing material, its husks for rope making, its shells for drinking vessels, and the young terminal buds are eaten under the name of "palm cabbages." Like citrus trees, coconut palms bloom and fruit year around. Ten to thirteen times a year a new flower spike emerges from the crown of the tree, developing into a cluster of six to twelve nuts. The individual coconuts require a year to reach full maturity from the time they first begin to take shape, but since new nuts are constantly being produced, there is a continuous yield. In some years an individual palm may bear two hundred coconuts, but a good annual harvest averages sixty coconuts. Cultivated trees start bearing in seven to ten years, produce mature crops from fifteen to fifty, and continue to bear up to seventy years of age.

It is the fruit, botanically classed as a drupe and not a nut, that gives the plant its greatest economic importance. The largest seed known, each nut is encased in a smooth outer layer, a fibrous middle layer, or coir, and a strong inner portion or shell, which encloses the single seed. Very buoyant and easily waterborne, coconuts have been carried on the

Gulf Stream to places as unlikely as Norway. Those appearing in markets have generally had the outer layers removed so that only the inner fibrous husk shows.

Buying Tips Coconuts may be found on the market all year, but October through December are the peak months. A quality nut is one that is heavy for its size and that sloshes with liquid when shaken. Do not choose one without liquid, as this indicates spoilage; also avoid those with moldy or wet "eyes," as these are unsound.

Culinary Uses The coconut's first dividends are reserved for those who live in its habitat. At six months, while the pulp is still green, the meat is gelatinous and no harder than that of a melon, with a fresh, fruity flavor, more nut-flavored than sugary. The unripe coconuts are preferred by natives over the solid ripe meat; it is eaten with a spoon, fed to babies, and used as a healing food. Ripe coconuts have a meat that is solid, pure white, and very sweet. To crack the coconut, pierce the soft spots or "eyes" at the top of the shell with an ice pick or other sharp object, and then drain the liquid. Tap all around the hard shell with a hammer until the shell cracks and falls away, or heat it in the oven at 350°F for thirty minutes, and the shell will easily break away. Coconut flesh can be eaten fresh out of hand, grated with a grater, or chopped in the blender. The fresh coconut is more flavorful and less expensive than packaged coconut, and is free of the additives used to preserve it in cans. Coconut can also be purchased dried, desiccated, flaked, shredded, or as coconut cream. Keep these in the refrigerator or freezer, or store in an airtight jar and

Coconut

Nutritional Value Per 100 g Edible Portion

	Raw	Dried Unsweetened	Raw Cream	Raw Milk	Raw Water
Calories	354	660	330	230	19
Protein	3.33 g	6.88 g	3.63 g	2.29 g	0.72 g
Fat	33.49 g	64.52 g	34.68 g	23.84 g	0.20 g
Fiber	4.27 g	5.31 g	n/a	n/a	0.02 g
Calcium	14 mg	26 mg	11 mg	16 mg	24 mg
Iron	2.43 mg	3.32 mg	2.28 mg	1.64 mg	0.29 mg
Magnesium	32 mg	90 mg	n/a	37 mg	25 mg
Phosphorus	113 mg	206 mg	122 mg	100 mg	20 mg
Potassium	356 mg	543 mg	325 mg	263 mg	250 mg
Sodium	20 mg	37 mg	4 mg	15 mg	105 mg
Zinc	1.100 mg	2.010 mg	0.960 mg	0.670 mg	0.100 mg
Copper	0.435 mg	0.796 mg	0.378 mg	0.266 mg	0.040 mg
Manganese	1.500 mg	2.745 mg	1.304 mg	0.916 mg	n/a
Beta Carotene (A)	0 mg	0 mg	0 mg	0 mg	0 mg
Thiamine (B_1)	0.066 mg	0.060 mg	0.030 mg	0.026 mg	0.030 mg
Riboflavin (B_2)	0.020 mg	0.100 mg	0 mg	0 mg	0.057 mg
Niacin (B_3)	0.540 mg	0.603 mg	0.890 mg	0.760 mg	0.080 mg
Pantothenic Acid (B_5)	0.300 mg	0.800 mg	n/a	n/a	0.043 mg
Pyridoxine (B_6)	0.054 mg	0.300 mg	n/a	n/a	0.032 mg
Folic Acid (B_9)	26.4 mcg	9 mcg	n/a	n/a	n/a
Ascorbic Acid (C)	3.3 mg	1.5 mg	2.8 mg	2.8 mg	2.4 mg
Tocopherol (E)	0.73 mg	n/a	n/a	n/a	n/a

Lore and Legend

In New Guinea, a native belief holds that the coconut palm originated by sprouting from the head of the first man to die. Thousands of miles away in northern India, the coconut is considered the sacred fruit of the "Tree of Life." A symbol of prosperity and fertility, shrines often keep a supply of coconuts to be given by priests to women who wish to conceive. In Bali, however, women are forbidden to touch coconut palms lest the fertility of the tree be drained off into the fertility of the woman. Do not pick up what looks to be an abandoned coconut lying by the road in Samoa unless you are looking for trouble; somebody knows it is there and has proprietary rights to it. On the Nicobar Islands in the Indian Ocean, whole coconuts comprised the local currency until the early twentieth century, with the value of goods reckoned in number of coconuts. Discs carved from coconut shells formed part of the shell-money strings that served as currency on some islands in the Carolines and in the Bismarck Archipelago in the South Pacific. According to an old South Sea proverb: "He who plants a coconut tree plants food and drink, vessels and clothing, a habitation for himself, and a heritage for his children."

use quickly, as the high oil content makes them prone to rapid rancidity. Shredded or flaked coconut is a wonderful garnish for cakes and candies, and makes a tasty addition to baked goods, granolas, and vegetable and rice dishes. Coconut is especially useful in Indonesian and West Indian dishes, where it is an important ingredient in curries, chutneys, and stews. Avoid coconut that is sweetened and has glycerine (a coal tar product) added.

Health Benefits Coconuts contain the organic iodine necessary to prevent thyroid gland problems. It digests best when combined with salads and cooked vegetables; with starches or sugars, including honey, it digests with difficulty. Coconut milk is warming, sweet, and quenches thirst.

Byproducts

Coconut milk is the liquid that is extracted from grating the fresh kernel, mixing it with water, and then straining the mixture. It is an important food commodity for millions of people throughout the tropical world, and used in place of oil, fat, and butter. Coconut milk can be used in cooking and baking, or as a liquid refreshment. In chemical balance it compares to mother's milk, and is a complete protein food when taken in its natural form.

Coconut oil is obtained by directly processing wet kernels or crushed good quality copra (shredded coconut). Fluid in warm tropical climates, at temperatures below 73°F the oil changes to a solid fat with the consistency of butter. In its liquid state, the oil has for thousands of years been used for cooking; in a semisolid state, the oil is a substitute for lard, but coconut fats are easily digested and metabolized and do not tend to cause weight gain. Most coconut oil is not sold in its unrefined state, however, but has been further refined by bleaching, deodorizing, and hydrogenating it into a clear liquid that has neither the taste nor the odor of the coconut. This refined oil has an astonishingly high percentage of saturated fat—over 90 percent, which is even higher than the animal fats butter and lard. Since it is quite resistant to oxidation, coconut oil is frequently used in ice cream, salad dressings, confections, as a spray oil on crackers, and especially for nondairy coffee creamers and whipped toppings (where it is better at raising blood cholesterol than cream). High-quality unrefined oil is said to be useful in mitigating muscular aches when massaged into the affected area, in preventing stretch marks during pregnancy, for healing cuts and scratches as well as burns (including sunburns), and has been recommended as a facial massage and wrinkle remover. Coconut oil is 86.50 percent saturated, 5.80 percent monounsaturated, and 1.80 percent polyunsaturated. It also contains 0.04 mg iron and 0.80 mg tocopherol (vitamin E) per 100 grams of oil.

Coconut water is the liquid found inside the coconut upon opening. Ripe coconuts have a liquid that is cloudy, aromatic, and pleasing to the taste and body. That of unripe coconuts is clear, light, and tastes both delicious and cleansing. Both the ripe and unripe liquids are either drunk straight from the shell or used in tropical drinks, fruit shakes, cocktails, or as a flavoring for spiced vegetables.

Shredded or **Desiccated coconut** is made from the meat of the coconut, the white inner lining of the kernel. Following shelling, the reddish-brown skin is pared off the outside surface of the white meat; the meat is then washed, pasteurized, blanched, shredded, dried, and graded into extra fine, fine, medium, and coarse qualities. The finished product has a moisture content of less than three percent and an oil content of about sixty-eight percent. Although coconut meat has its own natural sweetness, some commercial shredded coconut makers add extra sugar and propylene glycol (a preservative) to retain moisture. If you cannot get whole fresh coconut, try to find unsweetened shredded or flaked coconut without additives.

Cola (*Cola nitida, C. acuminata*)

Cola is the native name for these nuts, while nitida means shiny or glossy, and acuminata means acuminate or long-pointed.

General Information A popular stimulant in West Africa, cola "nuts" are not really nuts but the interior part of the fleshy seeds of tropical trees. Following the harvest, the nuts are removed from the pods, fermented for a few days, then washed, cleaned, sun-dried, and stored in baskets lined with rot-resistant green leaves. From time to time the leaves must be changed; with proper care, the nuts can be stored for several months. The seeds may be pink, white, or purple, the preferred being white.

Lore and Legend

Among a number of tribal groups in West Africa, the cola nut is a symbol of hospitality, given to the guest either upon arrival or departure. In addition, sharing and partaking of cola is an integral part of many social ceremonies. It plays a significant role in early morning worship, childbirth, child naming, marriage, installation of chiefs, and at funerals. Prayers are generally said over the cola nut before it is shared; it is not looked upon as a luxury, but as a vital necessity of life. If the host does not present his guest with a cola nut, it is considered to be a serious breach of etiquette in many Nigerian communities.

Culinary Uses The taste at first is slightly bitter, but after moderate chewing, a sense of well-being is said to spread through the body, leaving a more pleasant taste in the mouth, which causes any food or drink consumed immediately thereafter to seem sweet. Pulverized and boiled in water, cola nuts formed part of a traditional, stimulating West African beverage. Their use in beverages accounted for the origin of the word "cola" in several of today's popular soft drinks. During the 1880s, Coca-Cola started out as a powerful, caffeine-rich, patent medicine, containing carbonated water mixed with a powder of ground cola nuts and an extract of coca (*Erythroxylon coca*) leaves from Peru. The coca leaves contain several alkaloids, including cocaine. Cocaine is not an ingredient today in any of the cola beverages in the United States, but extracts of the cola nut are still utilized for natural flavor in many cola-type soft drinks.

Health Benefits Small pieces of the nut, when masticated, are supposed to benefit the chewer by increasing mental activity, reducing fatigue, dulling appetite, and counteracting intoxication. As a medicine it is reputed to be an effective stimulant—a tonic that will allay thirst, promote digestion, give strength, and "stave off a porter's exhaustion during a forced march in the heat of the tropics while bearing an eighty-pound head load. It will prevent sleep," but will not induce a drug habit. The nuts have a similar effect to tea or coffee, since they contain the same alkaloid, caffeine. They also contain smaller amounts of theobromine—as does the related cacao "bean"—and kolanin, a heart stimulant.

Cottonseed Oil

General Information Cottonseed oil is derived from the small, pea-sized seeds of the cotton plant, fifty of which are found in each cotton boll (the fluffy white puff that becomes fiber for clothing). About one hundred pounds of cotton seed will yield sixteen pounds of oil; the remaining eighty-four pounds becomes lint and cottonseed meal, the latter used as livestock feed. The seeds are freed from the hulls, and the kernels crushed, heated, and subjected to high pressure or solvent extraction to produce a reddish raw oil that must be further refined. The final product, the cottonseed oil found on the market, is yellow and has a light flavor and color.

Culinary Uses A popular oil due to its comparatively low cost, a high percentage of the cottonseed oil produced is blended with safflower oil, soy oil, or other vegetable oils to produce a generic salad oil, margarine, or shortening.

Health Benefits Because cotton is not considered a food crop, residues from pesticides—which are heavily used in cotton cultivation—may be present in the oil, thus rendering it potentially unsafe for consumption. The oil also contains between 0.6 percent and 1.2 percent of a fatty acid known as cyclopropen that has toxic effects on the liver and gall bladder, slows down sexual maturity, and multiplies the power of the cancer-causing aflatoxin fungi; as well, it contains gossypol, a substance that irritates the digestive tract, causes water retention in the lungs, shortness of breath, and paralysis. Gossypol is also known to inhibit sperm function and is being investigated as the "male birth control pill." Its use as an antifertility agent began after studies demonstrated that men who had used substantial quantities of crude cottonseed oil over a number of years as their cooking oil had low sperm counts, followed by total testicular failure. Cottonseed oil is 25.90 percent saturated, 17.80 percent monounsaturated, and 51.90 percent polyunsaturated.

Flax Seed/Linseed (*Linum usitatissimum*)

Linum is the old classical name for the plant used by Theophrastus, from the Greek linon, *meaning cord or flax. The term* usitatissimum *means most useful. In the southern regions this plant was known as* linum; *in the northern regions it was known as* flahs, *from the Old German, referring to the process of flailing or flaying the fibers.*

General Information Flax is a graceful little plant with turquoise blue blossoms that grows up to four feet in height. This highly valuable plant is said by some to be native to Egypt, while others believe it to have come from the elevated plains of central Asia. Flax was already being cultivated in Babylon around 5000 B.C., and flax seeds and pods, along with wall paintings depicting its cultivation, and cloth made of flax fiber (linen) were found in the oldest known burial chambers of the Egyptians (around 3000 B.C.). The French leader Charlemagne pronounced flax more sanitary than wool (because linen is so much easier to launder than woolen fabrics) and ordered his subjects to cultivate it. The plant was introduced into North America by European colonists, who processed it for cloth. Its economic importance grew as flax seed was used in a variety of products—from flax seed cakes, which were used for fattening cattle, to linseed oil, which was employed in making oilcloth and linoleum. This multipurpose herb offers something for the weaver, the painter, the physician, and the cook. Fibers from the stalk are spun into linen; oil from the seeds is used in paint and linoleum; both the seeds and the oil are used medicinally; and the seeds are combined with other ingredients to bake into a wholesome bread. Until the eighteenth century, when cotton came to the forefront, flax

Lore and Legend

In Teuton mythology, flax is said to be under the protection of the goddess Hulda, the watchful Guardian of Flax Fields, no doubt because it was she who taught mortals the arts of spinning and weaving. In Bohemia the spindly leaves of flax have the beneficent property of making homely girls beautiful, provided the girls dance among the leaves when precisely seventeen. But not on Saturday, for the plant belongs to the devil on that day. Even spinning is not done on Saturday. One Saturday, it is told, two old sisters defied the devil and went right on with their spinning. That night one of them died. The next Saturday the other sister sat again at her spindle. Toward evening she looked up, and there beside her stood the dead woman, enveloped in flames. She had returned from hell to show the punishment that awaited those who dared spin on Saturday. Young women getting married in Thuringia place flax in their shoes as a charm against poverty, and tie a flaxen string around their left leg so the marriage will thrive. To the ancient Egyptians, white linen (woven flax) was a symbol of divine light and purity associated with the great mother-goddess Isis. Linen was worn as a symbol of purity by Greek, Hebrew, and Egyptian priests, and in Egyptian tombs the mummies of Pharaohs lay wrapped in fine linen bindings for thousands of years. Detailed wall paintings in the tombs represent the history of flax in the Nile valley, and show that its basic cultivation, processing, and weaving into fabric has changed little through the ages. The Cherokee Indians regarded flax as one of their most nourishing and healing herbs, and the plant was as sacred to them as the eagle feather. They believed that flax seed oil captured energies from the sun that could then be released and utilized in the body's metabolic processes.

Flax Seed

Nutritional Value Per 100 g Edible Portion

	Dried
Calories	450
Protein	17.3-31.6 g
Fat	31.9-44.7 g
Fiber	24.0-31.6 g

was the most important vegetable fiber in the Western world, being used to produce linen as well as ropes and high grade paper. About A.D. 750, a paper superior to papyrus or parchment was created of flax fibers in Samarkand, still part of the Moslem Empire. During the next five centuries the Moors built paper mills and introduced flax from Cairo to Morocco and Sicily. The Crusaders during the Middle Ages brought the art of paper-making from flax fibers to Europe. The introduction of mechanical printing about the middle of the fifteenth century increased the demand for paper far beyond possible flax production, and the French naturalist Rene de Reaumur suggested that paper be manufactured from wood pulp as an alternative. By 1800, mills were producing wood-based paper in France, and the demand for flax in paper production decreased.

Culinary Uses Flax seeds are the tiny, shiny, oval-shaped, brown seeds of the flax plant. Their smooth, nutty flavor makes them a tasty and crunchy addition to freshly baked bread, and an excellent addition to casseroles, sauces, and salads. When placed in water the seeds readily soften, swell, and dissolve, producing a gel. This gelatinous effect accounts for the ability of soaked and cooked flax seed to be whipped up like egg white. Flax seed meal keeps fresh only a few days because of its high oil content, after which it is rancid to the point of being harmful. Flakes are now available that have been stabilized to prevent spoilage. The oil pressed from the seeds, called linseed oil, is used as a kitchen oil, but also goes rancid within just a couple hours. If you use the oil as a topping for baked potatoes, pasta, or vegetables, do not heat it.

Health Benefits Decongestant, demulcent, emollient, expectorant, laxative, purgative. Flax seed has been used in medicine since antiquity for liniments, cough syrups, and salves with which to treat boils and similar infections. This simple domestic herb helps to alleviate the problems of constipation, distension, and discomfort in the abdominal region. The seeds have a thick outer coating of cells that abound in a viscous matter, which in hot water forms a thick mucilaginous fluid. Eating the seeds intact is useful for constipation, as the seeds swell to three times their dry volume in the intestines and encourage elimination by increasing the volume of fecal matter. Flax seeds are also energizing, help to relieve asthma and chronic cough, enrich the blood, and strengthen the nerves, and are reputedly good for dry, brittle hair. They are one of the best vegetarian sources of Omega-3, the fatty acid typically found in fish oil that has been shown to reduce serum triglyceride levels in heart patients. Flax also contains up to 60 percent LNA (linolenic acid), which has been shown to inhibit the production of tumor-promoting acid in the body and helps maintain the integrity of cell walls, along with all eight essential amino acids and lecithin. Ancient Indian scriptures state that in order to reach the highest state of contentment and joy, flax seeds must be eaten daily.

Flax seed flour and defatted flax seed meal, because of their high content of lignans, are being used for investigations into the association between high lignan consumption and lowered risk for sex-hormone-dependent cancers such as breast cancer. Plant lignans are converted into enterolactone and enterodiol by intestinal bacteria. These hormone-like substances produce a number of protective effects against breast cancer. Studies show that omnivorous women with breast cancer typically excrete much lower levels of lignans in their urine than do vegetarian women. Lignans are also found in many other seeds, grains, and legumes. High in potassium, magnesium, calcium, phosphorus, iron, niacin, lecithin, and vitamin E.

Byproducts

Linseed oil The oil pressed from flax seeds is called linseed oil and has the dubious distinction of turning rancid faster than any other vegetable oil. When first pressed from the seeds, linseed oil is a thick, sticky fluid, but when exposed to oxygen from the air it gradually hardens and dries. Painted on wood or other surfaces, linseed oil makes a pliant but strong protective coating. Oilcloth, first produced in the United States in 1809, was in bygone days made into tablecloths, shelf paper, floor and wall coverings, rain gear, and carrying bags. Paints and varnishes had a linseed-oil base, and linseed oil was a common finish for furniture and other woodwork. In 1863 it was discovered that boiled linseed oil, when mixed with cork, applied to a burlap backing, and rolled into sheets, made an excellent floor covering. Within a decade, linoleum decorated most of the floors in North America (until vinyl superseded flax).

Fresh linseed oil is known for its rich golden color, delicate nutty taste, and ease of digestion. Avoid any oil that tastes bitter, acrid, or scratchy, as it has turned rancid. The fresh oil rapidly spoils when exposed to light, oxygen, and heat, and thus special care must be taken in pressing, filling, and storing operations. The spoilable "impurities" are the two nutritionally essential fatty acids LA (linoleic acid)and LNA (linolenic acid), found in such high quantities (over 70 percent) that if they were removed, very little oil would be left. LNA helps disperse hardened deposits of saturated fatty acids and cholesterol from cellular membranes, and plays an essential role in keeping veins and arteries soft and pliable. Another unique feature is that the oil contains a substance resembling the prostaglandins, which regulate blood pressure and arterial function, and also play an important role in calcium and energy metabolism. Linseed oil has been found to lower high cholesterol and high triglyceride levels, and has also been found therapeutic in treating mood disorders, low vitality, liver disorders, and cancer. Many women find that the use of flax seed oil with a good balanced diet and other nutritional support has cleared up PMS symptoms as well as prevented stretch marks from developing after having children. Flax seed oil helps to initiate cell renewal after a radiation burn, as it provides the essential fatty acids as well as vitamin A, minerals, lecithin, and other vital nutrients. The oil is 9.40 percent saturated, 20.20 percent monounsaturated, and 66.00 percent polyunsaturated.

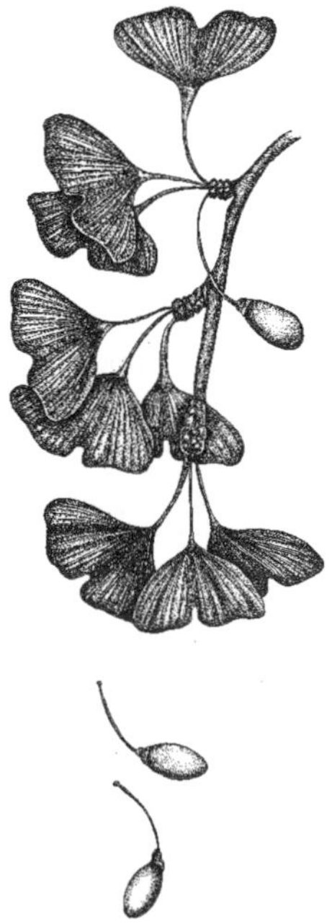

Ginkgo Nut (*Ginkgo biloba*)

Due to its unusual leaf shape, the ancient Chinese called the ginkgo tree Ya-chio, *meaning duck's foot, which got anglicized to the English* ginkgo. *The term* biloba *means bi-lobed.*

General Information The celebrated ginkgo tree is a "living fossil" of the distant past, the only surviving member of the Ginkgoaceae, a tree family dominant in the vegetation of the Northern Hemisphere 125 million years ago

Lore and Legend

Ginkgo nuts have a ritual significance in China and Japan, where they are consumed at feasts and weddings as an oriental delicacy called "silverfruits." The leaf is a widely-used motif in traditional Japanese art, frequently turns up on jewelry, kimonos, and family crests, and is the official emblem of Tokyo University.

Ginkgo

Nutritional Value Per 100 g Edible Portion	Raw	Dried
Calories	182	348
Protein	4.32 g	10.35 g
Fat	1.68 g	2.00 g
Fiber	0.50 g	0.98 g
Calcium	2 mg	20 mg
Iron	1.00 mg	1.60 mg
Magnesium	27 mg	53 mg
Phosphorus	124 mg	269 mg
Potassium	510 mg	998 mg
Sodium	7 mg	13 mg
Zinc	0.340 mg	0.670 mg
Copper	0.274 mg	0.536 mg
Manganese	0.113 mg	0.220 mg
Beta Carotene (A)	558 IU	1,091 IU
Thiamine (B_1)	0.220 mg	0.430 mg
Riboflavin (B_2)	0.090 mg	0.176 mg
Niacin (B_3)	6.000 mg	11.732 mg
Pantothenic Acid (B_5)	0.160 mg	1.345 mg
Ascorbic Acid (C)	15 mg	29.3 mg

when dinosaurs were still roaming the earth. Probably native to northern China, the ginkgo tree is no longer found in the wild, but for over a thousand years it has been cultivated as a sacred tree in Buddhist temple courtyards around China. Each year it bears drupe-like fruit: round, plum-sized, and brown. The fleshy, foul-smelling pulp encloses the seed or nut, which is cream-colored, oval, and one-half to three-quarters of an inch long, within a smooth, thin, white shell.

Culinary Uses The ginkgo nut is only edible cooked, when it has a pleasant flavor similar to mild Swiss cheese. The color also changes, from a soft pale yellow to a pale yellowish-green. Not yet popular among Westerners, they are consumed for the most part by the Chinese and Japanese. Most are eaten as appetizers, but they also appear in any "eight-jeweled" Chinese dish. Skewered and grilled, or fried and added to other dishes, they contribute color and a mild, sweet, crisp flavor. While fresh ginkgo nuts appear in the autumn markets, boiled and canned nuts are also available.

Health Benefits Ginkgo nuts have a high starch content of over 60 percent. They are said to promote digestion and diminish the effects of too much drinking.

Hazelnut and Filbert *(Corylus avellana, C. maxima)*

The genus name Corylus *comes from the Greek* korys, *meaning a helmet or hood, and refers to the shape of the husk enclosing the nut. The specific epithet* avellana *is said to be derived either from the name of an Asian valley or the town of Abella Italy, while* maxima *means largest. The English word* hazel *is derived from the Anglo-Saxon word* haesel, *meaning head-dress or bonnet, which is a good description of the way the short nut fits inside its covering. The word* filbert *is thought by some to have originated from the German* vollbart, *or full-beard; others claim the name is taken from the Frankish Abbot Saint Philibert, whose feast day in England on August 20 coincides with the time the nut matures.*

General Information Filbert and hazel trees are small shrubby trees of the birch family. Their clustered, green-skinned nuts once rivaled the popularity of the acorn in Europe. Many species grow wild in temperate areas, but only three are cultivated as a cash crop: the Turkish hazel, the Mediterranean filbert, and the Old World cobnut. Traditionally, the smaller round nuts not entirely covered by the husk were known as hazels or cobs; cob because they were thought to look like a short, stout English horse called a cob. The larger and longer nuts were known as filberts and they had a tubular husk, often fringed, that completely covered and often extended beyond the end of the oblong nut. Once the nuts were shelled, though, it was difficult to distinguish them. Filbert trees grow wild all across the northern temperate zones of the United States and are grown commercially in Oregon and Washington.

Culinary Uses Filberts and hazelnuts have smooth, reddish-brown shells, which are thin and brittle. The tasty kernels are among the most popular nuts (for humans and squirrels both) with their pleasant, somewhat toasty flavor. Used mainly in baking and confectionery, they can also be added to stuffings, ice creams, butters, and nut loaves. The nuts yield a fair amount of oil when pressed, which is often used in the preparation of cosmetics and perfumes.

Health Benefits Filberts are a rich food for those with good digestion, are good for the teeth and gums, and aid in normalizing the metabolism. Like most other nuts, filberts and hazelnuts have an acidic reaction on the system and should be eaten only in moderation.

Lore and Legend

The nut-bearing hazel has long been associated with mystic rites and the occult, and the trees are emblematic of justice, reconciliation, and love. Virgil praised the filbert, stating that it was accorded more honors than the vine, the myrtle, and even the bay tree. In Greek mythology the two sons of Jupiter—Apollo, the god of harmony, and Mercury, the god of eloquence exchanged gifts with which they would be empowered to provide a better life for humanity. Apollo received a lyre made of tortoiseshell, whose tone would free the artistic spirit of mankind, while Mercury received a winged wand made of hazel, whose touch would enable men to express their thoughts through words. The winged hazel rod, entwined with two serpents, is even today the symbol of communication, reconciliation, and commerce. Among ancient Romans the hazel was intimately connected with marriage, and it was their custom to burn hazel torches during the wedding night to insure a peaceful and happy union of the newlywed couple.

In Nordic and Teutonic mythology the hazel was dedicated to Thor and Donar, gods of thunder, war, and strength. In Celtic and Old Irish legend it was the Tree of Wisdom, and linked with the magic number nine: the nine hazels of wisdom signify all knowledge of the arts and sciences, the hazel was the ninth tree in the Old Irish tree alphabet, and a symbol of the ninth month (August 6 to September 2). So honored was it that anyone caught cutting down a hazel tree could be put to death. In Sweden, hazelnuts were reputed to have the power of making a person invisible, and their magical properties placed them in great demand for divination. In France and Germany young girls danced under the hazelnut tree to attract suitors; courting under the tree was the best opportunity to have one's love returned, even by those who had shown no love elsewhere. The cracking of the nuts on All Hallow's Eve, accompanied by fortune telling, was a traditional amusement linked with British folklore—October 31 was called "Nut crack Night." Chinese lore relates the hazelnut as being one of the five sacred nourishments bestowed on humans, and the nuts have been cultivated continuously in China for over 4,500 years.

Hazelnut, Filbert

Nutritional Value Per 100 g Edible Portion	Dried, Unblanched
Calories	632
Protein	13.04 g
Fat	62.64 g
Fiber	3.80 g
Calcium	188 mg
Iron	3.27 mg
Magnesium	285 mg
Phosphorus	312 mg
Potassium	445 mg
Sodium	3 mg
Zinc	2.400 mg
Copper	1.509 mg
Manganese	2.016 mg
Beta Carotene (A)	67 IU
Thiamine (B_1)	0.500 mg
Riboflavin (B_2)	0.110 mg
Niacin (B_3)	1.135 mg
Pantothenic Acid (B_5)	1.148 mg
Pyridoxine (B_6)	0.612 mg
Folic Acid (B_9)	71.8 mcg
Ascorbic Acid (C)	1.0 mg
Tocopherol (E)	23.92 g

Byproducts

Hazelnut oil, with its delicate flavor and bouquet, is considered to be the finest gourmet cooking oil, and is preferred by many Gold Medal chefs for creating fine dishes and desserts. Produced mainly in France, it is expensive and should be used sparingly. Its delicate flavor is lost when heated, but the oil can be whisked into a sauce at the last minute or used for baked goods in combination with hazelnuts. Exceptional on salads and pasta as well as in pancakes, waffles, and muffins, hazelnut oil is rich in monounsaturated fatty acids. Traditionally the oil has been used as a massage oil and in the treatment of tuberculosis, urinary disease, and colitis. Because it is easily digested, it is recommended to people recovering from disease, the elderly, pregnant women, and diabetics. Hazelnut oil is 7.40 percent saturated, 78.00 percent monounsaturated, and 10.20 percent polyunsaturated.

Heart Nut *(Juglans ailanthifolia, J. sieboldiana cordiformis)*

The generic term Juglans *is a contraction of the Latin* Jovis glans, *nut of Jupiter, or nut of "the Gods," after the ancient belief that the gods dined on walnuts.* Ailanthifolia *means having leaves like the Ailanthus tree (Tree of Heaven);* sieboldiana *is in honor of Philipp Franz von Siebold (1796–1866);* cordiformis *means heart-shaped.*

General Information One of the "other walnuts" of the walnut family, its common English name is derived from the shape of the nut, both before and after hulling. Native to Japan, it is known also as the **Japanese walnut** and the **Siebold walnut**. The nuts, about one inch in diameter, are smaller than the butternut, and are easily cracked to remove the kernel.

Culinary Uses The flavor is mild and pleasant, resembling that of the butternut. Introduced into the United States from Japan in the 1860s, the heart nut did well for a time, but in the early twentieth century was nearly decimated by the walnut bunch disease, and has been replaced for the most part by the Persian or English walnut.

Hickory Nut *(Carya)*

Carya comes from the Greek name karya for the hickory tree. The Algonquin Indians in Virginia in the mid-seventeenth century called the nuts pokahickery, which the colonial settlers shortened to hickory.

Hickory Nut

Nutritional Value Per 100 g Edible Portion

	Dried
Calories	657
Protein	12.72 g
Fat	64.37 g
Fiber	3.24 g
Calcium	61 mg
Iron	2.12 mg
Magnesium	173 mg
Phosphorus	336 mg
Potassium	436 mg
Sodium	1 mg
Zinc	4.310 mg
Copper	0.738 mg

General Information Hickory trees are a native North American tree of the walnut family. Although all species of hickory trees bear nuts, the only commercially important one is the pecan, which is covered separately. Second in importance is the shagbark hickory (*Carya ovata*), so named for its loose, shaggy bark, which hangs in long strips. Though few are cultivated, this nut with its thin, flattened, light-tan shell is the northern equivalent of the pecan. Another closely related hickory is the shellbark, which produces similar nuts. A natural hybrid nut, called hican, is produced by crossing an edible hickory variety with a pecan tree. The result is a nut larger than the pecan but still as tasty as a hickory.

Culinary Uses Hickory nuts can be eaten raw but are especially good when baked in cookies.

Jack Nut *(Artocarpus heterophyllus)*

Artocarpus comes from the Greek words artos, meaning bread, and carpos, meaning fruit; heterophyllus means having leaves of more than one form. The English name jack was given to this fruit by the Portuguese in the sixteenth century since it sounded like the Malayan name for the plant, tsjaka.

General Information This tropical evergreen tree is believed indigenous to the rain forests of India and the Malayan Peninsula. The fruits grow sporadically on the trunk and large branches, a somewhat unusual habit called cauliflory, which also occurs in the cacao tree. Under normal conditions, a single tree may bear 150 to 250 huge fruits per year. The interior is complex, consisting of large bulbs of yellow flesh enclosing a smooth oval seed, massed among narrow ribbons of tougher tissue and surrounding a central pithy core. There may be up to five hundred large, starchy, kidney-shaped, edible seeds of medium size contained within the edible flesh. See also reference for **Jackfruit** under **Fruits.**

Jack Nut

Nutritional Value Per 100 g Edible Portion

	Fresh	Dried
Protein	6.6 g	n/a
Fat	0.4 g	n/a
Fiber	1.5 g	n/a
Calcium	0.05-0.55 mg	0.13%
Iron	0.002-1.200 mg	0.005%
Phosphorus	0.13-0.23 mg	0.54%

Culinary Uses The raw seeds or "nuts" are indigestible due to the presence of a powerful trypsin inhibitor, and have a slightly unpleasant flavor that is removed by boiling or roasting, after which they taste much like European chestnuts. Once cooked, the seeds can be added to soups, stewed with meat, or made into a starchy flour.

Health Benefits Jack nuts have an unusually low fat content of less than one percent, even lower than chestnuts. The Chinese consider jackfruit pulp and seeds to be tonic, cooling, nutritious, and useful in overcoming the influence of alcohol on the system.

Jojoba Nut *(Simmondsia chinensis)*

When the British naturalist H.F. Link landed in Baja California in 1822 and gathered botanical specimens of jojoba, he named the plant Simmondsia *in honor of another British botanist, T.W. Simmonds, who had died several years earlier in Trinidad. Subsequently, Link visited China to carry out further plant exploration. When he shipped a box of Chinese botanical specimens back to England, his Mexican jojoba was accidentally mixed in with his Chinese botanical collection; thus the plant was erroneously given the specific name* chinensis. *The English name* jojoba *is of Mexican-Spanish origin.*

General Information A hardy desert shrub native to the Sonora Desert, the jojoba is usually found at elevations between 2,000 and 4,000 feet. "Female" plants bear fruit capsules that contain one to three oily, chocolate-brown seeds or nuts, about the size of small hazelnut kernels. Mature plants yield between three and twelve pounds of seed per year.

Culinary Uses Indians of the desert Southwest gathered the nuts and ate them, raw or roasted; their flavor is reminiscent of the hazelnut, but more bitter. Jojoba nuts contain about fifty percent oil and thirty percent protein. The plant is now the object of a major crop development program, because jojoba seed oil is the only natural substitute for sperm whale oil in the production of liquid wax.

Lotus Seed *(Nelumbo nucifera)*

Nelumbo *comes from the name of the plant in Singhalese (Sri Lanka), and* nucifera *means nut bearing. The English word* lotus *is derived from the Hebraic* lot, *meaning* myrrh.

General Information The spinning top-shaped seed-bearing receptacle of the lotus plant contains ten to thirty marble-sized white fruits that look rather like cooked chickpeas, each of which encloses a single seed. When the receptacle dries out and shrinks away from the hardening fruits, the seeds become loose and rattle in their cavities. During harvesting, the edible seeds are removed from the receptacles and the extremely bitter green embryos removed. The seeds are preferably picked unripe for the best flavor.

Culinary Uses Immature lotus seeds are eaten raw like nuts, at which stage they have a pleasant nutty flavor. Mature seeds are generally roasted or boiled; soak them for several hours, then boil them alone for an hour. Once cooked, many people prefer to push out the bitter center portion of the seeds with a wooden pick before eating them. The starchy lotus seeds are popular ingredients in many Asian meat and vegetable dishes, as well as in puddings, pastes, and candies. They also may be ground into flour, or dried for storage.

Health Benefits Lotus seed increases energy, promotes vitality, and aids digestion.

Lotus Seed

Nutritional Value Per 100 g Edible Portion

	Raw	Dried
Calories	89	332
Protein	4.13 g	15.41 g
Fat	0.53 g	1.97 g
Fiber	0.65 g	2.42 g
Calcium	44 mg	163 mg
Iron	0.95 mg	3.53 mg
Magnesium	56 mg	210 mg
Phosphorus	168 mg	626 mg
Potassium	367 mg	1368 mg
Sodium	1 mg	5 mg
Beta Carotene (A)	13 IU	50 IU
Thiamine (B_1)	0.171 mg	0.640 mg
Riboflavin (B_2)	0.040 mg	0.150 mg
Niacin (B_3)	0.429 mg	1.600 mg

Macadamia Nut *(Macadamia integrifolia, M. tetraphylla)*

Also Known As: Queensland Nut.

The tree was named Macadamia *in 1857 by Baron Ferdinand von Mueller, Director of the Royal Botanical Gardens in Melbourne and the foremost botanist of Australia, after his friend John Macadam, M.D. (1827–1865), Secretary of the Philosophical Institute of Victoria (Australia). Dr. Macadam died of pleurisy aboard the ship taking him to New Zealand, where he intended to sample the nut that bore his name. The term* integrifolia *means entire-leaved, while* tetraphylla *means four-leaved.*

Lore and Legend

Since the aborigines had informed Walter Hill, a Scottish botanist and Director of the Botanic Gardens at Brisbane (as well as a friend of von Mueller's) that macadamia nuts were poisonous, he was horrified to find his assistant (who had been instructed to crack the shells and plant them) eating the kernels and proclaiming them delicious! A few days later, when the boy did not sicken or die, Hill himself tasted the kernels and was so favorably impressed by their flavor that he immediately became an enthusiastic promoter of macadamia nuts. In 1858 Hill planted what is believed to be the first cultivated macadamia tree on the banks of the Brisbane River in Queensland, which as of 1984 was still alive and producing.

General Information The macadamia is an evergreen tree indigenous to the coastal subtropical rain forests of southeast Queensland and northern New South Wales in eastern Australia. The trees are not truly everbearing, although they put forth a few blossoms and nuts throughout the year. Cone-shaped clusters of about twenty nuts form on the tree, each nut having a brown leathery husk that splits when ripe, causing the nut to fall. The macadamia nut is a rarity—a "new" crop that was domesticated for the first time in 1858 in Australia, and is

Macadamia Nut

Nutritional Value Per 100 g Edible Portion

	Dried
Calories	702
Protein	8.3 g
Fat	73.72 g
Fiber	5.28 g
Calcium	70 mg
Iron	2.41 mg
Magnesium	116 mg
Phosphorus	136 mg
Potassium	368 mg
Sodium	5 mg
Zinc	1.710 mg
Copper	0.296 mg
Beta Carotene (A)	0 IU
Thiamine (B_1)	0.350 mg
Riboflavin (B_2)	0.110 mg
Niacin (B_3)	2.140 mg

the only indigenous Australian plant ever developed as a commercial food crop. They are cultivated on a large scale, however, only in the Hawaiian Islands, where the trees have thrived in the rich volcanic soil since being introduced in 1882 by William Herbert Purvis. Macadamias are the third-largest crop of Hawaii; pineapples and sugar cane are the leaders. The island of Hawaii, known as the Big Island, provides 99 percent of the Hawaiian macadamias and 95 percent of the world supply.

Culinary Uses The large (one inch in diameter), spherical, light beige macadamia kernel has a crunchy, sweet, delicate taste and a creamy, rich texture. Given their hard shells, a tendency to mildew in the shell, and high oil content, they are almost always sold shelled in vacuum-packed jars. Once the container is opened, the nuts should be consumed quickly, which is usually not a problem. Raw macadamias should be refrigerated or frozen in air-tight containers and used within two months. Most macadamias are processed by stripping their husks, and dehydrating them to remove almost every bit of moisture, followed by a roasting in coconut oil and a dunk in salt powder. They are mainly eaten as cocktail nibbles straight from the can, but are also occasionally used in salads, casseroles, confectionery, sweet dishes, and baked goods.

Health Benefits Macadamia nuts help rejuvenate the liver, and discourage the craving for alcohol. They are among the highest in fat (about 70 percent) and calories of the nuts, so should be eaten in moderation.

Olives and Olive Oil *(Olea europaea)*

The Romans knew this tree as Olea *from the root word* oleum, *meaning oil, since the fruits provide large quantities of this important commodity. The term* europaea *means European. The English word* olive *derives from the Greek* elaia.

General Information Asia Minor is credited as the original home of one of the oldest fruit trees known to humanity, the olive tree. Cultivated in the Near East and eastern Mediterranean regions since the Neolithic Age, records show that this evergreen tree was being cultivated by the ancient Egyptians in the seventeenth century B.C., and olives were one of the chief staples of husbandry and trade since the early days of Minoan Crete (3000 B.C.). The Spanish brought olives to America, the trees being among the first planted in the West Indies, to provide oil for the colonists. The first recorded planting in North America was at the mission of San Diego de Alcola about 1769 by Jesuit priests. Hand-picking is still the most reliable method for gathering olives, since the fruit does not ripen simultaneously and picking by hand is least likely to damage them. Spain produces mostly green olives, while Italy produces mainly black olives.

Culinary Uses Unlike most raw fruits, tree-ripened olives are too bitter to eat, and require such manner of preparation that one wonders how they were ever discovered to be edible. Fresh unprocessed olives are used for the production of olive oil, and the only ones

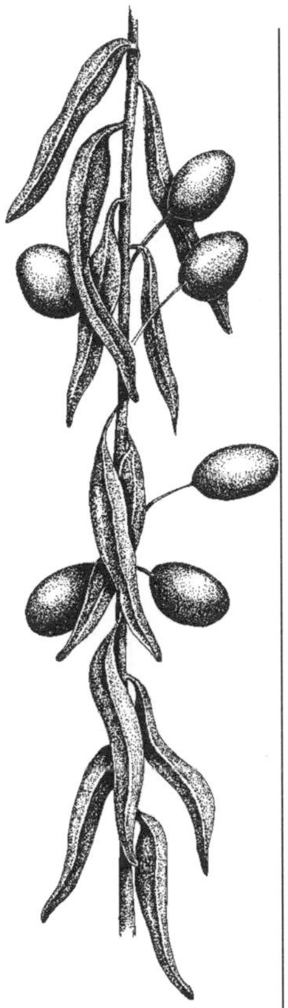

sold for eating are pickled. Of the two types, green and black, the green are the less oily of the two. Olive variety, growing conditions, and region all affect the olive's flavor and quality. Those grown in a particular geographic area generally share a similar character, but are by no means identical, due to the profound influence of each microclimate as well as other variables. Olives tend to retain chemical tastes and smells, so organically grown olives in any region are preferred over non-organic. The best olives are sun-dried; revive them in water and then place them back in olive oil. Used mainly as finger foods, olives can also be used in pizzas, salads, and cooked savory dishes. Olive oil, with its smooth and fruity taste, greatly enlivens salads, pastas, and vegetables. It also works well for sautéing, baking, salad dressings, and unheated sauces. Try the many different varieties: brilliant green Italian Tuscan oils usually taste rich and fruity with peppery accents; southern Italian oils are generally more delicate and mellow; while Greek oils are typically robust and assertive. Even though the oil's vitamin E content helps to preserve it, freshness is important to its taste. Unlike most fine wines, olive oil peaks in its first year and does not benefit from aging. Store it away from heat or bright light, and preferably in a dark glass container, as plastic may impart an off taste. Kept in the refrigerator, it will keep longer but congeal, an annoyance because you have to bring it back to room temperature to pour it.

Olives and Olive Oil

Nutritional Value Per 100 g Edible Portion

	Black, Canned	Oil
Calories	81-115	884
Protein	0.84-0.97 g	0 g
Fat	6.87-10.68 g	100 g
Fiber	n/a	0 g
Calcium	88-94 mg	0.18 mg
Iron	3.30-3.32 mg	0.38 mg
Magnesium	4 mg	0.01 mg
Phosphorus	3 mg	1.22 mg
Potassium	8-9 mg	n/a
Sodium	872-898 mg	0.04 mg
Zinc	0.220 mg	0.060 mg
Copper	0.251 mg	0.226 mg
Manganese	0.020 mg	n/a
Beta Carotene (A)	346-403 IU	n/a
Thiamine (B_1)	0.003 mg	n/a
Riboflavin (B_2)	0 mg	n/a
Niacin (B_3)	0.022-0.037 mg	n/a
Pyridoxine (B_6)	0.009-0.012 mg	n/a
Folic Acid (B_9)	0 mcg	n/a
Ascorbic Acid (C)	0.9-1.5 mg	n/a
Tocopherol (E)	n/a	11.9 mg

Health Benefits Olive oil is easily digested and imparts a generally soothing and healing influence to the digestive tract. Used therapeutically, olive oil is beneficial for the gall bladder and liver, strengthens and develops body tissue, and is a general tonic for the nerves. Taken internally, it increases the secretion of bile, and acts as a laxative by encouraging muscular contraction in the bowels. Mild in its action, olive oil can be given to children where more potent laxatives or cathartics might be harmful. It is also soothing to mucous membranes and is said to help dissolve cholesterol deposits. Externally the oil is good for sunburn or other burns as well as dry skin, minor skin eruptions, and inflammations. Rich in vitamins that nourish the skin's epidermic layer, it may attract the sun's rays and tend to produce sunburns (unless 1 cup of olive oil is mixed with 10 drops of iodine and the juice of a lemon). A lotion made of warm olive oil and a squeeze of lemon juice will quickly undo the damage done to skin by heavy labor or too much scrubbing. Olive oil and lime water is recommended for burns. Olive oil is 13.50 percent saturated, 73.70 percent monounsaturated, and 8.40 percent polyunsaturated.

Varieties

Black and **Green olives** Most olives are picked green from the tree in October, and then held in brine for several months. Those to be sold green must be soaked in a lye

Lore and Legend

The olive tree in ancient times was so important that Moses exempted from military service all men who would work at its cultivation. In scriptural and classical writings, olive oil is symbolic of goodness and purity, and the tree of peace, happiness, and prosperity. The oil, in addition to its wide use in diet and healing, was burned in the sacred temple lamps. The Greeks prayed for prosperity and peace with green olive boughs held in their hands, garlands draped around their necks, and plaited crowns of olive leaves set upon their heads. When the Romans extended their power into Tunis they taxed the Tunisians 300,000 gallons of oil yearly, and special conduits were built for it down to the sea and the waiting ships. Among the Chinese, disputes or quarrels were settled by sending the offended person an olive wrapped in red paper.

In Greek legend, the as yet nameless newly founded city of Athens was being fought over by Athena and Poseidon, who both desired to become the city's patron. The rest of the gods decreed that the one who gave the best gift to humanity should have this honor. Poseidon struck the seashore with his trident and there sprang forth the horse; Athena smote the ground with her spear and the olive tree arose. Athena's gift, being a symbol of peace and agriculture, was deemed infinitely better for humanity than Poseidon's horse, an emblem of war, and thus Athena became the patron goddess of Athens.

solution before brining, while black olives can be brined immediately. Those that wind up black are bombarded continuously with jets of air, a technique that oxidizes the skin and meat to its dark color. Those that are to be marketed as ripe green olives are not aerated, but kept immersed in the lye and/or brine solution to prevent oxidation. In either case the final steps are the same: the olives are washed thoroughly to remove all traces of lye, and then packed in a dilute salt solution and canned. Green olives are often pitted and stuffed with various ingredients including almonds, pimientos, anchovies, capers, or onions.

Greek/Italian olives These olives are not picked until they are fully tree-ripened, at which time they are dark purple, soft, and juicy. They are then put down in rock salt and left for several months before being packed in olive oil and marketed. **Kalamata olives** are the most popular Greek olive. These purple-black olives are marinated in a wine-vinegar solution.

Spanish green olives. Following harvest these olives are placed in brine solution to which a little sugar has been added. A particular strain of bacteria may then be manually introduced, or the vats may be allowed to receive wild or natural bacteria from the air; the medium is selective, and only acid-forming bacteria will grow in it. They are then fermented for several days or weeks at a temperature of 100°F or more, until the correct amount of lactic acid is formed. The olives are then removed and packed in jars.

Byproducts

Olive oil comes from the same black or green olives you may eat as an appetizer. Tree-ripened olives are picked when their color changes from green to purplish-black and the skins look oily but are not too soft. The first pressing is done with gentle pressure, and temperatures produced are not much above room temperature. Oil thus extracted is sold as **extra virgin**, contains 1 percent or less oleic acid, and has an enticing fragrance and superb flavor. Oil from the second pressing is sold as **virgin**. **Fine virgin** contains no more than 1.5 percent acidity and is also delicious; **semi-fine virgin** may have up to 3 percent acidity, but still maintains a pleasant aroma and taste. Oil from subsequent pressings of pulp and pits is processed with high heat and chemical solvents, and is sold as **pure** or **refined** olive oil. Another category of olive oil to enter the market recently is **light** olive oil, which does not refer to fewer calories or fat, but rather to its lighter color and minimal taste. Also look for the appellation **cold-pressed** which states that the oil was mechanically pressed without heat or chemical treatments. Like wine, olive oil is distinguished by words such as smooth, full-bodied, round, fruity, sweet, light, and extra bouquet. A greenish cast to the oil indicates a less refined oil and one of higher quality. Used for centuries in Greek, French, and Italian cuisines, olive oil is a favorite for giving even ordinary dishes a Mediterranean flavor. It is excellent for sautéing, makes a rich, exotic mayonnaise, and is delicious when used in salad dressings, sauces, and spreads. Pure olive oil has excellent stability and can sometimes be stored without refrigeration for over a year, but virgin and extra virgin oils degrade more quickly.

Oyster Nut (*Telfairia pedata*)

The oyster nut tree was named in honor of Charles Telfair (1778–1833), an Irish botanist and plant collector who lived in Mauritius. Pedata *means footed or pedate. The name* oyster nut *is due to their resemblance in shape to oysters.*

General Information Native to tropical East Africa, this fast-growing, woody-stemmed, prodigious climbing vine of the gourd family reaches a height of sixty to seventy feet as it climbs and scrambles over tall trees. Individual branches may attain one hundred feet in length, while a single plant may overrun an area the size of a tennis court. The fruits are deeply ridged and shaped like large footballs, reach one to two feet in length, eight to twelve inches in diameter, and can weigh up to thirty pounds apiece. Often, the trees that originally supported the vines with their heavy gourds become smothered and crushed under the enormous weight. The fruits burst open when ripe, releasing over one hundred pale yellow seeds embedded in a golden yellow pulp. Large, flat, and circular, about one-and-one-half inches in diameter by one-half inch thick, the seeds are washed and dried in the sun for several days, after which they are opened in a manner much like shucking an oyster: they are cut around the edge and the bitter fibrous shells are pried open with a knife to extract the edible kernels.

Culinary Uses Raw or roasted, the oyster nut has a pleasant flavor somewhat similar to the Brazil nut. In East Africa, the kernels are used to make sweets, cakes, and soups, and are prepared with a variety of other foods.

Health Benefits Oyster nuts have a fat content of over 60 percent.

Palm Oil

General Information The oil palm, which looks similar to a coconut tree, is used to produce two types of oil: palm oil and palm kernel oil. Palm oil comes from the fibrous pulp (mesocarp) of the fruit and is used in commerce, for soap making, and—when ultrarefined—for margarine. Palm kernel oil is extracted from the nut contained within the fruit. Both oils are liquid when warm and solid at room temperature.

Culinary Uses Palm oil is common as the frying fat for potato chips and is used in margarine, gravies, and soups. Palm kernel oil is a familiar ingredient in nondairy coffee creamers, dressings, dips, whipped toppings, candies (especially carob), and in cookies and waffles as filler fat. For certain uses, such as snacks and confections, the oil is fractionated, a process that separates the unsaturated fatty acids from the saturated fatty acids to make the oil nearly 100 percent saturated. This prevents candy coatings from melting at room temperature or in your fingers.

Health Benefits Palm oil in its crude form is among the richest sources of beta carotene (three hundred times more than tomatoes, and fifteen times more than carrots) and has a high content of vitamin E. However, since all palm oil used in the western world is highly refined (crude palm oil has a reddish brown color, which most consumers would probably reject), most of the vital nutrients are destroyed. Palm oil contains 39 percent palmitic acid, the most palmitic acid of any food, and this is the common fatty acid that tends to raise blood cholesterol. Palm oil is 49.30 percent saturated, 37.00 percent monounsaturated, 9.30 percent polyunsaturated, and contains 19.1 mg per 100 grams tocopherol (vitamin E), while palm kernel oil is 81.50 percent saturated, 11.40 percent monounsaturated, 1.60 percent polyunsaturated, and contains 3.8 mg per 100 grams tocopherol (vitamin E).

Peanut *(Arachis hypogaea)*

Also Known As: Monkey Nuts, Groundnuts, Goobers, Pindars.

> Arachis *is a Greek term referring to the plant's hairy stem, which suggests the web of Arachne, the Lydian girl who challenged Athena to a weaving contest and was turned into a spider. The specific name* hypogaea *means growing beneath the ground. The English word* peanut *comes from the plant being a member of the pea (legume) family and the seeds looking like nuts.*

General Information The peanut, technically a legume rather than a nut, is the seed of a plant native to Peru and Brazil. It was cultivated extensively by the Mayans in Yucatan, by the Incas in Peru, and by various tribes in Brazil. It was spread by Portuguese explorers to East Africa and by Spanish explorers to the Philippines. Later, it came to North America via Africa and the slave trade. Rather low and bushy, the plant bears pods which have the peculiar habit of bending groundward and being pushed into the ground by the elongating branches. After the plant withers and dies back, the mature pods carrying between one and three peanuts each are ready to be dug. Only toward the end of the nineteenth century was the peanut extensively cultivated as an oil-producing plant. Before that they were grown almost solely for hog feed. A St. Louis physician named Ambrose Straub is credited with creating in 1880 what many consider to be the most exalted state of grace any ambitious nut can aspire to: peanut butter. Promoting his peanut butter as a readily digestible, healthy yet tasty high-protein food, the physician gained a loyal circle of consumers in the St. Louis

Peanut

Nutritional Value Per 100 g Edible Portion

	Unroasted, Raw	Boiled	Dry Roasted w/salt	Oil Roasted
Calories	567	318	585	581
Protein	25.80 g	13.50 g	23.68 g	26.35 g
Fat	49.24 g	22.01 g	49.66 g	49.30 g
Fiber	4.85 g	1.96 g	5.10 g	5.33 g
Calcium	92 mg	55 mg	54 mg	88 mg
Iron	4.58 mg	1.01 mg	2.26 mg	1.83 mg
Magnesium	168 mg	102 mg	176 mg	185 mg
Phosphorus	376 mg	198 mg	358 mg	517 mg
Potassium	705 mg	180 mg	658 mg	682 mg
Sodium	18 mg	751 mg	813 mg	433 mg
Zinc	3.270 mg	1.830 mg	3.310 mg	6.630 mg
Copper	1.144 mg	0.499 mg	0.671 mg	1.300 mg
Manganese	1.934 mg	1.023 mg	2.083 mg	2.062 mg
Beta Carotene (A)	0 mg	0 mg	0 mg	0 mg
Thiamine (B_1)	0.640 mg	0.259 mg	0.438 mg	0.253 mg
Riboflavin (B_2)	0.135 mg	0.063 mg	0.098 mg	0.108 mg
Niacin (B_3)	12.066 mg	5.259 mg	13.525 mg	14.277 mg
Pantothenic Acid (B_5)	1.767 mg	0.825 mg	1.395 mg	1.390 mg
Pyridoxine (B_6)	0.348 mg	0.152 mg	0.256 mg	0.255 mg
Folic Acid (B_9)	239.8 mcg	74.6 mcg	145.3 mcg	125.7 mcg
Ascorbic Acid (C)	0 mg	0 mg	0 mg	0 mg
Tocopherol (E)	8.33 mg	n/a	7.80 mg	6.94 mg

area. It gained exposure and popularity when he introduced it at the Chicago World's Columbian Exposition of 1893. Dr. Straub patented a machine to make peanut butter in 1903. Patent No. 721,651 was granted on February 14, 1903, for a "mill for grinding peanuts for butter." It was launched at the 1904 St. Louis World's Fair. Soon grocers across the country were stocking peanut butter in bulk in large wooden tubs to satisfy customer demand. During the same period Dr. John H. Kellogg, famous for breakfast cereals, prescribed peanut butter as nourishment for his convalescing patients. When the innovative agricultural scientist Dr. George Washington Carver developed an improved version of the butter it attracted even more enthusiasts to the fold. How seriously Americans regard peanut butter becomes quite clear when one notes the presence in Chicago of the American Museum of Peanut Butter History. Nearly half the peanuts grown in the United States are turned into peanut butter to satisfy the voracious American appetite, which currently runs about twelve pounds of peanuts per capita annually; the remainder is used primarily for oil and industrial uses. Three types of peanuts are grown: **Spanish**, which are a small, roundish nut; **Valencia**, which are a medium-sized, oval-shaped nut most often used for salted-in-the-shell peanuts; and **Virginia** (or **Jumbo**), which are the large nuts typically added to cocktail mixed nuts. All three varieties are used for peanut butter, candies, snacks, and home cooking.

Lore and Legend

In ancient Peru, pots of peanuts were buried with the dead for sustenance on their long journey into the next world. In Africa, gold peanuts hammered from crude ore were trophies of the sixteenth century, being presented by tribal chieftains to warriors, athletes, and hunters.

Culinary Uses Peanuts should not be eaten raw, because they contain a substance, readily destroyed by heat, that is believed to inhibit the body's ability to absorb nutrients. Avoid peanuts that have been salted in the shell, as this is done by adding salt to a detergent-like compound that transports the salt through the shell. Although their main use is for peanut butter and peanut oil, peanuts make an excellent sauce for serving with salads or lightly cooked vegetables; this sauce is made by reducing lightly roasted peanuts to a puree in a blender or food processor with chili pepper, garlic, and fresh coriander to taste, and adding enough milk, coconut milk, or stock to make a thick sauce. In Indonesia and many African countries, peanuts are often used as the basis of sauces, curries, and stews, and can also be used in any of the ways suggested with other nuts.

Health Benefits Unfortunately, peanuts are one of the most chemically adulterated crops, since the fields are rotated with cotton that, because it is a nonfood crop, is treated with chemicals too toxic to be allowed on food crops. These chemical residues remain to affect the following peanut crop. Furthermore, peanuts are highly susceptible to the aflatoxin mold (*Aspergillis flavus*), one of the most powerful liver carcinogens known. Aflatoxin is twenty times more toxic than DDT and has been linked to mental retardation and lowered intelligence. This mold is present in both raw and processed peanuts; roasting does not kill it. Peanut oils will not contain it because the strong alkalis used in processing neutralize the toxin. Organic peanuts not only contain fewer chemical residues, but are less subject to aflatoxin. In moderate amounts, peanuts can benefit the person with a fast metabolism; they tend to slow metabolic rate, so are not recommended for those with slow digestion. Peanuts also have a high content of phosphoric acid, and the combination of starch, protein, and phosphoric acid makes them a highly acid-forming food. For those trying to lose weight, the peanut should be avoided altogether due to its high fat content.

Byproducts

Peanut butter of the commercial variety often contains as little as 75 percent peanuts. The rest is made up of hydrogenized fats (to prevent oil separation), sugar (for added sweetness and to mask the taste of inferior peanuts), emulsifiers (against oil separation), texturizers (to aid spreadability and counteract the butter's natural tendency to stick to the roof of the mouth), and degermed peanuts (for infinite shelf life). Buy high-quality peanut butter from natural food stores (often made right in the store) or make your own. Americans consume over 800 million pounds of peanut butter annually, or three-plus pounds per person, most of this by children, 92 percent of whom eat peanut butter at least twice a week. According to a 1988 Peanut Advisory Board survey, women prefer chunky peanut butter by a margin of 43 to 39. The survey said most men have no preference.

Peanut flour is made solely of finely ground peanuts or from peanuts that are processed to remove a high proportion of the oil and calories, leaving a flour product that contains about sixty percent protein and less than one percent fat. It is becoming more popular as a protein extender in bakery and confectionery products, especially for diet-conscious consumers.

Peanut meal is the meal remaining after the peanuts have been processed for oil. It can be used as a substitute for chopped peanuts, or to boost the nutritional level of baked goods and lend a delicious taste. This meal is available both roasted or unroasted, with the roasted having a more distinctive nutty flavor.

Peanut oil Peanuts were one of the first native North American sources of vegetable oil, and can produce large quantities, since the nut is about 50 percent oil. Peanut oil is frequently used in combination with other vegetable oils to make an all-purpose cooking oil because it is light colored and bland. With its high smoke point, peanut oil lends itself particularly well to frying, and is often used for popping popcorn. However, the quality of commercial peanuts is doubtful, plus this oil is highly refined. Buy freshly pressed peanut oil, filtered rather than refined, without antioxidants, preservatives, and solvents. Peanut oil, according to tests at the University of Vienna, is an aid to the transportation of adrenalin, and has laxative properties. Peanut oil is 16.90 percent saturated, 46.20 percent monounsaturated, and 32.00 percent polyunsaturated. It also contains traces of calcium, iron, magnesium, potassium, sodium, zinc, and vitamin E.

Peanut

Nutritional Value Per 100 g Edible Portion

	Defatted Flour	Lowfat Flour	Commercial Peanut Butter Chunky	Commercial Peanut Butter Smooth
Calories	327	428	589	588
Protein	52.20 g	33.80 g	24.05 g	24.59 g
Fat	0.55 g	21.90 g	49.94 g	49.98 g
Fiber	4.05 g	n/a	2.50 g	2.41 g
Calcium	140 mg	130 mg	41 mg	34 mg
Iron	2.10 mg	4.74 mg	1.90 mg	1.67 mg
Magnesium	370 mg	48 mg	159 mg	157 mg
Phosphorus	760 mg	n/a	317 mg	323 mg
Potassium	1290 mg	1358 mg	747 mg	721 mg
Sodium	180 mg	1 mg	486 mg	478 mg
Zinc	5.100 mg	5.990 mg	2.780 mg	2.510 mg
Copper	1.800 mg	2.039 mg	0.515 mg	0.556 mg
Manganese	4.900 mg	4.231 mg	1.865 mg	1.536 mg
Beta Carotene (A)	0 mg	n/a	0 mg	0 mg
Thiamine (B_1)	0.700 mg	n/a	0.125 mg	0.136 mg
Riboflavin (B_2)	0.480 mg	n/a	0.112 mg	0.099 mg
Niacin (B_3)	27.000 mg	n/a	13.689 mg	13.090 mg
Pantothenic Acid (B_5)	2.744 mg	n/a	0.964 mg	0.920 mg
Pyridoxine (B_6)	0.504 mg	n/a	0.450 mg	0.378 mg
Folic Acid (B_9)	248.2 mcg	n/a	92.0 mcg	78.2 mcg
Ascorbic Acid (C)	0 mg	0 mg	0 mg	0 mg
Tocopherol (E)	n/a	n/a	n/a	n/a

Pecan (*Carya illinoinensis*)

The pecan was formerly known botanically as Hicoria pecan*—the Latin name of the genus* Hicoria *having been derived from* powcohicoria*, the American Indian name for a milky beverage made from pulverized hickory nuts and water.* Carya *comes from the Greek word* karyon*, which was their name for the tree. Towards the end of the French and Indian Wars, about 1760, fur traders introduced the pecan from the territory of the Illinois Indian to the Atlantic seaboard; thus it became known as the "Illinois" nut (*illinoinensis *means coming from Illinois). The English word* pecan *was the common name adopted for this nut, from the Algonquin Indian word* paccan*, a word which also included walnuts and hickories—referring to nuts so hard they had to be cracked with a stone.*

General Information A native North American tree belonging to the hickory family and a near relative of walnuts, the pecan tree is a large, stately deciduous tree which under favorable conditions may grow to over one hundred feet in height, with a trunk diameter of six feet and a limb spread of some one hundred feet. These trees are indigenous to the Mississippi River basin, growing as far north as Indiana and Illinois and west into Texas and Kansas. They are very long-lived, with some native trees in the southeast known to be over a thousand years old. The fruit, like that of the walnut, is enveloped in a hard woody husk, which opens when ripe, releasing four rounded oblong nuts with edible, oily kernels of excellent flavor. Each tree may yield up to one hundred pounds annually. Before the sixteenth century, no European had ever seen a pecan nut, and there was little commercial development of the trees until the 1850s, when a black slave known as Antoine developed the Centennial variety at a Louisiana plantation. It is claimed the oval-shaped pecan is the second most popular nut in the United States, after the peanut.

Pecan

Nutritional Value Per 100 g Edible Portion

	Dried	Flour/ Meal
Calories	667	329
Protein	7.75 g	31.87 g
Fat	67.64 g	1.43 g
Fiber	1.60 g	1.50 g
Calcium	36 mg	32 mg
Iron	2.13 mg	1.97 mg
Magnesium	128 mg	120 mg
Phosphorus	291 mg	274 mg
Potassium	392 mg	334 mg
Sodium	1 mg	1 mg
Zinc	5.470 mg	5.130 mg
Copper	1.182 mg	1.116 mg
Manganese	4.506 mg	4.249 mg
Beta Carotene (A)	128 IU	n/a
Thiamine (B_1)	0.848 mg	n/a
Riboflavin (B_2)	0.128 mg	n/a
Niacin (B_3)	0.887 mg	n/a
Pantothenic Acid (B_5)	1.707 mg	n/a
Pyridoxine (B_6)	0.188 mg	n/a
Folic Acid (B_9)	39.2 mcg	n/a
Ascorbic Acid (C)	2.0 mg	n/a
Tocopherol (E)	3.10 mg	n/a

Culinary Uses Pecan nutmeats have a sweet pulpy texture. They are great in fruit salads and, if toasted slightly, are a delicious topping for cooked grains or steamed green vegetables. Salted pecans are a delicacy, and the nuts are particularly enjoyed when ingredients of the infamous pecan pie, butter pecan ice cream, or of the praline—a brown sugar candy of French origin. In most recipes, they can be substituted directly for walnuts. Try mixing chopped pecans into your favorite nut loaf or bean burgers, or hide a few in sandwiches for a crunchy

Lore and Legend

Some North American Indians believed the pecan tree to be the manifestation of the Great Spirit and valued it so much that the early Spaniards in Florida were able to trade nuts for hides and mats. One tribe who lived in Texas, the Mariames, ate them as their only food for two months of every year.

surprise. Pecans are best purchased in the shell, for their high oil content predisposes them to turn rancid quickly after shelling.

Health Benefits Best characterized as rich, one fully developed pecan kernel has a fat content of almost 70 percent, and in every pound of shelled nuts there are a whopping 3,633 calories. Raw pecans are one of nature's richest source of readily assimilable organic pyridoxine (vitamin B6), an element that plays an essential role in converting the amino acids from consumed proteins into usable form for the body as well as being important to the nervous system; thus, raw pecans assist in the regeneration of damaged cells in diseased hearts.

Byproducts

Pecan meal is easily made by grinding these tender nuts in a blender, and the meal can be added to bread and cookie recipes for a nutty flavor and nutritional boost.

Pili Nut *(Canarium ovatum, C. luzonicum)*

Canarium perhaps refers to the Canary Islands, while ovatum means ovate or egg-shaped.

General Information Native to the Old World tropics of southeast Asia, the pili nut, also known as the **Java almond**, gets its common name from the Philippines and is indigenous to that island group. Female trees begin to produce in their sixtieth year, producing oblong, black, smooth fruits, which are about two and one-half inches in length, and grow in clusters. Each fruit contains within a fleshy husk a single, slender, triangular, sweet-tasting, cream-colored nut that is pointed at both ends.

Pili Nut

Nutritional Value Per 100 g Edible Portion

	Dried
Calories	719
Protein	10.80 g
Fat	79.55 g
Fiber	2.80 g
Calcium	145 mg
Iron	3.53 mg
Magnesium	n/a
Phosphorus	575 mg
Potassium	507 mg
Sodium	3 mg
Beta Carotene (A)	41 IU
Thiamine (B_1)	0.913 mg
Riboflavin (B_2)	0.093 mg
Niacin (B_3)	0.519 mg

Culinary Uses The pili has a delicious flavor, suggestive of the almond, and is used in the same manner. The thick, bony shell of the nut is hard to crack—so hard that it may be an obstacle to pili orchard development, even though the kernels are very popular locally. Eaten raw, or roasted and salted, in all cases the seed coat is removed before eating. A good-quality edible oil, suitable for culinary purposes, is expressed from the kernels; this oil also serves as a lamp oil in the Philippines.

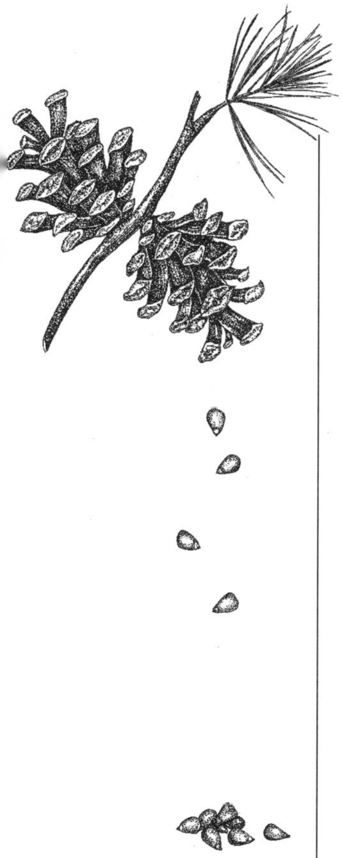

Pine Nut *(Pinus pinea, P. edulis, P. cembroides, P. koraiensis)*

Also Known As: Pignolias, Piñons.

Pinus *is the ancient Latin name for the tree;* pinea *means of or from the pine;* edulis *means edible;* koraiensis *means coming from Korea.* Pignolia *is the diminutive form of pine.*

General Information Pine nuts are the seeds from the cones of certain pine tree species. Most of those which are marketed under the name of pine nuts come from either the Italian stone pine (*P. pinea*), Colorado piñon (*P. edulis*), Mexican piñon (*P. cembroides*), or the Chinese nut pine (*P. koraiensis*). Many classical authors have written about pine nuts, which were valued as an article of food and as a dessert; all speak of the pine woods of Ravenna which, although much diminished, still remain today one of the greater areas of concentration of pine. The seeds do not appear on the Italian stone pine until their fifteenth year of growth, and the greatest production comes only after half a century of life. The Colorado piñon, inhabiting the drier mountainous regions from Colorado south and west into Mexico, does not begin bearing until it is twenty-five years of age, not reaching full production until it is seventy-five, and then it only bears large crops every third or fourth year.

Pine Nut

Nutritional Value Per 100 g Edible Portion

	Dried
Calories	515-568
Protein	11.57-24.00 g
Fat	50.70-60.98 g
Fiber	0.80-1.71 g
Calcium	8-26 mg
Iron	3.06-9.20 mg
Magnesium	234 mg
Phosphorus	35-508 mg
Potassium	599-628 mg
Sodium	1-72 mg
Zinc	4.250-4.280 mg
Copper	1.026-1.035 mg
Beta Carotene (A)	29 IU
Thiamine (B_1)	0.810-1.243 mg
Riboflavin (B_2)	0.190-0.223 mg
Niacin (B_3)	3.570-4.370 mg
Ascorbic Acid (C)	2.0 mg

Lore and Legend

The ancient Greeks held the stone pine sacred to the god Neptune, and both Greeks and Romans appreciated the taste of the nuts (most often preserved in honey). The piñon pine was an integral part of the mythology of many Indians of the southwest. The Navaho smeared piñon pitch on corpses before burial; the Hopi dabbed pitch on their foreheads as a protection against sorcerers before going out of doors in December; burning piñon gum provided incense for Navaho nocturnal ceremonies, and specially selected piñon branches served as ritual wands. In China and Japan the pine is symbolic of longevity, and the Chinese god of immortality is often pictured sitting beneath a pine tree.

Culinary Uses Pine nuts are a small, thin, white, pellet-shaped nutmeat or seed. Their delicate buttery taste and soft texture make them suitable, either raw or lightly roasted, for use in a variety of dishes and desserts. Probably best known for their appearance in pesto, they are also delicious when added to rice and eggplant dishes, East Indian curries, or used as a garnish for fruit and vegetable dishes. The nuts should either be purchased in the shell or kept refrigerated in an airtight glass container, as they spoil very quickly.

Health Benefits The pine nut is one of the best sources of protein in the nut family, and can easily take the place of the finest meats; a very small portion supplies all that the body needs of protein and fats. In general, European species of pine nuts are richer in protein and lower in fat than the American varieties, but American pine nuts offer more vitamins and minerals.

Pistachio *(Pistacia vera)*

Also Known As: Green Almond.

The Latin Pistacia *and the English name* pistachio *are derived from* pisteh, *the Persian name for this nut. The term* vera *means true, genuine, or standard.*

Pistachio

Nutritional Value Per 100 g Edible Portion	Dried
Calories	577
Protein	20.58 g
Fat	48.39 g
Fiber	1.88 g
Calcium	135 mg
Iron	6.78 mg
Magnesium	158 mg
Phosphorus	503 mg
Potassium	1093 mg
Sodium	6 mg
Zinc	1.340 mg
Copper	1.189 mg
Manganese	0.327 mg
Beta Carotene (A)	233 IU
Thiamine (B_1)	0.820 mg
Riboflavin (B_2)	0.174 mg
Niacin (B_3)	1.080 mg
Folic Acid (B_9)	58.0 mcg
Tocopherol (E)	5.21 mg

General Information The diminutive pistachio tree probably originated in the Levant, most notably Persia, from where it spread throughout Palestine, the Mediterranean region, and into certain areas of India and Russian Central Asia. Tradition says that the pistachio was brought to ancient Rome by the Emperor Vitellius, circa A.D. 50. Related to the sumac and cashew, this twenty-foot tall deciduous species of turpentine tree flourishes under adverse conditions, literally thriving in poor stony terrain where for most of the year there may be no rainfall, and tolerating long, hot summers with temperatures over 100 degrees; while resistant to both cold and wind, pistachios cannot tolerate excessive dampness or high humidity. Under favorable conditions, pistachio trees live and produce for centuries: in the Kerman region of Iran a seven hundred year old tree is still standing. Hard, off-white shells surround the uniquely colored pale green nutmeat. The green color is due to the presence of chlorophyll, and varieties of pistachio differ markedly in this respect, with the dark green kernels being the most highly valued and decorative. A Syrian immigrant introduced pistachios into the United States in the late 1890s. Before migrating to America, he was a nut salesman in Syria and Turkey, traveling his territory by camel. He first imported pistachios for his family and friends in New York, then in 1906 he became a dealer, and other East Coast competitors soon followed his lead. Ninety-eight percent of the world supply of pistachios is now consumed in the United States.

Culinary Uses The pistachio nut is so prized for its pleasant mild flavor and fetching green color that consumers are willing to pay exorbitant prices for it. The pistachio's shell is naturally tan, those that are red have been dyed to conceal mottled markings caused by the natural drying process, while those overly light may have been whitened with heavy coats of salt and corn starch; both should be avoided. The greenish kernel (the more pronounced the color the better the nut) is shaped somewhat like a small almond, and is

Lore and Legend

If bad weather or disease prevents the nuts from ripening so that the shells fail to split open, pistachio growers repeat an old Turkish expression, "Too bad, our pistachios are not smiling." The Queen of Sheba was especially fond of pistachio nuts and is said to have monopolized the limited pistachio output of Assyria for herself and her court favorites. By decree of the queen, no subject outside the royal household was allowed to keep any part of the pistachio harvest. Following a social call in Syria, the departing guest is frequently given a small bag of pistachio nuts as a gesture of good will; the nuts are also an important ingredient at wedding feasts. One gluttonous Emperor of Rome around A.D. 69, Vitellius, would finish off his meal by stuffing his mouth full of pistachios.

used to flavor and color ice cream, Turkish delight, and halva. They are also delicious in salads and stuffings, either coarsely chopped, in paste form, or both. Early Persians used to grind pistachios and other nuts and use the paste as a thickener. Because the shell splits during the drying process, the pistachio does not have as lengthy a shelf life as do other whole nuts.

Health Benefits Pistachio nuts are rich in oil, with an average oil content of about 55 percent, all in a form very easily digested and assimilated. It contains no indigestible cellulose or fiber, and is inclined to be alkaline-forming. Raw pistachios are beneficial for constipation, and help purify the blood and tone the liver and kidneys.

Poppy Seed *(Papaver somniferum hortense, P. rhoeas)*

Papaver *is a classical Latin name for the poppy plant.* Somniferum *means sleep-bearing, and is derived from* Somnus, *the Roman god of sleep. The term* hortense *means belonging to a* hortus *or garden;* rhoeas *comes from the Greek name* rhoias *for the corn poppy.*

General Information Poppies are native to Eurasia, and have been grown in the Near East since ancient times. The tiny seeds are so small that it takes nearly ten million of

Lore and Legend

The sedative properties of opium were used by the ancient Egyptians, and by the women of Crete, who worshipped a Poppy Goddess in 1400 B.C. The Greeks, who regarded sleep as the greatest of all physicians and the most powerful consoler of humanity, crowned all their nocturnal gods with a wreath of poppy blossoms. The plant was dedicated to Nix, goddess of night; to Thanatos, god of death; to his twin brother Hypnos, god of sleep; and to the son of Hypnos, Morpheus, god of dreams. The poppy was also an attribute of the love goddess, Aphrodite. When Pluto, god of the Underworld, stole Persephone from her mother Ceres, the wheat was neglected and her mother's ceaseless wanderings brought her to Sicily where, nearly exhausted, she climbed Mount Etna to light her torch so she might continue her journey at night. The gods, noting her desperate drive to continue despite extreme fatigue, caused poppies to grow around her feet. Ceres inhaled their fragrance, nibbled on the seeds, and fell into a much-needed, long, peaceful sleep. Once Ceres was properly rested, the wheat began to flourish once again. Thereafter, the seeds were offered to the dead to insure their peaceful sleep. The poppy is a Christian symbol of fertility, ignorance, and indifference, although when carved on the end of church benches and pews it is supposed to designate heavenly sleep (though preferably not during the services). The red corn poppy, considered the emblem of eternal sleep and oblivion, was believed to spring up on every battleground where men fought and died, deriving its red color from the blood of slain warriors. The battle-torn fields and desolate farms of Flanders were robed in red after one season of calm following the Battle of Waterloo and again after the First World War. The flower was thus chosen as the emblem of remembrance of fallen war heroes, and the *Poppies of Flanders* were adopted as the emblem of the U.S. Armistice Day, in memory of America's armed forces.

Poppy Seed

Nutritional Value Per 100 g Edible Portion	Dried
Calories	533
Protein	18.04 g
Fat	44.70 g
Fiber	6.26 g
Calcium	1448 mg
Iron	9.40 mg
Magnesium	331 mg
Phosphorus	848 mg
Potassium	700 mg
Sodium	21 mg
Zinc	10.230 mg
Copper	1.633 mg
Manganese	6.833 mg
Beta Carotene (A)	trace
Thiamine (B_1)	0.849 mg
Riboflavin (B_2)	0.173 mg
Niacin (B_3)	0.976 mg
Pyridoxine (B_6)	0.444 mg

them to make a single pound. The most notorious of poppies is the garden or opium poppy (*P. somniferum*), with white or bluish-purple blooms. The drug opium is contained in the juicy cell walls of the ripening capsule up to twenty days after flowering. The seeds, however, contain no drug, as the opium-yielding power of the plant is lost before the seeds ripen.

Culinary Uses Poppy seeds have a pleasantly nutty flavor and aroma. The seeds are frequently sprinkled on breads and rolls and included in recipes for cakes and pastries, salad dressings, and vegetable dishes. Poppy seed butter adds extra flavor and aroma to noodles, rice, vegetables, and fish.

Psyllium Seed (*Plantago psyllium*)

Plantago *is derived from* planta, *the sole of the foot, and refers to the broad shape of the leaves. The specific name* psyllium *is derived from the Greek word for flea,* psylla, *an allusion to the seed's small size.*

General Information Psyllium is an annual herb related to the plantain, and which is native to the Mediterranean regions of southern Europe, the Canary Islands, northern Africa, and as far east as western Pakistan. It is widely cultivated in Pakistan, India and parts of Europe, and is now being grown in North America as well. The plant grows low to the ground and produces small white flowers. The seeds, which are the part of the plant used, are smooth, dull ovals, varying from one-sixteenth to one-eighth of an inch long, and are colored pinkish-brown or pinkish-white. Each seed is enveloped in a thin, white, translucent husk. The seeds have neither taste nor odor, but when soaked in water will swell to from eight to fourteen times their original volume. This is due to the presence of mucilage, complex carbohydrates that attract and hold water.

Culinary Uses There are two forms of psyllium seed sold—the husks and the meat. The husks are coarse like bran, while the meat made from the husked seed is gentler and easier to digest. While the Greeks simply chewed the seeds, other options include blending them in a vegetable juice cocktail, or sprinkling the whole or ground seeds on cereal or yogurt.

Health Benefits Laxative. Both psyllium husks and meat are non-irritating, but the meat surrounds any food that may be consumed with the seed and renders it impermeable by the digestive fluids. As the seeds swell, they create a mucilaginous bulk that expands and sweeps through the entire intestinal

Psyllium Seed

Nutritional Value Per 100 g Edible Portion	Dried
Calories	235
Protein	1.5 g
Fat	3.7 g
Fiber	0.3 g
Calcium	334 mg
Iron	20.0 mg
Magnesium	51 mg
Phosphorus	63 mg
Potassium	811 mg
Sodium	54 mg
Zinc	2.100 mg
Manganese	1.600 mg
Beta Carotene (A)	4023 IU
Thiamine (B_1)	0 mg
Riboflavin (B_2)	0 mg
Niacin (B_3)	0 mg
Ascorbic Acid (C)	0 mg

tract, pushing out food from blocked areas, pockets and crevices on its way. They are said to relieve an ailment known as autointoxication, in which the body poisons itself by reabsorbing from impacted areas of the colon an excess of intestinal waste products. The husks are most often used for laxative purposes, since they contain a very soothing indigestible substance with little crude fiber, and either take up water from a loose stool or add moisture when it is too dry and hard. In India, psyllium is used as a diuretic, while in China related species are used to treat bloody urine, coughing, and high blood pressure.

Pumpkin Seed *(Cucurbita pepo, C. maxima)*

Also Known As: Pepito.

> Cucurbita *is the old classical Latin name for a gourd; the term* maxima *means largest;* pepo *comes from the Greek word* pepon, *meaning sun-ripened or mellow. The English name* pumpkin *is a derivative of the Greek* pepon, *with the diminutive '-kin' ending.*

General Information Pumpkins are members of the cucumber family, which includes melons, gourds, and squashes. All pumpkin or squash seeds are edible. Most varieties produce seeds that are enclosed in teardrop-shaped shells thin enough to crack open with your teeth. Some pumpkin varieties have hull-less seeds and are grown specifically for this purpose, but their flesh reportedly is stringier and tastes inferior to other pumpkins. In the early 1970s, the U.S. Department of Agriculture released a new, high-yielding pumpkin cultivar called Lady Godiva, which got its name because its rounded, dark green, "naked" seeds have no seed coat. These attractive shell-less seeds are suitable for consumption as a snack food.

Culinary Uses Although mainly used as a source of oil, hulled or hull-less pumpkin seeds can be used just like any other nut or seed. Either raw or toasted, pumpkin seeds are excellent as a snack on their own, in salads of all kinds, or added to casseroles, breads, and nut loaves. Try them ground into a meal and added to pancakes and other baked goods, or mixed with peanut butter for a protein-rich spread.

Health Benefits Anthelmintic. Pumpkin seeds are nature's most nourishing food for the male prostate gland due to their high magnesium and zinc content, and also are valuable sources of Omega-3 fatty acids. These seeds have been used worldwide as an aid to remove intestinal worms. The effectiveness of pumpkin seeds as a vermifuge has been attributed to mechanical effects and to a rare amino acid (3-amino-3 carboxypyrrolidine, or cucurbitin) found only in certain *Cucurbita* species. Another constituent of pumpkin is myosin, the chief protein constituent of nearly all muscles in the body, which

Pumpkin Seed

Nutritional Value Per 100 g Edible Portion

	Dried
Calories	541
Protein	24.54 g
Fat	45.85 g
Fiber	2.22 g
Calcium	43 mg
Iron	14.97 mg
Magnesium	535 mg
Phosphorus	1174 mg
Potassium	807 mg
Sodium	18 mg
Zinc	7.460 mg
Copper	1.387 mg
Beta Carotene (A)	380 IU
Thiamine (B_1)	0.210 mg
Riboflavin (B_2)	0.320 mg
Niacin (B_3)	1.745 mg
Ascorbic Acid (C)	173 mg

plays an important role in the chemistry of muscular contraction. The seed oil is helpful for healing burns and wounds.

Byproducts

Pumpkin seed oil Pumpkin seed or squash seed oil has been used throughout history in India, Europe and the Americas. This dark green oil is quite tasty and should be used raw, poured directly onto vegetables, pasta, and other dishes. One of the most nutritious of oils, with a good proportion of both the Omega-3 and Omega-6 essential fatty acids, it has similar properties to the seeds and has been used to nourish and heal the digestive tract, fight parasites, improve circulation, help heal prostate disorders, help prevent dental caries, and is commonly recommended for pregnant and lactating women due to its essential fatty acid content.

Quandong Nut *(Eucarya acuminata)*

Acuminata *means acuminate or long-pointed.*

General Information Also known as the Australian "native peach," quandong is the aboriginal name for the small trees or shrubs native to and abundant in the southwest and central desert regions of Australia, where there is little rainfall. The tree produces fruits that are globular, about one-half to three-quarters of an inch in diameter, and usually bright red in color. The edible pulp, rich in vitamin C, may be eaten raw, used as a pie filling, or made into preserves and jellies with a flavor similar to that of the guava.

Culinary Uses Within the pitted stone is an edible oily kernel or nut, with a hard shell that is difficult to crack. The kernels, harshly aromatic in flavor, have been prized by the aborigines for many centuries, but are virtually unknown outside of Australia. Although unusually delectable, the flavor of the quandong kernel tends to be too pungent and overpowering for some palates.

Safflower Oil

General Information Safflower oil is extracted from the seeds of the safflower (*Carthamus tinctorius*), a plant native to the semi-arid Mediterranean region as well as the mountainous regions of southwest Asia and Ethiopia. Botanically related to lettuce, sunflowers, and daisies, this annual plant was apparently originally domesticated for its flowers, which were used for a dye, and only later for its oil-rich seeds.

Culinary Uses Safflower oil is probably the most versatile vegetable oil; in its unrefined form, it has a deep amber-yellow color and slightly nutty, earthy flavor. Because of its high fat content, it has a tendency to go rancid much quicker than other oils, and should be stored in the refrigerator. Refined safflower oil is typically a very pale yellow with a bland taste. Often used for deep-fat frying, sautéing, and baking, it is also used as an ingredient in salad dressings and mayonnaise.

Health Benefits Safflower oil probably has the highest percentage of unsaturated fats of all the oils and is highest in linoleic acid (78 percent). Although widely touted because of its high content of polyunsaturated fatty acids, safflower oil is considered by many to be excessively irritating and capable of provoking or aggravating a wide variety of disorders. High-linoleic safflower oil (greater than 70 percent) is 9.10 percent saturated, 12.10 percent monounsaturated, and 74.50 percent polyunsaturated, while high-oleic safflower oil (greater than 70 percent) is 6.10 percent saturated, 75.30 percent monounsaturated, and 14.20 percent polyunsaturated.

Sapucaya Nut *(Lecythis usitata)*

Also Known As: Paradise Nut

> *The generic name* Lecythis *is from the Greek for oil jar, a rather accurate description of the appearance of the fruit, which looks like a jar complete with a neatly-fitting lid;* usitata *means useful.* Sapucaya *is an Amazonian Indian word meaning chicken, since the nut was frequently fed to chickens. The alternate name* Paradise nut *owes its origin to the high quality of the nut, said to be even more delicious than the Brazil nut.*

General Information Native to the Amazonian rain forests of northeastern Brazil and the neighboring Guiana region, there are some fifty species of *Lecythis* in northern South America, of which the Brazil nut and the paradise nut are the most widely known. The tree produces large woody fruits about eight inches long and ten inches wide which are suspended upside-down from the ends of the branches. When mature, the lid of the fruit drops off; the nuts then gradually become detached and fall to the ground. A single fruit contains thirty to forty irregularly oblong, wrinkled seeds (nuts), each about two inches long, resembling Brazil nuts, although the paradise nuts are more rounded, have a lighter brown color, and a thinner, softer shell.

Culinary Uses The nut kernels are ivory white with a creamy texture, and an unusual, delicate, sweet flavor considered by some connoisseurs to be the finest among nuts. They may be eaten raw or roasted and are utilized to a limited extent in making candies and cakes. An excellent pale yellow, edible oil is expressed from the kernels, and is employed by natives of the Amazon to produce soap and illuminants.

Health Benefits Containing about 62 percent fat and 20 percent protein, the nuts are highly nutritious. Precautions should be taken in gathering and eating paradise nuts: there are harrowing reports about the fruits of certain poisonous species of *Lecythis* in tropical America which, when eaten, can cause severe nausea, diarrhea, dramatic (if temporary) loss of scalp and body hair, and the shedding of fingernails.

Sesame Seed *(Sesamum indicum)*

> *The English name* sesame *can be traced back through the Arabic* simsim *and Coptic* semsem *to the early Egyptian* semsemt, *a name mentioned in the Ebers Papyrus (c. 1800 B.C.), which indicates how long humanity has known and used the herb. The term* indicum *means from India.*

General Information Sesame seeds come from a tall annual herb native to the East Indies whose single hairy stalk can grow as high as seven feet, although a two- to four-foot stalk is much more common. The heavy glistening stems support variable leaves and rose-colored flowers. The flowers become four-celled capsules containing many tiny black and white seeds; when ripe, the seeds burst suddenly with a pop from the capsule and scatter. Sesame was one of the very earliest plants to be used by man both for the seed and for the oil contained in the seeds. The oil today is still the main source of fat used in cooking in the Near and Far East.

Culinary Uses Sesame seeds have a pleasant nut-like aroma and flavor which is heightened by toasting. Whole unhulled sesame seeds are dark, the hulled seeds are white, and tan seeds have been hulled and roasted. The darker variety of sesame have a stronger taste and smell, and are worth seeking out (but beware the dyed variety). You can judge the freshness of the seeds by their color: fresh sesame seeds should be white or light yellow, while old and rancid seeds acquire a muddy gray look. The best season to buy them is between September and April, when the new crops have been harvested. Sesame seeds can be sprinkled over breads and cereals, used in salads and biscuits, or processed into tahini, gomasio, or other products.

Health Benefits Emollient, laxative. Sesame seeds will often help relieve local swelling or tumors, and their high vitamin E content strengthens the nerves and heart. Since the sesame seed hull contains 2 to 3 percent oxalic acid—a compound that can interfere with calcium utilization—and has a bitter flavor, the hull is often removed. Like most nuts and seeds, sesame contains lignans. Sesamin, a lignan that exists exclusively and abundantly in sesame, has demonstrated remarkable antioxidant effects and has been put to good use in stabilizing sesame products. In studies with rats, sesamin has been shown to inhibit the absorption of cholesterol from the diet and to inhibit the manufacture of cholesterol in the liver. Sesame seeds are hard to digest, even when properly chewed, which in itself can be difficult since they are so small.

Sesame Seed

Nutritional Value Per 100 g Edible Portion

	Whole Dried	Kernels Dried	Flour
Calories	573	588	526
Protein	17.73 g	26.38 g	30.78 g
Fat	49.67 g	54.78 g	37.10 g
Fiber	4.60 g	2.96 g	6.39 g
Calcium	975 mg	131 mg	159 mg
Iron	14.55 mg	7.80 mg	15.17 mg
Magnesium	351 mg	347 mg	361 mg
Phosphorus	629 mg	776 mg	807 mg
Potassium	468 mg	407 mg	423 mg
Sodium	11 mg	40 mg	41 mg
Zinc	7.750 mg	10.250 mg	10.670 mg
Copper	4.082 mg	1.460 mg	n/a
Manganese	2.460 mg	1.430 mg	n/a
Beta Carotene (A)	9 IU	66 IU	69 IU
Thiamine (B_1)	0.791 mg	0.722 mg	2.684 mg
Riboflavin (B_2)	0.247 mg	0.085 mg	0.286 mg
Niacin (B_3)	4.515 mg	4.682 mg	13.369 mg
Pantothenic Acid (B_5)	0.050 mg	0.681 mg	2.928 mg
Pyridoxine (B_6)	0.790 mg	0.146 mg	0.152 mg
Folic Acid (B_9)	96.7 mcg	n/a	30.8 mcg
Ascorbic Acid (C)	0 mg	n/a	n/a
Tocopherol (E)	2.27 mg	n/a	n/a

Byproducts

Gomasio is made by finely grinding roasted sesame seeds and adding sea salt (five to eight parts sesame to one part salt). Also known as sesame salt, gomasio is widely used in Japan and macrobiotic diets, and its nutty flavor makes it a delicious addition to any dish.

Sesame butter is made of whole (unhulled) roasted sesame seeds, and may or may not have salt added. It may be used interchangeably with peanut butter. Differing from tahini, a better-known product, in that it is made from roasted seeds rather than raw, sesame butter is a heavier product with fewer culinary uses. Because of its high vitamin E content, sesame butter has a longer shelf life than other nut butters. Once opened, it should be refrigerated. If it causes a harsh or slight burning sensation in the back of the throat, it is rancid and should be discarded.

Black sesame butter is sesame butter made from black sesame seeds with their richly intense sesame flavor. It

> **Lore and Legend**
>
> In *The Thousand and One Nights*, the story of Ali Baba and the forty thieves, a password was needed to open the door of the robbers' den. The magical command "Open Sesame" may have been chosen because ripe sesame seeds bursting from their pods sound much like the sharp sudden pop of a lock springing open.

has recently become available in some specialty food stores and is worth experimenting with at least once. This black, gooey spread has no comparable match in our culinary tradition, and likely poses no threat to the peanut butter industry.

Sesame oil One of the oldest vegetable oils used, sesame oil is pressed from the seeds of the sesame plant. These edible, oil-rich seeds are one of the few seeds capable of yielding a commercially acceptable oil without being exposed to high heat or being put through a high-pressure expeller process. Unrefined sesame oil is dark yellow to amber in color and has a pleasant, mild, nutty flavor. A richer, darker, more flavorful oil is made by roasting the seeds before the process of oil extraction. Since the seeds contain sesamol, a natural preservative, the oil pressed from them is very stable and highly resistant to oxidation (rancidity). Highly refined sesame oil is pale yellow and has a bland taste. Sesame oil is utilized in the production of margarine, salad oils and good quality cooking oils, and is the traditional oil for Asian and macrobiotic cooking. It is also good for sautéing vegetables, grains and noodles, and for making salad dressings, spreads, pasta toppings, and mayonnaise. Sesame oil is rich in monounsaturated and polyunsaturated fatty acids, is rich in lecithin, which helps build the nervous system and brain cells, and has been used to help depression and stress as well as improve circulation. Externally, the oil may be used as a massage oil, and for soothing and healing in cases of sunburn or other burns, as well as for minor eruptions of the skin. Sesame oil is 14.20 percent saturated, 39.70 percent monounsaturated, and 41.70 percent polyunsaturated.

Sesame milk is made by blending sesame seeds and water, and then straining to remove the hulls. For flavoring, add any of the following singly or in combination: one tablespoon carob powder, six dates, a banana, stewed raisins, and apple or cherry concentrate. Highly nutritious, sesame milk is wonderful for gaining weight, and for lubricating the intestinal tract.

Sesame salt (see **Gomasio**, above).

Tahini is a light and creamy spread made from hulled and ground sesame seeds. The roasted variety tastes nuttier; the unroasted is sweeter. Both kinds may contain salt. Commercial tahini is made from seeds that are hulled in caustic chemical baths, neutralized, and bleached; these tahinis tend to be bitter and have a faintly soapy taste. Quality tahini is made from mechanically hulled seeds. This high-protein spread is a staple in Middle Eastern and Asian cookery, and is favored in dressings, sauces, and desserts. As well, it may serve as an oil, egg, or milk replacement in recipes; mixed with peanut butter or honey it makes a delicious spread; or add it to nut or soy milk, cream soups, and baby foods. Containing approximately 45 percent protein and 55 percent oil, it is easy to digest and very nutritious, especially for bones and teeth.

Souari Nut *(Caryocar nuciferum)*

> Caryocar *is from the Greek word for nut, while* nuciferum *means nut-bearing. The unusual vernacular name, applied to several species, comes from the Cariban Indian word* sawarie; *it is spelled in a number of different ways. To add to the confusion, the British often refer to the tree as "butternut," since the nuts have a high oil content of about sixty percent.*

General Information The souari is native to northern Brazil and the adjoining Guiana region. The trees produce fruits that are round, soft-wooded capsules, about six inches in diameter. When ripe, these capsules crash to the ground and burst on impact, loosening the nuts they contain (two to five in number), which are large, brown, kidney-shaped, and about the size of a hen's egg. Surrounding the nuts is an oily, yellow pulp which may be cooked and eaten as a vegetable. The souari nut is found mainly in European and South American seaports, and few people in the United States have had the opportunity to sample them.

Culinary Uses The nuts have a hard, woody, warty shell, about one-quarter of an inch thick, which is difficult to crack. The kernels are somewhat larger than Brazil nuts, pure white and soft, and are rich and oily with a sweet, almond-like flavor. Souari nuts are eaten raw or roasted and also serve as a source of cooking oil.

Sunflower Seed *(Helianthus annuus)*

The sunflower's botanical name is truly descriptive of the plant: Helianthus comes from the Greek words helios, meaning sun, and anthos, meaning flower; the species name, annuus, is derived from the Latin word for annual. The English word sunflower is simply the translation of its Latin name.

General Information The sunflower originated somewhere in the southwestern part of the United States, and has been raised for centuries for its nutritious seeds. More than any other flower, the sunflower proclaims summer. Wild, it bedecks roadways and gilds whole fields with sun-colored mandalas. Cultivated in home gardens it towers to impressive heights of fifteen feet or more and boasts a flower up to two feet in diameter. A single plant may yield several hundred plump nut-like kernels, which are actually the fruit of the flower. These teardrop-shaped seeds may be white, brown, black, or black with white stripes. The seeds have long been used as a staple article of diet by American Indians, but were only introduced to Europeans in the sixteenth century. The stalks, when treated like hemp, produce a fine, silky fiber.

Sunflower Seed

Nutritional Value Per 100 g Edible Portion

	Kernels Dried	Flour
Calories	570	326
Protein	22.78 g	48.06 g
Fat	49.57 g	1.61 g
Fiber	4.16 g	5.19 g
Calcium	116 mg	114 mg
Iron	6.77 mg	6.62 mg
Magnesium	354 mg	346 mg
Phosphorus	705 mg	689 mg
Potassium	689 mg	67 mg
Sodium	3 mg	3 mg
Zinc	5.060 mg	4.950 mg
Copper	1.752 mg	1.713 mg
Manganese	2.020 mg	1.975 mg
Beta Carotene (A)	50 IU	n/a
Thiamine (B_1)	2.290 mg	3.187 mg
Riboflavin (B_2)	0.250 mg	n/a
Niacin (B_3)	4.500 mg	7.313 mg
Pantothenic Acid (B_5)	n/a	6.595 mg

Culinary Uses Whole sunflower seeds are available, raw or roasted, with or without hulls. Raw sunflower seeds have an oily taste that is pleasantly nutty, and have virtually no aroma; roasting brings out the nutty flavor further. The best-quality seeds are bought in the hull and then either sprouted or eaten; pre-hulled raw or roasted sunflower seeds are almost always rancid. Whole or chopped sunflower seed kernels can be substituted for other nuts in any recipe. Sprinkle a few on top of a casserole before baking, or mix them into vegetable or fruit salads. Sauté the seeds with chopped onion and toss with a cooked vegetable just before serving. They are also a good addition to quick breads and muffins, but if used in a recipe that calls for baking soda, they will frequently turn the finished product green.

Health Benefits Diuretic, expectorant. The sunflower seed nourishes the entire body, supplying it with many vital elements needed for growth and repair. It is a rich source of protein of high biological value, being richer than most meats, eggs, and cheese (with no putrefying bacteria). As a source of vitamin D, sunflower seeds are superior to cod liver oil, which has many objectionable features. In addition to vitamin D, these seeds are richer in the B complex vitamins than an equivalent amount of wheat germ and also contain vitamins E and K. Fresh sunflower seeds contain pectin, which binds radioactive residues and removes them from the body, and the seeds have been found to relieve farsightedness, eyestrain, and extreme sensitivity to light. As well, they strengthen fingernails that are brittle or peeling.

Lore and Legend

As though magnetized by the sun's rays, the great floral disc of the sunflower follows the solar orb in its course through the heavens. Significantly in the Indian hunting calendar, the buffalo were said to be fat with plenty of good meat when sunflowers were tall and in full bloom. The Plains Indians of the prairie regions of North America placed ceremonial bowls filled with sunflower seeds on the graves of their dead for food to sustain them on their long and dangerous journey to their Happy Hunting Grounds. When Francisco Pizarro fought his way into Peru in 1532, he found there the giant sunflower, venerated by the Indians of the Inca empire as the sacred image of their sun-god. In the early eighteenth century, Peter the Great took the sunflower to Russia, where a historical quirk caused it to become an important food plant. The Holy Orthodox Church of Russia decreed very strict dietary regulations during Lent and the forty days preceding Christmas: nearly all foods rich in oil were proscribed by name and forbidden. Since the sunflower had only recently been introduced to the country and was virtually unknown, it was not on the prohibited list and the sharp-eyed laity eagerly adopted it as a food item and source of oil, thus making the plant very popular yet all the while complying with Church regulations.

Byproducts

Sunflower seed meal is made from ground sunflower seeds, and is easily made at home. Because of its high oil content, the meal needs to be kept refrigerated and used within a couple of days. Sunflower seed meal can be used as a substitute for some of the flour in baked goods, or it makes a delicious addition to soups, cereals, and casseroles. If you prefer, toast the seeds before grinding for a nuttier flavor.

Sunflower seed oil Although 40 to 65 percent of the United States sunflower crop consists of oil varieties, only 20 to 25 percent of this is used in domestic consumption—10 percent as vegetable oil and 15 percent as livestock feed. Unrefined sunflower oil is light amber in color and has a distinctive flavor; refined oil is pale and bland tasting. Often used as an extender for more expensive oils, sunflower oil is frequently used for baking and sautéing, and adds a wonderfully delicate nutty flavor to salads, baked goods, and other dishes. Be sure to buy pressed sunflower seed oil rather than additive-filled, chemically extracted commercial oil. Rich in polyunsaturated fatty acids, lecithin, linoleic acid, and vitamin E, sunflower oil has a long history of being used to help the endocrine and nervous systems, and to reduce cholesterol levels. Many naturopathic physicians believe that sunflower oil helps the formation of healthy tissue and generally aids resistance to disease. The consumption of sunflower seed oil (one teaspoonful three times a day) has cured paralysis stemming from polyneuritis, and greatly reduced symptoms from multiple sclerosis. Low-linoleic sunflower oil (less than 60 percent) is 10.10 percent saturated, 45.40 percent monounsaturated, and 40.10 percent polyunsaturated, while high-linoleic sunflower oil (greater than 60 percent) is 10.30 percent saturated, 19.5 percent monounsaturated, and 65.70 percent polyunsaturated. Both also contain traces of calcium, iron, magnesium, sodium, and vitamin E.

Tallow Nut *(Ximenia americana)*

Also Known As: False Sandalwood.

This tree is named after Francisco Ximenes, a Spanish friar who translated into Spanish a Latin manuscript describing the Mexican flora and fauna in 1615; americana *because it was found on the American continent.*

General Information The juicy, fleshy pulp of the yellow or reddish-colored, egg-shaped fruit is plum-like in character. Although the fruits have an acid taste like sour apples, they are eaten either raw or cooked, and can be made into an excellent jelly. Each contain a large, oily seed, the kernel of which is white.

Culinary Uses and **Health Benefits** Reports on the palatability of the tallow nut vary: some extol its flavor, comparing it to the filbert; others warn that the nuts are strongly purgative and should be eaten only a few at a time. The kernels are rich in protein, and have a high fat content of about 66 percent; they may be eaten raw or roasted.

Tiger Nut (*Cyperus esculentus*)

Also Known As: Chufa, Earth Almond, Earth Nut, Rush Nut, Zulu Nut.

> Cyperus *is an ancient Greek name which perhaps refers to the island of Cyprus, while* esculentus *means esculent or edible.*

General Information Tiger "nuts" are not really nuts, but edible, underground tubers of the creeping rootstock of the grass-like sedge indigenous to the Mediterranean region and western Asia. When dried, these tough-skinned corms, about one inch long by one-half inch in diameter, look like large, wrinkled peas.

Culinary Uses Tiger nuts possess an agreeable, slightly sweet, nutlike flavor. The fibrous nuts may be eaten raw out of hand, but they are usually roasted or cooked and added to soups. In confectionery, the roasted nuts may be substituted for almonds.

Tiger Nut

Nutritional Value Per 100 g Edible Portion	
Calories	403
Protein	4.3 g
Fat	23.8 g
Fiber	n/a
Calcium	48 mg
Iron	3.20 mg
Phosphorus	210 mg
Potassium	14 mg
Sodium	1 mg
Thiamine (B1)	0.230 mg
Riboflavin (B2)	0.100 mg
Niacin (B3)	1.100 mg
Ascorbic Acid (C)	6 mg

Health Benefits In Sierra Leone there is a native belief that the tiger nut has an aphrodisiac effect, and when a Zulu maiden wants to hasten the inception of menstruation, she eats a porridge in which tiger nuts have been mashed. Chufa oil, considered to be a superior table oil that compares favorably to olive oil, is also employed in soap-making.

Walnut (*Juglans regia, J. nigra*)

> *The generic term* Juglans *is a contraction of the Latin* Jovis glans, *nut of Jupiter, or nut of "the Gods," after the ancient belief that the gods dined on walnuts. The specific epithet* regia *means royal, both because of the tree's attractive appearance and because of its historical importance as a source of timber and food.* Nigra *means blackish. The English name* walnut *is partly of Teutonic origin, the Germans naming the nut* wallnuss, *or* welsche nuss, welsche *signifying foreign; another possibility is that the* wal *of walnut is derived from the Anglo-Saxon word* wealh, *meaning foreign or alien. The suffix* nut *comes from the Anglo-Saxon* hnutu, *meaning nut.*

General Information The Romans considered the walnut tree to be of Persian origin, but the tree is now so widespread that it is impossible to discern whether this is true. The majority opinion today seems to be that while Persia does fall within the area where the walnut was cultivated earliest, it covered a great deal more ground, ranging from south-

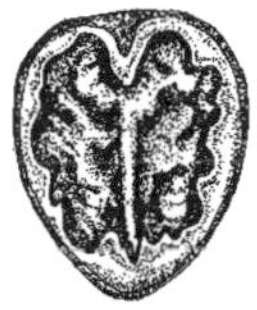
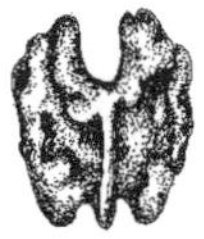

eastern Europe and/or Asia Minor to the Himalayas. Ancient Greeks pressed the nuts for their oil; they seem to have been using them nearly a century before the Romans, about the beginning of the fourth century B.C. The first walnuts planted in California were probably brought from Chile around 1770 by Franciscan fathers. Walnut trees are large, often growing one hundred feet high with trunks that may be up to twelve feet in diameter. There are about fifteen species of *Juglans*, the walnut genus; all are edible, but *J. regia*, known as the Persian or English walnut, is probably the most delicious, and certainly the most important. Other less commercially cultivated varieties are the **Black walnut, Chinese walnut, Japanese walnut,** and **White walnut** more commonly called **Butternut.** The nuts are harvested when the green outer husk begins to crack, the thin divider separating the halves of the kernel is no longer leathery but brittle, and the kernel itself still quite moist. The nuts are then mechanically hulled, washed, and dried to 8 percent moisture.

The European variety became known as **English walnuts** because when England became a powerful trading nation in the mid-fourteenth century, English trading ships transported walnuts from the Mediterranean countries to markets all over the world. This variety has a thin shell that can be easily crushed, with curly nutmeat halves. A good part of their flavor comes from the golden to dark-brown papery skin, which is both bitter and astringent. Spanish missionaries introduced English walnuts to North America via California, much as they did almonds, and a commercial orchard of two hundred trees was planted in 1869.

Eastern black walnuts are a native American walnut (*J. nigra*). Related to the English variety, they have a dark skin covering the white nutmeat, and hard, protective, sticky hulls that are difficult to remove. The shells require a cement floor and heavy hammer to crack (some people run over them with their cars). Once split, each morsel of nutmeat needs to be coaxed from the still-unyielding shell. During this process the oil leaves an indelible brown stain on fingers, fabric, and even cement. The amount of meat per nut is small, but its flavor is considered far superior to that of either the butternut or the English walnut, having a satisfyingly full, rich, "nutty" flavor. The black walnut is less popular for nibbling on its own, because the kernel's flavor is considered too strong by most people, but the flavor is prized when the nuts are combined with other ingredients for baking, in batter and icing, and for the manufacture of both candies and ice cream.

Lore and Legend

Roman lore claimed that in the "Golden Age" when people lived on acorns, the gods feasted upon walnuts, which were considered far superior to other such vulgar nuts as acorns, beechnuts, and chestnuts. Credited with bringing good health, warding off disease, and increasing fertility, it was customary at Roman weddings for the bridegroom to toss handfuls of walnuts—much as we now throw rice—to be scrambled for by young boys. By flinging the nuts away, the bridegroom showed he had laid aside childish amusements and was fully mature. In Romania, however, a bride who does not wish to bear children immediately places one roasted walnut in her bodice for every year she wishes to remain childless. During the Middle Ages, Europeans believed that evil spirits lurked in walnut branches; thus the walnuts themselves were thought useful in warding off lightning, fevers, witchcraft, the evil eye, and epileptic fits. In China, where the cricket has traditionally been considered a creature of good omen, musically-trained singing crickets were carried about in intricately carved walnut shells.

Walnut

Nutritional Value Per 100 g Edible Portion	English Dried	Black Dried
Calories	642	607
Protein	14.29 g	24.35 g
Fat	61.87 g	56.58 g
Fiber	4.60 g	6.46 g
Calcium	94 mg	58 mg
Iron	2.44 mg	3.07 mg
Magnesium	169 mg	202 mg
Phosphorus	317 mg	464 mg
Potassium	502 mg	524 mg
Sodium	10 mg	1 mg
Zinc	2.730 mg	3.420 mg
Copper	1.387 mg	1.020 mg
Manganese	2.898 mg	4.271 mg
Beta Carotene (A)	124 IU	296 IU
Thiamine (B_1)	0.382 mg	0.217 mg
Riboflavin (B_2)	0.148 mg	0.109 mg
Niacin (B_3)	1.042 mg	0.690 mg
Pantothenic Acid (B_5)	0.631 mg	n/a
Pyridoxine (B_6)	0.558 mg	n/a
Folic Acid (B_9)	66 mcg	n/a
Ascorbic Acid (C)	3.2 mg	n/a
Tocopherol (E)	2.62 mg	n/a

Culinary Uses Walnuts are extremely versatile, and may be used at different stages of their growth. Freshly shelled walnuts should be brittle and will snap if broken, showing a clean white interior; shriveled or rubbery nuts are already stale or rancid, and should be avoided. Some shelled walnuts are darker than others; the darker color develops in those that grow on the sunnier side of the tree, and these are richer and more flavorful. Because of their high oil content, walnuts are prone to rancidity and are best bought in the shell and stored in either the refrigerator or freezer. Whole walnuts stored in a cool, dry environment can be stored for up to one year. Shelled commercial walnuts are frequently treated with ethylene gas, fumigated with methyl bromide, dipped in hot lye or a solution of glycerine and sodium carbonate to loosen their skins, and then rinsed in citric acid. The result is a uniform, pale nut that is obviously less healthful than an organic nut. Besides the familiar multitude of dessert uses, walnuts are increasingly used in salads, where they provide a flavorful balance to fruits and strong greens like watercress. The nuts combine especially well with dill, garlic, and parsley. Walnuts are reduced to a paste to bind and thicken certain sauces, usually garlic sauces such as pesto. In the United States, the walnut is returning to the role of a full-fledged food in vegetarian dishes, due to its high protein content.

Health Benefits Walnuts are a warming and laxative food used to strengthen the kidneys and lungs, to lubricate the large intestine, and to improve metabolism. Black walnuts contain the essential arachidonic fatty acid, associated with alleviating symptoms of bursitis.

Byproducts

Dried walnuts are the type most often eaten, and are simply an older version of wet walnuts from which the moisture has been allowed to evaporate. A dried walnut is more than half oil, with the pressed oil frequently used for salads. Dried walnuts can be added to salads, savory dishes, cakes, and breads.

Green walnuts, which have not yet developed a hard shell, are still a quarter or more water. They must be peeled before eating, or the bitter skin produces a somewhat painful reaction in the mouth. Picked in June or July, green walnuts are used to make pickles (a British delicacy), ketchups, and chutneys. Green walnuts can also be made into walnut marmalade or nut brandy, added to jams, or preserved whole in syrup.

Walnut milk is made from blanched, pulverized walnuts soaked in water and then strained. This makes a tasty milk alternative and was drunk in many early European households that had no access to or could not afford regular milk.

Walnut oil is cold pressed from ripe walnuts and produces an aromatic, subtly delicious oil. In southern Europe, especially in France, walnut oil has long been a popular cooking oil, one frequently substituted for olive oil, and is also good on salads and vegetables. It is said that at one time, half the oil used in France was walnut oil. Walnuts from Perigord and Dordogne in France are said to produce the best oil; in those regions, walnuts are strictly graded for quality and production is small. Heavy, sweet, and characteristically aromatic, the oil loses its fluidity and thickens gradually over several months into a sort of jelly. The unsaturated oils in walnuts are prone to rancidity, and so must be used quickly. Since most of the walnut oils currently available in stores are heavily processed and refined, they cannot be recommended for use. Walnut oil is 9.10 percent saturated, 22.80 percent monounsaturated, and 63.30 percent polyunsaturated. It also contains a small amount of vitamin E.

Wet walnuts are those which are newly picked in early autumn. These have moist kernels with a hard outer shell; their delicious and fragrant flavor is marvelous in savory dishes.

Watermelon Seed *(Citrullus lanatus)*

> Citrullus *is the diminutive form of* citrus, *said to be in allusion to the shape of the fruits and color of flesh. The term* lanatus *means woolly.*

General Information The edible watermelon seeds vary considerably: they may be black, white, yellow, or reddish, but are generally smooth, flat, and up to five-eighths of an inch long by one-quarter inch wide. A thin shell encloses the oily, nutritious kernel. In some districts of western tropical Africa, watermelons with bitter flesh are grown solely for their edible seeds, and a yellow edible oil, extracted from the seeds, is employed for table use instead of peanut oil. These nutritious but neglected seeds might find a modest place in the growing snack nut trade.

Culinary Uses Although watermelon seeds are not generally considered a delicacy in this country, in other parts of the world they are eaten just like peanuts—either raw or roasted—following removal of the seedcoat. The Chinese have for centuries enjoyed watermelon seeds preserved in salt, and in the Near East, roasted watermelon seeds are sold in bags like popcorn. To make a seed milk drink, combine the seeds and water in a blender, grind, and strain.

Health Benefits Watermelon seeds are great for the kidneys. They are tranquilizers for the body and wonderful for the nervous system. The seeds contain cucurbocitrin, a compound that dilates capillaries and lowers high blood pressure, as well as improving kidney function. Watermelon seeds are also a remedy for constipation, and are nearly as efficacious as pumpkin seeds in their ability to expel worms.

Watermelon Seed

Nutritional Value Per 100 g Edible Portion

	Kernels, Dried
Calories	557
Protein	28.33 g
Fat	47.37 g
Fiber	3.04 g
Calcium	54 mg
Iron	7.28 mg
Magnesium	515 mg
Phosphorus	755 mg
Potassium	648 mg
Sodium	99 mg
Beta Carotene (A)	0 mg
Thiamine (B_1)	0.190 mg
Riboflavin (B_2)	0.145 mg
Niacin (B_3)	3.550 mg
Folic Acid (B_9)	57.9 mcg
Ascorbic Acid (C)	0 mg

Herbs, Spices, and Other Foods

"Awake, O north wind;
And come, thou south;
That the spices may flow out."

— Song of Solomon

HERBS, SPICES, and OTHER FOODS

Herbs, Spices, and Other Foods

FROM THE DAWN OF CIVILIZATION THOUSANDS OF YEARS AGO, herbs and spices have been used to bring flavor and color to foods, as well as for medicinal purposes. They played an important role in religious life, being used as ingredients in holy anointing oils and incense, and as strewing plants. Taxes were often collected in the form of spices, which during some periods of history were valued as highly as gold. The name *herb* comes from the Latin word *herba,* meaning grass or herbage, and technically refers only to those plants which do not have a woody stem, or a plant or plant part that is used for medicinal purposes. The name *spice* derives from the Latin *species,* meaning "something of a kind" or "to sort things out" into recognizable types. During the Middle Ages, the four most common *species* sold by grocers were saffron, cloves, cinnamon, and nutmeg. However, the terms herb and spice intermingle so much that for the purposes of this book, the two groups will be discussed together.

During the Dark Ages, the accumulated knowledge of the Persian, Greek, and Roman herbalists was nearly lost to humanity. In the sixth century, the community of Benedictine monks at Monte Cassino in Italy was one of the very few that owned a library of herbal manuscripts, or that cultivated an herb and vegetable garden, in all of Europe. These monks copied the gardening and agricultural books in their possession time and again for other monasteries, and thus kept the ancient science of the medicinal and nutritional values of plants alive. In later years it became a rule in every monastery that at least one of the monks acquire a thorough knowledge of plants, their use and cultivation. Finally, it took the invention of the printing press in the fifteenth century to popularize this knowledge throughout western Europe and England.

Personal fame, the glory of God, and a share in the spice trade—an unbeatable combination in fifteenth-century terms—all played a part in sending Columbus off on the voyage that was to end in the discovery of the New World. For the admiral himself, the first prospect was perhaps the most enticing. Luis de Santangel, the financier who lent Queen Isabella of Castile the money to subsidize the voyage, seems to have been more interested in the second. But it was the possibility of breaking into the highly lucrative spice trade that almost certainly swung the balance for Isabella, whose treasury was dangerously depleted by the campaign against the last Muslim garrisons in Spain.

One word of warning: conventionally grown and produced herbs, seasonings, and spices may contain some or all of the following: fillers, anti-caking agents, artificial colorings, preservatives, monosodium glutamate (MSG), and pesticide residues. Reactions to these various extraneous substances may occur. Look for organically grown, non-irradiated herbs and spices in your local natural foods and herb stores; the possible price difference is well worth it.

Agar-Agar *(Gelidium amansii, G. corneum, G. cartilagineum)*

Also Known As: Kanten, Chinese Grass, Ceylon Moss, "Vegetable Jello-O."

> Gelidium *is influenced in meaning by the Latin* gelare, *meaning to freeze or congeal. The term* corneum *means horn-bearing;* cartilagineum *means like cartilage in texture. The English word* agar *comes from a Malayan term for alga.*

General Information Agar-agar, or simply agar, is the product of mucilage from several species of Far Eastern seaweeds collectively classed as agarophytes. Three or more agarophytes are usually combined into one agar formula. This group of seaweeds, growing at varying depths between fifteen and two hundred feet, includes some of the world's most beautiful. Most grow in brown, red, or purple fern-like fronds up to three feet long. The colors of the red seaweeds, ranging from a soft rosy pink to a striking purplish-red, are due to pigments that camouflage their green chlorophyll. These pigments serve to soak up light, which is scarce, since they inhabit deep, dark waters. Within their plant cells lies an odorless, tasteless, colorless, and transparent substance that is processed out to become agar. Commercially harvested in Japan since 1769, the flat, fernlike seaweed is washed, sun-bleached, and dried. The strips are then boiled in water, the mucilaginous solution strained through a cloth, and the liquid allowed to harden and dry in the sun; this becomes a papery, whitish-clear product and is sold as bars, flakes, or granules. One of its most interesting properties is that agar is indigestible by practically all bacteria; hence, it is an excellent base on which to control the growth of laboratory bacterial cultures; the bacteria consume the medium in which they are grown, but not the agar itself.

Agar-Agar

Nutritional Value Per 100 g Edible Portion

	Raw	Dried
Calories	26	306
Protein	0.54 g	6.21 g
Fat	0.03 g	0.30 g
Fiber	0.45 g	0.70 g
Calcium	54 mg	625 mg
Iron	1.86 mg	21.40 mg
Magnesium	67 mg	770 mg
Phosphorus	5 mg	52 mg
Potassium	226 mg	1,125 mg
Sodium	9 mg	102 mg
Manganese	0.373 mg	4.300 mg
Beta Carotene (A)	0 IU	0 IU
Thiamine (B_1)	0.005 mg	0.010 mg
Riboflavin (B_2)	0.022 mg	0.222 mg
Niacin (B_3)	0.055 mg	0.202 mg
Ascorbic Acid (C)	0 mg	0 mg

Culinary Uses Agar has virtually no taste or smell, and can be used as a thickening and jelling agent for salads and desserts, substituting for gelatin derived from animal sources or pectin. Agar is available in powder, flakes, bars, and sticks; the powder dissolves the easiest and is the most concentrated. Bars and sticks are generally harder to find. One teaspoon of agar powder or two teaspoons of flakes firmly gel one cup of liquid. Use less for a softer gel, or for a less rubbery result use one part agar to three parts arrowroot powder. Add agar to a cool liquid, bring the mixture to a boil, lower the heat, and then simmer for about two minutes to fully activate. As it cools, the mixture will gel; at room temperature this takes from twenty to thirty minutes, while in the refrigerator the process takes only half as long. Jellies and jams made with agar rather than commercial pectin need less sweetener, since most of the sugar called for in recipes is required to compensate for the sourness of the pectin product and not the fruit. Commercially, agar is used in the manufacture of silk, textiles, and foods such as ice cream, jelly beans, and preserves. Because it is indigestible by humans, it is a common ingredient of packaged diet foods, filling the stomach without adding calories.

Health Benefits Demulcent, emollient, hydrophilic, laxative. At 75 percent carbohydrate, agar is high in a form of fiber that passes through the body undigested. Useful in cases of constipation, its high concentration of polysaccharide mucilage swells to many times its bulk upon reaching the intestines, absorbing moisture rapidly and supplying soft fibrous bulk and lubrication, thereby increasing peristaltic action and relieving constipation without painful griping. As well, it is believed to bond with toxins (including heavy metals and radioactive substances) and carry them out of the system.

Ajowan *(Carum ajowan, C. copticum, Trachyspermum ammi)*

Also Known As: Ajwain, Bishop's Weed.

> Carum *is probably derived from the region Caria in Asia Minor,* Trachyspermum *means shaggy seeded, and* ammi *means of sandy places.*

General Information Native to southern India, ajowan is a pretty plant resembling wild parsley that is closely related to caraway and cumin, although it tastes strongly of thyme. It has seeds that range from light brown to red in color.

Culinary Uses The seeds look similar to large celery seeds, and the taste, in addition to the thyme-like flavor, is hot and bitter. Indian breads such as nan, pakora, and paratha, are made with ajowan, which imparts a distinctive flavor to the dough.

Health Benefits Digestive. Besides flavor, ajowan helps control flatulence. Ajowan's essential oil, thymol, is used as a germicide and antiseptic.

Ajowan

Nutritional Value Per 100 g Edible Portion

	Seeds
Protein	15.0-18.5 g
Fat	21.8-33.5 g
Fiber	21.2-22.9 g
Calcium	1525-1647 mg
Iron	17.8-29.9 mg
Phosphorus	443-478 mg
Sodium	56-61 mg
Zinc	4.3 mg
Copper	0.910 mg
Manganese	3.31 mg
Beta Carotene (A)	0.070-0.080 mg
Thiamine (B_1)	0.210-0.230 mg
Riboflavin (B_2)	0.280-0.300 mg

Allspice

Nutritional Value Per 100 g Edible Portion

	Dried, Ground	1 tsp.
Calories	263	5
Protein	6.09 g	0.12 g
Fat	8.69 g	0.17 g
Fiber	21.64 g	0.41 g
Calcium	661 mg	13 mg
Iron	7.06 mg	0.13 mg
Magnesium	135 mg	3 mg
Phosphorus	113 mg	2 mg
Potassium	1,044 mg	20 mg
Sodium	77 mg	1 mg
Zinc	1.010 mg	0.020 mg
Copper	0.553 mg	n/a
Manganese	2.943 mg	n/a
Beta Carotene (A)	540 IU	10 IU
Thiamine (B_1)	0.101 mg	0.002 mg
Riboflavin (B_2)	0.063 mg	0.001 mg
Niacin (B_3)	2.860 mg	0.054 mg
Ascorbic Acid (C)	39.20 mg	0.75 mg

Allspice *(Pimenta officinalis, P. dioica)*

Also Known As: Clove Pepper, Jamaican Pepper, Pimento.

The Spanish called the tree bearing the allspice berries pimienta, *meaning pepper, because the berries resembled peppercorns. The term* Pimenta *comes from the medieval term* pigmentum, *meaning spicy.* Officinalis *means of the workshop, alluding to apothecaries' shops, and signifying that the plant was once part of the official pharmacopeia of Rome.* Dioica *means dioecious, having male and female flowers borne on different plants. The English name* allspice *was coined by a gentleman named Ray in 1693 due to the berry's taste, which has been described as a combination of cloves, juniper berries, cinnamon, and pepper.*

General Information Allspice is made from the dried berries of the West Indian pimento or allspice tree, native to the West Indian island of Jamaica especially, but also to Central and South America. This evergreen member of the myrtle family often grows to great heights of forty feet or more, depending on the climate. In July and August the tree produces clusters of half-inch, fleshy, sweet round berries that are purplish-black and rough-surfaced when ripe, a little larger than peppercorns, and contain two kidney-shaped seeds. Since the berries lose their aroma and volatile oil upon ripening, they are collected as soon as they have attained their full size. The unripe green berries are then dried in the hot tropical sun until they turn a dark reddish-brown. Considered among the most aromatic of spices, the Jamaican variety is held to be of higher quality, as the berries are smaller and more aromatic. Allspice, or pimento, should not be confused with pimientos, the fruits of certain *Capsicum* garden peppers.

Culinary Uses With its hint of many flavors, allspice can add a warm, rich taste to many meals. Ground allspice is found in many of the blended spice mixtures and can be used on its own in pickles, fruitcakes, plum pudding, spicy cakes and cookies. Just a pinch will add zip to carrots or other sweet vegetables. Two or three whole berries add a warm spicy flavor to green pea or other soups.

Health Benefits Aromatic, carminative, stimulant, stomachic. Allspice promotes digestion and removes gases from the upper intestinal tract. Applying the crushed berries to painful muscles and joints works as an effective pain reliever, and the oil may

Lore and Legend

In their quest for black pepper, the Spanish discovered the island of Jamaica, which was covered with trees bearing aromatic berries that somewhat resembled peppercorns. Although it is hard to believe that the explorers actually thought the berries were peppercorns, the trees and their small berries were nonetheless called *pimiento* (Spanish for pepper). They were long regarded and feared as an aphrodisiac, and Peter the Venerable in 1132 forbade the monks under his charge at Cluny to eat pimento (allspice) because it was"provokative to lust." The leaves of the allspice tree are used in the production of bay rum, and at one time the white bark was sold as clove cinnamon.

be applied directly to painful teeth and gums as an anesthetic and/or first aid until professional care can be obtained.

Aloe Vera *(Aloe vera, A. barbadensis, A. ferox)*

> Aloe *is derived from the Arabic* alloeh, *meaning bitter and shiny substance;* vera *means true;* barbadensis *means coming from Barbados;* ferox *means ferocious or thorny.*

General Information Aloe vera is a desert plant belonging to the lily family, a succulent native to East and South Africa. In the sixth century A.D., Arab traders carried aloe from Spain to Asia and introduced it to India's traditional Ayurvedic physicians, who heralded its healing properties. References to the healing benefits of aloe are found in Egyptian, Roman, Chinese, Greek, Italian, Algerian, Moroccan, Arabian, Indian, and Christian history. The plant grows extremely well in dry soils and requires little or no care, propagating itself by means of suckers, small plants growing out from the roots of the parent plant. The basal leaves are long and narrow, fleshy with a spiny margin about two inches in thickness. Decorative as well as medicinal, aloe is particularly effective as a center of floral designs. Some varieties make excellent houseplants, especially for those without green thumbs.

Lore and Legend

Aloe is one of the few non-narcotic plants to cause a war. When Alexander the Great conquered Egypt in 332 B.C., he heard stories of a plant growing on an island off Somalia with amazing wound-healing powers. Intent on healing his soldiers' wounds—and denying this healer to his enemies—Alexander sent an army to seize the island of Socotra to gain access to the plant, which turned out to be aloe.

Culinary Uses The leaves of aloe vera are pressed into juice and administered for liver ailments. Fresh or prepared aloe is sold in various forms: as juices, gel caps, powders, and other formulas. Fresh juice is readily obtained by breaking off a leaf and squeezing the juice out.

Health Benefits Antibiotic, demulcent, emollient, healing, purgative, vulnerary. Aloe vera is one of the oldest healing remedies known to man. Most of its tissue does not contain any medicinally active substance, but inside the outer layer of the leaf is a crystal-clear mucilaginous gel. When applied externally, the gel is quickly absorbed, soothing and relieving pain, burning, and itching; it provides a natural protection for the skin, seems to reduce scar tissue formation, does not stain, and has no unpleasant odor. As well, there seems to be some unknown substance that acts as a "wound hormone" to accelerate the healing process of injured surfaces. Documented cases of radiation burn victims show more rapid healing when using aloe than with any other method of burn treatment. If turmeric is added to the gel, the healing process is even faster. Taken

Aloe Vera

Nutritional Value Per 100 g Edible Portion

	Dried
Calories	280
Protein	5.7 g
Fat	0.80 g
Fiber	17.7 g
Calcium	460 mg
Iron	4.1 mg
Magnesium	93 mg
Phosphorus	94 mg
Potassium	85 mg
Sodium	51 mg
Zinc	1.100 mg
Manganese	0.600 mg
Beta Carotene (A)	5,080 IU
Thiamine (B_1)	0.080 mg
Riboflavin (B_2)	trace
Niacin (B_3)	6.400 mg
Ascorbic Acid (C)	626 mg

internally, aloe vera will purify the blood and liver and regulate and cleanse the colon, as well as soothe ulcers and hemorrhoids. In Java, aloe juice is massaged into the hair and scalp to improve its condition and stimulate growth. The fresh gel is frequently used in cosmetic skin care products as an emollient, and might well be worth a try, as the beautiful Cleopatra is known to have massaged it into her skin.

NOTE: Pregnant women and diabetics are cautioned not to take aloe vera internally.

Angelica *(Angelica archangelica, A. sinensis, A. atropurpurea, A. sylvestris)*

Also Known As: Wild Celery, Masterwort, Archangel.

There are several versions of how this plant got its name Angelica. *One group claims the name comes from the old Roman name* herba angelica, *meaning angelic herb, because it was thought to possess powers against poison and plague. Another possibility is that because angelica often blooms around May 8, the feast day of St. Michael the Archangel, the plant was named in his honor. My personal favorite is a legend that holds that during the bubonic plague of 1665, a monk dreamt he met an angel who showed him an herb (angelica) that could cure the scourge; the monk then duly named the plant in honor of the angel in his dream.* Archangelica *means archangel,* sinensis *means originating in China,* atropurpurea *signifies dark purple, and* sylvestris *means pertaining to the woods or growing wild.*

General Information Angelica is a member of the carrot family resembling celery; its roots and fruit furnish a flavorful oil. The European variety (*Angelica archangelica*), with its preference for cold, moist climates, is native to the north of Europe, while the American variety (*Angelica atropurpurea*) grows in meadows and marshy woods from Canada to the Carolinas. Of the several different species of angelica, the one most sought after comes from China; commonly known as **Dong quai,** and botanically as *Angelica sinensis*, this species is used as a flavorful cooking spice and as a potent herbal medicine. Other species of angelica that come from Europe are used for flavoring wines, perfumes, and liqueurs, as well as being used in folk medicine.

Culinary Uses Angelica has a flavor reminiscent of licorice and juniper berries that most people enjoy; its sweet hardy flavor permeates the fresh or dried leaves, stem, root, and seeds of the plant. The most celebrated part of angelica is its stem. Fresh stems can be cooked and eaten as a fresh herb, used for seasoning fish, or made into syrup for pudding and ice cream toppings. Candied or crystallized stems are used as a confection, and their sweet flavor was once widely known and enjoyed (especially in fruitcake). Savor the stems alone, or use them to decorate cakes, tarts, and other sweet pastries. Fresh leaves provide a slightly sweet, zesty accent to fruit or vegetable soups and green salads. Dried ground leaves reduce the need for sweetener when making pies or sauces, and add zip to desserts and pastries. The dried ground root has a taste similar to the leaves, but is bolder and earthier; this flavor works well in yeasted and quick breads, cakes, muffins, and cookies.

Angelica

Nutritional Value Per 100 g Edible Portion

	Chinese, Dried (Dong quai)
Calories	320
Protein	13.0 g
Fat	1.8 g
Fiber	17.2 g
Calcium	282 mg
Iron	88 mg
Magnesium	265 mg
Phosphorus	334 mg
Potassium	1070 mg
Sodium	trace
Zinc	trace
Manganese	2.600 mg
Beta Carotene (A)	2,010 IU
Thiamine (B_1)	trace
Riboflavin (B_2)	0.340 mg
Niacin (B_3)	6.800 mg
Ascorbic Acid (C)	30.4 mg

Health Benefits Aromatic, carminative, expectorant, stimulant, stomachic, tonic. Angelica has been highly regarded in Europe and Asia for centuries due to its medicinal properties. Angelica stimulates many functions of the body: it strengthens the heart and lungs, opens passageways in the liver and spleen to allow them to function better, reduces gas in the intestines, relieves heartburn and sour stomach, and promotes perspiration and the production of urine. The root is widely used in treating stomach and bowel disorders. In small doses, angelica root decreases the production of gastric juices, which is good for ulcer sufferers; in larger doses, it increases the production of gastric juices, thus stimulating the appetite. With the regular use of angelica, there seems to arise a distaste for alcoholic drinks.

Lore and Legend

European peasants made angelica leaf necklaces to protect their children from illness and witchcraft. The presence of angelica in a woman's garden or cupboard was once used as a defense against spurious charges of witchcraft, as it was reputedly the only herb never used by witches.

NOTE: Fresh angelica roots contain poisonous elements only eliminated by thorough drying. Unless you are a confident field botanist, do not collect angelica in the wild, as it is too easy to confuse the plant with the extremely poisonous water hemlock (Cicuta maculata).

In China, the ten different angelica species collectively known as dong quai have been used for several thousand years and are considered second only to ginseng in importance. The brown, fleshy root looks much like gentian root, while its odor is strong, resembling celery, but the taste is warm, sweetish, and aromatic. Ranking next to licorice in frequency of use, it is much prescribed for female complaints, colds, flu, and a large number of other complaints. Dong quai was introduced into Western medicine in 1899 by the Merck company in the form of a liquid extract sold under the name of Eumenol, and recommended for menstrual disorders. The active constituents of dong quai appear to be aromatic volatile oils that affect the uterus, liver, heart, blood pressure, and nervous system.

Anise/Aniseed *(Pimpinella anisum)*

Pimpinella *possibly derives from the Latin* bipinnula, *meaning bipinnate (having similar parts arranged on opposite sides). The early Arabic name for the plant was* anysum, *from which was derived the Greek* anison *or* anneson, *the Latin* anisum, *and the English* anise.

General Information Anise is an annual oil-bearing seed plant of the carrot family native to western Asia and Egypt. This dainty annual reaches two feet in height and has feathery leaves divided into many leaflets and umbrella-like clusters of tiny white or yellow flowers, which bloom in mid-summer and produce small, downy, ribbed fruits (seeds) in late

Anise/Aniseed

Nutritional Value Per 100 g Edible Portion

	Whole	Seed
Calories	337	7
Protein	17.60 g	0.37 g
Fat	15.90 g	0.33 g
Fiber	14.60 g	0.31 g
Calcium	646 mg	14 mg
Iron	36.96 mg	0.78 mg
Magnesium	170 mg	4 mg
Phosphorus	440 mg	9 mg
Potassium	1,441 mg	30 mg
Sodium	16 mg	trace
Zinc	5.300 mg	0.110 mg
Copper	0.910 mg	n/a
Manganese	2.300 mg	n/a

Lore and Legend

Anise was so important as a spice and cash crop for ancient cultures that it was frequently used as a medium of exchange and for the payment of taxes. Clay tablets found in Assyria contain praise for the medicinal properties of anise, while ancient Greeks valued its purported effectiveness as an aphrodisiac. The Romans cultivated the herb extensively and anise was one of several spices used to flavor a cake called *mustaceum,* often served as a dessert and digestive aid at feasts. In medieval England the spice was so popular as a flavoring, medicine, and perfume that in 1305 King Edward I placed a special import tax on it to raise money to repair the London Bridge. For some reason, mice seem to find anise quite irresistible, and if a better mouse trap is ever developed, it just may use anise as the bait.

summer. The whole plant has a fragrant odor and the pungent seeds taste warm, sweet, and reminiscent of licorice when chewed.

Culinary Uses Anise is used both as a seed and a leafy herb. Before the seed heads are produced, the leaves and stalks can be used as a salad herb; they have a sweet licorice-like taste and are delicious served freshly chopped into salads and cream sauces, or they can be steamed or sauteed with a bit of olive oil, garlic, and lemon juice. Aniseeds are classed as one of the four great hot seeds. Available either whole or powdered, aniseed has a sweet yet spicy aroma and flavor of licorice, and is used to flavor cakes and cookies, pickles, salad dressings, and soups. Using the whole seed is preferable, since many of the volatile oils quickly become lost after grinding. Try adding just a dash to applesauce for a delightful change.

Health Benefits Antispasmodic, aphrodisiac, aromatic, carminative, diuretic, stimulant, stomachic, tonic. Medicinally, anise has warming and moistening properties, and has traditionally been used in European herbal medicine as a mild diuretic, a slight stimulant for vital bodily organs, to treat flatulence and indigestion, to sweeten the breath, and to increase mother's milk. It is mildly expectorant and thus appears frequently as a flavoring and active ingredient in cough syrups and lozenges. Chewing aniseed will help induce sleep and alleviate cramps and nausea. To make a pleasant digestive remedy, bruise two teaspoonfuls of aniseeds well in a mortar, then put them in a jug and pour in half a pint of boiling water. Cover and leave to get cold, then bottle. Adults should take two teaspoonfuls, while half a teaspoonful will be sufficient for a very young child.

Annatto *(Bixa orellana)*

Also Known As: Achiote, Bija, Bijoul, Roucou.

Bixa *is derived a South American name for the plant.*

Annatto

Nutritional Value Per 100 g Edible Portion	Fresh
Calories	54-346
Fat	0.3-1.9 g
Fiber	0.5-3.2 g
Calcium	7.0-45.0 mg
Iron	0.8-5.0 mg
Phosphorus	10-64 mg
Beta Carotene (A)	0.090-0.600 mg
Riboflavin (B_2)	0.050-0.300 mg
Niacin (B_3)	0.30-1.90 mg
Ascorbic Acid (C)	2.0-13.0 mg

General Information The annatto tree is an attractive small flowering tree that grows throughout the Caribbean, Mexico, and Central and South America. It bears large pink flowers that resemble wild roses. However, it is the orange dye from the pulp, which surrounds the fifty or so seeds inside the heart-shaped, prickly scarlet fruits that makes the tree commercially important. The warlike Carib Indians used the dye to paint their bodies, and it was also used by the ancient Mayans in Guatemala. Annatto was introduced to the Philippines by the Spaniards, and it has since become an important ingredient in many dishes.

Culinary Uses Annatto is exploited to its fullest in the cooking of the Caribbean and Latin American cultures, where it is used primarily as a coloring although also as a gentle flavoring. It is an ingredient in the spicy sauce that is served over the Jamaican national dish of akee and salt cod. In Mexico, annatto seeds are ground with other herbs and spices for a seasoning mixture that has a fragrant and flowery taste. In Europe and North America, annatto is used to color butter and cheese. The seeds, if brick red, will keep indefinitely in a cool dark place.

Arrowroot *(Maranta arundinacea)*

The botanical name Maranta *was given by Plumier in 1559 to honor a famous Venetian physician and botanist, Bartommeo Maranto. The term* arundinacea *means reed-like. The English name* arrowroot *actually originates from an American Indian name for all flour-giving roots,* araruta.

General Information Arrowroot powder is a fine, starchy flour extracted from the beaten pulp of tuberous rootstocks of a tropical plant native to South America and the West Indies. There are red and white varieties, of which the former is the most esteemed. Most of our arrowroot comes from the West Indian island of St. Vincent. The roots, which were once believed to cure wounds from poisoned arrows, are ground, sun-dried, and powdered.

Arrowroot

Nutritional Value Per 100 g Edible Portion

	Powder
Calories	357
Protein	0.30 g
Fat	0.10 g
Fiber	n/a
Calcium	40 mg
Iron	0.33 mg
Magnesium	3 mg
Phosphorus	5 mg
Potassium	11 mg
Sodium	2 mg
Zinc	0.070 mg
Copper	0.040 mg
Manganese	0.470 mg
Beta Carotene (A)	n/a
Thiamine (B_1)	0.001 mg
Riboflavin (B_2)	0 mg
Niacin (B_3)	0 mg
Pantothenic Acid (B5)	0.130 mg
Pyridoxine (B_6)	0.005 mg
Folic Acid (B_9)	7.0 mcg
Ascorbic Acid (C)	0 mg

Culinary Uses A fine silky powder without the chalkiness of cornstarch or the graininess of flour, arrowroot can be used to thicken fruits, soups, and gravy. Although it will keep almost indefinitely when stored in a cool, dry cupboard, the general recommendation is that it be used within a year of purchase. One tablespoon of arrowroot powder will thicken a cup of liquid; for a thicker mixture, use two tablespoons per cup. Dissolve the powder by stirring it into an equal amount of cool liquid before adding it to the dish being prepared; stir the mixture in during the last minutes of cooking time. It does not have to reach the boiling point to thicken. Use 1 1/2 teaspoons of arrowroot to replace 1 tablespoon of either cornstarch or flour in recipes. It works especially well for fruit desserts and other preparations that require little or no cooking. One precaution: arrowroot-thickened sauces tend to break down if overcooked or allowed to stand too long before serving.

Health Benefits Arrowroot is easily digested and more nutritious than cornstarch. The powder of choice for diaper rash, this absorbent, soothing, natural, and nontoxic powder reduces friction, prevents irritation, and keeps skin dry by absorbing water.

Asafoetida *(Ferula assafoetida, F. foetida regel)*

Also Known As: Hing, Stinking Gum, Devil's Dung, Food of the Gods.

> Ferula *is an old Latin name for the plant, likely derived from the verb* ferire, *to strike, because its stems were used as ferules (an instrument, i.e. a flat piece of wood, used to punish children).* Assafoetida *derives from the Persian* aza, *meaning mastic or resin, and the Latin* foetida, *meaning fetid or bad smelling. The* regel *part of the name perhaps refers to Eduard von Regel (1815-1892), the German founder of Gartenflora, and Director of the Botanic Gardens in St. Petersburg, Russia.*

General Information Asafoetida comes from a brown resinous substance, known as gum asafoetida, contained in two varieties of the giant fennels native to Persia and Afghanistan. These are unrelated to the garden and wild fennels, though somewhat similar in appearance, and have a dreadful stink (said by some to resemble rotting garlic) due to their sulphur compounds. In ancient Persia this plant was highly regarded and known as "Food of the Gods." The leaves and stems were used as a vegetable; the odor evidently disappearing once the plant was boiled. The Romans, who knew asafoetida as Persian Sylphium, valued it for medicinal purposes and as a flavoring for sauces and wines. An expensive imported spice, it became more so when a money-hungry government found it worth taxing, as happened in second century A.D. Alexandria. For a natural pesticide to ward off deer and rabbits, mix 1 ounce of powdered asafoetida with 1½ quarts water and shake hard, then apply around plants.

Lore and Legend

As its name suggests, asafoetida in any quantity has a strong repulsive smell and a nauseating taste—characteristics that also burdened it with the name devil's dung. In the Middle Ages, a small piece of the gum was worn around the neck to ward off disease; whatever effectiveness it had was probably due more to the antisocial properties of the amulet rather than any medicinal virtue.

Culinary Uses Asafoetida is available in solid wax-like pieces or in powder form. Used sparingly, it will give a flavor redolent of garlic and shallots to vegetables, stews, gravies and sauces, and goes especially well with fresh or salted fish. The repellent smell quickly disappears with cooking. A frequent ingredient in Indian cooking, it is especially popular in bean dishes and sauces, where it helps lower their gas-producing tendencies. It is also worth noting that among the ingredients of that long-lived modern favorite, Worcestershire sauce, there are very small quantities of asafoetida. In Afghanistan and Iran, the leaves and stems are eaten as a vegetable.

Health Benefits Anthelmintic, aphrodisiac, carminative, diaphoretic, diuretic, emmenagogue, expectorant, laxative, stimulant, tonic. Asafoetida will produce a sensation of warmth without any rise in body temperature, and stimulate digestion and the mucous membranes, particularly the alimentary canal, acting like a natural laxative and detoxicant. Occasionally, those who are not accustomed to asafoetida may develop a puzzling diarrhea after ingestion.

Baking Powder

General Information Baking powder is a mixture of the "slow-acting" leavening agent baking soda, and a "fast-acting" leavening agent such as calcium acid phosphate (monocalcium phosphate monohydrate), calcium sulfate, or cream of tartar. Those containing sodium aluminum sulphate are viewed with concern, since excessive amounts of aluminum in the body are not desirable. "Double-acting" indicates that the baked product will rise both when the batter is prepared as well as during baking. Rumford baking powder was invented by two scientists in 1854 (one of them Eben Horsford, a professor who held the Rumford Chair of Applied Science at Harvard University) and named after Count Rumford, formerly known as Benjamin Thompson of Massachusetts (1753–1814). Count Rumford was a politician and inventor; the Leonardo da Vinci of the kitchen, he was the founder of home economics, invented the first kitchen range and other useful kitchen items, and was a pioneer in studies of light and heat, guns and explosives, ship design, and many other areas. It was Rumford who conceived the idea of an American military academy, but he was denied a role in establishing West Point due to his British sympathies during the Revolution.

Baking Powder

Nutritional Value Per Tablespoon

	Calumet Brand	Brand with Cream of Tartar
Calories	3	7
Protein	0 g	0 g
Fat	0 g	0 g
Fiber	n/a	n/a
Calcium	241 mg	0 mg
Iron	0 mg	0 mg
Magnesium	0 mg	0 mg
Phosphorus	83 mg	0 mg
Potassium	0 mg	361 mg
Sodium	426 mg	694 mg
Zinc	0 mg	0 mg

Culinary Uses Baking powders have been in use for more than one hundred years as a yeast substitute. When baking powder is mixed into a batter, carbon dioxide gas is released from the sodium or potassium bicarbonate by the action of an acid or an acid salt. It is this gas which gives volume (rise) and a lighter texture to the finished product. Easily made at home, baking powder can be put together from two parts cream of tartar, one part baking soda, and two parts arrowroot powder.

Health Benefits Most commercially available baking powders contain aluminum compounds that are deleterious to health as well as flavor, imparting a bitter aftertaste. Look for aluminum-free baking powders instead. Baking powder depletes baked goods of the B vitamins thiamine and folic acid, and creates a type of alkalinity in the body that eradicates vitamin C.

Baking Soda *(Sodium bicarbonate)*

General Information Baking soda was developed by John Dwight and his brother-in-law Dr. Austin Church in 1846. Called Dwight's Saleratus (acerated salts), the powder was made from carbon dioxide-treated soda ash, and completely revolutionized the baking industry. Baking soda today is produced by the Solvay method, in which a brine solution is run into saturation tanks, where it mixes with ammonia gas; this ammonia brine is then injected with carbon dioxide to produce bicarbonate of soda. The newly formed soda is insoluble, so it is precipitated out, drawn off, filtered, washed in cold water, dried, and milled into the refined

Baking Soda

Nutritional Value Per 100 g Edible Portion

		1 tsp.
Calories	0	0
Protein	0 g	0 g
Fat	0 g	0 g
Fiber	0 g	0 g
Sodium	27,360 mg	1,259 mg

white powder we are all familiar with. Baking soda is used as a leavening agent in quick breads, which do not require kneading and rising before baking, but also in cookies, cakes, pies, pancakes, and any other baked goods using pastry wheat flours or flours other than hard wheat.

Culinary Uses Baking soda must be used in conjunction with an acid; when mixed in the proper proportions with a liquid, they almost completely neutralize each other, forming water and carbon dioxide gas, which lifts the batter and creates a light, smooth-textured product. A few blandly flavored salts remain of the original baking soda. The most familiar use for baking soda is as an ingredient in baking powder. When cooked with garbanzo or black beans, baking soda makes them lighter and facilitates the cooking process.

Health Benefits Baking soda depletes baked goods of the B vitamins thiamine and folic acid, and creates a type of alkalinity in the body that eradicates vitamin C. An excellent use of baking soda is as a dentrifice, as its highly alkaline properties neutralize plaque acids and eliminate the bacteria that cause tooth decay. It also helps stop the major cause of tooth loss—gum infection and inflammation such as gingivitis and pyorrhea—better than most commercial toothpastes. Another excellent use is as a treatment for athlete's foot: dust feet liberally in the morning and then put on cotton or wool socks. Baking soda relieves skin infections, hives and rash, and maintains the health and hygiene of the skin. A paste of baking soda and water can soothe the itch of a mosquito bite; one-quarter to one-half cup added to a warm bath can soothe itchiness due to hives, eczema, or minor sunburn, as well as promote circulation and make the skin soft. A pinchful with one cup of warm water and the juice of one-half lemon relieves stomach acidity, gas, and indigestion. An excellent external treatment in every form of radiation exposure is a bath of sea salt and baking soda. Add 1 pound each of sea salt and baking soda to a warm bath, and soak for 20 minutes; rinse with cool water. Repeat three times a week for one month in cases of serious exposure.

Balm (*Melissa officinalis*)

Also Known As: Sweet Balm, Lemon Balm, Melissa.

> *Until the fifteenth century this plant was considered important only as a bee-attracting plant and was known as either* melissophyllon, *Greek for bee leaf, or* apiastrum, *Latin for bee plant. Its modern botanical name,* Melissa, *meaning bee, reflects this early association.* Officinalis *means of the workshop, alluding to apothecaries' shops, and signifying that the plant was once part of the official pharmacopeia of Rome. The English name* balm *comes from the Greek* balsamon, *meaning balsam, an oily, fragrant resin; since this plant does not actually exude a balsam, the name probably refers to its fragrant aroma and its ability to soothe and calm the nerves.*

General Information Balm originated in the Middle East but soon found its way to the Mediterranean countries, where it was cultivated for its fragrant lemony-scented leaves. A rather coarse low herb, it is always popular due to its pleasant fragrance and is the special joy of honeybees, who are forever delving into its small white or yellowish flowers. An important herb in the monastic apothecary gardens, balm has a venerable history of use as both a healing herb and as part of a drink to ensure longevity.

Balm

Nutritional Value Per 100 g Edible Portion	Seed
Protein	29.3 g
Fat	11.5 g

Culinary Uses Balm has a lemony scent, and imparts a lemon-mint, honey-sweet flavor to salads, salad dressings, iced tea, and fruit drinks. The leaves can also be used for flavoring or garnish in soups, stews, custards, puddings, or cookies.

Health Benefits Antibacterial, antispasmodic, astringent, calmative, carminative, diaphoretic, emmenagogue, relaxant, stomachic, tonic. Leaves of balm have been used to dress and heal wounds since ancient times, due to their antibacterial properties. Recommended for troubles involving the liver, spleen, kidneys, or bladder, balm will help the digestion and relieve nausea and vomiting. Tea made from the fresh or dried leaves is said to soothe menstrual cramps and headaches, relieve insomnia, act as a sedative, quiet vomiting, relieve colic, and reduce fever. The leaves contain a volatile oil that is used in the manufacture of perfumes and cosmetics.

Basil (*Ocimum basilicum, O. sanctum*)

Also Known As: Sweet Basil, St. Josephwort.

Ocimum *is from an old Greek name for the plant, while* basilicum *means royal or magnificent, and* sanctum *means holy. The common name* basil *is an abbreviation of* basilikon phuton, *Greek for kingly herb.*

General Information Basil is another member of the mint family, a bushy annual with broad, light green, oval leaves that release a spicy scent when bruised. Native to India, there are many different varieties, including sweet basil, lemon basil, licorice basil, cinnamon basil, and purple basil. Basil makes a safe and natural insect repellent for the garden and house, repelling houseflies, mosquitoes, and cockroaches.

Basil

Nutritional Value Per 100 g Edible Portion	Fresh	Dried	1 tsp.
Calories	27	251	4
Protein	2.54 g	14.37 g	0.20 g
Fat	0.61 g	3.98 g	0.06 g
Fiber	n/a	17.76 g	0.25 g
Calcium	154 mg	2,113 mg	30 mg
Iron	n/a	42.00 mg	0.59 mg
Magnesium	81 mg	422 mg	6 mg
Phosphorus	69 mg	490 mg	7 mg
Potassium	462 mg	3,433 mg	48 mg
Sodium	4 mg	34 mg	trace
Zinc	0.850 mg	5.820 mg	0.080 mg
Copper	0.290 mg	1.367 mg	n/a
Manganese	1.446 mg	3.167 mg	n/a
Beta Carotene (A)	n/a	9,375 IU	131 IU
Thiamine (B1)	0.026 mg	0.148 mg	0.002 mg
Riboflavin (B2)	0.073 mg	0.316 mg	0.004 mg
Niacin (B3)	0.925 mg	6.948 mg	0.097 mg
Pantothenic Acid (B5)	0.238 mg	n/a	n/a
Pyridoxine (B6)	0.129 mg	n/a	n/a
Folic Acid (B9)	64.0 mcg	n/a	n/a
Ascorbic Acid (C)	n/a	61.22 mg	0.86 mg

Lore and Legend

Ancient lore seems to have accorded basil somewhat mixed attributes. In India, the herb flourishes freely and from time immemorial has been sacred to the Hindus, consecrated to their god Vishnu, and to his popular incarnation, Krishna (especially *Ocimum sanctum*, "holy basil"). They call it *tulasi*, after the goddess Tulasi, the wife of Vishnu, who when she came to earth took the form of this lowly herb. Thus the plant is revered, and no sprig of it may be broken off except for a worthy reason, and only then gathered with a prayer to Tulasi and Vishnu for forgiveness, for the heart of Vishnu is sorely agitated and tormented when so much as a leaf is broken from the stalk of his wife Tulasi. Yet these leaves are necessary, for no Hindu could rest in his grave unless his head had been bathed with tulasi water just before burial, and a tulasi leaf laid on his breast. According to Greek mythology, basil was named for the baneful basilisk, a fabulous creature half lizard and half dragon born of serpents, that was believed to inhabit the deserts of Africa, and whose very look was fatal. Because the plant was regarded as magical protection against this monster, no one carrying a sprig could be injured by his look, breath, or even by his bite if a leaf were quickly applied to the wound. In more enlightened days, when the lizard-dragon basilisk had passed into fable, basil leaves became very naturally an antidote for the bite of any venomous creature, even a mad dog. Later Greeks and Romans had a curious belief that, because the herb was a symbol of hostility and insanity, to grow truly fragrant basil one had to shout and swear angrily and outlandishly while sowing its seeds. Even today in French, "sowing basil" (*semer le basilic*) means "ranting."

Culinary Uses The flavor of fresh basil is rich and spicy, almost peppery and rather like cloves, with a strong, pungent, sweet smell. The dried leaves taste more like curry. Its pungency, unlike most other herbs, actually increases with cooking, so handle with care. The sweet clove-like flavor and aroma give basil infinite uses, but it is probably best known for its use with tomato dishes, especially pizza. It combines especially well with rosemary, sage, and summer savory and is used in pasta salads, Mediterranean-style dishes, and herb breads. When purchasing basil, look for crisp, vibrant green leaves with no sign of decay. A successful way of storing the fresh leaves is by placing them in a jar with a pinch of salt and covering them with olive oil. Dried basil can be used if fresh basil is not available.

Health Benefits Antiseptic, antispasmodic, appetizer, carminative, emmenagogue, stomachic. Traditionally classified as a warming and moistening herb, basil is regarded as slightly antiseptic, and a mild nervine and emmenagogue. It has a good affinity with the stomach, where it will stimulate the appetite, digestion and nerves; as well it counteracts flatulence, stomach cramps, nausea, vomiting, and constipation. Tea made from the leaves is recommended for nausea, gas pains, and dysentery.

Bay (*Laurus nobilis*)

Its botanical name emphasizes the respect with which the ancient held this plant: Laurus *from the Latin meaning to praise, and* nobilis *meaning renowned or famous. The English word* bay *derives from the Latin* baca, *meaning berry.*

General Information The stately, fragrant bay tree is indigenous to the Mediterranean basin, growing especially near the coasts of the three continents surrounding the Mediterranean Sea, but also extending its range inland and northeast to the Black Sea coast of Turkey. It was so highly valued in all the Mediterranean regions that a Roman gold coin of 342 B.C. has a laurel wreath modeled upon its surface. Usually a shrub or small tree, the leaves are dark green and somewhat glossy, as leathery and as thin as when they are dried. The leaves are gathered by hand in mid- to late summer by mountain peasants—picked in the morning and dried in the shade lest they turn brown. Leaves from the American bay (*Umbellularia californica*) have a camphor-and-paint smell and an awful taste. These are sometimes sold for culinary uses, but should be avoided. Instead, seek out the best European bay you can find.

Culinary Uses Bay leaves have an aromatic perfume and strong spicy flavor reminiscent of pine, nutmeg, and pepper. When the leaves are shredded or crushed, the aroma and flavor are even more apparent. Fresh leaves are strongly scented, bitter, and not to everyone's taste. They are best left to dry and mellow for a few days, although not for too long, as old dried leaves will be quite flavorless. Newly dried leaves are sweet in the sense that cinnamon and clove are sweet, with a grassy freshness. Popular in Mediterranean cooking, bay leaves are usually used when preparing meats, but can also be added to stews, casseroles, and soup stocks. By their very nature, bay leaves provide support to other seasonings. They should be used sparingly due to their strong flavor, with one-half to one leaf all that is needed for a medium-sized pot of soup or stew. The whole leaves do not cook down and should be removed before the dish is served.

Bay leaves appear to repel roaches, moths, and fleas. Put a whole leaf in a canister of flour to keep insects out, or put whole leaves on the floor of your closet, in drawers where woolen clothes are stored, or around the drain under the sink in your kitchen.

Bay

Nutritional Value Per 100 g Edible Portion

	Dried Crumbled	1 tsp.
Calories	313	2
Protein	7.61 g	0.05 g
Fat	8.36 g	0.05 g
Fiber	26.32 g	0.16 g
Calcium	834 mg	5 mg
Iron	43.00 mg	0.26 mg
Magnesium	120 mg	1 mg
Phosphorus	113 mg	1 mg
Potassium	529 mg	3 mg
Sodium	23 mg	trace
Zinc	3.700 mg	0.020 mg
Copper	0.416 mg	n/a
Manganese	8.167 mg	n/a
Beta Carotene (A)	6,185 IU	37 IU
Thiamine (B_1)	0.009 mg	trace
Riboflavin (B_2)	0.421 mg	0.003 mg
Niacin (B_3)	2.005 mg	0.012 mg
Ascorbic Acid (C)	46.53 mg	0.28 mg

Lore and Legend

Legend has it that we owe the bay laurel to Apollo, Greek god of prophecy, poetry, and medicine. It seems that one day Apollo scolded Cupid for some unseemly conduct and called him a mere child. The usually charming but mischievous Cupid decided to avenge the insult, and succeeded in shooting Apollo with a golden arrow to induce passionate longing for the first woman he saw; Cupid then loosed a second arrow of lead to cause that woman to be equally repelled. While traversing the verdant forest, Apollo came upon the lithe and lovely wood nymph Daphne, and the effect of the golden shaft was immediate. He saw before him not merely a wood nymph but a goddess of superb beauty with attributes of wisdom and charm beyond all description. However, Daphne felt such repugnance that she fled in panic. Apollo eagerly pursued and entreated her, but she refused to stop; when the capture seemed inevitable, Daphne prayed urgently to the gods to take from her the physical form that had so enchanted Apollo, and under his grasping hands her feet were rooted into the ground, her body and upraised arms thickened into a tree trunk and limbs covered not with silky skin but rough bark, and her blowing hair turned into rustling leaves. The amazed Apollo was inconsolable but determined that his unrequited love would take another form, and thus decreed that the tree would remain green during both summer and winter, and that its leaves would be the badge of honor and glory for those who excelled in courage or accomplishment. Laurel wreaths were given the victors in the Pythian Games and at the first Olympics in 776 B.C. in honor of Apollo.

It was believed that laurel endowed prophets with vision, and the Pythian priestesses at Delphi, the oracle dedicated to Apollo, chewed laurel leaves to induce oracular powers. Since the leaves are mildly narcotic in large doses, they may have induced the required trance states. When the ancient Greek civilization flourished, bay branches from the sacred groves near the healing temples were gathered and woven into wreaths to honor great artistic figures, victors, heroes, and athletes. Physicians, upon completing their studies, were crowned with wreaths of berried laurel branches, the "baca lauris," and students even today receive their baccalaureate degrees.

Health Benefits Antiseptic, relaxant. Bay has an ancient reputation of being beneficial to the health and happiness of man. A pleasant tonic that gives tone and strength to the digestive organs, bay is especially good for soothing the stomach, relieving abdominal cramps, and relieving flatulence. Bay oil is said to benefit sprains, bruises, and skin rashes; studies show that it has bactericidal and fungicidal properties, as well as having narcotic and sedative effects on mice.

Beebalm *(Monarda didyma)*

Also Known As: Bergamot, Oswego Tea.

> *The name* Monarda *honors the Spanish physician and medical botanist Dr. Nicolas Monardes of Seville, who wrote his herbal on the flora of America in 1569,* Joyful Newes Out of the New Founde World. *Dr. Monarda called this herb* bergamot *because its leaf scent resembles that of the Italian bergamot orange.* Didyma *refers to the leaves, which grow in pairs. It received its English name* beebalm *because bees seem especially attracted to its fragrant flowers.*

General Information Beebalm is a member of the mint family native to swampy, moderately acid woodland soils of eastern North America. In Europe beebalm is an introduced plant, first raised in 1745 by Peter Collinson from seed collected from the shores of Lake Ontario. The flowers are a startling red, borne in heads with red bracts between each floret so that the whole plant resembles a sparkling firework. Used by Native Americans, the plant has a citrus-like fragrance.

Culinary Uses Beebalm's flavor has a bright tang, reminiscent of citrus and mint, with a soft mingling of orange and lemon. Wherever you need a little zip or a little color, throw in some beebalm flowers: into a salad, or float them in a bowl of punch as a bright, colorful garnish. Use the fresh leaves in cooking or dried leaves in tea blends. Its citrusy flavor naturally complements many fruits: strawberries, apples, oranges, and melons, as well as working well in combination with other mints.

Health Benefits Herbalists recommend an infusion of beebalm for coughs, sore throats, nausea, flatulence, and menstrual cramps. A tea made from the leaves is used as a gentle febrifuge. Scientists have found that the oil contains thymol, which is antiseptic and effective against fungi, bacteria, and some parasites. In lotions and baths, infusions of beebalm stimulate the skin.

Bitter Root *(Lewisia rediviva)*

Also Known As: White Mountain Rose, Spatlum.

> *The genus* Lewisia *commemorates Captain Meriwether Lewis (1774–1809) of the Lewis and Clark expedition;* rediviva *means restored, or brought back to life. The English name* bitter root *was given because the root is intensely bitter when raw.*

General Information Bitter root is a member of the purslane family native to the western United States, from Montana, Wyoming, and Utah west to the Pacific.

Probably because of its importance to the American Indians and early settlers, it was made the state flower of Montana, and the high range of mountains between Montana and Idaho received their name from this plant. This stemless perennial is amazingly tenacious. After being uprooted and dried for weeks or even months, it has the power of reviving when placed in water or in the ground, putting forth leaves and flowers. Its dark-colored roots are white and floury inside and resemble arrowroot when boiled; they have great vitality and are capable of a large yield when cultivated.

Culinary Uses Although the fleshy roots are intensely bitter when raw, this property is chiefly removed when cooked, and they become quite succulent. From the roots the California Indians make a flour known as *spatlum* (or *spatulum*) which is surprisingly nourishing, with one ounce said to provide sufficient nourishment for a meal.

Borage *(Borago officinalis)*

Borage gets its name from the Latin root borra *or* burra, *meaning rough hair or short wool.* Officinalis *means of the workshop, alluding to apothecaries' shops, and signifying that the plant was once part of the official pharmacopeia of Rome.*

General Information Borage is originally a wild plant from Syria, a member of the forget-me-not family now widely spread over Europe and North America. It was spread by the Arabs in the Middle Ages, and became popular as a culinary herb and as food for bees. A decorative plant, it has coarse woolly hairs that cover its stems and leaves. In centuries past, borage was most widely known as a bee-plant and for its handsome blue or purplish racemose flowers. There is an old saying that "a garden without borage is like a heart without courage."

Lore and Legend

Borage has an ancient reputation for having a wonderfully positive effect on the mind and body, and is believed to drive away sorrow, increase joyfulness, and strengthen the heart. According to old folktales, borage was sometimes smuggled into the drink of prospective husbands to give them the courage to propose marriage.

Culinary Uses Borage has a fresh, slightly salty, cucumber flavor. The leaves are best when picked young and finely chopped to minimize their hairy texture. They can then either be used in salads, or cooked and served like spinach. Do not cook borage in an aluminum or iron pot, because the tannins can react with the metal to discolor both pot and borage. If the hairy leaves are not appealing, the stalk can be peeled and cut into chunks. The leaves and stalk are excellent added to lettuce, cucumber, or potato salads, or used to enhance the flavor of iced tea and fruit drinks. The dried leaves have much less flavor than the fresh ones. The vivid blue flowers are also edible and make a tasty salad ingredient or garnish, are decorative in beverages, or can be candied and eaten as a sweet.

Borage

Nutritional Value Per 100 g Edible Portion

	Raw	Cooked
Calories	21	25
Protein	1.80 g	2.09 g
Fat	0.70 g	0.81 g
Fiber	0.92 g	1.07 g
Calcium	93 mg	102 mg
Iron	3.30 mg	3.64 mg
Magnesium	52 mg	57 mg
Phosphorus	53 mg	55 mg
Potassium	470 mg	491 mg
Sodium	80 mg	88 mg
Beta Carotene (A)	4,200 IU	4,385 IU
Thiamine (B_1)	0.060 mg	0.059 mg
Riboflavin (B_2)	0.150 mg	0.165 mg
Niacin (B_3)	0.900 mg	0.940 mg
Ascorbic Acid (C)	35.0 mg	32.5 mg

Health Benefits Diaphoretic, diuretic, emollient, tonic. This bland, cooling herb is a valuable remedy for reducing high fever, soothing irritation of skin and mucous membranes, restoring vitality, and for chronic catarrh. The leaves can be used as a poultice on inflammatory swellings due to their mucilaginous qualities and the healing powers of their natural salts (especially potassium nitrate and calcium oxalate). Borage also seems to have some calming effect on the central nervous system that make it useful for nervous conditions.

NOTE: Internal consumption of large amounts of borage has recently been questioned for safety due to its alkaloid pyrrolizidine.

Byproducts

Borage seed oil was first used during the Middle Ages, when it was recommended to insure good blood quality. High in gamma-linolenic acid, borage seed oil has been used to help those struggling with illnesses. This oil should only be used in small amounts, from one-quarter to one-half teaspoon daily, taken plain by mouth or poured directly onto food. It should never be used for cooking and must be kept refrigerated.

Burdock (*Arctium lappa*)

Also Known As: Beggar's Button, Cockleburr, Great Burdock, Burr, Lappa.

The name of the genus, Arctium, *is derived from the Greek* arktos, *a bear, in allusion to the roughness of the burrs;* lappa, *the specific name, is derived from the Celtic word* llap, *meaning a hand, on account of its prehensile properties. The plant's English name* burdock *is a combination of* bur, *from the Latin* burra *meaning a lock of wool such as is often found entangled with the plant when sheep have passed by, and* dock, *an Old English word for plant.*

General Information A native of Europe, burdock is a coarse composite herb growing to four feet in height. The sticky seedballs of burdock hitchhike everywhere, and have even begged a lift across the Atlantic at some stage in the past. The plant has since become naturalized in all regions of North America, where it grows alongside roads, among rubbish, and in cultivated fields. Well known for its propensity of attaching burrs to any and all who brush by, the plant seems to grow well under most any conditions.

Culinary Uses Tender young burdock leaves have a slightly bitter flavor but are delicious in salads, and the stems of older plants can be peeled, steamed, and served like asparagus. The long grayish-brown roots can be grated into salads, steamed as a vegetable, or sliced into soups, stews, and stir-fried dishes. They can also be boiled, then buttered and served like turnips or potatoes. Do not cook burdock in an aluminum or iron pot, because the pigments can react with the metal to discolor both pot and plant.

Health Benefits Cholagogue, demulcent, diaphoretic, diuretic, tonic. Burdock contains high concentrations of vitamins and minerals, especially iron, and is actually higher in minerals than beets, carrots, potatoes, or turnips. It contains between 27 percent and 45 percent inulin, a form of starch that is easily digested, and which is the source of most of its curative powers. Volatile oils in the fresh roots account for the diaphoretic and urinary tonic effects. Used both as folk medicine and in homeopathic remedies, burdock is said to neutralize and eliminate poisons from the body, promote the flow of secretions from the glands to cleanse and normalize their inner membranes, stimulate the action of the stomach, increase perspiration and the flow of urine, and cleanse and eliminate impurities from the blood. The Chinese also consider burdock to be a strengthening aphrodisiac. Burdock root is perhaps the most widely used of all blood purifiers, and the most important herb for treating chronic skin problems. Dried burdock root is sometimes sold in health food stores as *lappa*, which is used to make burdock tea, and the tea when taken freely will help heal all kinds of skin diseases, boils, and carbuncles.

Burdock

Nutritional Value Per 100 g Edible Portion

	Dried
Calories	205
Protein	10.6 g
Fat	0.70 g
Fiber	7.2 g
Calcium	733 mg
Iron	147 mg
Magnesium	537 mg
Phosphorus	437 mg
Potassium	1,680 mg
Sodium	152 mg
Zinc	2.20 mg
Manganese	6.00 mg
Beta Carotene (A)	7,500 IU
Thiamine (B_1)	1.100 mg
Riboflavin (B_2)	0.340 mg
Niacin (B_3)	1.300 mg
Ascorbic Acid (C)	8.5 mg

Burnet (*Sanguisorba minor, S. officinalis*)

The Latin name Sanguisorba *means blood absorber, from* sanguis, *blood, and* sorbeo, *to staunch, an indication of its use on battlefields to staunch bleeding wounds.* Minor *is the lesser or smaller burnet, while* officinalis *means of the workshop, alluding to apothecaries' shops, and signifying that the plant was once part of the official pharmacopeia of Rome. The English name* burnet *comes from the French diminutive for brown,* brunette, *in reference to its chestnut brown color.*

General Information The burnets are pleasantly aromatic members of the rose family that are native to Eurasia but were introduced into North America and now are widely naturalized. A hardy perennial, they are of an ornamental character with their odd-pinnate leaves and little heads of flowers with drooping stamens. You can tell the two varieties apart by their flowers: garden or salad burnet (*S. minor*) has light green to yellow-green flowers, while greater burnet (*S. officinalis*) has red ones. Garden burnet (*Poterium sanguisorba*) is also edible.

Burnet

Nutritional Value Per 100 g Edible Portion

	Fresh
Protein	11.1 g
Fat	9.4 g
Fiber	7.6-24.4 g

Lore and Legend

In Hungary, burnet is considered a mystic plant, and called "Chaba's salve." Tradition says that long ago, King Chaba fought a sanguinary battle with his brother, who was attempting to usurp the throne. Fifteen thousand of Chaba's soldiers were wounded, and the good king cured every one of them with the leaves of burnet. Soldiers fighting in the American Revolution dosed themselves with a tea made from burnet on the night before a battle, on the theory that if they suffered a wound in battle the next day, the burnet in their system would keep them from bleeding to death.

Culinary Uses Burnet leaves are pleasantly aromatic, with a slightly nutty cucumber-like flavor. Since the flavor fades when the leaves dry out, pick the tenderest leaves and use them as soon as possible in salads, soups, and casseroles, in herb butters, and as a garnish for fancy dishes or cool summer drinks. Burnet blends especially well with rosemary, tarragon, basil, and thyme.

Health Benefits Astringent, carminative, stomachic, tonic. Burnet has antiseptic and astringent qualities, making it useful for wounds and abrasions. Added to unfamiliar foods along with other herbs, burnet will help prevent digestive upsets. Tea made from its dried leaves is one of the best remedies for a sour stomach, and is very useful for cleansing the chest, lungs, and stomach. The roots, rich in tannin, are used as an astringent and are valuable in the treatment of dysentery and enteritis. In weaker doses, a tisane of the leaves or dried roots serves as a stomachic.

Calamus Root (*Acorus calamus*)

Also Known As: Sweet Flag.

Acorus *comes from a Greek word meaning pertaining to the eye, and* calamus *is a Greek word for reed canes.*

General Information Calamus is native to southern Asia. It was apparently brought to Europe via the Balkans by Turks, Tartars, and perhaps even the Crusaders. As early as the seventeenth century it was a popular medicine as well as a culinary herb. A relative of skunk cabbage and jack-in-the-pulpit, this highly aromatic reed-like plant resembles the cattail in appearance and frequently grows in the same locations: swamps, marshy grounds, and along sluggish streams. Grown for thousands of years for its rhizomes, which were traded as articles of commerce in the Near East, the fleshy rootstalks grow in closely matted masses often many feet in extent. The sword-shaped leaves, which smell of tangerine when bruised, resemble those of the iris, but are glossy and yellow-green, while those of the iris are bluish-green and dull. The interior of the stalk is sweet—hence the name Sweet flag.

Culinary Uses The entire calamus plant has a spicy citrus fragrance. Used to flavor milk (left to soak like a vanilla pod), the leaves impart a delicious taste to creams and custards. The fleshy rootstock has a warm, pungent, rather bitter taste; it is sometimes used as a substitute for ginger, cinnamon, or nutmeg because of its spicy nature, or can be candied as a sweetmeat by confectioners. The root should not be peeled, for the vital principles lay just under the surface.

Health Benefits Carminative, expectorant, stimulant, tonic. The rhizome contains an aromatic essential oil, tannins, and bitter principles and it is these constituents that have a medicinal effect. Calamus was recommended

Calamus Root

Nutritional Value Per 100 g Edible Portion

	Fresh
Calcium	704 mg
Iron	35.0 mg
Magnesium	110 mg
Potassium	1,600 mg
Sodium	45.9 mg
Zinc	trace
Copper	0.4 mg
Manganese	30.9 mg

to the French and British armies during the Crimean War in 1854 as a remedy against marsh pestilence, since quinine was in short supply. The pungent powder may be taken into the nose like snuff to relieve sinus congestion, common colds, or sinus headache. It acts on the higher cerebral functions and brain tissue to help expand and bring clarity to the consciousness. In Ayurvedic medicine, calamus is used to help restore mental acuity after damage done by drugs or other causes. An alcohol extract is used externally as a rub to alleviate tired and sore muscles and as a stimulating agent in baths. The dried root is the best antidote for the ill effects of marijuana, which is toxic to the liver and brain cells; better yet is chewing the dried root, because it will cause nausea in those who smoke and thus destroy the taste for tobacco.

Calendula (*Calendula officinalis*)

It was the Romans who recorded that calendulas were usually in bloom on the first day, or calends, of every month; from this observation came the Latin generic name Calendula. Officinalis *means of the workshop, alluding to apothecaries' shops, and signifying that the plant was once part of the official pharmacopeia of Rome. The plant received its alternative English name* pot marigold *in the fourteenth century, called "Mary's gold" by early Christians after Mary, mother of Jesus, and the color of its flowers, which are bright gold.*

General Information The genus *Calendula* is native to the Mediterranean region from the Canary Islands to Iran. Grown for ornament, as food for bees, and for its medicinal properties, the first record of its cultivation dates from the twelfth century by the Abbess Hildegarde von Bingen. The flowerheads, either whole along with the green outer bracts but without the stalk, or else only the outer ray florets from the flowerheads, are used in medicines.

Calendula

Nutritional Value Per 100 g Edible Portion

	Fresh
Protein	0.64 g
Fat	26.0-45.0 g
Calcium	3,040 mg
Ascorbic Acid (C)	133-310 mg

Culinary Uses The brightly colored flowers of calendula used to be frequent additions to cookery. Sown with spinach, they were often cooked along with it. In the eighteenth century, no serious soup in the Netherlands was served without calendula petals, and it was even used to flavor oatmeal. Cooks made calendula puddings, dumplings, even wine. Used either fresh or dried, the petals impart a delicate aromatic bitterness and strong coloring to dishes. Petals and young leaves can be eaten in salads, to decorate or color various dishes, or used in cakes, cheeses, or butter.

Lore and Legend

The history of calendula is filled with poetry and symbolism, most of that has been in reaction to an unusual characteristic which has fascinated poets and prose writers alike since early times. The golden-orange blossoms rise and open at dawn with the sun, creating the poetic image of a "weeping" flower; the flowers then brighten the day until evening, when they close down again for the night. According to German folklore, if the flowers remain closed after seven o'clock in the morning, there is a strong indication of rain.

Health Benefits Antiseptic, stimulant, tonic, vulnerary. Powdered calendula petals mixed with arrowroot powder, cornstarch, or pure talc, is a pleasant way to soothe skin rashes for both adults and children. The crushed petals can also be soaked in olive oil or ointment and used to speed the healing of cuts, burns, old wounds or scars, and as a general tonic for the complexion. Bathing with calendula petals or an infusion made from them promotes the granulation of damaged tissue and has been successfully used in the treatment of minor burns, frostbite, and varicose ulcers. The plant is a good source of organic iodine, which accounts for its beneficial antiseptic qualities.

Cane Sugar and Palm Sugar

General Information Granulated cane sugar from sugar cane juice is a mechanically processed, chemical-free product that physically resembles light brown sugar. This unrefined product has existed in certain tropical areas for five thousand years, and is made simply by evaporating the water from whole sugar cane juice. It contains between 80 and 85 percent sucrose, but vitamins, minerals, and other nutrients present in the original cane are still intact. Although cane sugar was previously difficult to export because of fermentation resulting from its moisture content, in recent years drier, non-fermenting products are being produced in the West for the first time. One popular brand is **Sucanat**. Sucanat is a trade name that stands for sugar cane natural. These fine brown granules have a faint molasses flavor and are more complete than regular brown or turbinado sugar (although still processed), containing up to 2.5 percent mineral salts, vitamins, and trace minerals. It is used just like regular refined sugar, but should be stored away from excess humidity, as the granules will clump and possibly ferment. Occasionally whole sugar cane can be purchased; take it home and chew on the core for a while—it is quite delicious, yet not overly sweet.

Cane Sugar

Nutritional Value Per 100 g Edible Portion

Protein	1.10 g
Calcium	165 mg
Chromium	40 mcg
Phosphorus	50 mg
Beta Carotene (A)	1600 IU
Thiamine (B_1)	20 mcg
Riboflavin (B_2)	20 mcg
Niacin (B)	20 mcg

Palm sugar was used long before cane sugar, and is made from the sugary sap of the sugar palm (*Arenga pinnata* or *Borassus flabellifer*), or by tapping the tender, unopened inflorescence of the coconut, date, or toddy palms. This sweet liquid can be drunk fresh or boiled down (like maple sap) to make palm sugar. Not highly refined, palm sugar retains most of its mineral content, and is available from Indian and Middle Eastern grocery stores. It is frequently sold compressed into round or rectangular shapes (which may need to be grated or melted before use), in round, slightly domed cakes, or as a thick paste. With a maple sugar-like flavor and color that varies by brand, palm sugar is sold in Asian markets under a variety of names. Mexican *piloncillo* and Indian *jaggery* are sometimes available in ethnic or natural foods markets.

Culinary Uses Cane sugar and palm sugar are easily substituted for refined white sugar. One popular use for the molded sugar is to melt it in a saucepan, strain, and then pour over pancakes or waffles.

Health Benefits Because this type of sweetener is unrefined, it contains many more vitamins and minerals than refined white sugar.

Caper *(Capparis spinosa)*

Capparis *and the English* caper *come from the Greek word* kapparis, *said by some to have been derived from the Arabic name for the plant.* Spinosa *means full of spines.*

General Information Capers are the unopened flowerbuds of a low straggling, spiny shrub that grows wild on mountain slopes, principally those that border the Mediterranean Sea. They frequently inhabit old walls and cliffs, on which they provide a graceful ornament. Native to northern Africa, where it is known as the Sahara caper tree, the plant is clearly designed for desert existence, remaining green, with its stems and leaves juicy with sap even when the soil around its roots is completely dried up. The greenish flower buds or young berries are most often pickled to bring out their strong aromatic flavor (due to the presence of capric acid).

Caper

Nutritional Value Per 100 g Edible Portion

	Fresh
Protein	19.0-22.0 g
Fat	31.6-36.0 g

Culinary Uses The strongly aromatic caper is most often available pickled, although raw capers may sometimes be found. Like green olives, capers develop their unique flavor in the brine marinade. The little buds are small, but explode with a burst of lemony tang. Capers form the basis of the piquant caper sauce as well as many other sauces and dressings, are useful additions to salads and hors d'oeuvres, and will make an attractive garnish.

Health Benefits Because pickled capers are high in sodium they may increase the body's retention of fluids and raise blood pressure. For salt-free capers, grow your own bushes, which thrive in mild winter climates.

Lore and Legend

Centuries ago caraway was believed to have retentive properties. Love potions were laced with caraway to attract and magnetize a person's love; people also mingled caraway seeds with their prized possessions, in the hope that the seeds would protect their goods from theft, or magically hold any would-be thief in place until the owner returned.

Caraway *(Carum carvi)*

Carum *is probably derived from the region Caria in Asia Minor, and* carvi *from the Latin* carui *meaning dear or costly. The English name* caraway *comes from the ancient Arabic name* karawya, *by which it is still known.*

General Information Of unknown origin, the oldest caraway seeds found to date were discovered in Neolithic lake settlements in Switzerland. The ancient Romans may first have received caraway from Gaul, where it was used to season sausages. These flavorful seeds were introduced to Britain during the Victorian age by Prince Albert, who was extremely fond of them. A member of the carrot family, caraway is also sometimes called "Roman cumin" because the ground seed has a flavor similar to, but lighter than, ground cumin. Although found in many meadow plant communities in Eurasia, the caraway used for culinary and medicinal purposes is not obtained from plants found wild, but only from those especially cultivated for this purpose. The plant's thin crescent-

Caraway

Nutritional Value Per 100 g Edible Portion

	Whole Seed	1 tsp.
Calories	333	7
Protein	19.77 g	0.42 g
Fat	14.59 g	0.31 g
Fiber	12.65 g	0.27 g
Calcium	689 mg	14 mg
Iron	16.23 mg	0.34 mg
Magnesium	258 mg	5 mg
Phosphorus	568 mg	12 mg
Potassium	1351 mg	28 mg
Sodium	17 mg	trace
Zinc	5.500 mg	0.120 mg
Copper	0.910 mg	n/a
Manganese	1.300 mg	n/a
Beta Carotene (A)	363 IU	8 IU
Thiamine (B_1)	0.383 mg	0.008 mg
Riboflavin (B_2)	0.379 mg	0.008 mg
Niacin (B_3)	3.606 mg	0.076 mg

shaped seeds have a strong flavor that gives rye bread and kummel (a popular liqueur) their characteristic tastes, a flavor that not everyone enjoys.

Culinary Uses The flavor of caraway is pleasantly warm and spicy, but rather sharp, seeming to combine both anise and dill but with a tang and surprising nuttiness. A popular feature of German and Austrian cooking, caraway is used in sauerkraut, baked goods, cheese spreads and dips, vegetable dishes, and sweet pickles. Add caraway seeds after the dish is cooked, since long cooking may turn its flavor bitter. The seeds can also be ground and used as a substitute for cumin in homemade curry or chili powders. Young caraway leaves have a stronger dill flavor than the seeds, and can be used to add flavor to many kinds of salads, soups, and cheeses. The root is also edible, generally boiled and served as parsnips would be, and having a slightly carrot-like taste.

Health Benefits Antispasmodic, carminative, emmenagogue, expectorant, stomachic. Caraway is said to strengthen and tone the stomach, prevent fermentation in the stomach, aid the digestion of heavy starches, promote the onset of menstruation, and relieve uterine and intestinal cramping. For flatulent infant colic or for a general stomach settler (child and adult alike), caraway is especially recommended. The main medicinal constituent of the seeds is an essential oil that contains carvone, limonene, and other substances.

Cardamom *(Elettaria cardamomum)*

> Elettari *was the name of the plant in Malabar, a region in India where the best quality is still grown.* Cardamomum *comes from the Greek* kardamon, *peppergrass, and* anomon, *fragrant spice plant.*

Cardamom

Nutritional Value Per 100 g Edible Portion

	Ground	1 tsp.
Calories	311	6
Protein	10.76 g	0.21 g
Fat	6.70 g	0.13 g
Fiber	11.29 g	0.23 g
Calcium	383 mg	8 mg
Iron	13.97 mg	0.28 mg
Magnesium	229 mg	5 mg
Phosphorus	178 mg	4 mg
Potassium	1,119 mg	22 mg
Sodium	18 mg	trace
Zinc	7.470 mg	0.150 mg
Copper	0.383 mg	n/a
Manganese	28.000 mg	n/a
Beta Carotene (A)	trace	n/a
Thiamine (B_1)	0.198 mg	0.004 mg
Riboflavin (B_2)	0.182 mg	0.004 mg
Niacin (B_3)	1.102 mg	0.022 mg

General Information The cardamom plant is a tropical shrub of the ginger family native to India and Ceylon. It is the world's third most expensive spice, behind saffron and vanilla, because each seedpod must be hand picked. Sold whole or ground, the pods may be either green (dried indoors in large kilns and milder flavored), or a creamy white (bleached; these have the least flavor). Brown cardamom pods are not true cardamom but a related variety, with a flavor and texture not as delicate or pleasant as the green variety. The Vikings brought this exotic spice back to their homeland from their long voyages to the spice centers of the East and it is a popular feature in Scandinavian and other northern European cuisines. Since cardamom contains the same chemical, eucalyptol, that is found in bay leaves, it may help repel household pests. Try a few seedpods in your flour canister; even if it doesn't work, at least the flour smells wonderful.

Culinary Uses Cardamom has a delightfully pleasant aroma, faintly reminiscent of pine and eucalyptus. The flavor is rich and deep yet airy, ginger-like with a touch of lemon. Because it rapidly loses flavor when ground, this spice is best purchased whole, in its pods. The dark brown or black seeds can then be removed from within the pods and ground as needed. The seed may also be roasted to heighten its warming sweetness. Cardamom's most frequent use is in baked goods and desserts, especially Danish pastries, but it is also a frequent addition to curries, rice dishes, and spiced wine.

Health Benefits Carminative, stimulant. The seeds contain essential oils that make cardamom a stimulant like cinnamon or ginger. Chewing on the seeds is said to relieve flatulence and indigestion, relieve pain, sharpen the mind, open the bronchial tubes, warm the body, and sweeten the breath.

Carob (*Ceratonia siliqua*)

> Ceratonia *comes from the Greek word* keras*, meaning horn, in reference to the large pod;* siliqua *is Latin for pod or husk. The Arabic word for sweetness,* kharru bah*, is generally believed to be the origin for the English word* carob.

General Information The carob tree is native to southwestern Europe and western Asia, but is also widely cultivated in the Mediterranean region. Peasants have virtually lived on the pods during times of famine, but the tree is valued mostly for providing great amounts of pods for livestock feed. Spanish missionaries introduced the carob into Mexico and southern California, and groves of carob still grow in these regions. This dome-shaped evergreen tree, with its dark green glossy leaves and small clustered red flowers, can grow to heights of fifty feet. A ten- or twelve-year-old tree can bear up to one hundred pounds of pods annually. Each long brown seedpod holds five to fifteen seeds within sweet pulp; those grown in Sicily have particularly sweet fleshy pulp. The pods are harvested in September by shaking the branches of the tree with long sticks; after being sun-dried, the seeds are removed from the pods and the pulp ground into carob powder. The seeds are the source of locust bean gum (carob gum), an additive used in ice creams, cheeses, and confections to improve the texture by thickening and stabilizing the food. To make carob syrup, the powder is dissolved in water and boiled until it is the consistency of honey.

Lore and Legend

Legend has it that Saint John the Baptist once survived in the wilderness by eating locust beans (carob pods) and wild honey, hence carob's nickname of "Saint John's Bread." The word "locust" was originally applied only to the carob tree; later it was also applied to migratory and other grasshoppers, along with a number of other leguminous trees with pinnate leaves and oblong pods. The seeds at one time served as the original 'carat' weight measurement for goldsmiths.

Culinary Uses The big, handsome, brown carob pods can be eaten fresh and unprocessed out of hand. They are sweet and chewy, something like hard dates. Broken pods smell faintly like Limburger cheese but taste much better. Generally the pods are roasted and ground

Carob

Nutritional Value Per 100 g Edible Portion

	Flour	1 Tbsp.
Calories	180	14
Protein	4.62 g	0.37 g
Fat	0.65 g	0.05 g
Fiber	7.19 g	0.58 g
Calcium	348 mg	28 mg
Iron	2.94 mg	0.24 mg
Magnesium	54 mg	4 mg
Phosphorus	79 mg	6 mg
Potassium	827 mg	66 mg
Sodium	35 mg	3 mg
Zinc	0.920 mg	0.070 mg
Copper	0.571 mg	0.046 mg
Manganese	0.508 mg	0.041 mg
Beta Carotene (A)	14 IU	1 IU
Thiamine (B_1)	0.053 mg	0.004 mg
Riboflavin (B_2)	0.461 mg	0.037 mg
Niacin (B_3)	1.897 mg	0.152 mg
Pantothenic Acid (B_5)	0.047 mg	0.004 mg
Pyridoxine (B_6)	0.366 mg	0.029 mg
Folic Acid (B_9)	29.0 mcg	2.3 mcg
Ascorbic Acid (C)	0.20 mg	0 mg

into a powder (flour) that is used in place of chocolate, owing to the similarity of color, texture, and cooking properties. Both raw and roasted forms of carob powder may be available; the raw is preferred for baking, since it will be more flavorful when cooked for the first time. Roasted carob powder is generally used for mixing in liquids to produce carob-flavored drinks, hot or cold. It is a good substitute for hot cocoa or for chocolate flavoring in milk shakes and smoothies. Substitute equal amounts of carob powder for cocoa in recipes. When substituting for chocolate, use three tablespoons of carob powder plus one tablespoon of water for each 1 ounce square of chocolate. Since carob powder is 46 percent natural sugar, less sweetener should be used than when using cocoa or unsweetened chocolate. Chips made from carob are made from barley malt, corn malt, carob powder, and lecithin; since they contain no refined sugar or dairy solids, they are preferred by many for baking over chocolate chips. The roasted seeds have served as a substitute for or adulterant of coffee in Europe.

Health Benefits Carob powder contains pectin, which is good for regulating digestion. Unlike chocolate, it contains a negligible amount of fat, is naturally sweet, contains no caffeine, and encourages the absorption of calcium. It does, however, contain a notable level of tannin—as do cocoa, coffee, and tea—which inhibits the absorption of protein.

Cassia (*Cinnamomum cassia*)

The scientific name Cinnamomum *derives from the Hebraic and Arabic term* amomon, *meaning fragrant spice plant, and with the prefix* kin *means fragrant spice plant of China. The English name* cassia *is of Semitic origin.*

Cassia

Nutritional Value Per 100 g Edible Portion

	Dried
Protein	4.3 g
Fat	3.5 g
Fiber	27.0 g
Calcium	490-1,357 mg
Iron	2.5-42.1 mg
Magnesium	77-168 mg
Phosphorus	100 mg
Potassium	302-1,550 mg
Sodium	4.2-28.7 mg
Zinc	0.4-1.0 mg
Copper	0.2-1.0 mg
Manganese	16.7-60.0 mg
Thiamine (B_1)	0.100 mg
Riboflavin (B_2)	0.100-0.200 mg
Ascorbic Acid (C)	30.9 mg

General Information Cassia is the bark of an evergreen tree related to true cinnamon, *Cinnamomum zeylanicum*. It grows wild, especially in the Chinese province of Kwangsi, and in Tonkin and Annam in Indochina. Cassia has a stronger scent than cinnamon and instead of tan is a reddish brown color. Sticks of true cinnamon look like quills, forming a single tube, while those of cassia are rolled from both sides toward the center so that they look like scrolls. Cassia buds, the dried fruit of the cassia tree, are highly aromatic spices that look like cloves; in China, they are used for adding a cinnamon flavor to candy and sweet pickles. Cassia blossoms sold in Asian markets are not truly the blossoms of the cassia tree, but are from a member of the jasmine family (*Osmanthus fragrans*). The yellow flowers are sold preserved in a sweetened brine, and are used to perfume sweets such as lotus seed soup, various pastries, steamed pears, and Chinese teas and wines. They are also sold embalmed in a sugary paste called cassia blossom jam.

> ### Lore and Legend
> One Chinese legend tells of the celestial World Tree, a cassia or cinnamon tree, that has been growing since time immemorial to an incredible height in Paradise, a garden located far up in the Tibetan Mountains at the source of the Hwang-Ho, or Yellow River. Whoever enters Paradise and eats of the fruit of this tree will gain bliss and immortality.

Culinary Uses The taste of cassia has been described as warm and very spicy, yet coarser than true cinnamon, with an odor recalling that of the bedbug. If you were to taste plain cassia and plain cinnamon, you would find cassia bitter, and cinnamon warm and sweet. Never sold under its own name, cassia bark may be ground and mixed with cinnamon to be marketed as "ground cinnamon" or rolled and sold as "cinnamon sticks." The leaves also have a cassia flavor and can be used as a flavoring like bay leaves. The buds, which look a little like cloves, are useful where a slight cinnamon flavor is needed. While we tend to associate cinnamon (and thus cassia) with sweets, it was first valued as a meat preservative. According to ancient texts, its culinary value lay with its ability to "eliminate the stench of raw flesh"; it does contain phenols which inhibit the bacteria responsible for putrefaction.

Health Benefits Similar properties as cinnamon, but weaker.

Catnip *(Nepeta cataria)*

Also Known As: Catmint, Catswort, Field Balm.

> *The name* Nepeta *may derive from the city of Nepi (called Nepete by the Etruscans) in Tuscany, where catnip once grew in great profusion and where it was highly valued.* Cataria *derives from the Latin* catus, *meaning cat. The English name* catnip *came from the habit of cats nipping off the leaves to chew with relish.*

Catnip

Nutritional Value Per 100 g Edible Portion

	Dried
Calories	n/a
Protein	9.8 g
Fat	n/a
Fiber	n/a
Calcium	616 mg
Iron	138 mg
Magnesium	207 mg
Phosphorus	241 mg
Potassium	2,350 mg
Sodium	trace
Zinc	trace
Manganese	37.400 mg

General Information Catnip is a temperate herb of the mint family that originated in the milder climes of Europe, Asia, and Africa. The herb was brought to North America about 1620 by a certain Captain John Mason, who considered it one of eleven essential herbs for the fisherman's garden in Newfoundland, and was used frequently for a popular everyday tea. Upon its introduction, it quickly escaped from cultivated gardens and spread rapidly across the continent. The plant secretes an oil to ward off insects, but it attracts cats who, in their ecstatic rolling and rubbing, may completely demolish the plants. Although many people think of this herb only in connection with cats, it has a

Lore and Legend

Early Americans settlers believed eating dried catnip roots made even the kindest person mean. Thus, executioners and hangmen would eat it to ensure the courage and proper mood necessary to carry out their duties.

long history of human use. It was a popular garden herb earlier in European history, and was used for many centuries in cooking and for medicinal use. Catnip tea was a popular beverage before the importation of Indian and Chinese tea to Europe. Catnip is also helpful around the house, ridding it of pesky ants if you sprinkle their trails with some crushed leaves. They evidently dislike the smell and will leave your house alone.

Culinary Uses Catnip leaves can be used to add a minty flavor to salads. The young leaves can also be used in the manner of basil to make a flavorful pesto. To get the most flavor from the leaves, chop or rub them against the side of a colander or sieve to release the flavorful oils.

Health Benefits Aromatic, antispasmodic, carminative, diaphoretic, emmenagogue, tonic. Catnip benefits the body by quieting the nervous system. Tea made from the steeped (not boiled) leaves is beneficial for relieving stomach gas or cramps, aids in digestion, helps clean out excess mucus in the body, and is efficacious in the treatment of iron-deficiency anemia, menstrual and uterine disorders, and dyspepsia. Well into this century, a simmering pot of catnip tea was a fixture on the back burner of many American homes, awaiting colds, fevers, stomach upset, or sleeplessness. Chewing a leaf reportedly relieves headaches. Some find that hot catnip tea taken at bedtime works as a mild sedative, and thus helps them sleep better.

Cayenne (*Capsicum annuum, C. minimum*)

Cayenne

Nutritional Value Per 100 g Edible Portion

	Dried Ground	1 tsp.
Calories	318	6
Protein	12.01 g	0.22 g
Fat	17.27 g	0.31 g
Fiber	24.88 g	0.45 g
Calcium	148 mg	3 mg
Iron	7.80 mg	0.14 mg
Magnesium	152 mg	3 mg
Phosphorus	293 mg	5 mg
Potassium	2014 mg	36 mg
Sodium	30 mg	1 mg
Zinc	2.480 mg	0.050 mg
Copper	0.373 mg	n/a
Manganese	2.000 mg	n/a
Beta Carotene (A)	41,610 IU	749 IU
Thiamine (B_1)	0.328 mg	0.006 mg
Riboflavin (B_2)	0.919 mg	0.017 mg
Niacin (B_3)	8.701 mg	0.157 mg
Ascorbic Acid (C)	76.44 mg	1.38 mg

The word capsicum *arrived on the scene in 1700 under the auspices of Joseph Pitton de Tournefort, early plant taxonomist and plant-hunter for the spectacular gardens of Louis XIV. It most likely derives either from the Latin* capsa, *meaning box, for the hollow box-like shape of the fruit, or from the Greek* kapto, *meaning to bite, for the pepper's acrid, tongue-searing pungency. The term* annuum *signifies an annual plant, while* minimum *means very small, pertaining to some of the fruit's diminutive size. The English name* cayenne *came from the ground dried chili peppers called* kian *native to the Cayenne Island, capital of French Guiana.*

General Information Cayenne peppers are native to the warmer regions of Asia and America, and are cultivated in almost all parts of the world. With its oddly shaped fruit and its colorful presence, the shrubby cayenne plant looks as unusual as it is biting to the tongue. The hot pungent spice is made from the dried pods, although other spices are often added to the powder in its commercial form. Varying in color from orange-red to deep red, cayenne is sometimes labeled simply "red pepper." Cayenne from Sierre Leone in Africa is said to be the most pungent and medicinal. Used as a fumigant, cayenne is safe and effective in ridding buildings of vermin. Put a heaping tablespoon of the dried and powdered pepper in a shallow pan over a low flame and allow the fumes to pervade the air. Mice, rats, even cockroaches

abhor the fumes, which are quite harmless to humans and domestic pets. Another good use is to sprinkle a little in your shoes to warm up cold toes.

Culinary Uses Cayenne is very hot and should therefore be used delicately and respectfully. Cayenne can be added to impart a spark to most any dish, but its most common uses are in white sauces, soups, and stews. Common paprika is the mildest form of cayenne, and is also the form with the highest vitamin C content. Cayenne peppers are available in various forms: whole fresh, whole dried, crushed dried, or ground. Select according to recipe specifications.

Health Benefits Appetizer, digestive, stimulant, tonic. Cayenne is said to be the purest and most certain stimulant producing a natural warmth and improving circulation. It helps the digestion when taken with meals, arouses all the secreting organs, helps heal stomach and intestinal ulcers, has a cleansing action upon the large intestine and sweat glands, and helps to evacuate the bowel and destroy worms and parasites. Cayenne is good for colds, coughs, and congestion, and produces a natural warmth when used as a poultice such as for pneumonia and other acute congestions. For travelers, a container of red cayenne pepper or a small bottle of pepper sauce (cayenne in vinegar) is a sensible protection when you travel in countries where the preparation and serving of food is not always sanitary, and protects against amoebic dysentery.

Celery Seed (*Apium graveolens*)

Apium *derives either from the Latin* apis, *meaning bee, because bees go dotty over its tiny white flowers, or from a prehistoric Indo-European word for water, which would also be appropriate since celery prefers wet soils and salt marshes.* Graveolens *means heavy-scented. The common name* celery *derives from its remedial reputation—from the Latin* celer, *meaning quick-acting or swift.*

Celery Seed

Nutritional Value Per 100 g Edible Portion

	Whole Seeds	1 tsp.
Calories	392	8
Protein	18.07 g	0.36 g
Fat	25.27 g	0.50 g
Fiber	11.85 g	0.24 g
Calcium	1,767 mg	35 mg
Iron	44.90 mg	0.90 mg
Magnesium	440 mg	9 mg
Phosphorus	547 mg	11 mg
Potassium	1,400 mg	28 mg
Sodium	160 mg	3 mg
Zinc	6.930 mg	0.140 mg
Copper	1.370 mg	n/a
Manganese	7.567 mg	n/a
Beta Carotene (A)	52 IU	1 IU
Ascorbic Acid (C)	17.14 mg	0.34 mg

General Information Celery seeds are the dried fruit of a variety of wild celery popularly known as "smallage." They are the smallest of all the seeds used as flavorings, needing about 760,000 seeds to make just one pound. The seeds are much more intensely aromatic than the leaves or stalks of the plant because they contain proportionally more of the flavorful oil. The wild plant itself is tough and inedible, with an acrid, unpleasant taste. During the seventeenth century, Italian gardeners developed both the familiar stalk celery and celeriac from the wild plant.

Lore and Legend

The ancient Greeks prized celery and gave awards of celery or celery wine to winning athletes. Celery elixirs have been used in healing throughout history, and legend has it that celery was an ingredient of the love potion that had such dire effects on Tristan and Isolde. Medieval magicians, it was believed, tucked celery seeds into their shoes in order to fly.

Culinary Uses Celery seed can be used in almost any dish calling for fresh celery. It gives an added zest to thousands of salads, roasts, sauces and stews. They are also found ground and mixed with salt to make "celery salt."

Health Benefits Carminative, diuretic, stimulant, tonic. Pharmacologists confirm that celery seed is a carminative, effective for the relief of gas pains, and that the seeds may also have a sedative action. This herb has been highly recommended for rheumatism, flatulence, and as an appetite stimulant.

Chamomile (*Chamaemelum nobile, Anthemis nobilis, Matricaria recutita*)

Also Known As: Camomile, Matricaria, Anthemis, Ground Apple.

Because of the apple-scented characteristic noted by the Greeks, they named it ground apple—from chamai, *on the ground, and* melon, *an apple—the origin of the name* Chamomile. Anthemis *comes from the Greek word* anthemon, *meaning flower, in reference to the great number of flowers the plant produces.* Nobile *and* nobilis *mean noble or famous. The name* Matricaria *is either from the Latin root words* mater *and* cara, *meaning beloved mother, or from* matrix, *meaning womb, after its use for treating female disorders.* Recutita *means skinless or apparently bare of epidermis.*

Chamomile

Nutritional Value Per 100 g Edible Portion

	German, Dried
Calories	299
Protein	11.5 g
Fat	3.9 g
Fiber	7.2 g
Calcium	672 mg
Iron	17 mg
Magnesium	292 mg
Phosphorus	322 mg
Potassium	1,320 mg
Sodium	258 mg
Zinc	trace
Manganese	5.200 mg
Beta Carotene (A)	365 IU
Thiamine (B_1)	0.080 mg
Riboflavin (B_2)	0.430 mg
Niacin (B_3)	14.900 mg
Ascorbic Acid (C)	26.7 mg

General Information Actually, chamomile is not one herb, but two botanically unrelated plants of the daisy family which produce the same light blue oil used in healing since ancient times. Both have downy stems, pale green feathery leaves, daisylike flowers with yellow centers and white rays, and a distinct apple-like fragrance and flavor. The flowers are the only edible parts of the plants. Roman chamomile (*Chamaemelum nobile* or *Anthemis nobilis*) is native to western Europe. A perennial plant that rarely exceeds nine inches, it is often used as a ground cover for garden paths. It forms a carpet of fine, ferny foliage that can be mowed, and will stay lush if mowed a few times during the summer. The plant does best when occasionally stepped on, since walking on it releases the herb's lovely apple fragrance and does not hurt the plant. German chamomile (*Matricaria recutita*, also known as Sweet False Chamomile) is believed native to southern Europe, and is an annual that reaches three feet in height. It is the German variety that is most frequently used herbally because it is less expensive than the Roman, and more concentrated in valuable chemical constituents. Most Roman chamomile is somewhat bitter, and its primary use is in potpourri rather than tea.

Culinary Uses Only the flowers of chamomile are used, and they can be added fresh or dried to a salad or steeped to make an apple-scented tea. Fresh flowers or a well-sealed tea bag contain the most medicinal value, as the volatile oils dissipate rapidly. As a flavoring agent, chamomile appears in alcoholic beverages such as vermouth and some bitter tonics, as well as in a variety of teas, desserts, and candies.

> **Lore and Legend**
>
> Chamomile was cherished by the ancient Egyptians, who claimed that its aromatic tea was a mild elixir of youth. They dedicated it to the sun and worshiped it above all other herbs for its healing properties. In Beatrix Potter's classic "Tale of Peter Rabbit," after Peter was chased from Mr. MacGregor's garden, he went scurrying home in great fright. When he arrived, his mother sent him to bed with a cup of soothing chamomile tea to calm his fear.

Health Benefits Antispasmodic, aromatic, carminative, tonic. Chamomile soothes, deodorizes and cleanses wherever there is chaos in the form of flatulence, disturbed metabolism, congestion, cramps, diarrhea, insomnia, or anxiety. The major effects of chamomile are due to its volatile oils, actions that are strongest on the liver and kidneys, where the oils stimulate the organs to purge themselves of toxins. These oils (including azulene) are bactericidal and fungicidal, especially against certain Staph bacteria and Candida albicans. A cup of chamomile tea, probably the most popular herbal tea, made from three or four fresh flowers to a cupful of boiling water, will soothe and calm fevers and colds, headaches, upset stomachs, flatulence and colic, menstrual cramps, pain and swelling caused by arthritis or injury, and diarrhea. It is an excellent children's remedy, gently calming colicky infants and teething babies. When kids are cranky and irritable, give them a warm chamomile bath by brewing a large pot of tea and pouring the strained tea into the bathtub. When used as a topical remedy, chamomile soothes the skin and promotes healing, helps soothe burns, sunburn, diaper rash, and even radiation burns. Chamomile is also a frequent ingredient in rinses for blond hair.

NOTE: This herb is not recommended during pregnancy, as some herbalists consider it too relaxing to the uterus. Also, some people with hayfever who are sensitive to ragweed, asters, or related plants may be sensitive to chamomile.

Chervil *(Anthriscus cerefolium)*

Also Known As: Skirret.

> Anthriscus *derives from the Greek* anthriskos, *probably referring to an anther or beard of grain.* Cerefolium *means wax-leafed. The English name* chervil *comes from a Greek word meaning leaf of rejoicing or cheerleaf.*

> **Lore and Legend**
>
> Because chervil's flavor and fragrance resemble the myrrh brought by the wise men to the baby Jesus, and because chervil symbolized new life, it became traditional in Europe to serve chervil soup on Holy Thursday.

General Information Chervil is of eastern European and Russian origin, and was introduced into the Mediterranean region around 400 B.C. The Greeks used it, as we do today, to flavor other foods, but the Romans also cooked it by itself as a vegetable in its own right. The Romans later introduced it to France and Britain, where it found enthusiastic favor in the kitchen. A fernlike annual plant related to carrots, chervil may have either curly or flat leaves; both have the same pleasant flavor, but the curled leaf makes a more decorative garnish. It has been called "gourmet's parsley," since it has a more delicate flavor than parsley, and is sweeter and more aromatic, with a scent some say resembles tarragon.

Chervil

Nutritional Value Per 100 g Edible Portion

	Dried	1 tsp.
Calories	237	1
Protein	23.20 g	0.14 g
Fat	3.90 g	0.02 g
Fiber	11.30 g	0.07 g
Calcium	1,346 mg	8 mg
Iron	31.95 mg	0.19 mg
Magnesium	130 mg	1 mg
Phosphorus	450 mg	3 mg
Potassium	4,740 mg	28 mg
Sodium	83 mg	trace
Zinc	8.800 mg	0.050 mg
Copper	0.440 mg	n/a
Manganese	2.100 mg	n/a
Pyridoxine (B_6)	1.225 mg	0.007 mg

Culinary Uses Chervil is a subtly aromatic herb that provides a mild, slightly sweet, tender flavor of part anise and part parsley. Its taste and fragrance fill the senses the way warmth does, slowly, softly, subtly. Although available dried, for the very best results it should be used fresh—either finely chopped or in tiny sprigs. Its delicate flavor is destroyed when cooked, so it is best used raw or added when the dish is nearly ready. Chervil is an essential ingredient in French cooking, lending its sweet fragrance and flavor to salads and salad dressings, herbal soups, sauces, and vegetables. Use it generously in the kitchen; it never overpowers, but rather enhances and improves the combination of other herbal flavors.

Health Benefits Digestive, diuretic, expectorant, stimulant. Chervil has long been used as a spring tonic; it is said to have blood cleansing and diuretic qualities, as well as having a mild stimulant effect on all functions of the metabolism.

Chickweed (*Stellaria media*)

This little plant got its Latin name Stellaria *due to the star-like (*stella*) shape of its delicate white flowers.* Media *means medium or intermediate, serving to distinguish this plant from both larger and smaller relatives. The plant in English is called* chickweed *(and was formerly called* chickenweed*) because chickens and other birds relish the seeds and young foliage. Its ancient Latin name was* Morsus gallinae*, meaning a bite or morsel for hens.*

General Information The ubiquitous chickweed has changed little since neolithic times. Before written history it was gathered on the plains of India, as it was gathered later in Greece and Rome, because it was an edible green that provided food through the colder months. In Elizabethan days the plant was gathered to feed falcons, because it had been observed that flocks of wild birds sought out patches of it as winter feed. Although its arrival in America is not recorded, Puritan housewives most likely brought it with them to grow in their dooryard gardens. The New England climate proved extremely hospitable, and now the prolific weed is easily found in gardens, fields, waste places, cultivated grounds, or woods over most of the country. Chickweed is so common because it blooms as early as March and continues blooming throughout the summer months, with its seeds easily scattered by the wind.

Culinary Uses Chickweed has no scent, a pleasantly salty taste, and a flavor of mild cabbage. Some eat it cooked like spinach as a vegetable, while others prefer it raw as a salad green. The young leaves are the best tasting, and the plant should only be used when fresh.

Chickweed

Nutritional Value Per 100 g Edible Portion

	Dried
Calories	213
Protein	21.7 g
Fat	4.8 g
Fiber	10.8 g
Calcium	1,210 mg
Iron	253 mg
Magnesium	529 mg
Phosphorus	448 mg
Potassium	1,840 mg
Sodium	147 mg
Zinc	5.200 mg
Manganese	15.300 mg
Beta Carotene (A)	7,229 IU
Thiamine (B_1)	0.210 mg
Riboflavin (B_2)	0.130 mg
Niacin (B_3)	4.700 mg
Ascorbic Acid (C)	6.9 mg

Health Benefits Carminative, demulcent, emollient, laxative, refrigerant. Chickweed is a mild-acting herb that is probably best known as a kidney herb, since it is one of the traditional country herbs taken to cleanse the kidneys and liver after a winter of heavy eating. Healing and soothing anything it comes in contact with, chickweed dissolves plaque in blood vessels and carries out toxins. Its most popular use is as a poultice on external abscesses and rashes, where it removes the heat of infection and draws out poisons. It is a mild diuretic, but the effect is only temporary, as the body produces cholesterin to neutralize this effect after about a week.

Chicory (*Cichorium intybus*)

Also Known As: Coffeeweed, Blue Sailors, Wild Endive, Blue Dandelion, Succory.

Cichorium *(from the Greek* kichoreia*) and* intybus *both come from old names of unknown meaning for the plant. The English name* chicory *derived from the Greek through the French* chicoree.

General Information Chicory is native to temperate and northern subtropical regions of Europe, western Asia, and North Africa. The plant came early to North America with the colonists as a medicinal herb, but Thomas Jefferson and others grew it as a forage crop, as had been done in Europe. Because it does not dry well for hay, it was usually cut and fed green to horses, cattle, sheep, poultry, and rabbits. Chicory quickly escaped from cultivation and became a naturalized weed in pastures and fields, and now grows along much of the country's roadsides. Its leaves resemble those of the dandelion sufficiently to have earned it the occasional nickname "blue dandelion," and its delicate blue flowers open and close again with clocklike regularity in the morning hours. Chicory came prominently before the public in the late 1890s and early 1900s, when it was widely cultivated as an adulterant and substitute for coffee. However, the principal consumers of chicory coffee insisted that the European root was superior to the American, and thus American-grown chicory faded back into obscurity. Growers have developed dozens of improved cultivars that scarcely resemble the scrawny roadside weed, including heading chicories such as radicchio; looseleaf chicory; root chicory, grown either for cooking like parsnips or for roasting to make a coffee substitute; and witloof, or Belgian endive, the roots of which are forced to produce elongated shoots called chicons.

Lore and Legend

According to folktale, the flowers of chicory are a beautiful clear blue because they are the transformed eyes of a young maiden weeping for her lover's ship, which was lost at sea, never to return. Because the plant's sky-blue flowers can be counted on to open and close at precisely the same time every day, the Swedish botanist Carolus Linnaeus included it in the floral clock he planted at Uppsala, Sweden.

Chicory

Nutritional Value Per 100 g Edible Portion

	Raw Leaves	Raw Roots
Calories	23	73
Protein	1.70 g	1.40 g
Fat	0.30 g	0.20 g
Fiber	0.80 g	1.95 g
Calcium	100 mg	41 mg
Iron	0.90 mg	0.80 mg
Magnesium	30 mg	22 mg
Phosphorus	47 mg	61 mg
Potassium	420 mg	290 mg
Sodium	45 mg	50 mg
Beta Carotene (A)	4,000 IU	6 IU
Thiamine (B_1)	0.060 mg	0.040 mg
Riboflavin (B_2)	0.100 mg	0.030 mg
Niacin (B_3)	0.500 mg	0.400 mg
Ascorbic Acid (C)	24.0 mg	5.0 mg

Culinary Uses Young chicory leaves have a slightly bitter tang and are best used in

salads. The white underground parts of the earliest leaves are good in salad or cooked as a potherb. Later leaves are apt to be bitter, but cooking and serving them as spinach makes them quite tasty. The roots when cooked taste like parsnips, but are almost too skinny to bother with. They may also be chopped and added to salads. Dried chicory root is frequently roasted and used as a coffee substitute; in fact, chicory is the secret ingredient that made Creole New Orleans' coffee "black as sin and sweet as love."

Health Benefits Diuretic, laxative, tonic. Chicory shares many of the medicinal and culinary uses of its relative the dandelion. Its tasty bitter leaves act as a stimulant to the appetite and internal organs, toning up the system in general. The root has inulin as a primary component (up to 20 percent), the easily digestible carbohydrate that gives Jerusalem artichokes their characteristic flavor. When roasted, this inulin is converted to oxymethylfurfurol, which smells like coffee but has none of the harmful caffeine. Root extracts have been used as a diuretic and laxative, and to treat fevers and jaundice. Laboratory research has shown these root extracts to be antibacterial, anti-inflammatory, and slightly sedative. Leaf extracts have similar effects but are weaker. Chicory is also recommended in herbal tea mixtures that help purify the blood. These are taken mainly in spring to help cleanse the body of residues from heavy food eaten over the cold winter months.

Chili Powder

Chili Powder

Nutritional Value Per 100 g Edible Portion

	Dried Ground	1 tsp.
Calories	314	8
Protein	12.26 g	0.32 g
Fat	16.76 g	0.44 g
Fiber	22.23 g	0.58 g
Calcium	278 mg	7 mg
Iron	14.25 mg	0.37 mg
Magnesium	170 mg	4 mg
Phosphorus	303 mg	8 mg
Potassium	1,916 mg	50 mg
Sodium	1010 mg	26 mg
Zinc	2.700 mg	0.070 mg
Copper	0.429 mg	n/a
Manganese	2.165 mg	n/a
Beta Carotene (A)	34,927 IU	908 IU
Thiamine (B_1)	0.349 mg	0.009 mg
Riboflavin (B_2)	0.794 mg	0.021 mg
Niacin (B_3)	7.893 mg	0.205 mg
Ascorbic Acid (C)	64.14 mg	1.67 mg

General Information Chili powder is a blend of spices created in the American Southwest by a New Braunfels, Texas German, Willie Gebhardt, in 1892, and is the basis of the fabled chili con carne. A representative chili powder is mostly red (cayenne) pepper, plus cumin, oregano, paprika, salt, and garlic powder. It gets its bite chiefly from capsaicin, the most pungent chemical in cayenne peppers.

Culinary Uses Since the fire of capsaicin does not dissolve in cold water, ice water just will not do to quench the burning of a hotly spiced chili-flavored stew. What works best is a glass of cold milk or a chilled beer, since both milk fat and alcohol are capable of dissolving capsaicin to relieve the stinging in your mouth. You can enrich the flavor of any chili powder and make it more interesting by adding a pinch of one of the "sweet" spices: allspice, cinnamon, cloves, or onion.

Health Benefits Diaphoretic, irritant. Virtually all the effects of chili powder on the body are due to the capsaicin in the red pepper. This irritates the mucous membranes lining the nose and throat, causing them to weep a watery secretion. It also irritates the stomach lining, stimulating the flow of gastric juices, and triggering the contractions we call hunger pains. The small amount of garlic also adds its antimicrobial powers, while cumin enhances the digestive powers. Eating food spiced with moderate amounts of chili powder may be helpful when you have hay fever or a cold, because it makes it easier to clear the accumulated mucus.

Chive *(Allium schoenoprasum, A. tuberosum)*

Allium *is the ancient Latin name for the garlic family;* schoenoprasum *is derived from two Greek words—*schoinos, *meaning reed-like, and* prason, *meaning leek;* tuberosum *means tuberous. The English name* chive *derives from the Latin* cepa, *meaning onion, which became* cive *in French.*

General Information Native to Asia and Europe, chives have been known for almost five thousand years. The cultivated variety is very closely related to a wild Alpine variety; other wild varieties grow widely over the Northern hemisphere. A well-known member of the onion family, chives grow six to eight inches in height, and make dense mats of narrow hollow leaves similar to slender scallions, but without the swollen bulbs. Their purple clover-like blossoms come in the early spring, often blooming off and on again all summer. Garlic chives (*Allium tuberosum*) are a garlic flavored chive also called Chinese chives; these can be used in the same way as ordinary chives. They have grayish, straplike leaves with white flowers in flat clusters.

Chive

Nutritional Value Per 100 g Edible Portion

	Fresh, Raw
Calories	30
Protein	3.27 g
Fat	0.73 g
Fiber	n/a
Calcium	92 mg
Iron	1.60 mg
Magnesium	42 mg
Phosphorus	58 mg
Potassium	296 mg
Sodium	3 mg
Zinc	0.560 mg
Copper	0.157 mg
Manganese	0.373 mg
Beta Carotene (A)	4,353 IU
Thiamine (B_1)	0.078 mg
Riboflavin (B_2)	0.115 mg
Niacin (B_3)	0.647 mg
Pantothenic Acid (B_5)	0.324 mg
Pyridoxine (B_6)	0.138 mg
Folic Acid (B_9)	105.0 mcg
Ascorbic Acid (C)	58.1 mg

Culinary Uses Unlike most of its onion relatives, chive tops are the only usable part of the plant. These hollow, flat, narrow green leaves are snipped and used as a culinary herb, either fresh or dried. If cut regularly, more will grow and the stalks will remain tender; those left too long have a tendency to become tough and go to seed. Once flowers appear, the leaves become much less flavorful, but the young pink, lavender, purple, or white flower clusters are edible if used before seeds form. Chives have a soft springtime flavor, only mildly oniony, and more delicate than that of scallions. They do not benefit from long cooking but should be chopped finely and added at the last moment to soups, vegetables, omelets, sauces, and salads. Garlic chives are frequently used in Asian dishes to give them their characteristic flavor.

Health Benefits Antiseptic, appetizer, digestive. Like the rest of the onion family, chives are an antiseptic due to their content of sulphur-containing oil, but have none of the former's digestion disturbing tendencies. Chives have a stimulating effect on the appetite, fight intestinal fermentation, and are energizing to the stomach and liver. They are also good for the kidneys and help lower blood pressure.

Chocolate and Cocoa *(Theobroma cacao)*

The high regard in which chocolate had come to be held is readily apparent in the scientific name assigned to cacao in 1720 by the Swedish botanist, Carolus Linnaeus, during his monumental classification of the world's plant life: Theobroma cacao, *from the Greek* theos *meaning god, and* broma *meaning food—hence the free translation "cacao, food of the gods." The English name* chocolate *comes from the Mexican* chocolatl, *while cacao is from* cacauatl. *Both the tree and its beans are called cacao; the powder manufactured from roasted cacao beans after a portion of their butterfat has been removed is called cocoa.*

General Information The cacao tree is a tree native to tropical America that grows up to thirty feet tall and starts bearing fruit in its fourth year. The tree has the unusual habit of bearing its flowers, and subsequently its pods, on the trunk as well as on its branches. Ripe pods are seven to twelve inches in length, and dark reddish-brown or purple in color; the tough, thick rind encloses a mass of slippery, whitish pulp that surrounds the almond-sized cacao beans. After hand-picked harvesting, the pods are cut open to remove the pulp and bean seeds (twenty to fifty per pod, four hundred to a pound), and the seeds are placed in fermentation tanks to cure. Freshly-picked raw seeds are very bitter and have no chocolate taste; fermentation causes them to become more reddish and less bitter. Later the beans are cleaned, sorted, roasted, and cracked to remove their hard shells. The "cocoa nibs" are then ground into a thick, oily paste called chocolate liquor, and blended according to the desired specifications of chocolate and cocoa manufacturers. The cocoa fat—more than 50 percent of a cocoa bean—is rendered into yellowish cocoa butter. Unlike most fats, it is not greasy. It also has a pleasant odor and does not easily become rancid, and thus is prized for use in soaps, other toiletry products, and soothing ointments. The fat-free powdered residue is cocoa; mixed with sugar and either hot milk or water, it makes the energizing drink that most people love.

Chocolate and Cocoa

Nutritional Value Per 100 g Edible Portion

	Unsweetened Cocoa Powder	Cocoa Butter
Calories	229	884
Protein	19.6 g	n/a
Fat	13.7 g	100.0 g
Fiber	5.2 g	n/a
Calcium	128 mg	n/a
Iron	13.86 mg	n/a
Magnesium	499 mg	n/a
Phosphorus	734 mg	n/a
Potassium	1,524 mg	n/a
Sodium	21 mg	n/a
Zinc	6.810 mg	n/a
Copper	3.788 mg	n/a
Manganese	3.837 mg	n/a
Beta Carotene (A)	20 IU	n/a
Thiamine (B_1)	0.078 mg	n/a
Riboflavin (B_2)	0.241 mg	n/a
Niacin (B_3)	2.185 mg	n/a
Pantothenic Acid (B_5)	0.254 mg	n/a
Pyridoxine (B_6)	0.118 mg	n/a
Folic Acid (B_9)	32.0 mcg	n/a
Ascorbic Acid (C)	0 mg	n/a
Tocopherol (E)	n/a	1.80 mg

It is chiefly to the Aztecs that we owe our knowledge of cocoa. They roasted the beans in pots, then crushed them between stones and formed the paste into cakes. This paste could then be diluted with water and spiced with annatto and anise seeds, crushed long red peppers, and cinnamon. The mixture was beaten and stirred slowly over a low fire until it became a foamy, bubbling liquid: a sort of hot, spicy, deluxe chocolate shake. It was on his fourth voyage, in 1502, that Columbus discovered cacao beans in what is today Nicaragua and sent some back to Spain, to general indifference; probably no one knew how to rid them of their forbidding bitterness. But in 1519, Hernando Cortez tasted chocolate as the Aztecs prepared it—both in drink form and in some form of paste. He not only brought back more beans, but also the knowledge of how the Aztecs prepared them. They were given to a monastery, where the roasted ground beans, dampened into a paste, were mixed with cane sugar (another novelty in Europe at that time). The resulting product was so appreciated that Spain attempted to keep its origin and preparation secret. France acquired chocolate when Jews expelled from Spain settled in the region of Bayonne and began to process chocolate there. France regarded chocolate as at best a barbarous product and at worst a noxious drug, and Bayonne forbade making chocolate within the city limits. In 1550, only thirty years after the first white men tasted cocoa in Montezuma's palace, chocolate factories of considerable size were operating in Lisbon, Marseilles, Bayonne, Turin, Genoa and many other cities throughout southern Europe. The first chocolate factory in the United States was opened in 1765 in Dorchester, Massachusetts, and funded by Dr. James Baker. Baker's chocolate became part of American folklore, and the factory is still in existence today. Switzerland was a late bloomer in chocolate, only starting commercial production toward the middle of the nineteenth century. The Swiss were short on chocolate and sugar, but had plenty of milk, so in 1876 milk chocolate was introduced to the rest of the world, a concoction developed by M. Daniel Peter. Milton Snaveley Hershey invented the candy bar in 1894 after seeing a German chocolate-making machine at the 1893 Chicago World's Columbian Exposition. He ordered one of the German machines and began experimenting, loosing on the market a couple of candy bars that are still popular today: the Hershey's Milk Chocolate Bar and the Hershey's Milk Chocolate with Almonds Bar.

Lore and Legend

The cacao beans are so important to the Ecuadorian economy that they are still called *pepe de oro*, or seeds of gold. The Aztecs used the cacao bean as currency, the unit 8,000 indicated by a sack holding 8,000 cacao beans, and the Mayans did likewise. In fact, the Mayans even had trouble with "counterfeiters" of cacao beans, the con men filling hollowed beans with dirt and passing them off as the real thing. The emperor Montezuma convinced Europeans that chocolate was ambrosia for the gods; however, this royal drink was forbidden to the women of the court, much to the dismay of the ladies, who had to go to unladylike lengths to get it. Chocolate became more popular than ever with lovers after a Swiss named M. Daniel Peter invented milk chocolate in 1876. Since then it has become the foremost of Valentine gifts, and on St. Nicholas Eve (December 5th) Dutch lovers exchange chocolate initials, or use them as place cards at the dinner table.

Culinary Uses The enticing taste of chocolate has been cherished for centuries in Mexico and the West Indies, and today it is one of the most popular ingredients in candies and baked goods, with people in the United States consuming an estimated one million tons of cocoa products every year. Chocolate and cocoa are invariably sweetened with some form of sugar to mask the natural bitterness, in some cases with up to an equal amount of sugar.

Health Benefits There is very little to recommend chocolate for the health conscious. It contains about 50 percent saturated fat and the stimulants caffeine (230 mg) and theobromine (2,057 mg), along with tannic and oxalic acids. Cocoa butter is 59.7% saturated, 32.9% monounsaturated, and 3.0% polyunsaturated fat. One reason that chocolate is so popular is because it is rich in phenylethylamine, a chemical the brain manufactures when stimulated by the emotion of love. Thus a box of chocolates eases the edge for the unrequited lover, or sets the stage for the suitor.

Cinnamon (*Cinnamomum zeylanicum*)

The botanical name Cinnamomum *derives from the Hebraic and Arabic term* amomon, *meaning fragrant spice plant, and with the prefix* kin *means fragrant spice plant of China.* Zeylanicum *means of Ceylonese origin. This spice is known as "true cinnamon," to distinguish it from the similar looking and tasting cassia (*Cinnamomum cassia*).*

Lore and Legend

Cinnamon was highly prized in ancient times as a perfume, medicine, preservative, and flavoring spice; small quantities of the precious quills were considered gifts fit for kings. The Arabs, who first brought cinnamon to the West, shrouded its origins in grotesque mysteries to frighten off rival traders. Herodotus, in a credulous mood, reproduced one Arabian account of the cinnamon harvest:

> 'Where it comes from and what country produces it, they do not know. What they say is that the dry sticks, which we have learned from the Phoenicians to call cinnamon, are brought by large birds (Phoenixes) which carry them to their nests, made of mud, on mountain precipices which no man can climb, and that the method the Arabians have invented for getting hold of them is to cut up the bodies of dead oxen, or donkeys, or other animals, into very large joints which they carry to the spot in question and leave on the ground near the nests. They then retire to a safe distance and the birds fly down and carry off the joints of meat to their nests which, not being strong enough to bear the weight, break and fall to the ground. Then the men come along and pick up the cinnamon, which is subsequently exported to other countries.'
>
> —Herodotus, III, iii.

There were equally disarming action-packed tales about frankincense and cassia featuring flying snakes and belligerent bats.

General Information Cinnamon is the dried aromatic inner bark of a tropical evergreen laurel species native to India and Sri Lanka (Ceylon). Only small groves of cinnamon trees grew in Arabia, where the spice was so prized that only priests were permitted to gather it, offering the first bundle gathered to the Sun God. After the bark is peeled from the tree's shoots during the rainy season, when it is juicy with sap, it is left to dry and ferment for twenty-four hours. Then the outer layer of the bark is scraped off, leaving the inner light-colored layer, which curls into quills as it dries. Removing the outer bark makes the cinnamon less biting and mellows its aroma. Ancient travelers introduced the aromatic herb to the Egyptians, who added it enthusiastically to their embalming mixtures; it was partly the Egyptian demand for cinnamon, as well as the desire for pepper, that provided the chief impetus for the spice trade and world exploration. It was the Arabs, strategically situated, who monopolized most of the spice traffic with the East until the first century A.D. Much of the cinnamon bark came by the long and hazardous route from Malaya and Indonesia to Madagascar (4,500 miles of open sea in double outrigger canoes), and then on up the coast of East Africa to the Red Sea. The Arabs knew very well where cinnamon came from, and how, but since there was nothing wrong with their commercial instincts, they took care to protect their middleman's profit by giving currency to a number of magical myths about its origins.

Culinary Uses Cinnamon has a fragrant spicy flavor that is slightly sweet, and which becomes stronger when ground. Available in either quills or powder, the thinnest bark is the best quality and has the finest aroma. Cinnamon is best purchased whole and ground as needed, or purchased ground in small quantities and constantly replaced, as it quickly becomes stale. Frequently used in baked goods, cinnamon also adds a warm flavor to mulled wine, puddings, fruit pies, curries, pilafs, and creams. Much of the cinnamon sold is actually partly **Cassia,** a related plant of lesser quality (see separate reference).

Health Benefits Antiseptic, aromatic, astringent, carminative. Cinnamon is a good detoxifying herb, as it creates freshness and strengthens and energizes the tissues; it also acts as a pain reliever, promotes digestion, and has a natural cleansing action. Cinnamon contains a substance that kills various fungi, bacteria and other microorganisms, including *Staphylococcus aureas* (staph infections), *Clostridium botulinum* (botulism), *Aspergillus parasiticus* (many molds) and *A. flavus* (which produces the poison aflatoxin). Cinnamon, ginger, cardamom, and clove are used together as a tea to relieve cough and congestion and to promote digestion. The aroma of cinnamon has also proven to be an aphrodisiac in a recent study (by Alan Hirsch, M.D., at the Smell and Taste Treatment and Research Foundation in Chicago) in which male subjects sniffed a variety of odors. Freshly baked cinnamon rolls scored the highest response of the ten odors tested.

Cinnamon

Nutritional Value Per 100 g Edible Portion

	Dried, Ground	1 tsp.
Calories	261	6
Protein	3.89 g	0.09 g
Fat	3.18 g	0.07 g
Fiber	24.35 g	0.56 g
Calcium	1,228 mg	28 mg
Iron	38.07 mg	0.88 mg
Magnesium	56 mg	1 mg
Phosphorus	61 mg	1 mg
Potassium	500 mg	11 mg
Sodium	26 mg	1 mg
Zinc	1.970 mg	0.050 mg
Copper	0.233 mg	n/a
Manganese	16.667 mg	n/a
Beta Carotene (A)	260 IU	6 IU
Thiamine (B_1)	0.077 mg	0.002 mg
Riboflavin (B_2)	0.140 mg	0.003 mg
Niacin (B_3)	1.300 mg	0.030 mg
Ascorbic Acid (C)	28.46 mg	0.65 mg

Clove *(Eugenia aromatica, Syzygium aromaticum, E. caryophyllata)*

This tree was given the genus Eugenia *in honor of Prince Eugene of Savoy.* Aromatica *means simply aromatic;* caryophyllata *was a name given this plant by Pliny, and refers to its nut-shaped leaves. The English name* clove *comes from the Latin* clavus, *meaning nail, which the buds resemble.*

General Information Cloves are the dried aromatic flower buds of a tropical evergreen tree of the Myrtle family. Picked just before opening into pinkish-green blossoms, the buds are dried for 48 hours in the sun, so that they change color from rose to brown. The buds are then separated from their husks and dried for several more days. Clove trees are believed to have originated in China, and are now most commonly found in southeast Asia. First cultivated by the Dutch in the Moluccas (Spice Islands), they were smuggled out to Mauritius and the West Indies with intricate subterfuge by spice-hungry colonialist nations. In line with the centuries-old battle for a monopoly on cloves, Zanzibar made it a capital offense in 1972 to smuggle cloves out of the country. Fifteen persons were actually sentenced to death for this crime that year. The whole tree is highly aromatic, although the only commercially useful part is the flower buds. Since they are small and lightweight, it takes five thousand to seven thousand dried cloves to make a pound of spice. A major portion of the world's clove production goes to Indonesia for use in kretak cigarettes, which contain a mixture of two parts tobacco to one part cloves.

Lore and Legend

Chinese officials during the Han dynasty of 207 B.C. to A.D. 220 were allowed to approach their monarch only when holding cloves in their mouths to mask their unpleasant breath.

Culinary Uses Step into any spice shop and breathe deeply. Chances are that the dominant fragrance comes from rich, warm-smelling cloves. Good quality cloves should be plump, oily, not easily broken, and have

Clove

Nutritional Value Per 100 g Edible Portion

	Dried, Ground	1 tsp.
Calories	323	7
Protein	5.98 g	0.13 g
Fat	20.06 g	0.42 g
Fiber	9.62 g	0.20 g
Calcium	646 mg	14 mg
Iron	8.68 mg	0.18 mg
Magnesium	264 mg	6 mg
Phosphorus	105 mg	2 mg
Potassium	1,102 mg	23 mg
Sodium	243 mg	5 mg
Zinc	1.090 mg	0.020 mg
Copper	0.347 mg	n/a
Manganese	30.033 mg	n/a
Beta Carotene (A)	530 IU	11 IU
Thiamine (B_1)	0.115 mg	0.002 mg
Riboflavin (B_2)	0.267 mg	0.006 mg
Niacin (B_3)	1.458 mg	0.031 mg
Ascorbic Acid (C)	80.81 mg	1.70 mg

a pungent, spicy taste. Ideally, they should be bought as whole buds and the central head ground as needed, but pre-ground cloves (which are less pungent) are also available. Cloves are excellent added to baked goods and spiced drinks. A few cloves brewed with Oriental tea add an enticing flavor, as well as giving a carminative effect, while clove-spiced mulled wine offers a more exciting way to aid digestion than most commercial concoctions. Whole fresh cloves can be pushed into a thin-skinned orange until the entire orange is covered. The orange can then be rolled in ground cinnamon, wrapped in tissue paper, and set to dry for several weeks to make a beautifully scented pomander ball for the home.

Health Benefits Anesthetic, antiseptic, carminative, rubefacient. Cloves aid the digestion and utilization of food, promoting the flow of saliva and gastric juices. A natural pain reliever, clove oil has an anesthetic effect, relieving pain and spasms as it travels throughout the body. Oil of cloves can be used to relieve toothaches, as a decongestant, and to benefit circulation. Tinctures of clove oil are effective against many fungi, among them the one that causes athlete's foot. Eating cloves is said by some to work as an aphrodisiac. Tea, made by steeping the buds in boiling water, is said to cure nausea and to rid the stomach and intestines of gas.

Clover, Red (*Trifolium pratense*)

Trifolium *comes from the Latin* tres, *meaning three, and* folium, *meaning leaf, referring to its trifoliolate leaves.* Pratense *means growing in meadows, its frequent habitat. The English word* clover *comes from the ancient German word* kleo.

Lore and Legend

Because of its importance in early agriculture, red clover has a long history as a religious symbol. The ancient Greeks, Romans, and Celts of pre-Christian Ireland all revered it. In pre-Christian times the three-leafed clover was associated with the triad goddesses of Greek and Roman mythology and with the sacred sun wheel of the Celts. The rare four-leaf clover, also a Christian symbol with its four leaves representing the form of the cross, was said to enable its wearer to ward off evil (including witches), to see fairies and various spirits, to heal illnesses, to have good fortune, and to escape military service. According to an old medieval folk rhyme, each leaf of a four-leaf clover represents a different aspect of happiness. The first leaf stood for fame; the second, wealth; the third for a faithful lover; and the fourth for excellent health. Together these qualities could be said to represent the epitome of good fortune, a completely happy life. The extremely rare five-leaf clover was believed to be unlucky.

General Information Clover is a member of the legume family and native to the Mediterranean and Red Sea areas. From there, it wandered north and westward throughout Europe with the Roman legions, who called it "clava" because its three-petaled leaf reminded them of Hercules' club. By the late twelfth century, red clover was well established as a dependable forage crop in the Rhine valley. Albertus Magnus, a Dominican priest and scholar with a deep interest in natural science, cultivated red clover in Cologne during the middle of the thirteenth century. In 1240 he built the first greenhouse in the history of horticulture, and gave a large dinner party to demonstrate his invention, which made it possible to grow plants throughout the winter. Unfortunately, this miniature plot of spring in the midst of a snowy winter landscape made him suspect of sorcery, but his reputation suffered no permanent damage: in 1931 he was canonized, and is now sometimes referred to as Saint Albert the Great. By the sixteenth century red clover was cultivated throughout much of Italy. Europe's first botanical garden opened at the University of Padua (Italy), and Prosper Alpinus, who had been appointed to the chair of botany, took a particular interest in red clover. By 1750 red clover had been introduced into the English colonies on the Atlantic coast and was growing on scattered farms as forage. It grows in fields, along roadsides, and in waste places in all temperate climates. Children of all ages love looking for four-leaf clovers and picking the pretty blossoms.

Clover, Red

Nutritional Value Per 100 g Edible Portion

	Dried
Calories	326
Protein	11.5 g
Fat	3.6 g
Fiber	9.9 g
Calcium	1,310 mg
Iron	0.035 mg
Magnesium	349 mg
Phosphorus	322 mg
Potassium	2,000 mg
Sodium	16 mg
Zinc	trace
Manganese	5.900 mg
Beta Carotene (A)	2,008 IU
Thiamine (B_1)	0.420 mg
Riboflavin (B_2)	0.330 mg
Niacin (B_3)	12.500 mg
Ascorbic Acid (C)	296.6 mg

Culinary Uses The leaves of red clover are used as salad greens, in tacos, sandwiches, and coleslaw. Blossoms should be picked when near or in full bloom and immediately eaten in a salad or dried for tea-making.

Health Benefits Antispasmodic, depurative. Red clover benefits the entire body, purifying the blood, promoting healing, soothing the nerves, and offering relief for those with coughs or bronchial conditions. Clover heads, dried quickly, retain their fragrance and color and make a pleasing and effective curative powder. Red clover tea may be imbibed as freely as water; it is pleasant steeped alone, or with another aromatic herb.

Comfrey *(Symphytum officinale, S. peregrinum)*

Also Known As: Knitbone, Bruisewort, Boneset.

> *The genus name* Symphytum *is derived from the Greek word* sympho, *meaning to unite or grow together, referring to comfrey's healing and mending properties.* Officinale *means of the workshop, alluding to apothecaries' shops, and signifying that the plant was once part of the official pharmacopeia of Rome;* peregrinum *means foreign or wandering. The English name* comfrey *derives from the Latin* conferva *meaning knitting or growing together.*

General Information Comfrey is a very popular herb of the borage family suited to almost every climate. Native to Europe, it was introduced into North America by early settlers and now grows wild throughout much of the continent. The plant sends its taproots over ten feet deep into the subsoil to raise moisture and valuable minerals to the upper levels. A perennial crop lasting up to twenty years, comfrey grows well in drought-prone regions, and brings the subsoil into the fertility cycle much faster than alfalfa, as well as growing where alfalfa will not. Easily grown, a simple root cutting will produce enormous plants up to four feet high and just as wide, with leaves up to thirty-nine inches long and eight inches wide. The rampant tubers run wild, and produce offshoot plants at random. The most commonly used comfrey comes from the

Comfrey

Nutritional Value Per 100 g Edible Portion

	Leaves	Root, Dried
Calories	n/a	217
Protein	22 g	9.4 g
Fat	n/a	1.7 g
Fiber	n/a	7.2 g
Calcium	n/a	1,130 mg
Ironn	/a	81 mg
Magnesium	n/a	170 mg
Phosphorus	n/a	211 mg
Potassium	n/a	1,590 mg
Sodium	n/a	351 mg
Zinc	n/a	0.28 mg
Manganese	n/a	6.70 mg
Beta Carotene (A)	n/a	11,000 IU
Thiamine (B_1)	0.500 mg	0.120 mg
Riboflavin (B_2)	1.000 mg	0.720 mg
Niacin (B_3)	5.000 mg	6.700 mg
Cobalamin (B_{12})	0.700 mg	n/a
Ascorbic Acid (C)	100.0 mg	13.2 mg
Tocopherol (E)	30.0 mg	n/a

plant *Symphytum officinale*; a less well known variety is Russian comfrey, *Symphytum peregrinum*.

Culinary Uses Comfrey leaves are somewhat bitter, but quite edible (see note below). They wilt rapidly after picking, so they should be used immediately in salads, steamed lightly as cooked greens, or juiced with other vegetables for a green drink. The leaves can also be dried, ground, and added to baked goods. The stalks, if blanched, make a good substitute for spinach, while the mild-flavored, spindle-shaped root can be used finely chopped in a salad, or ground for use as the base of seed-nutmeat loaves, or fruit-carob candies. Comfrey root, along with dandelion and chicory roots, can be made into a coffee substitute without the harmful effects of coffee.

Health Benefits Astringent, demulcent, emollient, expectorant, nutritive, vulnerary. Comfrey is among the most nutritionally healthful plants, and probably used for more different purposes than any other herb. With more protein in its leaf structure than any other known member of the vegetable kingdom, it is also the only land plant discovered so far that contains traces of vitamin B_{12}. Comfrey is an excellent detoxicant, especially effective on liver and lung tissues, creating richer, cleaner blood cells that are capable of carrying greater amounts of oxygen and nourishment. All parts of the comfrey plant contain allantoin, a substance which promotes the healthy proliferation of red blood cells, increases blood circulation, and rapid healing of injured bone and muscle tissue; it also has pepsin and other enzymes to aid digestion. Comfrey, combined with alfalfa, feeds the pituitary gland. Rich in a watery but slightly viscous fluid which forms a paste easily and sets quickly, poultices made of the leaves and root are applied to swellings, bruises, broken bones, or sore breasts. As a tea, comfrey has been found helpful in healing and soothing the inner body as well as loosening mucus. About one-quarter to one-half cup of strong comfrey tea with a teaspoon of honey can end an asthmatic or allergic night cough and bring restful sleep.

NOTE: The FDA suggests that comfrey be used only in topical ointments and salves, due to questions about its suitability for human consumption.

Coriander and Cilantro (*Coriandrum sativum*)

Also Known As: Chinese Parsley, Mexican Parsley.

> *The name* Coriandrum, *used by Pliny, comes from the Greek* koris, *a name for an ill-smelling bug or bedbug; it was given to this plant because of the peculiar odor produced when struck or broken.* Sativum *refers to the fact that this plant has long been cultivated.* Cilantro *is the Spanish name for the plant.*

General Information Coriander is most probably indigenous to the Mediterranean regions of Africa and Asia. One of the most ancient of herbs still in use today, coriander seeds have been found in Bronze Age ruins on the Aegean islands and in the tombs of

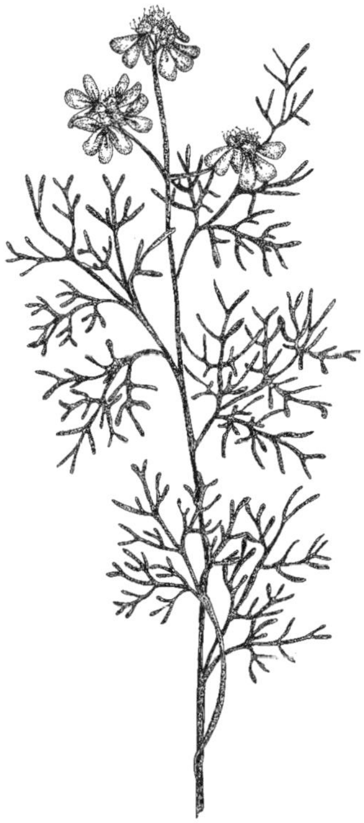

the Pharaohs. Cultivated in Egyptian gardens thousands of years before the birth of Christ, coriander was steeped in wine to increase its intoxicating power. Coriander was introduced into Latin America by the Spaniards shortly after they encountered the New World, and won instant favor with the Indians. Later, it was passed on by them to the American Indians of what is today the southwestern United States.

Cilantro is the name used for the young, flat, feathery leaves of the coriander plant, a member of the carrot family. The plant grows one to three feet in height, with glabrous, strong-smelling leaves divided into almost thread-like divisions. Sometimes confused with parsley, this plant has a distinctly different taste. The aroma of the whole plant has a disagreeable smell until the active principles in the volatile oil reach their apogee and the seeds are fully ripened; then, the disagreeable element changes and becomes pleasant and aromatic. The seeds are gathered from the small white or purple-tinged flowers of the plant and dried to bring out the characteristic sweet aroma. The small seeds are pale green to cream or brown in color, round and ridged. The dried seeds of the plant are sold as the spice coriander.

Coriander

Nutritional Value Per 100 g Edible Portion

	Whole Seed	1 tsp.
Calories	298	5
Protein	12.37 g	0.22 g
Fat	17.77 g	0.32 g
Fiber	29.12 g	0.52 g
Calcium	709 mg	13 mg
Iron	16.32 mg	0.29 mg
Magnesium	330 mg	6 mg
Phosphorus	409 mg	7 mg
Potassium	1,267 mg	23 mg
Sodium	35 mg	1 mg
Zinc	4.700 mg	0.080 mg
Copper	0.975 mg	n/a
Manganese	1.900 mg	n/a
Beta Carotene (A)	trace	trace
Thiamine (B_1)	0.239 mg	0.004 mg
Riboflavin (B_2)	0.290 mg	0.005 mg
Niacin (B_3)	2.130 mg	0.038 mg

Cilantro

Nutritional Value Per 100 g Edible Portion

	Fresh, Raw	Dried	1 tsp.
Calories	20	279	2
Protein	2.36 g	21.83g	0.13 g
Fat	0.59 g	4.76 g	0.03 g
Fiber	0.80 g	10.39 g	0.06 g
Calcium	98 mg	1,246 mg	7 mg
Iron	1.95 mg	42.46 mg	0.25 mg
Magnesium	26 mg	694 mg	4 mg
Phosphorus	36 mg	481 mg	3 mg
Potassium	542 mg	4,466 mg	27 mg
Sodium	28 mg	211 mg	1 mg
Copper	n/a	1.786 mg	n/a
Manganese	n/a	6.355 mg	n/a
Beta Carotene (A)	2,767 IU	n/a	n/a
Thiamine (B_1)	0.074 mg	1.252 mg	0.008 mg
Riboflavin (B_2)	0.120 mg	1.500 mg	0.009 mg
Niacin (B_3)	0.730 mg	10.707 mg	0.064 mg
Ascorbic Acid (C)	10.5 mg	566.71 mg	3.40 mg

Culinary Uses Often confused with some types of parsley, coriander leaves, called cilantro, have a fresh zesty orange and parsley flavor and are an important ingredient in Mexican, Indian and Asian dishes due to their cooling effect. They go especially well with green chili peppers and form the basis of many Mexican salsas as well as Indian curries and chutneys. Best used fresh, the leaves make excellent additions to salads or sauces, or can be used as a garnish for soups.

Coriander seeds have a distinctive, sweetly aromatic flavor and spicy scent when crushed. They are more intensely flavored than the leaves, with a rich earthy blend of lemon and sage that is brought out even further by toasting and grinding. Unripe coriander seeds have an unpleasant odor that becomes warm and spicy when the seed matures; this is one spice that actually improves with age. A basic spice in Indian curries along with cayenne pepper, turmeric, and ginger, coriander is also used for pickles and sweet dishes, including certain types of cakes and baked goods. It

Lore and Legend

Coriander seeds were frequently among the funeral offerings found in Egyptian tombs. The Chinese cultivated coriander as a valuable culinary and medicinal plant as early as the fourth century B.C., and the plant acquired a reputation for bestowing immortality on those who ate the seeds during a state of spiritual purity. Other herbalists developed aphrodisiac concoctions from coriander with lust in mind, for they believed that it aroused passion, a rumor which may have been started by the Arabian fantasy, *The Thousand and One Nights*, in which coriander was referred to as an aphrodisiac.

has a well-established place in the food industry as a seasoning that not only improves the flavor and aroma of food, but also makes heavier meats and pickled vegetables more digestible; it has the same effect when used in making breads and as an ingredient of curry powder. Coriander roots taste more like the leaves than the seeds, but with an added nutty flavor; they are most often minced and used fresh.

Health Benefits Antispasmodic, aromatic, carminative, diuretic, stomachic, refrigerant. Warm, spicy coriander has been used as an herbal digestive aid for thousands of years. It is a natural diuretic, has cooling properties, helps purify the blood and strengthen the heart, and is also useful for gas, indigestion, nausea, and vomiting. A soothing drink is made by infusing half a teaspoon of the crushed seeds in one cup of hot water; if sipped half an hour before meals this will greatly improve digestion. The leaves may be pulped and applied to the skin to relieve burning sensations.

Cream of Tartar

Nutritional Value Per 100 g Edible Portion

		1 tsp.
Calories	258	8
Protein	0 g	0 g
Fat	0 g	0 g
Calcium	8 mg	0.2 mg
Iron	3.72 mg	0.11 mg
Magnesium	2 mg	0 mg
Phosphorus	5 mg	0 mg
Potassium	16,500 mg	495 mg
Sodium	52 mg	2 mg
Zinc	0.420 mg	0.013 mg
Copper	0.195 mg	0.006 mg
Manganese	0.205 mg	0.006 mg

Cream of Tartar *(Potassium bitartrate)*

General Information Cream of tartar is a by-product of the wine-making industry. The sediment (called crystals of argolis) that forms on the sides and bottoms (lees) of wine barrels during the fermentation process contain tartaric acid. These crystals are ground, purified, dried, and re-ground to product cream of tartar. The powder was used as the acid counterpart to baking soda in the early formulas for baking powder.

Culinary Uses The best known use for cream of tartar is in baking powder, where it combines with baking soda to release carbon dioxide. The cream of tartar is a "fast-acting" leavening agent that encourages the release of carbon dioxide at room temperature, while baking soda is a "slow-acting" leavening agent that releases its carbon dioxide later, when the batter is heated in the oven. Baking powders that contain baking soda and cream of tartar are called "double acting" baking powders.

Cubeb *(Piper cubeba)*

Piper *is an ancient Latin name for the plant.* Cubeba *derives from an Indonesian word* cabe *meaning pepper. The Sanskrit word* pippali *meant berry and also long pepper, and because long pepper* (P. longum) *was at first the most highly regarded pepper, it became the root of the word* pepper *in European languages.*

General Information The cubeb berry is a drupe from a climbing shrub native to the Indonesian Islands, mainly Java, and now grown in other parts of southeastern Asia and

India. The dried black berry is the size of the largest allspice berries and comes with its stem attached (giving rise to one of its other names of tailed pepper). In England in 1307, a pound of cubebs for the "King's Wardrobe" cost nine shillings. Cubebs were used then to season meats and other dishes in a highly spiced, even sugared, Moslem-influenced style that would probably unsettle modern palates. This relative of black pepper has long since fallen out of use, and is extremely difficult to find in the West.

Culinary Uses The flavor of cubeb is reminiscent of tea with a mild muskiness and spice. Ground in a mortar, the berries release an aroma of nutmeg and cumin. Cooking alters the scent to something more currylike, persistent and still slightly floral, with scarcely a trace of the heat of black pepper. This spice is a feature of Indonesian cuisine, lending a distinctive taste more akin to allspice than pepper.

Health Benefits Cubeb berries contain substances that have been used as antiseptics, carminatives, and diuretics. Oil of cubeb is a constituent of some throat lozenges. The original use of cubeb was medicinal, mainly as a treatment for respiratory problems and for male reproductive difficulties.

Cumin (*Cuminum cyminum, Nigeria sativa, Nigella sativa*)

The name cumin *is of Semitic origin, but unknown meaning.* Nigeria *means of or from Nigeria;* sativa *means cultivated.*

General Information Cumin is native to the eastern Mediterranean, especially the upper reaches of the Nile. The seeds resemble caraway in appearance, but are slightly longer, lighter in color, and have quite a different flavor, being hot and pungent. The white variety is the most common, but if you shop in Indian grocery stores, you may run across black cumin (*Nigeria sativa*), an unrelated plant also known as nutmeg flower or Roman coriander. The black cumin is easier to grow than regular cumin and produces pods with small, dark seeds that smell like fennel and taste something like peppery nutmeg. They can be ground and used like pepper, but the flavor is quite distinctive, so try a little before you season a whole dish.

Culinary Uses Cumin has a strongly aromatic spicy taste, even a little bitter, but pleasantly so. When darkened several shades by toasting in a hot dry skillet, the seed releases its gentle perfume and the taste becomes richer and mellower. In Biblical times, cumin seeds were valued for their digestive properties and were used for flavoring bread and other dishes during periods of

Cumin

Nutritional Value Per 100 g Edible Portion

	Whole Seed	1 tsp.
Calories	375	8
Protein	17.81 g	0.37 g
Fat	22.27 g	0.47 g
Fiber	10.50 g	0.22 g
Calcium	931 mg	20 mg
Iron	66.35 mg	1.39 mg
Magnesium	366 mg	8 mg
Phosphorus	499 mg	10 mg
Potassium	1,788 mg	38 mg
Sodium	168 mg	4 mg
Zinc	4.800 mg	0.100 mg
Copper	0.867 mg	n/a
Manganese	3.333 mg	n/a
Beta Carotene (A)	1,270 IU	27 IU
Thiamine (B_1)	0.628 mg	0.013 mg
Riboflavin (B_2)	0.327 mg	0.007 mg
Niacin (B_3)	4.579 mg	0.096 mg
Ascorbic Acid (C)	7.71 mg	0.16 mg

Lore and Legend

Cumin was so highly valued in the time of Christ that it had become negotiable for the payment of taxes. It is also supposed to induce a pallid complexion, and Pliny tells of the students of Porcius Patro, the celebrated master of oratory, who consumed cumin to achieve that pallid "studious" look. In early Roman times, cumin was the symbol of cupidity and avarice; because he was judged to possess these characteristics, Marcus Aurelius was nicknamed "Cumin." Later, cumin was associated with being a tightwad, and in an era when profligacy was the rule, the exceptional thrift of Emperor Antonius Pius was ridiculed by dubbing him "the cumin splitter."

ceremonial fasting to make up for the lack of meat. Available in both seed and powdered form, cumin is most frequently used in commercial curry powder, but also makes appearances in Mexican-style rice or bean dishes, relishes, soups and salads, curries, and baked goods. A true Texan would not consider cooking his pinto beans without cumin (or *comino*), which also serves as the major ingredient in his chili powder; the Indian or Pakistani also regards cumin as an essential ingredient in *dahl*, the staple dish made from dried beans or peas that is taken with nearly every meal.

Health Benefits Aromatic, carminative. Cumin is one of the best aromatic spices to strengthen digestion and improve the taste of food while aiding the secretion of digestive juices. It also stimulates circulation, relieves pain and cramping in the abdomen, and helps prevent and relieve flatulence. Roasted cumin powder is effectively used in intestinal disorders such as diarrhea or dysentery.

Curry Powder

The word curry *is derived from the original south Indian* kari, *meaning sauce.*

Curry Powder

Nutritional Value Per 100 g Edible Portion

	Powder	1 tsp.
Calories	325	6
Protein	12.66 g	0.25 g
Fat	13.81 g	0.28 g
Fiber	16.32 g	0.33 g
Calcium	478 mg	10 mg
Iron	29.59 mg	0.59 mg
Magnesium	254 mg	5 mg
Phosphorus	349 mg	7 mg
Potassium	1,543 mg	31 mg
Sodium	52 mg	1 mg
Zinc	4.050 mg	0.080 mg
Copper	0.815 mg	n/a
Manganese	4.289 mg	n/a
Beta Carotene (A)	986 IU	20 IU
Thiamine (B_1)	0.253 mg	0.005 mg
Riboflavin (B_2)	0.281 mg	0.006 mg
Niacin (B_3)	3.467 mg	0.069 mg
Ascorbic Acid (C)	11.41 mg	0.23 mg

General Information Curry is a combination of spices that may consist of a mixture of as few as five or as many as fifty ingredients. At Indian meals, several curries—each of them with different flavors—may be served during the course of one meal. The color of most curry powders is derived from the goldenrod yellow of turmeric. True Indian curry bears very little resemblance to the parodies of it served in the West. For Indians, curry is a sauce intended to add relish—no more—to bland basic fare like rice or the wheaten pancakes known as chapatis. A little of it goes, and is meant to go, a long way.

Culinary Uses Commercially prepared curry powder usually contains fifteen or twenty spices, herbs, and seeds. It is prepared by grinding slightly roasted, dried chili-peppers to a powder, mixing it with ground turmeric for color, and adding coriander along with other spices, which may include one or more of the following: allspice, anise, bay leaves, caraway, cardamom, celery seed, cinnamon, cloves, cubeb berries, cumin, curry leaves, dill, fennel, fenugreek (seeds and leaves), garlic, ginger, juniper berries, mace, mint, mustard, nutmeg, pepper (white and/or black), poppy seeds, saffron, sumac seeds, and salt. The pungency is dependent on the amount of chili pepper used. If you wish to make your own curry powder, combine six parts turmeric, four parts cumin, and one part each of cardamom, coriander, cinnamon, black pepper, ground fenugreek, and ginger. This combination will provide maximum flavor but minimal heat.

Health Benefits Because curry powder promotes perspiration, which acts as a natural air conditioner to cool the body as the moisture evaporates on the skin, curry powder is a popular seasoning in warm climates. Its pungency may also be helpful to clear the head and nose during a head cold.

Dandelion (*Taraxacum officinale*)

The derivation of the name Taraxacum *is clouded by several points of view. Some botanists claim that* Taraxacum *derives from the Persian word* tark hashgun, *or wild endive. Others believe that it was taken from an Arabian alteration of a Greek word meaning edible. The more common theory is that the name is taken from the Greek* taraxos, *meaning disorder, and* akos, *meaning remedy, alluding to its ability to correct a multitude of disorders.* Officinale *means of the workshop, alluding to apothecaries' shops, and signifying that the plant was once part of the official pharmacopeia of Rome. The English name* dandelion *comes from the French term* dent de lion, *quite literally lion's tooth, from the jagged leaves, which look like the teeth of a lion.*

General Information Dandelions probably originated in Asia Minor, but spread throughout the known world long before written history. They were first mentioned in the writings of Arabian physicians in the tenth and eleventh centuries. European settlers deliberately introduced it to North America. Perhaps the world's most famous weed, this ubiquitous plant makes its appearance in nearly every country around the world and is the winner of a rogue's reputation, for it grows indiscriminately in lawns, pastures, fields, and gardens. The lowly dandelion is an extremely hardy plant, one which some believe will be among the few to survive all the herbicides we have dumped on this planet. Although lawn owners so feverishly dig it up, the dandelion actually heals the earth by transporting minerals (especially calcium) upward from deep layers, even from underneath hardpan. The dandelion's beautiful golden flower head is made up of tiny blossoms that soon turn to fluffy parachutes tipped by dark seeds—thirty-five thousand of them to the ounce. All parts of this jagged-leaved plant are quite edible, and there is now even a cultivated variety, which produces greens

Dandelion

Nutritional Value Per 100 g Edible Portion

	Greens, Raw	Cooked	Dried
Calories	45	33	265
Protein	2.70 g	2.00 g	16.50 g
Fat	0.70 g	0.60 g	1.60 g
Fiber	1.60 g	1.30 g	8.90 g
Calcium	187 mg	140 mg	614 mg
Iron	3.10 mg	1.80 mg	96 mg
Magnesium	36 mg	n/a	157 mg
Phosphorus	66 mg	42 mg	362 mg
Potassium	397 mg	232 mg	1,200 mg
Sodium	76 mg	44 mg	113 mg
Beta Carotene (A)	14,000 IU	11,700 IU	14,000 IU
Thiamine (B_1)	0.190 mg	0.130 mg	trace
Riboflavin (B_2)	0.260 mg	0.175 mg	0.210 mg
Niacin (B_3)	n/a	n/a	3.310 mg
Ascorbic Acid (C)	35.0 mg	18.0 mg	37.6 mg
Tocopherol (E)	2.50 mg	n/a	n/a

with a milder flavor than the wild. Early spring and fall (after the first frosts of autumn) are the best times to "harvest" dandelions; the plants in summer have matured to the point of being tough and bitter.

Culinary Uses Wild dandelions have more flavor than cultivated ones because they are richer in vitamins and mineral salts. All parts of the dandelion are edible, but be sure to pick early, as the plant gets quite bitter as it matures. Tender young leaves can be chopped and added raw to salads, or steamed and seasoned with onion, vinegar, lemon, or herbs, to be served like spinach. Unopened buds are excellent nut-like morsels, delicious in salads and as a tea for tonic and indigestion. Fried in butter, they taste much like mushrooms. Dandelion root has a stronger flavor than the highly cultivated vegetables most of us are accustomed to, with a marked taste that is both slightly sweet and bitter. Young roots are good chopped and added to salads, peeled and sauteed to be served as a tasty vegetable, or dried, roasted, and ground to be used as a caffeine-free coffee substitute. A kind of beer can be made from the leaves, and from the crushed flowerheads a light golden dandelion wine is made that has a taste suggestive of sherry and a reputation as an excellent tonic for the blood.

Lore and Legend

The feathery seed balls of dandelions were used in olden times as oracles by lovers. Young maidens would blow three times on the fluff to determine if their sweethearts were thinking of them; the maiden was not forgotten if a lone feather remained. Dandelion greens were so highly prized by the Apache Indians that they would spend days or weeks searching the surrounding countryside for them.

Health Benefits Cholagogue, diuretic, laxative, stomachic, tonic. One of the oldest and most versatile of the healing herbs, dandelion is regarded as a blood cleanser, tonic, and digestive aid. This is due to its content of mucilages, which soothe the digestive tract, absorb toxins from ingested food, and regulate intestinal bacteria. Dandelion root is regarded as one of the finest liver remedies, both as a food and as a medicine. The root contains bitter principles which enhance the flow of bile, improving such conditions as liver congestion, bile-duct inflammation, hepatitis, gallstones, and jaundice. Its action in increasing bile flow is twofold: it has a direct effect on the liver, causing an increase in bile production and flow to the gallbladder (choleretic effect); and it has a direct effect on the gallbladder, causing contraction and release of stored bile (cholagogue effect). In the spring, the root contains levulose, a sugar easily assimilated by diabetics; by autumn, this sugar has changed to inulin, an easily assimilated starch. Dandelion leaves are many times richer in vitamin C, potassium (which makes them bitter), and calcium than leaf lettuce or even spinach. The young greens are also an excellent liver cleanser, stimulate the activity of the pancreas and spleen, and detoxify any poisons throughout the body. Because it cleanses toxins, dandelion has a beneficial effect on any skin disorders, jaundice, menstrual troubles, and blood pressure irregularities.

Dandelion juice is an excellent tonic used to counteract hyperacidity, to help normalize the alkalinity of the system, and is beneficial for the teeth and gums. Juice from the broken stems of spring or summer dandelions is reputed to cure warts (autumn and winter juice will not work). Touch the wart with the milky juice and leave on to dry; repeat frequently. In a few days, the wart will turn black and fall off. The tea is used as a remedy for fatigue, a diuretic, a tonic, to promote bowel regularity, and to nourish the liver.

Dill (*Anethum graveolens*)

Anethum *is from an ancient Greek name for the dill plant,* anethom; graveolens *means heavy-scented. The English name* dill *is a derivative of the old Norse word* dilla, *which means to lull.*

General Information Dill is a member of the parsley family native to the Mediterranean region and southern Russia. Used since time immemorial, it makes its first written appearance in an Egyptian medical work of about 3000 B.C. Among the Greeks it was used as a food, a perfume, and an incense. The Romans chewed dill seeds to promote digestion, and they hung dill garlands in their dining halls, believing the herb would prevent stomach upset. The plant yields two different herbs: dill seed (the fruit of the plant) and dill weed, the top eight inches of the graceful feathery leaves. Dill is highly prized in Scandinavian, Russian, and Polish cooking, but is used in the United States primarily in pickles, potato salad, and sauerkraut.

Culinary Uses Dill is a fragrant, decorative plant whose delicate flavor cannot be matched by any other herb. The green feathery leaves have a subtle piquant flavor, similar to mild caraway, and enhance the natural flavors of cucumbers, green salads, vegetables, soups and stews. Dill seeds have a slightly sharper taste than the leaves, and are quite plainly bitter. They are used in pickles, cheese dishes, salad dressings,

Dill

Nutritional Value Per 100 g Edible Portion

	Leaves, Fresh	Leaves, Dried	Leaves, 1 tsp.	Whole Seed	Seed, 1 tsp.
Calories	43	253	3	305	6
Protein	3.46 g	19.96 g	0.20 g	15.98 g	0.34 g
Fat	1.12 g	4.36 g	trace	14.53 g	0.31 g
Fiber	n/a	11.93 g	0.12 g	21.09 g	0.44 g
Calcium	208 mg	1,784 mg	18 mg	1,516 mg	32 mg
Iron	n/a	48.77 mg	0.49 mg	16.32 mg	0.34 mg
Magnesium	55 mg	451 mg	5 mg	256 mg	5 mg
Phosphorus	66 mg	543 mg	5 mg	277 mg	6 mg
Potassium	738 mg	3,308 mg	33 mg	1,186 mg	25 mg
Sodium	61 mg	208 mg	2 mg	20 mg	trace
Zinc	0.910 mg	3.300 mg	0.030 mg	5.200 mg	0.110 mg
Copper	0.146 mg	0.490 mg	n/a	0.780 mg	n/a
Manganese	1.264 mg	3.950 mg	n/a	1.833 mg	n/a
Beta Carotene (A)	n/a	n/a	n/a	53 IU	1 IU
Thiamine (B_1)	0.058 mg	0.418 mg	0.004 mg	0.418 mg	0.009 mg
Riboflavin (B_2)	0.296 mg	0.284 mg	0.003 mg	0.284 mg	0.006 mg
Niacin (B_3)	1.570 mg	2.807 mg	0.029 mg	2.807 mg	0.059 mg
Pantothenic Acid (B_5)	0.397 mg	n/a	n/a	n/a	n/a
Pyridoxine (B_6)	0.185 mg	1.461 mg	0.015 mg	n/a	n/a
Folic Acid (B_9)	150 mcg	n/a	n/a	n/a	n/a

Lore and Legend

Hanging a bunch of dill over the doorway was said to protect the house from witches. In the American colonies dill (and fennel) seeds were called "meetin' seeds" because they were carried to church by mothers for restless and hungry children to chew on during the interminable sermons.

potato salads, and occasionally in cakes and pastries. Fresh dill leaves and seeds are preferable to the dried forms.

Health Benefits Antispasmodic, aromatic, carminative, diuretic, stimulant, stomachic. Dill contains an essential oil that includes carvone and other components that give it its inimitable fragrance. Both leaves and seed have a mild soporific effect, and in England a soothing dill water was once given to babies. Herbalists regularly use dill leaves and seeds to dispel flatulence, stimulate the appetite and settle indigestion, induce sleep, and increase mother's milk. Try chewing a few seeds to help clear up halitosis. Seasoning food with dill makes it more appetizing and digestible, with the added bonus of a high vitamin content.

Epazote

Nutritional Value Per 100 g Edible Portion

	Fresh
Calories	42-295
Protein	3.8-30.9 g
Fat	0.7-5.4 g
Fiber	1.3-12.1 g
Calcium	304-2456 mg
Iron	5.2-55.7 mg
Phosphorus	52-403 mg
Sodium	1.0-6.9 mg
Beta Carotene (A)	3.5-43.6 mg
Thiamine (B_1)	0.060-0.540 mg
Riboflavin (B_2)	0.300-2.500 mg
Niacin (B_3)	0.600-18.500 mg
Ascorbic Acid (C)	11-610 mg

Epazote (*Chenopodium ambrosioides*)

Also Known As: Mexican Tea, Wormseed, Jerusalem Oak.

Chenopodium *is a Greek word meaning goosefoot and alludes to the shape of the leaves;* ambrosioides *means ambrosial.*

General Information Epazote is native to tropical America and grows wild in the Americas and parts of Europe.

Culinary Uses This herb has an aroma similar to that of turpentine or menthol, and is used as a green herb in Mexican cooking and as a tisane in Europe. When combined with beans, epazote helps to reduce intestinal gas. Because pests are deterred by the leaves, they are stuffed in mattresses and sachets in Brazil.

Health Benefits Oil from the seeds is used to expel worms, but overdoses have caused death in infants due to its toxic alkaloid. The tea is used by herbalists to treat dysentery. Only use this herb in small quantities.

Fennel (*Foeniculum vulgare dulce, F. piperitum, F. azoricum*)

Also Known As: Finocchio, Carosella, Florence Fennel.

The Romans named the plant foeniculum, *which means little hay. The name eventually evolved into the more familiar* fennel. Vulgare dulce *means commonly found sweet plant;* piperitum *means resembling peppermint, or being sharply fragrant/flavored;* azoricum *means from the Azores.*

General Information Fennel was originally a maritime plant from southern Europe. The Romans employed all parts of this aromatic plant—roots, stems, leaves, and seeds—eaten either raw or cooked. It was introduced into western North America by Spanish priests, and still grows wild around their old missions. Early English settlers brought the plant to the eastern coast. A rather unusual looking vegetable with a celery-like base and feathery dill-like leaves, its small yellow flowers each produce two green or yellow-brown seeds about 1/8- to 5/16-inch long, oval in shape, ribbed, and greenish-gray. These diminutive seeds are said by some to resemble miniature watermelons. There are several varieties of fennel, including Florence fennel (*F. piperitum*), which produces thick stalks that can be eaten like celery; sweet fennel (*F. vulgare dulce*), whose seeds are used as an herb; and finocchio (*F. azoricum*), which is grown for its bulbous stalk base.

Fennel

Nutritional Value Per 100 g Edible Portion

	Whole Seed	1 tsp.
Calories	345	7
Protein	15.80 g	0.32 g
Fat	14.87 g	0.30 g
Fiber	15.66 g	0.31 g
Calcium	1,196 mg	24 mg
Iron	18.54 mg	0.37 mg
Magnesium	385 mg	8 mg
Phosphorus	487 mg	10 mg
Potassium	1,694 mg	34 mg
Sodium	88 mg	2 mg
Zinc	3.700 mg	0.070 mg
Copper	1.067 mg	n/a
Manganese	6.533 mg	n/a
Beta Carotene (A)	135 IU	3 IU
Thiamine (B1)	0.408 mg	0.008 mg
Riboflavin (B2)	0.353 mg	0.007 mg
Niacin (B3)	6.050 mg	0.121 mg

Culinary Uses Fennel is one of the newer arrivals in North American supermarkets. This strange looking plant has a flavor slightly reminiscent of anise and licorice, but softer and nuttier. The leaves, tender stems, and seeds are used from the milder sweet fennel variety, while the stalks and bulbs are used from Florence fennel and finocchio. The bulb and stems are eaten like celery; the stalk, stripped of its skin and dressed in vinegar and pepper, makes a tasty celery-like salad called *cartucci* that is popular in the plant's native Mediterranean area. Feathery leaves of dark green are a tasty addition to mayonnaise, vinaigrette sauces, salads, and soups. Finocchio is used as a vegetable, most often in salads. Fennel seeds can be used in a wide range of dishes, from apple pies to curries and vinegars. Toss a few fennel seeds in your next pot of baked beans, as they will help cut down on the flatulent aftereffects.

Health Benefits Aromatic, antispasmodic, carminative, diuretic, expectorant, stimulant, stomachic. Fennel has been used to soothe the stomach and intestines, relieve

Lore and Legend

Early Greeks believed that fennel had slimming powers and was able to give a man strength, courage, and long life. The plant's name in Greek was *marathon*; the place where the famous battle with the Persians in 490 B.C. was fought was so called because the soil there was overgrown with fennel. Romans believed that fennel was an aid in sharpening vision and was a symbol of success. The giant variety grown by the Romans was used to flog reluctant students, with the hope that, perhaps by osmosis, new insights and abilities would result. As far back as Pliny there was a belief that serpents ate the leaves of fennel to renew their youth and thus enable them to shed their skins. It was also believed that serpents constantly haunted fennel patches because its strong licorice odor improved their vision, which at best is never very keen. During the Middle Ages people ate fennel seeds to stave off hunger during Church fasts. In sixteenth-century Europe, the expression "to give fennel" meant to flatter or give false compliments; just as fennel allayed hunger for a while, bringing no lasting nourishment, a false compliment flatters temporarily but brings no real satisfaction to its recipient.

flatulence, expel pinworms, sweeten the breath, as a gargle, an eyewash, to regularize menstrual periods, and to increase milk in nursing mothers. Its volatile oils are responsible for most of its medicinal properties. Many of these oils are antimicrobial. Tea made from its crushed seeds is used to treat indigestion and cramps, and has been proven scientifically to contain antispasmodic properties. Chew the leaves, bulb, or seeds for a pleasant, refreshing taste and breath sweetener, as well as an appetite suppressant. To bathe the eyes, put a teaspoonful of the leaves in a cup, pour in boiling water, allow to cool, and then gently drop the strained liquid into the eyes. Fennel has a specific affinity for the bloodstream, and builds strong blood plasma. Other benefits include being an excellent obesity fighter, since it accelerates the digestion of fatty foods.

Fenugreek (*Trigonella foenum-graecum*)

Also Known As: Greek Hay, Foenugreek.

> *The name* Trigonella *is derived from the old Greek name denoting three-angled, due to the form of its corolla. The English name* fenugreek *comes from* foenum-graecum, *a Latin phrase meaning Greek hay; the plant being used to scent inferior hay. Early Greeks mixed the plant into moldy or insect-damaged animal forage to make it more palatable to their animals, and in the process discovered that sick horses and cattle would eat fenugreek when they would not eat anything else.*

Fenugreek

Nutritional Value Per 100 g Edible Portion

	Whole Seed	1 tsp.
Calories	323	12
Protein	23.00 g	0.85 g
Fat	6.41 g	0.24 g
Fiber	10.07 g	0.37 g
Calcium	176 mg	6 mg
Iron	33.53 mg	1.24 mg
Magnesium	191 mg	7 mg
Phosphorus	296 mg	11 mg
Potassium	770 mg	28 mg
Sodium	67 mg	2 mg
Zinc	2.500 mg	0.090 mg
Copper	1.110 mg	n/a
Manganese	1.228 mg	n/a
Beta Carotene (A)	n/a	n/a
Thiamine (B_1)	0.322 mg	0.012 mg
Riboflavin (B_2)	0.366 mg	0.014 mg
Niacin (B_3)	1.640 mg	0.061 mg
Folic Acid (B_9)	57.0 mcg	2.1 mcg
Ascorbic Acid (C)	3.00 mg	0.11 mg

General Information Fenugreek is a member of the leguminous bean family cultivated for its seeds, and is one of the oldest culinary and medicinal plants. Indigenous to Mediterranean shores and western Asia, fenugreek plants resemble white clover but produce pods, each of which contain between ten and twenty aromatic seeds. Each seed is about one-quarter inch long, brownish-yellow, and marked with an oblique furrow along half its length. The plant was introduced into central Europe by Benedictine monks, and Charlemagne himself promoted its use during the ninth century. Fenugreek was introduced to the Chinese during the Sung Dynasty (c. 1057 A.D.), and the Chinese have since made much use of the plant. The seeds in their natural state have little or no odor; they acquire some when dried, a little more when ground, and a final increment when heated.

Culinary Uses Young shoots of fenugreek are chopped and added to salads, while the leaves are used as a vegetable. The yellow seeds have a slightly bitter yet pleasant taste, reminiscent of celery and maple, with a similar odor. For cooking, the seeds are best dry-roasted before use to remove their bitter flavor, although over-roasting will leave them just as unpleasant. These seeds can be sprouted like mustard and cress, and will make a tasty, crunchy addition to salads. Ground fenugreek seed is an important ingredient in Indian curry powder, chutneys, and the Jewish sweet dish halva. The seeds are so hard, however, that they cannot be ground in a mortar, but only with a special poppyseed grinding mill. The oil of fenugreek has a maple flavor and can be used for a maple flavoring in cooking and syrups.

Health Benefits Emollient, expectorant, mucilaginous, tonic. Fenugreek is one of the oldest medicinal plants, dating back to the ancient Egyptians and the Greek Hippocrates. Early Egyptians prepared a thick paste by soaking the seeds in water; this was used to prevent fevers, soothe stomach disorders, and to treat diabetics. The seeds are high (40 percent) in mucilage, as well as an emollient soothing to the skin, and are used as an emulsifier in drugs and food. They are also rich in fixed oils that are often compared to cod liver oil preparations, as they contain choline and vitamin A (and upon oxidizing produce a distinct "fishy" odor). Nourishing and body-building, fenugreek aids digestion, intestinal inflammation, mucous membranes, ulcers, lung problems, and allergies. Fenugreek tea helps lubricate the intestines, cleaning out poisonous toxins that build up in the body's system, and helps relieve lower back pain and that general feeling of tiredness often associated with stomach and intestinal troubles. The seeds also contain saponins and spogenins consisting of diosgenin and yamogenin, which are starting materials for the synthesis of steroid hormones and related drugs. Diosgenin is important in the synthesis of oral contraceptives and sex hormone treatments, as it can be converted to pregnenolone (a steroid formed during the synthesis of hormones) and progesterone, the anti-estrogen hormone secreted by pregnant women.

Lore and Legend

Arab women from Libya to Syria ate roasted fenugreek seeds to gain weight and attain the shapely Rubenesque proportions synonymous with beauty from ancient times through the nineteenth century. The lord of the harem, meanwhile, ate them as an aphrodisiac. In many places, fenugreek is still considered a potent aphrodisiac. Nursing mothers in Ethiopia increase their intake of fenugreek, for it is believed to promote the production of milk (it does provide a generous 180 mg of calcium per 100 grams of seed). Fenugreek was a major ingredient in Lydia E. Pinkham's famous Vegetable Compound, introduced to the American public in 1875 as a remedy for "female complaints;" the compound also contained a comforting syrup that was about 18 percent alcohol.

Galangal *(Alpinia galanga)*

The genus Alpinia *was named after Prosper Alpinus, an Italian botanist.*

General Information Galangal resembles ginger, to which it is related, but its rhizomes are larger and pale yellow with zebra-like markings and pink shoots. Called galingale in England, it was popular throughout Europe in the Middle Ages, but disappeared from Western cooking when the heavy use of spices went out of favor in the eighteenth century. Dried, ground galangal (often called *laos*, its Indonesian name) can frequently be found in Asian groceries.

Culinary Uses The fresh root is not to be eaten on its own, because it has a fiery medicinal taste and the texture of a wood chip. Pounded fresh in a mortar with seasonings such as lemon grass, chili peppers, shallots, and garlic, galangal has a much more appealing flavor and is an important ingredient in Thai curry pastes. Dried, ground galangal is added to soups, stews, and curries.

Health Benefits Galangal is reputed to curb nausea and settle the stomach as well as ginger, and grated galangal with lime juice is an all-purpose tonic in southeast Asia.

Garam Masala

The name of this Indian spice literally translates as "hot mixture."

General Information Garam masala is an aromatic mixture of toasted, ground spices used as a basic seasoning for many Indian dishes. Although freshly blended and ground in India and the East, here in the West it is bought ready-prepared and may contain such "warm" spices as allspice, cinnamon, coriander, peppercorns, cloves, cumin, and chili pepper.

Culinary Uses and **Health Benefits** The primary use of garam masala is in bean dishes, where it adds a great deal of energy and flavor. Garam masala has all the beneficial properties of its constituent spices.

Garlic (*Allium sativum, A. scorodoprasum*)

Garlic

Nutritional Value Per 100 g Edible Portion

	Raw	Powder	1 tsp.
Calories	149	332	9
Protein	6.36 g	16.80 g	0.47 g
Fat	0.50 g	0.76 g	0.02 g
Fiber	1.50 g	1.87 g	0.05 g
Calcium	181 mg	80 mg	2 mg
Iron	1.70 mg	2.75 mg	0.08 mg
Magnesium	25 mg	58 mg	2 mg
Phosphorus	153 mg	417 mg	12 mg
Potassium	401 mg	1,101 mg	31 mg
Sodium	17 mg	26 mg	1 mg
Zinc	n/a	2.630 mg	0.070 mg
Copper	n/a	0.147 mg	n/a
Manganese	n/a	0.545 mg	n/a
Beta Carotene (A)	0 IU	trace	n/a
Thiamine (B_1)	0.200 mg	0.466 mg	0.013 mg
Riboflavin (B_2)	0.110 mg	0.152 mg	0.004 mg
Niacin (B_3)	0.700 mg	0.692 mg	0.019 mg
Folic Acid (B_9)	3.1 mcg	n/a	n/a
Ascorbic Acid (C)	31.2 mg	n/a	n/a
Tocopherol (E)	0.01 mg	n/a	n/a

Allium *is the ancient Latin name for the garlic family, and may derive from the Celtic* all, *meaning pungent.* Sativum *refers to the fact that this plant has long been cultivated. The English name* garlic *is derived from the Middle English* gar, *meaning spear, and* leac, *meaning pot herb. During the Middle Ages bald men were called* pilgarlics, *a term meaning peeled garlics.*

General Information The origin of garlic is unknown, though it is believed to have originated somewhere near Siberia and to have spread from there into the Middle East and Europe. This member of the lily family has a compact bulb divided into a varied number of white or purplish-colored almond-shaped segments called cloves, each one wrapped in its own papery skin. Mentioned in the literature of all the great ancient world kingdoms—Babylon, Medo-Persia, Greece, and Rome—garlic has a long history that has always been tied to the working class. A ruffian with a heart of gold and a wealth of talents—serving in the kitchen, the medicine chest, and the vegetable garden—garlic is totally undistinguished of appearance, and its smell (to some) is coarse and offensive. California produces 90 percent of the United States crop (more than 250 million pounds); some of the best is reported to be cultivated around Gilroy. In years when frost strikes the garlic crop, the cloves turn out firmer and

Lore and Legend

There has never been a time when humanity ignored garlic, nor has there ever been an herb called upon to play such disparate roles. The entire ancient world from Spain to China revered garlic; in fact, the cultivation of garlic in China is of such ancient origin that it has an ideogram to itself. During the time of the Pharaohs, when Egypt was at the peak of its power, garlic was given to the laborers and slaves who were building the great pyramids in order to increase their stamina and strength as well as to protect them from disease. In the fifth century A.D., the Greek historian Herodotus wrote that on one of the pyramids there is an inscription describing the amount of garlic, onions, and radishes consumed by those building the great pyramid of King Khufu (Cheops). The use of garlic was evidently not limited solely to slaves, as Herodotus called all Egyptians "the stinking ones" because of their redolent garlic aroma. The Greeks greatly admired garlic and made much of it, and Greek criminals were given garlic to eat in order to purify them of their crimes. However, common folk who smelled of garlic were not allowed to enter the temple of Cybele, the mother goddess of the earth and goddess of untellable name, worshipped throughout the Near East. Among the Romans garlic was fed to laborers to make them strong and to the army to give it courage, since the plant was dedicated to the war god Mars. They even attributed their success in conquering the world to garlic because "no invader would come into the country that smelled so strong." The lowly bulb was not considered with much favor by the richer classes, however, who viewed garlic breath as a sign of low birth, a belief that lasted well into the twentieth century. In India the priestly brahmins were forbidden to eat garlic, while in the first days of Islam, the Prophet Muhammed—fearful of offending his hosts by rejecting a dish liberally laced with garlic—explained disarmingly, "I am a man who has close contact with others." Sir John Harrington, in *The Englishman's Doctor*, written in 1609, summarized garlic's virtues and faults thus: "Garlic then have power to save from death; Bear with it though it maketh unsavory breath; And scorn not garlic like some that think; It only maketh men wink and drink and stink." Garlic has an age-old reputation as a stimulant to the sexual appetites and rambunctious thoughts. In many Eastern religious traditions, yogis, monks, and nuns eliminate garlic from their diets for these reasons.

smoother. **Elephant garlic** (*Allium scorodoprasum*) cloves are roughly the size of quail eggs. Each slips nicely out of its papery skin, and in theory, one clove of the big stuff is equal to about eighteen to twenty cloves of the normal-sized garlic. They are milder than regular garlic and have none of the aftereffects. Elephant garlic provides essence and mild taste, but not the pungency.

Culinary Uses Sold fresh or dried into flakes and powder, garlic is probably the most popular flavoring. It is important in most of the world's cuisines and adds dimension to all foods except desserts; preparing such foods as eggplant, tomatoes, Caesar salads, and pesto is absolutely unthinkable without garlic. Raw garlic has a vibrantly sharp, biting flavor, which some find too strong for their palate. Cooking eliminates the bite and softens the flavor, while roasting garlic gives it a smooth, mild, nutty flavor. Unpeeled cloves are roasted for about 15 minutes at 350°F, then peeled, mashed, and used in purees, sauces, and soups.

Health Benefits Antibacterial, antiseptic, antispasmodic, antithelmintic, aromatic, carminative, diaphoretic, digestive, expectorant. Garlic—and its less potent botanical relatives onions, scallions, leeks, chives, and shallots—ranks among the world's oldest medicines. An Egyptian medical papyrus from the sixteenth century B.C. lists twenty-two remedies employing garlic for everything from heart disease and worms, to tumors, headaches, and bites. Biochemists have confirmed the ancient use of garlic as an antibiotic and fungicide, isolating allicin as the active component. It is this agent that emits the characteristic smell; however, allicin appears only in freshly cut or crushed raw garlic. If the aroma—hence allicin—is destroyed, as in cooking or other processing, garlic is no longer a microbe killer, although it can perform other therapeutic tricks such as lowering cholesterol and acting as a decongestant. One raw crushed clove contains the antibiotic equivalent of one hundred thousand units of penicillin, and has proven more effective than either penicillin and tetracycline in suppressing certain types of disease-carrying agents. Dr. Albert Schweitzer, deep in the

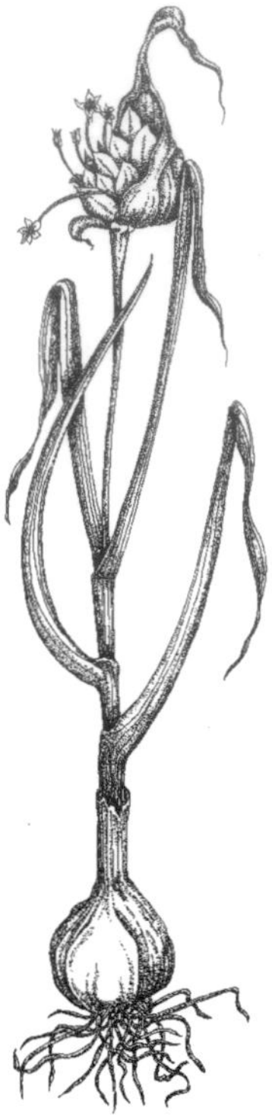

jungle, with his mainstream pharmaceuticals depleted, gave his patients garlic for amoebic dysentery; in Japan a cold-processed, odorless raw garlic substance called Kyolic serves as an antibiotic; and in the former Soviet Union, where garlic is known as "Russian penicillin," officials on one occasion imported some five hundred tons to combat an outbreak of influenza.

Garlic is one of the most beneficial foods for the digestive system and has a strong effect on the lymphatic fluid and tissue, aiding in the elimination of noxious waste matter. In fact, European studies show garlic helps eliminate lead and other toxic heavy metals from the body. Garlic is also effective in ridding the alimentary canal of worms and other parasites, boosting immunological functions, purifying the bloodstream by removing sticky inorganic deposits in the blood vessels, and regularizing the action of the liver and gallbladder. For protection against dysentery, such as when traveling in foreign countries, chew a clove of garlic before consuming suspected food or water. To ward off mosquitos, eat garlic at least once daily. As a remedy for athlete's foot, spread freshly crushed garlic over the affected area (which will feel warm for about five minutes) and leave on for a half hour before washing with plain water. Do this once a day for a week. If the skin burns, wash immediately with plain water and try later with less garlic. Another method is to sprinkle powdered garlic daily on wet feet and let dry before wearing socks. Raw garlic, when eaten to very great excess, may cause various digestive problems. It may also result in burns in the mouth, throat, esophagus, and stomach. Garlic is high in sulphur and iodine.

Geranium, Scented (*Pelargonium graveolens*)

The genus name Pelargonium *is Greek for stork, because the peculiarly shaped fruit is long and slender like a stork's bill;* graveolens *means heavy-scented. The English name* geranium *derives from the Greek diminutive word for crane,* geranos.

General Information The rose geranium, an annual plant grown for its small lavender flowers and wonderful rose aroma, originated in South Africa and was introduced to Europe in 1690. There are also geraniums that smell like apples, cinnamon, coconut, lemon, and mint; these plants are collectively known as "scented geraniums." The unusual foliage, pretty blossoms, easy cultivation, and delightful aromatic properties of these herbs have endeared them to gardeners the world over. The French perfume industry first demanded large-scale cultivation of rose geraniums for their essential oil in 1847.

Culinary Uses Leaves from all the scented geraniums can be used to add an enticing aroma and delicate sweet flavor to fresh salads, desserts, baked goods, jellies, and jams. The larger the leaves, the more fragrant they will be. For drinks the leaves may be added whole to cool fruit drinks, crushed in warm water to make a tea, or added to other herb brews, such as peppermint tea. Jars of homemade jam are sealed with a large leaf, or one or two leaves are placed in jars of apple or blackberry jelly before storing. Rose geranium leaves have the delicate taste and aroma of roses, with just a hint of spice.

Ginger *(Zingiber officinale)*

Ginger gets its Latin and English names from the Latin translation of the Sanskrit word sringavera, *which means horn-root, from the fancied resemblance of its misshapen flattened rhizome to the horns of an animal.* Officinale *means of the workshop, alluding to apothecaries' shops, and signifying that the plant was once part of the official pharmacopeia of Rome.*

General Information Ginger, a distant relative of the banana, is an exotic tropical plant that originated in India. First mentioned in China about 400 B.C., the plant has since been naturalized and cultivated in Jamaica, Africa, and the West Indies. It was a popular import item in Europe from the eleventh to thirteenth centuries. Cultivated for its edible root, the ginger plant thrives in warm, humid climates, growing up to three feet high with wide, erect, stalkless leaves and highly aromatic flowers shooting up from the tuberous underground rhizomes. The best ginger reputedly comes from the island of Jamaica, while the most highly prized of the several varieties of ginger rhizomes has a light brown skin and creamy yellow to light green fibrous flesh.

Culinary Uses Fresh ginger root is juicy, hot, and fibrous, with a pungent almost peppery flavor and a refreshing sharpness. The flavor and texture of ginger root varies according to the season in which it is gathered and the length of time it is stored. The older roots tend to be tough, fibrous, and strong tasting, whereas the younger roots are mild and tender. If ginger is young and fresh, the skin will be thin and unnecessary to peel; if the skin is tough or shriveled, the skin needs to be peeled with a paring knife before using. Choose tubers that are fresh-looking and firm. The little sprouts that appear on the sides of the root are more delicate in flavor than the main section. Store fresh ginger in the refrigerator. Peeled and ground to a pulp, ginger is a popular ingredient in many curries, grains, and vegetable dishes. Try adding a few bits of ginger to a pot of chamomile tea for a treat; to butter before pouring over vegetables; or to rice as it cooks for a delicate, mysterious flavor. Ginger is

Ginger

Nutritional Value Per 100 g Edible Portion

	Fresh Raw	Dried Powdered	1 tsp.
Calories	69	347	6
Protein	1.74 g	9.12 g	0.16 g
Fat	0.73 g	5.95 g	0.11 g
Fiber	1.03 g	5.91 g	0.11 g
Calcium	18 mg	116 mg	2 mg
Iron	0.50 mg	11.52 mg	0.21 mg
Magnesium	43 mg	184 mg	3 mg
Phosphorus	27 mg	148 mg	3 mg
Potassium	415 mg	1342 mg	24 mg
Sodium	13 mg	32 mg	1 mg
Zinc	n/a	4.720 mg	0.080 mg
Copper	n/a	0.480 mg	n/a
Manganese	n/a	26.500 mg	n/a
Beta Carotene (A)	0 IU	147 IU	3 IU
Thiamine (B_1)	0.023 mg	0.046 mg	0.001 mg
Riboflavin (B_2)	0.029 mg	0.185 mg	0.003 mg
Niacin (B_3)	0.700 mg	5.155 mg	0.093 mg
Pantothenic Acid (B_5)	0.203 mg	n/a	n/a
Pyridoxine (B_6)	0.160 mg	n/a	n/a
Ascorbic Acid (C)	5.0 mg	n/a	n/a

Lore and Legend

Ancient Indians used their native ginger as a physical and spiritual cleanser. They shunned strong-smelling garlic and onion before religious celebrations for fear of offending their deities, but ate lots of ginger because it left them smelling sweet, and therefore presentable to the gods. Ancient Chinese sailors chewed ginger root to prevent seasickness, and when the root arrived in ancient Greece it was used as a stomach soother. Physicians prescribed it wrapped with bread, eventually leading to the world's first cookie, gingerbread, and later to a folk remedy for upset stomach that is still popular today: ginger ale. Beginning with the twelfth century, gingerbread was a favorite confection in England, but the cost was sufficient to largely confine its pleasure to royalty and the wealthy. The gingerbread man, beloved of children and adults alike, is the impersonalized descendant of the aristocratic gingerbread portraits of the Elizabethan court, when Elizabeth I employed a chef-artist to fashion portraits of honored guests in gingerbread. Being the subject of such attention must have been very flattering, if it didn't presage a more realistic beheading.

also available dried and ground to a powder, canned, crystallized in sugar, or preserved in syrup. Candied ginger root, a favorite treat of children, has recently regained some of its popularity, largely because it is very nearly as healthful as it is pleasurable to eat. Powdered or dried ginger, used primarily in baking, gives a completely different flavor to foods, and cannot be substituted for fresh ginger. Dried, powdered ginger adds a delicious flavor to stewed fruit and puddings, baked goods, and other desserts.

Health Benefits Antispasmodic, appetizer, astringent, carminative, diaphoretic, diuretic, expectorant, stimulant, stomachic. Ginger rhizomes produce the volatile oil that contains such aromatic substances as camphene, phellandrene, zingiberene, and zingerone. These, along with several other chemicals, have made ginger one of the world's oldest and most popular medicinal spices, used in folk medicine almost everywhere. Ginger is regarded as promoting overall circulation of energy in the body and acting as a stimulant for those who are debilitated, lethargic, or convalescing from an illness. It promotes heat, neutralizes toxins, and aids the digestion and assimilation of food, as well as affecting a systematic cleansing through the skin, bowels, and kidneys. Recent research has shown that ginger is helpful in preventing motion sickness and vertigo. Ginger tea, made by boiling pieces of fresh ginger root in water, promotes cleansing of the system through perspiration, and is also said to be useful for menstrual cramps, bloating or suppressed menstruation. Try some warm ginger tea at the onset of a cold or flu to ease the effects of the usual symptoms. The tea is also gentle enough to use during pregnancy to help ease morning sickness or alleviate colds. Finally, chew the peeled root to stimulate the flow of saliva and to soothe a sore throat.

NOTE: Germany's Commission E recommends that dried powdered ginger not be taken for morning sickness during pregnancy; traditional Chinese medicine also recommends against using ginger during pregnancy.

Ginseng *(Panax ginseng, P. quinquefolius, Eleutherococcus senticosus)*

The genus name Panax, *like the word panacea, is derived from the Greek words* pan, *meaning all, and* akos, *meaning remedy, thus* panakeia *means all-healing, in reference to the miraculous virtue ascribed to it by the Chinese, who consider it a sovereign remedy in almost all diseases. The ancient Chinese called the plant* jen shen, *or "essence of the earth in the form of a man," which became the English* ginseng. *The term* quinquefolius *means five-leaved.* Eleutherococcus *comes from the Greek words* eleutheros, *meaning free, and* coccus, *meaning a berry, seed, or grain.*

General Information Ginseng is the aromatic root of an unassuming ivy-like ground cover that commonly grows to a length of two feet or more. Asiatic ginseng (*Panax* *ginseng*) grows in the damp woodlands of Manchuria and is cultivated primarily in Korea. American ginseng (*Panax quinquefolius*) is a perennial plant which at one time was found wild in the rich, cool woodlands of eastern North America, from Quebec west to Manitoba and south to northern Florida and Alabama. It is most abundantly found in the Cumberland Gap region of southern Appalachia. Siberian ginseng (*Eleutherococcus senticosus*) has a habitat of primarily Siberia, thus its vernacular name; it is not a true ginseng, but is part of the same family as the other two ginsengs and contains similar active chemicals. All three varieties of ginseng are used interchangeably, and as its high reputation in Asia ensures constant demand, world trade consists almost exclusively of cultivated plants. Esteemed by the Chinese above all other botanicals as a cure-all, it has primarily been their centuries-old demand which provoked incredible market fluctuations, astronomical prices, overharvesting, and a lingering curiosity. This curious root, with its distinctive trunk and extremities, which approximate human arms and legs, remains as important in Chinese folk medicine as ever. A Jesuit missionary named Joseph Lafitau in Montreal, Canada during the early 1700s realized that American ginseng was nearly identical to a medicinal plant much in demand in China, and almost overnight a brisk export trade developed. The first American ship to reach China in 1784, Major Samuel Shaw's *Emperor of China*, carried a cargo of American ginseng, and made quite a tidy profit. Popular demand for the roots nearly wiped out the wild supply, and ginseng is now protected by law in many states because of previous overharvesting.

Ginseng

Nutritional Value Per 100 g Edible Portion

	Asian, Dried
Calories	274
Protein	10.9 g
Fat	1.77 g
Fiber	7.2 g
Calcium	288 mg
Iron	trace
Magnesium	48.1 mg
Phosphorus	52.8 mg
Potassium	243 mg
Sodium	2.4 mg
Zinc	trace
Manganese	1.90 mg
Beta Carotene (A)	trace
Thiamine (B_1)	0.170 mg
Riboflavin (B_2)	0.180 mg
Niacin (B_3)	8.000 mg
Ascorbic Acid (C)	0 mg

Culinary Uses Ginseng lovers claim that the fabled herb has a mild licorice flavor, which adds a delightful accent to tea, coffee and other beverages and dishes. The Chinese have traditionally chewed the root and brewed it into a tea and spring tonic, but today ginseng is available in powder, capsule, honey, liquid, and natural form.

Health Benefits Chinese medical practitioners classify Asian ginseng as yang (warming/male) and use it for increasing *ch'i* (energy), strength, and blood volume; promoting life and appetite; and quieting the spirit and giving wisdom. This variety of ginseng is best avoided by those who are well-muscled and quick to anger. American ginseng is considered a yin (cooling/female) tonic whose action is to reduce heat of the respiratory or digestive systems, reduce fatigue, enhance reproductive performance and immunity, and is well suited for those with an aggressive constitution. In North America, American ginseng was an important medicine among many Indian tribes. It was to induce easy childbirth, treat nosebleeds, increase female fertility, and as a general mental tonic. Siberian ginseng is used for increasing *ch'i*, treating energy deficiencies that result in lower back pain and kidney problems, and normalizing body functions. It is noted for protecting against the mental and physical effects of stress.

Lore and Legend

Ginseng is one of the most fabled ancient healing plants, a plant cloaked in mystery and superstition. According to ancient beliefs, ginseng represented the crystallization of the unseen spirit of nature in the form of a man who dwells in its root. Thus, ginseng roots that were clearly man-shaped held the spirit and power of God and were effective in curing disease and strengthening the weak. In one legend, ginseng began as a divine gift to a deserving but miserable young wife who, after several years of marriage, had no children and was frantic with disappointment. Custom made her situation particularly bitter, because after three childless years her husband would be permitted to take a concubine. One night she dreamed about an old man in the mountains who could assist her; searching him out, she took the herbal remedy he offered and soon bore a child. Later, when she made the journey back to see and thank him, she thanked him so prettily that he (who was actually a deity in disguise) filled the woods with this miraculous plant. The plant was ginseng, and has become a Chinese symbol of strength, vigor, long life, and clear judgment. Surpassing even the truffle throughout history as a precious aphrodisiac, one Chinese emperor reputedly paid $10,000 for a perfect man-figure ginseng root. Like mandrake, the most potent ginseng roots are said to be shaped like a man's body, and the Chinese believe that even better results are obtained when the root is dug up at midnight during a full moon.

Chinese records verify the fact that the renowned Chinese herbalist Li Chung Yun reached 256 years of age. He was born in 1677, and in 1933 the *New York Times* announced the death of this remarkable man. Professor Li gave a course of twenty-eight lectures on longevity at a Chinese university when he was over the age of 200. Those who saw him declared that he did not appear older than a man of fifty-two; that he stood straight and strong, and had his own natural hair and teeth. It is claimed that Li Chung Yun's longevity was due to his strictly vegetarian diet, his calm and serene attitude toward life, and the fact that he regularly used powerful rejuvenating herbs prepared as teas. These herbs were Fo-ti (*Polygonum multiflorum*), gotu kola (*Centella asiatica*), and ginseng. With the exception of the ginseng *root*, Li would eat only food that was produced above the ground.

Russian studies have demonstrated enhanced adaptation to darkness and temperature extremes, and increased reactivity of certain types of brain cells in response to stress among persons taking ginseng root extracts. They also showed that ginseng stimulates the central nervous system and respiratory system, and reduces blood sugar, serum cholesterol, and blood pressure. Extracts of Asian ginseng root have been shown to counteract the toxic effects of chloroform, amphetamines, and other toxins, and to prolong the lives of mice exposed to X-rays.

Ginseng has been said to be a general panacea, with the ability to promote healing in all ailments—everything from conquering cancer to rejuvenating male sexuality. It is the only plant used routinely by so great a number of more or less healthy individuals for stimulation, added energy and a sense of well-being. The main active constituents of ginseng are a group of fifteen ginsenosides, each of which acts differently, stimulating or sedating depending on the particular metabolic needs of the individual. Hence the term adaptogen is used to describe ginseng, for it helps the body restore and maintain internal homeostasis. Tests have shown that ginseng stimulates the central nervous system and various secretory glands, promotes increased motor coordination, stamina and endurance, mental alertness, adaptability and agility, sensual perception, and learning ability. It has also been found to afford protective medicinal action against radiation exposure.

NOTE: Germany's Commission E, a division of the German Federal Health Agency, recommends that Siberian ginseng not be used in cases of high blood pressure.

Gum Karaya (*Sterculia urens*)

Sterculia *comes either from Sterculius of Roman mythology, or from* stercus, *meaning manure, because the leaves and fruits of some species have a particular odor;* urens *means burning or stinging. The English term* gum karaya *is due to the plant's exuding a gummy substance, while* karaya *is from a Hindi term* karayal, *meaning resin.*

General Information Every spring, harvesters enter the forests of the subtropical Himalayas in search of the soft-wooded trees called karaya. Avoiding the large leaves, which resemble the leaves of grapevines except that their stalks are armed with stinging hairs, they selectively wound some of the larger trees, cutting away two sheets of the smooth bark. A gummy, brownish, vinegary-smelling sap begins to flow, solidifying into ropy strips or huge tears, some of which may weigh as much as ten pounds. The hardened sap is a polysaccharide—a complex form of carbohydrate—whose individual molecules have been reported to outweigh those of water by more than 500,000 times. When it comes in contact with water, the absorbent granules of the dried gum swell up like sponges to as much as one hundred times their original size. The paper industry uses karaya as a fiber binder in tissue paper; in construction, it is used to bind the particles of some composition boards.

Culinary Uses Gum karaya is used as a stabilizer for salad dressings, a binder for meat products, a gummy base for candies, and a thickener of meringue, ice cream sticks, sherbets, whipped cream, and cheese spreads.

Health Benefits Laxative. In the intestines, gum karaya swells and triggers peristalsis, pushing food through the digestive system. Dentists use the powdered gum as a denture adhesive that is resistant both to bacteria and to the enzymes of the mouth.

Honey, Raw

General Information Honey is one of the oldest sweeteners known to humans. People collected and ate this sweet, golden substance before they knew how to raise cereal grains or keep dairy animals. Originally, honey was collected by smoking bees from their nests, a method illustrated in Egyptian tomb reliefs of the third millennium B.C., but dating back much earlier. Made throughout the world by only five varieties (*Apis mellifica*) of the ten thousand bee species recorded, honey is the product of the blossom nectar gathered by bees and converted into a sweet sticky liquid. It takes 160,000 bees numerous trips to two million flowers to gather the four pounds of nectar required to produce just one pound of honey; a single honeybee will produce only one teaspoonful in its entire lifetime. Until the end of the Middle Ages honey was the sweetener par excellence in much of the world, although by no means the only one. Some countries used date syrup or fig syrup, others malted grains, still others grape juice, and a few had sugar cane. Having discovered the pleasant flavor and energy-giving properties of honey, people soon found that it had other virtues. Since the golden substance is almost pure sugar and ferments very readily, even the debris of a honeycomb left to soak in water is enough to produce a delicious and mildly intoxicating liquid. Honey ale, generally known as mead, was to be popular for thousands of

Honey

Nutritional Value Per 100 g Edible Portion

	Strained
Calories	304
Protein	0.3 g
Fat	0 g
Fiber	n/a
Calcium	6 mg
Iron	0.42 mg
Magnesium	2 mg
Phosphorus	4 mg
Potassium	52 mg
Sodium	4 mg
Zinc	0.220 mg
Copper	0.036 mg
Manganese	0.080 mg
Beta Carotene (A)	0 IU
Thiamine (B_1)	0 mg
Riboflavin (B_2)	0.038 mg
Niacin (B_3)	0.121 mg
Pantothenic Acid (B_5)	0.068 mg
Pyridoxine (B_6)	0.024 mg
Folic Acid (B_9)	2 mcg
Ascorbic Acid (C)	0.5 mg

years, especially in countries where grapes did not grow and ale-making grains were scarce. In England, honey did not lose its hold until the sixteenth century and the dissolution of the monasteries (monks were the primary beekeepers—they used the wax for votive candles and the honey as a commercially valuable by-product).

Lore and Legend

Milk and honey are frequently mentioned as offerings to gods, or as food of the gods, which indicates how important they were to the ancients. In Greek mythology, the young Zeus was rescued from his father Cronus and brought up secretly by the nymphs Amalthea and Melissa, who fed him milk and honey. Aristotle thought honeydew was the nectar of the gods fallen to earth, and had something to do with rainbows; Pliny the Elder thought it a sweet liquid of the heavens, saliva from the stars or juice produced when air purified itself. The Koran teaches that the disappearance of honey would be Allah's punishment of men: "The first good that God will take from man will be honey." As told in an ancient Egyptian legend, one day long ago the god Ra wept, and the tears that dropped from his eyes turned into bees that promptly set about making honeycomb and gathering nectar from the flowers. An old custom is the practice of placing a few drops of honey on the first book presented to a child. The child would lick the honey off the book, thus forever associating books with sweetness.

Culinary Uses Honey is the only food that will not spoil; it will crystallize, but is easily brought back to a fluid state by heating. There are quality considerations in selecting honey. The lighter colored honeys are mildest in flavor, while darker honeys are stronger flavored and have a greater nutritional value. The three most commercially prevalent types are alfalfa, clover, and buckwheat. Alfalfa and clover honey are usually light colored and mild flavored; pure buckwheat honey is dark brown and strong flavored, similar to sorghum. Good honey should be unfiltered (or strained only through cheesecloth to remove any extraneous material) and uncooked; filtering removes the pollen that gives good honey its cloudiness and valuable nutrients. The U.S. Department of Agriculture grades honey according to its clarity, which is a reflection of how much it is filtered. In typical government fashion, the honeys with the greatest clarity receive the highest grades: Grade A or Fancy honey has been screened and filtered to death. Lower grades are B (Choice), C (Standard), and D (Substandard). These grades imply nothing about the quality of the honey or its source, but only indicate the degree of fineness of the screen through which the honey has been filtered. The word "uncooked" on the label should tell what temperature was employed during the processing. Temperatures up to 145°F can be used with "uncooked" still permitted as a description, but to be meaningful the word should mean not heated over 104°F, just enough to encourage free flowing, but not high enough to destroy vitamins and enzymes. When honey is heated to high temperatures or cooked, its attributes are altered and the resultant product can clog the digestive tract and create toxins within the body by its acidic nature. Truly uncooked honey begins to crystallize at room temperature within several weeks after bottling, and if necessary can be reliquified by setting the jar or can into a pan of warm water. Honey has a sweetening power 140 percent greater than white sugar, so less is needed.

Health Benefits Antiseptic, laxative. Because of its content of potassium and formic acid, honey has the characteristic of being antiseptic. It is hygroscopic, meaning that honey draws every bit of moisture out of germs, thus killing them. Universally applied to dress external wounds and sores to keep them sterile, honey also hastens the healing process. Honey creates heat in the body, is good for healing internal and external ulcers, carries the medicinal properties of herbs to the bodily tissues, is an excellent blood purifier, and is good for the eyes and teeth. Mixed with lemon juice or vinegar, it makes a soothing cough syrup; taken with water, the combination energizes the body and helps to flush the kidneys. Honey is probably the best natural source of energy available to man due to its pure sugar content, which is very easily assimilated by the body. Since honey has the complexity of a whole food, the blood-sugar race it triggers will be conducted at a slower speed than the one triggered by processed sugar. Buy from quality sources only, and avoid those producers who feed their bees antibiotics, sugar syrup, sulphur drugs, or whose honey contains pesticides or other toxic residues. Darker honeys are generally richer in minerals than light honey.

NOTE: Do not give honey to children under one year of age, as it has been known to cause botulism in infants.

Hyssop *(Hyssopus officinalis, Agastache foeniculum)*

> Hyssopus *comes from the Greek* hyssopos *and the Hebrew* ezobh, *meaning holy herb, because it was traditionally used for cleaning sacred places.* Officinalis *means of the workshop, alluding to apothecaries' shops, and signifying that the plant was once part of the official pharmacopeia of Rome.* Agastache *is derived from the Greek words* agan, *meaning very much, and* stachys, *meaning ear of grain.* Foeniculum *means anise-like or anise-scented.*

General Information Hyssop is a perennial shrub of the mint family that is native to southern Europe and temperate Asia. Easily grown, it produces small purple flowers and narrow, pungent leaves. In Elizabethan and Tudor gardens, the plant is frequently clipped into miniature hedges for knot gardens. In seventeenth century Europe, hyssop was a popular strewing herb; crushed leaves and flower tops were scattered around homes to mask odors at a time when people rarely bathed and when farm animals often shared human living quarters. When bathing became popular and strewing ceased, hyssop was placed in scent baskets in sickrooms. Hyssop has also been used for centuries as a potherb and for salads. Anise hyssop (*A. foeniculum*) is neither anise nor hyssop, but another completely separate member of the mint family.

Lore and Legend

So powerful is hyssop's fragrance that elderly women in Switzerland and Bavaria are said to press its flowers in their psalm books in the hopes that its strong odor will prevent them from falling asleep during boring sermons.

Culinary Uses Hyssop has provided a culinary seasoning for many centuries, with its evocative, spicy and slightly bitter, minty flavor. Although hyssop is too pungent for most modern palates, the Romans liked its taste and made an herbal wine from it; medieval monks also favored the herb, and spiced soups and sauces with it. Hyssop's strong flavor is best used in small quantities, adding a few leaves to salads, breads and soups, or it can be used as a decorative garnish. Anise hyssop has fragrant licorice and anise-scented leaves that can be used for teas and seasonings. The violet blue flowers are used fresh or dried to garnish fruit dishes or desserts.

Health Benefits Antiseptic, aromatic, astringent, carminative, depurative, emmenagogue, expectorant, stimulant, tonic, vermifuge. Hyssop aids the digestion of fat, and is recommended for use with greasy meats and fish. It acts as a general cleansing tonic, improves blood quality and circulation, and benefits the bronchial and stomach linings. A tea prepared from the flower tops is used for respiratory problems, easing coughs, hoarseness, sore throats, and loosening phlegm. When the leaves are ground and applied to cuts or wounds, they exert an antiseptic quality and speed healing. Hyssop is used in essentially the same way as sage, with which it is sometimes combined.

Juniper Berry *(Juniperus communis)*

> Juniperus *is the classical name for this plant.* Communis *means common.*

General Information Juniper is an evergreen shrub that, unlike most conifers, produces spicy blue-black or purplish berries. The common Juniper is a native of Europe, but has been introduced into some parts of the United States, where it has

Juniper Berry

Nutritional Value Per 100 g Edible Portion

	Dried
Calories	341
Protein	18.2 g
Fat	5.6 g
Fiber	12.0 g
Calcium	849 mg
Iron	15.0 mg
Magnesium	93 mg
Phosphorus	90 mg
Potassium	957 mg
Sodium	trace
Zinc	trace
Manganese	6.30 mg
Beta Carotene (A)	2,026 IU
Thiamine (B_1)	0.120 mg
Riboflavin (B_2)	0.060 mg
Niacin (B_3)	1.200 mg
Ascorbic Acid (C)	0 mg

become naturalized. The bushes carry berries at all different stages of development since the berries take three years to fully ripen. All parts of the plant contain a volatile oil, which imparts an aromatic scent. The berries were at one time popular as a strewing herb to sweeten stale air in overcrowded rooms or hospital wards. Potency of the berries varies by region, with juniper from southern Europe being the most flavorful.

Culinary Uses Juniper berries, used either fresh or dried, are aromatic, spicy, and taste slightly of pine. Most people consider them too pungent to be eaten fresh. Frequently used to remove the strong gamey taste of wild game, and to add flavor to sauerkraut, pickles, and chutneys, just a few berries added to stews, casseroles, and vegetable dishes add an intriguing flavor. When dried, they may be ground in a pepper mill like peppercorns. Oils and extracts of juniper are used in many foods (including gin) and as a fragrance in soaps and perfumes.

Health Benefits Antiseptic, carminative, diuretic, stimulant, stomachic, tonic. Ripe juniper berries contain a component-rich, aromatic essential oil similar to turpentine oil. They will gently stimulate the appetite, increase the production of hydrochloric acid, counteract flatulence, and help remedy gastrointestinal infections, inflammations, and cramps. An infusion of berries in wine is an appetite stimulant. The berries are used by herbalists for treating some kidney infections, but in conjunction with more cooling herbs.

Lore and Legend

Juniper often figures in stories and legends as a magical plant. During the Middle Ages, Europeans believed planting a juniper beside the front door kept witches out; however, the tree did not provide complete protection, as a witch could still enter if she correctly guessed the number of its needles. Parents burned juniper branches during childbirth in the belief that its smoke prevented the fairies from substituting a changeling for their newborn baby.

NOTE: Taken in large quantities, the berries occasionally produce irritation of the urinary passages. They are not recommended for pregnant women.

Kudzu *(Pueraria lobata, P. thunbergiana)*

Also Known As: Kuzu.

This plant received its genus name in honor of M.N. Puerari, a botanist from Geneva. Lobata *means divided into lobes;* thunbergiana *is given in honor of Carl Peter Thunberg, 1743–1822, a Swedish botanist. The English name* kudzu *is derived from* kuzu, *the plant's name in Japan.*

General Information Kudzu is a prostrate Asian leguminous vine whose root has been known for its medicinal and culinary properties in Japan and China for over one thousand years. This "giant of roots" weighs an average of two hundred pounds, and grows up to seven feet in length. The traditional way of preparing the starch is a labor-intensive process taking up to 120 days. The root is dug out of the ground during the winter when the sap is concentrated there; this root is then cleaned, chopped, and pounded into a mash. Eventually a crude fibrous paste forms which is washed, filtered through cloth, and allowed to settle out in broad, shallow settling ponds. This process is repeated up to fifty times until ultimately a pure white starch is obtained; after the last settling the water is drained off and the damp layer of starch is cut into small blocks and allowed to air dry naturally for up to two months. There is no way to speed up this drying process since direct sunlight and ovens are too hot, and alter the starch's ability to dissolve in water during use. After drying, the cubes are crumbled and packaged for use.

Kudzu was introduced to the United States from Indochina and Japan in 1876. Exhibited at the Philadelphia Centennial Exposition, it was admired by Americans as an attractive ornamental and planted as a shade vine. Between 1910 and 1935, kudzu was widely used in the South as livestock fodder and pasturage and was renamed King Kudzu. However, by 1955 the plant was considered a noxious weed because the fast-growing vine had spread far beyond desired boundaries, covering crops, pastures, and forest. A single vine can grow one hundred feet or more in a single season, pulling down and/or killing everything in its path.

Culinary Uses Kudzu is used as a thickener in much the same way as cornstarch or arrowroot, or as a gelling agent like agar and gelatin. It adds a subtle sweetness and smoothness to sauces, desserts, and confections. The odorless, tasteless white starch is unequaled in producing transparent, smooth and tasty sauces, but does not have the elastic texture or raw, starchy flavor often noticeable in cornstarch-thickened mixtures. Usually sold in chunks, the pieces work best when first crushed to a fine consistency so that they will dissolve more readily. Like cornstarch, kudzu must be dissolved in cold liquid before using. Once dissolved, it can be added to the liquid being used and brought to a boil.

Health Benefits As a kitchen remedy, kudzu helps develop an alkaline condition within the body, and provides relief from intestinal and digestive disorders, headaches, fever, colds, and hangovers.

Lambsquarter (*Chenopodium album*)

Also Known As: Wild Spinach, Goosefoot.

> Chenopodium *is a Greek word meaning goosefoot and alludes to the shape of the leaves;* album *means white.*

General Information Lambsquarter is a relative of garden spinach and beets, and grows in gardens and cultivated fields in most temperate climates. The plant seems to have a special affinity for potato fields, coming up after cultivation has ceased. Native to Europe and Asia, and introduced early into North America, it is now found everywhere except the extreme northern section of the country. Not necessarily an attractive plant, it has historically been used for "spring greens," since it was found in abundance and easily collected. When small, six to ten inches high, the plants are succulent and tender.

Lambsquarter

Nutritional Value Per 100 g Edible Portion	Raw	Cooked
Calories	43	32
Protein	4.20 g	3.20 g
Fat	0.80 g	0.70 g
Fiber	2.10 g	1.80 g
Calcium	309 mg	258 mg
Iron	1.20 mg	0.70 mg
Phosphorus	72 mg	45 mg
Beta Carotene (A)	11,600 IU	9,700 IU
Thiamine (B_1)	0.160 mg	0.100 mg
Riboflavin (B_2)	0.440 mg	0.260 mg
Niacin (B_3)	1.200 mg	0.900 mg
Ascorbic Acid (C)	80.0 mg	37.0 mg

Culinary Uses Both the foliage and seeds of lambsquarter are edible. Young, tender leaves or shoots may be used raw in salads; the older leaves and immature seeds can be steamed and served as spinach. Fully ripened seeds may be eaten raw, or dried and ground into a meal to make bread. Both leaves and seeds can be dried for winter use.

Health Benefits Antiscorbutic.

Lavender (*Lavandula officinalis, L. vera, L. angustifolia*)

Lavandula *is derived from the Latin* lavandus, *meaning to be washed, because it was used in ancient times to perfume bath water.* Officinalis *means of the workshop, alluding to apothecaries' shops, and signifying that the plant was once part of the official pharmacopeia of Rome.* Vera *means true, perhaps in reference to the existence of false or inferior lavenders.*

General Information Lavender originated in the mountainous regions of the Mediterranean, and covers vast tracts of dry barren land in Spain and Italy. A perennial plant with narrow gray-green leaves and long purple-flowered spikes, lavender became popular in ancient Rome as a sensual fragrance for the bath. It was used for a variety of healing purposes in medieval Europe, and in many parts of Europe stalks of lavender leaves and flowers were set in linen closets to impart their fragrance to sheets, pillowcases, blankets, and comforters. Though used in a more limited manner today, lavender still scents sachets, perfumes, and soaps. The dried flowers or sprigs will keep moths away from stored linens and clothes, while the fresh flowers can be rubbed over the skin to deter obnoxious insects.

Lore and Legend

Lavender has long had a reputation as an antiaphrodisiac (counter-stimulant), with one old belief advocating sprinkling lavender on your head as an aid in maintaining chastity. In sixteenth century England, women and men had the spicy-smelling flowers of lavender quilted into their hats to "comfort the braines."

Culinary Uses Lavender flowers have a strong fragrant odor, and an aromatic, warm, bitterish taste. The fragrant leaves and flowers can be used fresh in salads and fruit dishes, or added to beverages, cooked sauces, candies and baked goods. When dried, the leaves are most often used in jellies.

Health Benefits Aromatic, carminative, diuretic, sedative, stimulant, tonic. Lavender is a wonderfully refreshing and delightfully scented plant with a long history of medicinal use. Its strong scent, like that of mint, is a remedy for dizziness and fainting. The plant has been attributed calmative and sedative properties and used to soothe the nerves, relieve nervous headaches and depression, stimulate the appetite, relieve stomach or intestinal flatulence, and soothe colic. A few sprigs in the evening bath will calm jaded nerves and inhibit germs. Crushed leaves can be used as an antiseptic wash for wounds, and are quite effective on snake bites.

Lecithin

The name lecithin *is derived from the Greek word for egg yolk because that is the source from which it was first isolated.*

General Information A phosphorized fat molecule (phospholipid) that moves well through both fat and water, lecithin is a necessary structural component of all cell membranes in living organisms. Found in many natural foods, including whole grains, nuts and seeds, and unrefined vegetable oils, lecithin is also produced routinely in the body. Soybeans are the primary commercial source of lecithin (phosphatidylcholine). Unrefined soy oil contains approximately 3 percent lecithin. During refining, the lecithin is removed as an "impurity" and then sold for use in baked goods, prepared foods, and pharmaceutical preparations. Lecithin is available in both liquid and granulated form.

Lecithin

Nutritional Value Per 100 g Edible Portion	
Calories	763
Fat: Saturated	15.01%
Monounsaturated	11.00%
Polyunsaturated	15.32%

Culinary Uses Granulated lecithin resembles waxy or oily millet seeds, although it is more golden. These slightly nutty flavored granules can be sprinkled on cereals, added to beverages, or used in baked goods, where they result in a better texture and tenderer crust and also act as a preservative. Commercially, lecithin is usually referred to as an emulsifier, stabilizer, or thickener, and holds together everything from margarine and mayonnaise to baked goods, salad dressings, and cosmetics.

Health Benefits Lecithin is an important constituent of all the bodily organs. It aids in the breakdown, absorption, and utilization of fats as well as vitamins A, D, E, and K. Lecithin has demonstrated positive effects in lowering cholesterol levels, by preventing cholesterol from collecting and attaching to the walls of blood vessels, and is actually said to reduce harmful cholesterol levels in the body. It also improves liver and gallbladder function, helps eliminate liver spots, repairs various neurological disorders, and is beneficial in cases of dry skin and psoriasis. Lecithin also provides choline, which is necessary for both liver and brain function, along with phosphorus and inositol.

Lemon Grass (*Cymbopogon citratus, C. flexuesus*)

Cymbopogon *comes from the Greek* kumbo, *meaning a cup, and* pogon, *a beard.* Citratus *means citrus-like and refers to the pleasant citrusy aroma;* flexuesus *means flexuous, tortuous, or zig-zagged. Its English name* lemon grass *is due to its scent and appearance.*

General Information The term lemon grass refers to several species of grass native to southeast Asia, all possessing the flavor of lemon due to the presence of citric oils. These are perennial plants with tall gray-green grass-like leaves that grow best in cooler tropical climates. A relative of citronella, these plants have long been cultivated for their aromatic oil, which is used in cosmetics and fragrances. Fresh lemon grass is sold by the stalk, which is two feet in length and looks something like a scallion, though it

Lemon Grass

Nutritional Value Per 100 g Edible Portion	Dried
Calories	389
Protein	8.2 g
Fat	7.1 g
Fiber	n/a
Calcium	368 mg
Iron	54.3 mg
Magnesium	331 mg
Phosphorus	214 mg
Potassium	2300 mg
Sodium	64 mg
Zinc	trace
Manganese	10.40 mg

is fibrous to the point of being woody. Only the bulb-like six- to eight-inch base of the stalk is used, after the top is trimmed and a layer of tough outer leaves peeled off.

Lore and Legend

In Indonesia, young girls are sent to cut lemon grass, because of an old belief that the grass is at its most fragrant when harvested by someone with a virgin's pure thoughts.

Culinary Uses Lemon grass has a light, airy, floral aroma combining lemon and lime peel with fresh cut hay. Available dried, powdered (when it is known as **Sereh powder**), and fresh, this plant is frequently used in southeast Asian cooking to impart a lemony flavor and aroma. The straw-like fresh stalks can lend their flavor to soups and stews or used for steaming, but need to be removed before the dish is served, as they are too harsh-textured to be eaten. It is the inner part of the stalk, a pale, tubular core resembling a firm scallion bulb, that is tender enough to be eaten. This is finely slivered into dishes, adding its inimitable lemony pungency. Since fresh lemon grass is powerful and develops with cooking, use it sparingly until its potency is understood. The dried herb possesses only a wisp of its former seasoning power, and must be soaked before use. One teaspoon of ground powder is roughly equivalent to one stalk.

Licorice (*Glycyrrhiza glabra*)

The etymology of Glycyrrhiza, *the botanical name of licorice, derives from the Greek words* glukos, *meaning sweet, and* riza, *meaning root, an appropriate description. The term* glabra *means glabrous or smooth. The Romans changed* glycyrrhiza *to* liquiritia, *which evolved into the English word* licorice.

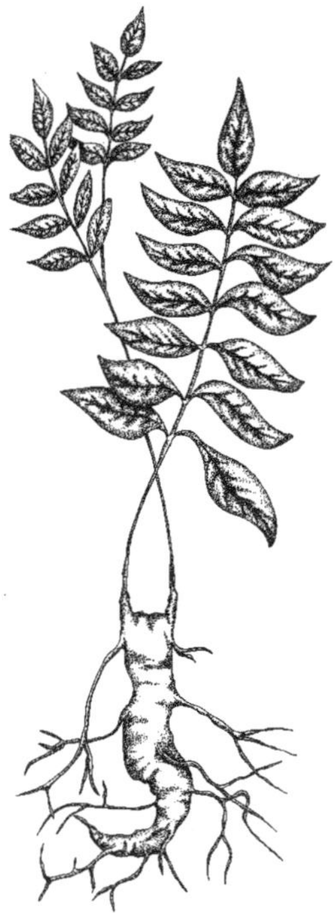

General Information Licorice is true to its Greek name, as it is 50 times sweeter than sugar. A member of the pea (and thus legume) family that grows wild in southern Europe and Asia, licorice is a graceful plant with light, spreading pinnate foliage presenting an almost feathery appearance from a distance. Taproots may sink three or four feet, and should be harvested in the fall. The use of licorice has been known since ancient times. It was introduced to the Greeks by the Scythians, and was also used by the Chinese and Indians. Great quantities of licorice were found with the fabulous treasures of King Tut and other Egyptian rulers; the Egyptians believed that the licorice could be used to prepare a sweet drink ("maisus") in the next world. Licorice is cultivated for its sweet-tasting rhizomes (underground stems) and roots, which are used as flavorings. Ninety percent of all natural licorice imported is employed as a conditioning and flavoring agent in tobacco.

Culinary Uses Sweet and slightly astringent, licorice can be purchased as the whole dried root, sliced, or powdered. Some people use the powder in fruit smoothies or on their food as a seasoning. Licorice flavoring is used in soft drinks, ice cream, candy, desserts, cakes, and confectionery. Licorice candy, which rarely contains more than 2 percent natural licorice extract, is more likely to be flavored with anise (which is unrelated to licorice) or with a synthetic licorice flavoring. Licorice extracts are used extensively as ingredients in cough drops and syrups, tonics, laxatives, anti-smoking lozenges, and as flavoring agents to mask bitter, nauseous, or other undesirable tastes in medicine.

Health Benefits Demulcent, diuretic, expectorant, laxative. The main active component in licorice root is a saponin-like glycoside called glycyrrhizin, which is fifty times sweeter than sugar. Its use as a non-caloric sweetener is limited, however, because of the strong taste it imparts to food. Licorice root cleanses the mouth and teeth, arrests tooth decay due to its germicidal action, promotes salivation and increases secretions in the gastro-intestinal tract. Known to improve circulation and cleanse the blood, it is also good for hypoglycemia and the removal of age spots and drugs from the body. Research indicates that licorice may counteract various viruses, including herpes simplex I and HIV. Licorice tea is a mild laxative, a natural expectorant and decongestant, will aid digestion, help the liver discharge toxins, and strengthen both the heart and circulatory system. This is the most common herb in Chinese herbal combinations, as it is thought that licorice helps to harmonize the action of all other herbs. Septic or non-healing wounds will be healed by the application of licorice tea or licorice ghee.

Licorice

Nutritional Value Per 100 g Edible Portion

	Dried
Calories	268
Protein	11.0 g
Fat	1.0 g
Fiber	8.4 g
Calcium	878 mg
Iron	88 mg
Magnesium	965 mg
Phosphorus	79 mg
Potassium	1,140 mg
Sodium	818 mg
Zinc	0.30 mg
Manganese	4.70 mg
Beta Carotene (A)	trace
Thiamine (B_1)	0.210 mg
Riboflavin (B_2)	0.160 mg
Niacin (B_3)	7.000 mg
Ascorbic Acid (C)	62.6 mg

NOTE: Glycyrrhizin increases fluid and sodium retention and promotes potassium depletion if licorice is used for long periods. Persons with cardiac problems and hypertension should avoid consumption of significant quantities.

Lovage *(Levisticum officinale, Ligusticum scoticum)*

The botanical name Levisticum *is a corruption of the earlier name* Ligusticum*, named after Liguria, Italy (a region that includes the Italian Riviera), where lovage once grew in abundance.* Officinale *means of the workshop, alluding to apothecaries' shops, and signifying that the plant was once part of the official pharmacopeia of Rome.* Scoticum *denotes a variety that comes from Scotland. The English name* lovage *is a corruption of the Latin name.*

General Information Lovage is a tall plant with large, dark green leaves, native to the Balkans and Mediterranean area. The Romans, who used lovage as a medicinal herb, introduced it to much of Europe and Great Britain. In the Middle Ages it was used as a cure-all for most illnesses. This relative of dill, angelica, and parsley sometimes looks, smells, and tastes more like celery than celery itself.

Lovage

Nutritional Value Per 100 g Edible Portion

	Fresh
Protein	20.0 g
Fat	14.7 g

Culinary Uses The flavor of lovage is similar to strong celery with a bit of anise; some compare it to that of brewer's yeast. Used as a celery substitute, the leaves, stems, and stalks will add a slightly spicy taste to every dish. Tender, young leaves are best for salads, while older leaves can be used in soups, stews, and casseroles. It is excellent in potato salads and other salads; in soups and stews its strong flavor persists even after long cooking. The stems, like angelica, may be candied, but the flavor is inferior. If lovage goes to seed, use the seeds for making breads, herb butters, chicken salads, and candy.

Health Benefits Carminative, diuretic, emmenagogue, expectorant, stimulant, stomachic. Lovage contains a volatile oil called angelic acid, which has antiseptic qualities, plus strong resins and oils that act on the kidneys and bladder and relieve menstrual disorders. This herb is mostly used for its diuretic properties in cases of water retention and urinary difficulties, but also has a beneficial cleansing effect on the system, remedies digestive difficulties, eases flatulence, and can be applied externally to wounds due to its antiseptic qualities.

NOTE: Because it promotes the onset of menstruation, lovage should not be used by those who are pregnant.

Mallow *(Malva rotundifolia, M. sylvestris)*

Also Known As: Malva, Cheese Plant, Low Mallow.

> *This plant got its botanical name* Malva *from the Greek* malake, *meaning soft, due to its soft emollient leaves.* Rotundifolia *means round-leaved;* sylvestris *means from the woods and forests. The English word* mallow *is a corruption of the Latin name.*

General Information Common or high mallow (*M. sylvestris*) and dwarf mallow (*M. rotundifolia*) are ancient herbs native to Europe and Asia that have been cultivated since the era of the Romans, and which now grow wild in North America. Centuries ago, Pliny wrote of the wonders of low mallow, to the effect that whoever ate a spoonful of it every day would be free of disease. Other related species having many uses for hundreds of years are hollyhock, okra, and marsh mallow.

Culinary Uses Mallow produces small, round leaves that can be added to salads, boiled and eaten as a vegetable, or brewed into a delicately flavored tea. Its shoots, green seed capsules (known as cheeses) and pink flowers can be chopped and added to salads.

Health Benefits Astringent, demulcent, emollient, expectorant. Mallow contains the healing substances of asparagin, pectin, and mucilage, all beneficial for the respiratory, alimentary, and urinary organs. It is also an emollient, so it softens and soothes sensitive tissues. American Indians and modern herbalists have recommended poultices made from the plant's leaves to relieve the pain of sores, insect stings and bites, and swellings. Mallow taken either in the form of soup or tea can overcome stubborn constipation.

Maple Syrup and Maple Sugar *(Acer saccharum)*

General Information Maple syrup and maple sugar are made only in the United States and parts of Canada, from the sap of sugar maples. American Indians on the northeast coast made maple syrup for centuries before the coming of Europeans. The Algonquins called it *sinzibuckwud,* "drawn-from-the-wood." Trees grown elsewhere do not produce enough sap to make syrup, since they require a climate with a long winter that goes from below freezing during the night to above freezing the next day, a condition common in New England and eastern Canada. The sap starts flowing from the trees' roots to the branches in late winter and early spring, bringing nourishment for budding leaves. Collectors drill holes into the tree trunks and insert a spout to divert the clear, tasteless, watery sap into buckets. Each tree averages twelve gallons of sap per season. Boiled in large vats to evaporate the water, between thirty and forty gallons of sap are needed to make one gallon of syrup, which is why pure maple syrup is so expensive. Buy organic maple syrup to avoid formaldehyde, chemical anti-foaming agents, and mold inhibitors.

Maple Syrup and Maple Sugar

Nutritional Value Per 100 g Edible Portion

	Syrup	Sugar
Calories	262	354
Protein	0 g	0.1 g
Fat	0.2 g	0.2 g
Fiber	0 g	0 g
Calcium	67 mg	90 mg
Iron	1.20 mg	1.61 mg
Magnesium	14 mg	19 mg
Phosphorus	2 mg	3 mg
Potassium	204 mg	274 mg
Sodium	9 mg	11 mg
Zinc	4.160 mg	6.060 mg
Copper	0.074 mg	0.099 mg
Manganese	3.298 mg	4.422 mg
Beta Carotene (A)	n/a	n/a
Thiamine (B_1)	0.006 mg	0.009 mg
Riboflavin (B_2)	0.010 mg	0.013 mg
Niacin (B_3)	0.030 mg	0.040 mg
Pantothenic Acid (B_5)	0.036 mg	0.048 mg
Pyridoxine (B_6)	0.002 mg	0.003 mg
Folic Acid (B_9)	0 mcg	0 mcg
Ascorbic Acid (C)	0 mg	0 mg

Culinary Uses Buy only high quality (Pure or Fancy) maple syrup, avoiding those "maple-flavored" syrups that contain mostly additives and as little as 3 percent real syrup. The syrup should be refrigerated after the container has been opened. Highest grade (AA or Fancy) maple syrup has the sweetest, most delicate flavor and is best used as a topping. Darker, stronger-flavored grades are ideal for cooking and baking. **Maple sugar** is maple syrup taken a few steps further, boiled down until it crystallizes and sets solid in sugar cakes. This is then usually pulverized into sugar crystals, with a light tan color and a concentrated maple flavor. Maple sugar can be reconstituted back into maple syrup with the addition of water. Both maple syrup and granules make a good white sugar substitute for cooking and baking, and add a warm, rich flavor to the finished product.

Health Benefits Valued for its flavor rather than its nutritive qualities, maple syrup is composed primarily of simple carbohydrates and some trace minerals.

Marjoram

Nutritional Value Per 100 g Edible Portion

	Dried	1 tsp.
Calories	271	2
Protein	12.66 g	0.08 g
Fat	7.04 g	0.04 g
Fiber	18.11 g	0.11 g
Calcium	1,990 mg	12 mg
Iron	82.71 mg	0.50 mg
Magnesium	346 mg	2 mg
Phosphorus	306 mg	2 mg
Potassium	1,522 mg	9 mg
Sodium	77 mg	trace
Zinc	3.600 mg	0.020 mg
Copper	1.133 mg	n/a
Manganese	5.433 mg	n/a
Beta Carotene (A)	8,068 IU	48 IU
Thiamine (B_1)	0.289 mg	0.002 mg
Riboflavin (B_2)	0.316 mg	0.002 mg
Niacin (B_3)	4.120 mg	0.025 mg
Ascorbic Acid (C)	51.43 mg	0.31 mg

Marjoram (*Origanum majorana, Majorana hortensis*)

The botanical name Origanum *is from the Greek words* oros *and* ganos, *meaning mountain glamor, or joy of the mountain, after the attractive appearance and aroma of the bushy flowering plant, which adorned the hilly Mediterranean landscape.* Majorana *or* maiorana *is a very old name of unknown derivation by which the plant was known when first introduced to Europe in the Middle Ages.* Hortensis *means belonging to a* hortus, *or garden.*

General Information Native to North Africa and southwest Asia, this member of the mint family is now naturalized in the Mediterranean region and cultivated in North America. Marjoram is so closely related to oregano that botanists sometimes use the same botanical name to describe both plants; most distinguish between them by using the name *Majorana hortensis* for the sweet-scented marjoram and the *Origanum majorana* or *Origanum vulgare* for the sharper-flavored oregano.

Culinary Uses The flavor of sweet marjoram is delicate, sweet, and spicy, rather similar to thyme, but sweeter and more scented. The leaves and flowers are used fresh or dried in salads, soups, stuffings, quiches and pies, omelets and potato dishes. Marjoram's delicate flavor destroyed by heat, so it is best added just before the dish is ready or used in lightly-cooked dishes. It complements especially well the herbs bay, garlic, onion, thyme, and basil.

Health Benefits Antispasmodic, calmative, carminative, diaphoretic, expectorant, stimulant, stomachic, tonic. Marjoram will benefit a sour stomach or loss of appetite,

Lore and Legend

There are many stories regarding the origin of marjoram, but all of them hold the plant as a symbol of youth, beauty, and happiness. Greek legend holds that the plant owes its beginnings to Aphrodite, who was inadvertently wounded by one of Cupid's arrows one day in her garden. Quickly she looked about for a cure to counteract the love-dart, but found none at hand. Causing sweet marjoram to spring up, she gave it the wrong magic in her haste, making it enhance the damage rather than cure it. From that day forward sweet marjoram was endowed with great potency as a love plant. Greek couples wore marjoram wreaths at their weddings because of its association with Aphrodite, and young girls placed marjoram in their beds so that Aphrodite would visit their dreams and reveal the identity of their future spouses.

Another legend of its origin comes from the island of Cyprus. The king of the island lived in a beautiful marbled palace looking out to the sea. As ruler, he expected instant obedience and efficient service from his many servants; any laxity or carelessness was met with stern punishment. One day a new page named Amarakos was given a large urn of costly perfume to carry to the king's quarters. As he attempted to shift the heavy burden from one shoulder to the other the urn slipped, falling and shattering on the floor. The boy, seeing the puddling perfume and remembering the demanding reputation of his king, was so paralyzed with fright that he fell dead to the wet floor. As custom demanded, the boy was duly buried, but upon his grave grew a beautiful plant that exuded the same fragrance as the rich perfume he had spilled, which was then named sweet marjoram.

increase white blood corpuscles, improve circulation, relieve abdominal cramps, and ease respiratory ailments. When added to the bath, it can promote a calming effect and relieve insomnia.

Matrimony Vine *(Lycium chinense)*

> Lycium *is derived from the Greek* lykion, *a name given to a* Rhamnus *from Lycia and later transferred by Linnaeus to this genus.* Chinense *means belonging to China. It received its English name of* Matrimony Vine *because it was related to a Western species that is so named.*

General Information Shoots of this spiny shrub are increasingly available at Asian produce stands. The thorny stalk is discarded and the leaves used. Traditionally, the leaves are eaten in the spring, the flowers in the summer, the berries (called wolfberries) in the fall, and the root in the winter. The berries look like small, pointed reddish-orange raisins and have a sweet, slightly licorice flavor. There are evidently abundant matrimony vine extracts, tinctures, and pills, and even the dried parts of the plant itself, for sale in Chinese herbal shops.

Culinary Uses The peppermint-flavored leaves are stirred into rich soups just before they are served, or they are traditionally cooked with pork. In China and Japan the leaves are also used to make tea.

Health Benefits The berries have a reputation for improving eyesight and kidney function. Children in Chinese apothecary shops are often given a handful as a quick, tonic snack.

Mint *(Mentha viridis, M. spicata, M. piperita)*

> *The genus* Mentha *is named after the Greek nymph Minthe.* Viridis *means green;* spicata *means spicate or having spikes;* piperita *means sharply fragrant or flavored. The English name* spearmint *is a corruption of "spire-mint," its tall flower spikes resembling the spires of weathered churches; the name* peppermint *is due to this variety's peppery flavor.*

General Information Originally natives of the Near East, the many varieties of mint spread across the globe in part because of their aggressive growth characteristics, but also due to the great esteem in which they were held by all who came in contact with them. All mints are relatively pungent because of their volatile oil containing menthol, carried in resinous dots on the stems and leaves. Best known to most people of the more than two thousand varieties are **Spearmint** *(M. viridis, M. spicata)* and **Peppermint** *(M. piperita)*. Spearmint is the oldest variety of mint, and while the leaves closely resemble those of peppermint, the flavor does not; peppermint has more oils and a very strong taste of menthol that is not found in spearmint. The high menthol content accounts for its characteristic sensation of coolness, which invades the mouth after the original pungency has died away. Because it is strongly aromatic, a bouquet of mint

Mint

Nutritional Value Per 100 g Edible Portion

	Peppermint, Dried
Calories	302
Protein	24.8 g
Fat	5.4 g
Fiber	11.4 g
Calcium	1,620 mg
Iron	60 mg
Magnesium	661 mg
Phosphorus	772 mg
Potassium	2,260 mg
Sodium	195 mg
Zinc	trace
Manganese	6.10 mg
Beta Carotene (A)	39,579 IU
Thiamine (B_1)	1.210 mg
Riboflavin (B_2)	3.890 mg
Niacin (B_3)	11.400 mg
Ascorbic Acid (C)	20.1 mg

hung indoors will pleasantly scent the whole house and give an impression of coolness. The commercial demand for the extracted volatile oil of mint is so great that in a town named Mentha, Michigan, growing this herb is the principal industry.

Buying Tips Many mints are now widely available fresh in grocery stores. This is the preferred form. If fresh mints are not available, the dried leaves or extracts also provide good flavor.

Culinary Uses All mints have a distinctive flavor and refreshing aroma. Mint leaves can be used fresh or dried (although fresh is better) as a tasty addition to potato salads, bean dishes, vegetable and fruit salads, fruit drinks, jellies, and sauces. Peppermint's volatile oil, which contains menthol, is employed in the manufacture of medicines, candies, liqueurs, cigarettes, and other products. Spearmint's pleasant but less potent flavor comes from its leaves and oil, and is an ingredient in mint sauces and jellies, as well as flavoring chewing gum and candy, iced teas, liqueurs and other drinks, and baked goods.

Health Benefits Antiseptic, antispasmodic, aromatic, carminative, stimulant, stomachic, tonic. Peppermint is considered a general stimulant, cleansing and strengthening the entire body. A strong cup of peppermint tea will act more powerfully on the system than any liquor stimulant, quickly diffusing itself throughout the entire system and bringing back to the body its natural warmth and glow. Because it can allay nausea, peppermint is suggested for use against seasickness. Spearmint is neither as versatile nor popular as peppermint, and is used primarily for flavoring foods. The refreshingly cool, stimulating scent and taste of mint has been valued since antiquity in cooking and healing. Mint of any kind is a balm for

Lore and Legend

In early Palestine, mint was one of the accepted forms for tax payment. Greeks, and Athenians in particular, believed mint to have the aroma of strength, and they would rub leaves over their arms to bolster their endurance. Peppermint oil was mentioned by Aristotle as an aphrodisiac, and the use of wild mint by soldiers of Alexander the Great was forbidden because he felt it so aroused them erotically that it took away all desire to fight. The Romans spread mint on the floors during feasts, as the fragrant aroma was believed to cause humans to rejoice and incline them toward eating (plus, it had the added benefit of frightening away mice). The Arabs have also used mint for centuries, partaking of mint tea as a social drink as well as a virility stimulant. The familiar after-dinner mints evolved from the ancient custom of concluding feasts with a sprig of mint to soothe the stomach.

Pluto, the god of the Greek underworld, fell in love with the beautiful nymph Minthe. His wife soon discovered the romantic affair and went into a fury, which culminated when she threw Minthe to the ground and stamped her to death. Although Pluto could not bring Minthe back to life, he changed her form into that of the fragrant plant. Another tale relates the story of two strangers who were walking through Phrygia. Snubbed by the villagers, who offered them neither food nor drink, the two knocked at the humble house of Philemon and Baucis, and asked for food. The old couple quickly made them welcome and looked around for ways to enhance their plain environment. Gathering some mint that was growing by the door, they used it to scrub the table and impart a sweet fragrance to the room. Upon serving their guests the food intended for their own meal, a radiance soon revealed the true identities of their guests—Zeus and Hermes. The gods richly rewarded Philemon and Baucis for their hospitality, changing their home into a beautiful temple where priests were assigned to serve the humble pair for the rest of their lives.

the entire digestive tract, regulating the stomach, liver, gall bladder, and intestines; it also regulates the sexual functions of both men and women. It is effective against stomach gas or spasms, vomiting, intestinal parasites, excessive acidity, and colic. The volatile oil of mint, menthol, is a time-honored and clinically-proven aid to digestion, and also a mild antispasmodic that is useful for relieving menstrual cramps and nausea. The utilization of menthol in upper respiratory ailments and as a soothing rub for sore muscles is easily verified by a trip to the local pharmacy, where the labels of many respiratory preparations and rubs indicate its presence. Menthol has also been shown to have antimicrobial properties. The deodorant properties of mint have been capitalized on as well, as they make frequent appearances in mouthwashes and toothpastes to sweeten the breath.

Molasses

The English name molasses *comes from the Latin term* mellaceus, *meaning like honey.*

General Information Molasses is the thick, dark syrup that remains after sugar crystals are removed during the process of sugar refining. The color and flavor differ depending on whether it results from early or later extractions. In Britain and western Europe, molasses is often called black treacle.

Molasses

Nutritional Value Per 100 g Edible Portion

	Regular	Blackstrap	Sorghum
Calories	266	235	290
Protein	0 g	0 g	0 g
Fat	0.1 g	0 g	0 g
Fiber	n/a	n/a	0.1 g
Calcium	205 mg	860 mg	150 mg
Iron	4.72 mg	17.50 mg	3.80 mg
Magnesium	242 mg	215 mg	100 mg
Phosphorus	31 mg	40 mg	56 mg
Potassium	1,464 mg	2,492 mg	1,000 mg
Sodium	37 mg	55 mg	8 mg
Zinc	0.290 mg	1.000 mg	0.410 mg
Copper	0.487 mg	2.040 mg	0.130 mg
Manganese	1.530 mg	2.610 mg	n/a
Beta Carotene (A)	0 IU	0 IU	n/a
Thiamine (B_1)	0.041 mg	0.033 mg	0.100 mg
Riboflavin (B_2)	0.002 mg	0.052 mg	0.155 mg
Niacin (B_3)	0.930 mg	1.080 mg	0.100 mg
Pantothenic Acid (B_5)	0.804 mg	0.880 mg	n/a
Pyridoxine (B_6)	0.670 mg	0.700 mg	n/a
Folic Acid (B_9)	0 mcg	1 mcg	n/a
Ascorbic Acid (C)	n/a	n/a	n/a

Varieties

Blackstrap molasses (sulphured) is the waste residue left after the third extraction of sugar from the sugar cane or beet. It contains all the nutrients that were stripped away from sugar during the refining process; it also contains all the residues from chemicals used in growing and refining the sugar—pesticides, lead, and sulphur, to name just a few. Very aromatic, blackstrap molasses has a strong, deep, slightly bitter licorice flavor, and is not the kind of syrup you would want to eat straight from the container. It imparts its unique dark flavor to fruit cakes, toffees, gingerbreads, and cookies. Blackstrap molasses is 55 percent sucrose.

Light molasses is the residue left after the first extraction of sugar crystals, and is quite sweet (65 percent sucrose).

Medium or **Dark molasses** is obtained from the second extraction and is moderately sweet.

Sorghum molasses, also called **Unsulphured, West Indies**, or **Barbados molasses,** is made from the sweet sorghum plant (*Horcus sorghum saccara*), grown specifically for making molasses.

This plant grows to a height of fifteen feet and forms a stalk (cane) that is topped by clusters of seeds, much like its relative millet. The stalks of the plant are cut and pressed through rollers, and the sweet, dark, thick liquid released is cooked and clarified into a dark syrup. It takes eight to twelve gallons of sorghum sap to make one gallon of "finished" syrup. Good quality sorghum is a clear amber color, with little sediment and no gritty or grainy feel in the mouth. It will have a rich, hearty, smoky and bittersweet taste, and is from 65 to 70 percent sucrose. Because sorghum molasses is not a by-product of sugar refining, it contains none of the sulphur dioxide, a fairly dangerous chemical used in the manufacturing of white sugar. However, it is usually difficult to find a pure cane syrup since its shelf life is fairly short, and for this reason many additives are often used to help preserve it. Traditionally, sorghum molasses is used on pancakes, corn muffins, and other breads, but it is also a suitable substitute for other sweeteners (using one-half to three-quarters the amount of sweetener called for) in most recipes, where it adds a unique taste. Sorghum can ferment, so refrigerate it if you do not use it often.

Mustard *(Brassica nigra, B. juncea, Sinapis alba)*

Brassica *is the old classical Latin name for this family of plants. The term* nigra *means black;* juncea *means rush-like;* alba *means white. The English name* mustard *is derived from the Latin* mustum ardens*, or burning must, which refers to the early French practice of grinding the pungent mustard seeds with grape must (the still-fermenting juice of wine grapes).*

General Information There are many varieties of mustard, but the three species used for the condiment are the black (*Brassica nigra*), the brown (*B. juncea*), and the white (*Sinapis alba*). The husk of the black seed is a dark purplish red-brown; the husk of the brown may vary from brown to black, yet also yellow; the husk covering the white seed is actually a pale tan yellow. Black mustard originated in Asia Minor and Iran, and has scarcely been grown for the past twenty-five years because it is difficult to harvest. The brown seed, which originated in the Himalayan area, has replaced the black both in England and America; it is the mustard of North American Chinese restaurants, and certain varieties are grown for salad greens. White mustard is an eastern Mediterranean native. It is the kind used in the ubiquitous American ballpark mustard, dyed bright yellow. All three kinds have become so thoroughly naturalized in North America that they now grow over much of southern Canada and nearly all of the United States. Mustard seeds contain two chemical compounds, myrosin and sinigrin, which when mixed with water produce a volatile oil that may cause skin blisters or burns upon contact. No mustard has either flavor or fire until the cells are broken and water added, and then it takes a few moments for the potency to show and achieve full force.

Lore and Legend

In India, where mustard is symbolic of rebirth or reincarnation, there was a beautiful little temple inhabited by the lovely nymph Bakawali. For twelve years she occupied the temple, but the structure fell into disrepair, was dismantled, and the earth over the site plowed and planted with mustard. One day a young couple, who remained childless despite much prayer and the advice of many wise men, walked by the mustard field and picked some of the leaves to take home. After cooking and eating the leaves, the wife discovered she was pregnant. When the tiny, nymph-like infant was born, she was named Bakawali in honor of the original nymph, who may have changed form once more.

White mustard heats only the tongue; black and brown can also be felt on the tongue, but they rise memorably to the nose, eyes, and even the forehead, with a pungency that is more intense and longer-lasting than the white.

Early Romans pounded mustard seeds and mixed them with wine to make an early version of our table mustard. Dijon mustard, made in Dijon, France, was heavily regulated. Mustard seed had to be soaked in and mixed with only good vinegar and aged for twelve days before it could be ground and sold. After grinding, the husks were filtered out of the wet mustard to create a smooth yellow paste. If the husks are left in and ground fine, mustard is brown, as are coarse mustards from dark seed. Jeremiah Colman, who gave his name to the famous English mustard business, early mastered the skill of grinding mustard fine without heating it and bringing out the oil. His company thrived, and in 1866 Colman's was appointed mustard maker to Queen Victoria.

Buying Tips Mustard can be purchased in either form: greens and seeds. The seeds are available whole; as ground, powdered seeds; and as prepared mustard.

Culinary Uses Mustard is a thoroughly economical plant, as its leaves, flowers, and seed pods are all edible. The most common mustard greens are from brown mustard (*B. juncea*), with soft, slightly fuzzy, thin oval leaves of brilliant parrot or emerald green, frilled or scalloped around the edge, and attached to fairly long stems. They have a taste very similar to that of prepared mustard, with just a hint of radish, and a pleasant perfumy edge. Slivered mustard greens (the stems are not used) lend depth and brilliance to soups, or they can be cooked on their own like spinach and served with butter. Flowers and seed pods can be used in salads to add a bright taste.

The tiny mustard seed provides a disproportionate amount of spicy flavor for its size due to its hot-tasting volatile oils. White mustard seeds are milder than the black variety, and have a pleasant, mild, nutty flavor. Used primarily for mustard powder, they should not be substituted in recipes calling for dark mustard seeds, becuase their flavor is quite different. Mustard seed is used for a wide range of dishes, including curries, cocktail dips, sandwich spreads, relishes, cheese dishes, and dressings. So popular is prepared mustard in the United States that it ranks second only to black pepper. Because of its acidity and salt, a store-bought jar of mustard does not spoil, but slowly loses flavor as well as fire, even in a vacuum-sealed jar. Heat and pungency begin to decline as soon as they reach their peak twenty minutes after mixing. Plan on buying small jars and using quickly, or your mustard will taste more acidic than flavorful.

Mustard

Nutritional Value Per 100 g Edible Portion

	Whole Seed	1 tsp.
Calories	469	15
Protein	24.94 g	0.82 g
Fat	28.76 g	0.95 g
Fiber	6.55 g	0.22 g
Calcium	521 mg	17 mg
Iron	9.98 mg	0.33 mg
Magnesium	298 mg	10 mg
Phosphorus	841 mg	28 mg
Potassium	682 mg	23 mg
Sodium	5 mg	trace
Zinc	5.700 mg	0.190 mg
Copper	0.410 mg	n/a
Manganese	1.767 mg	n/a
Beta Carotene (A)	62 IU	2 IU
Thiamine (B_1)	0.543 mg	0.018 mg
Riboflavin (B_2)	0.381 mg	0.013 mg
Niacin (B_3)	7.890 mg	0.260 mg

Health Benefits Appetizer, counterirritant, digestive, emetic, laxative, rubefacient, stimulant. Mustard is pungent, sharp, penetrating, and oily. It stimulates the appetite, increasing salivation by as much as eight times. Used as a domestic spice, it promotes digestion and neutralizes toxins, as well as prevents indigestion, distension of the abdomen, and the discomfort caused by improper digestion. Mustard contains sulphur, one of the best known treatments for skin diseases, as it rids the blood of excess impurities and slows the activities of the sebaceous glands, which throw off cellular debris. Oil of mustard is a rubefacient, irritating the skin and dilating the small blood vessels underneath. This increases the flow of blood to the skin, turns it red and makes it feel warm, and the increased blood flow carries away any toxic products.

Byproducts

Mustard powder is a mixture of ground brown and white seeds combined with turmeric or saffron, which adds flavor and color. Dry mustard powder can be added to innumerable dishes, and when used sparingly gives an excellent flavor.

Prepared mustard is a ready-to-use blend of mustard seeds, salt, other spices, and vinegar (an acid that acts as a fixative so the mustard retains its strength and flavor). You can easily make your own by boiling together 1 cup of apple cider vinegar, 2 tablespoons of honey, 1/8 teaspoon of turmeric, and 1/2 teaspoon of salt. While the mixture is still hot, pour it into a blender, add 1/2 cup yellow mustard seed, and grind. When it has achieved a smooth consistency, add 1 tablespoon of olive oil.

Nasturtium (*Tropaeolum majus, T. minus*)

Tropaeolum *comes from a Greek word meaning to twine. The terms* majus *and* minus *differentiate the larger and smaller varieties. The English name* nasturtium *is derived from the Latin words* nasus tortus *(a convulsed nose) on account of its pungency.*

General Information Nasturtium is an annual twining vine originally from Peru with decorative, round, light-green leaves and colorful flowers that bloom almost continuously. Both nasturtium and its botanical cousin watercress get their spicy, peppery flavor from mustard oils.

Nasturtium

Nutritional Value Per 100 g Edible Portion	Fresh Leaf/Stalk
Calories	48-350
Protein	1.8-13.2 g
Fat	1.2-8.8 g
Fiber	0.5-3.6 g
Calcium	211-1540 mg
Iron	1.3-9.5 mg
Phosphorus	85-620 mg
Beta Carotene (A)	9.0-66.5 mg
Thiamine (B_1)	0.090-0.650 mg
Riboflavin (B_2)	0.350-2.550 mg
Niacin (B_3)	1.000-7.500 mg
Ascorbic Acid (C)	200-465 mg

Culinary Uses The leaves, petals, and seeds of nasturtium have a crisp, pungent, peppery taste. Stems, leaves, and flowers can be chopped and added to salads, or the leaves can be cooked and served as a vegetable. The brilliantly-hued blossoms make stunning additions to special sandwiches, green salads, or can be floated in bowls of punch for a garnish. The still-green seeds may be pickled in vinegar and served as a substitute for capers.

Health Benefits Antiscorbutic, antiseptic, expectorant, stimulant, tonic. Medicinally, nasturtium builds stronger blood by promoting the formation of blood cells, breaks up congestion in the respiratory passages and chest during colds, is good for nervous depression and constipation, and helps clear the skin and eyes. With its high sulphur content, it is especially good for older people and greatly increases their energy. Nasturtium also has a reputation for arousing sexual appetites.

Nettle, Stinging *(Urtica dioica)*

Urtica is from the Latin uro, meaning to burn. Dioica refers to its dioecious character (having separate male and female plants). The English name nettle is said to derive from the Latin nassa, meaning fish net, because the stems were woven into strong nets.

General Information The stinging nettle is a native of Eurasia. Introduced into America with imported cattle by the first English settlers, it is commonly found in wet waste places. In 1672, the nettle was mentioned in *New England Rarities Discovered*, the first book about the flora and fauna of America. It is a perennial plant with persistent, spreading roots that can grow up to seven feet in height. With bristly hairs on its square stems, sawtoothed leaves, and small clusters of dull greenish flowers sprouting near the joints of the leaves and stems, the common nettle is not the prettiest plant. Easily recognized by anyone who has come into contact with it, each tiny flower and hair contains sharp hypodermic-like points that can easily penetrate the skin and insert their virulent venom derived from formic acid. Generally regarded as an ugly weed, they do have some redeeming characteristics. Nettles are frequently the preferred food of goats, chickens become ecstatic when offered fresh nettles, and when made into hay it makes excellent feed for cattle and horses. In Scotland and in parts of Europe, the nettle was treated much like flax, the fibers making a cloth similar to linen. In World War I, with cotton imports cut off, the Germans utilized nettle for weaving. This should come as no surprise, since nettles are closely related to hemp, which makes a top-quality fiber.

Lore and Legend

In Scandinavian mythology, nettles are sacred to the thunder god Thor. Thus they were thrown on the fire during thunderstorms to protect the home from being destroyed by lightning. When carried about the person, it was believed to give courage to the bearer and drive away fear in times of danger.

Culinary Uses Young shoots and leaves (picked with gloves on) provide a good spring green, cooked in the manner of spinach and served with salt, pepper, and a little vinegar or lemon juice. The leaves are tender, with a rather salty, earthy flavor. A famous pudding made of nettles combined with leeks, broccoli, or cabbage and rice, and then boiled in a muslin bag, comes from Scotland; a nettle cream soup is a specialty in Ireland; and nettle beer is made in regions of Britain. The leaves, with the addition of a little salt, can curdle milk, and can be put to use as a substitute for rennet. The poisonous property of the hair disappears with either cooking or drying.

Health Benefits Diuretic. A number of references to nettle refer to an infusion of the leaves as a treatment for rheumatism. The seeds also have been given as an infusion for coughs and shortness of breath. The high content of iron, silicic acid, and vitamins A and C in young spring

Nettle, Stinging

Nutritional Value Per 100 g Edible Portion

	Dried
Calories	n/a
Protein	10.2 g
Fat	2.3 g
Fiber	n/a
Calcium	2,900 mg
Iron	41.8 mg
Magnesium	860 mg
Phosphorus	447 mg
Potassium	1,750 mg
Sodium	4.9 mg
Zinc	4.70 mg
Manganese	7.80 mg
Beta Carotene (A)	15,700 IU
Thiamine (B_1)	0.540 mg
Riboflavin (B_2)	0.430 mg
Niacin (B_3)	5.200 mg
Ascorbic Acid (C)	83 mg

nettle shoots explains the effectiveness of nettle tea, which is said to be good for kidney disorders and to improve the function of the liver, gallbladder, and intestines. Tea made from the seeds is used in modern herbal medicine as a hair tonic and growth stimulant as well as an anti-dandruff shampoo. An old practice to abate gout and rheumatism was to thrash afflicted joints with nettle shoots; the possible improvement was due to the increased flow of blood to that region. Pressing the boiled leaves against a wound will stop the bleeding and at the same time purify the blood.

Nigella (*Nigella sativa*)

Also Known As: Kalonji.

> Nigella *is the diminutive form of the Latin term* niger, *meaning black, and refers to the color of the seeds;* sativa *means that the plant has long been cultivated.*

General Information Nigella is native to western Asia, the Middle East, and southern Europe, though today it is grown primarily in India. The pretty plant love-in-a-mist, with its feathery foliage and attractive blue flowers, is a very close relative, and the two are frequently called by the same name. This hardy annual grows to about two feet in height, and its seeds must be gathered before they are fully ripe; otherwise, the pods will burst and the seeds will be lost. The seeds are very small and black and look rather like onion seeds.

Nigella

Nutritional Value Per 100 g Edible Portion

	Seed
Protein	21.2-27.2 g
Fat	35.5-41.6 g
Fiber	5.5 g
Calcium	1,060 mg
Iron	14.0 mg
Potassium	582 mg
Sodium	98 mg
Ascorbic Acid (C)	257.7 mg

Culinary Uses The small black seeds are lightly aromatic, with a peppery flavor. They are a familiar ingredient in many spice mixtures of the Indian area and are frequently found sprinkled on breads, including those of Turkey and other Middle Eastern countries. They can usually be purchased in specialty grocery stores under their Indian name, *kalonji*. In Western dishes, use nigella as a pepper substitute; the taste will be slightly more spicy and bitter. To bring out the most flavor, dry-roast the seeds in a skillet before use. Added to buttered vegetables such as zucchini or cabbage, nigella gives an exotic flavor and pleasant crunchy texture.

Nutmeg and Mace (*Myristica fragrans*)

> Myristica *is from the Greek word* myrrha, *which refers to the aromatic qualities of the plant;* fragrans *means fragrant. The English word* nutmeg *derives from the Latin* nux, *meaning nut, and* muscat, *meaning musky;* mace *derives from the Greek* makir.

General Information Nutmeg is native to Indonesia, the dried seed of a fruit resembling a peach or apricot from a slow-growing evergreen tree of the myrtle family. When the nutmeg fruit is harvested, its outer husk is broken open and the red fibrous covering (aril) is separated by hand from the seed shell inside, while the seed kernel (nutmeg) is left to dry inside the shell. The broken pieces of the aril are dried to develop their strong aroma, then ground to make the powder we call mace. If mace comes from

Indonesia, it is generally orange in color, while that from the West Indies is yellowish-brown. Arab traders brought nutmeg to the eastern spice markets and introduced it to European palates, but it took several hundred years for Westerners to develop both taste and pocketbook for this spice. So expensive was this fragrant, nut-like seed that, in the fourteenth century, a pound of it could be exchanged for two calves, three sheep, or half a cow. Where nutmeg is grown, people eat the fruit or preserve it in syrup, but the seed is dried for export.

Buying Tips Nutmeg can be purchased as the whole or ground seed, while mace is available as a ground powder. Whole nutmeg is best, because once ground it rapidly loses its volatile oils, thus altering its flavor.

Culinary Uses Both nutmeg and mace have a warm, sweet, spicy fragrance and warm, slightly sharp, pervasive flavor. Grated nutmeg is used for cakes, custards, pies (especially pumpkin), and in milk puddings, cream soups, and hot drinks. The more pungent mace is used in pickles and preserves, cheese dishes, stewed fruit, and mulled wine, and especially complements dishes with either cherries or chocolate.

Lore and Legend

Because nutmeg was so costly, it became fashionable in Europe for ladies and gentlemen alike to carry their own nutmeg, along with tiny graters. At fashionable eating establishments, the diners would bring out their nutmeg and graters to flavor wine or food. Predictably, since the graters were carried about and displayed when used, special designs and shapes were created. Some were made of silver and embossed, some folded inside a case to be worn as a pendant, some were pierced in intricate patterns, but all imparted to their users a status of fashion-conscious elegance.

Health Benefits Aromatic, carminative, stimulant. Nutmeg is used for general weakness, diarrhea, gas and dull aching pain in the abdomen, for liver and spleen disorders, and for improving appetite and digestion. Taken with milk, it serves as a tonic for the heart, brain, and reproductive organs.

NOTE: Both nutmeg and mace can produce severe toxicity at doses exceeding one teaspoon. Nausea, vomiting, and dizziness accompanied by hallucinations, feelings of unreality, and delusions are some of the symptoms that may develop.

Nutmeg and Mace

Nutritional Value Per 100 g Edible Portion

	Nutmeg Ground	Nutmeg 1 tsp.	Mace Ground	Mace 1 tsp.
Calories	525	12	475	8
Protein	5.84 g	0.13 g	6.71 g	0.11 g
Fat	36.31 g	0.80 g	32.38 g	0.55 g
Fiber	4.02 g	0.09 g	4.77 g	0.08 g
Calcium	184 mg	4 mg	252 mg	4 mg
Iron	3.04 mg	0.07 mg	13.90 mg	0.24 mg
Magnesium	183 mg	4 mg	163 mg	3 mg
Phosphorus	213 mg	5 mg	110 mg	2 mg
Potassium	350 mg	8 mg	463 mg	8 mg
Sodium	16 mg	trace	80 mg	1 mg
Zinc	2.150 mg	0.050 mg	2.300 mg	0.040 mg
Copper	1.027 mg	n/a	2.467 mg	n/a
Manganese	2.900 mg	n/a	1.500 mg	n/a
Beta Carotene (A)	102 IU	2 IU	800 IU	14 IU
Thiamine (B_1)	0.346 mg	0.008 mg	0.312 mg	0.005 mg
Riboflavin (B_2)	0.057 mg	0.001 mg	0.448 mg	0.008 mg
Niacin (B_3)	1.299 mg	0.029 mg	1.350 mg	0.023 mg

Oregano (*Origanum vulgare*)

The botanical name Origanum *means joy of the mountain, derived from the Greek words* oros, *meaning mountain, and* ganos, *meaning joy. Those who have visited Greece, where oregano covers the hillsides and scents the warm summer air, would emphatically agree.* Vulgare *means common or vulgar.*

General Information Oregano is a member of the mint family, a relative of basil and marjoram. Native to Europe, oregano is a branching perennial growing about two feet tall and bearing pink or purple flowers. This "pizza herb" has highly aromatic small leaves and young shoots that can be used fresh like those of sweet marjoram, or dried for later use.

Oregano

Nutritional Value Per 100 g Edible Portion

	Dried	1 tsp.
Calories	306	5
Protein	11.00 g	0.17 g
Fat l	0.25 g	0.15 g
Fiber	14.96 g	0.22 g
Calcium	1,576 mg	24 mg
Iron	44.00 mg	0.66 mg
Magnesium	270 mg	4 mg
Phosphorus	200 mg	3 mg
Potassium	1,669 mg	25 mg
Sodium	15 mg	trace
Zinc	4.430 mg	0.070 mg
Copper	0.943 mg	n/a
Manganese	4.667 mg	n/a
Beta Carotene (A)	6903 IU	104 IU
Thiamine (B_1)	0.341 mg	0.005 mg
Riboflavin (B_2)	n/a	n/a
Niacin (B_3)	6.220 mg	0.093 mg

Culinary Uses Oreganos vary in flavor, from the mild common oregano to the more strongly flavored Greek and Spanish oregano, all the way to Mexican oregano (also known as Mexican marjoram or Mexican wild sage), which is the strongest of all, strong enough to be used in chili powders and dishes flavored with chili peppers. Oregano is often available fresh, which is the preferred form. If the fresh herb is not available, the whole dried leaves are the best remaining alternative. One of the most frequently used dried herbs, oregano has a hot, peppery flavor. Both oregano and its cousin marjoram are popular in Mediterranean cooking and are best known for their appearance in tomato sauce; oregano also enhances mushrooms, eggplant, and zucchini dishes, various salads, pasta sauces, cabbage, broccoli, and onions. Its flavor combines well with those of garlic, thyme, parsley, and olive oil.

Health Benefits Carminative, choleretic, emmenagogue, stimulant, tonic. Oregano will help rid the body of poisons, strengthen the stomach, and expel gas from the gastrointestinal tract. Herbalists have noted that its warming qualities have made it useful as a liniment and rubefacient, and the oil is a frequently mentioned toothache remedy. Oregano also makes a refreshing and invigorating bath additive to treat rheumatic pains and skin infections, in a dilution of two tablespoons dried leaves per two liters of water.

Pandanus Leaf (*Pandanus odorus*)

Also Known As: Screw Pine Leaf.

Pandanus *is the Latinized form of a Malayan name for the plant;* odorus *means fragrant. The alternate name* Screw Pine, *given the plant by European sailors traveling in the South Pacific, leads one to think the plant looks like a pine tree, when in fact it is more akin to palm trees.*

General Information The bush-sized plant produces thin, pointed leaves that are used as a seasoning in Thailand, Malaysia, Indonesia, and elsewhere in southeast Asia. Leaves up to twenty inches in length are increasingly available in Asian produce stands. Look for leaves that are shiny green on one side; they lose luster as they dry and age.

Culinary Uses The flavor is best described as new-mown hay with a floral dimension. Typically one or two leaves are cooked in a sugar syrup that is then strained as a first step in turning out various puddings, cakes, and custards made with rice, tapioca, and even mung bean flours. The leaves color the syrup and resultant product green.

Paprika, Sweet Hungarian (*Capsicum tetragonum*)

Our word capsicum *arrived on the scene in 1700 under the auspices of Joseph Pitton de Tournefort, early plant taxonomist and plant-hunter for the spectacular gardens of Louis XIV. The name is thought to come from either the Latin* capsa, *meaning box, for the hollow box-like shape of the fruit (at least in some cases), or the Greek* kapto, *meaning to bite, for the pepper's acrid tongue-searing pungency.* Tetragonum *means four-angled, referring to the shape of the pods used for this powder. By the 1560s,* capsicum *peppers had reached the Balkans, where they were called* peperke *or* paparka*—and the Hungarians, by a short linguistic jump, had acquired their famed* paprika *by 1569.*

General Information Paprika always refers to a ground product prepared of highly colored, mild red pods of one or more varieties of capsicums used to flavor and color foods. Sweet paprika is mostly pericarp with more than half of the seeds removed, while hot paprika contains some seeds, placenta, calyces, and stalks, depending on the grade. The Hungarian powder is ground from dried pods of the long podded type, and is more pungent than the Spanish paprika, which uses a tomato-shaped pepper.

Culinary Uses Paprika is traditionally used in Hungarian goulash, but is also used in cheese dishes, cocktail dips, dressings, sauces, and soups, or makes an attractive and tasty garnish.

Health Benefits Antibacterial, stimulant. The capsicum in paprika is one of the best stimulants; when the body is properly stimulated, the healing and cleansing process starts, allowing the body to function normally. Paprika normalizes blood pressure, improves the entire circulatory system, boosts secretion of saliva and stomach acids, increases peristaltic movement, and feeds the cell structure of the arteries, veins, and capillaries so they will regain elasticity.

Paprika

Nutritional Value Per 100 g Edible Portion

	Dried	1 tsp.
Calories	289	6
Protein	14.76 g	0.31 g
Fat	12.95 g	0.27 g
Fiber	20.89 g	0.44 g
Calcium	177 mg	4 mg
Iron	23.59 mg	0.50 mg
Magnesium	185 mg	4 mg
Phosphorus	345 mg	7 mg
Potassium	2,344 mg	49 mg
Sodium	34 mg	1 mg
Zinc	4.060 mg	0.080 mg
Copper	0.607 mg	n/a
Manganese	0.843 mg	n/a
Beta Carotene (A)	60,604 IU	1,273 IU
Thiamine (B_1)	0.645 mg	0.014 mg
Riboflavin (B_2)	1.743 mg	0.037 mg
Niacin (B_3)	15.320 mg	0.322 mg
Ascorbic Acid (C)	71.12 mg	1.49 mg

Parsley *(Petroselinum crispum)*

The ancient Greek Dioscorides named this plant petroselinum *from the Greek words* petros, *meaning rock, and* selinon, *meaning celery.* Crispum *means curled;* sativum *refers to the fact that this plant has long been cultivated. The English word* parsley *is a corruption of the original Latin.*

General Information Parsley is believed to be indigenous to Sardinia, Turkey, Algeria, and Lebanon, where it still grows wild. A member of the carrot family, there are more than thirty-seven different varieties, including broad-leaved, curly-leaved, Hamburg and Neapolitan (Italian) parsley. The mild curly-leaf is prettier as a garnish, but the flat-leaf (Italian) is tenderer and has a stronger, more intense flavor.

Culinary Uses Parsley has a tangy, sweet flavor that helps bring out the flavor of other herbs and seasonings, particularly in soups and stews. The stems have a stronger flavor than the leaves, but both are used to flavor sauces, soups, salads, omelets, and stuffings, and can be used as a decorative garnish for virtually any dish. Parsley is also available in the form of dried flakes, although these are nowhere near as good as the fresh. Due to the high vitamin C and iron content of this herb, it should be added to foods whenever possible. Parsley's high chlorophyll content works to absorb odors and thus makes an effective after-dinner breath "mint."

Health Benefits Antispasmodic, carminative, emmenagogue, expectorant, diuretic. Raw parsley facilitates oxygen metabolism, cleanses the blood, dissolves sticky deposits in veins, maintains elasticity of blood vessels, will facilitate removal of

Lore and Legend

Parsley is one of the first herbs to appear in spring, and has been used for centuries in the Seder, the ritual Jewish Passover meal, as a symbol of new beginnings. In Greek mythology, parsley sprang from the blood of Opheltes, infant son of King Lycurgus of Nemea, who was killed by a serpent while his nanny directed some thirsty soldiers to a nearby spring. One of the soldiers, the seer Amphiarus, seeing the child's death as a bad omen predicting his own death in an upcoming battle, gave Opheltes the surname Archemorus, meaning "first to die." For centuries Greek soldiers believed any contact with parsley before battle signaled impending death. Because of this association, parsley was planted on Greek graves, a custom that ironically led to its rehabilitation. To honor the memory of important figures, the Greeks held the Nemean Games, crowning the winners of the athletic contests with wreaths of parsley. Over a few centuries, the herb lost its association with death and came to symbolize strength. The Romans fed it to their horses on the theory that it made them swift, and wore curly-leafed parsley garlands in their hair, not only because they were attractive but because they believed that nibbling on parsley sprigs enabled one to drink more wine without becoming drunk.

In medieval times, parsley was thought to belong to the devil, with Good Friday being the only day of the year on which it could be sown successfully, and then only if the moon was rising. Before the plant would grow, the seed was thought to go to the Devil and back seven times, and would only grow successfully if the woman was master of the household. In Devonshire parsley is considered a most unlucky plant. One may break off a few leaves, for that is of benefit to the plant, but if one should pull up a stalk, even to transplant it, the sprites who guard the parsley-beds would be seriously offended, and would have their revenge by sending death to some member of the family.

Parsley

Nutritional Value Per 100 g Edible Portion

	Fresh, Raw	Dried	1 tsp.	Freeze-Dried	1 Tbsp.
Calories	36	276	1	271	1
Protein	2.97 g	22.42 g	0.07 g	31.30 g	0.13 g
Fat	0.79 g	4.43 g	0.01 g	5.20 g	0.02 g
Fiber	n/a	10.32 g	0.03 g	10.06 g	0.04 g
Calcium	138 mg	1,468 mg	4 mg	176 mg	1 mg
Iron	6.20 mg	97.86 mg	0.29 mg	53.90 mg	0.22 mg
Magnesium	50 mg	249 mg	1 mg	372 mg	1 mg
Phosphorus	58 mg	351 mg	1 mg	548 mg	2 mg
Potassium	554 mg	3,805 mg	11 mg	6,300 mg	25 mg
Sodium	56 mg	452 mg	1 mg	391 mg	2 mg
Zinc	1.070 mg	4.750 mg	0.010 mg	6.110 mg	0.020 mg
Copper	0.149 mg	0.640 mg	n/a	0.459 mg	0.002 mg
Manganese	0.160 mg	10.500 mg	n/a	1.338 mg	0.005 mg
Beta Carotene (A)	5,200 IU	23,340 IU	70 IU	63,240 IU	253 IU
Thiamine (B_1)	0.086 mg	0.172 mg	0.001 mg	1.040 mg	0.004 mg
Riboflavin (B_2)	0.098 mg	1.230 mg	0.004 mg	2.260 mg	0.009 mg
Niacin (B_3)	1.313 mg	7.929 mg	0.024 mg	10.400 mg	0.042 mg
Pantothenic Acid (B_5)	0.400 mg	n/a	n/a	2.516 mg	0.010 mg
Pyridoxine (B_6)	0.090 mg	1.002 mg	0.003 mg	1.375 mg	0.006 mg
Folic Acid (B_9)	152.0 mcg	n/a	n/a	1,535.4 mcg	6.1 mcg
Ascorbic Acid (C)	133.0 mg	122.04 mg	0.37 mg	149.0 mg	0.6 mg
Tocopherol (E)	1.74 mg	n/a	n/a	n/a	n/a

moderately sized kidney stones and gallstones, stimulates the bowel, benefits the sexual system, and stimulates adrenal sections. Chewed after eating a meal heavy in garlic, it will eliminate halitosis (bad breath) due to its chlorophyll content. Parsley tea strengthens the teeth and makes a face lotion to increase circulation and bring color to the skin. Stir one teaspoonful of parsley leaves in a cup of hot water, cool, stir, and strain before drinking or using as a wash.

NOTE: Furocoumarins (toxic crystalline acids) present in the volatile oil are phototoxic, and may cause skin inflammations and contact dermatitis in sensitive individuals.

Pepper, Black *(Piper nigrum)*

Piper *is an ancient Latin name for the plant;* nigrum *means black. The Sanskrit word* pippali *meant berry and also long pepper, and because long pepper (*P. longum*) was at first the most highly regarded pepper,* pippali *is the root of the word* pepper *in European languages.*

General Information Pepper is the small berry of a tropical vining shrub from the Malabar coast of India that for over three thousand years has been the world's most important spice, and was probably the earliest spice known to man. It was first cultivated probably around 1000 B.C., and a thousand years later carried by Hindu immigrants to Malaysia and Indonesia, where it was established in such places as Malacca, Sarawak, Java, Sumatra, and the Moluccas (Spice Islands). The pepper berries are borne on two- to six-inch spikes, fifty to sixty berries per spike. On average, eight to ten thousand black peppercorns make a pound. Pepper was the spice par excellence of the classical world and was well known in Greece by the fifth century B.C., although less for cooking than as an item in the official pharmacopoeia. In medieval Europe it was so precious that it was classed with gold, silver, and gems. **Black peppercorns** are berries that are picked when full-sized but unripe and allowed to dry in the sun to

Lore and Legend

Indian pepper was so important that it was numbered among the five "essential luxuries" on which the whole foreign trade of the Roman empire were said to have been based (the others were Chinese silk, African ivory, German amber, and Arabian incense). Of the five, only pepper came nearest to being a true essential, not because spices were vital to Roman cuisine but because they transformed the food (often quite bland and boring) of everyday life. Many spices influenced the ebb and flow of history, but it was pepper that launched one of the grandest series of dramas in recorded history. Desire for a readier access to pepper and other spices instigated European attempts to find alternative routes to India, and Columbus' search for a western route ended in the discovery of America. Like other spices, peppercorns were valuable because they were small, easily transported, and lasted indefinitely at normal temperatures. So high a price did the spice command in medieval times that it was used in payment of levies and taxes instead of coins. Pepper represented a more stable medium of exchange than gold or silver in days when every petty sovereign (and a number of important cities as well) struck his own coins and only an Archimedes could assess their content of precious metal, even without taking into account the common habit of scraping or clipping some of it off as money passed from hand to hand. Today the phrase "peppercorn rent" is sometimes used to denote a nominal sum, but in late medieval times there was nothing nominal about it; a pound of pepper was the barter equivalent of two or three weeks' labor on the land, and worth a pound of gold. The habit even arose in medieval times of expressing a man's wealth not in terms of the amount of land in his estate, but of the amount of pepper in his pantry. One way of saying a man was poor was to say that he lacked pepper. The wealthy kept large stores of pepper in their houses, and let it be known that it was there: it was a guarantee of solvency. In 408 A.D. Alaric, king of the Visigoths, demanded three thousand pounds of pepper as part of the ransom for the city of Rome.

develop their color and flavor. The outer flesh, which contains most of the aromatic power of the spice, shrinks to become the wrinkled black skin; the blackening is caused by enzymes within the berries. **White peppercorns** are berries that are allowed to mature to their fully ripe red stage before being picked; after harvesting they are soaked in water, washed of the soft outer layer to reveal the smooth whitish core, and allowed to dry and bleach in the sun. **Green peppercorns** are harvested in their green unripe stage and packed in vinegar or brine, or else freeze-dried or dehydrated. The dehydrated green peppercorns are more flavorful than the freeze-dried and are preferred for pepper mills. The spiciness and moderate heat of green peppercorns suggest a less concentrated version of black pepper (which is picked at the same stage). **Red** or **Pink peppercorns** come from *Schinus terebinthifolius*, a plant called variously the Brazilian pepper tree, Christmas berry, and Florida holly. This plant is native to Brazil and has become a pest in Florida. The dried spice is usually slightly larger than a peppercorn, with the red to pink skin dried to a thin brittle shell loosely surrounding a single seed. The flavor is at first sweet, almost citrusy, and then somewhat menthol and resinous; there is slight bitterness and little if any heat. These novelty peppercorns have caused adverse reactions in some people, and for a time were banned from sale by the FDA.

Culinary Uses Although not as ubiquitous as water or salt, pepper is probably the third most common addition to food. Pepper can be purchased as whole peppercorns, or ground into a powder. Whole peppercorns hold their flavor and volatile oils better than ground pepper, which eventually begins to taste bitter. Black pepper has a very characteristic fragrant aroma with a hot, biting, pungent flavor; white pepper is somewhat milder and more warmly aromatic than the black. Green peppercorns have a fresh and pungent flavor and are usually sold pickled in brine. Pepper flavors nearly all dishes other than desserts, and though it needs to be used sparingly, can make an enormous difference to the flavor of foods. Lacking the strictly defined personalities of most other spices, pepper enhances and at the same time is submissive. It blends easily with meat, fish, and vegetables; its heat teases gently, and burns only when used in ludicrous quantities. Freshly ground pepper is a must, as the aromatic qualities of pepper are fleeting, and pepper turns bitter if pre-ground too far in advance. As a general rule, white pepper is added for aesthetic reasons to pale-colored foods and sauces where little specks of black pepper would spoil the appearance. Whole peppercorns are added to pickles, marinades, and bouillon.

Another beneficial use of pepper is as a pest deterrent. Pepper contains piperine, which is a natural insecticide considered

Pepper

Nutritional Value Per 100 g Edible Portion

	Black, Whole	1 tsp.	White, Whole	1 tsp.
Calories	255	5	296	7
Protein	10.95 g	0.23 g	10.40 g	0.25 g
Fat	3.26 g	0.07 g	2.12 g	0.05 g
Fiber	13.13 g	0.28 g	4.34 g	0.10 g
Calcium	437 mg	9 mg	265 mg	6 mg
Iron	28.86 mg	0.61 mg	14.31 mg	0.34 mg
Magnesium	194 mg	4 mg	90 mg	2 mg
Phosphorus	173 mg	4 mg	176 mg	4 mg
Potassium	1,259 mg	26 mg	73 mg	2 mg
Sodium	44 mg	1 mg	5 mg	trace
Zinc	1.420 mg	0.030 mg	1.130 mg	0.030 mg
Copper	1.127 mg	n/a	0.910 mg	n/a
Manganese	5.625 mg	n/a	4.300 mg	n/a
Beta Carotene (A)	190 IU	4 IU	trace	n/a
Thiamine (B_1)	0.109 mg	0.002 mg	0.022 mg	0.001 mg
Riboflavin (B_2)	0.240 mg	0.005 mg	0.126 mg	0.003 mg
Niacin (B_3)	1.142 mg	0.024 mg	0.212 mg	0.005 mg

more toxic to houseflies than pyrethrins, the natural insecticide derived from chrysanthemums. Black pepper has been proven toxic against a number of agricultural and household pests, including ants, potato bugs, silverfish, and some roaches and moths. To protect your plants, spray them with a solution of one-half teaspoon freshly ground pepper in one quart of warm water. Or sprinkle ground pepper in areas insects frequent.

Health Benefits Stimulant. Most commercial ground pepper is roasted and is an irritant rather than a stimulant. Make your own fresh ground pepper with a pepper mill and whole peppercorns. Because pepper is hot and pungent, it acts as a digestive stimulant, increasing the secretion of digestive juices,improving the taste of food, and alleviating that uncomfortable heavy feeling after a large meal. Meanwhile, it irritates the mucous membranes inside the nose and throat, causing them to weep a watery secretion that makes it easier to cough up mucus or blow the nose. Pepper also makes you perspire, and because perspiration acts as a natural air conditioner, cooling the body as the moisture evaporates from the skin, peppery foods are popular in warm climes. Pepper has demonstrated impressive antioxidant and antibacterial properties. The overuse of pepper, however, can provoke chronic hypersecretion followed by a burning sensation in the stomach. A pinch of pepper mixed with ghee and applied externally relieves disorders such as dermatitis and hives.

Pepper, Indian Long *(Piper longum)*

Piper *is an ancient Latin name for the plant;* longum *means long. The Sanskrit word* pippali *meant berry and also long pepper, and because long pepper (*P. longum*) was at first the most highly regarded pepper,* pippali *is the root of the word* pepper *in European languages.*

General Information Indian long pepper is native to India. The philosopher Theophrastus, pupil of Aristotle along with Alexander the Great, wrote, "Pepper is a fruit, and there are two kinds. One is round . . . and it is reddish; the other is elongated and black and has seeds like those of a poppy. And this kind is much stronger than the other" (Behr, *The Artful Eater*, p. 68). The entire pod of long pepper is used as the spice; it is about an inch and a half long, less than a quarter inch wide, and slightly tapered. Like black pepper, it is harvested unripe and dried in the sun. Long pepper was much more common in ancient and medieval times than today, probably because white and black pepper were scarcer. It is possible to find long pepper in Indian markets if you ask in the stores that specialize in food from the Bombay region, or in southeast Asian markets.

Culinary Uses and **Health Benefits** The sweet smell of ground long pepper gives no warning of its hot pungency. The taste suggests something of black pepper, wintergreen, cinnamon, and clove. Someone once compared it to the candies called Red Hots. The unripe dried berry is used mainly in parts of India and Indonesia, where it is added whole to curries and pickles.

Peppergrass (*Lepidium virginicum*)

Also Known As: Cress, Land Cress, Bird's Pepper.

The botanical term Lepidium *is a Greek term meaning little scales, alluding to the small flat pods;* virginicum *means from Virginia. The English name* peppergrass *comes from its taste.*

General Information Peppergrass is an annual herb of the mustard family that grows in temperate to hot climates. The foliage and pods have an aromatic peppery flavor; the herbage of some species is used as a salad herb, and the pods are sometimes fed to tame birds (whence the name "bird's pepper").

Culinary Uses The spicy, pungent flavor of peppergrass leaves and seeds greatly enhances soups, coleslaws and salads, green drinks, seed- or nut-meat loaves, and pizzas. It should be added when the dish is ready to serve, as it should not be cooked.

Health Benefits Herbalists use peppergrass to clear lung congestion.

Peppergrass

Nutritional Value Per 100 g Edible Portion

	Raw	Cooked
Calories	32	23
Protein	2.60 g	1.90 g
Fat	0.70 g	0.60 g
Fiber	1.10 g	0.90 g
Calcium	81 mg	61 mg
Iron	1.30 mg	0.80 mg
Magnesium	n/a	n/a
Phosphorus	76 mg	48 mg
Potassium	606 mg	353 mg
Sodium	14 mg	8 mg
Beta Carotene (A)	9,300 IU	7,700 IU
Thiamine (B_1)	0.080 mg	0.060 mg
Riboflavin (B_2)	0.260 mg	0.160 mg
Niacin (B_3)	1.000 mg	0.800 mg
Pyridoxine (B_6)	0.247 mg	n/a
Ascorbic Acid (C)	69.0 mg	23.0 mg
Tocopherol (E)	0.70 mg	n/a

Plantain (*Plantago major, P. media*)

The botanical name Plantago *has as a root element the Latin word* planta, *meaning the sole of the foot, and referring to the broad shape of the leaves.* Major *means large or great, referring to the leaf size;* media *means medium or intermediate. The English name* plantain *is a corruption of the Latin* plantago.

General Information Plantain is a humble perennial Eurasian weed with an ancient reputation in both Oriental, European, and Native American medicine. There are many varieties of plantain, but the most familiar is common plantain (*P. major*), characterized by its rosette of ribbed, ovate leaves and spiked stalk. This variety is commonly found in waste places, lawns, dooryards, and roadsides all over North America and Europe. Another variety (*P. psyllium*), known as psyllium seed, is becoming more well known, as the seeds are used for medicinal purposes and are frequent ingredients in laxatives and intestinal cleansing products. See psyllium's separate reference under **Nuts, Seeds, and Oils.**

Plantain

Nutritional Value Per 100 g Edible Portion

	Fresh
Protein	18.8 g
Fat	10.0-22.0 g
Fiber	19.0 g
Potassium	460 mg
Ascorbic Acid (C)	trace

Culinary Uses Plantain's young tender leaves have a sour-sharp taste, and are used in salads or lightly steamed like spinach.

Health Benefits Antiseptic, astringent, demulcent, expectorant, hemostatic, vulnerary. The medicinal part of plantain is contained in the broad, ribbed leaves; these contain such an effective soothing, mucilaginous fluid that a poultice made of the freshly bruised or ground leaves applied to wounds and sores will often check bleeding. Not only is plantain excellent for cuts, skin infections, and chronic skin problems, but the freshly crushed leaves are used on stings and bites, and will give relief when rubbed on poison ivy. They also contain tannin, and are thus an astringent or able to draw tissues together. Plantain is an excellent blood purifier, and works to improve the functioning of the kidneys. It also helps prevent gas and diarrhea.

Lore and Legend

According to legend, plantain was once a maiden who spent so much time by the roadside watching and waiting for her absent lover that she eventually was transformed into this common roadside plant. The ancient Saxon Alfric's leech book *Lacuna* considered plantain one of the nine sacred herbs, while for early Christians the plant symbolized the well-trodden path of the multitude who sought Christ. American Indians called it White Man's Foot because the plant, resembling miniature cattails to some extent, seemed to follow the white settlers wherever they went.

Purslane *(Portulaca oleracea)*

Also Known As: Pussley, Indian Cress, Portulaca, Verdolaga.

Portulaca *is most likely derived from the Latin* porto, *to carry, and* lac, *milk, ultimately meaning "milk carrier," due to the plant's milky sap.* Oleracea *means oleraceous, or a vegetable garden herb used in cooking. The English name* purslane *is derived from the Latin* portulaca.

General Information A native of India and Africa, purslane was introduced into Europe by the Arabs as a salad plant during the fifteenth century. There are two varieties of purslane: the wild form is a sprawling plant that grows no more than two inches high and has reddish-green or purple-tinted stems with greenish purple leaves; cultivated purslane has larger leaves of a golden yellowish color. Both varieties have thick fleshy branches and succulent stems that ooze milky fluid when squeezed. During colonial times, it was naturalized in America and has spread over this country and into Mexico and South America, acting like a native in the southwestern United States. The purslane most favored by the North American Indians is the white mountain rose or bitterroot (*Lewisia rediviva*), discussed separately.

Culinary Uses Purslane has a sharp yet not unpleasant taste similar to watercress that blends well with other herbs. The leafy new growth is the tastiest part to eat. In salads, purslane leaves are delicious, and the yellow-leafed variety adds a spark of color.

Purslane

Nutritional Value Per 100 g Edible Portion

	Raw	Cooked
Calories	16	18
Protein	1.30 g	1.49 g
Fat	0.10 g	0.19 g
Fiber	0.80 g	0.81 g
Calcium	65 mg	78 mg
Iron	1.99 mg	0.77 mg
Magnesium	68 mg	67 mg
Phosphorus	44 mg	37 mg
Potassium	494 mg	488 mg
Sodium	45 mg	44 mg
Beta Carotene (A)	1,320 IU	1,852 IU
Thiamine (B_1)	0.047 mg	0.031 mg
Riboflavin (B_2)	0.112 mg	0.090 mg
Niacin (B_3)	0.480 mg	0.460 mg
Ascorbic Acid (C)	21.0 mg	10.5 mg

The whole plant can be used if cooked as a green; boil or steam for only five minutes and serve garnished with butter and a touch of lemon. It also goes well in stir-fries, or is delicious pickled. Purslane's mucilaginous texture gives it thickening power and makes a welcome addition to many soups; use it instead of okra in gumbos and creole dishes.

Health Benefits Antiscorbutic. Purslane leaves contain tannin, phosphates, urea, and various minerals. They have been used to counteract inflammation and destroy bacteria in bacillary dysentery, diarrhea, and hemorrhoids.

Rose and Rose Hip *(Rosa pomifera, R. rugosa, R. canina)*

Also Known As: Brier Rose, Dog Rose.

The genus name Rosa *is derived from the Greek word* rodon, *meaning red.* Pomifera *means bearing pome-like fruits;* rugosa *means rugose or wrinkled;* canina *means pertaining to a dog. The epithet* dog *is only incidentally derogatory, coming originally from the* cynorrodon *of Pliny and* Rosa canina *of the Middle Ages after a supposed ability of the root to cure "mad-dog bites" or rabies.*

General Information Prized since the dawn of history, the rose is queen of the flowers. But in herbal healing, this plant becomes noteworthy only after the velvety petals have fallen away, revealing the rusty-colored, cherry-shaped rose hips or "false fruit" left after the bloom has died—"false fruit" because in fact the fruits are inside it, each one containing a seed. Almost all varieties of roses produce valuable hips, but only some of those produced are pleasant tasting. The others are inclined to be astringent. The best rose hips come from the rugosa rose. Pick fruits when they are fully colored. Do not allow them to become overripe (soft and wrinkled). The plant became important during World War II, because Britain was short of the fruit providing vitamin C, and schoolchildren were sent to gather rose hips so that the hips could be boiled down to make a syrup issued as a dietary supplement.

Rose Hip

Nutritional Value Per 100 g Edible Portion

	Hips, Dried
Calories	341
Protein	13.3 g
Fat	1.9 g
Fiber	30.0 g
Calcium	810 mg
Iron	trace
Magnesium	139 mg
Phosphorus	256 mg
Potassium	827 mg
Sodium	4,600 mg
Zinc	trace
Manganese	4.000 mg
Beta Carotene (A)	7,015 IU
Thiamine (B_1)	0.380 mg
Riboflavin (B_2)	0.720 mg
Niacin (B_3)	6.800 mg
Ascorbic Acid (C)	740 mg

Culinary Uses The small apple-like rose hips have a pleasant flavor that is both fruity and spicy, almost cranberrylike, and many people enjoy eating them fresh, straight off the bush. They are best when left on the bush until the first frost has touched them, and then picked when bright red and slightly soft to the touch. The seeds inside the vase-like receptacle of the fruit are covered with small, irritating hairs (used by mischievous schoolchildren to make an itching powder) and should be removed. Rose hips are used to make syrups, jellies and jams, teas, wines, soups (especially in Scandinavian cultures), purees, pies, tarts, quick breads, and muffins. Fresh rose petals and leaves tossed either in or on top of a fruit or vegetable salad provide elegance as well as extra nutrition. Petals can also be used in omelets, fried in batter, crystallized, or made into jam. The Arab countries have many sweets made with roses, and in the eighteenth century there was a rage for dousing everything with rosewater, from meats to sauces.

Lore and Legend

According to Greek myth, one cloudy morning Chloris, the deity of flowers, walked through the woods and found the body of a beautiful nymph. Saddened to see such a lovely creature deprived of life, she decided to transform the nymph into a beautiful flower surpassing all others in charm and beauty. She called on the other deities to help with her task: Aphrodite, to give beauty; the three Graces, to bestow brilliance, joy, and charm; her husband Zephyrus, the West Wind, to blow away the clouds so that Apollo, the Sun, could send his blessing through his rays; and Dionysius, the deity of wine, to give nectar and fragrance. When the new flower was finished, the gods rejoiced over its charming beauty and delicate scent. Chloris collected a diadem of dewdrops and crowned the new flower queen of all flowers. Aphrodite then presented the rose to her son Eros, the deity of love. The white rose became the symbol of charm and innocence, and the red rose of love and desire. When Eros in turn gave the rose to Harpocrates, the deity of silence, to induce him to conceal the weaknesses of the gods (especially the amorous affairs of his mother), the rose became the emblem of silence and secrecy. A rose hung in a room or over a table meant that all information spoken was to be kept secret or *sub rosa*—under the rose.

There is another pretty legend about the rose, this one Rumanian, of a princess going to bathe in her garden pool. The Sun, passing overhead, fell so in love with her beauty that he stopped still in the heavens to watch her. Hours passed, and there he remained. This fretted the Moon, for she wanted her own chance to parade across the sky; complaining, she approached the god of Night and Day, who promptly changed the princess into a rosebush, so the Sun would go on about his business. The roses were originally white, but when the Sun appeared the next day those nearest him began to blush; and at midday, under his ardent rays, the topmost ones blushed deeply—thus the Rumanians have white, pink, and red roses. The Greeks relate that it was Cupid, dancing among them one day, who dashed a goblet of wine over some of them and stained them red. Another legend says that roses were stained red from the blood of Aphrodite, who pricked her foot on a thorn while trying to aid her beloved dying Adonis. The Turks, on the other hand, claim the red rose is stained from the blood of Muhammad; Christian legend says the red rose is colored from the blood of martyrs. The thorns are also attributed to Cupid who, flying over the garden, saw one very lovely rose and alighted to kiss it. However, there was a bee within which angrily stung him on the lip. Crying with indignity, he flew to his mother for comfort; she gave him a quiver of arrows tipped with captive bees, and he shot them at the bush, their stings remaining to this day as thorns on the roses.

Roses were a favorite of the ancient Egyptians, who used the fragrant petals as air fresheners and rose water as perfume. When Cleopatra invited Mark Anthony to her palace, she had the floors covered knee-deep in rose petals so that their scent would rise above him as he walked toward her—such was her belief in the romantic powers of their perfume. In Greece and Rome, the rose was the favorite flower of the goddess of the flowers, the Greek Chloris, and her Roman counterpart Flora. In festivals for these goddesses, people bedecked themselves and their animals with flowers, using mostly roses. At Roman banquets roses were used lavishly for decoration; the Emperor Nero once used millions of the blooms to decorate a hall for a single banquet, with rose water-saturated pigeons fluttering overhead to sprinkle the guests with scent. For Teutonic peoples, the rose was the flower of the northern goddess of love, Freyja, who was known for her ability to keep secrets. In Scandinavia the rosebush is under the special protection of elves and dwarfs, and it is only by gently asking their permission for each flower taken that one may gather the roses; but one must never pluck a leaf, for it is the leaves that hide the elves from mortal eyes.

A rose by any name signifies joy, beauty, and love; its perfect blossom is associated with love, beauty, youth, perfection, and even immortality; its thorns with the pain of love and guilt; its withering blossom with the ephemeral nature of beauty and youth. The specific meaning of roses depends on the color of the flower: red is for passion and desire; pink for simplicity and happy love; white for innocence and purity; yellow for jealousy and perfect achievement.

Lore and Legend

Rosemary's legendary origin is in the steep, barren cliffs of Sicily, where the evil Woman of Etna cast a jealous spell over the island, destroying love and peace and causing only the poisonous mandrake, henbane, and belladonna to grow. The people despaired, and the surrounding sea grew turbulent in anger, but so great was the Woman of Etna's power that she quelled the ocean's rage. But as the last wave crashed upon the cliffs, a maiden was drawn back into the swirling waters crying "Remember, remember;" with these words, where her fingers grappled helplessly with the wet rocks, a beautiful plant burst forth—the rosemary.

Rosemary's ability to preserve meats led to the belief that it helped preserve memory, and Greek students frequently wore garlands of rosemary when going into examinations. It was believed that rosemary would only grow in the gardens of righteous people, and because it was associated with memory, became the symbol of fidelity, friendship, and affectionate remembrance. Rosemary was also deemed popular with the fairy and elfin folk: should a mortal be so fortunate as to find a four-leaf clover that some fairy has touched and thus given magic sight in passing, he might see whole rows of young fairies perched on rosemary branches while their elders danced amid the thyme.

Steeped in Christian tradition, rosemary has a place as a symbol of fidelity and remembrance in two of the holiest of Christian ceremonies: weddings and funerals. Sprigs were dipped in scented water, and then woven into bridal bouquets or exchanged by the newlyweds as a token of their troth; sprigs were also richly gilded and bound in multicolored ribbons, then presented to the wedding guests as reminders of love and virtuous fidelity. At funerals, rosemary sprigs were tossed into the grave as a pledge that the life and good deeds of the departed would not soon be forgotten. Regarded as a powerful defense against evil, sprigs were frequently placed in churches and even used as incense.

The flowers of this pleasant herb were once a dull white, according to Spanish legend. When the Virgin Mary and the Christ child were fleeing from the soldiers of Herod, a thick stand of rosemary bushes parted to enable them to take shelter and rest. Mary remained in that sheltered spot for some time, the sweet pungence of rosemary's fragrance so reviving her that as she left she bestowed upon the flowers the glorious color of her light blue mantle. The flowers were then called the roses of Mary or rosemary. For centuries people thought that a rosemary plant would grow no higher than six feet in thirty-three years, so as not to stand taller than Christ.

Health Benefits Antiscorbutic. Rose hips are an important source of vitamin C. Do not bring them into contact with any metal except stainless steel, for they will quickly lose their color and the precious store of vitamin C will be depleted. They also contain a high amount of carotene (vitamin A precursor), vitamin P (bioflavonoids), B-complex vitamins, and rutin. Rose hips are excellent for the skin, help stop infection, dizziness, cramps, colds, stress, and are also known to be a blood purifier. Rose hip tea is made by boiling or steeping one teaspoonful of the crushed hips per one cup of water, which is then poured through a sieve to remove the irritating hairs on the fruits. Four to six cups of this tea may be drunk daily. A handful of rose petals thrown into the bath will do wonders for rheumatic pains. Symptoms of sore and irritated eyes are relieved by steeping a few rose petals in a cup of hot water; this is carefully filtered and the liquid applied to each eye four or five times a day. Rose vinegar can be prepared (a handful of fresh rose petals steeped in vinegar) and used as a rub, cleansing the skin, and acting as a disinfectant for pimples and sores.

Rosemary *(Rosmarinus officinalis)*

The botanical name Rosmarinus *comes from the Latin words* ros, *meaning dew, and* marinus, *of the sea. Like the fabled rosmarine, a walrus-like creature that scaled ocean cliffs to feed on the dew, rosemary thrives best on "dew of the sea." Sometime during the Middle Ages the word* rosmarinus *was changed to* rosemary *in honor of Mary, the mother of Jesus, whose name was then linked to the flower.* Officinalis *means of the workshop, alluding to apothecaries' shops, and signifying that the plant was once part of the official pharmacopeia of Rome.*

General Information Rosemary is an evergreen shrub of the mint family native to the Mediterranean region, where it often grows by the ocean, a fact which is reflected in its botanical name. It likes arid growing conditions and seems to prefer watering only by the evanescent humidity that drifts in from the sea; it is true that rosemary is never so richly flavored as when it grows by the ocean. This relative of basil and oregano often grows to heights of six feet, with dark green, silver-tipped, aromatic leaves that look like tiny pine needles. A natural insecticide, rosemary protects other plants in the garden by its presence, and sachets of rosemary, either alone or in combination with lavender and ground lemon peel, will repel moths if placed throughout the wardrobe.

Rosemary

Nutritional Value Per 100 g Edible Portion

	Dried	1 tsp.
Calories	331	4
Protein	4.88 g	0.06 g
Fat	15.22 g	0.18 g
Fiber	17.65 g	0.21 g
Calcium	1,280 mg	15 mg
Iron	29.25 mg	0.35 mg
Magnesium	220 mg	3 mg
Phosphorus	70 mg	1 mg
Potassium	955 mg	11 mg
Sodium	50 mg	1 mg
Zinc	3.230 mg	0.040 mg
Copper	0.550 mg	n/a
Manganese	1.867 mg	n/a
Beta Carotene (A)	3,128 IU	38 IU
Thiamine (B_1)	0.514 mg	0.006 mg
Riboflavin (B_2)	n/a	n/a
Niacin (B_3)	1.000 mg	0.012 mg
Ascorbic Acid (C)	61.22 mg	0.74 mg

Culinary Uses Rosemary contains oil of camphor, which gives it a wonderful scent and pleasantly pungent flavor, sometimes described as a cross between sage and lavender with a touch of ginger. These small needle-shaped leaves are used fresh; they should be crushed or minced to bring out their full flavor before sprinkling over or rubbing into foods. Whole sprigs can be placed in olive oil for an excellent alternative to butter, and the pale blue flowers make a wonderful addition to salads. Being extremely versatile, its fame spreads from breads and meats to jams and desserts, and it especially complements the herbs bay, chervil, chives, parsley, and thyme in recipes. Store-bought dried rosemary has lost most of its oil and fragrance.

Health Benefits Antiseptic, aromatic, astringent, carminative, diaphoretic, emmenagogue, nervine, stimulant, tonic. Rosemary has a reputation for miracles that is not totally unjustified, for the herb has a wide spectrum of powers. Due to its high essential oil content, rosemary has many effects similar to those of other members of the mint family. It helps alleviate nervous conditions, headaches, and respiratory troubles, corrects and improves the function of the liver and gall bladder, strengthens and tones the muscles of the stomach, acts to raise blood pressure and improve circulation, and even helps with potency disturbances. Its diuretic action is effective in alleviating rheumatism and gout, as well as kidney stones. Like thyme, rosemary makes a healthful tea that can be drunk throughout the day with tangible benefits. The tea, because of the oils, is also wonderful for the hair if applied externally as a rinse; it combats dandruff and makes hair more manageable and easier to comb, as well as stimulating new growth. Rosemary has cleansing and antiseptic properties when burned, similar to juniper and cedar. During World War II in French hospitals, rosemary and juniper were used as incense to kill germs in the air. A sprig of rosemary in the bath water is highly stimulating (some even find it works as an aphrodisiac), and is invaluable in the treatment of slow-healing wounds and rheumatic pains. Rosemary is high in easily assimilable calcium and benefits the entire nervous system.

Rue (*Ruta graveolens*)

The name Ruta *derives from the Greek word* reuo, *meaning to set free, due to its efficaciousness in various diseases;* graveolens *means heavy-scented. The English name* rue *comes from a mistaken association with the verb to rue, or have regret.*

General Information Rue is native to southern Europe and northern Africa, and was introduced into Britain by the Romans, who needed it to flavor their wine. A hardy evergreen, rue tends to be shrubby in growth but reaches about three feet in height. Glands distributed over the entire plant contain a volatile oil that accounts for both its unusual smell and bitter taste. This distinctive fragrance is found pleasant and attractive by some, while others find it objectionable. The oil has the odd power of photo-sensitizing the skin of some people, causing small water blisters to break out.

Rue

Nutritional Value Per 100 g Edible Portion

	Fresh
Fat	37.0 g
Beta Carotene (A)	94.4 mg
Ascorbic Acid (C)	479 mg

Culinary Uses Rue has a strong aromatic scent and a pungent acrid taste. Young chopped leaves can be added to salads in small quantities as a strong seasoning. The most common use for rue is for the leaves to be ground up and used as a bug deterrent.

Health Benefits Antispasmodic, aromatic, emmenagogue, irritant, stimulant, stomachic, tonic. Aromatic rue is a valuable stimulant and tonic when taken in small doses only, relieving flatulence and congestion of the uterus, and beneficial in menstrual difficulties. It has also been employed as an anthelmintic (to destroy intestinal worms), and the oil used externally as a rubefacient. The medicinally important flavonol rutin was isolated for the first time from rue, thus its name.

NOTE: This plant should not be boiled, used if you are pregnant, nor used in large doses as it can cause violent gastrointestinal pains and vomiting, possible abortion, and toxic poisoning. Contact with the sap from the cut stems may cause a skin rash or edema in sensitive people.

Lore and Legend

The Greeks regarded rue as an anti-magical herb, because it served to remedy the nervous indigestion, attributed to witchcraft, that they suffered when eating before strangers. They also wore rue as protection against spells and the evil eye. According to mythology, it was the herb given to Ulysses by Mercury to overcome the charms of Circe, as an antidote for her potion and a preserver of chastity. During the Middle Ages, rue was grown in monastery gardens because of its ability to counteract amatory tendencies, and its use prescribed for monks who wished to preserve their purity. Shakespeare called it the Herb of Grace, because at one time holy water was sprinkled from brushes bound from rue at the ceremony "Asperges," usually preceding Sunday celebration of High Mass. It was also used for many centuries as an antidote to poisons, insect bites, and infections, with judges carrying it into court as one of a bouquet of herbs to guard them against infection from prisoners. In the first century B.C., King Mithradates VI of Asia Minor apparently ate rue to immunize himself against being poisoned by enemies, taking the herb in gradually increasing doses. However, this scheme worked so well that it backfired when he attempted suicide by poisoning himself and failed—in the end, he had to persuade a slave to stab him. Both Leonardo da Vinci and Michelangelo claimed that, owing to rue's metaphysical powers, their eyesight and creative inner vision had been improved.

Saffron (*Crocus sativus*)

The Latin genus Crocus *is from* krokos, *the Greek name for the plant.* Sativus *refers to the fact that this plant has long been cultivated. The Arabs, who introduced the cultivation of the saffron crocus into Spain as an article of commerce, bequeathed to us its modern title of* zafara, *or* saffron.

General Information Saffron is a small perennial plant native to Asia Minor. Cilicia was its most abundant area of cultivation, Sicily produced a good deal of it, but Mount Tobus in Phrygia was, in the general opinion, the site which produced the best saffron of the ancient world. Saffron is supposed to have entered China when that country was invaded in the thirteenth century by the Mongols, who made considerable use of it in their cooking. The cultivation of saffron was well established in Rome before the birth of Christ, and Pliny the Elder notes that it was an important product of Sicily by the year A.D. 1. A valuable (and extremely costly) dye plant in early Europe and the Orient, saffron produced golden-yellow cloth for the exclusive use of the rich and noble. The plant is now cultivated in many places, but particularly in France, Spain, Sicily, and Iran. The spice saffron, made from the dried stigmas, is said to be the most expensive spice in the world. Each saffron flower has only three stigmas, which must be handpicked as soon as the flowers open. It takes nearly one hundred thousand flowers to yield enough flat, tubular, threadlike stigmas to make two pounds of dried saffron; over 4,300 flowers are necessary for just one ounce. Paradoxically, this expensive spice is prevalent in the diets of the Pennsylvania Dutch. Since they grow their own saffron and eat it themselves, however, its price on the world market is a negligible factor. Schwenkfelder cake, a recipe found in almost all Pennsylvania Dutch cookbooks, comes from the Schwenkfelder family, who emigrated to the United States in the eighteenth century, bringing with them the materials of the business they had been pursuing in Germany—growing saffron. Saffron flourished in their new home, and the Schwenkfelders and their neighbors acquired such a taste for it that today it is one of the most common spices in Pennsylvania Dutch country.

Saffron

Nutritional Value Per 100 g Edible Portion

	Dried	1 tsp.
Calories	310	2
Protein	11.43 g	0.08 g
Fat	5.85 g	0.04 g
Fiber	3.87 g	0.03 g
Calcium	111 mg	1 mg
Iron	11.10 mg	0.08 mg
Phosphorus	252 mg	2 mg
Potassium	1,724 mg	12 mg
Sodium	148 mg	1 mg
Copper	0.328 mg	n/a
Manganese	28.408 mg	n/a

Culinary Uses Saffron is available as either whole or ground threads, with the whole thread having the best flavor and least chance of being adulterated. True saffron has a characteristic penetrating scent with a spicy, aromatic, pungent, and slightly bitter taste. Very little is required to give color and flavor to food; too much saffron overpowers and borders on an unpleasant medicinal flavor. Commercial saffron is frequently adulterated due to its cost; turmeric can be used as an inexpensive substitute. Saffron is a traditional ingredient in the classic Spanish dish "paella," and is also used in soups, rice dishes, cakes, and biscuits.

Lore and Legend

According to Greek legend, the crocus flower was born of the unfulfilled love of a beautiful youth called Crocus. Consumed by his ardor for a beautiful shepherdess of the hills named Smilax, Crocus pined away and died. Upon his death, the gods changed him into the flower which bears his name. The orange-yellow tones of its dyestuff have held sacred positions in widespread areas of the world. The gods, goddesses, heroes, and nymphs of Greek myths and poetry wore robes dyed golden-yellow with saffron. Then there are the saffron robes of the Buddhist monks; the saffron cloaks once worn by Irish kings; and the saffron shirts alloted to noblemen of the Hebrides through the seventeenth century. The ancients often used this flower to adorn their marriage beds because according to the Greek poet Homer, the crocus plant was one of the flowers of which the couch of Zeus and Hera was composed. In ancient Rome during the time of Nero, the crocus was considered to be a great cordial, a tonic for the heart, and a potent love potion. The luxury-loving Romans of that time were so fond of the blossom that they would strew them throughout their banquet halls, fountains, and the small streams that flowed through their gardens and courtyards, filling the air with a beautiful fragrance.

Returning Crusaders introduced the saffron crocus to the table of King Henry I of England (1068–1135), who quickly became very fond of it. When the court ladies started to use up the entire saffron supply to dye their hair, the King forbade this use of his favorite spice by severe punishment. In the fifteenth century, Henry VIII made two demands at his royal table: enormous quantities of food, and dishes flavored with saffron. To eliminate much of the competitive demand for this scarce spice, he issued an edict banning the practice of using saffron to dye beards and hair orange (they soon found a suitable substitute—marigold). He also forbade the Irish to use saffron as a linen dye, because the populace believed that saffron had some manner of sanitary virtue and cloth dyed with it was therefore not as frequently washed. The temptation to adulterate saffron has always been strong, and in the fifteenth century regular saffron inspections were held in Nuremberg. Those unfortunates who had extended their saffron for profit were burned at the stake or buried alive—along with their impure saffron.

In Kashmir, saffron cultivation flourished under the monopoly of the rajah. Ownership by others, much less exportation of even a single bulb, carried a penalty of death. Nevertheless, during the reign of Edward III, a traveler disguised as a monk managed to conceal a bulb in his hollow pilgrim's staff and brought it to England. The bulb was planted in the soil of Walden, near London, and thrived. So much saffron was produced in this area from the single original bulb that the place was named Saffron Walden, and the arms of Saffron Walden bear three crocus flowers yet today.

Health Benefits Anodyne, antispasmodic, aphrodisiac, appetizer, choleretic, emmenagogue, expectorant, sedative. Saffron contains the only water-soluble carotene, crocetin, a dark orange carotene responsible for much of the color, and which performs potent antioxidant and anticancer activities. Saffron in small quantities is a pure and natural digestive aid, soothing the entire digestive tract, and has a balancing and calming effect on the entire system. It will also promote perspiration, and help relieve gout and arthritis.

NOTE: In substantial doses, saffron produces a pleasant mania with sudden changes from hilarity to melancholia. In excessive quantity, it can create headaches, cough, and even hemorrhaging, with detrimental effects on the central nervous system and kidneys.

Sage (*Salvia officinalis*)

The botanical name Salvia *is derived either from the Latin* salvus, *meaning health and salvation, or from the Latin* salvere, *meaning to save, both alluding to its powerful healing properties.* Officinalis *means of the workshop, alluding to apothecaries' shops, and signifying that the plant was once part of the official pharmacopeia of Rome. The English word* sage *derives from the French name,* sauge.

General Information Sage is indigenous to northern Mediterranean regions, where it prefers the arid soil of hillsides, especially if it is chalky. Another member of the enormous mint family, this aromatic woody evergreen shrub has violet blue flowers and woolly, gray-green leaves. Like many other foods, sage got into the pantry via the medicine chest. Its health-protecting advantages have been forgotten by many, but along the way most people have learned to like its flavor. The French produced so much sage at one time that they exported it in the form of tea; the Chinese became so fond of sage tea that they traded four pounds of their tea for one pound of sage.

Culinary Uses Sage is available as fresh or dried leaves, the dried being generally preferred over the fresh leaves. Dried sage is either "rubbed" or ground; "rubbed" sage has gone through a minimum grinding into a fluffy, velvety powder, while ground sage is more finely ground. The flavor of sage may be described as warm, pungent, slightly bitter yet lemony, with just a hint of camphor. Chopped fresh or dried leaves are added to salads, kebabs, stuffings, squash dishes, beans, pickles, and cheese. The most popular use of sage is as an ingredient in stuffing at Thanksgiving, but it should be used throughout the year.

Health Benefits Antiseptic, astringent, expectorant, tonic, vermifuge. Sage is one of those herbs that has been used to cure a multitude of ills. One of its properties is to aid in the digestion of heavy greasy meats, preventing their oxidation, and thus is a common ingredient in pork, sausage, and duck recipes. It has long been regarded as a tonic that keeps the stomach, intestines, kidneys, liver, spleen, and sexual organs healthy (although it may temper sexual desire). Sage is stimulating and cleansing to the skin and scalp, soothing to sore muscles, and restorative to aging skin and hair, encouraging hair growth if the roots have not been destroyed. Its stimulating qualities increase circulation and relieve headaches, break fevers, and help reduce respiratory congestion and other cold symptoms. For sparkling teeth, rub them with fresh sage leaves; this will not only whiten and clean them, it will also strengthen the gums and make the breath

Sage

Nutritional Value Per 100 g Edible Portion

	Dried, Ground	1 tsp.
Calories	315	2
Protein	10.62 g	0.07 g
Fat	12.74 g	0.09 g
Fiber	18.05 g	0.13 g
Calcium	1,652 mg	12 mg
Iron	28.12 mg	0.20 mg
Magnesium	428 mg	3 mg
Phosphorus	91 mg	1 mg
Potassium	1,070 mg	7 mg
Sodium	11 mg	trace
Zinc	4.700 mg	0.030 mg
Copper	0.757 mg	n/a
Manganese	3.133 mg	n/a
Beta Carotene (A)	5900 IU	41 IU
Thiamine (B_1)	0.754 mg	0.005 mg
Riboflavin (B_2)	0.336 mg	0.002 mg
Niacin (B_3)	5.720 mg	0.040 mg
Ascorbic Acid (C)	32.38 mg	0.23 mg

Lore and Legend

In the tenth century, the medical school at Salerno, Italy, coined the aphorism "Cur moriatur homo cui Salvia crescit in horto?" or "Why should a man die when sage grows in his garden?" To those of the ancient world, sage was associated with immortality, or at least longevity, and was credited with increasing mental capacity, as well as relied upon to cure all manner of ills—from colds to worms, from excessive sexual desire to sexual debility, from nerves to dandruff and even graying hair. The ancient Druids believed that it possessed curative powers so magical that it could even resuscitate the dead. One belief held that sage, like rosemary, flourished in the garden only when the woman dominated the house; another belief was that the plants reflected the fortunes of the man of the house, flourishing when he prospered and withering when he did not. One fanciful legend has it that if young maidens at twilight on Midsummer's Eve go to a pond in a lonely wood, pick a twig of sage, and wave it around their heads seven times while repeating an incantation, their bridegrooms will appear to them at midnight.

pleasant. Sage extracts have powerful antioxidant activity due to the presence of phenolic acids, especially labiatic and carnosic acids. Its volatile oil contains thujone, camphor, cineole (eucalyptus fragrance), and borneol, all of which are antimicrobial and antispasmodic. The carminative property of the oil results from its ability to stimulate the production of digestive fluids and relax smooth muscles. Sage tea is very soothing and quieting to the nerves; has been used as an antidote against sore throat, cold sores, fevers and congestion; as a tonic for the hair and scalp; will regulate hormones, bringing on a late or suppressed menses and helping lessen an excessively heavy menstrual flow; works to expel worms; and when taken cold will help dry up milk in nursing mothers (when desired). To make sage tea, steep two or three leaves in one cup of hot water; strain and add one teaspoon of powdered ginger.

Salt (*Sodium chloride*)

Sodium *derives from the English term* soda*;* chloride *comes from the Greek term* chlorid*, meaning greenish-yellow chemical. The English word* salt *comes from the Roman god of health, Salus, who gave to the English language such words as "salutary" and "salute," as well as "salvation."*

General Information One of the most traditional of food flavorings, salt is composed of 40 percent sodium and 60 percent chloride. The mineral in the form of sodium chloride is extracted either from sea water or from underground deposits. Prior to refinement, salt contains over seventy different elements, a composite of all these elements as they occur in sea water. The process of refining is typically accomplished with the use of chemicals and extremely high heat, reducing salt from a whole food to an ultra-refined compound. According to the standards of the United States Food Chemicals Codex, commercial salt must be 97.5 percent pure sodium chloride to qualify for food use. Most commercial brands are iodized, which means that potassium iodide, an essential nutrient removed during the refining process, has been re-added. There may also be other ingredients added: sodium silicoaluminate, dextrose, sodium bicarbonate, magnesium carbonate, plus other chemicals to absorb moisture and make the salt flow freely.

Salt

Nutritional Value

	1 tsp.
Calories	0
Calcium	14 mg
Iron	trace
Phosphorus	3 mg
Potassium	trace
Sodium	2,100-2,300 mg

Throughout history, there have been groups of people who have not used salt. The fact is that these people who astonished observers by not eating salt *did* eat salt; what they did not eat was *added* salt. They were either great drinkers of milk (the Bedouins), or great consumers of animal proteins (the Eskimos), or both. Cow's milk contains 1.6 grams of salt per liter (three times as much as human milk), while meat averages between 0.1 to 0.15 grams of salt per 100 grams of weight. Thus these people's diet provided the necessary salt for their survival; only upon changing to a more cereal and vegetable-based diet was there a need for supplemental dietary salt.

For every one hundred pounds of salt produced each year, only five go into your salt shaker or prepared food products. The rest is used for packing meat, feeding livestock (both large and small), building roads and keeping them free of winter's ice and snow, tanning leather, and industrial uses such as the manufacture of glass and soap. Of the many salt works in existence during the eighteen and nineteenth centuries, very few are still in existence today; the suffix *-wich* in an English place name (Norwich, Middlewich, Greenwich) bears testimony to the sites of saltworks or brine springs.

Lore and Legend

Salt has often been associated with magic due to its puzzling properties. A rock rather than a plant, salt can alter the taste of food more powerfully than any organic herb or spice; it will also preserve delicate food, yet destroy solid metal. Because salt is pure (and therefore good), spilling it brought bad luck; and since the Devil hated salt, all you had to do was throw some into his face (he could generally be found lurking over your left shoulder), and all would be well again. In some cultures salt is sprinkled on the threshold and in the corners of new homes to rid the premises of evil influences. Roman Catholics once used salt as part of the baptism rite, placing it on the baby's tongue for protection. Salt was so important in imperial Rome that soldiers were paid with it or given the money to buy it: salt money, *salarium*, was the predecessor of our "salary." Those lacking in mercenary skill were thought to not be worth their salt. In ancient China, a favored way of committing suicide was to eat a pound of salt. For all Semitic peoples, an offer of salt was an offer of hospitality, with all its attendant duties; this obligation could be avoided by strewing salt across the sill of a house or the entrance of a tent to warn strangers that they were not welcome.

Culinary Uses Salt's potency for heightening and enhancing the taste of food is unmatched. It deepens flavors and unites them, balancing acidity and sweetness. Without salt, breads, potatoes, and grains would taste flat and metallic. In the majority of bread recipes, salt is almost a necessity, as it strengthens the gluten (the building fiber of wheat) and helps to form a crisp crust. It also conveniently lowers the freezing point of water in the salt and ice mixture of old-fashioned ice cream freezers. Salt is extremely useful to the food industry, since it acts as a natural preservative. It can mask the flavor of odorous foods, help inhibit the growth of molds and bacteria, and bleaches and "improves" food color. It is a processing aid in peeling, sorting, and floating; it is useful in drying and freezing foods; and whets the appetite to consume even more processed foods and beverages. Brining, pickling, curing, and salting are processes that produce especially high salt content in foods. Cured ham is 20 times saltier than fresh pork, and potato chips contain 340 times the sodium found naturally in raw potatoes of the same weight. Additional sodium may be ingested from unsuspected sources such as soft drinks, sparkling water, and desserts. Most current guidelines for daily salt consumption recommend about 3,000 milligrams, while the average American takes in approximately 17,000 milligrams, or about 3 1/2 teaspoonfuls of highly refined salt each day. An estimated 70 percent of the sodium in the American diet comes from processed foods, and Americans now use over one million tons of salt annually for food preparation or processing; this averages out to a horrendous 10 pounds per person.

Health Benefits Carminative, stimulant. Many people use salt simply to improve the taste of food; however, it also has medicinal properties. Salt is necessary for converting carbohydrates into fat, for ridding the body of carbon dioxide, and for heart and muscle contractions. The chloride in salt is needed by the body to produce hydrochloric acid—the main digestive juice in the stomach—as well as to balance the body's acid-alkaline level, and to stimulate the liver. Salt relieves gas and distention of the abdomen, cleanses the mouth, stimulates secretions in the digestive canal, and aids digestion. Insufficient sodium can result in symptoms similar to heat stroke: faintness, nausea, vomiting, weakness, and muscle cramps. Too much salt, though, may result in water weight gain, because salt can cause water retention and make you thirsty. It can also contribute to hypertension, high blood pressure, the risk of heart disease, and all the calcium deficiency problems. Although we would die without the 3 1/2 ounces of salt our bodies contain, few people are in danger of dying from insufficient sodium, but rather risk death daily by overconsumption. A tablespoon of salt dissolved in a cup of warm water is a quick emetic to administer in case of poisoning. A bath of sea salt and baking soda is an excellent external treatment in every form of radiation exposure. Add one pound of both sea salt and baking soda to a warm bath and soak for twenty minutes; rinse with cool water. This can be repeated up to three times a week for one month in cases of serious exposure.

Varieties

Flavored salts such as garlic, onion, and celery salts are available. This is just salt that has been combined with a proportion of flavoring agent.

Iodized salt contains not more than 0.01 percent potassium iodine, a mineral needed for proper thyroid functioning. Iodine was added to salt in the early 1900s to prevent goiters, caused from deficiency in this mineral, but iodine is now generally plentiful in the diets of North Americans.

Rock salt is obtained from underground land deposits where millions of years ago there were probably living sea waters. Although rock salt is less refined than table salt, the passage of time has removed all trace minerals and left the pure chemical sodium chloride. This is the kind most often sold in the United States.

Sea salt comes either in crystalline or granular form, and is obtained by vacuum-drying sea water. This salt, with all its mingled salts of the sea and correspondingly less plain sodium chloride than refined salt, has the stimulating flavor of the ocean. Unrefined, it contains an abundance of trace minerals (iodine in particular) that make it superior to the pure chemical sodium chloride of land-mined salt. The sea salt most rich in minerals is gray in color. Most sea salt sold in the United States is every bit as refined as rock salt, however, unless you can find imported unprocessed salt. Europeans generally prefer sea salt to rock salt, saying that it produces a better flavor in foods. Even with the trace minerals in unprocessed sea salt, in order to benefit from them, you would have to eat far more than is desired. You would get more benefit nutritionally by simply eating fresh fruit and vegetables. Sodium is found in good quantities in many other foods, including all seaweeds, beets, turnips, and greens such as chard, spinach, and parsley.

Table salt has been commercially processed to be 99.99 percent sodium chloride, and contains a number of extra additives to make it more "manageable" and keep it from hardening. One such chemical is YPS (sodium ferrocyanide), which causes small tentacles to form on each grain, preventing them from sticking together.

Savory (*Satureja hortensis, S. montana*)

In ancient days, savory plants were believed to be under the protection of the Satyrs, hence the name Satureja. *The term* hortensis *means belonging to a* hortus *or garden;* montana *means pertaining to mountains, and thus to snow and winter. The plant got its English name from the Saxons, who named it* savory *for its pleasantly spicy, pungent taste.*

General Information Summer savory (*S. hortensis*) is a small, compact plant with pink or white flowers that grows only during the summer months. This aromatic plant was brought to England by the Romans, but died out during the Dark Ages, and then was reintroduced during the sixteenth century. The ground savory sold in stores is summer savory. Winter savory (*S. montana*) is a small hardy evergreen perennial from the mountains of southern Europe and North Africa. It looks similar to summer savory with its white or blue flowers, but has stiff, dark green, pointed leaves. Also known as Spanish savory, this variety is not generally available in stores.

Savory

Nutritional Value Per 100 g Edible Portion

	Dried, Ground	1 tsp.
Calories	272	4
Protein	6.73 g	0.09 g
Fat	5.91 g	0.08 g
Fiber	15.27 g	0.21 g
Calcium	2132 mg	30 mg
Iron	37.88 mg	0.53 mg
Magnesium	377 mg	5 mg
Phosphorus	140 mg	2 mg
Potassium	1,051 mg	15 mg
Sodium	24 mg	trace
Zinc	4.300 mg	0.060 mg
Copper	0.847 mg	n/a
Manganese	6.100 mg	n/a
Beta Carotene (A)	5,130 IU	72 IU
Thiamine (B_1)	0.366 mg	0.005 mg
Riboflavin (B_2)	n/a	n/a
Niacin (B_3)	4.080 mg	0.057 mg

Culinary Uses Summer savory's small green leaves have a pungent spicy aroma and peppery flavor reminiscent of thyme. In Europe, savory is called "the bean herb" because not only does it complement the flavor of beans, but it also greatly diminishes their flatulent tendencies. Egg dishes profit as well by the addition of summer savory, as do nearly all kinds of meat (especially sausage), stuffings, salads, soups, and stews. In many dishes it makes a flavorful substitute for salt. Winter savory has a stronger, sharper, more piney taste than summer savory, and is best used with strong game meats and pâtés.

Health Benefits Antiseptic, astringent, carminative, expectorant, stimulant, stomachic. Although not as strong as others in the mint family, the savories make a pleasant digestive aid. Both varieties contain a strong volatile oil that aids digestion, and are therefore recommended in dishes that are known to be difficult to digest, such as game, dried beans and peas. Savory tea is a safe remedy for most stomach and intestinal disorders, including cramps, nausea, indigestion, and lack of appetite. The leaves can be chewed to sweeten the breath, or crushed and applied to a bee sting to reduce swelling and pain. Savory also has a long reputation as an "herb of love," and men who nibble on savory swear that their amorous abilities increase tenfold. The Roman naturalist Pliny called summer savory an aphrodisiac and the winter variety a sexual depressant (not surprisingly, summer savory was more popular). The famous French herbalist, Maurice Messegue, often used summer savory instead of ginseng to help couples retrieve their marital bliss.

Lore and Legend

For reasons lost to history, the ancient Romans linked summer savory to the mythological licentious satyrs—the lustful, half-man, half-goat creatures who roamed the ancient forests playing their pipes, and who disported endlessly with the nymphs in debauched orgies in honor of Dionysus, god of wine. As a result of this association, savory was forbidden in monastic physic gardens for many centuries.

Shepherd's Purse (*Capsella bursa-pastoris*)

Also Known As: Lady's Purse, Pepper and Salt, Rattleweed, Pastor's Purse, Purselet.

Capsella *is the diminutive form of* capsa, *Latin for box, and* bursa-pastoris *means bag or purse belonging to a shepherd. This plant takes both its Latin and English names from the shape of its flat and rather triangular seedpods, which were commonly compared to the leather pouches in which shepherds carried their food.*

Shepherd's Purse

Nutritional Value Per 100 g Edible Portion

	Fresh
Calories	330-280
Protein	4.2-35.6 g
Fat	0.3-36.0 g
Fiber	1.1-10.2 g
Calcium	208-1763 mg
Iron	4.8-40.7 mg
Phosphorus	60-729 mg
Potassium	394-3339 mg
Beta Carotene (A)	0.260-2.200 mg
Thiamine (B_1)	0.250-2.120 mg
Riboflavin (B_2)	0.170-1.440 mg
Niacin (B_3)	0.400-3.400 mg
Ascorbic Acid (C)	36.0-550.0 mg

General Information Shepherd's purse is a native of the Old World that now thrives around the globe. It is well suited for survival: a single plant can produce up to forty thousand seeds. This small common evergreen plant with arrow-shaped leaves and clusters of small white flowers easily adapts to mild and extreme climates alike. When broken, the foliage has a peculiar and unpleasant odor and somewhat biting taste. In mild temperate climates, this member of the mustard family grows year-round and is commonly found in waste areas with sandy, gravely soil.

Culinary Uses The leaves of shepherd's purse have a peppery taste, and serve both as a vegetable and salad The mature seeds can be used in breadmaking, soups, and salads.

Health Benefits Antiscorbutic, diuretic, stimulant, styptic, tonic, vasoconstrictor. Shepherd's purse regularizes blood pressure and heart action, whether the pressure is high or low. It is effective for various menstrual problems, including difficult menstruation, and will temper the sometimes excessive menstrual flow of pubescent girls or menopausal women. Shepherd's purse is sometimes used to promote uterine contractions during childbirth, and can promote bowel movements with a similar effect on the intestines. An extract applied to internal or external bleeding works as an effective blood coagulant.

Shiso (*Perilla frutescens*)

Also Known As: Perilla, Beefsteak Plant.

Perilla *is said to be a native name in India, while by others it is believed a Greek or Latin proper name.* Frutescens *means shrubby or bushy.*

General Information This cousin of basil and mint was eaten by the Chinese as a vegetable over fifteen hundred years ago, and they valued the oil from its seeds for cooking. For some reason, however, the Chinese gave up on shiso as a food staple centuries ago, but the Japanese—to whom they introduced the plant—still eat two varieties: green (*ao-jiso*) and red (*aka-jiso*). Found packed in brine in Japanese groceries, the large red leaves' main culinary use is for pickling plums into umeboshi. The smaller green leaves are sometimes sold fresh in small plastic packages.

Culinary Uses The smaller green leaves are used as a garnish and sometimes fried whole in tempura batter. Most often they are used as an aromatic addition to sushi rolls. The larger red leaves seem to be strictly for umeboshi.

Health Benefits The Chinese materia medica cites shiso as an antidote to fish poisoning.

Sorrel *(Rumex acetosa, R. acetosella, R. scutatus)*

Also Known As: Sheep Sorrel, Sour Grass, Little Vinegar.

> Rumex *is an old Latin name for the plant. Both* acetosa *and* acetosella *comes from the Latin word for vinegar, and implies its acid and/or sour character, mainly from oxalic acid;* scutatus *means carrying a shield. The English name* sorrel *derives from the Germanic* sur *and Old French* surele, *both meaning sour.*

General Information Sorrel is a perennial plant native to Europe and Asia. From the Middle Ages up until the 1700s, sorrel's jade-green leaves were a regular feature of European vegetable gardens. This relative of rhubarb is commonly found in damp meadows and along roads and shorelines in both Europe and Asia, but is only found sparingly in North America. There are several varieties, but the main ones are garden sorrel (*R. acetosa*), sheep sorrel (*R. acetosella*), and French sorrel (*R. scutatus*). The leaves of garden sorrel are arrowhead shaped, with the detached points at the base parallel to the stem. Leaves up to about six inches long are young enough to use for salads; older leaves are coarse and more sour. Sheep sorrel has leaves that are no more than two inches long, in the same arrowhead shape as garden sorrel, but with base lobes that splay outward from the stem. The plant is said to have come to America as a weed mixed in with other seed or with hay brought over from Europe to feed shipboard animals. Sorrel has a high content of the chemical salt binoxalate of potash, which imparts the highly acidic taste. Oxalic acid was formerly known as "salts of sorrel" and used as a stain remover.

Culinary Uses Sorrel has a refreshing, slightly bitter, spinach-like taste; the French variety has just a hint of citrus flavor. Use fresh leaves if you can, as the dried leaves have lost most of their distinctive citrus-like flavor. Fresh young leaves can be combined with other herbs in salads or cooked and served like spinach, usually in combination with either Swiss chard or spinach. It may also be used to enliven soups, as a garnish and flavoring in small amounts to season eggs and meat, as an ingredient in sauces, or as one of a variety of herbs on which fish is steamed. Once cooked, it wilts into a flavorful purée. For most preparations, the leaves are washed and the stems pulled off to remove any coarse veins. Then about two dozen leaves are laid parallel in a neat pile, rolled into a fat cigar, and the compressed leaves shredded crosswise with a knife. Place the shreds in a pan with a generous teaspoon of butter—or a little water, olive oil, or cream—to a quarter pound of leaves. Over

Sorrel

Nutritional Value Per 100 g Edible Portion

	Fresh
Protein	5.6-9.6 g
Fat	1.7-3.6 g
Calcium	1,620 mg
Magnesium	1,085 mg
Phosphorus	1,126 mg
Potassium	2,293 mg
Ascorbic Acid (C)	50-1200 mg

low heat with occasional stirring the leaves will melt into an olive green puree in about fifteen minutes. If the dish they are to be used in is elegant or if the leaves are coarse, the puree is put through a fine strainer. Sorrel should not be cooked in an iron pan, as it will draw out a potentially harmful and very unpleasant metallic taste. The juice of the leaves can have the same action upon milk as rennet, forming a junket.

Health Benefits Antiscorbutic, astringent, diuretic, nutritive, tonic. Sorrel is used as a preventive tonic against scurvy, and the tea given to reduce fevers and quench thirst. Tea made from the leaves also works as a wound cleanser, for treating chronic skin diseases, as a blood purifier, and works especially well as a remedy for kidney trouble, helping properly regulate their function and expelling stones.

NOTE: The herb's sharp taste is due to its oxalic acid and vitamin C content. Because even small amounts of oxalic acid are toxic to some extent, sorrel should not be served indiscriminately. In large quantities, oxalic acid is extremely poisonous. Persons with gout, rheumatism, or kidney ailments should avoid eating this plant, as it will tend to aggravate those conditions.

Spirulina *(Spirulina platensis, S. maxima)*

The term Spirulina *was given due to the algae's growth pattern of tiny spiraling wires.* Maxima *means largest.*

General Information Spirulina is one of a variety of blue-green algae often found in saline—usually highly alkaline—natural lakes like Lake Texcoco near Mexico City and Lake Chad in Africa. It has been used for centuries by the Africans and was a major protein source for the Aztec culture. It is also cultivated in man-made tanks in the United States, Korea, and Japan. Spirulina grown in man-made tanks can have its mineralization altered toward the maximum values for human nutrition. The algae grows in single cells that resemble filaments—tiny spiral wires—to about one millimeter in length. Its size is measured in microns (millionths of a meter). Natives of the Sahara dry it with grains, vegetables, and seasonings to form *dihe*, practically a meal in itself. Another micro-algae is wild blue-green (*Aphanizomenon flos-aquae*), which grows wild in Oregon's Klamath Lake.

Culinary Uses This bland, extremely fine green powder is used most frequently as a food supplement, and often combined with nutritional yeast, comfrey, ginseng powder, or bee pollen. It can be added (up to 10 percent by volume) to cereals and other food products to boost their nutritional profile without changing the flavor or creating objectionable tastes.

Health Benefits Micro-algae exists on the edge between the plant and animal kingdoms, and offers some unique nutritional advantages. In its dried state—the usual commercial form—spirulina contains the highest sources of protein, beta carotene, and nucleic acids of any animal or plant food. All of its nutrients are in a form easy to digest and absorb. Its very large store of nucleic acids (RNA and DNA) is known to benefit cellular

Spirulina

Nutritional Value Per 100 g Edible Portion

	Raw	Dried
Calories	26	290
Protein	5.92 g	57.47 g
Fat	0.39 g	7.72g
Fiber	0.34 g	3.64 g
Iron	n/a	28.50 mg
Magnesium	n/a	195 mg
Phosphorus	11 mg	118 mg
Potassium	127 mg	1,363 mg
Sodium	98 mg	1,048 mg
Beta Carotene (A)	n/a	250,000 IU
Thiamine (B_1)	0.222 mg	2.380 mg
Riboflavin (B_2)	0.342 mg	3.670 mg
Niacin (B_3)	1.196 mg	12.820 mg
Pantothenic Acid (B_5)	0.325 mg	3.480 mg
Pyridoxine (B_6)	0.034 mg	0.364 mg
Ascorbic Acid (C)	0.9 mg	10.1 mg

regeneration and to reverse aging. Too much nucleic acid, however, can raise the uric acid level in the body, causing calcium depletion, kidney stones, and gout. One of the most outstanding of spirulina's nutritional features for curing deficiency is its exceptionally high level of the fatty acid GLA. It also contains substantial Omega-3 alpha-linolenic acid. GLA is important for growth and development, and is found most abundantly in mother's milk; spirulina is the next highest whole food source. Thus spirulina is often recommended for people who were never breast-fed, in order to foster the hormonal and mental development that may not have occurred because of lack of proper nutrition. Spirulina is richly supplied with the blue pigment phycocyanin, a biliprotein that has been shown to inhibit cancer-colony formation. Spirulina protects the kidneys against injury that occurs from taking strong prescription medication, and helps the liver regenerate after severe damage from malnutrition, alcoholism, or the consumption of nutrient-destroying food or drugs. In recent years, researchers have increasingly studied micro-algae such as spirulina because they contain anti-fungal and anti-bacterial biochemicals not found in other plant or animal species.

Wild blue-green algae has the most extreme properties of the commonly available micro-algae, and one needs to take precautions when using it. Under certain conditions, wild blue-green can transform into an exceptionally toxic plant. Experts claim this toxic state has never been found in Oregon's Klamath Lake, and the companies that harvest there monitor the product closely. Wild blue-green is bitter, cooling, drying, mildly diuretic, a neurostimulant, antidepressant, and a relaxant. Because bitter substances can focus the mind, certain foods, including wild blue-green algae and peyote, have been used to improve concentration during meditation and prayer.

Star Anise *(Illicium verum, I. anisatum)*

> *The Latin name* Illicium *means allurement or that which entices, given because of the very pleasant scent of the tree and fruit. The term* verum *means true, genuine, or standard;* anisatum *means anise-scented. The shape of the fruits as they open account for the "star" in star anise's name. The "anise" comes from the fact that star anise tastes and smells like anise, although the two plants are not botanically related.*

General Information Star anise is a small evergreen tree indigenous to southern Chile. The tree grows to a height of about twenty-six feet, and does not bear fruit until approximately six years of age, but can continue to bear for the next century. Its yellow flowers are followed by brown fruit that opens, when ripe, into star shapes. Each point of the star contains a shiny brown seed that is less aromatic than the pod. These star-shaped fruits with their six to eight points are collected while still green and then sun-dried until they become woody and reddish brown. Both the pod and the shiny, golden-brown, oval seeds contain the same essential oils as anise. Long used as a spice in the East, star anise was not seen in Europe until 1588, when a sample was brought from the Philippines to London. For many years, star anise made the journey from the east via the China-Russia tea route (and was called Siberian cardamom because of it), but is now quite popular in Western countries.

Culinary Uses The spicy sweet flavor of star anise is stronger and more pungent than ordinary anise. The pod is used whole as a garnish, and can be broken or crushed to intensify the flavor. A frequent addition to Asian cooking, spicy dishes, casseroles, baked goods, and drinks, star anise adds a delicate aniseed flavor; it is one of the main ingredients of Chinese five-spice powder. Despite the fact that they come from different plants, anise and star anise contain the same essential oil (anethole), have the same composition and flavor, and are considered to be widely interchangeable.

Health Benefits Carminative, diuretic, expectorant, stimulant. Star anise is used particularly in China, where it is believed to have a beneficial effect on the digestive system, and where it is common to chew a piece after meals to sweeten the breath and relieve flatulence. It has a reputation as being mildly sleep-inducing.

Stevia (*Stevia rebaudiana*)

Stevia *was named in honor of P.J. Esteve (1556), a Spanish botanist.*

General Information The stevia plant, first cultivated in Paraguay, has been used as an herbal sweetener for centuries in South America. The Guarani Indians of Paraguay have long used stevia to make a sweet tea, and the dried leaves and twigs of the plant are commonly sold in local markets and pharmacies. Also called sweet leaf or sweet herb, an extract is made of the leaves and flowers. Stevia contains a very sweet component called stevioside, with a sweetening effect similar to cane sugar. In Japan, where the government approved the herb in 1970, stevia and its extracts make up 40 percent of the sweetener market, and it is used by companies such as Coca-Cola and Beatrice to sweeten various products such as Diet Coke. In 1991, the U.S. FDA placed an import ban on stevia, declaring that there is "not adequate evidence to establish that such use in food is safe." This ban was reversed late in 1995, although it still is required to be sold as a nutritional supplement rather than as a sweetener.

Stevia

Nutritional Value Per 100 g Edible Portion

	Dried
Calories	254
Protein	11.2 g
Fat	1.9 g
Fiber	15.2 g
Calcium	544 mg
Iron	3.9 mg
Magnesium	349 mg
Phosphorus	318 mg
Potassium	1,780 mg
Sodium	89.2 mg
Zinc	trace
Manganese	14.700 mg
Beta Carotene (A)	12,440 IU
Thiamine (B_1)	trace
Riboflavin (B_2)	trace
Niacin (B_3)	trace
Ascorbic Acid (C)	11 mg

Culinary Uses Powdered stevia looks similar to parsley flakes. The powdered leaf can be made into a simple extract by mixing one teaspoon in a cup of water and allowing it to soak overnight. The liquid extract is much better tasting and easier to use than the powdered form. Only a few drops will sweeten a cup of tea; it is also delicious in yogurt, cereal, and baked goods. Stevia's sweet flavor is not affected by heat, thus it can be used in teas and other beverages, in canning fruits, and when baking all kinds of desserts.

Health Benefits Tests have shown the sweetening agent, the glycoside stevioside, is thirty times sweeter than granulated table sugar. Because it is a whole herbal food, stevia contains other properties that nicely complement its sweetness. A report from the Hiroshima University School of Dentistry indicates that stevia actually suppresses dental bacteria growth rather than feeding it as other sugars do. Japanese and Latin American scientists have discovered other attributes as well, including its use as a tonic, diuretic, to combat mental and physical fatigue, to harmonize digestion, regulate blood pressure, and assist in weight loss.

Lore and Legend

Sweet cicely is believed to quicken a dull mind, make the heart merry, aid the memory, and give the aged a new lease on youth.

Sweet Cicely *(Myrrhis odorata)*

The generic name Myrrhis *is derived from the Greek word* myrrha*, meaning fragrant or perfume, because of its myrrh-like smell;* odorata *means fragrant or odorous. Until the sixteenth century this plant was known as* seseli*, a name first used by Dioscorides. It is usually prefaced by "sweet" due to the sweet taste of the leaf.*

General Information Sweet cicely is a graceful decorative plant, probably native to central and southern Europe, with lacy fern-like leaves and small white flowers. The soft green leaves have a myrrh-like scent with overtones of moss, woodland, and a hint of anise. Sweet cicely was very popular in England during the sixteenth and seventeenth centuries, and held a highly regarded place in the old kitchen gardens, for its leaves, flowering tops, seeds, and fragrant roots were all used in salads, broths, and baked goods. In the north of England, the plant was rubbed on beehives to attract bees, and the seeds used for polishing furniture. Nowadays, sweet cicely is not in demand, and few supermarkets carry it.

Culinary Uses Sweet cicely smells slightly like anise and has a sugary sweet flavor with licorice overtones. The leaves, flowers, and stem tips can be used fresh in salads, added to soups and stews, or boiled to make a licorice-flavored liquid used in fruit pies and compotes. If the liquid is added to cream, the cream will lose its fatty taste and become sweeter. Sweet cicely's nutty, licorice-flavored small green or black seeds can be used raw in salads and fruit dishes. Roots are also edible, steamed, simmered, or cooked and puréed like parsnips.

Health Benefits Aromatic, carminative, expectorant, stomachic. Sweet cicely is used in much the same manner as anise—for coughs, indigestion, flatulence, mucous congestion, and lack of appetite. The fresh roots are antiseptic, while the distilled liquid is a diuretic. It acts as a gentle stimulant for weak or debilitated stomachs, and makes a natural sweetener for diabetics and others who have to avoid sugar.

Szechuan Pepper *(Zanthoxylum piperitum)*

Also Known As: Fagara, Anise Pepper, Chinese Pepper.

Zanthoxylum *comes from two Greek words:* xanthos*, meaning yellow, and* xylon*, meaning wood.* Piperitum *means pepper-scented. Szechuan pepper got its English name because it is native to that province.*

General Information Szechuan pepper is made from the dried rusty-brown seed pods of an ornamental woody prickly ash tree native to Japan, Korea, and northern China. This plant is a member of the citrus family and grows in any temperate climate. Completely unrelated to black pepper, most parts of the plant, but especially the fruits, emit a strong aromatic odor when bruised. The 3- to 4-millimeter berry has a rough reddish-brown shell that splits open to reveal a black seed inside. The black seed is bitter and can be discarded; the red shell is the part used culinarily. Szechuan pepper was once a standard table condiment in China to the point that even wines were flavored with it. During the Tang Period (618–907 A.D.) it was the vogue to take Szechuan pepper with tea and clotted cream. When black pepper was introduced from the tropics, Szechuan pepper fell out of favor and has never fully regained its popularity.

Culinary Uses Szechuan pepper has a hot, aromatic flavor that provides a sharp accent to foods. The rusty-brown peppercorns are not piping hot, but spicy, mildly piquant, and fragrant. The dried pods make useful additions to soups, stews and sauces, are delicious on roasted fish, and are a frequent ingredient in five-spice powder. The Chinese often mix this peppery spice with salt, sometimes roasting it first to release its full woodsy flavor. Available pre-crushed or in pods, the pods are crushed to a coarse powder or ground in a pepper mill over foods. Seeds and inner bark are cooked or pickled, and fresh leaves are added to soup.

Tamarind (*Tamarindus indica*)

Tamarindus *comes from the Arabic* tamr-hindi *meaning Indian date.* Indica *means coming from India.*

General Information Tamarind is the dried fruit of the leguminous tamarind tree native to East Africa. Known as "Indian dates" because of their sticky, fibrous appearance, the fruit is a cinnamon-colored oblong pod from three to eight inches long, with a thin, brittle shell enclosing a soft, brownish, acidulous pulp. When ripe, the fruit possesses a sweet yet sour taste. It is peculiar of the fruit that it contains more acid and, at the same time, more sugar than any other fruit. Although often referred to as "tamarind seed," it is in fact the pulp around the seeds that is used.

Tamarind

Nutritional Value Per 100 g Edible Portion

	Pulp
Calories	115
Protein	3.10 g
Fat	0.10 g
Fiber	5.6 g
Calcium	35-170 mg
Iron	1.3-10.9 mg
Phosphorus	54-110 mg
Potassium	375 mg
Sodium	24 mg
Beta Carotene (A)	15 IU
Thiamine (B_1)	0.160 mg
Riboflavin (B_2)	0.070 mg
Niacin (B_3)	0.600-0.700 mg
Ascorbic Acid (C)	0.7-3.0 mg

Culinary Uses When fresh and tender, tamarind's spicy date-apricot pulp can be eaten raw, or cooked with rice and fish. When purchased dried, the fruit is first soaked in water and the soaking liquid used (the seeds are discarded). Tamarind's spicy pulp is used to add a sour, fruity taste to seasonings, curries, chutneys, and various drinks.

Health Benefits Anthelmintic, laxative, refrigerant. The principal use of the ripe, sweet-sour, stringy pulp throughout the Americas and Caribbean is as a mild laxative. The pulp of the fruit contains citric, tartaric, and malic acids, which give it cooling properties; therefore, it is a useful drink for those ill with fever, as well as being a popular cooling beverage in hot countries.

Tansy (*Tanacetum vulgare*)

The generic name Tanacetum *means quite literally a bed of tansy;* vulgare *means common or vulgar. The English word* tansy *is derived from the Greek* athanatos, *meaning immortal, tansy having been the plant the gods employed when they granted eternal life to human beings.*

General Information Tansy is an attractive plant with fern-like delicate leaves native to temperate regions of Europe and Asia. The Benedictine monks at Saint Gall in

Lore and Legend

Ancient Greeks and Romans regarded tansy as a symbol of immortality, and it was a critical ingredient in a potion that conferred immortality upon a handsome Greek boy named Ganymede, who became the eternal cupbearer for the god Zeus. It developed into a symbolic and pragmatic component in Easter rites, being embraced as one of the Bitter Herbs of Passover. In the belief that tansy could rejuvenate the human body after a long winter's subsistence on salted meat and fish, and purify the humors of the body after the sparsities of Lent, tansy cakes and other tansy-flavored foods were made as traditional fare after the Lenten fasts were over.

Switzerland were cultivating tansy in their medicinal gardens as early as 1265. By the fifteenth century it was commonly used as a medicine in both France and England, but old herbals caution about its careless use. Used as an embalming agent from ancient days until the time of the American Revolution, tansy was also used to preserve meat from the ravages of storage in pre-refrigeration times. The plant is a natural insecticide, repelling flies, mosquitoes, ants, and other insects; plant it by doorways or sprinkle the dried leaves in cellars and attics to deter pests.

Culinary Uses The flavor of tansy is hot and peppery, bitter, and largely disliked. Once used as a substitute for pepper, tansy now plays a minor role in flavoring baked goods, salad dressings, and omelets. Among its better known uses is in the manufacture of the liqueur Chartreuse. It is best used sparingly, due to its strong flavor.

Health Benefits Anthelmintic, emmenagogue, stimulant, tonic. Tansy is an old remedy used to tone up the system, soothe the bowels, expel parasites, and strengthen a weak heart. American Indians made a tea from the entire plant to promote suppressed menstruation and induce abortion.

NOTE: In the small quantity used by the cook, the juice of the crushed leaves does little or no harm; in any quantity, however, the volatile oils are toxic. The strength of the poison greatly increases at flowering and seed time. Tansy leaves can no longer be sold for tea-making purposes in the United States because they are considered to be poisonous.

Tarragon (*Artemisia dracunculus*)

Tarragon was named in honor of the Greek goddess Artemis, daughter of Zeus and sister to Apollo, the virgin huntress and goddess of wild life, childbirth, and protectress of all young things. Dracunculus *means little dragon. Ibnal Baithar, an Arabian botanist and pharmacist living in Spain in the thirteenth century, mentioned tarragon by the name of* tarkhun, *meaning little dragon; the Spanish called it* taragoncia *(also meaning little dragon), and from this name the English word* tarragon *was derived.*

General Information Tarragon is a tall weedy plant, one of the very few that was relatively unknown in ancient times. Perhaps the fact that it is native to Siberia and Mongolia accounts for its anonymity, since those places were not on the trade routes and

Tarragon

Nutritional Value Per 100 g Edible Portion

	Dried, Ground	1 tsp.
Calories	295	5
Protein	22.76 g	0.36 g
Fat	7.24 g	0.12 g
Fiber	7.41 g	0.12 g
Calcium	1,139 mg	18 mg
Iron	32.30 mg	0.52 mg
Magnesium	347 mg	6 mg
Phosphorus	313 mg	5 mg
Potassium	3,020 mg	48 mg
Sodium	62 mg	1 mg
Zinc	3.900 mg	0.060 mg
Copper	0.677 mg	n/a
Manganese	7.967 mg	n/a
Beta Carotene (A)	4,200 IU	67 IU
Thiamine (B1)	0.251 mg	0.004 mg
Riboflavin (B2)	1.339 mg	0.021 mg
Niacin (B3)	8.950 mg	0.143 mg

Lore and Legend

Tarragon was once believed to cure the bites of mad dogs and venomous creatures, because in medicinal lore and legend any plant with a serpentine root system is given credit for treating snakebite. By many it was also considered an aphrodisiac.

their inaccessibility left them isolated. It is believed to have reached the West with the invading Mongols. Tarragon was unknown in Europe until the latter part of the fifteenth century, but was later brought to America by the colonists. Affectionately known in most western languages as "little dragon" in reference to its dragon-like roots, the plant may actually strangle itself if not divided frequently. In the United States, the plant most often sold as tarragon is actually False or Russian tarragon (*A. dracunculoides*), which is nearly tasteless.

Culinary Uses Tarragon's long, delicate, polished gray-green, aromatic leaves have a sweet yet slightly bitter flavor. Although some say that tarragon has a slight flavor of licorice, others find no hint of this. The young shoots and tips of the plants were cooked and eaten as a vegetable in earlier times; they are still served as an appetizer in the Near East. Because tarragon's flavorful oil evaporates when the leaves are dried, fresh tarragon is much more flavorful than dried; the dried leaves also take on a musty hay-like quality. Add the leaves to salads, dressings, sauces, and to vegetable, poultry, and fish dishes. Those who make their own tartar sauce will find this herb indispensable. Tarragon can easily take the place of salt, pepper, and vinegar, if necessary, and can also replace garlic. Because it is strongly flavored, tarragon should be used with discretion. Fresh or dried, heat intensifies the flavor.

Health Benefits Diuretic, emmenagogue, hypnotic, stomachic. A simple infusion of tarragon leaves will stimulate the appetite, relieve flatulence and colic, regulate menstruation, balance the body's acidity, alleviate the pain of arthritis, rheumatism and gout, and expel worms from the body. Tarragon is also regarded as a mild, non-irritating diuretic that helps the system flush out toxins produced by the digestion of heavy proteins. Drinking tarragon tea before going to bed helps to overcome insomnia. The fresh leaf or root when applied to aching teeth, cuts, or sores, is said to act as a local anesthetic.

Thyme (*Thymus vulgaris*)

> *It is said that the botanical name* Thymus *is connected with the Greek word* thymon*, meaning to fumigate, as it was used for incense in temples; another derivation is from the Greek* thymos*, which signifies courage and strength, the plant being held in ancient and medieval days to be a great source of invigoration, its cordial qualities inspiring courage.* Vulgaris *signifies common or vulgar.*

General Information Thyme is a member of the mint family that originally was grown as a decorative rather than culinary herb in the Mediterranean. Used by the Sumerians, its history goes back to at least 3500 B.C. Thyme has woody stems, clusters of small lavender flowers, and short oval gray-green leaves. There are more than one hundred varieties of thyme, all developed from wild thyme (*T. serphyllum*), the so-called "mother of thyme"; each looks slightly different and has a different flavor and aroma. Thyme from England has broad leaves; French thyme has narrow leaves; and winter thyme from Germany stays green all winter. There are also thymes that taste and smell like lemon, mint, pine, licorice, caraway, or nutmeg. Thyme has long been associated with bees and honey, as the plant attracts bees in great profusion and is thus excellent for orchards. This low, creeping plant was invariably planted along walkways, so that it might creep over the sun-warmed stones and impart its delicious aroma when walked upon. Thyme, especially the lemon scented variety, is a mild pest repellent.

Thyme

Nutritional Value Per 100 g Edible Portion

	Dried, Ground	1 tsp.
Calories	276	4
Protein	9.10 g	0.13 g
Fat	7.43 g	0.10 g
Fiber	18.63 g	0.26 g
Calcium	1,890 mg	26 mg
Iron	123.60 mg	1.73 mg
Magnesium	220 mg	3 mg
Phosphorus	201 mg	3 mg
Potassium	814 mg	11 mg
Sodium	55 mg	1 mg
Zinc	6.180 mg	0.090 mg
Copper	0.860 mg	n/a
Manganese	7.867 mg	n/a
Beta Carotene (A)	3,800 IU	53 IU
Thiamine (B_1)	0.513 mg	0.007 mg
Riboflavin (B_2)	0.399 mg	0.006 mg
Niacin (B_3)	4.940 mg	0.069 mg

Culinary Uses The gray-green leaves of fresh thyme smell resinous and sweet and have a bright, sharp taste. It can easily overpower other, more delicate flavors with its strong aromatic flavor, so should be used with discretion. Dried, it loses some of its fragrance and gains pungency. Lemon thyme is milder, with a lemony tang, and blends better in dishes for which garden thyme is too sharp. Thyme especially complements vegetables of the cabbage family, but also goes well with potatoes, tomatoes, zucchini, and eggplant. This herb improves the digestion of food, so it is often found with fatty meats such as lamb or pork, or with bean dishes.

Health Benefits Antiseptic, aromatic, carminative, diaphoretic, expectorant, tonic, vulnerary. Thyme is an excellent natural tranquilizer because it contains carvacrol, which has a tonic effect on the nerve centers, and also helps retard hair loss by improving the superficial blood vessels of the scalp, whose job it is to feed the roots of the hair. Its carminative properties are attributed to its volatile oils, which irritate the gastrointestinal lining, thus stimulating the production of gastric fluids. Oil of thyme (thymol) has a powerful antiseptic action and was used in World War I as an antiseptic as well as a local anesthetic and deodorant. The tea sweetened with honey is an excellent soothing cough mixture, and is helpful in fevers, relieves headaches, acts as a mood elevator, expels gas, and increases perspiration.

Lore and Legend

Thyme has not always been a seasoning herb, or even primarily so. History records its cultivation for decorative, ceremonial, aphrodisiac, and medicinal purposes. Long valued as an herb of courage, elegance, and grace in Greece, the highest compliment that could be paid a man was to tell him that he smelled of thyme. Indeed it was very popular as a bath scent and was used in other ways as a male cosmetic. Thyme was held sacred to both Mars and Venus (respectively, Roman god of war and goddess of love); in the Middle Ages, thyme sprigs or thyme-embroidered kerchiefs and scarves were given by ladies to their favorite knights in order to protect them in battle. If a young girl wore a corsage of wild thyme flowers, it meant that she was looking for a sweetheart; if a bashful boy drank enough wild thyme tea it would give him the courage to take her up on it. Due to its antiseptic qualities it was included in the embalming fluids used by the Egyptians and the posies carried by European judges and nobility to protect them from the odors and diseases of the common people. Early anatomists named the lymph gland in the chest the thymus because it reminded them of a thyme flower. A bed of thyme was thought to be a favorite for fairies, who would creep out late in the evening and frolic in the garden. Gardeners once set aside a patch of the herb especially for them, much as we provide birdhouses. According to legend, at midnight on Midsummer's Eve the king of the fairies and his followers dance in beds of wild thyme.

Turmeric *(Curcuma longa)*

Curcuma *comes from an Arabic name for the plant,* kurkum, *meaning saffron or crocus;* longa *means long. The English name* turmeric *comes from the Medieval Latin phrase* terra merita, *meaning deserving earth.*

Turmeric

Nutritional Value Per 100 g Edible Portion

	Dried, Ground	1 tsp.
Calories	354	8
Protein	7.83 g	0.17 g
Fat	9.88 g	0.22 g
Fiber	6.71 g	0.15 g
Calcium	182 mg	4 mg
Iron	41.42 mg	0.91 mg
Magnesium	193 mg	4 mg
Phosphorus	268 mg	6 mg
Potassium	2,525 mg	56 mg
Sodium	38 mg	1 mg
Zinc	4.350 mg	0.100 mg
Copper	0.603 mg	n/a
Manganese	7.833 mg	n/a
Beta Carotene (A)	trace	n/a
Thiamine (B_1)	0.152 mg	0.003 mg
Riboflavin (B_2)	0.233 mg	0.005 mg
Niacin (B_3)	5.140 mg	0.113 mg
Ascorbic Acid (C)	25.85 mg	0.57 mg

General Information Turmeric is an East Indian tropical herb of the ginger family. It flourishes in the rich, moist soils of Java, China, India, and Bangladesh and is a valuable cash crop in many other tropical areas of the Far East. Like ginger, it is the underground rhizome of the plant which is used, but it is both sweeter and more fragrant than ginger. This aromatic, vivid yellow spice is prepared by washing, peeling, drying, and grinding the thick root.

Culinary Uses Turmeric is sometimes available fresh, when it looks similar to fresh ginger, but is normally bought dried, either whole or ground. Eaten raw in southern India, the bright yellow, aromatic root has a delicate, buttery, slightly peppery and mustard-like taste (some compare it to horseradish) which is clean and refreshing. One of the basic curry spices, turmeric gives a pleasantly warm and rich undertone to food, as well as adding its unmistakable coloring. It can be added to any curried dish, or used alone to lend color and subtle spice to grains, beans, chutneys, cream sauces, and mayonnaise. Turmeric may be used as a cheap substitute for saffron, but the flavor is stronger. If you wish to make your own curry powder, combine six parts turmeric, four parts cumin, and one part each of cardamom, coriander, cinnamon, black pepper, ground fenugreek, and ginger. This combination will provide maximum flavor but minimal heat.

Health Benefits Antifungal, cholagogue, choleretic. Turmeric is noted as a blood purifier, has a soothing action on respiratory ailments, improves liver function, benefits the circulation, helps regulate the menstrual cycle, and works as a restorative after loss of blood at childbirth. It also helps the body to digest proteins, and when combined with coriander and cumin it aids in the digestion of complex carbohydrates. Turmeric has antifungal properties and helps heal wounds both internally and externally. For an abrasion, bruise or traumatic swelling, a half-teaspoon of turmeric and a pinch of salt may be made into a paste with water or ghee and applied to the affected area. The most active component in turmeric is curcumin (the yellow pigment), which has been found effective as an anti-inflammatory and anti-microbial agent, as well as a cardiovascular and gastrointestinal aid. Turmeric is considered to have beneficial effects on the skin, and it is said that Indian women owe their velvety complexions to the daily intake of turmeric in their foods.

Lore and Legend

The Persian sun worshippers held the golden crocus sacred as the representation on earth of the sun, and used saffron to dye their holy garments and color their skins. The availability of saffron, however, was not sufficient to supply all their needs, so a substitute of equally vibrant color was deemed acceptable for use: turmeric. Even today, turmeric is used as a dye and cosmetic. The faces of Hindu brides are made more glowing by being painted with turmeric, and many ladies use it in place of rouge to add radiance to the skin.

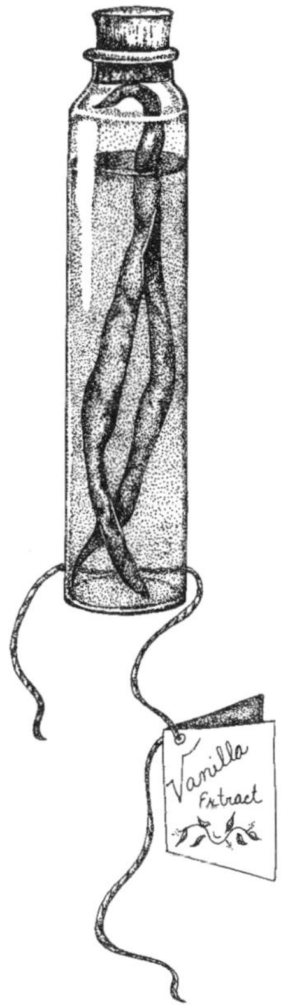

Vanilla (*Vanilla planifolia, V. tahitensis, V. fragrans*)

Vanilla derives both its Latin and English name from the Spanish vaina, *meaning sheath or pod; therefore* vainilla *is a diminutive meaning small sheath, with reference to the thinness of the black capsuled fruit. The Spanish word goes further back etymologically, to the Latin* vagina, *which was what the shape of the bean suggested to a number of people, giving it an aphrodisiac reputation.* Planifolia *means flat-leaved;* tahitensis *means coming from Tahiti;* fragrans *means fragrant.*

General Information Vanilla beans are the unripe dried fruits of the only member of the orchid family used as a foodstuff. One of the most expensive spices after saffron, vanilla is grown throughout most tropical areas within twenty degrees of the equator. The plant will grow elsewhere but not produce pods. In the wild of Mexico, vanilla vines climb trees in the shade of the jungle canopy and reach up for 250 feet or more. Under cultivation the vines are looped over specially planted trees or training stakes seven or eight feet tall to keep them within reach. Flowering lasts two months, with each blossom producing a single bean. The pods hang in banana-like bunches, growing for eight to nine months before they are harvested. The long thin pods are filled with a pulpy substance in which are embedded a multitude of all but invisible black seeds—the tiny black specks you may see, for instance, in vanilla ice cream. In its natural environment, a tiny bee called the melipone pollinated the vanilla orchid, but this insect is now extinct due to pesticide usage. All vanilla is now hand-pollinated, and pollination must occur within a few hours of the flower's opening. When mature, the pods must be picked just before the moment when, thoroughly ripened, they would split open by themselves. Without curing, the vanilla pod develops no great culinary interest. The aroma and flavor develop as a result of a complicated curing process that lasts five to six months or more after harvest. Bourbon beans are first "killed" by dipping baskets of them briefly into near-boiling water; in Mexico, the beans are first dried in sheds for several weeks. Next, the beans are laid out on wool blankets in the sun to bake until they are too hot to touch. At night they are wrapped in their blankets and sealed up indoors to "sweat;" this routine may continue for several weeks. The beans shrivel, become flexible, and darken, eventually turning chocolate brown to black. They are then dried for two to three months more in the shade before being tied in bundles and packed away for conditioning.

Vanilla

Nutritional Value Per 100 g Edible Portion

	Cured
Protein	2.6-10.0 g
Fat	4.7-21.2 g
Fiber	15.3-26.3 g
Calcium	1,900 mg
Phosphorus	70 mg

There is not enough natural vanilla in the world to supply even the American demand alone, which has intensified during the last decades due to the growing popularity of vanilla ice cream. Vanilla accounts for over 50 percent of all ice cream sales, and vanilla is also a constituent of many other flavors of ice cream. The United States alone imports 100,000 pounds (in 1980) of vanilla annually from Mexico, and enough from several other small tropical countries to exercise an appreciable effect on their economies. That part of the demand which genuine vanilla cannot meet is furnished by substitutes.

Bourbon vanilla is named after the French island of Reunion in the Indian Ocean, formerly known as Ile de Bourbon after the royal family. Most of it is actually grown on the northeastern coast of Madagascar, with smaller amounts coming from relatively nearby Reunion and the Comoro Islands. Madagascan vanilla is particularly smooth and rich, while Reunion has more sweetness and spice. **Mexican vanilla** is the traditional vanilla. It produces a fine flavor, with just a hint of sharpness or pungency. The best Mexican vanilla comes from the state of Veracruz, and where it grows the air is richly scented. **Tahitian vanilla** (*V. tahitensis*) vines produce fatter, thicker skinned, and more strongly flowery-scented beans compared with the more traditional Mexican vanilla. The plant was taken to Tahiti from Manila in 1848, and botanists still argue whether the specific strain was produced intentionally or by a chance mutation of nature. All the vanilla produced in Tahiti used to be exported to France, but the United States now imports half the crop.

Culinary Uses Vanilla pods should be chocolate-brown or coal-black in color, flexible, and covered with a frosting of aromatic crystals (*givre*, the French word for frost). The pods can be reused after making vanilla extract if washed and dried each time. They should be stored in a tightly sealed glass jar so that they lose no further moisture or volatile essence. Once they have reached the dry, brittle stage, they have lost their flavor and incomparable character. Vanilla has a wide range of uses in confectionery, being used as a flavoring in sauces, cakes and desserts, creams, baked goods, ice creams, and custards. The primary quality that vanilla adds is sweetness, although this is usually overwhelmed by the sweetness of sugar.

Extract is made by circulating a mixture of alcohol and water heated to 70 degrees Fahrenheit through chopped beans in a sealed vat, and then aging the resultant product for three to six months. The vanilla extract manufactured and sold in Mexico is frequently fortified with coumarin, a toxic natural flavoring obtained from the tonka bean. Coumarin contains no vanillin, but adds a sweet, smooth flavor close enough to true vanilla to fool most people. Unless you are certain of the purity, it is advisable to avoid buying extract in Mexico. Until 1954, when coumarin was banned in the United States for health reasons, its very sweet flavor was widely employed in artificial and blended vanilla extracts. **Pure vanilla extract** contains 35 percent alcohol by volume. **Vanilla flavoring** contains less alcohol, has the same taste components, but is less concentrated than vanilla extract. **Imitation vanilla** is, at best, made from a sulfite waste byproduct (vanillin) of soft-wood pulp used in the paper industry; at worst, it is a totally synthetic product (hydroxy-4 methoxy-3 benzaldehyde). By law, any vanilla product containing vanillin must be labeled as imitation. Although imitation vanilla simulates the flavor of pure vanilla to some degree, it is in comparison harsh, abrasive, and lacks the well-rounded, sweet flavor and aroma. There is nothing to recommend the use of imitation vanilla—real vanilla is worth any extra cost you might pay.

Health Benefits Choleretic. The medicinal value of vanilla has declined over the years but it was at one time considered to be a stimulant, an aid to digestion, and an aphrodisiac.

Verbena *(Verbena officinalis, Aloysia triphylla)*

The English name verbena *means green bough, and refers to the sacred branches of laurel, myrtle, or olive carried by heralds and certain priests.* Officinalis *means of the workshop, alluding to apothecaries' shops, and signifying that the plant was once part of the official pharmacopeia of Rome.* Aloysia *comes from the name Louisa, the plant being named after Maria Louisa, wife of King Charles IV of Spain;* triphylla *means three-leaved.*

General Information Verbena (*Verbena officinalis*) is native to the Mediterranean region, but early on spread throughout Eurasia. Even though it is rather undistinguished in appearance and not rare, verbena was long regarded with awe throughout its natural range. The plant was brought to North America by the Puritans, and now is widely naturalized throughout temperate North America. Lemon verbena (*Aloysia triphylla*) is an unassuming woody shrub with narrow, shiny, pale green leaves that taste like lemon and smell like a combination of lemons and limes. This plant charmed the Spanish explorers who happened upon it in Argentina and Chile with its delicate lemony aroma. Verbenas wound their way into the hearts of colonial gardeners because they provided both color for the eye and satisfaction for the nose, as well as a savory herb tea that relieved colds and fevers in a pleasant manner. Although people seem to find the fragrance intimate, this and other lemon-scented plants appear to act as natural insect repellents.

Culinary Uses Lemon verbena leaves are particularly useful because they will not lose their lemony flavor or aroma when dried or cooked. The leaves brighten the taste of vegetable marinades, salad dressings, jams, puddings, beverages, or anything else that needs just a touch of lemon.

Health Benefits Antispasmodic, aphrodisiac, astringent, diaphoretic, diuretic, sedative, tonic. Scientists have recently substantiated verbena's folk use as a diuretic, gout remedy, and anorexic (appetite suppressant). In southern Europe, it is recommended as a remedy for exhaustion and depression. Verbena corrects minor menstrual irregularities, its diuretic properties eliminate edemas caused by cardiovascular disorders, and it is used in the treatment of inflammation of the spleen and liver.

Lore and Legend

The European verbena or vervain plant was sacred to Mars, the ancient Roman god of war, and it was believed that the plant had the properties of repelling the enemy. Heralds bore crowns of verbena when dispatched to other nations carrying messages of peace, or to give defiance and challenge to an enemy. Verbena was also considered a great purifying plant, and its green leaves were used to cleanse tables and altars in festivities to honor Zeus and lesser gods. In ancient Gaul and Britain the plant was held in great veneration. It was both an ingredient of medieval witches' love potions and a charm against their evil spells; it even made its way into Christian lore as the plant used to staunch Christ's wounds on Calvary. The Druids regarded the vervain as a plant of spells and enchantment, and used it as a sacred food in their rituals, holding it in great reverence because they saw in its leaves a resemblance to those of the oak. In the north, vervain was sacred to Thor, the god of lightning.

Vinegar

The English name vinegar *comes from the French* vin aigre*, or sour wine, reflecting its first major source.*

General Information Vinegar is a sour liquid obtained by acetic fermentation, a natural process that occurs when a liquid containing less than 18 percent alcohol is exposed to the air. Bacteria present in the air react with the alcohol to produce a thick skin over the surface of the liquid, the "mother," which is a layer of yeast cells and bacteria that converts the alcohol into a natural acetic acid. This acid gives vinegar its characteristic sharpness. The most common sources of fermentable sugar are wine, apples, and grains. Like salt, vinegar is one of the oldest condiments used to season, preserve, and tenderize food. Vinegars owe their specific characteristics largely to their source and sometimes to fermentation techniques. In addition to different degrees of sourness or tartness, acidity, and other traits, a vinegar's essence can be tinged with the sweetness of fruits, the tang of an herb, the fragrance of a spice, or a blend of all three.

Varieties

Apple cider vinegar, when raw and unpasteurized, has a bright, crisp flavor, and is generally used for marinades, salad dressings, and sauces. It has about 5 to 6 percent acetic acid and a pronounced apple-acid flavor.

Vinegar

Nutritional Value Per 1 Tablespoon

	Apple Cider	Distilled
Calories	2	2
Protein	trace	trace
Calcium	1 mg	n/a
Iron	0.1 mg	n/a
Phosphorus	1 mg	n/a
Potassium	15 mg	2 mg
Sodium	trace	0 mg

Balsamic vinegar is made from grapes, pressed and cooked into a dark sweet liquid. This "must" is mixed with wine vinegar and aged in wooden barrels. Named for the Italian word for "balm," for its smooth, mellow character, this dark vinegar makes a delicious salad dressing with olive oil. Balsamic vinegar has a 6 percent acidity and is lustily sweet and woodsy, one of the most flavorful vinegars.

Malt vinegar is usually made from malted barley. Most often used for pickling onions and other vegetables, its strong flavor is overly harsh for use in salad dressings, but it combines well with fish and chips.

Rice vinegar is distilled from rice, has less sharpness than cider vinegar, and just a hint of sweetness. The Japanese use it to make sushi, dipping sauces, and many pickled dishes, but it is also good for marinating tofu (with soy sauce and ginger), and in grain and bean salads.

White distilled vinegar is the product of fermenting ethyl alcoholic fluids. Strong, acidic, and too sharp for dressings and regular cooking, it is good for washing windows and little else. Substitute lemon, tomato, or grapefruit juice in recipes where white vinegar is called for.

Wine vinegars have a 5 percent acidity, and may derive from red, white, or rosé wines. They are robust and perceptibly fruity and combine well with salads, sauces, and dressings.

Health Benefits Distilled vinegar should not be used internally, as it is highly demineralizing, leaching out phosphorous, overstimulating the thyroid gland, and rapidly destroying red blood corpuscles. Quality vinegars for internal use contain more of their own minerals; even so, these are potent and should be used sparingly. Like all fermented products, vinegar suspends salivary digestion, and thus prevents the proper assimilation of food. Apple cider vinegar has been used as a folk remedy for many types of disorders. However, one must continue to use vinegar to benefit chronic conditions. This vinegar dependency may be overcome with improved diet and lifestyle.

Vinegar neutralizes poisons in the body and thus is good for food poisoning. Take 1/4 teaspoonful every fifteen minutes until relieved. Soaking feet daily in vinegar will help clear up athlete's foot. Apply vinegar directly to insect bites or stings to relieve pain. Added to bath water, vinegar stimulates circulation and keeps the pores open. Used as a rinse, it gives hair a glossy appearance and soft texture. Apple cider vinegar brings immediate relief from burns and will retard scarring if applied immediately.

Lore and Legend

Greek legend attributes the violet to Jupiter, who changed his beloved Io into a white heifer for fear of Juno's jealousy. When Io shed tears over the coarseness of the common grass she was forced to feed upon, Zeus decided to create a new and more suitable plant for the delicate creature. From her fallen tears he caused to spring forth a sweet-smelling dainty flower, and gave it her name. Ancient Athenians held the plant in high regard for its power both to moderate anger and to cure insomnia. In Greek burials it was the custom to cover the dead with violets as a symbol of both the beauty and the transitory quality of life. The Greeks chose the violet as a symbol for Athens, dedicated this seductively-scented flower to Aphrodite, and from it made vast quantities of violet wine, as well as conserves and cosmetics. The flower became so popular that it was cultivated on a large scale to supply the needs of all the Mediterranean countries. In Toulouse, France, violets were given as a poetry prize during the age of troubadours, and in southern Germany during the Middle Ages, the appearance of the first spring violet was celebrated with dancing. The violet (posy) was a love token between Napoleon Bonaparte and Josephine, and later became his political emblem. He sometimes was known as Corporal Violet because of his fondness for the flower, and wearing a violet became a symbol of support among his followers while he was exiled on Elba. Upon his return to power in Paris, violets were strewn along the parade route.

Violet, Sweet (*Viola odorata*)

Viola *is the Latin form of the Greek name* Ione; odorata *means fragrant or odorous.* Violet *is the diminutive of the Latin* viola.

General Information Violets come originally from Europe, and since the days of Hippocrates have been used in medicines, perfumes, love potions, and sweets. Sweet violet, which has heart-shaped leaves, deep purple flowers, and root stalks that creep along the ground, is one of the most fragrant of the more than six hundred species of violets. Suggestive of soft kisses, violets are one of the tenderest of flowers, with an elusive fragrance.

Culinary Uses Violet flowers are highly fragrant and have a sweet aromatic flavor. The purple flowers can be candied or used fresh as a garnish in salads. Crystallized flowers are a familiar sight on violet-flavored sweets and chocolates. Violet water, made by weighting and steeping leaves and petals in water until fragrant, is used in tea breads, cupcakes, puddings, ices, fruit compotes, and chilled soups.

Health Benefits Antiseptic, diuretic, expectorant. Violet flowers contain an abundance of vitamins A and C. The leaves are mildly laxative and contain glucosides that are antiseptic; the roots and seeds are purgatives and emetics, causing severe gastric upset including nausea and vomiting. The flowers are now principally used as a coloring agent, as a fragrance in perfumes, and in cough syrups.

Wintergreen (*Gaultheria procumbens*)

This plant received its name in honor of Dr. Gaultier, a prominent physician in Quebec. Procumbens *means procumbent, laying face down, or having stems that trail along the ground without rooting. The English name* wintergreen *was given because this plant stays green and does not lose its leaves throughout the winter.*

General Information Wintergreen is a low-growing evergreen plant native to southern Canada and the United States. A member of the heath family, it has white flowers and spicy red berries. The leaves are sharply astringent and aromatic on account of the volatile oil, known as oil of wintergreen. Anyone who has ever sought relief from a muscle ache and reached for the Ben-Gay has experienced the soothing qualities of wintergreen's active constituent. Even more familiar is the refreshing minty taste of oil of wintergreen, a popular flavoring for gum, candy, and toothpaste.

Culinary Uses Wintergreen's shiny leaves may be nibbled on for a natural chewing gum—but only for half a minute or so because the sweet, aromatic taste soon turns bitter. The bright red berries are prized for their sweet and refreshing flavor, and can be eaten as a special treat on their own, with other fruit, or blended with honey to make a wintergreen spread.

Health Benefits Aromatic, astringent, carminative, diuretic, rubefacient, stimulant. The medicinal virtues of wintergreen leaves reside essentially in the oil of wintergreen which can be obtained by steam distillation. The oil consists primarily of methyl salicylate, one of the ingredients of aspirin. Not surprisingly then, the leaves have long been used for headaches and other aches and pains, inflammations, and rheumatism. Wintergreen tea will stimulate the stomach and respiration, and is beneficial as a gargle.

Yeast Extracts (*Saccharomyces cerevisiae*)

Saccharomyces *derives from the Latin* saccharus, *meaning sweet, and the Greek* myces, *meaning fungus or mushroom.*

General Information Yeasts are living organisms, microscopic, non-identical, single-celled fungi with as many as one hundred billion cells per ounce. These tiny plants, which occur naturally in honey, soil, and on rinds or peelings of fruits such as grapes, metabolize (digest) sugars and produce alcohols and carbon dioxide as by-products. They differ from other plant cells because they are not surrounded by cellulose, which must be destroyed either by proper mastication (chewing), cooking, or fermentation before the cell can be useful as food. Yeast probably came into human use by a happy accident, but is now widely utilized. The two main functions of commercial yeast are for fermentation and for growing nutrients. Fermenting yeasts include those used in baking and in brewing wine or beer. Nutrient-growing yeasts produce vitamins, enzymes, amino acids, and other microbial nutrients used in scientific research studies as well as for human or animal consumption. At the end of the growth period, the culture is pasteurized to kill the yeast.

Yeast Extracts

Nutritional Value

	Baker's Dry Active 1 pkg.	Brewer's Dry 1 Tbsp.	Torula 1 oz.
Calories	20	25	79
Protein	3 g	3 g	10.9 g
Fat	trace	trace	0.3 g
Fiber	n/a	n/a	n/a
Calcium	3 mg	6-60 mg	120 mg
Iron	1.1 mg	1.4 mg	5.5 mg
Phosphorus	90 mg	140 mg	486 mg
Potassium	140 mg	152 mg	580 mg
Sodium	4 mg	10 mg	4 mg
Beta Carotene (A)	trace	trace	trace
Thiamine (B_1)	0.160 mg	1.250 mg	3.970 mg
Riboflavin (B_2)	0.380 mg	0.340 mg	1.430 mg
Niacin (B_3)	2.600 mg	3.000 mg	12.600 mg
Ascorbic Acid (C)	trace	trace	trace

The "natural" B vitamins proclaimed in yeast are from synthetic vitamins fed the culture during its growth stage, and then the end product is further fortified. This allows a yeast of any B vitamin potency desired to be produced and used to formulate vitamin pills with "B vitamins derived from yeast." Ammonia also is generally added to the growth medium of the yeast, just as it is used in chemical farming—as a nitrogen fertilizer to increase protein content in the finished product.

Culinary Uses Nutritional yeast extracts have an agreeable taste, somewhat like cheese, but with a more refreshing aftertaste. For many it is an acquired taste; those who are nauseated by yeast or who find its taste disagreeable should avoid it. Fresh yeast should not be ingested except when the stomach is empty. It should be eaten by itself, allowed to dissolve slowly in the mouth, or mixed with warm water or milk—never with anything else. The best times to take fresh yeast are early in the morning, one hour before the evening meal, or at bedtime. Yeasts are used mostly in sandwich spreads or hot drinks, but are also used to flavor soups and stews.

Health Benefits Yeast is one of the most valuable antidotes against acid or toxic bile, and neutralizes irritation in the bowels, soothes inflamed surfaces, and restores normal bowel movements. Since it contains certain vitamins that help the deranged liver to oxidize fats properly (incompletely oxidized fats in the diet clog the oil and sebaceous glands and thus cause acne), yeast has a beneficial effect on the skin, and has long been used as a remedy for pimples and acne. In their raw state, yeasts are a rich source of the B vitamins and alkaline elements, especially sodium and potassium; cooking partially destroys these nutrients. What B_{12} there is in yeast is either included as an additive at the end of its manufacture, or else the yeast is grown in a B_{12}-enriched medium; not all contain the vitamin. Yeasts do have their disadvantages though: they are high in nucleic acids, which when metabolized are converted to uric acid crystals that tend to settle throughout the body and cause gout or kidney stones. They are exceptionally rich in certain nutrients, and deficient in others that are needed for balance; if not properly balanced with other foods, yeasts can cause deficiencies. Another problem with yeast is that microorganisms of this sort tend to induce unhealthy amounts of candida-type yeasts in the body, especially in more susceptible individuals.

Varieties

Baker's yeast is used to give lift and lightness to baked products. When given a moist, warm environment, the yeast cells start to grow and outgas carbon dioxide, causing bread to rise. If temperatures are too cold or too hot, the yeast will not function properly, and the baked product will be dense and heavy. Baker's yeast works best with hard wheat flours, not with the softer pastry wheats or other grains, because hard wheat is the only grain with sufficient gluten to trap the gases produced by yeast and induce rising. Other grains like rye, barley, and corn have to be mixed with hard wheat flour or gluten flour if you expect them to rise well with yeast. Baker's yeast is available in two forms: compressed or dry. **Compressed yeast** is a fresh, soft yeast obtainable in one-pound blocks from most bakeries. Extremely perishable, it should be stored in the refrigerator and used within a week, although it can be frozen successfully for longer periods of time. When its light gray color turns to brown, it is too old to use. There are also small cakes wrapped in foil, but this size also must be kept refrigerated and used within a week. **Dry yeast** generally comes in small foil packets and will keep for about six months. Many commercial baking yeasts contain BHT (butylated hydroxytoluene), a petroleum base antioxidant that is best avoided. Baker's yeast, since it is active, should not be used as a nutritional supplement. Live yeast feeds on the foods in the intestinal tract, and may cause health problems.

Brewer's yeast, now called **Nutritional yeast,** was originally the byproduct of beer production, hence its name. The original yeast was grown on barley malt, rice, corn or corn syrup, and hops. Now most nutritional yeast is grown on a molasses or sugar beet solution for use solely as a nutritional supplement. Once grown, the yeast is removed from the vats, debittered, and reduced to a powder by being sprayed through drying chambers kept at a temperature of 250 degrees Fahrenheit—which kills and sterilizes, as well as giving it the characteristic "chicken soup" flavor. The resulting product keeps well, but is classed as a "dead" yeast because it will not leaven dough. Nutritionally, brewer's yeast has some strong points and some weak points. It contains a full complement of amino acids, iron, and B vitamins, as well as a few hard-to-get trace elements like selenium and chromium. However, the heating not only reduces the vitamin content, but also changes its organic salts into inorganic salts, rendering it acidic to the body. Also, yeast is a high phosphorus food, and as such needs to be balanced out by some sort of calcium supplementation, and it is high in purines, which produce uric acid, a prime factor in gout, a painful disease of the joints. Unlike fresh yeast, nutritional yeast is compatible with any kind of food and causes less flatulence. To most people, it has a pleasant-tasting, cheesy flavor, and can be used directly on vegetables, baked potatoes, popcorn, and other foods as a condiment.

Torula yeast is frequently (but not always) grown on food-grade ethyl alcohol, a by-product of petroleum refining and paper making. It is frequently added to processed foods such as dessert toppings and pastries, and is used as a meat substitute in extenders. This type of yeast has been found to irritate some people. Torula yeast is not considered by many nutritionists to be a true food.

Yellow Dock *(Rumex crispus)*

Rumex is an old Latin term for lance, in reference to the shape of its leaves; crispus means curled. The English name dock most likely comes from the Scottish Gaelic dogha, meaning burdock.

Yellow Dock

Nutritional Value Per 100 g Edible Portion

	Raw	Cooked	Dried
Calories	22	20	284
Protein	2.00 g	1.83 g	20.30 g
Fat	0.70 g	0.64 g	4.10 g
Fiber	0.80 g	0.73 g	12.20 g
Calcium	44 mg	38 mg	1,000 mg
Iron	2.40 mg	2.08 mg	76 mg
Magnesium	103 mg	89 mg	320 mg
Phosphorus	63 mg	52 mg	757 mg
Potassium	390 mg	321 mg	1,220 mg
Sodium	4 mg	3 mg	7.7 mg
Manganese	n/a	n/a	14.5 mg
Beta Carotene (A)	4,000 IU	3,474 IU	37,432 IU
Thiamine (B_1)	0.040 mg	0.034 mg	0.810 mg
Riboflavin (B_2)	0.100 mg	0.086 mg	1.080 mg
Niacin (B_3)	0.500 mg	0.411 mg	5.400 mg
Ascorbic Acid (C)	48.0 mg	26.3 mg	405.4 mg

General Information Yellow dock is a perennial plant of the *Rumex* genus, a group of plants that includes sorrel, rhubarb, and buckwheat. It is native to Europe and Asia, but was early introduced into America, and is now found nearly everywhere throughout the United States, most often as a troublesome weed in fields and waste places. It quickly inhabits cultivated ground and grows along roadsides, producing copious quantities of seed each fall. Its slender, curly leaves are used as a vegetable and potherb, and are best gathered in the spring so that they are young and tender. The most medicinal part is the root.

Culinary Uses Young leaves of yellow dock have a sharp, bitter flavor similar to that of spinach, but with a slight tinge of lemon. Like dandelion greens, the leaves are tasty only when young and tender, and again after autumn frost has removed the leaves' bitterness. The new leaves make a pleasant steamed green on their own or mixed with spinach, especially when seasoned with a little garlic and olive oil. It is recommended to cook the leaves before eating due to their high oxalic content; they are relatively safe when boiled in water that has been changed twice, since this cooks away much of the acid.

Health Benefits Antiscorbutic, astringent, laxative, tonic. Known as a medicinal plant since ancient times, yellow dock (both leaves and root) has been used as a laxative or mild astringent tonic, strengthening the circulatory system, purifying the blood, and cleansing the lymphatic system. A good liver and spleen herb, yellow dock also stimulates the elimination channels (especially the skin) and promotes the elimination of excess lymph fluid. During the nineteenth century, it gained popularity as a remedy for jaundice and as a tonic for the liver and gall bladder, and has since been included in nearly all herbal liver remedies. The active principles in yellow dock are the astringent tannins and purgative anthraquinone glycosides, based on emodin and chrysophenic acid, which have antimicrobial properties. Decoctions of the plant are useful in scrofulous diseases of the skin, including psoriasis and eczema. Its astringent and antimicrobial properties also explain the use of the powdered root as an abrasive dentrifice, especially in cases of spongy gums. Ointments or herbal bath treatments with yellow dock make effective treatments for skin conditions such as eczema, itches, sores, hives, and ringworm.

COOKING TIMES AND PROPORTIONS

Grains

(1 CUP DRY MEASURE)	WATER	COOKING TIME	YIELD
Amaranth	2 1/2 cups	20–25 minutes	2 1/2 cups
Barley			
Whole (hulled)	3 cups	1 hour, 25 minutes	3 1/2 cups
Scotch	3 cups	50–55 minutes	3 1/2 cups
Pearled	2 1/2 cups	40–45 minutes	3 1/2 cups
Grits	4 cups	20 minutes	3 2/3 cups
Rolled	3 cups	30 minutes	2 2/3 cups
Buckwheat			
Groats/Kasha	2 cups	15 minutes	2 1/2 cups
Grits	3 cups	10–15 minutes	2 1/3 cups
Corn			
Cornmeal	3–4 cups	15 minutes	3 3/4 cups
Grits	5 cups	25–30 minutes	3 cups
Polenta	4 cups	25 minutes	3 1/2 cups
Job's Tears	4 cups	70 minutes	2 1/2 cups
Kamut			
Whole berries	3 cups	1 1/2 hours	2 2/3 cups
Flakes	3 cups	20 minutes	3 cups
Millet	2 1/2 cups	30 minutes	4 cups
Oats			
Whole	3 1/2 cups	45–60 minutes	3 cups
Groats	3 cups	60 minutes	3 cups
Steel–cut	3 1/2 cups	40–45 minutes	3 cups
Rolled (oatmeal)	2 cups	10 minutes	1 3/4 cups
Quinoa	2 cups	15 minutes	3 1/2 cups
Rice			
Brown	2 1/2 cups	40–60 minutes	3 cups
White and Converted	2 cups	15–20 minutes	3 cups
Wild	3 1/2 cups	1 hour	4 cups
Rye			
Berries	3 1/4 cups	2 hours	2 1/2 cups
Flakes	3 cups	30 minutes	2 2/3 cups
Grits	3 cups	45 minutes	2 2/3 cups
Sorghum	3 cups	1 hour	~3 cups
Spelt			
Whole berries	3 cups	1 1/2 hours	2 2/3 cups
Flakes	3 cups	20 minutes	3 cups
T'ef	3 cups	15 minutes	3 cups
Triticale			
Whole berries	3 cups	70 minutes	2 1/2 cups
Cracked	3 cups	25 minutes	3 cups
Wheat			
Whole berries	3 cups	1 1/2 hours	2 2/3 cups
Bulgur (steep in hot water)	2 cups	15–20 minutes	2 1/2 cups
Cracked	3 cups	25 minutes	3 cups
Couscous	2 cups	15 minutes	2 1/2 cups
Farina	2 1/2 cups	3 minutes	2 1/2 cups
Flakes	3 cups	20 minutes	3 cups

Legumes

(1 CUP MEASURE)	WATER	COOKING TIME	YIELD
Aduki Beans	3 1/2 cups	45–60 minutes	3 cups
Black–Eyed Peas	3 cups	1 hour	2 cups
Broad/Fava Beans	4 cups	1 hour	2 cups
Chickpeas (Garbanzos)	4 cups	3 hours	2 cups
Kidney Bean Family	3 cups	2 hours	2 cups
Lentils	3 cups	30–60 minutes	2 1/4 cups
Lima Beans			
Large	2 cups	1 1/2 hours	2 cups
Baby	2 cups	1 hour	1 3/4 cups
Mung	3 cups	1 hour	2 cups
Dried Peas	3 1/2 cups	1 hour	2 1/4 cups
Pigeon Peas	3 cups	90 minutes	3 cups
Scarlet Runner Beans	3 cups	75 minutes	3 cups
Soybeans	4 cups	3+ hours	2 cups
Soy grits	2 cups	15 minutes	2 cups

GLOSSARY OF TERMS USED

Adaptogen An herb that maintains health by increasing the body's ability to adapt to environmental and internal stress, generally by strengthening the immune system, nervous system, and/or glandular system.

Amino Acids The chief components of proteins, synthesized by living cells or obtained as essential components of the diet.

Analgesic An herb that relieves pain without causing loss of consciousness. Some analgesics are also antispasmodics, relieving pain by reducing cramping in muscles; others affect the nerves directly, reducing the pain signals to the brain.

Anodyne A substance that soothes, calms, or comforts.

Anesthetic An agent that induces loss of feeling or reduces pain in an area by desensitizing the nerves.

Anthelmintic An agent that tends to kill and/or expel intestinal parasitic worms. Plants containing substances that are obnoxious to the worms or which act as cathartics have been used for this purpose. Chamomile and tansy are two such examples.

Anthocyanidins The anthocyanidins (and proanthocyanidins) are the flavonoids responsible for the red to blue colors of blueberries, blackberries, cherries, grapes, hawthorn berries, and many flowers. These flavonoids are found in the flesh of the fruit as well as the skin. They are able to increase vitamin C levels within the cells, decrease the leakiness and breakage of small blood vessels, protect against free-radical damage, and support our joint structures.

Antibacterial Any substance that has the ability, even in dilute solutions, to destroy or inhibit the growth or reproduction of bacteria and other microorganisms; used especially in the treatment of infectious diseases.

Antibiotic An organic substance that is capable of killing viruses, bacteria, or other microorganisms and is used to combat infections or disease. While many herbal antibiotics have direct germ killing effects, their primary action is the stimulation of the body's own immune response.

Antidote A remedy to counteract or neutralize poisons and toxins.

Antioxidants Substances that oppose oxidation or inhibit reactions promoted by oxygen or peroxides.

Antiscorbutic A substance that prevents the disease scurvy, caused by a deficiency of vitamin C.

Antiseptic A substance that prevents sepsis, or putrefaction and decay, by arresting the growth or action of noxious microorganisms, either by inhibiting their activity or by destroying them. The term antiseptic generally refers to agents applied to living tissue; the term disinfectant to those used on inanimate objects such as floors, walls, or clothing.

Antispasmodic A relaxant or nervine that relieves or prevents involuntary muscle contractions or "spasms," such as those occurring in epilepsy, painful menstruation, intestinal cramping, or muscle "shock." Antispasmodics are included in most herb formulas to relax the body and allow it to use its full energy for healing.

Aphrodisiac A substance believed to arouse sexual desire and improve sexual potency and power.

Aromatic An herb with a strong, volatile, and fragrant aroma. Medicinally, aromatics are used to relieve flatulence, open nasal passages, or eliminate phlegm, although many people regard them merely as pleasant fragrances, which are often added to medicines to improve their palatability.

Astringent An agent that causes a constricting, drawing together or binding effect such as dehydration, thus checking the discharge of mucous or blood, or that closes skin pores, tightens muscles, and the like.

Balsamic A substance that has the odor of an aromatic substance called balsam, which is derived from various plants and used in medicinal preparations to heal or soothe.

Butyric Acid This short-chain fatty acid (SCFA) provides an important energy source for cells that line the colon. In fact, butyrate is the preferred source for energy metabolism in the colon, and its production may be responsible for the anticancer properties of dietary fiber.

Carminative An agent that checks the formation of gas in the gastrointestinal tract and aids in dispelling whatever gas has already formed. The after-dinner mint is the most familiar carminative. Among other herbs and spices used as carminatives are anise, caraway, cloves, dill, and ginger.

Carnitine This vitamin-like compound stimulates the breakdown of long chain fatty acids by mitochondria (energy-producing units in cells). Carnitine is essential in the transport of fatty acids into the mitochondria; it is synthesized from the amino acid lysine in the liver, kidney, and brain. Carnitine increases HDL (good) cholesterol levels, while decreasing triglyceride and LDL (bad) cholesterol levels.

Carotene Carotenes or carotenoids represent the most widespread group of naturally occurring pigments in nature. They are a highly colored (red to yellow) group of fat-soluble compounds that function in plants to protect against damage caused during photosynthesis. Carotenes are best known for their capacity for conversion into vitamin A; for their antioxidant activity; and for their correlation with the maximum life-span potential of humans, other primates, and mammals. The leading sources of carotenes are dark green leafy vegetables and yellow-orange fruits and vegetables.

Catarrh An inflammation of any mucous membrane, but especially one affecting the respiratory tract.

Cathartic An agent (laxative or purgative) that causes the evacuation of the bowels. A laxative provides a gentle stimulation and quickening of peristaltic action, while a purgative stimulates the secretions of the intestines, is much more forceful, and used only in stubborn conditions.

Chlorophyll Chlorophyll is the green pigment of plants found in the chloroplast compartment of plant cells. In the chloroplast, electromagnetic energy (light) is converted into chemical energy through the process known as photosynthesis. The natural chlorophyll found in green plants is fat-soluble, and is used as a vulnerary.

Cholagogue An agent that stimulates the gallbladder and biliary duct to discharge bile into the small intestine and increase the body's excretion of cholesterol.

Choleretic An agent that stimulates the liver to increase its production of bile, which helps emulsify fats in the duodenum and increase peristalsis.

Choline Choline performs the vital function of making the main components of the cell membranes, such as phosphatidylcholine (lecithin) and sphingomyelin. Choline is also required for the proper metabolism of fats; without choline, fats become trapped in the liver and block metabolism.

Contraindication This is a certain condition for which the specific herb (or other plant) is not recommended.

Corm A solid, swollen part of a stem, usually underground, protected by a thin layer of scale leaves. It differs from a true bulb in that it is solid and sends down a root when a new growing season begins. Usually starchy and edible.

Decoction A preparation made by simmering roots, bark, seeds, or stems of herbs in water.

Demulcent An agent that is soothing to the intestinal tract, usually of an oily or mucilaginous nature, and which provides a protective coating and allays irritation. Also soothes and softens the part to which it is applied, acting to relieve irritation. Glycerin and olive oil are well-known examples.

Depurative Having cleansing properties, but especially a blood purifier.

Diaphoretic An herb or substance taken internally to increase perspiration, usually through expansion of capillaries near the skin. Such medicines are also called **sudorifics**, and have been used along with sweat baths throughout history to promote general and specific health.

Dietary Fiber Originally the definition of dietary fiber was restricted to the sum of plant compounds that are not digestible by the secretions of the human digestive tract. For everyday purposes, however, the term refers to the components of plant cell walls as well as to the indigestible residues. The composition of the plant cell wall varies according to the species of plant. Most contain 35 percent insoluble fiber, 45 percent soluble fiber, 17 percent lignans, 3 percent protein, and 2 percent ash.

Diuretic An agent which increases the secretion and discharge of urine. Notable herbs are dandelion, juniper berries, and lemon juice.

Ellagic Acid One of ellagic acid's primary actions is to protect against damage to our chromosomes and to block the cancer-causing actions of many pollutants. Ellagic acid is a potent antioxidant and has shown an ability to increase many of the body's antioxidant compounds.

Emetic An agent that causes or promotes vomiting.

Emmenagogue A substance that promotes the onset of menstruation. Some emmenagogues, such as pennyroyal, are so strong that they have been used to induce abortion.

Emollient An agent that will soften and soothe the surface of the body when applied locally to the skin or other exposed tissue. Similar to **demulcents**, emollients are used externally on the skin.

Expectorant A medicinal substance that helps in the expulsion of mucus or phlegm from the throat or lungs (by coughing, sneezing, or spitting).

Fatty Acids Any of numerous acids that occur naturally, usually in the form of esters in fats, waxes, and essential oils. Omega-3 fatty acids are polyunsaturated fats that may help reduce the risk of heart disease.

Febrifuge An agent that reduces fever.

Flavonoid The flavonoids are a group of plant pigments largely responsible for the colors of fruits and flowers. In plants, flavonoids protect against environmental stress, while in humans, they seem to function as "biological response modifiers." Flavonoid molecules are unique in being active against a wide variety of oxidants and free radicals. Bioflavonoids are flavonoids with recognized biological activity.

Galactogogue Substances that increase the secretion of milk.

Glycoside Glycosides are complex organic substances that when hydrolyzed (split by the action of water, acids, or enzymes) separate into two parts: a sugar (glycone) component and a nonsugar (aglycone) component. Glycosides also include saponins, a characteristic of which is that they produce a soapy foam.

Hemostatic Any substance that prevents bleeding, arrests hemorrhaging, or promotes clotting of blood.

Hydrogenation The process of adding hydrogen to unsaturated oils to turn them into semi-solid fats, destroying the double bonds in the fatty acids and saturating the carbon atoms with hydrogen; the resulting fats contain more saturated fat than the liquids from which they were made.

Infusion A preparation made by pouring boiling water on dried or fresh flowers or leaves, and then steeping. All herbal infusions and decoctions should be freshly prepared and used within twelve hours.

Inositol Inositol functions quite closely with choline. It is a primary component of cell membranes, where it is bound as phosphatidylinositol. Like choline, inositol promotes the flow of fat to and from the liver, and has shown some promise as a treatment in diabetic neuropathy. Good sources include citrus fruits, whole grains, nuts and seeds, and legumes.

IU The abbreviation for **International Unit**, a quantity of something (such as a vitamin) that produces a particular biological effect agreed upon as an international standard.

Laxative An herb, food, or medicine that causes elimination of the feces. Laxatives work by stimulating peristaltic action of the intestinal wall, by moistening the colon, by increasing the secretion of bile, or by relaxing intestinal cramps.

Lignan Lignans are compounds found in high-fiber foods that show important properties, such as anticancer, antibacterial, antifungal, and antiviral activity. Flax seeds are the most abundant source of lignans, but other seeds, grains, and legumes are also good sources.

Mucilage Mucilages are generally found within the inner layer (endosperm) of grains, legumes, nuts and seeds. Guar gum, found in most legumes, is the most widely studied plant mucilage. Guar gum and other mucilages, including psyllium seed husk and glucomannan, are perhaps the most potent cholesterol-lowering agents of gel-forming fibers. In addition, mucilage fibers have been shown to reduce fasting and after-meal glucose and insulin levels in both healthy and diabetic subjects.

Mucilaginous These herbs are full of or secrete a sticky or slimy, gelatin-like substance that is soothing to inflammations. Mucilages and gums form gels when mixed with water and are used externally to soothe inflamed skin, while internally their bulking effect is laxative and cleansing.

Nervine An herb that relaxes the whole body or a part of the body by affecting the nervous system, and which gives a feeling of healthy well-being.

Nutritive A substance that is thought to gradually increase some function of the body, generally by supplying nutrients, rather than by stimulation of the nervous or circulatory system.

Pectin Pectins are found in all plant cell walls, as well as in the outer skin and rind of fruits and vegetables. For example, the rind of an orange contains 30 percent pectin; an apple peel 15 percent; and onion skins 12 percent. The gel-forming properties of pectin are well known to anyone who has made jelly or jam. Pectins also lower cholesterol levels, by binding it along with bile acids in the intestines and promoting their excretion.

Phytochelatins Large plant molecules that lock around minerals and hold them, thus removing toxic minerals (such as cadmium, copper, mercury, and lead) from the body.

Phytoestrogens Plant estrogens that seem to act as a key to unlock and potentiate existing estrogen within the body, eliminating or easing many of the symptoms of low estrogen.

Purgative A cleansing agent that will purge the bowels, such as a strong laxative.

Refrigerant An old medical term referring to plant drugs that cool the blood and reduce fever.

Rhizome An elongated, thickened, usually horizontal, underground plant stem that sends out roots below and shoots above. It is differentiated from ordinary rootstock by the presence of nodes, buds, and occasionally scale-like leaves.

Rubefacient A substance that increases blood circulation to the area where it is applied (turning it red), usually on the skin but sometimes internally. Its function is to draw inflammation and congestions from deeper areas.

Saponins These compounds form stable froths or foams when shaken in water. Their healing effect resides in their capacity to break up red blood cells.

Sedative Herbs that greatly quiet the nervous system.

Stimulant An agent that produces a temporary increase in the various functional actions of the body, such as quickening digestion or raising body temperature. It does this quickly, unlike a tonic, which stimulates general health over a period of time. Unlike a narcotic, it does not necessarily produce a feeling of general well-being, which a narcotic produces by depressing nerve centers. Among the best known plant stimulants are cinnamon, cloves, ginger, horseradish, pepper, peppermint, and sage.

Stomachic An agent that gives strength and tone to the stomach or stimulates the appetite by promoting digestive secretions. Stomachics can also stimulate the secretion of hydrochloric acid.

Tannin Tannins are organic substances of diverse composition with pronounced astringent properties that react with protein. One of the best known uses of tannins is in preserving animal hides by turning them into leather; tannins also soothe inflamed mucous membranes and promote wound healing and the formation of new skin.

Tincture An alcohol or water/alcohol fluid extraction of medicinal herbs that concentrates herbal properties and can be kept at full potency for years. Tinctures were particularly popular with herbalists during the late nineteenth and early twentieth centuries. Usually a specified number of drops of tincture are mixed with a small amount of water or juice, and this mixture is taken according to directions.

Tonic An herb usually used by itself to strengthen or tone the body or some part of the body gradually by stimulating the nutrition of tissues within the body. Bitter tonics stimulate the flow of gastric juices, increasing the appetite, and promoting the intake of food. Tonics are usually slightly stimulating, as opposed to being only nutritive. Whether an herb is regarded as a tonic, a nutritive builder, or a stimulant often has to do more with the dose or quantity used than with its actual properties. When tonics are used in formulas they are often referred to as neutrals (balancers).

Vermifuge Any substance that destroys and expels intestinal worms and similar intestinal parasites upon ingestion or repeated ingestion. Also called an **anthelmintic**.

Vulnerary Any plant or substance used to treat wounds, usually an antibiotic or antiseptic, that promotes healing through cell regeneration and repair. These were extremely important herbs in the days of hand-to-hand combat.

ANNOTATED BIBLIOGRAPHY

Airola, Paavo. *Are You Confused?* Phoenix, Ariz.: Health Plus Publishers, 1971. Broad health overview, somewhat dated and dogmatic.

Andrews, Jean. *Peppers: The Domesticated Capsicums.* Austin, Tex.: University of Texas Press, 1984. Scientific and historical overview of the Capsicum genus, with lots of pictures.

Appleton, Nancy, Ph.D. *Lick The Sugar Habit.* New York: Avery Publishing Group, 1988. Exposé on sugar addiction and allergic responses; interesting information and very pertinent to our Western culture.

Baggett, Nancy, Ruth Glick, and Gloria Kaufer Greene. *Eat Your Vegetables!* New York: Times Books, 1985. A brief history and recipes for the more common vegetables.

Bailey, Adrian (editor). *Cook's Ingredients.* Pleasantville, N.Y.: Reader's Digest Association, 1990. Very brief overview, with lots of pictures of kitchen ingredients, including meats.

Bailey, Liberty H. *How Plants Get Their Names.* New York: Dover Publications, 1963. I used the list of specific Latin names from the Appendix. The rest of the book is slanted toward the horticulturist or botanist.

———. *Standard Cyclopedia of Horticulture.* New York: Macmillan, 1922. A discussion of all plants known to cultivation at the time. Encompassing six large volumes, it has a lot more information than most people would ever want or need to know. I used it for the history of plant names.

Baker, Elton, and Elizabeth Baker. *Bandwagon to Health.* Col.: Drelwood Publications, 1984. Deals with transitional diet from processed to raw foods, and leads through steps.

———. *The UnCook Book.* Wash.: Drelwood Publications, 1980. Excellent book on raw foods and food combining, with delicious recipes.

Balch, James F., M.D., and Phyllis A. Balch, CNC. *Prescription for Nutritional Healing.* New York: Avery Publishing Group, 1990. Fairly comprehensive self-help guide organized by ailment.

Ballentine, Rudolph, M.D. *Diet & Nutrition: A Holistic Approach.* Honesdale, Penn.: Himalayan International Institute, 1982. A comprehensive study of nutrition and diet, and an overview of Ayurvedic principles.

Ballister, Barry. *Barry Ballister's Fruit and Vegetable Stand.* Woodstock, N.Y.: Overlook Press, 1987. Overview of fruits and vegetables written from the greengrocer's view. Some nutritional information and recipes.

Behr, Edward. *The Artful Eater: A Gourmet Investigates the Ingredients of Great Food.* New York: Atlantic Monthly Press, 1992. Origins and uses of some familiar ingredients.

Bianchini, Francesco, Francesco Corbetta, and Marilena Pistoia. Translated by Italia and Alberto Mancinelli. *The Complete Book of Fruits and Vegetables.* New York: Crown Publishers, 1975. Beautiful illustrations, text leans heavily toward botany.

Bieler, Henry G., M.D.. *Food is Your Best Medicine.* New York: Ballantine Books, 1982. Discusses the body and its operations, the genesis of diseases, and how foods can rebuild the body. Tends to ramble.

Bragg, Paul C. *The Shocking Truth About Water.* Desert Hot Springs, Cal.: Health Science, 1975. Explains why water is a prime requisite for health, what actions it performs within the body, the best types of water, and how to find them. Very fascinating little book, well worth reading.

Brandt, Johanna. *The Grape Cure.* St. Catherines, Ontario, Canada: Provoker Press, 1967. Story of her miraculous recovery from cancer, and her attempts to help others in the United States.

Brothwell, Don and Patricia. *Food in Antiquity: A Survey of the Diet of Early Peoples.* New York: Frederick A. Praeger, 1969. Interesting historical and botanical information on various foods written from an anthropological viewpoint.

Bruder, Roy. *Discovering Natural Foods.* Santa Barbara, Cal.: Woodbridge Press, 1982. Nice, well-written, and informative introduction to natural foods, written by a former store owner.

Bumgarner, Marlene Anne. *Book of Whole Grains.* New York: St. Martin's Press, 1976. A beginner's book on grains, has a wide selection of recipes (not vegan).

Carroll, Anstice, and Embree de Persiis Vona. *The Health Food Dictionary with Recipes.* New York: Weathervane Books, 1973. Encyclopedic style of foods, primarily slanted toward a person new to nutrition and healthful eating.

Carper, Jean. *The Food Pharmacy.* New York: Bantam Books, 1988. Discoveries about diet's impact on disease. Goes through fifty-five foods that have had medicinal properties investigated, and gives research reports and conclusions. From a traditional scientific/medical background and perspective.

Castleman, Michael. *The Healing Herbs.* Emmaus, Penn.: Rodale Press, 1991. Reputable herbalist; list of possible side effects and contraindications.

Cituk, Kathy and John Finnegan. *Natural Foods and Good Cooking.* Mill Valley, Cal.: Elysian Arts, 1989. A conservative approach to healthier living. Very basic.

Clute, Willard N. *The Common Names of Plants and Their Meanings.* Indianapolis, Ind.: Willard N. Clute & Co., 1942. A small, rambling book about how plants get their names and some of their meanings.

Coon, Nelson. *Using Plants For Healing.* Emmaus, Penn.: Rodale Press, 1979. History of medicinal plants, preparation, and glossary.

Cost, Bruce. *Bruce Cost's Asian Ingredients.* New York: William Morrow and Co., 1988. A guide to the fresh, preserved, and bottled ingredients arriving in our markets from Asia. Recipes for most ingredients.

Creasy, Rosalind. *The Complete Book of Edible Landscaping.* San Francisco: Sierra Club Books, 1982. Deals mostly with fruit and nut trees.

Cusumano, Camille. *The New Foods.* New York: Henry Holt and Company, 1989. A guide to some of the newer foods (and some that are now very familiar).

Davidson, Alan. *Fruit: A Connoisseur's Guide and Cookbook.* New York: Simon & Schuster, 1991. An informative account of the edible fruits and nuts of the world. The organization is a little unusual, but the illustrations are stunning, and there is a complete index if you get lost.

Davis, Ben. *Rapid Healing Foods.* West Nyack, N.Y.: Parker Publishing Co, 1980. Foods that cleanse the body of poisons and help relieve multiple ailments. Many personal stories, very little scientific research cited.

Dawson, Adele G. *Health, Happiness and the Pursuit of Herbs.* Brattleboro, Vt.: Stephen Greene Press, 1980. Arranged more for gardeners, but still an interesting book.

Diamond, Harvey and Marilyn. *Fit for Life.* New York: Warner Books, 1985. Basics on health and nutrition, diet plan for transition to healthier eating, good recipes. Would highly recommend for any and all to read.

———. *Living Health.* New York: Warner Books, 1987. Continuation of Fit for Life program, additional information and recipes.

Diamond, Marilyn. *American Vegetarian Cookbook.* New York: Warner Books, 1990. Completely vegan, good basic book with simple recipes. Lots of information regarding foods, nutrients. Substitute chart for old-style cooking.

Doyle, Harrison. *Golden Chia: Ancient Indian Energy Food.* Vista, Cal.: Hillside Press, 1975. An rambling story about the author's experience with both eating and growing Chia seeds.

Dyer, T.F. Thiselton. *The Folk-lore of Plants.* New York: D. Appleton and Co., 1889. Contains some good information, but difficult to read and not well organized.

Editors of the East West Journal. *Shopper's Guide to Natural Foods.* Garden City Park, N.Y.: Avery Publishing Group, 1987. A beginner's introduction to natural foods and food stores.

Elkort, Martin. *The Secret Life of Food: A Feast of Food and Drink History, Folklore, and Fact.* Los Angeles, Cal.: Jeremy P. Tarcher Inc., 1991. A fun book full of historical information, anecdotes, and definitions.

Elliot, Rose. *The Complete Vegetarian Cuisine.* New York: Pantheon Books, 1988. Beautifully illustrated book, half reference and half cookbook. European-style cookery.

Esser, William L. *Dictionary of Foods.* Bridgeport, CT: Natural Hygiene Press, 1953, 1983. Have both old and new versions; makes for a nice encyclopedic listing of natural foods. Ideologies are in line with Herbert Shelton's writings.

Fielder, Mildred. *Wild Fruits: An Illustrated Field Guide & Cookbook.* Chicago, Ill: Contemporary Books, 1983. Identifies and provides recipes for seventy-eight North American wild fruits.

Finnegan, John. *The Facts about Fats.* Mill Valley, Cal.: Elysian Arts, 1992. Role of fats and oils in diet, how processed, uses and abuses.

Friedlander, Barbara. *The Vegetable, Fruit & Nut Book: Secrets of the Seed.* New York: Grosset & Dunlap, 1974. An eclectic gathering of facts, history and myths, and other items of interest about these plants.

Gledhill, D. *The Names of Plants.* New York: Cambridge University Press, 1989. An excellent dictionary of botanical terms and their meanings.

Grieve, Maude. *A Modern Herbal, vols. 1 and 2.* New York: Dover Publications, 1971. An old-style listing of primarily English botanical herbs with some spices. Wouldn't recommend for the novice reader.

Griggs, Barbara. *The Food Factor.* Middlesex, England: Viking Books, 1986. The fascinating history of nutrition, vitamins, government policy, and the health pioneers.

Grigson, Sophie. *Gourmet Ingredients.* New York: Van Nostrand Reinhold, 1991. Foods from a British point of view, some foods still unseen in North America.

Halpin, Anne Moyer (editor). *Unusual Vegetables.* Emmaus, Penn.: Rodale Press, 1978. Interesting book on some lesser known and obscure vegetables, as well as some more familiar ones.

Haughton, Claire Shaver. *Green Immigrants: The Plants That Transformed America.* New York: Harcourt Brace Jovanovich, 1978.A fascinating book about many botanical immigrants to America. Well worth reading for those interested in plant history.

Healey, B.J. *A Gardener's Guide to Plant Names.* New York: Charles Scribner's Sons, 1972. Deals primarily with flower names, but there are a smattering of other ones thrown in.

Heifetz, Jeanne. *Green Groceries: A Mail-Order Guide to Organic Foods.* New York: HarperCollins, 1992. An excellent sourcebook for mail-ordering any sort of organic food items; in fact, this is the only book I have seen that has put all these sources together in one place.

Heinerman, John. *Encyclopedia of Fruits, Vegetables and Herbs.* West Nyack, N.Y.: Parker Publishing Company, 1988. From a medical anthropologist, an alphabetical listing of common fruits, vegetables, and herbs, and some of their health-promoting uses. Very useful home remedy book.

Heiser, Charles B., Jr. *Seed to Civilization: The Story of Food.* San Francisco, Cal.: W.H. Freeman and Company, 1981. A quick history of agriculture and food crops.

Hendrickson, Robert. *Foods for Love.* New York: Stein and Day, 1974. A guide to aphrodisiac edibles, their history, and curious anecdotes. Strange and unusual, but interesting.

Hurd, Frank J. and Rosalie. *A Good Cook . . . Ten Talents.* Chisholm, Minn.: Frank J. Hurd, 1985. Excellent food-combining cookbook (no dairy, eggs, sugars) and health manual. Some religious dogma.

Jensen, Bernard, and Mark Anderson. *Empty Harvest.* Garden City Park, N.Y.: Avery Publishing Group, 1990. A somber picture of how interconnected humans are to this earth, and how this connection is being destroyed. Offers range of prac--tical solutions still available to mend nature's broken links.

Jensen, Bernard. *Foods That Heal.* Garden City Park, N.Y.: Avery Publishing Group, 1993. A guide to understanding and using the healing power of some of the common foods, including their history of use, buyer's tips, therapeutic benefits, nutrient information, and recipes.

———. *Tissue Cleansing Through Bowel Management.* Escondido, Cal.: Bernard Jensen Press, 1981. Very graphically shows the power of fasting and colonics.

Kadans, Joseph M., Ph.D. *Encyclopedia of Fruits, Vegetables, Nuts and Seeds.* West Nyack, N.Y.: Parker Publishing, 1973. Alphabetical listing, some interesting information.

Kilham, Christopher S. *The Bread & Circus Whole Food Bible.* Reading, Mass.: Addison-Wesley Publishing Co., 1991. How to select and prepare whole foods. Good for beginners.

Kloss, Jethro. *Back to Eden.* Loma Linda, Cal.: Back to Eden Books Publishing Co., 1992. Originally printed in 1939 and updated for a Fiftieth Anniversary Edition. Fairly comprehen-sive, lots of stories, some dogma but quite readable.

Kraft, Ken and Pat. *Exotic Vegetables.* New York: Walker and Company, 1977. Older book with brief discussion of vegetables, some gardening tips, and a few recipes for each.

Kulvinskas, Viktoras. *Sprouts For The Love Of Every Body.* Wethersfield, Conn.: Omango D'Press, 1978(?). Nutritional values of sprouts and wheatgrass. Benefits of including sprouts in diet.

Larkcom, Joy. *The Salad Garden.* New York: Viking Press, 1984. Various information on salad plants and gardening.

Lehner, Ernst and Johanna. *Folklore & Odysseys of Food & Medicinal Plants.* New York: Farrar, Straus & Giroux, 1973. Brief history of many plants and resultant products. Lots of old, interesting illustrations.

———. *Folklore and Symbolism of Flowers, Plants and Trees.* New York: Tudor Publishing Co, 1960. A brief overview of many of the sacred plants, lore and legends surrounding them, and the language of flowers. A small, older book, but still interesting.

Levy-Bacon, Josephine. *Exotic Vegetables A–Z.* Topsfield, Mass.: Salem House Publishers, 1988. Information on some of the lesser known vegetables.

Liebman, Malvina W. *From Caravan to Casserole: Herbs and Spices in Legend, History, and Recipe.* Miami, Fla.: E.A. Seemann Publishing, 1977. A brief history of better-known herbs and spices, along with recipes.

London, Sheryl and Mel. *The Versatile Grain and the Elegant Bean.* New York: Simon & Schuster, 1992. Covers most of the available grains and beans, giving a brief history and description, as well as cooking instruction with lots of recipes for each one (non-vegetarian). List of mail order sources for most products.

Loewenfeld, Claire and Phillippa Back. *The Complete Book of Herbs and Spices.* New York: G.P. Putnam's Sons, 1974. Older British book, but with very good concise information. Well laid out and easy to read. Nice sections on description, habitat, cultivation, as well as flavor, culinary and medicinal uses. Would be a welcome addition to any culinary or herbal library.

Lovelock, Yann. *The Vegetable Book: An Unnatural History.* New York: St. Martin's Press, 1973. Fascinating information about not only the more common vegetables, herbs, and spices, but also about unusual ones, which were once popular but now forgotten. From a British perspective; some information gets rather technical and tedious. For somebody interested in botany and the historical significance of names, this is an excellent book.

Lucas, Richard. *Common and Uncommon Uses of Herbs for Healthful Living.* West Nyack, N.Y.: Parker Publishing, 1969. Presents herbal folk remedies, history and uses of herbs.

Lust, John. *The Herb Book.* New York: Bantam Books, 1974. Catalog of plants and various uses. Some history and folklore.

Margen, Sheldon (editor). *The Wellness Encyclopedia of Food and Nutrition.* New York: Random House, 1992. Covers the basics on how to buy, store, and prepare most every common variety (plus a few newer ones) of fresh food. Nicely categorized by section. Promotes no particular lifestyle; has sections on meat, fish, and dairy.

Medsger, Oliver Perry. *Edible Wild Plants.* New York: Macmillan Company, 1966. Guide to identification and preparation of North American edible wild plants. A perusal of these pages makes clear just how little most of us know about the plants around us.

Messegue, Maurice. Translated by Clara Winston. *Maurice Messegue's Way to Natural Health and Beauty.* New York: Macmillan Publishing Co, 1974. Foods and nutrition from a French point of view. Entertaining to read; some of the information is a little old, but a fun book.

Meyerowitz, Steve. *Juice Fasting and Detoxification.* Great Barrington, Mass.: The Sprout House, 1992. Detoxification through juice fasting; programs and remedies. Fun and easy to read.

Morton, Julia F. *Fruits of Warm Climates.* Miami, Fla., 1987. An exceptionally complete book for identifying and growing any of the warm-weather fruits.

Murray, Michael T. *The Healing Power of Foods: Nutrition Secrets for Vibrant Health and Long Life.* Rocklin, Cal.: Prima Publishing, 1993. Explains the components of a healthful diet and the health-promoting properties that specific foods possess. Section on specific food prescriptions for common health problems.

National Academy of Sciences. *Underexploited Tropical Plants with Promising Economic Value.* Washington, D.C., 1975. From U.S. Government, so technical, but still interesting reading.

Neal, Bill. *Gardener's Latin.* Chapel Hill, N.C.: Algonquin Books, 1992. A lexicon giving the origins, lore, and meanings of botanical names.

Null, Gary. *The Vegetarian Handbook: Eating Right for Total Health.* New York: St. Martin's Press, 1987. Reminiscent of John Robbins' books.

Ortiz, Elizabeth Lambert. *The Encyclopedia of Herbs, Spices, and Flavorings.* London: Dorling Kindersley, 1992. A beautifully illustrated book on herbs, spices, and flavorings for the kitchen.

Pedersen, Mark. *Nutritional Herbology.* Bountiful, Utah: Pedersen Publishing, 1991. Nutritional profiles of 106 commonly used herbs and foods.

Pennington, Jean A.T. *Food Values of Portions Commonly Used.* New York: Harper & Row, 1989. Food composition tables.

Pitchford, Paul. *Healing with Whole Foods.* Berkeley, Cal.: North Atlantic Books, 1993. Oriental traditions and modern nutrition.

Pizer, Vernon. *Eat The Grapes Downward: An Uninhibited Romp Through the Surprising World of Food.* New York: Dodd, Mead & Company, 1983. Fascinating facts and insights into the colorful world of food. Examines the role of food in history, religion, politics, the arts, and sex, and probes its influence on nations and cultures.

Poole, Gray Johnson. *Nuts from Forest, Orchard, and Field.* New York: Dodd, Mead & Company, 1974. A quick look at each of the common nuts and their place in history as well as the kitchen.

Price, Weston A. *Nutrition and Physical Degeneration.* New Canaan, Conn.: Keats Publishing, 1989. This nutrition classic is a must-read for anybody seriously interested in good health. Price's research was primarily for dentistry, but applies equally for all medical and nutritional fields. Shows how a modern poor diet changes body shape and form, dental structure, and quality of teeth and health, including mental health.

Quinn, Vernon. *Leaves: Their Place in Life and Legend.* New York: Frederick A. Stokes Co, 1937. An interesting little book about leaves, their many uses and legends.

Reader's Digest. *Herbs (Home Handbook).* Pleasantville, N.Y.: Reader's Digest Assoc. Inc, 1990. A basic book on herbs and their various uses.

———. *Magic and Medicine of Plants.* Pleasantville, N.Y.: Reader's Digest Assoc. Inc, 1986. A fun book on herbs and other plants.

Reich, Lee. *Uncommon Fruits Worthy of Attention: A Gardener's Guide.* Reading, Mass.: Addison-Wesley Publishing Co, 1991. Guide to the history, cultivation, and use of uncommon but easy-to-grow fruits.

Reid, Daniel P. *Tao of Health, Sex & Longevity.* New York: Simon & Schuster, 1989. Excellent in-depth book on food, its effects on health and longevity. This is the book that started my quest for information regarding food and health.

Riely, Elizabeth. *A Feast of Fruits.* New York: Macmillan, 1993. Has descriptions and over 340 recipes for 36 different kinds of fruits.

Rinzler, Carol Ann. *The Complete Book of Herbs, Spices and Condiments.* New York: Facts on File, 1990. Orthodox medical viewpoint on herbs, showing nutritional value, medical benefits, adverse effects and nontraditional uses.

Robbins, John. *Diet For A New America.* Walpole, N.H.: Stillpoint Publishing, 1987. How our food choices affect our health

and the health of the planet. A very convincing argument to reduce or eliminate the consumption of meat.
———. *May All Be Fed.* New York: William Morrow, 1992. A continuation of *Diet For A New America.* Much of the same information.
Robertson, Laurel, Carol Flinders, and Bronwen Godfrey. *Laurel's Kitchen.* Petaluma, Cal.: Nilgiri Press, 1976. Basics on vegetarianism, lots of nutritional facts, tables, and recipes.
Robertson, Laurel, Carol Flinders, and Brian Ruppenthal. *The New Laurel's Kitchen: A Handbook for Vegetarian Cookery and Nutrition.* Berkeley, Cal.: Ten Speed Press, 1986. Lots of nutritional information, recipes include lots of dairy and eggs.
Rodale Press. *The Rodale Herb Book.* Emmaus, Penn.: Rodale Press, 1974. Lots of good herbal information for cooking, aromatics, herbal medicines, history, etc.
———. *Rodale's Illustrated Encyclopedia of Herbs.* Emmaus, Penn.: Rodale Press, 1987. Features entries on more than 140 herbs, including history and lore, cultivation and storage. Accompanied by kitchen tips, charts, and other information. A good reference book.
Roehl, Evelyn. *Whole Food Facts.* Rochester, Vt.: Healing Arts Press, 1988. Excellent book on foods; no medicinal uses, but fairly complete otherwise; foods in sections by classes (grains, fruit, etc).Would recommend for general info.
Rogers, Ford. *Nuts: A Cookbook.* New York: Fireside, 1993. A beautifully photographed cookbook with a wide assortment of dishes to try. Has a short but nice introduction to the major nuts.
Rohe, Fred. *The Complete Book of Natural Foods.* Boulder, Col.: Shambhala Press, 1983. Very basic level primer on whole foods, and how to make the transition to a more wholesome diet based on whole foods.
Rombauer, Irma S., and Marion Rombauer Becker. *The Joy of Cooking.* New York: Bobbs-Merrill Company, 1975. An American household classic covering everything. Not even remotely vegetarian; I use it as a reference base.
Root, Waverley. *Food.* New York: Simon and Schuster, 1980. An enormous but fascinating tome on the history and dictionary of world foods.
Rosengarten, Frederic Jr. *The Book of Edible Nuts.* New York: Walker Publishing Co., 1984. Discusses botany, ecology, history, and processing. Recipes for many of the nuts. For anyone seriously interested in learning more about nut trees, nuts, and their uses, an excellent book to read.
———. *The Book of Spices.* New York: Livingston Publication Co., 1969. Beautiful, albeit older, book on common spices.
Rosenthal, Sylvia. *Fresh Food.* New York: E.P. Dutton, 1978. How to select, buy, and store the freshest food.
Rupp, Rebecca. *Blue Corn and Square Tomatoes.* Pownal, Vt.: Storey Communications, Inc., 1987. Unusual facts about common garden vegetables. Fun and informative narratives tracing the origin of scientific and common names, investigating poor reputations of many of our now most popular vegetables, some nutritional values. List of seed suppliers.
Sanecki, Kay N. *The Complete Book of Herbs.* New York: Macmillan, 1974. More herbal information for the beginner.
Schauss, Alexander. *Diet, Crime and Delinquency.* Berkeley, Cal.: Parker House, 1981. Explains connection between poor nutrition and antisocial behavior, and how proper nutrition can dramatically change behavior.
Schmid, Dr. Ronald F. *Traditional Foods are Your Best Medicine.* Stratford, Conn.: Ocean View Publications, 1987. Reviews traditional diet of longest-lived cultures. Proposes we put more emphasis on fish, meat, and fowl of good quality. Strongly emphasizes benefits of fish and fish oils upon health. Downplays role of fruits and vegetables.
Schneider, Elizabeth. *Uncommon Fruits and Vegetables: A Commonsense Guide.* New York: Harper & Row, 1986. Some of these are not so uncommon anymore. A light, easy to read, interesting review of the more unusual fruits and vegetables. Comes with description and several recipes for each. For anybody seriously interested in experimenting with these foods, it is well worth buying.
Shannon, Sara. *Diet for the Atomic Age.* Wayne, NJ: Avery, 1987. How to protect yourself from the radiation that is all around us.
Shelton, Herbert M., M.D.. *Superior Nutrition.* San Antonio, Tex.: Willow Publishing, 1982. Hard-to-read tome, heavy with dogma.
Sokolov, Raymond. *Fading Feast: A Compendium of Disappearing American Regional Foods.* New York: Farrar, Straus & Giroux, 1981. Twenty-four pieces on regional foods.
Spencer, Colin. *The New Vegetarian.* New York: Viking Penguin Inc, 1986. European-style (some very strange foods) cookbook, with nice illustrated section on herbs, spices, vegetables, etc.
Stanchich, Lino. *Power Eating Program.* Miami, Fla.: Healthy Products Inc, 1989. Details the importance of chewing your food properly (mastication) and the resultant beneficial effects on your health. Promotes macrobiotic lifestyle, stress reduction.
Staten, Vince. *Can You Trust a Tomato in January?* New York: Simon & Schuster, 1993. An entertaining and revealing trip through the supermarket, revealing things you always wanted to know about food in the grocery store (and a few you didn't).
Stearn, William T. *Botanical Latin.* North Pomfret, Vt.: David & Charles, 1983. Very helpful for finding Latin terminology.
———. *Stearn's Dictionary of Plant Names for Gardeners.* London: Cassell Publishers Ltd., 1992. Used to help find botanical names.
Steinman, David. *Diet for a Poisoned Planet.* New York: Harmony Books, 1990. Guide to common foods, with lists of pesticides and chemical residues found in them. Short detoxification section. Large appendices for sources on organic products, activist groups, certification groups, and testing laboratories.
Stuart, Malcolm (editor). *The Encyclopedia of Herbs and Herbalism.* New York: Crescent Books, 1979. History of herbalism, biology and chemistry of plants, medicinal, culinary, and other uses. Encyclopedic section organized bythe Latin botanical name.
Tannahill, Reay. *Food in History.* New York: Crown Publishers, 1988. A world history of food from prehistoric times to today; traces the way in which food (or lack of) has influenced the entire course of human development. Fascinating reading; follows culture's perception of diet and nutrition from ancient day until the present.
U.S. Department of Agriculture, Human Nutrition Information Services. *Composition of Foods: Fruits and Fruit Juices; Raw, Processed, Prepared.* Agriculture Handbook No. 8–09, 1982.
———. *Composition of Foods: Nut and Seed Products; Raw, Processed, Prepared.* Agriculture Handbook No. 8–12, 1984.
———. *Composition of Foods:Vegetables and Vegetable Products; Raw, Processed, Prepared.* Agriculture Handbook No. 8-11, 1984.
———. *Composition of Foods: Legumes and Legume Products; Raw, Processed, Prepared.* Agriculture Handbook No. 8-16, 1986.

———. *Composition of Foods: Fats and Oils; Raw, Processed, Prepared.* Agriculture Handbook No. 8-04, 1979.
———. *Composition of Foods: Cereal Grains and Pasta; Raw, Processed, Prepared.* Agriculture Handbook No. 8-20, 1989.
———. *Composition of Foods: Snacks and Sweets; Raw, Processed, Prepared.* Agriculture Handbook No. 8-19, 1991.
———. *Composition of Foods: Spices and Herbs.* Agriculture Handbook No. 8-2, 1977.
———. *Composition of Foods: 1989 Supplement.*
———. *Composition of Foods: 1990 Supplement.*
Waldstein, Steve. *How to Choose the Diet That's Right for You.* New York: Crossing Press, 1984. Vegetarianism, diets, foods and nutrition. Good section on vitamins and minerals.
Walker, N.W. *Colon Health: The Key to a Vibrant Life.* Phoenix, Ariz.: O'Sullivan Woodwide & Co, 1979. Explains how health of colon affects rest of body.
———. *Natural Way to Vibrant Health.* Phoenix, Ariz.: O'Sullivan Woodside & Co, 1983. Basics of digestion and nutrition; written in typical rambling Walker style.
Watt, B.K., and A.L. Merrill. *Composition of Foods . . . Raw, Processed, Prepared.* U.S. Department of Agriculture, Agriculture Handbook No. 8, 1963. This is the older version of the Agriculture Handbooks.
Weiner, Michael. *Weiner's Herbal.* New York: Stein and Day, 1980. An okay book, heavy on the botanical descriptions.
Wigmore, Ann. *The Sprouting Book.* Wayne, N.Y.: Avery Publishing Group, 1986. Lots of good information on sprouts, setting up home sprouting, recipes for using sprouts.
Wood, Rebecca. *The Whole Foods Encyclopedia.* New York: Prentice Hall Press, 1988. Encyclopedic style; some good information but not very in-depth.

INDEX OF ENGLISH NAMES

INDEX OF BOTANICAL NAMES

…ed from front endpaper

TIME LINE: THE HISTORY OF EARLY CHILDHOOD EDUCATION

1952 Jean Piaget's *The Origins of Intelligence in Children* was published in English translation.

1955 Rudolf Flesch's *Why Johnny Can't Read* criticized the schools for their methodology in teaching reading and other basic skills.

1957 The Soviet Union launched *Sputnik*, sparking renewed interest in other educational systems and marking the beginning of the "rediscovery" of early childhood education.

1958 The National Defense Education Act was passed to provide federal funds for improving education in the sciences, mathematics, and foreign languages.

1960 Katharine Whiteside Taylor founded the American Council of Parent Cooperatives for those interested in exchanging ideas in preschool education; it later became the Parent Cooperative Preschools International.

1960 The Day Care and Child Development Council of America was formed to publicize the need for quality services for children.

1964 At its Miami Beach conference, the NANE became the National Association for the Education of Young Children (NAEYC).

1964 The Economic Opportunity Act of 1964 was passed, marking the beginning of the War on Poverty and the foundation for Head Start.

1965 The Elementary and Secondary Education Act was passed to provide federal money toward programs for educationally deprived children.

1965 The Head Start program began with federal money allocated for preschool education; the early programs were known as child development centers.

1966 The Bureau of Education for the Handicapped was established.

1967 The Follow Through program was initiated to extend Head Start into the primary grades.

1968 B. F. Skinner wrote *The Technology of Teaching*, which outlined a programmed approach to learning.

1968 The federal government established the Handicapped Children's Early Education Program to fund model preschool programs for children with disabilities.

1970 The White House Conference on Children and Youth was held.

1971 The Stride Rite Corporation in Boston was the first to start a corporate-supported child care program.

1972 The National Home Start Program began for the purpose of involving parents in their children's education.

1975 Public Law 94-142, the Education for All Handicapped Children Act, was passed, mandating a free and appropriate education for all children with disabilities and extending many rights to parents of such children.

1979 The International Year of the Child was sponsored by the United Nations and designated by Executive Order.

1980 The first American lekotek (toy-lending library) opened its doors in Evanston, Illinois.

1980 The White House Conference on Families was held.

1981 The Head Start Act of 1981 (Omnibus Budget Reconciliation Act of 1981, Public Law 97-35) was passed to extend Head Start and provide for effective delivery of comprehensive services to economically disadvantaged children and their families.

1907 Maria Montessori started her first preschool in Rome called Children's House; her now-famous teaching method was based on the theory that children learn best by themselves in a properly prepared environment.

1909 Theodore Roosevelt convened the first White House Conference on Children.

1911 Arnold Gesell, well known for his research on the importance of the preschool years, began child development study at Yale University.

1911 Margaret and Rachel McMillan founded an open-air nursery school in Great Britain in which the class met outdoors; emphasis was on healthy living.

1912 Arnold and Beatrice Gesell wrote *The Normal Child and Primary Education*.

1915 Eva McLin started the first U.S. Montessori nursery school in New York City.

1915 The Child Education Foundation of New York City founded a nursery school using Montessori's principles.

1918 The first public nursery schools were started in Great Britain.

1919 Harriet Johnson started the Nursery School of the Bureau of Educational Experiments, later to become the Bank Street College of Education.

1921 Patty Smith Hill started a progressive, laboratory nursery school at Columbia Teachers College.

1921 A. S. Neill founded Summerhill, an experimental school based on the ideas of Rousseau and Dewey.

1922 With Edna Noble White as its first director, the Merrill-Palmer Institute Nursery School opened in Detroit, with the purpose of preparing women in proper child care; at this time, the Institute was known as the Merrill-Palmer School of Motherhood and Home Training.

1922 Abigail Eliot, influenced by the open-air school in Great Britain and basing her program on personal hygiene and proper behavior, started the Ruggles Street Nursery School in Boston.

1924 *Childhood Education*, the first professional journal in early childhood education, was published by the IKU.

1926 The National Committee on Nursery Schools was initiated by Patty Smith Hill at Columbia Teachers College; now called the National Association for the Education of Young Children, it provides guidance and consultant services for educators.

1926 The National Association of Nursery Education (NANE) was founded.

1930 The IKU changed its name to the Association for Childhood Education.

1933 The Work Projects Administration (WPA) provided money to start nursery schools so that unemployed teachers would have jobs.

1935 First toy-lending library, Toy Loan, was founded in Los Angeles.

1940 The Lanham Act provided funds for child care during World War II, mainly for day care centers for children whose mothers worked in the war effort.

1943 Kaiser Child Care Centers opened in Portland, Oregon, to provide twenty-four-hour child care for children of mothers working in war-related industries.

1944 The journal *Young Children* was first published by the NANE.

1946 Dr. Benjamin Spock wrote the *Common Sense Book of Baby and Child Care*.

1950 Erik Erikson published his writings on the "eight ages or stages" of personality growth and development and identified "tasks" for each stage of development; the information, known as "Personality in the Making," formed the basis for the 1950 White House Conference on Children and Youth.

continued on back endpaper

Early Childhood Education Today

Early Childhood Education Today

8th Edition

George S. Morrison

University of North Texas

Merrill
Prentice Hall

Upper Saddle River, New Jersey
Columbus, Ohio

Library of Congress Cataloging in Publication Data
Morrison, George S.
Early childhood education today / George S. Morrison—8th ed.
p. cm.
Includes bibliographical references and index.
ISBN 0-13-019131-0
1. Early childhood education—United States. I. Title.
LB1139.25.M66 2001
372.21—dc21

00-035515

Vice President and Publisher: Jeffery W. Johnston
Executive Editor: Ann Castel Davis
Editorial Assistant: Pat Grogg
Development Editor: Gianna Marsella
Production Editor: Linda Hillis Bayma
Copy Editor: Sally Jaskold
Photo Coordinators: Sherry Mitchell and Lori Whitley
Design Coordinator: Diane C. Lorenzo
Text and Cover Designer: Ceri Fitzgerald
Cover photo: © SuperStock
Electronic Text Management: Marilyn Wilson Phelps, Karen L. Bretz, Melanie N. Ortega
Production Manager: Laura Messerly
Director of Marketing: Kevin Flanagan
Marketing Manager: Amy June
Marketing Services Manager: Krista Groshong

This book was set in Goudy Old Style by Prentice Hall. It was printed and bound by Von Hoffman Press, Inc. The cover was printed by Von Hoffman Press, Inc.

Photo Credits: p. 245 by Bill Aron/PhotoEdit; p. 500 by D. Berry/PhotoDisc, Inc.; p. 66 by Corbis Bettmann; p. 395 by Vic Bider/PhotoEdit; p. 29 by Michelle Bridwell/PhotoEdit; p. 202 by M. Brodskaya/Impact Visuals Photo & Graphics, Inc.; p. 7 by David Buffington/PhotoDisc, Inc.; p. 404 by Robert Burke/Tony Stone Images; p. 304 by Cleo Freelance Photo; pp. 56, 82, 347 by Paul Conklin/PhotoEdit; pp. 6, 21, 73, 100, 103, 104, 107, 108, 130, 134, 135, 139, 143, 210, 264, 268, 296, 300, 310, 328, 346, 351, 358, 360, 362, 416, 430, 459, 464, 510 by Scott Cunningham/Merrill; p. 335 by Custom Medical Stock Photo, Inc.; p. 12 by Robert E. Daemmrich/Tony Stone Images; p. 237 by Laima Druskis/PH College; pp. 427, 472 by Laura Dwight/PhotoEdit; p. 112 by Esbin/Anderson/Omni-Photo Communications, Inc.; pp. 150, 232 by Tony Freeman/PhotoEdit; p. 155 by Chip Henderson/Tony Stone Images; p. 285 by Hope Foundation; p. 180 by Richard Hutchings/PhotoEdit; p. 384, IBM Corporation; p. 116 by Russell Illig/PhotoDisc, Inc.; p. 70 by Indiana University Photographic Services; p. 188 by K. B. Kaplan/Index Stock Imagery, Inc.; p. 442 by Ken Lax/Photo Researchers, Inc.; p. 492 courtesy of Lynchburg, VA Police Department; pp. 75, 197 by Anthony Magnacca/Merrill; p. 217 by Lawrence Migdale/Photo Researchers, Inc.; p. 84 by Margaret Miller/Photo Researchers, Inc.; pp. 308, 448 by Will & Deni McIntyre/Photo Researchers, Inc.; p. 400 by Modern Curriculum Press; pp. 41, 54, 253, 283, 496 by Michael Newman/PhotoEdit; p. 2 by Mike Peters/Silver Burdett Ginn; p. 401 by Prentke Romich; p. 486 by Suzanne Szasz/Photo Researchers, Inc.; p. 412 by Arthur Tilley/FPG International LLC; p. 176 by Uniphoto Picture Agency; p. 48 by Alan S. Weiner/Liaison Agency, Inc.; p. 285 by Todd Yarrington/Merrill; pp. 167, 354, 373, 422, 504 by David Young-Wolff/PhotoEdit; p. 36 by Shirley Zeiberg/PH College.

Merrill
Prentice Hall

10 9 8 7 6 5 4 3 2
ISBN: 0-13-019131-0

For Betty Jane—who has made many sacrifices, all in the name of deepest love

About the Author

George S. Morrison, Ed.D., is professor of early childhood education and holder of the Velma E. Schmidt Endowed Chair in early childhood education at the University of North Texas. Dr. Morrison's accomplishments include a Distinguished Academic Service Award from the Pennsylvania Department of Education, an Outstanding Alumni Award from the University of Pittsburgh School of Education, and Outstanding Service and Teaching Awards from Florida International University.

Dr. Morrison is the author of many books on early childhood education, child development, curriculum, and teacher education, including *Fundamentals of Early Childhood Education*, Second Edition, and *Teaching in America*, Second Edition.

His professional affiliations include the National Association for the Education of Young Children (NAEYC), the Society for Research in Child Development (SCRD), the Association for Supervision and Curriculum Development (ASCD), the American Educational Research Association (AERA), the Association of Teacher Educators (ATE), the American Psychological Society (APS), and the Southern Early Childhood Association (SECA).

Dr. Morrison's professional interests include the application of neuroscience and developmental research to early childhood programs. Dr. Morrison and his associates have developed *Success For Life*, a research-based curriculum and program for children from birth to six years of age.

Preface

This is my eighth preface to *Early Childhood Education Today*. I've always tried to begin with words of encouragement and challenge, and this edition is no exception. This is an exciting time to be in the field of early childhood education. In fact, I can think of only one other time during my career when there was so much excitement and challenge: 1965, with the implementation of Head Start. The excitement and possibility in the air at that time was similar to that of today because of the current emphasis on brain and developmental research and a renewed interest in the importance of the early years.

Early childhood education is in the public spotlight. We are in the golden age of early childhood education for young children, parents, families, and professionals, and this age brings with it both possibilities and challenges. The possibilities are endless for you as an early childhood education professional, in what you can do for children and families and to change and remake the early childhood profession. An important question is, "What will you and others do with this 'prime time' for early childhood education?"

I believe that how you and I respond to the opportunities we have in front of us will determine how long the current golden age of early childhood education lasts. You and other early childhood professionals must be creative in responding to the opportunities for helping young children, extending the interest in young children, and providing the support that they and their families need.

Goals of the Text

The primary goal of *Early Childhood Education Today,* Eighth Edition, is to help you meet the challenges of early childhood education and to help you be the best early childhood professional you can be. I believe this edition will give you the knowledge, skills, and insights necessary to confidently and appropriately assume your goal of being a leader in educating children, parents, and families.

I wrote *Early Childhood Education Today* to meet preservice teachers' desire for a learning text that is practical and based upon current ideas about what teaching young children is like today. Six main core themes are integrated throughout the text and provide a framework for reading and study. These themes are as follows:

- *Theory to Practice*. This text will help you understand how theories of learning and educating young children are translated into practice by teachers and programs. The "Voice from the Field" and "Program in Action" sections provide real-life insights into how teachers in programs across the United States endeavor to apply early childhood theories to their everyday practices. In other words, you will read firsthand about professional colleagues who make theories come alive in concrete ways that truly help children succeed in school and life.
- *Diversity*. The United States is a nation of diverse people, and this diversity is reflected in every early childhood classroom and program. You and your colleagues must have the knowledge and sensitivity to teach all students well, and you must understand how culture and language influence teaching and learning. In addition to two full chapters on diversity (chapter 14, "Multiculturalism: Education for Living in a Diverse Society," and chapter 15, "Children with Special Needs: Appropriate Education for All"), every other chapter of this edition emphasizes the theme of diversity through narrative examples and program descriptions.
- *Family-Centered, Community-Based Practice*. To effectively meet children's needs, you and other early childhood professionals must collaborate with families and communities. Today, teaching is not an isolated endeavor in which one seeks to practice the craft of early childhood education in isolation from colleagues and others in the school and community. Successful partnerships at all levels are essential for effective teaching and learning. In addition to a chapter on this important topic (chapter 16, "Parent, Family, and Community Involvement: Cooperation and Collaboration"), every other chapter provides examples of successful partnerships and their influences on teaching and learning.
- *Timeliness*. This edition is a book for the twenty-first century. The information it contains is timely, reflective of the very latest trends and research. Every chapter has been thoroughly revised to reflect the changes in the field. I take great pride in ensuring that you and other readers will be well versed in the current state of early childhood education after reading this text.
- *Developmentally Appropriate Practice*. The theme of developmentally appropriate practice runs throughout this text. Developmentally appropriate practice is the foundation for all that early childhood professionals do. It is important, therefore, that you as an early childhood education professional understand developmentally appropriate practice and become familiar with how to implement it in your teaching. Appendix B reprints NAEYC's guidelines for developmentally appropriate practice, and every chapter provides examples and illustrations of how to apply developmentally appropriate practice.
- *Technology Applied to Teaching and Learning*. Technological and information literacy is essential for living and working in contemporary society. This edition provides readers the information and skills that they need to integrate technology effectively into the curriculum and use new teaching and learning styles enabled by technology. In addition to chapter 13, "Technology and Young Children: Education for the Information Age," margin notes direct readers to related information on the Companion Website for this textbook, located at http://www.prenhall.com/morrison. Websites are also integrated into the content of every chapter. Additionally, included at the end of each chapter is a "Linking to Learning" section that provides an annotated list of Websites.

In this way, you and others are supported in using the Internet and new technologies as sources of professional growth and development.

Organization and Coverage of the Text

Early Childhood Education Today, Eighth Edition, provides a thorough introduction to the field of early childhood education in a straightforward and engaging style. The book analyzes current issues and ideas and applies practical, developmentally appropriate strategies and models to the practice of early childhood education. This edition has been extensively revised to reflect the changes in society, research, and the practice of early childhood education. The text is comprehensive in its approach to the profession and is organized into five parts:

- Part I, "Early Childhood Education and Professional Development," begins with a chapter on professional development. This chapter has been extensively revised and is designed to place professional practice at the heart of being a good teacher. Chapter 1 will help you engage in professional, ethical practice and sets the tone for what being an early childhood professional is all about. Chapter 2 provides you with an understanding of the current issues of early childhood education today and gives you insight into the research issues and political agendas shaping contemporary practice and programs.
- Part II, "The Development of Early Childhood Programs," provides a historical overview of the field of early childhood education and descriptions of Montessori and Piagetian theories, ideas, and practices. These chapters also show how the past influences the present and how the two major theories of Montessori and Piaget influence programs for young children today. Chapter 6 is new to this edition and provides a comprehensive look at models of early childhood curricula and how they function.
- Part III, "Developmentally Appropriate Programs and Practices," provides a comprehensive overview and discussion of children's development from infancy through the primary grades. In addition, these chapters provide guidelines for how to teach young children in developmentally appropriate ways and how to develop and implement programs that are developmentally appropriate.
- Part IV, "Guiding and Assessing Young Children," provides practical guidelines for observing and authentically assessing young children, shows how to most effectively observe and assess, and explains how to apply the results of observation and assessment to your early childhood practice. How to guide children's behavior is also an important topic in early childhood education today. Chapter 12 suggests ideas for guiding children and helping them be responsible for their own behavior. These ideas will enable you to confidently manage classrooms and other early childhood settings.
- Part V, "Meeting the Special Needs of Young Children," begins with a chapter on technology and young children. Technology is an important part of this information age, and it is imperative that young children learn to use it and that you and other teachers use it to support your teaching and children's learning. Chapters 14 and 15 address issues of multiculturalism, diversity, and children's special needs. These two chapters help you meet children's special needs in developmentally appropriate and authentic ways. Chapter 16 stresses the importance of cooperation and collaboration with family and community citizens. This chapter helps you learn how to develop partnerships and

confidently interact with parents, families, and communities to provide the best education for all children.

Appendix A, "The NAEYC Code of Ethical Conduct," provides the basis for teaching in an ethical and professional manner, and Appendix B, "NAEYC Guidelines for Developmentally Appropriate Practice in Early Childhood Programs," helps assure that you teach and develop programs so that they meet the developmental and educational needs of children in ways that are appropriate to them as individuals.

Special Features

- *Programs in Action.* One of the hallmarks of this edition of *Early Childhood Education Today* is its practical nature and its ability to translate theory into practice. "Programs in Action" in almost every chapter enable you to experience actual programs designed for children in real-life classrooms and early childhood programs throughout the United States. I can think of no better way for you to understand what early childhood education in practice is like than to learn about real programs in action. These real examples of schools, programs, classrooms, and teachers enable you to explore the best practices of early childhood education and see up close what teaching is like. They also offer special opportunities to spotlight current topics such as early and family literacy, multiage and bilingual classrooms, early gifted education, inclusion, and early intervention. This approach enables you to make the transition from thinking about being a teacher to becoming a competent professional.
- *Voices from the Field.* I believe it is important for the teacher's voice to be heard in and throughout *Early Childhood Education Today*, Eighth Edition. "Voices from the Field" provide real teachers the opportunity to explain to you their philosophies, beliefs, and program practices. These teachers mentor you as they relate how they practice early childhood education. Among the contributors are four teachers who have recently received "Teacher of the Year" honors.
- *Video Viewpoints.* Integrated throughout this edition are feature boxes that ask you to respond to questions requiring reflective thought and decision making. These "Video Viewpoints" are linked to the video segments in the ABC News/Prentice Hall video library. The segments and the "Video Viewpoint" activities address current issues in early childhood education, help connect theory to practice, and bring to life important topics relating to young children and families.

New to This Edition

- *New Chapter on Observation and Assessment.* Users of the seventh edition suggested the inclusion of a chapter devoted to observing and assessing young children. Chapter 11, "Observing and Assessing Young Children: Effective Teaching Through Appropriate Evaluation," responds to this user need and brings together these two important topics. The addition of this chapter should facilitate your efforts at observing and assessing young children and using the results of those efforts to guide your practice.
- *New Chapter on Model Early Childhood Programs.* Chapter 6, "Early Childhood Programs: Applying Theories to Practice," is also new to this edition. This chapter brings together the major models of early childhood education that are used today, including but not limited to Head Start, High/Scope, and Reggio Emilia. Having all the models in one chapter enables you to compare/contrast and evaluate these programs and

helps you make decisions about which models you think are most appropriate for young children.

- *Emphasis on Professional Practice.* Chapter 1 is now entirely devoted to professional practice and sets the tone and context for the entire text. By beginning with professional practice, students understand the importance of the early childhood educator's role in shaping the future. They also recognize that their own professional development is an ongoing responsibility and a necessary part of helping children grow and develop as happily and successfully as possible.
- *Integrated Technology.* Web resources and URLs are integrated throughout the text of each chapter, and margin notes cue students to additional resources that can be found on the Companion Website for this text, located at http://www.prenhall.com/morrison. These links will help enrich and extend your learning. In addition, at the end of each chapter there is a "Linking to Learning" section that provides a list of annotated Web addresses for further research, study, and reflection.
- *Full-Color Text.* The eighth edition of *Early Childhood Education Today* is a full-color text. Whereas the seventh edition had color inserts only, the full-color format is now carried throughout the book. This format enhances the visual appeal and readability of the text and supports its contemporary nature.

Supplements to the Text

The supplements package for the eighth edition has also been thoroughly revised and upgraded with some exciting new ancillaries:

- *Instructor's Manual.* The Instructor's Manual provides professors with a variety of useful resources, including chapter overviews, teaching strategies, and ideas for classroom activities, discussions, and assessment that will assist them in using this text. The manual also includes a comprehensive print testbank containing both multiple-choice and essay questions.
- *Computerized Testbank Software.* The computerized testbank software gives instructors electronic access to the test questions printed in the *Instructor's Manual,* allowing them to create and customize exams on their computer. The software can help professors manage their courses and gain insight into their students' progress and performance. Computerized testbank software is available in both Macintosh and PC/Windows versions.
- *ABC News/Prentice Hall Video Library.* Available free to instructors, *Current Issues in Early Childhood Education, volumes 1 and 2,* contain a total of eleven video segments, four of which are new to the eighth edition. Video segments cover a variety of topics and vary in length for maximum instructional flexibility. The "Video Viewpoint" feature boxes in the chapters can be used to link the segments to the text and to promote thoughtful classroom discussion of current issues in early childhood education. A special table of contents identifies topics discussed and their locations in the text.
- *Companion Website.* (NEW!) Located at *http://www.prenhall.com/morrison*, the Companion Website for this text includes a wealth of resources for both students and professors. The Syllabus Manager™ enables professors to create and maintain the class syllabus on-line while also allowing the student access to the syllabus at any time from any computer on the Internet. Focus Questions help students review chapter content.

Students can test their knowledge by taking interactive Self-Tests—multiple-choice quizzes that provide immediate feedback with a percentage score and correct answers—or responding to essay questions that can be submitted to instructors or study partners via e-mail. The Linking to Learning feature contains hot links to all the Websites mentioned in the margins of the text and assists students in using the Web to do additional research on chapter topics and key issues. The Programs in Action module provides hot links to many of the Web pages of the Programs in Action featured in the text and extends students' learning via Web-based activities. The Glossary helps students familiarize themselves with key vocabulary. Both the Message Board and Chat features encourage student interaction outside the classroom. The Professional Development Checklist will help students monitor their progress toward becoming accomplished early childhood educators. Finally, the Resources module links to Merrill Education's early childhood education resources supersite.

- *Student Study Guide*. (NEW!) The *Student Study Guide* provides students with additional opportunities to review chapter content and helps them learn and study more effectively. The study guide leads readers through each chapter and helps them identify key concepts and information. Each chapter of the guide contains a number of helpful review resources, including a self-check quiz.

Acknowledgments

In the course of my teaching, service, and consulting, I meet and talk with many professionals who are deeply dedicated to doing their best for young children and their families. I am always touched, heartened, and encouraged by the openness, honesty, and unselfish sharing of ideas that characterize these professional colleagues. I thank all the individuals who contributed to "Voices from the Field," "Programs in Action," and other program descriptions. They are all credited with their personal accounts of their lives, their children's lives, and their programs.

I am also very grateful to reviewers Audrey W. Beard, Albany State University; Elizabeth Engley, Jacksonville State University; Anne Federlein, State University of New York at Oneonta; and Frank Miller, Pittsburg State University (Kansas) for their helpful feedback.

My editors at Merrill continue to be the best in the industry. It is a pleasure working with Ann Davis. She is astute and visionary and continually develops ways to keep *Early Childhood Education Today* the leader in the field. Gianna Marsella is creative, facilitative, and cheerful. As the development editor, she brings a can-do attitude to the developmental process. Linda Bayma is patient, persistent, and helpful. I greatly appreciate her attention to detail in her role as production editor. She always smooths out the bumps of the production process. Sally Jaskold is a thorough copy editor, and I appreciate her good efforts. Together, Ann, Gianna, Linda, and Sally have made this eighth edition one of exceptional quality.

Discover the Companion Website Accompanying This Book

The Prentice Hall Companion Website: A Virtual Learning Environment

Technology is a constantly growing and changing aspect of our field that is creating a need for content and resources. To address this emerging need, we have developed an online learning environment for students and professors alike—Companion Websites—to support our textbooks.

In creating a Companion Website, our goal is to build on and enhance what the textbook already offers. For this reason, the content for each user-friendly website is organized by chapter and provides the professor and student with a variety of meaningful resources. Common features of a Companion Website include:

For the Professor

Every Companion Website integrates **Syllabus Manager™**, an online syllabus creation and management utility.

- **Syllabus Manager™** provides you, the instructor, with an easy, step-by-step process to create and revise syllabi, with direct links into Companion Website and other online content without having to learn HTML.
- Students may logon to your syllabus during any study session. All they need to know is the web address for the Companion Website, and the password you've assigned to your syllabus.
- After you have created a syllabus using **Syllabus Manager™**, students may enter the syllabus for their course section from any point in the Companion Website.
- Clicking on a date, the student is shown the list of activities for the assignment. The activities for each assignment are linked directly to actual content, saving time for students.
- Adding assignments consists of clicking on the desired due date, then filling in the details of the assignment—name of the assignment, instructions, and whether or not it is a one-time or repeating assignment.
- In addition, links to other activities can be created easily. If the activity is online, a URL can be entered in the space provided, and it will be linked automatically in the final syllabus.
- Your completed syllabus is hosted on our servers, allowing convenient updates from any computer on the Internet. Changes you make to your syllabus are immediately available to your students at their next login.

For the Student

- **Chapter Objectives** – outline key concepts from the text
- **Interactive Self-quizzes** – complete with hints and automatic grading that provide immediate feedback for students

  After students submit their answers for the interactive self-quizzes, the Companion Website **Results Reporter** computes a percentage grade, provides a graphic representation of how many questions were answered correctly and incorrectly, and gives a question by question analysis of the quiz. Students are given the option to send their quiz to up to four email addresses (professor, teaching assistant, study partner, etc.).

- **Message Board** – serves as a virtual bulletin board to post—or respond to—questions or comments to a national audience
- **Chat** – real-time chat with anyone who is using the text anywhere in the country—ideal for discussion and study groups, class projects, etc.
- **Web Destinations** – links to www sites that relate to chapter content
- **Additional Resources** – access to chapter-specific or general content that enhances material found in the text

To take advantage of these resources, please visit the *Early Childhood Education Today,* 8th edition, Companion Website at

www.prenhall.com/morrison

Brief Contents

Contents

PART II: THE DEVELOPMENT OF EARLY CHILDHOOD PROGRAMS

CHAPTER 3

CHAPTER 4

CHAPTER 9

CHAPTER 10

CHAPTER 14

Multiculturalism: Education for Living in a Diverse Society 417

CHAPTER 15

Children with Special Needs: Appropriate Education for All 449

CHAPTER 16

Parent, Family, and Community Involvement: Cooperation and Collaboration 493

Note: Every effort has been made to provide accurate and current Internet information in this book. However, the Internet and information posted on it are constantly changing, so it is inevitable that some of the Internet addresses listed in this textbook will change.

Special Features

Video Viewpoints

Programs in Action

Voices from the Field

Early Childhood Education Today

PART I

Early Childhood Education and Professional Development

CHAPTER 1
You and Early Childhood Education:
What Does It Mean To Be a Professional?

CHAPTER 2
Early Childhood Education Today:
Understanding Current Issues

CHAPTER 1

I believe the impulse to teach is fundamentally altruistic and represents a desire to share what you value and to empower others. I am not talking about the job of teaching so much as the calling to teach. Most teachers I know have felt that calling at some time in their lives.

HERBERT KOHL

You and Early Childhood Education

What Does It Mean To Be a Professional?

Focus Questions

1. Who is an early childhood professional?
2. What can you do to embody the personal, educational, professional practice, and public dimensions of professionalism?
3. What is the terminology of early childhood education?
4. How can you prepare for a career in early childhood education?
5. What does the future hold for the early childhood professional?

To review the chapter focus questions online, go to the Companion Website at http://www.prenhall.com/morrison and select chapter 1.

Just as early childhood education was in the spotlight at the end of the twentieth century, it will continue to be at the center of public attention and discussion well into this century. The issues and opportunities of the new millennium will be exciting and challenging for you and all who work with young children and their families.

The public increasingly recognizes the importance of children's early years in learning and development. Today, more than ever, the public and politicians are interested in improving the quality of education and teaching. As a result, you and other early childhood professionals have a wonderful opportunity to develop new and better programs and to advocate for best practices. You can be a leader in helping the early childhood profession make the American dream a reality for all children. Being the best professional you can will enable you to be a partner in making teaching a high-quality profession.

Who Is an Early Childhood Professional?

To check your understanding of this chapter with the online Study Guide, go to the Companion Website at http://www.prenhall.com/morrison, select chapter 1, then choose the Study Guide module.

You are preparing to be an early childhood professional, to teach children from birth to age eight. You are going to work with families and the community to bring a high quality of education and services to all children. How would you explain the term *early childhood professional* to others? What does *professional* mean?

An early childhood professional has the personal characteristics, knowledge, and skills necessary to teach and conduct programs so that all children learn and the ability to inform the public about children's and family issues. Professionals are those who promote high standards for themselves, their colleagues, and their students—they are continually improving and expanding their skills and knowledge. A professional is a multidimensional person.

Figure 1.1 outlines professional categories as identified by the National Association for the Education of Young Children (NAEYC). These categories reflect the association's efforts to continually enhance the concept of professionalism in early childhood education. As you identify the differences in these professional areas, reflect about their meaning for you and the ways you can start to develop the necessary knowledge and skills for success at whatever level you select.

The Dimensions of Professionalism

While Figure 1.1 helps you understand the different levels of professionalism, it doesn't tell you who a professional is and what a professional needs to know and be able to do. There is much more to being a professional than degrees and experiences. Professionalism has many dimensions, all of which are important and integrated. Let's consider the various dimensions of professionalism and the implications they have for you. These dimensions are shown in greater detail in Figure 1.2.

There are four dimensions to being a high-quality professional: personal characteristics, educational attainment, professional practice, and public presentation. Each of these dimensions plays a powerful role in determining who and what a professional is and how professionals implement practice in early childhood classrooms. Let's review each of these dimensions and see how you can apply them to your professional practice.

- **Early Childhood Professional Level VI**

Successful completion of a Ph.D. or Ed.D. in a program conforming to NAEYC guidelines; OR
Successful demonstration of the knowledge, performance, and dispositions expected as outcomes of a doctoral degree program conforming to NAEYC guidelines.

- **Early Childhood Professional Level V**

Successful completion of a master's degree in a program that conforms to NAEYC guidelines; OR
Successful demonstration of the knowledge, performance, and dispositions expected as outcomes of a master's degree program conforming to NAEYC guidelines.

- **Early Childhood Professional Level IV**

Successful completion of a baccalaureate degree from a program conforming to NAEYC guidelines; OR
State certificate meeting NAEYC/ATE certification guidelines; OR
Successful completion of a baccalaureate degree in another field with more than 30 professional units in early childhood development/education including 300 hours of supervised teaching experience, including 150 hours each for two of the following three age groups: infants and toddlers, 3- to 5-year olds, or the primary grades; OR
Successful demonstration of the knowledge, performance, and dispositions expected as outcomes of a baccalaureate degree program conforming to NAEYC guidelines.

- **Early Childhood Professional Level III**

Successful completion of an associate degree from a program conforming to NAEYC guidelines; OR
Successful completion of an associate degree in a related field, plus 30 units of professional studies in early childhood development/education including 300 hours of supervised teaching experience in an early childhood program; OR
Successful demonstration of the knowledge, performance, and dispositions expected as outcomes of an associate degree program conforming to NAEYC guidelines.

- **Early Childhood Professional Level II**

Successful completion of a one-year early childhood certificate program.
Successful completion of the CDA Professional Preparation Program; OR
Completion of a systematic, comprehensive training program that prepares an individual to successfully acquire the CDA Credential through direct assessment.

- **Early Childhood Professional Level I**

Individuals who are employed in an early childhood professional role working under supervision or with support (e.g., linkages with provider association or network or enrollment in supervised practicum) and participating in training designed to lead to the assessment of individual competencies or acquisition of a degree.

Figure 1.1
Definitions of Categories of Early Childhood Professionals

Source: "NAEYC Position Statement: A Conceptual Framework for Early Childhood Professional Development, 1994," Young Children, *49(3), p. 74. Copyright © 1994 by the National Association for the Education of Young Children. Reprinted by permission.*

The Personal Dimension

The personal dimension of professionalism includes all the qualities, behaviors, and attitudes that you demonstrate as a professional. Let's focus on four areas of the personal dimension in particular, for they are of highest importance: personal character, emotional qualities, physical health, and mental health.

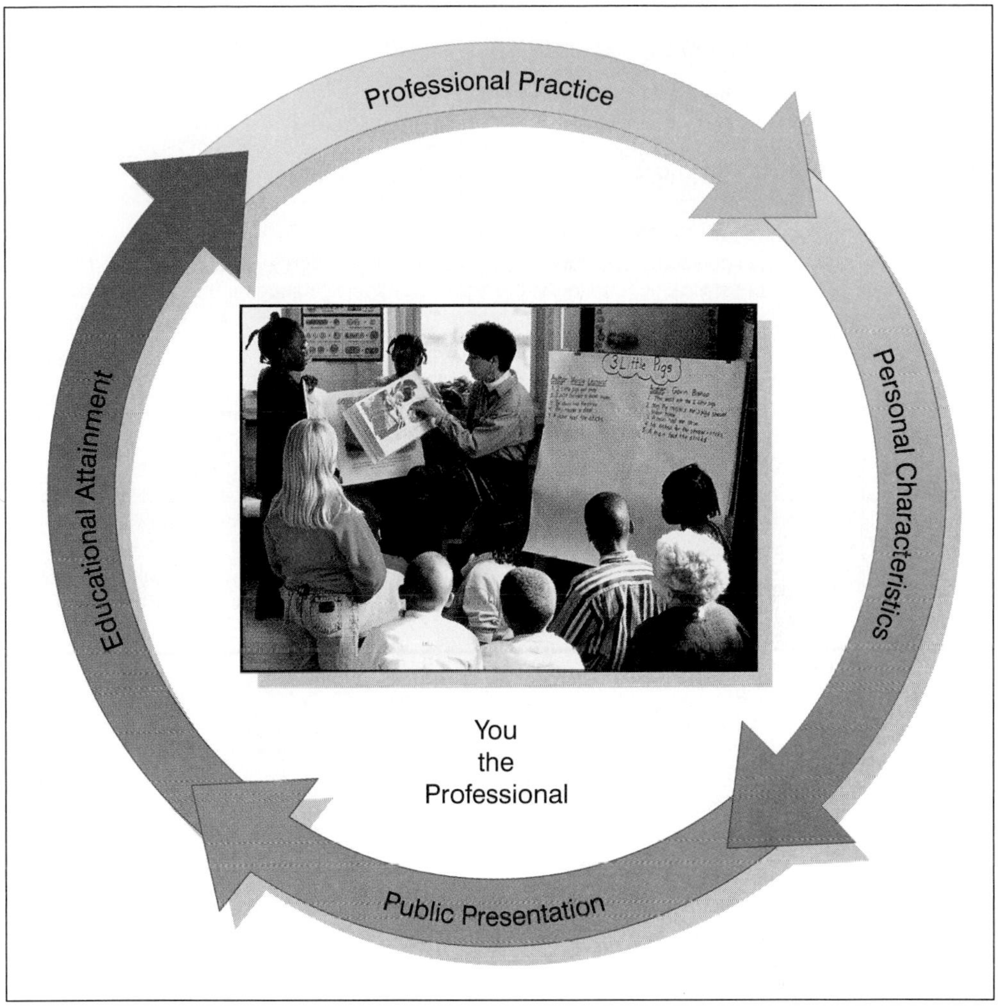

Figure 1.2
The Four Dimensions of Professionalism

For more information about NAEYC and other similar organizations, go to the Companion Website at http://www.prenhall.com/morrison, select chapter 1, then choose the Linking to Learning module to connect to their home pages.

PERSONAL CHARACTER. One very important quality of your personal character is ethical behavior—having high morals and values. Professional teachers conduct their practices in ways that are legally and ethically proper. Professionals want to do what is right in their relationship with students, colleagues, and parents. They base their knowledge on a code of professional ethics. Many professions, such as medicine and law, have unified and universal codes of ethics that govern practice. Although the teaching profession lacks such a code, professional organizations, such as the NAEYC, have developed codes of ethics that help inform and guide professional practice. You can review the NAEYC Code of Ethical Conduct in Appendix A.

A second important personal characteristic is civility, which includes compassion, patience, and acts of kindness and helpfulness. An example of civil behavior is mannerly and courteous interaction with children, parents and families, colleagues, and others.

In addition, early childhood professionals should demonstrate the following personal character traits: courtesy, dedication, respect, enthusiasm, honesty, intelligence, and motivation. Home and early school experiences are critical for developing these character qualities.

So if we want these qualities in our future professionals, we need to promote them now, in our teaching of young children.

EMOTIONAL QUALITIES. Some emotional qualities that are critical to being a successful early childhood professional are love and respect for children, understanding of children and their families, compassion, empathy, friendliness, kindness, sensitivity, trust, tolerance, warmth, and caring.

For an early childhood professional, the most important of these emotional qualities is caring. Good professionals care about children. They accept and respect all children and their cultural and socioeconomic backgrounds. As a professional, you will work in classrooms, programs, and other settings where things do not always go smoothly—for example, children do not always learn ably and well, and they are not always clean and free from illness and hunger. Children's and their parents' backgrounds and ways of life will not always be the same as yours. If you truly care, being an early childhood professional is not easy. Caring means you will lose sleep trying to find a way to help a child learn to read, that you will spend your own money to buy supplies, that you will spend long hours planning and gathering materials. Caring also means you will not leave your intelligence, enthusiasm, or talents at home but will bring them into the center, classroom, administration offices, boards of directors' meetings, and wherever you can make a difference in the lives of children and their families.

PHYSICAL HEALTH. Being healthy and fit are important parts of professional practice. When you are healthy, you can do your best and be your best. When you practice good health habits, such as eating a well-balanced diet and staying physically fit, you also set a good example for your students. Wellness and healthy living are vital for the energy, enthusiasm, and stamina that teaching requires and demands.

MENTAL HEALTH. Good mental health is as important as good physical health. Good mental health includes having a positive outlook on life, the profession, and the future. Hav-

Early childhood professionals are often role models for the children they teach. Therefore, if we want children to be caring, kind, tolerant, and sensitive individuals, the adults in their lives should model those behaviors.

ing good mental health enables professionals to instill in children good mental health habits. Some of these characteristics are optimism, attentiveness, self-confidence, and self-respect. If you have good mental health, you continue to try and try again, and you believe the glass is half full rather than half empty.

The Educational Dimension

The educational dimension of professionalism involves having essential knowledge regarding the profession and professional practice. This includes knowing the history of the profession and the ethics of the profession, understanding the ways children develop and learn, and keeping up-to-date on public issues that influence early childhood and the profession.

A major challenge facing all areas of the early childhood profession is the training and certification of those who care for and teach young children. Training and certification requirements vary from state to state, but more states are tightening personnel standards for child care, preschool, kindergarten, and primary personnel. Many states have mandatory training requirements that individuals must meet before being certified. The curriculum of these training programs frequently specifies mandatory inclusion of topics. For example, in Texas, all child care personnel must complete the Department of Health and Rehabilitation Services' twenty-hour child care training course. The course is composed of four modules:

1. State and local rules and regulations governing child care
2. Health, safety, and nutrition
3. Identifying and reporting child abuse and neglect
4. Child growth and development

In addition, all child care personnel must complete an annual eight-hour in-service training program.

Many states have career ladders that specify the requirements for progressing from one level of professionalism to the next. Figure 1.3 illustrates the career pathway for early childhood professionals in Texas.

DEGREE PROGRAMS

Associate Degree Programs. Many community colleges provide training in early childhood education that qualifies recipients to be child care aides, primary child care providers, and assistant teachers. For example, Massachusetts Bay Community College in Wellesley Hills, Massachusetts, offers a two-year Associate's Degree in Early Childhood Education. Courses in the program include child development, early childhood education, children's literature, art and music for young children, and health and emergency care. Access the school's Web site at mbcc.mass.edu to review the entire program of study.

Baccalaureate Programs. Four-year colleges provide programs that result in early childhood teacher certification. The ages and grades to which the certification applies vary from state to state. Some states have separate certification for prekindergarten programs and nursery schools; in other states, these certifications are "add-ons" to elementary (K–6, 1–6, 1–4) certification.

Master's Degree Programs. Depending on the state, individuals may gain initial early childhood certification at the master's level. Many colleges and universities offer master's-level programs for people who want to qualify as program directors or assistant directors or may want to pursue a career in teaching.

THE CDA NATIONAL CREDENTIALING PROGRAM. At the national level, the Child Development Associate (CDA) National Credentialing Program offers early childhood professionals the opportunity to develop and demonstrate competencies for meeting the needs of young children. A CDA is one who is "able to meet the specific needs of children

Competency Level Eight

- Hold a Doctorate in Child Development/Early Childhood Education

or

- Hold a Doctorate in a related field with 30 college credits in Early Childhood Education/Child Development.

Competency Level Seven

- Hold a Master's Degree in Child Development/Early Childhood Education

or

- Hold a Master's Degree in a related field with 24 college credits in Early Childhood Education/Child Development.

Competency Level Six

- Hold a Bachelor's Degree in Child Development/Early Childhood Education

or

- Hold a Bachelor's Degree in a related field with 12 college credits in Early Childhood Education/Child Development and a state endorsement in Early Childhood.

Competency Level Five

- Hold an Associate's degree in Early Childhool or Child Development.

Competency Level Four

- Hold a Texas child development early childhood certificate from a community college, trade school, or vocational education school.

Competency Level Three

- Hold a Child Development Associate's Credential or its equivalent.

Competency Level Two

- Meet all the requirements for Level One, *plus*
- Complete a minimum of 60 clock hours of training which addresses theTexas Core Knowledge and Skills for Early Care and Education

or

- Complete a three-hour semester credit course which addresses the Texas Core Knowledge and Skills for Early Care and Education from a community college, trade school, or vocational education school.

Competency Level One

- Have a minimum of 8 hours of Texas Department of Protective and Regulatory Services-approved pre-service training and
- be 16 years of age, and
- be working on a GED or high school diploma, and
- be enrolled in a training program approved by the TDPRS-approved by the TDPRS Child Care Licensing Division.

or

- Complete a minimum of 8 hours of TDPRS-approved pre-service training, and
- have a high school diploma or GED, and
- be at least 18 years of age, and
- be participating in a training program which addresses the Texas Core Knowledge and Skills for Early Care and Education

Figure 1.3
Texas Career Path for the Early Care and Education Practitioner

Source: Texas Core Knowledge and Skills in Early Care and Education, Application Packet, Texas Early Care and Education Career Development System Initiative, Texas Head Start–Collaboration Office, Charles A. Dana Center at the University of Texas at Austin, 1998, pp. 21–27. Reprinted by permission.

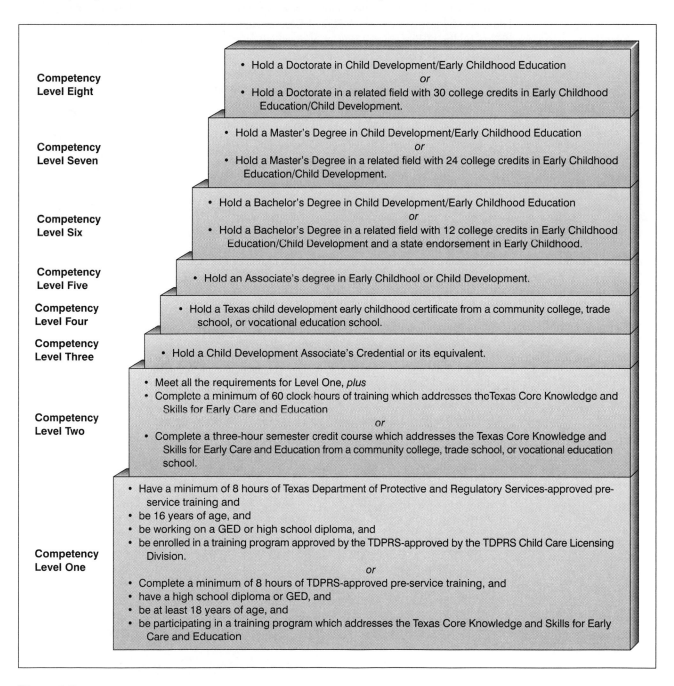

and who, with parents and other adults, works to nurture children's physical, social, emotional, and intellectual growth in a child development framework."[1]

The CDA program, which began in 1971, is a major national effort to evaluate and improve the skills of caregivers in center-based preschool settings, center-based infant/toddler settings, family day care homes, home visitor settings, and programs that have specific goals for bilingual children. The CDA National Credentialing Program is operated by the Council for Early Childhood Professional Recognition, which offers two options for obtaining the CDA credential. One option, the CDA Professional Preparation Program-P3, allows candidates to work in postsecondary institutions as part of the credentialing process. The second option is the direct assessment method, which is designed for candidates who have child care work experience in combination with some early childhood education training.

A candidate for the CDA credential in any setting must be eighteen years old or older and hold a high school diploma or equivalent. To obtain the CDA national credential, candidates under the direct assessment option must meet these additional eligibility requirements:

- 480 hours of experience working with children within the past five years
- 120 clock hours of training with at least ten hours in each of eight CDA training areas, with an emphasis in either infant/toddler or preschool concerns:
  - Health and safety
  - Physical and intellectual development
  - Social and emotional development
  - Relationships with families
  - Program operation
  - Professionalism
  - Observing and recording children's behavior
  - Child growth and development

The candidate must then demonstrate competence in the six CDA competency areas (see Table 1.1).

The CDA Professional Preparation Program. To obtain credentialing by means of this option, the candidate must meet the two general eligibility requirements of age and education and must also identify an advisor to work with during the year of study, which is made up of three phases: fieldwork, coursework, and final evaluation.

Fieldwork involves study of the council's model curriculum, *Essentials for Child Development Associates Working with Young Children*. This curriculum includes the six competency areas listed in Table 1.1. In the second phase, coursework, the candidate participates in seminars offered in community colleges and other postsecondary institutions. These seminars are designed to supplement the model curriculum and are administered by a seminar instructor. The third phase is the final evaluation, which takes place in the candidate's work setting or field placement.

For more information about becoming an early childhood professional, go to the Companion Website at http://www.prenhall.com/morrison, select any chapter, then choose Topic 1 of the ECE Supersite module.

The results of all three phases are sent to the council office for review and determination of whether the candidate has successfully completed all aspects of the CDA Professional Preparation Program. To date, more than fifty thousand persons have been awarded the CDA credential.

For additional information, you may visit the National Network for Child Care on the Web at www.nncc.org/Evaluation/cdacb.html.

The Professional Practice Dimension

Professional practice involves doing what professionals do—teaching and caring for children, working with parents and families, collaborating with community partners, and assuming all

Table 1.1
CDA Competency Goals and Functional Areas

CDA Competency Goals	Functional Areas
I. To establish and maintain a safe, healthy learning environment	1. Safe: Candidate provides a safe environment to prevent and reduce injuries. 2. Healthy: Candidate promotes good health and nutrition and provides an environment that contributes to the prevention of illness. 3. Learning environment: Candidate uses space, relationships, materials, and routines as resources for constructing an interesting, secure, and enjoyable environment that encourages play, exploration, and learning.
II. To advance physical and intellectual competence	4. Physical: Candidate provides a variety of equipment, activities, and opportunities to promote intellectual competence. 5. Cognitive: Candidate provides activities and opportunities that encourage curiosity, exploration, and problem solving appropriate to the development levels and learning styles of children. 6. Communication: Candidate actively communicates with children and provides opportunities and support for children to understand, acquire, and use verbal and nonverbal means of communicating thoughts and feelings. 7. Creative: Candidate provides opportunities that stimulate children to play with sound, rhythm, language, materials, space, and ideas in individual ways and to express their creative abilities.
III. To support social and emotional development and to provide positive guidance	8. Self: Candidate provides physical and emotional security for each child and helps each child to know, accept, and take pride in himself or herself and to develop a sense of independence. 9. Social: Candidate helps each child feel accepted in the group, helps children learn to communicate and get along with others, and encourages feelings of empathy and mutual respect among children and adults. 10. Guidance: Candidate provides a supportive environment in which children can begin to learn and practice appropriate and acceptable behaviors as individuals and as a group.
IV. To establish positive and productive relationships with families	11. Families: Candidate maintains an open, friendly, and cooperative relationship with each child's family, encourages their involvement in the program, and supports the child's relationship with his or her family.
V. To ensure a well-run, purposeful program responsive to participant needs	12. Program management: Candidate is a manager who uses all available resources to ensure an effective operation. The candidate is a competent organizer, planner, record keeper, needs communicator, and a cooperative coworker.
VI. To maintain a commitment to professionalism	13. Professionalism: Candidate makes decisions based on knowledge of early childhood theories and practices; promotes quality in child care services; and takes advantage of opportunities to improve competence, both for personal and professional growth and for the benefit of children and families.

Source: The Council for Professional Recognition, Essentials for Child Development Associates Working with Young Children *(Washington, DC: Author, 1991), p. 415. Used by permission.*

Early childhood educators are professionals who—in addition to teaching and caring for children—plan, assess, report, collaborate with colleagues and families, and behave in ethical ways.

the other roles and responsibilities involved in the profession. This dimension includes knowing children; developing a philosophy of education; planning; assessing; reporting; reflecting and thinking; teaching; collaborating with parents, families, and community partners; engaging in ethical practice; and seeking continued professional development opportunities.

Child development is the *what* of early childhood. Early childhood education is the *how* of the profession. Learning how to teach is as important as knowing what to teach. You really can't have one without the other. Early childhood professionals must be able to do the following:

- Demonstrate a basic understanding of the early childhood profession and make a commitment to professionalism.
- Demonstrate a basic understanding of child development and apply this knowledge in practice.
- Observe and assess children's behavior for use in planning and individualizing curriculum.
- Establish and maintain an environment that ensures children's safety and their healthy development.
- Plan and implement a developmentally appropriate program that advances all areas of children's learning and development, including intellectual, social, emotional, and physical competence.
- Establish supportive relationships with children and implement developmentally appropriate techniques of guidance and group management.

- Establish positive and productive relationships with families.
- Support the uniqueness of each child, recognizing that children are best understood in the context of family, culture, and society.[2]

These items represent the core knowledge of the profession. Every professional, at the moment of entry into the field and at every level, undertakes the responsibility to engage in increasing levels of preparation and knowledge acquisition.

KNOWING CHILDREN. Two kinds of knowledge are essential for professional practice: knowledge of child development and knowledge of how to teach.

Child development knowledge enables you to know how children grow and develop across all developmental levels—the cognitive, linguistic, social, emotional, and physical. Quality professionals really know the children they care for. This knowledge of individual children, combined with knowledge of child growth and development, enables you to provide care that is appropriate for each child. Such knowledge is essential for understanding how to conduct developmentally appropriate practice, which is the recommended teaching practice of the profession. I will discuss developmentally appropriate practice in more detail in chapters 8 and 9. Appendix B contains NAEYC's Guidelines for Developmentally Appropriate Practice in Early Childhood Programs.

DEVELOPING A PHILOSOPHY OF EDUCATION. Professional practice includes teaching with and from a philosophy of education, which acts as a guidepost to help you base your teaching on what you believe about children.

A philosophy of education is a set of beliefs about how children develop and learn and what and how they should be taught. Your philosophy of education is based on your philosophy of life. What you believe about yourself, about others, and about life infuses and determines your philosophy of education. Knowing what others believe is important and useful, for it can help you clarify what you believe, but, when all is said and done, *you* have to decide what you believe. Moment by moment, day by day, what you believe influences what you will teach and how you will teach it.

A philosophy of life and education is more than an opinion. A personal philosophy is based on core values and beliefs. Core values of life relate to your beliefs about the nature of life, the purpose of life, your role and calling in life, and your relationship and responsibilities to others. Core beliefs and values about education and teaching include what you believe about the nature of children and the purpose of education, about learning styles and the role of teachers, and about what you think is worth knowing.

Your philosophy of education will guide and direct your daily teaching. Your beliefs about how children learn best will determine whether you individualize instruction or try to teach the same thing in the same way to everyone. Your philosophy will determine whether you help children do things for themselves or whether you do things for them. The following paragraphs describe ways you can begin now to develop your philosophy.

Read widely in textbooks, journals, and other professional literature to get ideas and points of view. A word of caution: When people refer to philosophies of education, they often think only of historic influences. This is only part of the information available for writing a philosophy. Make sure you explore contemporary ideas as well, for these will also have a strong influence on you as a professional. The resources at the end of the chapter will help you get started.

As you read through and study this book, make notes and reflect about your developing philosophy of education. The following headings will help get you started:

- I believe the purposes of education are . . .

- I believe that children learn best when they are taught under certain conditions and in certain ways. Some of these are . . .
- The curriculum of any classroom should include certain "basics" that contribute to children's social, emotional, intellectual, and physical development. These basics include . . .
- Children learn best in an environment that promotes learning. Features of a good learning environment are . . .
- All children have certain needs that must be met if they are to grow and learn at their best. Some of these basic needs are . . .
- I would meet these needs by . . .
- A teacher should have certain qualities and behave in certain ways. Qualities I think important for teaching are . . .

Once you have determined your philosophy of education, write it down, and have other people read it. This helps you clarify your ideas and redefine your thoughts, because your philosophy should be understandable to others (although they do not necessarily have to agree with you).

Talk with successful teachers and other educators. The accounts of the information from teachers and others in the "Voice from the Field" features throughout this text are evidence that a philosophy can help you be an above-average teacher. Talking with others exposes you to different points of view and stimulates your thinking.

Finally, evaluate your philosophy against this checklist:

- Does my philosophy accurately relate my beliefs about teaching? Have I been honest with myself?
- Is it understandable to me and others?
- Does it provide practical guidance for teaching?
- Are my ideas consistent with one another?
- Does what I believe make good sense?
- Have I been comprehensive, stating my beliefs about (1) how children learn, (2) what children should be taught, (3) how children should be taught, (4) the conditions under which children learn best, and (5) what qualities make up a good teacher?

PLANNING. Planning is also an essential part of practicing the art and craft of teaching. Planning consists of setting goals for children and selecting and developing activities to help you achieve your teaching goals. Without planning you can't be a good teacher. Planning will help ensure that all children will learn, which is one of the most important and meaningful challenges you will face as an early childhood professional. You may have heard it said that all children can learn. What is important is believing that all children *will* learn and acting on this basic belief. Some essential steps in the planning process are as follows:

- Stating what your children will learn and be able to do. These objectives can come from a number of sources. Currently, forty-nine states have developed or are developing standards regarding what students should know and be able to do in kindergarten through grade three. Standards for preschool education are on the way. Program goals represent a second source of objectives. These goals are carefully thought out by staff and families and provide direction for what and how children will learn.

... voice from the field

Philosophy of Education

NORMA JACKSON, 1998–1999 TEXAS TEACHER OF THE YEAR

I can't remember a time when I didn't want to be a teacher. My parents tell stories of me "instructing" second grade friends for hours from my classroom on the steps of our front porch. While the details of those lazy afternoons elude me, I clearly remember an unwavering desire to become a real teacher.

While I grew up surrounded by teachers, including my father and several aunts and uncles, my real passion for teaching was ignited by my students. My first practicum as an undergraduate student was with mentally challenged students. If someone had asked me at the time what I learned most from this experience, I would have replied that it uncovered my talent for analyzing concepts and breaking them down into fun, manageable steps. These special children taught me the pure, unselfish joy that comes from helping someone grasp a difficult concept, but I would realize later that they laid the foundation for a far more valuable lesson.

Another of my toughest, most defining experiences was student teaching in a classroom for emotionally disturbed children. Needless to say, they were not as eager as the "class" I greeted on the front steps of my childhood home. These often angry, distraught children taught me to look beyond the obvious. I still have a note from one of these students. It serves as a powerful, though humorous, reminder that every child can learn, but sometimes you have to meet other more basic needs first:

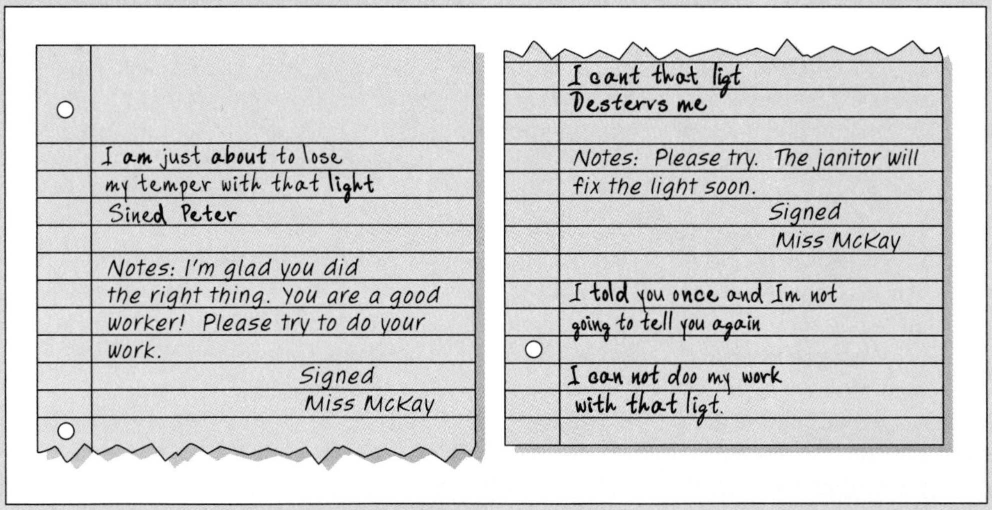
I am just about to lose
my temper with that light
Sined Peter

Notes: I'm glad you did
the right thing. You are a good
worker! Please try to do your
work.
Signed
Miss McKay

I cant that ligt
Desterys me

Notes: Please try. The janitor will
fix the light soon.
Signed
Miss McKay

I told you once and Im not
going to tell you again

I can not doo my work
with that ligt.

Peter *did* complete his work that day, but even more remarkable, he was able to control his volatile temper by venting on paper instead of hitting and screaming. This note is a treasure I continue to save as an important record of my own growth. I was learning to listen with more than my ears. Writing was a new coping skill for Peter, and he needed acknowledgment of his efforts. Peter was teaching me to appreciate and value the learner as much as the learning.

These early learning experiences formed the cornerstone of my philosophy of education, summed up simply as "Children first." How lucky I was to discover this so early in my career—without this insight, the many demands in education might have become overwhelming. Instead, when inundated with a myriad of issues and events, I find direction by refocusing on solutions that most directly meet my students' needs.

If "children first" is the foundation of my philosophy, then "practice what you preach" is the framework around which I shape my instruction. I believe that all truly great teachers are themselves passionate learners. As a teacher, I am a partner in learning for my students, with my students, and through my students. Teaching is a new learning adventure each and every day.

Students often think of me as the Ben Franklin of the classroom, as I frequently quote proverbs or adages which reflect the principles I hold dear. For over ten years, the first words out of my mouth as I address a new class of students is the riddle "How do you eat an elephant?" As I go on to share the answer, "One bite at a time," I explain that even when something we are learning seems as large and overwhelming as an elephant, each one of them will learn it by taking it one step at a time. This lesson is intended to help them understand that though we won't all learn everything easily or at the same pace, we can all learn if we keep at it. I am a "can do" teacher and I know that students who learn the value of perseverance and determination face life with more confidence and self-assurance that they will find the answers they seek.

"If you give a man a fish, he eats for a meal. If you teach a man to fish, he eats for a lifetime." My role as a teacher is to help students become independent learners who can continue their quest for knowledge even without me. Every opportunity is used to point out when students exemplify what "good mathematicians," "good scientists," "good readers," or "good citizens" do to solve problems. For example, when a student reread a page to determine the meaning of an unknown word, I praised him and pointed out that he was doing what all good readers do: use picture clues, sound clues, and context clues to figure out the words they don't understand. When another child discovered water on the floor by the drinking fountain and took the initiative to wipe it up before someone slipped, I complimented her on doing what good citizens do: look out for the welfare of others, as well as their own. It is important that children recognize their ability to learn and think for themselves. This builds self-reliance and provides a foundation for applying their knowledge in new situations. Being a risk-taker and problem-solver myself, I use a teaching approach that fosters a safe environment for students to take risks and solve problems as well.

I hold high expectations for myself and for my students. It is never enough to do the minimum. Students are always encouraged to "Go the extra mile," to find and ask their own questions, then seek the answers using available resources. Activities have either a stated challenge or an open-ended challenge which invites students to continue learning beyond my lesson. My students don't just stay busy, they stay mentally engaged in learning. They actively seek knowledge and understanding.

This strong work ethic is reinforced by a story I tell about my childhood. When I was a little girl visiting my grandmother, she would let me have coffee. Actually it was more like milk with a teaspoon of coffee, but I felt quite grown up all the same. Every morning upon rising, my grandmother would say, "First we work, then we play." We would get dressed, make the beds, and pick up before enjoying biscuits and coffee together. Today Grandma's Rule prevails in my classroom, as well. My students begin most days gathered together at the back of the room to discuss the day's activities. Even though I have prepared lesson plans, I invite students to help sequence activities, set deadlines, and establish goals for the day. This helps them learn how to prioritize and establish goals of their own. My students develop pleasure and pride in working hard and accomplishing difficult tasks.

Regardless of how supportive my classroom may be, sometimes students experience frustrations or setbacks. I cannot shield them from these disappointments, but I can teach them the value of a positive attitude. When something goes wrong or gets in the way of a goal of mine, an individual student, or the class, I cheerfully begin "Oh well . . . " and we repeat in unison, "If life gives you lemons, make lemonade." Then we make a game of finding the good in the situation or creative ways to work around the problem. Learning requires perseverance and perseverance requires a positive attitude.

Still they sometimes lose sight of what's important. I've taught second graders for 24 years, so I consider myself somewhat of an authority on seven- and eight-year-olds. They are wonderful little people with expressive eyes and snaggle-tooth grins eager to burst from their lips at the slightest provocation. But they also experience disappointments with the same reckless abandon. Sometimes eight-year-old hands can't quite manage the grand ideas that an eight-year-old mind envisions, prompting quite a theatrical scene. When a child is in tears over a hole he just rubbed in his paper, I pull him up close and ask, "What's more important: people or things?" Though the child may be reluctant to admit it, I lead him to see that the paper is a thing. It can be fixed or replaced or forgotten. People are the only things in this world that are worth worrying about.

About five years ago, my principal gave everyone on our faculty a Children First pin which resulted in a ritual I perform each morning before declaring my primping complete. I do not skip this ritual no matter how late I may be running or how frustrated I feel over a bad-hair day. As I pick up my Children First pin to put it on, I pause to think about the little boy who seems to have lost his smile over the last few days, the little girl who's struggling with reading, or the child who is having trouble getting along. My thoughts become a prayer and a recommitment to put the children I touch before meetings, deadlines or even curriculum. My pin becomes a touchstone—a reminder that people are more important than things.

I want my students to see me as a teacher who finds joy in learning and who sees day-to-day challenges as exciting problems to solve, but who never loses sight of them as respected, cherished individuals. My philosophy is reflected in life lessons designed to take my students beyond knowledge and inspire them to set their own high expectations, to be unswervingly determined, and to maintain a positive outlook. I want my students to view their own learning as a life-long adventure that will bring them joy and enable them to bring joy into the lives of others, as well.

- Selecting developmentally appropriate activities and materials and ones that are based on children's interests.
- Deciding how much time to allocate to an activity.
- Deciding how to assess activities and the things that children have learned.

ASSESSING. Assessment is the process of gathering information about children's behavior and achievement and, on the basis of this data, making decisions about how to meet children's needs. Chapter 11, "Observing and Assessing Young Children," provides you with practical skills and ideas for how to conduct developmentally appropriate assessment.

REPORTING. Reporting to parents and others in an understandable and meaningful way serves several purposes. First, it answers every parent's question, "How is my child doing?" Sec-

ond, information about children's achievement helps you, as a professional, be accountable to the public in fulfilling your role of helping children learn and be successful. Chapters 5 through 11 provide specific ideas and examples for reporting children's progress to parents and others.

REFLECTING AND THINKING. A professional is always thinking about and reflecting on what he has done, is doing, and will do. A good guideline for thinking and reflecting is this: Think before you teach, think while you are teaching, and think after you teach. This constant cycle of *reflective practice* will help you be a good professional and will help your children learn.

TEACHING. If you asked most teachers what they do, they would tell you they have a job description that requires them to wear many hats and that their jobs are never done. Teachers' responsibilities and tasks are many and varied. Teaching involves making decisions about what and how to teach, planning for teaching, engaging students in learning activities, managing learning environments, assessing student behavior and achievement, reporting to parents and others, collaborating with colleagues and community partners, and engaging in ongoing professional development. You might feel a little overwhelmed. However, you will have a lot of help and support on your journey to becoming a good teacher. Your teacher preparation program, your instructors, participating classroom teachers, and this textbook will help you learn how to meet the many responsibilities of becoming a good teacher.

COLLABORATING WITH PARENTS, FAMILIES, AND COMMUNITY PARTNERS. Parents, families, and the community are essential partners in the process of schooling. Knowing how to effectively collaborate with these key partners will serve you well throughout your career. Chapter 16, "Parent, Family, and Community Involvement: Cooperation and Collaboration," will help you learn more about this important topic.

Family education and support is an important role of the early childhood professional. Children's learning begins and continues within the context of the family unit, whatever that family unit may be. Learning how to comfortably and confidently work with parents is as essential as teaching children.

ENGAGING IN ETHICAL PRACTICE. Ethical conduct—the exercise of responsible behavior with children, families, colleagues, and community members—enables you to confidently engage in exemplary professional practice. A professional is an ethical person. As previously indicated, the profession of early childhood education has a set of ethical standards to guide your thinking and behavior. NAEYC has developed a Code of Ethical Conduct (see Appendix A) and a Statement of Commitment. Following is the Statement of Commitment:

> As an individual who works with young children, I commit myself to furthering the values of early childhood education as they are reflected in the NAEYC Code of Ethical Conduct. To the best of my ability I will:
>
> > Ensure that programs for young children are based on current knowledge of child development and early childhood education.
> >
> > Respect and support families in their task of nurturing children.
> >
> > Respect colleagues in early childhood education and support them in maintaining the NAEYC Code of Ethical Conduct.
> >
> > Serve as an advocate for children, their families and their teachers in community and society.
> >
> > Maintain high standards of professional conduct.
> >
> > Recognize how personal values, opinions, and biases can affect professional judgment.
> >
> > Be open to new ideas and be willing to learn from the suggestions of others.

... voice from the field

My Philosophy of Teaching

LAURIE SYBERT, 1999 MISSOURI TEACHER OF THE YEAR

I believe that teaching should be a challenging and rewarding experience for both the teacher and the student. I want to challenge students to live effectively in a society that is culturally and ethnically diverse. Because of our school's high student mobility rate (45 percent), it is a constant challenge to reevaluate my classroom make-up and modify lessons to make them relevant to each student. I strive to blend all subjects together in a thematic way to help students see how everything is interconnected.

I use a variety of thematic techniques in my teaching to help facilitate learning in consideration of the very diverse educational backgrounds of the students. Students share the morning responsibilities of passing out papers, watering plants, checking the moisture in the toad habitat, feeding the fish, and taking the messages to the office. We feed the toads live crickets once a month. The students absolutely love gathering around the aquarium and watching them eat. It serves as a marvelous writing opportunity or as an opportunity to solve real-life math problems. My fish habitat consists of a large Rubbermaid tub with cattails growing at one end. The children enjoy sitting by this habitat when they are reading their books during silent reading time.

I incorporate language by encouraging students to write stories, plays, and journal entries and through partner work. We have written and illustrated several large "animal shape" books that have been distributed to various area doctors' offices. We tied these books into our thematic days that we celebrate each month. In reading we have a wonderful unit on animals, their tracks, and their habitats. This gives me an opportunity to take the children to the outdoor classroom and look for signs of the animal home and tracks. We are fortunate to have an outdoor classroom that is home to various animals, such as deer, raccoon, birds, and rabbits. We draw pictures of habitats, write about the animals that live there, and make plaster-of-paris models of the tracks. For the past two years I have arranged to have the 2nd grade classes go to the Runge Nature Center in Jefferson City to look at the animals [and] nature displays, and walk the nature trails. It is a great conclusion to our reading unit.

"Math Their Way" techniques allow me to explore numbers by using manipulatives, the overhead, math books, and journals. I try to give the students real-life situations that are relevant to them. One such situation might be to figure out how many cups, quarts, or gallons it would take to fill an aquarium. The students may be given an example of what the aquarium would look like if it contains "X" amount of cups of water and then they figure out how many the entire container would hold. Of course, after several students have what they feel is the correct answer, the answers are discussed and the true amount measured.

Science is my absolute love and generally is the basis for most daily themes. We put together habitats, visit the outdoor classroom, go for nature walks, cook "bugs" in the cooking lab (not real), etc. Some of the outdoor classroom activities that the students enjoy are our nature scavenger hunt, making a spider web print, putting together a "soil sundae," collecting colorful leaves, and adopting a classroom tree to watch change during the four seasons.

One of the year-long experiments that the students enjoy is planting trash. It always amazes me what a second grader's viewpoint is on exactly what happens to the leaves and dead animals that they see alongside the road or in their yards. The children and I collect

items to put in our container of dirt. Then we water it and check it once a month to see if everything is still there. This gives us an opportunity to talk about changes in the contents of the container and why they are occurring.

Another experiment that I do each Thanksgiving is to plant corn in the way the Native Americans showed to the early pioneers. I get several dead minnows from a local bait shop and each student plants a dead minnow with three kernels of corn. We also plant corn without the fish. We write the date on the aquarium and wait for it to grow. The students keep a journal on the growth of their corn and these results are graphed and discussed. Both these experiments are great for understanding decomposition and replacing nutrients in the soil.

Using a thematic approach to learning helps the child have hands-on experiences and to better see how everything in everyday life is interconnected. The child stops receiving only pieces of the puzzle, but instead begins to see a realistic picture of how to use the information that [he has] been given to solve real-life problems.

Continue to learn, grow, and contribute as a professional.

Honor the ideals and principles of the NAEYC Code of Ethical Conduct.[3]

You can also review NAEYC's Code of Ethical Conduct on-line (http://www.naeyc.org/about/position/pseth98.htm) and begin now to incorporate professional ethical practices into your interactions with children and colleagues.

SEEKING ONGOING PROFESSIONAL DEVELOPMENT OPPORTUNITIES. When, if ever, does a person become a "finished" professional? It makes the most sense to say that a person is always in the process of becoming a professional. A professional is never a "finished" product; you will always be involved in a process of studying, learning, changing, and becoming more professional. The Teachers of the Year who share with you their philosophies and beliefs are always in the process of becoming more professional.

Becoming a professional means you will participate in training and education beyond the minimum needed for your present position. You will also want to consider your career objectives and the qualifications you might need for positions of increasing responsibility. The NAEYC has established the National Institute for Early Childhood Professional Development, which conducts efforts to achieve an articulated, coordinated professional development system and helps make the discipline of early childhood education even more professional.

The Public Dimension

The fourth dimension of professional practice is the public dimension. This dimension includes advocacy, articulation, and representation.

ADVOCACY. Advocacy is the act of pleading the causes of children and families to the profession and the public. There is no shortage of issues to advocate for in the lives of children and families. Some of the issues that are in need of strong advocates involve quality programs, abuse and neglect prevention, children living in poverty, good housing, and health. Some things you can do to advocate include the following:

A professional is never a "finished" product. Collaborating with other professionals who share your philosophies is an excellent way to continue your professional development. What are some other ways?

- Join an early childhood professional organization such as the National Association for the Education of Young Children, the Association for Childhood Education International (ACEI), and the Southern Early Childhood Association (SECA). These organizations have student and local affiliates. They are very active in advocating for young children, and you can serve on a committee or be involved in some other way.
- Organize an advocacy group in your program or as a part of your class. Select a critical issue to study, and develop strategies for increasing public awareness about this issue.

ARTICULATION. Being articulate about what you do and what the profession does and speaking to parents and the public is essential for helping children and families be successful. Early childhood professionals must be knowledgeable and informed about the profession and the issues it faces. At the same time, they have to be able to discuss these issues with the public, the media, families, and others in the community.

REPRESENTATION. Representation is the process of acting in the best possible ways on behalf of children and families. It involves being a role model for what a professional is and stands for, including how you dress, how you groom, and how you talk and act. It is important for professionals to make a good impression. We cannot practice our profession well or expect and receive the respect of parents and the public if we don't always put our best foot forward. How we look and how we behave does make a difference. And like it or not, first impressions count with many people. How we appear to others often sets the tone for interpersonal interactions. So, you should always look your best, do your best, and be your best.

To monitor your progress toward professionalism using the online version of the Professional Development Checklist, go to the Companion Website at http://www.prenhall.com/morrison, select any chapter, then choose the Resources module.

These, then, are the four dimensions of professionalism—personal, educational, professional, and public. If you add these dimensions to whom and what you are now, you should be able to represent yourself and the profession very well. You can enhance your professional development by completing the Professional Development Checklist shown in Figure 1.4 now.

Desired Professional Outcome	High Level of Commitment and Accomplishment	Satisfactory Level of Commitment and Accomplishment but Need Improvement
1. I have thought about and written my philosophy of teaching and caring for young children.		
2. I have a professional career plan for the next year that includes goals and objectives I will endeavor to meet as a professional.		
3. I engage in study and training programs to improve my knowledge and competence related to teaching and caring for young children.		
4. I am a teachable person. I am willing to change my ideas, thinking, and practices based on study, new information, and the advice of colleagues and professionals.		
5. I have worked or am working on a degree or credential (CDA, A.A., B.S.) to enhance my personal life and my life as a professional.		
6. I try to improve myself as a person by engaging in a personal program of self-development.		
7. I practice in my own life and model for others good moral habits and ethical behavior. I encourage others to act ethically.		
8. I act professionally and encourage others to do the same.		
9. I place the best interests of children, parents, and the profession first in decisions about what constitutes quality teaching and caregiving.		
10. I know about and am familiar with my profession's history, terminology, issues, contemporary development, and trends.		
11. I consciously and consistently find ways to apply concepts and knowledge about what is best for children to my teaching and caregiving.		
12. I belong to a professional organization and participate in professional activities such as celebrations, study groups, committees, and conventions.		
13. I am an advocate for and on behalf of my profession and the needs and rights of children and families.		
14. I involve parents in my program and help and encourage parents in their roles as children's primary caregivers and teachers.		
15. I seek the advice of and cooperate with other professionals and professional groups in my work with young children, parents, and families.		

Figure 1.4
Fifteen Steps to Becoming a Professional: A Professional Development Checklist

Little or Low Commitment and Accomplishment—Need Considerable Improvement	Evidence of Commitment and Accomplishment (*Specify what you have done and are doing to meet these professional criteria*)	Action Plan for Commitment and Accomplishment (*Specify what you plan to do to improve in this area*)	Target Date for Completing Action Plan or Demonstrating Increased Commitment and Accomplishment

What Is the Terminology of Early Childhood Education?

For a complete online glossary of early childhood education terms, go to the Companion Website at http://www.prenhall.com/morrison, select any chapter, then choose the Glossary module.

As an early childhood professional, you will need to know and use the terminology of the profession (Tables 1.2 and 1.3). The following paragraphs discuss key terms.

The term *professional* refers to all who work with, care for, and teach children between birth and age eight. Using this term avoids the obvious confusion of trying to distinguish between *caregiver* and *teacher*. The caregiving and teaching roles are now blended, so a person who cares for infants is teaching them as well. However, in the preschool, kindergarten, and primary years, the term *teacher* will continue to be used to designate these professionals. Also, the early childhood profession is trying to upgrade the image and role of all those who work with young children. Referring to everyone with the designation *professional* helps achieve this goal.

The term *early childhood* refers to the period from birth to age eight, the standard and accepted definition used by NAEYC.[4] (At the same time, professionals recognize that prenatal development is a critical period that influences all of human development.) The term also frequently refers to children who have not yet reached school age, and the public often uses it to refer to children in any type of preschool program.

Early childhood programs provide "services for children from birth through age eight in part-day and full-day group programs in centers, homes, and institutions; kindergartens and primary schools; and recreational programs."[5]

Early childhood education consists of the services provided by early childhood professionals. It is common for professionals to use the terms *early childhood* and *early childhood education* synonymously. *Preschool* generally means any education program for children prior to their entrance into kindergarten. *Preschool programs* for three- and four-year-old children are rapidly becoming a part of the public school system, particularly those designed to serve low-income children and their families. For example, the Dade County, Florida, public schools operate approximately 220 preschool programs for three- and four-year-old children. *Kindergarten* is for five- and six-year-old children prior to their entry into first grade. Public school kindergarten is now almost universal for five-year-old children (see chapter 9) and is now part of the elementary grades kindergarten through six.

The term *prekindergarten* refers to programs for four-year-olds attending programs prior to kindergarten. Another term, *transitional kindergarten*, designates a program for children who are not ready for kindergarten and who can benefit from another year of educational and other experiences. *Transitional* also refers to grade school programs that provide additional opportunities for children to master skills associated with a particular grade. Transitional programs do not usually exist beyond the second and third grades.

Junior first grade, or *pre–first grade*, are transitional programs between kindergarten and first grade designed to help five-year-olds get ready to enter first grade. Not all children are equally "ready" to benefit from typical first grade because of their range of mental ages and experiential backgrounds, and children frequently benefit from such special programs. The goal of many early childhood professionals is to have all children learning at levels appropriate for them.

Preprimary refers to programs for children prior to their entering first grade; *primary* means first, second, and third grades. In some school districts, primary grade children are taught in classes that include two grade levels. In these split, or nongraded, classes, first and second graders and second and third graders are taught in a single class. Split classes are seldom composed of upper-elementary children. Reasons for split classes include increasing or decreasing school enrollments and teacher contracts that limit class size.

A *parent cooperative* preschool is a school formed and operated by parents for their children. Programs of this type are generally conducted democratically, with the parents hiring

the staff. Often, some of the parents are hired to direct or staff the program. Being part of a cooperative means parents have some responsibility for assisting in the program.

The term *child care* encompasses many programs and services for preschool children. *Day care* is a term used for *child care*, but it is almost universally regarded as outmoded. *Child*

Table 1.2
Types of Early Childhood Programs

Program	Definition and Purpose	Ages Served
Early childhood program	Multipurpose	Birth to grade 3
Child care	Play/socialization; baby-sitting; physical care; provides parents opportunities to work; cognitive development; full-quality care	Birth to 6 years
High school child care programs	Provides child care for children of high school students, especially unwed parents; serves as an incentive for student/parents to finish high school and as a training program in child care and parenting skills	6 weeks to 5 years
Drop-off child care centers	Provides care for short periods of time while parents shop, exercise, or have appointments	Infancy through the primary grades
Before- and after-school care	Provides care for children before and after school hours	Children of school age; generally K–6
Family day care	Provides care for a group of children in a home setting; generally custodial in nature	Variable
Employer/corporate child care	Different settings for meeting child care needs	Variable; usually as early as 6 weeks to the beginning of school
Proprietary care	Provides care and/or education to children; designed to make a profit	6 weeks to entrance into first grade
Nursery school (public or private)	Play/socialization; cognitive development	2 to 4 years
Preschool (public or private)	Play/socialization; cognitive development	2½ to 5 years
Parent cooperative preschool	Play/socialization; preparation for kindergarten and first grade; baby-sitting; cognitive development	2 to 5 years
Prekindergarten	Play/socialization; preparation for kindergarten	3½ to 5 years
Junior kindergarten	Prekindergarten program	Primarily 4-year-olds
Kindergarten	Preparation for first grade; developmentally appropriate activities for 4½ – to 6-year olds; increasingly viewed as the grade before the first grade and a a regular part of the public school program	4 to 6 years
Pre–first grade	Preparation for first grade; often for students who "failed" or did not do well in kindergarten	5 to 6 years
Interim first grade	Provides children with an additional year of kindergarten and readiness activities prior to and as preparation for first grade	5 to 6 years

continued

Table 1.2, continued
Types of Early Childhood Programs

Program	Definition and Purpose	Ages Served
Developmental kindergarten	Same as regular kindergarten; often enrolls children who have completed one or more years in an early childhood special education program	5 to 6 years
Transitional kindergarten	Extended learning of kindergarten; preparation for first grade	Variable
Preprimary	Preparation for first grade	5 to 6 years
Primary	Teaches skills associated with grades 1, 2, and 3	6 to 8 years
Toy lending libraries	Provides parents and children with games, toys, and other materials that can be used for learning purposes; housed in libraries, vans, or early childhood centers	Birth through primary years
Lekotek	Resource center for families who have children with special needs; sometimes referred to as a *toy library* or *play library* (*lekotek* is a Scandinavian word that means "play library")	Birth through primary years
Infant stimulation programs (also called parent/infant stimulation)	Programs for enhancing sensory and cognitive development of infants and young toddlers through exercise and play; activities include general sensory stimulation for children and educational information and advice for parents	3 months to 2 years
Multiage grades or groups	Groups of classes of children of various ages; generally spanning 2 to 3 years per group	Variable
Dual-age classroom	An organizational plan in which children from two grade levels are grouped together; maintains reasonable student–teacher ratios; another term for multiage grouping	Variable
Learning families	Another name for multiage grouping; however, the emphasis is on practices that create a family atmosphere and encourage living and learning as a family; the term was commonly used in open educational programs; its revival signifies the reemergence of progressive and child-centered approaches	Variable
Junior first grade	Preparation for first grade	5 to 6 years
Split class	Teaches basic academic and social skills of grades involved	Variable, but usually primary
Head Start	Play/socialization; academic learning; comprehensive social and health services; prepares children for kindergarten and first grade	2 to 6 years

care is a more accurate and descriptive term because it focuses on children themselves. The primary purpose of child care programs is to care for young children who are not in school and for school-age children before and after school hours. Programs may have a total quality orientation or an educational orientation, and some may offer primarily baby-sitting or custodial care. Many programs have a sliding-fee schedule based on parents' ability to pay. Quality

Program	Definition and Purpose	Ages Served
Follow Through	Extended Head Start services to grades 1, 2, and 3	6 to 8 years
Department of Children, Youth, and Families	A multipurpose agency of many state and county governments; usually provides such services as administration of state and federal monies, child care licensing, and protective services	All
Health and Human Services	Same as Dept. of Children, Youth, and Families	All
Health and Social Services	Same as Dept. of Children, Youth, and Families	All
Home Start	Provides Head Start services in the home setting	Birth to 6 or 7 years
Laboratory school	Provides demonstration programs for pre-service teachers; conducts research	Variable; birth through senior high
Child and Family Resource Program	Delivers Head Start services to families	Birth to 8 years
Montessori school (preschool and grade school)	Provides programs that use the philosophy, procedures, and materials developed by Maria Montessori (see chapter 4)	1 to 8 years
Magnet school	Specializes in subjects and curriculum designed to attract students; usually has a theme (e.g. performing arts); designed to give parents choices and to integrate schools	5 to 18 years

child care programs are increasingly characterized by comprehensive services that address children's total physical, social, emotional, linguistic, creative, and intellectual needs. Today, parents, the public, and the profession understand that *child care* means providing physical care and educational programs for the whole child.

A large number of *family day care* programs provide child care services in the homes of caregivers. This alternative to center-based programs usually accommodates a maximum of four to five children in a family day care home. Formerly custodial in nature, there is a growing trend for caregivers to provide a full range of services in their homes.

Church-related or *church-sponsored* preschool and elementary programs are quite common and are becoming more popular. These programs usually have a cognitive, basic skills emphasis within a context of religious doctrine and discipline. These programs, which often charge tuition, are popular because of their emphasis on the basic skills and a no-nonsense approach to learning and teaching.

Head Start is a federally sponsored program for children from low-income families. Established by the Economic Opportunity Act of 1964, Head Start is intended to help children and their families overcome the effects of poverty. *Follow Through* extends Head Start programs to children in grades one through three and works with school personnel rather than apart from the schools.

Public and private agencies, including colleges, universities, hospitals, and corporations, operate many kinds of early childhood programs. Many colleges and universities with schools of education have a *laboratory school* used primarily for research in teaching methods, demonstration of exemplary programs and activities, and teacher training. Many of these

Table 1.3
Early Childhood Professionals

Title	Description
Early childhood professional	This is the preferred title for anyone who works with young children in any capacity. The designation reflects the growing belief of the early childhood profession that people who work with children at any level are professionals and as such are worthy of the respect, remuneration, and responsibilities that go with being a professional.
Early childhood educator	Works with young children and has committed to self-development by participating in specialized training and programs to extend professional knowledge and competence.
Early childhood teacher	Responsible for planning and conducting a developmentally and educationally appropriate program for a group or classroom of children; supervises an assistant teacher or aide; usually has a bachelor's degree in early childhood, elementary education, or child development.
Early childhood assistant teacher	Assists the teacher in conducting a developmentally and educationally appropriate program for a group or classroom; frequently acts as a coteacher but may lack education or training to be classified as a teacher (many people who have teacher qualifications serve as an assistant teacher because they enjoy the program or because the position of teacher is not available); usually has a high school diploma or associate degree and is involved in professional development.
Early childhood associate teacher	Plans and implements activities with children; has an associate degree and/or the CDA credential; may also be responsible for care and education of a group of children.
Aide	Assists the teacher and teacher assistant when requested; usually considered an entry-level position.
Director	Develops and implements a center or school program; supervises all staff; may teach a group of children.
Home visitor	Conducts a home-based child development/education program; works with children, families, and staff members.
Child development associate	Has completed a CDA assessment and received the CDA credential.*
Caregiver	Provides care, education, and protection for the very young in or outside the home; includes parents, relatives, child care workers, and early childhood teachers.
Parent	Provides the child with basic care, direction, support, protection, and guidance.
Volunteer	Contributes time, services, and talents to support staff. Usually are parents, retired persons, grandparents, and university/college/high school students.

**CDA National Credentialing Program,* Child Development Associate Assessment System and Competency Standards *(Washington, DC: CDA National Credentialing Program, 1985), p. 551.*

schools also develop and distribute model curricula, and some have programs for children with physical and learning disabilities.

As the name implies, a *toy library* makes toys and other learning materials available to children, parents, child care providers, and teachers. Toy libraries may be housed in libraries, shopping malls, churches, preschools, and mobile vans. Many toy libraries are supported by user fees and parent and community volunteers.

For further definitions of early childhood education terminology, see Tables 1.2 and 1.3.

How Can You Prepare Yourself for a Career in Early Childhood Education?

A career as an early childhood professional can be greatly rewarding. The following are some things you can do to make your career happy and productive for yourself and the children and families with whom you work.

DEVELOP A PHILOSOPHY OF EDUCATION AND TEACHING. As discussed earlier, your philosophy of education is based on your philosophy of life. See the previous discussion in the section "The Professional Practice Dimension" about the importance of developing a philosophy of education to guide your classroom practice.

EXAMINE YOUR WILLINGNESS TO DEDICATE YOURSELF TO TEACHING. Acquaint yourself thoroughly with what teaching involves. Visit many different kinds of early childhood programs. Are these programs ones in which you want to spend the rest of your life? Talk with several professionals to learn what is involved in teaching. Ask yourself, "Am I willing to work hard? Am I willing to give more time to teaching than a teaching contract may specify? Are teachers the kind of people with whom I want to work? Do I have the physical energy for teaching? Do I have the enthusiasm necessary for good teaching?"

ANALYZE YOUR ATTITUDES AND FEELINGS TOWARD CHILDREN. Do you really want to work with young children, or would you be happier in another field? During your interactions with children, constantly test your attitudes toward them and their families. If you decide that working with children is not for you because of how you feel about them, then by all means do not teach.

Honestly analyze your feelings and attitudes toward working with young children. Not everyone has the skills or temperament required for effective teaching of young children.

BELIEVE THAT ALL CHILDREN ARE CAPABLE OF LEARNING. Some parents lament that those who work with young children act as though their children cannot learn because of their cultural or socioeconomic background. All children have the right to be taught by a professional who believes they are capable of learning and will learn to their fullest capacity.

IMPROVE YOUR SKILLS AND INCREASE YOUR KNOWLEDGE. Many professionals choose to improve their skills and increase their knowledge by enrolling in continuing education classes, attending professional meetings and conferences, and participating in other professional activities. Reading is also one method of self-improvement. Whatever method you choose, you should recognize the need for constant retraining. While some school districts and early childhood programs do provide opportunities for retraining, most of the responsibility will be yours. Learning is considered a lifelong process. All early childhood professionals are expected to engage in a process of continuous learning, growth, and development throughout their life span. As professionalism demands higher levels of competence, we will see an intensification of training. It is important for you to keep up to date with changing issues, changing children, and a changing knowledge base.

TRY NEW THINGS. Learning about and trying new methods is an important dimension of professionalism. As a developing professional you will want to consider and explore the possibilities for you and your children to get involved in and try new things. Some professionals and some early childhood programs waste potential and miss opportunities because of unwillingness to adjust to changing circumstances and conditions.

BE ENTHUSIASTIC FOR TEACHING. Time and again the one attribute that seems to separate the good professional from the mediocre is enthusiasm. Trying to be enthusiastic will help a great deal on your professional journey.

EXPLORE THE POSSIBILITIES FOR EDUCATIONAL SERVICE IN FIELDS OTHER THAN THE PUBLIC SCHOOL. Do not limit your career choices and alternatives because of your limited conception of the professional's role. Some believe that teacher education prepares one only for a teaching role. On the contrary, other opportunities for service are available in religious organizations; federal, state, and local agencies; private educational enterprises; hospitals; and libraries and in social work. Do not feel pressured to choose a major during your first year or two in college. Take a variety of electives that will help you in career choices, and talk to vocational counselors. Do not make up your mind too quickly about teaching a certain grade level or age range. Many teachers find out, much to their surprise, that the grade level they thought was best for them was not. Remain flexible about what grade or subject to teach.

SEIZE EVERY EDUCATIONAL OPPORTUNITY TO ENHANCE YOUR TRAINING PROGRAM AND CAREER. Through wise course selection, you can strengthen your weaknesses and explore new alternatives. For example, if your program of studies requires a certain number of social science credits, use them to explore areas such as sociology and anthropology, which have fascinating relationships to education. Good electives to take in college are keyboarding, first aid, audiovisual aids and media, behavior modification/management, special education, creative writing, and arts and crafts. And of course, as a teacher, you can never have too strong a background in child development.

SEEK EVERY OPPORTUNITY FOR EXPERIENCES WITH ALL KINDS OF CHILDREN IN ALL KINDS OF SETTINGS. Individuals often limit themselves to experiences in one setting (e.g., the public schools) and ignore church schools, child care programs, pri-

vate and nonprofit agencies (e.g., March of Dimes, Easter Seal Society), and baby-sitting as venues to broaden and expand their knowledge of children. These experiences may often be work related and can be quite rewarding. You will not only broaden your knowledge, but such work may also help you determine the ages and kinds of children you want to work with and the settings you are comfortable in.

GO WHERE THE OPPORTUNITIES ARE. Sometimes people lock themselves into a particular geographic area or age range of children. Some locations may have an oversupply of professionals; other areas, especially urban school districts and programs, have a chronic shortage of professionals. Cities usually offer challenging and rewarding opportunities. There will always be a job for you if you are willing to go where the jobs are.

What Does the Future Hold for the Early Childhood Professional?

In preparing to undertake the professional challenges of the twenty-first century, many have attempted to forecast what life then will be like. As a result, essential features of the future have become evident that will influence and determine the nature of the professional's necessary core knowledge, skills, and behaviors:

- The population of the United States will become even more diverse than it is today. Diversity training must be an essential part of the training of early childhood professionals, enabling them to work with children, parents, and families from all cultural and socioeconomic backgrounds.
- More services to children will be delivered in and through the family system. This means that early childhood professionals will need to know more about adult growth and development and how to meet adult needs.
- Early childhood programs will continue to serve more young children with disabilities, from birth to age five, in programs designed to meet their and their families' needs. This means new programs will be developed, and teachers will be trained or retrained to provide appropriate services. The two fields of early childhood education and early childhood special education are fast becoming one. As more children with disabilities are included in more programs, professionals have to be trained in both areas to appropriately meet the needs of all children and their families.
- Public sector spending for educating young children and their families will increase. Early childhood education will continue to be a source of great interest and the focus of the public's attention. Business and industry will play larger roles than at present in educating young children and their families and in supporting services that achieve this goal. Early childhood professionals must be prepared to work cooperatively and collaboratively as professionals with the public sector. Indeed, these linkages provide a challenging opportunity to expand and enrich early childhood programs.
- Technology will play an even greater role in young children's learning. Part of your professional development includes developing technological literacy and a willingness to foster technological literacy in all children.
- The role of early childhood professionals will continue to be reconceptualized. Teachers will be trained to work with parents, design curriculum materials, plan programs for

To take an online self-test on this chapter's contents, go to the Companion Website at http://www.prenhall.com/morrison, select chapter 1, then choose the Self Test module.

paraprofessionals, and work cooperatively with community agencies, including business and industry. In addition, early childhood professionals will reconceptualize their roles and responsibilities to children and their families. This reconceptualization is critical for the professional in the twenty-first century. For example, early childhood professionals seldom think of themselves as part of one of the most effective crime prevention programs, but it is so. In one case, the High/Scope Perry Preschool Study found that children born in poverty who participated in a high-quality, active-learning preschool program at ages three and four have fewer criminal arrests than adults who received no preschool program as children.[6]

- There will be an even stronger movement toward the professionalization of teaching, already evident from our previous discussion of professionalism. This professionalization is part of the national effort to improve education. The public recognizes, albeit belatedly, that real and lasting changes in education will occur when teachers are trained and treated as professionals. The emphasis on professionalism will require you to assume more responsibility for your own behavior and professional development. A higher degree of professionalism will bring greater responsibility and decision-making opportunities.

For additional Internet resources or to complete an online activity for this chapter, go to the Companion Website at http://www.prenhall.com/morrison, select chapter 1, then choose the Linking to Learning or Making Connections module.

- Professionals and community agencies will develop more collaborative, cooperative relationships. Teaching is an integral part of the broader range of human services and helping professions. The sharp lines that have traditionally separated social work, the health professions, and education are gradually blurring. There is also a trend toward resolving social problems through interdisciplinary programs, to which each profession contributes its particular expertise.

Involvement in the early childhood profession can be a joyful experience for you. The profession demands, and young children deserve, the best teachers have to offer. Becoming a good professional requires a lot of hard work and dedication. All who call themselves "professional" must accept the challenges and responsibilities that are part of the title.

Activities for Further Enrichment

Applications

1. Recall the teachers who had a great influence on you. Which of their characteristics do you plan to imitate?
2. Put your philosophy of education in writing, and share it with others. Have them critique it for comprehensiveness, clarity, and meaning. How do you feel about the changes they suggested?
3. Metaphors are an effective way of expressing meanings and ideas. They are also a good way to think about yourself, your beliefs, and teaching. For example, some of the metaphors my students have identified for themselves are teacher as leader, coach, and facilitator. Add to this list and then identify one metaphor that best describes your metaphor for teaching at this time. Use these and other metaphors to help you develop your philosophy of education.

Field Experiences

1. Attend local meetings of an early childhood professional organization in your area, such as NAEYC or ACEI. What issues are local professional groups addressing? How are the groups meeting the needs of their members? Of children and families? Would you join the organizations you visited?
2. Many local school districts elect and honor their teachers of the year. Contact these teachers and have them share with you the ideas and attitudes that caused their colleagues to elect them as a teacher of the year. Plan for how you will integrate these qualities into your professional development plan.

Research

1. Interview preschool and kindergarten teachers about topics for in-service training they think would contribute to their professional development.
2. Interview five early childhood professionals to determine what they think constitutes professionalism and how professionals can be more involved in increasing professionalism.
3. Interview professionals about careers that relate to children and parents. How did they come to their jobs? Is there evidence that they planned for these careers? Do you think you would enjoy an alternative career in education? Why?
4. Interview teachers in various programs and agencies to determine their core beliefs about teaching and the essentials of being a professional. Make a list of these core beliefs and reflect on them as you continue to consider your philosophy of education.

Readings for Further Enrichment

Beatty, B. *Preschool Education in America.* Binghamton, NY: Yale University Press, 1995.

This comprehensive history describes policies and programs for the education of three, four, and five-year olds in the United States since the colonial era. It also traces efforts to make preschool education a part of the public school system and shows why these efforts have been rejected, despite increasing evidence that preschools are beneficial for all young children.

Catron, C. E., and Allen, J. *Early Childhood Curriculum: A Creative Play Model,* 2nd ed. Upper Saddle River, NJ: Prentice Hall, 1999.

This comprehensive guide provides information on planning programs with a play-based, developmental curriculum for children from birth to five years of age and covers basic principles and current research in early childhood curricula.

Fujawa, J. *(Almost) Everything You Need to Know About Early Childhood Education: A Book of Lists for Teachers and Parents.* Beltsville, MD: Gryphon House, 1998.

Filled with the imminently practical ("Creative Gift Ideas") to the philosophic ("Answers to: Why Read to My Child?") to the hilarious ("The 'F' Words Children Are Allowed to Use"), these lists cover nearly everything one needs to work with and raise young children.

Henniger, M. L. *Teaching Young Children: An Introduction.* Upper Saddle River, NJ: Merrill/Prentice Hall, 1999.

This coverage of child development—which includes discussions about guiding young children, working families, and celebrating diversity—will help teachers facilitate all aspects of the birth-to-eight-year-old child's growth.

Seefeldt, C. *The Early Childhood Curriculum: Current Findings in Theory and Practice,* 3rd ed. New York: Teachers College Press, 1999.

Includes chapters on inclusion and the multicultural world of the early childhood classroom, an overview of current developments in the field, and coverage of teaching strategies. This information will enable educators to make decisions about what curriculum content is appropriate for young children.

White, S. C., and Coleman, T. M. *Early Childhood Education: Building a Philosophy for Teaching.* Upper Saddle River, NJ: Merrill/Prentice Hall, 2000.

Discusses early childhood issues within the context of society, family, and classroom approaches that influence the care and education of children from birth through age eight to help teachers build their teaching philosophy. It is designed to help students develop a professional identity and confidence in their ability to respond to the educational needs of young children in contemporary society.

Wiles, J. W. *Curriculum Essentials: A Resource for Educators.* Boston: Allyn & Bacon, 1999.

Contains compilations of important dates and events, definitions of curriculum, names to know in curriculum study, and an introduction to the philosophies and theories influencing curriculum involvement.

Wiseman, D., Cooner, D., and Knight, S. *Becoming a Teacher in a Field Based Setting.* Stamford, CT: Wadsworth, 1999.

This text offers a traditional framework for a methods or education course, while adding the field-based component. Portfolio assessment is explained in the text and illustrated by various activities.

Linking to Learning

Related Web Sites

Center for Career Development in Early Care and Education

http://ericps.crc.uiuc.edu/ccdece/ccdece.html

The center's technical assistance, training delivery, research, and information dissemination activities are designed to help education institutions bring about systematic change to replace the currently fragmented training system with one that meets the needs of families, children, and the field.

Center for Early Childhood Leadership

http://nlu04.nl.edu/cecl

The center's activities encompass four areas: improving the knowledge of early childhood program directors, technical assistance to improve program quality, research on professional development issues, and public awareness of the role early childhood directors play in providing services for children and families.

Child Development Policy Institute

http://www.cdpionline.com

Advocacy group that lobbies on behalf of children in child care settings.

Children's Rights Council

http://www.vix.com/crc/

The Children's Rights Council focuses on work with individuals, parents, children, families, and communities to develop and strengthen the family as the building block of society.

Council for Early Childhood Professional Recognition

http://www.cdacouncil.org

Offers a nationally recognized, competency-based Child Development Associate credential that provides training, assessment, and certification of child care professionals. Bilingual specialization also available.

Early Childhood Education

http://www.tapr.org/~ird/Dimsdle/mnpage.html

A page designed as a gateway, a site that leads to resources on the Web for parents of young children and professionals who work with young children.

Early Childhood Education Online

http://www.ume.maine.edu/~cofed/eceol/welcome.shtml

This Web site exists to promote and facilitate information management and exchange and to serve as a resource and benefit for all children, their families, and all people who help them grow and learn.

Early Childhood Education Web Guide

http://www.ecewebguide.com

The Early Childhood Education Web Guide provides childcare professionals with the most up-to-date Internet resources. The sites on this guide are checked on a weekly basis to ensure their reliability and integrity.

Educating Policymakers About Children's Issues: Hit the Floor Running

http://www.jumpstartmich.com/educating.html

This article, written by Michele Strasz, gives many excellent pointers for educators on how to effectively lobby elected government officials on issues pertaining to children.

ERIC Clearinghouse on Elementary and Early Childhood Education

http://ericeece.org

Provides information to parents and educators on all subjects and grade levels, publishes free biannual newsletters, and sponsors a parent question answering service (E-mail: askeric@ericir.syr.edu) and electronic discussion groups.

National Association for the Education of Young Children

http://www.naeyc.org

Publishes brochures, posters, videotapes, books, and journals discussing teaching and program ideas, ways to improve parent–teacher relations, and resources for students about safety, language arts, and learning. National, state, and local affiliate groups offer training opportunities.

National Center for Early Development and Learning

http://www.fpg.unc.edu/~ncedl/

Research at the National Center for Early Development and Learning (NCEDL) focuses on enhancing the cognitive, social, and emotional development of children from birth through age eight.

National Resource Center for Family Centered Practice

http://www.uiowa.edu/~nrcfcp/new/index.html

The National Resource Center for Family Centered Practice provides technical assistance, staff training, research and evaluation, and information on family-based programs and issues to public and private human services agencies in states, counties, and communities across the United States.

Planet Daycare

http://www.thechildcarecircle.com/index.html

Connecting daycare, preschool, and early childhood education professionals together on the Web.

Teacher Information Network

http://www.teacher.com

With listings of organizations, resources, sites, and governmental departments, TIN is a one-stop gateway to all the resources a teacher could want on the Web. Chat with other teachers, sign up for free e-mail, or just keep abreast of the latest teaching trends, all at TIN.

Electronic Journals Related to Early Childhood Education

Children's Advocate

http://www.4children.org/childadv.htm

A bimonthly newsmagazine published by the Action Alliance for Children that covers California, national, and international policy issues affecting children. Highlights from the current issue and selected articles from past issues are available on the Web site.

Early Childhood News

http://www.earlychildhoodnews.com

A journal on professional development in early childhood education, Early Childhood News *is a valuable resource for anyone interested in the field of educating the leaders of tomorrow and the learners of today.*

Early Childhood Update

http://www.ed.gov/offices/OERI/ECI/newsletters/97fall/index.html

A quarterly newsletter of the National Institute of Early Childhood Development (Early Childhood Institute [ECI]) with articles of interest to the early childhood community.

The Future of Children
http://www.futureofchildren.org

The Future of Children *is an online child advocacy journal published three times a year by The Davis and Lucile Packard Foundation. Has online articles on issues pertaining to the health and well-being of children in our nation.*

Instructor Magazine
http://www.scholastic.com/inschool

Practical ideas for the classroom and information on teachers' professional development.

Teacher Magazine
http://www.edweek.org/tm/tm.htm

Addresses issues from preschool through grade twelve.

Professional Organization Contacts

The following agencies are devoted to improving professional practice. Contact them for information about their programs, position statements, and professional and child advocacy initiatives.

Association for Childhood Education International (ACEI)
11501 Georgia Ave., Suite 315
Wheaton, MD 20902
(301) 942-2443 or (800) 423-3563; fax (301) 942-3012
Contact: Marilyn Gardner, Director of Conferences and Marketing
E-mail: acei@aol.com
http://www.udel.edu/bateman/acei

National Association for the Education of Young Children (NAEYC)
1509 16th St. NW
Washington, DC 20036-1426
(202) 232-8777 or (800) 424-2640; fax (202) 328-1846
Contact: Pat Spahr, Information Services Director
E-mail: pubaff@naeyc.org
http://www.naeyc.org

National Association of Elementary School Principals (NAESP)
1615 Duke St.
Alexandria, VA 22314-3483
(800) 38-NAESP; fax (800) 39-NAESP
Contact: Gail Gross
E-mail: naesp@naesp.org
http://www.naesp.org/naesp.htm

National Early Childhood Technical Assistance System (NECTAS)
500 Nations Bank Plaza
137 E. Franklin St.
Chapel Hill, NC 27514-3628
(919) 962-2001; fax (919) 966-7463
E-mail: nectas@unc.edu
http://www.nectas.unc.edu

Southern Early Childhood Association (SECA)
P.O. Box 55930
Little Rock, AR 72215
(800) 305-7322; fax (501) 663-2114
E-mail:seca@arstotle.net
http://www.seca50.org

ENDNOTES

1. Carol Brunson Phillips, *Field Advisor's Guide for the CDA Professional Preparation Program* (Washington, D.C.: Council for Early Childhood Professional Recognition, 1991), 2.
2. Barbara Willer and Sue Bredekamp, "A 'New' Paradigm of Early Childhood Professional Development," *Young Children* 47, no. 3 (1993), 64.
3. S. Feeney and K. Kipnis, *Code of Ethical Conduct and Statement of Commitment* (Washington, DC: National Association for the Education of Young Children). Copyright © 1992 by NAEYC. Reprinted by permission.
4. National Academy of Early Childhood Programs, *Accreditation Criteria and Procedures* (Washington, DC: National Association for the Education of Young Children, 1984), x.
5. National Association for the Education of Young Children, *Early Childhood Teacher Education Guidelines* (Washington, DC: Author, 1982), xii.
6. Lawrence J. Schweinhart, H. V. Barnes, and David P. Weikart, *Significant Benefits: The High/Scope Perry Preschool Study through Age 27* (Ypsilanti, MI: High/Scope, 1993), xv.

CHAPTER 2

Our progress as a nation can be no swifter than our progress in education.

JOHN F. KENNEDY

Early Childhood Education Today

Understanding Current Issues

Focus Questions

1. What critical issues do children and families face today?
2. How do social, political, economic, and educational issues influence and change child rearing, early childhood education, and teaching?
3. What are some implications that contemporary issues have for curriculum, teaching, and the life outcomes of children and families?
4. How can early childhood programs and teachers help solve contemporary social problems?

To review the chapter focus questions online, go to the Companion Website at http://www.prenhall.com/morrison and select chapter 2.

Issues Influencing the Practice of Early Childhood Education

To check your understanding of this chapter with the online Study Guide, go to the Companion Website at http://www.prenhall.com/morrison, select chapter 2, then choose the Study Guide module.

Many contemporary social issues affect decisions that families and early childhood professionals must make about the education and care of young children. Problems of child abuse, poverty, low-quality care and education, inequality of programs and services, and society's inability to meet the needs of all children are perennial sources of controversy and concern to which our society continues to seek solutions. All of these problems dramatically and permanently affect the development and life outcomes of children. New ideas and issues relating to the education and care of young children and the quest to provide educationally and developmentally appropriate programs keep the field of early childhood education in a state of constant change. In fact, change is one constant of the early childhood profession. Early childhood professionals are constantly challenged to determine what is best for young children and their families given the needs and political demands of society today.

Issues facing children and families today are of concern to everyone. Daily newspapers provide ample evidence of the nation's interest in young children. Figure 2.1 shows recent newspaper headlines that call attention to young children, parents, families, and child service agencies.

Newspapers are full of articles relating to children and family news. These are just a few representative headlines that show the enormous range of topics. A good way to keep informed about such issues is to read daily newspapers.

- "Class Helps Moms, Dads Navigate Preschool Years" (*Chicago Tribune,* March 4, 1999)
- "Don't Leave Out the Littlest Learners" (*Chicago Tribune,* March 1, 1999)
- "Education Begins at Birth; So Should Support for Education" (*Chicago Tribune,* May 7, 1999)
- "Enhancing the Language Development of Young Children" (*Early Childhood News,* January/February 1999)
- "Full-day Preschool for New Jersey's Poorest" (*New York Times,* January 7, 1999)
- "Improving Child-Care Facilities" (*Chicago Tribune,* July 1, 1999)
- "More Parents Are Pitching in: Programs Forging Better Links Between Home and School" (*Boston Globe,* March 21, 1999)
- "Play as Curriculum" (*Early Childhood News,* March/April 1999)
- "Programs Designed to Help Infants, New Parents" (*Chicago Tribune,* February 2, 1999)
- "Should Boys Have War Toys?" (*Boston Globe,* May 20, 1999)
- "Study Links Good Day Care to Readiness for School" (*Los Angeles Times,* June 9, 1999)
- "Where Parents (at Home) Can Go for Expert Advice on Child Rearing" (*New York Times,* November 4, 1999)
- "Who Says Poor Children Can't Learn?" (*Christian Science Monitor,* June 8, 1999)
- "Quality Day Care Early Is Tied to Achievement as an Adult" (*New York Times,* October 22, 1999)

Figure 2.1
Examples of Recent Newspaper Headlines Relating to Early Childhood Issues

The NAEYC, with over 100,000 members, believes that "ensuring the well-being of all children and families must become the nation's most fundamental priority."[1] The following issues are some that you will want to consider as you pursue your professional career. We cannot ignore these issues or pretend they do not exist. We must be part of the solution to making it possible for all children to achieve their full potential. Education is very political, and politicians look to early childhood professionals to help develop educational solutions to social problems.

Changing Families

Families are in a continual state of change as a result of social issues and changing times. The definition of what a family is varies as society changes. Consider the following ways families changed in the twentieth century:

For more information about families and early childhood education, go to the Companion Website at http://www.prenhall.com/morrison, select any chapter, then choose Topic 10 of the ECE Supersite module.

1. *Structure.* Families now include arrangements other than the traditional nuclear family:

    single-parent families, headed by mothers or fathers

    stepfamilies, including individuals related by either marriage or adoption

    heterosexual, gay, or lesbian partners living together as families

    extended families, which may include grandparents, uncles, aunts, other relatives, and individuals not related by kinship

2. *Roles.* As families change, so do the roles that parents and other family members perform. For example:

    More parents work and have less time for their children and family affairs.

    Working parents must combine roles of both parents and employees. The number of hats that parents wear increases as families change.

3. *Responsibilities.* As families change, many parents are not able to provide or cannot afford to pay for adequate and necessary care for their children. Some parents find that buffering their children from social ills such as drugs, violence, and delinquency is more than they can handle. Also, some parents are consumed by problems of their own and have little time or attention for their children.

Families will certainly continue to change. You and other early childhood professionals must develop creative ways to provide services to children and families of all kinds.

FAMILIES AND EARLY CHILDHOOD. Two primary goals of early childhood education are how to best meet children's needs and how to best meet these needs in culturally appropriate ways. Early childhood professionals agree that a good way to meet the needs of children is through their families, whatever that family unit may be. Review Figure 2.2 now, which shows two methods for educating both children and families. Providing for children's needs through and within the family system makes sense for a number of reasons.

First, the family system has the primary responsibility for meeting many children's needs. So, helping families function means that everyone stands to benefit. Helping people in a family unit—mother, father, grandparents, and others—function better helps them and their children.

Second, professionals frequently need to address family problems and issues first in order to help children effectively. For example, helping parents gain access to adequate, affordable health care means that the whole family, including children, will be healthier.

Third, early childhood professionals can do many things concurrently with children and their families that will benefit both. Literacy is a good example. Early childhood profes-

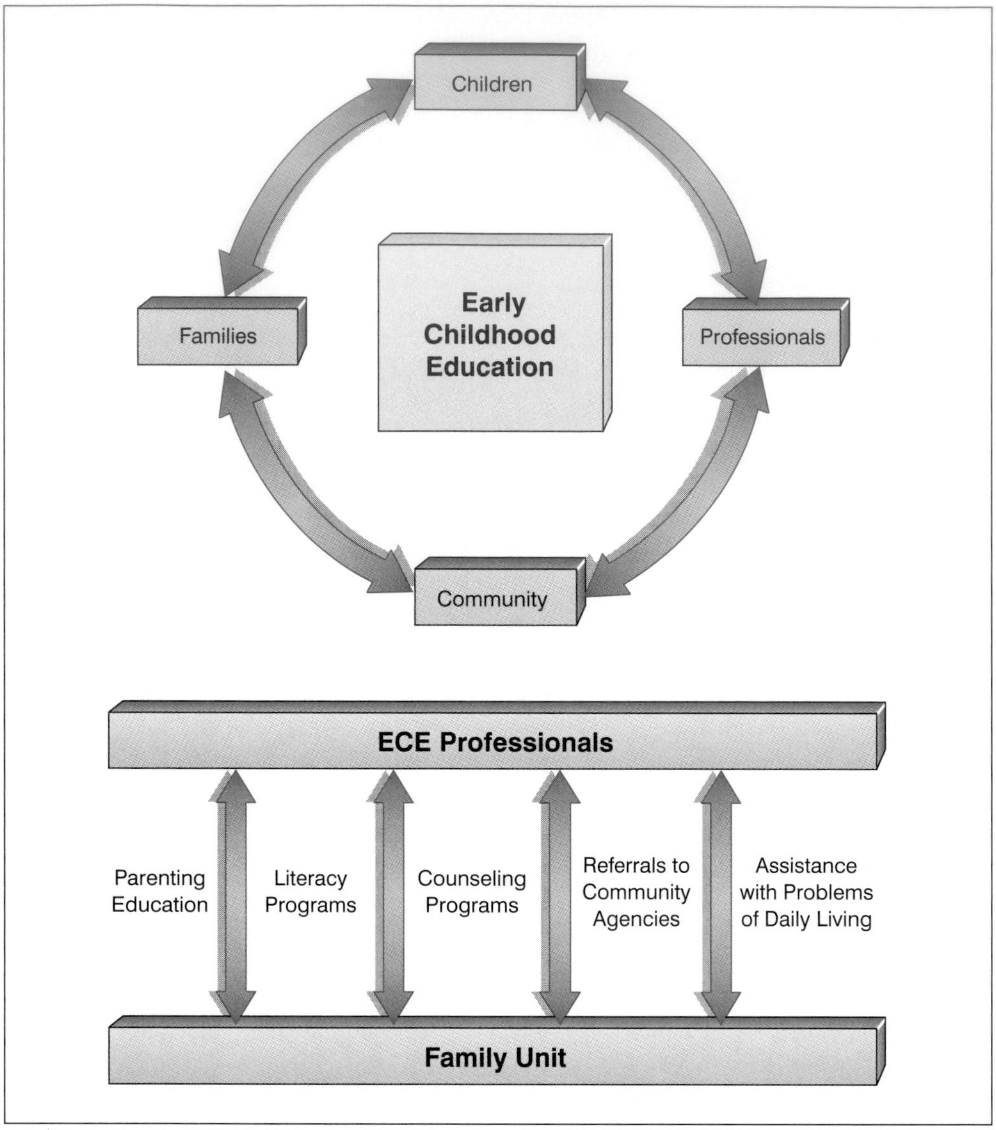

Figure 2.2
Two Models for Meeting the Needs of Children and Families

sionals are taking a family approach to helping children, their parents, and other family members learn how to read, write, speak, and listen. Teaching parents to read helps them understand the importance of supporting and promoting their children in the learning and teaching process.

Fourth, addressing the needs of children and their families as a whole (known as the holistic approach to education and the delivery of services) enables early childhood professionals and others to address a range of social concerns simultaneously. Programs that provide education and support for literacy, health care, nutrition, healthy living, abuse prevention, AIDS education, and parenting are examples of this family-centered approach. A major trend in early childhood education is that professionals will expand the family-centered approach to providing for the needs of children and families.

When families are involved in their children's education, everyone benefits. What are some culturally appropriate ways you can reach out to the families of the children in your care?

WORKING PARENTS. More and more families find that both parents must work to make ends meet. An increasing percentage of mothers with children under six are currently employed (nearly 65 percent in 1999; see Figure 2.3), which creates a greater need for early childhood programs. This demand brings a beneficial recognition to early childhood programs and encourages early childhood professionals to meet parents' needs. Unfortunately, the urgent need for child care has encouraged some ill-prepared people to establish programs that do not necessarily have children's or parents' best interests in mind. Demand is high enough that good programs have not yet had a chance to drive inferior ones from the child care marketplace. For their part, some parents are not able or willing to evaluate programs and select the best ones for their children, which also encourages poor-quality programs to stay in operation.

If you work as a professional, you will encounter several misconceptions about mothers who work outside the home: working mothers are somehow not good mothers; working mothers are less productive at work; and mothers' working has a negative impact on their children's behavior and development. Let's examine these issues.

First, according to a recent survey conducted by Lutheran Brotherhood, 52 percent of working parents say they are more productive at work because they are parents.[2] Several factors account for working parents' reporting they are more productive. Technology lets parents work at home and keep in touch with their work sites. Second, working parents also report that they work hard so they can have time to be with their families. Third, as for the criticism that children are harmed by their mothers working outside the home, this is not the case. Children are not significantly harmed when their mothers work outside the home. In fact, the income that mothers bring home positively affects children's behavior and academic achievement. This is particularly true in low-income families.[3] So, you and other early childhood professionals have the responsibility to help correct public misconceptions about the alleged negative influences of working parents on children's developmental and academic outcomes.

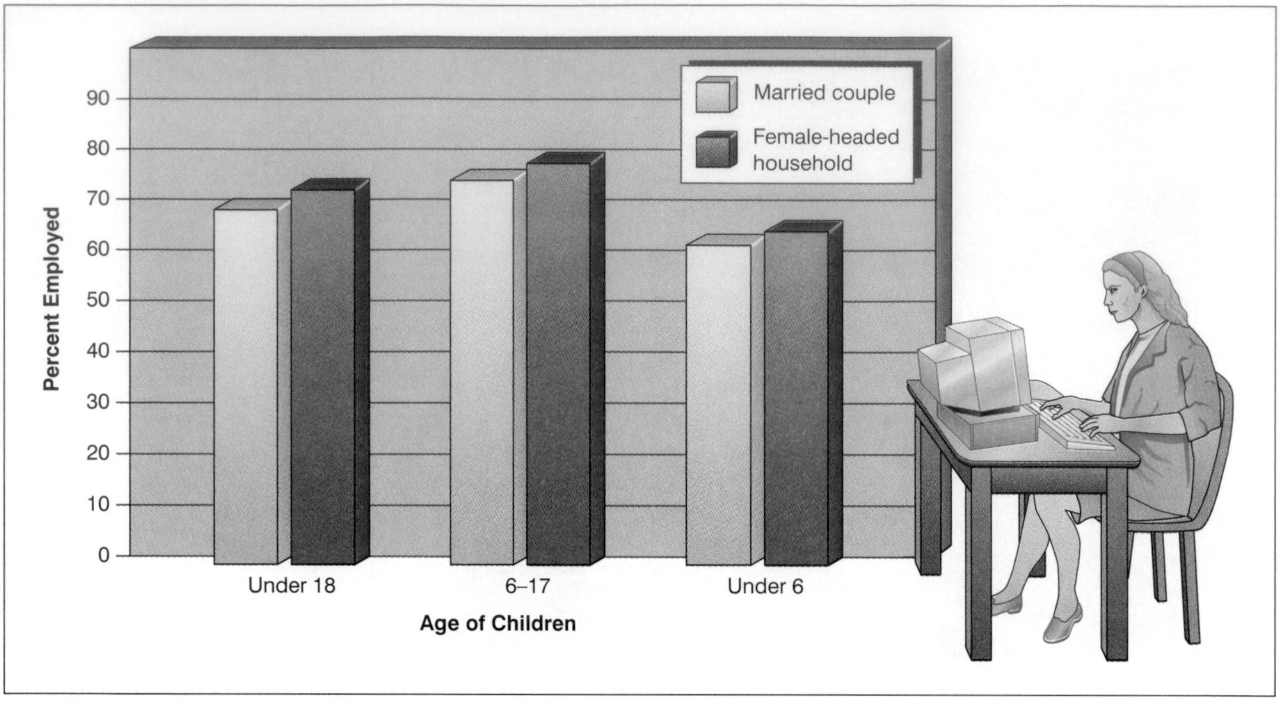

Figure 2.3
Mothers in the Workforce

Source: Data from National Bureau of Labor Statistics, 1999.

AFFLUENT FAMILIES. Many parents with middle- and upper-level incomes are willing to invest money in early education for their children. They look for nursery schools and preschool programs they feel will give their children a good start in life. Montessori schools and franchised operations such as Bright Horizons, Kindercare, and La Petite Academy have benefited in the process. Private preschool education is a booming business. Some parents of three- and four-year-olds spend almost as much in tuition to send their children to good preschools as parents of eighteen-year-olds do to send their children to state-supported universities.

Some parents have sufficient disposable income and are willing to spend it on enriching their lives and the lives of their children. Parents enroll themselves and their infants and toddlers in self-improvement programs promoted as physically and cognitively stimulating. Courses designed for expectant parents, new parents, and grandparents are now a standard part of the curriculum of many community colleges and community schools. During one semester at a local community college, for example, parents could select from these courses: Parent/Infant Enrichment, Play Activities with the Preschool Child, Discipline Strategies That Work, Movement and Play Activities, Creative Learning-Storytelling/Drama, Toilet Learning, Choosing a Preschool for Your Child, Building Your Child's Self-Esteem, and Developmental Screening for Infants. Many of the courses required registration of both parents and their young children!

Stimulation/enrichment programs help popularize the importance of the very early years. Infant–parent stimulation programs catch the fancy of young parents who want "the best" for their children and are willing to spend time, effort, and money to see that they get it. This allows early childhood professionals to address the importance of the early years. It also creates a climate of acceptance for very early education and an arena in which early childhood professionals are heard.

Infant stimulation programs stimulate more than infants. Parent groups discuss how to help children get along with others, how to provide safe learning environments, how to reduce stress in children's lives, how to nurture in the twenty-first century, how to accommodate diverse lifestyles, how to extend more rights to children, and how to parent in an electronic era, in which children seemingly see and know all.

FATHERS. These days, it is apparent that fathers are rediscovering the joys of parenting and working with young children. Not only have many fathers rediscovered parenting and child rearing, but early childhood education has discovered fathers! Men are playing an active role in providing basic care, love, and nurturance to their children. The definition of *fatherhood* has changed; a father is no longer stereotypically unemotional, detached from everyday responsibilities of child care, authoritarian, and a disciplinarian. Fathers no longer isolate themselves from child rearing because they are male. Men are more concerned about their role of fatherhood and their participation in family events before, during, and after the birth of their children. Fathers want to be involved in the whole process of child rearing. Because so many men feel unprepared for fatherhood, agencies such as hospitals and community colleges are providing courses and seminars to introduce fathers to the joys, rewards, and responsibilities of fathering.

Fathers no longer quietly acquiesce to giving up custody of their children in a divorce. Men are becoming single parents through adoption and surrogate childbearing. (Figure 2.4 shows the number of single-parent families headed by fathers among certain races.) Also increasing in number are stay-at-home dads. Estimates of the number of fathers who stay home with their children are as high as two million. Fathers are also receiving some of the employment benefits that have traditionally gone only to women, such as paternity leaves, flexible work schedules, and sick leave for family illness. Companies such as Texas Instruments, J.P. Morgan, Marriott, and Boeing offer parenting seminars for male employees.

Another program dedicated to the role of fatherhood in child rearing is the Fatherhood Project, the longest-running national initiative on fatherhood (you may visit its Web site at www.fatherhoodproject.org). Founded in 1981 at the Bank Street College of Education in New York City, it is now operated by the Families and Work Institute. The Fatherhood Pro-

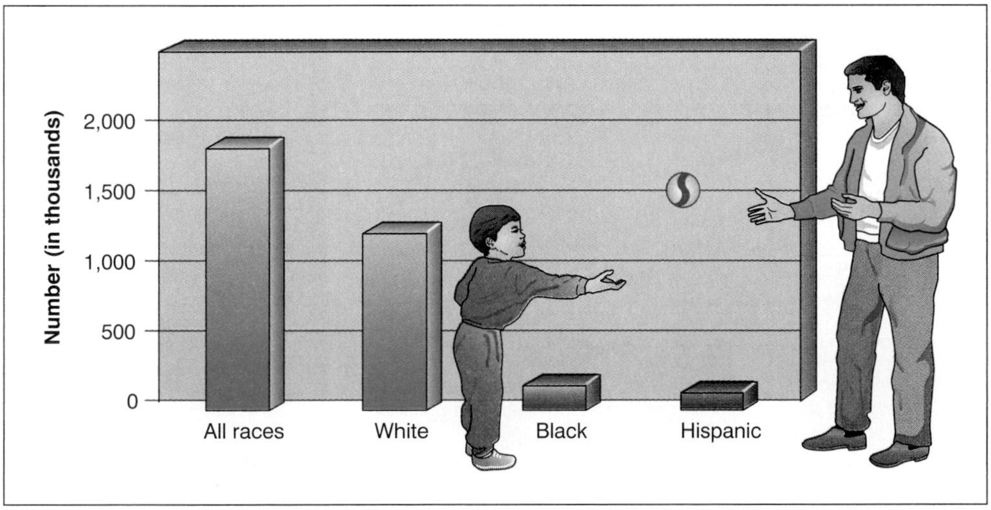

Figure 2.4
Single-Parent Families Headed by Fathers Among Certain Races

Source: Data from U.S. Bureau of the Census, Historical Time Series, *Families (FM-2), May 1998.*

ject is a national research and education project that is examining the future of fatherhood and developing ways to support men's involvement in child rearing. Components of the project include the following:

- Fatherhood USA: A two-part PBS documentary that examines what it takes for fathers to build or rebuild relationships with their children.
- Working Fathers: Ongoing research into "best practices" and strategies for creating a workplace that enables fathers to better balance work and family life while also enhancing business productivity and increasing women's equal opportunity. This research is routinely channeled into popularly accessible publications, seminars for employees and managers on DaddyStress/DaddySuccess, and executive briefings on Daddy Strategy.
- The Male Involvement Project: A national training initiative that helps Head Start and early childhood programs get fathers and other significant men involved in their programs and in the lives of children.
- State Initiatives on Responsible Fatherhood: An examination of policies and programs in all fifty states that will yield a new understanding of government's role in fostering responsible fatherhood.

SINGLE PARENTS. The number of one-parent families, male and female, continues to increase. Certain ethnic groups are disproportionately represented in single-parent families. Figures 2.4 and 2.5 illustrate these trends. These increases are attributable to several factors. First, pregnancy rates are higher among lower socioeconomic groups. Second, teenage pregnancy rates in poor white, Hispanic, and African American populations are sometimes higher because of lower education levels, economic constraints, and fewer life opportunities. In 1997, 22 percent of families were headed by females and 5 percent were headed by males.

People become single parents for a number of reasons. Half of all marriages end in divorce; some people choose single parenthood; and some, such as many teenagers, become single parents by default. In addition, liberalized adoption procedures, artificial insemination, surrogate childbearing, and increasing public support for single parents make this lifestyle an

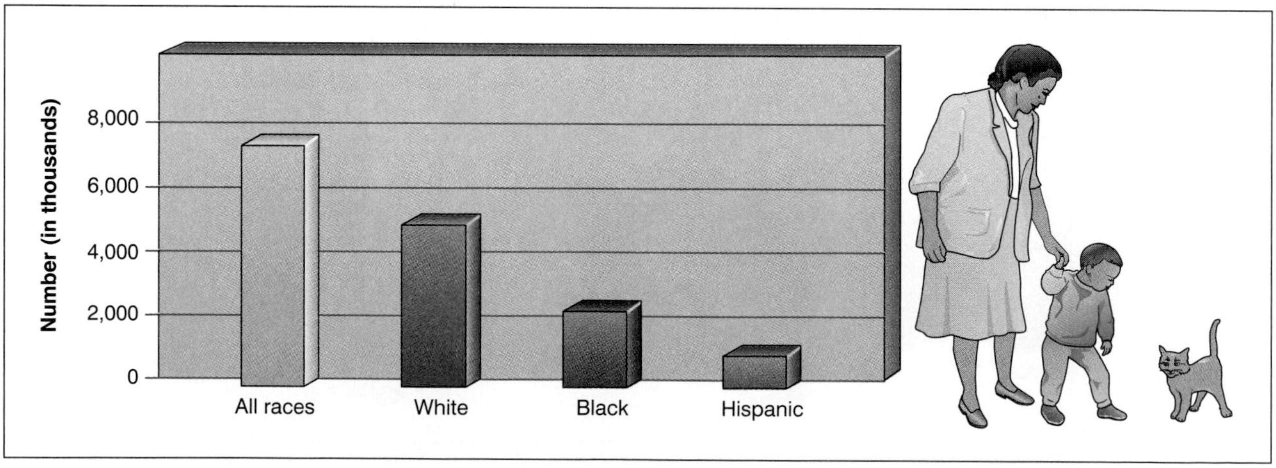

Figure 2.5
Single-Parent Families Headed by Mothers Among Certain Races

Source: Data from U.S. Bureau of the Census, Historical Time Series, *Families (FM-2), May 1998.*

attractive option for some people. The reality is that more women are having children without marrying.

No matter how people become single parents, the extent of single parenthood has tremendous implications for early childhood professionals. In response to growing single parenthood, early childhood programs are developing curricula to help children and their single parents. In addition to needing assistance with child care, single parents frequently seek help in child rearing, especially in regard to discipline. Early childhood professionals are often asked to conduct seminars to help parents gain these skills. Additionally, the increasing number of children living in single-parent families challenges early childhood professionals to find ways to help children grow up within this context. How well early childhood professionals meet the needs of single parents can make a difference in how successful single parents are in providing for the needs of children and other family members.

TEENAGE PARENTS. Teenage pregnancies continue to be a societal problem. Each year, one out of ten, or 1.1 million, teenagers becomes pregnant. The following facts about teenage pregnancy dramatically demonstrate its extent and effects:[4]

- In 1997, for women aged fifteen through nineteen, there were 52.3 births per 1,000, down from 62.1 in 1991.
- As a group, Latino teenagers have the highest birthrate, with 99.1 births per 1,000.
- Among states, Mississippi has the highest birthrate for teenagers, with 73.7 births per 1,000.

While the teenage birthrate has dropped over the last decade, concerned legislators, public policy developers, and national leaders view teenage pregnancy as a loss of human potential. They worry about the demand for public health and welfare services and an increased number of school dropouts. From an early childhood point of view, teenage pregnancies create greater demand for infant and toddler child care and programs to help teenagers learn how to be good parents. The staff of an early childhood program must often provide nurturance for both children and parents, because the parents themselves may not be emotionally mature. Emotional maturity is necessary for parents to engage in a giving relationship with children. Early childhood professionals must nurture and help teenage parents who lack parenting skills.

Wellness and Healthy Living

A major goal of all early childhood programs is to provide for the safety and well-being of children. A complementary goal is to help parents and other family members provide for the well-being of themselves and their children. It is almost a given in early childhood education that poor health and unhealthy living conditions are major contributors to poor school achievement and life outcomes. A number of health issues facing children today put their chances for learning and success at risk. As a society, we do not have a very good track record of providing for the health and safety of our children.

Poverty

Society and early childhood professionals know that poverty has serious negative consequences for children and families. Approximately 40 percent of the poor population is made up of children, even though only one-quarter of the population as a whole is children. Nearly 22 percent of children under six—over four million children—live in poverty (see Figure 2.6).

... *video viewpoint*

Children Growing Up Without Fathers

ABCNEWS

Living in homes without fathers is a reality that affects the lives of growing numbers of children in the United States. In 25 percent of American households, mothers are raising forty million children alone. These are children that may never see or have contact with their biological fathers.

Reflective Discussion Questions

Why are we as a society so concerned about the absence of fathers in children's formative years? From your own background and experiences, what are some consequences for children being reared in homes without fathers? What does research show are some outcomes for children who are reared in homes without fathers? Why is having two parents in the home important for children? What are some critical behaviors that fathers role model for their children? In what ways do fathers make a critical difference in the lives of children? Why is it important for mothers and fathers to tell their children "I love you"?

Reflective Decision Making

What can you as an early childhood professional do to make a difference in the lives of the children and their mothers living in homes without fathers? Make a list of community-based services that would be of help to families without fathers. How could you as an early childhood professional link children and their mothers to community-based services?

For children living in single-parent homes with female heads of household, poverty is a greater risk. More than one-half of these children (59.1 percent) live in poverty. Approximately 40 percent of African American children under the age of six live in poverty; this figure climbs to 61 percent in single-mother households. Poverty rates for Hispanic American children under the age of six are 38.3 percent overall and about 68 percent for those in single-mother homes.[5]

Living in poverty means you and your family don't have the income that allows you to purchase adequate health care, housing, food, clothing, and education services. In 1999, poverty for a nonfarm family of four meant an income of less than $16,400. The federal government annually revises its poverty guidelines, which are the basis for distribution of federal aid to schools and student eligibility for academic services such as Head Start, Title I (a program that provides additional help in math and reading), and free and reduced-price school breakfasts and lunches.

Children and youth have no control over the social, economic, and family conditions that contribute to the conditions of poverty. Living in a rural community and in a rural southern state increases the likelihood that families will live in poverty. Cities with the highest school-age poverty rate are in the South and East. As Table 2.1 illustrates, five of the ten states with the highest school-age poverty rates are in the South. In Mississippi, one-third of all children are poor, nearly twice the national average.[6]

Also, living in the inner city means that the chances of being poor are higher. With increases in rural and urban poverty go decreases in wealth and support for education. This in turn means that, as a whole, children living in poverty will attend schools that have fewer resources and poorer facilities.

The effects of poverty are detrimental to students' achievement and life prospects. For example, children and youth from low-income families are often older than others in their

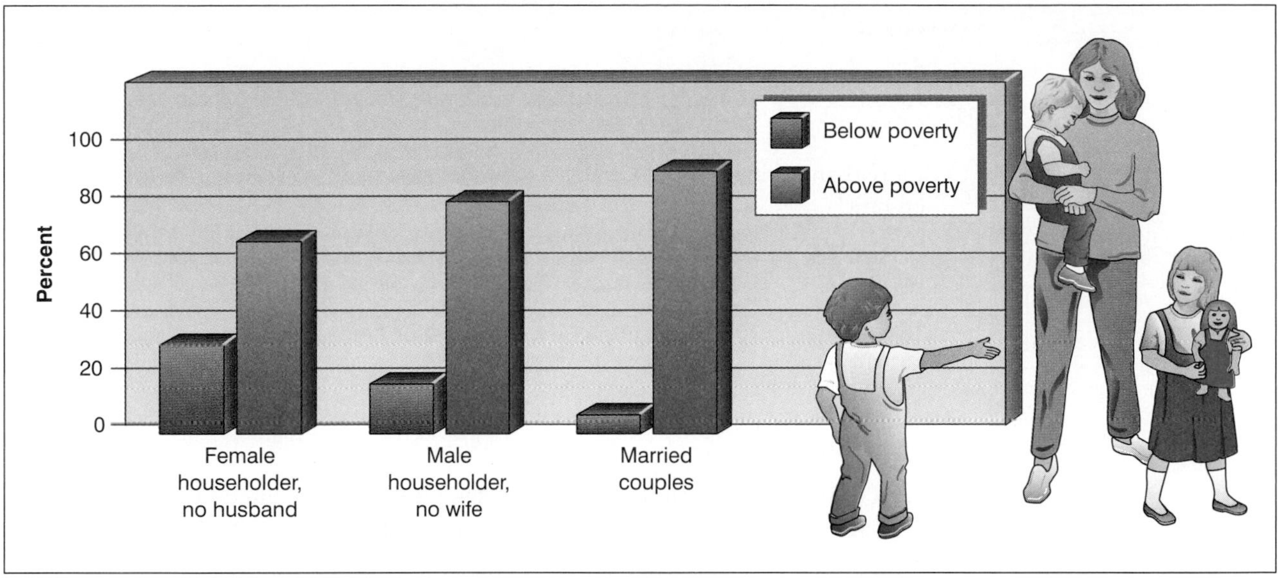

Figure 2.6
Families with Children Living in Poverty, 1998

Source: Data from U.S. Bureau of the Census, Historical Time Series, *Families, (FM-2), May 1998.*

grade level, move more slowly through the educational system, are more likely to drop out, and are less likely to find work.[7] Poor children are more likely to be retained in school, and students who have repeated one or more grades are more likely to become school dropouts.[8] Poverty affects students' health prospects as well. For example, more than one-half of all children who lack insured health care come from poor families.[9]

Children in poverty are more likely to have emotional and behavioral problems and are less likely than others to be "highly engaged" in school.[10] Also, parents of low-income families are less likely to help their children complete homework assignments.

Table 2.1
States and Washington, D.C., with Highest Percentage of People in Poverty, 1998

State	Population in Poverty
1. Washington, D.C.	22.73%
2. New Mexico	22.44
3. Louisiana	18.66
4. Mississippi	18.38
5. Arizona	18.19
6. West Virginia	17.64
7. Arkansas	17.24
8. New York	16.61
9. Montana	16.49
10. California	16.35

Source: U.S. Bureau of the Census, Current Population Survey, *March 1999.*

Housing

A major study of the effects of poor and substandard housing on children reveals the following:[11]

- More than 4.5 million children live in families that spend at least half of their income on rent.
- Almost 1.5 million apartments affordable to poor families have been lost over the last two years.
- 187 children die each year in house fires caused by faulty electrical equipment, particularly heaters.
- 21,000 children have stunted growth caused by health problems related to a lack of stable housing.
- 10,000 children between the ages of four and nine are hospitalized for asthma attacks each year because of cockroach infestation at home.
- 2.5 million collective IQ points are lost among children ages one to five from lead poisoning. This impaired intellectual functioning will affect children for the rest of their lives. Virtually all these children are poisoned at home.

Children's Illnesses

For more information about children's health and well-being, go to the Companion Website at http://www.prenhall.com/morrison, select chapter 2, then choose the Linking to Learning module to connect to the American Public Health Association site.

When you think of children's illnesses, what do you think of? I'll bet you think of such diseases as measles, rubella, and mumps. Guess again. Asthma, a chronic inflammatory disorder of the airways, is the most common chronic childhood illness in the United States. It is estimated that 1.3 million children under age five suffer from asthma. Asthma is caused in part by poor air quality, dust, mold, animal fur and dander, allergens from cockroaches and rodent feces, dust mites, and strong fumes. Many of these causes are found in poor and low-quality housing. You will want to reduce asthma-causing conditions in your early childhood programs and work with parents to reduce the causes of asthma in their homes. Some things you

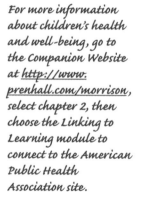

Poverty and substandard housing can adversely affect the health and well-being of children. Since children from such environments often have difficulties in school, the role of the early childhood educator in their lives is an especially important one.

can do include the following: prohibit smoking around children, keep the environment clean and free of mold, reduce or eliminate the amount of carpeting, have children sleep on mats or cots, and work with parents to ensure that their children are getting appropriate asthma medication.[12] For additional information about asthma, visit the Web sites of the Asthma and Allergy Foundation of America (www.aafa.org), the Allergy and Asthma Network/Mothers of Asthmatics, Inc. (www.aanma.org), the National Asthma Education and Prevention Program (www.nhlbi.nih.gov/about/naepp/index.htm), the American Academy of Pediatrics (www.aap.org and www.schoolhealth.org), and the American Lung Association (www.lungusa.org).

Lead poisoning is also a serious childhood disease. The Centers for Disease Control (CDC) estimates that approximately one million children between birth and age five have elevated blood lead levels. They also estimate that 20 percent of African American children living in housing built before 1946 have elevated blood lead levels. Lead has long been identified as a harmful environmental pollutant. The major source of lead poisoning is from old lead-based paint. Other sources are from batteries and from dust and dirt from polluted soil. Approximately 80 percent of homes built before 1978 have lead-based paint in them. Since then, lead has no longer been used in paint. Lead poisoning can cause learning disabilities, behavioral problems, and brain damage. Lead enters the body through inhalation and ingestion. Young children are especially vulnerable since they put many things in their mouths, chew on windowsills, and crawl on floors. Search the Web sites of the CDC (www.cdc.gov) and the National Safety Council (www.nsc.org) for more information about how to prevent lead poisoning at home and school, or call the National Lead Information Clearinghouse at 1-800-LEAD-FYI.

Brain Research

Although the field of neuroscience has been contributing to brain research for approximately twenty-five years, public interest in the application of this research to early childhood education has recently intensified. Media coverage of brain research and its implications for early childhood education is one factor contributing to this interest. Sharon Begley's *Newsweek* articles, "Your Child's Brain" and "How to Build a Baby's Brain," address the implications of brain research and how the findings of this research may be used to enhance children's early years.[13]

What specifically does brain research tell us about early childhood experiences? In many cases it affirms what early childhood educators have always intuitively known. Good parental care, warm and loving attachments, and positive age-appropriate stimulation from birth onward make a tremendous difference in children's cognitive development for a lifetime.

Brain research also tells us a great deal regarding stimulation and the development of specific areas of the brain. For example, brain research suggests that listening to music and learning to play musical instruments at very early ages stimulate the brain areas associated with mathematics and spatial reasoning. Brain research also suggests that gross motor activities and physical education should be included in a child's daily schedule throughout the elementary years. Regrettably, school systems often cut programs such as physical education and music in times of budget crisis, even though research shows that these programs are essential to a child's complete cognitive development.

New early childhood curricula are being developed based on the findings of brain research, and these programs strive to apply research findings in a practical way. One such program is Success For Life, developed by researchers and educators at the University of North Texas. The vision of Success For Life is to help children achieve a positive outlook on life through success in school and daily life. The goal of this interdisciplinary program is to integrate the findings of brain researchers with the best practices in early childhood education to provide support for healthy growth and to increase the cognitive and social competence of children. Children's needs—physical, social, emotional, cognitive, linguistic, nutritional, and health—are correlated with appropriate support and learning opportunities to create an optimal environment for growth and development. For additional information, visit the Web site of Success For Life at www.unt.edu/velma_schmidt.

Another program, Zero to Three, focuses on infants, toddlers, and families and is dedicated to promoting the healthy development of America's babies and young children. Zero to Three believes that a child's first three years are crucial for developing intellectual, emotional, and social skills. If these skills are not developed, the child's lifelong potential may be hampered. The organization supports professionals, parents, and policymakers and strives to increase public awareness, inspire leaders, and foster professional excellence through training, always emphasizing the first three years of a child's life. Visit the Zero to Three Web site at www.zerotothree.org.

Brain research and other studies are influencing our ideas about how children learn, how to teach them, and what they should learn. As a result, there is a major shift in basic educational premises concerning what children can achieve. Early childhood professionals have arrived at the following conclusions about young children:

1. The period of most rapid intellectual growth occurs before age eight. The extent to which children will become intelligent, based on those things by which we measure intelligence and school achievement, is determined long before many children enter school. The notion of promoting cognitive development implies that children benefit from enriched home environments that are conducive to learning and early school-like experiences, especially for children from environments that place them at risk of not developing their full potential.

2. It is increasingly evident that children are not born with fixed intelligences. This outdated concept fails to do justice to children's tremendous capacity for learning and change. In addition, evidence supports developmental intelligence. The extent to which individual intelligence develops depends on many variables, such as experiences, child-rearing practices, economic factors, nutrition, and the quality of prenatal and postnatal environments. Inherited genetic characteristics set a broad framework within which intelligence will develop. Heredity sets the limits, while environment determines the extent to which individuals achieve these limits.

3. Children reared in homes that are not intellectually stimulating may also lag intellectually behind their counterparts reared in more advantaged environments. Implications concerning the home environment are obvious. Experience shows that children who lack an environment that promotes learning opportunities may be at risk throughout life. On the other hand, homes that offer intellectual stimulation tend to produce children who do well in school.

4. Brain research findings suggest that good parental care, warm and loving attachments, and positive, age-appropriate stimulation from birth onward make a difference in children's overall development for a lifetime.[14] Even during the fetal stage, the kind of nourishment and care a child receives affects neural development (i.e., the development of brain nerve cells). The majority of recent research shows that much of a child's learning capacity is developed during the earliest years.

5. Positive interactions with caring adults stimulate children's brains profoundly in terms of establishing new synaptic connections and strengthening existing ones. For example, cuddling and signing to infants and toddlers stimulate brain connections and lay the foundation for learning throughout life. Those connections used over time become

permanent, and those that are not used wither and become dormant. If a child receives little stimulation during the early months and years, synapses will not develop, and the brain will have fewer cellular connections. Increasingly, researchers are showing how early stimulation sets the stage for future cognitive processes. In addition, positive emotional interactions, formations of secure attachments, and effective regulation of temperament and emotionality lay the foundation for healthy emotional development. Temperament-related genetic predispositions, early experiences, and learned behaviors greatly influence learning, processes of development, and the way one interacts with his or her environment over the life-span.

6. Early experiences during critical/sensitive periods and windows of opportunity are so powerful that they can completely change the way a person develops.[15] Research suggests that the right input at the right time is crucial for a child to fully develop his cognitive potential. Neurobiologists are still trying to understand exactly which kinds of experiences or sensory input wire the brain in particular ways. Research conducted in the area of visual perception suggests that the circuit for vision has a neuron growth spurt at two to four months of age, thus helping the child begin to notice the shape of objects, or the visual gestalt.[16] This neuron growth spurt peaks at eight months, when connections are established between these neurons, suggesting the importance of providing appropriate visual stimuli to establish connections in the brain's visual processing region.

Public Policy and Early Childhood Education

At no time in U.S. history has there been so much interest and involvement by early childhood professionals in the development of public policy. Public policy includes such things as laws, position statements of professional organizations, and court decisions. Public policies affect and influence the lives of children, parents, families, and professionals working in the field. Public policies determine at what ages children can enter school, what immunizations are required before children enter any program, how child care programs operate, and how to provide appropriate care and education for children with special needs.

For more information about public policy and early childhood education, go to the Companion Website at http://www.prenhall.com/morrison, select chapter 2, then choose the Linking to Learning module to connect to the Early Childhood Care and Development site.

Social issues have public policy implications for young children, families, and early childhood professionals. On Tuesday, April 20, 1999, two Columbine high school students walked into their high school in Littleton, Colorado, and engaged in a terrorism spree that left twelve high school students and one adult dead and another twenty students suffering from various gunshot wounds. Then they committed suicide. Such violence as this leads to proposals for how to provide violence-free homes and educational environments, how to teach children to get along nonviolently with others, and how to reduce violence on television, in the movies, and in video games. How to reduce violence presented on television, for example, in turn leads to discussions and proposals for ways to limit children's television viewing (such proposals include "pulling the plug" on television; using the V-chip, which enables parents to block out programs with violent content; boycotting companies whose advertisements support programs with violent content; and limiting violence shown during prime-time viewing hours). Early childhood professionals play important roles in these and other public policy debates and formulations. Throughout this text, you will find many other examples of how public policy affects programs for children and families and how they are implemented and funded.

Professional organizations issue position statements designed to influence public policy prior to its enactment and implementation. Child advocacy agencies draft position papers on topics ranging from developmentally appropriate practices for young children to the pros and cons of developing public school programs for four-year-olds. NAEYC, for example, is a strong advocate for developmentally appropriate practices in early childhood programs. Throughout this text you will read position statements issued by agencies that influence national and state legislation for programs to help children and families. For example, the Children's Defense Fund issues the Source Book, which is an annual report on the state of America's children; access this agency's Web site at www.childrensdefense.org to review its various advocacy initiatives on behalf of children and families. This political involvement of professional organizations is beneficial to all—children, parents, families, and early childhood professionals—for it helps ensure that policymakers will consider children's and families' best interests when making decisions that affect them.

Politics and Early Childhood Education

The more that the issue of early childhood is in the news, the more it generates public interest and attention; this is part of the political context of early childhood education. Whatever else can be said about education, one point holds true: education is political. Politicians and politics exert a powerful influence in determining what is taught, how it is taught, to whom it is taught, and by whom it is taught. Early childhood education is no exception.

An important political and educational event occurred in 1989 when President George Bush and the governors of all fifty states met at the University of Virginia to set national education goals. One result of this meeting was the release in 1991 of America 2000: An Education Strategy, which outlined six educational goals, or national standards. These, and two additional goals, were passed as part of the Goals 2000: Educate America Act in 1994. The eight goals, to have been achieved by the year 2000, are listed in Figure 2.7.

The Goals 2000: Educate America Act includes these eight goals, to be achieved by 2000:

1. All children in America will start school ready to learn.
2. The high school graduation rate will increase to at least 90 percent.
3. All students will leave grades four, eight, and twelve having demonstrated competency over challenging subject matter...,and [all students will be] prepared for responsible citizenship, further learning, and productive employment.
4. The nation's teaching force will have access to programs for the continued improvement of their professional skills.
5. U.S. students will be first in the world in mathematics and science achievement.
6. Every adult American will be literate.
7. Every school in America will be free of drugs and violence and will offer a disciplined environment conducive to learning.
8. Every school and home will engage in partnerships that will increase parental involvement and participation in promoting the social, emotional, and academic growth of children.

Figure 2.7
Goals 2000

Source: U.S. Department of Education, 1994.

These goals have generated a great deal of debate, particularly concerning what they mean and how best to achieve them. Goals 1, 2, 6, 7, and 8 will continue over the next decade to influence early childhood education. Goal 1 obviously affects children's readiness for school. Goal 2 is pertinent because the early childhood years are seen as the place to prevent school dropout. Many public school programs for three- and four-year-old children are funded specifically as beginning efforts to keep children in school at a later age. Goal 6 has encouraged many intergenerational literacy and family literacy programs in which children, their parents, and other family members are taught to read. Goal 7 supports the drug prevention programs implemented in early childhood programs, again on the premise that early prevention is much more effective than later treatment. Finally, goal 8 makes implicit as part of national policy the importance of home–school partnerships. Implementation of goal 8 is treated in detail in chapter 16.

What has been the progress of the Goals 2000 program so far? According to "The National Education Goals Report: Building a Nation of Learners, 1999," efforts toward achieving the goals are working. Significant improvement has been associated with goals 1, 3, 5, and 7. Regarding goal 1 (ready to learn), for instance, the percentage of families reading and telling stories to their children on a regular basis has increased; for goal 3 (student achievement and citizenship), the percentages of students who are proficient in mathematics have risen in grades 4, 8, and 12; and for goal 7 (safe, disciplined, and alcohol- and drug-free schools), the percentage of students who report that they have been threatened or injured at school has decreased. However, significant declines in national performance are associated with goals 4 (teacher education and professional development) and 7. For example, the percentage of secondary school teachers who hold a degree in their main teaching assignment has decreased; and the percentage of students reporting that someone has offered to sell or give them drugs at school has increased.

Although progress has not been the same for all the goals nor within each state, the program has inspired the educational system to improve performance at all levels. Here is a summary from the National Education Goals panel:

> We believe that the National Education Goals have moved America forward and, on balance, encouraged greater progress in education. We are clearer about what appropriate Goals are and how to measure progress toward them at the national and state levels. There is no doubt that the National Education Goals have encouraged a broad spectrum of educators, parents, students, business and community leaders, policymakers, and the public to work toward their attainment. . . . Can we do better? Of course we can. But we are convinced that our gains have been greater because we have had National Education Goals to guide our efforts. Ten years of progress have shown us that the Goals are working.[17]

SCHOOL READINESS. Goal 1, known as "the readiness goal," has generated particular interest in determining precisely what readiness means and how to best achieve this goal. As a result, we have reconceptualized what readiness is.

Previously, some viewed readiness as the process of children getting ready for school. From this perspective, readiness is viewed in relation to school and the ability to read and write. This conception places the responsibility for "getting ready" for school on children themselves. This concept of readiness also implies that if they are not ready, as judged by a test or some other criteria, they should not enter kindergarten or other programs. This practice often leads to keeping children out of school for a year while they "get ready" or failing them or holding them back in kindergarten or preschool.

Although the early childhood profession would like to curtail the use of the term *readiness* as typically used, it is a term widely used by the public and media. Today, professionals talk about readiness within the context of children's learning and development. The National

Education Goals Panel, the group charged with assessing the nation's progress toward achieving Goals 2000, has identified three critical objectives as crucial to meeting goal 1:

- Children will receive the nutrition, physical activity experiences, and health care needed to arrive at school with healthy minds and bodies and to maintain the mental alertness necessary to be prepared to learn; also, the number of low-birth-weight babies will be significantly reduced through enhanced prenatal health systems.
- Every parent in the United States will be a child's first teacher and devote time each day to helping his or her preschool child learn; also, parents will have access to the training and support they need.
- All children will have access to high-quality and developmentally appropriate preschool programs that help prepare children for school.[18]

These dimensions provide a fuller understanding of the concept and process of readiness. They enable early childhood professionals to focus on specific skills, behaviors, and attitudes that will enable children to be successful in school and life. For further information, you can visit the National Education Goals Panel's Web site at www.negp.gov.

State Involvement in Early Childhood Programs

A trend in the funding of educational programs is for the federal government, instead of directly funding programs, to provide monies to the fifty states to spend as they see fit.

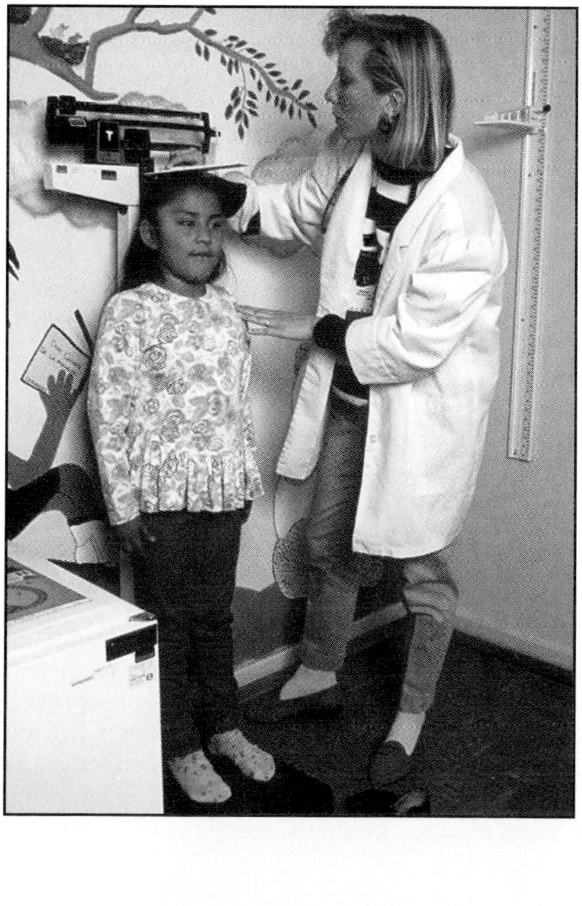

Readiness includes general health and physical growth, such as being well rested and fed and properly immunized. How does children's health status affect their readiness for learning?

As a result, all the states are taking a lead in developing programs for young children, stimulated by these budgetary changes. As federal dollars shift to other programs, states are responding by initiating programs of their own, funded from both federal allocations and other sources, including lottery monies and increased taxes on commodities and consumer goods such as cigarettes.

The Florida Department of Education, for example, has an office dedicated to early intervention and school readiness. One of its programs is Florida First Start, a home–school partnership designed to give children at risk of future school failure the best possible start in life and to support parents in their role as their children's first teachers. Emphasis is on enabling families to enhance their children's intellectual, physical, language, and social development by involving parents in their children's education during the critical first three years of life. Through early parent education and support services, the program lays the foundation for later learning and future school success, while fostering effective parent–school relationships. Further information on the program is available on the Internet at www.firn.edu/doe/bin00021/fs.htm.

In addition, instead of giving monies directly to specific programs, many federal dollars are consolidated into what are known as *block grants*—sums of money given to states to provide services according to broad general guidelines. In essence, the states, not the federal government, control the way the money is spent and the nature of the programs funded. As targeted federal support for early education becomes subject to different methods of funding, it may well be that states will finance replacement, alternative, and substitute programs. This involvement will grow and strengthen as the states make greater commitments to child care and early education programs, especially for children from low-income families. For example, the majority of states have appropriated monies for prekindergarten programs to serve at-risk four-year-old children.

This trend will accelerate. With direct funding comes control—when agencies contribute funding for programs, they also help determine the direction the programs will take, the policies that govern them, and the children and families they will serve. Federal support for early childhood and related programs will likely continue to be scarce, with the exception of Head Start. Increased support from private agencies, contributions, and volunteerism constitutes legitimate alternatives to federal funds.

Not everyone, however, agrees that declining federal support for early childhood and other programs is a good idea. Critics of the declining federal presence in early childhood programs maintain that the results are harmful for women, children, and families. They specifically cite increases in the number of women and children living in poverty and a higher infant mortality rate.

The Public Schools and Early Education

Traditionally, the majority of preschool programs were operated by private agencies or agencies supported wholly or in part by federal funds to help the poor, the unemployed, working parents, and disadvantaged children. But times have changed. All parents exert great pressure on public school officials and state legislatures to sponsor and fund additional preschool and early childhood programs. Increasingly, preschools are providing a full range of services for children and families with an emphasis on providing for the whole child.

Another trend involves preschool programs conducted in the public schools. Currently, California, Florida, New York, North Carolina, and Texas support preschools; nationwide, about 500,000 preschool children are enrolled in public school programs. As preschool programs admit more three- and four-year-olds nationwide, opportunities for teachers of young children will grow.

The spread of preschools reflects changing family patterns, especially the rise in single-parent families and families with two adult wage earners. Demand for preschools also relates to their use in early childhood intervention programs and to the popular belief that three- and four-year-old children are ready, willing, and able to learn.

Parents lobby for public support of early childhood education for a number of reasons. First, because working parents cannot find quality child care for their children, they believe the public schools hold the solution to child care needs. Second, the persistent belief that children are a nation's greatest wealth makes it seem sensible to provide services to avoid future school and learning problems. Third, many people believe that early public schooling, especially for children from low-income families, is necessary if the United States is to promote equal opportunity for all. They argue that low-income children begin school already far behind their more fortunate middle-class counterparts and that the best way to keep them from falling hopelessly behind is for them to begin school earlier. Fourth, some parents cannot afford quality child care. They believe preschools, furnished at the public's expense, are a reasonable, cost-efficient way to meet child care needs. A fifth reason for the demand for public school involvement relates to the "competent child"—parents want academic programs for their children at an earlier age and look, naturally, to the public schools to provide programs that will help their children succeed in life. Sixth, today's parents are the best educated in U.S. history. These well-educated parents are causing a boom in preschool programs that emphasize earlier and more comprehensive education for young children.

The alignment of the public schools with early childhood programs is becoming increasingly popular. Several arguments favor such a collaboration. First, some professionals think it is not wise to train nonteachers for preschool positions when trained professionals are available. Second, some professionals think it makes sense to put the responsibility for educating and caring for the nation's children under the sponsorship of one agency—the public schools. For their part, public school teachers and the unions that represent them are anxious to bring early childhood programs within the structure of the public school system.

Early public schooling is a reality for growing numbers of the nation's children. What societal changes are contributing to this trend toward early public schooling?

Third, many public schools have already moved into the area of child care and preschool programs for three- and four-year-old children.

There is by no means consensus that universal public schooling or even anything approaching it should be available for very young children. Critics of the effort to place preschool programs in the public schools give three reasons for their stance. First, they cite the failure of public education to do a good job of teaching young children for whom they currently provide programs. They ask, "How can public schools handle an expanded role if they have not done a good job with what they are already supposed to do?" Second, some critics say that public school teachers are not trained in the specific skills needed in Head Start, child care, and other preschool programs. A third, more convincing argument relates to money: having the public schools assume the responsibility of preschool programs would probably cost several billion dollars.

Nonetheless, it seems inevitable that the presence of the public schools in early childhood education will continue to expand. Given that so many public schools offer programs for three- and four-year-olds, can programs for infants and toddlers be far behind?

Business Involvement in Early Childhood Programs

Many corporations and businesses are finding that early childhood education is a good investment. Corporations are increasingly dissatisfied with the products of the nation's schools. They have to spend millions of dollars teaching their employees such basic skills as reading and writing. Corporate executives think it makes more sense to invest in literacy in the early rather than in the later years. In this sense, corporations see their investments in children and families as social investments; that is, investing in children and families pays dividends to all. This social investment approach to early childhood and other programs is also based in part on economics. A dollar invested in quality child care, drug prevention programs, literacy programs, and health programs (e.g., immunizations) will save money later by helping to produce drug-free, literate, healthy adults. (One formula that corporate executives and politicians often use is that $1 invested in the early childhood years saves $7 in the adolescent and adult years.)

Consequently, companies such as American Telephone & Telegraph and Johnson & Johnson are spending considerable amounts of money on early childhood programs. The Stride Rite Corporation in particular has a reputation as a leader in providing programs for children and families. Stride Rite was the first company to provide on-site child care for its employees (in 1971) and the first to offer intergenerational care for children and the elderly in the same facility. Additionally, many corporations (such as Barnett Bank and Glaxo Wellcome) provide on-site child care services.

Increasingly, the private and government sectors are asking businesses to help them assist underserved populations. For example, the federal government is seeking business aid in paying for a new pregnancy handbook designed to help reduce the infant mortality rate. The eighty-two-page *Health Diary* provides information on prenatal care and health care for children during the first two years of life. The $6.00 publication is also seen as a tool for empowering parents and actively involving them in their health and that of their children. Federal officials will use the money from businesses to distribute free copies of the *Health Diary* in fifteen cities participating in Healthy Start, a federal program begun in 1991 to improve prenatal care. You can find out more about Healthy Start at www.healthystart.net.

In short, early childhood education and young children have captured the attention of the nation. They compete with budget deficits, nuclear arms treaties, and summit meetings for prime-time media attention. Consequently, early childhood professionals must learn more about how to care for, educate, and rear children so they can advise parents, legislators, and those who formulate public policy in determining what is best for the nation's children.

Program in Action

The Stride Rite Intergenerational Day Care Center

Stride Rite's intergenerational day care center is the first center in American business to pair the care of children and the elderly.

On a Tuesday morning at the Stride Rite Corporation's headquarters in Cambridge, Massachusetts, an unusual scene is unfolding. Two elderly women, Eva DaRosa and Margaret Donovan, are ferrying preschoolers, two at a time, from their classroom to the lunchroom, where the staff is working with the children and elders to make a handprint mural. Everyone is enjoying the project, but the real fun of the day has turned out to be the ride in Margaret's wheelchair. Each pair of children takes turns riding in her lap and pushing the chair with Eva's help. One child gets to ride on the way out, the other on the way back to their classroom.

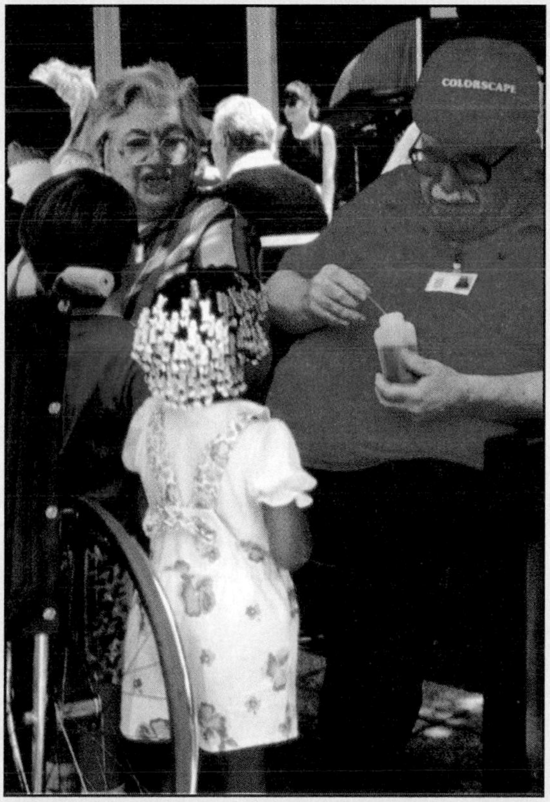

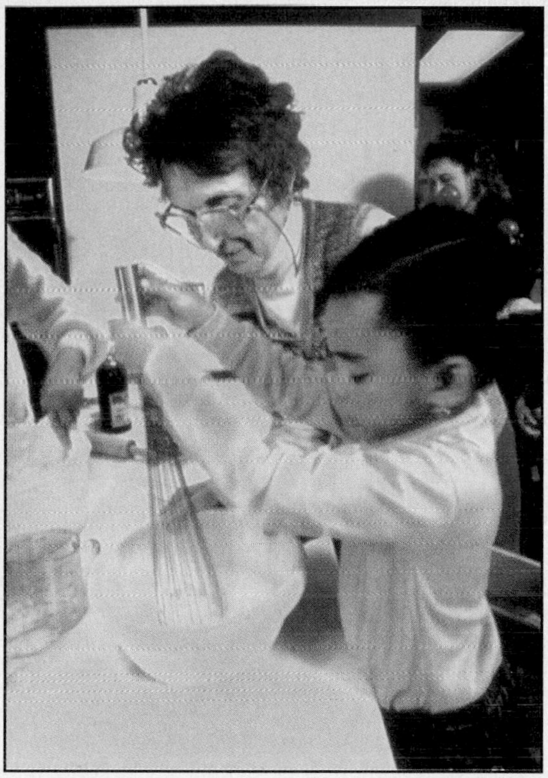

The women are enjoying the event almost as much and after a dozen runs have dubbed themselves the pony express.

The center's design allows a traffic pattern that encourages the informal interaction between children and elders while also providing privacy for each group. It is divided into two separate wings that are connected through a large central area. The children's wing has four classrooms for different age groups; the elders' wing has three rooms designed for a variety of quiet and noisy activities. The central core houses administrative offices, a kitchen and dining facility, and a resource center that includes conference rooms and a library. Among the special features of the facility are wide doorways to accommodate wheelchairs and floor surfaces that make mobility easier for frail elders.

An outdoor space was built to accommodate and stimulate both groups of clients.

The Stride Rite program meets the physical, social, and intellectual needs of each group through a carefully planned and supervised curriculum that fosters regular daily contact between the elders and children. Intergenerational curricula include (for children and elders separately and together) reading and writing stories, table games, celebrating holidays and birthdays, cooking and eating, arts and crafts, and taking field trips.

The intergenerational aspects are proving to be a great success for both children and elders. "The relationship between the children and the elders has really exceeded our expectations," says Karen Leibold, director, Work and Family Programs. "We thought we'd need to bring them together slowly, with a lot of staff direction and with specific projects to do. What we've found is that they're like magnets with each other. They just come together. They enjoy each other's company. Sometimes it can be for five minutes at the end of the day, when they meet in the entryway. Sometimes it's waving across the lunchroom at each other. Sometimes it can be an extended period of time, reading books together, or cooking, or making things with blocks or Play-Doh."

The intergenerational day care program is an outstanding example of how the needs of employees, employers, children, and elders can be met through collaborative planning.

Contributed by Stride Rite Corporation, Cambridge, Massachusetts; photos courtesy of Rick Friedman.

The Ecology of Early Childhood

Public policy initiatives and legislation are implemented in programs such as child care centers, public schools, and community agencies and within families and homes. It is therefore important for us to consider these environments. Ecology involves the study of how people interact with their environments and the consequences (good and bad) of these interactions. Early childhood professionals are very much interested in how children interact with their environments and how their environment affects them.

Early childhood ecological considerations apply to three levels. The first level is an examination of environments—how they are structured and arranged to promote children's maximum growth. For example, early childhood professionals are sensitive to the influence the child care environment has on health, safety, and physical and intellectual development. Sensitive professionals seek ways to structure environments so they are less stressful, more healthful, less dangerous, and more accommodating to children's developmental needs. Likewise, they arrange environments to welcome and support parents. For example, many early childhood programs provide parent rooms and lounges and furnish them with couches, comfortable chairs, parenting pamphlets, magazines, and other material that supports children's literacy development.

At the second level, early childhood professionals focus on how environments interact with each other. Professionals and parents are both part of children's environments, and how they interact affects children. For example, the extent to which a child's home and family supports her literacy development greatly influences how well she learns to speak, write, and read. An unfavorable ecological setting, one without printed materials—books, magazines, and newspapers—and that does not encourage language development, negatively influences a child's literacy development. Early childhood professionals who are attuned to the importance of the interaction between educational settings and homes will initiate programs of parent involvement and family support.

Political and social environments represent a third, more abstract level of interaction. For example, in Florida, kindergarten is compulsory for all children five years of age by Sep-

tember 1 (i.e., if a child is five years old by September 1 of a given year, he or she must begin to attend kindergarten). What effects does such political policy have on young children? Some people worry that children who are five by September 1 are "too old" when they enter kindergarten. Others are concerned about the cost and trauma parents undergo to find quality child care because their children were born a day or month too late. Others see an advantage to the September 1 age limit in that children are older when they come to school and therefore are more "ready" to learn. Early childhood professionals try to influence political processes so they are most beneficial to and supportive of children's and families' growth and development.

Ecological considerations interest early childhood and child development researchers in another way. They want to know how children's natural environments—their homes, families, child care centers, peer groups, and communities—influence their behavior. Today, for example, early childhood educators are very interested in how the home supports learning; one of the best predictors of whether a child is able to read is whether he or she is read to by parents in the home. Members of the early childhood profession, parents, social workers, legislators, and others are beginning to care about such ecological relationships. Such considerations will undoubtedly play an even more important role in early childhood as the years go by.

New Directions in Early Childhood Education

Because of the changing needs of society, including families, and because new knowledge is always surfacing, the field of early childhood education is constantly changing. Changes in the field of early childhood education affect what professionals believe and how they teach. Following are some important changes occurring in early childhood education today that will influence how you and others practice the profession of early childhood education:

- *Full day–full year services.* Parents want full day–full year services for a number of reasons. First, it fits in with their work schedule and lifestyle. Working parents in particular find it very difficult to patch together child care and other arrangements when their children are not in school. Second, parents believe that full day–full year services support and enhance their children's learning. More programs are responding positively to parents' desire for full day–full year services.
- *Family-centered programs.* Early childhood professionals are now working within the family system to provide the most meaningful education and services to children and their families.
- *Family education and support.* It will become a public priority as more programs come to be funded to provide families with child development and neuroscience information, parenting skills, and other resources that will help them get their children ready for schools and learning.
- *Two-generation programs.* It is common now for early childhood professionals to work with children and their parents, and in many cases grandparents, to develop such skills as literacy and parenting. Three-generational programs are becoming more commonplace.
- *Collaborative efforts with other agencies.* Increasing numbers of early childhood professionals are working cooperatively and collaboratively with professionals from other agencies to combine resources and to integrate their work. For example, many school

districts work with social workers to help children and families meet their needs regarding food, clothes, and school.

- *Support for intellectual development.* Early childhood professionals have always acknowledged that they must provide for all of children's needs—the physical, social, emotional, and especially intellectual. Today, as a result of brain and other research, there is a greater emphasis on supporting children's intellectual development. A recent report released by the National Institute of Child Health and Development (NICHD) concluded that one way to improve America's child care is to provide more intellectual stimulation for children.[19]
- *Early literacy learning.* New brain research has in turn created interest in the importance of early literacy development. For example, children's early conversational experiences with adults who are interested in them and who are willing to carry on conversations of interest are crucial in helping them produce a vocabulary necessary for language development and literacy. There is tremendous interest in helping children learn to read. This literacy emphasis will continue to accelerate in the coming years.
- *Professionals incorporating new curriculum initiatives into early childhood programs.* Two of the more popular programs involve wellness/healthy living and character/moral education.
- *Child-centered programs.* Increasingly, what early childhood professionals do in their programs focuses on the needs of children and their families rather than their own needs or those of their agencies. In addition, child-centered programs emphasize that actively involving children in learning is the preferred method of education and is the process by which children learn best. Today, the teaching–learning process centers on having children involved as active participants in their own learning and cognitive development as opposed to being passive recipients of knowledge through teacher-directed learning, worksheets, and the like. Active learning is in; passivity is out.

To take an online self-test on this chapter's contents, go to the Companion Website at http://www.prenhall.com/morrison, select chapter 2, then choose the Self Test module.

For additional Internet resources or to complete an online activity for this chapter, go to the Companion Website at http://www.prenhall.com/morrison, select chapter 2, then choose the Linking to Learning or Making Connections module.

Social changes that cause changes in the field of early childhood education also form the basis for public policy pronouncements and initiatives. For example, today we hear a lot about the debate between those who believe the family is the most important unit in children's care, education, and development and those who believe that it "takes a village"—the community—to adequately rear and provide for children. What is best for young children and what programs will achieve this goal are at the heart of public policy debates and formulations.

Activities for Further Enrichment

Applications

1. Review early childhood literature and daily newspapers to identify statements of public policy and issues relating to public policy. For example, a recent article in the *New York Times* discussed the issues involved in ending "social promotion," or the problems of promoting children who have not mastered grade-appropriate material. What are the issues involved in such problems? In what ways do you agree or disagree with these policies?
2. Interview single parents and determine what effects and influences they think single parenting has on children. In what ways is single parenting stressful to parents and children? How can early childhood programs support and help single parents? Search for and review research relating to this topic. How does the research agree or disagree with what parents report?
3. Find out what problems early childhood professionals in local preschools and child care centers face as a result of

divorce, abuse, and other types of stress in children's lives. How do they help with these problems?

Field Experiences

1. Visit corporations and businesses in your area and determine what they are doing to support education and family programs.
2. List at least five social, political, and economic conditions of modern society and explain how these conditions influence how people view, treat, and care for the very young.
3. List at least five significant contributions you believe good early childhood education programs can make in the lives of young children.

Research

1. Contact agencies that provide services to single parents, teenage parents, and families in need. How do these programs influence early childhood education programs in your local community?
2. Investigate the types of preschool programs available in your community. Who may attend them? How are they financed? What percentage of the children who attend have mothers working outside the home?
3. Over a period of several weeks or a month, collect articles from newspapers and magazines relating to infants, toddlers, and preschoolers and categorize them by topic (child abuse, nutrition, etc.). What topics were given the most coverage? Why? What topics or trends are emerging in early education, according to this media coverage? Do you agree with everything you read? Can you find instances in which information or advice may be inaccurate, inappropriate, or contradictory?

Readings for Further Enrichment

Arce, E. *Early Childhood Education: Perspective Series.* Boston: Houghton Mifflin, 1999.

This collection of articles gives the reader an authentic view of children's cultures, languages, and abilities. It examines issues regarding individual differences, policies that enhance the child, and societal changes that impact early childhood education.

Ballenger, C. *Teaching Other People's Children: Literacy and Learning in a Bilingual Classroom.* New York: Teachers College Press, 1998.

Explores how teachers who listen closely to children from other cultures can understand the approaches to literature that these children bring with them to school. Focuses on classroom behavior, concepts of print, and storybook reading.

Levine, J. *New Expectations: Community Strategies for Responsible Fatherhood.* New York: Fatherhood Project, 1999.

This latest release from the Fatherhood Project promotes a new way of thinking and acting to promote responsible fatherhood, including a jargon-free review of research, state-of-the-art review of community-based strategies, tips from leading practitioners, and a guide to more than three hundred programs nationwide and to one hundred of the most useful publications.

Levine, J., and Pittinsky, T. *Working Fathers: New Strategies for Balancing Work and Family.* New York: Harvest Books, 1998.

In this text, parenting expert James A. Levine, director of the Fatherhood Project at the Families and Work Institute, and Todd L. Pittinsky of the Harvard Business School present a groundbreaking examination of the work–family dilemma and offer a proven and effective game plan to help fathers as well as mothers, employees as well as managers, succeed in managing the competing demands of home and work.

Weiner, L. *Urban Teaching: The Essentials.* New York: Teachers College Press, 1998.

Provides invaluable "insider" recommendations for coping with school realities ranging from overcrowded classes and lack of appropriate materials to cultural diversity, frustrating bureaucracy, and school violence.

Linking to Learning

American Public Health Association

http://www.apha.org

Publishes material on topics including chemical toxicology, communicable diseases, natural disasters, food safety, breast-feeding, mental health, and nutrition.

Annie E. Casey Foundation

http://www.aecf.org

A friendly, newly updated resource, this Web site presents the latest information on issues affecting America's disadvantaged children.

Children Now

http://www.childrennow.org

Children Now works to translate the nation's commitment to children and families into action to improve conditions for all children. Recognized nationally for its policy expertise and up-to-date information on the status of children.

Early Childhood Care and Development

http://ecdgroup.harvard.net

An international, interagency group dedicated to improving the condition of young children at risk by keeping them on the agenda of policymakers, funders, and program developers.

National Center for Family Literacy

http://www.famlit.org

Advances and supports family literacy services through programming, training, research, advocacy, and dissemination of information about family literacy.

Stand for Children Action Center

http://www.stand.org

Establishes a process that enables and encourages people to become volunteers, defenders, and advocates for children. The center offers a toll-free 800 number, Web site, and monthly updates that feature success stories.

ENDNOTES

1 National Association for the Education of Young Children, *A Call to Action on Behalf of Children and Families* (Washington, DC: Author, 1995). [On-line]. Available: http://www.naeyc.org/about/position/pscall98.htm.

2 S. Armous, "On the Clock: Working Parents Take Issue," *USA Today*, May 27, 1999, 1B.

3 E. Harvey, "Short-term and Long-term Effects of Early Parental Employment on Children of the National Longitudinal Survey of Youth," *Developmental Psychology* 35(March 1999): 445–459.

4 U.S. Department of Health and Human Services, *Births: Final Data for 1997* (Washington, DC: Author, 1999). [On-line]. Available: http://www.cdc.gov/nchswww/releases/99news/99news/97natal.htm.

5 J. Dalaker and M. Naifeh, *U.S. Bureau of the Census, Current Population Reports, Series P60-201,* "Poverty in the United States: 1997" (Washington, DC: U.S. Government Printing Office, 1998), Table 2.

6 U.S. Bureau of the Census, *Current Population Survey,* March 1998.

7 National Center for Education Statistics, *The Condition of Education 1994* (Washington, DC: U.S. Department of Education, 1994).

8 National Center for Education Statistics, *The Condition of Education 1994* (Washington, DC: U.S. Department of Education, 1994), 1.

9 U.S. General Accounting Office, *Health Insurance for Children: Many Remain Uninsured Despite Medicaid Expansion* (Washington, DC: Author, 1995), 18.

10 J. Ehrle and K. Moore, *Snapshots of America's Families, Children's Environment and Behavior: Behavioral and Emotional Problems in Children* (Washington, DC: Urban Institute, 1999). [On-line]. Available: http://newfederalism.urban.org/nsaf/children_c6.html.

11 Boston Medical Center and Children's Hospital, *Not Safe at Home: How America's Housing Crisis Threatens Our Children* (Boston: Author, February 1998). [On-line.] Available: http://www.bmc.org/program/doc4kids/index.html.

12 Healthy Child Publications, *Asthma Resources* (Harbor Springs, MI: Author). [On-line]. Available: http://www.healthychild.net/Asthma9.html.

13 S. Begley, "Your Child's Brain," *Newsweek*, 19 February 1996, 55–62; and "How to Build a Baby's Brain," *Newsweek*, Spring/Summer Special Issue 1997, 28–32.

14 National Institute of Child Health and Development, *The NICHD Study of Early Child Care* (Washington, DC: Author, 1999). [On-line]. Available: http://www.nih.gov/nichd/publications/news/early-child/Early_Child_Care.htm.

15 H. Chugani, "Functional Brain Reorganization in Children," *Brain and Development* 18 (1996): 347–356.

[16] M. Lamb and J. Campos, *Development in Infancy* (New York: Random House, 1982).

[17] The National Education Goals Panel, "Goals Work!" [On-line]. Available: http:www.negp.gov/pages 1-5.htm.

[18] The National Education Goals Panel, "Goals 2000, Goal 1" (Washington, DC: Author, 1999). [On-line]. Available: http:www.negp.gov/pages3-3.htm.

[19] Chugani, "Functional Brain Reorganization in Children."

PART II

The Development of Early Childhood Programs

CHAPTER 3

The teacher is not in the school to impose certain ideas or to form certain habits in the child, but is there as a member of the community to select the influences which shall affect the child and to assist him in properly responding to these influences.

JOHN DEWEY

The Past and the Present

Prologue to the Future

Focus Questions

1. Why is it important to have an appreciation for the ideas, professional accomplishments, and contributions of great educators?
2. What are the basic beliefs of the following people who have influenced early childhood education: Luther, Comenius, Locke, Rousseau, Pestalozzi, Owen, Froebel, Montessori, Dewey, Piaget, Vygotsky, Maslow, Erikson, Gardner, and Hirsch?
3. How have the beliefs and ideas of great educators influenced early childhood programs?
4. How have people, agencies, and legislation been influenced by historical events?
5. How does the past of early childhood education influence its future?

To review the chapter focus questions online, go to the Companion Website at http://www.prenhall.com/morrison and select chapter 3.

Why Is the Past Important?

To check your understanding of this chapter with the online Study Guide, go to the Companion Website at http://www.prenhall.com/morrison, select chapter 3, then choose the Study Guide module.

By reading of the hopes, ideas, and accomplishments of people whom our profession judges famous, we realize that today's ideas are built on those of the past. There are at least five reasons to know about the ideas and theories of great educators who have influenced the field of early childhood education.

Rebirth of Ideas

Old ideas and theories have a way of being reborn. Good ideas and practices persist over time and tend to be recycled through educational thought and practices in ten- to twenty-year periods. For example, many practices popular in the 1970s—using phonics to teach reading; family grouping and multifamily grouping; child-centered education; and active learning—are now popular again at the beginning of the twenty-first century.

Old ideas and practices seldom get recycled exactly in their previous form. They are changed and modified as necessary for contemporary society and situations. Knowing about these former ideas and practices helps us recognize them when they do come around again. Most important, this knowledge enables you to be an active participant in the recycling process of applying good practices of previous years to contemporary practice. You can more fully appreciate this recycling if you understand the roots of the early education profession.

Build the Dream—Again

Many ideas of famous educators are still dreams, despite the advances we attribute to modern education. In this regard, we are the inheritors of the ideas of a long line of early childhood educators. We should acknowledge this inheritance and use it as a base to build meaningful teaching careers and lives for children and their families. We have an obligation to have bright visions for children and build on the dreams of others. You are both a builder of dreams and an implementer of dreams.

Implement Current Practice

Ideas expressed by early educators will help you better understand how to implement current teaching strategies, whatever they may be. For instance, Rousseau, Froebel, and Montessori all believed children should be taught with dignity and respect. This attitude toward children is essential to an understanding of good educational practice and contributes to good teaching and quality programs. Any program you are involved in should include respect—among many other attributes—as one of its core values.

Empower Professionals

Theories about how young children grow, develop, and learn decisively shape educational and child-rearing practices. Some parents and teachers may not realize, however, what assumptions form the foundations of their daily practices. Studying the beliefs of the great educators helps parents, you, and other early childhood educators clarify what to do and

gives insight into behavior and practice. In this sense, knowing about theories liberates the uninformed from ignorance and empowers professionals and parents. As a consequence, those who understand the theories are able to implement developmentally appropriate practices with confidence.

Inspire Professionals

Exploring, analyzing, and discovering the roots of early childhood education helps inspire professionals. Recurring rediscovery forces people to contrast current practices with what others have advocated. Examining sources of beliefs helps clarify modern practice, and reading and studying others' ideas make us rethink our own beliefs and positions. In this regard, the history of the great educators and their beliefs helps keep us current. When you pause long enough to listen to what they have to say, you frequently find a new insight or idea that will motivate you to continue your quest to be the best you can be.

Historical Figures and Their Influence on Early Childhood Education

Martin Luther

While the primary impact of the Protestant Reformation was religious, other far-reaching effects were secular. Two of these effects involved universal education and literacy, both topics very much in the forefront of educational practice today.

In Europe, the sixteenth century was a time of great social, religious, and economic upheaval, partly because of the Renaissance and partly because of the Reformation. Great emphasis was placed on formal schooling to teach children how to read, the impetus for which is generally attributed to Martin Luther (1483–1546) and the Reformation he spurred.

For links to many of Martin Luther's writings online, go to the Companion Website at http://www.prenhall.com/morrison, select chapter 3, then choose the Linking to Learning module to connect to the Martin Luther site.

The question of what to teach is an issue in any educational endeavor. Does society create schools and then decide what to teach, or do the needs of society determine what schools it will establish to meet desired goals? This is a question early childhood professionals wrestle with today. In the case of European education of that time, Luther emphasized the necessity of establishing schools to teach children to read. Simply stated, Luther replaced the authority of the hierarchy of the Catholic Church with the authority of the Bible. Believing that individuals were free to work out their own salvation through the Scriptures meant that people had to learn to read the Bible in their native tongue.

This concept marked the real beginning of teaching and learning in people's native language, or vernacular, as opposed to Latin, the official language of the Catholic Church. Before the Reformation, only the wealthy and those preparing for a religious vocation learned to read and write Latin. Luther translated the Bible into German. Other translations followed, finally making the Bible available to people in their own language. In this way, the Protestant Reformation encouraged and supported popular universal education.

Luther also believed the family was the most important institution in the education of children. To this end, he encouraged parents to provide religious instruction and vocational education in the home. Throughout his life Luther remained a champion of education, writing letters and treatises and preaching sermons on the subject.

Out of the Reformation evolved other religious denominations, all interested in preserving the faith through education and schooling. Today, many churches, synagogues, and

mosques operate child care and preK–12 programs. A growing number of parents want early childhood programs that support their religious values, beliefs, and culture. They look for and find such programs operated by religious organizations.

John Amos Comenius

For more information about how John Amos Comenius contributed to the "invention of childhood," go to the Companion Website at http://www.prenhall.com/morrison, select chapter 3, then choose the Linking to Learning module to connect to a Life magazine article honoring John Amos Comenius.

John Amos Comenius (1592-1670) was born in Moravia, a former province of the Czech Republic, and became a Moravian minister. He spent his life serving as a bishop, teaching school, and writing textbooks. Of his many writings, those that have received the most attention are *The Great Didactic* and the *Orbis Pictus* ("The World in Pictures"), considered the first picture book for children.

Comenius believed that humans are born in the image of God. Therefore, each individual has an obligation and duty to be educated to the fullest extent of one's abilities so as to fulfill this godlike image. Since so much depends on education, then, as far as Comenius was concerned, it should begin in the early years.

> It is the nature of everything that comes into being, that while tender it is easily bent and formed, but that, when it has grown hard, it is not easy to alter. Wax, when soft, can be easily fashioned and shaped; when hard it cracks readily. A young plant can be planted, transplanted, pruned, and bent this way or that. When it has become a tree these processes are impossible.[1]

Comenius also believed that education should follow the order of nature, which implies a timetable for growth and learning. Early childhood professionals must observe this pattern to avoid forcing learning before children are ready. Comenius also thought that learning is best achieved when the senses are involved and that sensory education forms the basis for all learning.

Comenius said that the golden rule of teaching should be to place everything before the senses—for example, that children should not be taught the names of objects apart from

(104)

LI.

Piſcatio.

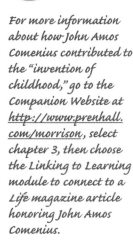

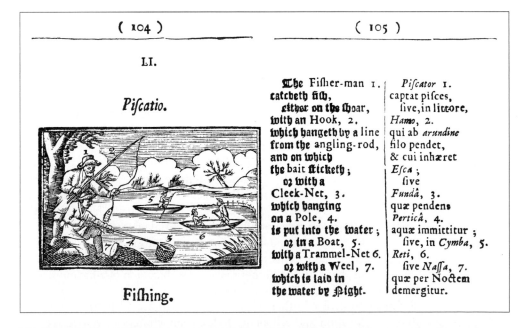

Fiſhing.

(105)

The Fiſher-man 1.	*Piſcator* 1.
catcheth fiſh,	captat piſces,
either on the Shoar,	ſive, in littore,
with an Hook, 2.	*Hamo*, 2.
which hangeth by a line	qui ab *arundine*
from the angling-rod,	filo pendet,
and on which	& cui inhæret
the bait ſticketh;	*Eſca*;
or with a	ſive
Cleek-Net, 3.	*Fundâ*, 3.
which hanging	quæ pendens
on a Pole, 4.	*Perticâ*, 4.
is put into the water;	aquæ immittitur;
or in a Boat, 5.	ſive, in *Cymba*, 5.
with a Trammel-Net 6.	*Reti*, 6.
or with a Weel, 7.	ſive *Naſſa*, 7.
which is laid in	quæ per Noctem
the water by Night.	demergitur.

This illustration from Orbis Pictus *demonstrates Comenius's emphasis on using sensory education as a means for teaching. What are some ways that early childhood professionals use children's senses to help them learn?*

the objects themselves or pictures of the objects. *Orbis Pictus* helped children learn the names of things and concepts, as they appeared during Comenius's time, through pictures and words. Comenius's emphasis on the concrete and the sensory is a pedagogical principle early childhood professionals still try to grasp fully and implement. Many contemporary programs stress sensory learning, and several early childhood materials promote learning through the senses.

A broad view of Comenius's total concept of education is evidenced by examining some of his principles of teaching:

> Following in the footsteps of nature we find that the process of education will be easy
>
> i. If it begins early, before the mind is corrupted.
> ii. If the mind be duly prepared to receive it.
> iii. If it proceeds from the general to the particular.
> iv. And from what is easy to what is more difficult.
> v. If the pupil be not overburdened by too many subjects.
> vi. And if progress be slow in every case.
> vii. If the intellect be forced to nothing to which its natural bent does not incline it, in accordance with its age and with the right method.
> viii. If everything be taught through the medium of the senses.
> ix. And if the use of everything taught be continually kept in view.
> x. If everything be taught according to one and the same method.
>
> These, I say, are the principles to be adopted if education is to be easy and pleasant.[2]

Comenius's two most significant contributions to today's education are books with illustrations and the emphasis on sensory training found in many early childhood programs. We take the former for granted and naturally assume that the latter is a necessary basis for learning.

John Locke

John Locke (1632–1704) popularized the tabula rasa, or blank tablet, view of children. More precisely, Locke developed the theory of and laid the foundation for environmentalism—the belief that the environment, not innate characteristics, determines what children will become. The extent of Locke's influence on modern early childhood education and practice is probably unappreciated by many who daily implement practices based on his theories.

For links to important works by John Locke, go to the Companion Website at http://www.prenhall.com/morrison, select chapter 3, then choose the Linking to Learning module to connect to the John Locke site.

Locke's assumption in regard to human learning and nature was that there are no innate ideas. This belief gave rise to his theory of the mind as a blank tablet, or "white paper." As Locke explains,

> Let us suppose the mind to be, as we say, white paper void of all characters, without ideas. How comes it to be furnished? Whence comes it by that vast store which the busy and boundless fancy of man has painted on it with an almost endless variety? Whence has it all the materials of reason and knowledge? To this I answer, in one word, from experience; in that all our knowledge is founded, and from that it ultimately derives itself.[3]

For Locke, then, environment forms the mind. The implications of this belief are clearly reflected in modern educational practice. The notion of the primacy of environmental influences is particularly evident in programs that encourage and promote early education as a means of overcoming or compensating for a poor or disadvantaged environment.

Based partly on the idea that all children are born with the same general capacity for mental development and learning, these programs also assume that differences in learning, achievement, and behavior are attributable to environmental factors such as home and family conditions, socioeconomic context, early education, and experiences. Programs of early schooling, especially the current move for public schooling for three- and four-year-olds, work on the premise that "disadvantaged" children fail to have the experiences of their "more advantaged" counterparts. In fact, it is not uncommon to provide public funding for early schooling for those who are considered disadvantaged and to design such programs especially for them.

Because Locke believed that experiences determine the nature of the individual, sensory training became a prominent feature in the application of his theory to education. Locke exerted considerable influence on others, particularly Maria Montessori, who developed her system of early education based on sensory training.

Jean-Jacques Rousseau

For more information about Jean-Jacques Rousseau, go to the Companion Website at http://www.prenhall.com/morrison, select chapter 3, then choose the Linking to Learning module to connect to the Jean-Jacques Rousseau site.

Jean-Jacques Rousseau (1712–1778) is best remembered by educators for his book *Émile,* in which he raises a hypothetical child from birth to adolescence. Rousseau's theories were radical for his time. The opening lines of *Émile* set the tone not only for Rousseau's educational views but many of his political ideas as well. "God makes all things good; man meddles with them and they become evil."[4]

Rousseau advocated a return to nature and an approach to educating children called naturalism. To Rousseau, naturalism meant abandoning society's artificiality and pretentiousness. A naturalistic education permits growth without undue interference or restrictions. Rousseau would probably argue against such modern practices as dress codes, compulsory attendance, minimum basic skills, frequent and standardized testing, and ability grouping, on the grounds that they are "unnatural."

There is some current tendency in American education to emphasize naturalism. For example, family grouping seeks to create a more natural family-like atmosphere in schools and classrooms, literacy programs emphasize literature from the natural environment (e.g., using menus to show children how reading is important in their everyday lives), and conflict resolution programs teach children how to get along with others.

According to Rousseau, natural education promotes and encourages qualities such as happiness, spontaneity, and the inquisitiveness associated with childhood. In his method, parents and teachers allow children to develop according to their natural abilities, do not interfere with development by forcing education, and tend not to overprotect children from the corrupting influences of society. Rousseau felt that Émile's education occurred through three sources: nature, people, and things. He elaborates:

> All that we lack at birth and need when grown up is given us by education. This education comes to us from nature, from men, or from things. The internal development of our faculties and organs is the education of nature. . . . It is not enough merely to keep children alive. They should learn to bear the blows of fortune; to meet either wealth or poverty, to live if need be in the frosts of Iceland or on the sweltering rock of Malta.[5]

Rousseau believed, however, that although parents and others have control over education that comes from social and sensory experiences, they have no control over natural growth. In essence, this is the idea of unfolding, in which the nature of children—what they are to be—unfolds as a result of maturation according to their innate timetables. We should observe the child's growth and provide experiences at appropriate times. Some educators interpret this as a laissez-faire, or "let alone," approach to parenting and education.

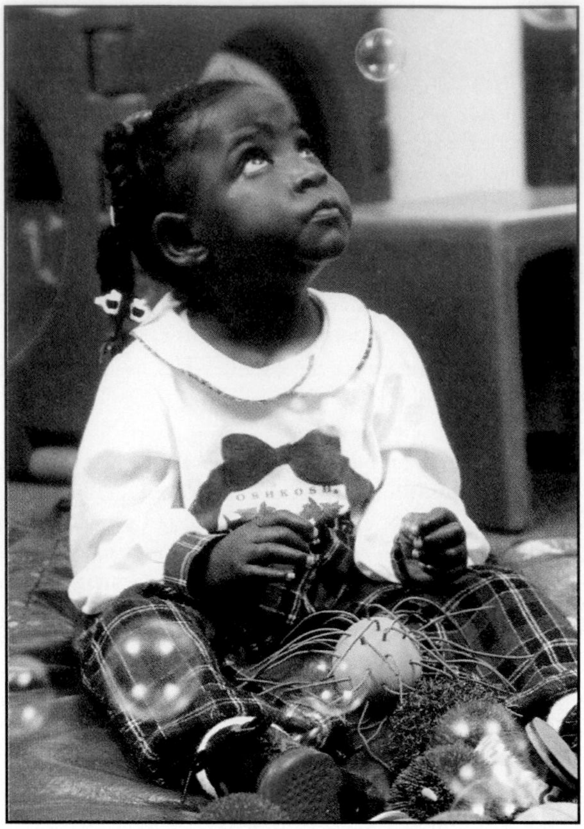

Rousseau maintained that a natural education encourages qualities such as happiness, spontaneity, and inquisitiveness. What should parents and teachers do to provide experiences where children can develop their natural abilities?

Perhaps the most famous contemporary example of the laissez-faire approach to child rearing and education is found in A. S. Neill's book *Summerhill,* which was also the name of his famous school. Neill presents a strong case for freedom and self-regulation. He and his wife wanted "to make the school fit the child—instead of making the child fit the school." Therefore,

> We set out to make a school in which we should allow children freedom to be themselves. In order to do this, we had to renounce all discipline, all direction, all suggestion, all moral training, all religious instruction. We have been called brave, but it did not require courage. All it required was what we had—a complete belief in the child as a good, not an evil, being. For almost forty years, this belief in the goodness of the child has never wavered; it rather has become a final faith.[6]

Educational historians point to Rousseau as dividing the historic and modern periods of education. Rousseau established a way of thinking about the young child that is reflected in innovators of educational practice such as Pestalozzi and Froebel. His concept of natural unfolding echoes Comenius's concept of naturalness and appears in current programs that stress promoting children's readiness as a factor in learning. Piaget's developmental stages also reinforce Rousseau's thinking about the importance of natural development. Educational practices that provide an environment in which children can become autonomous and self-regulating have a basis in his philosophy. The common element in all the approaches that advocate educating in a free, natural environment is the view of children as essentially good and capable of great achievement. It is the responsibility of early childhood professionals and parents to apply appropriate educational strategies at the right time, enabling all children to reach their full potential.

Johann Heinrich Pestalozzi

For more information about Johann Heinrich Pestalozzi, go to the Companion Website at http://www.prenhall.com/morrison, select chapter 3, then choose the Linking to Learning module to connect to the Johann Heinrich Pestalozzi site.

Johann Heinrich Pestalozzi (1746–1827) was so impressed by Rousseau's back-to-nature concepts that he purchased a farm and, in 1774, started a school called Neuhof. There Pestalozzi developed his ideas of the integration of home life, vocational education, and education for reading and writing.

Pestalozzi spent many years writing about his educational ideas and practices in such writings as *Leonard* and *Gertrude*. He became well known as a writer and educator, spending his later years developing and perfecting his ideas at various schools throughout Europe.

Rousseau's influence is most apparent in Pestalozzi's belief that education should follow the child's nature. His dedication to this concept is demonstrated by his rearing his only son, Jean-Jacques, using *Émile* as a guide. His methods were based on harmonizing nature and educational practices:

> And what is this method? It is a method which simply follows the path of Nature, or, in other words, which leads the child slowly, and by his own efforts, from sense-impressions to abstract ideas. Another advantage of this method is that it does not unduly exalt the master, inasmuch as he never appears as a superior being, but, like kindly Nature, lives and works with the children, his equals, seeming rather to learn with them than to teach them with authority.[7]

Unfortunately, Pestalozzi did not have much success rearing his son according to Rousseau's tenets, as evidenced by Jean-Jacques's inability to read and write by age twelve. This may be due to either his physical condition (he was thought to have epilepsy) or Pestalozzi's inability to translate Rousseau's abstract ideas into practice. Pestalozzi was able, however, to refine his own pedagogical ideas as a result of the process.

Probably the most important lesson from Pestalozzi's experience is that in the process of education, early childhood professionals cannot rely solely on children's own initiatives and expect them to learn all they need to know. For example, although some children do teach themselves to read, parents and others have created the climate and conditions for that beginning reading process. To expect that children will be or can be responsible for learning basic skills and appropriate social behaviors by themselves is simply asking too much.

Pestalozzi believed all education is based on sensory impressions and that through the proper sensory experiences, children can achieve their natural potential. This belief led to "object lessons." As the name implies, Pestalozzi thought the best way to learn many concepts was through manipulatives, such as counting, measuring, feeling, and touching. Pestalozzi believed the best teachers were those who taught children, not subjects. He also believed in multiage grouping. Pestalozzi anticipated by about 175 years the many family-centered programs of today that help parents teach their young children in the home. He believed mothers could best teach their children, and he wrote two books—*How Gertrude Teaches Her Children* and *Book for Mothers*—detailing procedures to do this. He felt that "the time is drawing near when methods of teaching will be so simplified that each mother will be able not only to teach her children without help, but continue her own education at the same time."[8]

Robert Owen

Quite often, people who affect the course of educational thought and practice are also visionaries in political and social affairs. Robert Owen (1771–1858) was no exception. Owen's influences on education resulted from his entrepreneurial activities associated with New Lanark, Scotland, a model mill town he managed. Owen was an environmentalist; that

is, he believed that the environment in which children are reared is the main factor contributing to their beliefs, behavior, and achievement. Consequently, he maintained that society and persons acting in the best interests of society can shape children's individual characters. He also was a Utopian, believing that by controlling the circumstances and consequent outcomes of child rearing, it was possible to build a new and perhaps more perfect society. Such a deterministic view of child rearing and education pushes free will to the background and makes environmental conditions the dominant force in directing and determining human behavior. As Owen explained it:

> Any character, from the best to the worst, from the most ignorant to the most enlightened may be given to any community, even to the world at large, by the application of proper means; which means are to a great extent at the command and under the control of those who have influence in the affairs of men.[9]

For a bibliography of writings by Robert Owen, go to the Companion Website at http://www.prenhall.com/morrison, select chapter 3, then choose the Linking to Learning module to connect to the Robert Owen site.

Owen believed that good traits were instilled at an early age and that children's behavior was influenced primarily by the environment. Thus, in Owen, we see influences of both Locke's blank tablet and Rousseau's ideas of innate goodness and naturalism.

To implement his beliefs, Owen opened an infant school in 1816 at New Lanark designed to provide care for about a hundred children, ages eighteen months to ten years,while their parents worked in his cotton mills. This led to the opening of the first infant school in London in 1818. Part of Owen's motivation for opening the infant schools was to get the children away from their uneducated parents. Owen opened a night school for his workers to provide them an education and transform them into "rational beings."

While we tend to think that early education for children from low-income families began with Head Start in 1965, Owen's infant school came over a hundred years before! Owen also had Utopian ideas regarding communal living and practice. In 1824, he pur-

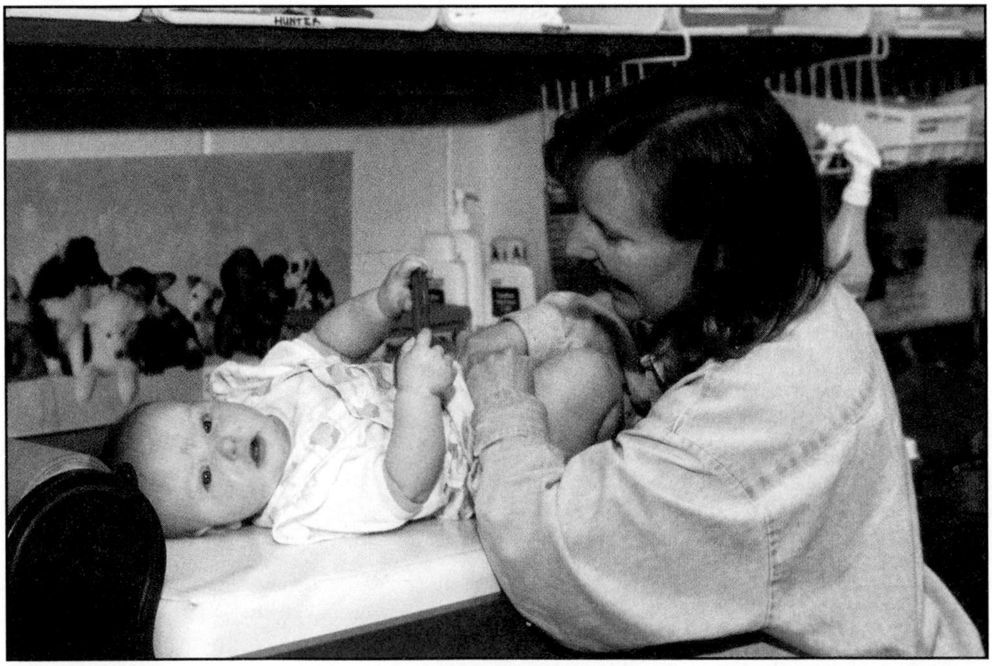

Robert Owen believed that infant schools were an ideal way to provide for the needs of young children while their families worked. What are some issues facing early childhood professionals today as they try to provide quality infant care for working parents?

chased the village of New Harmony, Indiana, for a grand experiment in communal living. Part of the community included a center for a hundred infants. The New Harmony experiment failed, but Owen's legacy lived on in the infant schools of England. These eventually developed into kindergartens, influenced by European educators.

Several things about Owen's efforts and accomplishments are noteworthy. First, his infant school preceded Froebel's kindergarten by about a quarter of a century. Second, Owen's ideas and practices influenced educators as to the importance of early education and the relationship between education and societal improvements, an idea much in vogue in current educational practice. In addition, early childhood professionals and other professionals today, not unlike Owen, seek through education to reform society and provide a better world for all humankind.

Friedrich Wilhelm Froebel

For a bibliography and biography of Friedrich Wilhelm Froebel, go to the Companion Website at http://www.prenhall.com/morrison, select chapter 3, then choose the Linking to Learning module to connect to the Friedrich Wilhelm Froebel site.

Friedrich Wilhelm Froebel (1782–1852) devoted his life to developing a system for educating young children. While his contemporary, Pestalozzi, with whom he studied and worked, advocated a system for teaching, Froebel developed a curriculum and educational methodology. In the process, Froebel earned the distinction "father of the kindergarten." As a result of his close relationship with Pestalozzi and his reading the works of Rousseau, Froebel decided to open a school and put his ideas into practice.

Froebel's primary contributions to educational thought and practice are in the areas of learning, curriculum, methodology, and teacher training. His concept of children and how they learn is based in part on the idea of unfolding, held by Comenius and Pestalozzi before him. The educator's role, whether parent or teacher, is to observe this natural unfolding and provide activities that will enable children to learn what they are ready to learn when they are ready to learn. The teacher's role is to help children develop their inherent qualities for learning. In this sense, the teacher is a designer of experiences and activities.

Consistent with his idea of unfolding, comparable to the process of a flower blooming from a bud, Froebel compared the child to a seed that is planted, germinates, brings forth a new shoot, and grows from a young, tender plant to a mature, fruit-producing one. He likened the role of educator to that of gardener. In his *kindergarten*, or "garden of children," he envisioned children being educated in close harmony with their own nature and the nature of the universe. Children unfold their uniqueness in play, and it is in the area of unfolding and learning through play that Froebel makes one of his greatest contributions to the early childhood curriculum.

> Play is the purest, most spiritual activity of man at this stage, and, at the same time, typical of human life as a whole—of the inner hidden natural life in man and all things. It gives, therefore, joy, freedom, contentment, inner and outer rest, peace with the world. It holds the sources of all that is good. A child that plays thoroughly, with self-active determination, persevering until physical fatigue forbids, will surely be a thorough, determined man, capable of self-sacrifice for the promotion of the welfare of himself and others. Is not the most beautiful expression of child-life at this time a playing child?—a child wholly absorbed in his play?—a child that has fallen asleep while so absorbed?
>
> As already indicated, play at this time is not trivial, it is highly serious and of deep significance. Cultivate and foster it, O mother; protect and guard it, O father! To the calm, keen vision of one who truly knows human nature, the spontaneous play of the child discloses the future inner life of the man.
>
> The plays of childhood are the germinal leaves of all later life; for the whole man is developed and shown in these, in his tenderest dispositions, in his innermost tendencies.[10]

Froebel knew from experience, however, that unstructured play represented a potential danger and that it was quite likely, as Pestalozzi learned with his son Jean-Jacques, that a child left to his own devices may not learn much. Without guidance, direction, and a prepared environment in which to learn, there was a real possibility that little or the wrong kind of learning would occur.

According to Froebel, the teacher is responsible for guidance and direction so children can become creative, contributing members of society. To achieve this end, Froebel developed a systematic, planned curriculum for the education of young children. Its bases were "gifts," "occupations," songs he composed, and educational games.

Gifts were objects for children to handle and use in accordance with teachers' instructions so they could learn shape, size, color, and concepts involved in counting, measuring, contrasting, and comparison (see Figure 3.1). The first gift was a set of six balls of yarn, each a different color, with six lengths of yarn the same colors as the balls. Part of the purpose of this gift was to teach color recognition. Froebel felt that the ball (meaning any spherical object) played an important role in education; consequently, he placed a great deal of emphasis on its use. Froebel said that "the ball itself has such an extraordinary charm, such a constant attraction for early childhood, as well as for later youth, that it is beyond comparison the first as well as the most important plaything of childhood especially."[11]

The second gift—consisting of a cube, a cylinder, and a sphere—were suspended in such a way that the children could examine their different properties by rotating, spinning, and touching. The sphere, because of its symmetry, had only one loop hole by which it was to be suspended. But the cube and cylinder had multiple loops, so the children could suspend the solids in different ways and examine the complexity of these seemingly simple shapes.

A significant idea behind the gifts is the importance for developing minds of examining things around them in a freely structured manner. It is not difficult to imagine a three- or four-year-old playing with the wooden solids and learning from their play.[12] Figure 3.1 shows all the ten gifts.

"Occupations" were materials designed for developing various skills, primarily psychomotor, through activities such as sewing with a sewing board, drawing pictures by following the dots, modeling with clay, cutting, stringing beads, weaving, drawing, pasting, and folding paper. Many of the games or plays Froebel developed were based on his gifts.

Froebel is called the father of the kindergarten because he devoted his life to developing both a program for young children and a system of training for kindergarten teachers. Many of the concepts and activities of the gifts and occupations are similar to activities that many kindergarten and other early childhood programs provide.

Froebel's recognition of the importance of learning through play is reinforced by contemporary early childhood professionals who plan and structure their programs around play activities. Other features of Froebel's kindergarten that remain are the play circle (where children sit in a circle for learning) and songs that are sung to reinforce concepts taught with gifts and occupations. Froebel was the first educator to develop a planned, systematic program for educating young children. He also was the first to encourage young, unmarried women to become teachers, a break with tradition that caused Froebel no small amount of criticism and was one reason his methods encountered opposition.

Maria Montessori

Maria Montessori (1870–1952) devoted her life to developing a system for educating young children. Her system has influenced virtually all subsequent early childhood programs. A precocious young woman who thought of undertaking either mathematics or engineering as a career, she instead chose medicine. Despite the obstacles to entering a field traditionally closed to women, she became the first woman in Italy to earn a medical degree. Following

Solids

- **First Gift: Color**
  Six colored worsted balls, about an inch and a half in diameter
- **Second Gift: Shape**
  Wooden ball, cylinder, and cube, one inch and a half in diameter
- **Third Gift: Number**
  Eight one-inch cubes, forming a two-inch cube (2 × 2 × 2)
- **Fourth Gift: Extent**
  Eight brick-shaped blocks (2 × 1 × ½), forming a two-inch cube
- **Fifth Gift: Symmetry**
  Twenty-seven one-inch cubes, three bisected and three quadrisected diagonally, forming a three-inch cube (3 × 3 × 3)
- **Sixth Gift: Proportion**
  Twenty-seven brick-shaped blocks, three bisected longitudinally and six bisected transversely, forming a three-inch cube
- **Seventh Gift: Surfaces**
  - Squares: Derived from the faces of the second or third gift cubes; entire squares—one and a half inches square of one-inch square and half-squares, squares cut diagonally.
  - Equilateral triangles: Length of side one inch or one inch and a half; entire triangles, half triangles—the equilateral triangle is cut in the direction of the altitude, yielding right scalene triangles, acute angles of 60 degrees and 30 degrees and thirds of triangles, in which the equilateral triangle is cut from the center to the vertices, yielding obtuse isosceles triangles, angles 30 and 120 degrees
- **Eighth Gift: Lines**
  - Straight: Splints of various lengths
  - Circular: Metal or paper rings of various sizes; whole circles, half circles, and quadrants
- **Ninth Gift: Points**
  Beans, lentils, or other seeds, leaves, pebbles, pieces of cardboard or paper, etc.
- **Tenth Gift: Reconstruction**
  The child has progressed from the solid to the point. This last gift enables the child to reconstruct the surface of a solid synthetically from the point. It consists of softened peas or wax pellets and sharpened sticks or straws.

Figure 3.1
Froebel's Gifts

Source: Winfried Miller and Johannes Froebel-Parker. Froebel Web, an online resource. Gifts and Occupations designed by Friedrich Froebel. [Online] http://www.geocities.com/froebelweb/web7010.html

this achievement, she was appointed assistant instructor in the psychiatric clinic of the University of Rome. At that time, it was customary not to distinguish between children with mental retardation and those who were mentally ill, and her work brought her into contact with mentally retarded children who had been committed to insane asylums. Although Montessori's first intention was to study children's diseases, she soon became interested in educational solutions for problems such as deafness, paralysis, and "idiocy."

At that time she said, "I differed from my colleagues in that I instinctively felt that mental deficiency was more of an educational than medical problem."[13] Montessori became

interested in the work of Edouard Seguin, a pioneer in the development of an educational system for children with mental retardation, and of Jean Itard, who developed an educational system for individuals who were both deaf and mute. Montessori credits Itard and Seguin with inspiring her to continue her studies with mentally retarded children. She wrote of her initial efforts at educating children:

> I succeeded in teaching a number of the idiots from the asylums both to read and to write so well that I was able to present them at a public school for an examination together with normal children. And they passed the examination successfully.[14]

This was a remarkable achievement that aroused interest in both Montessori and her methods. Montessori, however, was already considering something else:

> While everyone else was admiring the progress made by my defective charges, I was trying to discover the reasons which could have reduced the healthy, happy pupils of the ordinary schools to such a low state that in the intelligence test they were on the level with my own unfortunate pupils.[15]

For more information about how Maria Montessori's ideas apply to certain age groups, go to the Companion Website at http://www.prenhall.com/morrison, select chapter 3, then choose the Linking to Learning module to connect to the Maria Montessori School and Teacher Training Center site.

While continuing to study and prepare herself for the task of educating children, Montessori came upon the opportunity quite by chance to perfect her methods and implement them with nondisabled school-age children. In 1906 she was invited by the director general of the Roman Association for Good Building to organize schools for young children of families who occupied the tenement houses constructed by the association. In the first school, named the Casa dei Bambini, or Children's House, she tested her ideas and gained insights into children and teaching that led to the perfection of her system.

Montessori was profoundly religious, and a religious undertone is reflected throughout her work. She often quoted from the Bible to support her points. For example, at the dedication ceremonies of the first Children's House, she read from Isaiah 60:1–5 and ended by saying, "Perhaps this Children's House can become a new Jerusalem, which, if it is spread out among the abandoned people of the world, can bring a new light to education."[16] Her religious dedication to the fundamental sacredness and uniqueness of every child, and subsequent grounding of educational processes in a religious conviction, undoubtedly account for some of her remarkable achievements as a person and educator. Thus, her system functions well for those who are willing to dedicate themselves to teaching as if it were a religious vocation. We discuss Montessori's system in detail in chapter 4.

John Dewey

John Dewey (1859–1952) represents a truly American influence on U.S. education. Through his positions as professor of philosophy at the University of Chicago and Columbia University, his extensive writing, and the educational practices of his many followers, Dewey did more than any other person to redirect the course of education in the United States.

Dewey's theory of schooling, usually called *progressivism*, emphasizes children and their interests rather than subject matter. From this child-centered emphasis comes the terms *child-centered curriculum* and *child-centered school*. The progressive education philosophy also maintains that schools should be concerned with preparing children for the realities of today rather than some vague future time. As expressed by Dewey in *My Pedagogical Creed*, "Education, therefore, is a process of living and not a preparation for future living."[17] Thus, out of daily life should come the activities in which children learn about life and the skills necessary for living.

What is included in Dewey's concept of children's interests? "Not some one thing," he explained, "it is a name for the fact that a course of action, an occupation, or pursuit absorbs

For more information about John Dewey, go to the Companion Website at http://www.prenhall.com/morrison, select chapter 3, then choose the Linking to Learning module to connect to the Center for Dewey Studies site.

the powers of an individual in a thorough-going way."[18] In a classroom based on Dewey's ideas, children are involved with physical activities, utilization of things, intellectual pursuits, and social interaction. Physical activities include running, jumping, and being actively involved with materials. In this phase the child begins the process of education and develops other interest areas that form the basis for doing and learning. The growing child learns to use tools and materials to construct things. Dewey felt that an ideal expression for this interest was daily living activities, or occupations such as cooking and carpentry.

To promote an interest in the intellectual—solving problems, discovering new things, and figuring out how things work—children are given opportunities for inquiry and discovery. Dewey also believed that social interest, referring to interactions with people, was encouraged in a democratically run classroom.

While Dewey believed the curriculum should be built on the interests of children, he also felt it was the teacher's responsibility to plan for and capitalize on opportunities to integrate or weave traditional subject matter through and around the fabric of these interests. Dewey describes a school based on his ideas:

> All of the schools . . . as compared with traditional schools [exhibit] a common emphasis upon respect for individuality and for increased freedom; a common disposition to build upon the nature and experience of the boys and girls that come to them, instead of imposing from without external subject-matter standards. They all display a certain atmosphere of informality, because experience has proved that formalization is hostile to genuine mental activity and to sincere emotional expression and growth. Emphasis upon activity as distinct from passivity is one of the common factors.[19]

Teachers who integrate subjects, use thematic units, and encourage problem-solving activities and critical thinking are philosophically indebted to Dewey.

There has been much misinterpretation and criticism of the progressive movement and of Dewey's ideas, especially by those who favor a traditional approach that emphasizes the basic subjects and skills. Actually, Dewey was not opposed to teaching basic skills or topics. He did believe, however, that traditional educational strategies imposed knowledge on children, whereas their interests should be a springboard for involvement with skills and subject matter.

Dewey not only influenced educational thought and practice in the United States but also exerted a strong influence on the educational thought and practice of other countries that embrace his concept of incorporating work and education. The idea of "socially useful education" is still evident in contemporary China, Russia, and some Eastern European countries.

Jean Piaget

For more information about Jean Piaget, go to the Companion Website at http://www.prenhall.com/morrison, select chapter 3, then choose the Linking to Learning module to connect to the Jean Piaget Society site.

Jean Piaget (1896–1980) studied in Paris where he worked with Theodore Simon at the Alfred Binet laboratory, standardizing tests of reasoning for use with children. (Binet and Simon developed a scale for measuring intelligence.) This experience provided the foundation for Piaget's clinical method of interviewing, used in studying children's intellectual development. As Piaget recalls, "Thus I engaged my subjects in conversations patterned after psychiatric questioning, with the aim of discovering something about the reasoning process underlying their right, but especially their wrong, answers."[20] The emphasis on this method helps explain why some developers of a Piaget-based early childhood curriculum encourage the teacher's use of questioning procedures to promote thinking.

Following his work with children in Paris, which established the direction of his life work, Piaget became associated with the Institute J. J. Rousseau in Geneva and began study-

Program in Action

The City & Country School Today

The City & Country School, founded by Caroline Pratt in 1914, is an example of a progressive school that continues to educate children using the curriculum structure that was set forth over eighty years ago: "giving children experiences and materials that will fit their stage of development and have inherent in them unlimited opportunities for learning." Pratt, a teacher, sought to provide a school environment that suited the way children learn best—by doing.

BASIC, OPEN-ENDED MATERIALS

The younger groups (ages two through seven) use basic, open-ended materials to reconstruct what they are learning about the world and organize their information and thinking in meaningful ways. Materials such as blocks, clay, water, paint, and wood are chosen because of their simplicity, flexibility, and the challenging possibilities that they offer. The blocks, developed by Pratt, are the mainspring of the curriculum today as they were in the early days of the school. It is City & Country School's belief that an early childhood curriculum based on open-ended materials fosters independence, motivation, and interest, all essential components of learning.

THE JOBS PROGRAM

The Lower School curriculum provides a firm foundation for the more formal academic skills that children must master in later years. The Jobs Program was developed to play the central role in groups aged eight through thirteen. Each group has a specific job to perform related to the school's functioning as an integrated community. These jobs provide both a natural impetus for perfecting skills in reading, writing, spelling, and mathematics and a relevant framework for the exploration of social studies and the arts.

Beyond their work with blocks and jobs, children at City & Country are given opportunities to experience art, music, dramatics, foreign languages, science, computer, and woodworking, often integrated with their classroom work.

Located in the Greenwich Village district of New York City on 13th Street, the school currently has an enrollment of 240 students between the ages of two and thirteen. It continues to exemplify child-centered education.

Contributed by Kathleen Holz, principal of the City & Country School.

ing intellectual development. Piaget's own three children played a major role in his studies, and many of his consequent insights about children's intellectual development are based on his observations and work with them. Using his own children in his studies caused some to criticize his findings. His theory, however, is based on not only his research but also in literally hundreds of other studies involving thousands of children. Piaget came to these conclusions about early childhood education:

- Children play an active role in their own cognitive development.
- Mental and physical activity are important for children's cognitive development.
- Experiences constitute the raw materials children use to develop mental structures.
- Children develop cognitively through interaction with and adaptation to the environment.
- Development is a continuous process.

Piaget concluded that children's thinking is not "wrong" but qualitatively different from adult thought. Can you give two examples of how children's thinking is different from adult thinking?

- Development results from maturation and the transactions or interactions between children and the physical and social environments.

Piaget also popularized the age–stage approach to cognitive development and influenced others to apply the theory to other processes such as moral, language, and social development. He encouraged and inspired many psychologists and educators to develop educational curricula and programs utilizing his ideas and promoted interest in the study of young children's cognitive development. This, in turn, contributed to the interest in infant development and education. We discuss Piagetian education in detail in chapter 5.

Lev Vygotsky

For a bibliography of additional readings about Lev Vygotsky, go to the Companion Website at http://www.prenhall.com/morrison, select chapter 3, then choose the Linking to Learning module to connect to the Lev Vygotsky site.

Lev Vygotsky (1896–1934), a contemporary of Piaget, increasingly inspires the practices of early childhood professionals. Vygotsky's theory of development is particularly useful in describing children's mental, language, and social development. His theory also has many implications for how children's play promotes language and social development.

Vygotsky believed that children's mental, language, and social development is supported and enhanced by others through social interaction. This view is opposite from the Piagetian perspective in which children are much more solitary developers of their own intelligence and language. For Vygotsky, development is supported by social interaction. "Learning awakens a variety of developmental processes that are able to operate only when the child is interacting with people in his environment and in collaboration with his peers. Once these processes are internalized, they become part of the child's independent developmental achievement."[21] Vygotsky further believed that children seek out adults for social interaction beginning at birth; development occurs through these interactions.

For early childhood professionals, one of Vygotsky's most important concepts is that of the *zone of proximal development,* which Vygotsky defines as

> that area of development into which a child can be led in the course of interaction with a more competent partner, either adult or peer. [It] is not some clear-cut space that exists

> independently of the process of joint activity itself. Rather, it is the difference between what the child can accomplish independently and what he or she can achieve in conjunction with another, more competent person. The zone is thus created in the course of social interaction.[22]

From Vygotsky's point of view,

> Learning is not development; however, properly organized learning results in mental development and sets in motion a variety of developmental processes that would be impossible apart from learning. Thus, learning is a necessary part and universal aspect of the process of developing culturally organized, specifically human, psychological functions.[23]

For Vygotsky, learning is directly related to the course of child development.

Intersubjectivity is a second Vygotsky concept. Intersubjectivity is based on the idea that "individuals come to a task, problem, or conversation with their own subjective ways of making sense of it. If they then discuss their differing viewpoints, shared understanding may be attained. . . . In other words, in the course of communication participants may arrive at some mutually agreed-upon, or intersubjective, understanding."[24] Communication or dialogue between teacher and child literally becomes a means for helping children "scaffold," that is, develop new concepts and think their way to higher-level concepts.

This intersubjectivity is similar to Piaget's theory that disequilibrium sets the stage for assimilation and accommodation, and consequently, new schemes develop (see chapter 5). Furthermore, Vygotsky believed that as a result of teacher–child collaboration, the child uses concepts learned in the collaborative process to solve problems when the teacher is not present. As Vygotsky said, the child "continues to act in collaboration even though the teacher is not standing near him. . . . This help—this aspect of collaboration—is invisibly present. It is continued in what looks from the outside like the child's independent solution of the problem."[25] According to Vygotsky, social interactions and collaboration are essential ingredients in the processes of learning and development.

Many current practices such as cooperative learning, joint problem solving, coaching, collaboration, mentoring, and other forms of assisted learning are consistent with Vygotsky's theory of development.

Abraham Maslow

Abraham Maslow (1890–1970) developed a theory of motivation based on the satisfaction of needs. Maslow identified self-actualization, or self-fulfillment, as the highest need but maintained that self-actualization cannot be achieved until certain basic needs are met. These basic needs include life essentials such as food, safety, and security; belongingness and love; achievement and prestige; and aesthetic needs. We discuss Maslow's hierarchy of needs in greater detail in chapter 7.

For more information about Abraham Maslow's concept of self-actualization, go to the Companion Website at http://www.prenhall.com/morrison, select chapter 3, then choose the Linking to Learning module to connect to the Abraham Maslow site.

Erik Erikson

Erik H. Erikson (1902–1994) developed an influential theory of psychosocial development: Cognitive development occurs hand in hand with social development; you cannot separate the two. This is why Erikson's theory is so important. According to Erikson, children's personalities and social skills grow and develop within the context of society and in response to society's demands, expectations, values, and social institutions such as families, schools, and other child care programs. Adults, especially parents and teachers, are principal components of these environments and therefore play a powerful role in helping or hindering children in

their personality and cognitive development. For example, school-age children must deal with demands to learn new skills or risk a sense of incompetence—a crisis of "industry versus inferiority." We discuss Erikson's theory in more detail in chapter 7.

Howard Gardner

For more information about Howard Gardner's ideas, go to the Companion Website at http://www.prenhall.com/morrison, select any chapter, then choose Topic 3 of the ECE Supersite module.

Howard Gardner (b. 1943) is codirector of Harvard Project Zero and directs research on such themes as children's appreciation of figurative language, children's play and narrative abilities, the development of musical competence, and children's facility with media and technology, including television and computers.

Gardner personifies how the past, present, and future of children's education integrate with each other. As a contemporary theorist, he is changing our ideas about children's intellectual development and of how to promote their cognitive development. Gardner challenges early childhood professionals—indeed, all professionals—with his theory of *multiple intelligences*.

According to Piaget, mature biological thinking, or intelligence, consists of mainly logical/mathematical activities such as classification, seriation, numeration, time, and spatial relations. This view of intelligence as a single set of mental skills, measurable by an intelligence test, is the way it is generally conceived by educators and the public. Gardner, on the other hand, believes differently:

> a human intellectual competence must entail a set of skills of problem solving—enabling the individual to resolve genuine problems or difficulties that he or she encounters and, when appropriate, to create an effective product—and must also entail the potential for finding or creating problems: thereby laying the groundwork for the acquisition of new knowledge.[26]

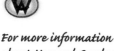

According to Gardner's theory of multiple intelligences, children demonstrate many types of intelligences. How would you apply his theory in the early childhood environment?

... video viewpoint

Emotional IQ

Researchers are now saying that the verbal intelligence of young children is not the only indicator of future success. Determining the emotional intelligence of people—including their reactions when they are angry, their ability to read others' nonverbal cues, and their self-control—may better identify individuals who can adapt to societal pressures and the demands of the workplace. Parents and early childhood professionals can play a role in helping children develop healthy emotional attitudes.

REFLECTIVE DISCUSSION QUESTIONS

Write down several examples of emotional intelligence. Give some examples of your personal emotional intelligence and how you manifest such emotions. How would you explain emotional intelligence to a parent? Why is impulse control so important in children's lives?

REFLECTIVE DECISION MAKING

How can you as an early childhood professional teach students about a healthy emotional intelligence? Give some examples of how you can role-play to demonstrate such emotions. What social skills can you help students learn to increase their emotional intelligence? What can you do to help children develop impulse control? Why is impulse control so important for success in life? What are some consequences of not being able to delay gratification and not being able to exercise impulse control? As an early childhood professional, how can you help children control their anger? Make a list of children's books and other materials that you could use to help children "read other children's emotions." What are some things that you can do to be your students' emotional tutor?

Based on this view, Gardner identifies eight intelligences: linguistic, musical, logical-mathematical, spatial, bodily-kinesthetic, interpersonal, intrapersonal, and naturalistic. He is considering the addition of a ninth intelligence, existential intelligence. This view of intelligence and its components has and will undoubtedly continue to influence educational thought and practice.

E. D. Hirsch

E. D. Hirsch Jr. (b. 1928), professor of English at the University of Virginia, is the contemporary articulator and proponent of an Essentialist Curriculum. Hirsch outlined his essentialist position in his manifesto, *Cultural Literacy: What Every American Needs to Know.* Cultural literacy, according to Hirsch, consists of those things that constitute the "common core" of a literate citizenry and that form the basis of American civilization. In other words, everyone should be culturally literate. Others who support cultural literacy include William Bennett, former U.S. secretary of education and author of the popular *Book of Virtues.*

Hirsch believes the lack of a cultural literacy curriculum contributes to children's general failure and poor school performance. He maintains, for example, that one reason children don't read with comprehension and understanding is because they have a limited cultural background—what Hirsch calls "cultural currency"—necessary to understand what they read. Hirsch argues, for example, that if a second-grader never heard of Alice as in

Program in Action

New City School

You don't have to be in early childhood education very long to hear a teacher say, "That boy is just soooo active." Indeed, this statement often has a "well, what can you do" tone to it. At New City School, an independent school in St. Louis with students 3 years old through 6th grade, both the tone and the words are different even though we certainly have lots of active boys. Our statement, "That's a very b-k kid," reflects our focus on Howard Gardner's Multiple Intelligences. We develop curriculum and look at children (and adults!) from the belief that there are at least eight intelligences: Bodily-Kinesthetic, Spatial, Logical-Mathematical, Musical, Linguistic, Naturalistic, Intra-Personal, and Inter-Personal. We believe children (and adults!) have strengths in all of these areas. We work to support children's growth in using their strengths and in understanding their particular strengths and those of others.

When New City teachers and administrators started working with Howard Gardner's Multiple Intelligences model about 10 years ago, we quickly agreed that our pre-school program had the fewest changes to make in order to reflect the Multiple Intelligences. Indeed, pre-school programs in general with their use of centers and choice time have traditionally given children many opportunities to explore and create. Puzzle areas and art centers offer spatial choices; pretending provides many inter-personal options; games and manipulatives offer logical-mathematical, spatial, and inter-personal choices; the list is long.

How then has our program changed? Two changes come quickly to mind. First, we now have a framework with which to plan centers and assessment. Our pre-school teachers use the Multiple Intelligences framework in planning centers and activities, checking themselves to make sure that children have opportunities to use and develop their various intelligences. Remember that b-k kid we talked about in the beginning? Rather than thinking about "containing him" with rules and time-outs, New City teachers plan centers making sure that there are bodily-kinesthetic activities available during choice time, not just at recess. Do we suddenly have an instant gym connected to our classroom? Definitely not! But, teachers now use adjacent halls and even classroom space for activities such as hopscotch, scooter boards, basketball, jumpropes and the like. Once children do activities, teachers provide parents and colleagues with assessment information using the Multiple Intelligence framework. Parents receive information about their children through multiple page progress reports and portfolio nights; here again, the Multiple Intelligences focus is used in showing the children's work and sharing their progress. So, the parents of that child with strong Bodily-Kinesthetic Intelligence learn that their child often chooses b-k related activities and that teachers use that bodily-kinesthetic strength in helping the child learn other things. Thus that child might practice counting while jumping rope or shooting baskets or learn letters by throwing bean bags at alphabet squares.

Secondly, we put a strong emphasis on the Personal Intelligences, Intra-Personal, knowing yourself, and Inter-Personal, knowing how to work and play with others. Believing strongly that these talents can be developed just as a musical or linguistic talent, New City teachers have developed activities and assessment techniques to support growth in the Personal Intelligences. In our 4/5s classrooms, for example, teachers regularly schedule "Buddy Days" during choice time. On a Buddy Day, children are paired up by the teachers and must then work together to choose activities for the morning. Teachers model, problem solve, comfort and support children as they learn to express their interests and accept the interests of their partners. Over the school year, these children learn to listen, negotiate, delay gratification and solve problems with a variety of peers. Parents recognize the importance we place on the Personals when they read our Progress Reports, where the first page is devoted entirely to the Personal Intelligences with assessment topics ranging from teamwork and appreciation for diversity to motivation and problem solving.

The Multiple Intelligences framework has allowed us to further develop an early childhood program where all of the Intelligences of the children are appreciated.

Contributed by Barbara James Thompson, New City School, St. Louis, Missouri.

Alice's Adventures in Wonderland, how can we expect the student to comprehend elements of a story that refers to Alice? Hirsch proposes that one solution is to teach students, beginning in kindergarten (indeed, even before, in the home), the names, dates, and events that constitute the core, the foundation of "our national cultural heritage" (see Figure 3.2).

a cappella
Aaron, Henry (Hank)
Abandon hope . . .
abbreviation
abdomen
abdominal cavity
Aberdeen
ABM
abolitionism
A-bomb
aborigines
abortion
Abraham and Isaac
abscess
Absence makes the heart grow fonder
absenteeism
absolute humidity
absolute monarchy
absolute power corrupts absolutely
absolute zero
abstract art
absurd, theater of the
AC
academic freedom
Academy, French
Academy, Plato's
Academy Awards
Acapulco
acceleration
accelerator, particle
according to Hoyle
accounting
acculturation
ace in the hole
Achilles
Achilles' heel
Achilles tendon
acid
acid rain
ACLU
acorns mighty oaks do grow, From little
Acquired Immune Deficiency Syndrome (AIDS)
acquittal
acronym
acrophobia
Acropolis
act of God
Actions speak louder than words
active site
active voice
actuary
acupuncture
acute angle
acute disease
A.D.
ad absurdum
ad hoc
ad hominem
ad nauseam
adagio
Adam and Eve
Adams, Henry
Adams, John
Adams, John Quincy
adaptation
Addams, Jane
Addis Ababa
Aden
adenoids
"Adeste Fidelis"
adhesion
adieu
adios
adipose tissue
Adirondack Mountains
adjective
Adonis
adrenal glands
adrenaline
Adriatic Sea
adsorption
adultery
Advent
Adventures of Huckleberry Finn, The
Adventures of Tom Sawyer, The
adverb
AEC
Aegean Sea
Aeneas
Aeneid
aerobic
aerodynamics
Aeschylus
Aesop's fables
aesthetics
affirmative action
affluent society
Affluent Society, The
Afghanistan
AFL-CIO
Africa
African National Congress (ANC)
African-American National Anthem
Agamemnon
Age cannot wither her, nor custom stale . . .
Age of Reason, The
Agnew, Spiro
agnosticism
agreement
agribusiness
Agriculture, Department of
Ahab, Captain
AI
Aida
AIDS
air, castles in the
air pollution
Air Quality Index
Akron
Alabama
Aladdin's lamp
Alamo
Alas, poor Yorick!
Alaska
Alaskan pipeline
Albania
Albany
albatross around one's neck
Albert, Prince
Alberta
Albuquerque
alchemy
alcoholism
Alcott, Louisa May
alderman
Aleutian Islands
Alexander the Great
Alexandria
algae
algebra
Alger, Horatio, Jr.
Algeria
Algiers
algorithm
Ali, Muhammad
Ali Baba
Alice's Adventures in Wonderland
Alien and Sedition Acts
alienation
alkali
All animals are equal . . .
All for one and one for all
All the news that's fit to print
All Quiet on the Western Front
All roads lead to Rome

Figure 3.2
Are You Culturally Literate?

Source: From Appendix, CULTURAL LITERACY *by E. D. Hirsch, Jr. Copyright © 1987 by Houghton Mifflin Company. Reprinted by permission of Houghton Mifflin Company. All rights reserved.*

After testing your knowledge of the above names, places, events, and terms, you may want to consult E. D. Hirsch's *Dictionary of Cultural Literacy: What Every American Needs to Know* for an A–Z description of what this essentialist thinks is important. Additionally, you may also want to review Hirsch's *First Dictionary of Cultural Knowledge: What Our Children Need to Know.* This revised second edition offers the common core of knowledge children should have by the end of grade school.

Hirsch is representative of the neoessentialists, who since the 1980s have led a revival in essentialist thinking and philosophy. He has established the Core Knowledge Foundation as a means of promoting a core essentialist curriculum. Many school districts and individual schools are teaching a core knowledge curriculum based on Hirsch's ideas. While Hirsch's revised benchmarks of cultural literacy include new books and topics that have a more multicultural perspective, he and his followers are criticized for Eurocentric views in which American cultural diversity is not acknowledged.

For essentialists, the teacher's role includes the following:

- Imparting knowledge. While it is a teacher's role to impart knowledge, it is the students' job to learn—whether or not they feel like it or like what they are learning.
- Initiating and promoting learning. In other words, the classroom is teacher directed, not student centered. The teacher is responsible for motivating students to learn and for maintaining the appropriate discipline for learning. Emphasis is placed on having students learn the basics they need for success in life.
- Engaging in teacher-directed activities characterized by discipline and teacher authority.

For essentialists, the student's role includes the following:

- Acquiring and using Western cultural knowledge
- Learning and using thinking skills
- Expending effort and devoting yourself to the learning process

From Luther to Hirsch: Basic Concepts Essential to Good Educational Practices

As They Relate to Children

For more information about how young children learn, go to the Companion Website at http://www.prenhall.com/morrison, select any chapter, then choose Topic 3 of the ECE Supersite module.

- Everyone needs to learn how to read and write.
- Children learn best when they use all their senses.
- All children are capable of being educated.
- All children should be educated to the fullest extent of their abilities.
- Education should begin early in life. Today especially there is an increased emphasis on beginning education at birth.
- Children should not be forced to learn but should be appropriately taught what they are ready to learn and should be prepared for the next stage of learning.
- Learning activities should be interesting and meaningful.

- Social interactions with teachers and peers are a necessary part of development.
- All children have many ways of knowing, learning, and relating to the world.

As They Relate to Teachers

- Teachers must show love and respect for all children.
- Teachers should be dedicated to the teaching profession.
- Good teaching is based on a theory, a philosophy, goals, and objectives.
- Children's learning is enhanced through the use of concrete materials.
- Teaching should move from the concrete to the abstract.
- Observation is a key way for determining children's needs.
- Teaching should be a planned, systematic process.
- Teaching should be child centered rather than adult or subject centered.
- Teaching should be based on children's interests.
- Teachers should collaborate with children as a means of promoting development.
- Teachers should plan so they incorporate all types of intelligence in their planning and activities.

As They Relate to Parents

- The family is an important institution in children's education and development. The family lays the foundation for all future education and learning.
- Parents are their children's primary educators. However, parents need help, education, and support to achieve this goal.
- Parents must guide and direct young children's learning.
- Parents should be involved in any educational program designed for their children.
- Everyone should have knowledge of and training for child rearing.
- Parents and other family members are collaborators in children's learning.
- Parents must encourage and support their children's many interests and their unique ways of learning.

Views of Children—Past and Present

How people view children determines how they teach and rear them and how society responds to their needs. As you read here about how people and society view children, try to clarify and change, when appropriate, what you believe. Also, identify social, environmental, and political factors that tend to support each particular view. Sometimes, of course, views overlap, so it is possible to synthesize ideas from several perspectives into a particular personal view.

Miniature Adults

Childhood has not always been considered a distinct period of life. During medieval times, the notion of childhood did not exist; little distinction was made between children and adults. The concept of children as miniature adults was logical for the time and conditions of medieval Europe. Economic conditions did not allow for a long childhood dependency. The only characteristics that separated children from adults were size and age. Children were expected to act as adults in every way, and they did so.

In many respects, at the beginning of the twenty-first century it is no different. Children are still viewed and treated as adults. Concern is growing that childhood as we knew or remember it is disappearing. Children are viewed as pseudoadults; they even dress like adults, in designer clothes and expensive footwear designed especially for them. Some believe that childhood is not only endangered but already gone. Others fear that, even when allowed a childhood, children are hurried and forced to grow up too fast too soon.

Reasons for society increasingly viewing children as adults are many and varied. Some contend that with more parents in the workforce, home and family life are more work centered than child centered. Children are given more responsibility at younger ages for their care, the care of siblings, and for household work. Also, children are being introduced to the adult world at earlier ages. Children attend R-rated movies, view adult programs on television, and encounter media violence at earlier ages. In many instances the boundaries between childhood and adulthood are blurred if not altogether eliminated.

Childhood and children are endangered in another way. In many countries of Latin America, Africa, and Asia, children are, of necessity, expected to be economically productive. They are members of the adult working world at age four, five, or six. The United Nations Educational, Scientific, and Cultural Organization (UNESCO) estimates that one hundred million children around the world work and live in city streets. In many countries children are involved in war as active participants and casualties. In the United States, as in many urban areas, children participate in gang-related and other activities as though they were adults. Almost daily, newspapers show these children dead or wounded and waiting for help.

In the United States, where child labor laws protect children from the world of adult work and exploitation, some people advocate allowing children to enter the workplace at earlier ages and for lower wages. In some rural settings, young children still have economic value. Approximately one million migrant children annually pick crops and help their parents earn a livelihood (see chapter 10). At the other end of the spectrum, child actors and models engage in highly profitable, and what some call glamorous, careers.

Encouraging children to act like adults and hurrying them toward adulthood causes conflicts between capabilities and expectations, particularly when early childhood professionals demand adultlike behavior from children and set unrealistic expectations. Problems associated with learning, behavior, and social skills can occur when children are constantly presented with tasks and activities that are developmentally inappropriate for them.

The Child as Sinful

Based primarily on the religious belief in original sin, the view of the child as sinful was widely accepted in the fourteenth through eighteenth centuries and particularly in colonial North America during the Puritan era of the sixteenth and seventeenth centuries. Misbehavior was a sign of this inherent sin. Those who sought to correct misbehavior emphasized forcing children to behave and using corporal punishment whenever "necessary." Misbehavior was taken as proof of the devil's influence, and "beating the devil out" of the child was an acceptable solution.

This view of inherent sinfulness persists, manifested in the belief that children need to be controlled through rigid supervision and insistence on unquestioning obedience to and respect for adults. Educational institutions are perceived as places where children can be taught "right" behavior. The number of private and religious schools that emphasize respect, obedience, and correct behavior is growing because of parents' hopes of rearing children who are less susceptible to the temptations of crime, drugs, and declining moral values. Also, many Christian religious conservatives advocate a "biblical" approach to child rearing, encouraging parents to raise their children to obey them. Disobedience is viewed as sinful, and obedience is promoted, in part, through strict discipline. With the emphasis on conservative child rearing, many parents are turning to biblically based approaches to child rearing.

Blank Tablets

The English philosopher John Locke (1632–1704) believed that children were born into the world as tabula rasae, or blank tablets. After extensive observations, Locke concluded, "There is not the least appearance of any settled ideas at all in them; especially of ideas answering the terms which make up those universal propositions that are esteemed innate principles."[27] Locke believed that children's experiences, through sensory impressions, determined what they learned and consequently what they became. The blank tablet view presupposes no innate genetic code or inborn traits; that is, children are born with no predisposition toward any behavior except what is characteristic of human beings. The sum of what a child becomes depends on the nature and quality of experience. In other words, environment is the primary determinant.

The blank tablet view has several implications for teaching and child rearing. If children are seen as empty vessels to be filled, the teacher's job is to fill them—to present knowledge without regard to needs, interests, or readiness for learning. What is important is that children learn what is taught. Children become what adults make of them.

This view de-emphasizes individual differences and assumes that as children are exposed to the same environmental influences, they will tend to behave and even think the same. This concept is the basis for many educational beliefs and practices in socialist countries. Children begin schooling early, often at six weeks of age, and are taught a standard curriculum that promotes a common political consciousness. They are expected to behave in ways that are consistent with and appropriate to how a citizen of the state should behave.

Growing Plants

A perennially popular view of children envisages them as growing plants, with the educator or parent acting as gardener. Classrooms and homes are greenhouses in which children grow and mature in harmony with their natural growth patterns. A consequence of growth and maturing is that children unfold, much as a flower blooms under the proper conditions. In other words, what children become results from natural growth and a nurturing environment. Two key ingredients of this natural unfolding are play and readiness. The content and process of learning are included in play, and materials and activities are designed to promote play.

Children become ready for learning through motivation and play. This concept prompts teaching subjects and skills when children reach the point at which they can benefit from appropriate instruction. Lack of readiness to learn indicates that the child has not sufficiently matured; the natural process of unfolding has not occurred.

Belief in this concept is evident in certain social and educational policies, such as proposals to raise the age requirements for entry into kindergarten and first grade so that chil-

dren have more time to mature and get ready for school (as discussed previously). Many people also believe each child's maturation occurs in accordance with an innate timetable, that there is a "best time" for learning specific tasks. They feel it is important to allow time for children's inner tendencies to develop and that teachers and parents should not "force" learning. This maturation process is as important as, if not more important than, children's experiences. Many contemporary programs operate on the unfolding concept, whether or not it is explicitly stated.

Evidence for the widespread view of children as growing plants is poignantly illustrated by one father's reflections on the results and implications of his son's kindergarten screening test. This father was struck by the fact that his son had performed adequately, but not perfectly, and wondered what relevance the kindergarten screening test actually had to his son's future school performance.

> We then went upstairs to water some late seedlings that go into our garden for fall. Radicchio . . . broccoli, lettuce and cauliflower. Noah ran his finger over the sprouts and giggled. They tickled. There they were, uncounted dozens of sprouts, all green, all about the same height.
>
> And it came to me.
>
> As I nurture and fertilize and pull the weeds that will want to clog this boy's growing-up years, he, too, will come to fruition. I'll have some control over that—some, not total, I realize. He may turn out to be the finest of the group, the biggest broccoli, the finest head of radicchio. He may command respect, praise and a high price in the marketplace of life.[28]

Property

The view that children are property has persisted throughout history. Its foundation is that children are the property of their parents or institutions. This view is justified in part by the idea that, as creators of children, parents have a right to them and their labors. Children are, in a real sense, the property of their parents. Parents have broad authority and jurisdiction over their children. Interestingly, few laws interfere with the right of parents to control their children's lives, although this situation is changing somewhat as children are given more rights and the rights they have are protected.

Laws (although difficult to enforce) protect children from physical and emotional abuse. Where there are compulsory attendance laws, parents must send their children to school. Generally, however, parents have a free hand in dealing with their children. Legislatures and courts are reluctant to interfere in what is considered a sacrosanct parent–child relationship. Parents are generally free to exercise full authority over their children. Within certain broad limits, most parents feel their children are theirs to do with as they please. Parents who embrace this view see themselves as their children's decision makers and may place their own best interests above those of their children.

Investments in the Future

Closely associated with the notion of children as property is the view that children represent future wealth or potential for parents and a nation. Since medieval times, people have viewed child rearing as an investment in the future. Many parents assume (not always consciously) that, when they are no longer able to work or must retire, their children will provide for them. Consequently, having children becomes a means to an end. Seeing that children are clothed and fed ensures their future economic contribution to their parents.

This view of children as investments, particularly in their parents' future, is being dramatically played out in contemporary society. More middle-age adults are becoming "parents" to their own aging and ill parents. This group, known as the "sandwich generation," also is taking care of their grandchildren, because their own children have surrendered responsibility for child rearing as a result of divorce, death, abandonment, or other circumstances. Many of these middle-age parents who thought they were investing in their future through their children may not have any investment at all.

Over the last several decades, some social policy in the United States has been based partly on the view that children are future investments for society in general. Many programs are built on the underlying assumption that preventing problems in childhood leads to more productive adulthood. An extension of this attitude is that preventing a problem is less expensive than curing one. Some local educational programs thus emphasize identifying the problems of children and their families early, to take preventive rather than remedial action. As professionals, we also know that besides being more expensive, remediation is not as effective as prevention.

Particularly during the 1960s, many federal programs were based on the idea of conserving one of the country's greatest resources—its children. Head Start, Follow Through, and child welfare programs are products of this view, which has resulted in a "human capital," or "investment," rationale for child care and other services.

The public believes a primary goal of education is to develop children who will be productive and help protect the nation against foreign competition. Therefore, the early education of young children in "good" programs is seen as one way to strengthen the United States economically. Thus, the country's best defense against outside economic forces is a well-educated, economically productive population. From this perspective, then, investing in children is seen as an investment in the country. Also, the view that children are our greatest wealth implies that we cannot and should not waste this potential.

Some believe, however, that this perspective of children as an investment in the future fails to consider children's intrinsic human worth. Trying to make a nation stronger through its children tends to emphasize national priorities over individuals. Also, solving a nation's problems is not and should not be viewed primarily as a "children's" problem.

Children as Persons with Rights

A contemporary legal and humanistic view recognizes children as individuals with rights of their own. While children are often still treated as economic commodities and individuals who need protection, their rights are beginning to be defined, promoted, and defended. Since children are not organized into political groups, others must act as their advocates. Courts and social service agencies are becoming particular defenders.

In 1989, the UN Convention on the Rights of the Child was adopted by 159 member states of the UN General Assembly. The convention, in reality a human treaty, went into effect on 2 September 1990, after ratification by more than twenty nations. It has the status of a legally binding treaty for all nations that sign it.

The convention contains fifty-four articles, and the highlights are printed in Figure 3.3. The articles convey a very strong view of the child as a family member and individual. You will note that the convention combines political, civil, economic, and cultural rights. In this sense, the convention acknowledges that health and economic well-being are also essential to political freedoms and rights. In addition, by extending rights to individual children, the convention challenges the view of children as property.

The National Education Association (NEA), the nation's largest teachers' professional organization, adopted the following Bill of Rights for Children as presented to the NEA Representative Assembly on 4 July 1991:

We, the People of the United States, in order to achieve a more perfect society, fulfill our moral obligations, further our founding ideals and preserve the continued blessings of liberty, do hereby proclaim this Bill of Rights for Children.

I. No child in a land of abundance shall be wanting for plentiful and nutritional food.

- Every child has the inherent right to life, and States shall ensure, to the maximum, child survival and development.
- Every child has the right to a name and a nationality from birth.
- When courts, welfare institutions or administrative authorities deal with children, the child's best interests shall be a primary consideration. The child's opinions shall be given careful consideration.
- States shall ensure that each child enjoys full rights without discrimination or distinctions of any kind.
- Children should not be separated from their parents, unless by competent authorities for their well-being.
- States should facilitate reunification of families by permitting them to travel into, or out of, their territories.
- Parents have the primary responsibility for a child's upbringing, but States shall provide them with appropriate assistance and develop child-care institutions.
- States shall protect children from physical or mental harm and neglect, including sexual abuse or exploitation.
- States shall provide parentless children with suitable alternative care. The adoption process shall be carefully regulated and international agreements should be sought to provide safeguards and assure legal validity if and when adoptive parents intend to move the child from his or her country of birth.
- Disabled children shall have the right to special treatment, education and care.
- The child is entitled to the highest attainable standard of health. States shall ensure that health care is provided to all children, placing emphasis on preventative measures, health education and reduction of infant mortality.
- Primary education shall be free and compulsory; discipline in schools should respect the child's dignity. Education should prepare the child for life in a spirit of understanding, peace and tolerance.
- Children shall have time to rest and play and equal opportunities for cultural and artistic activities.
- States shall protect the child from economic exploitation and work that may interfere with education or be harmful to health and well-being.
- States shall protect children from the illegal use of drugs and involvement in drug production or trafficking.
- All efforts shall be made to eliminate the abduction and trafficking of children.
- Capital punishment or life imprisonment shall not be imposed for crimes committed before the age of 18.
- Children in detention should be separated from adults; they must not be tortured or suffer cruel and degrading treatment.
- No child under 15 should take any part in hostilities; children exposed to armed conflict shall receive special protection.
- Children of minority and indigenous populations shall freely enjoy their own culture, religion and language.
- Children who have suffered maltreatment, neglect or detention should receive appropriate treatment for recovery and rehabilitation.
- Children involved in infringements of the penal law shall be treated in a way that promotes their sense of dignity and worth and that aims at reintegrating them into society.
- States should make the rights in the Convention widely known to both adults and children.

Figure 3.3
Highlights of the United Nations Convention on the Rights of the Child

Source: United Nations, Convention on the Rights of the Child *(New York: United Nations Department of Public Information, 1993), pp. 4–8. Reprint 4717—May 1993—20M. Publication Source DPI/1101, United Nations.*

II. A society as advanced in medical knowledge and abilities as ours shall not deny medical attention to any child in need.

III. Whereas security is an essential requirement for a child's healthy development, the basic security of a place to live shall be guaranteed to every child.

IV. To ensure the potential of the individual and nation, every child at school shall have the right to a quality education.

V. The government, whose primary role is to protect and defend at all levels, shall assure that children are safeguarded from abuse, violence, and discrimination.[29]

Although children of the world are gaining more rights, societal attitudes toward children's rights are often still ambivalent. Some children's rights supporters believe children need advocates to act on their behalf. They maintain that children are politically disenfranchised, economically disadvantaged, the personal property of their parents, vulnerable to abuse and exploitation because of their lack of experience, and have passive legal status. On the other hand, many people, including some parents, feel they should be allowed to raise their children as they think best, free of interference from children's rights advocates.

Rights are being extended to children in ways that would not have been thought possible even ten years ago. Particularly in the area of fetal rights, parents are encountering conflicts between their rights and the lives of their unborn children. Many states require places that sell liquor to post a sign reading, "Warning: Drinking alcoholic beverages during pregnancy can cause birth defects." Major controversies are arising between the right of the unborn and the rights of pregnant women. Such questions as "What rights of the pregnant woman supersede those of her unborn child?" and "Does the government or other agency have the right to intervene in a woman's life on behalf of her unborn child?" are not easy to answer. Controversy continues between those groups that advocate for the rights of the unborn fetus and groups that advocate for a mother's rights, including privacy, emotional and physical integrity, and self-determination. Viewpoints as to whose rights take precedence—the fetus's or the mother's—are becoming increasingly polarized.

The debate regarding children's rights will continue as the rights of children become further defined and clarified through the judicial system. The rights of all children will be examined, and more special interest groups will join the trend to gain even more rights for children.

A review of the ways we see children leads to some intriguing questions. In this generation, are parents and professionals as child centered as they should be? Are early childhood professionals interested in helping children receive the best so they can realize their best? What we know we should do and what we do are often two different things. Public and social policies often supersede our interest in children. Wars, national defense, and economics sometimes take precedence over questions of what is best for children.

The Return of Child-Centered Education

As early childhood professionals and the public increasingly view children as persons with rights, educators are implementing more child-centered approaches. The field of early childhood education has always been to a greater or lesser degree child centered, and today it is decidedly more so. This rediscovery and reemphasis on child-centered education is occurring for a number of reasons. First, society in general is much more interested in the whole child and efforts to address all of children's needs, not just their academic needs. As a result, there is much more concern for encouraging children to be healthy and lead healthy lifestyles. Consequently, interest in providing children with medical immunizations and seeing that all children are fully immunized by age two has received a lot of attention. Programs to help

To take an online self-test on this chapter's contents, go to the Companion Website at http://www.prenhall.com/morrison, select chapter 3, then choose the Self Test module.

children be free of drugs are common in early childhood and primary programs. Concern for the welfare of children in all areas of their growth and development is evident.

Evidence for the rebirth of child-centered approaches to early childhood education is also seen in such pedagogical practices as cooperative learning (see chapter 10), having children make choices about what they will learn and how, and the use of activities and strategies to promote children's thinking. Other child-centered approaches very much in evidence include programs designed to promote children's self-esteem; multiage grouping; having professionals stay with or teach the same group of children for more than one year; transition programs that help children move easily from program to program, grade to grade, and agency to agency; and concern for children's health, safety, and nutrition.

For additional Internet resources or to complete an online activity for this chapter, go to the Companion Website at http://www.prenhall.com/morrison, select chapter 3, then choose the Linking to Learning or Making Connections module.

All great educators have believed in the basic goodness of children—that is, that children by nature tend to behave in socially acceptable ways. They believed it was the role of the teacher to provide the environment for this goodness to manifest itself. Young children learn to behave in certain ways according to how they are treated, the role models they have to emulate, and the environments in which they have to grow. Children do not emerge from the womb with a propensity toward badness but tend to grow and behave as they are treated and taught.

A central point that Luther, Comenius, Pestalozzi, Froebel, Montessori, and Dewey sought to make about our work as educators, regardless of context—parent or early childhood professional—is that we must do it well and act as though we really care about those for whom we have been called to serve.

Activities for Further Enrichment

Applications

1. Reflect on your experiences in elementary school. What experiences were most meaningful? Why? What teachers do you remember best? Why?
2. Interview the parents of children who attend a private or alternative preschool, kindergarten, or elementary school. What are their reasons for sending their children to these schools? Do you agree or disagree with their reasons?
3. To what extent do religious beliefs determine educational practice? Give specific examples from your own experiences and from current accounts in newspapers and other media.
4. Reflect about how your philosophy of education has been or is being influenced by the ideas and contributions of great educators. Which of the ideas has influenced you the most? What ideas of yours have been most challenged by what you read in this chapter?

Field Experiences

1. Visit early childhood programs in your area. Observe to determine how they apply the basic ideas of the people you studied in this chapter.
2. As you visit schools, classrooms, and agencies, keep a journal in which you identify the philosophy or theory you think underlies the curriculum, teaching methods, and approach to learning. Reflect on your observations and consider the implications for your professional practice.
3. Develop an observation guideline based on Gardner's intelligences. Observe children and provide specific examples that demonstrate individual specific intelligences.

Research

1. Research journals, newspapers, the Internet, and other sources to determine how people, agencies, and legislation are influencing early childhood education. Do you think these influences will be long-lasting? Why? Why not?
2. A clipping file of newspaper, journal, and magazine articles relating to education is a great way to observe philosophies

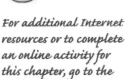

and theories in action. Many articles will critique how the schools are or are not implementing a certain reform or practice. As you read and review these articles, identify the ideas and philosophies that are influencing a particular point of view.

3. You have just been assigned to write a brief historical summary of the major ideas for the key educational pioneers you read about in this chapter. You are limited to fifty words for each person and are to write as though you were the person. For example:

   Locke: "At birth the mind is a blank slate and experiences are important for making impressions on the mind. I believe learning occurs best through the senses. A proper education begins early in life and hands-on experiences are an important part of education."

Readings for Further Enrichment

Dewey, John. *Experience and Education*. New York: Collier, 1938.

Dewey's comparison of traditional and progressive education. Provides a good insight into what Dewey believed schools should be like.

Fogarty, R., and Bellanca, J. *Multiple Intelligences: A Collection*. Boston: Allyn and Bacon, 1998.

Contains research and writing about Howard Gardner's multiple intelligences theory. Students will find that the articles explore practical applications of the theory and provide supporting evidence that teaching to the multiple intelligences is effective with all learners.

Gardner, Howard. *The Disciplined Mind: What All Students Should Understand*. New York: Collier, 1999.

In Gardner's latest text, he describes his "preferred path" for students in the K–12 grades to understand the wisdom of the ages. According to Gardner, schools should think of disciplinary knowledge and understanding as every child's birthright.

Hymes, J. L., Jr. *Twenty Years in Review: A Look at 1971–1990*. Washington, DC: National Association for the Education of Young Children, 1991.

A treasure trove of detail about recent history in early childhood education. Each chapter chronicles a year's history.

Montore, Will S. *Comenius and the Beginnings of Educational Reform*, 19th ed. New Hampshire: Ayer, 2000.

The author traces the reform movement in education before and up to Comenius, who was responsible for the movement's most significant contributions. He also talks about the life of Comenius and his educational writings.

Murphy, Daniel. *Comenius: A Critical Reassessment of His Life and Work*. Dublin: Irish Academy Press, 1995.

Murphy reexamines the principles of Comenius's pedagogic philosophy, giving particular attention to the learner-centered methods of teaching, which constitute his main legacy to world education.

Linking to Learning

Martin Luther

http://www.iclnet.org/pub/resources/text/wittenberg/wittenberg-home.html

Links to many of Luther's writings on-line.

John Amos Comenius

http://www.moravian.org/lifemag.htm

Comenius was honored in Life *magazine's 1997 "The Millennium" cover story under the title "The Invention of Childhood."*

John Locke

http://www2.msstate.edu/~src5/educator.html

A list of links to important works by Locke, including his personal epitaph, in which he states his philosophies of education.

Jean-Jacques Rousseau

http://www.infed.org/thinkers/et-rous.htm

Contains a brief statement by Rousseau on education, as well as a few links to other Rousseau sites.

Johann Heinrich Pestalozzi

http://www.infed.org/thinkers/et-pest.htm

From the same site as the above concerning Rousseau, a similar page about Pestalozzi.

Robert Owen

http://www.infed.org/thinkers/et-owen.htm

A bibliography of writings by Robert Owen.

Friedrich Wilhelm Froebel

http://www.infed.org/thinkers/et-froeb.htm

Biography and bibliography of the father of the kindergarten.

Maria Montessori

http://www.3000.com/montessori_sf/index.htm

The Web site of the Maria Montessori School and Teacher Training Center in San Francisco. This site contains brief descriptions of Montessori's ideas as they apply to various age groups.

John Dewey

http://www.siu.edu/~deweyctr/

The Center for Dewey Studies is housed at the University of Southern Illinois at Carbondale, and its Web site offers on-line documents about Dewey, numerous links, and instructions for joining the John Dewey Internet mailing list.

Jean Piaget

http://www.piaget.org/

The Jean Piaget Society's Web site is an excellent source of information regarding publications and conferences about the work and theories of Piaget.

Lev Vygotsky

http://www.bestpraceduc.org/people/LevVygotsky.html

An extensive bibliography of reading concerning Vygotsky.

Abraham Maslow

http://www.rebt.org/essays/achieve1.html

A detailed description of Maslow's concept of self-actualization.

Erikson Tutorial Home Page

http://www.snycorva.cortland.edu/~andersmd/erik/welcome.html

An introduction to and summary of Erik Erikson's eight stages of psychosocial development.

Howard Gardner

http://www.pz.harvard.edu/PIs/HG/html

A biography of Howard Gardner as well as his work on Harvard's Project Zero.

Engines for Education

http://www.ils.nwu.edu/~e_for_e/

Engines is a "hyper-book" written by Roger Schank, Director of ILS, and Chip Cleary, a graduate student of Dr. Schank, about what's wrong with the education system, how to reform it, and especially, about the role of educational technology in that reform. It includes links to articles by and about E. D. Hirsch Jr.

The History of Education and Childhood

http://www.socsci.kun.nl/ped/whp/histeduc/index.html

An international archive of links and source materials about the history of education and the history of childhood.

ENDNOTES

1 John Amos Comenius, *The Great Didactic of John Amos Comenius*, ed. and trans. M. W. Keating (New York: Russell & Russell, 1967), 58.

2 Ibid., 127.

3 John Locke, *An Essay Concerning Human Understanding*, ed. Peter H. Nidditch (Oxford: Oxford University Press, 1975), 104.

4 Jean-Jacques Rousseau, *Émile; Or, Education*, trans. Barbara Foxley (New York: Dutton, Everyman's Library, 1933), 5.

5 Jean-Jacques Rousseau, *Émile; Or, Education*, ed. and trans. William Boyd (New York: Teachers College Press, by arrangement with Heinemann, London, 1962), 11–15.

6 Alexander S. Neill, *Summerhill* (New York: Hart, 1960), 4.

7 Roger DeGuimps, *Pestalozzi: His Life and Work* (New York: Appleton, 1890), 205.

8 Ibid., 196.

9 S. Bamford, *Passages in the Life of a Radical* (London: London Simpkin Marshall, 1844), n.p.

10 Friedrich Froebel, *The Education of Man*, trans. M. W. Hailman (New York: Appleton, 1887), 55.

11 Friedrich Froebel, *Pedagogics of the Kindergarten*, trans. Josephine Jarvis (New York: Appleton, 1902), 32.

12 Froebel gifts and blocks, http://www.geocities.com/Athens/Forum/7905/fblgaben.html, 1999.

13 Maria Montessori, *The Discovery of the Child*, trans. M. J. Costelloe (Notre Dame, IN: Fides, 1967), 22.

14 Maria Montessori, *The Montessori Method*, trans. Anne E. George (Cambridge, MA: Bentley, 1967), 38.

15 Montessori, *The Discovery of the Child*, 28.

16 Ibid., 37.

17 Reginald D. Archambault, ed., *John Dewey on Education—Selected Writings* (New York: Random House, 1964), 430.

18 Henry Suzzallo, ed., *John Dewey's Interest and Effort in Education* (Boston: Houghton Mifflin, 1913), 65.

[19] Archambault, *John Dewey on Education,* 170–171.

[20] Edwin G. Boring, ed., *A History of Psychology in Autobiography,* vol. 4 (Worcester, MA: Clark University Press, 1952; New York: Russell & Russell, 1968), 244.

[21] L. S. Vygotsky, *Mind in Society* (Cambridge, MA: Harvard University Press, 1978), 244.

[22] Jonathan R. H. Tudge, "Processes and Consequences of Peer Collaboration: A Vygotskian Analysis," *Child Development* 63(1992): 1365.

[23] Ibid.

[24] Vygotsky, *Mind in Society,* 90.

[25] Tudge, "Processes and Consequences," 1365.

[26] Howard Gardner, *Frames of Mind* (New York: Basic Books, 1983), 60–61.

[27] John Locke, *An Essay Concerning Human Understanding* (New York: Dover, 1999), 92–93.

[28] Paul Wilkes, "The First Test of Childhood," *Newsweek* 114(1989), 8.

[29] National Education Association, *Bill of Rights for Children* (Washington, DC: Author, 1991).

CHAPTER 4

If education is always to be conceived along the same antiquated lines of a mere transmission of knowledge, there is little to be hoped from it. . . . For what is the use of transmitting knowledge if the individual's total development lags behind?

And so we discovered that education is not something which the teacher does, but that it is a natural process which develops spontaneously in the human being.

MARIA MONTESSORI

Montessori Education

Independence, Respect, and Self-Directed Learning

Focus Questions

1. Why are Montessori programs so popular?
2. What are the main philosophical and pedagogical principles of the Montessori program?
3. How do the prepared environment and learning materials support the Montessori method?
4. What are the essential roles of teachers and children in Montessori programs?
5. What are the basic characteristics of a good Montessori program?

To review the chapter focus questions online, go to the Companion Website at http://www.prenhall.com/morrison and select chapter 4.

If we were to single out one person to credit with the ongoing revival of early childhood education, it would be Maria Montessori. The Montessori method helped create and renew interest in early childhood education beginning about 1965. Today, when parents and professionals search for exemplary early childhood programs, Montessori is one of the models they turn to.

Why Are Montessori Programs So Popular?

To check your understanding of this chapter with the online Study Guide, go to the Companion Website at http://www.prenhall.com/morrison, select chapter 4, then choose the Study Guide module.

The Montessori system is popular, intriguing, and attractive to parents and others for a number of reasons. First, Montessori education has always been identified as a quality program for young children. Second, parents who observe a good Montessori program like what they see: orderliness, independent children, self-directed learning, a calm environment, and children at the center of the learning process. Third, Montessori's philosophy is based on the premise that education begins at birth, and the idea of early learning has been and remains popular with parents. Fourth, public schools include Montessori in their magnet programs, giving parents choices in the kind of program their children will have at a particular school. It is also used as a means of desegregation.

Over the past decade the implementation of Montessori education has increased tremendously in public school early childhood programs. Montessori would probably smilingly approve of the contemporary use of her method to once again help change the nature and character of early childhood education.

Principles of the Montessori Method

The following basic principles are a synthesis of Montessori ideas and practices. They fairly and accurately represent how Montessori educators implement the Montessori method in many kinds of programs across the United States.

Respect for the Child

Respect for the child is the cornerstone on which all other Montessori principles rest. As Montessori said:

> As a rule, however, we do not respect children. We try to force them to follow us without regard to their special needs. We are overbearing with them, and above all, rude; and then we expect them to be submissive and well-behaved, knowing all the time how strong is their instinct of imitation and how touching their faith in and admiration of us. They will imitate us in any case. Let us treat them, therefore, with all the kindness which we would wish to help to develop in them. And by kindness is not meant caresses. Should we not call anyone who embraced us at the first time of meeting rude, vulgar and ill-bred? Kindness consists in interpreting the wishes of others, in conforming one's self to them, and sacrificing, if need be, one's own desire.[1]

Because each child is unique, education should be individualized:

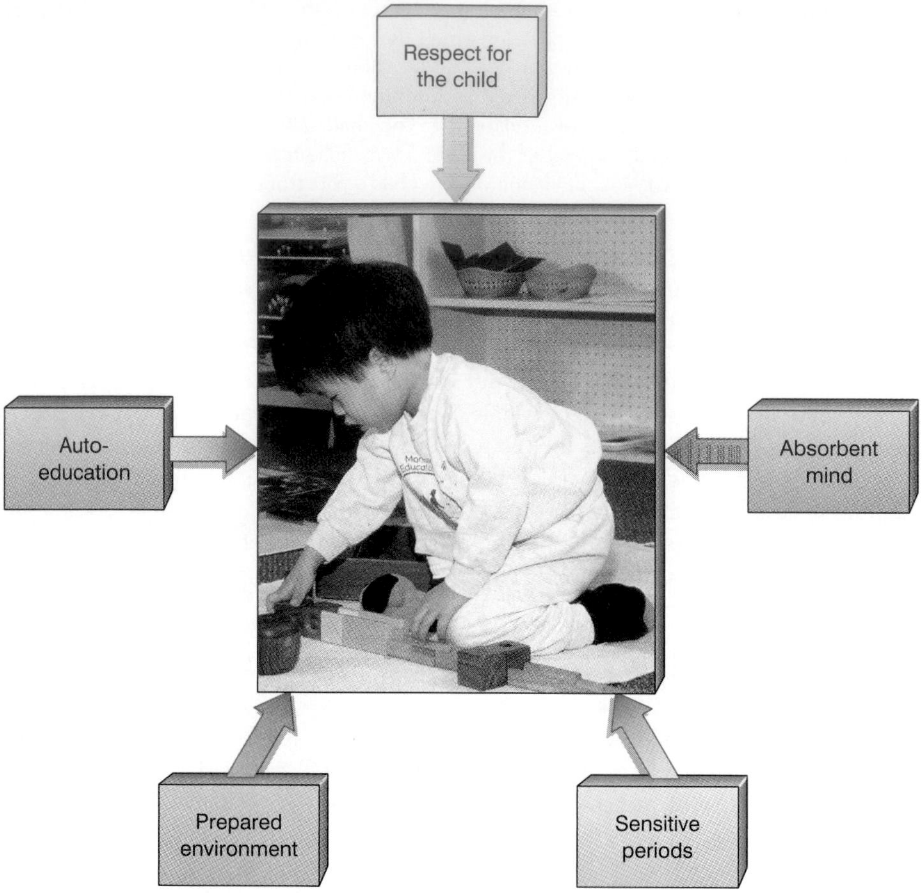

These basic principles are the foundation of the Montessori method. Taken as a whole, they constitute a powerful model for helping all children learn to their fullest.

Figure 4.1
Basic Montessori Principles

> The educator must be as one inspired by a deep worship of life, and must, through this reverence, respect, while he observes with human interest, the development of the child life. Now, child life is not an abstraction; it is the life of individual children. There exists only one real biological manifestation: the living individual; and toward single individuals, one by one observed, education must direct itself.[2]

Although we discussed in chapter 3 that today many children are viewed and treated as adults, we believe that children are not miniature adults and should not be treated as such. Montessori was firm in her belief that a child's life must be recognized as separate and distinct from that of the adult. She attributed most of the responsibility for restricting the education of young children to adults who impose their ideas and dreams on children, failing to distinguish between children's lives and their own.

> In their dealings with children adults do not become egotistic but egocentric. They look upon everything pertaining to a child's soul from their own point of view and, conse-

quently, their misapprehensions are constantly on the increase. Because of this egocentric view, adults look upon the child as something empty that is to be filled through their own efforts, as something inert and helpless for which they must do everything, as something lacking an inner guide and in constant need of direction. In conclusion we may say that the adult looks upon himself as the child's creator and judges the child's actions as good or bad from the viewpoint of his own relations to the child. The adult makes himself the touchstone of what is good and evil in the child. He is infallible, the model upon which the child must be molded. Any deviation on the child's part from adult ways is regarded as an evil which the adult hastens to correct.

An adult who acts in this way, even though he may be convinced that he is filled with zeal, love, and a spirit of sacrifice on behalf of his child, unconsciously suppresses the development of the child's own personality.[3]

Educators and parents show respect for children in many ways. Helping children do things and learn for themselves, for example, encourages and promotes independence. At the same time, it also demonstrates a basic respect for their needs as individuals to be independent and self-regulating. When children have choices, they are able to develop the skills and abilities necessary for effective learning, autonomy, and positive self-esteem. These practices are so much more respectful of children than always doing for them or insisting that they do things as adults want them to. (The theme of respect for children resurfaces in our discussion of guiding behavior in chapter 12.)

The Absorbent Mind

Montessori believed that children are not educated by others. Rather, one must educate oneself: "It may be said that we acquire knowledge by using our minds; but the child absorbs knowledge directly into his psychic life. Simply by continuing to live, the child learns to speak his native tongue."[4] This is the concept of the *absorbent mind*.

Many parents and professionals consider the Montessori approach to be ideal, as it encourages independence and responsibility in child-centered settings. What are three things about a Montessori program that appeal to parents?

There are unconscious and conscious stages in the development of the absorbent mind. From birth to three years, the unconscious absorbent mind develops the senses used for seeing, hearing, tasting, smelling, and touching. The child literally absorbs everything.

From three to six years, the conscious absorbent mind selects sensory impressions from the environment and further develops the senses. In this phase children are selective in that they refine what they know. For example, children in the unconscious stage merely see and absorb an array of colors without distinguishing among them; however, from three on, they develop the ability to distinguish, match, and grade colors. Montessori challenged the teacher to think through this concept of the absorbent mind:

> How does a child, starting with nothing, orient himself in this complicated world? How does he come to distinguish things, by what marvelous means does he come to learn a language in all its minute details without a teacher but merely by living simply, joyfully, and without fatigue, whereas an adult is in constant need of assistance to orient himself in a new environment to learn a new language, which he finds tedious and which he will never master with the same perfection with which a child acquires his own mother tongue?[5]

Montessori wanted us to understand that children cannot help but learn. Simply by living, children learn from their environment. Children are born to learn and they are remarkable learning systems. Children learn because they are thinking beings. What they learn depends greatly on the people in their environment, what those people say and do, and how they react. In addition, available experiences and materials also help determine the type and quality of learning—and thus the type and quality of the individual.

Early childhood professionals are reemphasizing the idea that children are born into the world learning and with constant readiness and ability to learn. We will discuss these concepts further in chapter 7.

Sensitive Periods

Montessori believed there are sensitive periods when children are more susceptible to certain behaviors and can learn specific skills more easily:

> A sensitive period refers to a special sensibility which a creature acquires in its infantile state, while it is still in a process of evolution. It is a transient disposition and limited to the acquisition of a particular trait. Once this trait or characteristic has been acquired, the special sensibility disappears. . . .
>
> A child learns to adjust himself and make acquisitions in his sensitive periods. These are like a beam that lights interiorly or a battery that furnishes energy. It is this sensibility which enables a child to come in contact with the external world in a particularly intense manner. At such a time everything is easy; all is life and enthusiasm. Every effort marks an increase in power. Only when the goal has been obtained does fatigue and the weight of indifference come on.
>
> When one of these psychic passions is exhausted, another area is enkindled. Childhood thus passes from conquest to conquest in a constant rhythm that constitutes its joy and happiness.[6]

The secret of using sensitive periods in teaching is to recognize them when they occur. While all children experience the same sensitive periods (e.g., a sensitive period for writing), the sequence and timing vary for each child. Therefore, it becomes the role of the directress (as Montessori teachers are often called) or the parent to detect times of sensitivity and pro-

vide the setting for optimum fulfillment. Observation thus becomes crucial for teachers and parents. Indeed, many educators believe that information gained by observation of children's achievement and behavior is more accurate than that acquired through the use of tests (see chapter 1). Chapter 11 will help you learn how to do this through guidelines for observing children.

The sensitive period for many learnings occurs early in life, during the time of rapid physical, language, and cognitive growth. Experiences necessary for optimum development must be provided at this time. Through observation and practice, for example, Montessori was convinced the sensitive period for development of language was a year or two earlier than originally thought.

Once the sensibility for learning a particular skill occurs, it does not arise again with the same intensity. For example, children will never learn languages as well as when the special sensitivity for language learning occurs. Montessori said, "The child grows up speaking his parent's tongue, yet to grownups the learning of a language is a very great intellectual achievement."[7]

Teachers must do three things: recognize that there are sensitive periods, learn to detect them, and capitalize on them by providing the optimum learning setting to foster children's development. Much of what early childhood professionals mean by readiness is contained in Montessori's concept of sensitive periods.

The Prepared Environment

Montessori believed that children learn best in a prepared environment, which can be any setting—classroom, a room at home, nursery, or playground. The purpose of the prepared environment is to make children independent of adults. It is a place in which children can *do things for themselves*. The prepared environment also makes learning materials and experiences available to children in an orderly format. The ideal classrooms Montessori described are really what educators advocate when they talk about child-centered education and active learning.

Following their introduction to the prepared environment, children can come and go according to their desires and needs, deciding for themselves which materials to work with. Montessori removed the typical school desks from the classroom and replaced them with tables and chairs at which children could work individually or in small groups. In a modern Montessori classroom, much of a child's work is done on the floor. Montessori saw no reason for a teacher's desk, since the teacher should be involved with the children where they are doing their work. She also introduced child-sized furniture, lowered chalkboards, and outside areas in which children could, at will, take part in gardening and other outdoor activities.

Her concept of a classroom was a place in which children could do things for themselves, play with material placed there for specific purposes, and educate themselves. She developed a classroom free of many of the inhibiting elements in some of today's classrooms. Freedom is the essential characteristic of the prepared environment. Since children within the environment are free to explore materials of their own choosing, they absorb what they find there.

Many adults fear that children will automatically abuse freedom or not know how to act in an environment in which they are responsible for governing their own actions. When a Montessori teacher anticipates inappropriate behavior, she quickly diverts the child to other materials or activities. Although the Montessori teacher believes in freedom for children and children's ability to exercise that freedom, children's choices are not unlimited. For example, children must know how to use materials correctly before they are free to choose them. Students are free to pick within the framework of choices provided by the teacher. Choice, however, is also a product of discipline and self-control that children learn in the prepared environment.

A Montessori environment is characterized by orderliness. The low shelving gives children ready access to materials to encourage their use. Why is it important to prepare such an organized environment?

Autoeducation

Montessori referred to the concept that children are capable of educating themselves as *autoeducation* (also known as self-education):

> The commonest prejudice in ordinary education is that everything can be accomplished by talking (by appealing, that is, to the child's ear), or by holding one's self up as a model to be imitated (a kind of appeal to the eye), while the truth is that the personality can only develop by making use of its own powers.[8]

Children who are actively involved in a prepared environment and exercising freedom of choice literally educate themselves. The role freedom plays in self-education is crucial:

> And this freedom is not only an external sign of liberty, but a means of education. If by an awkward movement a child upsets a chair, which falls noisily to the floor, he will have an evident proof of his own incapacity; the same movement had it taken place amidst stationary benches would have passed unnoticed by him. Thus the child has some means by which he can correct himself, and having done so will have before him the actual proof of the power he has gained: the little tables and chairs remain firm and silent each in its own place. It is plainly seen that the child has learned to command his movements.[9]

Our universal perception of the teaching–learning act is that the teachers teach and children learn, a view that overlooks the idea that everyone learns a great deal through their own efforts. Through the principle of autoeducation, Montessori focuses our attention on this human capability. The art of teaching includes preparing the environment so that children, by participating in it, educate themselves. Think of the things you learned by yourself and the conditions and circumstances under which you learned them. Your reflections will remind you of the self-satisfaction that accompanies self-learning and its power to generate further involvement.

Obviously, it is sometimes quicker, more efficient, and more economical to be told or shown what to do and how to do it. Teachers and parents need to understand, however, that autoeducation should have a more dominant role in education than we have been willing to give it. In this sense, education should become more child centered and less teacher centered.

The Role of the Teacher

Montessori believed that "it is necessary for the teacher to guide the child without letting him feel her presence too much, so that she may be always ready to supply the desired help, but may never be the obstacle between the child and his experience."[10]

The Montessori teacher should demonstrate certain behaviors to implement the principles of this child-centered approach, including the following:

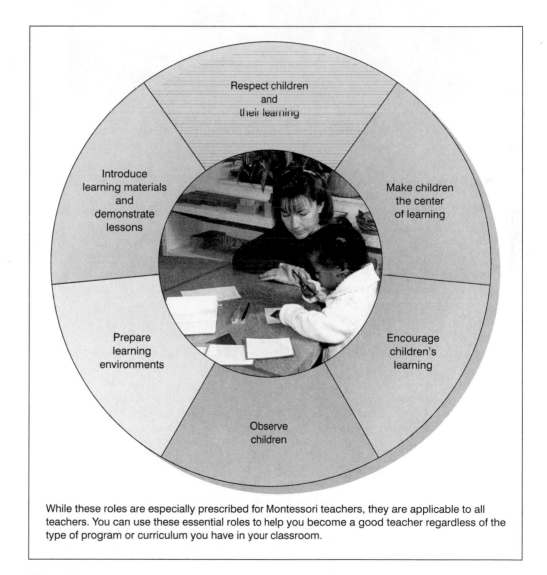

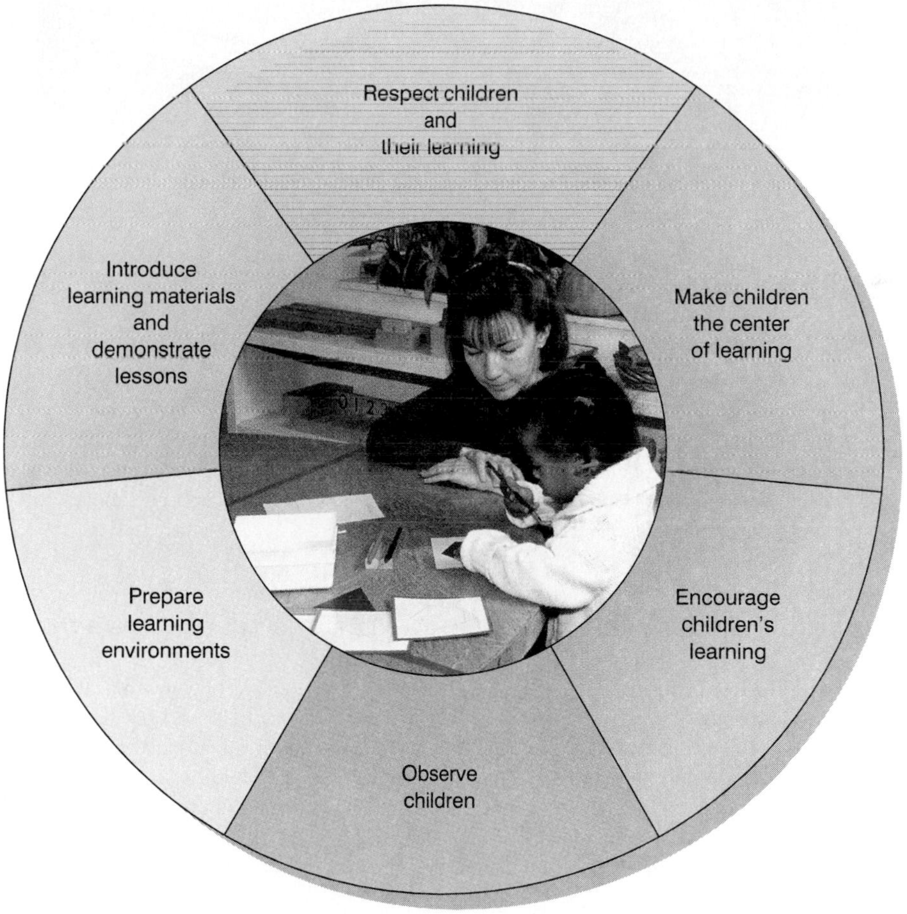

While these roles are especially prescribed for Montessori teachers, they are applicable to all teachers. You can use these essential roles to help you become a good teacher regardless of the type of program or curriculum you have in your classroom.

Figure 4.2
Teacher's Role in a Montessori Classroom

1. *Make children the center of learning.* As Montessori said, "The teacher's task is not to talk, but to prepare and arrange a series of motives for cultural activity in a special environment made for the child."[11]
2. *Encourage children to learn* by providing freedom for them in the prepared environment.
3. *Observe children* so as to prepare the best possible environment, recognizing sensitive periods and diverting inappropriate behavior to meaningful tasks.
4. *Prepare the learning environment* by ensuring that the learning materials are provided in an orderly format and that the materials provide for the appropriate experiences for all the children.
5. *Respect each child* and model ongoing respect for all children and their work.
6. *Introduce learning materials*, demonstrate learning materials, and support children's learning. The teacher introduces learning materials after observing each child. Presentation of materials is done in a manner so that children's interests are maintained and so that they are intrigued and captivated by the demonstration. Enthusiasm is as important in the presentation of materials as it is in all the dimensions of teaching. The "Voice from the Field" feature illustrates the importance of observation to the Montessori system and the way teachers introduce materials.

... voice from the field

Montessori Theory into Practice: Teachers Guide and Facilitate Learning

Dr. Montessori described her philosophy in three words: "Follow the child." To this end, one of the focal points of Montessori training is observation. Fine tuning observation skills allows the teacher to identify the true needs of each child as they occur. This, combined with a thorough understanding of child development and a knowledge of each child's abilities, provides the clues the teacher needs to plan appropriate activities for each child.

Throughout each day, the teacher observes children as they engage in social situations as well as with the materials set out in the room. She notes children's involvement or boredom, their concentration level or distractibility, their fine and gross motor skills and eye–hand coordination, their ability to learn abstract concepts, their need for less or greater challenge, their existing knowledge base, etc. With this information, the teacher then decides what material she could introduce to the child that would further his abilities. This material may already be in the class, or she may have to put it together.

All the activities in the room are designed in the same manner. The details of a task have been analyzed. The difficulties have been isolated so that there is only one in each activity, thus allowing the child to experience enough success to encourage him to continue through the challenging parts of the activity. The material is prepared in such a way that it follows a logical sequence. The activity incorporates a *control of error*—guiding points that enable a person to recognize when a mistake has been made. The activity is presented from the beginning, for example, choosing it, to its completion, where it is back on the shelf ready for the next child, thus demonstrating a complete cycle of activity. In addition, the language of the activity is presented, that is, the names and describing words of the items used—for example, thick cylinder.

At a time when Amani is not involved, the teacher approaches him and invites him to watch her do something she thinks he would especially like, based on her observations of his abilities and interests. As an example, he may have been watching another child engage in this activity, and this "watching" served as a direct preparation/initial conscious exposure to the activity. Her approach is one of mystery and intrigue, in order to capture and maintain his interest throughout her presentation of the activity. He watches her hands as they glide slowly and gracefully through the activity, emphasizing each movement to the fullest and stopping either to emphasize a specific point of clarification or to point something out verbally about the activity. Preschool children learn best when information is offered through one sense at a time, that is, visually watching actions involved in completing an activity. When done, she announces with excitement, "Now it's your turn!" and stays with Amani until he no longer needs her support and/or guidance on this activity.

Amani then begins a period of practice, using this activity first in the same way it was presented, to perfect the skill the activity is helping him develop. If the teacher has made an accurate decision presenting this material to him, he will choose this activity over and over until the skill is acquired; repetition is a natural tendency in humans as it helps them perfect desired skills. He may also engage in variations and extensions of that activity, experimenting, exploring, and making general applications of all the knowledge the material has to offer. Amani may also be asked to demonstrate the activity he has learned to another child, thus applying his knowledge and skill in a different way. In this way, knowledge and acquisition of skills are developed step by step, thus leading to more abstract concepts and higher levels of independence and skill. Once the skill becomes natural for Amani, the teacher will observe his readiness for a greater challenge and will introduce him to another activity more appropriate for his developing abilities at that time.

In this Montessori classroom, like many others, children learn continually from the teacher demonstrations, which occur a few times each week for each child. Due to the mixed age grouping, they also learn from other children providing indirect and direct exposure to various activities, and from hands-on exploration of, and experience with, the activities they choose to engage in on a daily basis. In addition, this teacher is continually learning from the children in her classroom—what they need, how best to introduce a material to each of them to maximize their learning, how to build on what each child already knows, how to keep the children's interest, how to maintain consistency in the environment while keeping it stimulating for the children in it, and so on—a most rewarding learning experience and challenge indeed!

This account by Janet Humphryes, director of education at Mile High Child Care, is based on the program and activities of the Mile High Child Care program at Edna Oliver Montessori Child Development Center in Denver, Colorado. There are six AMS (American Montessori Society)-certified directresses/teachers and an AMI (Association Montessori International)-certified director at this center.

How Does the Montessori Method Work?

In a prepared environment, materials and activities provide for three basic areas of child involvement: practical life or motor education, sensory materials for training the senses, and academic materials for teaching writing, reading, and mathematics. All these activities are taught according to a prescribed procedure.

For more information about the Montessori Curriculum model, go to the Companion Website at http://www.prenhall.com/morrison, select chapter 4, then choose the Linking to Learning module to connect to a variety of Montessori sites.

Practical Life

The prepared environment emphasizes basic, everyday motor activities, such as walking from place to place in an orderly manner, carrying objects such as trays and chairs, greeting a visitor, learning self-care skills, and other practical activities. For example, the "dressing frames" are designed to perfect the motor skills involved in buttoning, zipping, lacing, buckling, and tying. The philosophy for activities such as these is to make children independent of the adult and develop concentration. Water activities play a large role in Montessori methods, and children are taught to scrub, wash, and pour as a means of developing coordination. Practical life exercises also include polishing mirrors, shoes, and plant leaves; sweeping the floor; dusting furniture; and peeling vegetables.

Montessorians believe that as children become absorbed in an activity, they gradually lengthen their span of concentration; as they follow a regular sequence of actions, they learn to pay attention to details. Although most people assume that we learn practical life activities incidentally, a Montessori teacher shows children how to do these activities through precisely detailed instructions. Verbal instructions are minimal; the emphasis in the instructional process is on *showing how*—modeling and practice.

Montessori believed that children's involvement and concentration in motor activities lengthens their attention span. In a Montessori classroom, it is not uncommon to see a child of four or five polish his shoes or scrub a table for twenty minutes at a time! The child finds the activity intrinsically rewarding and pleasurable.

Practical life activities are taught through four different types of exercises. *Care of the person* involves activities such as using the dressing frames, polishing shoes, and washing hands. *Care of the environment* includes dusting, polishing a table, and raking leaves. *Social relations* include lessons in grace and courtesy. The fourth type of exercise involves *analysis and control of movement* and includes locomotor activities such as walking and balancing. Figures 4.3, 4.4, and 4.5 are directions for some of the practical life activities in a Montessori classroom. Notice the procedures and the exactness of presentation.

Sensory Materials

The following materials are among those found in a typical Montessori classroom (the learning purpose appears in parentheses):

- Pink tower (visual discrimination of dimension)—ten wood cubes of the same shape and texture, all pink, the largest of which is ten centimeters cubed. Each succeeding block is one centimeter smaller. Children build a tower beginning with the largest block.
- Brown stairs (visual discrimination of width and height)—ten blocks of wood, all brown, differing in height and width. Children arrange the blocks next to each other from thickest to thinnest so the blocks resemble a staircase.

Practical life activities help children learn about and practice everyday activities. Children enjoy doing practical, useful activities. Why do you think this is?

- Red rods (visual discrimination of length)—ten rod-shaped pieces of wood, all red, of identical size but differing in lengths from ten centimeters to one meter. The child arranges the rods next to each other from largest to smallest.
- Cylinder blocks (visual discrimination of size)—four individual wood blocks that have holes of various sizes; one block deals with height, one with diameter, and two with the relationship of both variables. Children remove the cylinders in random order, then match each cylinder to the correct hole.
- Smelling jars (olfactory discrimination)—two identical sets of white, opaque glass jars with removable tops through which the child cannot see but through which odors can pass. The teacher places various substances, such as herbs, in the jars, and the child matches the jars according to the smells.
- Baric tablets (discrimination of weight)—sets of rectangular pieces of wood that vary according to weight. There are three sets—light, medium, and heavy—which children match according to the weight of the tablets.
- Color tablets (discrimination of color and education of the chromatic sense)—two identical sets of small, rectangular pieces of wood used for matching color or shading.
- Sound boxes (auditory discrimination)—two identical sets of cylinders filled with various materials, such as salt and rice. Children match the cylinders according to the sound the fillings make.
- Tonal bells (sound and pitch)—two sets of eight bells, alike in shape and size but different in color; one set is white, the other brown. The child matches the bells by tone.
- Cloth swatches (sense of touch)—two identical swatches of cloth. Children identify them according to touch, first without a blindfold but later using a blindfold.

Materials: Tray, rice, two small pitchers (one empty, the other containing rice)

Presentation: The child must be shown how to lift the empty pitcher with the left hand and with the right, raise the pitcher containing rice slightly higher. Grasping the handle, lifting, and tilting are practiced. The spout of the full pitcher must be moved to about the center of the empty pitcher before the pouring begins. Set down both pitchers; then change the full one to the right side, to repeat the exercise.

When rice is spilled, the child will set the pitchers down, beside the top of the tray, and pick the grains up, one at a time, with thumb and forefinger.

Purpose: Control of movement.

Point of Interest: Watching the rice.

Control of Error: Hearing the rice drop on the tray.

Age: 2½ years.

Exercise: A container with a smaller diameter, requiring better control of movement. Control the amount of rice for the smaller container.

Note: Set up a similar exercise, using colored popcorn instead of rice.

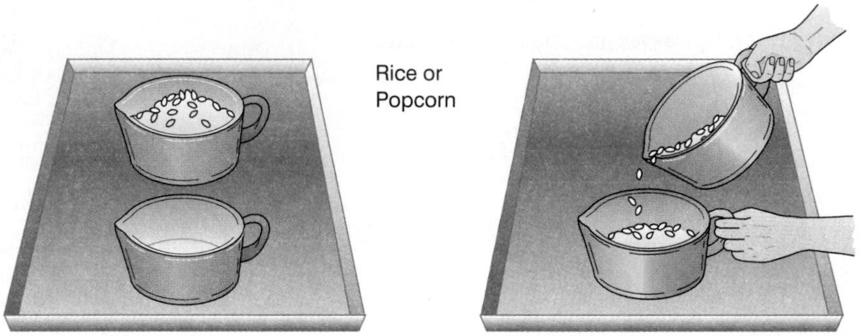

Figure 4.3
Pouring

Source: A Montessori Teacher's Manual, *by Elizabeth and Charles Caspari and Friends. © E. G. Caspari, 1974. All rights reserved. Used by permission.*

- Temperature jugs or thermic bottles (thermic sense and ability to distinguish between temperatures)—small metal jugs filled with water of varying temperatures. Children match jugs of the same temperature.

Materials for training and developing the senses have these characteristics:

- *Control of error.* Materials are designed so that children can see if they make a mistake; for example, if a child does not build the blocks of the pink tower in their proper order, she does not achieve a tower effect.
- *Isolation of a single quality.* Materials are designed so that other variables are held constant except for the isolated quality or qualities. Therefore, all blocks of the pink tower are pink because size, not color, is the isolated quality.

Materials: Apron, green-leafed plant, sheet of white freezer paper, basket with small sponge, caster, bottle of plant polish, orange stick, cotton ball

Presentation:

1. Lay out all the material in order of use from left to right.
2. Bring a plant to the table and place it on the paper.
3. Dampen the sponge at the sink and gently wipe off the top side of the leaf with forward strokes. Hold the leaf on the underside with the other hand. Stroke several leaves to remove the dust.
4. Pour small amount of polish into caster.
5. Wrap a small portion of the cotton ball on the orange stick.
6. Dip the stick in the polish and again stroke gently on the leaf in the manner described above.

Clean up:

1. Remove cotton from the stick and put it in the wastebasket.
2. Take the caster to the sink and wash and dry it.
3. Wash the sponge and bring it back to the table.
4. Place the material back in the basket.
5. Replace the plant on the shelf.
6. Fold the paper. Discard only if necessary.
7. Return basket and paper to the shelf.

Purpose: Coordination of movement; care of plants.

Point of Interest: Seeing the leaves get shiny.

Control of Error: Dull leaves and polish on white paper.

Age: 3 years and up.

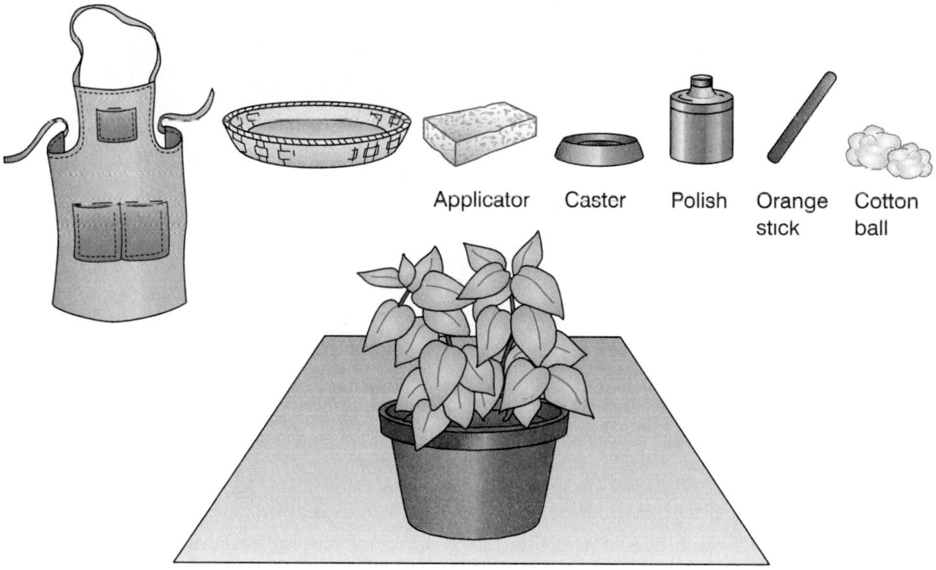

Figure 4.4
Plant Shining

Source: A Montessori Teacher's Manual, *by Elizabeth and Charles Caspari and Friends. © E. G. Caspari, 1974. All rights reserved. Used by permission.*

Materials: Basket with a duster, soft brush, and feather duster; table to be dusted

Presentation:
Look for dust, with the eyes at the level of the surface of the table. Start with one half of the table, the one immediately in front of you.
Wipe the surface first, as most of the dust will be lying on the top and will give the greatest result.
Always dust away from the body, starting at one end working progressively to the other end, using circular movements.
After the top dust the sides, after the sides dust the legs. Don't forget the corners, the insides of the legs, and underneath the tabletop. The brush is to be used for the corners.
Shake the duster over the wastebasket or outdoors.

Purpose: Coordination of movements, care of the environment, indirect preparation for writing.

Point of Interest: The dust to be found in the duster; shaking the dust off the cloth.

Control of Error: Any spot of dust left behind.

Age: $2^1/_2$ to $4^1/_2$ years.

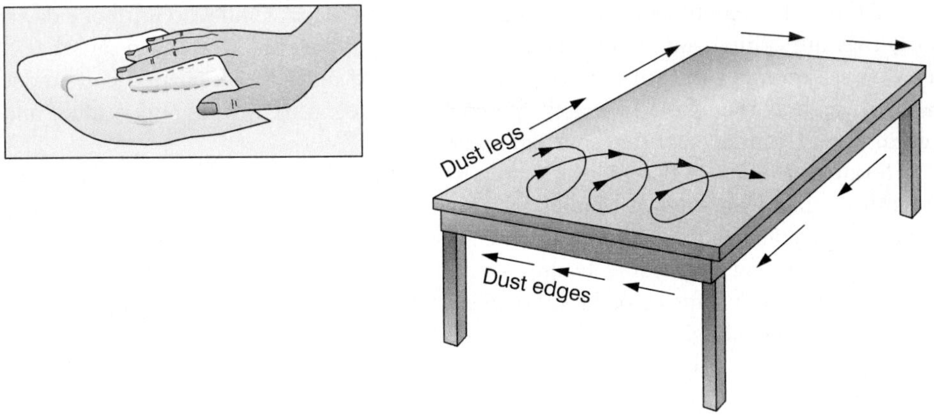

Figure 4.5
Dusting

Source: A Montessori Teacher's Manual, *by Elizabeth and Charles Caspari and Friends. © E. G. Caspari, 1974. All rights reserved. Used by permission.*

- *Active involvement.* Materials encourage active involvement rather than the more passive process of looking.
- *Attractiveness.* Materials are attractive, with colors and proportions that appeal to children.

BASIC PURPOSES OF SENSORY MATERIALS. One purpose of Montessori sensory materials is to train children's senses to focus on some obvious, particular quality; for example, with the red rods, the quality is length; with pink tower cubes, size; and with bells, musical pitch. Montessori felt it is necessary to help children discriminate among the many stimuli they receive. Accordingly, the sensory materials help make children more aware of the capacity of their bodies to receive, interpret, and make use of stimuli. In this sense, the Montessori sensory materials are labeled didactic, designed to instruct.

Second, Montessori thought that perception and the ability to observe details were crucial to reading. The sensory materials help sharpen children's powers of observation and visual discrimination for learning to read.

A third purpose of the sensory materials is to increase children's ability to think, a process that depends on the ability to distinguish, classify, and organize. Children constantly face decisions about sensory materials: which block comes next, which color matches the other, which shape goes where. These are not decisions the teacher makes, nor are they decisions children arrive at by guessing; rather, they are decisions made by the intellectual process of observation and selection based on knowledge gathered through the senses.

Finally, all the sensory activities are not ends in themselves. Their purpose is to prepare children for the occurrence of the sensitive periods for writing and reading. In this sense, all activities are preliminary steps in the writing–reading process.

Academic Materials for Writing, Reading, and Mathematics

The third area of Montessori materials is academic; specifically, items for writing, reading, and mathematics. Exercises are presented in a sequence that encourages writing before reading. Reading is therefore an outgrowth of writing. Both processes, however, are introduced so gradually that children are never aware they are learning to write and read until one day they realize they are writing and reading. Describing this phenomenon, Montessori said that children "burst spontaneously" into writing and reading. Montessori anticipated contemporary practices, such as the whole language approach, in integrating writing and reading and in maintaining that through writing children learn to read.

Montessori believed that many children were ready for writing at four years of age. Consequently, a child who enters a Montessori system at age three has done most of the sensory exercises by the time he is four. It is not uncommon to see four- and five-year-olds in a Montessori classroom writing and reading. Figures 4.6 and 4.7 show examples of children's writing.

Following are examples of Montessori materials that lay the foundation for and promote writing and reading:

Sensory training plays a major role in the Montessori method. What knowledge, skills, and concepts is this child learning through his involvement with modeling clay and cookie cutters?

Figure 4.6
Writing Sample by Montessori Student Miles Brooke

- *Ten geometric forms and colored pencils.* These introduce children to the coordination necessary for writing. After selecting a geometric inset, children trace it on paper and fill in the outline with a colored pencil of their choosing.
- *Sandpaper letters.* Each letter of the alphabet is outlined in sandpaper on a card, with vowels in blue and consonants in red. Children see the shape, feel the shape, and hear the sound of the letter, which the teacher repeats when introducing it.
- *Movable alphabet, with individual letters.* Children learn to put together familiar words.
- *Command cards.* These are a set of red cards with a single action word printed on each card. Children read the word on the card and do what the word tells them to do (e.g., run, jump).

The following are examples of materials for mathematics:

Figure 4.7
Writing Sample by Montessori Student Ella Rivas-Chacon

- *Number rods.* A set of red and blue rods varying in length from ten centimeters to one meter, representing the quantities one through ten. With the help of the teacher, children are introduced to counting.
- *Sandpaper numerals.* Each number from one to nine is outlined in sandpaper on a card. Children see, touch, and hear the numbers. They eventually match number rods and sandpaper numerals. Children also have the opportunity to discover mathematical facts through the use of these numerals.
- *Golden beads.* A concrete material for the decimal system. The single bead represents one unit. A bar made up of ten units in a row represents a ten; ten of the ten bars form

a square representing one hundred; and ten hundred squares form the cube representing one thousand.

Additional Features

Other features of the Montessori system are mixed-age grouping and self-pacing. A Montessori classroom always contains children of different ages, usually from two-and-a-half to six years. This strategy is becoming more popular in many classrooms and has long been popular in the British Infant Schools. Advantages of mixed-age groups are that children learn from and help each other, a range of materials is available for all children, and older children become role models and collaborators for younger children. Contemporary instructional practices of student mentoring and cooperative learning have their roots in and are supported by multi-age grouping.

In a Montessori classroom, children are free to learn at their own rate and level of achievement. They determine which activities to participate in and work at their own pace. Children are free to repeat and re-experience previously completed tasks to satisfy their intellectual and sensory needs for accomplishment and achievement. This explains why a variety of materials of varying levels is present in the classroom. However, children are not allowed to dally at a task. Through observation, the teacher determines when children have perfected one exercise and are ready to move to a higher level or different exercise. If a child does not perform an activity correctly, the teacher gives him or her additional help and instruction.

Table 4.1 outlines the basic characteristics of a good Montessori program that you can use as a guideline when you observe Montessori classrooms. Perhaps you can add other criteria you think would make a good early childhood program. Keep in mind that although details of educational programs vary from center to center, the basic constructs of a good Montessori program should be present.

Montessori as an Educational System

Montessori and the Public Schools

Patricia McGrath was the first to implement Montessori in the public schools. She taught a Montessori methods class in Philadelphia, Pennsylvania, at the Benjamin Franklin Elementary School from 1968 to 1974. Since then, Montessori programs have been implemented in many public school programs, especially preschool programs and kindergartens. Currently more than fifteen hundred public school classrooms offer Montessori programs.[12]

For more information about Montessori education, go to the Companion Website at http://www.prenhall.com/morrison, select chapter 4, then choose the Linking to Learning module to connect to a variety of Montessori sites.

A number of reasons account for the public school popularity of Montessori. First, Montessori is one of many programs of early childhood education that the public schools have used to *restructure*, or fundamentally change, the way they educate children. This restructuring of the schools is closely associated with the retraining of teachers; restructuring provides opportunities for retraining. So, a second reason for the growth of popularity of public school Montessori is that it is used as a means for retraining teachers. A successful Montessori program depends on well-trained teachers. Thus, by implementing a Montessori program, this provides the opportunity to train teachers in Montessori "new" and "alternative" approaches to educating young children.

Third, public school Montessori programs are often used as *magnet* schools. While the basic purpose of magnet schools is to integrate schools racially, at the same time they give parents a choice about what kind of program to give their children. Magnet schools as a

means of integration have enabled professionals to use federal dollars that otherwise would not be available to them. Without a doubt the availability of federal dollars has been a major factor for public school implementation of the Montessori program. If Montessori is implemented to the level it should be, the cost can be $20,000 a classroom.

Table 4.1
Basic Characteristics of a Montessori Program for Three- to Six-Year-Old Children

Growth in the Child	Program Organization	Adult Aspects
Toward independence and problem solving	Ungraded three-year age span: 2.6 to 6 years.	Certified Montessori teachers at the 3- to 6-year level
Toward the enjoyment of learning	Parental commitment to a three-year cycle of attendance	Continuing professional development
Toward the development of order, concentration, and coordination	Five-day week with a minimum daily three-hour session	Observational skills to match students' developmental needs with activities
Toward skills in oral communication	Personal and group instruction	Strategies to facilitate the unique and total growth of each individual
Toward respect for oneself, other people, and the planet	Child:adult ratio of 15:1	Leadership skills to foster a nurturing environment supportive of learning
Toward responsible group membership	Observational records of the child	A partnership developed with parents
	Regularly scheduled parent conferences	Supervision and education of auxiliary classroom personnel
	Public observation policy	

Learning Environment	Program Emphasis	Administrative Support
Diverse set of Montessori materials, activities, and experiences	To encourage intrinsic motivation, spontaneous activity, and self-education	Organized as a legally and fiscally responsible entity
Schedule that allows large blocks of uninterrupted learning time	To provide sensory education for intellectual development	Nondiscriminatory admissions policy
Classroom atmosphere that encourages social interaction	To encourage competencies through repetitive concrete experiences	Written educational policies and procedures
Space for personal, small group, and whole class learning activities	To encourage cooperative learning through peer teaching and social interaction	Adherence to state laws and health requirements
Lightweight, proportionate, movable child-sized furnishing	To provide learning opportunities through physical activity and outdoor work	Current school affiliation with AMS and other professional groups
Identifiable ground rules	To provide learning activities for creative expression	
Aesthetically pleasing environment		
Outdoor space to accommodate rigorous physical activity		

Source: American Montessori Society, "Basic Characteristics of a Montessori Program for Children Ages 3 to 6 Years," pamphlet (New York: Author, 1991). Copyright April 1991. Used by permission.

Fourth, inclusion of Montessori in the public schools is a way of giving parents choices in the kind of program their children will have at a particular school. Today, many early childhood and elementary programs specialize in a particular model, subject area, or program. This specialization enables many parents to select a school that teaches a curriculum they support.

Fifth, over the past decade parents who have had positive experiences with Montessori programs for their children have been strong advocates for the expansion of Montessori to public schools. This advocacy by parents has played a major role in both the popularity of Montessori and its growth.

Sixth, since Montessori developed her program for children with disabilities, some public schools see the Montessori method as an ideal inclusion of the learning needs of today's children with disabilities. Many Montessori programs practice *inclusion*, educating children with disabilities in regular education classrooms. More information about inclusion is provided in chapter 15.

The application of Montessori to the public school settings is so popular that these professionals have their own publication, the *Public School Montessorian* (published by Jola Publications, 2933 N. Second St., Minneapolis, MN 55411, http://www.jolapub.com).

Program in Action

A Day in the Life of a Child in a Full-Day Montessori Environment

In the heart of Denver's lowest-income neighborhood, Edna Oliver Montessori Child Development Center, one of Mile High Child Care's thirteen sites, offers a quality, full-day, Montessori program for eighty-three children, eight weeks to eight years of age. A staff member from each age group served (infants: birth to 18 months, toddlers: 18 months to 30/36 months, preschoolers: 2½/3 to 6 years, and schoolagers: 5 to 8 years) is there to greet children beginning at 6:30 every morning, and another to bid children farewell at 6:00 in the evening. Some children stay the full eleven and a half hours depending on the number of jobs the parents have and/or the shifts they work. All of the children eat breakfast, lunch, and dinner at the center five days a week, year round.

Preschool children arriving between 6:30 and 8 A.M. gather together in one of the two preschool classrooms to begin their day. Some of the first children to arrive seem as though they are still waking up, and find a soft corner or a quiet area to prepare themselves to join the group at their own pace. Others busy themselves with the tasks involved in readying the classroom for the day and seem to enjoy and take pride in their responsibilities. They turn on the calming music, open the shades covering the windows, wet all the sponges for each activity, fill the paint bucket with water, open and stir the paint in the paint jars with the paint brushes, slice two bananas into six unpeeled chunks and put them in the jar with the food preparation activity, feed the fish and gerbils and refill the water bottle in the gerbil cage, check activities to be sure they are supplied for the children's use that day, and set the table for breakfast. Some other children choose individual activities from the shelves, or find a friend to engage in an activity together. Children identify their own needs and choose appropriate experiences for themselves throughout the day; this is an integral part of the Montessori methodology.

While supervising the children's activities, the Montessori teacher greets arriving children and parents, and receives and relays pertinent messages about the children and program activities, for example, a mom who could be reached that day at a different number in case of emergency, the child who was returning from two days of illness, the field trip

to the museum the next week. At 7:00 an assistant arrives to help. Most staff work eight-hour staggered shifts to maintain an adequate teacher/child ratio throughout the day; some part-time staff are hired to help in the early morning and late afternoon.

When breakfast arrives in the classroom at 7:45 A.M., the children wash their hands, sit at the set tables, and join in a community meal, chatting about their plans for the day and sharing about their home life the night before, while they serve themselves and pass the food to the next child, family style. As they finish, each child pushes his chair in, scrapes the leftovers from his dish and puts it in the bucket, sweeps up any crumbs on the table or floor, wipes his place at the table, washes his hands and brushes his teeth, and goes off to choose an activity in that classroom, or the classroom down the hall, depending on which he belongs to. It is the job of two children on a rotating basis to assure the breakfast area is completely cleaned up, and the cart of leftovers and dirty dishes is returned to the cook in the kitchen.

By 8:30 A.M., the children are all engaged in various activities; some have chosen activities they will work on by themselves and some have chosen to interact with another child or a small group of children on some activity or project. Choices vary depending on what each child has been presented, personal learning styles, individual personalities, personal preferences, activities chosen as they may be for only one person, a suggestion from an adult or another child, the need to complete an activity that was begun previously, and so forth. The teacher involves herself in giving the children lessons on the various activities, one after another, while the assistant helps the children as needed, assuring they choose and follow through on activities appropriate for their abilities.

The guideline of respect for self, others and the environment has been established for the children: they know they need to ask the teacher for a lesson on an activity they have not yet been shown; they know to return activities to the shelf, clean and ready for another child to use them; they know to take care of the materials so they will stay beautiful; they know to not disturb another child's activity unless invited by that child. They know all this because this guideline of respect is continually reinforced by the teacher, the assistant, and the children.

Following a two-and-a-half-hour individual choice activity period, the children gather together for a fifteen-minute group activity. This teacher-directed time could include singing songs, reciting poetry, movement, dance, music, a group meeting or discussion, storytelling, etc. Many of the activities planned for this time connect to the monthly theme that may be botany, or ecology, or something else depending on the majority of the children's interests at the time.

A thirty- to forty-five-minute period outdoors on the playground occurs next. The children immediately seek their favorite outdoor activities such as trikes, swings, caring for the garden, sandbox, climbing structure, basketball, chatting in the shade under the trees, playing hide-and-seek. The teacher and assistant both interact with the children as they ensure their safety and encourage the development of both gross motor and social skills. Occasionally, this time is used for nature exploration (even in the city!) or a walk around the community, which helps build understanding and relationships, and a sense of connectedness with their neighborhood community.

At about 12 noon, children are approached, three to four at a time, to return inside and prepare for lunch. The first children inside wash their hands and help set up the tables, moving them together so that four to eight children sit at each, and setting out flatware, plates, glasses, napkins, pitchers of milk, serving utensils, and bowls of food at each table. As children sit at the table, they serve themselves and engage in discussions as they wait for everyone at their table to start eating together. Clean up for lunch occurs the same as breakfast. As children finish cleaning up, they each get their mat, sheet and blanket; make their bed/rest mat; get a book to look at/read; and lay down for a nap.

After twenty minutes of quiet, older children who are not needing a nap are invited to choose quiet activities until the other children wake up. This is a time the children generally engage in more advanced math and language activities with one or two other children, receiving more one-on-one guidance from the adult.

As children wake up, they put their mats, sheets and blankets away, and they are free to choose their own activities. In most cases, however, these full-day children choose to follow the lead of others, whether that be watching others as they do their activities, listening to a story read by an adult, finding pieces to a 100-piece puzzle over casual conversations, listening to classical music while gazing out the window, etc. Though children

of this age are quite capable of making good decisions regarding their own development and the activities that lead to that development, decisions do not come easily to them at this time of the day. Respect for their need to not direct themselves is facilitated by the teacher who has prepared this full-day environment to include opportunities for minimal participation and small group activities and prepared the schedule in such a way that this choice time in the afternoon is brief, 45 to 60 minutes in length.

At 3:45/4:00 P.M., the children again head outside to the playground. They return inside at 4:30 for dinner, in the same manner as before, a few children at a time. Following dinner, the children can again choose their own activities and/or participate in the closing of the classroom for the day. Their end-of-the-day responsibilities include cleaning the easel and brushes and closing the paints, replenishing paper and consumable supplies in the activities, sweeping the floor, emptying the trash and replacing the bag, putting children's dry art work into their folders, etc.

Staff greet parents as they come to retrieve their children between 5 and 6 P.M., and encourage the children to tell their parents about their day as they depart, giving them a specific reminder about something pertinent that occurred to them as a trigger for parent/child communication on the way home.

This account by Janet Humphryes, director of education of Mile High Child Care, is based on the program and activities of the Mile High Child Care program at Edna Oliver Montessori Child Development Center in Denver, Colorado. There are six AMS (American Montessori Society)-certified directresses/teachers, and an AMI (Association Montessori International)-certified director at this center.

Montessori and Contemporary Practices

The Montessori approach supports many methods used in contemporary early childhood programs. Some of these are the following:

- *Integrated curriculum.* Montessori provides an integrated curriculum in which children are actively involved in manipulating concrete materials across the curriculum—writing, reading, science, math, geography, and the arts. The Montessori curriculum is integrated in other ways, such as across age and developmental levels. Montessori materials are age appropriate for a wide age range of children.
- *Active learning.* In Montessori classrooms, children are actively involved in their own learning, as dramatized in the Program in Action feature, "A Day in the Life of a Child in a Full-Day Montessori Environment." Manipulative materials provide for active and concrete learning.
- *Individualized instruction.* Curriculum and activities should be individualized for children. Montessori does this through individualizing learning for all children. Individualization occurs through children's interactions with the materials as they proceed at their own rates of mastery.
- *Independence.* The Montessori environment emphasizes respect for children and promotes success, both of which encourage children to be independent. Indeed, independence has always been a hallmark of Montessori.
- *Appropriate assessment.* Observation is the primary means of assessing children's progress, achievement, and behavior in a Montessori classroom. Well-trained Montessori teachers are skilled observers of children and are adept at translating their observation into appropriate ways for guiding, directing, facilitating, and channeling children's active learning.

- *Developmentally appropriate practice.* From the preceding illustrations, it is apparent that the concepts and process of developmentally appropriate curricula and practice (see chapters 7 through 9) are inherent in the Montessori method. Indeed, it may well be that some of the most developmentally appropriate practices are conducted by Montessori practitioners.

Furthermore, I suspect that quality Montessori practitioners understand, as Maria Montessori did, that children are much more capable than some early childhood education practitioners think.

Infant Montessori Programs

Montessori for children under age three is growing ever more popular, as illustrated by the rapidly expanding Montessori infant programs. The Program in Action description of the Montessori Nido (Nest) provides an example of what is included in the Montessori infant program.

Program in Action
The Montessori Nido

A Nido consists of nine babies from two months to twelve to fourteen months (when a child is walking well). With three adults, a three-to-one child–caregiver ratio is maintained at all times. The Montessori Nido environment is divided into four main areas. The first area, the **movement area**, is equipped with a thin covered mattress with kiosks and bars the babies use for pulling up; other mattresses may be available around the room depending on the space. The movement area usually includes a stair as well.

The **sleeping area**, the second area of the Nido environment, is an isolated area with individual futons (the tiniest babies' futons are enclosed in a Plexiglas "crib" that sits on the floor). This area provides a quiet place for the babies to sleep whenever they need to, but it also has easy access to the rest of the environment so that when a baby awakens, he or she can crawl or walk to the adults. The children are free to go onto their futons when they are sleepy and come off when they are awake.

The third area, the **eating area**, is equipped with low, heavy "weaning" tables and chairs instead of high chairs. The children are capable of getting into and out of the chairs with ease. The adults sit on low stools facing the children when feeding them. This area is not carpeted; the children are encouraged to feed themselves as soon as possible but are never left to eat alone as eating

is a "social occasion." An area is provided for nursing moms to come and nurse their babies, and several adult areas are available for giving bottles to those babies who take them.

The last area, the **physical care area** (changing, bathing), is beside a water source. Elsewhere in the room there is a rocking chair for comforting babies. Most of the room is tiled—not carpeted—except for the sleeping area. This allows the babies to move around more easily and makes cleaning and sterilizing the floor possible. A low stool is used to accommodate children learning to change their own panties. Panties are used instead of diapers so that children can move more easily and become more aware of their bodily functions. This environment has no walkers, swings, playpens, cribs, or high chairs—none of the devices sold to "aid" a baby's movement. Babies are placed on the floor and move everywhere.

There is no program, so to speak, in the Nido. The children spend their time as they would at home: sleeping, being awake and interacting with adults and other children, using the materials provided for their development, moving about the environment, going outside—either in the garden or on a walk, eating, bathing, and so forth.

Contributed by Judith Orion, director, A. M. I. Assistance to Infancy Training, Denver, Colorado; photos provided by The Montessori Institute, Denver, Colorado.

Frequently Asked Questions

Does attending a Montessori program stifle a child's creativity? People who ask this question for some reason think the prepared environment and didactic materials somehow keep or prohibit children from becoming or being creative. A Montessori program, in and of itself, does not inhibit children's creative impulses or activities. How parents and teachers encourage, support, and promote children's behaviors determines how "creative" they are. Oddly, this "creativity" question is seldom asked about other programs.

After attending a Montessori program, do children have trouble adjusting to a regular program? Embedded in this question is the belief that children who engage in active, independent learning inherent in a Montessori program will have trouble adjusting to a more "rigid" public school program. Fortunately, as described, increasing numbers of public schools are implementing the Montessori system. In addition, transition programs—designed to help children make smooth adjustments from one school program to another—are growing in popularity and use. Most Montessori programs have such transition programs for children and their families.

How long should a child attend a Montessori program? I was recently asked this question by a university student whose sister has her child in a Montessori program. The sister's worry is based on her fears that her daughter will have problems adapting to a public school setting.

Public school administrators and teachers are responding to parents' demands for Montessori programs for preschool through grade six. Growing numbers of parents want the benefits of Montessori for their children throughout the elementary grades. So, some parents

For answers to additional frequently asked questions about Montessori education, go to the Companion Website at http://www.prenhall.com/morrison, select chapter 4, then choose the Linking to Learning module to connect to the American Montessori Society site, the national center for Montessori information.

address the adapting question by advocating for elementary Montessori programs. The answer to the question rests then both with the availability of the program and with how satisfied children and parents are with it.

Guidelines for Selecting a Montessori School

Parents frequently ask early childhood professionals for advice about placing their children in a Montessori program. Unfortunately, there is no guarantee that a given Montessori program is of the kind and quality advocated by Maria Montessori. Selecting a Montessori preschool is like making other consumer choices; the customer must beware of being cheated. No truth-in-advertising law requires operators of a Montessori school to run a quality program. Because the name has such appeal to parents, some schools call themselves Montessori without either the trained staff or facilities to justify their claim.

Not only do some schools misrepresent themselves, but some teachers do so as well. There is no requirement that a teacher must have Montessori training of any particular duration or by any prescribed course of instruction. The American Montessori Society (AMS) approves training programs that meet its standards for teacher training, and the Association Montessori International (AMI) approves teacher training programs that meet the standards of the international organization.

Early childhood professionals advise parents to consider the following points when selecting a Montessori program:

- Is the school affiliated with a recognized Montessori association (AMS or AMI)?
- Is the teacher a certified Montessori teacher or trained in the Montessori method?
- Are practices of the Montessori method part of the program?
- Contact parents of former students to determine their satisfaction with the program. Ask them, "Would you again send your child to this school? How is your child doing in first grade? How was the Montessori program beneficial to your child?"
- Compare tuition rates of the Montessori school with rates at other schools. Is any difference in tuition worth it?
- Why do you want your child to attend a Montessori school? Is it social status? Prestige? Do you feel your child will achieve more by attending a Montessori school? Visit other preschool programs to determine whether a Montessori program is best for your child.
- Interview the director and staff to learn about the program's philosophy, curriculum, rules and regulations, and how the program differs from others that are not Montessori.
- Following enrollment, pay attention to children's progress through visits, written reports, and conferences to be sure they are learning what will be needed for an easy transition to the next grade, program, or school.

Criticism of the Montessori Method

The Montessori system is not without critics. One criticism deals with the didactic nature of the materials and the program. Some say the system teaches a narrow spectrum of activities in

which concepts are learned in a prescribed manner, following prescribed methods, using a prescribed set of material. Montessori believed children learn best from materials when shown how to use them, which seems to make sense, rather than just allowed to mess around with them. In many Montessori programs but by no means all, children are encouraged to use and experiment with the materials in creative ways after they have mastered them. One Montessori teacher related that she has seen children use the pink tower blocks in over a hundred ways!

Critics also claim the Montessori classroom does not provide for socialization. They cite the lack of group play, games, and other activities normally present in traditional kindergarten programs. This criticism, of course, is no truer for a Montessori setting than for any other classroom. No method or teacher can stop social interactions unless the teacher is determined to do so or the children are afraid of her. Many Montessori activities promote and offer opportunities for sharing tasks, cooperation, collaboration, and helping. Also, outdoor time and lunchtime (when children eat in pairs, threes, or small groups) afford ample opportunity for social interaction.

A related criticism is that children do not have opportunities to participate in dramatic make-believe and pretend play. Montessori believed that "play is the child's work." As such, children's play sets the stage for later roles and functions necessary for successful adult living. Thus, according to Montessori, fantasy play had little value. This is one Montessori area professionals must examine in terms of our current knowledge of children and learning.

The charge is frequently heard that Montessori schools represent an elitist or middle-class system. This claim likely stems from the fact that many Montessori schools were at one time operated by individuals for profit with high tuition. In most towns and cities, the Montessori program is now widely used in many Head Start, day care, and public school programs.

One reason some parents and teachers feel the Montessori program is rigid is that its ideas and methodologies are so detailed. Another reason is that they have nothing to compare this system with other than the free-play programs they are more accustomed to. When parents and teachers compare the Montessori system, which organizes the environment and learning experiences in a specific, purposeful way, to a free-play setting, they tend to view the Montessori setting as rigid. Parents and teachers need to focus instead on the results of the system.

Further Thoughts

In many respects, Maria Montessori was a person for all generations, and her method is proving to be a program for all generations. Montessori contributed greatly to early childhood programs and practices. Through her method she will continue to do so. Many of her practices—such as preparing the environment, providing child-size furniture, promoting active learning and independence, and using multiage grouping—have been incorporated into many early childhood classrooms. As a result, it is easy to take her contributions, like Froebel's, for granted. We do many things in a Montessorian way without thinking too much about it.

To take an online self-test on this chapter's contents, go to the Companion Website at http://www.prenhall.com/morrison, select chapter 4, then choose the Self Test module.

As we have noted, today Montessori education is enjoying another rebirth, especially in the public schools' embracing of its method. What is important is that early childhood professionals adopt the best of Montessori for children of the twenty-first century. As with any practice, professionals must adapt approaches to fit the children they are teaching while remaining true to what is best in that approach. Respect for children is never out of date and should be accorded to all children regardless of culture, gender, or socioeconomic background.

We have the tremendous benefit of hindsight when it comes to evaluating and analyzing educational thought and practice. In this process we need to consider what was appropriate then and determine what is appropriate today. When appropriate, early childhood professionals need to make reasoned and appropriate changes in educational practice. This is what "growing" the profession is all about.

For additional Internet resources or to complete an online activity for this chapter, go to the Companion Website at http://www.prenhall.com/morrison, select chapter 4, then choose the Linking to Learning or Making Connections module.

More information about Montessori programs and training can be obtained by writing to the following organizations:

- The American Montessori Society, 281 Park Ave. South, 6th floor, New York, NY 10010-6102; 212-358-1250. http://www.amshq.org/
- Association Montessori International (this is the oldest international Montessori organization, founded by Maria Montessori in 1929). Address inquiries to AMI/USA, 410 Alexander St., Rochester, NY 14607; 716-461-5920
- North American Montessori Teachers' Association (NAMTA), 11424 Bellflower Rd. NE, Cleveland, OH 44106; 216-421-1905. http://www.montessori-namta.org/

Activities for Further Enrichment

Applications

1. Write three or four paragraphs describing how you think Montessori has influenced early childhood educational practice.
2. What features of the Montessori program do you like best? Why? What features do you like least? Why? What features are best for children?
3. A mother of a four-year-old asks your advice about sending her child to a Montessori school. What is your response?
4. Although there is a tremendous rise in the implementation of Montessori in the public schools, some educators think that this boom is not entirely good for either the Montessori system or the public schools. What do you think some of their concerns are?
5. Interview a Montessori school director to learn how to go about opening a Montessori school. Determine what basic materials are needed and their cost, then tell how your particular location would determine how you would "market" the program.

Field Experiences

1. Compare Montessori materials with those in other kindergartens and preschool programs. Is it possible for teachers to make Montessori materials? What advantages or disadvantages would there be in making and using these materials?
2. After visiting a Montessori classroom and talking with teachers, evaluate the criticisms of the system given in the chapter. Are the criticisms valid? Are there any you would add? Why? In addition, make a list of the aspects of the Montessori classroom you liked and disliked and explain why.

Research

1. Write to the ASM, AMI, and NAMTA for information about becoming a certified Montessori teacher. Compare the requirements for becoming a certified Montessori teacher with your university training. What are the similarities and differences?
2. Interview public and private school teachers about their understanding of the Montessori program. Do they have a good understanding of the program? What are the most critical areas of understanding or misunderstanding? Do you think all early childhood professionals should have knowledge of the Montessori program? Why?
3. Multiage grouping is one of the aspects of the Montessori program that appeals to many early childhood professionals. List the advantages and disadvantages of multiage grouping. What conclusions can you draw from your list?

Readings for Further Enrichment

Lawrence, L. *Montessori Read and Write: A Parent's Guide to Literacy for Children.* New York: Three Rivers Press, 1998.

Shows how you can teach your children to read and write using the famous Montessori system. The book is packed with ideas and age-specific activities and games that make learning easy and fun.

Spietz, H. A. *Montessori Resources: A Complete Guide to Finding Montessori Materials for Parents and Teachers.* Rossmoor, CA: American Montessori Consulting, 1999.

Contains in-depth reviews of products, information on where to buy supplies for integrated lesson planning, recommended com-

puter software, and reviews and recommendations of foreign language products.

Standing, E. M., and Havis, L. *Maria Montessori: Her Life and Works*. New York: Penguin USA, 1998.

Part biography and part exposition of her ideas, this engaging book is an ideal introduction that reveals through her letters and personal diaries Montessori's humility and delight in the success of her educational experiments.

Stephenson, S. M., and Stephenson, J. M. *The Joyful Child: Michael Olaf's Essential Montessori for Birth to Three*. Arcata, CA: Michael Olaf Company, 1998.

Contains valuable information on aiding the optimum development of the child from birth to three years and is used as an overview of this age in Montessori teacher training courses and other early childhood development courses. Included is a catalogue of books and materials.

Wentworth, R. A. *Montessori for the New Millennium*. Mahawah, NJ: Lawrence Erlbaum Associates, 1999.

This book elucidates the vital aspect of Maria Montessori's life work and shows how it applies to real-life teaching situations. Montessori believed that by transforming the process of children's education she could help to transform the attitudes for the adults they will later become.

Linking to Learning

American Montessori Society

http://www.amshq.org

AMS serves as a national center for Montessori information, both for its members and for the general public—answering inquiries and facilitating research wherever possible. To Montessori, a child's environment was a most important element in the learning process.

International Montessori Index

http://montessori.edu/

Montessori information for parents and teachers, links to Montessori school lists, conference lectures, organizations, educational materials, and other valuable sites.

International Montessori Society

http://www.wdn.com/trust/ims

Founded to support the effective application of Montessori principles throughout the world, the society provides a range of programs and services of the fundamental principles of (1) observation, (2) individual liberty, and (3) preparation of the environment.

Montessori Online

http://www.montessori.org/

Site for the Montessori Foundation, a nonprofit organization dedicated to the advancement of Montessori education. Offers programs and resources to anyone interested in learning about Montessori education.

Montessori Unlimited

http://www.montessori.com

Through this program, your child will learn the basis of Montessori—to respect oneself and one's environment. This basis, called practical life, is carried into other areas of learning, including language arts, math, and science.

ENDNOTES

[1] Maria Montessori, *Dr. Montessori's Own Handbook* (New York: Schocken, 1965), 133.

[2] Maria Montessori, *The Montessori Method,* trans. Anne E. George (Cambridge, MA: Bentley, 1967), 104.

[3] Maria Montessori, *The Secret of Childhood,* trans. M. J. Costello (Notre Dame, IN: Fides, 1966), 20.

[4] Maria Montessori, *The Absorbent Mind,* trans. Claude A. Claremont (New York: Holt, Rinehart & Winston, 1967), 25.

[5] Montessori, *The Secret of Childhood,* 48.

[6] Ibid., 46, 49.

[7] Montessori, *The Absorbent Mind,* 6.

[8] Ibid., 254.

[9] Ibid., 84.

[10] Montessori, *Dr. Montessori's Own Handbook,* 131.

[11] Ibid., 8.

[12] Interview 18 September 1996 with Denny Shapiro, editor of *The Public School Montessorian.*

CHAPTER 5

Children's minds, if planted in fertile soil, will grow quite naturally on their own.

JEAN PIAGET

Piaget and Others

Contributors to Constructivism

Focus Questions

1. How is an understanding of Piaget's theory of cognitive development important to early childhood professionals?
2. What cognitive processes did Piaget consider important for intellectual development?
3. What are the characteristics of children's thinking at each stage of cognitive development?
4. What are the major features and common concepts of educational curricula based on Piaget's theory?
5. What advantages and criticisms are associated with Piaget's theory?

To review the chapter focus questions online, go to the Companion Website at http://prenhall.com/morrison and select chapter 5.

While this chapter is mainly about the pioneering work of Jean Piaget, others have also contributed to our knowledge, understanding, and practice of constructivism, the theory according to which children literally construct their knowledge of the world and level of cognitive functioning. These include John Dewey, Lev Vygotsky, Howard Gardner, and Marian Diamond. Table 5.1 lists some of these educators' contributions to constructivism.

Jean Piaget was interested in how humans learn and develop intellectually, beginning at birth and continuing across the life span. He devoted his life to conducting experiments, observing children (including his own), and developing and writing about his theory, the *cognitive theory* approach to learning. Piaget has enriched our knowledge about children's thinking, and his influence on early childhood education continues to be significant. Many programs base their curricula squarely on Piaget's theory about how children learn.

Learning and Theories of Learning

Learning

To check your understanding of this chapter with the online Study Guide, go to the Companion Website at http://www.prenhall.com/morrison, select chapter 5, then choose the Study Guide module.

Reflect for a minute on your learning. How do you learn? How do children learn? We take learning for granted and frequently don't pay much attention to *how* learning occurs. But your answer to how children learn will play a major role in the curriculum you select for them and how you teach them. Think for a moment about how you would define *learning* and what learning means to you. For some, the ability to learn is a sign of intelligence. For others, it means the grades children bring home on their report cards. For many parents, learning is the answer to "What did you learn in school today?"

Table 5.1
Contributors to Constructivism

Contributor	Contributions to Curriculum and Teaching
John Dewey (1859–1952)	• Experiences stimulate learning. • Students should be involved in learning activities. • Build curriculum based on student's interests.
Jean Piaget (1896–1980)	• Learning involves discovery. • Manipulating objects promotes learning. • Interactions with people, places, and things leads to development of intellect and knowledge.
Lev Vygotsky (1896–1934)	• Learning is social and occurs through personal interactions. • More competent individuals help students scaffold learning. • Group work promotes learning.
Howard Gardner (b. 1943)	• Intelligence is multidimensional. • Human potential is the ability to solve problems. • There are many ways of knowing and expressing knowledge.
Marian Diamond (b. 1926)	• Brain development and early learning are important. • Enriched environments support brain development and learning. • Stimulating activities are essential for learning and brain development.

However, for our purposes, *learning* refers to the cognitive and behavioral changes that result from experiences, and the experiences that make up the curriculum are at the core of the learning process. So the experiences you provide for children should be based on a theory or theories of how children learn.

How will you know if and what children are learning? You can determine if learning occurs in a number of ways: by observing what Carolyn is doing; by noting how she is interacting with other children; by interpreting her results on her achievement test; and by reading her story of a visit to the zoo. I discuss these and other methods for observation and assessment of learning in chapter 11.

Theories

A *theory* consists of statements and assumptions about relationships, principles, and data designed to explain and predict a phenomenon. In our case, theories are used to explain how children learn. Many professionals use Piaget's theory of learning as a basis for curriculum and practice. His theory is very influential and is applied to many early childhood programs, several of which I discuss in this chapter. In fact, Piaget's theory is used more often than any other theory to explain children's thinking and learning and as a basis for program development.

Learning theories such as Piaget's are important for several reasons. First, they help us think about how children learn. Thinking about and understanding how children learn makes it easier for you and others to plan and teach. Second, theories enable you to explain to others, especially parents, how learning occurs and what you and they can expect of children. Explaining children's learning to parents when you are explaining it based on a theory of learning—Piaget's, Montessori's, or other theories—is easier and makes more sense than not having a theory on which to base your explanations. Third, theories enable you to evaluate children's learning because you have a basis on which to evaluate; for example, when you observe, you know what you are observing and why. Fourth, theories provide you with guidance in developing programs for children that support and enhance their learning.

Piaget's Theory of Learning

Piaget's theory is about cognitive development, which seeks to explain how individuals perceive, think, understand, and learn. His theory is basically a logicomathematical theory; that is, cognitive development is perceived as consisting primarily of logical and mathematical abilities. Review chapter 3, and compare Piaget's views with Lev Vygotsky's theory of social intelligence and Howard Gardner's theory of multiple intelligences.

For more information about Jean Piaget, go to the Companion Website at http://www.prenhall.com/morrison, select chapter 5, then choose the Linking to Learning module to connect to several sites about Jean Piaget.

Generally, the term *intelligence* suggests intelligence quotient, or IQ—that which is measured on an intelligence test. This is not what Piaget meant by intelligence; rather, *intelligence* is the cognitive, or mental, process by which children acquire knowledge; hence, *intelligence* is "to know." It is synonymous with *thinking* in that it involves the use of mental operations developed as a result of acting mentally and physically in and on the environment. Active involvement is basic to Piaget's cognitive theory; through direct experiences with the physical world, children develop intelligence. In addition, intelligence develops over time, and children are intrinsically motivated to develop intelligence.

Piaget conceived of intelligence as having a biological basis; that is, all organisms, including humans, adapt to their environments. You are probably familiar with the process of physical adaptation, in which an individual, stimulated by environmental factors, reacts and adjusts to that environment; this adjustment results in physical changes. Piaget applied the concept of adaptation to the mental level, using it to explain how intellectual development

One of Piaget's tenets is that children think differently at different stages of cognitive development. How would this affect the way you design learning experiences for children?

occurs as a result of children's encounters with parents, teachers, siblings, peers, and the environment. The result is cognitive development.

Constructivism and Cognitive Development

Piaget's theory is a *constructivist* view of development. The constructivist process

> is defined in terms of the individual's organizing, structuring and restructuring of experience—an ongoing lifelong process—in accordance with existing schemes of thought. In turn, these very schemes become modified and enriched in the course of interaction with the physical and social world.[1]

For more information about constructivism, go to the Companion Website at http://www.prenhall.com/morrison, select chapter 5, then choose the Linking to Learning module to connect to several sites about constructivism.

Children continuously organize, structure, and restructure experiences in relation to existing schemes of thought. As a result, children build their own intelligence.

In explaining the role of constructivism, Constance Kamii, a leading Piaget scholar, states, "Constructivism refers to the fact that knowledge is built by an active child from the inside rather than being transmitted from the outside through the senses."[2] Review now Figure 5.1, which lists the key concepts of constructivism.

Active Learning

Active learning as both a concept and a process is an inherent part of constructivism. As a concept, active learning means that children construct knowledge through physical and mental activity. As a process, active learning means that children are actively involved with a variety of manipulative materials in problem-setting and problem-solving activities. The majority of early childhood professionals support active learning as the preferred practice in early childhood programs.

Think for a minute what would happen if you gave six-month-old Emily some blocks. What would she try to do with them? More than likely she would put them in her mouth. She

- Children construct their own knowledge. They play the major role in their own cognitive development.
- Children better understand when they construct for themselves than when they are told the answers to problems.
- Mental and physical activity is crucial for construction of knowledge. Knowledge is built step-by-step through active involvement—that is, through exploring objects in their environment and through problem solving and interacting with others.
- Children construct knowledge best in the context of—out of—experiences that are of interest and meaningful to them.
- Autonomy is preferred to obedience.
- Cognitive development is a continuous process. It begins at birth and continues across the life span.

Figure 5.1
Basic Concepts of Constructivism

wants to eat the blocks. On the other hand, if you gave blocks to Emily's three-year-old sister Madeleine, she would try to stack them. Both Emily and Madeleine want to be actively involved with things and people as active learners. This active involvement comes naturally for them.

Cognitive Development and Adaptation

According to Piaget, the adaptive process at the intellectual level operates much the same as at the physical level. The newborn's intelligence is expressed through reflexive motor actions such as sucking, grasping, head turning, and swallowing. Through the process of adaptation to the environment via these reflexive actions, the young child's intelligence is developed.[3]

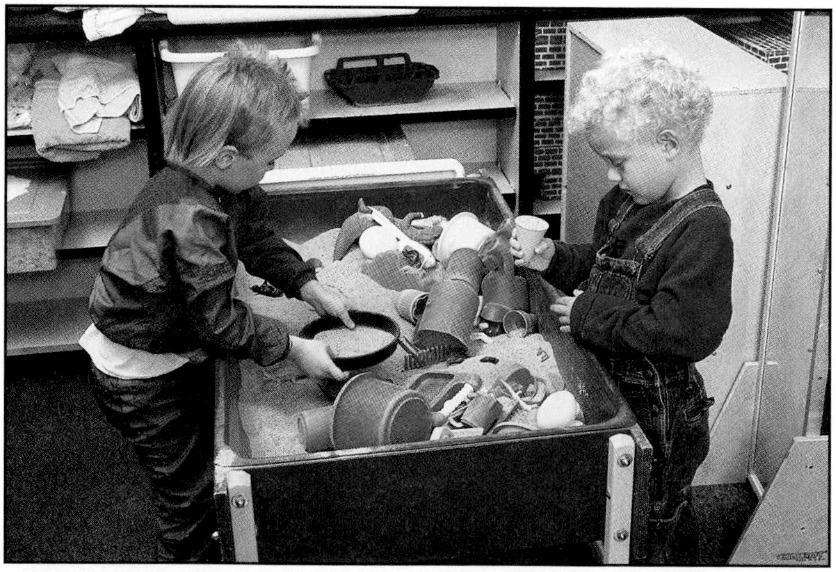

Piaget believed that the opportunity to be physically and mentally involved in learning is necessary to mental development in the early years. What are some examples of how children's active involvement contributes to their learning?

Through this interaction with the environment, children organize sensations and experiences. Obviously, therefore, the quality of the environment and the nature of children's experiences play a major role in the development of intelligence. For example, Zachary, with various and differing objects available to grasp and suck, and many opportunities for this behavior, will develop differentiated sucking organizations (and therefore an intelligence) quite different from that of Gary, who has nothing to suck but a pacifier.

Learning as the Adaptation of Mental Constructs

ASSIMILATION. Piaget believed that adaptation is an active process composed of two interrelated processes, assimilation and accommodation. *Assimilation* is the taking in of sensory data through experiences and impressions and incorporating them into knowledge of people and objects already created as a result of these experiences.[4] Through assimilation, children use old methods or experiences to understand and make sense of new information and experiences. Emily used assimilation when she put the block in her mouth and sucked on it. The block was fine for sucking, but not for eating.

ACCOMMODATION. *Accommodation* is the process by which individuals change their way of thinking, behaving, and believing to come into accord with reality. Accommodation involves changing old methods and adjusting to new situations. Whereas Emily tried to eat the blocks, Madeleine didn't want to eat them but wanted to stack them. This is accommodation. Robbie, who is familiar with kittens and cats because he has several cats at home, may, upon seeing a dog for the first time, call it a kitty. He has assimilated dog into his organization of kitty. However, Robbie must change (accommodate) his model of what constitutes "kittyness" to exclude dogs. He does this by starting to construct or build a scheme for dog and thus what "dogness" represents.[5]

The twin processes of assimilation and accommodation, viewed as an integrated, functioning whole, constitute *adaptation*.

EQUILIBRIUM. Equilibrium is another aspect of Piaget's theory of intelligence. Equilibrium is a balance between assimilation and accommodation. Children cannot assimilate new data without to some degree changing their way of thinking or acting to fit those new data. People who always assimilate without much evidence of having changed are characterized as "flying in the face of reality." Yet individuals cannot always accommodate old ideas to all the new information they receive. If they could, they wouldn't maintain any beliefs. A balance is needed between the two. Diagrammed, the role of equilibrium in the constructivist process looks something like that in Figure 5.2.

Upon receiving new sensory and experiential data, children assimilate, or fit, these data into their already existing knowledge (scheme) of reality and the world. If the new data can be immediately assimilated, then equilibrium occurs. If unable to assimilate the data, children try to accommodate and change their way of thinking, acting, and perceiving to account for the new data and restore the equilibrium to the intellectual system. It may well be that Robbie can neither assimilate nor accommodate the new data; if so, he rejects the data entirely. Figure 5.3 and accompanying text illustrate the construction of a new concept.

Rejection of new information is common if what children are trying to assimilate and accommodate is radically different from their past experiences and the data they have received. This partially accounts for Piaget's insistence that new experiences must have some connection or relationship to previous experiences. Child care and classroom experiences should build on previous life and school experiences.

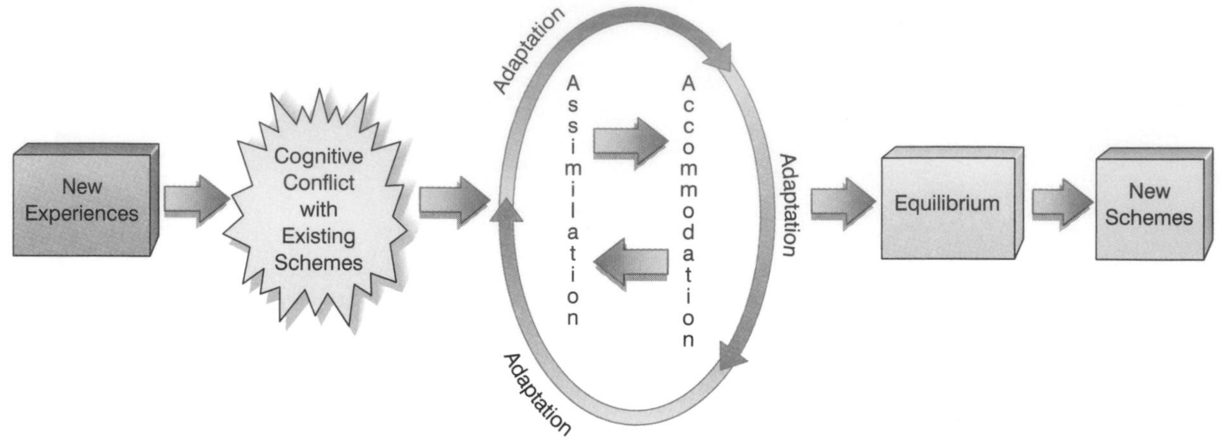

Intellectual functioning involves the mental changing of existing ideas, information, and knowledge to fit with new ideas and information as a result of experiences with people, places, and things.

Figure 5.2
The Constructivist Process

Schemes

Piaget used the term *scheme* to refer to units of knowledge that children develop through the adaptation process. (In reality, children develop many schemes.) Newborns have only reflexive actions. By using reflexive actions such as sucking (remember what Emily did with the blocks you gave her) and grasping, children begin to build their concept and understanding of the world. Review Figure 5.3 again to see how Robbie develops a new scheme for dog.

In the process of developing new schemes, Piaget ascribed primary importance to physical activity, which is important for developing such schemes. Physical activity leads to mental stimulus, which in turn leads to mental activity. Thus, it is not possible to draw a clear line between physical activity and mental activity in infancy and early childhood. Settings should provide for active learning by enabling children to explore and interact with people and objects. Early childhood professionals' understanding of this key concept helps explain their arranging infant and toddler settings so children can be active. It also helps explain the growth of programs that encourage and provide active learning for all children.

Everyone recognizes that children should play, but we have not always recognized the importance of play as the context in which children construct mental schemes to form a basis for all other schemes. Play, to Piaget, is a powerful process in intellectual development. Parents seem to sense this intuitively in wanting their children to play, particularly with other children. Many early childhood professionals have an understanding of the importance of play and include it in their curricula.

Stages of Intellectual Development

Figure 5.4 summarizes Piaget's developmental stages and provides examples of stage-related characteristics. Piaget contended that developmental stages are the same for all children, including the atypical child, and that all children progress through each stage in the same order. The ages are only approximate and should not be considered fixed. The sequence of

Figure 5.3
All children have schemes consisting of thoughts and actions. Robbie has a scheme for identifying kittens, which includes short ears and a fluffy tail. When he sees another animal, in this case a dog, that is similar to but different from his scheme for a kitty, disequilibrium occurs. However, through the processes of assimilation and accommodation, he develops a new scheme for dog that is separate from that for kitty.

Piaget believed that, developmentally, after children are capable of making one-to-one correspondence and classifying and ordering objects, they are ready for higher-level-thinking activities such as those that involve numeration and time and spatial relationships.

growth through the developmental stages does not vary; the ages at which progression occurs do vary.

SENSORIMOTOR STAGE. The sensorimotor stage is the first of Piaget's stages of cognitive development. During the period from birth to about two years, children use senses and motor reflexes to build knowledge of the world. They use their eyes to see, mouths to suck, and hands to grasp. When a child uses primarily reflexive actions to develop intellectually, he or she is in the *sensorimotor stage*. Reflexive actions help children construct a mental scheme of what is suckable and what is not (what can fit into the mouth and what cannot) and what sensations (warm and cold) occur by sucking. Children also use the grasping reflex in much the same way to build schemes of what can and cannot be grasped. Through these innate sensory and reflexive actions, they continue to develop an increasingly complex, unique, and individualized hierarchy of schemes. What children are to become physically and intellectually is related to these sensorimotor functions and interactions.

The sensorimotor period has these major characteristics:

- Dependence on and use of innate reflexive actions
- Initial development of object permanency, the idea that objects can exist without being seen, heard, or touched
- Egocentricity, whereby children see themselves as the center of the world and believe events are caused by them
- Dependence on concrete representations (things) rather than symbols (words, pictures) for information

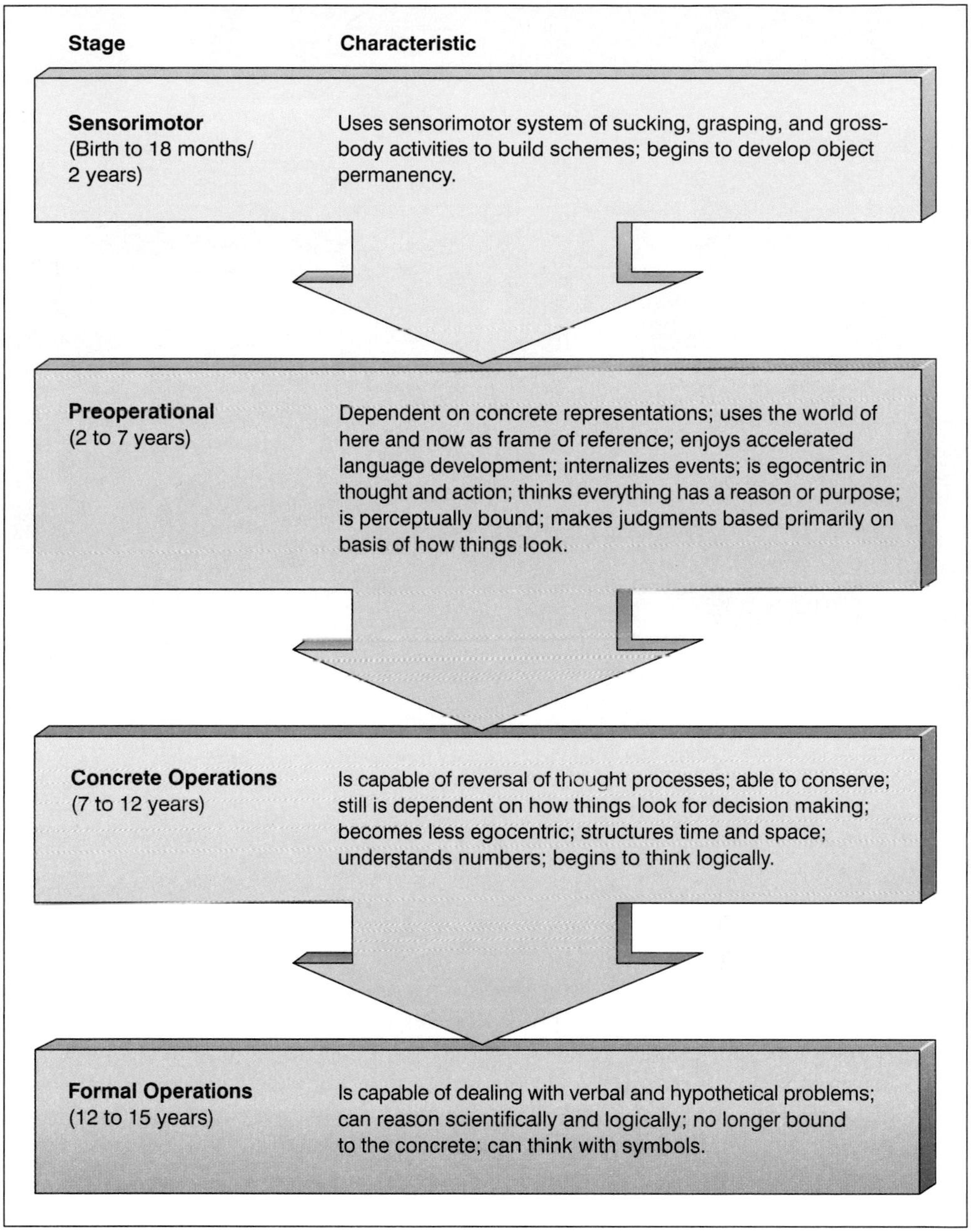
Stage
Characteristic
Sensorimotor
(Birth to 18 months/ 2 years)
Uses sensorimotor system of sucking, grasping, and gross-body activities to build schemes; begins to develop object permanency.
Preoperational
(2 to 7 years)
Dependent on concrete representations; uses the world of here and now as frame of reference; enjoys accelerated language development; internalizes events; is egocentric in thought and action; thinks everything has a reason or purpose; is perceptually bound; makes judgments based primarily on basis of how things look.
Concrete Operations
(7 to 12 years)
Is capable of reversal of thought processes; able to conserve; still is dependent on how things look for decision making; becomes less egocentric; structures time and space; understands numbers; begins to think logically.
Formal Operations
(12 to 15 years)
Is capable of dealing with verbal and hypothetical problems; can reason scientifically and logically; no longer bound to the concrete; can think with symbols.

Figure 5.4
Piaget's Stages of Cognitive Development

- By the end of the second year, less reliance on sensorimotor reflexive actions; beginning use of symbols for things that are not present

(We will discuss intellectual development in infants, toddlers, preschoolers, and primary grade children in more detail in later chapters.)

PREOPERATIONAL STAGE. The *preoperational stage*, the second stage of cognitive development, begins at age two and ends at approximately seven years. Preoperational children are different from sensorimotor children in these ways:

- Language development begins to accelerate rapidly.
- There is less dependence on sensorimotor action.
- These children have an increased ability to internalize events and think by using representational symbols such as words in place of things.

Preoperational children continue to be egocentric, expressing ideas and basing perceptions mainly on how they perceive or see things. Children learn to use symbols such as words or mental images to solve problems and think about things and people who are not present. How things look to preoperational children is the foundation for several other stage-related characteristics. First, when children look at an object that has multiple characteristics, such as a long, round, yellow pencil, they will "see" whichever of those qualities first catches their eye. Preoperational children's knowledge is based mainly on what they are able to see, simply because they do not yet have operational intelligence or the ability to think using mental images.

Second, the absence of operations makes it impossible for preoperational children to *conserve*, or determine that the quantity of an object does not change simply because some transformation occurs in its physical appearance. For example, show preoperational children two identical rows of checkers (see Figure 5.5). Ask whether each row has the same number of checkers. The children should answer affirmatively. Next, space out the checkers in each row, and ask whether the two rows still have the same number of checkers. They may insist that more checkers are in one row "because it's longer." Children base their judgment on what they can see—namely, the spatial extension of one row beyond the other row. This example also illustrates that preoperational children are not able to *reverse* thought or action, which requires mentally putting the row back to its original length.

For more information about child development, go to the Companion Website at http://www.prenhall.com/morrison, select any chapter, then choose Topic 2 of the ECE Supersite module.

Preoperational children believe and act as though everything happens for a specific reason or purpose. This explains children's constant and recurring questions about why things happen and how things work.

Preoperational children also believe everyone thinks as they think and acts as they do for the same reasons. Preoperational children have a hard time putting themselves in another's place, and it is difficult for them to be sympathetic and empathetic.

How preoperational children talk reflects their egocentrism. For example, in explaining about his dog that ran away, Matt might say something like this: "And we couldn't find him . . . and my dad he looked . . . and we were glad." Matt assumes you have the same point of view he does and know the whole story. The details are missing for you, not for Matt. Young children's egocentrism also helps explain why they tend to talk at each other rather than with each other. This dialogue between two children playing at a day care center reveals egocentrism:

Jessica: My Mommy's going to take me shopping.

Ashley: I'm going to dress this doll.

Jessica: If I'm good I'm going to get an ice cream cone.

Ashley: I'm going to put this dress on her.

The point is that egocentrism is a fact of cognitive development in the early childhood years. Our inability always to see clearly someone else's point of view is evidence that egocentrism in one form or another is part of the cognitive process across the life span.

CONCRETE OPERATIONS STAGE. Concrete operations is the third stage of Piaget's cognitive development plan. Piaget defined an operation as an action that can be carried out in thought as well as executed materially and that is mentally and physically reversible.

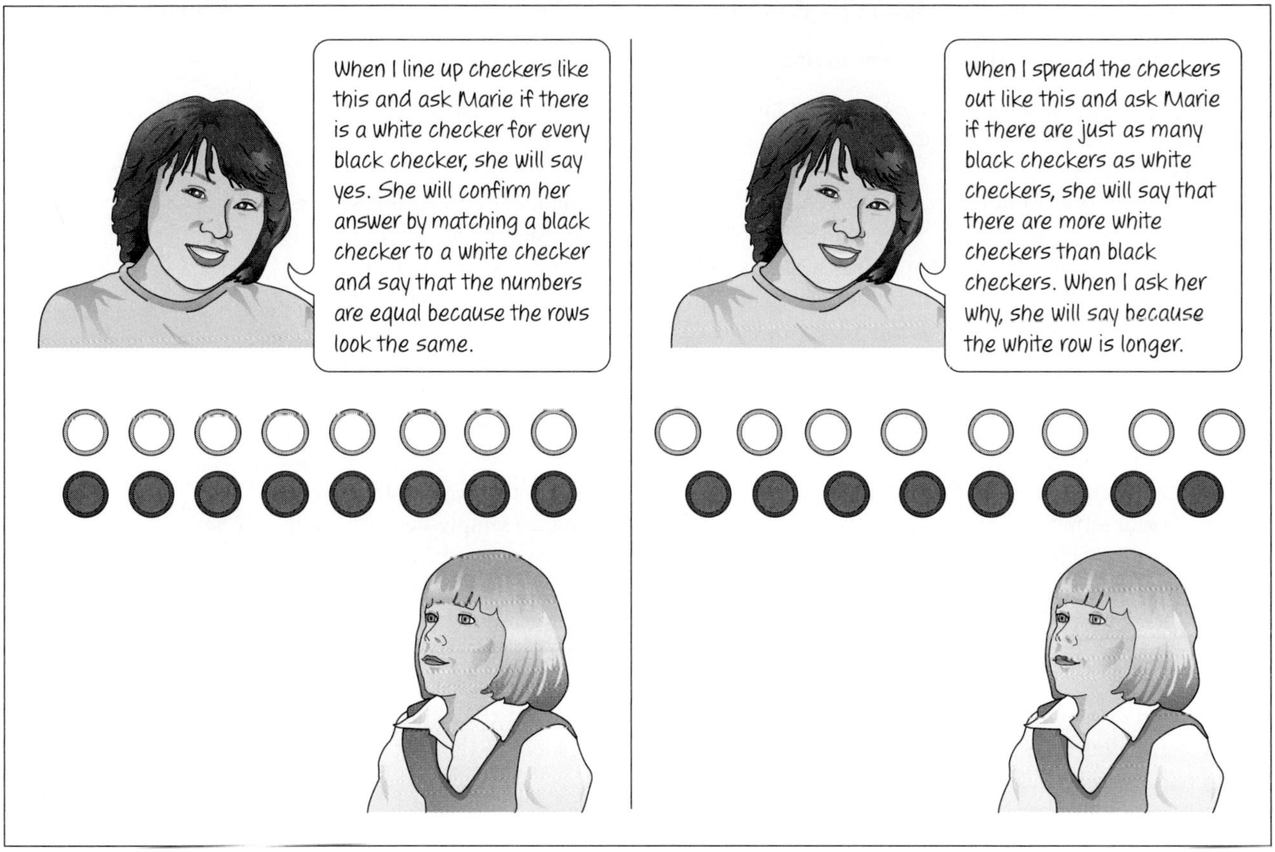

Figure 5.5
The absence of operations in preoperational children makes it impossible for them to determine that the quantity of a group of objects does not change because some changes occur in how the objects look. Try this checker experiment with several children and see how they are thinking and making sense of their world based on how things look to them.

Children in the *concrete operations stage*, from about age seven to about age twelve, begin to use mental images and symbols during the thinking process and can reverse operations. Teachers can encourage the development of mental processes during this stage through the use of concrete or real objects when talking about and explaining concepts.

Keep in mind, however, that telling is not teaching. Professionals should structure learning settings so children have experiences at their level with real objects, things, and people. Teachers often provide activities that are too easy rather than too difficult. For example, instead of just giving the children a basket of beads to play with, ask them to sort the beads into a red group, a blue group, a yellow group, and a green group.

Concrete operational children begin to develop the ability to understand that change involving physical appearances does not necessarily change quality or quantity. They also begin to reverse thought processes, by going back over and "undoing" a mental action just accomplished. Other mental operations children are capable of during this stage are these:

- One-to-one correspondence
- Classification of objects, events, and time according to certain characteristics
- Classification involving multiple properties of objects

Observation serves as a basis for assessing children's abilities, achievements, and stage of cognitive development. What do you think this teacher can learn about the child she is observing?

- Class inclusion operations
- Complementary classes

The concrete stage does not represent a period into which children suddenly emerge, after having been preoperational. The process of development from stage to stage is gradual and continual and occurs over a period of time as a result of maturation and experiences. No simple sets of exercises will cause children to move up the developmental ladder. Rather, ongoing developmentally appropriate activities lead to conceptual understanding.

FORMAL OPERATIONS STAGE. The second part of operational intelligence is formal operations, which is the fourth and final stage of cognitive development. The *formal operations stage* begins at about twelve years of age and extends to about fifteen years. Children become capable of dealing with increasingly complex verbal and hypothetical problems and are less dependent on concrete objects to solve problems. Thinking ranges over a wide time span that includes past, present, and future. Children develop the ability to reason scientifically and logically, and they can think with all the processes and power of adults. How a child thinks is thus pretty well established by age fifteen, although adolescents do not stop developing new schemes.

Piaget came to these conclusions about early childhood education:

- Children play an active role in their own cognitive development.
- Mental and physical activity are important for cognitive development.
- Experiences constitute the raw materials necessary to develop mental structures.
- Children develop cognitively through interaction with and adaptation to the environment.

- Development is a continuous process.
- Development results from maturation and the transactions, or interactions, between children and the physical and social environments.

Early childhood professionals use these tenets to guide their planning and teaching. The "Project Construct" Program in Action feature is one example of a program based on the constructivist theory.

Program in Action

Project Construct

WHAT IS PROJECT CONSTRUCT?

Project Construct is a process-oriented curriculum and assessment framework for working with children ages three through seven. In a process-oriented curriculum children are encouraged and supported to acquire skills for learning. These skills include questioning, discovering, exploring, observing, researching, making decisions, problem solving, and applying to everyday life what they are learning. Started by the Missouri Department of Elementary and Secondary Education in 1986, Project Construct incorporates theory-based curricula linked to state and national curriculum frameworks and standards.

Project Construct is based on constructivist theory, which states that children construct their own knowledge and values as a result of interactions with the physical and social world. Through "hands-on, minds-on" experiences, students in Project Construct classrooms attain deep understandings in the core content areas, while they also learn to work collaboratively with adults and peers and to be lifelong problem solvers.

WHY WAS PROJECT CONSTRUCT INITIATED?

Project Construct was developed to fulfill a need for a curriculum and assessment framework that supports young children's characteristic ways of learning, while at the same time providing teachers, parents, and administrators the information they need to make appropriate decisions regarding the education of young children.

WHAT ARE THE PRINCIPLES OF PROJECT CONSTRUCT AND HOW DO THEY GUIDE TEACHING PRACTICE?

Project Construct is built on the belief that the teacher is a professional whose day-to-day decisions in the classroom influence children's development. Within the framework for curriculum and assessment, the teacher has considerable autonomy to choose and design experiences that actively involve children and promote learning. Project Construct is based on four basic principles of child development and related teaching practices.

Principle 1. Children have an intrinsic desire to make sense of the world. What they genuinely need to know and are genuinely interested in knowing helps them learn.

Practices. Create learning activities that are meaningful and interesting to young children; create conditions in which children need to construct, develop, and apply additional knowledge or skills; provide activities that offer children choices and

opportunities to function as planners, decision makers, and creators; allow sufficient time for children to pursue their ideas.

Principle 2. Children actively construct knowledge and values by acting upon the physical and social world. Because their thoughts are still closely tied to action, they require a physically and mentally active learning environment.

Practices. Provide opportunities for exploration, interaction, and experimentation with peers, adults, and objects; help children reflect on and evaluate their thoughts and actions; create activities that allow children to make use of their knowledge in new situations; foster opportunities for children to cooperate and consider different points of view; permit children to use concrete actions to inform their decision making.

Principle 3. In young children's universal struggle to understand the world, their thinking will contain predictable errors.

Practices. Value children's imaginative and incorrect answers and ideas; encourage peer interaction to discuss, question, and challenge each other's ideas; allow all children to experience the consequences of their ideas and actions within reasonable constraints; facilitate children finding answers to their own questions; analyze how and why children respond in certain ways.

Principle 4. Developmental domains are interactive and interrelated, each influencing the other. It is within the sociomoral environment that cognition and language are developed.

Practices. Emphasize an integrated approach to teaching; integrate "academic" instruction within contexts that are meaningful to the child; promote curriculum goals through activities that promote various aspects of development; view learning as dynamic and organic rather than static and linear.

What Is the Role of Assessment in Project Construct?

The Project Construct Assessment System has two primary components: one part is based on informal assessment techniques and is designed to monitor students' day-to-day progress, while the other part reflects a more structured approach to assessment and is most useful for summative evaluation. Both components feature performance-based methods and promote developmentally appropriate assessment practices.

How Do the Project Construct Goals Relate to Other Educational Goals?

Throughout its development, Project Construct has remained dedicated to bringing together the educational goals of early childhood programs with those of elementary schools. Although Project Construct is not organized by traditional subjects, the foundations for academic learning are integrated throughout the framework. Thus, Project Construct provides a solid developmental foundation for later knowledge and skill acquisition. For example, sociomoral goals focus on children's understanding of the social world and the function of rules within a democratic society, cognitive goals reflect the development of logical thinking, and representational goals center on the child's emerging ability to understand and communicate ideas and feelings. The goals are based on two assumptions: positive learning outcomes result from the alignment of curriculum, instruction, and assessment; and all children can be successful in school.

For more information, visit Project Construct on-line at http://www.projectconstruct.org.

Piaget Reconsidered: Advantages and Criticisms

Like all things designed to advance our knowledge and understanding of children, theories must stand the tests of time, criticism, and review. Theories are subject to the scrutiny, testing, and evaluation of professionals. This is the way theories are accepted, rejected, modified,

and refined. Researchers have conducted thousands of studies to test the validity of Piaget's ideas. Following are descriptions of some advantages of using his theory and some criticisms.

Advantages

A powerful advantage of Piaget's theory is that it is an elegant explanation of four stages of cognitive development. It enables us to clearly track cognitive development through the four stages from birth to adolescence. Second, with each stage Piaget and others describe what children are and are not able to do. Third, Piaget's four stages offer a somewhat complete description of cognitive development from birth through adulthood. For over half a century, Piaget's theory has provided professionals and researchers with a theory on which to develop curricula and guide program development.

Criticisms

On the other hand, there are a number of things you must consider in applying Piaget's theory. First, Piaget seems to have underestimated the ages at which children can perform certain mental operations. In fact, it appears that he underestimated the intellectual abilities of all children, but particularly younger children. Children can understand more than Piaget believed based on the problems and tasks he gave them to perform. For example, children in the preoperational stage can perform tasks he assigned to the concrete operations stage. Additionally, recent advances in infant research suggest that infants have more cognitive tools than Piaget or others thought (more about this in a minute).

Second, Piaget's emphasis on a unidimensional view of intelligence as consisting primarily of logicomathematical knowledge and skills tends to de-emphasize other views. Professionals now recognize other definitions of intelligence and how it develops, such as Howard Gardner's multiple intelligences. You must consider varying definitions of *intelligence* when designing curricula and activities for children.

Third, Piaget's theory emphasizes that individual children are literally responsible for developing their own intelligence. In this regard, he likened children to "little scientists," engaged in a solitary process of intellectual development. With his emphasis on the role of the individual child, Piaget's approach to cognitive development tends to downplay the role of social interactions and the contributions of others to this process. On the other hand, Lev Vygotsky (see chapter 3) believed that people play a major role in children's cognitive development and that children are not alone in their development of mental schemes. For Vygotsky, children develop knowledge, attitudes, and ideas through interactions with more capable others—parents, teachers, and peers. Early childhood professionals' embracing of Vygotsky's ideas helps explain the popularity of many social-based learning processes such as cooperative learning, multiage grouping, child–teacher collaboration, and peer-assisted teaching.

Fourth, one characteristic of children's language and cognitive development is that children talk to themselves. Perhaps you have observed a four-year-old busily engrossed in putting a puzzle together and heard her say, "Which piece comes next?" Piaget called this self-directed talk "ego-centric speech" and believed it furnished additional evidence of children's egocentrism, that children are more preoccupied with their own needs and concerns rather than the views of others. Vygotsky, on the other hand, believed that children's private speech plays an important role in cognitive development. He thought that children communicate with themselves to guide their behavior and thinking. As children develop, their audible private speech becomes silent inner speech and continues to serve the important functions of helping to solve problems and guide behavior. By being attentive to children's private

speech, professionals can ask questions that will help children think and solve problems. Additionally, learning environments that permit children to be verbally active while solving problems support their cognitive development.

These and other views regarding the limitations of some of Piaget's ideas and observations do not invalidate his work. Rather, professionals must readjust their thinking and practices based on new discoveries about his ideas. While Piaget's theory is constantly reviewed and refined, and although other theories of intelligence are in the cognitive development spotlight, Piaget's contributions will continue to influence early childhood programs and professionals for decades to come. We have much more to learn from Piaget.

To take an online self-test on this chapter's contents, go to the Companion Website at http://www.prenhall.com/morrison, select chapter 5, then choose the Self Test module.

New Directions in Cognitive Development

As with most theories, new research and discoveries lead to modification and new directions. Since Piaget did his groundbreaking work, several advances have occurred that influence how we view children's cognitive development. First are the ongoing discoveries about genetic influences on cognitive development. These developments show, for example, that the genetic influences on verbal development were not as clearly established in Piaget's time as they are today. When I discuss infant language development in chapter 7, I will address this process in more detail.

Second, research in infant development clearly shows that infants possess a great many more cognitive skills than previously thought and that they are very actively involved in learning. For example, shortly after birth, neonates can discriminate and imitate happy, sad, and surprised facial expressions, indicating an innate ability to compare the sensory information of a visually perceived expression with the feedback of the movements involved in matching that expression. The developmental significance of such ability may be that it is the starting point of infant psychological development.[6]

For additional Internet resources or to complete an online activity for this chapter, go to the Companion Website at http://www.prenhall.com/morrison, select chapter 5, then choose the Linking to Learning or Making Connections module.

Activities for Further Enrichment

Applications

1. Now is a good time to review the philosophy you developed after reading chapter 1. How do your beliefs fit with Piaget's theory?

2 Compare Piaget's theory with another theory, such as Montessori's. How are they similar and different?

3. List five concepts or ideas about Piaget's theory that you consider most significant for how to teach and rear young children. Explain how learning about Piaget's beliefs and methods many be influencing your philosophy of teaching.

4. If an early childhood professional said that she did not think it was important to know about Piaget's theory, how would you respond?

Field Experiences

1. Constructivists believe that one of the main functions of teachers is to create a climate for learning. Interview early childhood teachers and ask them what they believe are important elements or features of classrooms that support learning. From this teacher data, develop a list of characteristics that you will use in your classroom. Place this list in your portfolio or learning file.

2. In a constructivist classroom, children's autonomy and initiative are accepted. Observe classrooms and give examples of how teachers are encouraging or discouraging initiative and autonomy in their classrooms. Based on your observations, develop plans for how you will support these two important factors in promoting learning.

3. Make a floor plan for what you think a classroom would look like that supports a constructivist approach. Have your professors and field experience teachers review your plan. After making appropriate revisions, place your plan in your learning file for future use.

Research

1. Observe three children—one six months old, one two years old, and one four years old. Note in each child's activities what you consider typical of behavior for that age. Can you find examples of behaviors that correspond to one of Piaget's stages?
2. Observe a child between birth and eighteen months. Can you cite any concrete evidence, such as specific actions or incidents, to support how the child is developing schemes of the world through sensorimotor actions?

Readings for Further Enrichment

Brooks, J., and Brooks, M. *In Search of Understanding: The Case for Constructivist Classrooms.* Alexandria, VA: Association for Supervision & Curriculum Development, 1999.

Builds a case for the development of classrooms where students construct deep understandings of important concepts. Presents new images for educational settings: student engagement, interaction, reflection, and construction.

Kamii, C., and Housman, L. *Young Children Reinvent Arithmetic: Implications of Piaget's Theory.* New York: Teachers College Press, 1999.

Describes and develops an innovative program of teaching arithmetic in the early elementary grades. Kamii bases her educational strategies on Piaget's scientific ideas of how children develop logicomathematical thinking.

Martin, D. *Elementary Science Methods: A Constructivism Approach.* Belmont, CA: Wadsworth, 2000.

This text's unique constructivist approach guides students in learning by doing. Geared to teachers of preschool through sixth grade students, it represents the cutting edge of elementary science teaching with up-to-date investigations into contemporary topics.

Oldfather, P., and West, J. *Learning Through Children's Eyes: Social Constructivism and the Desire to Learn.* Washington, DC: American Psychological Association, 1999.

The authors of this book show how teachers who take a social constructivist stance may enhance motivation and meaningful learning. The book illustrates the power of this theory by taking an interactive approach that includes discussion questions and case studies. Ideal for teacher education courses, professional development workshops, and independent use.

Linking to Learning

Building an Understanding of Constructivism

http://www.sedl.org/scimath/compass/v01n03/understand.html

A description of the basic tenets of constructivism and a list of resources.

Cognitive Skills Development Projects

http://www.ed.gov/pubs/EPTW/eptw10

This gopher site contains a complete list of projects on cognitive skills development approved by the U.S. Department of Education.

Computers as Learning Partners

http://www.clp.berkeley.edu/CLP.html

This project at the University of California at Berkeley presents information on project-based learning, technology-supported scaffolding, and descriptions of activities and applications.

Constructivism and the Five Es

http://www.miamisci.org/ph/lpintro5e.html

A description of constructivism and the "five Es"—Engage, Explore, Explain, Elaborate, and Evaluate.

The Constructivist

http://www.users.interport.net/~roots/act/ACT1.html

Web site for The Association for Constructivist Teaching, which provides a rich, problem-solving arena that encourages the learner's investigation, invention, and inference. Its mission is to enhance the growth of all educators and students through identification and dissemination of effective constructivist practices in both the professional cultures of teachers and the learning environment of children.

Easing into Constructivism

http://www.sedl.org/scimath/compass/v01n03/construct.html#const4

A brief discussion of how to begin the transition to constructivism in your program.

High/Scope Educational Research Foundation

http://www.highscope.org/

An independent nonprofit research, development, training, and public advocacy organization whose mission is to improve the life chances of children and youth by promoting high-quality educational programs. Activities include training teachers and administrators, conducting research projects on the effectiveness of educational programs, developing curricula for programs, and publishing books, videos, and other tools for educators and researchers.

Jean Piaget and Genetic Epistemology

http://www.gwu.edu/~tip/piaget.html

Detailed description of Piaget's theories concerning genetic epistemology. Site contains a QuickTime video clip of Piaget discussing this topic.

Jean Piaget and Intellectual Development

http://129.7.160.115/inst5931/PIAGET1.html

Discussion of Piaget's stages of intellectual development.

Jean Piaget Society

http://www.piaget.org/main.html

This society has an international, interdisciplinary membership of scholars, teachers, and researchers interested in exploring the nature of the developmental construction of human knowledge by providing an open forum through symposia, books, and other publications.

LiveText: The Home Page for Tech-Savvy Teachers

http://www.ilt.columbia.edu/k12/livetext/

A Web guide to the design of constructivist, cooperative learning projects.

Vygotsky and Thought and Language

http://129.7.160.115/inst5931/Vygotsky.html

Discussion of one of Vygotsky's books, in which he theorized that thought and language develop separately although they are similar processes.

ENDNOTES

1 David M. Brodzinsky, Irving E. Sigel, and Roberta M. Golinkoff, "New Dimensions in Piagetian Theory and Research: An Integrative Perspective," in *New Directions in Piagetian Theory and Practice,* ed. Irving E. Sigel, David M. Brodzinsky, and Roberta M. Golinkoff (Hillsdale, NJ: Erlbaum, 1981), 5.

2 Constance Kamii, "Application of Piaget's Theory to Education: The Preoperational Level," in *New Directions in Piagetian Theory and Practice,* ed. Irving E. Sigel, David M. Brodzinsky, and Roberta M. Golinkoff (Hillsdale, NJ: Erlbaum, 1981), 234.

3 Mary Ann Spencer Pulaski, *Understanding Piaget* (New York: Harper and Row, 1980), 9.

4 P. G. Richmond, *An Introduction to Piaget* (New York: Basic Books, 1970), 68.

5 Ibid.

6 A. Meltzoff and K. M. Moore, "Resolving the Debate About Early Imitation," *Reader in Developmental Psychology* (1999): 151–155.

CHAPTER 6

We begin with the hypothesis that any subject can be taught effectively in some intellectually honest form to any child at any stage of development.

JEROME BRUNER

Early Childhood Programs

Applying Theories to Practice

Focus Questions

1. Why is there a need for early childhood education models?
2. What are the basic features of early childhood education models?
3. What are the similarities, differences, and strengths of early childhood education models?
4. What implications do program models have for your practice as an early childhood professional?

To review the chapter focus questions online, go to the Companion Website at [*http://www.prenhall.com/morrison*](http://www.prenhall.com/morrison) *and select chapter 6.*

Parents want their children to attend high-quality programs that will provide them with a good start in life. They want to know that their children are being well cared for and educated. Parents want their children to get along with others, be happy, and learn. How to best meet these legitimate demands is one of the ongoing challenges of early childhood professionals.

The Growing Demand for Quality Early Childhood Programs

To check your understanding of this chapter with the online Study Guide, go to the Companion Website at http://www.prenhall.com/morrison, select chapter 6, then choose the Study Guide module.

Six thousand early childhood programs serving a half million children are accredited by the National Association for the Education of Young Children (NAEYC), the nation's largest organization of early childhood educators. An additional twelve thousand programs are in the process of being accredited. These programs are only a fraction of the total number of early childhood programs in the United States. Think for a minute about what goes on in these and other programs from day to day. For some children, teachers and staff have developed well thought-out and articulated programs that provide for their growth and development across all the developmental domains—cognitive, linguistic, emotional, social, and physical. In other programs, children are not so fortunate. Their days are filled with aimless activities that fail to meet their academic and developmental needs. At this time, when America is once again discovering the importance of the early years, the public is demanding more from early childhood professionals and their programs. On the one hand, the public is willing to invest more heavily in early childhood programs, but on the other hand, it is demanding that the early childhood profession and individual programs respond by providing meaningful programs. The public demands these things from early childhood professionals:

- Programs that will help ensure children's early academic and school success. The public believes that too many children are being left out and left behind.
- The inclusion of early literacy and reading readiness activities in programs and curricula that will enable children to read on grade level in grades one, two, and three. Literacy is the key to much of school and life success, and school success begins in preschool and before.
- Environments that will help children develop the social and behavioral skills necessary to help them lead civilized and nonviolent lives. In the wake of daily news headlines about shooting and assaults by younger and younger children, the public wants early childhood programs to assume an ever growing responsibility for helping get children off to a nonviolent start in life.

As a result of these public demands, there is a growing and critical need for programs that teachers and others can adopt and use. In this chapter we examine and discuss some of the more notable programs for use in early childhood settings. As you read about and reflect on each of these, think about their strengths and weaknesses and the ways each tries to best meet the needs of children and families. One thing is certain: in this new millennium, we will not be able to conduct business as usual. The public will demand more of us than that. The public will hold you and your colleagues accountable for programs that at a minimum meet the needs mentioned earlier. Pause for a minute and review Table 6.1, which outlines the models of early childhood education discussed in this chapter.

Table 6.1
Models of Early Childhood Education: Similarities and Differences

Program	Main Features	Theoretical Basis
High Scope	• Plan-do-review teaching–learning cycle • Emergent curriculum—curriculum is not established in advance • Children help determine curriculum • Key experiences guide the curriculum in promoting children's active learning	• Piagetian • Constructivist • Dewey
Reggio Emilia	• Emergent curriculum—curriculum is not established in advance • Curriculum based on children's interests and experiences • Project-oriented curriculum • Thousand Languages of Children—symbolic representation of work and learning • Active learning • *Atelierista* (teacher trained in the arts) • *Atelier* (art/design studio)	• Piagetian • Constructivist • Vygotskian • Dewey
Head Start	• Curriculum and program outcomes determined by performance standards • Broad spectrum of comprehensive services, including health, administrative support, and parent involvement • Parents play a key role in program operation • No national curriculum—curriculum developed at the local level	• Whole child • Maturationist • Intervention approach to addressing child and societal problems
Child Care	• Comprehensive services • Program quality determined by each program • Each program has its own curriculum	• Whole child • Maturationist
Montessori	• Prepared environment supports, invites, and enables learning • Children educate themselves—self-directed learning • Sensory materials invite and promote learning • Set curriculum regarding what children should learn—Montessorians try to stay as close to Montessori's ideas as possible • Multiage grouping • Students learn by manipulative materials and working with others • Learning takes place though the senses	• Montessori's beliefs about children

What Is Child Care?

For more information about child care, go to the Companion Website at http://www.prenhall.com/morrison, select chapter 6, then choose the Linking to Learning module to connect to several sites on child care.

Child care is a comprehensive service to children and families that supplements the care children receive from their families. Care is supplemental in that parents delegate responsibility to caregivers for providing care and appropriate experiences in their absence. It is comprehensive in that, although it includes custodial care such as supervision, food, shelter, and other physical necessities, it goes beyond these to include activities that encourage and aid learning and are responsive to children's health, social, and psychological needs. Child care is also educational. It provides for the intellectual needs of children and helps engage them in the process of learning that begins at birth. Quality child care does not ignore the educational needs of young children but incorporates learning activities as part of the curriculum. Furthermore, child care staff work with parents to help them learn how to support children's learning in the home. A comprehensive view of child

care considers the child to be a whole person; therefore, the major purpose of child care is to facilitate optimum development of the whole child and support efforts to achieve this goal.

Why Is Child Care Popular?

Child care is popular and in the center of the public eye for a number of reasons. One is that recent demographic changes have created a high demand for child care. There are more dual-income families and more working single parents than ever before. For example, nearly 62 percent of mothers with children under three are employed, and it is not uncommon for mothers to return to work as early as six weeks after giving birth. In 1998, over thirty-five million employed parents with young children reported significant work–family conflict, creating a general demand for infant and young child care.

Second, child care is an important part of many politicians' solutions to the nation's economic and social problems. In this regard, child care is an instrument of public policy. Child care can be used to address political and social issues. For example, child care is an essential part of work-training programs designed to get people off welfare and help them join the workforce. At the same time, many work-training programs train welfare recipients for child care jobs. So, many welfare recipients are moving from welfare to gainful employment as child care workers.

Quality child care is also seen by politicians and the public as a way of addressing many of the country's problems through early intervention in children's lives. The reasoning goes that if we provide children with quality programs and experiences early in life, we reduce the possibility that they will need costly social services later in life.

As the demand for child care increases, the challenge to you and other early childhood professionals is clear. You and the profession must participate in advocating for and creating quality child care programs that meet the needs of children and families.

Placements in Child Care Programs

Decisions to place children in child care are personal, individual, and complex. We can say with some assurance that because a parent works she places her child in child care. But it could also be the other way around. Because child care is available, a parent may choose to work. Decisions then relating to placement in child care are not necessarily straightforward but depend on many factors. Consider some of these interesting facts about child care placement:

- Three-fourths of families with working mothers use child care for children under five.
- One-third of children with nonworking mothers are placed in child care.
- Better-educated parents are more likely to place their children in child care than those who are not as well educated. Seventy-two percent of children with parents who attended some college are placed in child care, versus 42 percent of children whose parents have less than a high school diploma.
- As children grow older, their likelihood of being placed in child care increases.
- Children in the South are more likely to enter child care than children in the Northeast.
- Children who are white or Latino are less likely to be placed in child care.
- Parents are more likely to initiate child care when a child has a birthday.
- A child in a single-parent family is more likely to be placed in child care than is a child in a two-parent family.
- If a mother works during pregnancy, the likelihood of the child being placed in child care is four times higher than if the mother does not work during pregnancy.[1]

Types of Child Care Programs

Child care is offered in many places, by many persons and agencies that provide a variety of care and services. The options for child care are almost endless. However, regardless of the kinds of child care provided, the three issues of quality, affordability, and accessibility always are part of the child care landscape.

Child Care by Family and Relatives

Child care is most commonly arranged within nuclear and extended families or with friends. Parents handle these arrangements in various ways. In some cases, children are cared for by grandparents, aunts, uncles, or other relatives. These arrangements satisfy parents' needs to have their children cared for by people with similar lifestyles and values, and such care may be less costly. On average, child care provided by relatives costs about $1.63 an hour. Also, the caregiver-to-child ratio is low, and relatives will care for ill children.[2] These types of arrangements allow children to remain in familiar environments with people they know. Child care by family members provides children with continuity and stability parents desire for their children.

Family Care

When child care is provided in a child's own family or family-like setting, it is known as *family day care* or *family care*. In this arrangement an individual caregiver provides care and education for a small group of children in her or his home. Eleven percent of children under five in child care are in family day care. Family day care generally involves three types of settings: homes that are unlicensed and unregulated by a state or local agency, homes that are licensed by regulatory agencies, and homes that are licensed and associated with an administrative agency.

Family day care is the preferred method of child care. Parents like a program for their children that approximates a homelike setting. What are some characteristics of a homelike setting you can incorporate into your classrooms?

Both the quantity and quality of specific services provided in family homes vary from home to home and from agency to agency. However, almost 50 percent of caregivers spend a substantial amount of their time in direct interaction with children. Read the Program in Action, "Bridges Family Child Care," to see how good family day care is much more than baby-sitting.

Program in Action

Bridges Family Child Care

Welcome to the Bridges Community! Bridges is family child care. We work to model the child care experience after our natural human experience on earth. In a time when biological families now live great distances apart, we must develop relationships that we can depend on similar to the way that families have historically depended on each other. Modeling our program after the natural human experience influences our every decision in the design of our program, such as the number of children, the quality of food, the mix of ages, and the influence of the physical child care environment. With this as our "prime directive," we have incorporated what we know as early childhood educators to create a program that encourages exploration, challenges learning, emphasizes social and emotional development, offers wholesome and nutritious food, and provides quiet, restful spaces in a homelike, ecologically sensitive environment.

Bridges Child Care is committed to families by offering ongoing communication of the child's development and family concerns; sliding-scale fees that encourage accessibility, regardless of income; and networking with others for support services such as agencies that offer parent training, social support, and special needs support. Currently one-fourth of the children enrolled are children whose parents became pregnant as teenagers. We encourage parents in their parenting skills and share with them information on what has worked successfully for other families. We also try to keep current on community support services that they may be eligible to receive.

Ratios

Our child:adult ratios reflect our biological capabilities. We have eight children and two staff present, a similar ratio to our natural order of procreating. We believe that the low child:adult ratio is the single greatest factor in providing high-quality care. In a group setting it can be challenging to complete a learning opportunity with a child when other children may have the need for guidance at the same time. With the use of volunteers we are able to enhance our program further to offer one-on-one interactions.

Activities

By providing an environment with a range of self-directed options, children are able to determine what skills they would like to develop and work on. Opportunities such as a "help yourself project/art table" encourage creativity, as well as develop fine motor skills. Our cozy book area is stocked with pillows for quiet small group or even alone time for book exploration. An indoor cotton yoga swing (that doesn't hurt when a child gets bumped by it and is too thick to strangle anyone) provides large motor development and is in constant use! A permanently set up drum and percussion circle encourages regular sessions in music and rhythm and is located near the dramatic play area for chil-

dren to merge music, dance, and drama. We sing routinely, borrowing tunes from other songs and singing about what we are doing or the qualities of a child. We have a table for puzzles and games that has limited choices through regular equipment rotation. One area is reserved specifically for rotating themes such as setting up a hospital scene, store, post office, and such. This area is most often set up as a response to the children's interests or experiences. We also go on field trips, four to five times per week. Each morning at breakfast we share our ideas about what we could do. After the discussion of ideas we vote to determine where we'll head out for that day. We talk about street safety, and we take many opportunities to learn about the earth, animals, business, and politics, as well as doing many large-motor activities.

Self-Care

As the children grow they are encouraged to wash, dress, and toilet independently. The children at Bridges are encouraged to "help themselves" more and more as their skills develop. Self-care is a process: through repetitive and consistent reminders children become responsible for themselves. Self-care is evolutionary: what is an accomplishment for one child becomes an expectation for another as their skills develop.

Food and Nutrition

In an effort to ensure that the children are receiving the best nutrients and are safe from additives, hormones, and pesticides, we make a great effort to serve mostly organic, almost exclusively vegetarian and nonprocessed food. We are able to do this mostly because we have made it a priority, looking again at our natural experience on earth, this time in regards to food. We routinely involve the children in cooking, composting, and gardening.

Social–Emotional Development

At Bridges we feel that the one "job" of children in their early years is to learn how to live in the world with others. While each child differs in skill level of communication, each child is treated with great respect by the adults and is expected to treat others with respect. The conflict we deal with is a healthy part of development and is embraced at Bridges.

Inclusivity

Our program primarily serves children two to five years old. However, we make exceptions based on individual needs. Bridges alumni include children who are blind, autistic, have had cerebral palsy, and have had other physical differences. Currently we have a child with Down's syndrome who has been with us for five years, as well as a child who was born to a mother using crack.

The Environment

Bridges Child Care is located in a ninety-plus-year-old home. We have built a "school" addition using natural, nontoxic materials and recycled materials, which was designed by architects who specialize in environmentally friendly building designs and built in a communal setting. The children's "program" for those years evolved around exploring the work that had been done after child care hours, observing some of the process during construction, and "helping" when it was appropriate. We set up some small activities, such as mixing clay and straw, so they could get a sense of the process. We also talked about what other animals use to make homes and made bird nests from straw and clay. We made pumpkin pies from our gardens' harvest as "thank you" gifts for some of the folks who had helped. We now have separate spaces for learning and playing, eating, and resting. Having ample space in a well designed child care facility is like having an extra staff person because the room works for us, in a supportive and functional way!

Fair Compensation

Bridges Family Child Care is committed to paying a living wage to the employees, which includes health care for full-time staff and paid continuing education, holidays, vacation, and personal days for all the staff. We are also asking the community to help us reach our goal in attaining the sufficient

resources so that every staff member may be paid not just a living wage but a professional wage.

RESOURCES

We are continually evolving and developing our program to improve our service as well as enhance the resources. However, we feel that until public policy acknowledges that the cost of child care is a part of the cost of the greater societal infrastructure and contributes to our booming economy, the stability of child care will continue to be challenged. In Wisconsin, we have nearly an equal amount of licensed child care facilities open each year as we have close. Can you imagine if we operated our public school systems this way?

Visit Bridges Family Child Care on the Web at http://www.execpc.com/~bridges/home.htm.

Contributed by Vic McMurray, Bridges Family Child Care director, Madison, Wisconsin. Photos courtesy of Vic McMurray.

Intergenerational Child Care

Intergenerational child care programs take two forms. One kind integrates children and the elderly into an early childhood and adult care facility. The elderly derive pleasure and feelings of competence from helping care for and interact with children, and young children receive attention and love from older caregivers. In today's mobile society, families often live long distances from each other, and children may be isolated from the care that grandparents can offer. Intergenerational programs blend the best of two worlds: children and the elderly both receive care and attention in a nurturing environment.

For example, the Stride Rite Intergenerational Day Care Center (see chapter 2), located in Cambridge, Massachusetts, enables children and elders to come together for activities including reading, baking, and painting. The Intergenerational Center is the daytime home (7:30 A.M. to 5:30 P.M.) for elders over the age of sixty and children aged fifteen months to six years.

A second type of intergenerational child care utilizes older adults, often retirees, as employees and volunteers to help care for children. Valuable and often untapped resources of skills and knowledge, older citizens have much to offer children and programs.

Center Child Care

Center child care is conducted in specially designed and constructed centers and in churches, YMCAs and YWCAs, and other such facilities. Each state has its own definition of a center-based program, so you should research and become familiar with how your state defines center child care as well as the other types of child care discussed in this chapter. Many center programs are comprehensive, providing a full range of services. Some are babysitting programs, while some offer less than good custodial care. Search for your state's definitions and regulations regarding child care, center care, and other kinds of care. You can access the licensure regulations for all fifty states through this Web site: http://www.uchsc.edu/states.htm.

Employer-Sponsored Child Care

New responses to child care arise as more and more parents enter the workforce. The most rapidly growing segment of the workforce, in fact, is married women with children under one year of age. To meet the needs of working parents, employers are increasingly called on to

provide affordable, accessible, quality child care. Corporate-supported child care is one of the fastest-growing employee benefits, as identified by the U.S. Chamber of Commerce. Employer-sponsored child care is not new. The Stride Rite Corporation started the first on-site corporate child care program in Boston in 1971.

Employer-sponsored child care has become one of the more talked-about programs in child care. In fact, on-site child care is one of the most frequently asked-for benefits by employees. Corporations supply space, equipment, and child care workers. Some corporations contract with an outside agency to provide child care service. Some also maintain a list of family day care homes and contract for spaces. They may also assist in equipping the providers' homes for child care services.

OTHER WAYS BUSINESSES SUPPORT CHILD CARE. Today, almost everyone works, including women with young children. But many of society's institutions were designed during an era of male breadwinners and female homemakers. Workplace policies are now being put into place that ensure that women and men can participate fully in their jobs and careers and still have time and resources to invest in their children.

In addition to sponsoring child care programs, employers can provide child care services in a number of other ways, as shown in Figure 6.1. Many corporations have child care management programs operate their child care programs for them. Table 6.2 lists the top fifteen child care management organizations in the United States.

Proprietary Child Care

Some child care centers are run by corporations, businesses, and individual proprietors for the purpose of making a profit. Some for-profit centers provide custodial services and

- *Resource and referral services.* Corporations supply information and counseling to parents on selecting quality care and referrals to local child care providers. These services can be offered in-house (i.e., on site) or through community or national resource and referral agencies.
- *Direct aid.* Some companies provide a flat subsidy—a specific amount to their employees to help cover the cost of child care. For example, NationsBank, the largest bank in the South, pays its associates with limited incomes up to $35 per week to pay for child care.
- *Voucher systems.* Corporations give employees vouchers with which to purchase services at child care centers.
- *Vendor systems.* Corporations purchase spaces at child care centers and make them available to employees either free or at reduced rates.
- *Contributions to a child care center.* Corporations pay a subsidy to help reduce rates for employees at a particular center.
- *Parent-family leave.* Some corporations provide paid or subsidized leaves of absence for parents in lieu of specific child care services.
- *Other arrangements.* Employers can offer a flexible work schedule, so parents may need less or no child care. They may also offer maternity leave extension and paternity leaves and allow sick leave to include absence from work for a sick child.

Figure 6.1
How Businesses Support Child Care

Table 6.2
Top 15 Child Care Management Organizations in the United States

Organization/Headquarters	CEO	Contracted Centers	Office Park Centers	Licensed Capacity
Bright Horizons Family Solutions Nashville, TN	Marguerite Sallee	248	30	34,902
Children's Discovery Centers/ Knowledge Beginnings San Rafael, CA	Dr. Elanna Yalow	81	77	17,457
Childtime Learning Centers Farmington Hills, MI	Harold Lewis	35	17	5,782
ARAMARK Educational Resources Golden, CO	Duane Larson	30	12	5,100
KinderCare Learning Centers Portland, OR	David Johnson	43	0	4,989
Mulberry Child Care Centers Needham, MA	Clark Adams	15	23	4,784
La Petite Academy Overland Park, KS	James Kahl	29	0	3,600
Nobel Learning Communities Media, PA	Jack Clegg	3	15	2,450
Rainbow Rascals Learning Centers Lathrup Village, MI	Patrick Fenton	6	15	2,055
Kiddie Academy International Bel Air, MD	George Miller	0	16	1,920
Little People Day School Associates Collegeville, PA	Robert Sprague	3	9	1,728
The Sunshine House Greenwood, SC	Roseann/Dennis Drew	9	0	1,490
Next Generation Child Development Centers Carrollton, TX	Dr. Layton Revel	6	3	1,200
National Pediatric Support Services Fountain Valley, CA	Sheri Senter	9	0	723
The Learning Tree Schools Pittsburgh, PA	Dr. Jamie McIntyre- Southworth	5	0	600

NOTE: Organizations listed by total licensed capacity of all contracted and office park centers as of March 1, 1999. The "Contracted Centers" column displays centers operated under contract to a single employer. The "Office Park Centers" column displays centers operated in office parks or other commercial settings serving more than one employer. Based solely on information provided by organizations.

Source: Inside Child Care: Trend Report 2000. *Reprinted with permission from Child Care Information Exchange, P.O. Box 3249, Redmond, WA 98073. (800) 221-2864.*

preschool and elementary programs as well. Many of these programs emphasize their educational component and appeal to middle-class families who are willing to pay for the promised services. About 35 percent of all child care centers in the United States are operated for profit, and the number is likely to grow. Child care is a big service industry, with more and more entrepreneurs realizing that there is money to be made in caring for the nation's children. The child care industry is a $30 billion industry, and for-profit child care companies are

Program in Action

Bright Horizons Glaxo Wellcome Inc. Onsite Child Center

The standards at Bright Horizons Child Center focus on two primary aspects: the quality of our child-centered programming including interaction between faculty and families, and the quality of our faculty and the conditions in which they work. Guidelines have been created to continually assess our programs to assure that they exercise developmentally appropriate practices and that the delivery of our programs and design of our surroundings remain child centered.

Developmentally appropriate standards established by the National Association for the Education of Young Children form the basis of our program's curriculum. To develop our curriculum, we not only recognize the universal patterns and milestones of child development but also work to find in each individual child his or her unique pattern of developmental capabilities, temperamental characteristics, and learning styles. The intent of our curriculum, therefore, is to provide learning activities and materials that are real, concrete, and relevant to the lives and experiences of our young children.

The teacher's role in classrooms at Bright Horizons is to provide a variety of challenging activity choices for children and then facilitate children's engagement in the activities they select. A teacher's thoughtful input at the right moment can advance a child's competence and challenge a child's thinking. Small group sizes, intensive teacher:child ratios, and highly qualified and trained teachers provide assurance that each child

receives individual attention and develops a sense of belonging in the center. The development of self-esteem in each child is a fundamental goal. We believe that children develop a positive self-image when they are given opportunities to exercise the power of their own choices.

Essential to the Bright Horizons program is parent involvement and satisfaction. The center believes the systems created to support parent communication and involvement form the cornerstone of the Bright Horizon–Parent Partnership. The center emphasizes the important role parents play in the early learning and development of their children. As teachers of young children, staff at the center are able to share with parents aspects of their knowledge about child development and their particular insights about young children. To facilitate better communication, Bright Horizons issues a company-wide parent survey every year to solicit input with regard to all aspects of each center's program, such as program quality, faculty quality, and the level of satisfaction with the program. The faculty is surveyed as well.

In 1992, Bright Horizons established a task force to investigate the needs of families with both parents working and overall attitudes toward preschool education practices and school readiness. As a result of this undertaking, the center developed LANGUAGE WORKS!, a preschool pro-

gram that is a whole language learning experience to address the key element that contributes to a child's readiness for school and lifelong learning: language proficiency. LANGUAGE WORKS! is an expansion in Bright Horizon's developmental preschool education program to help children develop a foundation of social and cognitive skills. This program also offers opportunities for more parent participation, both in the classroom and at home, in order for children to enter elementary school "ready to learn."

Visit Bright Horizons on the Web at http://www.brighthorizons.com/.

Bright Horizons, based in Cambridge, Massachusetts, has managed Glaxo Wellcome Inc. child centers since late 1991. As a national child care management company, it manages 248 child care programs across the country. Photos provided by Bright Horizons.

growing in number and size. The five largest for-profit child care organizations are KinderCare Learning Centers, La Petite Academy, Children's World Learning Centers, Childtime Learning Centers, and Bright Horizons Family Solutions.[3]

Child Care for Children with Ongoing Medical Needs

As child care becomes more popular, it also is becoming more specialized. For most parents, balancing the demands of a job and the obligations of parenthood is manageable as long as children are healthy. But when children get sick, parents must find someone who will take care of them, or they must stay home. The National Child Care Survey data reveal that 35 percent of mothers employed outside the home reported that in the month previous to the survey their child was sick on a day they were supposed to work. Fifty-one percent of these women missed an average of 2.2 days of work per month because of sick children.[4]

Consequently, child care providers have begun to respond to parents' needs. More and more programs are providing care for children with medical needs, such as care when they have illnesses (both contagious and noncontagious) that keep them from attending other regular child care programs. Also, some children may have broken bones, which require special care and keep them from attending their programs. Some centers provide care for sick children as part of their program, and other providers are opening centers exclusively for the care of ill children. Ill children are cared for in the following ways:

- *In the home.* Child care aides go into homes to care for ill children.
- *Hospital based.* Some hospitals have programs providing for sick children.
- *Center based.* Ill child care is part of the program's services and is usually in a separate room or area.
- A *separate facility.* This facility is specifically designed, built, and staffed to provide child care as needed for sick children.
- *Family care.* Ill children are provided for in a family day care home.

Before-School and After-School Care

In many respects, public schools are logical places for before-school and after-school care. They have the administrative organization, facilities, and staff to provide such care. Many taxpayers and professionals have always believed that schools should not sit empty in the

afternoons, evenings, holidays, and summers. Using resources already in place for child care makes good sense. This is why in many communities public schools are helping meet the need for after-school child care. For example, the public schools in Dade County, Florida, provide before- and after-school care for over 23,000 students in 203 after-school centers and 3,300 students in 111 before-school centers. Special needs students are mainstreamed at 83 schools with well over 700 students in after-school care. Parents pay from $15 to $25 per week depending on the per-child cost at the individual school. Because the programs are school based and managed, the costs of services vary depending on the nature and cost of each program. Services begin at dismissal and end at 6 P.M. The curriculum includes Boy and Girl Scouts, 4-H, fun activities based on skills and concepts measured by state assessment tests for grades three and five, drama, and ballet.

According to the National Study of Before and After School Programs, about 1.7 million children in kindergarten through grade eight are enrolled in 49,500 programs.[5] The three most common sponsors of before- and after-school child care are the public schools, for-profit corporations, and nonprofit organizations. As child care grows and expands across the nation, it forces a number of critical issues. These are: how to maintain and provide high-quality care for *all* children; how to provide high-quality *affordable* care for all families; and how to ensure that high-quality, affordable care is *available* to all families that want and need it.

Model Programs

As you continue reading this chapter, review again Table 6.1 and compare and contrast the features of the models I discuss. I now discuss three highly regarded and widely adopted model programs: High/Scope, Reggio Emilia, and Head Start. A fourth, Montessori, I discussed at length in chapter 4. There is a good probability that you will be associated in some way as a teacher, parent, or advisory board member with one of these models. In any event, you will want to be informed about their main features and operating principles.

High/Scope: A Constructivist Approach

The High/Scope Educational Research Foundation is a nonprofit organization that sponsors and supports the High/Scope Educational Approach. The program is based on Piaget's intellectual development theory and

> seeks to provide broad, realistic educational experiences for children. The curriculum is geared to the child's current stage of development to promote the spontaneous and constructive processes of learning and to broaden the child's emerging intellectual and social skills.[6]

For more information about High/Scope, go to the Companion Website at http://www.prenhall.com/morrison, select chapter 6, then choose the Linking to Learning module to connect to the High/Scope Education Research Foundation site.

High/Scope identifies three fundamental principles:

- Active participation of children in choosing, organizing, and evaluating learning activities, which are undertaken with careful teacher observation and guidance in a learning environment replete with a rich variety of materials located in various classroom learning centers
- Regular daily planning by the teaching staff in accord with a developmentally based curriculum model and careful child observations
- Developmentally sequenced goals and materials for children based on the High/Scope "key experiences"[7]

Program in Action

High/Scope in Practice

The High/Scope educational approach for three- to five-year-olds is a developmental model based on the principle of active learning. The following beliefs underlie this approach:

- Children construct knowledge through their active involvement with people, materials, events, and ideas, a process that is intrinsically motivated.
- While children develop capacities in a predictable sequence, adult support contributes to children's intellectual, social, emotional, and physical development.
- Consistent adult support and respect for children's choices, thoughts, and actions strengthen the child's self-respect, feelings of responsibility, self-control, and knowledge.
- Careful observation of children's interests and intentions is a necessary step in understanding their level of development and planning and carrying out appropriate interactions with them.

In High/Scope programs these principles are implemented throughout the day, both through the structure of the daily routine and in the strategies adults use as they work with children. Staff of each program plan for the day's experiences, striving to create a balance between adult- and child-initiated activity.

As they plan activities, the staff considers five "factors of intrinsic motivation" that research indicates are essential for learning. These factors are enjoyment, interest, control, probability of success, and feelings of competence. During greeting circle and small group, staff members actively involve the children in decisions about activities and materials as a way of supporting their intrinsic motivation to learn. This emphasis on child choice continues throughout the day, even during activities initiated by adults.

A Day at a High/Scope Program

Each program implements the High/Scope approach in a different way. A typical day's activities at Giving Tree School follows.

The day begins with greeting time. Children gather as the teacher begins a well-known animal finger play, and join in immediately. Then the teacher suggests that the group make a circus of animals who are moving in many ways. Two children do not want to be animals, and the teacher suggests that these children may want to be the "audience." They get chairs and prepare to watch. Children suggest elephants, bears, and alligators as animals for the group to imitate. The children parade before the audience pretending to be animals and moving to the music. At the close of greeting time, the teacher suggests that children choose an animal to be as they move to the next activity, small-group time. During small-group time the children make "inventions" of their choice with recyclable materials a teacher has brought in and pine cones they collected the previous day.

As small-group activities are completed, planning begins. At this time, the teacher asks the younger children to indicate their plans for work time by going to get something they will use in their play. She asks the older children to draw or copy the symbols or letters that stand for the area in which they plan to play (each play area is labeled with a sign containing both a simple picture symbol and words for the area). To indicate his plan, Charlie, age three, gets a small hollow block and brings it to the teacher. "I'm going to make a train. That's all," he says. Aja, age four, brings a dress and a roll of tape. "I'm going to the playhouse to be the mommy, and then I'm going to the art area to make something with tape," she explains. Five-year-old Ashley shows the teacher her drawing of the tub table and the scoops she will use with rice at the table.

During work time, the teachers participate in children's play. Riding on Charlie's train, one

teacher shows Tasha how to make the numerals 3 and 5 for train "tickets," joins two children playing a board game, and listens to Aja as she explains how she made a doll bed out of tape and a box. One teacher helps Nicholas and Charlie negotiate a conflict over a block, encouraging them by listening and asking questions until they agree on a solution.

At recall time, the children gather with the small groups they met with at planning time. Standing in a circle, each group rotates a hula hoop (one of many such facilitating techniques) through their hands as they sing a short song. When the song ends, the child nearest the tape is first to recall his or her work time experiences. Charlie tells about the train they made out of blocks. Nicholas describes the special "speed sticks" he played with. Aja shows her doll bed, and Tasha describes her "tickets." After snack, the children get their coats on and discuss what they will do outside. "Let's collect more pine cones. We can use them for food for the baby alligators"; "Let's go on the swings. I just learned how to pump"; "Let's see if we can find more bugs hiding under the rocks. They go there for winter." The teacher responds, "I'd like to help you look for bugs."

KEY EXPERIENCES

As children play, they are actively involved in solving problems and participate in many of the High/Scope "key experiences." There are fifty-eight key experiences that fall into ten categories: *social relation and initiative, language, creative representation, music, movement, classification, seriation, numbers, space,* and *time.* Teachers use the fifty-eight key experiences as guides for understanding development, planning activities, and describing the thinking and actions involved in children's play.

The High/Scope approach to learning supports developmentally appropriate, active learning experiences for each child as it encourages decision making, creative expression, problem solving, and other emerging abilities.

Contributed by Betsy Evans, The Giving Tree School, Gill, MA, and Field Consultant, High/Scope Education Research Foundation.

Basic Principles and Goals of the High/Scope Approach

The High/Scope program strives to

> develop in children a broad range of skills, including the problem solving, interpersonal, and communication skills that are essential for successful living in a rapidly changing society. The curriculum encourages student initiative by providing children with materials, equipment, and time to pursue activities they choose. At the same time, it provides teachers with a framework for guiding children's independent activities toward sequenced learning goals.
>
> The teacher plays a key role in instructional activities by selecting appropriate, developmentally sequenced material and by encouraging children to adopt an active problem-solving approach to learning. . . . This teacher–student interaction—teachers helping students achieve developmentally sequenced goals while also encouraging them to set many of their own goals—uniquely distinguishes the High/Scope Curriculum from direct-instruction and child-centered curricula.[8]

The High/Scope approach influences the arrangement of the classroom, the manner in which teachers interact with children, and the methods employed to assess children. The High/Scope curriculum can be defined by looking at the five interrelated components shown in Figure 6.2. Review Figure 6.2 to see how active learning forms the hub of the "wheel of learning" and is supported by the key elements of the curriculum.

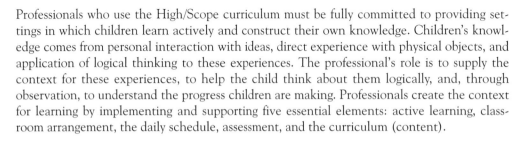

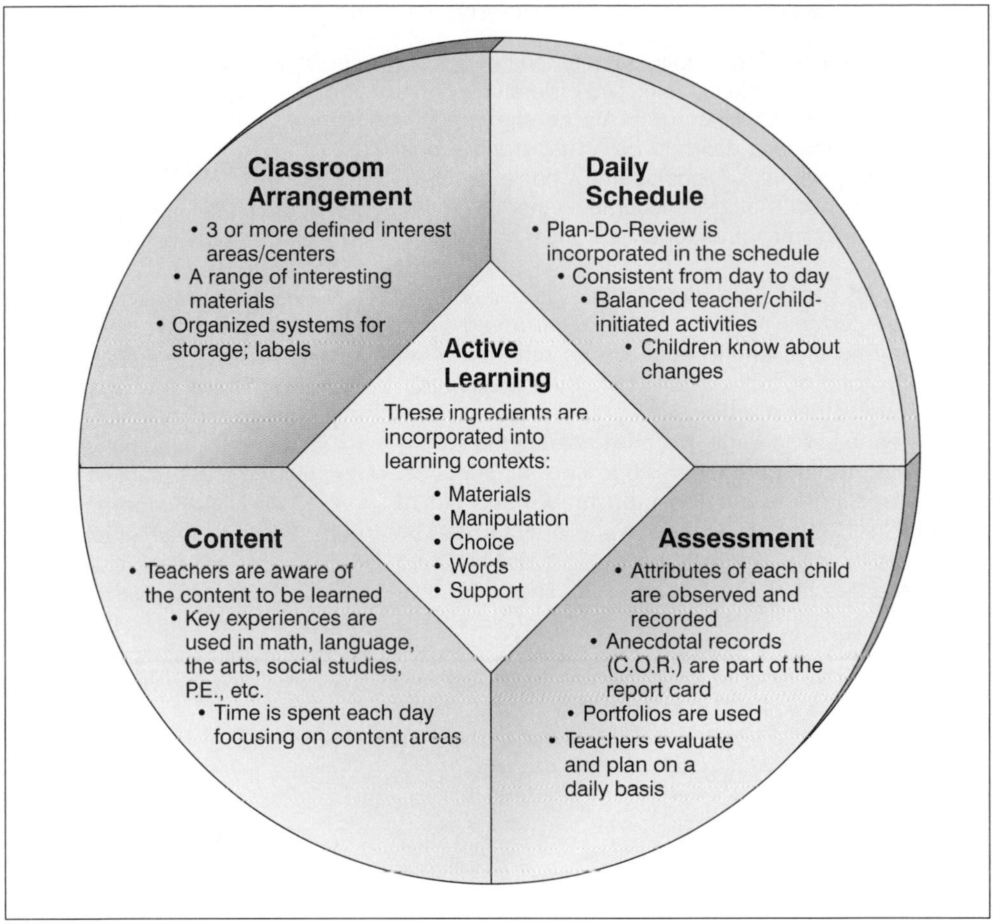

Figure 6.2
High/Scope Curriculum Wheel

Source: Used with permission of David P. Weikart, president, High/Scope Educational Research Foundation, 600 N. River St. Ypsilanti, MI 48198-2898.

The Five Elements of the High/Scope Approach

For more information about the High/Scope curriculum model, go to the Companion Website at http://www.prenhall.com/morrison, select any chapter, then choose Topic 4 of the ECE Supersite model.

Professionals who use the High/Scope curriculum must be fully committed to providing settings in which children learn actively and construct their own knowledge. Children's knowledge comes from personal interaction with ideas, direct experience with physical objects, and application of logical thinking to these experiences. The professional's role is to supply the context for these experiences, to help the child think about them logically, and, through observation, to understand the progress children are making. Professionals create the context for learning by implementing and supporting five essential elements: active learning, classroom arrangement, the daily schedule, assessment, and the curriculum (content).

ACTIVE LEARNING. The idea that children are the source of their own learning forms the center of the High/Scope curriculum. Teachers support children's active learning by providing a variety of materials, making plans and reviewing activities with children, interacting with and carefully observing individual children, and leading small- and large-group active learning activities.

Children can learn mathematics skills through activities that involve the manipulation of concrete objects, like blocks. What other active learning activities can you use to help children discover principles of mathematics?

CLASSROOM ARRANGEMENT. The classroom arrangement invites children to engage in personal, meaningful, educational experiences. In addition, the classroom contains five or more interest areas that encourage choice. Review Figure 6.3 to see a High/Scope room arrangement for kindergarten.

The classroom organization of materials and equipment supports the daily routine—children know where to find materials and what materials they can use. This encourages development of self-direction and independence. The floor plan in Figure 6.3 shows how room arrangement supports and implements the program's philosophy, goals, and objectives and how a center approach (books, blocks, computers, dramatic play, art, construction) provides space for large-group activities and individual work. In a classroom where space is at a premium, the teacher makes one area serve many difference purposes.

The teacher selects the centers and activities to use in the classroom based on several considerations:

- Interests of the children (e.g., kindergarten children are interested in blocks, housekeeping, and art)
- Opportunities for facilitating active involvement in seriation, number, time relations, classification, spatial relations, and language development
- Opportunities for reinforcing needed skills and concepts and functional use of those skills and concepts

Arranging the environment, then, is essential to implementing a program's philosophy. This is true for Montessori, for High/Scope, and for every other program.

DAILY SCHEDULE. The schedule considers developmental levels of children, incorporates a sixty- to seventy-minute plan-do-review process, provides for content areas, is as consistent throughout the day as possible, and contains a minimum number of transitions.

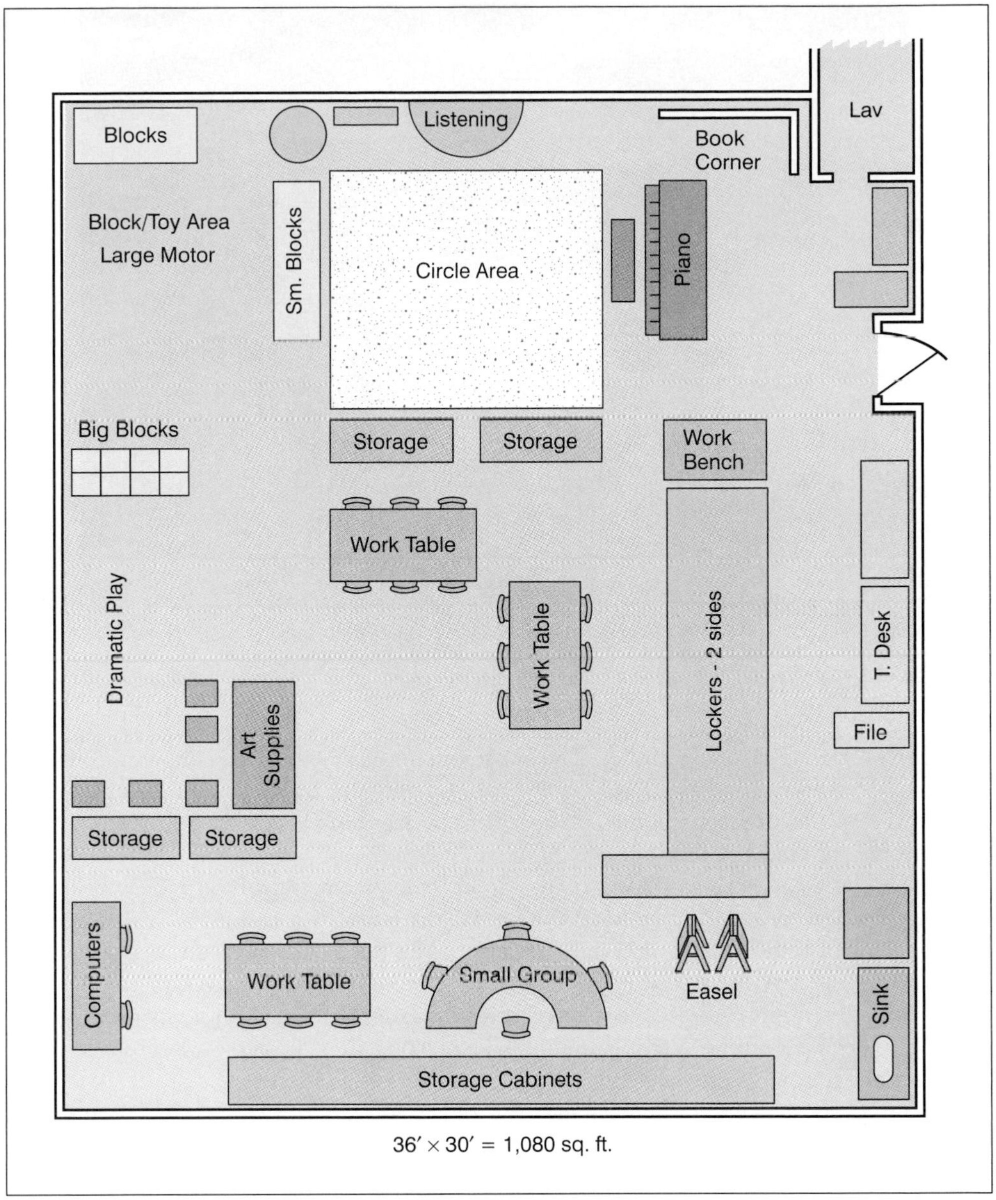

Figure 6.3
A High/Scope Kindergarten Classroom Arrangement

Source: Used with permission of David P. Weikart, president, High/Scope Educational Research Foundation, 600 N. River St. Ypsilanti, MI 48198-2898.

ASSESSMENT. Teachers keep notes about significant behaviors, changes, statements, and things that help them better understand a child's way of thinking and learning. Teachers use two mechanisms to help them collect data: the key experiences note form and a portfolio. The High/Scope Child Observation Record (see chapter 11) is also used to assess children's development.

CURRICULUM. The High/Scope curriculum comes from two sources: children's interests and the key experiences, which are lists of observable learning behaviors. (See Figure 6.4.)

Basing a curriculum in part on children's interests is very constructivist and implements the philosophies of Dewey and Piaget.

A Daily Routine That Supports Active Learning

The High/Scope curriculum's daily routine is made up of a plan-do-review sequence and several additional elements. The plan-do-review sequence gives children opportunities to express intentions about their activities while keeping the teacher intimately involved in the whole process. The following five processes support the daily routine and contribute to its successful functioning.

PLANNING TIME. Planning time gives children a structured, consistent chance to express their ideas to adults and to see themselves as individuals who can act on decisions. They experience the power of independence and the joy of working to be conscious of their intentions, and this supports the development of purpose and confidence.

The teacher talks with children about the plans they have made before the children carry them out. This helps children clarify their ideas and think about how to proceed. Talking with children about their plans provides an opportunity for the teacher to encourage and respond to each child's ideas, to suggest ways to strengthen the plans so they will be successful, and to understand and gauge each child's level of development and thinking style. Children and teachers benefit from these conversations and reflections. Children feel reinforced and ready to start their work, while teachers have ideas of what opportunities for extension might arise, what difficulties children might have, and where problem solving may be needed. In such a classroom, children and teachers are playing appropriate and important roles.

KEY EXPERIENCES. Teachers continually encourage and support children's interests and involvement in activities, which occur within an organized environment and a consistent routine. Teachers plan from key experiences that may broaden and strengthen children's emerging abilities. Children generate many of these experiences on their own; others require teacher guidance. Many key experiences are natural extensions of children's projects and interests. Refer again to Figure 6.4 to review key experiences that support learning in areas of speaking and listening, writing, and reading.

WORK TIME. This part of the plan-do-review sequence is generally the longest time period in the daily routine. The teacher's role during work time is to observe children to see how they gather information, interact with peers, and solve problems, and when appropriate they enter into the children's activities to encourage, extend, and set up problem-solving situations.

CLEANUP TIME. During cleanup time, children return materials and equipment to their labeled places and store their incomplete projects, restoring order to the classroom. All children's materials in the classroom are within reach and on open shelves. Clear labeling enables children to return all work materials to their appropriate places.

RECALL TIME. Recall time, the final phase of the plan-do-review sequence, is the time when children represent their work time experience in a variety of developmentally appropriate ways. They might recall the names of the children they involved in their plan, draw a picture of the building they made, or describe the problems they encountered. Recall strategies include drawing pictures, making models, physically demonstrating how a plan was carried out, or verbally recalling the events of work time. The teacher supports children's linking of the actual work to their original plan.

Speaking and Listening

Speaking their own language or dialect

Asking and answering questions

Stating facts and observations in their own words

Using language to solve problems

Participating in singing, storytelling, poetic and dramatic activities

Recalling thoughts and observations in a purposeful context

Acquiring, strengthening, and extending speaking and listening skills
- Discussing to clarify observations or to better follow directions
- Discussing to expand speaking and listening vocabulary
- Discussing to strengthen critical thinking and problem-solving activities

Writing

Observing the connections between spoken and written language

Writing in unconventional forms

Scribbles
- Drawing
- Letters—random or patterned, possibly including elements of names copied from the environment
- Invented spelling of initial sounds and intermediate sounds

Writing in conventional forms

Expressing thoughts in writing

Sharing writing in purposeful context

Using writing equipment (e.g., computers, typewriters)

Writing in specific content areas

Figure 6.4
Key Experiences in Language and Literacy for a High/Scope K–3 Curriculum

This review permits children to reflect on what they did and how it was done. It brings closure to children's planning and work time activities. Putting their ideas and experiences into words also facilitates children's language development. Most important, it enables children to represent to others their mental schemes.

Advantages

There are a number of advantages to implementing the High/Scope approach. It offers you and others a method for implementing a constructivist-based program that has its roots in Piagetian cognitive theory. Second, it is widely popular and has been extensively researched and tested. Third, there is a rather extensive network of training and support provided by the High/Scope Foundation. You can learn more about High/Scope through its Web site at www.highscope.org. This will further help you decide if High/Scope is a program you would consider implementing in your classroom.

Acquiring, strengthening, and extending writing skills
- Letter formation
- Sentence and paragraph formation
- Capitalization, punctuation, and grammatical usage
- Editing and proofreading for mechanics, content, and style

Expanding the forms of composition
- Expressive mode
- Transactional mode—expository, argumentative, descriptive

Poetic mode—narrative mode

Publishing selected compositions

Reading

Experiencing varied genres of children's literature

Reading own compositions

Reading and listening to others read in a purposeful context

Using audio and/or video recordings in reading experiences

Acquiring, strengthening, and extending specific reading skills
- Auditory discrimination
- Letter recognition
- Decoding—phonetic analysis (letter/sound associations, factors affecting sounds, syllabication), structural analysis (forms, prefixes, suffixes)
- Vocabulary development

Expanding comprehension and fluency skills
- Activating prior knowledge
- Determining purpose, considering context, making predictions
- Developing strategies for interpreting narrative and expository text
- Reading varied genres of children's literature

Reggio Emilia

Reggio Emilia, a city in northern Italy, is widely known for its approach to educating young children.[9] Founded by Loris Malaguzzi (1920–1994), Reggio Emilia sponsors programs for children from three months to six years of age.

For more information about Reggio Emilia, go to the Companion Website at http://www.prenhall.com/morrison, select chapter 6, then choose the Linking to Learning module to connect to the Reggio Emilia Approach to Early Childhood Education site.

Basic Principles of the Reggio Emilia Approach

Certain essential beliefs and practices underlie the Reggio Emilia approach. These basic features are what defines the Reggio approach, makes it a constructivist program, and defines it as a model being adapted and implemented in many U.S. early childhood programs.

BELIEFS ABOUT CHILDREN AND HOW THEY LEARN

Relationships. Education focuses on each child and is conducted in relation with the family, other children, the teachers, the environment of the school, the community, and the wider society. Each school is viewed as a system in which all these interconnected relationships are reciprocal, activated, and supported. In other words, as Vygotsky believed, children learn through social interactions. In addition, as Montessori indicated, the environment supports and is important to learning.

When preparing space, teachers offer the possibility for children to be with the teachers and many of the other children, or with just a few of them. Also, children can be alone when they need a little niche to stay by themselves.

Teachers are always aware, however, that children learn a great deal in exchanges with their peers, especially when they interact in small groups. Such small groups of two, three, four, or five children provide possibilities for paying attention, hearing and listening to each other, developing curiosity and interest, asking questions, and responding to them. Also, groups provide opportunities for negotiation and ongoing dynamic communication.

Time. Reggio Emilia teachers believe that time is not set by a clock and that continuity is not interrupted by the calendar. Children's own sense of time and their personal rhythm are considered in planning and carrying out activities and projects. The full-day schedule provides sufficient time for being together among peers in an environment that is conducive to getting things done with satisfaction.

Teachers get to know the personal rhythms and learning styles of each child. This really getting to know children is possible in part because children stay with the same teachers and the same peer group for three-year cycles (infancy to three years and three years to six years).

For more information about the Reggio Emilia curriculum model, go to the Companion Website at http://www.prenhall.com/morrison, select any chapter, then choose Topic 4 of the ECE Supersite module.

ADULTS' ROLE. Adults play a very powerful role in children's lives. Children's well-being is connected with the well-being of parents and teachers. Children have a right to high-quality care and education that supports the development of their potentials. Adults can provide these educational necessities. Parents have rights to be involved in the life of the school, and teachers have rights to grow professionally.

The Teacher. Teachers observe and listen closely to children to know how to plan or proceed with their work. They ask questions and discover children's ideas, hypotheses, and theories. They collaboratively discuss what they have observed and recorded, and they make flexible plans and preparations. Teachers then enter into dialogues with the children and offer them occasions for discovering and also revisiting and reflecting on experiences, since they consider learning an ongoing process. Teachers are partners with children in a continual process of research and learning.

***The* Atelierista.** An *atelierista,* a teacher trained in the visual arts, works closely with teachers and children in every preprimary school and makes visits to the infant–toddler centers.

Parents. Parents are an essential component of the program, and they are included in the advisory committee that runs each school. Parents' participation is expected and supported and takes many forms: day-to-day interaction, work in the schools, discussion of educational and psychological issues, special events, excursions, and celebrations.

THE ENVIRONMENT. The infant–toddler centers and school programs are the most visible aspect of the work done by teachers and parents in Reggio Emilia. They convey many messages, of which the most immediate is that this is a place where adults have thought about the quality and the instructive power of space.

The Physical Space. The layout of physical space, in addition to welcoming whoever enters, fosters encounters, communication, and relationships. The arrangement of structures, objects, and activities encourages choices, problem solving, and discoveries in the process of learning.

The centers and schools of Reggio are beautiful. Their beauty comes from the message the whole school conveys about children and teachers engaged together in the pleasure of learning. There is attention to detail everywhere: in the color of the walls, the shape of the furniture, the arrangement of simple objects on shelves and tables. Light from the windows and doors shines through transparent collages and weavings made by children. Healthy, green plants are everywhere. Behind the shelves displaying shells or other found or made objects are mirrors that reflect the patterns that children and teachers have created.

The environment is also highly personal. For example, a series of small boxes made of white cardboard creates a grid on the wall of a school. On each box the name of a child or a teacher is printed with rubber stamp letters. These boxes are used for leaving little surprises or messages for one another. Communication is valued and favored at all levels.

The space in the centers and schools of Reggio Emilia is personal in still another way: it is full of children's own work. Everywhere there are paintings, drawings, paper sculptures, wire constructions, transparent collages coloring the light, and mobiles moving gently overhead. Such things turn up even in unexpected spaces like stairways and bathrooms.

The Atelier. A special workshop or studio, called an *atelier*, is set aside and used by all the children and teachers in the school. It contains a great variety of tools and resource materials, along with records of past projects and experiences.

The activities and projects, however, do not take place only in the *atelier*. Smaller spaces called *mini-ateliers* are set up in each classroom. In the view of Reggio educators, the children's use of many media is not art or a separate part of the curriculum but an inseparable, integral part of the whole cognitive/symbolic expression involved in the process of learning.

Program in Action

Reggio Emilia

Reggio Emilia is a city in northern Italy. The excellent educational program the city offers its children, based on providing an educational environment that encourages learning, is known as the Reggio Emilia approach. Reggio Emilia sponsors infant programs for children three months to three years and programs for children three to six years.

Each of the Reggio schools can accommodate seventy-five children, with each group or class consisting of about twenty-five children with two co-teachers. Children of single parents and children with disabilities have priority in admission. The other children are admitted according to a scale of needs. Parents pay on a sliding scale based on income.

The Reggio Emilia approach is unique in that children are encouraged to learn by investigating and exploring topics that interest them. Learning is a social and cultural process that does not occur in isolation from other children, adults, and the environment. The Reggio school environment is designed to accommodate the child's developmental culture and provide a wide range of stimulating media and materials for children to express their learning, such as words, sounds and music, movement, drawing, painting, sculpting, and modeling clay or wire, making collages, using puppets and disguises, photography and more.

Reggio children typically explore topics by way of group projects. This approach fosters a sense of community, respect for diversity, and a collaborative approach to problem solving—both important aspects of learning. Two co-teachers are present during the project to guide the children and

widen the range of learning. This is the way Carina Rinaldi, *pedagogista* (consultant resource person), describes a project:

> A project, which we view as sort of an adventure and research, can start through a suggestion from an adult, a child's idea, or from an event such as a snowfall or something else unexpected. But every project is based on the attention of the educators to what the children say and do as well as what they do not say and do. The adults must allow enough time for the thinking and actions of children to develop.*

The children pictured here are working on a special "Shadows" project. The exploration of shadows has great attraction for children and many implications for learning with pleasure. Children discuss their ideas and formulate hypotheses about shadows' origins and destiny. Exploration of shadows in the schools of Reggio Emilia continues to be a favorite theme for children and teachers. In this specific episode, after exploring shadow outside (at different times of the day) and inside (with artificial light and flashlights), the teacher extends the interest of a child who has represented a little girl with a full skirt by posing a question-problem to her.

Additional resources for Reggio Emilia are available on-line at http://ericps.ed.uiuc.edu/eece/reggio/reglink.html.

Contributed by Lella Gandini, Northampton, Massachusetts. Photos from the city of Reggio Emilia, teachers, and children of the preprimary schools Diana and Gulliver, Tutto ha un ombra meno le formiche *(Everything but the ant has a shadow) (City of Reggio Emilia, Italy: Department of Education Via Guido do Castello, 1990), p. 12; photos provided by Lella Gandini.*

**Carina Rinaldi, "The Emergent Curriculum and Social Constructivism," in Carolyn Edwards, Lella Gandini, and George Forman, eds.,* The Hundred Languages of Children *(Norwood, NJ: Ablex, 1993), 108.*

PROGRAM PRACTICES. Cooperation is the powerful mode of working that makes possible the achievement of the goals Reggio educators set for themselves. Teachers work in pairs in each classroom. They see themselves as researchers gathering information about their work with children by means of continual documentation. The strong collegial relationships that are maintained with teachers and staff enable them to engage in collaborative discussion and interpretation of both teachers' and children's work.

Documentation. Transcriptions of children's remarks and discussions, photographs of their activity, and representations of their thinking and learning using many media are carefully arranged by the *atelierista*, along with the other teachers, to document the work and the process of learning. This documentation has five functions. First, to make parents aware of children's experience and maintain their involvement. Second, to allow teachers to understand children better and to evaluate their own work, thus promoting professional growth.

Third, to facilitate communication and exchange of ideas among educators. Fourth, to make children aware that their effort is valued. And fifth, to create an archive that traces the history of the school and the pleasure of learning by many children and their teachers.

Curriculum and Practices. The curriculum is not established in advance. Teachers express general goals and make hypotheses about what direction activities and projects might take. On this basis, they make appropriate preparations. Then, after observing children in action, teachers compare, discuss, and interpret together their observations and make choices that they share with the children about what to offer and how to sustain the children in their exploration and learning. In fact, the curriculum emerges in the process of each activity or project and is flexibly adjusted accordingly through this continuous dialogue among teachers and with children.

Projects provide the backbone of the children's and teachers' learning experiences. These projects are based on the strong conviction that learning by doing is of great importance and that to discuss in groups and to revisit ideas and experiences is the premier way of gaining better understanding and learning.

Ideas for projects originate in the experiences of children and teachers as they construct knowledge together. Projects can last from a few days to several months. They may start from either a chance event, an idea or a problem posed by one or more children, or an experience initiated directly by teachers.

CONSIDERATIONS. There are a number of things to keep in mind when considering the Reggio Emilia approach. First, its theoretical base rests within constructivism and shares ideas compatible with those of Piaget, Vygotsky, Dewey, Gardner, and Diamond (reflect on Table 5.1 again) and the concept or process of learning by doing. Second, there is no set curriculum. Rather, the curriculum emerges or springs from children's interests and experiences. This approach is, for many, difficult to implement and does not ensure that children will learn basic academic skills valued by contemporary American society. Third, the Reggio Emilia approach is suited to a particular culture and society. How this approach works and flourishes and meets the educational needs of children in an Italian village may not necessarily be appropriate for meeting the needs of contemporary American children. The Italian view of education is that it is the responsibility of the state, and the state provides high levels of financial support. While education is a state function in the United States, traditionally the local community control of education is a powerful and sacrosanct part of American education. Having said all of this, a number of schools and programs are implementing the Reggio approach. One that you can learn about is the Margaret Shadick Cyert Center for Early Education at Carnegie Mellon University in Pittsburgh, http://www.cmu.edu/cyert-center/.

Head Start

Head Start was implemented during the summer of 1965, and approximately 550,000 children in 2,500 child development centers were enrolled in the program. The first programs were designed for children entering first grade who had not attended kindergarten. The purpose of Head Start was literally to give children from low-income families a "head start" on their first grade experience and, hopefully, on life itself.

As of 1998, the National Head Start program has an annual budget of over $4.4 billion and serves some 794,000 low-income children and families. There are 1,456 Head Start programs nationwide, with a total of nearly 17,000 centers and over 42,000 classrooms. The average cost per child of the Head Start program is $4,882 annually. Head Start has a paid staff of 155,300 and 1,315,000 volunteers. A total of 16,892,000 children have been served by Head Start since it began.[10]

For more information about Head Start, go to the Companion Website at http://www.prenhall.com/morrison, select chapter 6, then choose the Linking to Learning module to connect to the National Head Start Association site.

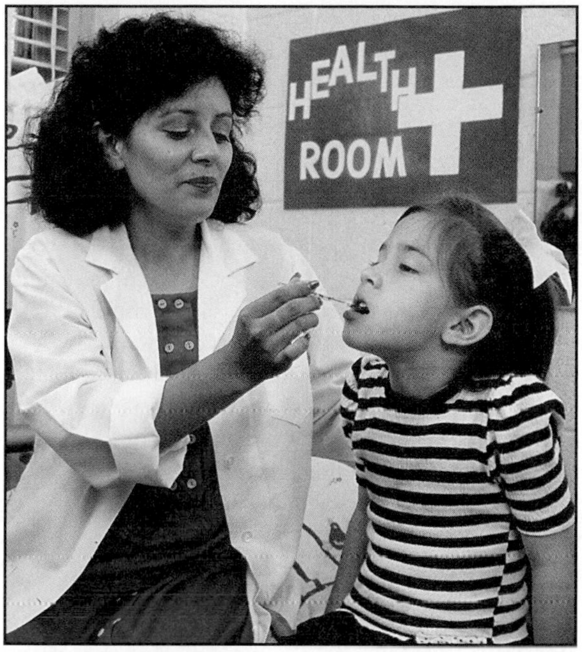

Head Start provides medical, dental, mental health, and nutrition services to preschool children. How does providing health services help achieve Head Start's goal of overall social competence for all children?

Program in Action

New Horizons

Located in rural Macon County, just minutes away from the Great Smokey Mountains, is our New Horizons Center for Children and Families. The foundation for New Horizons is a Head Start program that expanded to encompass a parent/child center, subsidized day care, developmental day care, and Head Start Wraparound services. Built on a longstanding commitment to quality, our Macon Program for Progress Head Start Centers are AA licensed and fully accredited by the National Association for the Education of Young Children (NAEYC).

Head Start performance standards were revised effective January 1998, for the first time in over twenty years. The new standards are based on three cornerstones: child development, community development, and staff development.

Implementing these standards has been a natural occurrence for us because the overall goal for MPP Head Start is *everyday excellence.* This goal is reflected in every aspect of our program, from curriculum development to collaboration with parents.

> I live in a very rural community with no family here. When the child care center first opened my daughter would not leave my sight. She had no idea how to play with other children. Now she looks forward to her school days more than anything.
>
> *T.M., parent*

Programs and facilities at New Horizons allow us to care for children ages six weeks to five years in four centers throughout Macon County. We are open year-round with child care available eleven and a half hours per day. We are fortunate to begin our services with a Head Start-funded 0–3 program that allows services to families from pregnancy through age three, when a child would normally enter Head Start.

FOCUS ON INFANT CARE AND DEVELOPMENT

Getting to know, enjoy, and care for each child on an individual basis is the curriculum for our 0–3 program. Caring for infants under the age of twelve months is more than bottles and diapers. Our teachers realize that they play an important role in the valuable learning experiences infants undergo in the first year of life.

Each infant has a primary caregiver. The selection of a primary caregiver is not necessarily by assignment. We find that personalities draw caregivers to infants.

We believe that the foundations of creativity develop in the early months of infant growth and are affected by the caregiver–child relationship. For example, it is very important for babies to feel good about themselves and things they are learning. We are excited about the things our babies accomplish. We praise them for pulling up, crawling, waving, smiling, and any number of small accomplishments they make during the day. Babies thrive on the attention and look to the caregivers for their approval. They learn they can make things happen and are delighted that the teacher is excited about it too!

The environmental considerations that we use to support individual development for infants are attachment, trust, mobility, senses, language, and health/safety.

- *Attachment* is a necessity for development and learning to occur. Comfortable chairs and floor areas encourage one-to-one interaction with babies and encourage attachment. Small group size and low teacher:child ratios also help promote attachment as teachers interpret and meet the diverse needs of each infant.
- *Trust* is developed by the familiarity of the environment and by association with the same small group and with the same caregiver. A trusting relationship between child and caregiver is necessary for exploration and learning to occur. Additionally, predictable and consistent routines are used to nurture and create a feeling of security.
- *Mobility* is encouraged by allowing babies to play freely on the floor and protecting less mobile babies with soft barriers.
- *Senses* are stimulated with colorful and soft, safe toys. Care is taken to prepare the environment to avoid sensory overload.
- *Language development* is fostered by songs and rhythm, interesting objects, views outside, pictures, and experiences in which adults talk to infants. We recognize that before babies talk they do a lot of listening. We too listen to the sounds infants are hearing and observe their body language; we then talk to the infants about how they are reacting to the sounds and about what they may be thinking.
- *Health and safety* awareness by all staff members is habit. We respect infants' knowing what they need so we provide a safe environment for their natural development. And, since we mainstream children with disabilities throughout the entire center, it is not unusual to have a baby with a heart monitor or other equipment. Differences in the needs of our children are embraced as a natural part of life.

SUPPORTING PARENTS AND PARENTING NEEDS

We recognize and encourage the fact that the parent is the best teacher in the child's life. Relationships are more intense with parents of infants than with older children. A deeper level of trust is involved, and teachers have a more intimate relationship with babies than they do with older children. It is imperative that we communicate in a collaborative manner with parents rather than take the role of the expert. Feeding schedules, for example, are completed and updated by the parent or guardian stating foods to be given along with preferred times and amounts. A daily feeding record is kept for each child along with times of diaper changes. Notations of a child's activities for the day are also recorded. The collaboration with parents comes with a commitment on our part to create and maintain effective communication and good relationships with parents.

Contributed by Betty De Pina, parent/child coordinator, and Sharon Franklin, lead teacher, 0–3 classrooms, New Horizons Center for Children and Families, Macon County, NC.

Basic Principles and Goals of Head Start

Head Start is based on the premise that all children share certain needs and that children of low-income families in particular can benefit from a comprehensive developmental program to meet those needs. The overall goal of Head Start is to bring about a greater degree of social competence enabling disadvantaged children to deal effectively with their environments and responsibilities in school and life.

Head Start is based on the philosophy that (1) a child can benefit most from a comprehensive, interdisciplinary program to foster development and remedy problems as expressed in a broad range of services; and that (2) the child's entire family, as well as the community, must be involved.[11] To this end, Head Start goals provide for:

- The improvement of the child's health and physical abilities.
- The encouragement of self-confidence, spontaneity, curiosity, and self-discipline, which will assist in the development of the child's social and emotional health.
- The enhancement of the child's mental processes and skills, with particular attention to conceptual and verbal skills.
- The establishment of patterns and expectations of success for the child, which will create a climate of confidence for his present and future learning efforts and overall development.
- An increase in the ability of the child and his family to relate to each other and to others in a loving and supporting manner.
- The enhancement of the sense of dignity and self-worth within the child and his family.

Program Management and Performance Standards

Head Start makes every effort to assure that the management and governance of programs is effective and supports its performance standards.

Since 1998, all Head Start programs operate their programs and services according to performance standards. I list and discuss some of these standards in our discussion of each service area. The full set of current Head Start Performance Standards appears in the 5 November 1996 issue of the *Federal Register* (online at http://www.nara.gov/fedreg/). Although the Head Start Bureau provides guidance on implementing the performance standards, local agencies are responsible for designing programs to best meet the needs of their children and families.

Head Start Services

Head Start offers the following program services: education and development, parent involvement, health services (including nutrition and mental health), staff development, and administration.

CHILD EDUCATION AND DEVELOPMENT. Performance standards for education and development for all children include the following guidelines:

- Provide children with a learning environment and the varied experiences that will help them develop socially, intellectually, physically, and emotionally in a manner appropriate to their age and state of development toward the overall goal of social competence.

- Integrate the educational aspects of the various Head Start components in the daily program of activities.

These educational objectives guide local agencies in developing their own programs that are unique and responsive to the children, families, and communities they serve. Thus, there is really no "national" Head Start curriculum.

Services to Children with Disabilities. At least 10 percent of Head Start enrollment must consist of children with disabilities. Nationally, 13.4 percent of all children enrolled in Head Start have a disability. (See chapter 14 for more information on educating children with disabilities.)

PARENT INVOLVEMENT/FAMILY PARTNERSHIPS. From the outset, Head Start has been dedicated to the philosophy that to improve children's lives, corresponding changes must be made in parents' lives as well. Head Start provides a program that recognizes parents as (1) responsible guardians of their children's well-being, (2) prime educators of their children, and (3) contributors to the Head Start Program and to their communities.

More than ever, Head Start is endeavoring to be in cooperative and collaborative relationships with families and communities by:

- Involving parents in educational activities of the program to enhance their role as the principal influence on the child's education and development
- Assisting parents to increase their knowledge, understanding, skills, and experience in child growth and development
- Identifying and reinforcing experiences that occur in the home that parents can utilize as educational activities for their children[12]

HEALTH SERVICES. Head Start assumes an active role in children's health. Children's current health status is monitored and reported to parents, and corrective and preventive procedures are undertaken with their cooperation. For example, if a child needs glasses, corrective orthopedic surgery, or dental care, services may be provided through the Head Start budget, although the program usually works with community social service agencies to provide services or money for health needs.

Head Start also seeks to direct children and parents to existing mental health delivery systems such as community health centers. It does not intend to duplicate existing services but to help its clientele become aware of and utilize available services.

Nutrition. In addition to arranging medical examinations and care, each Head Start program teaches children how to care for their health, including the importance of eating proper foods and caring for their teeth.

A basic premise of Head Start is that children must be properly fed to have the strength and energy to learn. This philosophy calls for teaching children good nutrition habits that will carry over for the rest of their lives and be passed on to their children. In addition, parents are given basic nutrition education so they, in turn, can promote good nutrition in their families.

Head Start programs must also design and implement a nutrition program that meets the nutritional needs and feeding requirements of each child, including those with special dietary needs and children with disabilities. Also, the nutrition program must serve a variety of foods that involve cultural and ethnic preferences and broaden the child's food experience.[13]

Promoting good nutrition for children and their families is an important part of the Head Start curriculum and helps establish lifelong attitudes toward healthy living.

Providing Head Start Services

Head Start services are provided to children and families through a comprehensive child development program in any of three Head Start–approved program options. These three options are center-based, home-based, and a combination of center-based and home-based visits. Locally designed program options, developed by the local program to specifically meet the needs of children and families, are also a possibility. One such option might be Head Start in family day care homes.

HOME-BASED OPTIONS. All Head Start programs are encouraged to explore ways to deliver services directly to children in their homes. This approach is based on the premise that the parent is the most important person in the child's life and the home the optimum place for growth and development.

Local agencies may choose home-based programs as a means of delivering Head Start services that children would normally receive in a center-based program. Today, 571 Head Start agencies and 4,562 home visitors serve more than 39,833 children and their families.

The home-based option has these strengths:

- Parent involvement is the very keystone of the program.
- Geographically isolated families have an invaluable opportunity to be part of a comprehensive child and family program.
- The individualized family plan is based on both a child and a family assessment.
- The family plan is facilitated by a home visitor who is an adult educator with knowledge and training related to all Head Start components.
- The program includes the entire family.[14]

Early Head Start

Early Head Start (EHS) is a federally funded, community-based program for low-income families with infants and toddlers and pregnant women. Its mission is to promote healthy prenatal outcomes for pregnant women, enhance the development of very young children, and promote healthy family functioning. Consequently, EHS enhances children's physical, social, emotional, and intellectual development; supports both parents in fulfilling their parental roles; and helps parents move toward economic independence. Programs are expected to offer certain core services, including high-quality early education (both in and out of the home) and family support services; home visits; parent education; comprehensive health and mental health services, including services for women prior to, during, and after pregnancy; nutrition; and child care. EHS programs have the flexibility to respond to the unique strengths and needs of their own communities and of each child and family within that community.

Among the program options are family child care, center-based care, and home visits. Several projects use combinations of these models. In response to specific needs identified in their communities, some projects emphasize certain program components such as services for teen parents, family literacy, life skills development, substance abuse treatment, and injury and accident prevention. All projects work with community partners to assure early, continuous, and comprehensive services.[15]

What Constitutes Quality Education and Care?

While there is much debate about quality and what it involves, we can nonetheless identify the main characteristics of quality programs that provide care and education for children and families.

Developmental Needs

Good care and education provides for children's needs and interests at each developmental stage. For example, infants need good physical care as well as continual love and affection and sensory stimulation. Toddlers need safe surroundings and opportunities to explore. They need caregivers who support and encourage active involvement.

Appropriate and Safe Environments

At all age levels, a safe and pleasant physical setting is important. Such an area should include a safe neighborhood free from traffic and environmental hazards; a fenced play area with well-maintained equipment; child-sized equipment and facilities (toilets, sinks); and areas for displaying children's work, such as finger painting and clay models. The environment should also be attractive and pleasant. The rooms, home, or center should be clean, well lit, well ventilated, and cheerful.

Caregiver:Child Ratio

The ratio of adults to children should be sufficient to give children the individual care and attention they need. NAEYC guidelines for the ratio of caregivers to children are 1:3 or 1:4 for infants; 1:3 or 1:4 for toddlers; and 1:8 to 1:10 for preschoolers, depending on group size.

Developmentally Appropriate Programs

Programs should have written, developmentally based curricula for meeting children's needs. A program's curriculum should specify activities for children of all ages that caregivers can use to stimulate infants, provide for the growing independence of toddlers, and address the readiness and literacy skills of four- and five-year-olds. All programs should include education to meet the social, emotional, and cognitive needs of all children.

Quality programs use developmentally appropriate practices to implement the curriculum and achieve their program goals.

Family Education and Support

Parents and other family members should know as much as possible about the program their children are enrolled in, their children's growth and development, and the curriculum program of activities. Parents need encouragement to make the program's services part of their lives, so they are not detached from it, its staff, or what happens to their children. Professionals must demonstrate to parents their competence in areas such as child development, nutrition, and planning and implementing developmentally appropriate curricula. They must also assure parents that they will maintain daily communication about the child's progress. Additionally, parents and professionals must agree on discipline and guidance procedures, and professionals and social service agencies need to guide parents about what constitutes good child rearing and appropriate discipline practices.

Staff Training and Development

All professionals should be involved in an ongoing program of training and development. The CDA program discussed in chapter 1 is a good beginning for staff members to become competent and maintain the necessary skills. Program administrators should have a background and training in child development and early childhood education. Knowledge of child growth and development is essential for caregivers. Professionals need to be developmentally aware and child oriented rather than self or center oriented.

Program Accreditation

In any discussion of quality, the question invariably arises, "Who determines quality?" Fortunately, NAEYC has addressed the issue of standards in its Center Accreditation Project (CAP). CAP is a national, voluntary accreditation process for child care centers, preschools, and programs that provide before- and after-school care for school-age children. Accreditation is administered through NAEYC's National Academy of Early Childhood Programs. NAEYC cites the following as benefits of accreditation:

- Accredited programs are recognized as quality programs.
- Parents will seek out accredited programs.
- The staff learns through the accrediting process.

The criteria addressed in the accreditation project include interactions among staff and children; curriculum, staff, and parent interactions; administration, staff, and parent interac-

tions; staff qualifications and development; staffing patterns; physical environment; health and safety; nutrition and food service; and program evaluation.[16]

The Effects of Care and Education on Children

Recent research reveals that high-quality early care and education has influences that last over a lifetime. High-quality care and education have these benefits:

- The high-quality day care children had higher cognitive test scores than the control group from toddler years to age twenty-one.
- Their academic achievement in both reading and math was higher from the primary grades through young adulthood.
- They completed more years of education and were more likely to attend a four-year college.[17]

In another study of program effectiveness, researchers found that quality care and education has a significant effect on school readiness and language skills. Children in high-quality programs have above-average scores on school readiness tests and are better able to express and understand language.[18] It is clear that professionals must provide high-quality programs and they must advocate for high quality with the public and state legislators.

To take an online self-test on this chapter's contents, go to the Companion Website at http://www.prenhall.com/morrison, select chapter 6, then choose the Self Test module.

... video viewpoint

Parenting: The First Years Last Forever (Early Head Start)

The federally funded Early Head Start program provides children younger than three in so-called at-risk families with the brain stimulation they need to grow and prosper and provides families with the support they need to raise healthy children.

REFLECTIVE DISCUSSION QUESTIONS

Why is it that some children seem smarter and learn faster than others? What difference do you think early intervention can make in a child's life? Why do you think the government has continued to expand the Head Start program over the past four decades?

REFLECTIVE DECISION MAKING

Visit the Department of Health and Human Services Web site (http://www.acf.dhhs.gov/) to learn more about Early Head Start. What are some of Early Head Start's goals and services? Are there any Head Start or Early Head Start programs in your area where you could visit or volunteer? Are there other resources in your community you could recommend to a parent in need?

For additional Internet resources or to complete an online activity for this chapter, go to the Companion Website at http://www.prenhall.com/morrison, select chapter 6, then choose the Linking to Learning or Making Connections module.

While all of the program models we have discussed in this chapter are unique, at the same time they all have certain similarities. All of them, regardless of their particular philosophical orientation, have as a primary goal the best education for all children.

As an early childhood professional, you will want to do several things now. First, begin to identify which features of the program models you can and cannot support. Second, decide which of these models and/or features of models you can embrace and incorporate into your own practice. An ongoing rule of the early childhood professional is to decide what you believe is best for children and families before you make decisions about what to teach.

Activities for Further Enrichment

Applications

1. Invite people from child care programs, welfare departments, and social service agencies to speak to your class about child care and education. Also, determine what qualifications and training are necessary to become a child care employee.
2. Which of the programs in this chapter do you think best meets the needs of young children? What accounts for this popularity? Would you implement one of them in your program? Why?

Field Experiences

1. Visit various child care programs, including center and home programs, and discuss similarities and differences in class. Which of the programs provides the best services? What changes or special provisions need to be made to improve the success of these kinds of programs?
2. Visit an employer-sponsored child care program and describe it to your classmates. List the pros and cons for parents and for employers of employer-sponsored child care.
3. Visit several Head Start programs and compare and contrast what you see. How are they similar and different? How do you account for this?

Research

1. Survey parents in your area to determine what service they desire from an early childhood program. Are most of the parents' child care needs being met? How is what they want in a child care program similar to and different from standards for quality child care discussed in this chapter?
2. Determine the legal requirements for establishing center and home child care programs in your state, city, or locality. What are the similarities and differences in regard to establishing home and center programs? What is your opinion of the guidelines? Why?
3. Link to NAEYC's Web site (www.naeyc.org) and review its Position Statement on Licensing and Public Regulation of Early Childhood Programs. Why does NAEYC believe licensing and regulation of child care are important processes?
4. Conduct a survey to learn the cost of child care services in your area. Arrange your data in a table. What conclusions can you draw?

Readings for Further Enrichment

Catron, C. E., and Allen, J. *Early Childhood Curriculum: A Creative Play Model*, 2nd ed. Upper Saddle River, NJ: Merrill/Prentice Hall, 1999.

This comprehensive guide provides information on planning programs with a play-based, developmental curriculum for children from birth to five years of age and covers basic principles and current research in early childhood curricula.

Eliason, C., and Jenkins, L. *Practical Guide to Early Childhood Curriculum*, 6th ed. Upper Saddle River, NJ: Merrill/Prentice Hall, 1999.

This popular text stresses the importance of a child-centered curriculum that encompasses the child's physical, social, emo-

tional, creative, and cognitive development. Contains lesson plans, activities, recipes, and lists of resources to help readers with planning and implementing a fully integrated childhood curriculum.

Kostelnik, M., Soderman, A., and Whiren, A. *Developmentally Appropriate Curriculum: Best Practices in Early Childhood Education*, 2nd ed. Upper Saddle River, NJ: Merrill/Prentice Hall, 1999.

Brings together the best information currently available for developing an integrated approach to curriculum and instruction in the early years. It is designed for current and future early childhood professionals working in formal group settings with young children ranging in age from three to eight.

Roopnarine, J., and Johnson, J. *Approaches to Early Childhood Education*, 3rd ed. Upper Saddle River, NJ: Merrill/Prentice Hall, 2000.

This up-to-date, comprehensive book, with contributions by major experts in the field, focuses on models, approaches, and issues that deal with prominent and tested practices in early childhood education today. Its major strengths are its pluralistic approach and the expertise of the authors.

Linking to Learning

Child Care Action Campaign

http://www.usakids.org/sites/ccac.html

A coalition of leaders from diverse organizations advocating for high-quality child care whose activities include education, information service, proposing possible solutions, and technical assistance to government offices.

Child Care Bureau

http://www.acf.dhhs.gov/programs/ccb

Information on the Child Care and Development Block Grant, links to other Administration on Children and Families sites and other information within the Department of Health and Human Services, with links to other related child care sites.

Electronic Policy Network

http://epn.org

A resource site, including information and links to national organizations working in child and family policy, welfare reform, health policy, and economic research.

Head Start Bureau

http://www2.acf.dhhs.gov/programs/hsb/

The Web site of Head Start includes a list of frequently asked questions concerning the program. Many of the program's research findings are viewable on-line.

High/Scope Education Research Foundation

http://www.highscope.org/

An overview of the High/Scope Foundation's educational program, research, and publications.

National Child Care Information Center

http://nccic.org

Sponsored by the Child Care Bureau, Administration for Children and Families, Department of Health and Human Services, this site provides a central access point for information on child care.

National Head Start Association

http://www.nhsa.org

The NHSA, composed of directors, staff, and parents, was created to provide a unified national voice for the Head Start community. The Web site contains information about the organization as well as the full text of the 1998 Head Start Amendments and other government documents related to Head Start.

National Resource Center for Health and Safety in Child Care

http://nrc.uchsc.edu

Funded by the Maternal and Child Health Bureau, Department of Health and Human Services, this site has the child care licensure regulations for each state. Also available are health and safety tips and full-text resources.

Reggio Emilia Approach to Early Childhood Education

http://www.cmu.edu/cyert-center

An overview of the Reggio Emilia approach.

ENDNOTES

1 Singer, J. D., Fuller, B., Keiley, M. K., and Wolf, A. "Early Child-Care Selection: Variation by Geographic Location, Maternal Characteristics, and Family Structure," *Developmental Psychology* 34, no. 5 (1998): 1129–1144.

2 "Relative Care: Closer Together," *Parenting*, June/July 1999, 123.

3 Child Care Information Exchange, "The Exchange Top 40: North America's Largest For-Profit Child Care Organizations." Reprinted with permission from Child Care Information Exchange, P.O. Box 3249, Redmond, WA 98073. (800) 221-2864.

4 Sandra L. Hofferth, April Brayfield, Sharon Deich, and Pamela Holcomb, *National Child Care Survey 1990* (Washington, DC: Urban Institute Press, 1991), 355.

[5] U.S. Department of Education, Office of Policy and Planning, Internet address www.ed.gov/offices/OUS/eval/esed/b4&aftr.html.

[6] High/Scope Education Research Foundation, *The High/Scope K-3 Curriculum: An Introduction* (Ypsilanti, MI: Author, 1989), 1.

[7] Ibid.

[8] Ibid., 3.

[9] This section is adapted from L. Gandini, "Foundations of the Reggio Emilia Approach," in J. Hendrick, ed., *First Steps Toward Teaching the Reggio Way* (Upper Saddle River, NJ: Merrill/Prentice Hall, 1997), 14–25.

[10] Administration for Children and Families, *Project Head Start Statistical Fact Sheet 1998* (Washington, DC: Author, 1998). [On-line]. Available: www2.acf.dhhs.gov/programs/hsb/research/98_hsfs.htm.

[11] U.S. Department of Health and Human Services, *Head Start Program Performance Standards* (45 CFR §1304) (Washington, DC: U.S. Government Printing Office, November 1984), 4.

[12] Ibid., 8–9.

[13] Ibid.

[14] E. Dollie Wolverton, "The Home-Based Option: Reinforcing Parents," *National Head Start Bulletin* (12):1.

[15] Early Head Start National Resource Center, www.ehsnrc.org.

[16] National Association for the Education of Young Children, *Accreditation by the National Academy of Early Childhood Programs* (Washington, DC: Author, 1991), 2.

[17] Jodi Wilgoren. "Quality Day Care, Early, Is Tied to Achievements as an Adult," *New York Times*, 22 October 22 1999, A16.

[18] Linda Jacobson. "Study: High-Quality Child Carc Pays Off," *Education Week*, 28 April 1999, 9.

PART III

Developmentally Appropriate Programs and Practices

CHAPTER 7

Babies are not just cute faces but are the greatest learning machines in the universe.

PATRICIA KUHL

Infants and Toddlers

FOUNDATION YEARS FOR LEARNING

Focus Questions

1. How is new brain research influencing the care and education of infants and toddlers?
2. What are the milestones in infant and toddler development?
3. How does Piaget's theory explain infant and toddler cognitive development?
4. What theories explain infant and toddler language and psychosocial development?
5. How can professionals provide quality programs for infants and toddlers?

To review the chapter focus questions online, go to the Companion Website at http://www.prenhall.com/morrison and select chapter 7.

As the new millennium begins, interest in infant and toddler care and education is at an all-time high; it will continue at this level well into the future. The growing demand for quality infant and toddler programs stems primarily from the reasons discussed in chapter 2. It is also fueled by parents who want their children to have an "early start" and get off on the "right foot" so they can be successful in life and work. The popularity of early care and education is also attributable to a changing view of the very young and the discovery that infants are remarkably competent individuals. Let's examine the ways that infants' and toddlers' early experiences shape their future development.

What Are Infants and Toddlers Like?

To check your understanding of this chapter with the online Study Guide, go to the Companion Website at http://www.prenhall.com/morrison, select chapter 7, then choose the Study Guide module.

Think for a minute about your experiences with infants. What characteristics stand out most in your mind? I know that infants never cease to amaze me!

Have you ever tried to keep up with a toddler? Everyone who tries ends up exhausted at the end of the day. A typical response is, "They are into everything!" The infant and toddler years between birth and age three are full of developmental milestones and significant events. Infancy, life's first year, includes the first breath, the first smile, first thoughts, first words, and first steps. Significant developments also occur during toddlerhood, the period between one and three years. Two of the most outstanding developmental milestones are walking and rapid language development. Mobility and language are the cornerstones of autonomy that enable toddlers to become independent. These unique developmental events are significant for children as well as those who care for and teach them. How you and other early childhood professionals and parents respond to infants' first accomplishments and toddlers' quests for autonomy helps determine how children grow and master life events.

Understanding the major development processes that characterize these formative years will help you and other early childhood professionals fully grasp your roles as educators and nurturers. To begin, we must recognize that infants and toddlers are not the miniature adults many baby product advertisements picture them to be. Children need many years to develop fully and become independent. This period of dependency and professionals' responses to it are critical for children's development. You must constantly keep in mind that "normal" growth and development milestones are based on averages, and the "average" is the middle ground of development (for example, Table 7.1 gives average heights and weights for infants and toddlers). To assess children's progress or lack of it, you must know the milestones of different stages of development. At the same time, you must consider the whole child to assess what is "normal" for each child. You must also take into account cultural and family background, including nutritional and health history, to determine what is normal for individual children. Also keep in mind that when children are provided with good nutrition, health care, and a warm, loving emotional environment, development tends toward what is "normal" for each child.

Young Brains: A Primer

In 1989, President George Bush declared the 1990s the "Decade of the Brain." Since then, as I indicated in chapter 2, brain and child development research has been a hot national topic. This research has created a great deal of interest in the first three years of life. As a result, there has been an explosion of further research regarding brain functioning and the ways that professionals and programs can help children get a good start in life. As we discuss these early years now, let's review some interesting facts about infant and toddler brain develop-

Table 7.1
Average Height and Weight of Infants and Toddlers

Age	Males		Females	
	Height (inches)	Weight (pounds)	Height (inches)	Weight (pounds)
Birth	19.9	7.2	19.6	7.1
3 months	24.1	13.2	23.4	11.9
6 months	26.7	17.3	25.9	15.9
9 months	28.5	20.2	27.7	18.9
1 year	30.0	22.4	29.3	21.0
1½ years	32.4	25.3	31.9	23.9
2 years	34.5	27.8	34.1	26.2
2½ years	36.3	30.1	35.9	28.5
3 years	38.0	32.4	37.6	30.7

Source: Based on data from P. V. V. Hamill et al., "Physical Growth: National Center for Health Statistics Percentiles," American Journal of Clinical Nutrition *32(1979), pp. 607–629.*

ment and consider the implications they have for how you practice as a professional. Also review Figure 7.1, which shows the regions of the brain and their functional processes.

The brain is a fascinating and complex organ. Anatomically, the young brain is like the adult brain, except it is smaller. The average adult brain weighs approximately 3 lb. At birth, the infant's brain weighs ¾ lb.; at six months, 1½ lb.; and at two years, 2¾ lb. So you can see

For more information about brain development, go to the Companion Website at http://www.prenhall.com/morrison, select chapter 7, then choose the Linking to Learning module to connect to the I Am Your Child site.

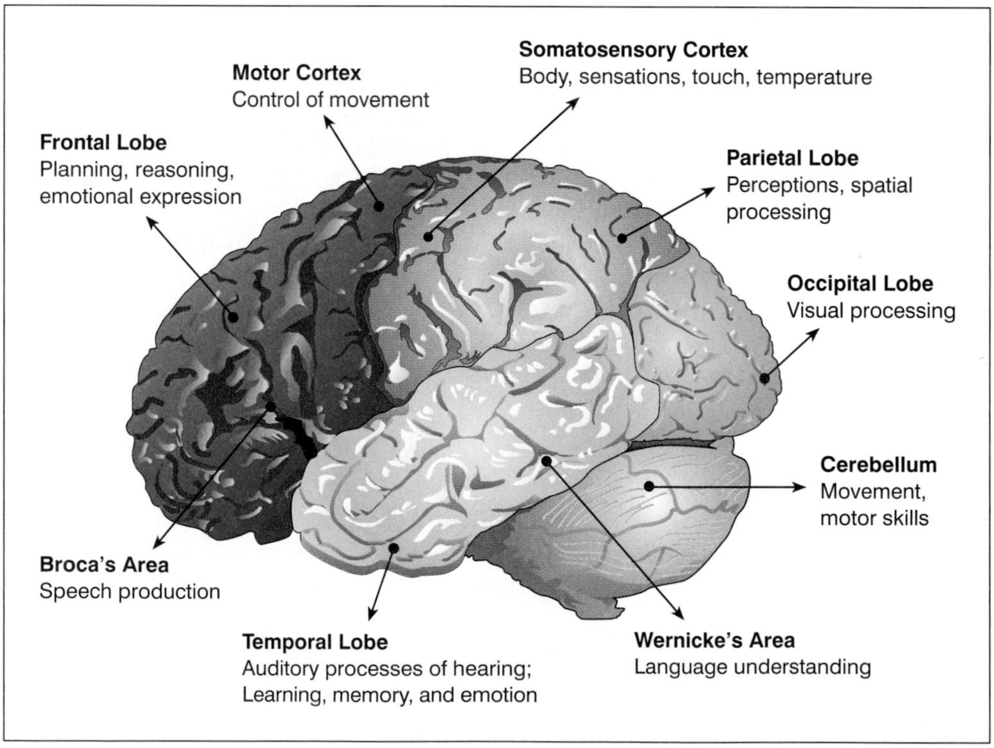

Figure 7.1
Brain Regions

that during the first two years of life the brain undergoes tremendous physical growth. The brain finishes developing at age ten, when it reaches its full adult size.

At birth, the brain has one hundred billion neurons, or nerve cells—all the brain cells it will ever have! That is why it is important for parents and other caregivers to play with, respond to, interact with, and talk to young children. It is through such processes that brain connections develop and learning takes place. As brain connections are repeatedly used, they become permanent. On the other hand, brain connections that are not used or used only a little may wither away. This withering away is known as neural *shearing* or *pruning*. Consequently, a child whose parents seldom talk or read to him may have difficulty with language skills later in life. This helps explain why children who are reared in language-rich environments do well in school, while children who are not reared in such environments may be at risk for academic failure.

For more information about the importance of the first three years of life, go to the Companion Website at http://www.prenhall.com/morrison, select chapter 7, then choose the Linking to Learning module to connect to the Zero to Three site.

Also by the time of birth, these billions of neurons have formed over fifty trillion connections, or synapses, through a process called *synaptogenesis*, the proliferation of neural connections; this process will continue to occur until the age of ten. But this is just the beginning. During the first month, the brain will form over one thousand trillion more synaptic connections between neurons. The forming of these connections and neural pathways is essential for brain development, and it is the experiences that children have that help form these neural connections. Experiences count. If children don't have the experiences they need to form neural connections, they may be at risk for poor developmental and behavioral outcomes. Incredibly, almost from birth, the brain begins to lose neurons.

Children need not just any experiences but the right experiences at the right times. For example, the critical period for language development is the first year of life. It is during this time that the auditory pathways for language learning are formed. Beginning at birth, an infant can distinguish the sounds of all the languages of the world. But at about six months, through the process of neuron pruning or shearing, infants lose the ability to distinguish the sounds of languages they have not heard. By twelve months, their auditory maps are pretty well in place.[1] It is literally a case of use it or lose it.

Having the right experiences at the right time also relates to *critical periods*, developmental "windows of opportunity" or *sensitive periods* (discussed in chapter 4) during which it is easier to learn something than it is at another time. (See Table 7.3 on page 207, which shows the progress of vocabulary development in the early years.) This is another example of how experiences influence development. An infant whose mother or other caregiver talks to her is more likely to have a larger vocabulary than an infant whose mother doesn't talk to her. Mothers who use different words and speak to their infants in complex sentences increase the infants' knowledge of words and their ability to speak in complex sentences.[2] Figure 7.2 identifies some major and critical facts about brain development in the early years.

There are several conclusions we can draw in our discussion about the brain:

- Babies are born to learn. They are remarkable learning instruments. Their brains make them so.
- Children's brain development and their ability to learn throughout life rely on the interplay between nature (genetic inheritance, controlled by eighty thousand genes) and nurture (the experiences they have and the environments in which they are raised).
- What happens to children early in life has a long-lasting influence on how children develop and learn.
- Critical periods influence learning positively and negatively.
- The human brain is quite "plastic." It has the ability to change in response to different kinds of experiences and environments.

- Neuroscience research findings suggest that good parental care, warm and loving attachments, and positive age-appropriate stimulation from birth onward make a difference in children's overall development for a lifetime.[1]
- Experiences during the early critical years of development are so powerful that they can greatly change the way a person develops.[2]
- Babies quickly revise their perceptions about people and the world in general based on new experiences. Their brains are less committed, or "cluttered," than adult brains, and they can revise their views of the world quite rapidly.[3]
- Auditory stimuli through word use in a particular language stimulate the formation of nerve connections. When children hear a phoneme (i.e., small unit of speech that distinguishes one sound from another) over and over, connections are being formed in the auditory cortex.[4]
- Sounds in different languages formulate different maps. Infants growing up in English-speaking homes have a different auditory map compared with those children from homes where other languages are spoken.[5]
- Eight-month-old infants have been shown to engage in long-term storage of words that occur frequently in speech after exposure to children's stories in comparison with children who had not been exposed to the stories.[6]
- Children who receive multivitamin supplements for ninety days have shown positive effects in relation to cognitive development.[7]
- Exercise supports learning. Increasing balance, spatial awareness, and motor coordination skills can enhance children's academic performance and learning.[8]
- Exposure to music has an impact on wiring the brain's neural network.[9]

Figure 7.2
The Importance of Brain Development in the Early Years

Sources: [1]*J. J. Newberger, "New Brain Development Research: A Wonderful Window of Opportunity to Build Public Support for Early Childhood Education,"* Young Children *(February 1997), 4–9;* [2]*H. Chugani, "Functional Brain Reorganization in Children,"* Brain and Development *18 (1996), 347–356;* [3]*P. Kuhl, "Early Language Acquisition: The Brain Comes Prepared," Parents as Teachers National Center (1999);* [4]*P. Kuhl, "Learning and Representation in Speech and Language,"* Current Opinion in Neurobiology 4 *(1994), 812–822, and S. Begley, "Your Child's Brain,"* Newsweek, *February. 19, 1996. [On-line.] Available: http://www.home.earthlink.net/~misbet/good.html* [5]*Ibid.;* [6]*P. W. Jusczyk and E. Hohne, "Infants' Memory for Spoken Words,"* Science *277 (1997), 1984–1986;* [7]*D. H. Fishbein and S. E. Pease, "Diet, Nutrition, and Aggression,"* Journal of Offender Rehabilitation *21 (1995);* [8]*R. T. Johnson, "Story Retelling in a Learning Technology Context,"* Early Child Development and Care *32 (1999), 53–58;* [9]*D. H. Atkins, "The Brain and Mind-Body Connections," Series of presentations to early childhood teachers, Velma E. Schmidt Programs, University of North Texas, and A. Kemp,* The Musical Temperament *(New York: Oxford University Press, 1996).*

- Prevention and early intervention are more beneficial than later remediation.
- The brain undergoes physiological changes in response to experiences.
- An enriched environment influences brain development. (Figure 7.6 on page 202 shows the characteristics of an enriched environment.)

Some Web sites you can access to learn more about the brain are shown in Figure 7.3.

Nature and Nurture

Today we hear a lot about nature, heredity, and genes. All of these are the influences that we enter the world with. Nurturing involves all the environmental influences that affect and play a

- About Brain Injury: A Guide to Brain Anatomy
  http://www.waiting.com/brainanatomy.html
  This site provides areas, functions, and associated signs and symptoms of the brain.
- The Brain Store
  http://www.thebrainstore.com
  Why a brain store? Revolutionary discoveries suggest how we can make changes to improve education, training, and our personal lives.
- Good Beginnings for All Children: From Brain Research to Action
  http://www.patnc.org/neuroforum.htm
  A growing body of research is shedding new light on the effects that early experiences have on the development and functioning of the brain.
- White House Conference on Early Childhood Development and Learning
  http://www.nncc,org/wh/whconf.html
  This site is focused on the practical applications of the latest scientific research on the brain, particularly for parents and caregivers.

Figure 7.3
Web Sites: Linking to the Brain

role in development. Which of these factors, nature (genetics) or nurture (environment) plays a larger role? This question is the focus of a never-ending debate. At this time there is no one right and true answer to the question. One reason for this is that the answer depends on many things. On the one hand, many traits are fully determined by heredity. For example, your eye color is a product of your heredity. Physical height is also largely influenced by heredity—as much as 90 percent. So we can say that many differences in individuals are due to heredity rather than to environmental factors. Certainly height can be influenced by nutrition, growth hormones, and other environmental interventions. But by and large, an individual's height is genetically determined. Other traits, such as temperament and shyness, are highly heritable.

... video viewpoint

Building Brains: The Sooner, the Better

Powerful research evidence exists that shows that the period from birth to age three is critical to a child's healthy growth and development and to later success in school and life.

Reflective Discussion Questions

Some policymakers are realizing that if they spend money on early intervention in a child's first few years of life, while their brains are most changeable, the government will save money down the line on special education, foster care, and prisons. What are some of the other costs to society when children do not receive the care they need when they are young?

Reflective Decision Making

What kind of interventions would most benefit the families in your neighborhood or school district? If you were to write a letter to your congressperson suggesting that your state enact early intervention legislation and programming, what would you recommend?

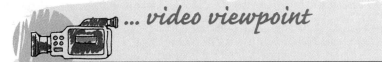

On the other hand, nurturing—the environment in which individuals grow and develop—plays an important role in what individuals are and how they behave. For example, the years from birth to age eight are extremely important environmentally. Some environmental factors that play a major role in early development include nutrition, quality of the environment, stimulation of the brain, affectionate relationships with parents, and opportunities to learn. Think for a moment about other kinds of environmental influences—such as family, environment, school, and friends—that affect development. Now review Figure 7.2, regarding what research says about brain development and the early years.

A decade or two ago, we believed that nature and nurture were competing entities and that one of these was dominant over the other. Today we understand that they are not competing entities; both are necessary for normal development, and it is the interaction between the two that makes us the individuals we are (see Figure 7.4).

How Does Motor Development Occur?

What would life be like if you couldn't walk, run, and participate in your favorite activities? Motor skills play an important part in all of life. Even more so, motor development is essential for infants and toddlers because it contributes to their intellectual and skill development. Table 7.2 lists infant and toddler motor milestones. Human motor development is governed by certain basic principles. Here are some for you to keep in mind:

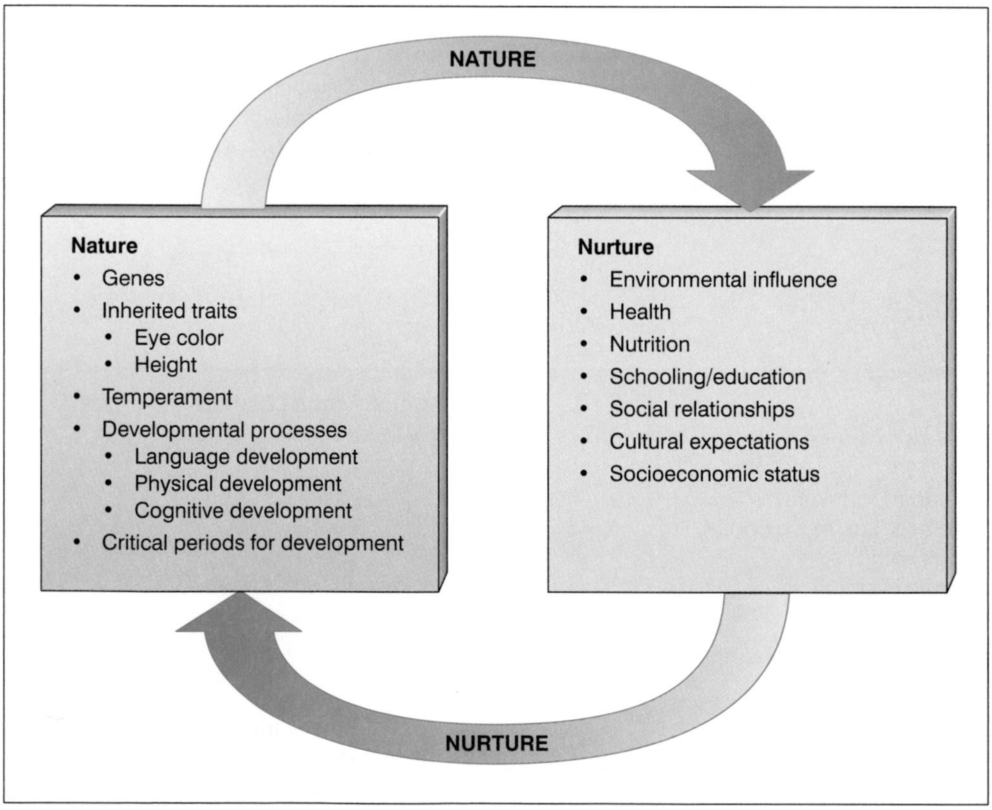

Figure 7.4
Nature and Nurture: Dimensions of Development

- Motor development is sequential.
- Maturation of the motor system proceeds from gross (large) to fine (small) behaviors. For example, as part of her learning to reach, Maria sweeps toward an object with her whole arm. Over the course of a month, however, as a result of development and experiences, Maria's gross reaching gives way to specific reaching, and she grasps for particular objects.
- Motor development is from *cephalo* to *caudal*—from head to foot (tail). This process is known as *cephalocaudal* development. At birth, Maria's head is the most developed part of her body; she holds her head erect before she sits, and her being able to sit precedes her walking.
- Motor development proceeds from the *proximal* (midline, or central part of the body) to the *distal* (extremities), known as *proximodistal* development. Maria is able to control her arm movements before she can control her finger movements.

Motor development plays a major role in social and behavioral expectations. For example, toilet training (also called *toilet learning* or *toilet mastery*) is a milestone of the toddler period. This process often causes a great deal of anxiety for parents, professionals, and toddlers. Many parents want to accomplish toilet training as quickly and efficiently as possible, but frustrations arise when they start too early and expect too much of children. Toilet training is largely a matter of physical readiness, and most child-rearing experts recommend waiting until children are two years old before beginning the training process.

The principle of toilet training is that parents and professionals help children develop control over an involuntary response. When an infant's bladder and bowel are full, the urethral and sphincter muscles open. The goal of toilet training is to teach children to control this involuntary reflex and use the toilet when appropriate. Training involves maturational development, timing, patience, modeling, preparing the environment, establishing a routine, and developing a partnership between the child and parents/professionals. Another necessary partnership is that between parents and professionals who are assisting in toilet training, especially when parents do not know what to do, are hesitant about approaching toilet training, or want to start the training too soon.

Table 7.2
Infant and Toddler Motor Milestones

Behavior	Age of Accomplishment for 90% of Infants/Toddlers
Chin up momentarily	3 weeks
Arms and legs move equally	7 weeks
Smiles responsively	2 months
Sits with support	4 months
Reaches for objects	5 months
Smiles spontaneously	5 months
Rolls over	5 months
Crawls	7 months
Creeps	10 months
Pulls self to stand	11 months
Walks holding onto furniture	13 months

Source: William K. Frankenburg, William Sciarillo, and David Burgess, "The Newly Abbreviated and Revised Denver Developmental Screening Test," Journal of Pediatrics *99 (December 1981), 996. Used by permission.*

Motor development plays a major role in cognitive and social development. For example, learning to walk enables young children to explore their environment, which in turn contributes to cognitive development. Can you think of other examples?

How Does Intellectual Development Occur?

Reflect on the discussion of cognitive development in chapter 5, and think about how a child's development of first schemata (schemes) are sensorimotor. According to Piaget, infants do not have "thoughts of the mind." Rather, they come to know their world by actively acting on it through their senses and through motor actions. Piaget said that infants *construct* (as opposed to absorb) schemes using reflexive sensorimotor actions.

For more information about infant and toddler development, go to the Companion Website at http://www.prenhall.com/morrison, select any chapter, then choose Topic 2 of the ECE Supersite module.

Infants begin life with only reflexive motor actions that they use to satisfy biological needs and their billions of neurons. In response to specific environmental conditions, they modify these reflexive actions through accommodation and adaptation to the environment. Patterns of adaptive behavior initiate more activity, which leads to more adaptive behavior, which in turn yields more schemes. Consider sucking, for example, an innate sensorimotor scheme. Kathy turns her head to the source of nourishment, closes her lips around the nipple, sucks, and swallows. As a result of experiences and maturation, Kathy adapts or changes this basic sensorimotor scheme of sucking to include both anticipatory sucking movements and nonnutritive sucking, such as sucking a pacifier or blanket.

Children construct new schemes through the processes of assimilation and accommodation. Piaget believed that children are active constructors of intelligence through *assimilation* (taking in new experiences) and *accommodation* (changing existing schemes to fit new information), which results in *equilibrium*.

Stages of Cognitive Development: Sensorimotor Intelligence

Sensorimotor cognitive development consists of six stages (shown in Figure 7.5 and described in the following subsections). Let's follow Madeleine through her six stages of cognitive development.

Stage	Age	Behavior
1. Reflexive action	Birth to 1 month	Reflexive actions of sucking, grasping, crying, rooting, swallowing Through experiences, reflexes become more efficient (e.g., amount of sucking required for nutrition) Little or no tolerance for frustration or delayed gratification
2. Primary circular reactions	1 to 4 months	Acquired adaptations form Reflexive actions gradually replaced by voluntary actions Circular reactions result in modification of existing schemes
3. Secondary circular reactions	4 to 8 months	Increased responses to people and objects Able to intitiate activities Beginning of object permanency

Figure 7.5
Stages of Sensorimotor Cognitive Development

STAGE 1: BIRTH TO ONE MONTH. During this stage, Madeleine sucks and grasps everything. She is literally ruled by *reflexive actions*. Reflexive responses to objects are undifferentiated, and Madeleine responds the same way to everything. Sensorimotor schemes help her learn new ways of interacting with the world. New ways of interacting promote Madeleine's cognitive development.

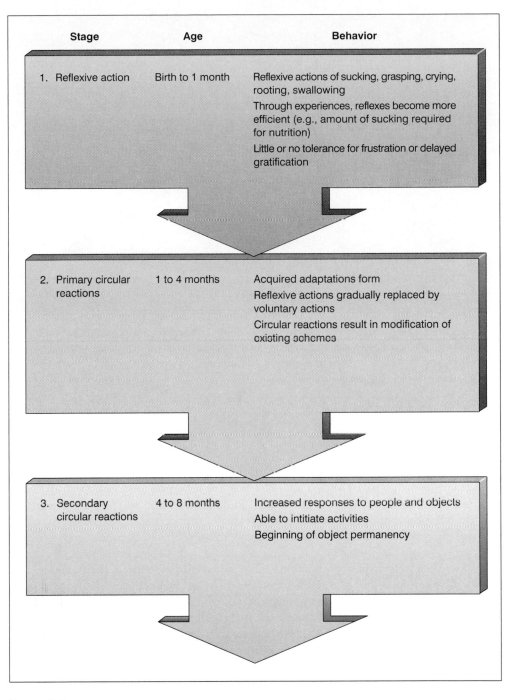

Stage	Age	Behavior
4. Coordination of secondary schemes	8 to 12 months	Increased deliberation and purposefulness in responding to people and objects First clear signs of developing intelligence Continuing development of object permanency Actively searches for hidden objects Comprehends meanings of simple words
5. Experimentation (tertiary circular reactions)	12 to 18 months	Active experimentation begins through trial and error Spends much time "experimenting" with objects to see what happens; insatiable curiosity Differentiates self from objects Realization that "out of sight" is not "out of reach" or "out of existence" Beginning of understanding of space, time, and causality
6. Representational intelligence (intention of means)	18 to 24 months	Development of cause–effect relationships Representational intelligence begins; can mentally represent objects Engages in symbolic imitative behavior Beginning of sense of time Egocentric in thought and behavior

Grasping is a primary infant sensorimotor scheme. At birth, the grasping reflex consists of closing the fingers around an object placed in the hand. Through experiences and maturation, this basic reflexive grasping action becomes coordinated with looking, opening the hand, retracting the fingers, and grasping, thus developing from a pure, reflexive action to an intentional grasping action. As Madeleine matures in response to experiences, her grasping scheme is combined with a delightful activity of grasping and releasing everything she can get her hands on!

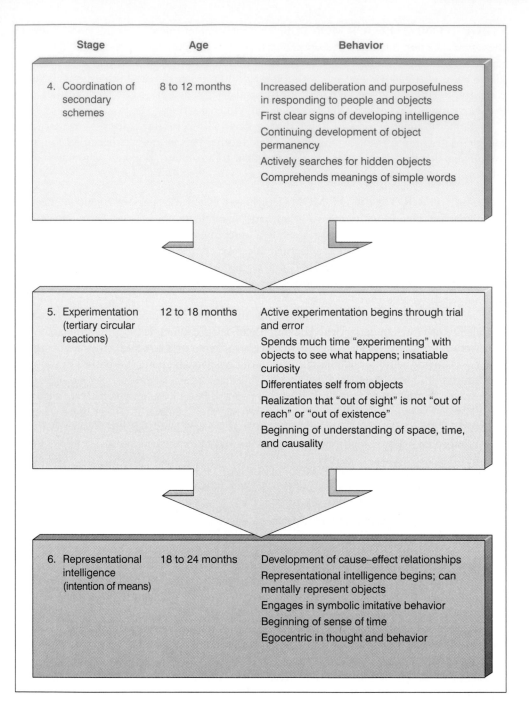

STAGE 2: ONE TO FOUR MONTHS. The milestone of this stage is the modification of the reflexive actions of stage 1. Sensorimotor behaviors not previously present in Madeleine's repertoire of behavior begin to appear: habitual thumb sucking (indicates hand–mouth coordination), tracking moving objects with the eyes, and moving the head toward sounds (indicates the beginning of the recognition of causality). Madeleine starts to direct her own behavior rather than being totally dependent on reflexive actions.

Primary circular reactions begin during stage 2. A circular response occurs when Madeleine's actions cause her to react or when another person prompts her to try to repeat the original action. The circular reaction is similar to a stimulus–response, cause-and-effect relationship.

STAGE 3: FOUR TO EIGHT MONTHS. Piaget called this stage of cognitive development "making interesting things last." Madeleine manipulates objects, demonstrating coordination between vision and tactile senses. She also reproduces events with the purpose of sustaining and repeating acts. The intellectual milestone of this stage is the beginning of *object permanence*. When infants in stages 1 and 2 cannot see an object, it does not exist for them—out of sight, out of mind. During later stage 3, however, awareness grows that things that are out of sight continue to exist.

Secondary circular reactions begin during this stage. This process is characterized by Madeleine repeating an action with the purpose of getting the same response from an object or person; for example, Madeleine will repeatedly shake a rattle to repeat the sound. Repetitiveness is characteristic of all circular reactions. *Secondary* here means that the reaction is elicited from a source other than the infant. Madeleine interacts with people and objects to make interesting sights, sounds, and events happen and last. Given an object, Madeleine will use all available schemes, such as mouthing, hitting, and banging; if one of these schemes produces an interesting result, she continues to use the scheme to elicit the same response. Imitation becomes increasingly intentional as a means of prolonging interest.

STAGE 4: EIGHT TO TWELVE MONTHS. During this stage, "coordination of secondary schemes," Madeleine uses means to attain ends. She moves objects out of the way (means) to get another object (end). She begins to search for hidden objects, although not always in the places they were hidden, indicating a growing understanding of object permanence.

STAGE 5: TWELVE TO EIGHTEEN MONTHS. This stage, the climax of the sensorimotor period, marks the beginning of truly intelligent behavior. Stage 5 is the stage of experimentation. Madeleine experiments with objects to solve problems, and her experimentation is characteristic of intelligence that involves *tertiary circular reactions*, in which she repeats actions and modifies behaviors over and over to see what will happen. This repetition helps develop understanding of cause-and-effect relationships and leads to the discovery of new relationships through exploration and experimentation.

Physically, stage 5 is also the beginning of the toddler stage, with the commencement of walking. Toddlers' physical mobility, combined with their growing ability and desire to experiment with objects, makes for fascinating and often frustrating child rearing. Madeleine and other toddlers are avid explorers, determined to touch, taste, and feel all they can. Although the term *terrible twos* was once used to describe this stage, professionals now recognize that there is nothing terrible about toddlers exploring their environment to develop their intelligence. What is important is that teachers, parents, and others prepare environments for exploration. As Madeleine's mom describes it, "I keep putting things up higher and higher because her arms seems to be getting longer and longer!" Novelty is interesting for its own sake, and Madeleine experiments in many different ways with a given object. For example, she will use any available item—a wood hammer, a block, a rhythm band instrument—to pound the pegs in a pound-a-peg toy.

STAGE 6: EIGHTEEN MONTHS TO TWO YEARS. This is the stage of transition from sensorimotor to symbolic thought. It is the stage of symbolic *representation,* which occurs when Madeleine can visualize events internally and maintain mental images of objects not present. Representational thought enables Madeleine to solve problems in a sensorimotor way through experimentation and trial and error and predict cause-and-effect relationships more accurately. She also develops the ability to remember, which allows her to try out actions she sees others do. During this stage, Madeleine can "think" using mental images and memories, which enables her to engage in pretend activities. Madeleine's representational thought does not necessarily match the real world and its representations, which accounts for her ability to have other objects stand for almost anything: a wooden block is a car; a rag doll is a baby. This type of play, known as *symbolic play*, becomes more elaborate and complex in the preoperational period.

In summary, we need to keep in mind several important concepts of infant and toddler development:

- The chronological ages associated with Piaget's stages of cognitive development are approximate. In fact, as we discussed in chapter 5, children can do things earlier than the ages Piaget assigned. You should not be preoccupied with children's ages but should focus on cognitive behavior, which gives a clearer understanding of a child's level of development. This is the true meaning of developmentally appropriate education and caregiving.
- Infants and toddlers do not "think" as adults do; they come to know their world by acting on it and need many opportunities for *active* involvement.
- Infants and toddlers are actively involved in *constructing* their own intelligence. Children's activity with people and objects stimulates them cognitively and leads to the development of mental schemata (schemes).
- Parents and early childhood professionals need to provide *environments* and *opportunities* for infants and toddlers to be actively involved. These are two important conditions for intellectual development. Reflexive actions form the basis for assimilation and accommodation, which enable cognitive structures to develop. You must ensure that infants and toddlers have experiences that support and contribute to successful intellectual construction.
- At birth, Madeleine and other infants do not know that there are objects in the world and, in this sense, have no knowledge of the external world. They do not and cannot differentiate between themselves and the external world. For all practical purposes, Madeleine *is* the world. All external objects are acted on through sucking, grasping, and looking. This acting on the world enables Madeleine to construct schemes of the world.
- The concept of *causality,* or cause and effect, does not exist at birth. Infants' and toddlers' concepts of causality begin to evolve only through acting on the environment.
- As infants and toddlers move from one stage of intellectual development to another, later stages evolve from, rather than replace, earlier ones. Schemes developed in stage 1 are incorporated and improved on by the schemes constructed in stage 2, and so forth.

Providing an enriched environment is a powerful way to promote infants' and toddlers' overall development. Figure 7.6 identifies some of the essential elements of an enriched environment.

An enriched environment:

- Includes a steady source of positive emotional support.
- Provides a nutritious diet with enough protein, vitamins, minerals, and calories.
- Stimulates all the senses (but not necessarily all at once!).
- Has an atmosphere free of undue pressure and stress but suffused with a degree of pleasurable intensity.
- Presents a series of novel challenges that are neither too easy nor too difficult for the child at his or her stage of development.
- Allows for social interaction for a significant percentage of activities.
- Promotes the development of a broad range of skills and interests that are mental, physical, aesthetic, social, and emotional.
- Gives the child an opportunity to choose many of his or her own activities.
- Gives the child a chance to assess the results of his or her efforts and to modify them.
- Is an enjoyable atmosphere that promotes exploration and the fun of learning.
- Above all, enriched environments allow the child to be an active participant rather than a passive observer.

Figure 7.6
Enriching the Environment

Source: Marian Diamond and J. Hopson, Magic Trees of the Mind: How to Nurture Your Child's Intelligence, Creativity, and Healthy Emotions from Birth through Adolescence *(New York: Dutton, 1998), pp. 107–108.*

All children are different, and early childhood educators must provide for the individual needs of each child. In what ways are the children in this photograph similar and different?

Language Development

Language development begins at birth. Indeed, some argue it begins before birth. The first cry, the first coo, the first "da-da" and "ma-ma," the first words are auditory proof that children are participating in the process of language development. Language helps define us as human and represents one of our most remarkable intellectual accomplishments. How does the infant go from the first cry to the first word a year later? How does the toddler develop from saying one word to several hundred words a year later? While everyone agrees that children learn language, not everyone agrees how. How does language development begin? What forces and processes prompt children to participate in one of the uniquely human endeavors? Let us examine some of the explanations.

... voice from the field

A View from the Classroom Door

What does good infant and toddler care and early education look like? Every director and principal spends at least some of his or her time each day looking into classroom doors and windows to see if things are going okay. Sometimes, this quick snapshot is where administrators get information about how the day is going for children and teachers. What should you expect to see? What are the indicators that matter during this snapshot view? Here are some of the things for me.

Continuity of teachers and children in the group. By far the first thing I look for is a familiar scene. Is everyone who should be in the classroom there? Are the people who are the most knowledgeable about the children in the group present to spend their day together? Are all of the children in the group present?

Familiar faces are crucial to high-quality care and early education for all children but particularly for infants and toddlers. Continuity of teacher and group members allows for an intense level of predictability and stability that facilitates children's adjustment to school. It also increases the likelihood that the separation and reunion process will be predictable and pleasant. Expect to see this continuity over time, up to three years. Keeping teachers and children together for longer periods of time allows teachers of infants and toddlers to create an experience that is similar to the child's family experience.

A sense of peace and tranquility. Perhaps one of the most frightening aspects of out-of-home care for parents of infants and toddlers is the valid concern that children's emotional needs will not be met. Parents report that they are afraid that their child will need attention and not get it because of the demands of having infants and toddlers in groups. This fear is magnified by the separation and reunion process, which is often (and quite normally) accompanied by crying and resistance. So parents may leave a crying child at the beginning of the day and return to a crying child at the end of the day—fueling fears that the time in the middle can't be very pleasant either.

So, classrooms for infants and toddlers need to have a sense of tranquility and peace—a sense that the underlying timbre of the classroom is calm and stable. I look for a classroom where crying children are getting prompt responses—at least a verbal connection ("I'm on my way as soon as I finish changing this diaper")if not a physical one—and for actions that

speak as loud as words do. Look to see if teachers have ideas about what children need now as well as what they might need later. See if teachers have planned to meet needs (are bottles being warmed? are security items labeled and available?). Look for evidence that teachers know each child's individual daily routine and respect it by offering a bottle or lunch before the child is too hungry or beginning a calm-down routine before the child gets too tired. And look for signs that the adults are calm, confident, relaxed, and unhurried.

A balance of new and familiar in a clean environment. In infant and toddler programs, cleanliness is crucial. Because infants and toddlers spend a great deal of time on the floor and exploring with their hands and mouths, the environment must be clean and without odors.

Environments must also be predictable, filled with familiar yet interesting things to look at and manipulate. Children need to be able to find things where they left them the last time they were at school—the same place for sleeping, eating, and reading books. But also expect to see novel and interesting things to do, objects to touch, places to be, things to dump and sort through, and things to be discovered by uncovering or unwrapping.

I look for space. Overcrowding is a problem with infant and toddler care because the room can be filled up with cribs and other furniture. Infants and toddlers need plenty of space—enough to always have another area to move or be moved to for exploration. They need places for different visual and tactile stimulation and a place to get away from stimulation and excitement when it gets to be too much. I look for babies to be on the floor or in adult arms—not restrained in swings, exer-saucers, or bouncy seats. Exploration and practice are powerful second teachers that emerge from an environment that does not restrain.

Engagement between children and teachers. One of the most critical components of quality care and early education for infants and toddlers is the interactive environment. Emotional connections between children and the adults who care for and educate them are formed through interactions. Sensitive responsiveness by teachers to cues and communication insulates children from getting overstimulated, too tired, too hungry, or too bored. These types of experiences can have significance for the remainder of children's lives, compensating for early deprivation or the stressful experiences caused by poverty, unskilled parenting, abuse, and neglect.

I look for teachers to be where children are and children to be where teachers are. Sometimes this means physical engagement like being together on the floor or sharing a book in a comfortable rocking chair, and sometimes it means emotional engagement during routine activities like diapering and eating. It can also mean eye contact that reconnects with a look that says—"Keep going, you are doing a good job!"

It means looking for evidence of emotional contact and connectedness—quick responses to cries, looking where the child looks and commenting on what is seen, checking in to see if you're needed, verbal exchanges that lead children to believe you mean what you say, and a sense of caring about what children are seeing, feeling, and doing.

Look to see if teachers treat children respectfully. See if the teacher asks a child if she is ready to be picked up before doing it. Observe whether she uses language to talk to children rather than at them. Expect her to narrate what is going to happen before it happens and as it happens.

Look to see if teachers are observing children. Careful observation is the source of recognition of developmental progress and the way to discover emergent skills and interests. It also ensures that teachers register and make changes as children change so that boredom does not set in.

Brain training. Experience is the chief architect of the brain—stimuli from people, places, and things provide the nutrients for healthy brain development. The kinds of brain training I look for are summarized by the following.

- *Time*—teachers who invest in the time it takes to provide responsive caregiving.
- *Touch*—teachers who send powerful messages to babies by touching them. Warm, soft touches send very different messages than do rough, insensitive touches. Holding hands is a powerful touching experience that stimulates communication between areas of the brain and improves coordination between the areas of the brain.
- *Talk*—the critical period for learning language begins to close as toddlers start using expressive language at about two. I look to see children included in communication—verbal and nonverbal, expressive and receptive. Encouraging functional language, language that gets needs met, is a crucial skill to see demonstrated by teachers.
- *Training*—repetition forms and strengthens connections in the brain. I look for teachers providing opportunities to repeat and practice familiar skills and activities and who repeat important social experiences to enhance children's interest in the human world.

Pace changes across the day. Because infants and toddlers in full-day care and early education can spend a majority of their day at school, pace changes are crucial—for both children and the adults who care for them. Look for things to change across the day. Positions are changed for young infants, all children get opportunities to go outside, music is added, window blinds are closed to create a sense of calm, then opened to let the sun shine in! Look for the pace to pick up and become energetic and active and then quiet down to become intimate and soothing.

Help with social problem solving. Children under three in school are not yet able to interact successfully for long periods of time in groups without facilitation and support. In the beginning this looks a lot like protection from others—keeping fingers out of mouths, helping children crawl around rather than over, supporting side-by-side play, and giving infants and toddlers opportunities to look at and watch other children doing interesting things. Later on, it includes facilitating emerging social skills like sharing resources, taking turns, perfecting skills like using an outstretched hand to ask for a toy without words, and using words to communicate needs and wants.

To make this happen, teachers need to be close to where children are—physically near them—so they are available to model, guide, or support children's initial and subsequent interactions. So I look for teachers to be on the floor where children are, at the table when children are eating, participating in the process of picking up and putting down interesting toys, and supporting emerging skills by example as well as with verbal and physical guidance.

Evidence of connections between home and school. Positive communication between home and school is a key ingredient of good programs. Excellent programs put parents at the center of the relationship—not on the periphery. Evidence of this connection should abound in infant and toddler rooms.

Pictures of mom and dad and other family members, security items that are protected from general use, cultural influences reflecting the children's family cultural experiences, lots of invitations to come in, sit, stay should welcome you from the door. I check to see if written communication systems are working. Teachers and parents need ways to communicate and

keep track of the myriad information that must be exchanged. Incomplete information, from the parent to the school or from the school to the parent, indicates that communication may be lacking. I check to see that parents are viewed as integral to the success of the child at school by looking for articles of interest about parenting, notes about children's accomplishments, photographs that celebrate experiences.

The view from the door is often a snapshot—and certainly not an in-depth program evaluation. But high-quality care and early education for infants and toddlers is very observable—the components that create a positive experience for parents, children, and their teachers can be seen in a view from the door.

Kay Albrecht, Ph.D., was the executive director of HeartsHome Early Learning Center, Houston, Texas, until December 1999. HeartsHome has over sixty infants and toddlers enrolled and has been accredited four times by the National Academy of Early Childhood Programs.

Language Acquisition

Heredity plays a role in language development in a number of ways. First, humans have the respiratory and laryngeal systems that make rapid and efficient vocal communication possible. Second, the human brain makes language possible. The left hemisphere is the center for speech and phonetic analysis and the brain's main language center. But the left hemisphere does not have the exclusive responsibility for language. The right hemisphere plays a role in our understanding of speech intonations, which enables us to distinguish between declarative, imperative, and interrogative sentences. Without these processing systems, language as we know it would be impossible. Third, heredity plays a role in language development in that some theorists believe that humans are innately endowed with the ability to produce language.

Theories of Language Development

Noam Chomsky is one proponent of the theory that humans are born with the ability to acquire language. He hypothesizes that all children possess a structure or mechanism called a *language acquisition device* (LAD) that permits them to acquire language. The young child's LAD uses all the language sounds heard to process many grammatical sentences, even sentences never heard before. The child hears a particular language and processes it to form grammatical rules.

Eric Lenneberg has studied innate language acquisition in considerable detail in many different kinds of children, including the deaf. According to Lenneberg,

> All the evidence suggests that the capacities for speech production and related aspects of language acquisition develop according to built-in biological schedules. They appear when the time is ripe and not until then, when a state of what I have called "resonance" exists. The child somehow becomes "excited," in phase with the environment, so that the sounds he hears and has been hearing all along suddenly acquire a peculiar prominence. The change is like the establishment of new sensitivities. He becomes aware in a new way, selecting certain parts of the total auditory input for attention, ignoring others.[3]

The idea of a sensitive period of language development makes a great deal of sense and had a particular fascination for Montessori, who believed there were two such sensitive periods. The first begins at birth and lasts until about three years. During this time, children

unconsciously absorb language from the environment. The second period begins at three years and lasts until about eight years. During this time, children are active participants in their language development and learn how to use their power of communication. Milestones of language development are listed in Table 7.3.

ENVIRONMENTAL FACTORS. While the ability to acquire language has a biological basis, the content of the language—syntax, grammar, and vocabulary—is acquired from the environment, which includes parents and other people as models for language. Development depends on talk between children and adults, and between children and children. Optimal language development ultimately depends on interactions with the best possible language models. The biological process may be the same for all children, but the content of their language will differ according to environmental factors. Children left to their own devices will not learn a language as well as children reared in linguistically rich environments.

The Sequence of Language Development

Regardless of the theory of language development we choose to adopt as our own, the fact remains that children develop language in predictable sequences, and they don't wait for us

Table 7.3
Language Development in Infants and Toddlers

Months of Age	Language
Birth	Crying
1½	Social smile
3	Cooing (long pure vowel sound)
5	"Ah-goo" (the transition between cooing and early babbling)
5	Razzing (child places tongue between lips and produces a "raspberry")
6½	Babbling (repetition of consonant sounds)
8	"Dada/Mama" (inappropriate)
10	"Dada/Mama" (appropriate)
11	One word
12	Two words
14	Three words
15	Four–six words
15	Immature jargoning (sounds like gibberish; does not include any true word)
18	Seven–twenty words
18	Mature jargoning
21	Two-word combinations
24	Fifty words
24	Two-word sentences
24	Pronouns (*I, me, you*; used inappropriately)

Source: A. J. Capute and P. J. Accardo, "Linguistic and Auditory Milestones During the First Two Years of Life," Clinical Pediatrics *17(11) (November 1978), 848. Used by permission.*

to tell them what theory to follow in their language development. They are very pragmatic and develop language regardless of our beliefs.

FIRST WORDS. Although the process of language development begins at the moment of birth, parents usually don't think of language as beginning until children say their first word. In a parent education session a young mother recently said to me, "Dr. Morrison, why should I talk to her when she can't talk to me?" Professionals have a responsibility to educate parents and other family members about the imperative of early language development. Children must have good language proficiency if they are to come to school ready to learn.

The first words of children are just that, first words. What are these first words? Children talk about people—dada, papa, mama, mummie, and baby (referring to themselves); animals—dog, cat, kitty; vehicles—car, truck, boat, train; toys—ball, block, book, doll; food—juice, milk, cookie, bread, drink; body parts—eye, nose, mouth, ear; clothing and household articles—hat, shoe, spoon, clock; greeting terms—hi, bye, night-night; and a few words for actions—up, no more, off.

HOLOPHRASIC SPEECH. Children are remarkable communicators without words. When children have attentive parents and professionals, they develop into skilled communicators, using gestures, facial expressions, sound intonations, pointing, and reaching to make their desires known and get what they want. Pointing at an object and saying, "uh-uh-uh" is the same as saying, "I want the rattle" or "Help me get the rattle." Responsive caregivers can respond by saying, "Do you want the rattle? I'll get it for you. Here it is!" One of the attributes of an attentive caregiver is the ability to read children's signs and signals, anticipating their desires even though no words are spoken.

The ability to communicate progresses from "sign language" and sounds to the use of single words. Toddlers are skilled at using single words to name objects, to let others know what they want, and to express emotions. One word, in essence, does the work of a whole sentence. These single-word sentences are called *holophrases*.

The one-word sentences children use are primarily *referential* (used primarily to label objects, such as "doll"), or *expressive* (communicating personal desires or levels of social interaction, such as "bye-bye" and "kiss"). The extent to which children use these two functions of language depends in large measure on the professional and parent. For example, children's early language use reflects their mother's verbal style. This makes sense and the lesson is this: how parents speak to their children influences how their children speak.

SYMBOLIC REPRESENTATION. Two significant developmental events occur at about the age of two. First is the development of symbolic representation. Representation occurs when something—a mental image, a word—is used to stand for something else not present. A toy may stand for a tricycle, a baby doll may represent a real person. Words become signifiers of things—ball, block, blanket.

This ability frees children from the here and now, from acting on concrete objects present only in the immediate environment. It enables their thoughts to range over the full span of time—past and present—and permits them to remember and project thoughts into the future. Concrete objects, the things themselves, need not be present for children to act on them. The ability to represent liberates the child from the present. He can imagine things as separate from himself. In this regard, mental representation literally frees the child of space and time.

The use of mental symbols also enables the child to participate in two processes that are characteristic of the early years: symbolic play and the beginning of the use of words and sentences to express meanings and make references.

VOCABULARY DEVELOPMENT. The second significant achievement that occurs at about two is the development of a fifty-word vocabulary and the use of two-word sentences. This vocabulary development and the ability to combine words mark the beginning of rapid

language development. Vocabulary development plays a very powerful and significant role in school achievement and success. Research repeatedly demonstrates that children who come to school with a broad use and knowledge of words achieve better than their peers who do not have an expanded vocabulary. Adults are the major source of children's vocabularies.

TELEGRAPHIC SPEECH. You have undoubtedly heard a toddler say something like "Go out" in response to a suggestion such as "Let's go outside." Perhaps you've said, "Is your juice all gone?" and the toddler responded, "All gone." These two-word sentences are called *telegraphic speech*. They are the same kind of sentences you would use if you wrote a telegram. The sentences are primarily made up of nouns and verbs. Generally, they do not have prepositions, articles, conjunctions, and auxiliary verbs.

MOTHERESE OR PARENTESE. Many recent research studies have demonstrated that mothers and other caregivers talk to infants and toddlers differently than adults talk to each other. This distinctive way of adapting everyday speech to young children is called motherese,[4] or parentese. Characteristics of such speech include the following:

- The sentences are short, averaging just over four words per sentence with babies. As children become older, the length of sentences mothers use also becomes longer. Mothers' conversations with their children are short and sweet.
- The sentences are highly intelligible. When talking to their children, mothers tend not to slur or mumble their words. This may be because mothers speak slower to their children than they do to adults in normal conversation.
- The sentences are "unswervingly well formed"—that is, they are grammatical sentences.
- The sentences are mainly imperatives and questions, such as "Give Mommie the ball" and "Do you want more juice?" Since mothers can't exchange a great deal of information with their children, their utterances are such that they direct their children's actions.
- Mothers use sentences in which referents ("here," "that," "there") are used to stand for objects or people: "Here's your bottle." "That's your baby doll." "There's your doggie."
- Mothers expand or provide an adult version of their children's communication. When a child points at a baby doll on a chair, the mother may respond by saying, "Yes, the baby doll is on the chair."
- Mother's sentences involve repetitions. "The ball, bring Mommie the ball. Yes, go get the ball—the ball—go get the ball."

GRAMMATICAL MORPHEMES. There is more to learning language than learning words. There is also the matter of learning grammar. Grammar is the way we change the meanings of sentences and place events and action in time: past, present, and future tense. Grammatical morphemes are the principal means for changing the meanings of sentences. A *morpheme* is the smallest unit of meaning it is possible to have in a language. A morpheme can be a word, such as "no," or an element of a word, such as "-ed." A morpheme that can stand alone, such as "child," is a *free morpheme*. A morpheme that cannot stand alone is a bound morpheme. "Kicked" consists of the free morpheme "kick" and the bound morpheme "-ed." Morphological rules include the rules governing tenses, plurals, and possessives.

The order in which children learn grammatical morphemes is well documented. The pattern of mastery is orderly and consistent. The first morpheme to be mastered is the present progressive (I drinking), followed by prepositions (in and on), plural (two dolls), past

irregular (toy fell), possessive (Sally's doll), uncontractible verb (there it is), articles (a block, the doll), past regular (Eve stopped), third-person regular (he runs), uncontractible auxiliary (I am going), contractible verb (that's a doll), and contractible auxiliary (I'm going).[5]

NEGATIVES. If you took a vote on the toddler's favorite word, "no" would win hands down. When children begin to use negatives, they simply add "no" to the beginning of a word or sentence ("no milk"). As their "no" sentences become longer, they still put "no" first ("no put coat on"). Later, they place negatives appropriately between subject and verb ("I no want juice").

When children move beyond the use of the one-word expression "no," the expression of negation progresses through a series of meanings. The first meaning conveys nonexistence, such as "no juice" and "no hat," meaning that the juice is all gone and the hat isn't present. The next level of negation is for the rejection of something. "No go out" is the rejection of the offer to go outside. Next, the use of "no" progresses to the denial of something the child believes to be untrue. If offered a carrot stick under the pretense it is candy, the child will reply, "No candy."[6]

By the end of the preschool years, children have developed and mastered most language patterns. The basis for language development is the early years, and no amount of later remedial training can make up for development that should have occurred during this sensitive period for language learning.

IMPLICATIONS FOR PROFESSIONALS. Professionals must attune themselves to children's developing language style and abilities. As children develop in their ability to use language, professionals can "mirror" that language back, adapting their way of talking to children in accordance with their growing use of language. Communicating with children provides a rich linguistic environment for children to learn language. Language that is short, direct, and grammatically correct supports children's efforts at language development. Expanding what the child says is also helpful.

Although it seems obvious to say that children can talk about what they know, some professionals act as though what they say to children makes little difference. Professionals should provide many experiences for children so they have something to talk about. Walks, encounters with other children and adults, field trips, and vicarious experiences through reading and tech-

The process of language development begins at birth—perhaps even before. What are some specific things parents, teachers, and caregivers can do to promote a child's language development?

nology all provide children with things to talk about. The other half of the equation, of course, is that children need professionals who will talk with them and provide opportunities for conversation. Having an opportunity to talk is as important as having something to talk about.

As noted earlier, children's first words are the names of things. Parents and professionals can teach children the names of things directly ("This is a ball") or indirectly ("Tell me what this is"). They can label, putting the name of the object on the object: "chair." They can use the names of things in their conversation with children ("This is a shoe; let's put your shoe on"). Children need to know the names of things if they are going to refer to them and talk about them.

Since children's first words are words for things, and since Piaget believed children need a mental representation of an object to match a name to it, it makes sense to give children experiences with real objects to lay the foundation for knowing their names. Experiences with toys, household objects, and people provide the basis for developing mental representations to which names can then be attached. On the other hand, a child whose environment lacks opportunities for experiences with real objects will have fewer mental representations and consequently a more limited vocabulary of the names of things.

Given the biological propensity for language development and the tremendous ability of children to learn language on their own even under the most difficult circumstances, there may be a tendency for some parents to treat language development with benign neglect and not do much to assist children with language acquisition. This approach is unfortunate and does a great disservice to children. The ability of children to teach themselves language flourishes best in a cooperative and supportive environment for language development.

Success in school is determined in part by how well children know and use language. Children who know the names of things, who can express themselves well, who can talk to the teacher, who understand the language of schooling, are children who, for the most part, will do well in school and life.

A high priority for early childhood professionals is to provide programs that support and facilitate children's language development. Providing children with professionals who are well trained and sensitive and responsive to children's language development is one place to start. Another is to provide a child–staff ratio that supports language development. For example, in a recent study of the effects of reduced child–staff ratio on children's development, researchers found that in programs with ratios of 1:4 for infants and 1:6 for toddlers, language proficiency improved dramatically from when ratios were higher.[7]

Figure 7.7 provides guidelines that will help you promote children's language development.

How Does Psychosocial Development Occur?

Erik H. Erikson (1902–1994) is noted for his *psychosocial theory* of development. According to Erikson, children's personalities grow and develop in response to social institutions such as families, schools, child care centers, and early childhood programs. Of course, adults are principal components of these environments and therefore play a powerful role in helping or hindering children in their personality development.

Stages of Psychosocial Development

Erikson's theory has eight stages, which he also classifies as *ego qualities*. These qualities emerge across the human life span. Erikson maintained that psychosocial development

results from the interaction between maturational processes such as biological needs and the social forces encountered in everyday living. Socialization provides the context for conflict and crisis resolution during the eight developmental stages. Four of these stages apply to children from birth to age eight (see Figure 7.8).

- Treat children as partners in the communication process. Many infant behaviors, such as smiling, cooing, and vocalizing, serve to initiate conversation, and professionals can be responsive to these through conversations.
- Conversations are the building blocks of language development. Attentive and caring adults are infants' and toddlers' best stimulators of cognitive and language development.
- Talk to infants in a soothing, pleasant voice, with frequent eye contact, even though they do not "talk" to you. Most mothers and professionals talk to their young children differently from the way they talk to adults. They adapt their speech so they can communicate in a distinctive way called *motherese* or *parentese.* Mothers' language interactions with their toddlers are much the same as with infants. When conversing with toddlers who are just learning language, it is a good idea to simplify verbalization—not by using "baby talk," such as "di-di" for diaper or "ba ba" for bottle, but rather by speaking in an easily understandable way. For example, instead of saying, "We are going to take a walk around the block so you must put your coat on," you would instead say, "Let's get coats on."
- Use children's names when interacting with them, to personalize the conversation and build self-identity.
- Use a variety of means to stimulate and promote language development, including reading stories, singing songs, listening to records, and giving children many opportunities to verbally interact with adults and other children.
- Encourage children to converse and share information with other children and adults.
- Help children learn to converse in various settings by taking them to different places so they can use their language with a variety of people. This approach also gives children ideas and events for using language.
- Have children use language in different ways. Children need to know how to use language to ask questions, explain feelings and emotions, tell what they have done, and describe things.
- Give children experiences in the language of directions and commands. Many children fail in school settings not because they do not know language but because they have little or no experience in how language is used for giving and following directions. It is also important for children to understand that language can be used as a means to an end—a way of attaining a desired goal.
- Converse with children about what they are doing and how they are doing it. Children learn language through feedback—asking and answering questions and commending about activities—which shows children that you are paying attention to them and what they are doing.
- Talk to children in the full range of adult language, including past and future tenses.

Figure 7.7
Promoting Language Development

Meeting Basic Human Needs

Abraham Maslow (1890–1970) identified a hierarchy of basic human needs (see Figure 7.9): (1) life essentials, (2) safety and security, (3) belongingness and love, (4) achievement and prestige, (5) aesthetic needs, and (6) self-actualization. All professionals must endeavor to provide the conditions, environments, and opportunities for children at all ages to have these basic needs met. Chapter 12 contains a comprehensive discussion of these needs and examples of how to provide for them, especially as a means of guiding children's behavior.

Quality Infant and Toddler Programs

Developmentally Appropriate Programs

Many issues I discuss in this book have implications for infant and toddler education. First is the issue of developmental appropriateness. All early childhood professionals who provide care for infants and toddlers—indeed, for all children—must understand and recognize this important concept, which provides a solid foundation for any program. The NAEYC defines *developmentally appropriate* as having three dimensions:

- What is known about child development and learning—knowledge of age-related human characteristics that permits general predictions within an age range about what activities, materials, interactions, or experiences will be safe, healthy, interesting, achievable, and also challenging for children;
- What is known about the strengths, interests, and needs of each individual child in the group to be able to adapt for and be responsive to inevitable individual variation; and
- Knowledge of the social and cultural contexts in which children live to ensure that learning experiences are meaningful, relevant, and respectful for the participating children and their families.[8]

For more information about Developmentally Appropriate Practice, go to the Companion Website at http://www.prenhall.com/morrison, select any chapter, then choose Topic 4 of the ECE Supersite module.

As part of the NAEYC's revised Developmentally Appropriate Practice in Early Childhood Programs, the following guidelines for making decisions about developmentally appropriate practice will help staff plan for activities:

Guidelines for Decisions about Developmentally Appropriate Practice

An understanding of the nature of development and learning during the early childhood years, from birth though age 8, generates guidelines that inform the practices of early childhood educators. Developmentally appropriate practice requires that teachers integrate the many dimensions of their knowledge base. They must know about child development and the implications of this knowledge for how to teach, the content of the curriculum—what to teach and when—how to assess what children have learned, and how to adapt curriculum and instruction to children's individual strengths, needs, and interests. Further, they must know the particular children they teach and their families and be knowledgeable as well about the social and cultural context.

The following guidelines address five interrelated dimensions of early childhood professional practice: creating a caring community of learners, teaching to enhance development and learning, constructing an appropriate curriculum, assessing children's development and learning, and establishing reciprocal relationships with families. (The word *teacher* is used to refer to any adult responsible for a group of children in any early childhood program, including infant/toddler caregivers, family child care providers, and specialists in other disciplines who fulfill the role of teacher.)

Stage	Approximate Age	Characteristics	Role of Early Childhood Educators	Outcome for Child
I. Basic Trust versus Mistrust: During this stage, children learn to trust or mistrust their environments and professionals. Trust develops when children's needs are met consistently, predictably, and lovingly.	Birth to 18 months	Infants learn to either trust or mistrust that others will care for their basic needs, including nourishment, sucking, warmth, cleanliness, and physical contact.	Meet children's needs with consistency and continuity.	Views the world as safe and dependable.
II. Autonomy versus Shame and Doubt: This is the stage of independence when children want to do things for themselves. Lack of opportunities to become autonomous and independent and professional overprotection result in self-doubt and poor achievement. As a result, instead of feeling good about their accomplishments, children come to feel ashamed of their abilities.	18 months to 3 years	Toddlers learn to be self-sufficient or to doubt their abilities in activities such as toileting, feeding, walking, and talking.	Encourage children to do what they are capable of doing; avoid shaming for any behavior.	Learns independence and competence.

Figure 7.8
Erikson's Stages of Psychological Development in Early Childhood

1. Developmentally appropriate practices occur within a context that supports the development of relationships between adults and children, among children, among teachers, and between teachers and families.
   A. The early childhood setting functions as a community of learners in which all participants consider and contribute to each other's well-being and learning.
   B. Consistent, positive relationships with a limited number of adults and other children are a fundamental determinant of healthy human development and provide the context for children to learn about themselves and their world and also how to develop positive, constructive relationships with other people.

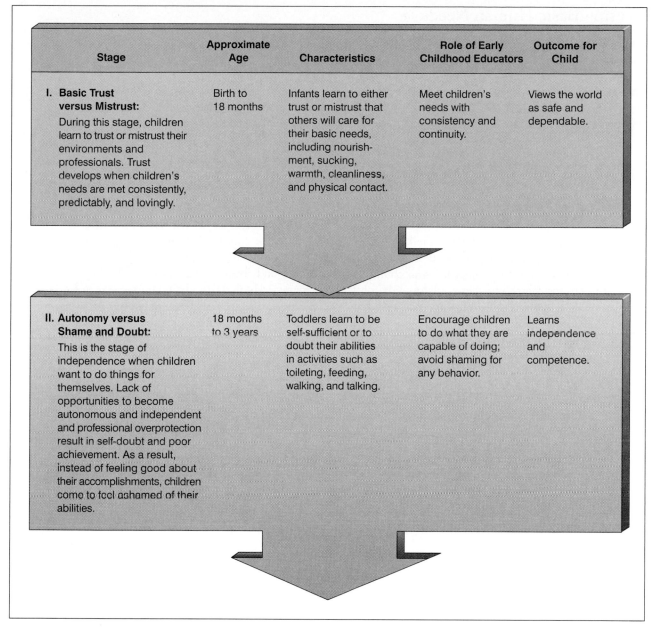

Stage	Approximate Age	Characteristics	Role of Early Childhood Educators	Outcome for Child
III. Initiative versus Guilt: During the preschool years children need opportunity to respond with initiative to activities and tasks, which gives them a sense of purposefulness and accomplishment. Erikson believes children can feel guilty when they are discouraged or prohibited from initiating activities and are overly restricted in attempts to do things on their own.	3–5 years	Children are learning and want to undertake many adultlike activities, sometimes overstepping the limits set by parents and thus feeling guilty.	Encourage children to engage in many activities; provide environments in which children can explore; promote language development.	Is able to undertake a task, be active and involved.
IV. Industry versus Inferiority: In this period, children display an industrious attitude and want to be productive. They want to build things, discover, manipulate objects, and find out how things work. Productivity is important during this stage. They also want recognition for their productivity, and adult response to children's efforts and accomplishments helps develop a positive self-concept. Feelings of inferiority result when children are criticized, belittled, or have few opportunities for productivity.	5–8 years	Children actively and busily learn to be competent and productive or feel inferior and unable to do things well.	Help children win recognition by producing things; recognition results from achievement and success.	Has feelings of self-worth and industry.

C. Social relationships are an important context for learning. Each child has strengths or interests that contribute to the overall functioning of the group. When children have opportunities to play together, work on projects in small groups, and talk with other children and adults, their own development and learning are enhanced.

D. The learning environment is designed to protect children's health and safety and is supportive of children's psychological needs for activity, sensory stimulation, fresh air, rest, and nourishment. The program protects children's psychological safety; that is, children feel secure, relaxed, and comfortable rather than disengaged, frightened, worried, or stressed.

E. Children experience an organized environment and an orderly routine that provides an overall structure in which learning takes place; the environment is dynamic and changing but predictable and comprehensible from a child's point of view.

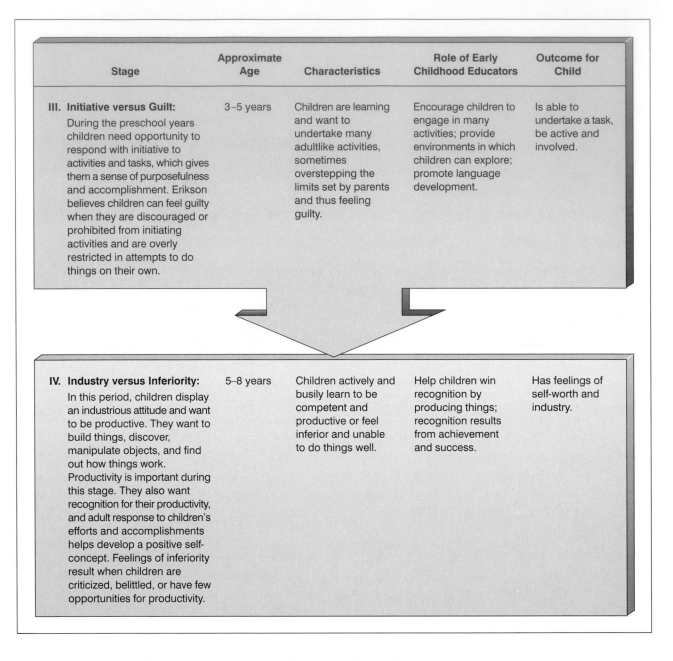

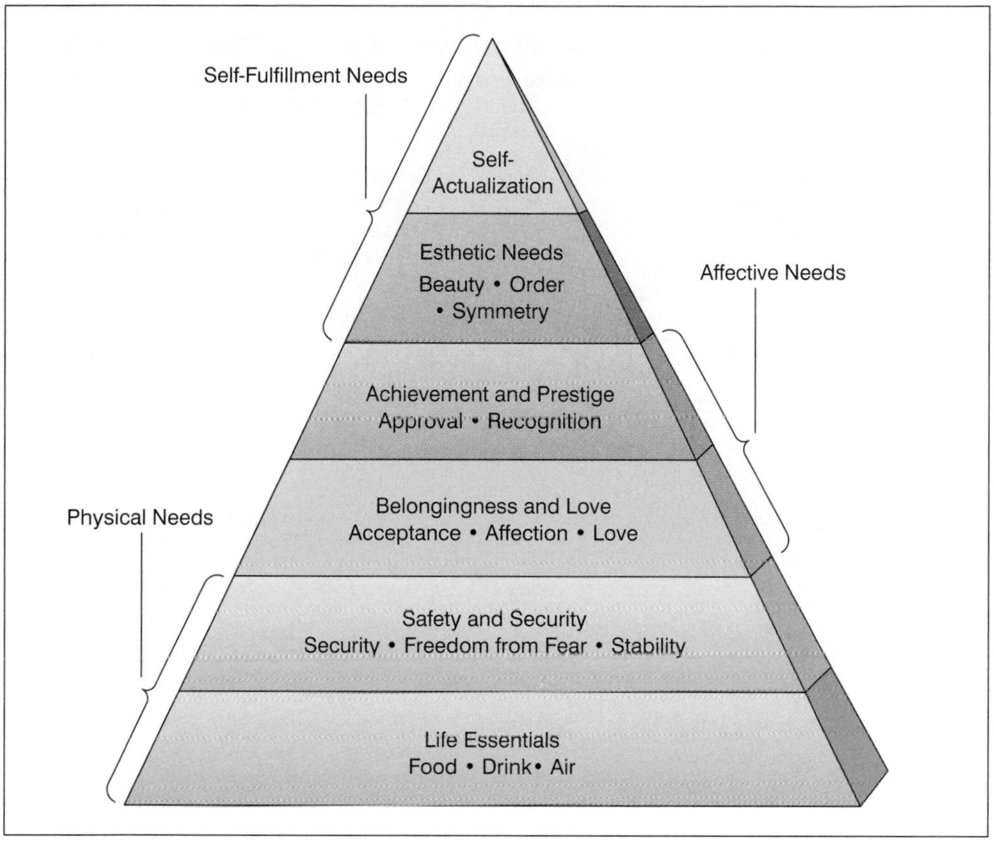

Figure 7.9
Hierarchy of Needs

Source: Maslow's hierarchy of needs data from Motivation and Personality, *3rd ed. by Abraham H. Maslow. Revised by Robert Frager et al. Copyright © 1954, 1987 by Harper & Row, Publishers, Inc. Copyright © 1970 by Abraham H. Maslow. Reprinted by permission of Addison-Wesley Educational Publishers, Inc.*

2. Adults are responsible for ensuring children's healthy development and learning.
   A. Teachers respect, value, and accept children and treat them with dignity at all times.
   B. Teachers make it a priority to know each child as well.
   C. Teachers create an intellectually engaging, responsive environment to promote each child's learning and development.
   D. Teachers make plans to enable children to attain key curriculum goals across various disciplines such as language arts, mathematics, social studies, science, art, music, physical education, and health.
   E. Teachers foster children's collaboration with peers on interesting, important enterprises.
   F. Teachers develop, refine, and use a wide repertoire of teaching strategies to enhance children's learning and development.
   G. Teachers facilitate the development of responsibility of self-regulation in children.
3. Constructing appropriate curriculum. The content of the early childhood curriculum is determined by many factors, including the subject matter of the disciplines, social or cultural values, and parental input. In developmentally appropriate programs, decisions about curriculum content also take into consideration the age and experience of the learners. Achieving success for all children depends, among other

When making decisions about child care, parents must consider five essential factors: the environment, quality professionals, staff–child ratios, the quality of care, and the curriculum.

essentials, on providing a challenging, interesting, developmentally appropriate curriculum. Constructing appropriate curriculum requires attention to at least the following guidelines for practice:

A. Developmentally appropriate curriculum provides for all areas of a child's development: physical, emotional, social, linguistic, aesthetic, and cognitive.

B. Curriculum includes a broad range of content across disciplines that is socially relevant, intellectually engaging, and personally meaningful to children.

C. Curriculum builds upon what children already know and are able to do (activating prior knowledge) to consolidate their learning and to foster their acquisition of new concepts and skills.

D. Effective curriculum plans frequently integrate across traditional subject-matter divisions to help children make meaningful connections and provide opportunities for rich conceptual development; focusing on one subject is also a valid strategy at times.

E. Curriculum promotes the development of knowledge and understanding, processes and skills, as well as the dispositions to use and apply skills and to go on learning.

F. Curriculum content has intellectual integrity, reflecting the key concepts and tools of inquiry of recognized disciplines in ways that are accessible and achievable for young children, ages 3 through 8.

G. Curriculum provides opportunities to support children's home culture and language while also developing all children's abilities to participate in the shared culture of the program and the community.

H. Curriculum goals are realistic and attainable for most children in the designated age range for which they are designed.

I. When used, technology is physically and philosophically integrated in the classroom curriculum and teaching.

4. Assessing children's learning and development. Assessment of individual children's development and learning is essential for planning and implementing appropriate curriculum. In developmentally appropriate programs, assessment and curriculum are integrated, with teachers continually engaging in observational assessment for the purpose of improving teaching and learning.
   A. Assessment of young children's progress and achievements is ongoing, strategic, and purposeful.
   B. The content of assessments reflects progress toward important learning and developmental goals.
   C. The methods of assessment are appropriate to the age and experiences of young children. Therefore, assessment of young children relies heavily on the results of observations of children's development, descriptive data, collections of representative work by children, and demonstrated performance during authentic, not contrived, activities. Input from families as well as children's evaluations of their own work are part of the overall assessment strategy.
   D. Assessments are tailored to a specific purpose for which they have been demonstrated to produce reliable, valid information.
   E. Decisions that have a major impact on children, such as enrollment or placement, are never made on the basis of a single developmental assessment or screening device but are based on multiple sources of relevant information, particularly observations by teachers and parents.
   F. To identify children who have special learning or developmental needs and to plan appropriate curriculum and teaching for them, developmental assessments and observations are used.
   G. Assessment recognizes individual variation in learners and allows for differences in styles and rates of learning. Assessment takes into consideration such factors as the child's facility in English, stage of acquisition, and whether the child has had the time and opportunity to develop proficiency in his or her home language as well as in English.
   H. Assessment legitimately addresses not only what children can do independently but what they can do with assistance from other children or adults. Teachers study children as individuals as well as in relationship to groups by documenting group projects and other collaborative work.
5. Establishing reciprocal relationships with families. Developmentally appropriate practices derive from deep knowledge of individual children and the context within which they develop and learn. The younger the child, the more necessary it is for professionals to acquire this knowledge through relationships with children's families.
   A. Reciprocal relationships between teachers and families require mutual respect, cooperation, shared responsibility, and negotiation of conflicts toward achievement of shared goals.
   B. Early childhood teachers work in collaborative partnerships with families, establishing and maintaining regular, frequent two-way communication with children's parents.
   C. Parents are welcome in the program and participate in decisions about their children's care and education. Parents observe and participate and serve in decision-making roles in the program.
   D. Teachers acknowledge parents' choices and goals for children and respond with sensitivity and respect to parents' preferences and concerns without abdicating professional responsibility to children.
   E. Teachers and parents share their knowledge of the child and understanding of children's development and learning as part of day-to-day communication and

planned conference. Teachers support families in ways that maximally promote family decision-making capabilities and competence.

F. To ensure more accurate and complete information, the program involves families in assessing and planning for individual children.

G. The program links families with a range of services, based on identified resources, priorities, and concerns.

H. Teachers, parents, programs, social service and health agencies, and consultants who may have educational responsibility for the child at different times should, with family participation, share developmental information about children as they pass from one level or program to another.[9]

The full text of the NAEYC's Position Statement on Developmentally Appropriate Practice in Early Childhood Programs is found in Appendix B.

Early childhood professionals must also understand the importance of providing programs for infants and toddlers that are uniquely different from programs for older children. NAEYC states the following about the necessity for unique programming for infants and toddlers:

> Developmentally appropriate programs for children from birth to age 3 are distinctly different from all other types of programs—they are not a scaled-down version of a good program for preschool children. These program differences are determined by the unique characteristics and needs of children during the first 3 years:
>
> - Changes take place far more rapidly in infancy than during any other period in life.
> - During infancy, as at every other age, all areas of development—cognitive, social, emotional, and physical—are intertwined.
> - Infants are totally dependent on adults to meet their needs.
> - Very young children are especially vulnerable to adversity because they are less able to cope actively with discomfort and stress.
>
> Infants and toddlers learn through their own experience, trial and error, repetition, imitation, and identification. Adults guide and encourage this learning by ensuring that the environment is safe and emotionally supportive. An appropriate program for children younger than three invites play, active exploration, and movement. It provides a broad array of stimulating experiences within a reliable framework of routines and protection from excessive stress. Relationships with people are emphasized as an essential contribution to the quality of children's experiences.[10]

Based on these dimensions, professionals must provide different programs of activities for infants and toddlers. To do so, early childhood professionals must get parents and other professionals to recognize that infants, as a group, are different from toddlers and need programs, curricula, and facilities specifically designed for them. It is then necessary to design and implement developmentally appropriate curricula. The early childhood education profession is leading the way in raising consciousness about the need to match what professionals do with children to children's development as individuals. We have a long way to go in this regard, but part of the resolution will come with ongoing training of professionals in child development and curriculum planning.

Finally, it is important to match professionals with children of different ages. Not everyone is emotionally or professionally suited to provide care for infants and toddlers. Both groups need adults who can respond to their particular needs and developmental characteristics. Infants need especially nurturing professionals; toddlers, on the other hand, need adults who can tolerate and allow for their emerging autonomy and independence.

Curricula for Infants and Toddlers

Curricula for infants and toddlers consist of all the activities and experiences they are involved in while under the direction of professionals. Consequently, early childhood professionals plan for all activities and involvement: feeding, washing, diapering/toileting, playing, learning and having stimulating interactions, outings, being involved with others, and having conversations. Professionals must plan the curriculum so it is developmentally appropriate. In addition to ideas derived from the NAEYC guidelines quoted previously, curriculum planning includes the following concepts:

- Self-help skills
- Ability to separate from parents
- Problem solving
- Autonomy and independence
- Assistance in meeting the developmental milestones associated with physical, cognitive, language, personality, and social development

Childproofing Homes and Centers

As infants become more mobile and as toddlers start their constant exploration, safety becomes a major concern. Professionals can advise parents about childproofing the home. In addition, professionals must childproof centers and other settings.

Home

- Remove throw rugs so toddlers do not trip.
- Put breakable objects out of toddlers' reach.

... *video viewpoint*

The First Three Years of Life

ABC NEWS

The Carnegie Corporation released a study of how important the first three years of life are for stimulation and nurturing and what being deprived of experiences and opportunities in those years can mean for the future of our children and our nation.

REFLECTIVE DISCUSSION QUESTIONS

Why is this such an important issue for professionals? for parents? How does poverty negatively influence children's environments and prevent them from fully developing in the early years?

REFLECTIVE DECISION MAKING

What are some things you can do to improve the quality of children's environments in the first three years of life? How can parents improve the quality of home environments? What are some things educators and parents can do to provide infants and toddlers with appropriate attention and stimulation?

- Cover electrical wall outlets with special covers.
- Remove electrical cords.
- Install gates in hallways and stairs (make sure gates are federally approved so the toddlers cannot get their heads stuck and strangle).
- Take knobs off stoves.
- Purchase medicines and cleaners with childproof caps.
- Store all medicines and cleaning agents out of reach; move all toxic chemicals from low cabinets to high ones (even things like mouthwash should be put in a safe place).
- Place safety locks that can be opened from the outside on bathroom doors.
- Cushion sharp corners of tables and counters with foam rubber and tape or cotton balls.
- If older children in the home use toys with small parts, beads, and so forth, have them use these when the toddler is not present or in an area where the toddler cannot get them.
- When cooking, turn all pot handles to the back of the stove.
- Avoid using cleaning fluids while children are present (because of toxic fumes).
- Place guards over hot water faucets in bathrooms so toddlers cannot turn them on.
- Keep wastebaskets on tops of desks.
- Keep doors to the washer and dryer closed at all times.
- Keep all plastic bags, including garbage bags, stored in a safe place.
- Shorten cords on draperies; if there are loops on cords, cut them.
- Immediately wipe up any spilled liquid from the floor.

Center

- Cover toddler areas with carpeting or mats.
- Make sure storage shelves are anchored well and will not tip over; store things so children cannot pull heavy objects off shelves onto themselves.
- Use only safe equipment and materials, nothing that has sharp edges or is broken.
- Store all medicines in locked cabinets.
- Cushion sharp corners with foam rubber and tape.
- Keep doors closed or install gates.
- Fence all play areas.

Providing Healthy Programs for Young Children

The spread of diseases in early childhood programs is a serious concern to all who care for young children. Part of the responsibility of all caregivers is to provide healthy care for all

Program in Action

A Changing Curriculum: A Necessity for the Toddler

The changing curriculum is a multifaceted environment consisting of an indoor play space designed to help children enjoy learning and an outdoor environment for extending learning opportunities. To produce happy, well-adjusted, intelligent young children, the daily environment, teachers, time frames, and schedules all must respond to children's developmental needs and desires. Children construct their knowledge by engaging in activities that are meaningful and purposeful to each unique individual. Each child becomes interested and absorbed in personally significant materials and ideas in achieving daily goals.

THE DAILY ENVIRONMENT

The indoor environment includes a covered walkway to the front door, a bridge of adjustment for toddlers as they prepare to say goodbye to mommy or daddy. The child enters the reception area with a parent where a caregiver takes health information.

A teacher or an aide greets children as they hang up their coats and escorts them to the main playroom. The room is divided into play areas for art, books, manipulative toys, small replicas and structures for role and dramatic play, indoor riding tracks, indoor wheel toys, small plastic construction sites, crawl-through play tunnels, slides, and a small indoor pond with toy ducks, frogs, and fish. Inviting pathways connect the areas to each other. Materials within are rotated often and changed frequently, with duplicated "favorites" available.

Materials and play equipment should be open ended and suggestive rather than directive. A chest containing throwaways that suggest, but do not dictate, are recommended: empty boxes, plastic bottles, various shaped containers, tubes, different articles of clothing with unusual textures and colors. Toddlers like to form their own imaginative ideas, unlike older preschoolers, who like to have structured activities imposed by an adult who suggests specific play or pretend situations. For example, four-year-olds like to have an adult suggest a tea party or a trip on a pirate ship. "Toddlers," "waddlers," and "talkers" prefer to create their own play situations.

Teachers here do not plan the curriculum; it is created each moment of the day as children respond to an environment carefully designed for interaction. The teacher observes, analyzes, and responds to each child's needs as the day progresses. As children are confronted with problems, the teacher attempts to answer or pose questions, select appropriate materials, and make suggestions to help children construct their own knowledge.

The following description of an imaginary child's morning in an ideal play center will help you visualize how a changing curriculum would operate.

LIBBY'S DAY IN THE CHANGING CURRICULUM

ENTERING THE RECEPTION AREA

A caregiver greets Libby and her mother at the door, saying, "Good morning, Libby. I'm glad to see you. Come, let me take your hand and we will talk with Miss Robyn. I know your mom wants to tell us what you had for breakfast, and how you slept last night." Miss Robyn is seated on a low chair so she can make eye contact and exchange smiles with all the arriving children. She writes on Libby's health chart (see Figure A) as Libby's mom speaks: ten hours of sleep; no bed wetting; bowel movement shortly after waking; no indication of fever, no rashes, eyes clear. Libby, while waiting, watches the water fountain nestled among the plants and walks over to pet a large toy pony statue on the head. As she becomes restless, an aide pulls a wagon in and Miss Robyn asks, "Libby, do you want a ride to the book corner?"

"I do," she responds.

THE DAY BEGINS

The wagon stops where books are on display and small chairs, pillows, and stuffed animals invite children into the area. From here, Libby can look out the window to see the rabbits in the cage on

Daily Health Check

Date: ____________________

Arrival Time: ____________ Departure Time: ____________

Accompanied By: ____________________

Breakfast: ____________ Supper: ____________ (previous evening)

No. Hours of Sleep: ____ Bath: Yes ____ No ____ Wet Bed: Yes ____ No ____ No. of Times: ____

Any Sleep Disturbance: ____________________

Bowel Movement: Yes ____ No ____ Normal: Yes ____ No ____

Nausea: ________ Eyes: ________ Temperature: ________

Skin Rash: ________ Other: ____________________

Happy: ______ Reserved: ______ Other Emotional Behaviors: ____________

Figure A
A Sample Health Card

Health information is recorded on a 5" x 8" prepared information card. A health aide or teacher looks at eyes and takes temperature using an aural thermometer, such as those manufactured by Thermoscan, as the daily health check is completed.

the patio, eating their breakfast of lettuce and chopped carrots. Libby watches for a very short time, then attends to the books.

Libby chooses one of her favorite books, *Good Night Moon,* stretches out on a large pillow, looks toward the ceiling, and calls out, "Can anyone get me a moon to play with?" At that moment, Brittany arrives and answers, "Sure, you know 'The Cow Jumped Over the Moon'? I bet she could." Libby jumps up from her pillow and says, "Where is that jumping cow, anyway?"

After two minutes of searching, Libby finds a plastic cow used as a prop in the recital of the nursery rhyme "The Cow Jumped Over the Moon." She says, "Hey, look, Miss Bone. He's dirty. A dirty cow can't find a moon if he is so dirty." Miss Bone replies, "Why don't you go wash the cow?" Libby is on her way to the bathroom, the cow under her arm, when she observes Daniel and Jessie playing with blocks and cars and trucks carrying small people.

"Hey, let me play," says Libby.

"No. You don't have no people," replies Daniel. Libby throws the cow over a doll's bed and proceeds to take "people" away from the two boys. Daniel and Jessie rebuff her intrusion, and Libby begins to cry. Miss Bone, who has been watching, intercedes, asking, "Libby, what happened to the cow that jumped over the moon?"

Libby replies, "I don't know. I want to ride on the tricycle."

THE DAY CONTINUES

During the day, the teachers take children outside a few at a time to explore the great outdoors (see Figure B). A patio is the bridge from the indoor to the outdoor environment, which again is defined by pathways leading to expanding physical activities that are both safe and manageable for toddlers.

Many trees, small shrubs, blooming flowers, sandboxes with spades, trucks, cooking utensils, boats, things to climb on or crawl through, and wagons to pull are available. Best of all, there are places and spaces to hide, with or without a friend, where children can fantasize and invent their own worlds. Children may move to a climbing apparatus, enclosed playhouses, old boats, shallow water with stepping stones, a water play area with hoses

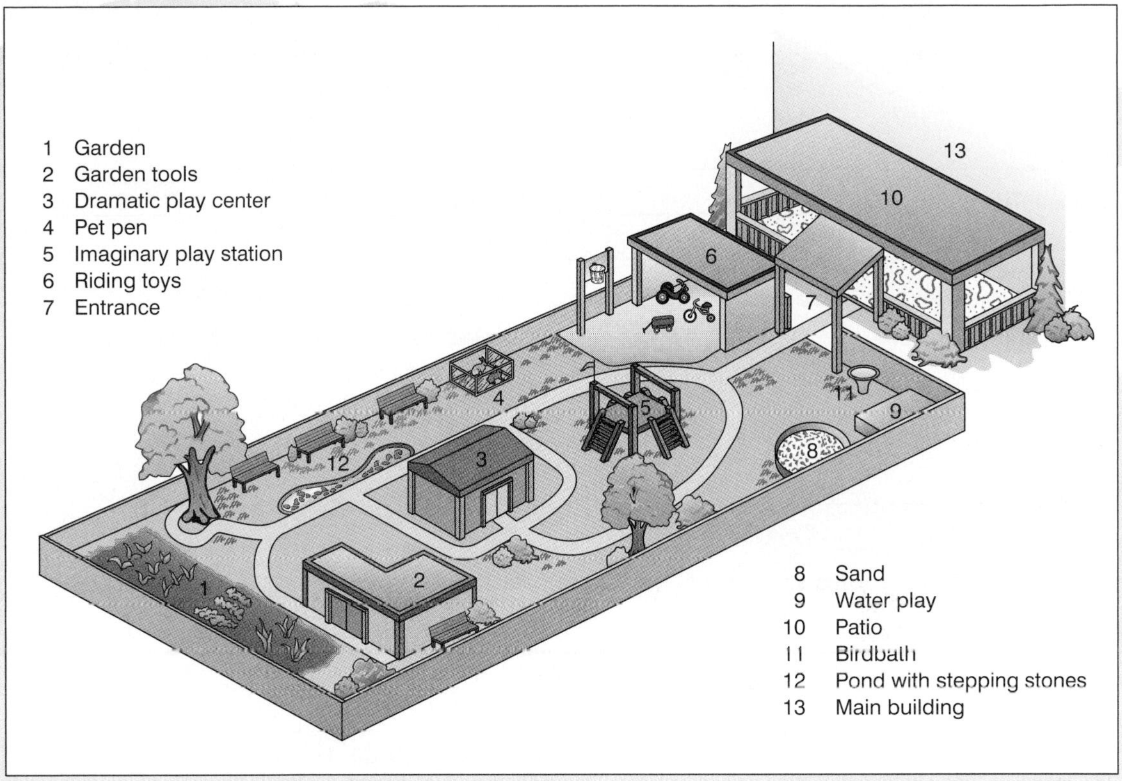

Figure B
A Typical Outdoor Environment

and sprinklers, or an imaginary play station. One covered area has wheel toys of various sizes, positioned adjacent to sand and water areas with plastic animals, trees, and barns. Nearby is a pen for live animals. These animals come to the center for short periods of time from pet stores or are brought by families to be shared.

One area has a garden, with fresh vegetables and flowers and fruit trees for children to observe and to sit beneath for rest periods or for private conversations. A tool shed here stores garden implements as well as other items that must be kept out of children's reach or protected from the weather. This shed has a large tub for washing toys and spaces for drying them as well.

A few minutes after Libby goes outside, Miss Bone appears with two clay pots and a small spade and asks, "Libby, do you want to help me dig some dirt to put in these pots?"

"What are we going to do with the dirt?" Libby asks.

Miss Bone replies, "We are going to plant bean seeds and watch them grow."

After helping for a minute or so, Libby asks, "Is it time to go now?"

"It's almost time for lunch," replies Miss Bone. "Do you want to go by the rabbits' cage as we go inside?"

Daniel, Jessie, Brittany, and Drew join Miss Bone and Libby as they walk toward the playroom. Each child waves and says, "Bye, Rabbit!"

The Changing Curriculum for Toddlers

We have shared our view of an ideal environment appropriate for toddlers both indoors and outdoors, a conceptual framework for the development of a curriculum unique to the individual programs and settings. You may adapt these suggestions to specific spaces and neighborhoods where programs exist for toddler care.

Your curriculum will not and cannot be successful with toddlers unless you understand the distinctive features of this special age group (16–36 months). You must carefully evaluate mate-

rials, activities, and encounters throughout the day, and must consider physical, social-emotional, and cognitive growth factors when constructing curricular opportunities.

For the curriculum to meet the needs of young children, content and presentation style must be modified to meet the rapid changes occurring in the structure of the brain, and to accommodate physical growth and personality adaptation. To assist in this, your curriculum structure should be stable, to promote assurance and trust. The curriculum and environment also should promote autonomy and self-reliance.

The toddler is seeking to understand who he is, what he is able to do with his body, where he should be, and why he is requested to perform certain actions throughout the day. Toddlers are able to understand and are eager to learn much more than previously thought. A competent professional will be able to guide, give explanations, demonstrate, provide stimuli, ask questions and pose problems, thus allowing young children to embrace new horizons.

A toddler's perceptual development is changing rapidly and is affected by experiences and cognitive maturity. Sensation, presented by caregivers, and actions on and within the environment provide the basis for your curriculum. The interactive physical, social, emotional, and cognitive stimulations should include sight, hearing, smell, taste, touch, as well as *proprioception* (body orientation, such as balance; ability to reach and stretch and to identify body parts; closing eyes and touching nose; sitting and standing with eyes closed; lifting, pushing, pulling). Children begin to construct their own knowledge as they test information for validity. When a child validates her own sensations, she can expand knowledge in innumerable ways, such as by understanding how to use information that is similar or different to solve problems or to express herself creatively.

Toddlers as well as adults live simultaneously in the worlds of reality and imagination. Children need to understand the fundamentals of their physical environment. This, the "real" world, is the primary content source for a curriculum for young children.

The world of imagination and make-believe is just as important to young children as the real world. It is difficult for toddlers to tell when one ends and the other begins. The make-believe world is less threatening and offers more possibilities for pure or uncontaminated development to occur. It is easier for children to use their imagination to deal with problems, thus creating their own learning and problem-solving techniques.

CONNECTING THE REAL AND IMAGINATIVE WORLDS

Storybooks can be a bridge as the curriculum moves back and forth from the imaginative to the real world. Select books because they connect with home or community activities. Many connecting activities emerge from community, seasons, family-specific events or holidays, family relationships, hobbies, and daily living.

For example, the Walt Disney version of the story *The Three Little Pigs*, where the pigs do not get eaten by the wolf but run from one house to the other until they are all secure in the brick house, provides a nonthreatening, real-life situation. Large cardboard boxes may become symbols for the three houses; two should be collapsible. Children may examine real bricks, sticks, and straw before building the structures.

In this version of the story, each pig was musically talented: one played the piano, one the flute, and one the violin. You may present these musical instruments by having children role play the pigs. You may also include singing and movement activities, and may record them on videotape. You may wish to use other props, such as a large black pot of the kind used to make soup, to hang in a make-believe fireplace. Another suggestion is to bring in a churn, which can be used to make butter to be served later.

These cardboard box houses may later be used on the patio for different purposes, such as developing Our Town, consisting of toy stores, book and video stores, bakeries, banks, and doctors' offices. A vegetable stand could also be placed near the patio, thus linking the covered space with the outdoor environment.

EVALUATION OF PROGRAM EFFECTIVENESS AND CHILDREN'S ACHIEVEMENT

AUTHENTIC DATA FILES

A variety of measurement tools are available to you. Your data collection for assessment must take place in a natural setting. The result should reflect your interpretation of each toddler's development based on the child's informal responses. Authentic assessment should also include notating unso-

licited responses and recording unanticipated events. Evidence of children's growth can be documented in a number of ways: pictorial, descriptive, audio, video, and in original samples of work.

ANECDOTAL RECORDS

Anecdotal records are a time-honored measurement device for young children. Anecdotal records are factual, nonjudgmental observations of a child's activity. Teachers and caregivers should record behaviors that relate to program and individual goals in addition to individual responses to the curriculum and environment. The anecdote should be kept in context, and include date, time, indoor or outdoor setting, and any other factual information necessary to facilitate understanding. For toddlers, the recording process must be kept simple.

CHECKLISTS AND RATING SCALES

Checklists and rating scales that reflect program and individual objectives can be designed to collect specific information. Screening instruments and development scales will assist you in considering changes in circular presentations and time frames.

BUILDING THE TODDLER DATA FILE

The authentic data file of each toddler in the program may include, but should not be limited to, the following:

- Birthdate; problems with pregnancies and early adjustments; note allergies, persons to contact in case of emergencies (giving relationship)
- Height, weight, and health status recorded at the initial registration and updated every three months
- Physical health, fine motor, gross motor, spatial orientation, with all data labeled and dated
- Children's scribbling and painting
- Photographs of play activities
- Videotapes of gross motor activities
- Audiotapes documenting the progression of language development through the waddler, toddler, and talker stages
- Teacher's notes from play encounters with children or from conversations and interviews conducted while playing games with children
- Videotapes of musical responses and sociodrama activities
- Special program, environment, and/or curriculum adaptations as discussed and mutually agreed upon by families, caregivers, and program directors

Contributed by Beverly Boals and Mildred B. Vance, professors of early childhood, Arkansas State University.

children. One of the most important things you can do to promote a healthy environment is to wash your hands properly. Figure 7.10 describes how to wash hands.

Diapering is another prime vehicle for germ transmission. The spread of germs can be greatly reduced through the use of sanitary diapering techniques. It is imperative that sanitary procedures be followed while diapering children. Figure 7.11 describes the steps of diapering children.

Community Collaboration

It is difficult for many families to provide for the total health needs of their children. Because families sometimes need help in rearing healthy children, communities in which these children live should also help in this regard. Through collaboration, it is possible to make healthy living a reality for all children. In many communities around the country, the public health community has combined efforts with the early childhood community in order to create the best care for children. Healthy Child Care America is an excellent example of this community collaboration in action.

- Always use warm, running water and a mild, preferably liquid soap. Antibacterial soaps may be used, but are not required. Premoistened cleansing towelettes do not effectively clean hands and do not take the place of handwashing.
- Wet the hands and apply a small amount (dime to quarter size) of liquid soap to hands.
- Rub hands together vigorously until a soapy lather appears and continue for at least 15 seconds. Be sure to scrub between fingers, under fingernails, and around the tops and palms of hands.
- Rinse hands under warm, running water. Leave the water running while drying hands.
- Dry hands with a clean, disposable (or single use) towel, being careful to avoid touching the faucet handle.
- Turn the faucet off using the towel as a barrier between your hands and the faucet handle.
- Discard the used towel in a trash can lined with a fluid-resistant (plastic) bag. Trash cans with foot-pedal operated lids are preferable.
- Consider using hand lotion to prevent chapping of hands. If using lotions, use liquids or tubes that can be squirted so that the hands do not have direct contact with the container spout. Direct contact with the spout could contaminate the lotion inside the container.
- When assisting a child in handwashing, either hold the child (if an infant) or have the child stand on a safety step at a height at which the child's hands can hang freely under the running water. Assist the child in performing all of the above steps and then wash your own hands.

Figure 7.10
How to Wash Hands

Source: "The ABC's of Safe and Healthy Child Care," http://www.cdc.gov.

The American Academy of Pediatrics coordinates the Healthy Child Care America campaign in partnership with the U.S. Department of Health and Human Services Child Care Bureau and the Maternal and Child Health Bureau. Healthy Child Care America is based on the principle that, through partnerships, families, child care providers, and health care providers can promote the healthy development of young children in child care and increase access to preventive health services and safe physical environments for children. Linking health care providers, child care providers, and families makes good sense—for maximizing resources, for developing comprehensive and coordinated services, and, most important, for nurturing children.

Goals of Healthy Child Care America include the following:

- Safe, healthy child care environments for all children, including those with special health needs
- Up-to-date and easily accessible immunizations for children in child care
- Access to quality health, dental, and developmental screening and comprehensive follow-up for children in child care
- Health and mental health consultation, support, and education for all families, children and child care providers
- Health, nutrition and safety education for children in child care, their families, and child care providers[11]

1. Organize needed supplies within reach:
   - Fresh diaper and clean clothes (if necessary)
   - Dampened paper towels or premoistened towelettes for cleaning child's bottom
   - Child's personal, labeled ointment (if provided by parents)
   - Trash disposal bag
2. Place a disposable covering (such as roll paper) on the portion of the diapering table where you will place the child's bottom. Diapering surfaces should be smooth, nonabsorbent, and easy to clean. Don't use areas that come in close contact with children during play, such as couches, floor areas where children play, etc.
3. If using gloves, put them on now.
4. Using only your hands, pick up and hold the child away from your body. Don't cradle the child in your arms and risk soiling your clothing.
5. Lay the child on the paper or towel.
6. Remove the soiled diaper (and soiled clothes).
7. Put disposable diaper in a plastic-lined trash receptacle.
8. Put soiled reusable diaper and/or soiled clothes WITHOUT RINSING in a plastic bag and give to parents.
9. Clean child's bottom with a premoistened disposable towelette or a dampened, single use disposable towel.
10. Place the soiled towelette or towel in a plastic-lined trash receptacle.
11. If the child needs a more thorough washing, use soap, running water, and paper towels.
12. Remove the disposable covering from beneath the child. Discard it in a plastic-lined receptacle.
13. If you are wearing gloves, remove and dispose of them now in a plastic-lined receptacle.
14. Wash your hands. NOTE: The diapering table should be next to a sink with running water so that you can wash your hands without leaving the diapered child unattended. However, if a sink is not within reach of the diapering table, **don't leave the child unattended on the diapering table** to go to a sink; wipe your hands with a premoistened towelette instead. **NEVER** leave a child alone on the diapering table.
15. Wash the child's hands under running water.
16. Diaper and dress the child.
17. Disinfect the diapering surface immediately after you finish diapering the child.
18. Return the child to the activity area.
19. Clean and disinfect:
   - The diapering area,
   - All equipment or supplies that were touched, and
   - Soiled crib or cot, if needed
20. Wash your hands under running water.

Figure 7.11
Recommended Procedure for Diapering a Child

Source: "The ABC's of Safe and Healthy Child Care," *http://www.cdc.gov.*

BLUEPRINT FOR ACTION. The purpose of the *Blueprint for Action* part of Healthy Child Care America is to provide communities with steps they can take to either expand existing public and private services and resources or to create new services and resources that link families, health care, and child care. Communities using *Blueprint for Action* are encouraged to identify their own needs and to adapt the ten steps as needed. The steps are not prioritized; communities can determine which step(s) should be implemented. The ten steps are as follows:

- Promote safe, healthy, and developmentally appropriate environments for all children in child care.
- Increase immunization rates and preventive services for children in child care settings.
- Assist families in accessing key public and private health and social service programs.
- Promote and increase comprehensive access to health screenings.
- Conduct health and safety education and promotion programs for children, families, and child care providers.
- Strengthen and improve nutrition services in child care.
- Provide training and ongoing consultation to child care providers and families in the areas of social and emotional health.
- Expand and provide ongoing support to child care providers and families caring for children with special health needs.
- Use child care health consultants to help develop and maintain healthy child care.
- Assess and promote the health, training, and work environments of child care providers.[12]

There are no quick and easy solutions to the challenges that families, child care providers, and health care providers face today in providing for and ensuring the healthy development of children. It is important that these three groups work together to expand and create partnerships. *Blueprint for Action* will help communities as they set priorities and goals that will lead to healthier child care in America. The following account is just one example of many regarding how one or all of the ten *Blueprint* steps are being implemented across the country.

To take an online self-test on this chapter's contents, go to the Companion Website at http://www.prenhall.com/morrison, select chapter 7, then choose the Self Test module.

HEALTHY BEGINNINGS, EARLY CHILDHOOD SERVICES, INC. This initiative provides onsite screening at licensed child care sites in seven counties in the northern Florida Panhandle. The Florida-based Early Childhood Services, Inc., administers a number of early childhood funding streams, including Head Start. Healthy Beginnings collaborated with Head Start's health and nutrition coordinator, with assistance from the Head Start Health Services Advisory Committee, to develop a coalition of health and safety providers. Health care professionals visit each licensed child care center in the seven-county area twice a year in a mobile medical van donated by two local hospitals. Only basic screenings (height, weight, heart, and dental) are completed because the coalition does not have funding for the liability coverage necessary for blood screenings. (Funding comes from the local Kiwanis Club through its national initiative to provide safe and healthy beginnings to children under 5.) The program is producing measurable results—approximately 20 percent of children screened for physical health problems and nearly 50 percent of those screened for dental health needs are referred for further services. The response from parents, particularly working parents who have difficulty scheduling routine health care for their children, is overwhelmingly positive. Recommendations for expanding Healthy Beginnings include funding for staff to oversee more intensive follow-up services, maintenance of a centralized database to track children's health as they move from setting to setting, and provision of onsite immunizations and blood screenings. You can read more about Healthy Child Care America and other successful examples at http://ericps.ed.uiuc.edu/nccic/hcca/action.html.

For additional Internet resources or to complete an online activity for this chapter, go to the Companion Website at http://www.prenhall.com/morrison, select chapter 7, then choose the Linking to Learning or Making Connections module.

Infants and toddlers are interesting and remarkably competent individuals. The developmental and educational milestones of these years are the foundations of all that follow throughout life. All professionals must use their knowledge, understanding, energy, and talents to assure that this foundation is the best it can be.

Activities for Further Enrichment

Applications

1. You have been asked to speak to a group of parents about what they can do to promote their children's language development in the first two years of life. Outline your presentation and list five specific suggestions you will make.
2. Observe children between the ages of birth and eighteen months. Identify the six stages of sensorimotor intelligence by describing the behaviors you observed. Cite specific examples of secondary and tertiary reactions. For each of the six stages, develop two activities that would be cognitively appropriate.
3. Why is motor development important in the early years? What are five activities professionals can include in their programs to promote motor development?
4. Identify at least ten games or activities that are beneficial to the developing infant and the growing toddler. Describe the benefits of each of the games or activities you list.

Field Experiences

1. Visit at least two programs that provide care for infants and toddlers. Observe the curriculum to determine whether it is developmentally appropriate. What suggestions would you make for improving the curriculum? Explain what you liked most and least about the program.
2. Visit centers that care for young children of different cultures. List the differences you find. What role does culture play in how we care for and educate children?

Research

1. In addition to the qualities cited in this chapter, list and explain five other qualities you think are important for professionals caring for infants and toddlers.
2. Identify customs that are passed down to infants and toddlers as a result of the family's cultural background. How do these customs affect young children's behavior?
3. Interview professionals who care for infants and toddlers. How are their rules similar and different? Which age group would you prefer to care for? Why?

Readings for Further Enrichment

Berk, L. *Infants and Children: Prenatal through Middle Childhood.* Needham Heights, MA: Allyn & Bacon, 1999.

In addition to its engaging style, this text combines the most recent scholarship with an outstanding pedagogical program to maximize learning. Numerous vignettes are presented throughout the text to engage student interest and foster connections to real life.

Diamond, M., and Hopson, J. *Magic Trees of the Mind: How to Nurture Your Child's Intelligence, Creativity, and Healthy Emotions from Birth through Adolescence.* New York: Dutton, 1998.

Based on interviews with noted scientists in the field and original surveys of thousands of parents and children, here are detailed analyses of cutting-edge programs designed to develop and expand your child's mind.

Golinkoff, R., and Pasek-Hirsh, K. *How Babies Talk: The Magic and Mystery of Language in the First Three Years of Life.* New York: Dutton, 1999.

The culmination of years of research, this text explains exactly how babies learn language in the first years of life. Outlines the milestones babies reach and how parents can help their babies reach them.

Karr-Morse, R. *Ghosts from the Nursery: Tracing the Roots of Violence.* Poulsbo, WA: Grove/Atlantic, 1999.

Cutting to the heart of the alarming trend of violence committed by children, Ghosts from the Nursery *gives startling new evidence that violent behavior is fundamentally linked to abuse and neglect in the first two years of life. Makes a convincing case for the revolution in our beliefs about the care of babies.*

Kreuger, A. *Parenting Guide to Your Baby's First Year.* New York: Ballantine Books, 1999.

With its timely, in-depth advice and hands-on guidance, Parenting *magazine brings you a comprehensive, up-to-the-minute guide to the all-important first year of your baby's life.*

Piper, T. *Language and Learning: The Home and School Years,* 2nd ed. Upper Saddle River, NJ: Merrill/Prentice Hall, 1998.

This book takes an integrative approach to how children learn language, how it is taught, and how the two are sometimes at odds. Gives balanced treatment to theory and practice, to first and second language acquisition, and to showing and telling.

Shore, R. *Rethinking the Brain: New Insights into Early Development.* New York: Families and Work Institute, 1997.

An outstanding, thorough, and highly accessible review of new research on the development of children from birth to five years. Was the source of inspiration, along with Carnegie Corporation's

Starting Points report issued in 1994, for the recent explosion in interest in young children's healthy development.

Warner, P. *Baby Play and Learn.* New York: Simon & Schuster, 1999.

A child development expert offers 160 specific suggestions for games and activities that will provide hours of development challenges and rewards for babies and parents.

Linking to Learning

Child Nutrition, Health, and Physical Activity
http://www.ificinfo.health.org/index3.htm

A series of files and web links to various resources concerning the health and nutrition of young children.

I Am Your Child
http://www.iamyourchild.org/

A national public awareness and engagement campaign to make early childhood development a top priority for our nation, I Am Your Child has educated millions of parents and professionals about breakthrough new discoveries in the process of brain development.

KidSource OnLine for Healthcare
http://www.kidsource.com/kidsource/pages/Health.html

Health care articles, online forums, and Web sites concerning the proper care of young children.

Zero to Three
http://www.zerotothree.org/

Concentrates exclusively on the miraculous first years of life, the critical period when a child undergoes the greatest human growth and development. Zero to Three's mission is to develop a solid intellectual, emotional, and social foundation for young children.

ENDNOTES

1 P. Kuhl, *Early Language Acquisition: The Brain Comes Prepared*, Parents as Teachers National Center (1996). [On-line.] Available: http://www.patnc.org/neuroforum.htm.

2 J. Huttenlocher, "Language Input and Language Growth," *Preventive Medicine: An International Devoted to Practice and Theory* (vol. 27, no. 2) (March–April 1998), 195–199.

3 Eric H. Lenneberg, "The Biological Foundations of Language," in Mark Lester, ed., *Readings in Applied Transformational Grammar* (New York: Holt, Rinehart & Winston, 1970), 8.

4 E. L. Newport, "Mother, I'd rather do it myself: Some Effects and Non-effects on Maternal Speech Style," in C. E. Snow and C. A. Ferguson, eds., *Talking to Children* (Cambridge, England: Cambridge University Press, 1977), 112–129.

5 R. Brown, *A First Language* (Cambridge, MA: Harvard University Press, 1973), 281.

6 L. Bloom, *Language Development: Form and Function in Emerging Grammars* (Cambridge, MA: MIT Press, 1970).

7 J. Portner, "Two Studies Link High-Quality Day Care and Child Development," *Education Week* (19 April 1995), 6.

8 Sue Bredekamp and Carol Copple, eds., *Developmentally Appropriate Practice in Early Childhood Programs,* rev. ed. (Washington, DC: National Association for the Education of Young Children, 1997), 9.

9 Ibid., 16–22.

10 National Association for the Education of Young Children, *Developmentally Appropriate Practice in Early Childhood Programs Serving Infants* (Washington, DC: Author, 1989), no. 547.

11 National Child Care Information Center, "Healthy Child Care America." (May 1995). [On-line.] Available: http://nccic.org/hcca/abthcca.html.

12 National Child Care Information Center, "Healthy Child Care America Blueprint for Action." (May 1995). [On-line.] Available: http://nccic.org/hcca/action.html.

CHAPTER 8

What I know of children I have learned from them.

CAROLINE PRATT

The Preschool Years

Getting Ready for School

Focus Questions

1. How has the history of preschool education influenced contemporary practice?
2. What are the characteristics of preschoolers' growth and development?
3. How does play promote children's learning?
4. What are the important issues concerning preschool programs?
5. How is the preschool curriculum changing?

To review the chapter focus questions online, go to the Companion Website at http://www.prenhall.com/morrison and select chapter 8.

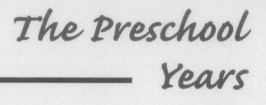

Early childhood professionals view the events of the preschool years as the cornerstone of later learning. The road to success in school and life begins long before kindergarten or first grade. The preschool years are assuming a more important place in the process of schooling these days. For many children, the preschool years are the beginning of a period of at least fourteen years during which their lives will be dramatically influenced by teachers and schooling. As a result, the preschool years are playing a more important role in the education process than at any time in history. The preschool years will continue to be the focus of public attention in the new millennium.

What Is Preschool?

To check your understanding of this chapter with the online Study Guide, go to the Companion Website at http://www.prenhall.com/morrison, select chapter 8, then choose the Study Guide module.

For our purposes, preschools are programs for three- to five-year-old children, before they enter kindergarten. Today it is common for many children to be in a school of some kind beginning as early as age two or three, and child care beginning at six weeks is becoming almost commonplace for children of working parents. Forty-one states currently invest in preschool education, whether as public preschools or as support for Head Start. Since 1997, New York has provided free early childhood education to every four-year-old whose parents want it. In Georgia, preschool programs are provided for all children. In 1999, the states spent $1.7 billion on preschool care and education. However, three-quarters of this spending was concentrated in just ten states—California, Florida, Georgia, Illinois, Massachusetts, Michigan, New Jersey, New York, Ohio, and Texas. Preschool education continues to grow, with greater numbers of four-year-olds entering preschools. Currently, about 725,000 three- to five-year-old children are in some kind of preschool program.

Why Are Preschools Growing in Popularity?

For more information about preschools, go to the Companion Website at http://www.prenhall.com/morrison, select chapter 8, then choose the Linking to Learning module to connect to several preschool sites.

A number of reasons help explain the current popularity of preschool programs. They include the following:

- Many parents are frustrated and dissatisfied with efforts to find quality and affordable care for their children. They view public schools as the agency that can and should provide care and education for their children.
- With changing attitudes toward work and careers, more parents are in the workforce than ever before. Additionally, many parents believe it is possible to balance family and career. This in turn places a great demand on the early childhood profession to provide more programs and services, including programs for three- and four-year-olds.
- Parents, public policy planners, and researchers believe intervention programs designed to prevent such social problems as substance abuse and dropout prevention work best in the early years. Research supports the effectiveness of this early intervention approach. Quality early childhood programs help prevent and reduce behavioral and social problems.
- With growing concern on the part of corporations and businesses about the quality of the American workforce, business leaders see early education as one way of developing

literate workers. Many preschool programs include work-related skills and behaviors in their curriculum. For example, learning how to be responsible and trustworthy are skills that are learned early in life. Likewise, being literate has its foundations in the early years as well.

- Advocacy exists for publicly supported and financed preschools as a means of helping ensure that all children and their families, regardless of socioeconomic background, are not excluded from the known benefits of attending quality preschool programs.
- It is becoming widely understood that the foundation for learning is laid in the early years and that three- and four-year-old children are ready, willing, and able to learn.

As preschool programs have grown in number and popularity over the last decade, they have also undergone significant changes in purposes. Previously, the predominant purposes of preschools were to help socialize children, enhance their social-emotional development, and get them ready for kindergarten or first grade. Today there is a decided move away from socialization as the primary function for preschooling. Preschools are now promoted as places to accomplish the following goals:

- Support and develop children's innate capacity for learning. The responsibility for "getting ready for school" has shifted from being primarily children's and parent's responsibilities to being a cooperative venture among child, family, home, schools, and communities. Review again the information on the importance of early learning for brain development discussed in chapter 7. The same reasons for providing early education to infants and toddlers also apply to preschool children and their curriculum.
- Use the public schools as a centralized agency to deliver services at an early age to all young children and their families.
- Deliver a full range of health, social, economic, and academic services to children and families. Family welfare is also a justification for operating preschools.
- Solve or find solutions for pressing social problems. The early years are viewed as a time when interventions are most likely to have long-term positive influences. Preschool programs are seen as ways of lowering the number of dropouts, improving children's health, and preventing serious social problems such as substance abuse and violence.

Given the changing nature of the preschool, it is little wonder that the preschool years are playing a larger role in early childhood education.

What Are Preschoolers Like?

Today's preschoolers are not like the children of previous decades. Many have already attended one, two, or three years of child care or nursery school. They have watched hundreds of hours of television. Many are technologically sophisticated. Many have experienced the trauma of family divorces or the psychological effects of abuse. Both collectively and individually, the experiential backgrounds of preschoolers are quite different from those of previous generations. But you and other early childhood professionals must understand precisely the impact and implications of this background to effectively meet preschoolers' needs.

For more information about preschoolers' development, go to the Companion Website at http://www.prenhall.com/morrison, select any chapter, then choose Topic 2 of the ECE Supersite module.

Physical and Motor Development

Understanding preschoolers' physical and motor development enables you to acknowledge why active learning is so important. To begin with, a noticeable difference between preschoolers and infants and toddlers is that preschoolers have lost most of their baby fat and taken on a leaner, lankier look. This "slimming down" and increasing motor coordination enables the preschooler to participate with more confidence in the locomotor activities so vitally necessary during this stage of growth and development. Both girls and boys continue to grow several inches per year throughout the preschool years. Table 8.1 shows the average height and weight for preschoolers.

Preschool children are learning to use and test their bodies. It is a time for learning what they can individually do and how they can do it. Locomotion plays a large role in motor and skill development and includes activities of moving the body through space—walking, running, hopping, jumping, rolling, dancing, climbing, and leaping. Preschoolers use these activities to investigate and explore the relationships among themselves, space, and objects in space.

Preschoolers also like to participate in fine-motor activities such as drawing, coloring, painting, cutting, and pasting. Consequently, they need programs that provide action and play, supported by proper nutrition and healthy habits of plentiful rest and good hygiene.

Cognitive Development

Preschoolers are in the preoperational stage of intelligence. As discussed in chapter 5, characteristics of the preoperational stage are (1) children grow in their ability to use symbols, including language; (2) children are not capable of operational thinking (an operation is a reversible mental action), which explains why Piaget named this stage *preoperational*; (3) children center on one thought or idea, often to the exclusion of other thoughts; (4) children are unable to conserve; and (5) children are egocentric.

Preoperational characteristics have particular implications for you and other early childhood professionals. You can promote children's learning during the preoperational stage of development by doing the following:

- *Furnish concrete materials to help children see and experience concepts and processes.* Children learn more from touching and experimenting with an actual object than they do from a picture, story, or video. If children are learning about apples, bring in a collection of apples for children to touch, feel, smell, taste, discuss, classify, manipulate, and

Table 8.1
Average Height and Weight of Preschoolers

	Males		Females	
Age	Height (inches)	Weight (pounds)	Height (inches)	Weight (pounds)
3 years	38.0	32.4	37.6	30.7
4 years	40.5	36.8	40.0	35.2
5 years	43.3	41.2	42.7	38.9

Source: Based on data from P. V. V. Hamill et al., "Physical Growth: National Center for Health Statistics Percentiles," American Journal of Clinical Nutrition *32(1979), pp. 607–629.*

It is essential that programs provide opportunities for children to engage in active play both in indoor and outdoor settings. What are some things that children can learn through participation in playground activities?

explore. Collections also offer children an ideal way to learn the names for things, classify, count, and describe.

- *Use hands-on activities that give children opportunities for active involvement in their learning.* When you encourage children to manipulate and interact with the world around them, they begin to construct concepts about relationships, attributes, and processes. Through exploration, preoperational children begin to collect and organize data about the objects they manipulate. For example, when children engage in water play with funnels and cups, they learn about concepts such as measurement, volume, sink/float, bubbles and the prism, evaporation, and saturation.
- *Give children many and varied experiences.* Diverse activities and play environments lend themselves to teaching different skills, concepts, and processes. Children should spend time daily in both indoor and outdoor activities. Give consideration to the types of activities that facilitate large and fine motor, social, emotional, and cognitive development. For example, outdoor play activities and games such as tag, hopscotch, and jump rope enhance large motor development; fine motor activities include using scissors, stringing beads, coloring, and writing.
- *Model appropriate tasks and behaviors, as the preoperational child learns to a great extent through modeling.* Children should see adults reading and writing daily. It is also helpful for children to view brief demonstrations by peers or professionals on possible ways to use materials. For example, after children have spent a lot of time in free exploration with math manipulatives, teachers and others can show children patterning techniques and strategies they may want to experiment with in their own play.
- *Provide a print-rich environment to stimulate interest and development of language and literacy in a meaningful context.* The physical environment should display room labeling, class stories and dictations, children's writing, and charts of familiar songs and fingerplays. There should be a variety of literature for students to read, including books,

magazines, and newspapers. Paper and writing utensils should be abundant to motivate children in all kinds of writing. Daily literacy activities should include opportunities for shared, guided, and independent reading and writing; singing songs and fingerplays; and creative dramatics. Children should be read to every day.

- *Allow children periods of uninterrupted time to engage in self-chosen tasks.* Children benefit more from large blocks of time provided for in-depth exploration in meaningful play than they do from frequent, brief ones. It takes time for children to become deeply involved in play, especially imaginative and fantasy play. Morning and afternoon schedules should each contain at least two such blocks of time.

Language Development

Children's language skills grow and develop rapidly during the preschool years. Vocabulary increases, and sentence length increases as children continue to master syntax and grammar. Infants and toddlers first use *holophrases*, single words that convey the meaning of a sentence. For example, a child may say "milk" to express, "I'd like some more milk, please."

At one year, infants know two or more words; by the age of two, about 275. During their second year, toddlers' language proficiency increases to include *telegraphic speech:* two- or three-word utterances acting as a sentence. "Amy go," for example, can mean that Amy wants her mother to take her for a walk in the stroller. During their third year or earlier, children add helping verbs and negatives to their vocabulary; for example, "No touch," or "I don't want milk." Sentences also become longer and more complex. During the fourth and fifth years, children use noun or subject clauses, conjunctions, and prepositions to complete their sentences.

During the preschool years, children's language development is diverse and comprehensive and constitutes a truly impressive range of learning. An even more impressive feature of this language acquisition is that children learn intuitively, without a great deal of instruction, the rules of language that apply to words and phrases they use. You can use many of the language practices recommended for infants and toddlers with preschoolers as well.

School Readiness: Who Gets Ready for Whom?

School readiness is a major topic of debate in discussions of preschool and kindergarten programs. The early childhood profession is reexamining "readiness," its many interpretations, and the various ways the concept is applied to educational practices.

For most parents, *readiness* means that their children have the knowledge and abilities necessary for success in preschool and for getting ready for kindergarten. Figure 8.1 shows what kindergarten teachers believe are important factors for kindergarten readiness. These are some of the things children should know and be able to do before coming to kindergarten. Thus they shape, influence, and inform the preschool curriculum and the activities of preschool teachers.

As discussed in chapter 2, goal 1 of the Goals 2000: Educate America Act, the readiness goal, states that by the year 2000 all children in America should start school ready to learn. This goal has three important subgoals:

- All children who are disadvantaged or who have disabilities will have access to high-quality and developmentally appropriate preschool programs that help prepare children for school.

Figure 8.1
What Kindergarten Teachers Believe Are Important Factors for Kindergarten Readiness

Source: Adapted from U.S. Department of Education, National Center for Education Statistics, Kindergarten Teacher Survey on Student Readiness, 1995.

- Physically healthy, rested, and well nourished
- Able to finish task
- Can count to twenty or more
- Takes turns and shares
- Has good problem-solving skills
- Is enthusiastic and curious in approaching new activities
- Is able to use pencils or paintbrushes
- Is not disruptive of the class
- Knows the English language
- Is sensitive to other children's feelings
- Sits still and pays attention
- Knows the letters of the alphabet
- Can follow directions
- Identifies primary colors and basic shapes
- Communicates needs, wants, and thoughts verbally in child's primary language

- Every parent in the United States will be a child's first teacher and will devote time each day helping his or her preschool child learn; parents will have access to the training and support they need.
- Children will receive the nutrition and health care needed to arrive at school with healthy minds and bodies, and the number of low-birth-weight babies will be significantly reduced through enhanced prenatal systems.

By 1999, according to the National Education Goals Panel, much progress was seen in achieving this goal: the proportion of infants born with one or more of four health risks had decreased; the percentage of two-year-olds who have been fully immunized against preventable childhood diseases had increased; the percentage of families who read and tell stories to their children on a regular basis had increased; and the gap in preschool participation between three- to five-year-olds from high- and low-income families had decreased.

Discussions about readiness have changed the public's attitude about what it means. Readiness is no longer seen as consisting of a predetermined set of capabilities children must attain before entering preschool or kindergarten. Furthermore, responsibility for children's early learning and development is no longer placed solely on the child or her parents but rather is seen as a shared responsibility among children, parents, families, early childhood professionals, communities, states, and the nation. The NAEYC has adopted the following position statement on school readiness:

> The National Association for the Education of Young Children (NAEYC) believes that those who are committed to promoting universal school readiness must be committed to
>
> 1. addressing the inequities in early life experience so that all children have access to the opportunities which promote school success;
> 2. recognizing and supporting individual differences among children; and

3. establishing reasonable and appropriate expectations of children's capabilities upon school entry.[1]

Maturation and Readiness

Some early childhood professionals and many parents believe that time cures all things, including a lack of readiness. They think that as time passes, a child grows and develops physically and cognitively and, as a result, becomes ready to achieve. This belief is manifested in school admissions policies that advocate children's remaining out of school for a year if they are not ready for school as measured by a school readiness test. Assuming that the passage of time will bring about readiness is similar to the concept of unfolding, popularized by Froebel. Unfolding implies that development is inevitable and certain and that a child's optimum degree of development is determined by heredity and a biological clock. Froebel likened children to plants, and he likened parents and teachers to gardeners whose task is to nurture and care for children so they can mature according to their genetic inheritance and maturational timetable. The concept of unfolding continues to be a powerful force in early childhood education and is based on the belief that maturation is predictable, patterned, and orderly. Inherent in this view of unfolding is the concept of developmental age to distinguish children's developmental growth from chronological age. For example, five-year-old Michael may have a developmental age of four because he demonstrates the behavioral characteristics of a four-year-old rather than a five-year-old. Parents and teachers make their greatest contribution to readiness by providing a climate in which children can grow without interference with their innate timetable and blueprint for development. The popularity of this *maturationist* view has led to a persistent sentiment that children are being hurried to grow up too soon too fast. Some critics of early education say that we should let children be children, allow them to enjoy the only childhood they will ever have, and not push them into schooling and learning. On the other hand, other parents and professionals believe that we have to educate children for the conditions and realities of contemporary society, not some past time. They maintain that the brain and developmental processes keep pace with our rapidly changing culture.

... video viewpoint

Improving Intelligence in Children

ABC NEWS

Scientists have discovered that if certain brain cells are not engaged by certain ages, the cells die off. They have also found some keys to helping children's brains to develop more fully.

REFLECTIVE DISCUSSION QUESTIONS

What are some consequences for society and for children of not providing them with the early stimulation they need to grow their brains? How does the phrase "use it or lose it" apply to children's neurological development? How early in life should parents begin to promote language development in their children?

REFLECTIVE DECISION MAKING

Make a list of things you can do to stimulate early language development. Interview a music educator regarding how exposing children to music stimulates logical thinking. What are some math games you can teach youngsters to promote higher-level thinking skills?

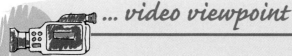

Important Readiness Skills

In all the rhetoric associated with readiness, readiness skills and behaviors are frequently overlooked. These skills and behaviors include language, independence, impulse control, interpersonal skills, experiential background, and physical and mental health.

LANGUAGE. Language is the most important readiness skill. Children need language skills for success in both school and life. Important language skills include receptive language, such as listening to the teacher and following directions; expressive language, demonstrated in the ability to talk fluently and articulately with teacher and peers, the ability to express oneself in the language of the school, and the ability to communicate needs and ideas; and symbolic language, knowing the names of people, places, and things, words for concepts, and adjectives and prepositions.

INDEPENDENCE. Independence means the ability to work alone on a task, take care of oneself, and initiate projects without always being told what to do. Independence also includes mastery of self-help skills, including but not limited to dressing skills, health skills (toileting, hand washing, using a handkerchief, and brushing teeth), and eating skills (using utensils and napkins, serving oneself, and cleaning up).

IMPULSE CONTROL. Controlling impulses includes working cooperatively with others; not hitting others or interfering with their work; developing an attention span that permits involvement in learning activities for a reasonable length of time; and being able to stay seated for a while. Children who are not able to control their impulses are frequently (and erroneously) labeled hyperactive or learning disabled.

INTERPERSONAL SKILLS. Interpersonal skills are those of getting along and working with both peers and adults. Asked why they want their children to attend preschool, parents frequently respond, "To learn how to get along with others." Any preschool program is an experience in group living, and children have the opportunity to interact with others to become successful in a group setting. Interpersonal skills include cooperating with others, learning and using basic manners, and, most important, learning how to learn from and with others.

EXPERIENTIAL BACKGROUND. Experiential background is important to readiness because experiences are the building blocks of knowledge, the raw materials of cognitive development. They provide the context for mental disequilibrium, which enables children to develop higher levels of thinking. Children must go places—the grocery store, library, zoo—and they must be involved in activities—creating things, painting, coloring, experimenting, discovering. Children can build only on the background of information they bring to a new experience. If they have had limited experiences, they have little to work with and cannot develop well. Varied experiences are the context in which children learn words, and the number and kinds of words children know is a major predictor of later school success.

PHYSICAL AND MENTAL HEALTH. Children must have good nutritional and physical habits that will enable them to participate fully in and profit from any program. They must also have positive, nurturing environments and caring professionals to help them develop a self-image for achievement. Today, more attention than ever is paid to children's health and nutrition. Likewise, the curriculum at all levels includes activities for promoting wellness and healthy living.

Dimensions of Readiness

Readiness has many dimensions that contribute to children's abilities to learn and develop. Readiness for life and learning begins at birth and is affected and influenced by many factors. Some things to keep in mind about readiness are these:

Readiness is never ending. It is not something that matters only in preschool, although we often think of it this way. Readiness is a continuum throughout life—the next life event is always just ahead, and the experiences children have today prepare them for the experiences of tomorrow.

All children are always ready for some kind of learning. Children always need experiences that will promote learning and get them ready for the next step. As early childhood educators, we should constantly ask such questions as What does this child know? What can I do to help this child move to the next level of understanding?

Schools and professionals should promote readiness for children, not the other way around. In this regard, schools should get ready for children and offer a curriculum and climate that allows for children's inevitable differences. Such schools are called Ready Schools. Ready Schools do the following:

1. Smooth the transition between home and school.
2. Strive for continuity between early care and education programs and elementary schools.
3. Help children learn and make sense of their complex and exciting world.
4. Are committed to the success of every child.
5. Are committed to the success of every teacher and every adult who interacts with children during the school day.
6. Introduce or expand approaches that have been shown to raise achievement.
7. Are learning organizations that alter practices and programs if they do not benefit children.
8. Serve children in communities.
9. Take responsibilities for results.
10. Have strong leadership.[2]

Public schools that want children to be ready for predetermined programs have their priorities reversed. Schools should provide programs based on the needs of children and families.

Readiness is individualized. Three-, four-, and five-year-old children exhibit a range of abilities. While we have said previously that all children are ready for learning, not all children are ready for learning the same thing at the same time. It is not abnormal for some children to be behind in certain skills and behaviors and others to be ahead. What is abnormal is to expect all children to be the same.

Readiness is a function of culture. Professionals have to be sensitive to the fact that different cultures have different values regarding the purpose of school, the process of schooling, children's roles in the schooling process, and what the family's and culture's roles are in promoting readiness. Professionals must learn about other cultures, talk with parents, and try to find a match between the process and activities of schooling and families' cultures. Providing culturally sensitive, supportive, and responsive education is the responsibility of all early childhood professionals. I discuss what you can do in this regard in more detail in chapter 13.

Play in Preschool Programs

Historically, play has been the heart of preschool programs, and using play is one way of implementing the preschool curriculum. There are many definitions of play and ideas about why children play. Children's play results in learning. Therefore, play is a process through which children learn. In this sense, play is a tool for learning.

Program in Action

The Harvard Emerging Literacy Project (HELP)

The Harvard Emerging Literacy Project (HELP) is an undergraduate organization at Harvard University. The program places volunteers in every Cambridge Head Start preschool and one Cambridge co-op preschool to read with the children once or twice a week for about an hour. Usually, two students go into a classroom together at the same time each week for a semester or, preferably, an entire year.

HELP's goal is not to teach children how to read but rather to promote literacy by showing them that reading books is a fun activity. For this reason, we ask teachers to schedule our visits during free-time periods in the classroom. As a result, the children can *choose* to read with our volunteers, instead of simply being assigned to that activity. Sometimes volunteers end up reading one-on-one with a child and sometimes they read to a small group; sometimes volunteers simply play games with the children. We firmly believe that one of HELP's greatest contributions to the classrooms is simply the additional personal attention and conversation our volunteers offer the students.

Volunteers do undergo training—four hours initially and two additional hours each semester—to learn productive reading strategies. These include techniques that subtly encourage the first baby steps of literacy (e.g., pointing out the author's and illustrator's names, asking for help in page turning, pointing out repetitive words for children to recognize as they are repeated), as well as ways to keep a child's attention.

Throughout the semester, HELP also hosts reflection sessions, where volunteers get together over dinner to discuss their experiences in the classrooms and any obstacles they have encountered (with reading to small children in general, a teacher's policies, or a particular child). Because up to six volunteers visit the same classroom and the demographics of the Cambridge classrooms tend to be similar, the brainstorming potential of these sessions can provide volunteers very specific and very relevant advice.

HELP has its own library of books that we encourage volunteers to bring to the classrooms, in order to give children options beyond the often limited classroom selection of books. HELP also actively seeks out grants and donations to put books directly into the Head Start classroom libraries. In addition, thanks to a grant from First Books, we have started an Incentive Program this year, where children earn books that they can take home and keep. By the end of the year, we hope to distribute six to eight books per child in each of the classrooms.

With a year-long commitment, an approach to literacy that emphasizes fun and freedom, and a steady supply of interesting and age-appropriate books, volunteers witness a tremendous amount of progress in the children. It starts with increased anticipation of volunteers' visits and an eagerness to spend time with them and develops into an earnest desire to participate in the reading process.

Visit the Harvard Emerging Literacy Project (HELP) on the Web at http://www.hcs.harvard.edu/~Lphelp.

Contributed by Amy Levin.

For more information about early childhood play, go to the Companion Website at http://www.prenhall.com/morrison, select any chapter, then choose Topic 5 of the ECE Supersite module.

The notion that children learn through play began with Froebel, who built his system of schooling on the educational value of play. As discussed in chapter 3, Froebel believed that natural unfolding (development) occurs through play. Since his time, most early childhood programs have incorporated play into their curricula or have made play a major part of the day.

Montessori viewed children's active involvement with materials and the prepared environment as the primary means through which they absorb knowledge and learn. John Dewey also advocated and supported active learning and believed that children learn through play activities based on their interests. Dewey thought, too, that children should have opportunities to engage in play associated with everyday activities (e.g., the house center, post office, grocery store, doctor's office). He felt that play helps prepare children for adult occupations. Many curriculum developers and teachers base play activities, such as a dress-up corner, around adult roles.

Piaget believed play promotes cognitive knowledge and is a means by which children construct knowledge of their world. He identified three kinds of knowledge: physical, logical-mathematical, and social. According to Piaget, through active involvement, children learn about things and the physical properties of objects; gain knowledge of the environment and their role(s) in it; and acquire logical-mathematical knowledge—numeration, seriation, classification, time, space, and number. Piaget believed that children learn social knowledge, vocabulary, labels, and proper behavior from others.

Unlike Piaget, Vygotsky viewed the social interaction that occurs through play essential to children's development. He believed that children learn through social interactions with others the language and social skills such as cooperation and collaboration that promote and enhance their cognitive development. Viewed from Vygotsky's perspective, adults' play with children is as important as children's play with their peers. Thus, play promotes cognitive development and provides a way to develop social skills.

Montessori thought of play as children's work and of the home and preschool as "workplaces" where learning occurs through play. This comparison conveys the total absorption, dedication, energy, and focus children demonstrate through their play activities. Children engage in play naturally and enjoy it; they do not select play activities because they intentionally set out to learn. Noah does not choose to put blocks in order from small to large because he wants to learn how to seriate, nor does he build an incline because he wants to learn the concept of "down" or the principles of gravity; however, the learning outcomes of this play are obvious. Children's play is full of opportunities for learning, but there is no guarantee that children will learn all they need to know when they need to know it through play.

Providing opportunities for children to choose among well-planned, varied learning activities enhances the probability that they will learn through play.

Purposes of Play

Children learn many things through play. Play activities are essential for their development across all developmental domains—the physical, social, emotional, cognitive, and linguistic. Play enables children to do the following:

- Learn concepts
- Develop social skills
- Develop physical skills
- Master life situations
- Practice language processes

Puppets and plays provide many opportunities for children to learn and interact with others.

... voice from the field

The Value of Play

Early childhood educators have long recognized the value of play for social, emotional, and physical development. Recently, however, play has attracted greater importance as a medium for literacy development. It is now recognized that literacy develops in meaningful, functional social settings rather than as a set of abstract skills taught in formal pencil-and-paper settings.

Literacy development involves a child's active engagement in cooperation and collaboration with peers; it builds on what the child already knows with the support and guidance of others. Play provides this setting. During observation of children at play, especially in free-choice, cooperative play periods, one can note the functional uses of literacy that children incorporate into their play themes. When the environment is appropriately prepared with literacy materials in play areas, children have been observed to engage in attempted and conceptual reading and writing in collaboration with other youngsters. In similar settings lacking literacy materials, the same literacy activities did not occur.

To demonstrate how play in an appropriate setting can nurture literacy development, consider the following classroom setting in which the teacher has designed a veterinarian's office to go along with a class study on animals focusing in particular on pets.

The dramatic play area is designed with a waiting room, including chairs; a table filled with magazines, books, and pamphlets about pet care; posters about pets; office hour notices; a "No Smoking" sign; and a sign advising visitors to "Check in with the nurse when arriving." On a nurse's desk are patient forms on clipboards, a telephone, an address and telephone

book, appointment cards, and a calendar. The office contains patient folders, prescription pads, white coats, masks, gloves, a toy doctor's kit, and stuffed animals for patients.

Ms. Meyers, the teacher, guides students in using the various materials in the veterinarian's office during free-play time. For example, she reminds the children to read important information they find in the waiting area, to fill out forms about their pets' needs, to ask the nurse for appointment times, or to have the doctor write out appropriate treatments or prescriptions. In addition to giving directions, Ms. Meyers also models behaviors by participating in the play center with the children when first introducing materials.

This play setting provided a literacy-rich environment with books and writing materials; modeled reading and writing by the teacher that children could observe and emulate; provided the opportunity to practice literacy in a real-life situation that had meaning and function; and encouraged children to interact socially by collaborating and performing meaningful reading and writing activities with peers. The following anecdotes relate the type of behavior Ms. Meyers observed in the play area.

Jessica was waiting to see the doctor. She told her stuffed animal dog, Sam, not to worry, that the doctor would not hurt him. She asked Jenny, who was waiting with her stuffed animal cat, Muffin, what the kitten's problem was. The girls agonized over the ailments of their pets. After a while they stopped talking and Jessica picked up the book *Are You My Mother?* and pretended to read to her dog. Jessica showed Sam the pictures as she read.

Preston examined Christopher's teddy bear and wrote a report in the patient's folder. He read his scribble writing out loud and said, "This teddy bear's blood pressure is twenty-nine points. He should take sixty-two pills an hour until he is better and keep warm and go to bed." At the same time he read, he showed Christopher what he had written so he could understand what to do.

When selecting settings to promote literacy in play, choose those that are familiar to children and relate them to themes currently being studied. Suggestions for literacy materials and settings to add to the dramatic play areas include the following:

- A fast-food restaurant, ice cream store, or bakery suggests menus, order pads, a cash register, specials for the day, recipes, and lists of flavors or products.
- A supermarket or local grocery store can include labeled shelves and sections, food containers, pricing labels, cash registers, telephones, shopping receipts, checkbooks, coupons, and promotional flyers.
- A post office to serve for mailing children's letters needs paper, envelopes, address books, pens, pencils, stamps, cash registers, and labeled mailboxes. A mail carrier hat and bag are important for children who deliver the mail and need to identify and read names and addresses.
- A gas station and car repair shop, designed in the block area, might have toy cars and trucks, receipts for sales, road maps for help with directions to different destinations, automotive tools and auto repair manuals for fixing cars and trucks, posters that advertise automobile equipment, and empty cans of different products typically found in service stations.

Contributed by Lesley Mandel Morrow, professor and coordinator of early childhood programs, Rutgers University.

- Develop literacy skills
- Enhance self-esteem
- Prepare for adult life and roles (e.g., learn how to become independent, think, make decisions, cooperate/collaborate with others)

Without the opportunity for play and an environment that supports it, children's learning is limited. Early childhood programs that provide time for play that promotes and supports learning increase and enhance children's opportunities for success in school and life.

Kinds of Play

SOCIAL PLAY. Much of children's play occurs with or in the presence of other children. Social play occurs when children play with each other in groups. Mildred Parten (children's play researcher, now deceased) developed the most comprehensive description and classification of the types of children's social play. They are as follows:

- *Unoccupied play.* The child does not play with anything or anyone; the child merely stands or sits, without doing anything observable.
- *Solitary play.* Although involved in play, the child plays alone, seemingly unaware of other children.
- *Onlooker play.* The child watches and observes the play of other children; the center of interest is other's play.
- *Parallel play.* The child plays alone but in ways similar to and with toys or other materials similar to those of other children.
- *Associative play.* Children interact with each other, perhaps by asking questions or sharing materials, but do not play together.
- *Cooperative play.* Children actively play together, often as a result of organization of the teacher. (This is the least frequently witnessed play in preschools.)[3]

Social play supports many important functions. First, it provides the means for children to interact with others and learn many social skills. Play provides a context in which children learn how to compromise ("OK, I'll be the baby first and you can be the mommy"), learn to be flexible ("We'll do it your way first and then my way"), resolve conflicts, and continue the process of learning who they are. Children learn what skills they have, such as those relating to leadership. Second, social play provides a vehicle for practicing and developing literacy skills. Children have others with whom to practice language and learn from. Third, play helps children learn impulse control; they realize they cannot always do whatever they want. And fourth, in giving a child other children with whom to interact, social play negates isolation and helps children learn how to have the social interactions so vital to successful living.

COGNITIVE PLAY. Froebel, Montessori, and Piaget recognized the cognitive value of play. Froebel through his gifts and occupations and Montessori through her sensory materials saw children's active participation with concrete materials as a direct link to knowledge and development. Piaget's theory influences contemporary thinking about the cognitive basis for play. From a Piagetian perspective, play is literally cognitive development (see chapter 6 and the High/Scope curriculum description). Piaget described four stages of play through which children progress as they develop: functional play, symbolic play, playing games with rules, and constructive play.

Functional Play. Functional play, the only play that occurs during the sensorimotor period, is based on and occurs in response to muscular activities and the need to be active. Functional play is characterized by repetitions, manipulations, and self-imitation. Piaget described functional play (which he also called *practice play* and *exercise play*) this way: "The child sooner or later (often even during the learning period) grasps for the pleasure of grasping, swings [a suspended object] for the sake of swinging, etc. In a word, he repeats his behavior not in any further effort to learn or to investigate, but for the mere joy of mastering it and of showing off to himself his own power of subduing reality."[4]

Functional play allows children to practice and learn physical capabilities while exploring their immediate environments. Very young children are especially fond of repeating movements for the pleasure of it. They engage in sensory impressions for the joy of experiencing the functioning of their bodies. Repetition of language also is common at this level.

Symbolic Play. The second stage is symbolic play, which Piaget also referred to as the "let's pretend" stage of play. During this stage, children freely display their creative and physical abilities and social awareness in a number of ways—for example, by pretending to be something else, such as an animal. Symbolic play also occurs when children pretend that one object is another—that a building block is a car, for example—and may also entail pretending to be another person—a mommy, daddy, or caregiver. As toddlers and preschoolers grow older, their symbolic play becomes more elaborate and involved.

Playing Games with Rules. This third stage of play begins around age seven or eight. During this stage, children learn to play within rules and limits and adjust their behavior accordingly, and they can make and follow social agreements. Games with rules are very common in middle childhood and adulthood.

Constructive Play. Piaget's fourth stage develops from symbolic play and represents children's adaptations to problems and their creative acts. Constructive play is characterized by children engaging in play activities to construct their knowledge of the world. They first manipulate play materials and then use these materials to create and build things (a sand castle, a block building, a grocery store) and experiment with the ways things go together.

INFORMAL OR FREE PLAY. Proponents of learning through spontaneous, informal play activities maintain that learning is best when it occurs in an environment that contains materials and people with whom children can interact. Learning materials may be grouped in centers with similar equipment: a kitchen center, a dress-up center, a block center, a music and art center, a water or sand area, and a free-play center, usually with items such as tricycles, wagons, and wooden slides for promoting large-muscle development.

The atmosphere of this kind of preschool setting tends to approximate a home setting, in which learning is informal, unstructured, and unpressured. Talk and interactions with adults are spontaneous. Play and learning episodes are generally determined by the interests of the children and, to some extent, professionals, based on what they think is best for children. The expected learning outcomes are socialization, emotional development, self-control, and acclimation to a school setting.

Three problems may result from a free-play format. First, some professionals interpret it to mean that children are free to do whatever they wish with whatever materials they want to use. Second, aside from seeing that children have materials to play with, some professionals do not plan for what special play materials to have, how children will interact with the materials, or what children are to learn while playing. Third, sometimes professionals do not hold children accountable for learnings from free play. They rarely question children about concepts or point out the nature of the learning. Such professionals are seldom part of the play process. They act as disinterested bystanders, their primary goal being to see that children do not injure themselves while playing. In a quality program of free play both indoors and outside, professionals are active participants. Sometimes they observe, sometimes they

play with the children, sometimes they help the children, but they never intrude or impose. Avoiding the possible pitfalls of the free-play format enables children to learn many things as they interact with interesting activities, materials, and people in their environment.

SOCIODRAMATIC (PRETEND) PLAY. Dramatic play allows children to participate vicariously in a wide range of activities associated with family living, society, and their and others' cultural heritage. Dramatic play is generally of two kinds: *sociodramatic* and *fantasy*. Sociodramatic play usually involves everyday realistic activities and events, whereas fantasy play typically involves fairytale and superhero play. Dramatic play centers often include areas such as housekeeping, dress-up, occupations, dolls, school, and other situations that follow children's interests. A skillful professional can think of many ways to expand children's interests and then replace old centers with new ones. For example, after a visit to the police station, a housekeeping center might be replaced by an occupations center.

In sociodramatic play, children have an opportunity to express themselves, assume different roles, and interact with their peers. Sociodramatic play centers thus act as a nonsexist and multicultural arena in which all children are equal. Professionals can learn a great deal about children by watching and listening to their dramatic play. For example, one professional heard a child remark to the doll he was feeding that "you better eat all of this 'cause it's all we got in the house." After investigating, the professional linked the family with a social service agency that helped them obtain food and assistance.

Professionals must assume a proactive role in organizing and changing dramatic play areas. They must set the stage for dramatic play and participate with children. They must also encourage those who "hang back" and are reluctant to play and involve those who may not be particularly popular with the other children. Surprisingly, because of their background and environment, some children have to be taught how to play. In other words, as in all areas of early childhood education, professionals must deal with children's dramatic play in an individual and holistic way.

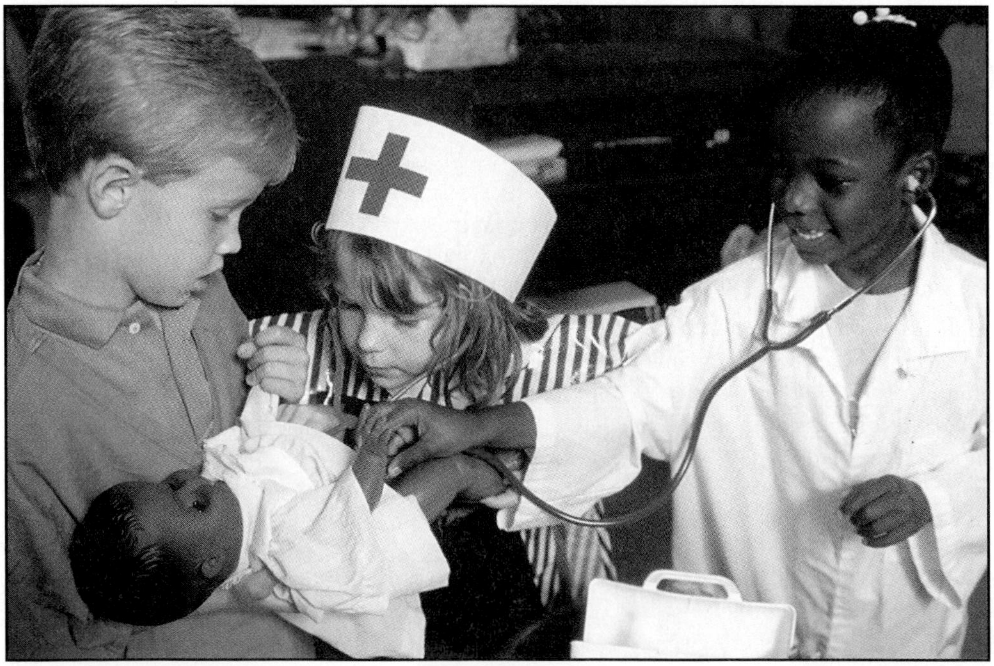

Dramatic play promotes children's understanding of concepts and processes. Here, play allows children to explore their feelings and ideas about medical practitioners and medical settings.

OUTDOOR PLAY. Children's play outside is just as important as that inside. Unfortunately, many consider outdoor play relatively unimportant and needed only as an opportunity for children to let off steam and get rid of excess energy. Children do need to relieve stress and tension through play, and outdoor activities provide this opportunity; however, professionals should plan for what children will do and what equipment will be available. Outdoor play is not a chance for children to run wild.

Outdoor environments and activities promote large- and small-muscle development and body coordination as well as language development, social interaction, and creativity. Professionals should plan for a particular child or group of children to move through progressively higher skill levels of running, climbing, and throwing. The outdoor area is a learning environment, and as such, the playground should be designed according to learning objectives.

Many teachers also enjoy bringing the indoor learning environment outdoors, using easels, play dough, or dramatic play props to further enhance learning opportunities. In addition, taking a group of children outdoors for story or music time, sitting in the shade of a tree, brings a fresh perspective to daily group activities. As with indoor activities, provisions for outdoor play involve planning, supervising, and helping children be responsible for their behavior.

ROUGH-AND-TUMBLE PLAY. All children, to a greater or lesser degree, engage in rough-and-tumble play. One theory of play says that children play because they are biologically programmed to do so; that is, it is part of children's (and adults') genetic heritage to engage in play activities. Indeed, there is a parallel in children's rough-and-tumble play and behaviors in the animal kingdom—for example, run-and-chase activities and "pretend" fighting. Rough-and-tumble play activities enable children to learn how to lead and follow, develop physical skills, interact with other children in different ways, and grow in their abilities to interact with children.

... video viewpoint

Wild About Learning

ABCNEWS

The NAEYC Guidelines for Developmentally Appropriate Practice recommend that young children have ample amounts of time and proper environments in which to play, since children do a great deal of learning when they play.

Reflective Discussion Questions

In what ways does play help a child's social, cognitive, emotional, and physical development? What is the role of structured play (team sport participation, music lessons, scouting, etc.) in relation to free play?

Reflective Decision Making

Visit a preschool, day care center, or grade school and observe a group of children at play. What are they doing? What learning is taking place? How do the activities, the people they interact with, the objects around them, and the immediate environment affect their play? Based on your observations, what could you do as an early childhood professional to promote meaningful learning experiences through play?

Early Childhood Professionals' Roles in Promoting Play

You and your colleagues are the key to promoting meaningful play, which promotes a basis for learning. What you do and the attitudes you have toward play determine the quality of the preschool environment and the events that occur there. You have the following responsibilities for supporting a quality play curriculum:

- Plan to implement the curriculum through play and integrate specific learning activities with play to achieve specific learning outcomes. Play activities should match children's developmental needs and be free of gender and cultural stereotypes. Professionals have to be clear about curriculum concepts and ideas they want children to learn through play.
- Provide time for learning through play. Include it in the schedule as a legitimate activity in its own right.
- Structure time for learning through play. Create both indoor and outdoor environments that encourage play and support its role in learning.
- Organize the classroom or center environment so that cooperative learning is possible and active learning occurs.
- Provide materials and equipment that are appropriate to children's developmental levels and support a nonsexist and multicultural curriculum.
- Educate assistants and parents about how to promote learning through play.
- Supervise play activities and participate in children's play. In these roles, help, show, and model when appropriate and refrain from interfering when appropriate.
- Observe children's play. Teachers can learn how children play and the learning outcomes of play to use in planning classroom activities.
- Question children about their play, discuss what children did during play, and "debrief" children about what they have learned through play.
- Provide for safety in indoor and outdoor play.

Providing a safe and healthy environment is an important part of an early childhood professional's responsibilities and applies to the playground as well as to the inside facilities. Outdoor areas should be safe for children to play in. Usually, states and cities have regulations requiring the playground to be fenced and have a source of drinking water, a minimum number of square feet of play area for each child, and equipment that is in good repair. The NAEYC advocates the following to ensure that children get the most out of playgrounds:

- *Children are carefully supervised.* The play area should be monitored by adults with a knowledge of injury prevention and first aid. Their responsibilities include scanning equipment, gates, and surfaces before children enter to check for stray animals, broken objects, and other hazards. Adults should set reasonable, appropriate rules for what children may do, such as sit down on the slide or wear sneakers to climb on monkey bars.
- *The space arrangement adds to children's safety.* Play areas should be inaccessible to streets, standing water, and other hazards. Equipment should be designed for a range of ages and abilities, and it should be installed with safety in mind. In a carefully constructed environment, children are able to roam between activities without getting into playground traffic jams.

- *Equipment is sturdy and engineered for safety*. The placement, size, height, and complexity of equipment must be tailored to the children who use it. For example, climbing equipment should not be taller than the children who climb.
- *Landing surfaces are resilient*. Playground equipment should never be placed on concrete or asphalt. Choose a material that is impact-absorbing to cover all areas where children may jump or fall.
- *Routine maintenance is scheduled and budgeted*. Parts of equipment that move should be checked and repaired regularly.
- *Appropriate choices are offered*. Children's bodies are at work when they play outdoors, and they are ripe to practice and learn new skills.[5]

The Preschool Curriculum and Goals

For more information about preschool curricula and teaching strategies, go to the Companion Website at http://www.prenhall.com/morrison, select any chapter, then choose Topic 6 of the ECE Supersite module.

How do we determine an appropriate curriculum for three- and four-year-olds? Some say the curriculum should stress academic skills related to reading, writing, and math as well as social skills and getting along with others. Others say the curriculum should be based on what children will learn and do in kindergarten and first grade. Still others say that individual children should determine the curriculum according to what each knows or does not know; thus, one should start with the needs and interests of children. These have always been three conflicting learning outcomes for preschool programs.

Increasingly, however, the responsibility for setting the preschool curriculum is being taken over by state departments of education through standards, statements of what preschoolers should know and be able to do. As attention to the preschool years increases, the public believes goals should state what preschoolers should know and be able to do.

Appropriate Preschool Goals

All programs should have goals to guide activities and on which to base teaching methodologies. Without goals, it is easy to end up teaching just about anything without knowing why. Goals of individual preschools vary, but all programs should have certain essential goals. Simply because programs have goals, however, does not necessarily mean their teaching methods support or achieve those goals. Many preschools suffer this weakness—there is a difference between what they say they do and what they actually do. Most quality preschools, however, plan goals in these areas: social and interpersonal skills, self-help and intrapersonal skills, learning how to learn and developing a love for learning, academics, thinking skills, learning readiness, language and literacy, character education, music and the arts, wellness and healthy living, and independence.

Social and Interpersonal Skills

- Helping children learn how to get along with other children and adults and how to develop good relationships with teachers
- Helping children learn to help others and develop caring attitudes

Self-Help and Intrapersonal Skills

- Modeling for children how to take care of their personal needs, such as dressing (tying, buttoning, zipping) and knowing what clothes to wear
- Eating skills (using utensils, napkins, and a cup or glass; setting a table)

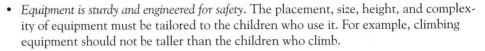

Although we want children to be involved in child-initiated and active learning, sometimes it is necessary to directly teach children certain concepts or skills. What concepts or skills is this teacher directly teaching the children?

- Health skills (how to wash and bathe, how to brush teeth)
- Grooming skills (combing hair, cleaning nails)

Learning to Learn

- Promoting self-help skills to help children develop good self-image and high self-esteem
- Helping children learn about themselves, their family, and their culture
- Developing a sense of self-worth by providing experiences for success and competence
- Teaching persistence, cooperation, self-control, and motivation

Academics

- Teaching children to learn their names, addresses, and phone numbers
- Facilitating children's learning of colors, sizes, shapes, and positions such as under, over, and around
- Facilitating children's learning of numbers and prewriting skills, shape identification, letter recognition, sounds, and rhyming
- Providing for small-muscle development

Thinking Skills

- Providing environments and activities that enable children to develop the skills essential to constructing schemes in a Piagetian sense—classification, seriation, numeration, and knowledge of space and time concepts. These form the basis for logical-mathematical thinking.
- Giving children opportunities to respond to questions and situations that require them to synthesize, analyze, and evaluate

Learning Readiness

- Facilitating readiness skills related to school success, such as following directions, learning to work alone, listening to the teacher, developing an attention span, learning to stay with a task until it is completed, staying in one's seat, and controlling impulses

Language and Literacy

- Providing opportunities for interaction with adults and peers as a means of developing oral language skills
- Helping children increase their vocabularies
- Helping children learn to converse with other children and adults
- Building proficiency in language
- Developing literacy skills related to writing and reading
- Learning the letters of the alphabet
- Being familiar with a wide range of books

Character Education

- Positive mental attitude
- Persistence
- Respect for others
- Cooperation
- Honesty
- Trustworthiness

Music and the Arts

- Using a variety of materials (e.g., crayons, paint, clay, markers) to create original work
- Using different colors, surface textures, and shapes to create form and meaning
- Using art as a form of self-expression
- Participating in music activities
- Singing a variety of simple songs
- Responding to music of various tempos through movement
- Engaging in dramatic play with others

Wellness and Healthy Living

- Providing experiences that enable children to learn the role of good nutritional practices and habits in their overall development
- Providing food preparation experiences
- Introducing children to new foods, a balanced menu, and essential nutrients

Independence

- Helping students become independent by encouraging them to do things for themselves
- Giving children reasonably free access to equipment and materials
- Having children be responsible for passing out, collecting, and organizing materials

The Daily Schedule

What should the preschool day schedule be like? While a daily schedule depends on many things—your philosophy, the needs of children, parents' beliefs, and state and local standards, the following descriptions illustrate what you can do on a typical preschool day.

This preschool schedule is for a whole-day program; many other program arrangements are possible. Some preschools operate half-day, morning-only programs five days a week; others operate both a morning and an afternoon session; others operate only two or three days a week. In still other programs, parents choose how many days they will send their children. Using creativity and meeting parent needs seem to be hallmarks of effective preschool programs. However, an important trend is toward full-day and full-year programs for young children. More preschools are following this trend.

Opening Activities. As children enter, the teacher greets each individually. Daily personal greetings make the child feel important, build a positive attitude toward school, and provide an opportunity to practice language skills. They also give the teacher a chance to check each child's health and emotional status.

Children usually do not arrive all at one time, so the first arrivals need something to do while others are arriving. Offering free selection of activities or letting children self-select from a limited range of quiet activities (such as puzzles, pegboards, or markers to color with) are appropriate. Some teachers further organize this procedure by having children use an "assignment board" to help them make choices, limit the available choices, and practice concepts such as colors and shapes and recognition of their names. Initially, the teacher may stand beside the board when children come and tell each child what the choices are. The teacher may hand children their name tags and help them put them on the board. Later, children can find their own tags and put them up. At the first of the school year, each child's name tag can include her or his picture (use an instant camera) or a symbol or shape the child has selected.

Group Meeting/Planning. After all children arrive, they and the teacher plan together and talk about the day ahead. This is also the time for announcements, sharing, and group songs and for children to think about what they plan to learn during the day.

Learning Centers. After the group time, children are free to go to one of various learning centers, organized and designed to teach concepts. Table 8.2 lists types of learning centers and the concepts each is intended to teach.

Bathroom/Hand Washing. Before any activity in which food is handled, prepared, or eaten, children should wash and dry their hands.

Snacks. After center activities, a snack is usually served. It should be nutritionally sound and something the children can serve (and often prepare) themselves.

Outdoor Activity/Play/Walking. Ideally, outside play should be a time for learning new concepts and skills, not just a time to run around aimlessly. Children can practice climbing, jumping, swinging, throwing, and using body control. Teachers may incorporate walking trips and other events into outdoor play.

Bathroom/Toileting. Bathroom/toileting times offer opportunities to teach health, self-help, and intrapersonal skills. Children should also be allowed to use the bathroom whenever necessary.

Lunch. Lunch should be a relaxing time, and the meal should be served family style, with professionals and children eating together. Children should set their own tables and decorate them with place mats and flowers they can make in the art center or as a special project. Children should be involved in cleaning up after meals and snacks.

Table 8.2
Learning Centers

Center	Concepts	Center	Concepts
• Housekeeping	Classification Language skills Sociodramatic play Functions Processes	• Woodworking	Following directions Functions Planning Whole/part
• Water/sand	Texture Volume Quantity Measure	• Art	Color Size Shape Texture Design Relationship
• Blocks	Size Shape Length Seriation Spatial relations	• Science	Identification of odors Functions Measure Volume Texture Size Relationship
• Books/language	Verbalization Listening Directions How to use books Colors Size Shapes Names	• Manipulatives	Classifications Spatial relationships Shape Color Size Seriation
• Puzzles/perceptual development	Size Shape Color Whole/part Figure/ground Spatial relations		

Relaxation. After lunch, children should have a chance to relax, perhaps to the accompaniment of stories, records, and music. This is an ideal time to teach children breathing exercises and relaxation techniques.

Nap Time. Children who want or need to should have a chance to rest or sleep. Quiet activities should be available for those who do not need to or cannot sleep on a particular day. Under no circumstances should children be forced to sleep or lie on a cot or blanket if they cannot sleep or have outgrown their need for an afternoon nap.

Centers or Special Projects. Following nap time is a good time for center activities or special projects. (Special projects can also be conducted in the morning, and some may be more appropriate then, such as cooking something for snack or lunch.) Special projects might involve cooking, holiday activities, collecting things, work projects, art activities, and field trips.

Group Time. The day can end with a group meeting to review the day's activities. This meeting develops listening and attention skills, promotes oral communication, stresses that learning is important, and helps children evaluate their performance and behavior.

How you structure the day for your children will determine in part how and what they learn. You will want to develop your daily schedule with attention and care.

Selecting a Good Preschool

Parents often wonder how to select a good preschool or other early childhood program. They will ask you for your suggestions and advice. You can use the following guidelines to help parents and others arrive at an appropriate preschool decision. In addition, you can use these guidelines to help ensure that quality is part of the program:

1. What are the physical accommodations like? Is the facility pleasant, light, clean, and airy? Is it a physical setting you would want to spend time in? (If not, children will not want to, either.) Are plenty of materials available for the children to use?
2. Do the children seem happy and involved? or passive? Is television used as a substitute for a good curriculum and quality professionals?
3. What kinds of materials are available for play and learning? Is there variety and an abundance of materials? Are there materials (like puzzles) that help children learn concepts and think?
4. Is there a balance of activity and quiet play and of individual, small-group, and group activities? child-directed and professional-directed activities? indoor and outdoor play?
5. Is the physical setting safe and healthy?
6. Does the school have a written philosophy, objectives, and curriculum? Does the program philosophy agree with the parents' personal philosophy of how children should be reared and educated? Are the philosophy and goals age appropriate for the children being served?
7. Is there an emphasis on early literacy development? Do teachers read to children throughout the day? A general rule of thumb is that teachers should read to children at least twenty minutes a day. Are there books and other materials that support literacy development? Another rule of thumb is that preschool children should be familiar with seventy-five to one hundred books by the time they enter kindergarten.
8. Is there a written curriculum designed to help children learn skills for literacy, math, and science? Does the curriculum provide for skills in self-help; readiness for learning; and cognitive, language, physical, and social-emotional development?
9. Does the staff have written plans? Is there a smooth flow of activities, or do children wait for long periods "getting ready" for another activity? Lack of planning indicates lack of direction. Although a program whose staff does not plan is not necessarily a poor program, planning is one indicator of a good program.
10. What is the adult:child ratio? How much time do teachers spend with children one-to-one or in small groups? Do teachers take time to give children individual attention? Do children have an opportunity to be independent and do things for themselves?
11. How does the staff relate to children? Are the relationships loving and caring?
12. How do staff members handle typical discipline problems, such as disputes between children? Are positive guidance techniques used? Are indirect guidance techniques used (e.g., through room arrangement, scheduling, and appropriate activity planning)? Is there a written discipline philosophy that agrees with the parents' philosophy?
13. Are staff personnel sensitive to the gender and cultural needs and backgrounds of children and families? Are the cultures of all children respected and supported?
14. Are there opportunities for outdoor activities?

15. How is lunchtime handled? Are children allowed to talk while eating? Do staff members eat with the children? Is lunchtime a happy and learning time?
16. Is there a low turnover rate for teachers and staff? Programs that have high and constant turnovers of staff are not providing the continuity of care and education children need.
17. What kind of education or training does the staff have? The staff should have training on how to develop the curriculum and teach young children.
18. Is the director well trained? The director should have at least a bachelor's degree in childhood education or child development (refer to chapter 1, Figure 1.1). Can the director explain the program? Describing a typical day can be helpful. Is she or he actively involved in the program?
19. How does the staff treat adults, including parents? Does the program address the needs of children's families? As I have indicated previously, staff should provide for the needs of families as well as children.
20. Is the program affordable? If a program is too expensive for the family budget, parents may be unhappy in the long run. Parents should inquire about scholarships, reduced fees, fees adjusted to income level, fees paid in monthly installments, and sibling discounts.
21. Are parents of children enrolled in the program satisfied? One of the best ways to learn about a program is to talk to other parents.
22. Do the program's hours and services match parents' needs? Too often, parents have to patch together care and education to cover their work hours.
23. What are the provisions for emergency care and treatment?
24. What procedures are there for taking care of ill children?

Making Successful Transitions

A transition is a passage from one learning setting, grade, program, or experience to another. Young children face many such transitions in their lives. You can help ensure that preschool children make transitions from home to preschool to kindergarten happy and rewarding experiences.

The transition from home to preschool to kindergarten influences positively or negatively children's attitudes toward school and learning. Children with special needs who are making a transition from a special program to a mainstreamed classroom need extra attention and support, as we will discuss in chapter 14.

Parents and preschool professionals can help preschool children make transitions easily and confidently in several ways:

- Educate and prepare children ahead of time for any new situation. For example, children and teachers can visit the kindergarten program the children will attend. Also, as time to enter the kindergarten approaches, children can practice certain routines as they will do them when they enter their new school or grade.
- Alert parents to new and different standards, dress, behavior, and parent–teacher interactions. Preschool professionals, in cooperation with kindergarten teachers,

should share curriculum materials with parents so they can be familiar with what their children will learn.

- Let parents know ahead of time what their children will need in the new program (e.g., lunch box, change of clothing).
- Provide parents of special needs children and bilingual parents with additional help and support during the transition.
- Offer parents and children an opportunity to visit programs. Children will better understand the physical, curricular, and affective climates of the new programs if they visit in advance. Professionals can then incorporate methods into their own program that will help children adjust to new settings.
- Cooperate with the staff of any program the children will attend, to work out a "transitional plan." Continuity between programs is important for social, emotional, and educational reasons. Children should see their new setting as an exciting place where they will be happy and successful.
- Additionally, what happens to children before they come to preschool influences the nature and success of their transitions to kindergarten. Three areas are particularly important in influencing the success of transitional experiences: children's skills and prior school-related experiences; children's home lives; and preschool classroom characteristics. Research demonstrates the following in relation to these three areas:
  - Children who are socially adjusted have better transitions. For example, preschool children whose parents initiate social opportunities for them are better adjusted socially.
  - Rejected children have difficulty with transitions.
  - Children with more preschool experiences have fewer transition adjustments to make.
  - Children whose parents expect them to do well in preschool and kindergarten do better than children whose parents have low expectations for them.
  - Developmentally appropriate classrooms and practices promote easier and smoother transitions for children.
- The nature, extent, creativity, and effectiveness of transitional experiences for children, parents, and staff will be limited only by the commitment of all involved. If professionals are interested in providing good preschools, kindergartens, and primary schools, then we will include transitional experiences in the curricula of all these programs.
- Exchange class visits between preschool and kindergarten programs. Class visits such as these are an excellent way to have preschool children learn about the classrooms they will attend as kindergartners. Having kindergarten children visit the preschool and tell the preschoolers about kindergarten provides for a sense of security and anticipation.
- Work with kindergarten teachers to make booklets about their program. These booklets can include photographs of children, letters from kindergarten children and preschoolers, and pictures of kindergarten activities. These books can be placed in the reading centers where preschool children can read about the programs they will attend.
- Hold a "kindergarten day" for preschoolers in which they attend kindergarten for a day. This program can include such things as riding the bus, having lunch, and participating in kindergarten activities.

Preschool Issues

In addition to the issues we included in our previous discussion, a number of other issues face preschool children, families, and society.

"Pushing" Children

Many preschool programs are academic in nature; the curriculum consists of many activities, concepts, and skills traditionally associated with kindergarten. Critics think this kind of program puts too much pressure on children because they are not developmentally ready. A persistent and long-standing issue in early childhood education, "pushing" children usually revolves around overemphasis on learning basic skills and other skills associated with school success. The issue is complex. First, we need a precise understanding of what it means to "push" children. Some children are able to do more than others at earlier ages; some respond better to certain kinds of learning situations than others. Some parents and children are able to be involved in more activities than are others. So, we must always relate the topic of pushing to individual children and their family contexts.

Research data is emerging about the effects of pushing young children. Researchers at Temple University, for example, found that children of mothers "who pushed them to attain academic success in preschool were less creative, had more anxiety about tests, and, by the end of kindergarten, had failed to maintain their internal academic advantage over their less-pressured peers."[6] Given this kind of data, both parents and early childhood educators must remember to provide opportunities for children to learn and develop at their own rates.

Access to Quality Preschools

Access to preschool is another issue facing children, families, and society. Currently, many children do not have access to preschools because there are not enough public preschools available. Many parents cannot afford to pay the tuition at private preschools. Rather than a comprehensive national program of preschools, children and families are confronted with a patchwork of fragmented public and private services that meet the needs of only some children. Additionally, available good programs are not equitably distributed.

Accordingly, the Carnegie Corporation proposes universal preschools for all three- and four-year-olds to promote their readiness and meet the need for school success. Its report said in part that "academic self-image is shaped between the ages of 3 and 10."[7] As preschools become more available and accessible to young children, they and their families will be included in the schools' programs. Parents are a vital link in creating the learning climate that all children need for life success.

For more information about early intervention, go to the Companion Website at http://www.prenhall.com/morrison, select any chapter, then choose Topic 9 of the ECE Supersite module.

Whom Are Preschools For?

An important question is this: Should all three- and four-year-old children attend public preschools? As you might expect, there is more support for four-year-old attendance than for three-year-olds. Some think that preschool programs should be for all children, not just for those who are at risk for school failure. However, not all agree. Others believe that attendance of all children is too costly. Some school districts, such as Dade County, Florida, provide public preschools for three- and four-year-olds, but they charge parents tuition for their children's attendance. Still others think that inclusion of children with disabilities in public preschool programs places too many demands on other children and early childhood profes-

sionals. However, it is the children who are at risk for school failure and children with disabilities who are most likely to benefit from taxpayer support of public preschools.

Teacher Training and Education

The problem of providing quality early childhood professionals for all preschool children in all programs is an ongoing issue. The growing number of preschools for three- and four-year-olds has created a need for more teachers and teacher assistants. Unfortunately, programs often hire unqualified personnel. In the public's efforts to provide programs for all children, we must continually advocate for quality and high standards. The public has moral, ethical, and legal obligations to support children and provide them with teachers of the highest quality. Part of this issue involves teacher certification: people who work with or teach preschoolers should have specific training and/or certification for that age group. To allow someone with inappropriate education to teach preschoolers does an injustice to the concept of a developmentally appropriate curriculum. Review chapter 1 regarding professional qualifications and qualities.

To take an online self-test on this chapter's contents, go to the Companion Website at http://www.prenhall.com/morrison, select chapter 8, then choose the Self Test module.

The Future of Preschool Education

The further growth of public preschools for three- and four-year-old children is inevitable. This growth, to the point where all children are included, will take decades, but it will happen. Most likely, the public schools will focus more on programs for four-year-old children and then, over time, include three-year-olds. A logical outgrowth of this long-term trend will be for the public schools to provide services for even younger children and their families. One thing is certain: preschool as it was known a decade ago is not the same today, and ten years from now it will again be different. Your challenge is to develop your professional skills so that you may assume a leadership role in the development of quality universal preschool programs.

For additional Internet resources or to complete an online activity for this chapter, go to the Companion Website at http://www.prenhall.com/morrison, select chapter 8, then choose the Linking to Learning or Making Connections module.

Activities for Further Enrichment

Applications

1. Visit preschool programs in your area. Determine their philosophies and find out what goes on in a typical day. Which would you recommend? Why?
2. Tell how you would promote learning through a specific preschool activity. (For example, what learning outcomes would you have for a sand/water area?) What, specifically, would be your role in helping children learn?
3. Develop a detailed daily schedule you would use in your preschool.

Field Experiences

1. Collect examples of preschool curricula and activities from textbook publishers, teachers, and others. Place these in your files for future reference and use.
2. Develop a file of activities you can use in a preschool program. Use the following headings to help organize your file: Activity Name; Objective; Description; Materials Needed. Is it easier to find materials for some areas than for others? Why?

Research

1. Observe children's play, and give examples of how children learn through play and what they learn.
2. Survey preschool parents to learn what they expect from a preschool program. How do parents' expectations compare with the goals of preschool programs you visited?

3. Read and review five articles that relate to today's trend in establishing quality preschool programs. What are the basic issues discussed? Do you agree with these issues?

Readings for Further Enrichment

Beaty, J. *Skills for Preschool Teachers*, 6th ed. Upper Saddle River, NJ: Merrill/Prentice Hall, 2001.

This text presents both theoretical background and ideas for practical applications in working with young children and their families. The content is built around the thirteen functional areas of the Child Development Associate (CDA) credential.

Cromwell, E. *Nurturing Readiness in Early Childhood Education: A Whole-Child Curriculum for Ages 2-5.* Upper Saddle River, NJ: Prentice Hall, 1999.

This is a practical guide to creating a whole-child curriculum organized into three parts: child development, the PLAN curriculum, and the environment. Featuring the author's PLAN model (Play, Learning, the Arts, and Nurturing), this early childhood curriculum system effectively connects and integrates theory, philosophy, and practice and advocates an open, interactive, child-centered environment.

Kostelnik, M., Soderman, A., and Whiren, A. *Developmentally Appropriate Curriculum: Best Practices in Early Childhood Education,* 2nd ed. Upper Saddle River, NJ: Merrill/Prentice Hall, 1999.

This comprehensive book brings together the best information currently available for developing an integrated approach to curriculum and instruction in the early years. The book creates a bridge between the worlds of child care and early education, as well as between preprimary and primary programs.

Soderman, A., Gregory, K., O'Neill, L., and C'Neill, L.T. *Scaffolding Emergent Literacy: A Child-Centered Approach for Preschool Through Grade 5.* Needham Heights, MA: Allyn & Bacon, 1999.

This book offers a sensitive approach to helping children become more strategic in their building of literacy skills and concepts. Underscored by rich child development theory, developmentally appropriate practices, and sound research, the book offers a comprehensive array of literacy activities to support children's emergent-to-fluent literacy.

Taylor, B. *A Child Goes Forth: A Curriculum Guide for Preschool Children,* 9th ed. Upper Saddle River, NJ: Merrill/Prentice Hall, 1998.

This highly successful curriculum planner explores basic developmental characteristics of children ages two to five and shows how these characteristics influence instructional planning, curriculum, and expectations. The text provides a wealth of practical and meaningful tasks, games, and activities students can take with them into their classrooms. Contains excellent coverage of computer use by young children.

Tompkins, G. *Literacy for the Twenty-first Century: A Balanced Approach,* 2nd ed. Upper Saddle River, NJ: Merrill/Prentice Hall, 2001.

Literacy for the Twenty-first Century *offers a readable, field-tested, and practical approach based on four contemporary theories of literacy learning—constructivist, sociolinguistic, interactive, and reader response. The text demonstrates how to implement a literature-based reading program with skills and strategies taught using a whole-part-whole approach.*

Linking to Learning

The Perpetual Preschool

http://www.perpetualpreschool.com

This site was built to celebrate the creativity and dedication of all those who contribute to the perpetual education of young children. It includes ideas for different kinds of plays and other activities.

Preschool Planning Ideas

http://members.xoom.com/Theme_ideas/lesson.htm

This is a site for all preschool/nursery school teachers, to help with curriculum plans, art project ideas, and integration of our themes into our centers.

Preschool Teacher

http://www.bv.net/~stormie

This Web site is dedicated to pre-K teachers. It is not necessarily for an expert in early childhood education, but the goal is to share ideas used in the classrooms, and to provide a place where peers can share theirs.

ENDNOTES

[1] National Association for the Education of Young Children, "NAEYC Position Statement on School Readiness," *Young Children* 46 (1) (November 1990), 21.

[2] "Creating 'Ready Schools,' Tips for School Leaders," *Reading Today,* October/November 1998, 14.

[3] Mildred Parten, "Social Play Among Preschool Children," *Journal of Abnormal and Social Psychology* 27 (1933), 243–269.

[4] Jean Piaget, *Play, Dreams, and Imitations in Childhood* (London: Routledge & Kegan Paul, 1967), 162.

[5] National Association for the Education of Young Children, *Playgrounds: Keeping Outdoor Learning Safe* (Washington, DC: Author, 1996).

[6] *New York Times,* 16 September 1996, A13.

[7] Ibid.

CHAPTER 9

Children are like tiny flowers; they are varied and need care, but each is beautiful alone and glorious when seen in the community of peers.

FRIEDRICH FROEBEL

Kindergarten Education

Learning All You Need to Know

Focus Questions

1. What is the history of kindergarten programs from Froebel to the present?
2. What are appropriate goals, objectives, and curriculum for kindergarten programs?
3. What issues confront kindergarten education today?

To review the chapter focus questions online, go to the Companion Website at http://www.prenhall.com/morrison and select chapter 9.

Perhaps the title of this chapter struck you as a little odd or puzzling. I got the idea from Robert Fulghum's book *All I Really Need to Know I Learned in Kindergarten*. Fulghum says that the following suggestions form the essentials of kindergarten education:[1]

> Share everything.
> Play fair.
> Don't hit people.
> Put things back where you found them.
> Clean up your own mess.
> Don't take things that aren't yours.
> Say you're sorry when you hurt somebody.

Hardly anyone would argue with these learning outcomes. But today, most people expect more of kindergarten programs. Kindergarten is seen as an essential year, perhaps *the* essential year in the schooling experience. And for this reason expectations are high for kindergarten children to learn the social, linguistic, behavioral, and academic knowledge and skills necessary for success in school and life.

The History of Kindergarten Education

To check your understanding of this chapter with the online Study Guide, go to the Companion Website at http://www.prenhall.com/morrison, select chapter 9, then choose the Study Guide module.

Froebel's educational concepts and kindergarten program were imported into the United States in the nineteenth century, virtually intact, by individuals who believed in his ideas and methods. Froebelian influence remained dominant for almost half a century, until John Dewey and his followers challenged it in the early 1900s. While Froebel's ideas still seem perfectly acceptable today, they were not acceptable to those in the mid-nineteenth century who subscribed to the notion of early education. Especially innovative and hard to accept was that learning could be based on play and children's interests—in other words, that it could be child centered. Most European and American schools were subject oriented and emphasized teaching basic skills. In addition, Froebel was the first to advocate a communal education for young children outside the home. Until Froebel, young children were educated in the home, by their mothers. Froebel's ideas for educating children as a group in a special place outside the home were revolutionary.

Margarethe Schurz established the first kindergarten in the United States. After attending lectures on Froebelian principles in Germany, she returned to the United States and in 1856 opened her kindergarten at Watertown, Wisconsin. Schurz's program was conducted in German, as were many of the new kindergarten programs of the time, since Froebel's ideas of education appealed especially to bilingual parents. Schurz influenced Elizabeth Peabody, the sister-in-law of Horace Mann, when, at the home of a mutual friend, Schurz explained the Froebelian system. Peabody was not only fascinated but converted.

Peabody opened her kindergarten in Boston in 1860. She and her sister, Mary Mann, also published *Kindergarten Guide*. Peabody almost immediately realized that she lacked the necessary theoretical grounding to adequately implement Froebel's ideas. She visited kindergartens in Germany, then returned to the United States to popularize Froebel's methods. Peabody is generally credited as kindergarten's main promoter in the United States.

One element that also helped advance the kindergarten movement was the appearance of appropriate materials. In 1860, Milton Bradley, the toy manufacturer, attended a lec-

ture by Peabody, became a convert to the concept of kindergarten, and began to manufacture Froebel's gifts and occupations (refer to chapter 3, especially Figure 3.1). In 1869 Bradley published Froebel's *Paradise of Childhood,* America's first book on the kindergarten.

The first public kindergarten was founded in St. Louis, Missouri, in 1873 by Susan E. Blow, with the cooperation of the St. Louis superintendent of schools, William T. Harris. Elizabeth Peabody had corresponded for several years with Harris, and the combination of her prodding and Blow's enthusiasm and knowledge convinced Harris to open a public kindergarten on an experimental basis. Endorsement of the kindergarten program by a public school system did much to increase its popularity and spread the Froebelian influence within early childhood education. In addition, Harris, who later became the U.S. commissioner of education, encouraged support for Froebel's ideas and methods.

Training for kindergarten teachers has figured prominently in the development of higher education. The Chicago Kindergarten College was founded in 1886 to teach mothers and train kindergarten teachers. In 1930, the Chicago Kindergarten College became the National College of Education. In 1888, Lucy Wheelock opened a kindergarten training program in Boston. Known as the Wheelock School, it became Wheelock College in 1949.

The kindergarten movement in the United States was not without growing pains. Over a period of time, the kindergarten program, at first ahead of its time, became rigid and teacher centered rather than child centered. By the turn of the twentieth century, many kindergarten leaders thought that programs and training should be open to experimentation and innovation rather than rigidly following Froebel's ideas. Susan Blow was the chief defender of the Froebelian approach. In the more moderate camp was Patty Smith Hill, who thought that while the kindergarten should remain faithful to Froebel's ideas, it should nevertheless be open to innovation. She believed that the kindergarten movement, to survive, had to move into the twentieth century, and she was able to convince many of her colleagues. More than anyone else, Hill is responsible for kindergarten as we know it today.

Hill's influence is evident in the format of many present-day preschools and kindergartens. Free, creative play, in which children can use materials as they wish, was Hill's idea and represented a sharp break with Froebelian philosophy. She also introduced large blocks and centers where children could engage in housekeeping, sand and water play, and other activities.

Were Froebel alive today, he would probably not recognize the program he gave his life to developing. Many kindergarten programs are subject centered rather than child centered as Froebel envisioned them. Furthermore, he did not see his program as a "school" but a place where children could develop through play. Although kindergartens are evolving to meet the needs of society and families, we must nonetheless acknowledge the philosophy and ideals on which the first kindergartens were based.

What Are Kindergarten Children Like?

Kindergarten children are like other children in two ways. They have developmental, physical, and behavioral characteristics that are the same and characterize them as kindergartners—children ages five to seven. Yet, at the same time, they have characteristics that make them the unique individuals they are.

Most kindergarten children, especially those who have been to preschool, are very confident, are eager to be involved, and want to and can accept a great deal of responsibility. They like going places and doing things, such as working on projects, experimenting, and working with others. Socially, kindergarten children are at the same time solitary and independent workers and growing in their ability and desire to work cooperatively with others.

For more information about kindergarteners' development, go to the Companion Website at http://www.prenhall.com/morrison, select any chapter, then choose Topic 2 of the ECE Supersite module.

Today, kindergarten is a universal part of schooling, enrolling children from different cultures and socioeconomic backgrounds and, subsequently, different life experiences. How can professionals help ensure that kindergarten experiences meet the unique needs of each child?

Their combination of a "can do" attitude and their cooperation and responsibility make them a delight to teach and work with.

Kindergarten children are energetic. They have a lot of energy, and they want to use it in physical activities such as running, climbing, and jumping. Their desire to be involved in physical activity makes kindergarten an ideal time to involve children in projects of building—for example, making learning centers to resemble a store, post office, or veterinary office.

Kindergarten children are in a period of rapid intellectual and language growth. They have a tremendous capacity to learn words and like the challenge of learning new words. This helps explain kindergarten children's love of big words and their ability to say and use them. This is nowhere more apparent than in their fondness for dinosaurs and words such as *brontosaur.* Kindergarten children like and need to be involved in many language activities.

Additionally, kindergartners like to talk. Their desire to be verbal should be encouraged and supported with many opportunities to engage in various language activities such as singing, telling stories, being involved in drama, and reciting poetry.

From ages five to seven, children's average weight and height approximate each other. For example, at six years, boys, on average, weigh forty-six pounds and are forty-six inches tall, while girls, on average, weigh forty-three pounds and are forty-five inches tall. At age seven, boys weigh around fifty pounds and are about forty-eight inches tall; girls weigh about forty-eight pounds and are about forty-eight inches tall (see Table 9.1).

Who Attends Kindergarten?

Froebel's kindergarten was for children three to seven years of age. In the United States, kindergarten is for five- and six-year-old children before they enter first grade. Since the age at which children enter first grade varies, the ages at which they enter kindergarten also differ. Many parents and professionals support an older rather than a younger kindergarten entrance age because they think older children are more "ready" for kindergarten and will learn better. Whereas in the past children had to be five years of age prior to December 31

Table 9.1
Average Height and Weight for Kindergarten Children

Age	Males		Females	
	Height (inches)	Weight (pounds)	Height (inches)	Weight (pounds)
5 years	43	41	43	39
5 ½ years	45	43	44	41
6 years	46	46	45	43
6 ½ years	47	48	46	45
7 years	48	50	48	48

Source: Based on data from P. V. V. Hamill et al., "Physical Growth: National Center for Health Statistics Percentiles," American Journal of Clinical Nutrition *32(1979), pp. 607–629.*

for kindergarten admission, today the trend is toward an older admission age; many school districts require that children be five years old by September 1 of the school year.

Should Kindergarten Be Compulsory?

There is wide public support for compulsory and tax-supported public kindergarten. On one recent Gallup poll, 80 percent of respondents favored "making kindergarten available for all those who wish it as part of the public school system," 71 percent favored compulsory kindergarten attendance, and 70 percent thought children should start school at ages four or five (29 percent favored age four and 41 percent favored age five).[2] In keeping with this national sentiment, most children attend kindergarten, though it is mandatory in only twelve states (Arkansas, Delaware, Florida, Oklahoma, South Carolina, Ohio, Kentucky, Maryland, New Mexico, Rhode Island, West Virginia, and Tennessee) and the District of Columbia.

Kindergarten has rapidly become universal for the majority of the nation's five-year-olds. Today, kindergarten is either a whole- or half-day program and within the reach of most of the nation's children. As with four-year-olds, the number of children attending kindergarten has risen steadily.

Readiness and Placement of Kindergarten Children

The Escalated Curriculum

After reading this chapter, you may be amazed about how kindergartens are changing. Perhaps you have visited a kindergarten program and left thinking, "Wow, a lot of what they're doing in kindergarten I did in first grade!" Many early childhood professionals would agree. More is expected of kindergarten children today than ever before, and this trend will continue.

A number of reasons account for the "escalated" curriculum. First, beginning in the 1980s there has been a decided emphasis on "academics" in U.S. education, particularly early childhood education, as discussed in chapter 2. Second, some parents believe an academic approach to learning is the best way to succeed in school and the work world. They may also see academics as one of the ways to compensate for the lack of experiences and opportunities prior to their children's entry into school. Third, some first grade teachers are demanding

Children are born to learn. Learning is not something children "get ready for" but is a continuous process. What factors do you think are critical to support children's readiness to learn?

children who are grounded in academics. And fourth, the standards and high-quality education reform movement encourages—indeed, demands—greater emphasis on academics.

These higher expectations for kindergarten children are not necessarily bad. For several decades, in many kindergarten programs, children did not learn the skills needed for success in the primary grades. This is especially true of minority children and children from low socioeconomic backgrounds. What many early childhood professionals are realizing is that we can no longer fail to teach children what they need in order to be ready to learn. How to achieve this goal in a developmentally appropriate way is one of the major challenges of early childhood professionals.

Alternative Kindergarten Programs

It is not surprising, given the changing kindergarten curriculum, that some children may not be ready for many of the demands that will be placed on them. As a result, professionals have developed alternative kinds of kindergarten programs.

DEVELOPMENTAL KINDERGARTENS. The developmental kindergarten is a pre-kindergarten for developmentally or behaviorally delayed kindergarten children. It is seen as a means of helping at-risk children succeed in school. There is a specific procedure and rationale for placing children in such a program. Although the process may differ from program to program, the following are some of the ways placements are made in these developmental programs:

- Test kindergarten-eligible children prior to their entrance to kindergarten to determine which children are at risk (developmentally delayed).
- Give at-risk children an extra year to develop by placing them in a less cognitively oriented kindergarten classroom in which developmental needs can be addressed.

- Promote children to a regular kindergarten classroom the following year.
- As a result of having had an extra year to mature in the developmental kindergarten, a reduction in later school failure will be achieved.[3]

TRANSITION CLASSES. A transition class is designed to give children the time they need to achieve what is required for entry into another grade. Children are really getting two years to achieve what they normally would achieve in one. A transition class is different from a nongraded program in that the transition class consists of children of the same age, whereas the nongraded classroom has multiage children.

The concept and practice of transition classes implies and should involve linear progression. Children are placed in a transition class so that they can continue to progress at their own pace. The curriculum, materials, and teaching practices should be appropriate for each child's developmental age or level.

Proponents of transitional programs believe they offer the following advantages:

- Placement in a transition program promotes success, whereas retention is a regressive practice that promotes failure.
- The program provides for children's developmental abilities.
- Children are with other children of the same developmental age.
- The program provides children with an appropriate learning environment.
- The program puts children's needs ahead of the need to place a child in a particular grade.
- The program provides time for children to integrate learning. This extra time is often referred to as "the gift of time."

On the other hand, opponents of such programs make these points:

- Transition programs are another form of suggesting failure and are really retention in disguise.
- Transition programs are really another form of tracking in which the less ready children are removed from their more able peers.
- Transition programs can reinforce a basic skills orientation to kindergarten.

Some school districts have eliminated or prohibit transitional programs.

MIXED AGE/MULTIAGE GROUPING. Multiage grouping provides another approach to meeting the individual and collective needs of children. In a mixed-age group there is a diversity of abilities, at least a two-year span in children's ages, and the same teacher. The context of multiage groups provides a number of benefits and serves several functions:

- Provides materials and activities for a wider range of children's abilities.
- Creates a feeling of community and belonging. Most mixed-age groups have a feeling of family, and this is supported because children spend at least two years in the mixed-age group.
- Supports children's social development by providing a broader range of children to associate with than they would in a same-age classroom. Children have more and less socially and academically advanced peers to interact with. Also, the mixed-age classroom provides a sustained and close relationship with children and teachers. In the

mixed-age classroom, the teacher encourages and supports cross-age academic and social interactions. Furthermore, older children act as teachers, tutors, and mentors. Younger children are able to model the academic and social skills of their older class members.

- Supports the scaffolding of learning.
- Provides for a continuous progression of learning.

Program in Action

Individualizing and Innovating in Multiage Classrooms

The learning community at Sycamore Elementary School in Claremont, California, believes multiage classes offer particular advantages to its students. Beginning in kindergarten, teachers give students the opportunity to make responsible choices, to have input in designing curriculum, to understand the importance of accountability, and to take advantage of the many different resources that support their learning. Sycamore teachers firmly believe when students in a multiage class are directly involved in the teaching/learning process and are held accountable, they establish high expectations for lifelong learning.

The broad scope of curricular expectations by teachers in a multiage classroom affords all its members the opportunity to better support one another and to build on each other's strengths. Students see a wider spectrum of learning, work cooperatively with peers of different ages, and pursue individual investigations and interests to greater depth. A nongraded setting benefits teachers by allowing them to be more responsive to the developmental needs of their students. The continuity of instructional and interpersonal relations among students, parents, and teachers is increased over the several years they work together. Since teachers encourage students to make many choices many times a day, the students experience firsthand that being responsible and accountable for their decisions is important and respected.

Individualized instruction is much easier to accomplish in a multiage setting. Since children develop readiness for learning at varying rates, their age or grade is not the determining factor—their learning levels are. In a multiage setting very capable younger children often choose to join an older group for instruction. Similarly, older students have the option to work at whatever instructional level is appropriate. Students are often unaware of grade levels because they are working on parallel tasks. Many older students recall when they needed assistance and return the favor by being patient, supportive, and knowing guides for the younger learners. In a manner consistent with their teachers' influence and the role-modeling of older, more mature peers, all students have a frame of reference from which to learn and instruct with confidence and competency.

An important goal when placing incoming kindergarten students is to create classes where a variety of learning styles are represented. This goal has even greater significance in the multiage setting, where students frequently spend several years with one teacher. Interest in the multiple intelligences (see Figure A) prompted Sycamore's primary teachers to make more valid the process they use to place new students in classes. Wanting an open-ended process to identify the different learning styles of their students, teachers devised a Play-Based Observation method. In late August, before the school year starts, teachers create an environment that allows the observation of the social, verbal, emotional, and academic characteristics of the students.

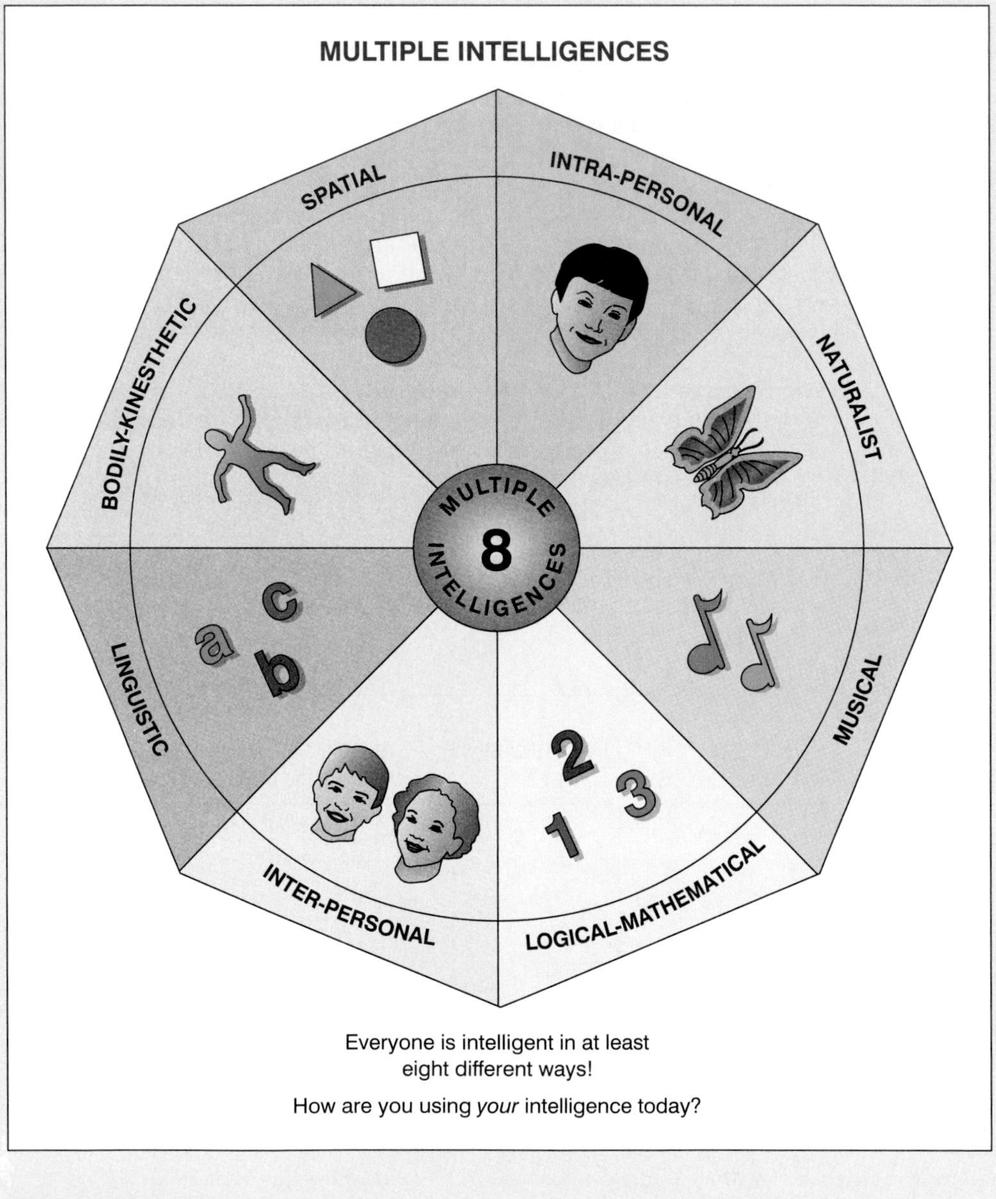

Figure A
A poster-size replica of this chart hangs in every classroom.

Groups of five to seven students attend forty-five-minute sessions, which are observed by all faculty teaching kindergarten that year. After introductions and instructions, teachers invite the students to choose from twelve to fourteen activities. Each activity reflects one or more of the eight intelligences and allows teachers to observe the students' aptitude for math, interest in music, kinesthetic agility, curiosity for reading and writing, best communication style (inter- or intrapersonal), spatial reasoning, and inquisitiveness about the natural world.

Teachers observe and document the activities that each child chooses, noting the frequency of activity change, the extent of peer interactions, and the level of independence displayed (see Figure C on the next page). The teachers talk with students to assess their verbal skills. After the last session, the kindergarten team begins the process of placing children with teachers and other students who will best support their individual learning styles. Notes, observations, and perceptions gleaned from the Play-Based Observation form the basis of these placements.

In a multiage classroom, student voice is more frequently solicited and incorporated into planning learning activities. Sycamore teachers and the principal developed a concept called Family Curricular Planning. During forty-five- to sixty-minute sessions held each semester both during the day and evening, small clusters of students and parents use a Sycamore-designed matrix to develop thematic units in a curriculum area selected by the students (see Figure B).

The matrix enables participants to identify what is to be learned, the resources needed, and how student progress will be assessed. Small cluster groups brainstorm and record a wide variety of curricular ideas. Each group then sorts, prioritizes, and presents their suggestions to classmates. Using the consensus model, students identify those units that they want to study in greater depth. This process demonstrates how meaningful curriculum results from the interaction of concerned, informed parents; engaged, attentive students; and skilled teacher facilitators. By validating student choice and increasing family involvement in classroom learning experiences, Sycamore teachers are able to draw upon many untapped resources that are available in the community. Two years ago Sycamore teachers guesstimated that a fall Family Curriculum Planning Session involving fifteen classes elicited over $8,500 in community-generated resources, materials, and curricular extensions (e.g., study trips to local businesses and museum visits).

SYCAMORE ELEMENTARY SCHOOLS/SYCAMORE COMMUNITY LEARNING CENTER
FAMILY CURRICULUM PLANNING SESSION

CURRICULUM FOCUS ______________________________

LEARNING EXPERIENCES	ADULT SUPPORT & RESOURCES	MATERIALS NEEDED	TIMELINE/ AVAILABILITY	ASSESSMENT/ LEARNING DEMONSTRATIONS

Figure B
Designed by Sycamore teachers Mary Worland and Elaine Haley to assist teachers in charting their observations during a play-based observation session. First used in 1996.

PLAY OBSERVATION: MULTIPLE INTELLIGENCES FOCUS

Child's Name ______________________________

DOB ________________ Today's Date ________________

Observer(s) ______________________________

Time-sample: Five-minute intervals

ACTIVITIES	1	2	3	4	COMMENTS
beanbags					
hula hoops					
marble roll					
puppets					
balance scale					
100-number board					
puzzles					
blocks					
plasticene					
scissors/paper/glue (which?)					
CD player/music					
instruments					
books					
paper/pencil					
listening center					
seashells					
rocks					

CODE:

1 = child's first activity choice
✓ = child's subsequent choices or number in order (five-minute time sample)
✗ = child interacts w/peer
✓ = child interacts w/adult
0 = child-initiated interaction

LANGUAGE USE:

Figure C
Originally designed by Sycamore principal Tom Cooper with input from staff. This chart is enlarged and used by parents and students to guide their curriculum planning sessions.

Sycamore Elementary School first opened its doors over a century ago as a one-room schoolhouse. As the city grew, the school district hired more teachers and built more schools based on standard single-age groupings. Sycamore parents, teachers, and administrators, however, chose to maintain their multiage philosophy. Children learn by doing what is modeled for them by their peers and by taking risks and asking questions of other learners. Their teachers incorporate multiple intelligence strategies in all situations and involve parents and students in the curriculum planning process. Today the Sycamore learning community still believes that multiage classes offer advantages in innovation, individualized instruction, and helping students learn to make choices.

Visit Sycamore Elementary on the Web at http://www.cusd.claremont.edu/~sycamore/

Contributed by teacher Elaine Haley and principal Thomas Cooper. Photos courtesy of Diane Rus and Elaine Haley.

LOOPING. Looping occurs when a teacher spends two or more years with the same group of same-age children. In other words, a teacher involved in looping would begin teaching a group in kindergarten and then teach the same group as first graders and perhaps second graders. Another teacher might do the same with second, third, and fourth graders. Advantages of looping include the following:

- Looping provides freedom to expand the curriculum vertically and horizontally over a two-year period.
- The teacher has the opportunity to monitor a child's progress more closely over a two-year period before seeking child study team input.
- A teacher's familiarity with his or her children contributes to fostering a family-like atmosphere in the classroom.
- Teachers can get into the curriculum earlier in the school year because the children know what is expected of them.
- Looping allows for individualized instruction because teachers are more familiar with the strengths and weaknesses of each child in the class.
- Looping provides children with stability.
- Looping grants teachers an opportunity to stay fresh and grow professionally by changing their grade-level assignments every year.[4]

RETENTION. Along with the benefits of early education and universal kindergarten come political issues as well. One of these is the issue of retention. Retained children, instead of participating in kindergarten graduation ceremonies with their classmates, are destined to spend another year in kindergarten. Many of these children are retained or failed because teachers judge them to be immature, or they fail to measure up to districts' or teachers' standards for promotion to first grade. Children are usually retained in the elementary years because of low academic achievement or low IQ. (In comparison, reasons for retention are different at the junior high level, at which students are generally retained because of behavior problems or excessive absences.)

When well-meaning early childhood education professionals fail children, they do so in the belief that they are doing them and their families a favor. These professionals feel that children who have an opportunity to spend an extra year in the same grade will do better the

second time around. Teachers' hopes, and consequently parents' hopes, are that these failed children will go on to do as well as (many teachers hold out the promise that they will do even better than) their nonretained classmates. But is this true? Do children do better the second time around?

Despite our intuitive feelings that children who are retained will do better, the research evidence is unequivocally to the contrary: children do not do better the second time around. In addition, parents report that retained children have a more pessimistic attitude toward school, with a consequently negative impact on their social-emotional development.[5]

The ultimate issue of retention is how to prevent failure and promote success. To achieve those goals, professionals will have to change their views about what practices are best for children and how to prevent the risk factors that create a climate for unsuccessful school experiences.

What Should Kindergarten Be Like?

All early childhood teachers have to make decisions regarding what curriculum and activities they will provide for their children. When making decisions about what kindergarten should be like, you can consider and compare the ideas and philosophies of the historic figures discussed in chapter 3 with contemporary practice. Consider Froebel, for example:

For more information about kindergarten curricula and teaching strategies, go to the Companion Website at http://www.prenhall.com/morrison, select any chapter, then choose Topic 6 of the ECE Supersite module.

> The Kindergarten is an institution which treats the child according to its nature; compares it with a flower in a garden; recognizes its threefold relation to God, man and nature; supplies the means for the development of its faculties, for the training of the senses, and for the strengthening of its physical powers. It is the institution where a child plays with children.[6]

By comparing Froebel's vision of the kindergarten with today's kindergartens, we see that many of today's kindergartens are much different than what Froebel envisioned. This situation is entirely appropriate in many ways, for society is vastly different today than it was in Froebel's time. What this means is that you have to develop your own vision of what our kindergarten will be like.

Additionally, NAEYC identifies the following ten signs of a good kindergarten:[7]

1. Children are playing and working with materials or other children. They are not aimlessly wandering or forced to sit quietly for long periods of time.
2. Children have access to various activities throughout the day, such as block building, pretend play, picture books, paints and other art materials, and table toys such as LEGOs, pegboards, and puzzles. Children are not all doing the same things at the same time.
3. Teachers work with individual children, small groups, and the whole group at different times during the day. They do not spend time only with the entire group.
4. The classroom is decorated with children's original artwork, their own writing with invented spelling, and dictated stories.
5. Children learn numbers and the alphabet in the context of their everyday experiences. Exploring the natural world of plants and animals, cooking, taking attendance, and serving snacks are all meaningful activities to children.
6. Children work on projects and have long periods of time (at least one hour) to play and explore. Filling out worksheets should not be their primary activity.
7. Children have an opportunity to play outside every day that weather permits. This play is never sacrificed for more instructional time.
8. Teachers read books to children throughout the day, not just at story time.

9. Curriculum is adapted for those who are ahead as well as for those who need additional help. Because children differ in experience and background, they do not learn the same things at the same time in the same way.
10. Children and their parents look forward to school. Parents feel safe sending their child to kindergarten. Children are happy; they are not crying or regularly sick.

Developmentally Appropriate Practice

For more information about Developmentally Appropriate Practice, go to the Companion Website at http://www.prenhall.com/morrison, select any chapter, then choose Topic 4 of the ECE Supersite module.

This book has emphasized that, in all things early childhood professionals do for and with children, their efforts should be *developmentally appropriate*. Developmentally appropriate practice—that is, teaching and caring for young children—facilitates learning that is in accordance with children's physical, cognitive, social, and linguistic development. Understanding professionals will help children learn and develop in ways that are compatible with how old they are and who they are as individuals (e.g., their background of experiences, culture). Those early childhood professionals who embody the qualities of good kindergarten teachers will tend to be those who teach in developmentally appropriate ways.

Talking about developmentally appropriate practice is one thing; putting it into practice is another. Here are some of the implications of such practice for kindergarten programs (indeed, all programs involving young children):

- Learning must be meaningful to children and related to what they already know. Children find things meaningful when they are interesting to them and they can relate to them.
- Children do not learn in the same way, nor are they interested in learning the same thing as everyone else all the time. Thus, teachers must individualize their curriculum as much as possible. Montessori understood this point (see chapter 4), and the High/Scope educational approach provides for it (see chapter 6).

... video viewpoint

Playgrounds

One of NAEYC's guidelines for developmentally appropriate practice is that children have ample opportunities to play safely. Unsupervised playground areas and improperly maintained equipment can put children at risk.

Reflective Discussion Questions

How can you create an environment that is conducive to safe and meaningful outdoor play? What kinds of play ideas and equipment can you provide to create an optimum play environment?

Reflective Decision Making

Visit the Web site of the Consumer Product Safety Commission (http://www.cpsc.gov/cpscpub/pubs/playtips.html) to review its guidelines for safe playgrounds. Then visit a nearby schoolyard or park playground and examine the equipment and the play environment. What did you find out about the safety level of the playground you visited? Share your observations with your classmates.

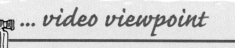

- Learning should be physically and mentally active; that is, children should be actively involved in learning activities by building, making, experimenting, investigating, and working collaboratively with their peers.
- Children should be involved in *hands-on* activities with concrete objects and manipulatives. Emphasis is on real-life activities as opposed to workbook and worksheet activities.

Full- or Half-Day Kindergarten

Both half- and full-day kindergarten programs are available. A school district that operates a half-day program usually offers one session in the morning and one in the afternoon, so that one teacher can teach two classes. Although many kindergartens are half-day programs, there is no general agreement that this system is best. Those who argue for it say that this is all the schooling the five-year-old child is ready to experience and that it provides an ideal transition to the all-day first grade. Those in favor of full-day sessions generally feel that not only is the child ready for and capable of a program of this length but also that such an approach allows for a more comprehensive program. Kindergartens are about evenly divided between whole- and half-day programs across the United States (thus, descriptions of both appear in this chapter).

The general trend is toward full-day kindergarten programs for all five-year-old children. However, essentially two factors stand in the way of a more rapid transition to full-day programs: tradition and money. Kindergartens have been historically and traditionally half-day programs, although there is ample evidence of full-day programs for four- and five-year-old children. As time passes and society's needs begin to point to full-day programs to prepare children for living in an increasingly complex world, more kindergarten programs will become full-day.

Money is the most important obstacle to the growth of full-day kindergarten programs. Without a doubt, it takes twice as many teachers to operate full-day programs as half-day programs. But as society continues to recognize the benefits of early education and as kindergartens and early childhood programs are seen as one means for solving societal problems, more funding will be forthcoming.

Program in Action

Longfellow Elementary School for the Performing Arts

An excellent example of restructuring at work in the early childhood arena is Longfellow Elementary School in Kansas City, Missouri, a magnet school for the visual and performing arts. Yvonne Clay's twenty-two kindergartners engage in an all-day program of basic skill instruction and drama, dance, music, and movement. Visual arts include painting, sketching, modeling with clay, and creative writing; the performing arts entail music, theater, and dance.

Drama plays a significant role in the curriculum and life of the kindergarten classroom. As Yvonne explains, "Drama and the other performing arts give children exposure to and experience with topics and people they would not otherwise have. Drama is in many ways a mirror of real-life events. I use drama to help children learn many important skills, concepts, and values. Drama is also a natural way of helping children learn through their bodies."

Yvonne gives these examples of drama activities in her kindergarten: "One of my groups reads in their basal reader a story of the rabbit and the hare. After the reading, the children acted out the story. We emphasized expression and how the human voice—their voices—sounds in certain situations. Also, during Black History Month in February, the children did a "Readers Theater" of the *Rosa Parks Story*. One group read the story and another group acted out the events. The children had a lot of fun getting ready. They made bus stop signs, made costumes out of clothing from the Salvation Army, and made a bus out of cardboard boxes with chairs for seats. I revised an existing script for the children who had reading parts. It was a great learning activity!"

Yvonne teaches readiness skills, reading (many of the children are reading at a first grade level or above by the end of the school year), math, social studies, science, writing, and creative movement—all integrated with drama. Support teachers provide instruction in art, music, physical education, computers, and Suzuki violin.

"I integrate academics into everything I do," explains Yvonne. "The visual and performing arts give children experiences to build their academics on. The arts also give children a chance to appreciate their self-worth at many levels and in different ways. Take, for example, a child like Alex, who struggles in reading. He really excels in dance. The experiences of being good in this area are a great benefit to him."

A number of important activities support the curriculum and make this kindergarten program unique.

Artist-in-Residence Program

The school district has an artist-in-residence program through which artists come into the school and classrooms to perform and teach. For example, a local, well-known puppeteer gave a performance, then taught the children about puppets. He worked with the children in making puppets and helped them give a performance with their puppets.

Field Trips

The kindergarten children go every other month to various performing arts functions. These include trips to the ballet, symphony orchestra, plays, and other performances throughout the Kansas City area. Following the field trips, children's experiences are integrated into the curriculum. For example, after a trip to the zoo, some children may create an art product and others may choose to write about the experience.

Community support for the Longfellow Magnet School is strong. According to Dee Davis, coordinator for the Kansas City Public Schools, "Families are enthusiastic about schools of choice for their children. They want and like to make choices on behalf of their children. Parents feel children do better in school when they study what interests them most." The curriculum of the kindergarten program, with its focus on song and dance, is in many ways reminiscent of that supported by Froebel and other great educators. It is also significant that a school named for one of the nation's most celebrated poets—Henry Wadsworth Longfellow—should be involved in promoting learning through the arts.

Literacy Education and Kindergarten Children

Literacy education is an important and highly visible topic today. Literacy is discussed in virtually all educational circles, and early childhood educators are talking about how to promote it. If they are not, they should be. Literacy has replaced reading readiness as the main objective of many kindergarten and primary programs. *Literacy* means the ability to read, write, speak, and listen, with emphasis on reading and writing well. To be literate also means reading, writing, speaking, and listening within the context of one's cultural and social setting.

Literacy education is a hot topic in educational circles for a number of reasons. First, the National Adult Literacy Survey estimates that over fifty million Americans are function-

1. Children have opportunities to expand their use and appreciation of oral language.
2. Children have opportunities to expand their use and appreciation of printed language.
3. Children have opportunities to hear good stories and informational books read aloud daily.
4. Children have opportunities to understand and manipulate the building blocks of spoken language.
5. Children have opportunities to learn about and manipulate the building blocks of written language.
6. Children have opportunities to learn the relationship between the sounds of spoken language and the letters of written language.
7. Children have opportunities to learn decoding strategies.
8. Children have opportunities to write and relate their writing to spelling and reading.
9. Children have opportunities to practice accurate and fluent reading in decodable stories.
10. Children have opportunities to read and comprehend a wide assortment of books and other texts.
11. Children have opportunities to develop and comprehend new vocabulary through wide reading and direct vocabulary instruction.
12. Children have opportunities to learn and apply comprehension strategies as they reflect upon and think critically about what they read.

Figure 9.1
Twelve Essential Components of Research-Based Programs for Beginning Reading Instruction

Source: Texas Reading Initiative, Beginning Reading Instruction. *Austin, TX: Texas Education Agency Publications Division.*

ally illiterate—at or below a fifth grade reading level. Furthermore, when we compare the U.S. literacy rate with that of other countries, we do not fare too well—many industrialized countries have higher literacy rates.[8] Consequently, educators and social policy planners are always concerned about the inability of the schools to teach all children to read at more than a functional level. As we have discussed, how to get all children to read is a major national concern. Figure 9.1 outlines twelve essential components of research-based programs designed to promote reading.

Second, businesses and industry are concerned about how unprepared the nation's workforce is to meet the demands of the workplace. Critics of the educational establishment maintain that many high school graduates do not have the basic literacy skills required for today's high-tech jobs. Therefore, schools, especially at the early grades, are feeling the pressure to adopt measures that will give future citizens the skills they will need for productive work and meaningful living.

Third, state governments are in the forefront of making sure that all children learn to read well and that they read on level by third grade. For example, the State of Texas conducted Kindergarten Teacher Reading Academies designed to provide teachers with knowledge and skills that promote early reading success. All kindergarten teachers attended four days of training and were paid $150 a day. These academies focused on research-based approaches to early literacy and reading.

What all of this means is that the goals for kindergarten learning are higher than they have been in the past (see Figure 9.2).

Kindergarten Accomplishments

- Knows the parts of a book and their functions.
- Begins to track print when listening to a familiar text being read or when rereading own writing.
- "Reads" familiar text emergently (i.e., not necessarily verbatim from the print alone).
- Recognizes and can name all uppercase and lowercase letters.
- Understands that the sequence of letters in a written word represents the sequence of sounds (phonemes) in a spoken word (alphabetic principle).
- Learns many, though not all, one-to-one letter–sound correspondences.
- Recognizes some words by sight, including a few very common ones (the, I, my, you, is, are).
- Uses new vocabulary and grammatical constructions in own speech.
- Makes appropriate switches from oral to written language styles.
- Notices when simple sentences fail to make sense.
- Connects information and events in texts to life and life experiences to text.
- Retells, reenacts, or dramatizes stories or parts of stories.
- Listens attentively to books the teacher reads to class.
- Can name some book titles and authors.
- Demonstrates familiarity with a number of types or genres of text (e.g., storybooks, expository texts, poems, newspapers, and everyday print such as signs, notices, labels).
- Correctly answers questions about stories read aloud.
- Makes predictions based on illustrations or portions of stories.
- Demonstrates understanding that spoken words consist of phonemes.
- Given spoken sets like "dan, dan, den," can identify the first two as the same and the third as different.
- Given spoken sets like "dak, pat, zen," can identify the first two as sharing one identical sound.
- Given spoken segments, can merge them into a meaningful target word.
- Given a spoken word, can produce another word that rhymes with it.
- Independently writes many uppercase and lowercase letters.
- Uses phonemic awareness and letter knowledge to spell independently (invented or creative spelling).
- Writes (unconventionally) to express own meaning.
- Builds a repertoire of some conventionally spelled words.
- Shows awareness of distinction between "kid writing" and conventional orthography.
- Writes own name (first and last) and the first names of some friends or classmates.
- Can write most letters and some words when they are dictated.

Figure 9.2
What Should Kindergarten Children Know?

Source: Adapted, with permission, from M. S. Burns, P. Griffin, and C. E. Snow, Starting Out Right: A Guide to Promoting Children's Reading Success. *Copyright 1999 by the National Academy of Sciences. Courtesy of the National Academy Press, Washington, D.C.*

The nation has set a goal of having all children read and write at or above level by grade three. What are some activities and practices you can implement that will help ensure that all children achieve this national goal?

Emergent Literacy and Reading

Today, early childhood professionals place a high priority on children's literacy and reading success. Literacy involves reading, writing, speaking, and listening. Professionals view literacy as a process that begins at birth (perhaps before) and continues to develop across the life span, through the school years and into adulthood. Thus, with the first cry, children are considered to begin language development (see chapter 7 for a discussion of linguistic development). Throughout discussion about literacy, reading, and the ways to promote them, the terms in Figure 9.3 will prove useful to your study of the process.

Emergent literacy involves a range of activities and behaviors related to written language, including those undertaken by very young children who depend on the cooperation of others, and/or on creative play, to deal with the material. It involves reading- and writing-related activities and behaviors that change over time, culminating in conventional literacy during middle school.[9]

Many literacy themes emphasize using environmental and social contexts to support and extend children's reading and writing. Children want to make sense of what they read and write. The meaningful part of reading and writing occurs when children talk to each other, write letters, and read good literature or have it read to them. All of this occurs within a print-rich environment, one in which children see others read, make lists, and use language and the written word to achieve goals. Proponents of whole language maintain that this environment is highly preferable to previous approaches to literacy development.

The process of becoming literate is also viewed as a natural process; reading and writing are processes that children participate in naturally, long before they come to school. No doubt you have participated with or know of toddlers and preschoolers who are literate in many ways. They "read" all kinds of signs (McDonald's) and labels (Campbell's soup) and scribble with and on anything and everything.

Alphabet knowledge: The knowledge that letters have names and shapes and that letters can represent sounds in language

Alphabetic principle: Awareness that each speech sound or phoneme in a language has its own distinctive graphic representation, and an understanding that letters go together in patterns to represent sounds

Comprehension: In reading, the basic understanding of the words and the content or meaning contained within printed material

Orthographic awareness: Familiarity with written symbols and an understanding of the relationships between these symbols and the sounds they represent

Onset-rime: The onset is the part of the syllable that precedes the vowel, while the rime is the remaining part of the syllable

Phoneme: The smallest unit of speech that makes a difference to meaning

Phonemic awareness: The ability to deal explicitly and segmentally with sound units smaller than the syllable

Phonological awareness: The ability to manipulate language at the levels of syllables, rhymes, and individual speech sounds

Print awareness: The recognition of conventions and characteristics of a written language

Figure 9.3
Reading/Literacy Instructional Terminology

The concept of emergent literacy, then, is based on the following beliefs about literacy and about how children learn:

- Reading and writing involve cognitive and social abilities that children employ in the processes of becoming literate and gaining meaning from reading, writing, speaking, and listening.
- Most children begin processes involved in reading and writing long before they come to school; they do not wait until someone teaches them. They should not have to wait to be taught. (Remember what Montessori said about early literacy.)
- Literacy is a social process that develops within a context in which children have the opportunity to interact with and respond to printed language and to other children and adults who are using printed language. In this context, children bring meaning to and derive meaning from reading and writing. Teachers and classrooms should encourage discussing and sharing knowledge and ideas through reading and writing.
- The cultural group in which children become literate influences how literacy develops and the form it takes. Children should also have opportunities to read the literature of many cultural groups in addition to their own.

Emergent reading involves reading-related activities and behaviors, especially those prior to a child's achieving the capacity to read fluently and conventionally. This includes (a) the attentive presence of a child while another writes according to the child's intentions, (b) the execution of acts with materials related to reading (e.g., page turning, letter naming), and (c) the pretense of processing and/or comprehending written language.[10]

The emergent literacy and reading models view reading and written language acquisition as a continuum of development. Think of children as being on a continuous journey toward full literacy development!

... voice from the field

Qualities of a Good Teacher

ANDY BAUMGARTNER, 1999
NATIONAL TEACHER OF THE YEAR

Quality teaching involves establishing a rapport that makes effective communication possible between the teacher and student, teacher and home, and home and student. It requires a teacher to be an effective listener who is willing to learn from his students and their families and to use that newly gained information to upgrade his instructional competence with each student. A good teacher has a personal, well-defined, but flexible yearly instructional plan that agrees with the philosophies of his school and system. He must be able to readily communicate this plan to his students and their parents, other teachers, administrators, and various members of the community.

When working with very young students, as I do, teachers must possess sensitivity, patience, energy, enthusiasm, and creativity. Early childhood educators must be prepared to combat very short attention spans, compete with an entertainment-oriented society, and always keep a sense of humor about themselves and their charges. We must also provide a loving, nurturing classroom environment in which students can feel safe and happy.

I try hard to bring these qualities to my work, and my students, their parents, my peers, and my supervisors often thank or commend me for them!

I have always kept an "open door" policy to any visitor and attempt to maintain a friendly and supportive relationship with parents that encourages them to visit and enables them to seek attention from me about any question or concern.

Believing in lifelong learning, I am constantly involved in classes, staff development, seminars, and workshops, and I pursue new personal experiences, such as ballroom dancing and furniture refinishing. This keeps my teaching fresh, since I never fail to gain some insight about technique or style that I can adapt and use in my classroom with my students. Returning to the position of student also reminds me to attend to the basic needs of *my* own students and their comfort in the classroom.

Because young children are so active and their attention spans are so short, early childhood educators must constantly switch channels and move to new activities. For this reason, I attempt to constantly replenish my "bag of tricks" with a new idea, a new song or poem, a picture that holds meaning or stimulates ideas, a game I've seen, or a book someone has shared with me. I gain the most enjoyment, however, by coming up with new ideas of my own! Sometimes, they may seem a bit off the wall or too big to handle, but nothing tried is nothing gained. Through this experimentation and change, my teaching grows each year. I am often amazed that I sometimes learn more from an activity that does not work out as I planned than I do from one that does. This is one of many important lessons that I try to help my students discover for themselves.

Most important, I believe that teaching has to be both exciting and enticing for students. I want my students to love learning and love school! I attempt to elicit creativity from my young charges by involving them in special activities like the following:

- *Young Author's Teas:* presented in the late fall and attended by parents, board members, other teachers, and visitors from the community. Our guests viewed numerous individual and group works totaling more than two hundred items, enjoyed refreshments, and were greeted with a welcome and introduction by each of the students. Student/Authors then read their works and signed autograph books. Experience in public speaking and the making of menus, invitations, programs, and decorations were all acquired from the teas.

- *Fairy Tales and Nursery Rhymes Productions:* plays complete with sets, costumes, lighting, music, singing, dancing, and memorized dialogue. In 1996, *Sleeping Beauty's Wedding* was presented, complete with attendants from favorite tales and rhymes, and enhanced by a lavish reception on the "castle lawn" with wedding cake, photographers, and rice. In 1997, the King and Queen of Hearts proclaimed a day of celebration throughout their kingdom for the *Knighting of Sir Jack.* Both of these shows also included slide presentations of student photographs, drawings, and subtitles (read to the audience with great gusto by members of the cast) that told the students' version of the stories of these famous characters. These successful events were popular with both the participants and the audiences and attracted many guests from the community.

- *Star Week and Celebrate the States Week:* schoolwide curriculum weeks that engaged students and faculty in whole school activities, as well as individual classroom instruction related to a central theme. Events included "kickoff programs" presented by the Augusta Opera and the Merry Players, units of study related to the topics, whole school writing projects, closed-circuit TV programs, Starlab and Earthdome tours, telescopes on the lawn, daily contests and quizzes, musical and literary presentations, and fun-filled, educational "curriculum nights" for students, parents, and guests from the community.

The rewards in teaching, for me, have always been in looking back over a year and identifying the successes of individual students, receiving appreciation from parents, or being recognized and thanked by students years after they have left my classroom. The biggest "kick" in teaching, however, comes when I look into the face of a young child and watch confusion turn to concentration, concentration to surprise, and, finally, surprise into the pride of accomplishment!

Developing Literacy and Reading in Young Children

Literacy and reading are certainly worthy national and educational goals, not only for young children but for everyone. However, how best to promote literacy has always been a controversial topic.

What do children need to know to become good and skillful readers? Research identifies the following:[11]

- Knowledge of letter names.
- Speed at which children can name individual letters.
- Phonemic awareness (letter sound awareness).

Basal approaches and materials used for literacy and reading development often emphasize a particular method. One of the most popular methods is the *sight word* approach (also called *whole-word* or *look-say*) in which children are presented with whole words (cat, bat, sat) and develop a "sight vocabulary" that enables them to begin reading and writing. Many early childhood professionals label objects in their classrooms (door, bookcase, etc.) as a means of teaching a sight vocabulary. Word walls are very popular in kindergarten and primary classrooms.

A second popular basal approach is based on *phonics* instruction, which stresses teaching letter–sound correspondence. By learning these connections, children are able to combine sounds into words (C-A-T). The proponents of phonics instruction argue that letter–sound correspondences enable children to make automatic connections between words and sounds and, as a result, they are able to sound out words and read them on their own. From the 1950s up until the present time (see chapter 3) there has been much debate about which of these two approaches to literacy development is best. Today, there is a

decided reemphasis on the use of phonics instruction. One reason for this emphasis is that the research evidence suggests that phonics instruction enables children to become proficient readers.[12]

Another method of literacy and reading development, the Language Experience Approach, follows the philosophy and suggestions inherent in progressive education philosophy (see chapter 3). This approach is child centered and maintains that literacy education should be meaningful to children and should grow out of experiences that are interesting to them. Children's own experience is a key element in such child-centered approaches. Many teachers transcribe children's dictated "experience" stories and use them as a basis for writing and for reading instruction.

Beginning about 1980, early childhood practitioners in the United States were influenced by literacy education approaches used in Australia and New Zealand as well as by approaches from Great Britain that were popular during the open education movement of the 1960s. These influences gradually developed into what is known as the *whole language* approach to literacy development. Since whole language is a philosophy rather than a method, its definition often depends on who is using the term. This approach nonetheless advocates using all aspects of language—reading, writing, listening, and speaking—as the basis for developing literacy. Children learn about reading and writing by speaking and listening; they learn to read by writing, and they learn to write by reading. Basic philosophical premises of whole language are the following:

- It is *child centered*—children, rather than teachers, are at the center of instruction and learning. Thus, children's experiences and interests serve as the context for topics and as a basis for their intrinsic motivation to read, write, and converse. In this way, literacy learning becomes meaningful and functional for children.
- Social interaction is important and part of the process of becoming literate. Lev Vygotsky (see chapter 3) stressed the social dimensions of learning. He proposed that through interaction with others, especially with more confident peers and through interactions and conversations with teachers, children are able to develop higher cognitive learning. This process of learning through social interaction is referred to as *socially constructed knowledge*.
- Spending time on the processes of reading and writing is more important than spending time on learning skills for getting ready to read. Consequently, from the moment they enter the learning setting, children are involved in literacy activities—that is, being read to; "reading" books, pamphlets, magazines, etc.; scribbling; "writing" notes; and so forth.
- Reading, writing, speaking, and listening are taught as an integrated whole, rather than in isolation.
- Writing begins early. This means that children are writing from the time they enter the program.
- Children's written documents are used as reading materials.
- Themes or units of study are used as a means of promoting interests and content. Generally, themes are selected cooperatively by children and teachers and are used as a means of promoting ongoing intrinsic interest in literary processes.

Whole language dominated early childhood practice from about 1990 through 1995. However, growing numbers of critics of this approach, including parents and the public, maintain that because it is a philosophy rather than a specific approach, it does not teach

children skills necessary for good reading. Additionally, some teachers have difficulty explaining the whole language approach to parents, and some find it difficult to implement as well. Further, some research has indicated that whole language approaches do not result in the high levels of reading achievement claimed by its supporters. As a result, proponents of phonics instruction are aggressively advocating a return to this approach as one which will best meet the needs of parents, children, and society.

A Balanced Approach

As with most things, a balanced approach is probably the best, and many early childhood advocates are encouraging literacy approaches that provide a balance between whole language methods and phonics instruction and that meet the specific needs of individual children. One thing is clear: systematic instruction that enables children to acquire skills they need to learn to read is very much in evidence in today's early childhood classrooms. It is likely that the debate over "the best approach" will continue. At the same time, there will be increased efforts to integrate the best of all approaches into a unified whole to make literacy education a reality for all children.

Supporting Children's Learning to Read

A primary goal of kindergarten education is for children to learn how to read. Teachers must instruct, support, and guide children in helping them learn what is necessary for them to be successful in school and life. Figure 9.4 lists some of the things you can do to motivate children's learning. Also, stop for a minute and reflect on what we said in chapter 3 about Vygotsky's theory of scaffolding children's learning. Figure 9.5 will help you learn how to scaffold children's literacy development.

Kindergarten Children and Transitions

A transition is a passage from one learning setting, grade, program, or experience to another. Young children face many such transitions in their lives. They are left with baby-sitters and enter child care programs, preschools, kindergarten, and first grade. Depending on how adults help children make these transitions, they can be either unsettling and traumatic or happy and rewarding experiences.

The transition from home to preschool to kindergarten influences positively or negatively children's attitudes toward school. Under no circumstances should the transition from preschool to kindergarten or from kindergarten to first grade be viewed as the beginning of "real learning." Leaving kindergarten to enter first grade is a major transition. The transition may not be too difficult for children whose kindergarten classroom is housed in the same building as the primary grades. For others whose kindergarten is separate from the primary program or who have not attended kindergarten, the experience can be unsettling. Children with special needs who are making a transition from a special program to a mainstreamed classroom need extra attention and support, as we will discuss in chapter 15.

Parents and kindergarten professionals can help children make transitions easily and confidently in several ways:

- Educate and prepare children ahead of time for any new situation. For example, children and teachers can visit the kindergarten or first grade program the children will attend. Also, toward the end of the preschool or kindergarten year, or as the time to

- Include a variety of different types of books, such as picture books without words, fairy tales, nursery rhymes, picture storybooks, realistic literature, decodable and predictable books, information books, chapter books, biographies, big books, poetry, and joke and riddle books.
- Provide other types of print such as newspapers, magazines, and brochures.
- Introduce and discuss several books each week (may be theme-related, same authors, illustrators, types of books, etc.).
- Have multiple copies of popular books.
- Include books in children's home languages.
- Have an easy-to-use system for checking out books.
- Provide a record-keeping system for keeping track of books read (may include a picture-coding system to rate or evaluate the book).
- Showcase many books by placing them so the covers are visible, especially those that are new, shared in read-aloud sessions, or theme-related.
- Organize books on shelves by category or type (may color code).
- Provide comfortable, inviting places to read (pillows, rugs, a sofa, large cardboard boxes, etc.).
- Encourage children to read to "friends" (include stuffed animals and dolls for "pretend" reading).
- Have an Author's Table with a variety of writing supplies to encourage children to write about books.
- Have a Listening Table for recorded stories and tapes.

Figure 9.4
Suggestions for Motivating Children to Read

Source: Adapted from L. M. Morrow, Literacy Development in the Early Years: Helping Children Read and Write, *3rd ed. Needham Heights, MA: Allyn & Bacon, 1997.*

enter the kindergarten or first grade approaches, children can practice certain routines as they will do them when they enter their new school or grade.

- Alert parents to new and different standards of dress, behavior, and parent–teacher interactions. Preschool professionals, in cooperation with kindergarten teachers, should share curriculum materials with parents so they can be familiar with what their children will learn. Kindergarten professionals can do the same with first grade teachers.
- Let parents know ahead of time what their children will need in the new program (e.g., lunch box, change of clothing).
- Provide bilingual parents and parents of special needs children with additional help and support during the transition.
- Offer parents and children an opportunity to visit programs. Children will better understand the physical, curricular, and affective climates of the new programs if they visit in advance. Professionals can then incorporate methods into their own program that will help children adjust to new settings.
- Cooperate with the staff of any program the children will attend to work out a "transitional plan." Continuity between programs is important for social, emotional, and educational reasons. Children should see their new settings as an exciting place where they will be happy and successful.

Scaffolding Script

Child	Teacher
	Can you tell us a story about your photo?
Ummmm. . . . . .[Child has difficulty beginning]	
	[Wait 5–10 seconds] Can you tell us what was happening here?
[No response]	
	[Wait 10 seconds] Who is that in the picture? (uses questions and prompts)
This is me . . . and my Mom . . . and my grandma.	
	Where were you when this was taken? (uses questions and prompts)
Outside, behind my house.	
	Yes, I see that you were outside . . . on the patio, and it was a beautiful sunny day. (recasts and expands) What were you all doing?
It was my grandma's birthday. We made her a big cake.	
	That was very thoughtful of you. It looks delicious! What kind of cake was it? (provides feedback, uses questions and prompts)
Chocolate. With little flowers and it said her name.	
	Chocolate? Yum. That's my favorite flavor! So you decorated the cake with flowers and wrote a name on it. Whose name did you write? (recasts and expands)
Rose. It said "Happy Birthday Rose."	
	Rose? Who is Rose? (requests clarification)
My grandmother . . . [hesitates to tell more]	
	You said before that you baked your grandmother's birthday cake. Can you tell us how you did that? (uses questions and prompts)
Yes. I made it with my Mom. We went to the store and got all the stuff to put in it and I helped.	
	Well, I know you're a great helper. I'll bet you mixed the ingredients together. Am I right? (recasts and expands, adding)
Yes. And it fell on the floor and made a big mess!	
	Hmmm. I'm not sure I understand. Can you tell us exactly what happened? (requests clarification)
Ummm . . . well . . . I was mixing the 'gredients and Spot . . . Spot's my dog, he came by and scared me and I jumped . . . and . . . and the flour fell down and got all over the floor and . . . and it got on Spot's nose and my mom laughed.	
	What a great story! I like how you told us that Spot is your dog . . . that helped us understand a lot better (provides feedback). Boys and girls, would any of you like to ask [name] a question about her photo? (promotes questions and conversation among children)

Figure 9.5
Scaffolding Children's Learning

Source: Adapted from Texas Education Agency, Kindergarten Teacher Reading Academies, *1999.*

Additionally, what happens to children *before* they come to kindergarten influences the nature and success of their transitions. Three areas are particularly important in influencing the success of transitional experiences: children's skills and prior school-related experiences; children's home lives; and preschool and kindergarten classroom characteristics. Research demonstrates the following in relation to these three areas:[13]

- Children who are socially adjusted have better transitions. For example, kindergarten children whose parents initiate social opportunities for them are better adjusted socially.
- Rejected children have difficulty with transitions.
- Children with more preschool experiences have fewer transition adjustments to make.
- Children whose parents expect them to do well in kindergarten do better than children whose parents have low expectations for them.
- Developmentally appropriate classrooms and practices promote easier and smoother transitions for children.

The nature, extent, creativity, and effectiveness of transitional experiences for children, parents, and staff will be limited only by the commitment of all involved. If we are interested in providing good preschools, kindergartens, and primary schools, then we will include transitional experiences in the curricula of all these programs.

Issues Related to Kindergarten

In addition to literacy and curriculum issues, a number of other issues swirl around kindergarten practices and challenge professionals to make the kindergarten experience a meaningful one for all children. For several reasons, there is a growing tendency for upwardly mobile parents to hold their children (especially sons) out of kindergarten for a year. First, when boys, who tend to be less mature than girls, have a birthday that makes them one of the youngest children in the class, they may not do as well as their parents expect. These parents want their children to be the oldest members of the kindergarten class, not the youngest. They reason that the older children will be the class leaders, will get more attention from the teacher, and have another year of school under their belt and therefore will be able to better handle the pushed-down curriculum. In other words, these children will be at the top of their class in all respects.

Second, parents who keep their children out of kindergarten for a year can afford to do this. Less well-to-do parents, on the other hand, want their children in school because they cannot afford day care or baby-sitters.

To take an online self-test on this chapter's contents, go to the Companion Website at http://www.prenhall.com/morrison, select chapter 9, then choose the Self Test module.

The Future of Kindergarten

From our discussions in this chapter, you may have several ideas about how kindergarten programs will evolve in the twenty-first century. Add your ideas to the ones cited here:

- The trend in kindergarten education is toward full-day, cognitive-based programs. Kindergartens give public schools an opportunity to provide children with the help they need for later success in school and life. Children come to kindergarten programs knowing more than their counterparts of twenty years ago. Children with different

abilities and a society with different needs require that kindergarten programs change accordingly.

- Kindergarten curricula will include more writing and reading. This literacy emphasis is appropriate and flows naturally out of the realization that success in readiness plays a major role in school success. The challenge for all professionals is to keep literacy development from becoming a rigid, basic skills approach.
- Technology (see chapter 13) will be included more in both preschool and kindergarten programs. This technology inclusion is in keeping with the current growth of technology in all grade levels. However, as with many things, we think that earlier is better, so introducing technology early is seen as one way of making children in the United States computer literate. The Program in Action in chapter 13, describing the kindergarten instructional program at the Alexander D. Henderson University School, illustrates and emphasizes the following points: (1) technology as an instructional model exists in growing numbers of early childhood programs, (2) technology is no longer something that can be feared or ignored by early childhood professionals, and (3) children are and can be very comfortable with, and adept at, technological applications to their lives and learning.

For additional Internet resources or to complete an online activity for this chapter, go to the Companion Website at http://www.prenhall.com/morrison, select chapter 9, then choose the Linking to Learning or Making Connections module.

Activities for Further Enrichment

Applications

1. Do you think as a teacher you are oriented toward cognitive skills or social-emotional play? Explain your reasons, and compare your response with those of your classmates.
2. As a teacher, would you support an earlier or later entrance age to kindergarten? If your local legislator wanted specific reasons, what would you tell him or her? Ask other teachers and compare their viewpoints.
3. Compare the curriculum of a for-profit kindergarten, a parochial school kindergarten, and a public school kindergarten. What are the similarities and differences? Which would you send your child to? Why?
4. You have been asked to speak to a parent group about the pros and cons of contemporary approaches to literacy development in kindergarten. What major topics would you include?

Field Experiences

1. Give examples from your observations of kindergarten programs to support one of these opinions: (1) Society is pushing kindergarten children. (2) Many kindergartens are not teaching children enough.
2. Develop a list of suggestions for how parents can promote literacy in the home.

Research

1. Interview parents to determine what they think children should learn in kindergarten. How do their ideas compare with the ideas in this chapter? With your ideas?
2. State the pros and cons for why you think kindergarten should be mandatory for all five-year-old children. At what age should it be mandatory?

Readings for Further Enrichment

Cunningham, P. *Teachers in Action: The K-5 Chapters from Reading and Writing in Elementary Schools.* Reading, MA: Addison Wesley Longman, 2000.

Using an imaginary school, the authors follow a class of children from kindergarten through fifth grade to show how different teachers use a variety of approaches to make literacy a reality for all students.

Fields, M. *Let's Begin Reading Right: A Developmental Approach to Emergent Literacy*, 4th ed. Upper Saddle River, NJ: Merrill/Prentice Hall, 1999.

This text is written from a constructivist viewpoint, employing a balanced approach to teaching early literacy learning. Combines

developmentally appropriate early childhood practice with the current views of emergent and holistic literacy.

O'Donnell, M. *Becoming a Reader: A Developmental Approach to Reading Instruction*, 2nd ed. Needham Heights, MA: Allyn & Bacon, 1999.

This text provides a developmental perspective of learning as a way to understand the literacy process. Describes how children become skilled through five stages: emergent reading, initial reading, transitional, basic literacy, and refinement.

Small, L. *Fundamentals of Phonetics: A Practical Guide for Students.* Needham Heights, MA: Allyn & Bacon, 1999.

Emphasizes issues tied to linguistic phonetics (with an introduction to clinical phonetics) and issues involving dialectal variations of speech, a topic missing or dated in most texts. With free audio CD.

Linking to Learning

Connect for Kids

http://www.connectforkids.org/

Provides virtual information for adults who want to make their communities better places for kids; links to pertinent books, Web sites, and resources related to early child care.

Development Tracker—Kindergarten

http://www.familyplay.com/toolkit/tracker/kindergarten

A toolkit from the Crayola Corporation to help gauge a child's progress through kindergarten.

Early Childhood Education Online

http://www.ume.maine.edu/~cofed/eceol/welcome.shtml

The community offers support and opportunities for information exchange to all educators: families, teachers, caregivers, and others interested in providing quality care and learning situations for young children.

Early (or Late) Kindergarten—Hoagies' Gifted Education Page

http://hoagiesgifted.org/kinder.htm

A series of articles detailing the specifics concerning the assessment and placement of gifted children in their earliest years.

Experts: Kindergarten

http://www.parentsplace.com/expert/elementary/kindergarten

A forum of experts who explain about types of schools and programs, discipline, social and cognitive development, and behavior.

Family Education Network

http://familyeducation.com/topic/front/0,1156,27-2247,00.html

Tips, activities, and expert advice you need to keep your kindergartner on the path to academic success.

Inside Kindergarten

http://www.geocities.com/Athens/Aegean/2221

The personal homepage of kindergarten teacher Addie Gaines of the nationally renowned Seneca Elementary, MO.

KIDS Inc.

http://www.kidsinc.com

KIDS, Inc. is committed to quality products and resources for early childhood educators and parents of preschool and kindergarten-age children.

Kindergarten Connection

http://www.kconnect.com

The Kindergarten Connection is dedicated to providing valuable resources to primary teachers. Each week they offer new hints, tips, and information.

National Kindergarten Alliance

http://www.kconnect.com/nka.html

The National Kindergarten Alliance is the result of a summit of leaders from various kindergarten associations, organizations, and interest groups from across the nation that met in January 2000. It is a national organization that serves kindergarten teachers throughout the United States.

Parent Education Resources

http://www.parent-education.com

An online handbook to surviving the kindergarten years, for both children and parents. It includes a forum of links, workshops, and a question-and-answer feature.

What Counts as Quality in Kindergartens?

http://www.ero/govt.nz/Publications/eers1997/97no1hl.htm

A government evaluation of the structure of kindergarten maintenance and administration.

ENDNOTES

1 From Robert L. Fulghum, *All I Really Need to Know I Learned in Kindergarten* (New York: Villard, 1988), 6. Copyright © 1986, 1988, by Robert L. Fulghum. Reprinted by permission of Villard Books, a division of Random House, Inc.

2 Alec M. Gallup, "The 18th Annual Gallup Poll of the Public's Attitudes toward Public Schools," *Phi Delta Kappan* 68 (1), 55–56.

[3] Jeffrey Burkart, "Developmental Kindergarten—In the Child's Best Interest?" *National Association of Early Childhood Teacher Educators* 10 (1989), 9–10.

[4] Marilyn Bellis, "Look Before You Loop," *Young Children* (May 1999), 72.

[5] P. Mantzicopoulos and D. Morrison, "Kindergarten Retention: Academics and Behavioral Outcomes through the End of Second Grade," *American Educational Research Journal* 29 (1), 182–198.

[6] Friedrich Froebel, *Mother's Songs, Games and Stories* (New York: Arno, 1976), 136.

[7] Copyright © 1996 by the National Association for the Education of Young Children, *Early Years are Learning Years Series,* "Top Ten Signs of a Good Kindergarten Classroom," on NAEYC Web site at http://www.naeyc.org/resources/eyly/1996/12.htm.

[8] Literacy Volunteers of America, *Facts on Literacy* (Syracuse, NY: Author, 1994).

[9] National Research Council, *Starting Out Right: A Guide to Promoting Children's Reading Success* (Washington, DC: National Academy Press, 1999) 148.

[10] Ibid.

[11] Marilyn Jager Adams, *Beginning to Read: Thinking and Learning about Print* (Urbana, IL: The Reading Research and Education Center, 1990), 36–38.

[12] Ibid., 8.

[13] K. L. Maxwell and S. K. Elder, "Children's Transition to Kindergarten," *Young Children* 49 (6), 56–63.

CHAPTER 10

We place a strong emphasis on raising academic standards, early childhood learning opportunities, reading, smaller classes, up-to-date classrooms, more after-school and summer school programs, and proven prevention efforts to keep our schools safe.

RICHARD RILEY, U.S. SECRETARY OF EDUCATION

The Primary Grades

Preparation for Lifelong Success

Focus Questions

1. What are the physical, cognitive, language, psychosocial, and moral developmental characteristics of primary children?
2. How are the primary grades being restructured?
3. How is the curriculum of the primary grades changing?
4. What are contemporary issues involved in primary education?

To review the chapter focus questions online, go to the Companion Website at http://www.prenhall.com/morrison and select chapter 10.

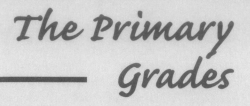

In contrast to the renewed interest in infants and preschoolers discussed in the previous chapters, one might almost say that the years from six to eight are the forgotten years of early childhood. In many ways, primary children are frequently overlooked in terms of early childhood education. Although the profession defines *early childhood* as the period from birth to age eight, children from birth through kindergarten receive most of the attention; primary grade children are more often thought of as belonging to the elementary years. Indeed, the years from six to twelve are often referred to as the middle years or middle childhood, the years between early childhood and adolescence.

Accordingly, one of the major challenges facing the early childhood profession is to reclaim the years from age six through eight. Early childhood professionals cannot focus research and training almost exclusively on the years up to age five as we presently do. Lives are shaped in the primary years as well as in the early years.

Having said this, we will see throughout this chapter that the primary curriculum is changing. Some of these changes include more and higher standards; high-stakes testing and more emphasis on reading, mathematics, and science; character education; and wellness and healthy living.

What Are Primary Children Like?

Throughout this text, we stress the uniqueness and individuality of children who also share common characteristics. The common characteristics of children guide our practice of teaching them. However, we must always account for the individual needs of children. All children are unique in many ways.

To check your understanding of this chapter with the online Study Guide, go to the Companion Website at http://www.prenhall.com/morrison, select chapter 10, then choose the Study Guide module.

Physical Development

Two words describe the physical growth of primary age children: *slow* and *steady*. Children at this age do not make the rapid and obvious height and weight gains of infants, toddlers, and preschoolers. Instead, they experience continual growth, develop increasing control over their bodies, and explore the things they are able to do. Primary children are building on the development of the earlier years.

From ages five to eight, children's average weight and height approximate each other, as shown in Table 10.1. The weight of boys and girls tends to be the same until about age nine, when girls pull ahead of boys in both height and weight. Wide variations appear in both individual rates of growth and development and among the sizes of children in each classroom. These differences in physical appearance result from genetic and cultural factors, nutritional intake and habits, health care, and experiential background.

For more information about the development of children in the primary grades, go to the Companion Website at http://www.prenhall.com/morrison, select any chapter, then choose Topic 2 of the ECE Supersite module.

Motor Development

Primary children are adept at many motor skills. Six-year-old children are in the initiative stage of psychosocial development; seven- and eight-year-old children are in the industry stage. Not only are children intuitively driven to initiate activities, they are also learning to be competent and productive individuals. The primary years are thus a time to use and test developing motor skills. Children at this age should be actively involved in activities that enable them to use their bodies to learn and develop feelings of accomplishment and competence. Their growing confidence and physical skills are reflected in games involving running,

Table 10.1
Average Height and Weight for Primary Children

Age	Males		Females	
	Height (inches)	Weight (pounds)	Height (inches)	Weight (pounds)
6 years	46	46	45	43
6 1/2 years	47	48	45	45
7 years	48	50	48	48
7 1/2 years	49	53	49	51
8 years	50	56	50	55
8 1/2 years	51	59	50	58

Source: Based on data from P. V. V. Hamill et al., "Physical Growth: National Center for Health Statistics Percentiles," American Journal of Clinical Nutrition *32 (1979), pp. 607–629.*

chasing, and kicking. A nearly universal characteristic of children in this period is their almost constant physical activity.

Differences between boys' and girls' motor skills during the primary years are minimal—their abilities are about equal. Teachers, therefore, should not use gender as a basis for limiting boys' or girls' involvement in activities. On the contrary, we should promote all children's involvement in age-appropriate activities. During the primary years we see evidence of continuing refinement of fine-motor skills in children's mastery of many of the tasks they previously could not do or could do only with difficulty. They are now able to dress themselves relatively easily and attend to most of their personal needs such as using utensils, combing their hair, and brushing their teeth. They are also more proficient at school tasks that require fine-motor skills, such as writing, making artwork, and using computers. In addition, primary children want to and are able to engage in real-life activities. They want the "real thing." This makes teaching them in many ways easier and more fun, since many activities have real-life applications, as discussed in the school-to-work program later in the chapter.

Cognitive Development

Children's cognitive development during the primary school years enables them to do things as first, second, and third graders that they could not do as preschoolers. A major difference between these two age groups is that older children's thinking has become less egocentric and more logical (see chapter 8). Concrete operational thought is the cognitive milestone that enables children between seven and eleven to think and act as they do. Logical operations, although more sophisticated than in preoperational children, still require concrete objects and referents in the here and now. Abstract reasoning comes later, in the formal operations stage during adolescence.

Moral Development

Jean Piaget and Lawrence Kohlberg are the leading proponents of a developmental concept of children's moral growth. Piaget identified the two stages of moral thinking typical of children in the elementary grades as *heteronomy*—being governed by others regarding right and wrong—and *autonomy*—being governed by oneself regarding right and wrong.

Heteronomy is characterized by relations of constraint. In this stage, children's concepts of good and bad and right and wrong are determined by the judgments pronounced by

Although children in the primary grades do not grow as rapidly physically as when they were younger, the years between six and eight are important ones for cognitive growth. What role should professionals play in these formative years for children?

adults. An act is "wrong" because a parent or teacher says it is wrong. Children's understanding of morality is based on the authority of adults and those values that "constrain" them.

Gradually, as children mature and have opportunities for experiences with peers and adults, moral thinking may change to relations of cooperation. This autonomy stage of personal morality is characterized by exchange of viewpoints among children, and between children and adults, as to what is right, wrong, good, or bad. Autonomy is not achieved by authority but rather by social experiences within which children may try out different ideas and discuss moral situations. Autonomous behavior does not mean that children agree with other children or adults but that autonomous people exchange opinions and try to negotiate solutions.

Recall that in chapter 3 we discussed Lev Vygotsky's zone of proximal development and the importance of having children collaborate with more competent peers and adults for cognitive and social development. According to Vygotsky, social interactions provide children opportunities for "scaffolding" to higher levels of thinking and behavior. Furthermore, Vygotsky said that part of the professional's pedagogical role was to challenge and help children move to higher levels of thinking and, in this case, moral development.

For more information about character education, go to the Companion Website at http://www.prenhall.com/morrison, select chapter 10, then choose the Linking to Learning module to connect to the Character Education: A General Introduction site.

The stage of relations of constraint is characteristic of children up through first and second grades, while the stage of relations of cooperation is characteristic for children in the middle and upper elementary grades. The real criterion for determining which developmental stage a child is operating in, however, is how that child is thinking, not how old she is. We can also see in Kohlberg's theory the importance of social interactions and collaboration of adults and peers in children's moral development. Kohlberg, a follower of Piaget, believed children's moral thinking occurs in developmental levels. Kohlberg conceptualized three levels of moral development: preconventional, conventional, and postconventional.[1] Children in early childhood are at the preconventional stage.

PRECONVENTIONAL LEVEL. When children are at this level, morality is basically a matter of good or bad, based on a system of punishments and rewards as administered by

adults in authority positions. In stage 1, the punishment and obedience orientation, children operate within and respond to physical consequences of behavior. Good and bad are based on the rewards they bring, and children base judgments on whether an action will bring pleasure.

In stage 2, the instrumental-relativist orientation, children's actions are motivated by satisfaction of needs. Consequently, interpersonal relations have their basis in arrangements of mutual convenience based on need satisfaction. ("You scratch my back; I'll scratch yours.")

Just as Piaget's cognitive stages are fixed and invariant for all children, so too are Kohlberg's moral levels. All individuals move through the process of moral development beginning at level 1 and progress through each level. No level can be skipped, but each individual does not necessarily achieve every level. Just as intellectual development may become "fixed" at a particular level of development, so may an individual become fixed at any one of the moral levels. You can learn more about Kohlberg's stages of moral development by accessing www.vgernet.net/diogenes/ex/lists/moraldev.html.

IMPLICATIONS FOR CLASSROOMS. The theories of Piaget, Kohlberg, and other programs for promoting moral education and character education have the following implications for primary grade classroom practice:

- All professionals must like and respect children.
- The classroom climate must support individual values. Respect for children means respect for and acceptance of the value systems children bring to school.
- Professionals and schools must be willing to deal with issues, morals, and value systems children bring to school.
- A sense of justice must prevail in the schools, instead of the injustice that may arise from imposing arbitrary institutional values.
- Children must have opportunities to interact with peers, children of different age groups and cultures, and adults to enable them to move to the higher levels of moral functioning.
- Students must have opportunities to make decisions and discuss the results of decision making. Children do not develop a value system through always being told what to do or through infrequent opportunities for making choices and decisions. Responsibility, for example, grows from being given opportunities to be responsible.

The Contemporary Primary School

As this text indicated a number of times, reform is sweeping across the educational landscape. Nowhere is this more evident than in the primary grades. Although the beginning of this chapter mentioned that the earlier years often receive the majority of attention, the primary grades *are* changing. Grassroots efforts, led by parents, teachers, and building- or program-level administrators, are aimed at changing how schools operate and are organized, how teachers teach, how children are taught and evaluated, and how schools involve and relate to parents and the community. At the same time, the top-down process is also at work. State governments are specifying the curriculum and testing agendas. Accountability and collaboration are in; schooling as usual in the primary grades is out.

Schooling in the primary years has become a serious enterprise for political, social, and economic reasons. First, educators, parents, and politicians are realizing that solutions to illiteracy, a poorly prepared work force, and many social problems begin in the first years of school or even before. Second, the public is not happy about continuing declines in educational achievement. It wants the schools to do a better job teaching children the skills that business and industry will need in the twenty-first century. Third, parents and the public in general want the schools to help solve many of society's problems (substance abuse, crime, violence, etc.) and to turn around what many see as an abandonment of traditional American and family values.

The Integrated Curriculum

For more information about primary curricula and teaching strategies, go to the Companion Website at http://www.prenhall.com/morrison, select any chapter, then choose Topic 6 of the ECE Supersite module.

A lot of change has occurred in the primary grades since the 1990s, with more on the way. Single-subject teaching and learning are out; integration of subject areas is in. Curriculum leaders want to help students relate what they learn in math to what they learn in science, and they want them to know that literacy is applied across the curriculum. Helping students make sense of what they learn to all areas of the curriculum and to apply it to life is one goal of contemporary curriculum reform.

Students sitting in single seats, in straight rows, solitarily doing their own work are out; learning together in small groups is in. Textbooks are out; projects and hands-on, active learning are in. The teacher as director of all and "the sage on center stage" is out; facilitation, collaboration, cooperative discipline, and coaching are in. However, direct, systematic instruction is becoming more popular as teachers strive to teach children the skills they need for success. Letter grades and report cards are still very popular, although narrative reports (in which professionals describe and report on student achievement), checklists (which describe the competencies students have demonstrated), parent conferences, portfolios containing samples of children's work, and other tools for reporting achievement are used to supplement letter grades.

In many respects, Dewey's progressive education ideas are still growing in the fertile ground of the hearts and minds of early childhood professionals. However, there is a decided back-to-basics movement in the United States today, and it is influencing the primary curriculum. The primary grades are also involved in the swinging pendulum of education change that is moving from less rigorous learning to academics. Figure 10.1 shows some of the critical features of an effective primary classroom. In addition to the content curriculum areas shown, add the curriculum programs discussed in this chapter.

Figure 10.1
Features of an Effective Primary Classroom

Source: Reprinted with permission from Toni S. Bickart, Judy Jablon, and Diane Dodge, Building the Primary Classroom, *page 9, © Teaching Strategies, Inc., Washington, DC, 1992. For more information please contact Teaching Strategies, Inc., PO Box 42243, Washington, DC 20015, 800-637-3652 or visit our Web site at http:www.TeachingStrategies.com.*

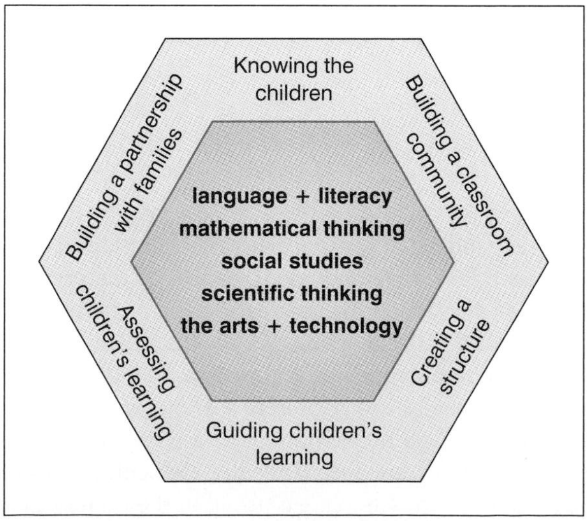

Prosocial and Conflict Resolution Education

There is a growing feeling among early childhood professionals that the ill effects of many societal problems, including uncivil behavior and violence, can be reduced or avoided. They believe efforts to achieve this goal should begin in the primary and preschool years. Consequently, they place emphasis on prosocial behaviors—teaching children the fundamentals of peaceful living, kindness, helpfulness, and cooperation. You can do several things to foster development of prosocial skills in the classroom:

- Be a good role model for children. You must demonstrate in your life and relationships with children and other adults the behaviors of cooperation and kindness that you want to encourage in children. Civil behavior begins with courtesy and manners. You can model these and help children to do the same.
- Provide positive feedback and reinforcement when children perform prosocial behaviors. When they are rewarded for appropriate behavior, children tend to repeat that behavior. ("I like how you helped Tim get up when you accidentally ran into him. I bet that made him feel better.")
- Provide opportunities for children to help and show kindness to others. Cooperative programs between primary children and nursing and retirement homes are excellent opportunities to practice kind and helping behaviors.
- Conduct classroom routines and activities so they are as free of conflict as possible. Provide opportunities for children to work together and practice skills for cooperative living. Design learning centers and activities for children to share and work cooperatively.
- When real conflicts occur, provide practice in conflict resolution skills. These skills include taking turns, talking through problems, compromising, and apologizing. A word of caution regarding apologies: too often, an apology is a perfunctory response on the part of teachers and children. Rather than just saying the often empty words "I'm sorry," it is far more meaningful to help one child understand how another is feeling. Encouraging empathic behavior in children is a key to the development of prosocial behavior.
- Conduct classroom activities based on multicultural principles that are free from stereotyping and sexist behaviors (see chapter 14).
- Read stories to children that exemplify prosocial behaviors, and provide such literature for them to read.
- Counsel and work with parents to encourage them to limit or eliminate children watching violence on television, attending R-rated movies, playing video games with violent content, and buying CDs with objectionable lyrics.
- Help children feel good about themselves, build strong self-images, and be competent individuals. Children who are happy, confident, and competent feel good about themselves and are more likely to behave positively toward others.

Teaching Thinking

We generally think of basic skills as reading, writing, and arithmetic, and many elementary schools give these subjects the major share of time and teacher emphasis. Yet some critics of education, and advocates of basic education, do not consider the "three Rs" the ultimate

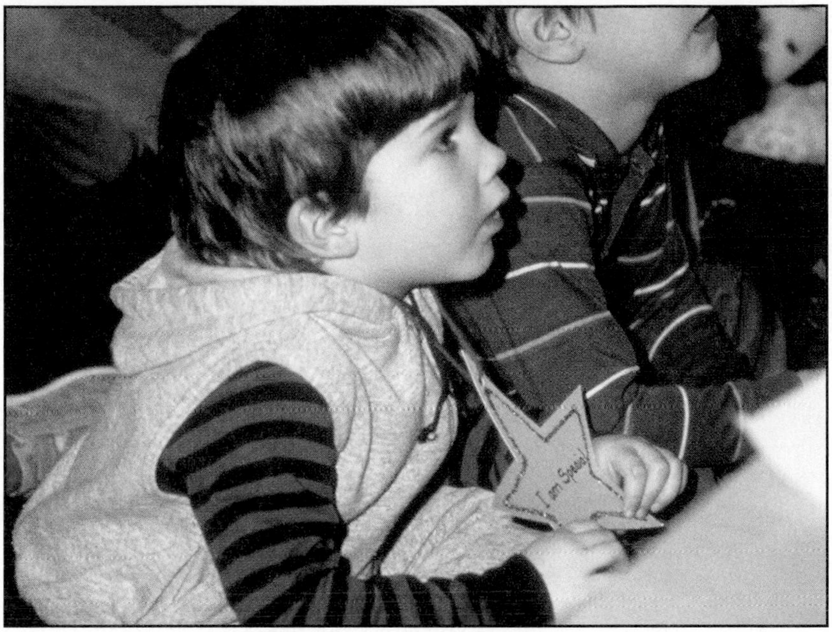

Teaching about self-esteem is less important than enabling children to learn how to assume responsibility for their learning and to succeed through their own efforts. What are some things you can do to help students be more successful?

"basics" of sound education. Rather, they feel the real basic of education is *thinking*. The rationale is that if students can think, they can meaningfully engage in subject matter curriculum and the rigors and demands of the workplace and life. Increasingly, thinking and problem-solving skills are coming to be regarded as no less "basic" than math facts, spelling, knowledge of geography, and so on.

As a result, teachers are including the teaching of thinking in their daily lesson plans, using both direct and nondirect methods of instruction to teach thinking skills. A trend in curriculum and instruction today is to infuse the teaching of thinking across the curriculum and to make thinking a part of the culture of a classroom, as they are trying to do with literacy.

> To talk about a classroom culture of thinking is to refer to a classroom environment in which several forces such as language, values, expectations, and habits work together to express and reinforce the enterprise of good thinking. In a classroom culture of thinking, the spirit of good thinking is everywhere. There is the sense that "everyone is doing it," that everyone including the teacher is making the effort to be thoughtful, inquiring, and imaginative, and that these behaviors are strongly supported by the learning environment.[2]

In classrooms that emphasize thinking, students are encouraged to use their power of analysis, when teachers ask higher-level questions. Table 10.2 shows examples of questions teachers can use following Benjamin Bloom's hierarchy of questioning levels. One teaching objective is to ask students questions across—from top to bottom—the hierarchy. Teachers are being encouraged to challenge their children to think about classroom information and learning material rather than to merely memorize acceptable responses. Instead of asking children to recall information, teachers ask them to think critically about information, solve problems, and reflect, teaching them skills such as the following:

COMMONLY TAUGHT THINKING SKILLS

- *Analyzing*—examining something methodically; identifying the parts of something and the relationships between those parts.
- *Inferring*—drawing a reasonable conclusion from known information.
- *Comparing and contrasting*—noting similarities and differences between two things or events.
- *Predicting*—forecasting what will happen next in a given situation, based on the circumstances.
- *Hypothesizing*—developing a reasonable explanation for events, based on an analysis of evidence.
- *Critical thinking*—examining evidence and arguments carefully, without bias, and reaching sound conclusions.
- *Deductive reasoning*—applying general principles to specific cases.
- *Inductive reasoning*—deriving general principles from an analysis of individual cases.
- *Organizing*—imposing logical order on something.
- *Classifying*—putting things into groups based on shared characteristics.
- *Decision making*—examining alternatives and, for sound reasons, choosing one.
- *Problem solving*—analyzing a difficult situation and thinking creatively about how to resolve it.[3]

INDUCTIVE AND DEDUCTIVE REASONING. Other basic building blocks are reasoning skills, which include the following intellectual activities:

- Enumeration, listing
- Grouping
- Labeling, categorizing
- Identifying critical relationships
- Making inferences
- Predicting consequences, explaining unfamiliar phenomena, hypothesizing
- Explaining and/or supporting the predictions and hypotheses
- Verifying predictions[4]

These skills are used in inductive reasoning (thinking from the particular to the general, or drawing a logical conclusion from instances of a case) and in deductive reasoning (inferring specifics from a general principle, or drawing a logical conclusion from a premise).

CRITICAL THINKING SKILLS. Critical thinking skills are used in everyday life activities to help determine the accuracy of information and to make decisions regarding choices. Critical thinking is the process of logically and systematically analyzing problems, data, and solutions to make rational decisions about what to do or believe. Skills involved in critical thinking include the following:

Table 10.2
Applying Bloom's Taxonomy to Early Childhood Classrooms

Competence	Skills Demonstrated	Sample Questions
Knowledge	• Observation and recall of information • Knowledge of dates, events, places • Knowledge of major ideas • Mastery of subject matter • *Question Cues*: List, define, tell, describe, identify, show, label, collect, examine, tabulate, quote, name, who, when, where, etc.	• How would you describe the size of an elephant? • Tell me three things that you can do with a soccer ball.
Comprehension	• Understanding information • Grasp meaning • Translate knowledge into new context • Interpret facts, compare, contrast • Order, group, infer causes • Predict consequences • *Question Cues:* Summarize, describe, interpret, contrast, predict, associate, distinguish, estimate, differentiate, discuss, extend	• How are sounds different (contrasting)? • What is the main idea or point of the book we just read together? Explain.
Application	• Use information • Use methods, concepts, theories in new situations • Solve problems using required skills or knowledge • *Question Cues*: Apply, demonstrate, calculate, complete, illustrate, show, solve, examine, modify, relate, change, classify, experiment, discover	• Construct two buildings in the math area, one tall building and one short building. • How would you organize your paintings to show your mother which one you painted first and which one you painted last?

- Identify central issues or problems.
- Compare similarities and differences.
- Determine which information is relevant.
- Formulate appropriate questions.
- Distinguish among facts, opinion, and reasoning judgment.
- Check consistency.
- Identify unstated assumptions.
- Recognize stereotypes and cliches.
- Recognize bias, emotional factors, propaganda, and semantic slanting.
- Recognize different value systems and ideologies.
- Evaluate the adequacy of data.
- Predict probable consequences.[5]

Competence	Skills Demonstrated	Sample Questions
Analysis	• Seeing patterns • Organization of parts • Recognition of hidden meanings • Identification of components • Question Cues: Analyze, separate, order, explain, connect, classify, arrange, divide, compare, select, explain, infer	• What are the parts of the clarinet? Why do you think the bottom of the clarinet is bell-shaped? • If you see your friend lying down on the playground, crying, what do you suppose happened that caused your friend to do that?
Synthesis	• Use old ideas to create new ones • Generalize from given facts • Relate knowledge from several areas • Predict, draw conclusions • *Question Cues*: Combine, integrate, modify, rearrange, substitute, plan, create, design, invent, what if?, compose, formulate, prepare, generalize, rewrite	• Can you create a new color by mixing paints? Predict what color the new color will be most like. • Imagine yourself as a Pilgrim boy or girl. How would your life be the same as it is now? How would your life be different than it is now?
Evaluation	• Compare and discriminate between ideas • Assess value of theories, presentations • Make choices based on reasoned argument • Verify value of evidence • Recognize subjectivity • *Question Cues*: Assess, decide, rank, grade, test, measure, recommend, convince, select, judge, explain, discriminate, support, conclude, compare, summarize	• Let's decide what the three most important rules of our classroom should be. • Which one of your paintings is your favorite? Why?

Source: Used with permission of Counseling Services—University of Victoria, "Learning Skills Program," http://www.coun.uvic.ca/learn/program/hndouts/bloom.html. Copyright 1996.

The goal of teaching critical thinking is to encourage students to question what they hear and read and to examine their own thinking. Teachers cultivate critical thinking by providing learning environments in which divergent perspectives are respected and free discussion is allowed.

CREATIVE PROBLEM-SOLVING STRATEGIES. Problem solving in any content area rests on thinking skills and critical thinking. Problem-solving skills can be taught directly through process strategies. For example, one system teaches problem-solving strategies using the acronym *IDEAL* as a mnemonic for a five-step process:

I Identify the problem.

D Define and represent the problem.

E Explore possible strategies.

A Act on the strategies.

L Look back and evaluate the effects of your activities.[6]

Critical thinking is necessary for successful participation in many life- and work-related activities. What are some ways that you will integrate critical thinking into your curriculum?

Other effective problem-solving strategies include teaching students brainstorming techniques, imaging strategies, and ways to represent problems visually as an aid to finding a solution.

IMPLICATIONS FOR PROFESSIONALS. Professionals who want to promote critical and creative thinking in children need to be aware of several things. First, children need the freedom and security to be creative thinkers. Many teachers and school programs focus on helping children learn the right answers to problems, so children soon learn from the process of schooling that there is only one right answer. Children may be so "right answer" oriented that they are uncomfortable with searching for other answers or consider it a waste of time.

Second, the environment must support children's creative efforts. Teachers must create classroom cultures in which children have the time, opportunity, and materials with which to be creative. Letting children think creatively only when all their subjects are completed, or scheduling creative thinking for certain times, does not properly encourage it.

Third, creative and critical thinking must be integrated into the total curriculum so that children learn to think during the entire school day and throughout their lives.

Cooperative Learning

You can probably remember how, when you were in primary school, you competed with other kids. You probably tried to see whether you could be the first to raise your hand. You leaned out over the front of your seat, frantically waving for your teacher's attention. How-

ever, in many of today's primary classrooms, the emphasis is on cooperation, not competition. Cooperative learning is seen as a way to boost student achievement and enhance self-esteem.

Cooperative learning is an instructional and learning strategy that focuses on instructional methods in which students are encouraged or required to work together on academic tasks. Students work in small, mixed-ability learning groups of usually four members wherein each member is responsible for learning and for helping all members learn. In one form of cooperative learning called "Student Teams—Achievement Division," four students—usually one high achiever, two average students, and one low achiever—participate in a regular cycle of activities such as the following:

- The teacher presents the lesson to the group.
- Students work to master the material using worksheets or other learning materials. Students are encouraged not only to complete their work but also to explain their work and ideas to group members.
- Students take brief quizzes.[7]

Children in a cooperative learning group are assigned certain responsibilities; for example, there is a group leader, who announces the problems or task; a praiser, who praises group members for their answers and work; and a checker. Responsibilities rotate as the group engages in different tasks. Children are also encouraged to develop and use interpersonal skills such as addressing classmates by their first names, saying "Thank you," and explaining to their groupmates why they are proposing an answer. At the classroom level, teachers must incorporate five basic elements into the instructional process for cooperative learning to be successful:

1. *Positive independence.* The students have to believe they are in the learning process together and that they care about one another's learning.
2. *Verbal, face-to-face interaction.* Students must explain, argue, elaborate, and tie what they are learning now to what they have previously learned.
3. *Individual accountability.* Every member of the group must realize that it is his or her own responsibility to learn.
4. *Social.* Students must learn appropriate leadership, communication, trust-building, and conflict resolution skills.
5. *Group processing.* The group has to assess how well its members are working together and how they can do better.[8]

Proponents and practitioners of cooperative learning are enthusiastic about its benefits:

- It motivates students to do their best.
- It motivates students to help one another.
- It significantly increases student achievement.[9]

Supporters of cooperative learning maintain that it enables children to learn how to cooperate and that children learn from each other; and because schools are usually such competitive places, it gives children an opportunity to learn cooperative skills.

Research shows that higher achievement results when children are engaged in cooperative learning tasks. How can you include cooperative learning in your classroom practices?

Not all teachers agree that cooperative learning is a good idea. They maintain that it is too time-consuming and that a group may take longer than an individual to solve a problem. Other critics charge that time spent on cooperative learning takes away time from learning the basic skills of reading, writing, and arithmetic.

Given the new approaches in primary education, it makes sense that professionals would want to use a child-centered approach that increases student achievement. Furthermore, school critics say that classrooms are frequently too competitive and that students who are neither competitive nor high achievers are left behind. Cooperative learning would seem to be one of the better ways to reduce classroom competitiveness and foster "helping" attitudes.

School-to-Work

Today, one of the emphases in all of education is to devise ways to help students apply what they learn in school to real life and real work situations. School-to-Work is a federal program authorized under the School-to-Work Opportunities Act of 1994. This act provides money to states in order to fund local school district initiatives for developing curricula and programs that will help students learn work-related skills. The basic work-related skills are literacy skills—reading, writing, and speaking. In addition, thinking and working cooperatively with others are also work-related skills. School-to-Work is a K–12 program, and many early childhood teachers participate in it. The early childhood level School-to-Work initiatives include helping students learn job-related skills—making change, using technology, etc.—and career awareness.

For example, in the Western Dubuque (Iowa) Community Elementary Schools, one K–6 elementary school researched careers. Kindergartners made a video in which they described what skills they each would need to do their job and what salary they expected. They also made a computer slide show with pictures they had taken. These students actually learned how to program their own photos into the computer to be included in their papers. They then typed the information on their picture pages, and these were printed as books. Each grade had a completed career book by the end of the year. For the past three years, counselors have developed Career Portfolios on each child to build a record of the activities

Program in Action

The Montrose School-to-Career Education Partnership

THEORY

Third graders are eager to learn about the world of work, and they love field trips and classroom visitors. Teachers are eager to keep the curriculum fresh and relevant. Businesses are eager to support schools, to share their expertise and sites. Combine this energy and desire to build a dynamic relationship among elementary students, teachers, and local business: an Education Partnership with curriculum punch.

HISTORY

In 1996–1997 Montrose school district (Montrose, Colorado) prioritized development of a School-to-Career component for elementary education. To ensure community support and buy-in, the district's School-to-Career leadership formed a lively, mutually respectful partnership with the Montrose Chamber of Commerce.

PROCESS

The chamber's Education Committee linked with School-to-Career to expand their Education Partnership program. The Education Committee guides the entire program using district input and technical assistance from the School-to-Career coordinator. Third grade teachers are invited to participate and asked to identify what type of business or government entity would be the best match for their classroom. The committee recruits businesses based on the teachers' desires and the committee's knowledge of the community.

The committee pairs a business with one or two elementary classrooms, targeting third grade. The business partners agree to participate in a minimum of three classroom activities during the school year. They host at least one field trip, which includes a visit to the worksite. The school district assumes financial responsibility for field trip costs.

The Education Committee facilitates two yearly meetings among principals, teachers, and businesspersons. These meetings orient all participants, evaluate activities, and make program recommendations. However, the main agenda item is brainstorming, which nourishes ideas for classroom curriculum links and activities. Teachers and their business partners use the "Education Partnership Panning Guide," which formalizes activity plans for the school year.

Program emphasis for teachers is on meshing the in-place curriculum with the expertise and knowledge of their chosen partner. The emphasis for business is on bringing relevancy to the classroom by showcasing the skills, equipment, and occupations within its organizational structure. For students the emphasis is on understanding how what they are learning in school is useful and necessary in the world of work.

Teachers and business partners discover curriculum possibilities and implement them according to student ability. The bottom line, the main goal, is to expand students' knowledge and basic skills with *immediate* application in the classroom curriculum.

EXAMPLES

Banking. Norwest Bank links money management to the math curriculum and sponsors an in-depth tour of the bank, including seeing lots of money and the safe. Norwest brings tellers, the CEO, the head of security, the maintenance supervisor, and loan officers to the classroom to share their workday responsibilities. Students count and sort money, learn basic budgeting, and write practice checks. One field trip was to a bank client, Reclamation Metals, where the students observed recycling in progress and began to understand the relationship banks have to community projects.

Aerospace Industry. Scaled Technology is a partner with a class that is participating in a project involving students collecting data for the Citizen Explore Satellite. Scaled Technology engineers talk about how satellites orbit and what the word *orbit* means. Students collect data using aerosol and ultraviolet meters. The business partner helps the students learn how the instruments work and how to collect and record data. Lessons about the scientific method are also part of what employees of

the company will teach. The field trip will be to the manufacturing plant where satellite parts are designed and built.

Newspapers. A journalist partners a class. She meets with students in groups of two or three, assisting with writing, editing, inspiring, and some classroom publishing. This partnership enhances language arts curriculum and the district's literacy efforts.

City Government. The City of Montrose partnership meshes perfectly with the social studies curriculum. In preparation for a tour of all departments at City Hall the students discuss job opportunities at the city level. From information provided about each employee, the students choose a job to write about. The first hour includes all departments housed at City Hall. Students meet the city manager, mayor, and department heads of Planning, Engineering, Legal, Information Technology, Human Resources, and so on. Once, the city planner explained his current assignment to study the population growth and find correct placement for a new elementary school. He provided the students with a colorful map containing all the pertinent demographic information and asked the students to formulate a recommendation to the school board on the new school site. Students leave city Hall eagerly anticipating the second field trip, which includes the City Shop, Animal Shelter, and Wastewater Treatment Plant. A third activity involves the students conducting a city council meeting by role playing city council members and staff in the actual council chambers.

Bureau of Land Management. Bureau of Land Management (BLM), like many public agencies, has a mission statement requiring interaction with

communities. The BLM leads its classroom partners into the world of environmental issues by having the students study and do experiments about soil types. Erosion and land management practices are the topics of discussion when students visit a site that illustrates soil issues.

County Government. The district judge partners with a class by linking to the social studies and health curricula. He discusses the judicial functions of government with students and encourages them to lead a drug-free and crime-free life. The students tour the criminal justice center courtroom, jail, and police headquarters.

Fire Department. The Fire Department partnership enhances the students' use of math, understanding of electricity, and health issues while also providing a Service Learning Project. The students conducted a neighborhood survey of smoke detector use. The results were analyzed by finding the mean, median, and mode. The department provided batteries to the students to distribute to the elderly. The class also inventoried the school's use of electrical outlets and learned why overloaded circuits can start fires. As part of health study, the students learned about CPR, first aid, and the dangers of smoking. The students made fire hats and were in charge of an actual fire drill at the school. The trip to the fire station was almost anticlimactic after all this excitement!

Natural Resources Conservation Service. A specialist with the NRCS visits the class throughout the year and brings fresh ideas to parts of the science curriculum that touch on natural resources. A study of the nutrient cycle, for instance, resulted in the students building worm bins in jars, then studying how worms help decompose almost anything. Field trips to habitat reclamation projects enliven the classroom activities.

CONCLUSION

In this elementary School-to-Career program, the Chamber of Commerce and school district discovered that a generous definition of the word *business* strengthens program diversity and community involvement. They actively recruit employers outside the normal school support loop. The data supports this and other strategies: participation in the first year included six schools and four businesses; participation in the second year involved sixteen classrooms and twelve businesses.

The elementary level School-to-Career program energizes and provides focus for the curriculum. It generates close school and community collaboration, increases mutual understanding about the daily challenges of education, and promotes program ownership. The Montrose Education Partnership firmly believes that curriculum-linked, reality-based experiences in the world of employment successfully launches students' dreams for a productive future.

Visit the Department of Education's School-to-Work Learning Center Web site at http://stw.ed.gov/.

Text and photos contributed by Carol Parker.

completed. All first graders used the new portfolios and the National Career Guidelines to track career awareness. Third graders visited area businesses and then created newspaper ads based on the information they learned about them. These were published in the local paper and paid for by each business.[10]

Character Education

Character education is rapidly becoming a part of many elementary classrooms (and middle and senior high schools as well) across the United States, for several reasons. While everyone believes children have to learn how to count, growing numbers of individuals also believe that schools have to teach children *what* counts. Character education is becoming a higher priority for everyone. Heated debates rage about whether teachers should teach values. But in the future, character education curricula designed to teach specific character traits will become commonplace. For example, all school districts in the state of Georgia are required to implement a comprehensive character education program for all children. Some traits included in this curriculum are honesty, fairness, responsibility for others, kindness, cooperation, self-control, and self-respect.

For more information about character education curricula, go to the Companion Website at http://www.prenhall.com/morrison, select chapter 10, then choose the Linking to Learning module to connect to the Character Education Institute site.

Schools should "provide guidance that helps develop occupational and life skills. That guidance will help students develop moral ethics, self-discipline and self-esteem," says Nanthana Wong-in, an educational psychology professor at Srinakharinwirot University in Thailand.[11] While educators may argue over what character traits to teach, there will no longer be a debate over whether they should be taught. During the 1960s, teachers abrogated their right and responsibility for teaching values. The twenty-first century will not be such a time. The first decade of this century will be a decade of the six Rs: reading, writing, arithmetic, reasoning, respect, and responsibility. Parents and families will increasingly take part in teaching life skills to children. "Socialization, which is the process of nurturing the helpless, psychologically unformed babe into a competent, participating member of society, is no longer the prerogative of parents. Schools, whether they are preschools, primary, or secondary schools, are seen by parents and society as agents of children's socialization, along with parents."[12]

Character education is an example of a curricular application of developmental approaches to learning. Programs aim to help students acquire positive character traits, such

Program in Action

The Giraffe Heroes Program for Character Education

The Giraffe Heroes Program for six- to eight-year-olds provides K–2 teachers with teaching assistants—Stan and Bea Tall, twin giraffes who go through the program with the class, learning character, service, active citizenship, social skills, and emotional intelligence along with the children. Stan and Bea are young friends trying, as the children are, to figure out how the world works and what their roles in it are.

Stan and Bea don't come into the classroom with lists of character traits or lectures on the importance of honesty or perseverance. They just go where the children are and help them move from there to experiences that bring forth the children's own innate compassion and their desire to contribute to their world. Stan, Bea, and the children learn together to be brave, caring, and responsible. As classroom puppets and as voices on audiotapes, Stan and Bea tell the children stories that give them models of meaningful lives. The heroes of these stories are giraffes because they stick their necks out to make the world a better place. The teacher's guide includes print, audio, and video stories of over thirty human giraffes, filling the children with stories of real heroes. The stories are from the files of the nonprofit Giraffe Project, which has been finding and commending real heroes since 1982.

Hearing these stories, kids understand what real heroism is about, despite the cultural messages that tell them that heroes are bulletproof cartoon figures, athletes, or entertainers. That's stage I of the program, Hear the Story.

In stage II, Tell the Story, the children look in their studies, in the media, and in their communities for real heroes and tell these stories to the class. Then comes putting all they've learned into action—Become the Story, Stage III. Stan and Bea guide the children through a process called Seven Neckbones (because giraffes' and humans' necks all have just seven bones).

Doing Neckbones takes students from looking at problems that concern them through successfully creating and carrying out a service project that addresses one of those problems. Key to the program is the respect given to children's concerns and ideas; they drive the program. The effect on the children is powerful as they realize that their unvoiced concerns can be voiced, that their participation in their community is wanted and valued.

In contrast to the lukewarm response sometimes evoked by being directed into a service program, the enthusiasm of students is high when they invent their own programs. As in all good programs that include service learning, students experience the practical value of academic skills as they carry out their projects. An independent study of the program's contents to determine the essential learnings it contains yielded this list:

Communications

- 1.2 Listen and observe to gain and interpret information
- 1.3 Check for understanding by asking questions and paraphrasing
- 2.1 Communicate clearly to a range of audiences
- 2.2 Develop content and ideas
- 2.3 Use effective delivery
- 3.1 Use language to interact effectively
- 3.2 Work cooperatively as a member of a group
- 3.3 Seek agreement and solutions through discussion
- 4.3 Analyze mass communications

Civics

1.3 Examine representative government and citizen participation

4.1 Understand individual rights and accompanying responsibilities

4.2 Identify and demonstrate rights of U.S. citizenship

4.3 Explain how citizen participation influences public policy

Social Studies

3.1 Identify and examine people's interactions with the environment

3.3 Examine cultural differences

Math

5.3 Relate mathematical concepts and procedures to real-life situations

Science

1.3 Environmental and resource issues

Kids who have done the Giraffe Heroes Program know that they are more than consumers of cereal, cartoons, CDs, and sneakers—they are brave, caring young people who can make good things happen in their world.

In reviewing the Giraffe Heroes Program, Dee Dickerson, founder of New Horizons for Learning, said, "It is never too early to help children develop the character traits the world needs so urgently—altruism, compassion, generosity, and responsible citizenship. The Giraffe Heroes Program for K–2 offers an engaging, age-appropriate series of lessons that are creative, interesting, humorous, and highly motivating. This program can fit easily into any curriculum, and can facilitate the learning of reading, writing, and communication skills. What a great start for lifelong learning!"

Former teacher Paula Mirk, now of the Institute for Global Ethics, said in her review, "Every time I imagine the children who get to experience this approach I think how lucky they are and how much I'd have used something like this if I'd had it in my own classroom. I predict it will become a significant cornerstone in character education for very young children. What I like best about it is the consistent attention to respecting 'where young children are at' throughout. Text directed at the teacher constantly reminds us that young children deserve very special handling, and then the structure of the curriculum makes such care very easy and a matter of course. The layout and organization of the curriculum is very simple and easy to follow."

Teachers are given lesson plans, scheduling suggestions, ideas on using the program for standard curriculum goals, handout masters, overhead transparencies, and templates for visuals. The guide includes a video about the Giraffe Project from public television that can be used for teacher and parent orientation, and it also includes two audiotapes for the classroom. There are thirty giraffe heroes stories, each with a photograph.

Visit the Giraffe Heroes Project on the Web at http://www.giraffe.org.

Text contributed by Jennifer Sand, education director; photos courtesy of Kathy Frazier.

as initiative, diligence, loyalty, tact, kindness, generosity, courage, and other traits believed to be good by society in general.[13] In 1997, the Georgia State Board of Education approved Georgia's Quality Core Curriculum (QCC), a list of core values to be taught in the Georgia public schools. These values include citizenship, respect for others, respect for self, self-esteem, and the work ethic. More information concerning Georgia's Quality Core Curriculum is available on its Web site (http://www.doe.k12.ga.us/).

... voice from the field

Teaching Character in Everything You Do

CAROL CATES, 1999 NORTH CAROLINA EDUCATOR OF THE YEAR

When I began my teaching career, many students received moral instruction from their home or church. However, times change over the years. I realized that there was a strong need for the teaching of values in schools. When character education was introduced into our school system, I was asked to be on the task force to develop plans for developing a curriculum. It was exciting to know that our system valued strong ethics and that we would be encouraged to integrate them into our curriculum.

Schoolwide Initiatives. Teaching with puppets was just one of the techniques I adopted to model concepts to my students and as a method to share character education with the entire school. By working with the school administrators, the guidance counselor, and the elementary grade teachers, I was able to organize a puppet team. We set up first- and second-semester teams to provide opportunities for more students to participate.

I write the skits using ideas from Thomas Lickona's book *Educating for Character,* William Bennett's *Book of Virtues,* and other literature that stresses morals, along with suggestions made by students and faculty. Using school puppets and ethnic-appropriate materials of my own, the skits are performed five to six times a year at our Terrific Kids assemblies, which are sponsored by the local Kiwanis Club. Each assembly emphasizes a monthly character word.

This project has also led to the start of two other programs that reinforce positive values: the Kids for Character Club, which meets monthly, and the Hillcrest Hornet TV News, a video shown to our entire school each Friday. Two Kids for Character Club representatives are chosen each semester by their teachers. A student who already models good behavior and one who may need more assistance in demonstrating good character skills consistently are selected to participate. The club activities include decorating character education bulletin boards, making cards for the Skilled Nursing Home of Burlington, and planting flower bulbs on the school grounds. The club members have also encouraged their classmates to fill shoe boxes for distribution to needy children. These opportunities have provided Hillcrest students with opportunities to develop their character skills. As a result, parents and educators who visit our school have noticed the positive environment. The students are polite to each other and respectful of adults, and everyone takes care of our facility.

Character Education in My Classroom. Although I enjoy these opportunities to promote character education throughout the school, my top priority is teaching twenty-two lively first graders. Character education is woven into all of our basic curriculum activities. Children become aware of the positive impact they have on others by demonstrating good character skills.

So children can broaden their perception of the world, I help them understand that their world is larger than their immediate neighborhood. I read books to the children that teach character traits, often referring to the list of traits adopted by our school system. We read the daily newspaper, locating cities and countries on our world and state maps. We use the special kids sections of the *Times News* (Character Counts and the Kids Scoop pages) to help students understand the importance of good character skills. Visitors and artifacts from other states and countries are used to help students compare where they live with other areas so they can appreciate the similarities and the differences. As we experience the variety of

cultures and countries, we try to eliminate prejudice and accept cultural differences. We also study the traditions of other cultures and have international tasting parties with food, games, folktales, or stories about the cultures. We also write letters to soldiers for several holidays, including Veterans Day.

Students make encouragement cards and small gifts for the cafeteria workers, maintenance workers, and office staff. Children send thank you notes and remembrance cards to parents and grandparents for sharing items or time with our class. We also write to other classes and school groups to express gratitude and encouragement when they have performed for our school.

In report cards, parents are given an update on their child's character development. I write notes to parents to keep them abreast of their children's progress. Students also write to their parents when they have disturbed the class with inappropriate behavior. The note indicates the character skill that was not demonstrated (e.g., "I did not show respect"), and the child finishes the note explaining how he or she will improve the next time that situation occurs. Students also take home "good" notes that I have made and ones we write together.

The "Moral" of the Story. Character development is an ongoing process. It needs to be a part of each day's expectations, and children need to learn how to practice virtues and ethics at an early age. When teachers expect and stress values in their classrooms, children understand and use methods for problem solving. Students know they are to practice character skills during transition times each day, and these skills continue at home and in the community.

What is the value of teaching character skills all day every day in every way? Consistently teaching children character values interwoven with all of the curriculum areas helps children realize that character is a part of everything they do in life and that demonstrating good character is a gift they can share with others.

Character education seeks to directly teach character traits, while moral education seeks to foster moral reasoning through discussions and values clarification activities. A comprehensive approach to character education might include the following teacher practices:

- Create a moral community. Act as a caregiver, model, and mentor, helping students know one another as persons, respect and care about one another, and feel valued membership in, and responsibility to, the group.
- Practice moral discipline, using the creation and enforcement of rules as opportunities to foster moral reasoning, voluntary compliance with rules, and respect for others.
- Create a democratic classroom environment, involving students in decision making and giving them responsibility for making the classroom a good place to be and learn.
- Teach values through the curriculum, using the ethically rich content of academic subjects such as literature, history, and science, including multicultural perspectives.
- Use cooperative learning to develop students' appreciation of others, ability to take different perspectives, and ability to work with others toward common goals.

- Develop the "conscience of craft" by fostering students' appreciation of learning, capacity for hard work, commitment to excellence, and sense of work as affecting the lives of others.
- Encourage moral reflection through reading, researching, essay writing, journal keeping, discussing, and debating.
- Teach conflict resolution so that students acquire the essential moral skills of solving conflicts fairly and without force.
- Foster caring beyond the classroom, using positive role models to inspire altruistic behavior and providing opportunities at every grade level to perform school and community service.
- Create a positive moral culture in the school, developing a schoolwide ethos that supports and amplifies the values taught in classrooms.
- Recruit parents and the community as partners in character education, letting parents know that the school considers them their child's first and most important moral teacher.[14]

Character Education Resources, an organization based in New Hampshire, provides a wealth of information about character education (http://www.charactereducationinfo.org/).

Character education is seen as a way of reducing, and possibly preventing, societal problems. "Character is broadly conceived to encompass the cognitive, emotional, and behavioral aspects of the moral life. Good character consists of understanding, caring about, and acting upon core ethical values."[15]

Character education programs seek to teach a set of traditional core values that will result in civic virtue and moral character, including honesty, kindness, respect, responsibility, tolerance for diversity, racial harmony, and good citizenship. Efforts to promote character qualities and values are evident in statewide efforts.

It is likely that there will be a great deal more emphasis in the near future on teaching character traits because parents and society are increasingly concerned about the life direction of children and youth. As previously indicated, students not only have to know how to count but also what counts in life.

Literacy and Reading

Just as in preschool and kindergarten, today's primary classroom decidedly emphasizes literacy development and reading. In fact, this emphasis is apparent in all the elementary grades, pre-K to 6. Society and parents want children who can speak, write, and read well.

A HOLISTIC APPROACH. As discussed in chapter 9, more professionals are adopting a balanced approach to promoting children's literacy and reading development. One such approach is holistic literary education, which advocates a complete system of children's literacy development. The following are characteristic of a holistic approach: [16]

- Teachers integrate the teaching of the language arts into a single period. They recognize the interrelatedness of reading, writing, speaking, and listening. . . . Holistic teachers therefore provide children with opportunities to talk, write, listen, and speak to each other and to the teacher.
- Teachers use children's oral language as the vehicle for helping them make the transition to the written language. Children are given opportunities to write messages, let-

ters, and stories, using their own words and sentence patterns, even before they can accurately read, write, or spell.

- Teachers encourage students to write as soon as they enter school. Children may dictate experiences or stories for others to write, as is done in the Language Experience Approach to reading instruction; however, holistic teachers emphasize children's doing their own writing, following their belief that children's writing skills develop from scribbling to invented spellings to eventual mature writing.
- In addition to using children's written documents as reading material, holistic teachers frequently use literature books, rejecting vocabulary-controlled, sentence-controlled stories in favor of those containing predictable language patterns. They choose the best children's literature available to read to and with children.
- Holistic teachers organize literacy instruction around themes or units of study relevant to students. Children use all of the language arts (listening, speaking, reading, and writing) as they study a particular theme. Many teachers also integrate the teaching of music, art, social studies, and other subjects into these units of study.
- Holistic teachers believe in intrinsic motivation, and when children enjoy good literature, create stories, write letters, keep personal journals, and share their written documents with others, language learning becomes intrinsically rewarding.
- Holistic teachers believe that literacy development depends on having opportunities to communicate. Since communication is not possible without social interaction, these teachers give children opportunities to read other children's compositions, and to write, listen, and speak to each other.
- Holistic teachers give children opportunities to both teach and learn from each other. They often work collaboratively on a common interest or goal. They react to each other's written products, and they share favorite books with each other.
- Holistic teachers control literacy instruction. It may be student centered, but it is also teacher guided. . . . [H]olistic teachers recognize that some direct instruction, including instruction in phonics, is not incompatible with student empowerment.
- Teachers emphasize holistic reading and writing experiences—children spend most of the classroom time available on meaningful reading and writing experiences.

Wellness and Healthy Living in the Primary Years

Three major health problems face young children and their families today—lead poisoning, asthma, and obesity.

Lead Poisoning

According to the Centers for Disease Control (CDC), nearly one million children in the United States have elevated levels of lead in their blood. This is known to cause brain damage, learning disabilities, and physical impairments. Major sources of lead exposure include lead-based paints found in many older houses and apartments, dust and soil contaminated

with lead from many environmental sources (including batteries), emissions from leaded gasoline, and old lead paint.[17]

Asthma

The CDC also reports that 4.8 million children suffer from asthma. Asthma is now considered the number one childhood disease. Unfortunately, asthma is incurable and disproportionately affects children who are poor and live in urban areas. Asthma is also considered to be one of the most common reasons that children miss school. Asthma is caused in part by poor air quality, dust, mold, animal fur and dander, allergens from cockroaches and rodent feces, dust mites, and strong fumes. Many of these causes are found in poor and low-quality housing. Asthma prevention is a major health issue in early childhood programs.[18]

Obesity and Nutrition

Nutrition for young children is a major concern of both school and society.[19] At least one child in five is overweight, and the number of overweight children continues to grow. Early childhood professionals are trying to help ensure that children gain the nutrition and wellness knowledge and behaviors they need to lead a healthy lifestyle. Educating children is only one part of the process. Helping them apply it to their lives is the other part. There are basically three reasons children become overweight. Genetic factors play a role. That is, some children may be genetically predisposed to be heavier than other children. Two factors that you, as an early childhood professional, have some control over are children's lack of physical activity and unhealthy eating habits.

WHAT DO CHILDREN EAT? The foods that two- to six-year-old children eat most often are somewhat different from foods eaten by older children and adults. For example, more of their meat group servings come from ground beef and luncheon meats, less from fish. Young children are more likely than adults to eat ready-to-eat cereals. Also, in comparison to older children and adults, young children are less likely to eat lettuce salads and more likely to eat green beans. They are also more likely to drink fruit juice than to eat whole fruit.

Overall, most young children are not consuming the recommended number of servings from the vegetable, fruit, grain, and meat groups. For example, two- to six-year-old children eat only about one and a half servings per day of vegetables, in comparison to the recommendation that they eat three servings a day. (Older children and adults also fail to eat the recommended number of servings of vegetables, eating only about two and a half of their recommended three to five servings per day.)

The federal government has published the Food Guide Pyramid for Young Children that is shown in Figure 10.2. This figure will help you help your students learn how to eat healthy and, hopefully, as a result, stay healthy. You can get further information about the Food Guide Pyramid and children's nutrition on the following Web site: http://www.usda.gov/cnpp/KidsPyra/index.htm. In addition, there are other things you can do to help children. For example, children who watch less television have less body fat, so perhaps you can influence your students to watch less television and participate in more physical activities.

The Future of Primary Education

Although the educational system in general is slow to meet the demands and dictates of society, it is likely the dramatic changes seen in primary education will continue in the next decade. The direction will be determined by continual reassessment of the purpose of educa-

Figure 10.2
Good Nutrition for Young Children

Source: U.S. Department of Agriculture.

tion and attempts to match the needs of society to the goals of schools. Substance abuse, child and family abuse, violence, and illiteracy are some of the societal problems the schools are being asked to address in significant ways.

Increasingly, schools are asked to prepare children for their places in the world of tomorrow. All early childhood programs must help children and youth develop the skills necessary for life success. Even with the trend toward having children spend more time in

... *video viewpoint*

They Are What They Eat

Children are not born with a taste for high-fat food. It is a learned behavior. But children are not often given better choices. Parents are appalled at what their children do not know about nutrition and at food manufacturers that do not necessarily offer the healthiest choices in their kid-attractive packages. Let loose in a supermarket to make their own choices, children will often choose high-calorie, high-fat food.

REFLECTIVE DISCUSSION QUESTIONS

Why do you think that, when given the opportunity, children select high-calorie, high-fat foods rather than "healthy" foods? Why do you think manufacturers produce and sell foods with higher fat content for children than adults? How are children's cartoon characters used to market children's foods? How does television advertising steer children toward "bad food choices"? What are some reasons children are eating more "unhealthy" foods? What is your reaction to the comment that there are no good or bad foods, that, eaten in moderation, any food is part of a well-balanced diet?

REFLECTIVE DECISION MAKING

Visit a local supermarket and read the fat, salt, and sugar content for foods marketed specifically for children. Make a list of the top fat, salt, and sugar foods for children. How can you work with parents to help them provide good nutritional meals for their children and other family members? What can you do in preschool and other early childhood settings to help children learn good nutritional practices? Conduct a survey of the foods that young children eat during the day. How many total grams of fat do you estimate they eat during a typical day? How does this compare with the 50 to 60 grams of fat recommended by nutritionists? Give specific examples of how manufacturers use food to promote and sell a particular product. What could you do as an early childhood educator to get children to eat more fruits and vegetables rather than fatty snacks?

school, we know that learning does not end with school and that children do not learn all they will need to know in an academic setting. It makes sense, therefore, to empower students with skills they can use throughout life in all kinds of interpersonal and organizational settings. Such skills include the following:

- The ability to communicate with others, orally and in writing.
- The ability to work well with people of all races, cultures, and personalities.
- The ability to be responsible for directing one's behavior.
- The desire and ability for success in life—measured not by earning a lot of money but by becoming a productive member of society.
- The desire and ability to continue learning throughout life.

End of Social Promotion

Not surprisingly, with the new directions in primary education there is also a new look at grade failure and retention practices. Retention as a cure for poor achievement or nonachievement is popular, especially with many professionals and the public. Despite the use of retention as a panacea for poor achievement, "the evidence to date suggests that achievement-based promotion does not deal effectively with the problem of low achievement."[20] Better and more helpful approaches to student achievement include the following strategies:

- Use promotion combined with individualized instruction.
- Promote to a transition class in which students receive help to master skills not previously achieved.
- Use after-school and summer programs to help students master skills.
- Provide children specific and individualized help in mastery of skills.
- Work with parents to teach them how to help their children work on mastery skills.
- Identify children who may need help before they enter first grade so that developmental services are provided early.
- Use multiage grouping as a means of providing for a broader range of children's abilities and to provide children the benefits that come from multiage grouping.
- Have a professional teach or stay with the same group of children over a period of several years as a means of getting to know children and their families and, as a result, better provide for children's educational and developmental needs. This approach is also called sustained instruction.
- Use a nongraded classroom. The nongraded classroom and nongraded institution go hand in hand. In the nongraded classroom, individual differences are recognized and accounted for. The state of Kentucky mandates that grades one through three be nongraded.

To take an online self-test on this chapter's contents, go to the Companion Website at http://www.prenhall.com/morrison, select chapter 10, then choose the Self Test module.

Advocates of nongraded classrooms offer the following advantages:

- Opportunities for individualized instruction.
- An enhanced social atmosphere—older children help younger children, and there are more opportunities for role modeling.
- Reduced or few, if any, retentions.
- Students do not have to progress through a grade-level curriculum in a lock-step approach with their age peers.

For additional Internet resources or to complete an online activity for this chapter, go to the Companion Website at http://www.prenhall.com/morrison, select chapter 10, then choose the Linking to Learning or Making Connections module.

Any effort to improve student achievement must emphasize helping children rather than using practices that threaten to detract from their self-image and make them solely responsible for their failure.

One thing is clear about the future of the primary grades: There will be more emphasis on academics, higher achievement, and helping students be successful.

Activities for Further Enrichment

Applications

1. Identify five contemporary issues or concerns facing society, and tell how teachers and primary schools could address each of them.
2. Explain how first grade children's cognitive and physical differences make a difference in how they are taught. Give specific examples.
3. Of the three primary grades, decide which you would most like to teach, and explain your reasons.
4. What do you think are the most important subjects of the primary grades? Why? What would you say to a parent who thought any subjects besides reading, writing, and arithmetic were a waste of time?

Field Experiences

1. Gather information from the Web sites provided in this chapter. Organize these by topics (e.g., character education). Put these in your teaching portfolio for future use.
2. Inquire whether there are schools in your area that have character education programs, use cooperative learning, or incorporate other curricula that seek to help children be better learners, persons, and citizens. Put information from these programs in your activity file or portfolio.

Research

1. Interview parents and teachers to determine their views pro and con of nonpromotion in the primary grades. Summarize your findings. What are your opinions on retention?
2. Compile a list of character traits that you believe are most important for teaching young children. Ask parents and community members what they believe are the most important traits. Compile a complete list.

Readings for Further Enrichment

Cunningham, P. *Phonics They Use: Words for Reading and Writing*, 3rd ed. Reading, MA: Addison Wesley Longman, 2000.

This text offers a coherent collection of practical, hands-on activities to help students develop reading and spelling skills. Stresses a balanced reading program—incorporating a variety of strategic approaches—tied to the individual needs of children.

Cunningham, P., and Allington, R. *Classrooms That Work: They Can All Read and Write*, 2nd ed. Reading, MA: Addison Wesley Longman, 1999.

Designed for courses that focus on instructional reading methods for at-risk and culturally diverse student populations, this inexpensive text assists preservice and in-service teachers in enriching the learning and reading skills of all children.

Glazer, J. *Literature for Young Children*, 4th ed. Upper Saddle River, NJ: Merrill/Prentice Hall, 2000.

This broad introduction to early childhood literature focuses on literary analysis and specific techniques and methods of effective literature-based education. Includes a number of valuable methods and suggestions that are designed to enhance both understanding and enjoyment of literature.

Ruddell, R. *Teaching Children to Read and Write: Becoming an Influential Teacher*, 2nd ed. Needham Heights, MA: Allyn & Bacon, 1999.

Central to this text is the real-world classroom; thus, theory and research is applied to literacy teaching through examples, instructional strategies, and illustrations—all intended to guide and support readers toward the goal of becoming an influential literacy teacher.

Linking to Learning

Baltimore County Public School

http://www.bcps.org

This program integrates the teaching of values throughout all curricular areas. Local school values committees are responsible for identifying a common core of values to be stressed for their school population. Materials include How to Establish a Values Education Program in your School: A Handbook for School Administrators.

Character Education

http://www.indiana.edu/~eric_rec/ieo/bibs/characte.html

An introductory exploration of Internet sources, journals, and books addressing the topic of character education.

Character Education Institute

www.charactereducationinfo.org

This organization distributes a character education curriculum designed to help pre-kindergarten through middle school students build self-esteem, avoid substance abuse, and develop critical thinking skills.

ENDNOTES

[1] Lawrence Kohlberg, "The Claim to Moral Adequacy of a Highest Stage of Moral Judgment," *Journal of Philosophy* 70(18), 630–646.

[2] S. Tishman, D. Perkins, and E. Jay, *The Thinking Classroom* (Boston: Allyn & Bacon 1995), 2.

[3] Adapted from "You CAN Teach Thinking Skills," by Scott Willis, from *Instructor,* February 1993. Copyright © 1993 by Scholastic, Inc. Reprinted by permission.

[4] Hilda Taba, *Teacher's Handbook for Elementary Social Studies* (Reading, MA: Addison-Wesley, 1967), 92–109.

[5] P. Kneedler, "California Assesses Critical Thinking." In A. Costa (ed.), *Developing Minds: A Resource Book for Teaching Thinking* (Alexandria, VA: Association for Supervision and Curriculum Development, 1985), 277.

[6] A. Woolfolk, *Educational Psychology* (Boston: Allyn & Bacon, 1995), 292.

[7] R. E. Slavin, "Cooperative Learning and the Cooperative School," *Educational Leadership* 45(1987), 7-13.

[8] R. Brandt, "On Cooperation in Schools: A Conversation with David and Roger Johnson," *Educational Leadership* 45(1987), 14-19.

[9] Slavin, "Cooperative Learning," 8-9.

[10] School-to-Work Initiative: http://www.stw.ed.gov/expsrch.cfm.

[11] T. Dansilp, "Teaching Students How to Become People No Simple Task," *The Nation* (October 12, 1999), C4.

[12] C. H. Keng, "Blame Parents for Delinquent Teens," *The Nation* (October 12, 1999), C4.

[13] C. Bennett, *Comprehensive Multicultural Education: Theory and Practice,* 4th ed. (Boston: Allyn & Bacon, 1998), 13. Copyright © 1998 by Allyn & Bacon. Reprinted by permission.

[14] The Character Education Partnership, *Eleven Principles of Effective Character Education,* 1997: (30 August 1997).

[15] Ibid.

[16] J. Lloyd Eldredge, *Teaching Decoding in Holistic Classrooms* (Upper Saddle River, NJ: Merrill/Prentice Hall, 1995), 5–6. Adapted by permission of Prentice Hall, Upper Saddle River, New Jersey.

[17] Centers for Disease Control and Prevention, http://www.cdc.gov.

[18] Ibid.

[19] Obesity is a Weighty Problem Among Children, http://wral-tv.com/features/healthteam/1998/0217-overweight-kids/

[20] Daniel Arnoux, Lauderhill (Florida) Middle School; Ilene Allgood, Adult Education Center, West Palm Beach, Florida; Gina Eyerman, Blanche Ely High School, Pompano Beach, Florida; Bradley Bluhm, Olympic Heights High School, Boca Raton, Florida; Carol Rivera, Park Ridge Elementary School, Pompano Beach, Florida; Ana Baez, Belle Glade, Florida. Personal communications, 1997.

PART IV

Guiding and Assessing Young Children

CHAPTER 11
Observing and Assessing Young Children:
Effective Teaching Through Appropriate Evaluation

CHAPTER 12
Guiding Children's Behavior:
Helping Children Become Responsible

CHAPTER 11

How we assess young children and the principles that frame such assessments need special attention. What works for older children or adults will not work for younger children; they have unique needs that we, as adults, are obliged to recognize if we are to optimize their development.

THE NATIONAL EDUCATION GOALS PANEL

Observing and Assessing Young Children

Effective Teaching Through Appropriate Evaluation

Focus Questions

1. What is assessment and why is it important?
2. Why is it important for professionals to know how to assess?
3. What are the purposes and uses of observation and assessment?
4. What are some major ways to assess children's development, learning, and behavior?
5. What issues are involved in assessment?

To review the chapter focus questions online, go to the Companion Website at http://www.prenhall.com/morrison and select chapter 11.

Kindergarten teacher Jesse Jones wants to make sure Amanda knows the initial beginning sounds that he has taught the class the last two weeks. First grade teacher Mindy McArthur wants to see how many words on the class word wall César is familiar with. Third grade teacher José Gonzalez wants to know if his class can apply what they're learning to real-life situations. Decisions, decisions, decisions.

The minutes, hours, and days are filled with assessment decisions. Questions abound: "What is Jeremy ready for now?" "What can I tell Maria's parents about her language development?" "The activity I used in the large group time yesterday didn't seem to work well. What could I have done differently?" Appropriate assessment can help you find the answers to these and many other questions relating to how to teach and what is best for children in all areas of development.

What Is Assessment?

To check your understanding of this chapter with the online Study Guide, go to the Companion Website at http://www.prenhall.com/morrison, select chapter 11, then choose the Study Guide module.

Much of children's lives are subject to and influenced by your assessment and the assessment of others. As an early childhood professional, assessment will influence your professional life and will be a vital tool of your professional practice. Assessment well done is one of your most important responsibilities, and it can benefit your children's learning.

Assessment is the process of collecting information about children's development, learning, health, behavior, academic progress, need for special services, and attainment. Figure 11.1 outlines the purposes of assessment.

Assessment occurs primarily through the following processes: observation, administration of commercial and teacher-made tests, and examination of students' products. You will probably use all three of these assessment procedures in your teaching. Keep in mind that all assessment procedures should help you inform your instruction so you can provide the best for all children. Your goal is to help children be successful.

What Is Appropriate Assessment?

For more information about the uses and abuses of assessment, go to the Companion Website at http://www.prenhall.com/morrison, select chapter 11, then choose the Linking to Learning module to connect to the Pathways to School Improvements site.

Today, early childhood professionals do their best to use assessment in appropriate ways—that is, to support children's learning. On the other hand, assessment and the results of assessment are often used inappropriately. One such example is the use of *high-stakes* assessment testing to make life-changing decisions about children. Two examples are noteworthy. In some cases, children are either admitted or not admitted to kindergarten or first grade based on the outcome of a test. In other cases, decisions about whether to promote children are based on the results of a national standardized test.

With so much emphasis on tests, it is understandable that the issue of testing and assessment raises many concerns on the part of parents and professionals. Critics maintain that the standardized testing movement reduces teaching and learning to the lowest common denominator—teaching children what they need to know to get the right answers. Many early childhood professionals believe that standardized tests do not measure children's thinking, problem-solving ability, creativity, or responsibility for their own learning. Furthermore, critics believe that group-administered, objectively scored, skills-focused tests—which dominate much of U.S. education—do not support (indeed, may undermine) many of the curricular reforms taking place today. Figure 11.2 identifies general principles of assessment of young children.

Purposes of Assessment As It Relates To:

Children

- Identify what children know
- Identify children's special needs
- Determine appropriate placement
- Select appropriate curricula to meet children's individual needs
- Refer children and, as appropriate, their families for additional services to programs and agencies

Families

- Help determine effectiveness of child's program

Early Childhood Professionals

- Make policy decisions regarding what is and what is not appropriate for children
- Determine how well and to what extent programs and services children receive are beneficial and appropriate

Early Childhood Programs

- Make lesson and activity plans
- Select materials
- Make decisions about how to implement learning activities
- Report to parents and families about children's developmental status and achievement
- Improve teaching–learning process

The Public

- Inform the public regarding children's achievement
- Provide information relating to students' schoolwide achievements
- Provide a basis for public policy (e.g., legislation, recommendations, and statements)

Figure 11.1
Purposes of Assessment

What Is Authentic Assessment?

Authentic assessment, also referred to as *performance-based assessment*, is conducted through activities that require children to demonstrate what they know and are able to do. Meaningless facts and isolated information are considered unauthentic. Authentic assessment has the following traits:

- *Assesses children on the basis of their actual work.* Work samples—often in a portfolio—exhibitions, performances, learning logs, journals, projects, presentations, experiments, and teacher observations are essential components of authentic assessment.
- *Provides for ongoing assessment over the entire school year.* Children's performance and achievement are continuously assessed, not just at the end of a grading period or at the end of the year through a standardized achievement test.

For more information about authentic assessment, go to the Companion Website at http://www.prenhall.com/morrison, select chapter 11, then choose the Linking to Learning module to connect to the Assessment and Standards on the Web site.

The following general principles should guide both policies and practices for the assessment of young children:

- **Assessment should bring about benefits for children.**
  Gathering accurate information from young children is difficult and potentially stressful. Formal assessments may also be costly and take resources that could otherwise by spent directly on programs and services for young children. To warrant conducting assessments, there must be a clear benefit—either in direct services to the child or in improved quality of educational programs.
- **Assessments should be tailored to a specific purpose and should be reliable, valid, and fair for that purpose.**
  Assessments designed for one purpose are not necessarily valid if used for other purposes. In the past, many of the abuses of testing with young children have occurred because of misuse. The recommendations in the sections that follow are tailored to specific assessment purposes.
- **Assessment policies should be designed recognizing that reliability and validity of assessments increase with children's age.**
  The younger the child, the more difficult it is to obtain reliable and valid assessment data. It is particularly difficult to assess children's cognitive abilities accurately before age 6. Because of problems with reliability and validity, some types of assessment should be postponed until children are older, while other types of assessment can be pursued, but only with necessary safeguards.
- **Assessment should be age-appropriate in both content and the method of data collection.**
  Assessments of young children should address the full range of early learning and development, including physical well-being and motor development; social and emotional development; approaches toward learning; language development; and cognition and general knowledge. Methods of assessment should recognize that children need familiar contexts to be able to demonstrate their abilities. Abstract paper-and-pencil tasks may make it especially difficult for young children to show what they know.
- **Assessment should be linguistically appropriate, recognizing that to some extent all assessments are measures of language.**
  Regardless of whether an assessment is intended to measure early reading skills, knowledge of color names, or learning potential, assessment results are easily confounded by language proficiency, especially for children who come from home backgrounds with limited exposure to English, for whom the assessment would essentially be an assessment of their English proficiency. Each child's first- and second-language development should be taken into account when determining appropriate assessment methods and in interpreting the meaning of assessment results.
- **Parents should be a valued source of assessment information, as well as an audience for assessment.**
  Because of the fallibility of direct measures of young children, assessments should include multiple sources of evidence, especially reports from parents and teachers. Assessment results should be shared with parents as part of an ongoing process that involves parents in their child's education.

Figure 11.2
General Principles of Assessment of Young Children

Source: The National Education Goals Panel, "Principles and Recommendations for Early Childhood Assessments," (December 14, 1998), pp. 5–6.

- *Is curriculum embedded.* Children are assessed on what they are actually doing in and through the curriculum.
- *Is a cooperative and collaborative process involving children, teachers, and in many cases parents.* This is an attempt to move away from teacher-focused assessment and to make assessment more child centered.
- *Is intended to help professionals and parents learn more about children.* All areas—social-emotional, language, cognitive, and physical—are assessed. The whole child is evaluated rather than a narrow set of skills. In this sense, it is child centered and humane.

- *Assesses what individual children are able to do.* Authentic assessment evaluates what they as individuals are learning, as opposed to comparing one child with another or children with children, as is so often the case.
- *Makes assessment part of the leaning process.* For example, one third grader, as part of a project on the community, visited the recycling center. She made a presentation to the class in which she used the overhead projector to illustrate her major points, displayed a poster board with pictures she had taken of the center, and presented several graphs to show which products were recycled most. In this way, she was able to demonstrate a broader range of what she had learned.

PORTFOLIOS. Today many teachers use portfolios—a compilation of children's work samples, products, and teacher observations collected over time—as a basis for authentic assessment. Decisions about what to put in portfolios vary, but examples include written work, artwork, audiotapes, pictures, models, and other materials that attest to what children are able to do. Some teachers let children put their best work in their portfolios; others decide with children what will be included; still others decide for themselves what to include. Portfolios are very useful especially during parent–teacher conferences. Such a portfolio includes your notes about achievement, teacher- and child-made checklists, artwork samples, photographs, journals, and other documentation.

In addition, some teachers are using technology to develop digital portfolios. These can stand alone or supplement the traditional portfolio. Digital portfolios include books and journals that children keep on computers and then illustrate with digital cameras. An important point to remember, and one often overlooked, is that portfolios are only one part of children's assessment.

Assessment for School Readiness

Because of federal mandates and state laws, many school districts assess children in some manner before or at the time of their entrance into school. Table 11.1 shows formal and informal methods for assessment.

Some type of screening occurs at the time of kindergarten entrance to evaluate learning readiness. Unfortunately, children are often classified on the basis of how well they perform on these early screenings. When assessment is appropriate and the results are used to design developmentally appropriate instruction, it is valuable and worthwhile.

For more information about assessment of young children, go to the Companion Website at http://www.prenhall.com/morrison, select any chapter, then choose Topic 7 of the ECE Supersite module.

Screening Processes

Screening measures give school personnel a broad picture of what children know and are able to do, as well as their physical and emotional status. As gross indicators of children's abilities, screening procedures provide much useful information for decisions about placement for initial instruction, referral to other agencies, and additional testing that may be necessary to pinpoint a learning or health problem. Many school districts conduct a comprehensive screening program in the spring for children who will enter kindergarten in the fall, which can involve the following:

- Gathering information from parents about their children's health, learning patterns, learning achievements, personal habits, and special problems
- Doing a health screening, including a physical examination, a health history, and a blood sample for analysis

Table 11.1
Formal and Informal Assessment Measures Used in Early Childhood

Assessment Instrument	Age/Grade Level	Purpose
Battelle Developmental Inventory	Birth to age 8	Assesses key developmental skills in children up to age 8.
Boehm Test of Basic Concepts—Revised	Kindergarten to Grade 2	Assesses children's mastery of basic concepts that are fundamental to understanding verbal instruction and necessary for early school achievement.
Brigance® Diagnostic Inventory of Basic Skills	Kindergarten to Grade 6	Assesses basic readiness and academic skills, measures and records performance, and serves as an aid in individualizing instruction.
Child Observation Record (COR)	Ages 2.2 to 6	Helps teachers and caregivers determine the developmental status of young children.
Denver Developmental Screening Test—Revised	1 month to age 6	Identifies infants and preschool children with serious developmental delays.
Developmental Indicators for the Assessment of Learning—Revised (DIAL–R)	Ages 2 to 6	Identifies children who may have special educational needs.
Peabody Individual Achievement Test	Kindergarten to Grade 12	Provides wide-range assessment in the content areas of general information, reading recognition, reading comprehension, mathematics, spelling, and written expression.
Peabody Picture Vocabulary Test–Revised	Ages 2 1/2 to 40	Tests hearing vocabulary; available in two forms.
Stanford-Binet Intelligence Scale	Ages 2 to 17	Measures verbal reasoning, quantitative reasoning, abstract/visual reasoning, and short-term memory.
Wechsler Intelligence Scale for Children–Revised	Ages 6 to 16	Shows a specific pattern of strengths and weaknesses (based on three IQ scores) to indicate how well the child is able to learn and whether there are any specific learning disabilities.
Wechsler Preschool and Primary Scale of Intelligence	Ages 4 to 6	Measures intelligence of children ages 4 to 6 1/2 years.

Sources: ERIC/AE Test Locator, *http://ericae.net/testcol.htm;* What Tests Would the School Psychologist Use?, *http://edcen.ehhs.cmich.edu/~mnesset/tests.html;* Sample ASSIST Print-Out, *http://www.agsnet.com/assist/*

- Doing a vision, hearing, and speech screening
- Collecting and analyzing data from former programs and teachers, such as preschools and child care programs
- Administering a cognitive and/or behavioral screening instrument

Comprehensive screening programs are conducted in one day or over several days. Data for each child are usually evaluated by a team of professionals who make instructional placement recommendations and, when appropriate, advise additional testing and make referrals to other agencies for assistance.

Many school districts conduct a comprehensive screening for children entering kindergarten, which may include tests of vision, hearing, and speech.

Screening Instruments and Observation Records

Several screening instruments provide information for grouping and planning instructional strategies. Most can be administered by people who do not have specialized training in test administration. Parent volunteers often help administer screening instruments, many of which can be administered in about thirty minutes.

BRIGANCE® K AND 1 SCREEN. BRIGANCE® K and 1 screen is an evaluation for use in kindergarten and grade one. The kindergarten pupil data sheet for the BRIGANCE® K and 1 screen shows the skills, behaviors, and concepts evaluated in the kindergarten portion of the screening instrument (Figure 11.3).

DIAL-R. The DIAL-R (Developmental Indicators for the Assessment of Learning-Revised) is an instrument designed for screening large numbers of prekindergarten children. Requiring approximately twenty-five to thirty minutes to administer, it involves individual observation for motor skills, concepts, and language skills. The screening team consists of a coordinator, an operator for each of the skills areas screened, and aides or volunteers to register parents and children.

THE HIGH/SCOPE CHILD OBSERVATION RECORD. The High/Scope Child Observation Record (COR) for ages two and a half to six is used by teachers and other observers to assess young children's development by observing their typical classroom activities.[1] The COR measures young children's progress in all facets of their development, whether or not the teacher is using the High/Scope curriculum. The High/Scope COR assesses the full variety of processes of young children's development of initiative, social relations, creative repre-

A. Student's Name *Colin Killoran* — Date of Screening: Year *2000* Month *6* Day *15* — School/Program *Vinal School*

Parents/Guardian *Kristin Killoran* — Birth date: *95* *1* *10* — Teacher *Leslie Feingold*

Address *310 Locke Street* — Age: *5* *5* *5* — Assessor *Dennis Dowd*

Page	Assessment Number	B. Basic Screening Assessments — Skill *(Circle the skill for each correct response and make notes as appropriate.)*	C. Scoring — Number of Correct Responses	Point Value	Student's Score
3	1A	**Personal Data Response:** Verbally gives: (1) first name (2) full name (3) age 4. address (street or mailing) 5. birth date (month and day)	*3*x	2 points each	*6*/10
4 & 5	2A	**Color Recognition:** (1) red (2) blue (3) green (4) yellow (5) orange 6. purple (7) brown (8) black (9) pink 10. gray	*8*x	1 point	*8*/10
6	3A	**Picture Vocabulary:** Recognizes and names pictures of: (1) dog (2) cat (3) key (4) girl (5) boy (6) airplane (7) apple (8) leaf 9. cup 10. car	*8*x	1 point each	*8*/10
7	4A	**Visual Discrimination–Forms and Uppercase Letters:** Visually discriminates which one of four symbols is different: (1) ○ (2) □ (3) ○ (4) ⬡ (5)) (6) O 7. I (8) P 9. V 10. X	*7*x	1 point each	*7*/10
8	5A	**Visual-Motor Skills:** Copies: (1) — (2) ○ (3) + (4) □ 5. △	*4*x	2 points ea.	*8*/10
9 & 10	6A	**Gross-Motor Skills:** (1) Hops two hops on one foot. (2) Hops two hops on the other foot (3) Stands on one foot momentarily. (4) Stands on the other foot momentarily. (5) Stands on one foot for five seconds. (6) Stands on the other foot for five seconds. (7) Walks forward heel-to-toe four steps. 8. Walks backward toe-to-heel four steps. (9) Stands on one foot momentarily with eyes closed. 10. Stands on the other foot momentarily with eyes closed.	*8*x	1 pt. ea.	*8*/10
11	7A	**Rote Counting:** Counts by rote to: (Circle all numbers prior to the first error.) (1) (2) (3) (4) (5) (6) 7 8 9 10	*6*x	.5 point each	*3*/5
12	8A	**Identifies Body Parts:** Identifies by pointing to or touching: (1) chin (2) fingernails (3) heels (4) ankles (5) jaw (6) shoulders (7) elbows 8. hips (9) wrists 10. waist	*8*x	.5 point each	*4*/5
13 & 14	9A	**Follows Verbal Directions:** Listens to, remembers, and follows: (1) one-step direction 2. two-step direction	*1*x	2.5 points each	*2.5*/5
15	10A	**Numeral Comprehension:** Matches quantity with numerals: (2) (1) (4) (3) 5	*4*x	2 points ea.	*8*/10
16	11A	**Prints Personal Data:** (Prints first name) Reversals: Yes ____ No *✓*	*1*x	5 points	*5*/5
17	12A	**Syntax and Fluency:** (1) Speech is understandable. (2) Speaks in complete sentences.	*2*x	5 points ea.	*10*/10
			Total Score:		*77.5*/100

D. Observations:

1. Handedness: Right *✓* Left ____ Uncertain ____
2. Grasps pencil with: Fist ____ Fingers *✓*
3. Hearing appeared to be normal: (See p. vii) Yes ____ No *✓* Uncertain ____
4. Vision appeared to be normal: (See p. vii) Yes *✓* No ____ Uncertain ____
5. Record other observations on another sheet.

E. Recommendations:

Ask nurse to check hearing. Below cutoff (<92).

Factor score 13.5 below at-risk guideline (<18).

Presence of risk factors. Rescreen in 6–9 months.

Figure 11.3

A Completed Kindergarten Pupil Data Sheet from BRIGANCE® K and 1 Screen

Source: From BRIGANCE® K and 1 Screen *(revised 1997). Curriculum Associates, Inc. BRIGANCE® is a registered trademark of Curriculum Associates®, Inc. Used by permission.*

sentation, music and movement, language and literacy, and logic and mathematics. It is not limited, as typical tests are, to language and mathematics questions to which there is only one right answer. The teacher directs a test and, using the COR, observes young children's self-initiated activities.

The teacher using the COR begins by observing children's activities throughout the program day and in the classroom, writing notes to describe these activities in developmental terms. In addition to identifying the date and the child, each note describes an activity succinctly but with relevant details. A typical note under "Initiative," for example, would read:

> (10/25) LaTanya wrote her name three times on the turn list so she could have three turns at the new math computer game.

The teacher collects these notes throughout the reporting period, which could be as brief as a month or as long as a semester, recording them on forms supplied for this purpose or, in the computer version, in easily retrievable data files. Using a Parent Report Form, the teacher reports to parents selected notes about their young children's development. This report is an opportunity for telling parents what their children are doing in the classroom and at home and allows parents and teachers to work together as partners to contribute to young children's development.

After collecting the notes, the teacher also uses them to rate each child's development, from level 1 to level 5, on each of thirty items. These items encompass the various aspects of development, from engaging in complex play and making friends to showing interest in reading, sorting, and counting objects. The item on expressing choices, for example, has the following four levels:

1. Child does not yet indicate choices to others.
2. Child indicates a desired activity or place of activity by saying a word, pointing, or some other action.
3. Child indicates desired activity, place of activity, materials, or playmates with a short sentence.
4. Child indicates with a short sentence how plans will be carried out ("I want to make a road out of blocks with Sara and drive a truck on it.")

The resulting scores indicate children's development in the various areas. Comparing children's developmental status at the beginning and end of a period indicates the progress during that period. In a study of sixty-four Head Start teaching teams, the High/Scope COR demonstrated evidence of its reliability and concurrent validity.[2]

What Is Observation?

Observation is one of the most widely used methods of assessment. Table 11.2 provides information and guidelines on observation and other informal methods of assessment.

> There is only one basis for observation: children must be free to express themselves and thus reveal those needs and attitudes that would otherwise remain hidden or repressed in an environment that did not permit them to act spontaneously. An observer obviously needs something to observe; and if he must be trained to be able to see and recognize the truth, he must also have at his disposal children placed in such an environment that they can manifest their natural traits.[3]

... voice from the field

Evaluating the Learning Process

I have used student portfolios to evaluate my kindergarten students for fifteen years. Over time, however, I have redefined their purpose and identified several criteria to make more effective use of portfolios. I believe that the value of student portfolios is to provide a record of each student's process of learning and therefore collect student work based on the following criteria:

- Portfolio entries reflect a student's cognitive, social, emotional, and physical development.
- They provide a visual record of a student's process of learning over time.
- They encourage input from students, teachers, and parents.

My students and I together select the work samples. Each portfolio also includes a parent questionnaire, parent responses to conferences, individual assessment profiles, and anecdotal records. Because the volume of materials that can accumulate in a portfolio can become overwhelming, I use a table of contents in the format of a checklist stapled inside the folder, which makes it easy to examine the contents and determine at a glance what data I have to make wise instructional decisions and what information I still need.

The success of student portfolios as an evaluation tool depends on the appropriate assessment of individual students and on accurate, conscientious documentation of student growth.

Appropriate Assessment. Appropriate assessment is the process of observing, recording, and documenting the work children do and how they do it. In my classroom, assessments are ongoing and occur as children perform daily classroom routines and participate in group time, share time, center time, and recess. I note which activities the children choose, how long they work on specific activities, and their process for completing activities. I observe students' learning styles, interest levels, skill levels, coping techniques, strategies for decision making and problem solving, and interactions with other children. Observations, however, have little value unless they are accurately documented.

Accurate Documentation. To manage documentation more accurately and efficiently, I have developed or adapted a variety of forms to make systematic assessments. Throughout the year, I use these assessment tools to systematically record information on individual children in each area of their development. I use a symbol to date the occurrence of behaviors and describe and document skill proficiency as appropriate. Emphasis is on what each child can do, and each child's progress is compared with his or her prior work. A I review these individual assessments I am able to quickly detect areas of growth.

Symbol System

+ = Progress is noted

√ = Needs more time and/or experience

* = See comments

In addition to the individual student profiles, I have also developed several class evaluation forms that allow me flexibility in recording observations quickly yet accurately. These forms are especially useful in planning group and/or individual instruction, and they provide additional documentation that supports the individual assessment records. For example, I make anecdotal records (on Post-It notes) of unanticipated events or behaviors, a child's social interactions, and problem-solving strategies. I transfer these Post-Its to a class grid so I can determine at a glance which children I have observed. The anecdotal records, along with the individual assessment profiles, become a part of each student's portfolio to be used for instructional planning and communicating with parents.

Throughout the year samples of students' work are dated and included in the portfolios. Quarterly work samples that I select include some that illustrate abilities with cutting activities, writing numbers (each child decides how far he or she can write), writing letters of the alphabet, and any words or stories a child can write independently (using either invented or conventional spelling). The children select samples of artwork and creative writing (e.g., journal entries, letters or drawings they have done for parents).

Use of Information. I use the information from student portfolios to plan classroom instruction for individuals and groups, to identify children who may need special help, and to confer with parents and colleagues. During conferences, I share with parents the student's assessment profile for the different areas of development, and together we examine samples of the child's work that support the assessment. Even though progress is visually obvious, I can also point out less obvious progress as we view the samples. I give conference response forms to parents and ask for comments or suggestions for additional portfolio entries. Using the portfolio, I am satisfied that I have gleaned an accurate assessment of and appreciation for each child's total development.

Contributed by Linda Sholar, Sangre Ridge Elementary School, Stillwater, Oklahoma.

Professionals recognize that children are more than what is measured by any particular test. Observation is an "authentic" means of learning about children—what they know and are able to do, especially as it occurs in more naturalistic settings such as classrooms, child care centers, playgrounds, and homes. *Observation* is the intentional, systematic act of looking at the behavior of a child or children in a particular setting, program, or situation. Observation is sometimes referred to as "kidwatching" and is an excellent way to find out about children's behaviors and learning.

Purposes of Observation

Observation is designed to gather information on which to base decisions, make recommendations, develop curriculum, plan activities and learning strategies, and assess children's growth, development, and learning. For example, when professionals and parents sometimes look at children, they do not really see or concern themselves with what the children are doing or why as long as they are safe and orderly. However, the significance and importance of critical behaviors go undetected if observation is done casually and is limited to "unsystematic looking." The purposes of observation then are these:

Table 11.2
Informal Methods for Assessment and Evaluation

Method	Purpose	Guidelines
Observation Kid watching—looking at children in a systematic way.	Enables teachers to identify children's behaviors, document performance, and make decisions.	Plan for observation and be clear about the purposes of the observation.
Authentic Is performance-based and is based on real-life activities.	Helps determine if children are applying what they have learned to real-life situations (e.g., making change).	Make sure that what is assessed relates to real-life events, that the learner is involved in doing something, and that instruction has been provided prior to assessment.
Anecdotal Record Brief narrative account of an event or behavior.	Provides insight into a particular reason for behavior and provides a basis for planning a specific teaching strategy.	Record only what is observed or heard; should deal with the facts and should include the setting (e.g., where the behavior occurs) and what was said and done.
Running Record Focuses on a sequence of events that occurs over time.	Helps obtain a more detailed insight into behavior over a period of time.	Maintain objectivity and try to include as much detail as possible.
Event Sampling Focuses on a particular behavior during a particular event (e.g., behavior at lunchtime, behavior on the playground, behavior in a reading group).	Helps identify behaviors during a particular event over time.	Identify a target behavior to be observed during particular times (e.g., fighting during transition activities).

- *To determine the cognitive, linguistic, social, emotional, and physical development of children.* Using a developmental checklist is one way professionals can systematically observe and chart the development of children. Figure 11.4 shows a checklist for emergent literacy.
- *To identify children's interests and learning styles.* Today, teachers are very interested in developing learning activities, materials, and classroom centers based on children's interests, preferences, and learning styles.
- *To plan.* The professional practice of teaching requires planning on a daily, ongoing basis. Observation provides useful, authentic, and solid information that enables teachers to intentionally plan for activities rather than to make decisions with little or no information.
- *To meet the needs of individual children.* Meeting the needs of individual children is an important part of teaching and learning. For example, a child may be advanced cogni-

Method	Purpose	Guidelines
Time Sampling Record particular events or behaviors at specific time intervals (e.g., five minutes, ten minutes).	Helps identify when a particular child demonstrates a particular behavior. Helps answer the question, "Does the child do something all the time or just at certain times and events?"	Observe only during the time period specified.
Rating Scale Contains a list for a set of behaviors.	Enables teachers to record data when they are observed.	Select the type of rating scale that is appropriate for what is rated. Make sure that key descriptors and the rating scale are appropriate for what is being observed.
Checklist A list of behaviors identifying what children can and cannot do.	Enables teachers to easily observe and check off what children know and are able to do.	Make sure that the checklist includes behaviors that are important for the program and for learning (e.g., counts from 1 to 10, hops on one foot).
Work Sample Collections of children's work that demonstrate what they know and are able to do.	Provides a concrete example of learning; can show growth and achievement over time.	Make sure that work samples demonstrate what children know and are able to do. Let children help select what items they want to use as examples of their learning.
Portfolio Collections of children's work samples.	Provides documentation of a child's achievement in specific areas over time. Can include test scores, writing work samples, videotapes, etc.	A portfolio is not a dumpster but a thoughtful collection of materials that documents learning over time.
Interview Engaging children in discussion through questions.	Children can be asked to explain behavior, work samples, or particular answers.	Ask questions at all levels of Bloom's taxonomy (see Chapter 10) in order to gain insight into children's learning at all levels.

tively but overly aggressive and lacking the social skills necessary to play cooperatively and interact with others. Through observation, a teacher can gather information to develop a plan for helping him learn how to play with others.

- *To determine progress*. Systematic observation, over time, provides a rich, valuable, and informative source of information about how individuals and groups of children are progressing in their learning and behavior.
- *To provide information to parents*. Professionals report to and conference with parents on an ongoing basis. Observational information adds to other information they have, such as test results and child work samples, and provides a fuller and more complete picture of individual children.
- *To provide self-insight*. Observational information can help professionals learn more about themselves and what to do to help children.

Program in Action

Observing Will

Welcome to Ms. Liz's classroom. Will is the child you will be observing. He is the energetic young boy dressed in overalls and a yellow shirt. You are encouraged to learn as much as you can about Will, his peers, his teacher (Ms. Liz), and the classroom. Before you focus on individual photographs, observe the classroom in general. Reflect on the following questions:

- What general statements would you make regarding classroom arrangement, organization, materials, and equipment? Based on your observation, what recommendations would you make if this was your classroom? Would you arrange your classroom differently?
- Based on your observation of the children's involvement with materials and their peers, what can you say about their development, social competence, and play behavior? How do the children and Ms. Liz get along?
- Do the children in the classroom feel comfortable taking risks, working together, and expressing emotions?
- Do you think Ms. Liz operates a child-centered classroom? How does your observation support your answer?
- Do you think the children spend more time participating in hands-on experiences or teacher-related experiences?
- Can Ms. Liz's classroom be characterized as an active learning environment? How and why?
- What can you infer regarding gender equity and the way boys and girls are treated in Ms. Liz's classroom?
- List five things children learn from large-motor activities. How does outdoor play support children's learning?

P-1

Literacy development is important in early childhood programs. In P-1, what is Ms. Liz doing to support the children's literacy development? What can you infer from the children's behavior regarding their literacy development? Note in P-2 how Ms. Liz supports Will's autonomy and "what he can do for himself." Based on your observation of P-3, what are five things Will knows about read-

P-2

ing? What do you notice about the behavior of Will's peers? What does their behavior indicate to you?

P-3

Personal Reflection. Focus once again on P-2. Do you agree with Ms. Liz allowing Will to take the picture book from her? Would you have allowed Will to read the book to the other children? What can Ms. Liz do to involve the other children in Will's retelling of the story?

P-4

In P-4 you see Will and his friend Ryan building a tall tower. What can you tell about Will's willingness to engage in cooperative play with other children? What can you infer from Will's behavior and facial expression about the activity? Observe how the top of the red tower is falling on the child behind Will.

Personal Reflection. Would you allow Will and his peers to build their tower as high as they are building it? Why or why not?

In P-5, observe how Will responds to the accident of the falling tower. What does Will's behavior tell you? What can you tell about Ms. Liz's behavior? What can you say about the behavior of Ryan (the child in the background behind Ms. Liz)?

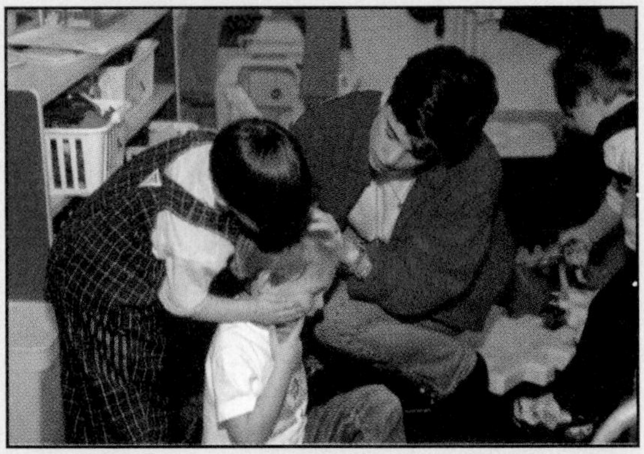

P-5

Personal Reflection. As a classroom teacher, how would you handle a situation in which a child was injured, though not seriously?

Personal Reflection. According to Mildred Parten (play researcher, now deceased) how would you categorize Will and Megan's play behavior in P-6? Based on your observation, what are some things that Will and Megan are learning? Are the materials appropriate for them to use?

P-6

Observe Will's determination and physical effort in P-7. What are some things you can learn through observation in the outdoors? What developmental skills is Will enhancing through his outdoor play?

P-7

Personal Reflection. What are some outdoor activities that you would include in your early childhood program? How would you provide for Will's safety and the safety of all children in outdoor play? What are some inferences you can make about outdoor safety?

P-8

In the parent–teacher conference depicted in P-8, observe Will's facial expression and body language. What do they tell you? Does Will's mother seem supportive of him?

Personal Reflection. Will is participating in the conference between Will's mother and Ms. Liz. Do you think he should be involved in the parent–teacher conference? Why or why not? Do you think Ms. Liz and Will's mother value Will's participation? What are the pros and cons of Will participating in the conference?

Merrill/Prentice Hall thanks Director Vicki Yun, Ms. Liz, Will Sims, and the children of LaPetite Academy in Dublin, Ohio. Photos by Anthony Magnacca.

Name:	Age	Observed	Not Observed
demonstrates visual acuity			
demonstrates hearing acuity			
Print Concepts			
recognizes left-to-right sequencing			
recognizes top, down directionality			
asks what print says			
connects meaning between two objects, pictures			
models reading out loud			
models adult silent reading (newspapers, books, etc.)			
recognizes that print has different meanings (informational, entertainment, etc.)			
Comprehension Behaviors			
follows oral directions			
draws correct pictures from oral directions			
recognizes story sequence in pictures			
interprets pictures			
sees links in story ideas			
links personal experiences with text (story, title)			
logically reasons story plot/conclusions			
sees patterns in similar stories			
Writing Behaviors			
makes meaningful scribbles (attempts to make letter-like shapes)			
draws recursive scribbles (rows of cursive-like writing)			
makes strings of "letters"			
uses one or more consonants to represent words			
uses inventive spellings			

Figure 11.4
Emergent Literacy Behaviors Checklist

Use this checklist to assess and date the student's progress as an emergent reader and writer.

Observing is an excellent way to find out about a child's behavior and how well he is learning. What do you think this teacher can learn about this child from watching him complete the puzzle?

Advantages of Intentional, Systematic Observation

There are a number of advantages to gathering data through observation:

- It enables professionals to collect information about children that they might not otherwise gather through other sources. A great deal of the consequences, causes, and reactions to children's behavior can be assessed only through observation. Observation enables you to gather data that cannot be assessed by formal, standardized tests; questioning; and parent and child interviews.
- Observation is ideally suited to learning more about children in play settings. Observation affords you the opportunity to note a child's social behavior in a play group and discern how cooperatively he or she interacts with peers. Observing a child at play gives professionals a wealth of information about developmental levels, social skills, and what the child is or is not learning in play settings.
- Observation allows you to learn a lot about children's prosocial behavior and peer interactions. It can help you plan for appropriate and inclusive activities to promote the social growth of young children. Additionally, your observations can serve as the basis for developing multicultural activities to benefit all children.
- Observation of children's abilities provides a basis for the assessment of what they are developmentally able to do. Many learning skills are developed sequentially, such as the refinement of large-motor skills before small-motor skills. Through observation, professionals can determine whether children's abilities are within a normal range of growth and development.
- Observation is useful to assess children's performance over time. Documentation of daily, weekly, and monthly observations of children's behaviors and learning provides a database for the cumulative evaluation of each child's achievement and development.

- Observation helps you provide concrete information for use in reporting to and conferencing with parents. Increasingly, reports to parents about children involve professionals' observations and children's work samples so parents and educators can collaborate to determine how to help children develop cognitively, socially, emotionally, and physically.

In summary, intentional observation is a useful, informative, and powerful means for informing and guiding teaching and for helping ensure the learning of all children.

Steps for Conducting Observations

The steps involved in the process of systematic, purposeful observation are listed in Figure 11.5. They include the following:

STEP 1: PLAN FOR OBSERVATION. Planning is an important part of the observation process. Everything you do regarding observation should be planned in advance of the observation. A good guide to follow in planning is to ask the questions *who*, *what*, *where*, *when*, and *how*.

Setting goals for observation is an important part of the planning process. Goals allow you to reflect on why you want to observe and thus direct your efforts to what you will observe. Stating a goal focuses your attention on the purpose of your observation. Goals, for example, that direct your attention to the effectiveness of your efforts in providing an inclusive classroom or program, and in fully including an exceptional child into the classroom, might read like this:

Goal 1: To determine what modifications might be necessary in the classroom to facilitate access to all parts of the classroom for Dana in her wheelchair.

Observing children at play enables teachers to learn about their developmental levels, social skills, and peer interactions. How might teachers use this information to plan future play-based activities?

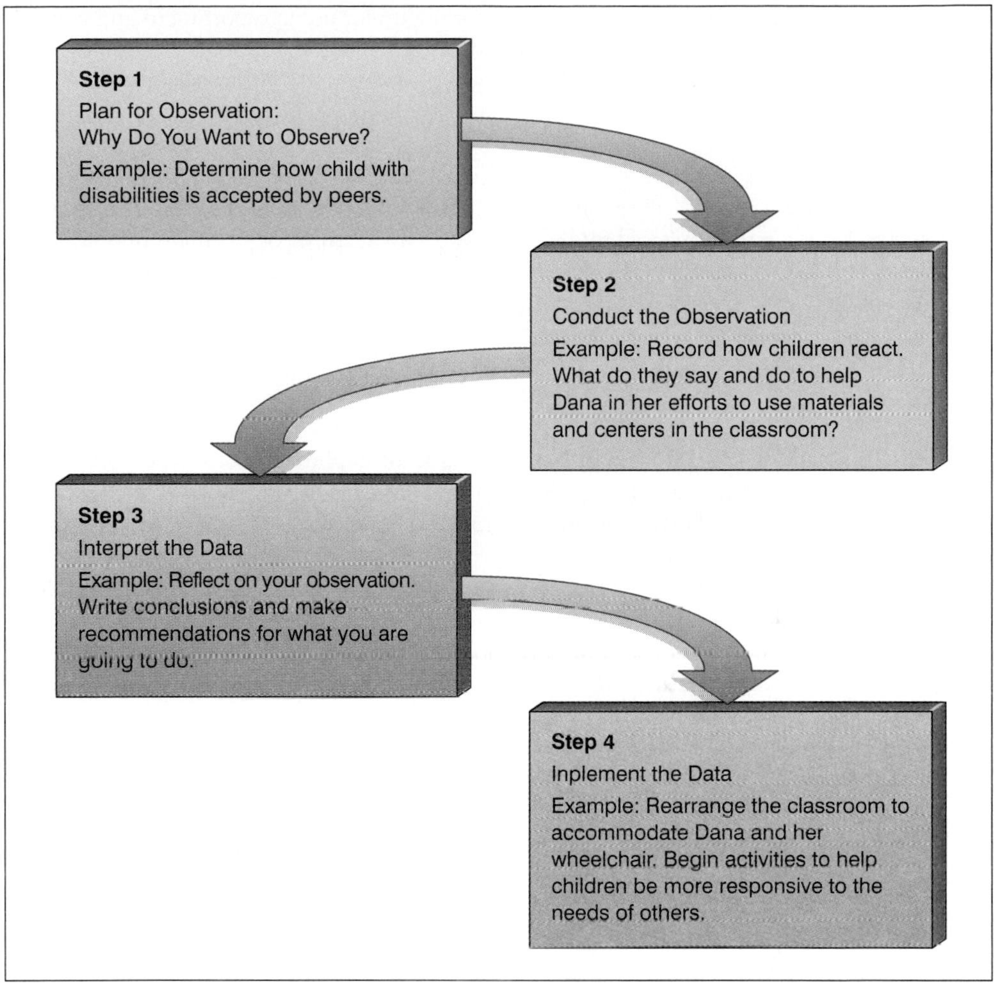

Step 1
Plan for Observation:
Why Do You Want to Observe?
Example: Determine how child with disabilities is accepted by peers.
Step 2
Conduct the Observation
Example: Record how children react. What do they say and do to help Dana in her efforts to use materials and centers in the classroom?
Step 3
Interpret the Data
Example: Reflect on your observation. Write conclusions and make recommendations for what you are going to do.
Step 4
Inplement the Data
Example: Rearrange the classroom to accommodate Dana and her wheelchair. Begin activities to help children be more responsive to the needs of others.

Figure 11.5
Four Steps for Effective Observation

Goal 2: To assess the development of prosocial behavioral characteristics that other children display to Dana while interacting in the classroom.

STEP 2: CONDUCT THE OBSERVATION. While conducting your observation, it is imperative that you be objective, specific, and as thorough as possible (see Figure 11.6). For example, during your observation of Dana and her peers you notice that there is not enough room for Dana to manipulate her wheelchair past the easel and shelf where the crayons are kept. None of her peers noticed that Dana could not reach the crayons and so did not help her get them. Dana had to ask one of the children to get the crayons for her.

STEP 3: INTERPRET THE DATA. All observations can and should result in some kind of interpretation. Interpretation serves several important functions. First, it puts your observations into perspective—that is, in relation to what you already know and do not know about events and the behaviors of your children. Second, interpretation helps you make sense of what you have observed and enables you to use your professional knowledge to

Several effective and efficient means for collecting observation information include:

- Carrying notecards and a pen for recording observations
- Developing and using a checklist of desired behaviors and actions
- Using a small, pocket-sized tape recorder for dictating your observations
- Finding areas in the classroom suitable for making observations
- Using a video camera to record your observations
- Sharing observation information, when appropriate, with the children, in order to probe the reasons behind their actions, behaviors, and language and to address their misconceptions about mathematics

Figure 11.6
Methods for Collecting Observation Information

Source: Thomasenia L. Adams, "Alternative Assessment in Elementary School Mathematics," Childhood Education *(Summer 1998), p. 222. Reprinted by permission of Thomasenia Adams and the Association for Childhood Education International, 17904 Georgia Avenue, Suite 215, Olney, MD. Copyright © 1998 by the Association.*

interpret what you have seen. Third, interpretation has the potential to make you learn to anticipate representative behavior indicative of normal growth and development under given conditions, and to recognize what might not be representative of appropriate growth, development, and learning for each child. Fourth, interpretation forms the foundation for the implementation, necessary adaptations, or modifications in a program or curriculum. In this observation, you can note that Dana's only exceptionality is that she is physically disabled. Her growth in other areas is normal, and she displays excellent social skills in that she is accepted by others, knows when to ask for help, and is able to ask for help. When Dana asks for help, she receives it.

STEP 4: IMPLEMENT THE DATA. The implementation phase means that you commit to do something with the results or the "findings" of your observation. For example, although Dana's behavior in your observation was appropriate, many of the children can benefit from activities designed to help them recognize and respond to the needs of others. The physical environment of the classroom as well requires some modification in the rearrangement of movable furniture to make it more accessible for Dana. Also, implementation means you report to parents or others. Implementing—that is, doing something with the results of your observations—is the most important part of the process.

Using an Observational Guide

Observation should help inform professionals and guide their teaching of young children. A sample observation form you can use is shown in Figure 11.7. You can also check other resources to develop more specific observation guides you could use as checklists to track developmental behaviors with individual children.

Reporting to and Communicating with Parents

Part of your responsibility as a professional is to report to parents about the growth, development, and achievement of their children. Some view reporting to parents as a bother and wish it was something they did not have to do. Nonetheless, reporting to and communicating with parents is one of the most important jobs of the early childhood professional. The fol-

Teacher's Name: ____________________

Date: ____________________

Time: ____________________

Location: ____________________

Classroom or Setting: ____________________

Purpose of Observing: ____________________

Prediction or Expectations of Findings: ____________________

Significant Events During Observation:

Reflective Analysis of Significant Events: (This reflection should include what you have learned.)

List at least three ways you can use or apply what you observed to your future teaching:

Figure 11.7
A Sample Observation Guide

lowing guidelines will help you meet this important responsibility of reporting your assessment information to parents:

- *Be honest and realistic with parents.* Too often, we do not want to hurt parents' feelings. We want to sugarcoat what we are reporting. However, parents need your honest assessments about what their children know, are able to do, and will be able to do.
- *Communicate to parents so they can understand.* What we communicate to parents must make sense to them. They have to understand what we are saying. Reporting to parents often has to be a combination of written (in their language) and oral communication.
- *Provide parents with ideas and information that will help them help their children learn.* Remember that you and parents are partners in helping children be successful in school and life.

Report your assessment findings accurately and honestly to the parents of your students. How might such communication build trust?

What Are the Issues in the Assessment of Young Children?

As with almost everything that has been talked about and will be talked about in this book, issues surround essential questions about what is good practice, what is inappropriate practice, and what is best for children and families. Assessment is no different regarding critical issues.

For more information about assessment issues that relate to young children, go to the Companion Website at http://www.prenhall.com/morrison, select chapter 11, then choose the Linking to Learning module to connect to the National Education Goals Panel site.

Assessment and Accountability

There is a tremendous emphasis on testing and the use of tests to measure achievement for comparing children, programs, school districts, and countries. This emphasis will continue for a number of reasons. First, the public, including politicians and legislatures, sees assessment as a means of making schools and teachers accountable for teaching the nation's children. Second, assessment is seen as playing a critical role in improving education. The view is that assessment results can be used as a guide for determining how the curriculum and instructional practices can be used to increase achievement. Therefore, as long as there is a public desire to improve teaching and achievement, we will continue to see an emphasis on assessment for accountability purposes.

High-Stakes Testing

We have previously talked about high-stakes testing. This kind of testing occurs when standardized tests are used to make important, and often life-influencing, decisions about chil-

To take an online self-test on this chapter's contents, go to the Companion Website at http://www.prenhall.com/morrison, select chapter 11, then choose the Self Test module.

dren. Standardized tests have specific and standardized content, administration and scoring procedures, and norms for interpreting scores. High-stakes outcomes include decisions about whether to admit children into programs (e.g., kindergarten) and whether to retain or promote children. Generally, the early childhood profession is opposed to high-stakes testing for children through grade three. However, as part of the accountability movement, many politicians and school administrators view high-stakes testing as a means of making sure that children learn and that promotions are based on achievement. Many school critics maintain that in the pre-K and primary grades there is too much social promotion—that is, passing children from grade to grade merely to enable students to keep pace with their age peers.

As an early childhood professional, part of your responsibility is to be an advocate for the appropriate use of assessment. You will make ongoing, daily decisions about how best to assess your children and how best to use the results of assessment.

Some states (at least ten) are tying teacher salaries to student achievement. This process is called "pay for performance." In 1999, Denver, Colorado, city schools became the first in the nation to tie student performance to teacher pay.[4] Many school districts allow their teachers to receive extra compensation or bonuses if their schools meet certain student achievement goals. These programs will increase in other states and school districts across the country. Such plans are based on measuring student achievement with standard tests, and this means more testing for all students at all ages.

For additional Internet resources or to complete an online activity for this chapter, go to the Companion Website at http://www.prenhall.com/morrison, select chapter 11, then choose the Linking to Learning or Making Connections module.

Test Bias

Many contend that many school district testing programs, as they are currently structured, do not allow all children to show what they are able to do. There are many gender and ethnic biases in test performance. What is needed are testing programs that include different ways of testing children so that all students are able to demonstrate what they know and are able to do.

Today there is a great deal of emphasis on accountability. Teachers are asked to be accountable to parents, legislators, and the public. Providing for and conducting developmentally appropriate assessment of young children and their programs is one of the best ways that you can be accountable for what you do. Conducting appropriate assessment not only enables you to be accountable to parents and the public, it also enables you to be accountable to young children. You have accepted a sacred trust and have dedicated your life to helping children learn and develop. Effective assessment practices will help you achieve this goal.

Activities for Further Enrichment

Applications

1. Create a developmental checklist similar to Figure 11.4. Watch an early childhood classroom and determine how effective you are at observing some aspect of children's development and learning.
2. Observe a particular child during play or another activity. Before your observation make sure you follow the steps reviewed in this chapter. Use the information you gathered to plan a learning activity for the child. As you plan, determine what information you need that you didn't gather through observation. When you observe again, what will you do differently?
3. Observe a program that is providing services for children with disabilities. Your purpose is to determine what accommodations need to be made for them.

Field Experiences

1. Interview several kindergarten and primary teachers and ask them for ideas and guidelines for how to assess with portfolios. Which ideas can you use?

2. Review the contents of several children's portfolios. How are they similar and different? What do the contents tell you about the children?

Research

1. Frequently there are articles in newspapers and magazines about assessment and testing. Over a two-week period, review these sources and determine what assessment and evaluation issues are "in the news." Put these materials in your portfolio or teaching file.

2. Visit pre-k–3 programs in several different school districts. Make a list of the various ways they assess and of the instruments and procedures they use. Compare them with the ones identified in this chapter. How and for what purposes are the tests used? What conclusions can you draw from the information you gathered?

Readings for Further Enrichment

Chase, C. *Contemporary Assessment for Educators.* New York: Longman, 1999.

This text focuses on providing a basic foundation of knowledge about assessment with strong applications to real classroom settings. Designed specifically to guide teachers in the creation and management of classroom assessment and to assist them in interpreting and understanding published assessment results.

Gredler, M. *Classroom Assessment and Learning.* New York: Longman, 1999.

The book redirects assessment—whether quantitatively or qualitatively based—back to the classroom. Students will benefit by learning how assessment models can be constructed and used to guide teacher decision making and student learning. Emphasizes the role assessment plays in stimulating cognitive advancement.

Puckett, M., and Black, J. *Authentic Assessment of the Young Child: Celebrating Development and Learning*, 2nd ed. Upper Saddle River, NJ: Merrill/Prentice Hall, 2000.

While retaining its strong emphasis on child growth and development, this edition has been expanded to include new information on learner-centered approaches. This text is based on the idea that teaching, learning, and assessment are parts of a single ongoing process that provides meaningful, authentic learning experiences for children.

Linking to Learning

ARCNet

http://tiger.coe.missouri.edu/~arcwww/arcnet.html

The Web site created for anyone interested in the world of assessment.

Assessment and Standards on the Web

http://www.kane.k12.il.us/Links/AssmtLinks.html#anchor41851014

Includes links to several Web sites on the topic of assessment. Sites include Appropriate and Authentic Assessment; *also links to topics regarding current standards on this issue.*

National Education Goals Panel

http://www.negp.gov/

Provides a variety of early childhood reports, including "Reconsidering Children's Early Development and Learning," "Getting a Good Start in School," "Ready Schools," "Principles and Recommendations for Early Childhood Assessments," and "Trends in Early Childhood Assessment Policies and Practices."

Pathways to School Improvement on the Web

http://www.ncrel.org/sdrs/areas/issues/students/earlycld/ea500.htm

A Web site containing information on current issues, including assessment of the progress and attainments of young children three to eight years of age and the uses and abuse of assessment.

ENDNOTES

1 High/Scope Educational Research Foundation, *High/Scope Child Observation Record (COR) for Ages 2½ to 6* (Ypsilanti, MI: Author, 1992).

2 L. J. Schweinhart, S. McNair, H. Barnes, and M. Larner, "Observing Young Children in Action to Assess Their Development: The High/Scope Child Observation Record Study," *Educational and Psychological Measurement,* 53(Summer), 445–455.

3 M. Montessori, *The Discovery of the Child* (New York: Ballantine Books, 1980), 46.

4 Ann Bradley, "Denver Teachers to Pilot Pay-for-Performance Plan," *Education Week* (September 22, 1999), 5.

CHAPTER 12

*Kind words are short and easy to speak,
but their echoes are truly endless.*

MOTHER TERESA

Guiding Children's Behavior

Helping Children Become Responsible

Focus Questions

1. Why is it important to help children guide their own behavior?
2. What are important elements in helping children guide their behavior?
3. Why is developing a philosophy of guiding children's behavior important?
4. What are different theories of guiding children's behavior?
5. What are important trends and issues in children's behavior guidance?

To review the chapter focus questions online, go to the Companion Website at http://www.prenhall.com/morrison and select chapter 12.

A glance at daily newspapers tells volumes about the crises of violence and crime facing children and society. Consider these news headlines:

"What Is Justice for a Sixth-Grade Killer?" *Time*, April 6, 1998

"12-Year-Old Accused in Los Angeles Murder, Rape," CNN, August 2, 1996

"Boys, 7 and 8, to Stand Trial in Beating Death," CNN, August 11, 1998

Additionally, recent U.S. juvenile crime statistics illustrate the seriousness of the problem. For example:

> Thirty-two percent of juvenile arrests have involved youths below the age of 15. These young juveniles were involved in 11 percent of all juvenile murder arrests, 38 percent of forcible rapes, 26 percent of robberies, 33 percent of aggravated assaults, 38 percent of burglaries, 42 percent of larceny-thefts, 26 percent of motor vehicle thefts, 31 percent of weapons carrying, 16 percent of drug law violation arrests, and 67 percent of arsons.[1]

This information paints a pretty grim picture of the nation's youth. Local and national news media underscore public and professional interest in children's behaviors at home, on the streets, and in early childhood programs. The public sees children, at ever younger ages, being mean and nasty to their peers and adults. We also see young children as victims of violence and crime by ever younger children.

Who is to blame? Certainly parents receive their share. The public believes parents have the responsibility for rearing their children well and with the manners and morals necessary for civilized living. But the public also blames the educational system for allowing and even promoting uncivilized behavior. Parents interpret children's misbehavior as one indicator that educators have gone "soft" on discipline. Schools are accused of not managing children's behavior and not teaching them the manners, morals, and behavior necessary for living in civilized society.

Contemporary society also receives its share of blame for the way children act. There is national concern about the breakup of the family, the breakdown of moral standards, violence on television, proliferation of R-rated movies, violent video games, objectionable song lyrics, widespread substance use, rampant crime, and general disrespect for authority. These trends are seen as evidence of parental and societal erosion of authority and discipline beginning in the earliest years. Again, many believe that current social ills are caused by parents' and educators' failure to discipline children.

The present and future behavior and misbehavior of children is the subject of much debate. Parents and the public look to early childhood professionals for assistance in helping children learn how to live cooperatively and civilly in a democratic society.

To check your understanding of this chapter with the online Study Guide, go to the Companion Website at http://www.prenhall.com/morrison, select chapter 12, then choose the Study Guide module.

What Is Guiding Behavior?

As a society, we believe discipline by parents and teachers is one solution to children's misbehavior. But what does the term *discipline* mean? *Discipline* comes from the Latin *disciplina*, which means "to instruct or teach." And this is the purpose of teaching and parenting—to teach children how to guide and direct their behavior and get along with others. The empha-

sis is on teaching children how to become responsible for guiding and directing their own behavior.

Guiding children's behavior is a process of helping children build positive behaviors. Discipline is not about compliance and control but involves *behavior guidance*, a process by which all children learn to control and direct their behavior and become independent and self-reliant. In this view, behavior guidance is a process of helping children develop skills useful over a lifetime. Professionals' and parents' roles in behavior guidance are to (1) help children solve problems, (2) help children be problem solvers, (3) guide children toward developing self-control, (4) encourage children to be independent, (5) meet children's intellectual and emotional needs, (6) establish expectations for children, (7) organize appropriate behaviors and arrange environments so self-discipline can occur, and (8) change their own behavior when necessary. The result will be *self-regulation*, whereby students are able to plan, monitor, and guide their own thinking, feeling, and behavior.

The goal of most parents and early childhood professionals is to have children behave in socially acceptable and appropriate ways that contribute to and promote living in a democratic society. Professionals should view guidance of children's behavior as a process of learning by doing. Children cannot learn to develop appropriate behaviors and learn to be responsible by themselves. Just as no one learns to ride a bicycle by reading a book on the subject, children do not learn to guide themselves by being told what to do all the time. Discipline is not telling but modeling and helping. Children must be shown and taught through precept and example. They need opportunities to develop, practice, and perfect their abilities to control and guide their own behavior. They need the guidance, help, support, and encouragement of parents and early childhood professionals.

How can professionals achieve these goals? Effective guidance of children's behavior at home and in early childhood programs consists of these essential elements:

- Know yourself.
- Know child development.
- Meet children's needs in individually and culturally appropriate ways.
- Help children build new behaviors and skills of independence and responsibility.
- Establish appropriate expectations.
- Arrange and modify the environment so that appropriate, expected behavior and self-control are possible.
- Model appropriate behavior.
- Provide guidance.
- Avoid creating or encouraging behavior problems.
- Develop a partnership with parents, families, and others who are responsible for children.
- Promote empathy and prosocial behavior.
- Teach cooperative living and learning.
- Use conflict management and resolution techniques.

Let us take a closer look at each of these essential elements in guiding children's behavior.

Parents and early childhood professionals have an obligation to help children learn correct behaviors by guiding their actions and modeling appropriate behavior. What role does setting rules play in guiding behavior?

Know Yourself

The first rule in guiding children's behavior is to know yourself. Unless you know your attitudes toward discipline and behavior, it will be hard to practice a rational and consistent program of guidance and discipline, and consistency plays a major role in teaching and guiding. Therefore, develop a philosophy about what you believe concerning child rearing, discipline, and children. There are many child-rearing/guidance approaches available. Knowing what you want for your children at home and school helps you decide which approach to select.

Knowing yourself and what you believe also makes it easier for you to share with parents, help them guide behavior, and counsel them about discipline. Today, many parents find the challenges of child rearing overwhelming. They do not know what to do and consequently look to professionals for help. Knowing what you believe, based on sound principles of how children grow, develop, and learn, enables you to work confidently with parents.

Know Child Development

It may be overstating the obvious, but the foundation for guiding all children is to know what they are like—how they grow and develop. Unfortunately, not all early childhood professionals are as knowledgeable about children as they should be. As a result, they may expect some children to behave in ways that are more appropriate for younger or older children. Here lies part of the problem of not being able to help children guide their behavior: children cannot behave well when adults expect too much or too little of them based on their development or when they expect them to behave in ways inappropriate for them as individuals. So, a key for guiding children's behavior is to *really know what they are like.*

Meet Children's Needs

Part of knowing children and child development is knowing and meeting their needs. Abraham Maslow felt that human growth and development was oriented toward *self-actualization*, the

striving to realize one's potential. Maslow felt that humans are internally motivated by five basic needs that constitute a hierarchy of motivating behaviors, progressing from physical needs to self-fulfillment. Maslow's hierarchy (see chapter 7 for a graphic representation of this hierarchy) moves through physical needs, safety and security needs, belonging and affection needs, and self-esteem needs, culminating in self-actualization. Let us look at an example of each of these stages and behaviors to see how we can apply them to guiding children's behavior.

PHYSICAL NEEDS. Children's abilities to guide their behavior depend in part on how well their physical needs are met. Children do their best in school, for example, when they are well nourished. Thus, parents should provide for their children's nutritional needs by giving them breakfast. Early childhood professionals should also stress the nutritional and health benefits of eating breakfast. Information on recent brain research provided in chapter 2 also informs us about nutrition and the brain. For example, the brain needs protein and water to function well. Many schools allow children to have water bottles at their desks and allow them to have frequent nutritional snacks.

The quality of the environment is also important. Children cannot be expected to "behave" if classrooms are dark and noisy and smell of stale air. Children also need adequate rest to do and be their best. The amount of rest is an individual matter, but many young children need eight to ten hours of sleep each day. A tired child cannot meet many of the expectations of schooling.

SAFETY AND SECURITY. Children can't learn in fear. They should not have to fear parents or professionals and should feel comfortable and secure at home and at school. Asking or forcing children to do school tasks for which they do not have the skills makes them feel insecure, and children who are afraid and insecure are under a great deal of tension. Consider also the dangers many urban children face, such as crime, drugs, and homelessness, or the insecurity of children who live in an atmosphere of domestic violence. So, in addition, part of guiding children's behavior includes providing safe and secure communities, neighborhoods, homes, schools, and classrooms.

BELONGING AND AFFECTION. Children need love and affection and the sense of belonging that comes from being given jobs to do, having responsibilities, and helping make classroom and home decisions. Love and affection needs are also satisfied when parents hold, hug, and kiss their children and tell them, "I love you." Professionals meet children's affectional needs when they smile, speak pleasantly, are kind and gentle, treat children with courtesy and respect, and genuinely value each child for whom she or he is. An excellent way to show respect for children and demonstrate to them belonging and affection is to greet them personally when they come into the classroom, center, or home. A personal greeting helps children feel wanted and secure and promotes feelings of self-worth. In fact, all early childhood programs should begin with this daily validation of each child.

SELF-ESTEEM. Children who view themselves as worthy, responsible, and competent act in accordance with these feelings. Children's views of themselves come primarily from parents and early childhood professionals. Experiencing success gives them feelings of high self-esteem, and it is up to parents and professionals to give all children opportunities for success. The foundations for self-esteem are success and achievement.

SELF-ACTUALIZATION. Children want to use their talents and abilities to do things for themselves and be independent. Professionals and parents can help children become independent by helping them learn to dress themselves, go to the restroom by themselves, and take care of their environments. They can also help children set achievement and behavior goals ("Tell me what you are going to build with your blocks") and encourage them to evaluate their behavior ("Let's talk about how you cleaned up your room").

These points highlight the basic needs professionals and parents must consider when guiding children and helping them develop responsibility for their behavior.

Help Children Build New Behaviors

Helping children build new behaviors means that we help them learn that they are primarily responsible for their own behavior and that the pleasures and rewards for appropriate behavior are internal, coming from within them as opposed to always coming from outside (i.e., from the approval and praise of others). We refer to this concept as *locus of control*—the source or place of control. The preferred and recommended locus of control for young and old alike is internal.

For strategies preschoolers can use to get along with others, go to the Companion Website at http://www.prenhall.com/morrison, select chapter 12, then choose the Linking to Learning module to connect to the National Network for Child Care site.

Children are not born with this desired inner-directed locus of control. The process of developing an internal locus of control begins at birth, continues through the early childhood years, and is a never-ending process throughout life. We want children to control their own behavior. When their locus of control is external, children are controlled by others; they are always told what to do and how to behave. Parents and professionals must try to avoid developing an external locus of control in children.

One criticism of programs and practices in which children's behaviors are constantly reinforced through praise and rewards is that this approach promotes an external locus of control. The argument goes that children behave only because someone else is telling them to and rewarding them for the behavior. However, rewards, such as genuine praise and other means of reinforcement, are entirely proper when used wisely and appropriately. Everyone likes praise, and there should be praise for honest efforts. I will discuss this point further shortly.

EMPOWER CHILDREN. Helping children build new behaviors creates a sense of responsibility and self-confidence. As children are given responsibility, they develop greater self-dis-

Helping children become more independent by warmly supporting their efforts is one of the most effective forms of guidance. Identify some ways professionals can support children's efforts to do things for themselves.

cipline, so early childhood professionals and parents have to provide less guidance. Some professionals and parents hesitate to let children assume responsibilities, but without responsibilities, children are bored and frustrated and become discipline problems—the very opposite of what is intended. Guidance is not a matter of adults getting children to please them by making remarks such as, "Show me how perfect you can be," "Don't embarrass me by your behavior in front of others," "I want to see nice groups," or "I'm waiting for quiet."

To reiterate, guiding behavior is not about compliance and control. Rather, it is important to instill in children a sense of independence and responsibility for their own behavior. For example, you might say, "You have really worked a long time cutting out the flower you drew. You kept working on it until you were finished. Would you like some tape to hang it up with?"

Parents and early childhood professionals can do a number of things to help children develop new behaviors that result in empowerment:

- *Give children responsibilities.* All children, from an early age, should have responsibilities—that is, tasks that are their job to do and for which they are responsible. Being responsible for completing tasks and doing such things as putting toys and learning materials away promote a positive sense of self-worth and convey to children that in a community people have responsibilities for making the community work well.
- *Give children choices.* Life is full of choices—some require thought and decisions; others are automatic, based on previous behavior. But every time you make a decision, you are being responsible and exercising your right to decide. Children like to have choices, and choices help them become independent, confident, and self-disciplined. Learning to make choices early in life lays the foundation for decision making later. Guidelines for giving children choices are as follows:
  - Give children choices when there are valid choices to make. When it comes time to clean up the classroom, do not let children choose whether they want to participate, but let them pick between collecting the scissors or the crayons.
  - Help children make choices. Rather than say, "What would you like to do today?" say, "Sarah, you have a choice between working in the woodworking center or the computer center. Which would you like to do?"
  - When you do not want children to make a decision, do not offer them a choice.
- *Support children.* As an early childhood professional, you must support children in their efforts to be successful. Arrange the environment and make opportunities available for children to be able to do things. Successful accomplishments are a major ingredient of positive behavior.

Making choices is key for children developing responsible behavior that internalizes their locus of control.

Establish Appropriate Expectations

Expectations relate to and set the boundaries for desired behavior. They are the guideposts children use in learning to direct their own behavior. Like everyone, children need guideposts along life's way.

Early childhood professionals and parents need to set appropriate expectations for children, which means they must decide what behaviors they expect of them. When children know what adults expect, they can better achieve those expectations. Up to a point, the more we expect of children, the more and better they achieve. Generally, we expect too little of most children.

In a High/Scope classroom (see chapter 6), children are encouraged to make choices about what activities they will engage in. Giving children choices is an excellent way to help them develop independence and responsibility.

However, having expectations for children is not enough. Early childhood professionals have to help children know and understand what the expectations are and help them meet these expectations. Some children will need little help in meeting expectations; others will need demonstration, explanation, encouragement, and support as they learn.

SET LIMITS. Setting limits is closely associated with establishing expectations and relates to defining unacceptable behavior. For example, knocking over a block tower built by someone else and running in the classroom are generally considered unacceptable behaviors. Setting clear limits is important for three reasons:

For more information about guiding children's behavior, go to the Companion Website at http://www.prenhall.com/morrison, select chapter 12, then choose the Linking to Learning module to connect to the Virginia Cooperative Extension site.

1. It helps you clarify in your own mind what you believe is unacceptable, based on your knowledge of child development, children, their families, and their culture. When you do not set limits, inconsistency can occur.
2. Setting limits helps children act with confidence because they know which behaviors are acceptable.
3. Limits provide children with security. Children want and need limits.

As children grow and mature, the limits change and are adjusted to developmental levels, programmatic considerations, and life situations.

CLASSROOM RULES. Although I like to talk about and think in terms of expectations and limits, some early childhood professionals think and talk about rules. This is fine, but here are some additional guidelines about rules.

Plan classroom rules from the first day of class. As the year goes on, you can involve children in establishing classroom rules, but in the beginning, children want and need to know what they can and cannot do. For example, rules might relate to changing groups and bathroom routines. Whatever rules you establish, they should be fair, reasonable, and appro-

priate to the children's age and maturity. Keep rules to a minimum; the fewer the better. For example, the following would be appropriate guidelines for four-year-olds:

1. Be gentle with your friends.
2. We are all friends at school.
3. Use an inside voice.
4. Use your words when you have a problem.

You would remind children of these rules and encourage them to conform to them. Four-year-olds can realistically be expected to follow these guidelines, so there is less chance for misbehavior. Children are able to become responsible for their own behavior in a positive, accepting atmosphere where they know what the expectations are. Review the rules, and have children evaluate their behavior against the rules. You can have expectations without having rules. If you have activities ready for children when they enter the classroom, you establish the expectation that on arriving, they should be busy.

Arrange and Modify the Environment

Environment plays a key role in children's ability to guide their behavior. For example, if parents want a child to be responsible for taking care of his room, they should arrange the environment so he can do so, by providing shelves, hangers, and drawers at child height. Similarly, arrange your classroom so children can get and return their own papers and materials, use learning centers, and have time to work on individual projects.

In child care centers, early childhood classrooms, and family day care homes, early childhood professionals arrange the environment so that it supports the purposes of the program and makes appropriate behavior possible. Room arrangement is crucial to guiding children's behavior, and appropriate room arrangements signal to children that they are expected to guide and be responsible for their own behavior. Additionally, the appropriate environment enables teachers to observe and provide for children's interests through their selection of activities. Furthermore, it is easier to live and work in an attractive and aesthetically pleasing classroom or center. We all want a nice environment—children should have one, too. The following guidelines can be helpful to you as you think about and arrange your classroom or program area to support your efforts toward helping children guide their own behavior.

- Have an open area in which you and your children can meet as a whole group. This area is essential for story time, general class meetings, and so on. Starting and ending the day with a class meeting allows children to discuss their behavior and say how they and others can do a better job.
- Center areas should be well defined and accessible to children and have appropriate and abundant materials for children's use. Also, center boundaries should be low enough so that you and others can see over them for proper supervision and observation.
- Provide for all kinds of activities, both quiet and loud. Try to locate quiet areas together (reading area and puzzle area) and loud centers together (woodworking and blocks).
- Locate materials so that children can easily retrieve them. When children have to ask for materials, this promotes dependency and can lead to behavior problems.

- Materials should be easily stored, and children should put them away. A general rule of thumb is that there should be a place for everything and everything should be in its place when not in use.
- Provide children with guidelines for how to use centers and materials.

THE CLASSROOM AS REINFORCER. You also can apply behavior modification strategies to the physical setting of the classroom, arranging it so that it is conducive to the behaviors you want to reinforce. If you want to encourage independent work, you must provide places and time for children to work alone. Disruptive behavior is often encouraged by classroom arrangements that force children to walk over other children to get to equipment and materials. You may find that your classroom actually contributes to misbehavior. The atmosphere of the classroom or the learning environment must be such that new behaviors are possible.

The same situation applies in the home. If parents want children to keep their rooms neat and clean, they must make it possible for them to do so. Children should also be shown how to take care of their rooms. Parents may have to lower shelves or install clothes hooks. When the physical arrangement is to children's sizes, they can learn how to use a clothes hanger and where to hang certain clothes. A child's room should have a place for everything, and these places should be accessible and easy to use.

A REWARDING ENVIRONMENT. The classroom should be a place where children can do their best work and be on their best behavior. It should be a rewarding place to be. The following are components of an environmentally rewarding classroom:

- Opportunities for children to display their work
- Opportunities for freedom of movement (within guidelines)
- Opportunities for independent work
- A variety of work stations and materials based on children's interests

Figure 12.1 also identifies characteristics of classrooms that support children in their learning self-regulation and guiding their own behavior.

TIME AND TRANSITIONS. Time, generally more important to adults than children, plays a major role in every program. The following guidelines relate to time and its use:

- *Do not waste children's time.* Children should be involved in interesting, meaningful activities from the moment they enter the center, classroom, or family day care home.
- *Do not make children wait.* When children have to wait for materials, their turn, and so forth, provide them with something else to do, such as listening to a story or playing in the block center. Problems can occur when children have to wait, because children like to be busy and involved.
- *Allow transition time.* Transitions are times when children move from one activity to another. They should be made as smoothly as possible, and as fun as possible. In one program, teachers sing, "It's Cleanup Time!" as a transition from one activity to cleanup and then to another activity.

ROUTINES. Establish classroom routines from the beginning. Children need the confidence and security of a routine that will help them do their best. A routine also helps prevent discipline problems, because children know what to do and can learn to do it without a

- Community and culture of caring
- Clear expectations
- High expectations
- Consistent behavior from teachers and staff
- Open communication between
    - children–children
    - teacher–children
    - children–teacher
    - teacher–parents
    - parents–teacher
- Sufficient materials to support learning activities
- Efficacious teachers, those who believe children can and will learn. Efficacious teachers also believe they are good teachers.
- Routines established and maintained
- Balance between cooperation and independent learning
- Atmosphere of respect and caring
- Parent, teacher, and child partnerships

Figure 12.1
Basic Features of Classrooms That Support Guidance and Self-Regulation

lot of disturbance. Parents need to establish routines in the home; a child who knows the family always eats at 5:30 P.M. can be expected to be there. As an early childhood professional, you must also be consistent. Consistency plays an important role in managing behavior in both the home and classroom. If children know what to expect in terms of routine and behavior, they will behave better.

Model Appropriate Behavior

We have all heard the maxim "Telling is not teaching." Nevertheless, we tend to teach by giving instructions, and, of course, children do need instructions. Professional educators soon realize, however, that actions speak louder than words.

Children see and remember how other people act. Observing another person, a child tries out a new behavior. If this new action brings a reward of some kind, she repeats it. Proponents of the modeling approach to learning believe that most behavior people exhibit is learned from the behavior of a model or models. They think children tend to model behavior that brings rewards from parents and early childhood professionals.

A model may be someone whom we respect or find interesting and whom we believe is being rewarded for the behavior he or she exhibits. Groups may also serve as models. For example, it is common to hear a teacher in an early childhood classroom comment, "I like how Cristina and Carlos are sitting quietly and listening to the story." Immediately following such a remark, you can see the group of children settle down to listen quietly to the story. Models children emulate do not necessarily have to be from real life; they can come from books and television. In addition, the modeled behavior does not have to be socially acceptable to be reinforcing.

You can use the following techniques to help children learn through modeling:

- *Show*. For example, show children where the block corner is and how and where the blocks are stored.
- *Demonstrate*. Perform a task while students watch. For example, demonstrate the proper way to put the blocks away and how to store them. Extensions of the demonstration method are to have children practice the demonstration while you supervise and to ask a child to demonstrate to other children.
- *Model*. Modeling occurs when you practice the behavior you expect of the children. Also, you can call children's attention to the desired behavior when another child models it.
- *Supervise*. Supervision is a process of reviewing, insisting, maintaining standards, and following up. If children are not performing the desired behavior, you will need to review the behavior. You must be consistent in your expectations of desired behavior. Children will soon learn they do not have to put away their blocks if you allow them not to do it even once. Remember, you are responsible for setting up the environment to enable the children's learning to take place.

As an early childhood professional, you will need to model and demonstrate social and group-living behaviors as well, including using simple courtesies (saying, "Please," "Thank you," "You're welcome," etc.) and practicing cooperation, sharing, and respect for others.

Provide Guidance

Children need help to act their way out of undesirable behavior. Parents and early childhood professionals may say, "You know how to act," when indeed a child does not know. Teachers also often say, "He could do better if he wanted to." The problem, however, is that the child may *not* know what he wants to do or may not know what is appropriate. In other words, he needs an organized procedure for how to act. Building new behavior, then, is a process of getting children to act in new ways.

A common approach to behavior management is "talking to" and reasoning. As children often do not understand abstract reasoning, it does not generally have the desired effect. The child is likely to behave the same way as before, or worse. This often leads to a punishment trap, in which the early childhood professional or parent resorts to yelling to get the desired results. The behavior we want children to demonstrate must be within their ability. For instance, children cannot pay attention to and be interested in a story that is based on concepts that are too advanced for their comprehension or that is read in a monotonic, unenthusiastic voice. Although *Charlotte's Web* is a children's classic, we cannot expect a group of three- and four-year-olds to sit still and listen attentively while we read it aloud. A book such as *If You Give a Pig a Pancake* would be more appropriate.

Avoid Problems

Parents and early childhood professionals can encourage children's misbehavior. Frequently, professionals see too much and ignore too little. Often parents expect perfection and adult behavior from children. If you focus on building responsible behavior, there will be less need to solve behavior problems.

Ignoring inappropriate behavior is probably one of the most overlooked strategies for managing an effective learning setting and guiding children's behavior. Ironically, some early childhood professionals feel guilty when they use this strategy. They believe that ignoring undesirable behaviors is not good teaching. While ignoring some inappropriate behavior can

Program in Action

Positive Discipline: Responsible, Motivated, Self-Directed Learners

When Grapevine (Texas) Elementary School opened in the fall of 1994, its staff had a vision. This vision emphasized the desire to encourage all learners to be responsible, intrinsically motivated, and self-directed in an environment of mutual respect. As we looked for a discipline management system that fit this philosophy, we recognized that we needed one that emphasized personal responsibility for behavior and cooperation instead of competition and that focused on developing a community of supportive members. We also discovered that we held several beliefs in common that should be the foundation for our discipline management plan:

1. All human beings have three basic needs—to feel connected (the ability to love and be loved), to feel capable (a sense of "I can" accomplish things), and to feel contributive (I count in the communities in which I belong).
2. Natural and logical consequences for poor choices encourage responsible behavior. Punishment, on the other hand, encourages rebellion and resentment.
3. Children can be creative decision makers and responsible citizens when given opportunities to direct the processes that affect the day-to-day environment in which they live.

Our desire was, and is, to address the needs of the whole child as we educate our children to be responsible citizens.

ADOPTING THE DISCIPLINE PLAN

After much research and deliberation, we, as a faculty and staff, decided to implement "Positive Discipline" as a discipline management system. The training of the staff occurred during the summer before the school opened. As we studied the book *Positive Discipline in the Classroom* by Jane Nelsen, Lynn Lott, and Stephen Glenn, teachers spontaneously began to discuss several rituals that normally occur in school routines that did not seem to fit the philosophy of the environment we were attempting to create. One of these was the concept of "rules." Teachers decided to establish a set of "Grapevine Star Responsibilities" in place of the more traditional concept of rules:

> I will be responsible for myself and my learning.
>
> I will respect others and their property.
>
> I will listen and follow directions promptly.
>
> I will complete my classwork and homework in a quality manner.

Furthermore, we decided that rewards—whether in the way of stickers, pencils, or award ceremonies—were not, on the whole, consistent with encouraging intrinsic motivation and the belief that all children should continuously monitor their own learning and behavior. Rather, reward for success should be based on what children find personally significant. Reward should come from within as children and classes celebrate achievement of personal and class goals.

In the summer before school began, teachers discussed the understanding that they should be role models. We understood that the decision to implement "Positive Discipline" would require a change in thinking and a change in behavior for teachers. Teachers would have to change from the role of arbitrator/referee to mediator; they would become facilitators of decision-making sessions instead of "general in command"; and they would have to consistently challenge themselves to think in terms of consequences instead of punishment. Instead of demanding, they would encourage self-evaluation by students. For example, teachers might ask, "What would responsible second grade behavior look like in this situation?" Teachers knew that the atmosphere of caring they created in their classrooms would determine whether their classrooms would build or hinder the development of community within each class and, in a larger context, the school.

ENGAGING STUDENTS

Throughout the course of the year, students set goals each six-week period (usually one academic goal and one behavioral goal) and conferred with their teachers at the end of the six weeks to determine the extent of their achievement toward that goal. At the end of our first year, students participated in a celebration of achievement. Each student chose the goal that held the most personal significance and received a certificate that detailed the goal. The principal read each chosen goal in grade-level celebrations as the student walked across the stage and shook hands with the principal. One second grader chose a goal that included developing two new friendships; a third grader chose a goal that reflected learning all of his multiplication facts; a kindergartner expressed delight in overcoming his fear of the class pet, a rat! Teachers, parents, and students all enjoyed this ceremony, which emphasized the worth of each individual and that learning was, and is, the ultimate goal of education and school (as opposed to a grade or series or marks on a report card).

Class meetings are the cornerstone of "Positive Discipline." The format of a class meeting is forming a circle, giving compliments, and addressing items that students or teachers have placed on the agenda. In the primary grades, agenda items include problems that students are having with one another or a teacher, decisions the class has to make, and concerns that the teacher might have. Before a class can begin to have meetings, children must begin to develop a basic understanding of the difference between consequences and punishment. Teachers must practice with their students skills such as active listening, the use of "I-messages," and brainstorming solutions to problems.

One of the most amazing and critical parts of a class meeting is the compliment time at the beginning. Children are encouraged to compliment others for specific actions or character traits, not the generic, "I like Joan because she is my friend." In any Grapevine Elementary kindergarten class, one could observe children as they pass a stuffed animal around the circle (whoever holds the stuffed animal is the speaker) and compliment one another with statements such as, "Thanks, Tim, for helping me pick up all the crayons I dropped this morning." If indeed the deepest craving of every soul is the need to be appreciated, this part of the class meeting proves magical. Children beam as their classmates compliment them. We often note that children who normally are left out become the target of compliments by responsible, caring leaders in the class without any prompting from teachers. This part of the class meeting is beneficial in and of itself because it encourages the atmosphere in which children can feel they are connected, capable contributors!

Problems identified by students and teachers are addressed in the meeting's agenda section. Each teacher has his own individualized method for developing a class agenda. In kindergarten, the children draw pictures on a class tablet to remind them of what the problem is; in second grade, children write the problem on a slip of paper and place it in the agenda box. The focus during the agenda section of the class meeting is on addressing problems and finding solutions, not placing blame or punishing. When the school year began, it was not unusual for children to suggest that others be "sent to the principal" for some act of unkindness or lack or responsibility. Gradually, children became extremely creative and often decided on solutions that astounded teachers.

In one third grade class, the children were having a continual problem with one student who was using inappropriate language and embarrassing students. They took turns telling this boy how his language and behavior was making them feel. The boy began to cry quietly. Rather than stopping the process, the children continued. When everyone had a turn at sharing, they each walked by the young boy, touched him gently on the knee or shoulder and told him something they appreciated about him and how glad they were that he was in the class. The boy's behavior changed, and the students were empowered by taking responsibility for communicating respectfully and for helping a fellow classmate.

Irene Boynton, a mixed-age (K-1) teacher, notes that a great deal of teaching and work is required to make class meetings successful. She spends times brainstorming feeling words because children often get stuck on the words *good* and *bad*. Role playing is used successfully in her class meetings to focus on issues such as pushing in line and "bothering" other students. Occasionally, she will purposefully tailor a cooperative learning activity immediately before a class meeting so that everyone can discuss issues of cooperation in the meeting itself while the experiences are fresh in the students' minds. Mrs. Boynton comments that "Positive Discipline" allows children to experience

the rewards of feeling confident and healthy about making respectful, responsible choices because it is the "right" thing to do, not because they will receive something for their choice.

THE BENEFITS

At Grapevine Elementary, it took children a while to move past wanting the teacher to make decisions for them, as had been done in the past, toward an understanding that they had the skills to solve their own problems. Now teachers consistently respond that the use of class meetings encourages children to be responsible for personal problem solving. When asked by a child to referee or arbitrate, they are often able to respond with, "Have you tried to work it out yourselves?" or, "Is this something that you need to place on the class agenda?" Tattling, too, has decreased dramatically as we continue to emphasize the difference between tattling and important telling and the use of "I-Care" language.

Kindergarten teacher Carol Matthews believes that class meetings are an excellent tool for teaching problem solving. Meetings encourage children to talk about their own feelings and to be aware of the feelings of others. For her, seeing children carry skills outside the classroom is exciting. A mother of one of her students once told Mrs. Matthews that her daughter responded in an interesting way when she and some other girls were squabbling over how to accomplish a task during an Indian Princess camp out, declaring, "C'mon you guys, we've got to solve this problem ourselves." The children went off to the side and talked through the problem without help from an adult. The process empowers children!

Teachers at Grapevine Elementary, when asked to comment on "Positive Discipline," say such things as, "Is there any other way to teach?" and, "We would never go back to playing referee again!" Students no longer ask, "What am I going to get?" in response to a request to go the extra mile for another student or while working on a project. They are developing respect for themselves and for the rights and needs of others. The skills learned in class meetings extend into academic areas, where we find that students are becoming more thoughtful, introspective, self-motivated, and effective problem solvers. We believe that we are fostering a safe, respectful community where children and adults thrive together in an atmosphere of mutual respect.

Visit Grapevine Elementary on the Web at http://www.gcisd-k12.org/schools/ges/index.html.

Contributed by Nancy Robinson, Grapevine Elementary, Grapevine, Texas. For more detailed information on implementing "Positive Discipline," refer to Positive Discipline in the Classroom, *by Jane Nelsen, Lynn Lott, and H. Stephen Glenn. Our implementation of this program was based on teachers' understanding of the book and other programs, not from direct training from any of the authors.*

be an effective strategy, it must be combined with positive reinforcement of desirable behavior. Thus, one ignores inappropriate behavior and at the same time reinforces appropriate behavior. A combination of positive reinforcement and ignoring can lead to desired behavior.

When children do something good or are on task, reward them. Use verbal and nonverbal reinforcement and privileges to help ensure that the appropriate behavior will continue. Catch children being good; that is, look for good behavior. This helps improve not only individual behavior but group behavior as well.

Writing contracts for certain work experiences is a great way to involve children in planning their own work and behavior. Follow these rules when contracting: (1) keep contracts short and uncomplicated, (2) make an offer the child cannot refuse, (3) make sure the child is able to do what you contract for, and (4) pay off when the contract is completed.

Develop a Partnership with Parents, Families, and Others

Involving parents and families is a wonderful way to gain invaluable insights about children's behavior. Furthermore, parents and early childhood professionals must be partners and work

For more information about working with families, go to the Companion Website at http://www.prenhall.com/morrison, select any chapter, then choose Topic 10 of the ECE Supersite module.

cooperatively in effectively guiding children's behaviors. In addition, involving other persons who are involved with your children is a good idea. Some of these significant others in the lives of children are other teachers, baby sitters, before- and after-school care providers, coaches, and club leaders.

Another important rule in guiding behavior is to *know your children*. A good way to learn about the children you care for and teach is through home visits. If you do not have an opportunity to visit the home, a parent conference is also valuable. Either way, you should gather information concerning the child's health history and interests; the child's attitude toward schooling; the parents' educational expectations for the child; what school support is available in the home (e.g., books, places to study); home conditions that would support or hinder school achievement (such as where the child sleeps); parents' attitudes toward schooling and discipline; parents' support of the child (e.g., encouragement to do well); parents' interests and abilities; and parents' desire to become involved in the school.

The visit or conference also offers an opportunity for you to share ideas with parents. You should, for example, express your desire for the child to do well in school; encourage parents to take part in school and classroom programs; suggest ways parents can help children learn; describe some of the school programs; give information about school events, projects, and meetings; and explain your beliefs about discipline.

Working with and involving parents also provides early childhood professionals with opportunities to help parents with parenting skills and child-related problems. The foundation for children's behavior is built in the home, and some parents unwittingly encourage and promote children's misbehavior and antisocial behavior. In many ways, parents promote antisocial behavior in their children by using punitive, negative, and overly restrictive punishment. In particular, when children are enrolled in child care programs at an early age, professionals have an ideal opportunity to help parents learn about and use positive discipline approaches to child rearing.

In your collaborative process of working with others to help children develop self-regulation, each group has certain basic rights. Figure 12.2 lists these basic rights. Perhaps as you read them you can think of others you want to include.

Promote Empathy and Prosocial Behavior

One trend in early childhood education is for professionals to focus on helping children learn how to share, care for, and assist others. We call these and similar behaviors *prosocial behaviors*.

Parents and early childhood professionals want to encourage altruistic behavior in children—that is, intentional behaviors that benefit others. Part of altruistic behavior involves empathy, the ability to vicariously feel another person's emotions and feelings. As mentioned in chapter 5, Piaget believed that young children are egocentric, which prevents them from having empathy for others. This is another area in which Piaget's theory is being modified and updated based on continuing research. We now know that children as young as two and three years of age are quite capable of empathy.

You can do a number of things to promote prosocial behaviors that will enable children to show concern for others; to help others through acts of kindness and sharing; and to respond to the conditions of others through affection, comfort, sympathy, joy, and love:

- *Model behaviors that are caring, loving, and helping.* When young children see adults helping others, sharing with others, and comforting others in distress, then they too learn that such behaviors are important and worthwhile. Provide children opportunities to see other children and adults modeling prosocial behaviors. Organizations such as

Children's Rights

Children have these rights in classrooms designed to promote self-regulation:

- To be respected and treated courteously
- To be treated fairly in culturally independent and gender-appropriate ways
- To learn behaviors necessary for self-guidance
- To have teachers who have high expectations for them
- To learn and exercise independence
- To achieve to their highest levels
- To be praised and affirmed for appropriate behaviors and achievements
- To learn and practice effective social skills
- To learn and apply basic academic skills

Teachers' Rights

- To be supported by administration and parents in appropriate efforts to help children guide their behavior
- To have a partnership with parents so they can be successful
- To be treated courteously and professionally by peers and others

Parents' Rights

- To share ideas and values of child rearing and discipline with teachers
- To be involved in and informed about classroom and school discipline policies
- To receive periodic reports and information about their children's behaviors
- To be educated and informed about how to guide their children's behavior

Figure 12.2
Children's, Teachers', and Parents' Rights That Support Positive Behavior

Junior Girl Scouts, Brownies, Cub Scouts, and others that traditionally engage in helping activities offer a social context for children to see people helping others and for them to do the same.

- *Provide opportunities to engage children in helping and giving service to others.* For example, beginning in the toddler years, children can visit with the elderly, bringing them treats and artwork. What is important is to offer children the chance to engage in helping others in meaningful ways.
- *Help children "put themselves in someone else's place."* Ask them what they think about a particular situation or event. For example, you might ask, "How do you think Laura feels because you won't share your toys with her?"

Parents and professionals want to promote the intrinsic development of empathy, a desire to engage in sympathetic behaviors, because it is the right and good thing to do. They should avoid rewarding children for these behaviors. When rewards are the consequences of empathy and helping, then children learn that acts of helping or kindness are based on these external rewards. Certainly children can and should be complimented for doing good things, and they should be encouraged to assist others. However, they should not learn that the reward is the reason for helping others. Helping and kindness are themselves rewards.

Teach Cooperative Living and Learning

Early childhood professionals can do a lot to promote cooperative living in which children help each other direct their behavior. Recall from chapter 3 our discussion of Vygotsky's theory of social relations. Children are born seeking social interactions, and social relations are necessary for children's learning and development. Peers help each other learn.

Children's natural social groups and play groups are ideal and natural settings in which to help children assist each other in learning new behaviors and being responsible for their own behavior. The classroom as a whole is an important social group. Classroom meetings in which early childhood professionals and children talk can serve many useful functions. They can talk about expected behaviors from day to day ("When we are done playing with toys, what do we do with them?"), review with children what they did in a particular center or situation, and help them anticipate what they will do in future situations ("Tomorrow morning when we visit the Senior Citizen Center . . . "). In all these situations, children are cooperatively engaged in thinking about, talking about, and learning how to engage in appropriate behavior. Furthermore, children can help identify a particular problem or misbehavior and discuss appropriate behavior.

Teachers and children also form an important social group that influences behavior. You can model a particular behavior, engage a child in a discussion of behavior, and compliment the child on behavior.

Early childhood professionals must initiate, support, and foster a cooperative, collaborative learning community in the classroom in which children are involved in developing and setting guidelines and devising classroom and, by extension, individual norms of behavior. Professionals "assist" children but do not do things for them, and they ask questions that make children think about their behavior—how it influences the class, themselves, and others. This process of cooperative living occurs daily. Discussions grow out of existing problems, and guidance is provided based on the needs of children and the classroom.

There are many social, cognitive, and behavioral benefits to children helping the elderly and the elderly helping children. (See "The Stride-Rite Intergenerational Day Care Center" in chapter 2.)

Use Conflict Management and Resolution Techniques

Quite often, conflicts result from children's interactions with others. Increasingly, early childhood professionals are advocating teaching children ways to manage and resolve their own conflicts.

Teaching conflict resolution strategies is important for several reasons. First, it makes sense to give children the skills they need to handle and resolve their own conflicts. Second, teaching conflict resolution skills to children enables them to use these same skills as adults. Third, the peaceful resolution of interpersonal conflicts contributes, in the long run, to peaceful homes and communities. In this sense, peace curricula and attempts to teach children behaviors associated with peacemaking begin with harmony in the child care and preschool classroom families. Children who are involved in efforts to resolve interpersonal behavior problems peacefully intuitively learn that peace begins with them.

Strategies used to teach and model conflict resolution include the following:

- *Talk it over*. Children can learn that talking about a problem often leads to a resolution and reveals that there are always two sides to an argument. Talking also helps children think about other ways to solve problems. Children should be involved in the solution of their interpersonal problems and classroom and activity problems.

- *Model resolutions*. Professionals can model resolutions for children: "Erica, please don't knock over Shantrell's building because she worked hard to build it"; "Barry, what is another way (instead of hitting) you can tell Pam that she is sitting in your chair?"
- *Teach children to say, "I'm sorry."* Saying "I'm sorry" is one way to heal and resolve conflicts. It can be a step toward good behavior. Piaget maintained that prior to the stage of concrete operations (before the age of seven), young children do not have the cognitive maturity to take another's point of view. Since they cannot "decenter," it is difficult for them to know how others feel and therefore to be sorry for something. Thus, the very young are not cognitively able to learn to say "I'm sorry" and have real conviction that they indeed are sorry. Nevertheless, children need to be reared in an environment in which they see and experience others being sorry for their inappropriate actions toward others.
- *Do something else*. Teach children to get involved in another activity. Children can learn that they do not always have to play with a toy someone else is playing with. They can get involved in another activity with a different toy. They can do something else now and play with the toy later. Chances are, however, that by getting involved in another activity they will forget about the toy they were ready to fight for.
- *Take turns*. Taking turns is a good way for children to learn that they cannot always be first, have their own way, or do a prized activity. Taking turns brings equality and fairness to interpersonal relations.
- *Share*. Sharing is good behavior to promote in any setting. Children have to be taught how to share and how to behave when others do not share. Children can be helped to select another toy rather than hitting or grabbing. Again, keep in mind that during the early years children are egocentric, and acts of sharing are likely to be motivated by expectations of a reward or approval such as being thought of as a "good" boy or girl.

It is increasingly important for early childhood professionals to help children learn how to resolve their differences, share, and cooperate. Because of this, curricula for helping children to peaceably resolve conflict are growing in popularity.

Behavior Modification Approaches to Guiding Behavior

A popular approach to guidance based on observable behavior rather than on feelings is *behavior modification*. An important concept of behavior modification is that all behavior has a cause. Everyone acts the way they do for reasons, although the reasons may not always be apparent; individuals themselves do not always know why they behave a certain way. How often have you heard the expressions, "He didn't know what he was doing," "I don't know why she acts like she does," "I can't understand why I did that," and "I didn't know what I was doing"?

A second basic concept is that behavior results from reinforcement received from the environment. Psychologist Edward L. Thorndike (1874–1949) observed that the consequences of one's behavior influence future behavior. He formalized this observation in his learning principle, *the law of effect*: if a satisfying condition follows a behavior, the individual tends to repeat that behavior, and the strength of the stimulus–response connection increases. If an unsatisfying condition follows a behavior, the individual tends not to repeat that behavior, and the stimulus–response connection weakens or disappears. The law of effect points out how important the quality of feedback is for behavior.

This law has gradually come to be known as *the imperial law of effect*, which says that the consequences of particular responses determine whether the response will be continued and therefore learned. In other words, what happens to a child *after* acting in a particular way determines whether he or she continues to act that way. If a child cries and is immediately given a cookie, and this happens several times, that youngster will probably learn that crying is a good way to get cookies. And the cycle continues: receiving cookies reinforces crying behavior. We should understand that this behavior is not always planned; a child does not necessarily think, "I'm going to cry because I know Mom will give me a cookie." The child may have cried, the mother gave a cookie to stop the crying, and the child associated the two events.

B. F. Skinner (1904–1990) is given credit for many of the technological and pedagogical applications of behavior modification, including programmed instruction. Skinner also emphasized the role of the environment in providing people with clues that reinforce their behavior.

In behavior management, we are concerned with behavior modification, or changing behavior. As used in our discussion, *behavior modification* means the *conscious* application of the methods of behavioral science, with the intent of changing children's behavior. Early childhood professionals and parents have always been concerned with changing children's behavior, but it is implicit in the term *behavior modification* that we mean the conscious use of techniques to change behavior.

Behaviorists maintain that all behavior is learned and, in this sense, all behavior is caused by reinforcers from which individuals gain pleasure of some kind. The problem, however, is that early childhood professionals and parents have usually changed children's behavior without realizing it. You must be aware of the effect you have on children's behavior. To use power ignorantly and unconsciously to achieve ends that are basically dehumanizing to children is not good teaching practice. For example, when a child first comes to school, she may not understand that sitting quietly is a desirable behavior that many schools and teachers have established as a goal. The teacher may scold the child until she not only sits quietly but sits quietly and bites her nails. The teacher did not intentionally set out to reinforce nail biting, but this is the child's terminal behavior, and the teacher is unaware of how it happened.

Reinforced Misbehavior

We must recognize that our behavior, attitudes, predisposition, and inclinations can cause a great deal of child misbehavior. Many children misbehave because their misbehavior is reinforced. For example, children enjoy receiving attention; therefore, when a child receives any kind of attention, it reinforces the behavior the child exhibited to get that attention. A child who is noisy receives attention by being scolded. The chances of his exhibiting the same behavior (such as talking to the child beside him) to elicit attention is greatly increased as a result of the reinforcement.

We sometimes encourage children to do sloppy work or hurry through an activity when we emphasize finishing it. We may give children a paper with six squares on it to color and cut out and say, "After you color all the squares, I will give you a pair of scissors so you can cut the squares out." The child may hurry through the coloring to get to the cutting. We would do better to concentrate on coloring first, then cutting.

Positive Reinforcement

When we talk about positive reinforcement, we are talking about providing *rewards* or *reinforcers* that promote behaviors we decide are desirable. *Positive reinforcement* involves maintaining or increasing the frequency of a behavior following a particular stimulus. What the child receives—whether candy, money, or a hug—is the reinforcer, the reinforcement, or the reward. Generally, a positive reinforcer is any stimulus that maintains or increases a particular behavior.

Verbal reinforcers include "Good," "Right," "Correct," "Wonderful," "Very good," "I like that," "That's great!" and "I knew you could do it." You can also use nonverbal behavior to reinforce children's behavior and learning. For example, giving a nod, a smile, a hug, or a pat on the head or shoulder; standing close to someone; making eye contact; paying attention; and even giving a wink show children that you approve of their behavior or are proud of what they are doing.

You can set up your classroom as a positively reinforcing environment. If it is organized to help make desired behaviors possible, provides opportunities for novelty and children's control over their environment, and reflects children's desires, interests, and ideas, children will tend to try to live up to the expectations the setting suggests.

Understanding Behavior

Another extremely important concept of behavior modification focuses on external behavior rather than the causes of behavior; that is, professionals and parents should generally not be concerned with *why* a child acts as he or she does. This idea usually takes some getting used to, because it is almost the opposite of what we have been taught. Early childhood professionals particularly feel it is beneficial to know why children act the way they do, and they spend a great deal of time and effort trying to determine motivations. If Gloria is fidgety and inclined to daydream, for example, her teacher may spend six weeks investigating the causes. He learns that Gloria's mother has been divorced three times and ignores her at home. On the basis of this information, he concludes that Gloria needs help but may be no closer to solving her problem than he was six weeks previously. As educators, our time and energy should be spent developing strategies to help children with their behavior. Sometimes, underlying causes help us deal with the behavior we wish to modify, but we need to recognize that the *behavior* a child exhibits is the problem, and it is behavior that we need to attend to.

Reinforcing Behavior

Appropriate Reinforcers

A reinforcer is only as effective as the child's desire for it. In other words, if the reinforcer has the power to reinforce the behavior that precedes it, then it will work. One method used to determine the nature of a reinforcer is the *Premack principle*. David Premack determined that behaviors with a high probability of occurrence can be used to reinforce behaviors with a low probability of occurrence. For example, activities children participate in when they have free time are often what they like to do best. You can use these activities to reinforce desired behaviors.

Using the chalkboard or art easels is a highly desirable activity in many early childhood classrooms. Therefore, you can provide extra time to use them to reinforce desired behavior. Rewards that children help select are most likely to have a desired effect on behavior. Privileges children often choose are watering the plants, feeding classroom pets, washing chalkboards, running errands, going outside, playing games with friends, leading games, enjoying extra recess, passing out papers and supplies, using audiovisual equipment, doing flash cards, and cutting and pasting. Figure 12.3 shows ways you can acknowledge and affirm children's efforts and accomplishments.

Praise as a Reinforcer

Giving praise is probably the most frequent method of rewarding or reinforcing children's behavior. Praise is either general or specific. Specific praise is more effective because it

Verbal (praise)

"I like the way you . . . "
"Great!"
"Right on!"
"Beautiful."
"Terrific."
"Wow!"
"Way to go."
"Super!"
"Excellent."
"Fantastic."
"Good job!"
"Tremendous!"
"Awesome!"
"Cool."
"You're working hard."

Nonverbal

Facial
Smile
Wink
Raised eyebrow
Eye contact

Gestures
Clapping of hands
Waving
Forming an okay sign (thumb + index finger)
Victory sign
Nodding head
Shrugging shoulders

Proximity
Standing near someone
Shaking hands
Getting down on child's level
Hugging, touching
Holding child's arm up

Social (occur in or as a result of social consequences)
Parties
Group approval
Class privileges

Figure 12.3
Ways of Affirming and Acknowledging Children's Behavior

describes the behavior we want to build. The child has no doubt that she is being praised and what she is being praised for. For example, if a child picks up her blocks and you say, "Good, Laura," she may or may not know what you are referring to, but if you say "Laura, you did a nice job of putting your blocks away," Laura knows exactly what you are talking about.

Parents and early childhood professionals should approach children positively. A positive approach builds self-esteem. We help build positive self-images and expectations for good behavior by complimenting children and praising them for the things they do well. Every child has praiseworthy qualities.

Contingency Management

Early childhood professionals frequently find it helpful to engage in *contingency contracting* or *contingency management* to reinforce behavior. With this strategy, you might tell a child, "If you put the materials away when you're done with them, you can use the chalkboard for five minutes." Sometimes, contingency management is accompanied by a written contract between teacher and student, depending, of course, on the child's age and maturity.

When parents and early childhood professionals manage a contingency, they must be sure they have thought through its consequences. For example, if a parent says, "If you don't clean up your room, you have to stay there until you do," the child may choose not to clean up his room but to stay there and play with his toys. In this case, he does not have to do as he was told and is rewarded for not doing it.

Token System

Reinforcement works best when it occurs at the time of the behavior we want to reinforce. Also, the sooner reinforcement follows the desired behavior, the better it works. Particularly when building new skills and shaping new behaviors, it is important to reinforce the child immediately. To provide immediate reinforcement, some professionals use tokens, such as plastic disks, buttons, trading stamps, or beans, which the child later trades for an activity. If children like to use the art easel, the teacher might allow them to exchange ten tokens for time at the easel. The child receives a token for performing appropriate tasks and exhibiting teacher-specified behavior.

Time-out

Time-out is another practice early childhood professionals and parents often use. In fact, it is the most favored form of discipline used by parents. *Time-out* is the removal of a child from an activity because that child has done something wrong. Presumably, the time-out gives the child an opportunity to think about the misbehavior. After a set amount of time or when the child says he or she can behave (which, of course, all children say), the child is allowed to return to the activity.

Early childhood professionals should use time-out only when it is appropriate to children's developmental levels. This strategy is inappropriate for infants' and toddlers' developmental levels, but infrequent use is sometimes effective with preschoolers. Time-out is generally not effective as a guidance technique, because it is debatable whether young children will "think" about what they did wrong. Additionally, time-out is usually irrelevant to the inappropriate behavior, so children do not make a connection between the poor behavior and the punishment.

Children are energetic and impulsive, so it is effective to use preventive guidance techniques that catch problems before they happen, or "prevent" them. Examples of *preventive*

guidance are appealing room arrangement, effective scheduling, minimal waiting time, and an interesting, active curriculum. These approaches are far more effective than using "Band-Aid" guidance strategies such as time-out.

Development of Autonomous Behavior

Implicit in guiding children's behavior is the assumption that they can be, should be, and will be responsible for their own behavior. The ultimate goal of all education is to develop *autonomy* in children, which means "being governed by oneself."

Early childhood educators need to conduct programs that promote development of autonomy. One aspect of facilitating autonomy is exchanging points of view with children.

> When a child tells a lie, for example, the adult can deprive him of dessert or make him write 50 times "I will not lie." The adult can also refrain from punishing the child and, instead, look him straight in the eye with great skepticism and affection and say, "I really can't believe what you are saying because . . . " This is an example of an exchange of points of view that contributes to the development of autonomy in children. The child who can see that the adult cannot believe him can be motivated to think about what he must do to be believed. The child who is raised with many similar opportunities can, over time, construct for himself the conviction that it is best eventually for people to deal honestly with each other.[2]

The ultimate goal of developing autonomy in children is to have them regulate their own behavior and make decisions about good and bad, right and wrong (when they are mature enough to understand these concepts), and the way they will behave in relation to themselves and others. Autonomous behavior can be achieved only when children consider other people's points of view, which can occur only if they are presented with viewpoints that differ from their own and are encouraged to consider them in deciding how they will behave. The ability to take another person's point of view is largely developmental. It is not until around age eight, when children become less egocentric, that they are able to decenter and see things from other people's points of view. Autonomy is reinforced when professionals and parents allow sufficient time and opportunities for children to practice and perform tasks for themselves. Independence is also nurtured when children are allowed to use problem-solving techniques and to learn from their mistakes.

Rewards and punishment tend to encourage children to obey others without helping them understand how their behavior was appropriate or inappropriate. Even more important, they have not had an opportunity to develop rules of conduct to govern their behavior. Children can be encouraged to regulate and be responsible for their own behavior through what Piaget referred to as "sanctions by reciprocity." These sanctions "are directly related to the act we want to sanction and to the adult's point of view, and have the effect of motivating the child to construct rules of conduct for himself, through the coordination of viewpoints."[3]

Examples of sanctions by reciprocity include exclusion from the group when children have a choice of staying and behaving or leaving; taking away from children the materials or privileges they have abused, while leaving open the opportunity to use them again if they express a desire to use them appropriately; and helping children fix things they have broken and clean up after themselves. A fine line separates sanctions by reciprocity and punishment. The critical ingredients that balance the scales on the side of reciprocity are your respect for children and your desire to help them develop autonomy rather than blind obedience.

Physical Punishment

Is it possible to guide children's behavior without physical punishment? More and more, early childhood professionals agree that it is. Whether parents and professionals should spank or paddle as a means of guiding behavior is an age-old controversy. Some parents spank their children, following a "No!" with a slap on the hand or a spank on the bottom. This form of punishment can be an effective means of controlling a child's behavior when used in moderation immediately following the misbehavior. Some parents and religious groups base their use of physical punishment on their religious beliefs. Yet, what some parents do with their child in the home is not acceptable for others to do outside the home, where spanking is considered an inappropriate form of guidance. In fact, in some places, such as Florida, physical punishment in child care programs is legislatively prohibited.

For more information about alternatives to punishment, go to the Companion Website at http://www.prenhall.com/morrison, select chapter 12, then choose the Linking to Learning module to connect to the Center for Effective Discipline site.

Several problems with spanking and other forms of physical punishment persist. First, physical punishment is generally ineffective in building behavior in children. Physical punishment does not show children what to do or provide them with alternative ways of behaving. Second, adults who use physical punishment are modeling physical aggression. They are, in effect, saying that it is permissible to use aggression in interpersonal relationships. Children who are spanked are thus more likely to use aggression with their peers. Third, spanking and physical punishment increase the risk of physical injury to the child. Spanking can be an emotionally charged situation, and the spanker can become too aggressive, overdo the punishment, and hit the child in vulnerable places. Fourth, parents, caregivers, and teachers are children's sources of security. Physical punishment takes away from and erodes the sense of security that children must have to function confidently in their daily lives. In short, the best advice regarding physical punishment is to avoid it; use nonviolent means for guiding children's behavior. (For more information on physical punishment, see the Web site http://www.parentsplace.com. This address links you to a community where parents can connect, communicate, and celebrate the adventures of parenting; share insights; search through extensive archives of feature articles; and pose questions to a panel of experts.)

In the long run, parents and early childhood professionals determine children's behavior. In guiding the behavior of children entrusted to their care, professionals and others must select procedures that are appropriate to their own philosophies and children's particular needs. Guiding children to help them develop their own internal system of behavior control benefits them more than a system that relies on external control and authoritarianism. Developing self-regulation in children should be a primary goal of all professionals. Figure 12.4 outlines other alternatives to physical punishment.

Trends in Guiding Children's Behavior

In this first year of the twenty-first century we can clearly see trends in the guidance and discipline of young children. As an early childhood professional, you can expect to be involved in the following:

- *Development of democratic learning environments.* In our efforts to help prepare all children to live effectively and productively in a democracy, we are placing increasing emphasis on giving students experiences that will help promote behavior associated with democratic living. As a result, more professionals are making efforts to run their classrooms as democracies. The idea of teaching this behavior through classrooms that are miniature democracies is not new. John Dewey was an advocate of this approach

- Set firm, consistent, age-appropriate, and acceptable limits.
- Teach children conflict resolution and mediation skills, including listening actively, speaking clearly, showing trust and being trustworthy, accepting differences, setting group goals, negotiating, and mediating conflicts.
- Reason and talk with children in age-appropriate ways. Verbal teacher–child interactions enhance children's cognitive ability.
- Model patience, kindness, empathy, and cooperation.
- Provide daily opportunities for children to practice rational problem solving and to study alternatives and the effect of each alternative.
- Encourage and praise children.
- Allow children to participate in setting rules—and identify consequences for breaking them.
- Provide consistency, structure, continuity, and predictability in children's lives.
- Encourage children's autonomy.
- Provide parents with information on child development and behavior management through workshops, mentoring, conferences, library books, newsletters, brochures, flyers, and bulletin board materials.
- Help establish ties between the school and community through mental health and family counseling programs to support families in stress.

Figure 12.4
Alternatives to Corporal Punishment

Source: Sureshrani Paintal, "Banning Corporal Punishment of Children," Childhood Education *(Fall 1999), 37–38.*

and championed democratic classrooms as a way of promoting democratic living. However, running a democratic classroom is easier said than done. It requires a confident professional who believes it is worth the effort. Democratic learning environments require that students develop responsibility for their and others' behaviors and learning, that classrooms operate as communities, and that all children are respected and respectful of others.

- *The use of character education as a means of promoting responsible behavior*. In chapter 10 we discussed reasons for character education and its importance and role in the contemporary curriculum. Providing character education will continue to grow as a means of promoting fundamental behaviors that early childhood professionals and society believe are essential for living in democratic society.
- *Teaching civility*. Civil behavior and ways to promote it are of growing interest at all levels of society. The specific teaching of *civil behavior*—how to treat others well and in turn be treated well—is seen as essential for living well in contemporary society. At a minimum, civil behavior includes manners, respect, and the ability to get along with people of all races, cultures, and socioeconomic backgrounds.
- *Early intervention*. We all know habits are hard to break and that a behavior once set is difficult to change. Early childhood professionals believe it is essential to help develop appropriate behaviors in the early years by working with parents and families to help

To take an online self-test on this chapter's contents, go to the Companion Website at http://www.prenhall.com/morrison, select chapter 12, then choose the Self Test module.

them guide their children's behavior. Waiting to address delinquent behavior is much more costly than promoting right behavior from the beginning of children's lives.

As we have emphasized in this and other chapters, cognitive and social development and behavioral characteristics are interconnected. More early childhood professionals recognize that it does not make sense to teach children reading, writing, and arithmetic and not also teach them skills necessary for responsibly guiding their own behavior.

For additional Internet resources or to complete an online activity for this chapter, go to the Companion Website at http://www.prenhall.com/morrison, select chapter 12, then choose the Linking to Learning or Making Connections module.

Activities for Further Enrichment

Applications

1. List five advantages and disadvantages of using rewards to stimulate and reinforce desired behaviors.
2. What is the difference between normal behavior and acceptable behavior? Give an example of when normal behavior may not be acceptable and another when acceptable behavior may not be normal.
3. Observe a primary classroom and identify aspects of the physical setting and atmosphere that could influence classroom behavior. Can you suggest improvements?
4. List five methods for guiding children's behavior. Tell why you think each is effective, and give examples.
5. Explain, with examples, why it is important for early childhood professionals and parents to agree on a philosophy of behavioral guidance.

Field Experiences

1. Observe an early childhood classroom. What reinforcement system (implicit or explicit) does the teacher use to operate the classroom? Do you think the teacher is aware of the systems of reinforcement in use?
2. List ten behaviors you think are desirable in toddlers, ten in preschoolers, and ten in kindergartners. For each behavior, give two examples of how you would encourage and promote development of that behavior. Place these ideas in your portfolio or idea file.

Research

1. Behavior modification is sometimes practiced by parents and early childhood professionals without their being aware of what they are doing or the processes they are using. Observe a mother–child relationship for examples of parental behavioral management. What rewards does she offer? What was the child's resultant behavior? After further observation, answer these questions for the early childhood professional–child relationship. In both situations, what are the ethical implications of the adult's actions?
2. Observe an early childhood classroom to see which behaviors earn the teacher's attention. Does the teacher pay more attention to positive or negative behavior? Why do you think the teacher does this?
3. Interview five parents of young children to determine what they mean when they use the word *discipline*. What implications might these definitions have for you if you were their children's teacher?

Readings for Further Enrichment

Beaty, J. *Prosocial Guidance for the Preschool Child.* Upper Saddle River, NJ: Merrill/Prentice Hall, 1999.

This book reflects the new approach to guidance in the preschool classroom, focusing on positive rather than inappropriate behaviors. It provides future and current teachers with the skills to create a prosocial physical environment, to anticipate and prevent inappropriate behavior from happening, and to help children manage their own behavior.

Charles, C. M. *Building Classroom Discipline*. New York: Longman, 1999.

For reducing the types of student misbehavior that impede learning and produce stress, this best-selling text presents solutions developed by some of the most influential thinkers of the past fifty years by analyzing twelve models of discipline, including two models new to this edition, and by inviting students to pick and choose the best of each model to create systems comfortable to them.

Nelsen, J., Erwin, C., and Delzer, C. *Positive Discipline for Single Parents: Nurturing, Cooperation, Respect, and Joy in Your Single-Parent Family*. Rocklin, CA: Prima Publishing, 1998.

Focuses on raising children with nonpunitive discipline, through clear communication techniques and child-positive approaches to problem solving.

Nelsen, J., Lott, L., and Glenn, H. *Positive Discipline in the Classroom*. Rocklin, CA: Prima Publishing, 1997.

Three parenting experts address the popular concept of class meetings, where students and teachers work together to solve problems.

Ryan, K., and Bohlin, K. *Building Character in Schools: Practical Ways to Bring Moral Instruction to Life*. San Francisco, CA: Jossey-Bass, 1998.

The authors outline the principles and strategies of effective character education and explain what schools must do to teach students the habits and dispositions that lead to responsible adulthood.

Linking to Learning

Center for Effective Discipline

http://www.stophitting.com

The Center for Effective Discipline (CED) is a nonprofit organization that provides educational information to the public on the effects of corporal punishment and on alternatives to its use.

National Network for Child Care

http://www.nncc.org

Preschoolers are delightful to have around but at times can be quite a challenge! This site suggests ways that a preschooler can learn to get along with others and that a caregiver can learn to guide and discipline that preschooler.

Virginia Cooperative Extension

http://www.ext.vt.edu

Shows several commonsense strategies for effectively guiding the behavior of young children so they can make positive choices, learn problem-solving skills, and learn values of respect and responsibility.

ENDNOTES

1 U.S. Department of Justice, "Juvenile Arrests," 1997. [On-line]. Available: http://ojjdp.ncjrs.org/ojstatbb/qa001.html.

2 Constance Kamii, *Number in Preschool and Kindergarten* (Washington, DC: National Association for the Education of Young Children, 1982), 23.

3 Ibid., 77.

PART V

Meeting the Special Needs of Young Children

CHAPTER 13

It is important to realize that using computers with young children is a process of exploration and discovery for both you and the children.

SUSAN W. HAUGLAND, PROFESSOR OF CHILD DEVELOPMENT, SOUTHEAST MISSOURI STATE UNIVERSITY

Technology and Young Children

Education for the Information Age

Focus Questions

1. What does technological literacy mean for the computer generation?
2. What challenges do young children face in terms of access to technology and technological equity?
3. How can technology help special populations of youngsters, such as very young children, students with disabilities, and those with limited English proficiency?
4. Why and how should educators integrate technology in the early childhood learning environment?
5. How has technology changed parents' roles in their children's education?

To review the chapter focus questions online, go to the Companion Website at <u>http://www.prenhall.com/morrison</u> and select chapter 13.

A recent front-page headline declared: "Software for Kids a Growing Proposition." The writer of the article was acknowledging what many people think as they wander the aisles of computer software stores—the fastest growing software category is for young children under five. With names like *Jumpstart Baby* and *Reader Rabbit Playtime for Baby*, parents spent more than $41 million on young children's software annually.[1]

The Computer Generation

To check your understanding of this chapter with the online Study Guide, go to the Companion Website at http://www.prenhall.com/morrison, select chapter 13, then choose the Study Guide module.

Perhaps you are wondering about your role as a teacher in the new millennium. You may also wonder how you can use technology to become a better teacher. One thing is certain: children today are technologically oriented. They are the "dot-com" generation. Their growth, development, and learning are intimately tied to large doses of television, videos, electronic games, and computers in the home and shopping center.

Every day, newspapers, television, and other forms of popular media chronicle the latest technological benefits to society. What once was exceptional is now commonplace. Computers were once huge, power-hungry machines that filled rooms the size of small houses. Today, powerful computers are small enough to sit on students' desks, and more and more students have laptop computers they easily carry back and forth between home and school.

Home computing has grown in popularity during the past decade and will continue. A host of computer manufacturers have introduced computers targeted for the home market. Manufacturers design software to entertain and educate adults and children at home. Publishers of educational software for school use now design many of their newest titles with families in mind as well.

We cannot speak or think about technology as though it were separate from what goes on in the everyday world. Technology influences all of society. The production of consumer goods—from automobiles to zwieback—depends on computers and other technology. The point is that technology is all around us. In addition, many children are very savvy about technology and its use. Therefore, early childhood professionals must incorporate computers and other technology into their programs and into children's lives.

Technology: A Definition

Technology is the application of scientific, material, and human resources to the solution of human needs. Using this definition, technology goes beyond computers and video games. Of course, the most common use of the term *technology* refers to electronic and digital technology—in other words, devices that you can plug in. Such tools commonly found in early childhood programs include computers, computer programs, television, videotapes, tape recorders, cassettes, and types of assistive technology. These forms of technology have many teaching applications. Consequently, as an early childhood professional you must consider the full range of technology that is applicable to your classroom, learning centers, and activities.

Technological Literacy

Technology is changing and in the process has changed the goals of education, what it means to be educated, and what literacy means. Literacy now has added dimensions. Students not only have to read, write, listen and speak—skills fundamental to participation in a democra-

tic society—they also have to learn to use technology to be truly literate. As a society, we increasingly feel that this *technological literacy*, the ability to understand and apply technology to meet personal goals, is as important as the traditional components of literacy—reading, writing, speaking, and listening.

The following are some of the many dimensions of technological literacy:

- Understanding the language and vocabulary of the technological world. Figure 13.1 will help you achieve this goal.
- Using navigational strategies to access and find information.
- Staying literate. In the technological context, being literate is not a one-time thing, nor is it static. The challenge for today's students and teachers is in constantly keeping up—staying literate. Today's technological skills and knowledge are soon made obsolete by rapid change and innovation.
- Developing critical thinking and analytical skills necessary to assess and evaluate the information that almost anyone can publish. The abilities to sort fact from error, truth from fiction, and clarity from distortion are essential. Just because information is online doesn't mean that it is valid or true.
- Comprehending and managing the various dimensions of how information is presented (e.g., CDs, Web sites, digital photographs).[2]

These dimensions of the new literacy affect not only how students learn but also how they will conduct their daily lives. Empowerment, or the lack of it, may well mean the difference between employment and unemployment.

Equity and Access to Technology

Many educators fear that the United States may be creating a new class of illiterates—children who do not have access to computers and other technology and who do not know how to use and apply technology. Tables 13.1 and 13.2 list the percentage of time that children use computers at home and school. Note how computer use varies by gender, culture, and socioeconomic background. Table 13.2 indicates that many children still do not use computers in the public schools, with African American children in particular using computers less than other children. These demographics of technological ownership, availability, and use have serious implications for children, families, and you. If one group, socioeconomic class, or gender is more comfortable with, skillful with, and proficient in technology, inequities and technological illiteracy result. We must avoid creating a generation of technology "have nots." As an early childhood educator, you should advocate for increased access to technology for you and your students.

For more information about how to close the gap between technology "haves" and "have nots," go to the Companion Website at http://www.prenhall.com/morrison, select chapter 13, then choose the Linking to Learning module to connect to the KidzOnline site.

Equity means that all students have the opportunity to become technologically literate. All students must have equitable access to technology that is appropriate for them. While some may think it a worthy goal for all students to spend the same amount of time on a computer, all students may not need the same exposure. Some students may have to spend more time to master the objectives of their particular grade and subject.

Equity also applies to teachers and students. While many students have access to the Internet and E-mail, the gap between students' and teachers' use and access remains great.

Bit: Abbreviation for *B*inary dig*it*. A bit is the smallest unit of computer data and is represented by single number in base 2 (i.e., a 0 or a 1).

Browser: A software program used to access World Wide Web (see definition) sites. Browsers can be text based (such as *Lynx*) or graphic (such as *Netscape* or *Internet Explorer*).

Bulletin Board System (BBS): A computerized meeting and announcement system that allows people to carry on discussions, upload and download files, and make announcements without the people being connected to the computer at the same time. There are many thousands of BBSs around the world; most are very small, running on a single IBM clone PC with one or two phone lines. Some are very large, and the line between a BBS and a system like CompuServe gets crossed at some point, but it is not clearly drawn.

Byte: A string of bits, usually eight bits in length. A byte represents a number or character. K is used to stand for 1,024 bytes. (K means 1,000.) One megabyte (MB) equals 1,000 K. (Mega means a million.) One gigabyte (GB) equals 1,000 MB. These designations are important because they are used to describe how large computer files are and are also used to describe the amount of internal memory (RAM) and the hard drive size of a computer. (See also *RAM*.)

CD-R, CD-RW (Compact Disc Recordable, Compact Disc-Rewriteable): A type of CD-ROM that may be used in a CD-R or CD-RW drive to record data or create multimedia or audio CDs. A CD-R may be written to only once, while a CD-RW can be erased and reused in similar fashion to a floppy disk.

CD-ROM (Compact Disc-Read Only Memory): A disk that looks like an audio CD that is used to store computer data (up to 650 megabytes). Many computer software packages are distributed on CD-ROM, and these programs may includes color graphics, text, sound, and full-motion video.

Cookie: A collection of information, usually including a username and the current date and time, stored on the local computer of a person using the World Wide Web, used chiefly by Web sites to identify users who have previously registered or visited the site.

Cyberspace: A term originally coined by author William Gibson in his novel *Neuromancer*; this term is often used today to refer to the Internet, the World Wide Web, or any other information resource accessed through a computer.

DVD (Digital Versatile Disk): A new storage medium that is the same physical size as a CD-ROM but holds a much greater amount of data (up to 5.2 gigabytes). The medium's most common content is motion pictures, but DVD computer games and educational software are beginning to appear with greater frequency. Consumer-level recordable DVD drives first appeared on the market in 1998.

E-mail: Messages or "mail" sent from one person to another via computer. For example, my E-mail address is morrison@coefs.coe.unt.edu. Any person linked to the Internet (see definition) can communicate with me through E-mail. E-mail is also the standard form of communication for many mailing lists. As a result, persons can "post" notices to mailing lists, often consisting of large numbers of subscribers, and read the responses through their E-mail.

Figure 13.1
Glossary of Technological and Internet Terms

Racial and Socioeconomic Equity

Although the overall number of schools connected to the Internet is climbing, low-income and minority students are still less likely to have access than are affluent, mainstream stu-

Ethernet: Common method of connecting computers in a Local Area Network (LAN). Typical ethernet data transfer rate is 10,000,000 bits per second, and ethernet will work with almost any computer, regardless of power or age.

FAQ (Frequently Asked Question): A common feature of many Web sites and bulletin boards, the FAQ is a resource where new users may find answers to the most common questions regarding a given service or topic.

Freenet: An organization that provides Internet access to the public for free or for a small contribution.

Gigabyte (GB): 1,000 megabytes, or one billion bytes.

Gopher: A very successful menu system developed at the University of Minnesota to make information stored on the Internet easier to access. While the World Wide Web and hypertext have largely supplanted Gopher, Gopher servers are accessible through Web browsers. Given the number of Gopher servers in place, they will probably still be in use for quite some time.

Graphics Interchange Format (GIF): A service mark used for a raster-based color graphics file format, often used on the World Wide Web to store graphics.

Hard disk drive: A sealed disk used to store data. It stores more information and runs much faster than a floppy disk. Hard drives come in many sizes, and the bigger the better, because much of today's software takes large amounts of disk space. Hard drives have become so large that their size is typically measured in gigabytes (GB).

Home page: Typically used to refer to the main page of the Web site of a business or organization.

Hypermedia: Software that enables the user to access or link to other media such as graphics, audio, video, animation, and so forth, through a process known as branching. For example, you could read a small biography on Mozart, click a button to hear a symphony, and click another button to read about the influence of his music on the film industry.

Hypertext: Refers to any text that, when clicked by the user, causes another document to be retrieved.

Hyper-Text Markup Language (HTML): A markup language used to structure text and multimedia documents and to set up hyperlinks between documents, used extensively on the World Wide Web.

Interactive: Describes communicating one-on-one with the computer. The person operating the computer gives the computer a command, the computer reacts, the operator gives another command, and so forth. An example of a noninteractive process is when the computer operator gives a command and the computer finishes the task, process, or program without further instructions from the operator. Typically, drill-type software for students is considered noninteractive, or passive. An open-ended product, such as a software drawing program, would be considered interactive.

dents. Students from affluent families (families with a high socioeconomic status) are more than three times as likely to own a computer than are less fortunate students.

The percentage of public schools with Internet access increased from 35 percent in 1994 to 78 percent in 1997.[3] In schools where minority enrollment is 50 percent or more, only 63 percent have access to the Internet. On the other hand, 84 percent of schools with a minority enrollment of less than 6 percent have Internet access. Seventy-three percent of white students have computers; only 33 percent of African American students have computers.[4]

Internet: A worldwide computer network that links the various computer systems at participating government agencies, educational institutions, and commercial and private entities. The Department of Defense started the network (then ARPANET) in 1969. Today, it is estimated that the Internet consists of well over 60,000 interconnected networks. Quite an electronic highway!

Internet Relay Chat (IRC): A very large, multiuser live Internet chat facility. Any user can create his or her own "channel," which may be either public or private.

Internet Service Provider (ISP): A company that provides other companies or individuals with access to, or presence on, the Internet. Most ISPs are also Internet Access Providers; extra services include help with design, creation, and administration of World Wide Web sites, training, and administration of intranets.

Java: A trademark used for a programming language designed to develop applications, especially ones for the Internet, that can operate on different platforms.

Joint Photographic Experts Group (JPEG or JPG): The standard algorithm for the compression of digital images.

Local Area Network (LAN): A network (usually ethernet) that connects computers that are close to each other, usually in the same building, linked by cable.

Megabyte (MB): 1,000 kilobytes, or one million bytes.

Modem (MOdulator/DEModulator): Hardware, either internal or external, that connects to a telephone line and converts computer language to be sent over telephone lines. The modem transforms the computer's digital signal(s) (0s and 1s) to analog signals (sound). Given this conversion process, modems are inherently slower than a direct digital connection, but are still cheaper and more readily available for home users. Modem speed is measured in kilobytes per second (typical are 28.8K bps and 56K bps speeds). So-called cable modems are becoming more popular and offer a performance increase of up to ten times more than the fastest analog modems.

Mouse: A device that enables users to manipulate the cursor by hand—by moving the mouse and clicking a switch—rather than by using keyboard commands. A trackball performs the same function but is stationary.

Multimedia: The integration of still pictures, motion pictures, text, and sound with reading, writing, drawing, problem solving, searching, and creating. This definition is different from a common use of the word to mean the use of various media hardware such as television, computers, projectors, and so forth.

Musical Instrument Digital Interface (MIDI): A standard for representing musical information in a digital format.

Netiquette: Used to refer to acceptable behavior or etiquette on the Internet. Acceptable behavior, of course, will vary greatly from one Internet site to another.

Newsgroup: Typically used to refer to a USENET (see definition) discussion group. There are thousands upon thousands of USENET discussion groups covering practically every conceivable topic.

Figure 13.1, continued

The Technological Gender Gap

A recent study by the American Association of University Women (AAUW) reports that technology represents the new gender gap for girls. "Girls have narrowed some significant gender gaps, but technology is now the new 'boys club' in our nation's public schools," said

Plug-in: A small piece of software that adds functionality to a larger piece of software. For example, to add audio and video features to a Web browser, a plug-in supporting the various media standards will need to be added to the browser. More popular formats (such as *RealAudio* and *Shockwave*) have plug-ins built into or shipped with the browser software.

RAM: Acronym for Random Access Memory, used to describe the amount of memory a computer has (e.g., 64 MB of RAM). RAM is important because software packages often specify how many megabytes of RAM they require.

Scanner: An input device that copies pictures and words into the computer by turning the visual representations (analog) into digital information. Once in the computer, the digital information may be manipulated, stored, and printed.

Software: The programs, systems, data, games, and information that are stored on various media used in computers and other hardware.

Sound-card: Hardware, either built into the computer or obtained as an additional accessory, used to produce sound through the computer. Sound may be played back or recorded onto the computer's hard drive through the sound card.

Spam: Refers to "junk" or bulk E-mail that the user did not request to receive. Spam typically takes the form of advertising or get-rich-quick schemes. Many E-mail software packages now have anti-Spam utilities.

Telecommunications: The process of using telephone lines and computers to communicate with other computers. Satellite dishes play an important role in telecommunications and in distance learning—that is, the delivery of classes in which the teacher is not physically present. Telecommunications, such as E-mail, involves a computer, modem, telephone line, and telecommunication software.

Uniform Resource Locator (URL): The unique Internet address that identifies Web pages and sites. For example, the URL of my Web site is http://www.unt.edu/velma_schmidt. The inclusion of a URL has become almost ubiquitous in print and television advertising.

USENET: The Internet's decentralized system of discussion groups, also known as newsgroups. Users are able to post, read, and respond to messages on virtually any imaginable topic.

Veronica (Very Easy Rodent Oriented Net-wide Index to Computerized Archives): Veronica, developed at the University of Nevada, is a constantly updated database of almost every menu item found on any Gopher server and can be searched from major Gopher menus.

Virtual reality: A computer-based simulated environment that users seem to enter and that seems real for the participant.

Virus: A cracker program that searches out other programs and "infects" them by embedding a copy of itself in them, so that they become Trojan horses. When these programs are executed, the embedded virus is executed too, thus propagating the "infection." This normally happens invisibly to the user.

World Wide Web (WWW): This term has essentially two meanings. It is often used (albeit incorrectly) to refer to the Internet itself but more correctly refers specifically to the vast number of linked hypertext servers (http servers) that allow text, graphics, and streaming audio and video to be mixed together.

AAUW Executive Director Janice Weinman. Despite the progress in certain areas, gaps persist. "The gender gaps we see are evidence that public schools are failing to fully prepare girls for the 21st century," according to Sandy Bernard, president of AAUW. "As student diversity changes the face of public education, and technology changes the workplace, schools must work smarter and harder to ensure that girls graduate with the knowledge and abilities they need to compete and succeed in the 21st century economy," said Maggie Ford, president of AAUW Educational Foundation.[5]

Program in Action

East Rock Magnet School's Technology Program

East Rock Magnet School (New Haven, Connecticut) is a pioneer in the field of technology for K–8 education. The school has a formal partnership with both Compaq Computer and Microsoft Corporation. In addition, East Rock is a model technology school for Compaq on the East Coast and a national model school for Microsoft for the use of NT, Internet Explorer, and many of their software programs. Recently, the school became a national model for Asante Technologies because of its unique, extensive, and elaborate networking design. Yale University and Comcast Cable are additional sponsors, contributing extensively in program development each year. The school also receives funding from the New Haven Public Schools and from various grants and sponsorships.

Mission Statement

East Rock Magnet: A Global Studies School is dedicated to increasing the students' awareness and knowledge of their world. Its goal is to equip students with information-processing skills of accessing, analyzing, and communicating information effectively. Emphasis is directed towards improving student achievement levels through an interdisciplinary curriculum that incorporates state-of-the-art technology.

Vision Statement

East Rock Global Studies Magnet School recognizes that a Balanced Literacy Program is the key to the future success of our students. The philosophy is integrated into the district's curriculum framework, the national standards, and the global studies/technology curriculum of East Rock. It ensures that our students learn the necessary information literacy skills to compete in a global, technological, and information-driven society for the next millennium. Our new technology provides the proper tools for:

- Teachers to facilitate learning
- Students to learn higher-level thinking skills and communicate ideas
- Teachers and students to access, organize, and process information; reinforce prior learning; and solve problems more creatively, effectively, and efficiently

The sizable collection of print, audiovisual materials, and technology resources, based on the school's global studies curriculum, promotes the success of resource-based teaching/learning and recreational reading. The Library Media Center serves as an extension of the classroom and is the educational hub of the school. Furthermore, the library contains a Technology Media Center and a Teacher Resource Area.

In addition, our students, staff members, parents, and members of the community have access to our state-of-the-art technology, which includes the automation of the Library Media Center, schoolwide accessible networking (WAN), and our diverse collection of references and literature. The Internet, the Library Media Center's On-line catalog (OPAC), the New Haven Free Public Library's On-line Catalog, and software programs can be accessed from anywhere in the school.

To plan thematic units, the staff works collaboratively with the Library Media Specialist, who further identifies the portion of the collection and technology that will enrich their instructional programs. The above is made feasible by a newly developed flex schedule and a mapping of all grades with a monthly list of all core objectives. The Library Media Center services our students, teachers, support staff, and parents throughout the regular school day, as well as during our extended school day program.

In addition, the Technology Facilitator/Systems Engineer and the two Curriculum Facilitators collaboratively plan with the Library Media Specialist to promote and enhance many of the goals and objectives of the core program. A full-time Technology Facilitator/Systems Engineer executes

all of the sophisticated network/software installations and maintenance as well as the teaching and correlation of software programs. Our Curriculum Facilitators advance the Magnet School concept by working with both teachers and students on various thematic unit projects, including a full-scale video production studio. As a result, the students are active, curious learners who excel in the fundamentals of education: literacy, math, and science.

INFRASTRUCTURE AND DESIGN OF NETWORK

The results of the computer implementation of East Rock exemplify the recent scholarly evaluations showing that the use of technology improves teaching and learning. Integrating computers into classroom instruction is increasing student achievement 20 to 40 percent each year.

East Rock is a highly connected network providing access to resources, tools, and information across disciplinary, institutional, and national and international boundaries. It is our hope that East Rock will remain one of the pioneers in computer technology and promote a new style of learning for the next millennium.

CONCLUSION

> As the world shrinks, all of its people and knowledge are reachable from any point. The globe, once so vast, becomes more village-like. Any village and any learner can touch all the globe. (*Marshall McLuhan*)

Children around the world are growing up in a global society. Most of us were educated throughout our lifetimes in a world quite different from the one that our children now know. Children need new literacy and technology skills to function productively in this unique and culturally rich environment.

Children who grow up seeing themselves as human beings related to all other human beings have the potential for developing responsive, humane institutions and technologies to enhance the human condition throughout the world. As they explore the nature of being human, they come to see that each person depends upon and is responsible for all other human beings.

Visit East Rock at http://eastrock.org on the Web.

Contributed by Domenic A. Grignano, Technology Facilitator and Systems Engineer, East Rock Magnet School, New Haven, Connecticut.

REASONS FOR THE GENDER GAP. What are some of the reasons this gender gap exists?

- *Society's expectations for women*. Society stresses that technology is not a "girl thing." The stereotype of a girl is a person who is smart and intelligent, yet she still can't be too involved in technology.[6] As a result of societal messages that are sent by parents and teachers, found in the media, and embedded in technology and software itself, girls may think that they are not as capable as boys at technological activities. It seems that, as a result, more boys use computers outside of schools than do girls.[7]
- *Stereotypes about traditional work roles*. Computer and technology classes in schools are attended mainly by boys rather than girls. If girls do enroll in computer classes, it is most likely that they will enroll in a class such as data processing, whereas boys will enroll in the advanced computer science courses. "High schools still tend to steer girls and boys into School-to-Work programs that prepare them for traditional occupations for their gender," said Sandy Bernard. Janice Weinman continued, "While boys program and problem solve with computers, girls use computers for word processing, the 1990s version of typing."[8]

Table 13.1
Percentage of Students Using Computers at Home (based on socioeconomic status)

Household Income	Prekindergarten and Kindergarten	Grades 1 to 8
Less than $5,000	1.1	4.1
$5,000 to $9,999	0.9	4.5
$10,000 to $14,999	4.6	6.4
$15,000 to $19,999	6.9	10.9
$20,000 to $24,999	7.4	13.1
$25,000 to $29,999	12.3	19.3
$30,000 to $34,999	18.7	20.5
$35,000 to $39,999	13.0	26.3
$40,000 to $49,999	21.6	32.9
$50,000 to $74,999	25.5	45.3
$75,000 or more	38.2	62.3

Source: U.S. Department of Education, Office of Educational Research and Improvement, Digest of Education Statistics 1997 *(Washington, DC: U.S. Government Printing Office, 1997).*

- *The computer geek stereotype*. According to Jane Margolis, a research scientist at Carnegie Mellon University, "One reason girls are less inclined to study computers is the geek stereotype—the idea that if you're interested in computer science, you don't have a social life."[9] Since girls are often more social than boys, this concern may prevent them from exploring technology as a hobby or possible career path.
- *Male-oriented technology*. Unfortunately, most software today is male oriented. This only adds to the technological gender gap. A review of software conducted by Children's Software Revue reported that computer games during 1996 and 1997 were mainly male oriented since the main characters were male instead of female.[10] Of course, private software companies have the right to make their game characters male if they choose, but consumers have the right to refuse to purchase software that includes gender and other biases.

CLOSING THE GENDER GAP. Although the gender gap in technology may seem large, it will not be around forever. Over the past hundred years, gender gaps in other areas have

Table 13.2
Percentage of Students Using Computers at School (based on gender and race)

Group	Prekindergarten and Kindergarten	Grades 1 to 8
Male	25.9	69.5
Female	26.5	68.4
White	29.4	73.7
Black	16.5	56.5
Hispanic	19.2	58.4

Source: U.S. Department of Education, Office of Educational Research and Improvement, Digest of Education Statistics 1997 *(Washington, DC: U.S. Government Printing Office, 1997).*

Many children come to school familiar with computers and other technology. Other children have very limited exposure. What can you do to ensure that all children's technological needs are met?

shrunk, and most likely so will the technology gender gap. Women have become leaders in math and science, have flown on space shuttle missions, and are successful leaders in all walks of life. For instance, one only has to think of Madame Curie or 1983 Nobel prize recipient Dr. Barbara McClintock to look at the hurdles women have overcome. The same shall hold true for technology.

To assist in closing the gender gap, many schools are now offering computer classes specifically for women. For example, WINDOWS (Women Inventing Notable Database Online Winning Self-esteem) is a computer course specifically for girls offered all over the country. The purpose of the class is to help deal with issues of self-esteem while learning advanced computer applications. Instead of learning nothing but theory, the class focuses on how to use computer science to help in other areas of learning, such as nutrition and career development. "The way computer science is usually taught—as an abstract subject in and of itself—also discourages girls from taking an interest," said Jane Margolis.[11] This is where the new gender-specific computer classes help, because not only do they help with self-esteem issues, they foster a different way to learn computer applications.

Choosing Nonbiased Technology-Based Materials

Society, parents, teachers, and policymakers must be leaders in helping ensure that there are no technological gender gaps and that all software is free of bias. As discussed in chapter 14 and elsewhere throughout this text, all professionals must take into consideration the diversity present in contemporary society. When professionals select materials, including computer software, videos, films, and other technologically based applications, they must make sure these materials include depictions of children and adults with differing abilities, ages, and ethnic backgrounds and that these materials are nonstereotypic of gender, culture, and socioeconomic class. The software industry has made progress in this regard but still has a long way to go to meet antibias criteria in their products. Professionals must evaluate all software they purchase and continually advocate for nonbiased software.

For help in choosing high-quality, appropriate software, go to the Companion Website at http://www.prenhall.com/morrison, select chapter 13, then choose the Linking to Learning module to connect to the SuperKids Educational Software Review site.

Susan Haugland, professor of child development at Southeast Missouri State University, offers the following suggestions when evaluating software:[12]

- Software should be available in multiple languages.
- Software should portray diverse environments and cultures as well as characteristics of all environments.
- Software should maintain gender equity; that is, both sexes are represented and there should be equity in their roles.
- Software should have heterogeneous representation (African Americans, Hispanics, Asians, etc.).

For more specific information on evaluating software, see Figures 13.2 and 13.3.

Technology and Special Childhood Populations

Technology can have a profound effect on children with special needs, including very young children, students with disabilities, and students who are bilingual or have limited English proficiency.

Technology and Infants, Toddlers, and Preschoolers

As already indicated, technology is a growing part of the world of very young children. Computers and other technology have a great deal to offer, and there is much that young children can learn via technology in all domains—cognitive, social, emotional, and linguistic. Software is being designed for children as young as nine months. This software is often referred to as "lapware" because children have to crawl onto parents' laps to use it, and it is intended to be used by parents and children together.

You will find many software programs out there for the very young. For instance, *Jumpstart Baby* (www.etoys.com) and *BabyWow* (www.babywow.com) are aimed specifically at children nine months to two years. *Jumpstart Baby* leads children through eight activities, including wood-block puzzles and nursery rhyme sing-alongs. *BabyWow* has three hundred pictures and corresponding vocabulary words in eight languages. Microsoft has a four-CD-ROM set called My *Personal Tutor* (www.microsoft.com/kids): *Preschool Workshop* emphasizes matching colors, shapes, and sizes; *Alphabet Playhouse* focuses on reading readiness; *Reader Railway* is a beginning reading program; and *Mathopolis* is devoted to mathematics.

The market for infant, toddler, and preschool software is growing, with an estimated $50 million spent each year. Programs designed for children under five represent the fastest growing educational software market. Not everyone believes that such software is developmentally appropriate, and the battle rages on in early childhood circles about how much time children should spend on computers and what kind of software they should use. Remember that not all software is good software. Good teachers have always evaluated the materials they use with their children. Now they must also assess the software that children use. Return to Figure 13.2 for one set of evaluative criteria that teachers may use. Then consult Figure 13.4, which contains highlights of NAEYC's position statement on technology and young children. How do you feel about NAEYC's position statement? Do you agree with all its statements?

Assistive Technology and Children with Disabilities

The field of early childhood education is undergoing dramatic changes through integration with the field of special education. As a result, early childhood professionals are adopting

HAUGLAND DEVELOPMENTAL SOFTWARE SCALE

REVISED EDITION

Title		Ages	
Publisher		Cost	
Date Evaluated	Hardware Evaluated On	Updated	
Evaluated by	Multiple Platforms	Copyright	

Description

Comments

PICTURE

Subscore ☐
Anti-Bias ☐
TOTAL ☐

Age Appropriate ☐	☐ Realistic concepts ☐ Appropriate methods
Child in Control ☐	☐ Actors not reactors ☐ Can escape ☐ Children set pace ☐ Trial and error
Clear Instructions ☐	☐ Picture choices ☐ Simple, precise directions ☐ Verbal instructions
Expanding Complexity ☐	☐ Low entry, high ceiling ☐ Learning sequence is clear ☐ Teaches powerful ideas
Independence ☐	☐ Adult supervision not needed after initial exposure
Non-Violence ☐	☐ Software is free of violent characters and actions ☐ Software models positive social values
Process Orientation ☐	☐ Discovery learning, not skill drilling ☐ Intrinsic motivation ☐ Process engages, product secondary
Real-World Model ☐	☐ Concrete representations ☐ Objects function ☐ Simple, reliable model
Technical Features ☐	☐ Animation ☐ Colorful ☐ Installs easily ☐ Operates consistently ☐ Prints ☐ Realistic corresponding sound effects or music ☐ Runs quickly ☐ Saves children's work ☐ Uncluttered realistic graphics
Transformations ☐	☐ Objects and situations change ☐ Process highlighter
Multiple Languages ☐	☐ Multiple languages
Universal Focus ☐	☐ Universal focus
Mixed Gender and Role Equity ☐	☐ Mixed gender and role equity ☐ Exempt
People of Diverse Cultures ☐	☐ People of diverse cultures ☐ Exempt
Differing Ages and Abilities ☐	☐ Differing ability or age ☐ Exempt
Diverse Family Styles ☐	☐ Diverse family styles ☐ Exempt

Figure 13.2

Haugland Developmental Software Scale

Not all software is appropriate for classroom use. As a teacher, you will have to evaluate printed materials and software you use with your students. This software rating scale will help you make informed decisions about whether you want to use a particular software.

Source: Susan W. Haugland, based on the Haugland/Shade Developmental Scale, 1997.

The Haugland Developmental Software Scale is designed to distinguish software that is developmentally appropriate for young children and is consistent with NAEYC Guidelines for Developmentally Appropriate Practices (Bredekamp, 1986) and the NAEYC Position Statement on Technology and Young Children, Ages 3 through 8 (NAEYC, 1996). The scale is based on ten criteria, which are listed in the left column, beginning with Age Appropriate and ending with Transformations. These are the ten important components of software. Each criterion consists of characteristics that are listed to the right of the criteria. If software has all the characteristics within the criterion, enter 1.0 in the center box for that criterion. If it has 50 percent or more of the characteristics, enter a score of .5. If it has a less than one-half the characteristics, enter a score of 0 for that criterion. Add the scores for the ten criteria and enter the subscore.

Next, an antibias deduction is calculated to ensure that the software reflects the diversity of society. All software is expected to have multiple languages and a universal focus. Software with humanized animals must also have mixed gender and role equity. Software representing people must have mixed gender and role equity and include people of diverse cultures and with differing abilities and ages. Software depicting families must represent diverse family styles. Calculate how many characteristics the software needs to have (ranging from 2 to 6) and then score the deduction based on the same method you used for the criteria. However, since it is a deduction, software receives a 0 if it has all the required characteristics, -.5 if it has half the characteristics or more, -1 if it has less than half. Enter the antibias deduction below the subscore and subtract. This will provide you the final score for the software.

Software must receive a score of 7.0 or above to be developmentally appropriate for young children. Do not be surprised if many of your scores are low. Only 20 percent of the software being marketed for young children is developmentally appropriate.

For more information on administering the scale, including definitions of characteristics and Guidelines for Internal Consistency (which ensures reliability in scoring), see the book *Young Children and Technology: A World of Discovery* by Susan Haugland and June Wright (1987). Also the Computers and Young Children Web site provides descriptions, publishers, scores, and so forth for the best software over the past two years. Each month features four new software reviews, including pictures of the programs. The Computer and Young Children Web site is located at estl.semo.edu/kidscomp.

Figure 13.3
Guidelines for Administering the Haugland Developmental Software Scale

Source: Susan W. Haugland, based on the Haugland/Shade Developmental Scale, 1997.

assistive technology to help children and their families. According to Public Law 100-407, the Technology-Related Assistance for Individuals with Disabilities Act of 1988 (Tech Act), *assistive technology* is "any item, device or piece of equipment, or product system, whether acquired commercially off the shelf, modified, or customized, that is used to increase, maintain, or improve functional abilities of individuals with disabilities."[13]

Assistive technology covers a wide range of products and applications, from simple devices such as adaptive spoons and switch-adapted battery-operated toys to complex devices such as computerized environmental control systems. You will have opportunities to use many forms of assistive technology and modified educational software with all ages of students with special needs.

Assistive technology is particularly important for students with disabilities who depend on technology to help them communicate, learn, and be mobile. For example, closed-circuit television can be used to enlarge print, a Braille printer can convert words to Braille, and audiotaped instructional materials can be provided for students with vision impairments.

Although there is considerable research that points to the positive effects of technology on children's learning and development, the research indicates that, in practice, computers supplement and do not replace highly valued early childhood activities and materials, such as art, blocks, sand, water, books, exploration with writing materials, and dramatic play. Research indicates that computers can be used in developmentally appropriate ways beneficial to children and also can be misused, just as any tool can. Developmentally appropriate software offers opportunities for collaborative play, learning, and creation. Educators must use professional judgment in evaluating and using this learning tool appropriately, applying the same criteria they would to any other learning tool or experience. They must also weigh the costs of technology with the costs of other learning materials and program resources to arrive at an appropriate balance for their classrooms.

- In evaluating the appropriate use of technology, NAEYC applies principles of developmentally appropriate practice and appropriate curriculum and assessment. In short, NAEYC believes that in any given situation, a professional judgment by the teacher is required to determine if a specific use of technology is age appropriate, individually appropriate, and culturally appropriate.
- Used appropriately, technology can enhance children's cognitive and social abilities.
- Appropriate technology is integrated into the regular learning environment and used as one of many options to support children's learning.
- Early childhood educators should promote equitable access to technology for all children and their families. Children with special needs should have access when this is helpful.
- The power of technology to influence children's learning and development requires that attention be paid to eliminating stereotyping of any group and eliminating exposure to violence, especially as a problem-solving strategy.
- Teachers, in collaboration with parents, should advocate for more appropriate technology applications for children.
- The appropriate use of technology has many implications for early childhood professional development.

Figure 13.4
NAEYC Position Statement on Technology and Young Children

Source: "NAEYC Position Statement: Technology and Young Children, Ages 3 Through 8," Young Children *(September 1996), pp. 11–16. Copyright © 1996 by the National Association for the Education of Young Children. Reprinted by permission from the National Association for the Education of Young Children.*

Closed-captioned television and FM amplification systems can assist students who are deaf or hard of hearing. Touch-screen computers, augmentative communication boards, and voice synthesizers can assist students with limited mobility or with disabilities that make communication difficult. Technology helps children with vision impairments see and children with physical disabilities read and write. Technology helps developmentally delayed children learn the skills they need to achieve at their appropriate levels and enables children with disabilities to substitute one ability for another and receive the special training they need. In addition, computer-assisted instruction provides software tools for teaching students at all ability levels, including programmed instruction for students with specific learning disabilities.

Opportunities for using many forms of assistive technology are available to even very young children, from birth to age three. Some of these include powered mobility, myoelectric prostheses, and communication devices. Infants as young as three months have interacted

For more information about assistive technology, go to the Companion Website at http://www.prenhall.com/morrison, select chapter 13, then choose the Linking to Learning module to connect to the Assistive Technology, Inc. site.

with computers, eighteen-month-old children have driven powered mobility devices and used myoelectric hands, and two-year-olds have talked via speech synthesizers. Children with severe physical disabilities learn how to use switches and scanning techniques.

Technology permits children with special needs to enjoy—through the process of learning—knowledge, skills, and behaviors that might otherwise be inaccessible to them. Technology empowers children with special needs; that is, it enables them to exercise control over their lives and the conditions of their learning. It enables them to do things previously thought impossible.

In addition, technology changes people's attitudes about children with disabilities. For example, some may have viewed children with disabilities as not being able to participate fully in regular classrooms; however, they may now recognize that instead of being segregated in separate programs, these children can be fully included with the assistance of technology.

JUDGING APPROPRIATENESS OF ASSISTIVE TECHNOLOGY. An extremely important issue in the use of assistive technology with young children is the appropriateness of such technology. It is considered appropriate if it meets the following criteria:

- First, a technology should respond to (or anticipate) specific, clearly defined goals that result in enhanced skills for the child.
- Second, a technology should be compatible with practical constraints, such as available resources or the amount of training required to enable the child, his family, and the early childhood educator to use the technology.
- Third, a technology should result in desirable and sufficient outcomes. Some basic considerations for children with disabilities are related to (1) ease of training the child and

Assistive technology enables children with disabilities to participate in regular classrooms and to learn skills and behaviors not previously thought possible. What are some examples of assistive technologies that would enable this child and others with disabilities to learn?

his family to use and care for the technology; (2) reasonable maintenance and repair, with regard to time and expense; and (3) monitoring of the technology's effectiveness.[14]

The mere application of technology is therefore not enough. Early childhood professionals have to be sensitive to the above criteria as they work with children, families, and other professionals in applying technology to learning settings and children's special needs.

Technology and Children with Limited English Proficiency

Whereas the bilingual/multicultural software market was once neglected, businesses now realize there is a growing need for programs and software to meet the needs of a diverse population.

For example, the Florida Department of Education, the Dade County, Florida, Public Schools, and the Jostens Learning Corporation in San Diego, California, cooperatively developed "Technology-Assisted Language Learning for K–12 ESOL Students." The program was designed to be appropriate for English for Speakers of Other Languages (ESOL) programs across the nation. Total development cost of this program exceeded $6 million. Happily, such collaborative efforts between software companies and school districts have become more commonplace.

One part of the program is designed to help Spanish-speaking students in kindergarten and primary grades become fluent in English. It introduces them to the sounds and rhythms of the English language through literature, rhymes, and songs. Eight thematic units include on- and off-line activities that work together to help nonindependent and beginning-level students acquire the basic vocabulary and concepts they need to succeed in the classroom. These units use animation, full-color graphics, sound, role plays, games, small-group activities, and collaborative groups. Figure 13.5 depicts the contents of the K–3 component and shows steps to English language development.

Assistive technology such as the Alpha Talker II™ helps this child learn and use a basic core vocabulary. By selecting an appropriate icon, the Alpha Talker II™ enables her to talk and communicate with others. This technology is easily programmed for new words.

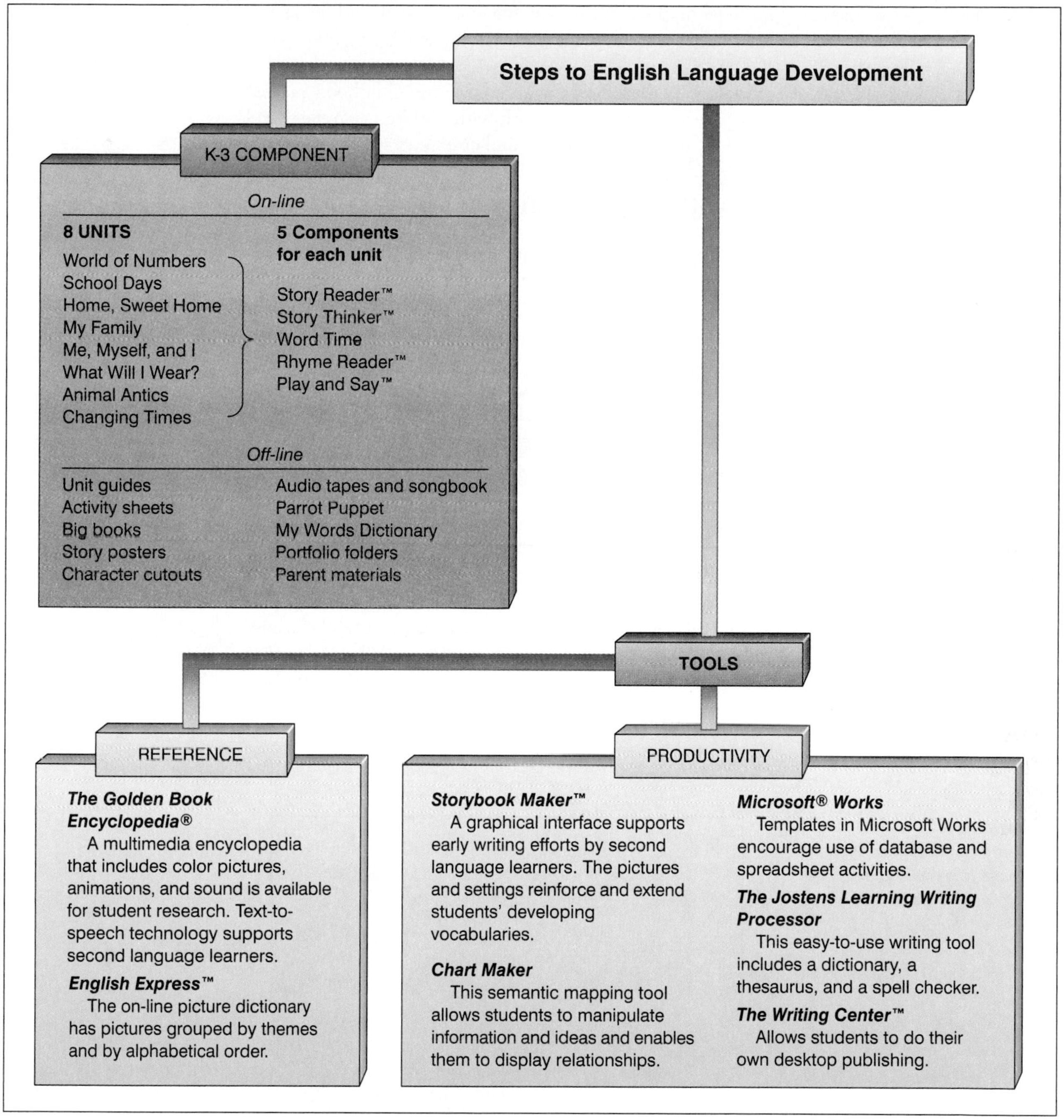

Figure 13.5

Steps to English Language Development

Business and industry are leaders in using technology to achieve their goals. As this figure illustrates, business and industry are collaborating with school districts to assist schools in using technology to achieve teaching and learning goals.

Source: Courtesy of Jostens Learning Corporation, San Diego, CA. Used by permission.

Implementing Technology in Early Childhood Education Programs

Three challenges confront early childhood teachers in implementing an effective program of computer instruction:

1. Their own personal acceptance of computers
2. Assurance that computers have a positive influence on children
3. Decisions about how to use computers in early childhood programs and classrooms

The next few sections of this chapter will help you address these challenges, because teachers cannot afford to decide not to use computers and technology. When they do, they risk having technologically illiterate children; denying children access to skills, knowledge, and learning; and not promoting an attitude of acceptance of technology into their everyday lives. Rather, they must promote access to technology and develop creative ways to involve children with technology.

Setting a Good Example: Your Personal Acceptance of Computers

As an early childhood educator, the first step in implementing an effective program of computer instruction is accepting technology and learning how to use it effectively and appropriately. Here are four guidelines for you to keep in mind: [15]

- Early childhood teachers must be aware of the potential benefits of computers and technology.
- Early childhood professionals must be open to the use of technology to help children learn new knowledge and skills.
- Early childhood teacher education and staff development programs must provide training in how to integrate technology into all areas of the early childhood curriculum.
- Early childhood programs must make computers available to all teachers and programs.

For links to topics of interest for early childhood educators, go to the Companion Website at http://www.prenhall.com/morrison, select chapter 13, then choose the Linking to Learning module to connect to the ECEOL (Early Childhood Education Online) site.

Your confidence and comfort level with technology will set a good example for the children in your care. As you use computers to access information through the Internet, send E-mail, and keep records of children's accomplishments, children will come to understand that computers are a natural part of the process of schooling and learning. Establishing positive attitudes toward technology is an important part of fostering an appropriate and inviting classroom environment.

Ensuring Positive Experiences: The Computer's Influence on Children

It is clear that technology can sometimes present challenges of organization and management and be controversial in terms of access and fair use. So why should educators introduce technology into the early childhood learning environment?

Research provides us with much valuable information about the influence of technology on children, their responses to technology, and how technology helps them learn. The results of these studies seem encouraging. In one study involving kindergarten and third grade children, researchers found that computers cultivated and sustained children's attention and concentration. Even while using television as a distracter during a twenty-seven-minute lesson, kindergarten children spent 69 percent and third graders 86 percent of their time attending to the computer. The researchers concluded the following:

> Computers can provide an intrinsically interesting learning environment for children that promotes attention, concentration to the task at hand, and reduced distractibility to competing environmental stimuli. Like television, computers appear to sustain attention by a rather effortless process. This effortless attentional process can be directed towards educational computer content that is worthy of children's sustained attention.[16]

Researchers have conducted many studies regarding the effects of technology on children's behavior, achievement, and literacy development. This research shows that technology and appropriate software, used in the right ways, promotes active learning, problem solving, literacy, and social-emotional development.[17] Furthermore, children exposed to developmental software—that is, software specifically identified as having the potential to support children's development—demonstrated gains in intelligence, nonverbal skills, structural knowledge, long-term memory, and complex memory. In addition, when developmental software is reinforced with supplemental activities, children also show gains in verbal skills, problem solving, abstractions, and conceptual skills.[18]

Making Decisions: How to Use Computers in Early Childhood Programs and Classrooms Effectively

As an early childhood educator, your next responsibility is to determine how to make the most of available technologies to spark your children's' learning and imagination. You should

Technology allows children to explore different worlds, access resources, and engage in learning activities. How can you use computers and other technology to appropriately support children's learning?

consider two learning goals for your students: learning *with* computers and learning *about* computers."[19] Decisions concerning what children learn about computers should be made not by asking, "What can we teach kids about computers?" but rather by asking, "What understandings about computers, their impact on our world, and their uses are developmentally appropriate for, and educationally relevant to, young children?"[20] This implies that lectures on the history of computers or rote memorization of computer components and terminology should not be included in the curriculum. Only when meaningful concepts can be actively learned should they be considered for inclusion.

When making decisions about how to use computers and computer-based technologies in the early childhood learning environment, there are a few questions to keep in mind: Is the technology developmentally appropriate? Are you meeting learners' individual needs when using technology? Does the technology promote the kind of learning you want to promote? Is the use of technology seamlessly integrated into the curriculum?

IS THE TECHNOLOGY DEVELOPMENTALLY APPROPRIATE? We have already noted the importance of children having a feeling of confidence and willingness to become involved with computers and computer technology. Such an attitude comes naturally when children are involved in developmentally appropriate technology-based activities.

Decisions about how to use technology in early childhood programs must always be based on developmentally appropriate practice. Review NAEYC's Position Statement on Technology and Young Children in Figure 13.4. Additionally, the NAEYC Position on Developmentally Appropriate Practice is found in Appendix B. It would be helpful for you to review these resources now as a means of developing your awareness about the use of technology and as background for making decisions about how to best provide for the technological needs of children.

Program in Action

Digital Literacy in the Kindergarten

Our challenge, as we saw it, was to use the computer to promote both computer literacy and reading skills without inhibiting creativity. In our kindergarten classroom we looked for ways in which technology would enhance or expand, in substantive ways, the limits of what could be accomplished. We were looking to do more than use a word processor to transcribe children's words or a drawing program to replace traditional handmade storybooks. Although we were aware that developing computer literacy would be a result of such a project, we were searching for ways in which the computer could creatively facilitate reading and writing literacy other than by imitating the traditional methods. We were also hoping that through the use of technology we could expand the type of projects possible in the classroom.

We used digital cameras to document trips and special projects, science experiments, and work done with blocks and in the creative play area as well as with manipulatives. The children continually surprised us with the skills they learned. They learned how to take pictures with the camera, download the pictures to the computer, use software to crop and alter their photos, sometimes adding an element of humor or surrealism to their work.

On a trip to Wave Hill Botanical Garden in the Bronx, we used this technique by having our students photograph the visit, print the pictures,

and annotate them. We used these pictures to create a bulletin board and later a book to share with their parents. Later in the year, after the children had gained enough keyboard proficiency and reading and writing skills to work more independently, we photographed a cooking class and produced another book that the students captioned using the computer—a project that lasted several weeks. In addition, the book became an extended exercise not only in literacy but also recall, verbalization of ideas, and creative writing practice—especially when the children condensed their commentary into captions that synthesized their thoughts and experiences. In another instance, we used this process to help a child who was a fluent reader but was reluctant to write. We encouraged him to make a photo essay of his school birthday party. This was enough to motivate him to experiment with the written word!

An important feature of these projects was that digital photos could be taken, downloaded, and printed in a matter of fifteen minutes. This allowed experiences to be on paper while they were still fresh in the children's minds. Some children learned to open their own files and start their own portfolios. However, this more advanced literacy led to questions of ethical behavior, integrity, honesty, and privacy. Children needed to be taught to work on only their own projects and not use their new profound computer proficiency to wreak havoc on a classmate's file.

Toward the end of the school year we utilized Kid Pix Companion Slide Show to create a presentation from photographs we'd taken, documenting the kindergarten experience. The slide show was an overview of the year's activities, which the children and parents could recall and reflect on. While the teachers initially set up the program as some students looked on, the students gradually took control of the program. As they learned, the children tutored each other on the workings of making a slide show. Each child in the class selected a photograph from our growing collection that was particularly relevant to him or her, brought the photograph into the program, and recorded an oral description of the activity pictured. This then became the student's personal frame in the show. The children also programmed the style of movement from one frame to the next. The entire class was enthusiastically involved in this project. The presentation that resulted was then shared with the parents at the annual Academic Fair. The children were able to show their parents their own personal slide show frame, as well as those of their classmates, and instruct the adults on the way to navigate the program.

For us as teachers, this project marked a milestone in attaining our goal of more creative use of technology in the classroom. Numerous benefits were reaped from this experience, including the following:

- The project involved *all* the children. Many who were formerly intimidated by computers became active, enthusiastic participants in this project.
- It gave the children a chance to highlight what they believed represented their interests, strengths, and talents.
- It gave the parents a window into school life.
- It allowed immediate documentation of learning experiences, which stimulated dialogue among the children.
- Digital photography captured images of experiences on the screen or on paper while they were still fresh in the children's minds. This became a great stimulus to writing.
- It allowed the children to express their artistic sensibilities through photography, image alteration, and layout.
- Through the manipulation of the software, the children became more comfortable using the computer and were able to explore the capabilities of the technology. The project stimulated the use of problem-solving strategies to overcome some of the technical challenges they faced.
- The children derived great satisfaction from their work. They were excited to share their school lives, through this media, with their families. The families were similarly excited to have a chance to see what went on during the school year.

Contributed by Ella Pastor, Emily Kerns, and Paula Reddy. Ella Pastor (epastor@juno.com) is head teacher of a kindergarten class; Emily Kerns (ekerns5285@aol.com) is an assistant teacher; and Paula Reddy is a computer specialist at Riverdale Country School, Bronx, New York. Together they designed this approach to fostering computer literacy for very young children.

ARE YOU MEETING LEARNERS' INDIVIDUAL NEEDS WHEN USING TECHNOLOGY? One additional aspect of ensuring that technology is being used most effectively in your classroom is making sure that children's individual needs are being met. You will want to take children's individual differences into account when making decisions about how to best involve them in learning activities with computers and other technology. Some children will need more help and encouragement than others, and some will intrinsically want to be more involved because of their learning style preference for using technology to learn.

Individual children will have different needs, interests, and abilities and, therefore, will learn different things about computers and will use them in different ways. This should be welcomed as well as accepted; no effort should be made to force all children to "master" all aspects of computer literacy. Instead of one definition of technological literacy for all, teachers should determine what computers can do to help a particular child reach a particular goal.

DOES THE TECHNOLOGY PROMOTE THE KIND OF LEARNING YOU WANT TO PROMOTE? Different educators have varying approaches to and philosophies of facilitating and promoting children's learning through computers. For some, the computer and software are seen as a central element of teachers teaching and children learning. On the other hand, some see computers as a means of providing open-ended discovery learning, problem solving, and computer competence. Different applications promote different kinds of learning experiences, and you will need to make intelligent decisions about which of these applications best suit your learners' needs and interests and your instructional objectives.

Drill Versus Discovery. A major controversy among early childhood professionals involves the purpose of computers in the classroom. On the one hand, some say that the more repetitive drill-and-practice programs have no place in the early childhood program. They say that only software that encourages learning by discovery and exploration is appropriate. On the other hand, some professionals see drill-and-practice software programs that emphasize helping children learn colors, numbers, vocabulary, and skills such as addition as a valuable means for children to learn concepts and skills they so desperately need to succeed in school.

Of course, in this case, as with so many things, a middle ground offers an appropriate solution. Many children like drill-and-practice programs and the positive feedback that often comes with them. Also, some children spend long periods of time working on such programs. However, not all children like or do well with skill-drill programs. Technological aids, as with other learning materials, require early childhood professionals to identify and address children's learning styles. What is important is that all children have access to a variety of software and instructional and learning activities that are appropriate to them as individuals. This is what a developmentally appropriate curriculum is all about, and it applies to technology and software as well.

Higher-Order Learning. Technology can support and facilitate critical educational and cognitive processes such as cooperative learning, group and individual problem solving, critical thinking, reflective practices, analysis, inquiry, process writing, and public speaking. Also, technology can promote metacognition—that is, encourage children to think about their thinking. One such technological application would be the use of *LEGO/Logo,* software that links the popular LEGO construction kit with the Logo programming language. Children start by building machines out of LEGO pieces, using not only the traditional building blocks but new pieces like gears, motors, and sensors. Then they connect their machines to a computer and write computer programs (using a modified version of Logo) to control the machines. For example, a child might build a LEGO house with lights and program them to turn on and off at particular times. Then the child might build a garage and program the door to open whenever a car approached.

LEGO/Logo engages children in thinking about their process of design and invention. Children have used this software to build and program a wide assortment of creative machines, including a programmable pop-up toaster, a "chocolate-carob factory" (inspired by the Willy Wonka children's stories), and a machine that sorts LEGO bricks according to their lengths.

The LEGO company now sells a commercial version of *LEGO/Logo,* used in more than a dozen countries, including more than 15,000 elementary and middle schools in the United States. The Epistemology and Learning Group is currently involved in developing programmable bricks—LEGO bricks with tiny computers embedded inside. With these new electronic bricks, children can build computational capabilities directly into their LEGO constructions.

IS THE USE OF TECHNOLOGY INTEGRATED INTO THE CURRICULUM? At best, technology should be integrated as fully as possible into the early childhood curriculum and learning environment, so its use can help promote cooperative learning and achieve learning outcomes for children.

Part of this integration involves making sure that all technology-based activities remain consistent with the beliefs, principles, and practices of the program. Another aspect of this integration is making sure technology use is not seen as a separate or add-on activity. There should not be a "computers" unit that is separate from work in social studies, science, language arts, and so on. Instead, you could create a computer/technology learning center in your classroom that children have access to as they would any other center. In this way, the technology would be used as much as possible. And, just as important, such a center should have software that enables children to work independently, with little or minimal adult supervision.

Finally, educational technology should not be something children get to use only when they have completed other tasks. It should not be used as a reward, nor should it be a supplemental activity. Technology should be an integrated part of your early childhood program.

Program in Action

Teaching and Learning with Computers: The Alexander D. Henderson University School

Technology is rapidly changing the way we conduct our daily lives. School systems across the country are incorporating technology into their instructional programs for young children. The Alexander D. Henderson University School, a K–8 public school in Boca Raton, Florida, is the perfect example of the successful incorporation of computers to foster learning. Learning at this school is accomplished through a series of related computer activities that involve all the child's senses. The program is called "Teaching and Learning with Computers," or TLC, and is a complete instructional model. At Henderson, students first encounter computers in kindergarten.

In Elaine Lewis's kindergarten class, students work with the literacy program *Writing to Read 2000*, which includes using books and audiotapes. They also spend time in a "Make Words" center that contains tactile letters of plastic and felt or stencils for creating letters and words.

The program at this stage is a useful diagnostic tool. Lewis says she often observes children as they work at the various centers to see eye–hand coordination and audio discrimination and if they are following directions.

In the first grade and higher, the TLC program expands to include science and mathematics programs as well. The incorporation of computers in these grades is more comprehensive.

Suzanne Sturrock, one of Henderson's first grade teachers, says her children are in learning centers all day. In the morning, she talks to the whole class for about thirty minutes to review what they did the day before. Then the students form small groups and begin moving through the room's five centers. At the end of the rotation, everyone gathers to talk about what they have done. At this point Sturrock evaluates the effectiveness of the tasks and assigns enrichment or review tasks for students as needed.

Additionally, Sturrock likes the integrated nature of the program, which addresses social, educational, and technological learning skills simultaneously. "It seems to meet the needs of all children by using a variety of activities. I can remediate slower learners and provide enrichment for gifted ones," she says. As the children progress through each grade, the program grows and changes with them to suit their needs. The technology component in the program provides an element of recency other educational materials cannot maintain.

Contributed by Barbara Bittner, Director, Alexander D. Henderson University School, Boca Raton, Florida; photos supplied by International Business Machines Corporation.

Parents and Technology

Technology has changed the way early childhood professionals teach and the way children learn, so it should come as no surprise to you that it has also changed parents' roles. With the help of technology, parents now have more resources for participating in, supervising, and directing their children's education. They also have additional responsibilities, like making sure the information their children have access to while surfing the Internet at home is developmentally appropriate.

To visit a Web site that encourages family literacy by posting original stories and articles for children, go to the Companion Website at http://www.prenhall.com/morrison, select chapter 13, then choose the Linking to Learning module to connect to the Parents and Children Together Online site.

Technology for Increasing Parent Participation

For most parents, parenting is a full-time proposition. In addition, many have demanding work schedules; many work two jobs to make ends meet. Juggling the demands of parenting and work causes anxiety and concern about parenting and children's school achievement. Parents' questions about and concerns for their children go well beyond the capability of teachers and school personnel to help them within the time constraints of the school day. In addition, many parents face constraints of time and mobility for getting to the school for par-

ent conferences, programs, and assistance. Technology offers a rich assortment of ways to exchange information, gain information, and get help and assistance.

The Bridge Project, for example, used in 285 schools around the country, is a computer-based voice messaging system used to exchange information between teachers and parents. Teachers record a brief message for parents that describes lessons taught, special learning events, homework assignments, and other vital information. Parents can call and hear the message at any time from any phone. Teachers also record "outcalls," which are automatically delivered by phone to students' homes. These messages relate to good news, organizational and emergency information, and attendance monitoring. Research on the model indicates positive parent attitudes and higher levels of parent interaction as well as improvement in math and reading scores.[21] The Bridge Project can be found on the web at www.peabody.vanderbilt.edu/depts/tandl/faculty/Bauch/bridge.html.

If the Pittsburgh public schools have their way, parents will soon be able to use the computer to check their children's test scores and attendance records and other information of interest to them and other stakeholders. Such access is part of the district's $25 million technology plan that will develop the databases, networks, and software to make such access possible. How do you feel about parents having access to such information? How will development of this kind of technology affect you as a beginning teacher?

Technology for Parental Supervision of Child Care

Technology will transform how parents access information about their children in other ways. Mary Manning, human resources manager for an engineering company in Norwalk, Connecticut, engages in virtual parenting by logging on to the Internet. By typing in a special password, she is able to view a picture of her son at his preschool.[22] Growing numbers of preschools and day care programs are installing cameras and systems that enable parents to access secure Web sites so they can monitor how their children are doing. A special user ID and password gives parents access. Preschools and child care programs generally pay about $6,000 for systems with names such as "Watch Me Grow!" (www.watch-me.com) and "I See You" (http://iseeu.com). Presently these programs offer silent still pictures that are periodically updated from a few seconds to a few minutes. Proponents of such access to preschool programs contend that they ease parents' minds about how their children are doing, promote communication between parents and programs, create closer bonds between parents and children, and are a safeguard against possible child abuse. On the other hand, critics say that it is another example of the intrusion of technology into the lives of children and families and that unauthorized people could get access to the system if parents are careless about their passwords or if they give them to others. What are your opinions regarding such technology? Would you want parents to have such access to your classroom? State your reasons, both pro and con.

Technology and Home Schooling

The Internet is also a valuable tool for parents who home school their children. Through the Internet, parents have access to educational information and resources and can be in contact with other parents and home-schooled children. Web sites for parents are becoming more numerous and contain curriculum resources and names of organizations and individuals offering help with home schooling and provide advice on legal matters. You can access some of these sites through this address: http://dir.yahoo.com/education/k_12/alternative/home_schooling/.

Parents and Supervision of Children's Internet Use

Parents face a technological challenge in trying to screen out the good from the bad on the Internet. One way is for parents to constantly monitor what their children access. However, for most parents, this is an impractical solution and one that many don't exercise. For example, as Figure 13.6 shows, only 24 percent of parents whose children have Internet access say they can always monitor their children's viewing.

Another way to monitor is through the use of a *filter*, a computer program that denies access to sites parents specify as inappropriate. One such program, *Cyber Sentinel*, blocks access to chat rooms, stops instant messages, and can be programmed to stop questions such as "What is your phone number?" Parents who use America Online can specify three levels of access—Kids Only (under twelve years), Young Teen (thirteen to fifteen), and Mature Teen (sixteen and seventeen). While many of these solutions are helpful, none can be considered 100 percent effective.

In 1998, Congress passed the Children's Online Privacy Act, which is designed to ensure privacy rights of children and protect them from unscrupulous individuals and firms. The act

To visit a Web site that features an online child safety forum, go to the Companion Website at http://www.prenhall.com/morrison, select chapter 13, then choose the Linking to Learning module to connect to the Safe Kids Homepage site.

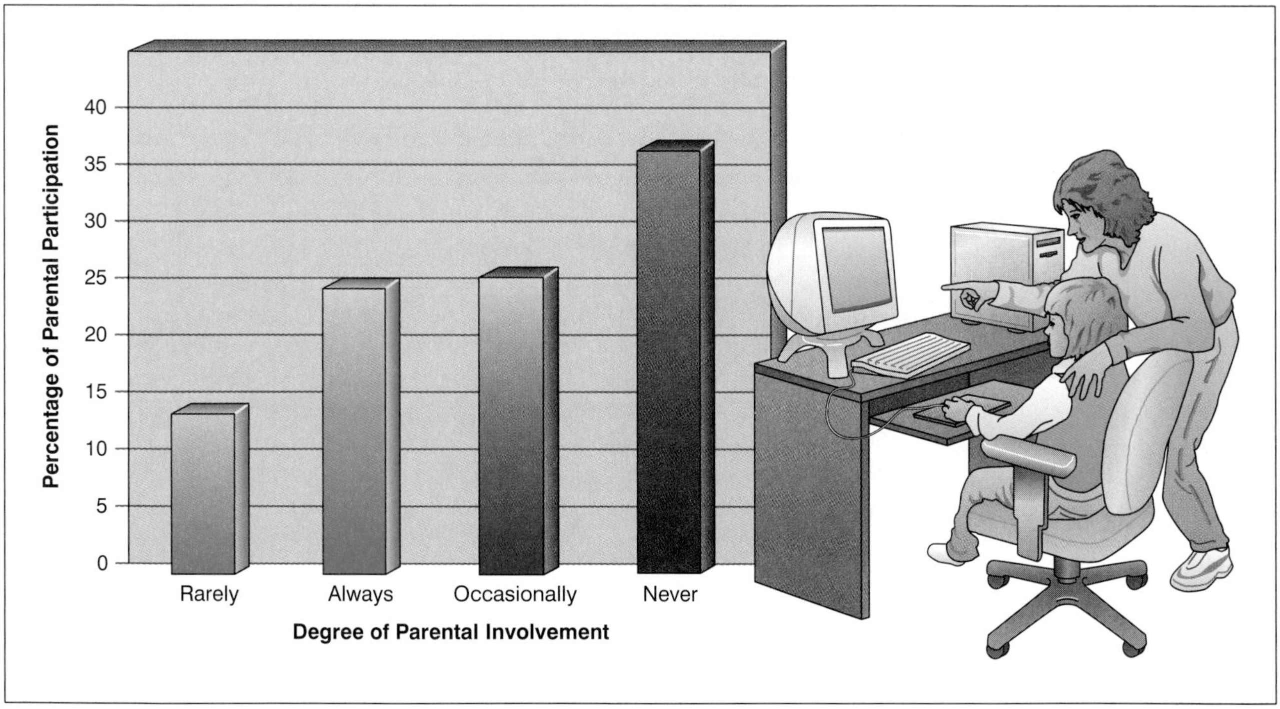

Figure 13.6
Percentage of Parents Who Participate with Their Children Ages 6 Through 17 on the Computer. Two issues facing teachers and parents is how much access children should have to the Internet and whether this access should be monitored. The majority of parents report that their children know more about the Internet than they do. Also, 36 percent of parents say that they never participate when their children use the Internet. How involved do you think parents should be in participating with and monitoring their children's Internet access? What other alternatives for monitoring do parents have?

Source: Market Facts/TeleNation for GTE Directories (1998). Data used with permission.

When parents and children team up to search the Internet together, it provides a fun and safe way for children to learn more about computers and technology. What are some of the dangers of letting children explore the Internet unsupervised?

To take an online self-test on this chapter's contents, go to the Companion Website at http://www.prenhall.com/morrison, select chapter 13, then choose the Self Test module.

requires World Wide Web operators to secure parental permission before they receive children's E-mail or home addresses. In *Privacy Online: A Report to Congress*, the Federal Trade Commission reported that of 212 children's Web sites, 90 percent collected personal information and only 1 percent obtained parental permission.[23] Federal Trade Commission Chairman Robert Pitofsky believes collecting information from children without parental permission is not acceptable. To alleviate any privacy concerns, many businesses such as America Online use mail-in parental notifications whereby parents can fill out an information card and mail it back in to the company.[24] Congress also passed the Child Online Protection Act, which calls for commercial Web site operators who offer "harmful" material to check the IDs of visitors. It is likely that Congress will continue to legislate ways to protect the privacy of children age twelve and under. How do you feel about such legislation? Do you believe it limits freedom of access?

You and the Technological Future

For additional Internet resources or to complete an online activity for this chapter, go to the Companion Website at http://www.prenhall.com/morrison, select chapter 13, then choose the Linking to Learning or Making Connections module.

Undoubtedly you have heard the saying "You haven't seen anything yet." This remark applies to technology and its application to all school settings—especially the early childhood years from birth to age eight. The vision that each child will acquire the foundational skills and competencies to succeed as an adult in the information age should involve children in the very early years.

What will have to happen to bring tomorrow to the classrooms today? First, early childhood professionals must decide themselves to use technology and gain the training necessary to be computer literate. Second, professionals must dedicate themselves to the developmentally appropriate use of technology and software. Third, professionals must recognize that technology and all its applications are not just add-ons to the curriculum, activities to do only when there is time, or rewards for good behavior or achievement. Technology, hardware and software, is here to stay, and can, like text-based materials, help children learn to their fullest potential.

Activities for Further Enrichment

Applications

1. Select at least four commercial educational software programs. Using the criteria from Figure 13.2, rate their suitability for use with children.
2. Develop a plan for how you would use Vygotsky's views (see chapter 3) to promote children's social interaction through computers.
3. Choose a particular theme and write a lesson plan to show how you would integrate technology relating to that theme into a subject you plan to teach.

Field Experiences

1. Visit classrooms in your local school district. What evidence of the integration of technology into the curriculum can you find? What conclusions can you draw?
2. Interview preK–3 teachers in a local district. What barriers do they say they must contend with in their efforts to include technology in the curriculum? What implications do these barriers have for what you may be able to accomplish as a teacher?
3. Visit classroom programs that provide services to students with disabilities. Cite five ways technology is used to implement curriculum, help teachers teach, and promote learning.
4. Some teachers and parents think children should not be introduced to computers at an early age. List reasons why they might feel this way. Then, interview five parents and teachers. Ask them the following questions: At what age should young children use computers? Why do you feel this age to be the best?
5. After reading the vignette on "Digital Literacy in the Kindergarten," E-mail Ella Pastor and Emily Kerns. Share your thoughts about how they teach literacy to their students. Ask them for on-line resources for you to use in your teaching.
6. Ask one or more of your professors to set up a "chat room" for your classes.
7. Investigate whether child care centers in your community have technologically advanced programs that enable parents to contact their children to see how they are doing.

Research

1. Read again the feature in this chapter called "Digital Literacy in the Kindergarten." List some advantages that the program has for children. Then try to think of alternatives to this program. What do you think would be more effective in helping the students learn?
2. Write a four-paragraph report in which you explain your views of the use of technology in preK–3 programs. Present this to a center director, school principal, or similar person for feedback. Set up a conference for discussion and reaction.
3. Review with several of your classmates the NAEYC Position Statement on Technology and Young Children (Figure 13.4). Tell how and in what ways you do or do not agree with the guidelines.
4. What can you do as a teacher to help ensure that the technological gender gap between boys and girls is eliminated? What evidence of this gender gap have you experienced in your own education? What can you do to combat this?

Readings for Further Enrichment

Hearne, B. *Story: From Fireplace to Cyberspace: Connecting Children and Narrative* (Allerton Park Institute Series Number 39). Chicago: University of Illinois, 1998.

These ten papers, presented at the Allerton Park Institute in 1997 on "Connecting Children and Narrative," are divided into four thematic areas: practice, theory, literature, and institutional culture.

Provenzo, E. F. *The Internet and the World Wide Web for Preservice Teachers*. Needham Heights, MA: Allyn and Bacon, 1999.

This handbook serves as an excellent resource to help beginning teachers use the Internet and the World Wide Web. By following the National Council for Accreditation of Teacher Education (NCATE) guidelines on "Technology and the New Professional Teacher," the author provides a practical and engaging introduction to using the Internet and the World Wide Web.

Roblyer, M. D., & Edwards, J. *Integrating Educational Technology into Teaching*, 2nd ed. Upper Saddle River, NJ: Merrill/Prentice-Hall, 2000.

This text presents effective theory and research-based strategies for integrating technology resources and technology-based methods into everyday classroom practices.

Linking to Learning

Assistive Technology, Inc.

http://www.assistivetech.com

Assistive Technology was founded in 1995 to develop innovative hardware and software solutions to increase opportunities for and

enhance the quality of life of people with disabilities. It provides innovative solutions to help people with learning, communication, and access difficulties lead more independent and productive lives.

Berit's Best Sites for Children

http://www.beritsbest.com

Offers links to many wonderful sites.

ECEOL (Early Childhood Education Online)

http://www.ume.maine.edu/~cofed/eceol/welcome.shtml

This site links to places and topics of interest to early childhood educators.

Education Links

http://school.discovery.com/schrockguide

A categorized list of sites for enhancing curriculum and teacher professional growth.

Kids Space

http://www.Kids-space.org

Children can contribute art to this site for display, as well as send in and read stories.

KidzOnline

http://www.kidzonline.org

KidzOnline is an educational organization dedicated to reducing the widening gap between the information "haves" and "have nots." They feel this can best be accomplished by having kids teach kids. The organization brings kids together electronically to share ideas, exchange viewpoints, and learn from each other.

Logo Foundation

http://lcs.www.media.mit.edu/groups/logo-foundation/

The Logo Foundation supports a "constructivist" approach to teaching math skills and other subjects through the use of "Logo programming environments," which educators have used since the late 1970s. Includes current information and tips.

New Parent Information Network

http://npin.org

This site offers up-to-date immunization schedules, lists of recalled toys, and other important information for parents and educators.

Parents and Children Together Online

http://www.indiana.edu/~eric_rec/fl/pcto/menu.html

The goal of this group is to further the cause of family literacy by bringing parents and children together through the magic of reading. PCTO features original stories and articles for children, suitable for reading aloud.

Safe Kids Homepage

http://www.safekids.com

This site, for children and educators, has a Child Safety Forum and links to other Web sites.

Stage Hand Puppets

http://www3.ns.sympatico.ca/onstage/puppets

This site discusses puppetry and patterns for puppets. Children are invited to create and stage puppet shows and send in scripts.

SuperKids Educational Software Review

www.superkids.com

This site offers teachers and parents objective reviews of educational software. Also has on-line activities for children.

Virtual Library

http://www.w3.org/

Choose from many subject categories.

ENDNOTES

[1] D. Addio, "Software for the Diaper Set," *Pittsburgh Post-Gazette,* July 12, 1998.

[2] J. M. Healy, "The 'Meme' That Ate Childhood," *Education Week* (October 7, 1998), 56.

[3] National Center for Education Statistics, *Internet Access in Public Schools* (Washington, DC: Government Printing Office, March 1998).

[4] National School Boards Association, "Equity Problems Persist," June 1998. [On-line]. Available: www.electronic-school.com.

[5] AAUW Educational Foundation, "Technology Gender Gap Develops While Gap in Math and Science Narrows, AAUW Foundation Report Shows," October 14, 1998. [On-line]. Available: www.aauw.org/2000/ggpr.html.

[6] C. J. Lee, "Educators Note Computer 'Gender Gap,'" *Pittsburgh Post-Gazette,* sec. C, September 27, 1998.

[7] "Technology Gender Gap Develops."

[8] Ibid.

[9] "Educators Note Computer 'Gender Gap.'"

[10] Children's Software Revue, "The Explosive Growth in Software for Girls," September 1997. [On-line]. Available: www.childrenssoftware.com.

[11] "Educators Note Computer 'Gender Gap.' "

[12] Susan W. Haugland, "Maintaining an Anti-Bias Curriculum," *Day Care and Early Education* (Winter 1992), 44–45.

[13] The Technology-Related Assistance for Individuals with Disabilities Act of 1988 (PL 100-407). [On-line]. Available: http://pursuit.rehab.uiuc.edu.

[14] L. Holder-Brown and H. Parette, "Children with Disabilities Who Use Assistive Technology: Ethical Considerations," *Young Children* (September 1992), 74–75.

[15] S. Haugland, "Will Technology Change Early Childhood Education?" *Day Care and Early Education* (Summer 1995), 45–46.

[16] Sandra L. Calvert, Caitlin Brune, Maria Eguia, and Jean Marcato, "Attention Inertia and Distractibility During Children's Educational Computer Interactions," poster session presented at the biennial meeting of the Society for Research in Child Development, Seattle, WA, April 1991.

[17] D. H. Clements, B. K. Nastasi, and S. Swaninathan, "Young Children and Computers: Crossroads and Directions from Research," *Young Children* (January 1993), 56–64.

[18] Susan W. Haugland, "The Effects of Computer Software on Preschool Children's Developmental Gains," *Journal of Computing in Childhood Education* 3 (1992), 15–30.

[19] Douglas H. Clements, *Computers in Early and Primary Education* (Needham Heights, MA: Allyn & Bacon, 1985), 52–53.

[20] Ibid.

[21] Peabody College, Betty Phillips Center for Parenthood Education, "The Bridge Project: Connecting Parents and Schools Through Voice Messaging," 1996. [On-line]. Available: www.peabody.vanderbilt.edu/-depts/tandi/faculty/Bauch/phillips.htm.

[22] J. Rabinovitz, "Logging on to the Baby's Day," *New York Times*, December 9, 1997, A19.

[23] P. Thibodeau, "Senate Weighs Online Privacy Rules for Tots," *Online News*, September 23, 1998 [On-line]. Available: www.onlinenews.com.

[24] America Online Inc., "Privacy Policy," 1998. [On-line]. Available: www.aol.com.

CHAPTER 14

We must learn together as brothers or perish together as fools.

MARTIN LUTHER KING, JR.

Multiculturalism

Education for Living in a Diverse Society

Focus Questions

1. What is multicultural education and what implications does a multicultural society have for schooling?
2. How do early childhood professionals infuse multicultural content in curriculum, programs, and activities?
3. What are contemporary issues relating to multiculturalism?
4. How can you educate both yourself and young children for living in a diverse society?

To review the chapter focus questions online, go to the Companion Website at http://www.prenhall.com/morrison and select chapter 14.

The population of the United States is changing and will continue to change. For example, the population will be less Caucasian. More students will be black and Hispanic. In addition, America will become even more a nation of blended races. Projections are that by 2050, 21 percent of the population will be of mixed ancestry. By 2025, almost one-fifth (20 percent) of the population will be Hispanic.

All these demographics have tremendous implications for increased multicultural education. Colleges of education must increase their efforts to recruit and educate minority teachers. As a result of changing demographics, more students will require special education, bilingual education, and other special services. Issues of culture and diversity will shape instruction and curriculum. These demographics have tremendous implications for how you teach and how your children learn. In part, how you respond to the multicultural makeup and needs of your children will determine how well they fulfill their responsibilities in the years to come. Because of the multicultural composition of society, as an early childhood educator you will want to promote multicultural awareness in your classroom.

Multicultural Awareness

To check your understanding of this chapter with the online Study Guide, go to the Companion Website at http://www.prenhall.com/morrison, select chapter 14, then choose the Study Guide module.

In its simplest form, *multicultural awareness* is the appreciation for and understanding of peoples' cultures, socioeconomic status, and gender. It also includes understanding one's own culture.

Bringing multicultural awareness to the classroom does not mean teaching about certain cultures to the exclusion of the cultures represented by children in the class. Rather, multicultural awareness programs and activities focus on other cultures while making children aware of the content, nature, and richness of their own. The terms and concepts for describing multicultural education and awareness (Figure 14.1) are not as important as the methods, procedures, and activities for developing meaningful early childhood programs. Learning about other cultures concurrently with their own culture enables children to integrate commonalities and appreciate differences without inferring inferiority or superiority of one or the other.

Who Are Multicultural Children?

For more information about diversity and early childhood education, go to the Companion Website at http://www.prenhall.com/morrison, select any chapter, then choose Topic 8 of the ECE Supersite module.

The population of young children in the United States reflects the population at large and represents a number of different cultures and ethnicities. Thus, many cities and school districts have populations that express great ethnic diversity, including Asian Americans, Native Americans, African Americans, and Hispanic Americans. For example, the Dade County, Florida, school district has children from 122 countries of the world, each with its own culture. Table 14.1 shows the proportion of minority students in the nation's ten largest school districts.

The great diversity of young children creates interesting challenges for early childhood educators. Many children speak languages other than English, behave differently based on cultural customs and values, and come from many socioeconomic backgrounds. Early childhood professionals must prepare themselves and their children to live happily and productively in this society.

Yet how to prepare children of all cultures for productive living is a major challenge for everyone. For instance, how can early childhood professionals use technology to help mil-

The following terms will assist you as you study this chapter:

Bias-free: Curriculum, programs, materials, language, attitudes, actions, and activities that are free from biased perceptions.

Bilingual education: Education in two languages. Generally, two languages are used for the purpose of academic instruction.

Cultural diversity: The diversity between and within various ethnic groups. The extent of group identification by members of ethnic groups varies greatly and is influenced by many factors such as skin color, social class, and professional experience.

Culturally fair education: Education that respects and accounts for the cultural backgrounds of all learners.

Cultural pluralism: The belief that cultural diversity is of positive value.

Diversity: Refers to and describes the relationships among background, socioeconomic status, gender, language, and culture of students, parents, and communities.

English as a Second Language (ESL): Instruction in which students with limited English proficiency attend a special English class.

Gender-balanced curriculum: Curriculum in which women are an integral part.

Gender-fair school: Learning environment in which male and female students participate equally and respond to similarly high expectations in all subjects.

Infusion: The process of having multiculturalism become an explicit part of the curriculum throughout all the content areas.

Mainstreaming: The educational and social integration of children with special needs into the schoolwide instructional process, usually the regular classroom.

Maintenance bilingual programs: Transitional bilingual programs that also infuse English into content area instruction with the goal of biliteracy.

Multicultural awareness: Ability to perceive and acknowledge cultural differences among people without making value judgments about these differences.

Multicultural education: Education that includes the relative perspective of all ethnic and cultural groups.

Multiculturalism: An approach to education based on the premise that all peoples in the United States should receive proportional attention in the curriculum.

Nonsexist education: Education that promotes attitudes and behaviors that convey that the sexes are equal.

Figure 14.1
Glossary of Multicultural Terms

lions of immigrant children become literate both in their native language and English? How can professionals help ensure that multicultural children will not become technological illiterates? The answers to these questions are not easy to give or implement.

Promoting multiculturalism in an early childhood program has implications far beyond the program itself. Multiculturalism influences and affects work habits, interpersonal relations, and a child's general outlook on life. Early childhood professionals must take these multicultural influences into consideration when designing curriculum and instructional processes for the impressionable children they will teach. One way to accomplish the primary goal of multicultural education—to positively change the lives of children and their families—is to infuse multiculturalism into early childhood activities and practices.

Program in Action

The Corcoran/Roberts Peace Corps Partnership Project

The Corcoran/Roberts Peace Corps Partnership Project is an activity of students at Corcoran High School and Roberts Elementaty School (K–8) in Syracuse, New York. Since 1983 the students have annually funded a Peace Corps Partnership Project through the Peace Corps. Peace Corps partnerships are small-scale, finite development projects proposed by Peace Corps volunteers in the field based on their villages' needs and requests.

Corcoran High School students select the project they wish to fund and then publish student-drawn note cards, which they sell nationwide to raise the necessary funds. As part of each partnership, the Corcoran students also go to Roberts School next door and work with the youngsters there. They teach a series of lessons about the culture of the village with whom they are working. They also engage the youngsters in an exchange of pictures, stories, and letters between Roberts and the partnership village children. These lessons may include ethnic music, language, children's games, ethnic food preparation, and art projects. Another activity in which the youngsters participate is the collection of pennies for funding a particular aspect of the partnership project. For example, the 1991 Roberts students collected 65,000 pennies and purchased a Braillewriter, which was then shipped to Bossangoa, Central African Republic. The Corcoran/Roberts project that year was funding the construction of a regional school for the blind (the first in all of Central Africa). River blindness is a common disease in central Africa.

In another project, in 1994, $10,000 was raised to fund construction of a primary school for nine Dogon villages in Mali. The Roberts students collected 20,000 pennies that year and purchased one dozen soccer balls for the villages that were participating in the primary school. These were the first real soccer balls any of the youngsters had ever had. The school, built of stone, was constructed at the foot of the Bandiagara cliffs. This necessitated bringing the stone down—one at a time, carried on the heads of the villagers—the 600-foot cliffs. The young men of the villages volunteered to bring them down although they were too old to attend the new school. Peace Corps volunteer Kris Hoffer organized a soccer tournament among the nine villages and awarded the new soccer balls to each village upon completion of the school construction. This is an example of unexpected dividends paid through the involvement of the young people.

In 1996, Corcoran students raised $14,500 to fund construction of a community kindergarten in Mensase, Ghana. The Roberts students exchanged drawings, stories, photographs, and letters with the youngsters of Mensase. They also collected 20,000 pennies, which were used to purchase eighty children's books in Ghana. The children of Mensase sent examples of their toys to the Roberts students.

For the community kindergarten project, the students wrote a series of lesson plans revolving around the Ashanti culture. Peace Corps volunteers are eager to share their knowledge of the culture in which they are immersed, and volunteer Renee Devereux sent the students a lot of materials. There were three lessons of approximately forty-five minutes in length spread over a four-week period. Two high school students taught each class. The introductory lesson included slides of the village and villagers. Subsequent lessons included music lessons, making paper masks, making Kente cloth designs on paper, and teaching traditional dances using a cassette tape of music sent by Renee. Plantain chips (similar to potato chips) were a big hit. The youngsters also drew pictures to illustrate the stories they told (printed beneath the pictures by the teachers).

Over the years, Roberts kindergarten classes have exchanged books of their illustrated stories

with each project's youngsters. These books have wallpaper covers, which make them more durable. The Peace Corps volunteer helps the village youngsters to print their illustrated stories in English.

The involvement of students, especially elementary students, in these small-scale development projects is a win–win–win situation. Schools, from administration to teachers and parents, love the positive publicity generated. The youngsters have a credible sense of accomplishment because of their involvement. They become more globally aware. Through the cross-cultural exchanges the young students begin to appreciate the lives of people from very different cultures and the values that are important to the villagers. The logistics of letter writing, penny collections, and the lessons created around the projects lend themselves to an entire school community involvement. Research projects, posters, and plays can all complement the project. Peace Corps volunteers will send pictures and cultural information throughout the partnership. Students, learning about the new culture and their new friends, can then return home and teach their own families what they have learned or teach lessons to other classes.

Peace Corps Partnership Projects are available for a commitment of as little as a few hundred dollars. The project can be accomplished within a school year, for the Peace Corps will advance the funds as soon as the commitment is received. This allows teachers to develop the cross-cultural exchange even as the project is being accomplished. For classes that don't wish to become involved in fund-raising (although events such as penny drives can easily become total-school activities), the Peace Corps World Wise Schools Program is the answer. This matches classes and schools with Peace Corps volunteers in the field primarily through the exchanges of letters.

Visit the Corcoran/Roberts Peace Corps Partnership Project on the Web at http://www.dreamscape.com/phatpc/peace; the Peace Corps Partnership Program at http://www.peacecorps.gov/contribute/partnership.html; and the World Wise Schools Program at http://www.peacecorps.gov/wws/index.html.

Contributed by Jim Miller, project adviser. Photos courtesy of Jim Miller.

Table 14.1

Proportion of Minority Students in the Ten Largest Public School Districts of the United States and Puerto Rico

Name of Reporting District	State or Commonwealth	Percentage of Minority Students
New York City Public Schools	NY	83.5
Los Angeles Unified School District	CA	88.7
Puerto Rico Department of Education	PR	100.0
City of Chicago School District 29	IL	89.2
Dade County School District	FL	85.8
Philadelphia City School District	PA	79.6
Houston Independent School District	TX	88.5
Broward County School District	FL	51.0
Hawaii Department of Education	HI	77.1
Detroit Public Schools	MI	94.3

Source: U.S. Department of Education, National Center for Education Statistics, Digest of Education Statistics 1997 *(Washington, DC: Office of Educational Research and Improvement, 1997). [On-line]. Available: www.nces.ed.gov/subs99/digest98/.*

Early childhood educators must consider the diverse needs of students—including gender, ethnicity, race, and socioeconomic factors—when planning learning opportunities for their classes. What are some ways diversity can enrich the curriculum?

What Is Multicultural Infusion?

For examples of multicultural education programs, go to the Companion Website at http://www.prenhall.com/morrison, select chapter 14, then choose the Linking to Learning module to connect to the Multicultural Education Programs site.

Infusion means that multicultural education permeates the curriculum to alter or affect the way young children and teachers look at diversity issues. In a larger perspective, infusion strategies are used to ensure that multiculturalism becomes a part of the entire center, school, and home. Infusion processes used by early childhood programs encompass a range of practices that embody the following precepts:

- Foster cultural awareness
- Promote and use conflict resolution strategies
- Teach to children's learning styles
- Welcome parent and community involvement
- Encourage cooperative learning

I discuss each of these practices in detail so you may fully understand how to apply them to your life and program. Keep in mind that as an early childhood professional, you will want to be constantly developing your multicultural awareness, attitudes, knowledge, and skills.

Foster Cultural Awareness

ASSESS YOUR ATTITUDES TOWARD CHILDREN. Before working with children to influence their multicultural awareness and education it is important for you to first assess their own attitudes toward young children and their families to help ensure that they are multiculturally sensitive. The following will help you assess your multicultural awareness level.

- Do you have different expectations of children from different neighborhoods? For example, do you expect a higher level of work from students who live in affluent neighborhoods than from those who live in trailer parks?
- With which children do you feel most comfortable? Are you influenced by what children wear? the positions their parents hold? the color of their skin? Some people believe men have higher levels of intelligence than women and that those with lighter skin colors are smarter than those with dark skin. Some people perceive those with an affluent, white-collar lifestyle as being "smarter, better, and more civilized" than those from working-class communities.
- What do you know about children's communities? To provide schooling relevant to students' lives, teachers need a sense of children's worldviews. What is it like living in the community? What roles and relationships are most important? Do you understand the nuances of students' verbal and nonverbal communication?
- What connections do you feel to the children's community? Society has changed drastically in the past quarter-century. Few children attend neighborhood schools in large urban districts; instead, many students of all ethnicities have become accustomed to long bus rides. In addition, few teachers teach in their own neighborhoods; they may instead drive ten miles or more to another community.
- Do you expect children to learn through your ways of teaching only, or do you find out in which modes of instruction children learn best? When teaching in a multicultural manner, do not try to mold children to fit your manner of teaching. Instead, learn about them and change your teaching to affirm them. As one effective strategy, use culturally familiar examples when discussing new concepts. For example, a teacher was giving a lesson in how people can provide themselves with complete proteins every day without eating meat. The teacher asked her predominantly Mexican American class what they ate for dinner. Some of the kids said, "Pizza." Other students said, "Spaghetti," while others yelled out, "Tortillas and beans!" The teacher then explained that when they ate tortillas, which are made from grains, with their beans, they were getting a complete protein. The example helped to make connections between an abstract scientific concept and students' personal lives.[1]

GUIDELINES AND PROCESSES FOR FOSTERING AWARENESS. As an early childhood professional, you must keep in mind that you are the key to a multicultural classroom. The following guidelines can help you in teaching multiculturalism:

- *Recognize that all children are unique.* They all have special talents, abilities, and styles of learning and relating to others. Provide opportunities for children to be different and use their abilities.
- *Promote uniqueness and diversity as positive.*
- *Get to know, appreciate, and respect the cultural backgrounds of your children.* Visit families and community neighborhoods to learn more about cultures and religions and the ways of life they engender.
- *Infuse children's culture (and other cultures as well) in your teaching.*
- *Use authentic situations to provide for cultural learning and understanding.* For example, a field trip to a culturally diverse neighborhood of your city or town provides children an opportunity for understanding firsthand many of the details about how people conduct

their daily lives. Such an experience provides wonderful opportunities for involving children in writing, cooking, reading, and dramatic play activities. What about setting up a market in the classroom?

- *Use authentic assessment activities to assess fully children's learning and growth.* Portfolios (see chapter 11) are ideal for assessing children in nonbiased and culturally sensitive ways. The point is that early childhood professionals should use varied ways of assessing children.
- *Infuse culture into your lesson planning, teaching, and caregiving.* Use all subject areas—math, science, language arts, literacy, music, art, and social studies—to relate culture to all the children and all you do.
- *Be a role model by accepting, appreciating, and respecting other languages and cultures.*
- *Use children's interests and experiences to form a basis for planning lessons and developing activities.* This approach makes students feel good about their backgrounds, cultures, families, and experiences. Also, when children can relate what they are doing in the classroom to the rest of their daily lives, their learning is more meaningful to them.
- *Be knowledgeable about, proud of, and secure in your own culture.* Children will ask about you, and you should share your background with them.

For more information about teaching with multicultural materials, go to the Companion Website at http://www.prenhall.com/morrison, select any chapter, then choose Topic 8 of the ECE Supersite module.

SELECT APPROPRIATE INSTRUCTIONAL MATERIALS. In addition to assessing your own attitudes and instituting guidelines for infusing personal sensitivity into a multicultural classroom, you need to carefully consider and select appropriate instructional materials to support the infusion of multicultural education. The following three sections offer suggestions.

Multicultural Literature. Choose literature that emphasizes people's habits, customs, and general living and working behaviors. This approach stresses similarities and differences regarding how children and families live their *whole* lives and avoids merely noting differences or teaching only about habits and customs. Multicultural literature today is more representative of various cultural groups than in the past and provides a more authentic language experience for young children. This literature is written by authors from particular cultures and contains more true-to-life stories and culturally authentic writing styles. The following books are representative of the rich selection now available:[2]

To preview existing and new multicultural education titles for educators, go to the Companion Website at http://www.prenhall.com/morrison, select chapter 14, then choose the Linking to Learning module to connect to the Multicultural Book Reviews site.

- *Miss Viola and Uncle Ed Lee,* by Catherine Stock (New York: Atheneum, 1999). On Bradley's day to tell a story at school, he describes his two neighbors, Miss Viola and Uncle Ed Lee. Although they are very different, they have become friends anyway. As Uncle Lee says, "Just because folks are different, don't mean they can't be friends."
- *A Band of Angels,* by Raul Colon (New York: Atheneum Books for Young Readers, 1999). Based on true events, this story tells of a freed slave's determination to receive an education. Ella Sheppard and the rest of the choral group at Fisk School must go on tour to earn money to save their school for freed slaves from closing.
- *Dance for the Land,* by Clemence McLaren (New York: Atheneum, 1999). When Kate's family moves from California to Hawaii, she tries to fit in. Some of the children at school threaten Kate because of her light coloring. While with her Native Hawaiian relatives, she struggles to learn Hawaiian Creole English. As Kate learns about her Hawaiian heritage, she comes to cherish it.
- *In the Moonlight Mist: A Korean Tale,* by Daniel San Souci (Honesdale, PA: Boyds Mills Press, 1999). This retelling of a Korean folktale concerns a caring young man who saves a deer from certain death. In gratitude, the deer grants him a wish. The only

thing the man can wish for is a wife and family but he must follow specific directions about what he must do until after the birth of the second son. The directions are not followed, and the man temporarily loses his family.

- *Mei-Mei Loves the Morning,* by Margaret Tsubakiyama (Morton Grove, IL: Albert Whitman, 1999). Typical morning events in the lives of a delightful little girl and her caring grandpa in a modern city in China are captured. With friends, they practice Tai-chi and drink warm tea before making their way back home through scenes of busy street life. This visit to Chinese culture allows readers to share a moment in a touching intergenerational relationship.

Themes. Early childhood professionals may select and teach through thematic units that help strengthen children's understanding of themselves, their culture, and the cultures of others. Thematic choices from a variety of cultures can help children identify cultural similarities and encourage understanding and tolerance, as with the following suggestions:

Getting to Know Myself, Getting to Know Others

What Is Special About You and Me?

Growing Up in the City

Growing Up in the Country

Tell Me About Africa (South America, China, etc.)

Personal Accomplishments. Add to classroom activities, as appropriate, the accomplishments of people from different cultural groups, women of all cultures, and individuals with disabilities.

The following criteria are most important when picking materials for use in a multicultural curriculum for early childhood programs:

- Make sure people of all cultures are represented fairly and accurately.
- Make sure to represent people of color, many cultural groups, and people with exceptionalities.
- Make sure that historic information is accurate and nondiscriminatory.
- Make sure the materials do not include stereotypical roles and language.
- Make sure there is gender equity—that is, that boys and girls are represented equally and in nonstereotypical roles.

AVOID SEXISM AND SEX-ROLE STEREOTYPING. Current interest in multiculturalism in general and nondiscrimination in particular has also prompted concern about sexism and sex-role stereotyping. *Sexism* is "the collection of attitudes, beliefs, and behaviors which result from the assumption that one sex is superior. *In the context of schools*, the term refers to the collection of structures, policies, practices and activities that overtly or covertly prescribe the development of girls and boys and prepare them for traditional sex roles."[3]

Title IX of the Education Amendments Acts of 1972, as amended by Public Law 93-568, prohibits such discrimination in the schools: "No person in the United States shall, on the basis of sex, be excluded from participation in, be denied the benefits of, or be subjected to discrimination under any education program or activity receiving Federal financial assistance."[4] Since Title IX prohibits sex discrimination in any educational program that receives federal money, early childhood programs as well as elementary schools, high schools, and uni-

versities cannot discriminate against males or females in enrollment policies, curriculum offerings, or activities.

There is yet another reason for the nation's interest in sexism. A recent survey conducted by the American Association of University Women (AAUW) reveals that four out of five students in grades eight to eleven are sexually harassed in school. Sexual harassment is defined as "unwanted and unwelcome sexual behavior which interferes with your life."[5] The AAUW research further revealed that

- Girls receive significantly less attention from classroom teachers than do boys.
- African American girls have fewer interactions with teachers than do white girls, despite evidence that they attempt to initiate interactions more frequently.
- Sexual harassment of girls by boys—from innuendo to actual assault—in our nation's schools is increasing.[6]

The AAUW results have many implications for early childhood professionals. First, the findings reveal the extent of sexual harassment. Second, 85 percent of girls surveyed and 76 percent of boys said that they have been sexually harassed. Some may think that sexual harassment is something only girls experience, but this data indicate the extent to which boys are also harassed. Third, the data from the survey reveal that the psychological effects of sexual harassment are more profound for girls than for boys; 70 percent of girls and 24 percent of boys reported that the experience made them very or somewhat upset.

These data should cause early childhood professionals to be concerned about the roots of sexism and sexual harassment and to realize that these practices have their beginnings in practices found in children's early years in homes, centers, and preschools. Early childhood professionals must continue to examine personal and programmatic practices, evaluate materials, and work with parents for the purpose of eliminating sexism and to ensure that girls—indeed, all children—will not be shortchanged in any way.

Parents and teachers should provide children with less restrictive options and promote a more open framework in which sex roles can develop. Following are some ways for you to provide a non–sex-stereotyped environment:

- *Provide opportunities for all children to experience the activities, materials, toys, and emotions traditionally associated with both sexes.* Give boys as well as girls opportunities to experience tenderness, affection, and the warmth of close parent–child and teacher–pupil relationships. Conversely, girls as well as boys should be able to behave aggressively, get dirty, and participate in what are typically considered male activities, such as woodworking and block building.
- *Examine the classroom materials you are using and determine whether they contain obvious instances of sex-role stereotyping.* When you find examples, modify the materials or do not use them. Let publishers know your feelings, and tell other faculty members about them.
- *Examine your behavior to see whether you are encouraging sex stereotypes.* Do you tell girls they cannot empty wastebaskets but they can water the plants? Do you tell boys they should not play with dolls? Do you tell girls they cannot lift certain things in the classroom because they are too heavy for them? Do you say that "boys aren't supposed to cry"? Do you reward only females who are always passive, well behaved, and well mannered?
- *Have a colleague or parent observe you in your classroom to determine what sex-role behaviors you are encouraging.* We are often unaware of our behaviors, and self-correction

You can combat the development of sexist attitudes by encouraging students in your classroom to engage in activities that challenge traditional gender-role stereotypes.

begins only after someone points out the behaviors to us. Obviously, unless you begin with yourself, eliminating sex-role stereotyping practices will be next to impossible.

- *Determine what physical arrangements in the classroom promote or encourage sex-role stereotyping.* Are boys encouraged to use the block area more than girls? Are girls encouraged to use the quiet areas more than boys? Do children hang their wraps separately—a place for boys and a place for girls? All children should have equal access to all learning areas of the classroom; no area should be reserved exclusively for one sex. In addition, examine any activity and practice that promotes segregation of children by sex or culture. Cooperative learning activities and group work offer ways to ensure that children of both sexes work together.

- *Counsel with parents to show them ways to promote nonsexist child rearing.* If society is to achieve a truly nonsexist environment, parents will be the key factor, for it is in the home that many sex-stereotyping behaviors are initiated and practiced.

- *Become conscious of words that promote sexism.* For example, in a topic on community helpers, taught in most preschool and kindergarten programs at one time or another, many words carry a sexist connotation. *Fireman*, *policeman*, and *mailman*, for example, are all masculine terms; nonsexist terms are *firefighter*, *police officer*, and *mail carrier*. You should examine all your curricular materials and teaching practices to determine how you can make them free from sexism.

- *Examine your teaching and behavior to be sure you are not limiting certain roles to either sex.* Females should not be encouraged to pursue only roles that are subservient, submissive, lacking in intellectual demands, or low paying. You can do the following specific things in your teaching:

- Give all children a chance to respond to questions. Research consistently shows that teachers do not wait long enough after they ask a question for most children, especially girls, to respond. Therefore, quick responders—usually boys—answer all the questions. By waiting longer you will be able to respond to more girls' answers.
- Be an active professional. Just as we want children to engage in active learning, so too professionals should engage in active involvement in the classroom. This helps ensure that you will get to interact with and give attention to all children, not to just a few.
- Help all children become independent and do things for themselves. Discourage behaviors and attitudes that promote helplessness and dependency. Discourage remarks such as "I can't because I'm not good at . . . "
- Examine your classroom management and behavioral guidance techniques (see chapter 12). Are you treating both sexes and all cultures fairly and in individual and culturally appropriate ways?
- Use portfolios, teacher observations, and other authentic means of assessing children's progress (see chapter 11) to provide bias-free assessment. Involving children in the evaluation of their own efforts also is a good way of promoting children's positive images of themselves.

- *Do not encourage children to dress in ways that lead to sex stereotyping.* Females should not be encouraged to wear frilly dresses, then forbidden to participate in an activity because they might get dirty or spoil their clothes. Children should be encouraged to dress so they will be able to participate in a range of both indoor and outdoor activities. This is an area in which you may be able to help parents if they seek your advice by discussing how dressing their child differently can contribute to more effective participation.

For more information about implementing an antibias curriculum, go to the Companion Website at http://www.prenhall.com/morrison, select any chapter, then choose Topic 8 of the ECE Supersite module.

IMPLEMENT AN ANTIBIAS CURRICULUM AND ACTIVITIES. The goal of an *antibias curriculum* is to help children learn to be accepting of others regardless of gender, race, ethnicity, socioeconomic status, and disability. Children participating in an antibias curriculum are comfortable with diversity and learn to stand up for themselves and others in the face of injustice. Additionally, in this supportive, open-minded environment, children learn to construct a knowledgeable, confident self-identity.

Young children are constantly learning about differences and need a sensitive teacher to help them form positive, unbiased perceptions about variations among people. As children color pictures of themselves, for example, you may hear a comment such as, "Your skin is white and my skin is brown." Many teachers are tempted, in the name of equality, to respond, "It doesn't matter what color we are—we are all people." While this remark does not sound harmful, it fails to help children develop positive feelings about themselves. A more appropriate response might be, "Amanda, your skin is a beautiful dark brown, which is just right for you; Christina, your skin is a beautiful light tan, which is just right for you." A comment such as this positively acknowledges each child's different skin color, which is an important step for developing a positive self-concept.

Through the sensitive guidance of caring teachers, children learn to speak up for themselves and others. By living and learning in an accepting environment, children find that they have the ability to change intolerable situations and can have a positive impact on the future. This is part of what empowerment is all about, and it begins in the home and in early childhood programs. It is important, then, that an antibias curriculum starts in early childhood and continues throughout the school years.

Program in Action

The Spady Way

S.D. Spady Elementary School in Delray Beach, Florida, made a fundamental change. The thirty-five teachers and 650 students began the process of converting the school from a traditional elementary to a Montessori magnet school. The change was gradual—one grade level per year. Some teachers had to take additional Montessori training covering both curriculum and teacher–student interactions.

The latter is an integral part of the Montessori approach. Maria Montessori stated, "If a teacher can clothe himself in the garment of humility, many delights are reserved for him that are denied to those who assume infallibility and authority in front of the class." Teacher training in conflict resolution, which was true to this Montessori spirit, was provided for all faculty.

What makes Spady Elementary unique is not simply that all teachers, or even a few students, have received training in conflict resolution and/or mediation. *Every* student in the school has received this training from members of the faculty or administration. The training is composed of two phases: (1) the practice phase tries to develop community outreach and self-concept development, and (2) the reactive phase teaches mediation skills to solve disputes among students once they occur.

Principal Denise Doyle set as a school goal a reduction by 50 percent of discipline referrals concerning conflicts among students. The school used to have forty-five such referrals each year. After all faculty and students went through conflict resolution and mediation training, referrals for conflicts among students dropped to twelve.

Montessori coordinator Kathy Brown emphasized that student training stresses "What are you going to do when his problem occurs again?" or "All actions have consequences." When Spady students have problems or disputes among themselves, they may select a fellow classmate to mediate or they may opt for a student mediator from another class. Ultimately, the program's goal is to change restraints on student behavior from external to internal ones.

Teacher Jesus Santiago comments that "it requires patience and respect for students' abilities to find their own answers. But in the end, it is well worth it." Spady's current principal, Denise Doyle, and the school's faculty and staff are committed to the notion that conflict resolution skills are as important as subject matter curriculum. Some faculty and staff have reported that "the Spady Way" has affected the way they interact with their own families.

Visit the Spady Way on the Web at http://www.palmbeach.k12.fl.us/SDSpadyES/.

Promote and Use Conflict Resolution Strategies

We all live in a world of conflict. Television and other media bombard us with images of violence, crime, and international and personal conflict. Unfortunately, many children live in homes where conflict and disharmony are ways of life rather than exceptions. Increasingly, early childhood professionals are challenged to help children and themselves resolve conflicts in peaceful ways. For this reason, *conflict resolution strategies* seek to help children learn how to solve problems, disagree in appropriate ways, negotiate, and live in harmony with others.

Part of your goal is to have children reach mutually agreeable solutions to problems without the use of power (fighting, hitting, pushing, shoving, etc.). You may wish to adopt the following strategies for helping children resolve conflicts:

Steps in Using the "No-Lose" Method of Conflict Resolution

1. Identify and define conflict in a nonaccusatory way. ("Vinnie and Rachael, you have a problem. You both want the green paint.")
2. Invite children to participate in fixing the problem. ("Let's think of how to solve the problem.")
3. Generate possible solutions with children. Accept a variety of solutions. Avoid evaluating them. ("Yes, you could both use the same paint cup. . . . You could take turns.")
4. Examine each idea for merits and drawbacks. With children, decide which to try. Thank children for thinking of solutions. ("Vinnie, that's a good idea—putting paint in the paper cups. Now both you and Rachel can use the green paint at the same time.")
5. Put plan into action. ("You might have to take turns dipping your brushes into the paint. . . . Try your idea.")
6. Follow up. Evaluate how well the solution worked. (Teacher comes back in a few minutes, "Looks like your idea of how to solve your green paint problem really worked.")[7]

Teach to Children's Learning Styles and Intelligences

For more information about multiculturalism and content-area instruction, go to the Companion Website at http://www.prenhall.com/morrison, select chapter 14, then choose the Linking to Learning module to connect to the Multicultural Awareness in the Language Classroom and Multicultural Perspectives in Mathematics Education sites.

Every child has a unique learning style. Although every person's learning style is different, we can cluster learning styles for instructional purposes. It makes sense to consider these various styles and account for them in early childhood programs when organizing the environment and developing activities.

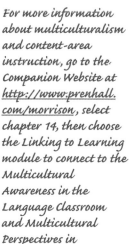

Not all children learn in the same way. As a result, it is important to assess each child's learning style and teach each child appropriately. What style of learning works best for you?

Program in Action

Brightwood Elementary School

Brightwood Elementary School (Greensboro, North Carolina) students, who are approximately 55 percent white and 45 percent African American, were scoring in the 30th percentile in mathematics and reading. The principal, Roland Andrews, decided to test Brightwood's students to determine their preferred learning styles. The results of the Learning Styles Inventory showed that the majority of Brightwood's students were "low auditory" learners and highly tactual and kinesthetic. The students preferred to learn more by touching and doing than by listening.

Teachers were shown how to begin lessons with tactual resources, such as objects to pass, and kinesthetic floor games, such as sentence trains. Later, teachers would reinforce lessons through students' less preferred learning style. Additional preferences considered in the new curriculum were the time of day students learned best, their mobility needs, and their desire to work independently or in cooperative learning groups. Learning style preferences are largely the product of socialization and/or child-rearing patterns, which are strongly influenced by cultural values and practices. For example, socialization patterns for Brightwood's African American students predisposed many of them to learn better in social contexts.

After learning styles were accommodated in teaching, discipline referrals dropped dramatically, from 143 to only 6.

Student scores on the California Achievement Test rose from the 30th percentile in reading and 40th percentile in math to the 74th percentile in reading and the 77th percentile in math. Both African American and white students at Brightwood were scoring in the 93rd percentile on the California Achievement Test. These scores were higher than those of peers in other elementary schools in the district and state.

Brightwood Elementary uses the North Carolina End of Grade Testing Program. According to Sally Voelker, guidance counselor at Brightwood Elementary, students at Brightwood are still scoring at or above the North Carolina state average for elementary students.

Teachers at Brightwood do their planning in teams. As new teachers join the faculty, those who are experienced in the learning styles teaching approach assist their newer colleagues in lesson planning. The school tries to provide learning styles in-service training every three to five years for the entire staff.

The case of Brightwood Elementary indicates that when student's learning styles are taken seriously, assessed, and incorporated into how they are taught, learning improves significantly, along with student satisfaction. This case suggests that when teaching is made more congruent with student learning styles, amazing results may occur.

DIFFERENT CHILDREN, DIFFERENT LEARNING STYLES. It makes sense to consider students' various learning styles and account for them when organizing the environment and developing activities. "Learning style is the way that students of every age are affected by their (1) immediate environment, (2) own emotionality, (3) sociological needs, (4) physical characteristics, and (5) psychological inclinations when concentrating and trying to master and remember new or difficult information or skills."[8]

Learning styles consist of the following elements:

- *Environmental*—sound, light, temperature, and design
- *Emotional*—motivation, persistence, responsibility, and the need for either structure or choice

- *Sociological*—learning alone, with others, or in a variety of ways (perhaps including media)
- *Physical*—perceptual strengths, intake, time of day or night energy levels, and mobility
- *Psychological*—global/analytic, hemispheric preference, and impulsive/reflective

There are many ways you can provide for children's learning styles while responding appropriately to diversity in your program. For example, Dunn et al. suggest the following ways to adapt the learning environment to children's individual learning styles.[9]

Noise Level. Provide earplugs or music on earphones (to avoid distractions for those who need quiet); create conversation areas or an activity-oriented learning environment separately from children who need quiet. *Or* establish silent areas: provide individual dens or alcoves with carpeted sections; suggest earphones without sound or earplugs to insulate against activity and noise.

Light. Place children near windows or under adequate illumination; add table or desk lamps. *Or* create learning spaces under indirect or subdued light away from windows; use dividers or plants to block or diffuse illumination.

Authority Figures Present. Place children near appropriate professionals and schedule periodic meetings with them; supervise and check assignments often. *Or* identify the child's sociological characteristics, and permit isolated study if self-oriented and peer groupings if peer oriented, or multiple options if learning in several ways is indicated; interact with collaborative professional.

Visual Preferences. Use pictures, filmstrips, films, graphs, single-concept loops, transparencies, computer monitors, diagrams, drawings, books, and magazines; supply resources that require reading and seeing; use programmed learning (if student needs structure) and written assignments and evaluations. Reinforce knowledge through tactile, kinesthetic, and then auditory resources. *Or* use resources prescribed under the perceptual preferences that are strong. Use several multisensory resources such as videotapes, sound-filmstrips, television, and tactile/kinesthetic material. Introduce information through child's strongest perceptual preference.

Tactile Preferences. Use manipulative and three-dimensional materials; resources should be touchable and movable as well as readable; allow children to plan, demonstrate, report, and evaluate with models and other real objects; encourage them to keep written or graphic records. Reinforce through kinesthetic, visual, and then auditory resources. *Or* use resources prescribed under the perceptual preferences that are strong. Use several multisensory resources such as videotapes, sound-filmstrips, television, and real-life experiences such as visits, interviewing, building, designing, and so on. Introduce information through activities such as baking, building, sewing, visiting, or acting; reinforce through visual, auditory, and kinesthetic methods. Introduce information through child's strongest perceptual preference.

Kinesthetic Preferences. Provide opportunities for real and active experiences in planning and carrying out objectives; visits, projects, acting, and floor games are appropriate activities for such individuals. Reinforce through tactile, visual, and then auditory resources. *Or* use resources prescribed under the preferences that are strong. Use several multisensory resources such as videotapes, sound-filmstrips, television, and tactile/manipulative materials. Introduce information through real-life activities (e.g., planning a part in a play or a trip); reinforce through tactile resources such as electroboards, task cards, learning circles, and so forth; then reinforce further visual and auditory resources.

Mobility. Provide frequent breaks, assignments that require movement to different locations, and schedules that permit mobility in the learning environment; require results, not immo-

bility. *Or* provide a stationary desk or learning station where most of the child's responsibilities can be completed without requiring excessive movement.

DIFFERENT CHILDREN, DIFFERENT INTELLIGENCES. Piaget's theory of intelligence (see chapter 5) is based primarily on one intelligence: logical-mathematical. In his book *Frames of Mind*, Gardner hypothesizes that rather than one overall intelligence, there are at least eight distinct intelligences (see chapter 3):[10]

- linguistic
- logical-mathematical
- spatial
- musical
- bodily-kinesthetic
- interpersonal
- intrapersonal
- naturalistic

Further, Gardner maintains that all children possess all eight of these intelligences, although some intelligences may be stronger than others. This accounts for why children have a preferred learning style; different interests, likes, and dislikes; different habits; preferred lifestyles; and preferred career choices.

These eight intelligences imply that students have unique learning styles appropriate to the particular intelligences. Consequently, early childhood professionals must consider children's learning styles and make efforts to accommodate their teaching styles, activities, and materials to them. Table 14.2 will help you make the connection using Gardner's theory. What this table also shows is how you can provide for children's intelligences while addressing issues of multiculturalism and technological equity.

Welcome Parent and Community Involvement

As an early childhood professional, you will work with children and families of diverse cultural backgrounds. As such you will need to learn about the cultural background of children and families so that you can respond appropriately to their needs. For example, let's take a look at the Hispanic culture and its implications for parent and family involvement.

For more information about family–school relations, go to the Companion Website at http://www.prenhall.com/morrison, select any chapter, then choose Topic 10 of the ECE Supersite module.

Throughout Hispanic culture there is a widespread belief in the absolute authority of the school and teachers. In many Latin American countries it is considered rude for a parent to intrude into the life of the school. Parents believe that it is the school's job to educate and the parent's job to nurture and that the two jobs do not mix. A child who is well educated is one who has learned moral and ethical behavior.

Hispanics, as a whole, have strong family ties, believe in family loyalty, and have a collective orientation that supports community life; they have been found to be field dependent with a sensitivity to nonverbal indicators of feeling.[11] Culturally, this is represented by an emphasis on warm, personalized styles of interaction, a relaxed sense of time, and a need for an informal atmosphere for communication. Given these preferences, a culture clash may result when Hispanic students and parents are confronted with the typical task-oriented style of most American teachers.

While an understanding of the general cultural characteristics of Hispanics is helpful, it is important to not overgeneralize. Each family and child is unique, and care should be

Table 14.2
Eight Styles of Learning Applied to Technology

	Highly developed in:	Students with a high degree:	May benefit from
Verbal/Linguistic Intelligence The capacity to use words effectively—either orally or in writing.	storytellers, orators, politicians, poets, playwrights, editors, and journalists	think in words; learn by listening, reading, and verbalizing; enjoy writing; like books, records, and tapes; have a good memory for verse, lyrics, or trivia	word processors that allow voice annotations; desktop publishing programs; programs with speech output; programs that encourage them to create poetry, essays, etc.; multimedia authoring; using videodiscs and barcode programs to create presentations; tape recorders; telecommunications/electronic networking
Visual/Spatial Intelligence The ability to perceive the world accurately and to perform transformations upon one's perceptions.	guides, interior designers, architects, artists, and inventors	think in images and pictures; like mazes and jigsaw puzzles; like to draw and design things; like films, slides, videos, diagrams, maps, and charts	drawing and painting programs; reading programs that use visual clues such as rebus method or color coding; programs that allow them to see information such as maps, charts, or diagrams (e.g., charting capability of spreadsheet program); multmedia programs; science probeware
Musical Intelligence The capacity to percieve, discriminate, transform, and express musical forms.	musical performers, aficionados, and critics	learn through rhythm and melody; play a musical instrument; may need music to study; notice nonverbal sounds in the environment; learn things more easily if sung, tapped out, or whistled	programs that combine stories with songs; reading programs that associate letter/sounds with music; programs that allow them to create their own song; constructing presentations using CD audio discs, videodisc player, and barcode program; sing-along videodisc programs that display words "karaoke" style
Logical/Mathematical Intelligence The capacity to use numbers effectively and to reason well.	mathematicians, tax accountants, statisticians, scientists, computer programmers, and logicians	reason things out logically and clearly; look for abstract patterns and relationships; like brain teasers, logical puzzles, and strategy games; like to use computers; like to classify and categorize	database and spreadsheet programs; problem-solving software; computer programming software; strategy game formats/simulations; calculators; multimedia authoring programs

Source: Adapted from Jack Edwards, "Multiple Intelligences and Technology." [On-line]. Available: http://www.firn.edu/~face/about/dec95/mult_int.html.

	Highly developed in:	Students with a high degree:	May benefit from
Bodily-Kinesthetic Intelligence Expertise in using one's whole body to express ideas and feelings, and facility in using one's hands to produce or transform things.	actors, mimes, athletes, dancers, sculptors, mechanics, and surgeons	process knowledge through bodily sensations; move, twitch, tap, or fidget while sitting in a chair; learn by touching, manipulating, and moving; like role playing and creative movement	software requiring alternate input such as joystick, mouse, or touch window; keyboarding and word processing programs; animation programs; programs that allow them to move objects around the screen; science probeware
Interpersonal Intelligence The ability to perceive and make distinctions in the moods, intentions, motivations, and feelings of other people.	Intelligence can include: sensitivity to facial expressions, voice, and gestures, as well as the ability to respond effectively to such cues	understand and care about people; like to socialize; learn more easily by relating and cooperating; are good at teaching other students	telecommunications programs; programs that address social issues; programs that include group presentation or decision making; games that require two or more players; TV production-team approach
Intrapersonal Intelligence Self-knowledge and the ability to act adaptively on the basis of that knowledge.	Intelligence can include: having an accurate picture of one's strengths and limitations, awareness of one's moods and motivations, and the capacity for self-discipline.	seem to be self-motivating; need their own quiet space; march to the beat of a different drummer; learn more easily with independent study, self-paced instruction, and individualized projects and games	computer-assisted instruction/ ILS labs; instructional games in which the opponent is the computer; programs that encourage self-awareness or build self-improvement skills; any programs that allow them to work independently; brainstorming or problem-solving software
Naturalist Intelligence The human ability to discriminate among living things (e.g., plants, animals) as well as sensitivity to other features of the natural world (e.g., clouds, rock configurations).	botanist, chef, biologist, veterinarian, and geologist	observe, understand, and organize patterns in the natural environment; show expertise in the recognition and classification of plants and animals	computer and other technology such as games involving birds, butterflies, insects; any software that provides opportunities for classifications of plant and animal species, programs that enable students to explore a geographic feature relating to mountains, oceans, and other geologic features; software that provides for study of the planets and exploration of the universe

At the heart of multiple intelligence theory is the concept that children are individuals with individual backgrounds, abilities, and needs. The eight separate intelligences develop in different children, in different times, and in different ways. Early childhood professionals are challenged on how to provide for children's ongoing and constantly developing intelligences. By integrating technology into the curriculum, teachers can provide learning activities that enable all children's intelligences to develop.

taken not to assume values and beliefs just because a family speaks Spanish and is from Latin America. It is important that teachers spend the time to discover the particular values, beliefs, and practices of the families in the community.

Based on this knowledge, you can use the following guidelines to involve Hispanic parents:

- *Use a personal touch.* It is crucial to use face-to-face communication in the Hispanic parents' primary language when first making contact. Written flyers or articles sent home have proven to be ineffective even when written in Spanish. It may also take several personal meetings before the parents gain sufficient trust to actively participate. Home visits are a particularly good way to begin to develop rapport.
- *Use nonjudgmental communication.* To gain the trust and confidence of Hispanic parents, teachers must avoid making them feel they are to blame or are doing something wrong. Parents need to be supported for their strengths, not judged for perceived failings.
- *Be persistent in maintaining involvement.* To keep Hispanic parents actively engaged, activities planned by the early childhood program must respond to a real need or concern of the parents. Teachers should have a good idea about what parents will get out of each meeting and how the meeting will help them in their role as parents.
- *Provide bilingual support.* All communication with Hispanic parents, written and oral, must be provided in Spanish and English. Many programs report that having bicultural and bilingual staff helps promote trust.[12]
- *Provide strong leadership and administrative support.* Flexible policies, a welcoming environment, and a collegial atmosphere all require administrative leadership and support. As with other educational projects and practices that require innovation and adaptation, the efforts of teachers alone cannot bring success to parent involvement projects. Principals must also be committed to project goals.
- *Provide staff development focused on Hispanic culture.* All staff must understand the key features of Hispanic culture and its impact on their students' behavior and learning styles. It is the educator's obligation to learn as much about the children and their culture and background as possible.
- *Conduct community outreach.* Many Hispanic families could benefit from family literacy programs, vocational training, ESL programs, improved medical and dental services, and other community-based social services. A school or early childhood program can serve as a resource and referral agency to support the overall strength and stability of the families.

Encourage Cooperative Learning

Cooperative learning is a teaching–learning process in which small groups or teams of children work together and help each other complete assignments. This method of learning continues to grow in popularity because of its ability to promote intergroup relations, encourage the acceptance of and respect for children with academic and physical special needs, and promote the ability of children to work cooperatively together. There are many forms of cooperative learning, but all of them involve children working together in heterogeneous small groups. Cooperative learning includes these key elements:

- Small group (four to six students) works together.
- Students help each other complete a group assignment.
- Group members contribute to the group project based on their talents, interests, and abilities.
- The final product is representative of the group effort. All students share in the praise and reward of the group product.

In addition to these benefits, cooperative learning provides students with involvement in and control over their learning activities. It also enables everyone to understand that all children have something to contribute to the learning process.

... voice from the field

Implications of Latino Child Development for Early Childhood Professionals

To provide appropriate programs and services to Latino populations (i.e., people whose origins are Mexican, Puerto Rican, Cuban, Central or South American, or some other Spanish origin) residing in the United States, early childhood professionals must begin to understand what aspects of the developmental process are "culturally specific" and what aspects are universal or common to all humans regardless of cultural background. This differentiation is not easily made. One of the primary reasons for our lack of understanding is the absence of systematic research targeting minority children in general. Much of what we know is often based on data that implicitly or explicitly compares low-income minority children against middle-class Anglo populations.

The problem with this approach is that minority children's development tends to be viewed as less optimal when compared with their middle-class counterparts. Rather, an understanding of minority children's development must be based within the contextual parameters of a particular culture. Given this guideline, what, as early childhood professionals, do we know about the Latino child's growth and development that is "culturally specific" and what implications does that knowledge have for how programs and services should be structured?

First, we know that cultural background and socioeconomic background are highly interrelated so that what we think may be "culturally specific" may be more a function of the group's adaptation to their socioeconomic conditions. When social class is similar, differences between middle-income Anglos and middle-income Latinos may decrease. For example, research shows that maternal teaching strategies are different when comparing low-income Latinos and middle-income Anglos. However, differences substantially decrease when comparisons are made between middle-income Latinos and middle-income Anglos.

Social class standing is an important indicator of available resources such as the quality of housing, employment opportunities, medical services, and, most important, educational programs. For Latinos residing in the United States, level of acculturation also plays an important role. *Acculturation* refers to the degree to which an individual is able to function

effectively in the dominant culture. This quality includes the ability to speak the language and knowledge of the dominant group's values and cultural expressions (e.g., foods, art). These factors play a major role in determining an individual's ability to adapt to the society. The early childhood professional must appreciate the relationship between social class standing and acculturation and those behaviors that stem from living in different socioeconomic situations.

Second, in understanding Latino child development, it is important to cultivate an awareness of Latino parents' orientation to children and examine how this affects the goals of child rearing. Previous research on parental beliefs suggests that cultural background is an important determinant of parental ideas. The type of competence parents expect of young children may vary from culture to culture. For low-income immigrant Latino parents, expectations for their children's skill development may differ from that of Latinos born in the United States; foreign-born Latinos perceive the behavioral capabilities of young children as developing later than do U.S.-born Latinos. It may be that low-income immigrant Latinos have a more maturational orientation to children's development so that the early emphasis on cognitive stimulation promoted in the United States is somewhat inconsistent with their expectations.

A maturational approach to child rearing may stem from the social and historic backgrounds of Latino groups living in the United States. In cultures in which children are expected to take part in the cultural activities of adults, such as sibling caretaking and economic maintenance of the family, certain parent–child interaction patterns will merge. Thus, in more rural, traditional cultures, parents may socialize their children by stressing observation and immediate assistance in task development rather then explicit instruction, which tends to be valued by middle-class U.S. parents. On the other hand, in U.S. culture children are segregated into age-graded classrooms in which information is given in bits and pieces over an extended period.

Early childhood professionals need to consider how parental orientation may differ from the specific goals and objectives of a particular intervention program. When working with immigrant families it is sometimes appropriate to indicate how the expectations of the school explicitly differ from the group's orientation. For many immigrant families, adaptation and innovation are a way of life, and accepting different ways of doing things is part and parcel of the immigrant experience. However, for second-generation or more acculturated groups reared in the United States, such explicit contrast may not suffice. In these instances, practitioners must become familiar with the degree of acculturation that characterizes the group and adjust their services accordingly.

Third, Latinos hold certain values and beliefs that are important for childhood socialization. The following sections present an overview of important core values and beliefs that will vary in individual families depending on their acculturation level, socioeconomic standing, and ethnic loyalty. It is very important to see these core values as broad generalizations subject to adaptations to local conditions.

Familialism

This value is viewed as one of the most important culture-specific values of Latinos. *Familialism* refers to strong identification and connection to the immediate and extended family. Behaviors associated with familialism include strong feelings of loyalty, reciprocity, and solidarity. Familialism is manifested through the following: (1) feelings of obligation to provide both material and emotional support to the family, (2) dependence on relatives for help and support, and (3) reliance on relatives as behavioral and attitudinal referents.

Respeto

Associated with familialism is the cultural concept of *respeto*, which is an extremely important underlying tenet of interpersonal interaction. Basically, *respeto* ("respect") refers to the deference ascribed to various members of the family or society because of their position. Generally speaking, respect is accorded to the position and not necessarily the person. Thus, respect is expected toward elders, parents, older siblings within the family, and teachers, clergy, nurses, and doctors outside the family. With respect comes deference; that is, the person will not question the individual in the authority position, will exhibit very courteous behavior in front of them, and will appear to agree with information presented to them by the authority figure.

Bien Educado

If a person exhibits the characteristics associated with *respeto*, then they are said to be *bien educado*. What is important here is that the term *educado* ("education") refers not to formal education but to the acquisition of the appropriate social skills and graces within the Latino cultural context. For traditional Latinos, someone having graduated with honors from Harvard University but who did not conform to this system of *bien educado* would be considered badly educated.

Incorporation of important cultural values and beliefs into the early childhood professional's semblance of cultural continuity maintains feelings of self-respect. The professional can accomplish this by demonstrating high degrees of courtesy, by understanding that indirect communication on the part of the child and parent is a reflection of *respeto* to teachers as authority figures, and by viewing the broader family configuration as an important resource for understanding Latino family dynamics. Within this general framework, the professional must accommodate individual differences and local community conditions.

Contributed by Marlene Zepeda, California State University, Los Angeles.

Program in Action

The Chinese American International School of San Francisco

THE SCHOOL: DESCRIPTION AND PHILOSOPHY

The Chinese American International School of San Francisco was established in 1981 by a multiethnic group of parents, educators, and civic leaders. It remains the nation's only full-time school from prekindergarten through eighth grade offering instruction in English and Mandarin Chinese as equal languages in all subjects.

The school's mission emphasizes fluency in both English and Mandarin Chinese, internationalism, intellectual flexibility, and the development of character, emotional, and social maturity as a foundation for active participation and leadership in the modern world.

No prior Chinese language knowledge is necessary for children to enter the program. Children of every ethnicity are enrolled in the school, with 95 percent of the families speaking no Mandarin Chinese at home.

The program is a 50/50 "foreign language immersion" program whereby all subjects in the curriculum are taught in and through Chinese Mandarin. Chinese Mandarin is an equal language of instruction and communication with English, and not simply the object of study itself, as in traditional foreign language classes.

Parents gravitate to this program for several different reasons: Asian Americans of second, third, or fourth generation seek an education with a link to their cultural and historical heritage; international business professionals want their children to enjoy the advantage of fluency in the language and culture; families who have studied research results send their children to the school for the social and cognitive benefits of bilingual education.

THE PREKINDERGARTEN AND KINDERGARTEN CHILDREN

Entering students in prekindergarten are immediately immersed in both English and Mandarin Chinese so that by the completion of kindergarten they have developed basic proficiency in both languages. Each class is taught by an English teacher and a Chinese teacher with the help of teaching assistants. All teachers are native speakers of the language they use for instruction.

The English kindergarten curriculum utilizes the Montessori method, allowing careful attention to each child's developmental level and individual learning style. Through lessons and everyday life skill experiences, the children develop a fine sense of order and enhanced ability to concentrate, following a complex sequence of steps. Hands-on learning materials make abstract concepts clear and concrete. Along with the opportunity to explore, it teaches them to be independent, responsible, caring individuals.

The Chinese prekindergarten and kindergarten curriculum provides similar opportunities for the children to grow and learn. It focuses on social interaction skills and respect for others as the children acquire listening and speaking skills in the foreign language. The Chinese immersion curriculum is concrete, multisensory, hands-on, and project oriented. A science class on flotation, for example, would require children to test and record flotation of real objects, enabling them to learn the objects' names as well as to express concepts related to flotation in the Chinese language.

In a typical school day, children will sing dramatized songs, produce art and craft projects, play games, listen to stories, and familiarize themselves with some written characters. The teacher uses Chinese exclusively, making use of movements, facial expressions, voice inflections, pictures, toys, and a myriad of props to ensure comprehension and participation. Children are allowed to demonstrate their understanding in multiple ways.

Together, the Chinese and English teachers in the prekindergarten programs encourage children to organize, hypothesize, explore, invent, discover, and test their experiences. An emphasis is placed on the development of each child's creativity, concentration, initiative, self-confidence, self-discipline, imagination, and love of learning. This lays the foundation for a challenging elementary school curriculum that emphasizes both oral and written communication in the two languages.

THE ELEMENTARY CURRICULUM

In elementary school, science, social studies, language arts, and mathematics share equal prominence in both the English and Chinese classes. In a 50/50 bilingual immersion program, students spend

half a day in an English classroom, learning in much the same way as students in a monolingual school would do. Then, in the second part of the day, they will enter a different classroom, filled with Chinese writing and media. They then study subjects from the Chinese teacher, just as they did in the morning, but expressing themselves in Chinese. On the following day, the model reverses itself, beginning with Chinese in the morning and English in the afternoon.

Close coordination between the English and the Chinese teachers allows the development of common themes for study materials and cultural celebrations. Teachers reinforce—but do not repeat or translate—each other's activities. For instance, while the Chinese teacher assumes the responsibility for the celebration of Chinese festivals such as Chinese New Year, the English teacher leads the celebration of American holidays like Thanksgiving. In the course of the celebrations, children can learn language and content simultaneously. Besides immersion in the culture, they acquire second-language vocabulary through cooking, costume designing, and dramatization of events.

PROFESSIONAL DEVELOPMENT

Current enrollment in the new San Francisco Civic Center campus has grown to four hundred students, with most grade levels incorporating multiple sections. The earliest graduates of the Chinese American International School are now enrolled in universities throughout the United States, most continuing their Chinese studies. Alumni in high school regularly serve as counselors and aids during the school's summer session. Summer sessions also serve as training periods for new faculty who work closely with a master/mentor teacher for several years before assuming full curricular responsibility.

The growing interest in teaching Chinese language at all age levels, and in the elementary curriculum in particular, led to the development of a separate unit of the school devoted to teacher training and curricular development. The Institute for Teaching Chinese Language and Culture is supported by two national foundations in its role as the creator of a graduate training program in the CAIS immersion methodology. The elementary school serves as the laboratory practicum for teachers coming for training from throughout the United States and Asia.

Visit the Chinese American International School on the Web at http://www.cie-cais.org/.

Text contributed by teacher Juliana Carnes and principal Shirley Lee; photos courtesy Emily Ching.

Programs That Support Multicultural Education

Bilingual Education

For most people, *bilingual education* means that children (or adults, or both) will be taught a second language. Some people interpret this to mean that a child's native language (often referred to as the *home language*)—whether English, Spanish, French, Italian, Chinese, Tagalog, or any of the other 125 languages in which bilingual programs are conducted—will tend to be suppressed. For other people, bilingual education means that children will be taught in both the home language and the primary language. The Bilingual Education Act, Title VII of the Elementary Secondary Education Act (ESEA), sets forth the federal government's policy toward bilingual education:

> The Congress declares it to be the policy of the United States, in order to establish equal educational opportunity for all children and to promote educational excellence (A) to encourage the establishment and operation, where appropriate, of educational programs

For more information about bilingual education, go to the Companion Website at http://www.prenhall.com/morrison, select chapter 14, then choose the Linking to Learning module to connect to the National Center for Bilingual Education site.

> using bilingual educational practices, techniques, and methods, (B) to encourage the establishment of special alternative instructional programs for students of limited English proficiency in school districts where the establishment of bilingual education programs is not practicable or for other appropriate reasons, and (C) for those purposes, to provide financial assistance to local educational agencies.[13]

REASONS FOR INTEREST IN BILINGUAL EDUCATION. Diversity is a positive aspect of U.S. society. Ethnic pride and identity have caused renewed interest in languages and a more conscious effort to preserve children's native languages. In the nineteenth and early twentieth centuries, foreign-born individuals and their children wanted to camouflage their ethnicity and unlearn their language because it seemed unpatriotic or un-American; today, however, we hold the opposite viewpoint.

A second reason for interest in bilingual education is an emphasis on civil rights. Indeed, much of the concept of providing children with an opportunity to know, value, and use their heritage and language stems from people's recognition that they have a right to them. Just as extending rights to children with disabilities is very much evident today, so it is with children and their languages, as part of the view of children as people with rights (see chapter 3).

Yet another reason for bilingual interest is the number of people who speak a language other than English. According to the Census Bureau, 31.8 million, or one in seven, residents of the United States speak a language other than English, with Spanish now the second most common language other than English. Table 14.3 shows the twenty-five most common languages (other than English) spoken in U.S. homes. Pay particular note to the fastest-growing languages, such as Mon-Khmer, spoken by Cambodians. Taken as a group, the Asian school-age population is expected to double by the year 2020.

These data show that the chances are increasing that you will work with parents, children, and families in a language other than English. They also give you some idea what languages parents and children you work with will speak. Moreover, these increases will necessitate a need to develop culturally appropriate material and activities. As individual

All classrooms must be places where people of all cultures, races, socioeconomic backgrounds, religions, and both genders are welcomed and accepted. If students learn to embrace diversity within the classroom, they will also embrace diversity outside of it.

professionals and as a body, we cannot ignore the need for appropriate curriculum materials for children of all cultures. To do so adds to the risk of language-minority children being cut off from mainstream life and from the "American dream." Finally, there is a need to develop training programs for early childhood professionals that will enable them to work in culturally sensitive ways with parents, families, and children.

PROGRAMS FOR STUDENTS WITH LIMITED ENGLISH PROFICIENCY. Early childhood programs and schools can make several responses to language learning for children with limited English proficiency (LEP). First, they can use an *immersion program*, in which children typically are placed in a program in which English is the exclusive language and all instruction is conducted in English. A teacher may or may not know the child's native language. The goal of an immersion program is to have children learn English as quickly and fluently as possible. Little if any effort is made to maintain or improve the child's native language ability.

Other than immersion, there are three broad categories of programs aimed at LEP students: English as a Second Language (ESL) programs, transitional bilingual education programs, and maintenance bilingual education programs. While there are variations within

Table 14.3
The Twenty-five Languages Other Than English Most Commonly Spoken at Home

Language	Total Speakers over 5 Years Old	Percentage Change from 1980
Spanish	17,339,172	50.1
French	1,702,176	8.3
German	1,547,049	–3.7
Italian	1,308,648	–19.9
Chinese	1,249,213	97.7
Tagalog	843,251	86.6
Polish	723,483	–12.4
Korean	626,478	127.2
Vietnamese	507,069	149.5
Portuguese	429,860	19.0
Japanese	427,657	25.0
Greek	388,260	–5.4
Arabic	355,150	57.4
Hindi, Urdu, and related	331,484	155.1
Russian	241,798	38.5
Yiddish	213,064	–33.5
Thai	206,266	131.6
Persian	201,865	84.7
French Creole	187,658	654.1
Armenian	149,694	46.3
Navajo	148,530	20.6
Hungarian	147,902	–17.9
Hebrew	144,292	45.5
Dutch	142,684	–2.6
Mon-Khmer	127,441	676.3

Source: U.S. Census Bureau, "Detailed Language Spoken at Home and Ability to Speak English for Persons 5 Years and Older" (Washington, DC: U.S. Government Printing Office, 1995).

each, the first two place value only on developing English language competency, and the third tries to create bilingual, biliterate students. (Note that bilingual programs may have different names in different states.)

English as a second language (ESL) programs generally provide a special English class for students learning the language along with sheltered English approaches to other subjects. *Sheltered English* involves a high degree of visualization of subject matter and a vocabulary adapted to the student's level of English proficiency.

Transitional bilingual programs have an ESL component and use the native language as a medium of instruction in the other subjects. As students learn more English, the native language use is de-emphasized until students fully adapt to a curriculum that uses English only.

Maintenance bilingual programs, like transitional ones, also teach English while using the native language to teach other subjects. As students learn more English, it is woven into content area instruction. What makes maintenance bilingual programs unique is that native language instruction is continued after students are fully functional in English. The goal of maintenance bilingual programs is to create students who are not only bilingual but also biliterate.

RESEARCH ON SECOND LANGUAGE LEARNING. Research increasingly points toward a consensus: children learn English faster and are more likely to excel academically if they are given several years of instruction in their native language first. A study endorsed by the National Academy of Sciences that followed two thousand Hispanic American schoolchildren concluded that "it is a myth that if you want children to learn English, you give them nothing but English."

Another commonly held misconception about acquiring English as a second language is that instruction in the student's first language will impair the acquisition of English. Research indicates that students who are literate and who understand grammar in their first language are more efficient learners of a second language than students who are not literate in their first language.

Research in second language acquisition since the 1970s has shown some surprising results:

- Early childhood is not necessarily the optimum period in which to acquire a second language; older children and adults can actually be better learners. Thus, the rush to immerse very young children in a second language may be inappropriate.
- Language proficiency is a configuration of many different kinds of language abilities. Though children may quickly acquire simple, everyday, social English, the English they need for academic success will take much longer to develop.
- Skills learned in one language transfer to another. Children with a good academic foundation in their first language will do better in a second language in the long run.
- Reading, especially for at-risk children, should first be taught in the native language. These skills will ultimately transfer into higher achievement in the second language.
- Children are not handicapped cognitively by bilingualism; some types of intelligence, such as creativity, may actually be enhanced by the child's being bilingual.

ISSUES IN BILINGUAL EDUCATION. As you might expect, programs for helping children learn English are controversial. Critics of immersion programs assert that when the focus is only on teaching English, children are at risk for losing the ability to speak and use their native language. On the other hand, proponents of immersion programs maintain that

English is the language of schooling and U.S. society, and it is in children's best interests to learn English as quickly and fluently as possible. Further, they maintain that it is the parents' responsibility to help maintain native language and culture. For their part, parents want their children to be successful in both school and society. Some regret that their children have not maintained their native language because of the role it plays in culture and religion.

Critics of transitional bilingual programs maintain that it takes children too long to learn English and that it is too costly to try and maintain a child's native language. On the other hand, proponents of transitional programs say it makes sense to help children learn English while preserving native language and culture.

To take an online self-test on this chapter's contents, go to the Companion Website at http://www.prenhall.com/morrison, select chapter 14, then choose the Self Test module.

Trends in Multicultural Education

As with most areas of early childhood education, we can identify trends that will affect multicultural curricula, programs, and practices. The following trends, and others to come, will affect how you teach young children:

- Multicultural curricula are becoming more pluralistic and are including knowledge and information about many cultures. Children learn to look at the world through the eyes of other cultures and ethnic groups. As a result, more children will examine a full range of cultures rather than looking at only two or three, as is often the current practice.
- More early childhood teachers are recognizing that just because children are young does not mean that they cannot learn about multicultural perspectives. Consequently, multicultural activities and content are being included in curricula from the time children enter preschool programs. For example, kindergarten children might be encouraged to look at Thanksgiving through the eyes of both Native Americans and Pilgrims instead of being taught only the Pilgrims' point of view.
- Many early childhood professionals are being challenged to preserve children's natural reactions to others' differences before they adopt or are taught adult stereotypical reactions. Young children are, in general, understanding and accepting of differences in others.
- Since the 1990s, increasing amounts of materials have become available to aid in teaching multicultural education. The amount and kind of multicultural materials will continue to increase, so teachers will have even more decisions to make regarding what kind of materials they want and can use. Because not all materials are of equal value or worth, this abundance will mean that professionals will need to be increasingly diligent when selecting appropriate materials for young children.
- There is a growing recognition that effective multicultural education is good for all. Whereas in the past some teachers and parents have resisted multicultural teaching, more and more the public is accepting and supportive of teaching multicultural education to all children.

While we have a long way to go to ensure that all classrooms and curricula provide for children's multicultural needs, we are making progress. You can be at the forefront of making even greater advances by educating both yourself and young children for living in a diverse society.

For additional Internet resources or to complete an online activity for this chapter, go to the Companion Website at http://www.prenhall.com/morrison, select chapter 14, then choose the Linking to Learning or Making Connections module.

Activities for Further Enrichment

Applications

1. The classroom environment and certain educational materials may promote sexism, and they play a powerful role in sex-role stereotyping. Examine the environment of selected classrooms and homes to determine the extent of sexist practices. Make recommendations based on your findings for minimizing or eliminating any such practices you find.
2. Effective educational programs provide children with opportunities to develop an understanding of other persons and cultures. Consider how you would accomplish the following objectives in your classroom:
   a. Provide children with firsthand, positive experiences with different cultural groups.
   b. Help children reflect on and think about their own cultural group identity.
   c. Help children learn how to obtain accurate information about other cultural groups.

Field Experiences

1. In addition to the books mentioned in this chapter, select ten children's books that have multicultural content. Decide how you would use these materials to promote awareness and acceptance of diversity. Read these books to children and get their reactions.
2. Survey ten teachers and your classmates, asking them what the term *multicultural* means. Ask them to share with you activities to promote multiculturalism. Put these activities in your teaching file.

Research

1. Examine children's books and textbooks to determine instances of sexism. What recommendations would you make to change such practices?
2. Stories and literature play an important role in transmitting to children information about themselves and what to expect in life.
   a. What books and literature played an important role in your growing up? In what way?
   b. Identify five children's books that you think would be good to use with children and indicate why you think so.

Readings for Further Enrichment

Bennett, C. *Comprehensive Multicultural Education: Theory and Practice*, 4th ed. Needham Heights, MA: Allyn & Bacon, 1999.

Bennett offers an in-depth, research-based treatment of the history of education for diversity in the United States and contemporary theory and methods in multicultural education.

Garrod, A., Ward, J., Robinson, T., and Kilkenny, R., eds. *Souls Looking Back: Life Stories of Growing Up Black*. New York: Routledge, 1999.

Each chapter—on social class and race, identity, and resistance and resilience—begins with an overview of the issue written by an African American scholar, followed by four to six personal narratives. The accounts are both thought provoking and extremely intimate.

Holliday, L., Lindroth, C., and Lindroth, J. *Children of the Dream: Our Own Stories of Growing Up Black in America*. New York: Pocket Books, 1999.

Offers first-person explorations of the lives of African Americans who came of age at the dawn of the Civil Rights era.

Howard, G. *We Can't Teach What We Don't Know: White Teachers, Multiracial Schools*. New York: Teachers College Press, 1999.

With lively stories and compelling analysis, this book takes readers on a journey of personal and professional transformation. From his twenty-five years of experience as a multicultural educator, the author looks deeply into the mirror of his own racial identity to discover what it means to be a culturally competent white teacher in racially diverse schools.

Nieto, S. *The Light in Their Eyes: Creating Multicultural Learning Communities*. New York: Teachers College Press, 1999.

Makes student learning the primary objective of multicultural education. Draws on a host of research in learning styles, multiple intelligences, and cognitive theories to portray the way students learn.

Toussaint, P., and Kadlecek, J. *I Call You Friend: Four Women's Stories of Race, Faith, and Friendship*. Nashville: Broadman & Holman Publishers, 1999.

Vivid, poignant, humorous, hard-hitting, and honest, four women—two black and two white—offer intimate portraits of how they grew from children to teens to adults against the backdrop of racial tension that ultimately shaped them into friends and unified them in the quest for racial reconciliation at its most personal level.

Valdez, A. *Learning in Living Color: Using Literature to Incorporate Multicultural Education into the Primary Curriculum.* Needham Heights, MA: Allyn & Bacon, 1999.

Through suggested ideas, the text promotes the reduction of race, class, gender, and ethnic divisions by helping students acquire knowledge, attitudes, and skills necessary for becoming active citizens in a democratic society and participating in social change.

Linking to Learning

Multicultural Awareness in the Language Classroom
http://www.wfi.fr/blair

This site contains excellent sources for language arts and English teachers.

Multicultural Book Reviews
http://www.isomedia.com/homes/jmele/homepage.html

This is a useful site for educators to preview existing and new titles in multicultural education.

Multicultural Education Programs
http://eric-web.tc.columbia.edu/families/index.html

This site provides examples of various multicultural education programs throughout the United States.

Multicultural Perspectives in Mathematics Education
http://jwilson.coe.uga.edu/DEPT/Multicultural/mathED.html

Explores multicultural dimensions of mathematics, a field often regarded as difficult to teach multiculturally.

National Clearinghouse for Bilingual Education
http://www.ncbe.gwu.edu

This site is operated by George Washington University and is an excellent source to explore the education and characteristics of limited-English-proficient students.

National Multicultural Institute
http://www.nmci.org

This site is operated by the Washington-based National Multicultural Institute and explores many facets of diversity.

ENDNOTES

1 Valerie Ooka Pang and Jesus Nieto, "Multicultural Teaching," *Kappa Delta Pi Record* 29 (1) (Fall 1992), 25–27.

2 J. Burnett, "Books for Children," *Childhood Education 176* (2, Winter 1999/2000), 108–109.

3 *Federal Register* (August 11, 1975), 33803.

4 *Federal Register* (June 4, 1975), 24128.

5 Millicent Lawton, "Four of Five Students in Grades 8 to 11 Sexually Harassed at School, Poll Finds," *Education Week* (June 9, 1993), 5.

6 American Association of University Women, "What the Research Reveals," *The AAUW Report: How Schools Shortchange Girls: Executive Summary* (Washington DC: Author, 1992), 2. Copyright © 1992, the American Association of University Women Educational Foundation.

7 Marian Marion, *Guidance of Young Children,* 4th ed. (Upper Saddle River, NJ: Merrill/Prentice Hall, 1995), 290–291.

8 Marie Cabo, Rita Dunn, and Kenneth Dunn, *Teaching Students to Read Through Their Individual Learning Styles* (Boston: Allyn & Bacon, 1991), 2.

9 Rita Dunn, Kenneth Dunn, and Gary Price, *Learning Styles Inventory (LSI)* (Lawrence, KS: Price Systems, 1987), 14–19. Adapted by permission.

10 Howard Gardner, *Frames of Mind* (New York: Basic Books, 1983).

11 N. Williams, *The Mexican American Family* (Dix Hills, NY: General Hill, 1990).

12 L. Espinosa, *Hispanic Parent Involvement in Early Childhood Programs* (Washington, DC: Office of Educational Research and Improvement, 1995).

13 Statute 2372, Section 703. Bilingual Education Act, Title VII of the Elementary Secondary Education Act, Statute 2268, Vol. 92 (November 1978).

CHAPTER 15

Inclusion involves all kinds of practices that are ultimately practices of good teaching. What good teachers do is to think thoughtfully about children and develop ways to reach all children.

DR. CHRIS KLIEWER

Children with Special Needs

Appropriate Education for All

Focus Questions

1. What are the appropriate terminology for and legal definitions of children with special needs?
2. What are reasons for contemporary interest in children with special needs?
3. What are the legal, political, moral, and social bases for mainstreaming and full inclusion of children in early childhood programs?
4. What issues relate to teaching children with special needs?
5. How do programs for the gifted meet children's needs?
6. What is the role of the early childhood professional in identifying and reporting child abuse?

To review the chapter focus questions online, go to the Companion Website at http://www.prenhall.com/morrison and select chapter 15.

Children with special needs are in every program, school, and classroom in the United States. As an early childhood professional, you will teach students who have a variety of special needs. They may come from low-income families or various racial and ethnic groups; they may have exceptional abilities or disabilities. Students with special needs are often discriminated against because of their disability, socioeconomic background, language, race, or gender. You and your colleagues will be challenged to provide for all students an education that is appropriate to their physical, intellectual, social, and emotional abilities and to help them achieve their best. Your challenge includes learning as much as you can about the special needs of children and collaborating with other professionals to identify and develop teaching strategies, programs, and curricula for them. Most of all, you need to be a strong advocate for meeting all children's individual needs.

Children with Disabilities

To check your understanding of this chapter with the online Study Guide, go to the Companion Website at http://www.prenhall.com/morrison, select chapter 15, then choose the Study Guide module.

Children with special needs and their families need education and services that will help them succeed. You will be a part of the process of seeing that they receive such services. Unfortunately, quite often children with disabilities are not provided appropriate services and fail to reach their full potential. This is one reason for laws to help ensure that schools and teachers will have high expectations for them and that they will have special education and related services. The federal government has passed many laws protecting and promoting the rights and needs of children with disabilities. One of the most important federal laws is PL 101-476, the Individuals with Disabilities Education Act (IDEA), passed in 1990. Congress has periodically updated IDEA, with the latest revision in 1997.

As with many special areas, the field of children with special needs has a unique vocabulary and terminology. The glossary in Figure 15.1 will help you as you read the chapter and as you work with children and families.

The Individuals with Disabilities Education Act (IDEA)

For more information about answers to frequently asked questions about IDEA, go to the Companion Website at http://www.prenhall.com/morrison, select chapter 15, then choose the Linking to Learning module to connect to the IDEA Practices site.

The purpose of the Individuals with Disabilities Education Act, as amended by PL 105-17 in 1997, is

> to ensure that all disabled children have available to them . . . a free appropriate public education which emphasizes special education and related services designed to meet their unique needs, to assure that the rights of disabled children and their parents or guardians are protected, to assist States and localities to provide for the education of all disabled children, and to assess and assure the effectiveness of efforts to educate disabled children.[1]

IDEA defines children with disabilities as those children

> with mental retardation, hearing impairments (including deafness), speech or language impairments (including blindness), serious emotional disturbance, orthopedic impairments, autism, traumatic brain injury, other health impairments, or specific learning disabilities; and who, by reason thereof, need special education and related services.[2]

Table 15.1 lists the number of persons from birth to age twenty-one with disabilities in the various categories. About 10 to 12 percent of the nation's students have disabilities.

Program in Action

The Play Bunch

INTRODUCE YOURSELF TO CORY

Cory is a young child with an orthopedic impairment who is an active member of the Play Bunch, an inclusive play group I started several years ago. Observe Cory as he moves about and interacts with the other children, as shown in these photos I've collected. What do you notice about how he is included in a variety of activities? What are the other children's relationships to Cory? How does Cory seem to relate to other children? What do you think the other children can learn from their interactions with Cory? What modifications in the learning environment might a teacher or a parent need to make in order for Cory to fully participate? How do you think the Play Bunch has contributed to Cory's confidence and independence?

THE BEGINNING

The Play Bunch was created because a need existed for positive, guided social interaction for preschoolers in an inclusive natural play setting. As a parent, I wanted my preschool daughter to become aware of exceptionalities and learn prosocial behaviors to interact with all peers. I wanted to be the catalyst in establishing feelings of acceptance and belonging, which are critical for becoming a functional and productive member of the future society. By collaborating with other parents and professionals, I located a group of families who shared my belief.

The group included children of various family structures, ethnicities, and abilities. Four families had households with two parents, one was headed by a single mother, and Grandma was a part of the extended family in another household. The children were of diverse ethnic heritage, including African American, Native American, and Spanish American. Exceptionalities of Down syndrome, spina bifida, and attention deficit were accepted by all. Our children became a play group participating and learning in developmentally appropriate and naturally inclusive environments. They played together on a tennis court with balls and balloons, at the beach, and in a park in the summer and fall. These children developed friendships and learned to be aware of others' feelings. The Play Bunch families accept exceptionalities and celebrate the diversity of our American society.

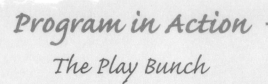

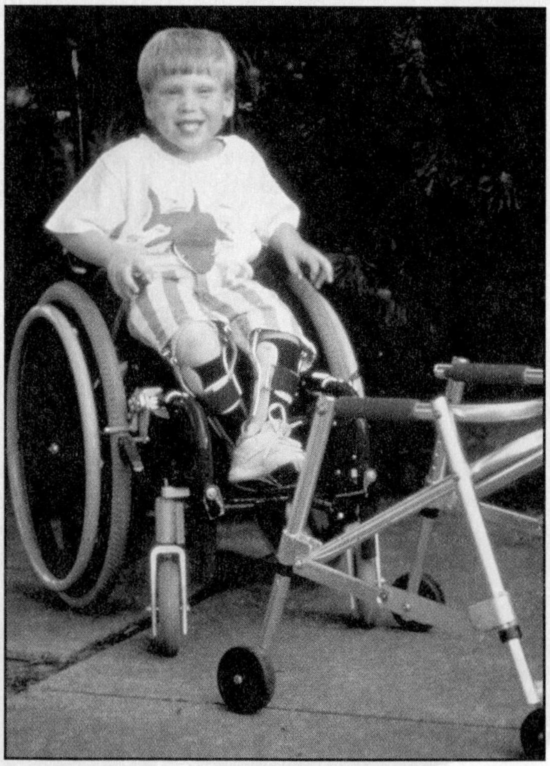

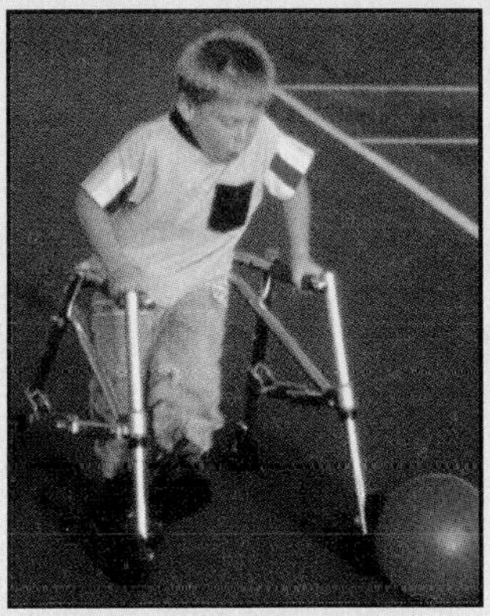

THE PHILOSOPHY

The Play Bunch concept celebrates exceptionalities in natural outdoor play and learning environments where preschool children are nurtured and guided in the development of feelings that they are accepted, liked, and wanted in community life. The Play Bunch children include various ethnic groups, family structures, and exceptionalities. The Play Bunch offers parents a model of an inclusive lifestyle option. These connections between parents and children in outdoor play and activities can enhance the quality of family life and continue the establishment of the acceptance of everyone's exceptionalities.

The new millennium presents educators and families with a society that is developing an awareness of exceptionalities and becoming increasingly ethnically, linguistically, and culturally diverse. Families of young children serve as the catalyst for establishing social acceptance of exceptionalities. Our basic educational belief system should also embody values for this future society. Our society will be remembered in history by the manner in which our children are nurtured and educated.

Learning to understand the feelings of others is critical in the social development of children. This learning is fostered when children are given opportunities to interact cooperatively with peers in developmentally appropriate inclusive activities. Educators can provide effective teaching strategies within a learning environment where children are guided in accepting their own exceptionalities. These strategies should be relevant to experiences with which children can identify.

Another aspect of being an educator of young children is realizing the need to empower families with ideas for promoting prosocial behaviors and understanding of others' feelings, thus developing social relationships outside the educational setting. Empowerment can begin by creating awareness of resources for building collaborative linkages and making community inclusion a reality. Parents can then make educated choices and be advocates for the nurturing of their children.

RESOURCES IN DEVELOPMENT

As an educator, I realized the importance of early reading and language stimulation with young children. I researched parent and special education resources and organizations throughout the country to find books showing inclusive play settings in a natural environment. There were no color picture books for the children to look at, be read to, and discuss. Clearly, such a need exists. I have made it my personal and professional goal to help other educators and parents by creating materials to use in or out of the classroom setting.

I am currently developing Play Bunch books and a video that can be used in a preschool educational setting to stimulate language through the discussion of feelings. Young children can look at pictures, be involved in reading activities, and discuss these examples of a diverse group of peers interacting with prosocial behaviors. Children can identify with outdoor play in a park, at a beach, or with balls and balloons. For an example related to your own professional training, introduce yourself to Cory.

It is my hope that, using the Play Bunch materials I am developing, educators will embody the values of nurturing, positive feelings and teaching prosocial behaviors to help children become functional members in their future society.

Visit the Play Bunch on the Web at Theplay bunch@aol.com.

Text and photos featuring the Play Bunch children of Sioux Falls, South Dakota, contributed by Debra A. Vande Berg.

IDEA'S SIX PRINCIPLES. IDEA establishes six principles for professionals to follow as they provide educational and other services to children with special needs:

1. *Zero reject:* a rule of educating all students and excluding none
2. *Nondiscriminatory evaluation:* a rule of fair evaluation to determine whether a student has a disability and, if so, what the student's education should consist of
3. *Appropriate education:* a rule of individualized education that benefits the student in making progress toward the national policy goals
4. *Least restrictive placement/environment:* a rule that students with disabilities must, to the maximum extent appropriate for each one, be educated with students who do not have disabilities (their education being in the academic, extracurricular, and other school activities that nondisabled students participate in)
5. *Procedural due process:* a rule that allows the schools and the parents to resolve their differences by mediation and, if not by that means, by having hearings before impartial hearing officers or judges
6. *Parental and student participation:* a rule of shared decision-making, where educators, parents, and students collaborate in deciding what the student's education should consist of[3]

Figure 15.2 (p. 456) lists the disabilities covered under IDEA.

Adaptive education: Modifying programs, environments, curricula, and activities in order to provide learning experiences that help all students achieve desired educational goals. The purpose of adaptive education is to respond effectively to student differences and to enhance each individual's ability to succeed in learning in such environments.

Children with disabilities: Replaces former terms such as *handicapped*. To avoid labeling children, do not use the reversal of these words (*i.e., disabled children*).

Co-teaching: The process by which a regular classroom professional and a special educator or a person trained in exceptional student education team teach, in the same classroom, a group of regular and mainstreamed children.

Disability: A physical or mental impairment that substantially limits one or more major life activities.

Early education and care settings: Promotes the idea that all children learn and that child care and other programs *should* be educating children birth to age eight.

Early intervention: Providing services to children and families as early in the child's life as possible in order to prevent or help with a special need or needs.

Exceptional student education: Replaces the term *special education*; refers to the education of children with special needs.

Full inclusion: The mainstreaming or inclusion of all children with disabilities into natural environments such as playgrounds, family daycare centers, child care centers, preschool, kindergarten, and primary grades.

Individualized education program (IEP): A written plan for a child stating what will be done, how it will be done, and when it will be done.

Integration: A generic term that refers to educating children with disabilities along with typically developing children. This education can occur in mainstream, reverse mainstream, and full-inclusion programs.

Least restrictive environment (LRE): Children with disabilities are educated with children who are not disabled, and that special classes, separate schooling, or other removal of children with disabilities from the regular educational environment occurs only when the nature or severity of the disability is such that education in regular classes with the use of supplementary aids and services cannot be achieved satisfactorily.

Limited English proficiency (LEP): Describes children who have limited English skills.

Mainstreaming: The social and educational integration of children with special needs into the general instructional process; usually a regular classroom program.

Merged classroom: A classroom that includes—merges—children with special needs and children without special needs and teaches them together in one classroom.

Natural environment: Any environment it is natural for any child to be in, such as home, child care center, preschool, kindergarten, primary grades, playground, and so on.

Normalized setting: A place that is "normal" or best for the child.

Reverse mainstreaming: The process by which typically developing children are placed in programs for children with disabilities. In reverse mainstreaming, children with disabilities are in the majority.

Typically developing children: Children who are developing according to and within the boundaries of normal growth and development.

Figure 15.1
Glossary of Terms Related to Children with Special Needs

Table 15.1
Persons Aged 0 to 21 Years Served in Federally Supported Programs by Type of Disability

Type of Disability	Numbers Served
All disabilities	5,339,400
Specific learning disabilities	2,723,094
Speech or language impairments	1,057,201
Mental retardation	587,334
Serious emotional disturbance	453,849
Hearing impairments	69,412
Orthopedic impairments	69,412
Other health impairments	192,218
Visual impairments	26,697
Multiple disabilities	106,788
Deaf-blind	1,670
Autism	42,715
Traumatic brain injury	10,679

Source: U.S. Department of Education, Office of Special Education Programs, Data Analysis System (DANS), June 4, 1997.

GUARANTEEING A FREE AND APPROPRIATE EDUCATION. IDEA mandates a free and appropriate education (FAPE) for all persons between the ages of three and twenty-one. To guarantee students a free appropriate public education, IDEA provides federal money to state and local educational agencies to help educate students in the following age groups:

1. From birth to age three (early intervention)
2. From age three to age six (early childhood special education)
3. From age six to age eighteen
4. From age eighteen to age twenty-one (transition or aging out of school)

The state and local agencies, however, must agree to comply with the federal law or else they will not receive federal money. Exceptional education and related services specified by IDEA are listed in Figure 15.3.

CREATING AN INDIVIDUALIZED EDUCATION PROGRAM. Exceptional student education laws currently mandate the creation of an Individualized Education Program (IEP), which requires a plan for the *individualization* of each student's instruction. This requires creating learning objectives and basing each student's learning plan on their specific needs, disabilities, and preferences, as well as on those of their parents. A collaborative team of regular and special educators creates these objectives. The IEP must specify what will be done for the child, how and when it will be done, and by whom, and this information must be in writing. In developing the IEP, a person trained in diagnosing disabling conditions, such as a school psychologist, must be part of the IEP team, as well as the parent and, when appropriate, the child.

For more information about IEPs, go to the Companion Website at http://www.prenhall.com/morrison, select chapter 15, then choose the Linking to Learning module to connect to the Individualized Education Plans site.

Function of the IEP. Using an individualized education plan with all children, not just those with disabilities, is gaining acceptance with all early childhood professionals. Individualizing objectives, methodology, and teaching helps ensure that the teaching process will become more accurate and accountable.

As an early childhood educator, you will have children with special needs in your classroom. The following disabilities qualify children for special education services under IDEA:

1. *Autism:* A developmental disability significantly affecting verbal and nonverbal communication and social interaction, generally evident before age three, that adversely affects educational performance.
2. *Deafness:* A hearing impairment which is so severe that a child is impaired in processing linguistic information through hearing, with or without amplification, which adversely affects educational performance.
3. *Deaf-blindness:* Simultaneous hearing and visual impairments, the combination of which causes such severe communication and other developmental and educational problems that a child cannot be accommodated in special education programs solely for children with deafness or children with blindness.
4. *Hearing impairment:* A hearing impairment, whether permanent or fluctuating, which adversely affects a child's educational performance but which is not included under the definition of "deafness."
5. *Mental retardation:* Significantly sub-average general intellectual functioning existing concurrently with deficits in adaptive behavior and manifested during the developmental period, which adversely affects a child's educational performance.
6. *Multiple disabilities:* Simultaneous impairments (such as mental retardation/blindness, mental retardation/orthopedic impairment, etc.), the combination of which causes such severe educational problems that the child cannot be accommodated in a special education program solely for one of the impairments.
7. *Orthopedic impairment:* A severe orthopedic impairment which adversely affects a child's educational performance. The term includes impairments caused by a congenital anomaly (e.g., clubfoot, absence of some member, etc.), impairments caused by disease (e.g., poliomyelitis, bone tuberculosis, etc.), and impairments from other causes (e.g., cerebral palsy, amputations, and fractures or burns which cause contractures).

Figure 15.2
Disabilities Covered Under IDEA

Public Law 101-476, October 30, 1990. Statute 1103.

The IEP has several purposes. First, it protects children and parents by ensuring that planning will occur. Second, it guarantees that children will have plans tailored to their individual strengths, weaknesses, and learning styles. Third, it helps professionals and other instructional and administrative personnel focus their teaching and resources on children's specific needs, promoting the best use of everyone's time, efforts, and talents.

Fourth, the IEP helps ensure that children with disabilities will receive a range of services from other agencies. The plan must not only include an educational component but also specify how the child's total needs will be met. If a child can benefit from special services such as physical therapy, for example, it must be written into the IEP. This provision is bene-

8. *Other health impairment:* Having limited strength, vitality or alertness, due to chronic or acute health problems such as a heart condition, tuberculosis, rheumatic fever, nephritis, asthma, sickle cell anemia, hemophilia, epilepsy, lead poisoning, leukemia, or diabetes, which adversely affects a child's educational performance. According to the Office of Special Education and Rehabilitative Services' clarification statement of September 16, 1991, eligible children with ADD may also be classified under "other health impairment."
9. *Serious emotional disturbance:* A condition exhibiting one or more of the following characteristics over a long period of time and to a marked degree, which adversely affects educational performance: (A) an inability to learn which cannot be explained by intellectual, sensory, or health factors; (B) an inability to build or maintain satisfactory interpersonal relationships with peers and teachers; (C) inappropriate types of behavior or feelings under normal circumstances; (D) a general pervasive mood of unhappiness or depression; or (E) a tendency to develop physical symptoms or fears associated with personal or school problems. The term includes children who have schizophrenia. The term does not include children who are socially maladjusted, unless it is determined that they have a serious emotional disturbance.
10. *Specific learning disability:* A disorder in one more of the basic psychological processes involved in understanding or in using language, spoken or written, which may manifest itself in an imperfect ability to listen, think, speak, read, write, spell, or to do mathematical calculations. The term includes such conditions as perceptual disabilities, brain injury, minimal brain dysfunction, dyslexia, and developmental aphasia. The term does not include children who have learning problems which are primarily the result of visual, hearing, or motor disabilities, of mental retardation, of emotional disturbance, or of environmental, cultural, or economic disadvantage.
11. *Speech or language impairment:* A communication disorder such as stuttering, impaired articulation, a language impairment, or a voice impairment, which adversely affects a child's educational performance.
12. *Traumatic brain injury:* An injury to the brain caused by an external physical force, resulting in total or partial functional disability or psychosocial maladjustment, or both, which adversely affects educational performance. The term does not include brain injuries that are congenital or degenerative, or brain injuries induced by birth trauma.
13. *Visual impairment, including blindness:* A visual impairment which, even with correction, adversely affects a child's educational performance. The term includes both children with partial sight and those with blindness.

ficial not only for children but for classroom professionals as well, because it broadens their perspective of the educational function.

Fifth, the IEP helps clarify and refine decisions as to what is best for children—where they should be placed and how they should be taught and helped. It also ensures that children will not be categorized or labeled without discussion of their unique needs.

Finally, review of the IEP at least annually encourages professionals to consider how and what children have learned, to determine whether what was prescribed is effective, and to prescribe new or modified strategies. Figure 15.4 shows a completed IEP.

IDEA FOR INFANTS AND TODDLERS. Under Part H of IDEA, funds are provided for infants and toddlers to receive early intervention services for the following purposes:

- To enhance the child's development and minimize the potential for any developmental delays.

1. "Audiology" includes identification of children with hearing loss; determination of the range, nature, and degree of hearing loss; and creation and administration of programs for [treatment and] prevention of hearing loss.
2. "Counseling services" means services provided by qualified social workers, psychologists, guidance counselors, or other qualified personnel.
3. "Early identification and assessment of disabilities in children" means the implementation of a formal plan for identifying a disability as early as possible in a child's life.
4. "Medical services" means services provided by a licensed physician to determine a child's medically related disability that results in the child's need for special education and related services.
5. "Occupational therapy" includes improving, developing, or restoring functions impaired or lost through illness, injury, or deprivation.
6. "Parent counseling and training" means assisting parents in understanding the special needs of their child and providing parents with information about child development.
7. "Physical therapy" means services provided by a qualified physical therapist.
8. "Psychological services" includes administering psychological and educational tests, and other assessment procedures; interpreting assessment results; obtaining, integrating, and interpreting information about child behavior and conditions relating to learning; consulting with other staff members in planning school programs to meet the special needs of children as indicated by psychological tests, interviews, and behavioral evaluations; and planning and managing a program of psychological services, including psychological counseling for children and parents.
9. "Recreation" includes assessment of leisure function, therapeutic recreation services, recreation programs in schools and community agencies, and leisure education.
10. "Rehabilitative counseling services" means services that focus specifically on career development, employment preparation, achieving independence, and integration in the workplace and community of a student with a disability.
11. "School health services" means services provided by a qualified school nurse or other qualified person.
12. "Social work services in schools" includes preparing a social or developmental history on a child with a disability, group and individual counseling with the child and family, working with those problems in a child's living situation (home, school, and community) that affect the child's adjustment in school, and mobilizing school and community resources to enable the child to learn as effectively as possible in his or her educational program.
13. "Speech pathology" includes identification, diagnosis, and appraisal of specific speech or language impairments, provision of speech and language services, and counseling and guidance of parents, children, and teachers regarding speech and language impairments.
14. "Transportation" includes travel to and from school and between schools, travel in and around school buildings, and specialized equipment (such as special or adapted buses, lifts, and ramps), if required to provide special transportation for a child with a disability.
15. Assistive technology and services are devices and related services that restore lost capacities or improve capacities.

Figure 15.3
Services Provided by IDEA

Exceptional Lives: Special Education in Today's Schools *by Turnbull/Turnbull/Shank/Leal, © 1995. Reprinted by permission of Prentice-Hall, Inc., Upper Saddle River, NJ.*

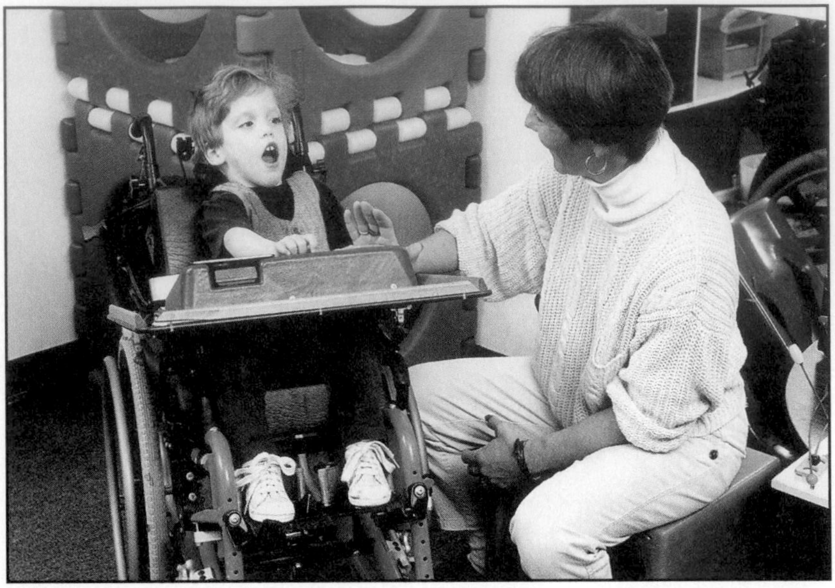

All early childhood programs should address the individual needs of children with disabilities. How can you use the IEPs to ensure that those needs are being met?

- To reduce the costs of educating the child by minimizing the need for special education when the child reaches school age.
- To minimize the likelihood that the family will institutionalize the child and increase the chances that the child, when an adult, will live independently.
- To enhance the family's capacities to meet the child's special needs.[4]

Services that can be provided under Part H include (but are not limited to) those listed in Figure 15.5.

The Individualized Family Service Plan. Under Part H, infants, toddlers, and their families have the right to an individualized family service plan (IFSP), which specifies what service children and their families will receive. Also, the IFSP is designed to help families reach the goals they have for themselves and their children. The IFSP provides for the following:

- Multidisciplinary assessment developed by a multidisciplinary team and the parents. Planned services must meet developmental needs and can include special education, speech and language pathology and audiology, occupational therapy, physical therapy, psychological services, parent and family training and counseling services, transition services, medical diagnostic services, and health services.
- A statement of the child's present levels of development; a statement of the family's strengths and needs in regard to enhancing the child's development; a statement of major expected outcomes for the child and family; the criteria, procedures, and timeliness for determining progress; the specific early intervention services necessary to meet the unique needs of the child and family; the projected dates for initiation of services; the name of the case manager; and transition procedures from the early intervention program into a preschool program.

Benefits of Family-Centered Services. As we have discussed, family-centered services are an important component of early childhood programming, and they will only become more

INDIVIDUALIZED EDUCATION PROGRAM

Student: Amy North Age: 9 Grade: 1 Date: Oct 17, 1999

1. ***Unique Characteristics or Needs: Noncompliance***

   Frequently noncompliant with teacher's instructions

   Present Levels of Performance

   Complies with about 50 percent of teacher's requests/commands

   Special Education, Related Services, and Modifications

   Implemented immediately, strong reinforcement for compliance with teacher's instructions (Example: "Sure I will" plan including precision requests and reinforcer menu for points earned for compliance, as described in The Tough Kid Book by Rhode, Jenson, and Reavis, 1992); within 3 weeks, training of parents by school psychologist to use precision requests and reinforcement at home.

   Objectives (including Procedures, Criteria, and Schedule)

   Within one month, will comply with teacher's requests/commands 90 percent of the time; compliance monitored weekly by teacher

   Annual Goals

   Will become compliant with teacher's requests/commands

2. ***Unique Characteristics or Needs: Reading***

   2a. Very slow reading rate
   2b. Poor comprehension
   2c. Limited phonics skills
   2d. Limited sight-word vocabulary

1. Present Levels of Performance

   2a. Reads stories of approximately 100 words on first-grade reading level at approximately 40 words per min.
   2b. Seldom can recall factual information about stories immediately after reading them
   2c. Consistently confuses vowel sounds, often misidentifies consonants, and does not blend sounds
   2d. Has sight-word vocabulary of approximately 150 words

2. Special Education, Related Services, and Modifications

   2a-2c. Direct instruction 30 minutes daily in vowel discrimination, consonant identification, and sound blending; begin immediately, continue throughout school year

   2a & 2d. Sight-word drill 10 minutes daily in addition to phonics instruction and daily practice; 10 minutes practice in using phonics and sight-word skills in reading story at her level; begin immediately, continue for school year

3. Objectives (including Procedures, Criteria, and Schedule)

   2a. Within 3 months, will read stories at her level at 60 words per minute with 2 or fewer errors per story; within six months, 80 words with 2 or fewer errors, performance monitored daily by teacher or aide

   2b. Within 3 months will answer oral and written comprehension questions requiring recall of information from stories she has just read with 90 percent accuracy (e.g., Who is in the story? What happened? Why?) and be able to predict probable outcomes with 80 percent accuracy; performance monitored daily by teacher or aide

   2c. Within 3 months, will increase sight-word vocabulary to 200 words, within 6 months to 250 words, assessed by flashcard presentation

4. Annual Goals

   2a-2c. Will read fluently and with comprehension at beginning-second-grade level

Figure 15.4
Sample Excerpt from an IEP
The IEP plays an important role in ensuring that children receive an individualized education through a range of services that are appropriate for them. How would an IEP help teachers work collaboratively with other professionals to guarantee that children receive the services they need?

Source: D. P. Hallahan and J. Kauffman, Exceptional Learners: Introduction to Special Education *(7th ed.). (Boston: Allyn & Bacon, 1997). Reprinted by permission.*

Figure 15.5
Services That Can Be Provided Under Part H of IDEA
Source: 34 Code of Federal Register (CFR) §303.12(d).

Assistive technology devices and services
Audiology
Family training, counseling, and home visits
Health services
Medical services for diagnosis or evaluation
Nursing services
Nutrition services
Occupational therapy
Physical therapy
Psychological services
Service coordination services
Social work services
Special instruction
Speech-language pathology
Transportation and related costs
Vision services

important. Programs that embrace and utilize family center services report results in the following areas:

- Improving child developmental and social adjustment outcomes;
- Decreasing parental stress as a result of support and assistance in accessing needed services for their child and themselves;
- Recognizing the family's role as decision maker and partner in the early intervention process on behalf of their children and themselves;
- Helping families to make the best choices for their children by providing comprehensive information about the full range of formal and natural resources in their communities;
- Accommodating individual child, family, and community differences through creative, flexible, and collaborative approaches to services;
- Valuing children and families for their unique capacities, experiences, and potential;
- Seeking meaningful and active family involvement in the planning and implementation of family-centered and community-based services; and
- Obtaining potential health care savings due to ongoing monitoring of health status and referral for primary health care and nutritional services.[5]

The following points should be kept in mind when striving for effective individual and family service plans:

- Methods and techniques of diagnostic and prescriptive teaching are essential as a basis for writing and implementing the IEP and the IFSP.
- Working with parents is an absolute must for every classroom professional. You should learn all you can about parent conferences and communication, parent involvement, and parents as volunteers and aides (see chapter 16).

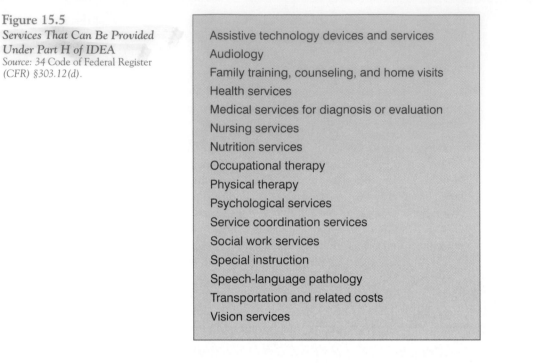

- Working with all levels of professionals offers a unique opportunity for the classroom professional to individualize instruction. Since it is obvious that all professionals need help in individualizing instruction, it makes sense to involve all professionals in this process.
- As individual education becomes a reality for all children and families, early childhood professionals will need skills in assessing student behavior and family background and settings.
- Professionals must know how to identify sources of, and how to order and use, a range of instructional materials, including the various media technologies. One cannot hope to individualize without a full range of materials and media. Professionals must regularly be concerned with students' visual, auditory, and tactile/kinesthetic learning styles. Some children in a classroom may learn best through one mode, others through another. The classroom professional can utilize media technologies in particular to help make teaching styles congruent with children's learning modalities.

... voice from the field

Strategies for Parent Involvement

Parents of students with special needs have been actively involved with teachers and administrators in their children's education for more than twenty years, as the diversity of their needs has been recognized and Individual Education Programs (IEPs) have been developed to meet them. In fact, many of the suggestions in this book have already been successful in meeting the concerns of families who have children with special needs.

Parents of children with special needs often feel isolated and uncertain about their children's future. Schools can help parents find the facts and support they need to understand that they are not alone and that help is available within the community as well as the school. Teachers can help parents feel comfortable discussing their children's future by listening to the parents—who know their children better than anyone else—and by explaining school programs and answering questions in words that parents can easily understand.

What Administrators Can Do

Teachers and parents need support from schools and the community to help children with special needs reach their full potential. School can be both a clearinghouse for information and a place where parents can gather to support one another.

Administrators can help teachers and parents by

- establishing parent resource centers to help parents and teachers develop good working relationships;
- providing basic training to help parents understand special education and the role of the family in cooperative planning, as well as offering workshops on topics requested by parents;
- making available up-to-date information and resources for parents and teachers; and
- encouraging creation of early childhood and preschool screening programs and other community services that can be centered in the schools.

What Teachers Can Do

The relationship between teachers and parents of children with special needs is defined by specific programs with specific guidelines too detailed to summarize here. In addition to these guidelines, there is some general advice for teachers, including the following:

- Make it clear to parents that you accept them as advocates who have an intense desire to make life better for their children.
- Provide parents with information about support groups, special services in the school and the community, and family-to-family groups.
- Offer parents referrals to helpful groups.
- Encourage parents to organize support systems, pairing families who can share experiences with each other during school activities.
- Involve parents in specific projects centered around hobbies or special skills that parents can share with students in one or several classes.
- Discuss a child's special talents with parents and use that positive approach as a bridge to discuss other issues.

Full Inclusion

Mainstreaming and full inclusion differ in that in full inclusion the student with disabilities is assumed to be in the natural environment from the beginning. It is important to know this when planning full-inclusion programs, because full-inclusion programs do not have separate exceptional education programs. The services formerly provided in separate exceptional education programs are now provided in full-inclusion programs in the natural environment by special educators and other special service providers.

Reaching All Families—Creating Family-Friendly Schools, *Office of Educational Research and Improvement, U.S. Department of Education, 1996.*

Full inclusion receives a lot of attention and is the subject of great national debate for several reasons:

- Court decisions and state and federal laws mandate, support, and encourage full inclusion. Many of these laws and court cases relate to extending to children and parents basic civil rights. For example, in the 1992 case of *Oberti* v. *Board of Education of the Borough of Clementon School District,* the judge ruled that Rafael, an eight-year-old child with Down syndrome, should not have to earn his way into an integrated classroom but that it was his right to be there from the beginning.
- Some parents of children with disabilities are dissatisfied with their children's attending separate programs. They view separate programs for their children as a form of segregation. In addition, they want their children to have the social benefits of attending classes in general education classrooms.

For more information about inclusion, go to the Companion Website at http://www.prenhall.com/morrison, select any chapter, then choose Topic 9 of the ECE Supersite module.

Inclusive classrooms educate students with disabilities in the least restrictive educational environment. What would you say to a parent of a child without a disability who questions the idea of an inclusive classroom?

Program in Action

Inclusion . . . Yours, Mine, Ours

Alimacani Elementary School is a National Model Blue Ribbon school located in Jacksonville, Florida, opening its doors in 1990. The faculty, staff, and community have consistently worked together to live up to their vision that "Alimacani is a place where education is a treasure and children are inspired to reach for their dreams."

The school serves preK–5 students that originally included self-contained classes for kindergarten children with varying exceptionalities. After several years of serving the youngsters using a traditional self-contained model and mainstreaming individually as appropriate, frustration ran high. Although the children with disabilities were occasional visitors to the kindergarten classes, they were never a part of the general classroom learning and social community. As our team of kindergarten teachers looked at this model of serving children, we brainstormed ideas of how to better meet the needs of individual students. After many difficult conversations, we agreed to focus on a

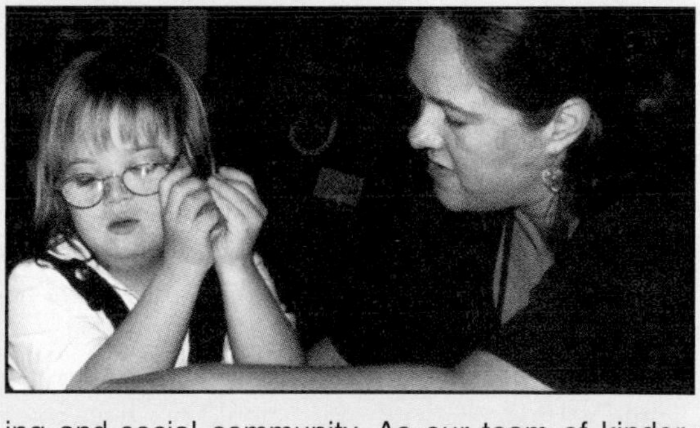

model that would best serve the needs of all of our children. We decided to take the entire population of children with special needs and include them in regular kindergarten classes, matching children with teacher strengths.

As our vision for inclusion was first formed, we were anxious and unsure. We would have to teach with other teachers and give up ownership of children and space. All of our roles would change. We had read about the benefits of collaboration with our colleagues, but we knew that the reality of so intimate a bond would require trust, respect, a great deal of faith, and a strong sense of humor!

Despite our reservations and uncertainty, we were full of enthusiasm! Our expectations changed daily. Even our assignments changed, as we enrolled and identified a record number of kindergarten children with special needs. In partnership with parents of the children with disabilities and with parents of typically developing children, we stretched, bent, and broadened our ideas. In most cases, visitors could not identify the children with disabilities in our classrooms from their typically developing peers. They also could not always identify general education teachers from special educators. Eighteen children with a variety of special needs were included in three different kindergarten classes during that initial year, including children with Down Syndrome, autism, mild physical and mental disabilities, attention deficit (hyperactivity) disorder, Asperger's Syndrome, Fetal Alcohol Syndrome, learning disabilities, and developmental delays.

To say that the first year was a success is an understatement. Without exception, we felt that we had done a better job of educating exceptional children than we had ever achieved in our self-contained model. We also learned that we did not have to sacrifice the many for the few. Our typically developing population of kindergartners thrived with the new responsibilities of helping their peers. As we came together to develop alternative methods of instruction for children with special needs, we found many of those same methods reaching our typically developing children. We were extremely proud of *all* of our kindergartners at the end of the year as they marched ahead into first grade.

This is not to say that there were no roadblocks, but we tried to turn each obstacle into an

opportunity. We detoured, we had traffic jams, and occasionally even head-on collisions, but we used each experience as a learning and building block. Out of one of our moments of frustration, we developed our Web site, http://www.rushservices.com/Inclusion, as a voice for teachers and parents to exchange information. We have logged on thousands of participants from all over the world who have willingly shared their insights and inspiration, their challenges and many successes.

Even with our own successes, we have come to believe that inclusion is not for everyone. We believe that there must continue to be an array of services to meet individual needs. We believe that we must learn to first look at the needs of our students, and then design programs and assign personnel to make learning successful.

We have chosen as our symbol the starfish. You may be familiar with the story of the person who comes upon a beach filled with starfish washed ashore. He spots a young man throwing starfish back into the ocean one at a time. He questions the young man as to why he is taking the time to throw the starfish back into the sea. After all, there is no way he can save all of the starfish on the beach. The young man answers that his efforts do make a difference to each starfish he is able to save. Well, that is how we feel at Alimacani. We are walking that same beach, making a real difference, one "starfish" at a time.

Visit the inclusive classrooms of Dayle Timmons, Marie Rush, Kerry Rogers, and Lori Medlock at http://www.rushservices.com/Inclusion.

Text contributed by Dayle Timmons, Marie Rush, Kerry Rogers, and Lori Medlock of Alimacani Elementary School; photos courtesy Kerry Rogers.

- Some parents believe their children are best served in separate special education settings. Many members of the public also do not support full-inclusion programs. In one public poll, 65 percent of respondents believed children with learning problems should be placed in special classrooms. Thirty-seven percent said that if students with learning problems are included in the same classrooms with other students, the effect of their inclusion on other students would be negative; 36 percent thought it would not make much difference. Forty percent believed that inclusion would have a negative effect on the students with learning problems.
- Some teachers feel they do not have the training or support necessary to provide for the disabilities of children in full-inclusion classrooms. These teachers also believe they will not be able to provide for children with disabilities, even with the assistance of aides and special support services.
- Some people believe the cost of full inclusion outweighs the benefits. There is no doubt that it costs more to educate students with disabilities than students who have no disabilities. The average cost of educating a regular classroom student nationally is $7,341, compared with $13,801 (1.88 times) for educating an exceptional education student in a special education program. (This cost can be more for some individual students and can cost more in some school districts.) Some professionals think that the money spent on separate special education facilities and programs can be better used for full-inclusion programs.

Program in Action

Bridges for Families Early Intervention Program

The Bridges for Families Early Intervention Program (Madison, Wisconsin) is a family-centered, community-based, birth to three years, early intervention program for infants and toddlers with disabilities and their families. Bridges is contracted by Dane County to ensure that the county meets its mandated requirements for Part C of the Individuals with Disabilities Education Act (IDEA). The program is housed within the Waisman Center University Affiliated Program, University of Wisconsin-Madison.

The program operates from the philosophy that:

- Parents and professionals are full partners in the planning, coordination, and implementation of early intervention services.
- The overall purpose of early intervention is to support families and enhance their abilities to meet the needs of their children with special needs.
- Services in Madison need to be a collaborative effort among agencies providing early intervention services.
- An early intervention program needs to be flexible, have an array of services and parent involvement options, and continually adapt to the changing needs of families and the community.

The program is community based and offers services to approximately 250 families a year in a variety of natural environments, including, but not limited to, family homes, family day care homes/centers, child care centers, early childhood programs, and other community sites where children and their families spend their days. Bridges has eighteen staff members, some who work part-time to accommodate individual preferences and family situations. Primary program staff include early childhood special education teachers, physi-

cal therapists, occupational therapists, speech and language pathologists, and social workers. At least two staff members have children with special needs, offering unique perspectives to families served by the program and insights to improve staff practices. Others such as grandparents, early childhood teachers, and child care providers are brought into the team for individual children as needed. Parents, program staff, and other community providers work together to develop Individualized Family Service Plans (IFSPs) for each child and family. These plans summarize the goals for each child and state the types, frequency, and duration of services to be provided to each child and family and the locations where they will be provided. The plans are based on the child's developmental needs and family concerns, priorities, and resources. Service coordinators then help identify and link families with community supports and resources.

On a typical day, a teacher or therapist will make three to five different home or community visits to work directly with a child in his or her family home or child care setting. Once or twice a week, staff conduct evaluations or meet with families to develop IFSPs. Time is built into the week for team meetings focused on program development and growth, case-based problem-solving discussions, routine staff meetings, and staff supervision and support. Commitment to this time has contributed to team functioning, program outcomes, and staff morale.

The program has established and maintained collaborative relationships with other community agencies working on behalf of children and families. A recent survey of community collaborators indicated that Bridges is positively perceived in the community and that collaborators perceive that families receive quality services from the program.

Being located at the Waisman Center with Wisconsin's personnel development system for birth to age three and other related early intervention training and technical assistance projects offers mutual benefits to each entity. The daily practices of Bridges staff inform statewide training efforts in early intervention, and vice versa. Bridges staff are frequently asked to participate in planning groups and present at statewide and local trainings. In addition, Bridges serves as a training site for university students from a range of academic departments to promote exemplary early intervention services.

Parents are actively involved in many aspects of the program. They participate on advisory boards, serve as family mentors for university students, speak at local and statewide early intervention training activities, speak at university courses, and participate in local and statewide parent leadership and support sessions. Annual family surveys indicate that families are satisfied with the Bridges program and report that their child with disabilities and their family benefited form the services they received. A survey of family mentors has indicated a high level of satisfaction from helping future providers experience family life with a young child with special needs—from the inside out.

Visit the Bridges for Families Early Intervention Program on the Web at: http://www.waisman.wisc.edu/earlyint/b_index.htm.

Contributed by Linda Tuchman, program director.

A CONTINUUM OF INCLUSIVE SERVICES. The policy of the Council for Exceptional Children (CEC), a professional organization of special educators, is as follows:

> CEC believes that a continuum of services must be available for all children, youth, and young adults. CEC also believes that the concept of inclusion is a meaningful goal to be pursued in our schools and communities. In addition, CEC believes children, youth, and young adults with disabilities should be served whenever possible in general education classrooms in inclusive neighborhood schools and community settings. Such settings should be strengthened and supported by an infusion of especially trained personnel and other appropriate supportive practices according to the individual needs of the child.[6]

A *continuum of services* means that a full range of services is available for individuals from the most restrictive to the least restrictive placements. This continuum implies a gradu-

ated range of services with one level of services leading directly to the next. For example, a continuum of services for students with disabilities would define institutional placement as the most restrictive and a general education classroom as the least restrictive. (Figure 15.6 shows this continuum of services.) There is considerable debate over whether providing such a continuum is an appropriate policy. Advocates of inclusion say that the approach works against developing truly inclusive programs. Figure 15.7 presents the policy on inclusion for the Division for Early Childhood of the Council for Exceptional Children.

There are many benefits for children in inclusive classrooms. They demonstrate increased acceptance and appreciation of diversity; develop better communication and social skills; show greater development in moral and ethical principles; create warm and caring friendships; and demonstrate increased self-esteem.

Given the great amount of interest in inclusion, discussions regarding its appropriateness and how best to implement it will continue for some time. As an early childhood professional, you will have many opportunities to participate in this discussion and to help shape the policies of implementation and classroom practice. You should fully participate in such processes.

Children with Attention Deficit Hyperactivity Disorder (ADHD)

Students with *attention deficit hyperactivity disorder (ADHD)* generally display cognitive delays and have difficulties in three specific areas: attention, impulse control, and hyperactivity. To be classified as having ADHD, a student must display for a minimum of six months before age seven at least eight of the characteristics outlined in Figure 15.8.

ADHD is diagnosed more often in boys than in girls and occurs in about 20 percent of all students. About half of the cases are diagnosed before age four. Frequently, the term *attention deficit disorder (ADD)* is used to refer to ADHD, but ADD is a form of learning disorder, whereas ADHD is a behavioral disorder.

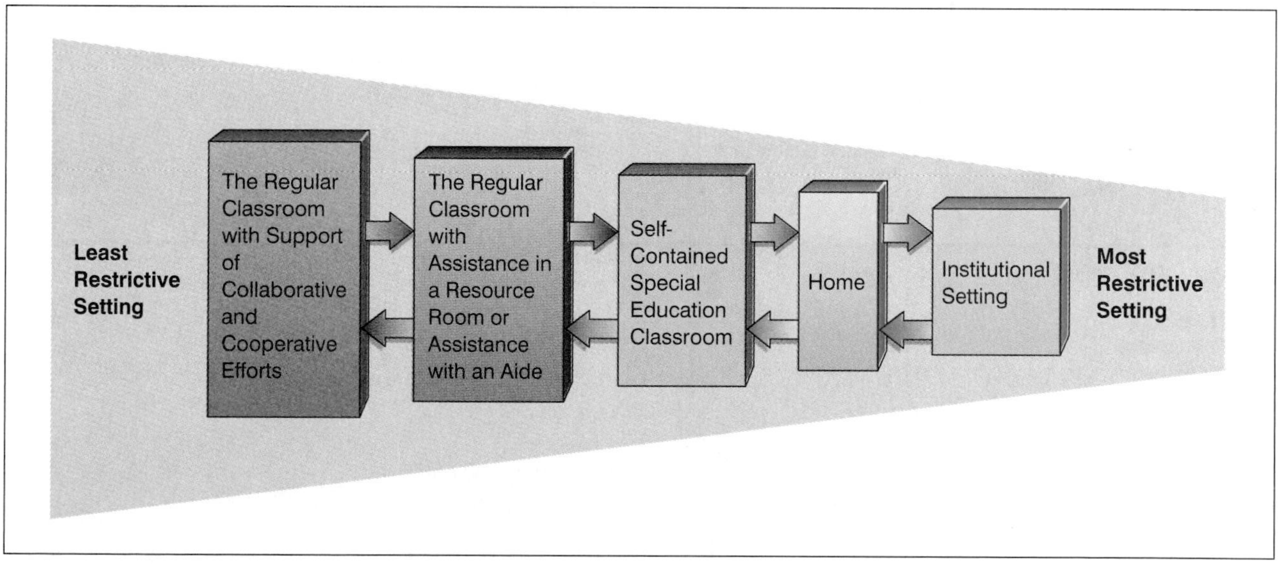

Figure 15.6
A Continuum of Services

Source: G. S. Morrison, *Teaching in America, 2nd ed.* (Needham Heights, MA: Allyn & Bacon, 2000), p. 182. Copyright © 2000 by Allyn & Bacon. Reprinted by permission.

Inclusion, as a value, supports the right of all children, regardless of their diverse abilities, to participate actively in natural settings within their communities. A *natural setting* is one in which the child would spend time had he or she not had a disability. Such settings include, but are not limited to, home and family, play groups, child care, nursery schools, Head Start programs, kindergartens, and neighborhood school classrooms.

DEC believes in and supports full and successful access to health, social service, education, and other supports and services for young children and their families that promote full participation in community life. DEC values the diversity of families and supports a family-guided process for determining services that are based on the needs and preferences of individual families and children.

To implement inclusive practices DEC supports:

a. The continued development, evaluation, and dissemination of full inclusion supports, services, and systems *so that options for inclusion are of high quality*;
b. The development of preservice and inservice training programs to prepare families, administrators, and service providers to develop and work within inclusive settings;
c. Collaboration among all key stakeholders to implement fiscal and administrative procedures in support of inclusion;
d. Research that contributes to our knowledge of state of the art services; and
e. The restructuring and unification of social, education, health, and intervention supports and services to make them more responsive to the needs of all children and families.

Figure 15.7
The Division for Early Childhood's Position Statement on Inclusion

Source: Division for Early Childhood of the Council for Exceptional Children, adopted April 1993, revised December 1993. Used by permission.

Strategies for Teaching Children with Disabilities

Sound teaching strategies work well for all students, including those with disabilities. You must plan how to create inclusive teaching environments. The following ideas will help you teach children with disabilities and create inclusive settings that enhance the education of all students:

For more information about teaching students with disabilities, go to the Companion Website at http://www.prenhall.com/morrison, select any chapter, then choose Topic 9 of the ECE Supersite module.

- *Accentuate the positive*. One of the most effective strategies is to emphasize what children can do rather than what they cannot do. Children with disabilities have talents and abilities similar to other children, and by exercising professional knowledge and skills you can help these and all children reach their full academic potential.
- *Use appropriate assessment, including work samples, cumulative records, and appropriate assessment instruments*. Discussions with parents and other professionals who have worked with the individual child are sources of valuable information and contribute to making accurate and appropriate plans for children.
- *Use concrete examples and materials.*
- *Develop and use multisensory approaches to learning.*

Attention deficit hyperactivity disorder has several types, including: (1) predominantly inattentive, (2) predominantly impulsive, or (3) combined. Individuals with this condition usually have many (but not all) of the following symptoms:

Inattention

- Often fails to finish what he starts
- Diagnosis of Attention Deficit Disorder
- Doesn't seem to listen
- Easily distracted
- Has difficulty concentrating or paying attention
- Doesn't stick with a play activity

Impulsivity

- Often acts without thinking and later feels sorry
- Shifts excessively from one activity to another
- Has difficulty organizing work
- Speaks out loud in class
- Doesn't wait to take turns in games or groups

Hyperactivity

- Runs about or climbs on things excessively
- Can't sit still and is fidgety
- Has difficulty staying in his seat and bothers classmates
- Excessive activity during sleep
- Always on the "go" and acts as if "driven"

Emotional Instability

- Angry outbursts
- Social loner
- Blames others for problems
- Fights with others quickly
- Very sensitive to criticism

Figure 15.8
Types and Characteristics of Attention Deficit Hyperactivity Disorder (ADHD)

Source: Reprinted with permission from the Diagnostic and Statistical Manual of Mental Disorders, *Fourth Edition. Copyright 1994 American Psychiatric Association. [On-line]. Available: www.cdipage.com/adhd.htm.*

- *Model what children are to do rather than just telling them what to do.* Have a child who has mastered a certain task or behavior model it for others. Ask each child to perform a designated skill or task with supervision. Give corrective feedback.
- *Let children practice or perform a certain behavior*, involving them in their own assessment of that behavior.
- *Make the learning environment a pleasant, rewarding place to be.*
- *Create a dependable classroom schedule.* Young children develop a sense of security when daily plans follow a consistent pattern. Allowing for flexibility also is important, however.
- *Encourage parents to volunteer at school and to read to their children at home.*
- *Identify appropriate tasks children can accomplish on their own* to create in them an opportunity to become more independent of you and others.

... video viewpoint

Teacher's Little Helper

As more children become more difficult for teachers to teach and control, teachers are increasingly recommending that children be placed on medication to control their behavior. This use of drugs to control children's behavior, rather than teaching children to control their own behavior, is a growing concern for many early childhood professionals. Growing numbers of professionals object to medication being part of the teacher's "bag of tricks."

REFLECTIVE DISCUSSION QUESTIONS

What are the controversies surrounding the use of Ritalin to control children's behaviors? What are some reasons why teachers would recommend that children should be placed on Ritalin? Would you as an early childhood professional consider Ritalin an appropriate alternative for use with young children? Do you think the use of Ritalin is an epidemic?

REFLECTIVE DECISION MAKING

Interview parents whose children are on Ritalin. Why was the child placed on Ritalin? Do the parents believe that Ritalin is helping their child? How? What advice would you give to a parent who asked you if you thought Ritalin was an appropriate response to children's destructive/aggressive/hyperactive behavior? What would be some activities you could recommend for controlling children's behavior without medication? Interview early childhood teachers and ask their opinions regarding the use of Ritalin. Based on your discussions, do you think they are pressuring parents into having Ritalin prescribed for their children?

- *Use cooperative learning*. Cooperative learning enables all students to work together to achieve common goals. Cooperative learning has five components:
  - *Positive interdependence*. Group members establish mutual goals, divide the prerequisite tasks, share materials and resources, assume shared roles, and receive joint rewards.
  - *Face-to-face interaction*. Group members encourage and facilitate each other's efforts to complete tasks through direct communication.
  - *Individual accountability/personal responsibility*. Individual performance is assessed, and results are reported back to both the individual and the group. The group holds each member responsible for completing his or her fair share of responsibility.
  - *Interpersonal and small-group skills*. Students are responsible for getting to know and trust each other, communicating accurately and clearly, accepting and supporting each other, and resolving conflicts in a constructive manner.
  - *Group processing*. Group reflection includes describing which contributions of members are helpful or unhelpful in making decisions and which group actions should be continued or changed.
- *Use Circle of Friends*. This technique helps students develop friendships with their classmates. Classmates volunteer to be part of a student's circle, and the circle meets as a team on a regular basis. The teacher coordinates the circle and helps the group solve

problems or concerns that arise. Students in the circle provide friendship and support so that no student is isolated or alone in the class.[7]

- *Use Classwide Peer Tutoring (CWPT) Program.* CWPT involves whole classrooms of students in tutoring activities that improve achievement and student engagement, particularly for at-risk, low-income students. Having opportunities to teach peers appears to reinforce students' own learning and motivation, according to Charles R. Greenwood, the program developer.[8]
- *Develop a peer buddy system.* In a peer buddy system, classmates serve as peer buddies (friends, guides, or counselors) to students who are experiencing problems. Variations are to pair an older student with a younger one who is experiencing a problem and to pair two students who are experiencing similar problems.[9]

A TRANSDISCIPLINARY TEAM. For young children with special needs, a *transdisciplinary team* approach consists of interdisciplinary involvement across and among various health and social services disciplines. Members of this team can include any of the following professionals: early childhood educator, physical therapist, occupational therapist, speech communication therapist, psychologist, social worker, and pediatrician. The rationale for the transdisciplinary team is that a unified and holistic approach is the most effective way to provide resources and deliver services to children and their families.

Members of the team diagnose, prescribe, share information, and work cooperatively to meet children's needs. One of the members, usually the early childhood educator, heads the team, and other members act as consultants. The team leader carries out the instructions of other team members. A variation of this model is to have members of the team, such as the

Because they have a great deal of knowledge about their children, parents should be involved in helping plan objectives and curricula for their children with disabilities. What are some things this teacher and parent may be discussing?

... voice from the field

Natural Settings Provide a Key for Inclusion

A visitor asked Andrea, the kindergarten teacher, what it was like having a child with a disability in her classroom. When Andrea looked puzzled, the visitor continued, "I mean, do you think he belongs here?" Andrea replied, "He's five, isn't he?" [1]

Andrea's response is a wonderful demonstration of her commitment to equitable inclusion for young children with disabilities into regular classrooms. For Andrea, it is not whether the child has disabilities that becomes the criterion for her acceptance or nonacceptance. The needs of the child dictate her choices.

In the past, many teachers concluded that children's disabilities prevented them from taking advantage of experiences that promote typical child development.[2] Research studies, however, indicate that young children with disabilities need developmentally appropriate services just as typically developing children do. Intervention services, including preventative, remedial, and compensatory efforts provided during the preschool years, increase the developmental and educational gains for young children with disabilities.[3] Studies also indicate that, in addition to intervention services, when young children with disabilities are enrolled in integrated educational settings, they make greater gains in language, cognitive, and motor development.[4] These children also demonstrate higher levels of social play and more appropriate social interactions than children with disabilities who are in special, self-contained classes.[5] Young children with disabilities need to experience inclusive practices in preschool programs.

What Are Practices for Inclusion in Preschool Settings?

Inclusion is . . . the underlying supposition that all children will be based in classrooms they would attend if they did not have a disability.[6] Inclusive practices accommodate the diverse needs of all children by "including" them in physical, social, and academic activities with typically developing children in regular classrooms or physical education environments—natural environments to the maximum extent possible. Natural environments are identified as any environment in which it would be natural for any young child to be, such as child day care centers, family day care centers, preschools, kindergartens, primary grades, and playgrounds. Inclusion of young children with disabilities in natural environments is an example of best practice.

Best practices in early childhood programming for children with disabilities have traditionally been based on a special education perspective.[7,8] As early childhood educational practice moves toward a more equitable inclusion of children with disabilities, professionals must integrate Early Childhood Special Education (ECSE) practices with Early Childhood Education (ECE) practices.[9] ECSE programs are oriented more toward teacher-directed activities, with a focus on behavioral learning, and are designed to meet individualized goals and objectives. Implicit in the ECSE design is that children with disabilities may not get to take advantage of typical environmental experiences and child-initiated activities promoted as more developmentally appropriate practice by professional organizations such as NAEYC. Thus, by its very nature and language, "best practices" generated by the field of special education has inadvertently communicated that what professionals do for children with disabilities must be somehow very different from the goals set for typically developing children by

the rest of the early childhood profession.[10] Early childhood professionals increasingly are proposing the creation of one system of early childhood education for all. Essentially this system would frame a plan based on what it takes to allow all young children to succeed. Practices that seem to be working for all children focus on developing language in inclusive, natural settings.

Inclusion and the Acquisition of Language

The acquisition of language forms the basis of all other forms of symbolic activity by humans.[11] When children in the first few years of life are given appropriate literacy opportunities, they make a remarkable, effortless acquisition of language. Conversely, delayed language development can be calamitous as it crosses over into other domains of development. Children learn what language is by learning what language can do.[12,13] In isolated settings we cannot expect children with disabilities to learn what language can do or how to use it well.

For some children with disabilities the greatest chance for success may be the implementation of specialized interventions within natural environments. In these environments children could be engaged in language development through both *milieu teaching* and *responsive interaction*. Milieu teaching differs from a didactic teaching methodology in that the topic and reinforcement used for communication is based on the child's immediate interest.[14] This milieu teaching follows a child's attentional lead and is based on the premise that a child's language production can be prompted, either indirectly through environmental arrangement or directly through explicit prompts. For example, an explicit prompt (called a *mand*, like demand) would have an adult say to a child who is handling a plastic dinosaur, "*This is a dinosaur. Say 'dinosaur.'*"

Responsive interaction focuses on increased responsiveness and decreased "directedness" of an adult conversation between an adult and a child. It also follows a child's lead but promotes more of a balance in the responsibility of a conversation between an adult and a child. For example, if a child who is physically able to enter and play in a home center picks up a cup, the adult might say, "*Let's pretend we are having tea. Do you want me to pour your tea into your cup? Tell me when you have enough.*"

One other strategy that also promises to engage children in typical childhood opportunities for language and play is *activity-based intervention*. Activity-based intervention asks the teacher to prepare an environment that is not only stimulating for all students but also considers how the classroom arrangement can develop functional skills and generalizable goals. In this approach, managing the environment to promote requests or comments by children is critical. One example of purposefully setting up the environment to promote language might be as follows: A preschool teacher arranges a center or physical environment with attractive materials and a high-interest activity. In this environmental arrangement, she prepares an activity that children have done previously with some frequency, such as cut and paste. However, this time as the teacher sets up the activity she purposefully leaves out some portion of the materials needed, such as scissors. Children have to communicate their need of scissors to complete the activity. By providing the materials requested by the child, the adult reinforces the child's use of language. In this kind of intervention strategy it becomes critical for the teacher or other adults to encourage children to initiate language as a means of gaining access to materials and getting help.[15]

Other activity-based intervention strategies can also be used to increase the chances that a child will use language skills. These might include the following: (1) any activity or material that increases the likelihood that children will get excited and need to talk about what is going on, (2) activities and materials that prompt children to respond to nonverbal

teacher cues, (3) materials that are slightly out of reach, (4) attractive materials that require adult assistance to use, (5) "sabotage," where materials are inadequate or missing, (6) activities that require children to make choices, and (7) activities or events that are unusual, discrepant, or silly. (One silly event might have a teacher putting a child's coat on inside out or a similar event that is inconsistently absurd compared with normal daily events.)[16]

Keys to success for these kinds of interventions are to use the environment to focus on making it a part of children's routines, provide adult and peer models who not only encourage children to use language but also respond to their attempts to do so, and establish a conditional relationship between access to materials and a need for assistance.[17] Activity-based intervention strategies involve planning activities or centers that help all children negotiate their environment satisfactorily, develop independence, and practice skills they will use in many different settings.

In Summary

All children benefit when children with and without disabilities are included in the same natural environment. Children with disabilities learn personal, language, cognitive, and social skills they might not otherwise learn in separate classrooms. Children who do not have disabilities demonstrate an increased self-concept, growth in social cognition, tolerance of others, and a decreased fear of differences in people.[18]

The references for this feature can be found after this chapter's Endnotes.

physical therapist, work directly with the child at specified times (e.g., twice a week) and provide activities and suggestions for the early childhood educator to implement at other times.

MAKING TRANSITIONS. Transitional experiences from one setting to another are a must for all special needs children, especially those who have attended preschool in a special setting or a separate public school facility from the elementary school. To help the special needs child make a transition, the staffs of the sending and receiving agencies must cooperate in arrangements, activities, and plans. Consider the following suggestions:

- Try to approximate certain features of the receiving environment. If the new classroom has a larger child–adult ratio, gradually get children used to working and functioning in larger groups.
- Help children become accustomed to social skills appropriate to the new environment. If children have been using a restroom inside the classroom but will have to go outside the classroom in the new school, help them practice this new routine.
- Use materials and activities as children will encounter them in the new setting. For example, get a set of textbooks and familiarize the child with the format and activities.
- Approximate the kind and length of instructional activities children will be expected to participate in and complete.
- Visit the new school with children and their parents.
- Communicate with the receiving professional to share information about the child.

- Structure a social setting in the receiving classroom. Arrange a "buddy system" with a child in the new classroom.
- After the child has made the transition, visit the classroom to demonstrate a supportive, caring attitude to the receiving professional, parents, and child.
- The receiving professional has reciprocal responsibilities to make the transition as stress free and rewarding as possible. Successful transitions involve all concerned—children, parents, professionals, administrators, and support personnel. (Other suggestions for transitional experiences are given in chapter 9.)

Figure 15.9 provides further information about what you will need to know and be able to do to be an effective teacher of children with disabilities.

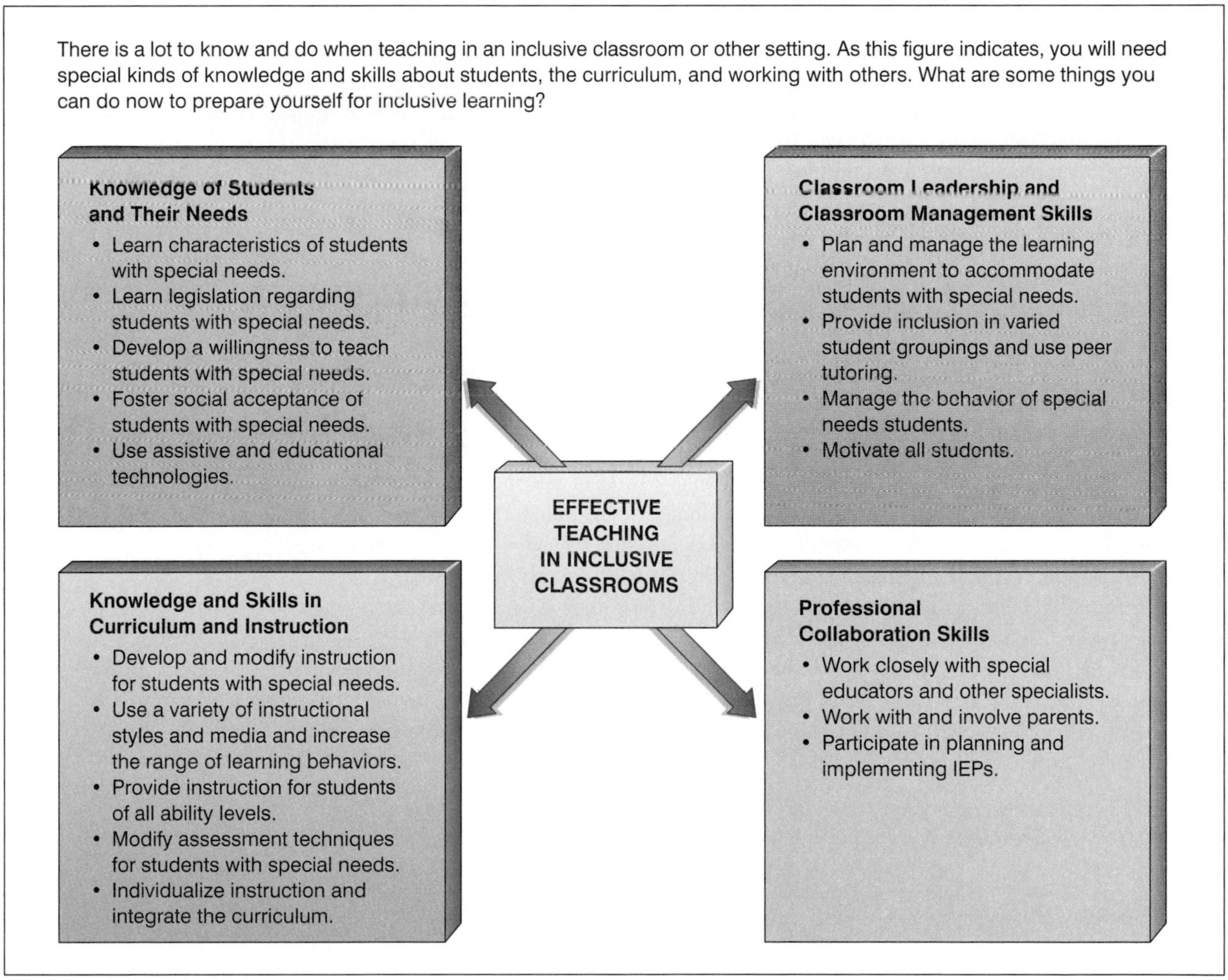

There is a lot to know and do when teaching in an inclusive classroom or other setting. As this figure indicates, you will need special kinds of knowledge and skills about students, the curriculum, and working with others. What are some things you can do now to prepare yourself for inclusive learning?
Knowledge of Students and Their Needs
• Learn characteristics of students with special needs.
• Learn legislation regarding students with special needs.
• Develop a willingness to teach students with special needs.
• Foster social acceptance of students with special needs.
• Use assistive and educational technologies.
Classroom Leadership and Classroom Management Skills
• Plan and manage the learning environment to accommodate students with special needs.
• Provide inclusion in varied student groupings and use peer tutoring.
• Manage the behavior of special needs students.
• Motivate all students.
EFFECTIVE TEACHING IN INCLUSIVE CLASSROOMS
Knowledge and Skills in Curriculum and Instruction
• Develop and modify instruction for students with special needs.
• Use a variety of instructional styles and media and increase the range of learning behaviors.
• Provide instruction for students of all ability levels.
• Modify assessment techniques for students with special needs.
• Individualize instruction and integrate the curriculum.
Professional Collaboration Skills
• Work closely with special educators and other specialists.
• Work with and involve parents.
• Participate in planning and implementing IEPs.

Figure 15.9
Knowledge and Skills for Effective Teaching in Inclusive Classrooms

Source: G. S. Morrison, Teaching in America, *2nd ed. (Needham Heights, MA: Allyn & Bacon, 2000), p. 173. Copyright © 2000 by Allyn & Bacon. Reprinted by permission.*

Gifted and Talented Children

In contrast to children with disabilities, children identified as gifted or talented are not covered under IDEA's provisions, and Congress has passed other legislation specifically to provide for these children. The Jacob K. Javits Gifted and Talented Students Education Act of 1988 defines *gifted and talented children* as those who "give evidence of high performance capabilities in areas such as intellectual, creative, artistic, or leadership capacity; or in specific academic fields, and who require services or activities not ordinarily provided by the school in order to fully develop such capabilities."[10] The definition distinguishes between *giftedness*, characterized by above-average intellectual ability, and *talented*, referring to individuals who excel in such areas as drama, art, music, athletics, and leadership. Students can have these abilities separately or in combination. A talented five-year-old may be learning disabled, and a student with orthopedic disabilities may be gifted.

For more information about the Gifted and Talented Students Education Act of 1999, go to the Companion Website at http://www.prenhall.com/morrison, select any chapter, then choose Topic 9 of the ECE Supersite module.

Although children may not display all these signs, the presence of several of them can alert parents and early childhood professionals to make appropriate instructional, environmental, and social adjustments. Figure 15.10 outlines characteristics displayed in each of the areas of giftedness. You can also use these to help you identify gifted children in your program.

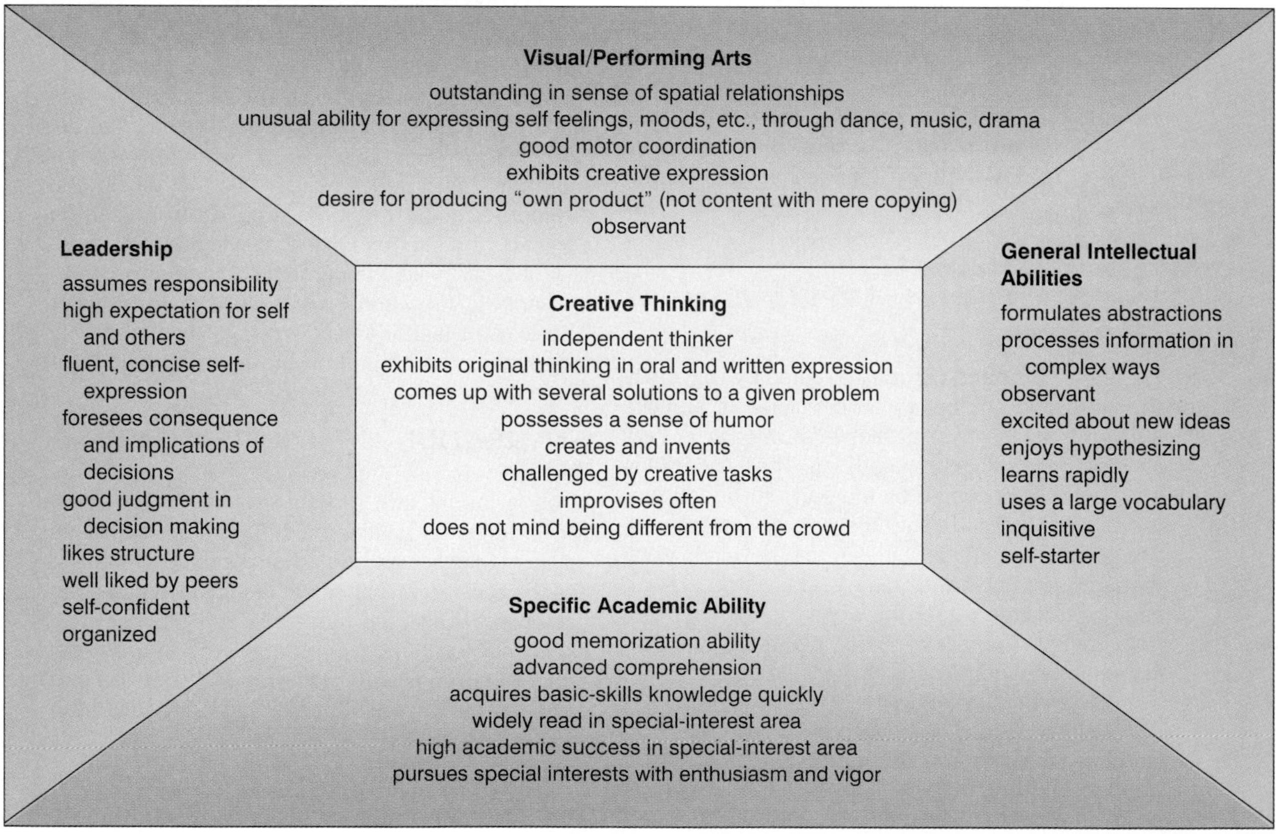
Visual/Performing Arts
outstanding in sense of spatial relationships
unusual ability for expressing self feelings, moods, etc., through dance, music, drama
good motor coordination
exhibits creative expression
desire for producing "own product" (not content with mere copying)
observant
Leadership
assumes responsibility
high expectation for self and others
fluent, concise self-expression
foresees consequence and implications of decisions
good judgment in decision making
likes structure
well liked by peers
self-confident
organized
Creative Thinking
independent thinker
exhibits original thinking in oral and written expression
comes up with several solutions to a given problem
possesses a sense of humor
creates and invents
challenged by creative tasks
improvises often
does not mind being different from the crowd
General Intellectual Abilities
formulates abstractions
processes information in complex ways
observant
excited about new ideas
enjoys hypothesizing
learns rapidly
uses a large vocabulary
inquisitive
self-starter
Specific Academic Ability
good memorization ability
advanced comprehension
acquires basic-skills knowledge quickly
widely read in special-interest area
high academic success in special-interest area
pursues special interests with enthusiasm and vigor

Figure 15.10
Characteristics of Various Areas of Giftedness

Source: Copyright © National Association for Gifted Children (NAGC), Washington, DC. This chart may not be further reproduced without the permission of NAGC.

Program in Action

University Primary School Early Childhood Gifted Education Program

MISSION AND PHILOSOPHY

University Primary School is an early childhood gifted education program serving children ages three to seven. The mission of University Primary School is to provide a site for the individuals at the College of Education of the University of Illinois at Urbana-Champaign to demonstrate, observe, study, and teach best practices in early childhood and gifted education, while at the same time providing a service to the community, especially to families with young children.

The philosophy of University Primary School is that young children are best served by teaching and curriculum practices that strengthen and support their intellectual growth and development, initiate them into basic skills, challenge them to increase their proficiency in academic tasks as well as intellectual processes, and at the same time fosters the development of their social competence.

INSTRUCTIONAL APPROACH AND CURRICULUM

The early childhood program adopted by University Primary School is based on principles of practice derived from the best available knowledge of how children grow, develop, and learn. These principles are generally accepted by the early childhood profession as appropriate to the age groups served. The basic assumption derived from developmental research is that in the early years, children learn best from active rather than passive experiences, from being in interactive rather than receptive roles in the learning context.

The curriculum is child-sensitive and responsive to individual patterns of growth, development, learning, and interests. Children have regular and frequent opportunities to work in informal groups on challenging tasks and to make decisions and choices.

The child's initiative, creativity, and problem solving are encouraged in all areas of the curriculum. By incorporating the Project Approach into the curriculum, children become actively involved in research and inquiry about topics worthy of their time and energy.

UNIQUE FEATURES OF UNIVERSITY PRIMARY SCHOOL

The daily schedule provides time for in-depth study and self-selected activities as well as small-group language arts and math instruction and an individualized reading program. These areas of the curriculum are described below.

ACTIVITY TIME AND PROJECT-WORK

Activity Time and Project-Work is highly valued in our curriculum. Activity Time allows students to make choices about their own learning and provides important school time to work in their interest areas. During this time period, teachers facilitate students' learning by building upon their ideas. Projects present learning to children in real-life contexts and integrate the acquisition and application of basic skills through inquiry modes of learning. Activity Time and Project-Work strive to foster "the love of learning" and provide an opportunity for teachers to engage in the learning with their students.

NUMERATION AND PROBLEM-SOLVING SKILLS

Math is taught with a problem-solving approach, with a focus on relating math to real-life situations using manipulatives and other concrete materials. Teachers facilitate learning in the following areas at the child's individual readiness level: conceptual skills, numeration, computation, measurement, problem solving, and geometry. Many of the student's projects will reflect integration of these mathematical skills.

LANGUAGE ARTS AND LITERACY

This program emphasizes a whole-language approach, where children learn to read by reading and to write by writing. Students are actively involved in both processes throughout the day.

Importance is placed on the "making sense" process. They learn within the whole context rather than parts. Early literacy involves three reading cue systems: contextual, grammatical, and phonetic. Teachers create a literacy-rich environment and model meaningful reading and writing.

ARTS AND AESTHETICS

The arts are integral to children's learning. Teachers guide students toward meaningful experiences in the arts with examples, materials, and cultural artifacts. Teachers promote sensitivity to and an appreciation of the environment.

SOCIAL AND EMOTIONAL GROWTH

Teachers take a proactive role in creating a classroom community that is open, honest, and accepting. To this end, discipline is designed around teachers structuring appropriate choices, students learning how to solve their own problems, and students sharing in the responsibility of developing a caring classroom community. Teachers encourage self-control and strive to develop both intellectual and emotional self-confidence.

Visit the University Primary School on the Web at http://www.uiuc.edu/ph/www/ups.

Contributed by Nancy B. Hertzog, Ph.D., director.

Nature or Nurture?

When identifying gifted and talented children, there is always the issue of how much giftedness is attributed to nature (genetic and biological factors) and how much is attributed to nurture (the environment). While experts agree that giftedness is attributable to both nature and nurture, they do not agree on what percentage each contributes. The following environmental factors, among others, contribute to giftedness—and to all good child rearing:

- Excellent early opportunities with encouragement from family and friends
- Superior, early, and continuing guidance and instruction
- Frequent and continual opportunity to practice and extend children's special abilities and to progress as they are able
- Close association with others of similar ability
- Opportunities for real accomplishment within their capabilities but with increasing challenge
- Provision for strong success experiences and recognition of successes[11]

Educating the Gifted and Talented

Professionals tend to suggest special programs and sometimes schools for the gifted and talented, which would seem to be a move away from providing for these children in regular classrooms. Regular classroom professionals can provide for gifted children in their classrooms through enrichment and acceleration. *Enrichment* provides an opportunity for children to pursue topics in greater depth and in different ways than planned for in the curriculum. *Acceleration* permits children to progress academically at their own pace.

In regular classrooms, early childhood professionals can encourage gifted children to pursue special interests as a means of extending and enriching classroom learning. They can use parents and resource people to tutor and work in special ways with these children and provide opportunities for children to assume leadership responsibilities themselves. For

example, they may be interested in tutoring other students who need extra practice or help. Tutoring can cut across grade and age levels. Students can also help explain directions and procedures to the class. Professionals can encourage them to use their talents and abilities outside the classroom by becoming involved with other people and agencies and can foster creativity through classroom activities that require divergent thinking ("Let's think of all the different uses for a paper clip").

Professionals must challenge children to think through the use of higher-order questions that encourage them to explain, apply, analyze, rearrange, and judge. Many schools have resource rooms for gifted and talented students, in which children can spend a half day or more every week working with a professional who is interested and trained in working with them. There are seven primary ways to provide for the needs of gifted and talented children:

1. *Enrichment classroom.* The classroom professional conducts a differentiated program of study without the help of outside personnel.
2. *Consultant professional.* A program of differentiated instruction is conducted in the regular classroom with the assistance of a specially trained consultant.
3. *Resource room pullout.* Gifted students leave the classroom for a short period of time to receive instruction from a specially trained professional.
4. *Community mentor.* Gifted students interact with an adult from the community who has special knowledge in the area of interest.
5. *Independent study.* Students select projects and work on them under the supervision of a qualified professional.
6. *Special class.* Gifted students are grouped together during most of the class time and are instructed by a specially trained professional.
7. *Special schools.* Gifted students receive differentiated instruction at a special school with a specially trained staff.[12]

Of these methods, resource room pullout is the most popular.

Children Who Have Been Abused or Neglected

Many of our views of childhood are highly romanticized. We tend to believe that parents always love their children and enjoy caring for them. We also envision family settings full of joy, happiness, and parent–child harmony. Unfortunately for children, their parents, and society, these assumptions are not always true. The extent of child abuse is far greater than we might imagine. In 1995, an estimated 3.1 million children were reported to Child Protective Services (CPS) agencies as alleged victims of child maltreatment (e.g., physical abuse, neglect, sexual abuse, emotional maltreatment). This means that forty-five children per thousand are reported each year; this number represents a 6 percent increase per year over the last decade.

Child abuse is not new, although it receives greater attention and publicity now than previously. Abuse, in the form of abandonment, infanticide, and neglect, has been documented throughout history. The attitude that children are property partly accounts for the history of abuse. Parents have believed, and some still do, that they own their children and can do with them as they please.

The extent to which children are abused is difficult to ascertain but is probably much greater than most people realize. Valid statistics are difficult to come by because the interest in reported child abuse is relatively new. In addition, definitions of child abuse and neglect differ from state to state and reports are categorized differently. Probably as many as one million incidents of abuse occur a year, but it is estimated that only one in four cases is reported.

Because of the increasing concern over child abuse, social agencies, hospitals, child care centers, and schools are becoming more involved in identification, treatment, and prevention of this national social problem. To do something about child abuse, those who are involved with children and parents have to know what abuse is. Public Law 93-247, the Child Abuse Prevention and Treatment Act, defines *child abuse and neglect* as the "physical or mental injury, sexual abuse, negligent treatment or maltreatment of a child under the age of eighteen by a person who is responsible for the child's welfare under circumstances which indicate that the child's health or welfare is harmed or threatened thereby as determined in accordance with regulations prescribed by the Secretary."[13]

In addition, all states have some kind of legal or statutory definition for child abuse and mistreatment. Many states are defining penalties for child abuse.

Just as debilitating as physical abuse and neglect is *emotional abuse*, which occurs when parents, teachers, and others strip children of their self-esteem and self-image. Adults take away children's self-esteem through continually criticizing, belittling, screaming and nagging, creating fear, and intentionally and severely limiting opportunities. Emotional abuse is difficult to define legally and, most certainly, difficult to document. The unfortunate consequence for emotionally abused children is that they are often left in a debilitating environment. Both abuse and neglect adversely affect children's growth and development.

The guidelines in Table 15.2 may help you identify abuse and neglect, and they provide for children's needs. However, you must remember that the presence of a single characteristic does not necessarily indicate abuse. You should observe the child's behavior and appearance over a period of time and should also be willing to give parents the benefit of the doubt about a child's condition.

Causes of Abuse

Why do parents and guardians abuse children? Those who have been responsible for a group of young children will better understand the reasons for child abuse than those who do not know young children. Child rearing is hard work; it requires patience, self-control, understanding, and restraint. It is entirely likely that most parents, at one time or another, have come close to behavior that could be judged abusive.

Stress is one of the most frequent causes of child abuse. Stressful situations arise from employment, divorce or separation, income, quality of family life, moving, death of a family member, violations of law, sickness or injury, and other sources. We are learning more about stress and its effect on health and the general quality of life. Parenting and teaching are stressful occupations, and parents and teachers often need support from professionals to manage stress.

Lack of parenting information is another reason parents abuse or neglect their children. Some parents do not know what to do or how to do it; these cases more frequently result in acts of omission or neglect than in physical violence. Frequently, the child does not receive proper emotional care and support because the parent is ignorant of this need. Lack of parenting information is attributable to several factors.

First, in this mobile population, young parents often live apart from their own parents, so grandparents have little opportunity to share child-rearing information.

Second, the greater number of teenage parents means that many parents are neither emotionally nor cognitively ready to have children; they are really children themselves. We

Table 15.2
Guidelines for Detecting Abuse and Neglect

Kind of Abuse	Child's Appearance	Child's Behavior	Parent or Caregiver's Behavior
Physical	Unusual bruises, welts, burns, or fractures Bite marks Frequent injuries, explained as "accidental"	Reports injury by parents Unpleasant, hard to get along with, demanding, often disobeys, frequently causes trouble or interferes with others; breaks or damages things; or is shy, avoids others, is too anxious to please, too ready to let other people say and do things to him or her without protest Frequently late or absent, or comes to school too early or hangs around after school Avoids physical contact with adults Wears long sleeves or other concealing clothing Version of how a physical injury occurred is not believable (does not fit type or seriousness of injury) Seems frightened of parents Shows little or no distress at separation from parents May seek affection from any adult	History of abuse as a child Uses unnecessarily harsh discipline Offers explanation of child's injury that does not make sense, does not fit injury, or offers no explanation Seems unconcerned about child Sees child as bad, evil, a monster, etc. Misuses alcohol or other drugs Attempts to conceal child's injury or protect identity of responsible party
Emotional	Less obvious signs than other types of mistreatment; behavior is best indication	Unpleasant, hard to get along with, demanding; frequently causes trouble, will not leave others alone Unusually shy, avoids others, too anxious to please, too submissive, puts up with unpleasantness from others without protest Either unusually adult or overly young for age (e.g., sucks thumb, rocks constantly) Behind for age physically, emotionally, or intellectually	Blames or belittles child Cold and rejecting Withholds love Treats children unequally Seems not to care about child's problems Misuses alcohol or other drugs Disorganized, upset home life Seems not to care what happens Isolated from friends, relatives, neighbors Does not know how to get along with others Long-term chronic illnesses History of neglect as a child Protective or jealous of child

Source: U.S. Department of Health, Education, and Welfare, Office of Human Development Services. Administration for Children, Youth, and Families, Head Start Bureau, Indian and Migrant Programs Division, New Light on an Old Problem, *DHEW Publication No. (OHDS) 78-31108 (Washington, DC: Author, 1978), 8–11.*

need a national effort to put parenting information into the curricula of every elementary and high school. Fortunately, a trend is beginning in this area.

A third reason for child abuse is the parent's cognitive and emotional state. How people are reared and what parenting attitudes were modeled for them have a tremendous influence on how they will rear their own children. Methods of child rearing are handed down

Kind of Abuse	Child's Appearance	Child's Behavior	Parent or Caregiver's Behavior
Neglect	Often dirty, tired, no energy Comes to school without breakfast, often does not have lunch or lunch money Clothes dirty or inappropriate for weather Alone often, for long periods Needs glasses, dental care, or other medical attention	Frequently absent Begs or steals food Causes trouble in school Often hasn't done homework Uses alcohol or drugs Engages in vandalism, sexual misconduct Withdrawn or engages in fantasy or babyish behavior	Misuses alcohol or other drugs Disorganized, upset home life Seems not to care what happens Isolated from friends, relatives, neighbors Does not know how to get along with others Long-term chronic illnesses History of neglect as a child
Sexual	Torn, stained, or bloody underclothing Pain or itching in genital area Has venereal disease	Poor relationships with other children Unwilling to participate in physical activities Engages in delinquent acts or runs away Says has been sexually assaulted by parent/caregiver	Protective or jealous of child Encourages child to engage in prostitution or sexual acts in presence of caregiver Misuses alcohol or other drugs Frequently absent from home

from generation to generation, and people who were abused as children are often abusive parents.

A fourth cause of abuse relates to unwanted and unloved children. We like to assume that every child is wanted and loved, but this is not the case. Some parents take out their frustration on their children, whom they view as barriers to their dreams and self-fulfillment. Or a parent may dislike a child because the child is a constant reminder of an absent spouse.

Some people believe a fifth reason for child abuse is the amount of violence in our society. Opponents of violence on television cite it as an example of people's callousness toward each other and decry it as poor role modeling for children.

A sixth cause of child abuse is parental substance abuse. Substance abuse creates a chaotic environment in which children cannot tell what to expect from their parents. Children of parents who use or abuse alcohol or drugs are often neglected because the parent is emotionally or physically absent when drunk or high. Substance-abusing parents may forget to go to the store for a week to buy food. Because children of drug-using parents may not be physically abused, the signs of abuse may be subtle. A teacher might pick up clues that something is wrong at home if the child is not bringing lunch, is wearing either the same clothes over and over again or clothes that do not fit, or has worn-out shoes because the parents have not noticed that new ones are needed. In general, drug use renders parents dysfunctional and unable to care for their children adequately.

To fully understand the causes and symptoms of abuse of children, we must consider the entire context of the family setting. Most abused children live in families that are dysfunctional. *Dysfunctional* families are characterized by parental mental instability, confused roles (a parent may function in the role of a child, which thus necessitates that the child function at an adult level), and a chaotic, unpredictable family structure and environment. Adults in such families are not functioning at a healthy level and are generally unable to care for and nurture a child's growth and development adequately.

Seeking Help

What can be done about child abuse? There must be a conscious effort to educate, treat, and help abusers and potential abusers. The school is a good place to begin. Another source of help is the federal government's National Center on Child Abuse and Neglect, which helps coordinate and develop programs and policies concerning child abuse and neglect. For information, call or write to any of the following:

For more information about child abuse and to link to the sites listed on this page, go to the Companion Website at http://www.prenhall.com/morrison, select chapter 15, then choose the Linking to Learning module.

- The National Center on Child Abuse and Neglect, Children's Bureau, Office of Child Development, Office of Human Development, Department of Health and Human Services, 200 Independence Avenue, W., Washington, D.C. 20201. http://www.acf.dhhs.gov/
- Child Help USA handles crisis calls and provides information and referrals to every county in the United States. Its hotline is 1-800-422-4453. http://www.childhelpusa.org/
- The National Committee to Prevent Child Abuse (NCPCA) is a volunteer organization of concerned citizens that works with community, state, and national groups to expand and disseminate knowledge about child abuse prevention. The NCPCA has chapters in all states; the address for its national office is National Committee to Prevent Child Abuse, 332 S. Michigan Avenue, Suite 1600, Chicago, IL 60604; telephone 312-663-3520. http://www.childabuse.org/

Figure 15.11 provides some information about reporting suspected abuse.

Child Abuse Prevention Curricula

Many curricula have been developed to help teachers, caregivers, and parents work with children to prevent abuse. The primary purposes of these programs are to educate children about abuse and to teach them strategies to avoid it. Before using an abuse prevention curriculum with children, staff and parents should help select the curriculum and learn how to use it. Parent involvement is essential. As with anything early childhood professionals undertake, parents' understanding, approval, and support of a program makes its goals easier to achieve. Parents and caregivers should not assume, however, that merely teaching children with an abuse prevention curriculum ends their responsibilities. A parent's responsibility for a child's care and protection never ends. Likewise, professionals have the same responsibility for the children entrusted to them.

Homeless Children

Walking down a city street, you may have encountered homeless men and women, but have you seen a homeless child? Homeless children are the neglected, forgotten, often abandoned segment of the growing homeless population in the United States. The National Coalition

You should be aware of the official policy and specific reporting procedures of your school system, and should know your legal obligations and the protections from civil and criminal liability specified in your state's reporting law. (All states provide immunity for mandated, good-faith reports.)

Although you should be familiar with your state's legal definition of abuse and neglect, you are not required to make legal distinctions in order to report. Definitions should serve as guides. If you suspect that a child is abused or neglected, you should report. The teacher's value lies in noticing conditions that indicate that a child's welfare may be in jeopardy.

Be concerned about the rights of the child—the rights to life, food, shelter, clothing, and security. But also be aware of the parents' rights—particularly their rights to be treated with respect and to be given needed help and support.

Bear in mind that reporting does not stigmatize a parent as "evil." The report is the start of a rehabilitative process that seeks to protect the child and help the family as a whole.

A report signifies only the *suspicion* of abuse or neglect. Teachers' reports are seldom unfounded. At the very least, they tend to indicate a need for help and support to the family.

If you report a borderline case in good faith, do not feel guilty or upset if it is dismissed as unfounded upon investigation. Some marginal cases are found to be valid.

Don't put off making a report until the end of the school year. Teachers sometimes live with their suspicions until they suddenly fear for the child's safety during the summer months. A delayed report may mean a delay in needed help for the child and the family. Moreover, by reporting late in the school year, you remove yourself as a continued support to both the child protective agency and the reported family.

If you remove yourself from a case of suspected abuse or neglect by passing it on to superiors, you deprive child protective services of one of their most competent sources of information. For example, a teacher who tells a [children's protective services] worker that the child is especially upset on Mondays directs the worker to investigate conditions in the home on weekends. Few persons other than teachers are able to provide this kind of information. Your guideline should be to resolve any question in favor of the child. When in doubt, report. Even if you, as a teacher, have no immunity from liability and prosecution under state law, the fact that your report is made in good faith will free you from liability and prosecution.

In the absence of guidance from the protective agency, the teacher can rely on several general rules for dealing with the abused or neglected child:

- Try to give the child additional attention whenever possible.
- Create a more individualized program for the child. Lower your academic expectations and make fewer demands on the child's performance—he or she probably has enough pressures and crises to deal with presently at home.
- Be warm and loving. If possible, let the child perceive you as a special friend to whom he or she can talk. By abusing or neglecting the child, someone has said in a physical way, "I don't love you." You can reassure the child that someone cares.
- Most important, remember that in identifying and reporting child maltreatment, you are not putting yourself in the position of autocrat over a family. The one purpose of your actions is to get help for a troubled child and family: the one goal is to reverse a situation that jeopardizes a child's healthy growth and development.

Figure 15.11
Suggested Responses to Suspected Abuse

Source: U.S. Department of Health, Education, and Welfare, Office of Human Development Services, Administration for Children, Youth, and Families, Head Start Bureau, Indian and Migrant Programs Division, New Light on an Old Problem, *DHEW Publication No. (OHDS) 78-31108 (Washington, DC: Author, 1978), 8–11.*

To take an online self-test on this chapter's contents, go to the Companion Website at http://www.prenhall.com/morrison, select chapter 15, then choose the Self Test module.

for the Homeless estimates there are between 500,000 and 750,000 homeless youth, living either in homeless families or on their own.

Homelessness has significant mental, physical, and educational consequences for children. Homelessness results in developmental delays and can produce high levels of distress. Homeless children observed in day care centers exhibit such problem behaviors as short attention spans, weak impulse control, withdrawal, aggression, speech delays, and regressive behavior. Homeless children are at greater risk than others for health problems. It is estimated that over 40 percent of homeless children do not attend school. If they do enter school, they face many problems relating to their previous school problems (grade failure) and attendance (long trips to attend school). Fortunately, more agencies are responding to the unique needs of homeless children and their families.

Public Law 100-77, the Stewart B. McKinney Homeless Assistance Act of 1987, provides that "each State educational agency shall assure that each child of a homeless individual and each homeless youth have access to a free, appropriate public education which would be provided to the children of a resident of a State."[14] PL 100-77 was amended in 1994 to extend the right to free, appropriate public preschool education to homeless preschoolers. It further provides that services to homeless children are not to replace a regular academic program or to segregate homeless children.

Childhood Stress

The scene of children being left at a child care center or preschool for the first time is familiar to anyone who has worked with young children. Some children quickly become happily involved with new friends in a new setting; some are tense, clinging fearfully to their parents. For many children, separation from the ones they are attached to is a stressful experience.

Children today are subjected to many stressful situations, including community environment, home life, and television. As early childhood professionals, what can we do to reduce or eliminate stresses that imperil children's lives and learning?

Crying, fear, and tension are children's *stress responses*, the symptoms or outward manifestations of children's stress.

Young children are subjected to an increasing number of situations and events that cause them fear and stress. Some of the *stressors* include their parents' divorce, being left at home alone before and after school, parents who constantly argue, the death of a parent or friend, being hospitalized, living in a dangerous neighborhood, family violence, poverty, and child abuse.

Parents and early childhood professionals are becoming aware of the effects stress can have on children: sickness, withdrawal, shyness, loss of appetite, poor sleep patterns, urinary and bowel disorders, and general behavior and discipline problems.

Many early childhood educators believe that one way to alleviate stress is through play. They feel children should be encouraged to play as a therapeutic antidote to the effects of stress. A second way to relieve stress in children is to stop hurrying and pressuring them. Many think children should be free from parental and social demands so they can enjoy their childhood. Unfortunately, society is as it is; we cannot and should not want to return to the "good old days." The tempo of life in the United States will continue to be hectic, and demands for individual achievement are increasing. As a result, the emphasis must be on helping children manage stress in their lives.

From preschool on, children should be taught stress reduction techniques, including relaxation and breathing exercises, yoga, physical exercises, meditation, and regular physical activity. Since we cannot slow the pace of society, we need to teach children coping skills. The amount and kinds of stress on children and its effect are causing more early childhood professionals to become involved in programs and agencies that work for solutions to societal issues that cause stress. In fact, reducing stress is one of the premier issues in early childhood education.

For additional Internet resources or to complete an online activity for this chapter, go to the Companion Website at http://www.prenhall.com/morrison, select chapter 15, then choose the Linking to Learning or Making Connections module.

Activities for Further Enrichment

Applications

1. Visit a center where children with special needs are included, and observe the children during play activities. Follow a particular child and note the materials available, the physical arrangement of the environment, and the number of other children involved. Try to determine whether the child is really engaged in the play activity. Hypothesize about why the child is or is not engaged. Discuss your observations with your colleagues.
2. Develop a file or notebook where you can keep suggestions for adapting curricula for children with special needs.
3. Visit an early childhood special education classroom and a regular preschool classroom and compare the types of behavior management problems and techniques found in each setting.

Field Experiences

1. Visit several public schools to see how they are providing individualized and appropriate programs for children with disabilities. What efforts are being made to involve parents?
2. Visit agencies and programs that provide services for people with disabilities. Before you visit, list specific features, services, and facilities you will look for.
3. How is curriculum and instruction in a class for gifted and talented students different from that in other classes? Get permission to visit and observe such a class. Then compare that class with others you have observed or experienced. On the basis of your observations, describe how you might teach a student who is gifted and talented within your inclusive classroom.
4. Contact local schools in your area and ask them what activities and services they provide for students before and after school. How are these designed to meet students' special needs?

Research

1. Interview parents of children with disabilities. What do they feel are their greatest problems? What do they consider the greatest needs for their children? List specific ways they have been involved in educational agencies. How have educational agencies avoided or resisted providing for their children's needs?
2. Spend some time in mainstreamed inclusive classrooms. What specific skills would you need to become a good professional in such settings?
3. What programs does the federal government support for children with special needs in your area? Give specific information.
4. Discuss with people of another culture their culture's attitudes toward children with disabilities. How are they similar or different from your attitudes?
5. How does a teacher modify the classroom environment, classroom routines, learning activities, student groupings, teaching strategies, instructional materials, assessments, and homework assignments to meet all students' needs? What human and material resources for successful inclusion are available to teachers and to students with special needs? How do students show social acceptance for their classmates with special needs? Visit an inclusive classroom and take notes on what you observe. Compare and discuss your observations with classmates who have visited different settings across all grade levels.
6. Visit the teacher resource center of a local school district or in the district where you plan to teach. Develop a list of resources that would be available to you in teaching students with special needs in your class.

Readings for Further Enrichment

Baldwin, A., and Vialle, W. *Many Faces of Giftedness.* Belmont, CA: Wadsworth, 1999.

Using the metaphor of masks, this text explores the many ways giftedness (intellectual potential) has been overlooked because of an individual's cultural group, handicap, or challenging condition. Readers are presented with practical suggestions to help "lift the masks" and provide a more appropriate education to develop the intellectual strengths of these children.

Cook, R. E., Tessier, F. A., and Klein, M. D. *Adapting Early Childhood Curricula for Children in Inclusive Settings,* 5th ed. Upper Saddle River, NJ: Merrill/Prentice Hall, 2000.

Reflects the most recent developments in the field, presenting the skills necessary for teachers to assist infants, young children, and their families to meet their special challenges and to develop to their fullest potential.

Friend, M., and Bursuck, W. *Including Students with Special Needs,* 2nd ed. Needham Heights, MA: Allyn & Bacon, 1999.

A practical guide for classroom teachers on teaching all students in inclusive classrooms. This book explains how to modify curricula, textbooks, classrooms, student groupings, assessments, and instruction to meet all students' learning needs.

Friend, M., and Cook, L. *Interactions: Collaboration Skills for School Professionals,* 3rd ed. Boston, MA: Addison Wesley Longman, 2000.

Provides a cutting-edge look at how teams of school professionals can effectively work together to provide a necessary range of services to students with special needs.

Gargiulo, R., Kilgo, J., and Graves, S. *Young Children with Special Needs: An Introduction to Early Childhood Special Education.* Belmont, CA: Wadsworth, 2000.

Focuses on children from birth to age five who are at-risk for school failure because of such factors as congenital disorders, developmental problems, and environmental factors such as poverty, abuse, and cultural and linguistic differences.

Hardman, M., Drew, C., and Egan, M. *Human Exceptionality: Society, School, and Family,* 6th ed. Needham Heights, MA: Allyn & Bacon, 1999.

An introductory textbook that guides the reader through the lives of individuals with exceptionalities in the school setting and beyond to cover the family, the community, and the challenges that face the individuals from birth through the adult years.

Howard, V. F., Williams, B. F., Port, P. D., and Lepper, C. *Very Young Children with Special Needs; A Formative Approach for the 21st Century,* 2nd ed. Upper Saddle River, NJ: Merrill/Prentice Hall, 2001.

Provides an introduction to early childhood professionals who plan to provide services and intervention to very young children with disabilities.

Mash, E., and Wolfe, D. *Abnormal Child Psychology.* Belmont, CA: Wadsworth, 1999.

This text achieves a balance among developmental, clinical-diagnostic, and experimental approaches to child and adolescent psychopathology. The authors focus on the child—not just the disorders—and include first-person accounts and cases to enrich the reader's understanding.

Raver, S. A. *Intervention Strategies for Infants and Preschoolers with Special Needs: A Team Approach,* 2nd ed. Upper Saddle River, NJ: Merrill/Prentice Hall, 1999.

Contains recommended practices in early intervention that are easy to implement for serving young children and their families. Features

contributions from leading professionals who have extensive experience with children who have special needs, birth to three years of age.

Rothstein, L. F. *Special Education Law,* 3rd ed. Boston, MA: Addison Wesley Longman, 2000.

Provides a comprehensive and current overview of the major federal laws, and judicial interpretations of those laws, that apply to the education of children with disabilities.

Sands, D., Kozleski, E., and French, N. *Inclusive Education for the 21st Century.* Belmont, CA: Wadsworth, 2000.

The authors challenge preservice special education and regular education teachers to develop the knowledge and skills to produce and support "inclusive school communities," which is both a process and an outcome, providing all students with access to broad educational opportunities.

Zepeda, S., and Langenbach, M. *Special Programs in Regular Schools: Historical Foundations, Standards, and Contemporary Issues.* Needham Heights, MA: Allyn & Bacon, 1999.

This book provides a comprehensive treatment of special programs in regular schools, a treatment predicated on a site-based, collaborative model that encourages a multidisciplined approach. Utilizes many of the special programs as parts of a more unified approach to meeting the needs of children and their families.

Linking to Learning

Council for Exceptional Children

http://www.cec.sped.org/

Publishes extremely up-to-date news regarding education-related legislation, and contains numerous links to other sites.

Council for Learning Disabilities

http://www.cldinternational.org

An international organization of and for professionals who represent diverse disciplines and who are committed to enhancing the education and lifespan development of individuals with learning disabilities. CLD establishes standards of excellence and promotes innovative strategies for research and practice through interdisciplinary collegiality, collaboration, and advocacy.

Disabilities Civil Rights

http://www.galaxy.com/galaxy/Government/Law/Constitutional-Law/Civil-Rights/Disabilities.html

Articles and directories of information concerning legal issues related to disabilities.

DisABILITY: Consumer Law/Searchable Index

http://consumerlawpage.com/resource/ability.shtml

List of links to on-line resources and a searchable index. This site also offers the opportunity for users to submit links to be added to the directory.

Disability Net: Feedback

http://www.disabilitynet.co.uk/

An interactive forum where questions can be posted and others' questions and responses may be viewed.

Frequently Asked Questions About Access to Technology for Students with Disabilities

http://www.resna.org/tap/aet_sfaq.htm

A list of numerous questions and detailed responses concerning technology and students with disabilities.

IDEA Practices

http://www.ideapractices.org

This site answers your questions about the Individuals with Disabilities Education Act, keeps you informed about ideas that work, and supports your efforts to help all children learn, progress, and realize their dreams.

Individualized Education Plans

http://www.neatschoolhouse.org/Library/Special_Education/Individualized_Education_Plans/Individualized_Education_Plans.htm

Contains links to other on-line resources, as well as a list of papers and other materials available on-line.

The National Information Center for Children and Youth with Disabilities

http://www.nichcy.org/

The National Information Center for Children and Youth with Disabilities (NICHCY) is the national information and referral center that provides information on disabilities and disability-related issues for families, educators, and other professionals.

The National Parent Network on Disabilities

http://www.npnd.org/

The National Parent Network on Disabilities (NPND) provides a presence and national voice for all families of children, youth, and adults with disabilities.

Office of Special Education and Rehabilitation Services

http://www.ed.gov/offices/OSERS/

The Office of Special Education and Rehabilitative Services (OSERS) supports programs that assist in educating children with special needs, provides for the rehabilitation of youth and adults with disabilities, and supports research to improve the lives of individuals with disabilities.

Special Child: For Parents of Children with Disabilities

http://www.specialchild.com

An online publication dedicated to parents of children with special needs, provided by the Resource Foundation for Children With Challenges (RFCC).

ENDNOTES

[1] Public Law 105-17, 1997.

[2] Ibid.

[3] A. Turnbull, H. Turnbull III, M. Shank, and D. Leal, *Exceptional Lives: Special Education in Today's Schools,* 2nd ed. (Upper Saddle River, NJ: Merrill/Prentice Hall, 1995), 64–71.

[4] Ibid., 84.

[5] National Early Childhood Technical Assistance System, *Helping Our Nation's Infants and Toddlers with Disabilities and Their Families, A Briefing Paper on Part H of the Individuals with Disabilities Education Act (IDEA)*, (Author, 1996). [On-line]. Available: http://www.nectas.unc.edu.

[6] Council for Exceptional Children, 1996. [On-line]. Available: http://www.cec.sped.org/

[7] J. Burnette, "Including Students with Disabilities in General Education Classrooms: From Policy to Practice," *The Eric Review* 4 (1996), 2-11.

[8] Ibid.

[9] Ibid.

[10] Jacob K. Javits Gifted and Talented Students Education Act of 1988.

[11] B. Clark, *Growing Up Gifted: Developing the Potential of Children at Home and School,* 5th ed. (Upper Saddle River, NJ: Merrill/Prentice Hall, 1991), 73-76.

[12] J. Gallagher, P. Weiss, K. Oglesby, and T. Thomas, *The Status of Gifted/Talented Education: United States Survey Needs, Practices, and Policies* (Los Angeles: National/State Leadership Training Institute on the Gifted and Talented, 1983).

[13] U.S. Statutes at Large, vol. 88, pt. 1 (Washington, DC: U.S. Government Printing Office, 1976), 5.

[14] Public Law 100-77, the Stewart B. McKinney Homeless Assistance Act, Title VII-B—Subtitle B-Education for Homeless Youth, July 1987.

ENDNOTES FOR "NATURAL SETTINGS PROVIDE A KEY FOR INCLUSION"

[1] Christine L. Salisbury, "Mainstreaming During the Early Childhood Years," *Exceptional Children*, (October/November 1991), 146.

[2] Karen E. Diamond, Linda L. Hestenes, and Caryn O'Connor, "Integrating Children with Disabilities into Preschool," *Eric Digest* (June 1994) EJ 365 981.

[3] B. J. Smith and P. S. Strain, "Does Early Intervention Help?" *Eric Digest* 455 (1988).

[4] R. R. Fewell and P. L. Oelwein, "The Relationship Between Time in Integrated Environments and Developmental Gains in Young Children with Special Needs," *Topics in Early Childhood Special Education* 10(Summer 1990), EJ 413 316.

[5] C. A. Peck, P. Carlson, and E. Helmstetter, "Parent and Teacher Perceptions of Outcomes for Typically Developing Children Enrolled in Integrated Early Childhood Programs: A Statewide Study," *Journal of Early Intervention* 16(Winter 1993), EJ 445 822.

[6] Salisbury, "Mainstreaming," 147.

[7] A. McDonnell and M. Hardman, "A Synthesis of 'Best Practice' Guidelines for Early Childhood Services," *Journal of Division for Early Childhood* 12(4), 1988.

[8] L. H. Meyer, J. Eichinger, and S. Park-Lee, "A Validation of Program Quality Indicators in Educational Services for Students with Severe Disabilities," *Journal of the Association for Persons with Severe Handicaps* 12(4), 1987.

[9] Gerald Mahoney, Cordelia Robinson, and Amy Powell, "Focusing on Parent–Child Interaction: The Bridge to Developmentally Appropriate Practices," 12(1, Spring), 1992, EJ 449 978.

[10] Salisbury, "Mainstreaming," 147.

[11] Steven F. Warren and Paul J. Yoder, "Communication and Language Intervention: Why a Constructivist Approach Is Insufficient," *Journal of Special Education* 28(3), 1994, 248.

[12] E. Bates, *The Emergence of Symbols: Cognition and Communication in Infancy* (New York: Academic Press, 1979).

[13] B. Hart, "Naturalistic Language Training Techniques." In S. F. Warren and A. Rogers-Warren (Eds.), *Teaching Functional Language* (Baltimore: University Park Press, 1985).

[14] Mary Louise Hemmeter and Ann P. Kaiser, "Enhanced Milieu Teaching: Effects of Parent-Implemented Language Intervention," *Journal of Early Intervention* 18(3), 1994.

[15] Michaelene M. Ostrosky and Ann P. Kaiser, "Preschool Classroom Environments That Promote Communication," *Teaching Exceptional Children* (Summer 1991).

[16] Ibid., 8–9.

[17] Ibid., 7.

[18] C. A. Peck, J. Donaldson, and M. Pezzoli, "Some Benefits Nonhandicapped Adolescents Perceive for Themselves from Their Social Relationships with Peers Who Have Handicaps," *Journal of the Association for Persons with Severe Handicaps* 15(2), 1990.

CHAPTER 16

It is well known that when families, educators, and communities all work together, schools get better and students get the high quality education they need to lead productive lives. Parents are the essential link in improving American education, and schools simply have to do a better job of reaching out to them.

RICHARD W. RILEY, SECRETARY OF EDUCATION

Parent, Family, and Community Involvement

Cooperation and Collaboration

Focus Questions

1. What changes in contemporary society and families influence children and early childhood programs?
2. Why is parent, family, and community involvement important in early childhood programs?
3. What are the benefits of involving parents and families in early childhood programs?
4. How is a personal philosophy of parent involvement important for success as an early childhood professional?
5. How can early childhood professionals and others encourage and support programs for involving families and communities?

To review the chapter focus questions online, go to the Companion Website at http://www.prenhall.com/morrison and select chapter 16.

One thing we can say with certainty about the educational landscape today is that parents, families, and communities are as much a part of the educational process as our children, teachers, and staff. At no time in U.S. educational history has support for family and community been so high. All concerned view the involvement of families and communities as critical for individual student success as well as for the success of the "American dream" of providing all children with an education that will meet their needs and enable them to succeed in school and be productive members of society. In this chapter, we look at some of the reasons why parent, family, and community involvement in education is so important and how you can confidently and productively contribute to the process.

Changes in Schooling

To check your understanding of this chapter with the online Study Guide, go to the Companion Website at http://www.prenhall.com/morrison, select chapter 16, then choose the Study Guide module.

Schooling used to consist mostly of teaching children social and basic academic skills. But as society has changed, so has the content of schooling. Early childhood programs have assumed many parental functions and responsibilities. Part of the broadening of the role and function of early education and schooling includes helping parents and families meet their problems and involving them in decisions regarding the ways programs function.

Goals 2000

As a result of goal 1 (the "readiness goal") of Goals 2000: Educate America (see chapter 2), early childhood professionals are now trying to help children come to school ready to learn. These efforts also focus attention on parents as the first teachers of their children. One of the first such programs is the state of Missouri's Parents as Teachers (PAT) program, a home-school partnership designed to give children a good start in life by maximizing their overall development during the first three years of life. PAT is a model for other programs throughout the country. It provides all parents with information about children's development and activities that promote language, intellectual, and social development.

Additionally, the partnership goal of Goals 2000 states, "Every school and home will engage in partnerships that will increase parental involvement and participation in promoting the social, emotional, and academic growth of children."[1] As a result, early childhood programs and public schools are mounting an unprecedented effort to truly make parents and community members collaborative partners.

Changing Attitudes

For more information about family–school relations, go to the Companion Website at http://www.prenhall.com/morrison, select any chapter, then choose Topic 10 of the ECE Supersite module.

Political and social forces have led to the strengthening of the relationship between families and schools. The accountability and reform movements of the past and present have convinced families that they should no longer be kept out of their children's schools. Families believe they should insist on effective instruction and care from schools and child care centers. They have become more militant in their demand for quality education, and schools and other agencies have responded by seeking ways to involve families in the quest for quality. Education professionals and families realize that mutual cooperation is in everyone's best interest.

In response to the changing landscape of contemporary society, early childhood professionals are working with parents to develop programs to help them and their children develop to their fullest and lead productive lives. Early childhood professionals are very supportive of such efforts. As Figure 16.1 shows, education professionals believe that involving parents is a high priority.

- Think parental involvement should occur both in the home and at school
- Want to see the level of parent involvement increase
- Believe the majority of parent contacts are positive
- Think parents are more willing than ever to be involved in their children's education
- Want parents to be informed about their schools
- Are somewhat reluctant to actively consult about what subjects should be taught and policy decisions
- Urban teachers are more critical of the level and quality of the parental involvement than are suburban teachers

Figure 16.1
What Teachers Believe About Parent/Family Involvement

Source: Louis Harris and Associates, Inc., The Metropolitan Life Survey of the American Teacher, 1998, Building Family–School Partnerships: Views of Teachers and Students *(New York: Author, 1998). Used with permission.*

Changing Families

The family of today is not the family of yesterday, nor will the family of today be the family of tomorrow. For example, households with children dropped from 45 percent in the 1970s to 26 percent in 1998. Figure 16.2 shows some of the other ways families have changed over the years. In addition, more young mothers are entering the workforce than ever before. This means that at an early age, often beginning at six weeks, children are spending eight hours a day or more in the care of others. Thus, working parents are both turning their young children over to others for care and spending less time with their children. Parents need more help with rearing their children at earlier ages. As a result, opportunities have blossomed for child-serving agencies, such as child care centers and preschools, to assist and support parents in their child-rearing efforts. One of the major trends of the next decade is that more programs will provide more parents with child development and child-rearing information.

For more information about changing families, go to the Companion Website at http://www.prenhall.com/morrison, select chapter 16, then choose the Linking to Learning module to connect to the Making Lemonade (run by a single mom) and Single and Custodial Father's Network site.

- Fifty-six percent of adults are married, compared with nearly 75 percent in 1972.
- Fifty-one percent of children live in a household with their two parents, vs. 73 percent in 1972.
- The percentage of households made up of unmarried people with no children is 33 percent, more than double the rate in 1972.
- The percentage of children living with single parents rose to 18.2 percent, vs. 4.7 percent in 1972.

Figure 16.2
How Families Have Changed

Source: Martha Irvine, "Married with Children: It's Down to Just 26%," Pittsburgh Post-Gazette *(November 24, 1999). Used with permission of the Associated Press.*

Families continue to change, and, as they do, early childhood professionals must adapt and adopt new ways of involving family members and providing for their needs. For example, what can professionals do to ensure the involvement of single fathers in their programs?

Implications of Family Patterns for Early Childhood Professionals

Given the changes in families today, there are a number of things you as an early childhood professional can do to help parents, including the following:

- *Provide support services.* Support can extend from being a "listening ear" to organizing support groups and seminars on single parenting. Professionals can help families link up with other agencies and groups, such as Big Brothers and Big Sisters and Families without Partners. Through newsletters and fliers, professionals can offer families specific advice on how to help children become independent and how to meet the demands of living in single-parent families, stepfamilies, and other family configurations.
- *Provide child care.* As more families need child care, early childhood personnel are logical advocates for establishing care where none exists, extending existing services, and helping to arrange cooperative baby-sitting services.
- *Avoid criticism.* Professionals should be careful not to criticize parents for the jobs they are doing. They may not have extra time to spend with their children or know how to discipline them. Regardless of their circumstances, families need help, not criticism.
- *Avoid being judgmental.* Similarly, professionals should examine and clarify their attitudes and values toward family patterns and remember that there is no "right" family pattern from which all children should come.

- *Arrange educational experiences*. Professionals need to address the issue of changing family patterns in the educational experiences they arrange. They must offer experiences children might not otherwise have because of their family organization. For example, outdoor activities such as fishing trips and sports events can be interesting and enriching learning experiences for children who may not have such opportunities.
- *Adjust programs*. Professionals need to adjust classroom and center activities to account for how particular children cope with their home situations. Children's needs for different kinds of activities depend on their experiences at home. For example, opportunities abound for role playing, and such activities help bring into the open situations that children need to talk about. Use program opportunities to discuss families and the roles they play. Make it a point in the classroom to model, encourage, and teach effective interpersonal skills.
- *Be sensitive*. There are specific ways to sensitively approach today's changing family patterns. For example, avoid having children make presents for both parents when it is inappropriate to do so and awarding prizes for bringing both parents to meetings. Replace such terms as *broken home* with *single-parent family*. Be sensitive to the demands of school in relation to children's home lives. For instance, when a professional sent a field trip permission form home with children and told them to have their mothers or fathers sign it, one child said, "I don't have a father. If my mother can't sign it, can the man who sleeps with her sign it?" Seek guidance and clarification from families about how they would like specific situations handled; for example, ask whether they want you to send notices of school events to both parents.
- *Seek training*. Request in-service training to help you work with families. In-service programs can provide information about referral agencies, guidance techniques, ways to help families deal with their problems, and child abuse identification and prevention. Professionals need to be alert to the signs of all kinds of child abuse, including mental, physical, and sexual abuse.
- *Increase parent contacts*. Finally, professionals should encourage greater and different kinds of parent involvement through visiting homes; talking to families about children's needs; providing information and opportunities to parents, grandparents, and other family members; gathering information from families (such as through interest inventories); and keeping in touch with parents. Make parent contacts positive.

Parent/family involvement is a process of helping families use their abilities to benefit themselves, their children, and the early childhood program. Families, children, and the program are all part of the process; consequently, all three parties should benefit from a well-planned program of family involvement. Nonetheless, the focus in parent/child/family interactions is the family, and you must work with and through families if you want to be successful.

For more information about involving families in children's education, go to the Companion Website at http://www.prenhall.com/morrison, select chapter 16, then choose the Linking to Learning module to connect to several sites with resources for working with families.

Education as a Family Affair

Education starts in the home, and what happens there profoundly affects the trajectory of development and learning. The greater the family's involvement in children's learning, the more likely it is that students will receive a high-quality education.

The central role families play in children's education is a reality that teachers and schools must address as they make plans for how to reform schools and increase student achievement. Partnering with parents is a process whose time has come, and the benefits far outweigh any inconveniences or barriers that may stand in the way of bringing schools and parents together.

Family-Centered Teaching

Family-centered teaching and learning focus on meeting the needs of students through the family unit, whatever that unit may be. Education professionals recognize that to most effectively meet the needs of students, they must also meet the needs of family members and the family unit. Family-centered teaching and learning make sense for a number of reasons. First, the family unit has the major responsibility for meeting children's needs. Children's development begins in the family system, and this system is a powerful determiner of developmental processes, both for better and worse. Therefore, helping parents and other family members meet their children's needs in appropriate ways means that everyone stands to benefit. Helping individuals in the family unit become better parents and family members benefits children and consequently promotes their success in school.

Second, it is frequently the case that to help children effectively, family issues and problems must be addressed first. For instance, helping parents gain access to adequate and affordable health care increases the chances that the whole family, including children, will be healthy.

Third, teachers can do many things concurrently with children and their families that will benefit both. Literacy is a good example. Adopting a family approach to literacy means that helping parents learn to read themselves, build literacy, and read aloud to their children helps ensure children's literacy development as well.

An example of family-centered teaching is Even Start, a federally funded family literacy program that combines adult literacy and parenting training with early childhood education to break cycles of illiteracy that are often passed on from one generation to another. Even Start is funded under Title I of the Improving America's Schools Education Act and is operated through the public school system. In particular, Even Start helps parents become full partners in the education of their children, assists children in reaching their full potential, and provides literacy training for parents. Even Start projects are designed to work cooperatively with existing community resources to provide a full range of services and to integrate early childhood education and adult education. Figure 16.3 diagrams family-centered teaching in action.

Family-Centered Curriculum and Instruction

Family-centered curriculum and instruction exist at three levels. First, programs and materials are designed to help parents be better parents and teachers of their children. To support parents in these roles, schools and teachers provide materials on parenting, conduct parenting classes, and furnish ideas about teaching their children reading and math skills through daily living activities. At a second level, instruction focuses on helping parents with everyday problems and issues of family living. For example, classes and information on tenant rights, nutritional meals, the importance of immunizations, and access to health services would be in keeping with the ideas of addressing families' daily living needs. At a third level, family-centered curriculum and instruction attempt to integrate students' classroom learning with learning in the home. For example, providing parents with books to read to their children at home would support efforts to link in-school learning with learning in the home.

Two-Generation and Intergenerational Programs

Two-generation programs involve parents and their children and are designed to help both generations and strengthen the family unit. *Intergenerational programs* involve grandparents and others as well. Two-generation delivery of services can and should begin before children's birth because many problems relating to child health can be prevented by good prenatal care.

Many educational and other services are delivered to children and families through the family unit. For example, many literacy programs work with children and with parents and use this opportunity to improve literacy within the entire family. What else can be taught to children and family members at the same time?

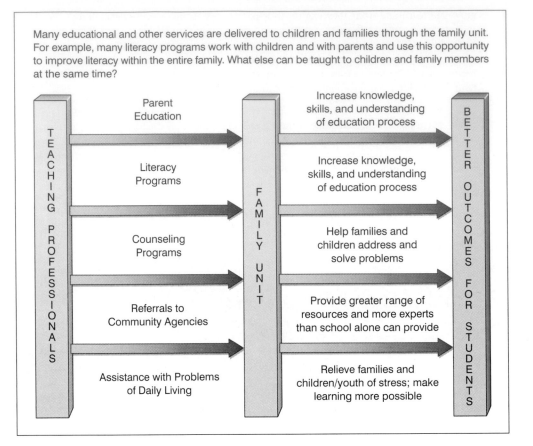

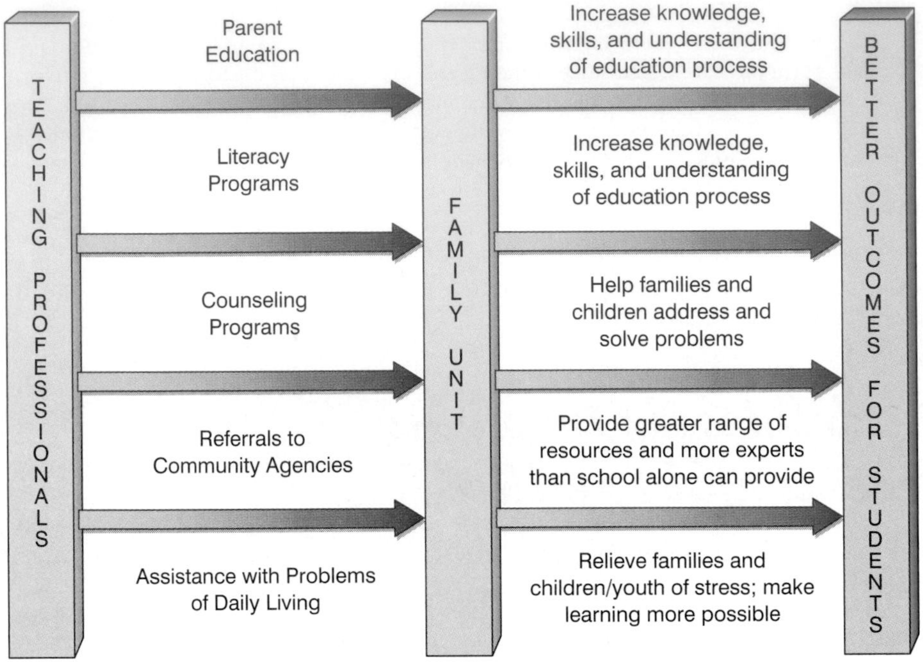

Figure 16.3
Family-Centered Teaching

Source: G. S. Morrison, Teaching in America, *2nd ed. (Needham Heights, MA: Allyn & Bacon, 2000), p. 227. Copyright © 2000 by Allyn & Bacon. Reprinted by permission.*

The preventive approach to maternal and prenatal health is reflected in the growing numbers of schools that have on-site health clinics. Services often include both health and education in which students and parents receive medical care and information that will support their efforts to lead healthy lives.

For example, Avance is a center-based parent support and education program serving low-income Hispanic families at three centers in San Antonio, Houston, and the Rio Grande valley in Texas. Parents and their children up to three years of age are enrolled through an aggressive door-to-door recruitment of families into the program. The heart of Avance is a nine-month parent education program in which parents are taught how they can be their children's first teachers and how to facilitate their children's development. To support parents in this effort, Avance provides transportation to the center, home visits, literacy development, employment training, family planning information, education in the use of community resources, and referrals and advocacy for other social service needs.

Mercedes Perez de Colon, Director of the National Family Resource Center for Avance, states the following:

> Our main goal has always been to help parents prepare their children for school success by focusing on the first three years of a child's life. We help parents understand how children

grow and learn and what they can do to maximize opportunities for their children. We provide a comprehensive array of services and opportunities to enable parents to become their children's first teachers. We try to help parents use resources available in the community and understand that helping their children to be prepared for school does not require money, it requires time and effort on the part of parents. We show parents how to help their children learn through language and through their five senses and through play.

We also stress healthy lifestyles for parents and children, so we focus on immunizations, nutrition, safety, and understanding the importance of healthy and preventive lifestyles. We have been very successful. Parents who attend our program increase their understanding of child growth and development, have a positive change in attitudes toward child rearing, and have better home environments for their children. We know that their children are meeting with success in school.[2]

Intergenerational programming also includes programs in which young people provide services to older persons, in which older persons provide services to youth, and in which two generations work cooperatively on a project.

Guidelines for Involving Parents and Families

As an early childhood professional, you can use the following tips to develop programs of parent and family involvement:

- Get to know your children's parents and families. One good way to do this is through home visits. This approach works better in early childhood programs where the number of students is limited. However, teachers who have large numbers of students find that visiting a few homes based on special circumstances can be helpful and informative.

Many programs are looking for ways to effectively integrate the care of both young children and the elderly into their programs. What are some advantages of providing for the education and care of young children and the elderly in the same program?

Program in Action

Los Niños Sunnyside Family Literacy Program

At first glance it's hard to tell the difference between the two classrooms in the portable building that is Los Niños Sunnyside Head Start in Tucson, Arizona. Both serve low-income families; both must follow federal standards of safety and cleanliness, being subject to numerous random inspections; both have state-of-the-art books, computers, and exploratory centers where children are actively engaged in learning and play; both have access to the spotless kitchen, which serves all the children two nutritious meals a day; both practice positive discipline and encourage parental involvement in their child's education. And the similarities don't end there.

The difference is that the children in one classroom, along with their parents, are students of Family Literacy. These children's parents don't go home after dropping their child off at Head Start—they head to Los Niños Elementary School for five hours of adult education (English or GED), vocational education, computers, parent time (parenting and leadership), and, perhaps most critical of all, parents and children together (PACT) time.

PACT time sets Family Literacy apart from other Head Start programs in that parents spend thirty to forty-five minutes every day in the early childhood classroom. Children plan ahead of time where they want to play and send the parent a note with this information. The goal is for parents to dedicate the entire period exclusively to their child, relinquishing control and learning to respect and understand their child's choices in play. To ease this often difficult transition, parents explore how to ask questions of their children to extend play, and they are encouraged to follow the staff's lead in using positive language and discipline.

What is the rest of the children's day like? After they arrive at Head Start, they are served a nourishing, sugar-free breakfast. They are encouraged to taste everything at least once and to drink their milk. They then do a dry brushing of their teeth. At 9:00 they go outside, and when they return forty-five minutes later they transition to group activity. At 10:00 they plan for PACT time and then sing and/or play music. Parents then arrive for PACT, which takes place between 10:30 and 11:00. During one PACT time a week, parents and children spend fifteen minutes reading together. At the end of PACT, everyone gathers in a circle for Circle Time, where we sing or read a story. Afterward, one parent stays to help set the tables and eat lunch with the children while the others go back to their room. After lunch, the children engage in a reading activity, write in their journals, and engage in "Do Time" work. At 12:55 they gather in a circle to review their day, and at 1:00 their parents come to take them home.

As mentioned above, positive guidance is a fundamental component of Head Start. Because children learn what they live, Head Start staff members guide children to make behavior decisions that are positive and safe for themselves and others. They do this by modeling positive language and actions in the classroom. For example, rules are started in positive terms: instead of "Don't run in the classroom!" teachers say, "Ramon, remember, we walk in the classroom. We run outside." Reasons are given: "So you won't hurt yourself and others." A very important rule is "Use your words when you want something." For many children, this is the first time they've experienced a consistently positive and supportive environment.

Head Start also stresses the importance of responsibility. Children have many responsibilities, from putting toys away to setting the table for breakfast and lunch. It's fascinating to watch a four- or five-year-old child set the table! Yet they do it with ease, having no trouble remembering where

things go. During lunch children serve themselves and pour their own milk. They are also responsible for bussing their dishes afterward, taking care to put the spoons in one container, the napkins in another, and the cups in another. Parents often comment that after being enrolled in Head Start, their preschoolers carry their dishes to the sink at home and are better at cleaning up after themselves in general.

For many parents, these are things that their children had heretofore been "unable" to do and so were never given the responsibility of doing. But Head Start strongly believes that we create self-esteem in our children by teaching them life skills. The ability to take care of oneself is certainly a skill that can increase a child's sense of competence. And as children become more self-confident, their self-esteem is given the chance to flower and grow.

Here at Los Niños, I have observed the effects of the Head Start/Family Literacy collaboration. Five children who were in the program last year are in kindergarten this year. Their teachers have told me how exceptionally well prepared these children were for kindergarten. Not only could they read and write, but they could also listen and follow rules. Longitudinal studies done by our office have shown that children who attend Family Literacy are consistently successful at school. And approximately 50 percent of former Family Literacy parents surveyed were still involved in their children's education by volunteering in their schools.

What makes Family Literacy stand above many preschool programs is the involvement of the whole family. This is Family Literacy's ninth year at Los Niños. Many lives have been turned around in that time, though gains are often slow. As the adult educator here, I often ask parents to share something good that's happened to them recently. Just this week one mom said she's yelling less at home now. Another said her fourth grade son, whose classroom she volunteers in two hours a week during her vocational time, told her he was proud of her. Another said that she now feels better able to help her older child with his homework. And the year just got started!

These are the small successes that add up to a program that has changed hundreds of lives. In the words of National Center for Family Literacy President Sharon Darling: "For more than ten years, the NCFL has been at the forefront of efforts to make the most important connection in education—giving parents the tools they need to be their child's first and best teacher. Recognized by academics and policymakers as invaluable to American education and multigenerational empowerment, family literacy . . . improves the lives of children and families like few other efforts." Family Literacy collaborates with other early childhood agencies besides Head Start, so see if there's a Family Literacy program in your area—and if not, start one!

Visit the National Center for Family Literacy on the Web at http://www.famlit.org/.

Contributed by Emily Creigh, adult educator at Los Niños Sunnyside Head Start. Photos courtesy of Emily Creigh.

- Ask parents what goals they have for their children. Use these goals to help you in your planning. Encourage parents to have realistically high expectations for their children.
- Build relationships with parents so you may communicate better with them.
- Learn how to best communicate with parents based on their cultural communications preferences. Take into account cultural features that can inhibit collaboration.

- Learn how families rear children and organize themselves. Political, social, and moral values of families all have implications for parent participation and ways to teach children.
- Support parents in their roles as first teachers of their children. Support can include information, materials, and help with parenting problems.
- Provide frequent, open communication and feedback on student progress, including good news.
- Train parents as mentors, classroom aides, tutors, and homework helpers. For example, communicate guidelines for helping students study for tests.
- Support fathers in their roles as parents. By supporting and encouraging fathers, you support the whole family.
- On the basis of parents' needs, identify resources they can use to help solve family and personal problems.
- Work with and through families. Ask parents to help you in working with and involving them and other parents. Parents respond positively to parents, so it makes sense to have parents helping families.

Four Approaches to Parent and Family Involvement

In looking at and designing programs of parent and family involvement, early childhood professionals may proceed in several different ways. For example, the National PTA has developed guidelines for improving family and parent involvement, which lead to student success (see Figure 16.4).

In 1997, the National PTA developed the National Standards for Parent/Family Involvement Programs to help schools, communities, and parenting groups implement effective parent involvement programs with the aim of improving students' academic performance. The standards include (1) regular communication between home and school, (2) support in parenting skills, (3) an emphasis on assisting student learning, (4) the promotion of volunteering at school, (5) parent involvement in school decision making and advocacy, and (6) collaborations with the community to provide needed resources.

The National PTA recommends that parents, educators, and community leaders work together in a cohesive way to implement the standards. The following steps outline a process for improving parent and family involvement and student success:

1. Create an action team.
2. Examine current practice.
3. Develop a plan of improvement.
4. Develop a written parent/family involvement policy.
5. Secure support.
6. Provide professional development for school/program staff.
7. Evaluate and revise the plan.

Figure 16.4
The National PTA's Standards for Family Involvement

Source: National PTA, "National Standards for Parent/Family Involvement Programs." Used by permission.

Parents can be involved in early childhood programs in many ways. Here a parent accompanies children on an outdoor field trip. How could you go about determining the best way to involve parents in your programs?

TASK APPROACH. The most common and traditional way to approach parent and family involvement is through a task orientation. This method seeks to involve parents to get assistance completing specific tasks that support the school or classroom program. In this orientation, faculty, staff, and administration work to involve parents and other family members as tutors, aides, attendance monitors, fund-raisers, field trip monitors, and clerical helpers. This is the type of parent and family involvement many professionals are comfortable with and the sort that usually comes to mind when planning for some kind of parent or family involvement. However, while this type of parent involvement has many benefits, by itself it does not represent a sufficient program of family involvement.

For more information about approaches to parent and family involvement, go to the Companion Website at http://www.prenhall.com/morrison, select chapter 16, then choose the Linking to Learning module to connect to the National Network of Partnership-2000 Schools site.

PROCESS APPROACH. In this approach, families are encouraged to participate in certain activities that are important to the educational process, such as curriculum planning, textbook review and selection, membership on task forces and committees, professional review and selection, and helping to set behavior standards. This approach is becoming popular because professionals realize the importance of sharing these processes and decisions with parents, family members, and members of the community. Parents and others need preparation and support for this kind of involvement. Some professionals may think parents lack the necessary skills to help in certain areas, but with some assistance and an opportunity to participate, many family members are extremely effective.

DEVELOPMENTAL APPROACH. This orientation seeks to help parents and families develop skills that benefit themselves, children, schools, professionals, and families and, at the same time, enhance family growth and development. This humanistic orientation is exemplified in such programs as cooperative preschools, community schools, and Head Start.

COMPREHENSIVE APPROACH. A comprehensive approach to parent and family involvement includes elements of all the preceding approaches, especially the developmental

approach (see Figure 16.5). It goes beyond the other three approaches, however, in that it makes the family the *center,* or *focus,* of activities. This method does not seek involvement from parent or family members for the sake of involvement or the benefit of a particular agency. Rather, it works with, in, and through the family system to empower, assist, and strengthen the family. As a result, all family members are helped, including children.

The comprehensive approach seeks to involve parents, families, and community persons in school processes and activities, including decisions about the school. The comprehensive approach may also provide parents choices about which school or program their children will attend. School choice programs are designed to enable parents to choose the school their children will attend, with certain limitations and within certain constraints. School choice is defined in a number of ways. At its most controversial level, it means giving families public funds to send their children to private schools. It also means giving parents the choice to send their children to other public schools across district lines and/or school attendance patterns. This process of giving parents the opportunity to choose schools for their children—and providing the means to do so through tax dollars—is a major issue in education today. In addition to creating much discussion, the school choice controversy has also reinforced and emphasized parents' roles and responsibilities for the education of their children. Furthermore, the debate has placed parents at the center of decision making about where children will attend school and what they will study and learn.

One expression of school choice is the voucher system. Vouchers are certificates good for certain amounts of money that parents can use to pay for some or all of their children's tuition at a private or public school. Vouchers are designed to support efforts at providing parents with choice. Proponents of vouchers say that they are a means of school reform and that they return decision making to parents. Opponents counter that the goal should be to make public schools better rather than going outside the public system. Critics also maintain that vouchers erode public school support and drain needed tax dollars from schools. Some opponents also claim that vouchers lead to resegregation of the schools.

A comprehensive program also provides involvement through family development and support programs. Many programs are not only encouraging involvement in family-centered programs, they are providing them. These family support programs include parenting programs, home visitations, substance abuse education and treatment programs, discussion and support groups, job training and referral programs, basic skills training programs, and parental links to existing community resource programs.

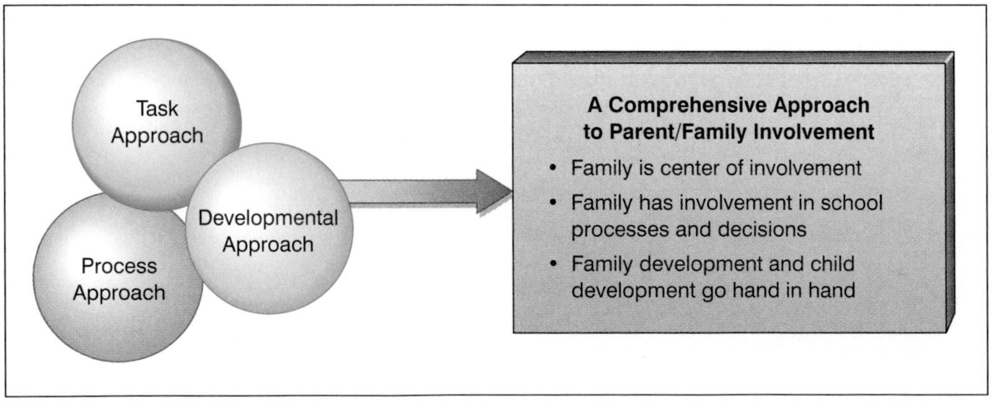

Figure 16.5
A Comprehensive Approach to Family Involvement

Activities for Involving Families

Unlimited possibilities exist for family involvement, but a coordinated effort is required to build an effective, meaningful program that can bring about a change in education and benefit all concerned: families, children, professionals, and communities. Families can make a significant difference in their children's education, and with early childhood professionals' assistance, they will be able to join teachers and schools in a productive partnership. Figure 16.6 lists some things you can do to help ensure you will be successful in your parent involvement activities. Also, the following are examples of activities that allow for significant family involvement.

Schoolwide Activities

- *Workshops*—to introduce families to the school's policies, procedures, and programs. Most families want to know what is going on in the school and would do a better job of parenting and educating if they knew how.
- *Family nights, cultural dinners, carnivals, and potluck dinners*—to bring families and the community to the school in nonthreatening, social ways.
- *Adult education classes*—to provide the community with opportunities to learn about a range of subjects.
- *Training programs*—to give parents, family members, and others skills as classroom aides, club and activity sponsors, curriculum planners, and policy decision makers. *When parents, family members, and community persons are viewed as experts, empowerment results.*
- *Support services such as car pools and baby-sitting*—to make attendance and involvement possible.
- *Fairs and bazaars*—to involve families in fund-raising.

The following are some things you can do to help make your involvement with parents successful:

- Make the school inviting.
- Strategize ways to involve parents in schools—many don't know how to become involved or feel intimidated because they haven't been in school since they were students themselves.
- Make parents equal partners with educators by allowing them a voice in school decisions.
- Avoid education jargon.
- Schedule meetings at times convenient for parents, even if those meetings aren't most convenient for educators.
- Show respect for parents' perspectives.
- Cultivate an open and civil atmosphere in which the principal is a facilitator.
- Keep parents well informed and encourage two-way communication.
- Celebrate parent participation.

Figure 16.6
Tips for Fostering Successful School–Parent Partnerships

Source: Karen Rasmussen (January 1998). "Making Parent Involvement Meaningful," Education Update *40 (1), 1, 6, 7. Reprinted with permission of the Association for Supervision and Curriculum Development.*

- *Performances and plays*—these, especially ones in which children have a part, tend to bring families to school; however, the purpose of children's performances should not be solely to get families involved.

Communication Activities

- *Telephone hotlines*. Hotlines staffed by families can help allay fears and provide information relating to child abuse, communicable diseases, and special events. Telephone networks are also used to help children and parents with homework and to monitor latchkey children.
- *Newsletters*. Newsletters planned with parents' help are an excellent way to keep families informed about program events, activities, and curriculum information. Newsletters in parents' native languages help keep language-minority families informed.
- *Home learning materials and activities*. Putting out a monthly calendar of activities is one good way to keep families involved in their children's learning.

Educational Activities

- *Participation in classroom and center activities*. While not all families can be directly involved in classroom activities, encourage those who can. Those who are involved must have guidance, direction, and training. Involving parents and others as paid aides is also an excellent way to provide employment and training. Many programs, such as Head Start, actively support such a policy.
- *Involvement of families in writing individualized education programs (IEPs) for special needs children*. Involvement in writing an IEP is not only a legal requirement but also an excellent learning experience (see chapter 15).

Service Activities

- *Resource libraries and materials centers*. Families benefit from books and other articles relating to parenting. Some programs furnish resource areas with comfortable chairs to encourage families to use these materials.
- *Child care*. Families may not be able to attend programs and become involved if they do not have child care for their children. Child care makes their participation possible and more enjoyable.
- *Respite care*. Some early childhood programs provide respite care for parents and other family members, which enables them to have periodic relief from the responsibilities of parenting a chronically ill child or a child with disabilities.
- *Service exchanges*. Service exchanges operated by early childhood programs and other agencies help families in their needs for services. For example, one parent provided child care in her home in exchange for having her washing machine repaired. The possibilities for such exchanges are endless.
- *Parent support groups*. Parents need support in their roles. Support groups can provide parenting information, community agency information, and speakers.
- *Welcoming committees*. A good way to involve families in any program is to have other families contact them when their children first join a program.

Decision Activities

- *Hiring and policymaking*. Parents and community members can and should serve on committees that set policy and hire staff.

- *Curriculum development and review.* Parents' involvement in curriculum planning helps them learn about and understand what constitutes a quality program and what is involved in a developmentally appropriate curriculum. When families know about the curriculum, they are more supportive of it.

Conducting Home Visits

Conducting home visits is becoming more commonplace for many teachers. In fact, California has a new $15 million initiative to pay teachers overtime for visiting students' homes. Teachers who do home visiting are trained prior to their going on the visits. Refer to Figure 16.7 for guidelines for how you can be successful at home visitation.

A home visiting program can show that the teachers, principal, and school staff are willing to "go more than halfway" to involve all parents in their children's education. Home visits help teachers demonstrate their interest in students' families and understand their students better by seeing them in their home environment.

These visits should not replace parent-teacher conferences or be used to discuss children's progress. When done early before any school problems can arise, they avoid putting any parents on the defensive and signal that teachers are eager to work with all parents. Teachers who have made home visits say they build stronger relationships with parents and their children, and improve attendance and achievement.

PLANNING

Administrators and teachers must agree to participate in the program and be involved in planning it.

These programs are successful when

- teachers' schedules are adjusted so that they have the necessary time;
- home visits are scheduled during just one month of the school year, preferably early; and
- visits are logged so that teachers and administrators can measure their benefits.

Strategies for successful home visits

Who does the visiting?—Wherever possible, teachers should visit homes of children in their classes. If this is not possible, the principal should ensure that every home that requests a visit receives one.

If teachers do not speak the parents' language, a translator needs to accompany them.

Figure 16.7
Home Visits

Source: Reaching All Families: Creating Family-Friendly Schools, *Office of Educational Research and Improvement, U.S. Department of Education, 1996.*

Conducting Parent–Professional Conferences

Significant parent involvement can occur through well-planned and well-conducted parent–early childhood professional conferences (informally referred to as *parent–teacher conferences*). Such conferences are often the first contact many families have with school. Conferences are critical both from a public relations point of view and as a vehicle for helping families and professionals accomplish their goals. The following guidelines will help you as an early childhood professional prepare for and conduct successful conferences:

- *Plan ahead.* Be sure of the reason for the conference. What are your objectives? What do you want to accomplish? List the points you want to cover and think about what you are going to say.

Scheduling—These suggestions may be helpful:

- Some schools have scheduled home visits in the afternoon right after school. Others have found that early evening is more convenient for parents. Some schedule visits right before a new school year begins. A mix of times may be needed to reach all families.
- Teachers should be given flexibility to schedule their visits during the targeted time period.
- Teachers of siblings may want to visit these children's homes together, but take care not to overwhelm parents.
- Some schools work with community groups (e.g., Boys and Girls Clubs, housing complexes, 4-H, Y's, and community centers) to schedule visits in neutral but convenient space.

Making parents feel comfortable—Here are some useful tips:

- Send a letter home to parents explaining the desire to have teachers make informal visits to all students' homes. Include a form that parents can mail back to accept or decline the visit.
- The letter should state clearly that the intent of this 15–30 minute visit is only to introduce the teacher and family members to each other, and not to discuss the child's progress.
- The letter might suggest that families think about special things their children would want to share with the teacher.
- The tone of the letter should try to lessen any parents' worries. One school included a note to parents which said, "No preparation is required. In fact, our homes need to be vacuumed and all of us are on diets!" This touch of humor and casualness helped to set a friendly and informal tone.
- A phone call to parents who have not responded can explain the plan for home visits and reassure parents that it is to get acquainted and not to evaluate students.
- Enlist community groups, religious organizations, and businesses to help publicize the home visits.

Many early childhood professionals conduct home visits to help parents learn how to support their children's learning at home. What useful information can parents provide professionals about children's learning, experiences, and growth and development?

- *Get to know the parents.* This is not wasted time; the more effectively you establish rapport with a parent, the more you will accomplish in the long run.
- *Avoid an authoritative atmosphere.* Do not sit behind your desk while the parent sits in a child's chair. Treat parents and others like the adults they are.
- *Communicate at the parent's level.* Do not condescend or patronize. Instead, use words, phrases, and explanations the parent understands and is familiar with. Do not use jargon or complicated explanations, and speak in your natural style.
- *Accentuate the positive.* Make every effort to show and tell the parent what the child is doing well. When you deal with problems, put them in the proper perspective: what the child is able to do, what the goals and purposes of the learning program are, what specific skill or concept you are trying to get the child to learn, and what problems the child is having difficulty in achieving. Most important, explain what you plan to do to help the child achieve and what specific role the parent can have in meeting the achievement goals.
- *Give families a chance to talk.* You will not learn much about them if you do all the talking, nor are you likely to achieve your goals. Professionals are often accustomed to dominating a conversation, and many parents will not be as verbal as you, so you will have to encourage families to talk.
- *Learn to listen.* An active listener holds eye contact, uses body language such as head nodding and hand gestures, does not interrupt, avoids arguing, paraphrases as a way of clarifying ideas, and keeps the conversation on track.
- *Follow up.* Ask the parent for a definite time for the next conference as you are concluding the current one. Having another conference is the best method of solidifying

gains and extending support, but other acceptable means of follow-up are telephone calls, written reports, notes sent with children, and brief visits to the home. While these types of contacts may appear casual, they should be planned for and conducted as seriously as any regular parent–professional conference. No matter which approach you choose, advantages of a parent–professional conference follow-up are these:

- Families see that you genuinely care about their children.
- Everyone can clarify problems, issues, advice, and directions.
- Parents, family members, and children are encouraged to continue to do their best.
- It offers further opportunities to extend classroom learning to the home.
- You can extend programs initiated for helping families and formulate new plans.

- *Develop an action plan.* Never leave the parent with a sense of frustration, not knowing what you are doing or what they are to do. Every communication with families should end on a positive note, so that everyone knows what can be done and how to do it.

CHILDREN AND CONFERENCES. A question frequently asked is, "Should children be present at parent–teacher conferences?" The answer is, "Yes, of course." The only caveat to this is, "if it is appropriate for them to be present," and in most instances it is appropriate and offers a number of benefits:

- Children have much to contribute. They can talk about their progress and behavior, offer suggestions for improvement and enrichment, and discuss their interests.
- The *locus of control* is centered in the child. Children learn they have a voice and opinions and that others think this is important and are listening.
- Children's self-esteem is enhanced because they are viewed as an important part of the conference and because a major purpose of the conference is to help them and their families.
- Children become more involved in their classroom and their education. "Students take pride not only in their own accomplishments and their ability to share them, but also in the opportunity to help each other prepare for and succeed at their conferences. A team spirit—a sense of community—can emerge and this can benefit the motivation and achievement of all."[3]
- Children learn that education is a cooperative process between home and school.

TELEPHONE CONTACTS. When it is impossible to arrange a face-to-face conference as a follow-up, making a telephone call is an efficient way to contact families (although, unfortunately, not all families have a telephone). The same guidelines apply as for face-to-face conferences. In addition, remember the following tips:

For more information about using the Web to increase communication with parents, go to the Companion Website at http://www.prenhall.com/morrison, select chapter 16, then choose the Linking to Learning module to connect to the nschool.com site.

- Since you cannot see someone on a telephone, it takes a little longer to build rapport and trust. The time you spend overcoming families' initial fears and apprehensions will pay dividends later.
- Constantly clarify what you are talking about and what you and the families have agreed to do, using such phrases as, "What I heard you say then . . . ," and, "So far, we have agreed that . . . "
- Do not act hurried. There is a limit to the amount of time you can spend on the phone, but you may be one of the few people who cares about the parent and the child. Your telephone contact may be the major part of the family's support system.

Involving Single-Parent Families

Sometimes, family involvement activities are conducted without much regard for single-parent families. Professionals sometimes think of single-parent families as problems to deal with rather than as people to work with. Involving single-parent families need not present a problem if you remember some basic points.

First, many adults in one-parent families are employed during school hours and may not be available for conferences or other activities during that time. Professionals must be willing to accommodate family schedules by arranging conferences at other times, perhaps early morning (breakfast), midmorning, noon (lunch), early afternoon, late afternoon, or early evening. Some employers, sensitive to these needs, give release time to participate in school functions, but others do not. Professionals and principals need to think seriously about going to families rather than having families always come to them. Some schools have set up parent conferences to accommodate families' work schedules, while some professionals find that home visits work best.

Second, you need to remember that such families have a limited amount of time to spend on involvement with their children's school and their children at home. When you confer with single-parent families, make sure that (1) the meeting starts on time, (2) you have a list of items (skills, behaviors, achievements) to discuss, (3) you have sample materials available to illustrate all points, (4) you make specific suggestions relative to one-parent environments, and (5) the meeting ends on time. One-parent families are more likely to need child care assistance to attend meetings, so child care should be planned for every parent meeting or activity.

Third, illustrate for single-parent families how they can make their time with their children more meaningful. If a child has trouble following directions, show families how to use home situations to help in this area. Children can learn to follow directions while helping families run errands, get a meal, or help with housework.

Fourth, get to know families' lifestyles and living conditions. An early childhood professional can easily say that every child should have a quiet place to study, but this may be an impossible demand for some households. You need to visit some of the homes in your community before you set meeting times, decide what family involvement activities to implement, and what you will ask of families during the year. All professionals, particularly early childhood professionals, need to keep in mind the condition of the home environment when they request that children bring certain items to school or carry out certain tasks at home. When asking for parents' help, you must be sensitive to parents' talents and time constraints.

Fifth, help develop support groups for one-parent families within the school, such as discussion groups and classes on parenting for singles. You must include the needs and abilities of one-parent families in your family involvement activities and programs. After all, single-parent families may be the majority of families represented in the program. Figure 16.8 provides some suggestions that can guide your involvement with single and working parents.

Involving Language-Minority Parents and Families

The developmental concept of family involvement is particularly important when working with language-minority families. *Language-minority parents* are individuals whose English proficiency is minimal and who lack a comprehensive knowledge of the norms and social systems in the United States. Language-minority families often face language and cultural barriers that greatly hamper their ability to become actively involved, although many have a great desire and willingness to participate in their children's education.

Because the culture of language-minority families often differs from the majority in a community, those who seek a truly collaborative community, home, and school involvement

An increasing number of children live in single-parent and step families. Many also live in foster families, and other non-traditional family forms. And in many two-parent families both parents work full days, so children come home to an empty house. Involving single and working parents presents many challenges to schools.

Communication

Communication with single-parent and other non-traditional families will be more effective if schools

- Avoid making the assumption that students live with both biological parents.
- Avoid the traditional "Dear Parents" greeting in letters and other messages, and instead use "Dear Parent," "Dear Family," "Friends," or some other form of greeting.
- Develop a system of keeping non-custodial parents informed of their children's school progress.
- Demonstrate sensitivity to the rights of non-custodial parents. Inform parents that schools may not withhold information from non-custodial parents who have the legal right to see their children's records.
- Develop a simple unobtrusive system to keep track of family changes, such as these examples:
  - ✓ At the beginning of the year ask for the names and addresses of individuals to be informed about each child and involved in school activities.
  - ✓ At mid-year send a form to each child's parents or guardians to verify that the information is still accurate. Invite the parents or guardians to indicate any changes.
- Place flyers about school events on bulletin boards of major companies in the community which are family-friendly to learning.

These approaches use different and more sensitive ways of communicating with non-traditional families, and do not require much more material resources.

Involvement

The following practices can make the involvement of single and working parents in school life more feasible:

- Hold parent-teacher conferences and other school events in the evenings.
- Welcome other children at such events, and provide organized activities or child care services.
- Provide teachers and counselors with in-service training that sensitizes them to special problems faced by children of single and working parents and the parents themselves.
- Gather information on whether joint or separate parent conferences need to be scheduled with parents.
- Sponsor evening and weekend learning activities at which parents can participate and learn with their children.
- Work with local businesses to arrange released time from work so that parents can attend conferences, volunteer or in other ways spend time at their child's school when it is in session.

Figure 16.8
Involving Single and Working Parents

Source: Reaching All Families—Creating Family-Friendly Schools, *Office of Educational Research and Improvement, U.S. Department of Education, 1996.*

must take into account the cultural features that can inhibit collaboration. Traditional styles of child rearing and family organization, attitudes toward schooling, organizations around which families center their lives, life goals and values, political influences, and methods of communication within the cultural group all have implications for parent participation.

Language-minority families often lack information about the U.S. educational system, including basic school philosophy, practice, and structure, which can result in misconceptions, fear, and a general reluctance to respond to invitations for involvement. Furthermore, this educational system may be quite different from what these families are used to. They may have been taught to avoid active involvement in the educational process, with the result that they prefer to leave all decisions concerning their children's education to professionals and administrators.

The U.S. ideal of a community-controlled and community-supported educational system must be explained to families from cultures in which this concept is not as highly valued. Traditional roles of children, professionals, and administrators also have to be explained. Many families, especially language-minority families, are quite willing to relinquish to professionals any rights and responsibilities they have for their children's education and need to be taught to assume their roles and obligations toward schooling.

Program in Action
A Partnership for Literacy

Located in Oakland's largely Latino Fruitvale neighborhood, Hawthorne—with more than 1,400 children—is the largest elementary school in the district. Eight-eight percent of the students qualify for a free or reduced lunch. The student population mirrors the state's diverse population. Students come from at least twelve different ethnic and cultural groups, and 74 percent of them speak only a limited amount of English. All communications with parents are written in six languages: Spanish, Vietnamese, Cantonese, Cambodian, English, and Lao.

Hawthorne's school reform history dates back more than fifteen years and spans three principals. With support from the state and the district, the school has implemented a wide range of programs for families and students in an effort to build a responsive, caring, and inclusive community. Programs and services include TRIBES (a process that builds respect for diversity and communication skills among children and adults), conflict mediation, a health and dental clinic, mental health services, and a parent center. As a result of these efforts, Hawthorne now serves as a model for how a school can meet the varied needs of its community in a respectful and resourceful way.

Hawthorne also is a Leadership School in the Bay Area School Reform Collaborative, the regional Annenberg reform initiative. This collaborative has stimulated and supported Hawthorne's reform work, in part with its vision for mutually accountable partnerships between school and community. The School Reform Collaborative's highest standards for partnerships serve as Hawthorne's guides:

- Whole community consensus building
- Partners in decision making and accountability
- Two-way communication and mutually beneficial relationships
- Partners in the substantive work of the school

An opportunity to build such a partnership has occurred recently at Hawthorne. In separate

meetings with teachers and administrators, parents of the Vietnamese and Cambodian students expressed concern about losing touch with their children as their children lose touch with their native language. In some cases, families literally could not communicate across the generations because the children now spoke only English and the parents spoke only their native language.

As a result of the meetings, the school has begun to offer after-school Vietnamese and Cambodian language classes. The school encourages children as well as parents to join the classes to build literacy skills.

Parents need to be informed about progress toward reform goals, but they also need to play a part in achieving them. To that end, Hawthorne has begun to test the theory that parents are more likely to become involved in the school and in their child's education if they develop a strong, trusting relationship with the child's teachers. Four teachers piloted an effort in this direction last year. The teachers were already working closely together to create a seamless continuum of expectations, curriculum, and relationships among their K-3 Spanish bilingual classes. The next step was to involve the parents of their students in a project they called Home-School Connections.

Activities included frequent information updates via phone and mail; family homework projects that encouraged reading at home; a series of family seminars on such topics as homework help, discipline, and reading; and social events. Parents felt free to visit the classrooms during and after school and to communicate with the teachers by phone. Through this pilot, parents got to know not only their child's current teacher but also the teachers their child would have in the next several years. Although it is difficult to assess the direct impact of this close family connection, last year the students in these classrooms had some of the highest reading scores in the school.

CULTURALLY SENSITIVE FAMILY INVOLVEMENT. The following suggestions for working with families are provided by Janet González-Mena, professor at Napa Valley College:[4]

- Know what each parent in your program wants for his or her child. Find out families' goals. What are their caregiving practices? What concerns do they have about their child? Encourage them to talk about all of this. Encourage them to ask questions. Encourage the conflicts to surface—to come out in the open.
- Become clear about your own values and goals. Know what you believe in. Have a bottom line, but leave space above it to be flexible. When you are clear, you are less likely to present a defensive stance in the face of conflict. When we are ambiguous, we come on the strongest.
- Become sensitive to your own discomfort. Tune in on those times when something bothers you instead of just ignoring it and hoping it will go away. Work to identify what specific behaviors of others make you uncomfortable. Try to discover exactly what in yourself creates this discomfort. A conflict may be brewing.
- Build relationships. When you do this, you enhance your chances for conflict management or resolution. Be patient. Building relationships takes time, but it enhances communications and understandings. You'll communicate better if you have a relationship, and you'll have a relationship if you learn to communicate.
- Become effective cross-cultural communicators. It is possible to learn these communication skills. Learn about communication styles that are different from your own. Teach your own communication styles. What you think a person means may not be

what he or she *really* means. Do not make assumptions. Listen carefully. Ask for clarification. Find ways to test for understanding.

- Learn how to create dialogue—how to open communication instead of shutting it down. Often, if you accept and acknowledge the other person's feelings, you encourage him or her to open up. Learn ways to let others know that you are aware of and sensitive to their feelings.
- Use a *problem-solving* rather than a *power* approach to conflicts. Be flexible—negotiate when possible. Look at your willingness to share power. Is it a control issue you are dealing with?
- Commit yourself to education—both your own and that of the families. Sometimes lack of information or understanding of each other's perspective is what keeps the conflict going.

Involving Teenage Parents

At one time, most teenage parents were married, but today the majority are not. Also, most teenage families elect to keep their children rather than put them up for adoption and are rearing them within single-parent families. Teenage families frequently live in extended families, and the child's grandmother often serves as the primary caregiver. Regardless of their living arrangements, teenage families have the following needs:

- *Support in their role as families.* Support can include information about child-rearing practices and child development. Regardless of the nature and quality of the information given to teenage families, they frequently need help in implementing the information in their interactions with their children.
- *Support in their continuing development as adolescents and young adults.* Remember that younger teenage parents are really children themselves. They need assistance in meeting their own developmental needs as well as those of their children.
- *Help with completing their own education.* Some early childhood programs provide parenting courses as well as classes designed to help teenage parent dropouts complete requirements for a high school diploma. Remember that a critical influence on children's development is the mother's education level.

As early childhood programs enroll more children of teenage families, they must be attentive to creatively and sensitively involving these families as a means of supporting the development of families and children.

Involving Fathers

More fathers are involved in parenting responsibilities than ever before. Over one-fifth of preschool children are cared for by their fathers while their mothers work outside the home.[5] The implication is clear: early childhood professionals must make special efforts to involve all fathers in their programs.

More professionals recognize that fathering and mothering are complementary processes. Definitions of nurturing are changing to include the legitimate and positive involvement of fathers in children's lives. Many fathers are competent caregivers, directly supervising children, helping set the tone for family life, providing stability to a relationship, supporting the mother's parenting role and her career goals, and personifying a masculine role model for the children. More fathers, as they discover or rediscover these parenting roles, turn to professionals for support and advice.

There are many styles of fathering. Some fathers are at home while their wives work; some have custody of their children; some are single; some dominate home life and control everything; some are passive and exert little influence in the home; some are frequently absent because their work requires travel; some take little interest in their homes and families; some are surrogates. Regardless of the roles fathers play in their children's lives, as an early childhood professional you must make special efforts to involve them, using the methods discussed in this chapter.

Involving Other Caregivers

Children of two-career families and single families often are cared for by nannies, au pairs, baby-sitters, or housekeepers. Whatever their title, these adults usually play significant roles in children's lives. Many early childhood programs and schools are reaching out to involve them in activities such as professional conferences, help with field trips, and supervision of homework. This involvement should occur with families' blessings and approvals for a cooperative working relationship.

Community Involvement and More

A comprehensive program of family involvement has, in addition to families, professionals, and schools, a fourth important component: the community. More early childhood professionals realize that neither they alone nor the limited resources of their programs are sufficient to meet the needs of many children and families. Consequently, early education professionals are seeking ways to link families to community services and resources. For example, if a child needs clothing, a professional who is aware of community resources might contact the local Salvation Army for assistance.

... video viewpoint

Feeding Hungry Children

Tired of the conditions she found in her city of Houston, Texas, Carol Porter organized an effort to feed hungry children. Her organization started out with just her family, who spent their life savings to set up Kid Care. Now Carol and her volunteers load up vans and head for Houston's poorest neighborhoods, feeding daily lunches to those who cannot provide for themselves.

REFLECTIVE DISCUSSION QUESTIONS

What effects do hunger and undernourishment have on children's learning? Why is seeing that children are well fed becoming a part of the early childhood curriculum?

REFLECTIVE DECISION MAKING

What can you do to help ensure that the children you teach are properly fed? What community agencies can you work with to help your children receive the food they need?

Using the Community to Teach

For more information about building stronger bonds between schools and communities, go to the Companion Website at http://www.prenhall.com/morrison, select chapter 16, then choose the Linking to Learning module to connect to the Communities in Schools of Washington D.C. site.

The community offers a vital and rich array of resources for helping you teach better and for helping you meet the needs of parents and their children. Schools and teachers cannot address the many issues facing children and youth without the partnership and collaboration of powerful sectors of society, including community agencies, businesses, and industry. Following are suggested actions you can take to learn to use your community in your teaching:

- *Know your students and their needs.* By knowing your students through observations, conferences with parents, and discussions with students, you can identify any barriers to their learning and learn what kind of help to seek.
- *Know your community.* Walk or drive around the community. Ask a parent to give you a tour to help familiarize you with agencies and individuals. Read the local newspaper and attend community events and activities.
- *Ask for help and support from parents and the community.* Keep in mind that many parents will not be involved unless you personally ask them. The only encouragement many individuals and local businesses will need is your invitation.
- *Develop a directory of community agencies.* Consult the business pages of local phone books, contact local chambers of commerce, and ask parents what agencies are helpful to them.
- *Compile a list of people who are willing to come to your classroom* to speak to or work with your students. You can start by asking parents to volunteer and for suggestions and recommendations of others.

Only by helping families meet their needs and those of their children will you create opportunities for these children to reach their full potential. For this reason alone, regardless of all the other benefits, family involvement programs and activities must be an essential part of every early childhood program. Families should expect nothing less from the profession, and we, in turn, must do our very best for them.

School–Business Involvement

One good way to build social capital in the community is through school–business involvement. More early childhood programs are developing this link as a means of strengthening their programs and helping children and families. For their part, businesses are anxious to develop the business–school connection in efforts to help schools better educate children. Basically, business involvement takes four forms:

- *Adopt-a-school.* Existing in about 40 percent of the elementary schools, this is the most popular type of involvement. Businesses provide tangible goods and services to schools such as guest speakers, employee tutors, small grants, and products. For example, companies such as Burger King and McDonald's provide professionals with coupons for food items. They in turn use these as incentives for achievement, appropriate behavior, literacy involvement, and so forth.
- *Project driven.* Businesses join with a school or program with the intent of bringing about change. The training of Head Start administrators illustrates this kind of involvement.

- *Reform oriented.* An individual company or a consortium gets involved to change a variety of practices throughout a district or agency.
- *Policy change.* Business leaders and organizations help develop or influence legislation and public policy. For example, one group known as the Business Roundtable seeks to promote programs of school choice in thirty states.

To take an online self-test on this chapter's contents, go to the Companion Website at http://www.prenhall.com/morrison, select chapter 16, then choose the Self Test module.

Additionally, many businesses are adopting family-friendly policies in the workplace, as in the following examples:

- Marriott International (Atlanta, Georgia). Because many service employees work non-traditional hours, Atlanta's Children's Inn will provide subsidized child care seven days a week, twenty-four hours a day. It will accommodate 250 children, and in addition to child care it will provide a variety of family services, including nutrition counseling, parenting education workshops, a community resource center, and a "Get Well" child care program for children with minor illnesses.
- U.S. Army units and installations have formed successful partnerships with local schools around the country since the mid-1980s. These partnerships are designed to improve the academic, social, and developmental skills of all children who are in need at the schools. Programs are tailored to meet specific local needs. An outstanding example of the army's partnerships can be found at Fort Hood in Killeen, Texas. The Parental Involvement Program is a huge success; after the program was piloted in 1994, the local district recorded great gains in student achievement.
- Pizza Hut Corporation has a history of helping improve reading. Its most recent addition is an effort to help motivate children to read during the summer, in conjunction with the U.S. Department of Education and Secretary Riley's Partnership for Family Involvement in Education. This effort, called Read*Write*Now!, encourages children to read thirty minutes a day and with a reading partner at least once or twice a week, learn a new vocabulary word a day, and obtain a library card. Children are rewarded at the end of the summer with a personal pan pizza. Pizza Hut also founded the BOOK IT! National Reading Incentive Program, a school-based program aimed at motivating children in grades K–6 to read by rewarding them for their reading accomplishment.
- Hewlett-Packard Company (Santa Rosa, California) teamed up with the Santa Rosa City School District to establish the first work site public school on the West Coast. The company's flextime policy enables its employees to take advantage of their proximity to the school by visiting their children during the day. The Hidden Valley Satellite School encourages parents to volunteer in the classroom, and teachers work with parents to determine the best type of help for each class.[6]

For additional Internet resources or to complete an online activity for this chapter, go to the Companion Website at http://www.prenhall.com/morrison, select chapter 16, then choose the Linking to Learning or Making Connections module.

The challenge to early childhood professionals is quite clear. Merely seeking ways to involve parents in school activities is no longer a sufficient program of parent involvement. Today, the challenge is to make families the focus of our involvement activities so that their lives and their children's lives are made better. Anything less will not help families and children access and benefit from the opportunities of the twenty-first century.

National Organizations

National programs dedicated to family involvement are a rich resource for information and support. Some of these are listed here:

Program in Action

New Kid on the Block for Parents

Parents for Public Schools (PPS), which was conceived in a Jackson, Mississippi, living room in 1989 by parents who were determined to resist middle-class flight and send their children to public schools, has come a long way in less than ten years.

The national network now has fifty-four chapters in twenty-six states, recruiting people to support public schools and advocating that parents be equal partners in making decisions about them. So when Kelly Allin Butler, the executive director of PPS, invited fifteen leading school reformers to join members at their May 1–3 national leadership conference, every one of them accepted.

The organization, based where it was founded, got a boost when it was featured in a report by the Annenberg Institute for School Reform, which examines public engagement efforts around the country.

Kristin Kurtenback of Millennium Communications Group in Washington, D.C., who conducted some of the research for the report, told PPS members that their network is unique because it's the only national organization focused solely on parents; it has both a national presence and connections in communities; its focus is systemwide, rather than on individual schools; and it's the only group actively recruiting people back into public schools.

In addition to giving parents information and providing them with a collective voice, PPS chapters can play a role as intermediaries in districts in turmoil.

While PPS expects to continue to grow, Ms. Butler said the organization is more concerned with signing up strong chapters than with sheer numbers. "It's not effective to sign up and hang out a banner and put out a newsletter," she said.

Visit Parents for Public Schools on the Web at http://www.parents4publicschools.com/.

For more information about the Institute for Responsive Education, the National Parent-Teacher Association, and other national organizations, go to the Companion Website at http://www.prenhall.com/morrison, select chapter 16, then choose the Linking to Learning module to connect to the IRE, PTA, and other Web sites.

- Institute for Responsive Education (IRE), 605 Commonwealth Ave., Boston, MA 02215; 617-353-3309.
- Center on Families, Communities, Schools and Children's Learning, 605 Commonwealth Ave., Boston, MA 02215; 617-353-3309. (The center's address and phone number are the same as IRE's.)
- Families United for Better Schools, 31 Maple Wood Mall, Philadelphia, PA 19144; 215-829-0442. This is an organization of families working to help other families work for better schools.
- National Committee for Citizens in Education (NCCE), 900 Second St., NE, Suite 8, Washington, D.C. 20002-3557; 800-638-9675. This organization seeks to inform families of their rights and to get them involved in the public schools.
- The Home and School Institute, 1201 16th St., NW, Washington, D.C. 20036; 202-466-3633.
- National Congress of Parents and Teachers (National PTA), 700 N. Rush St., Chicago, IL 60611; 312-787-0977.

THE FAMILY INVOLVEMENT PARTNERSHIP FOR LEARNING. The mission of the Family Involvement Partnership for Learning is to promote children's learning through the development of family/school/community partnerships. The national Family Involvement Partnership for Learning began as a cooperative effort between the U.S. Department of Education and the National Coalition for Parent Involvement in Education (NCPIE). NCPIE, a coalition of over one hundred national education and advocacy organizations, has been meeting for more than fifteen years to advocate the involvement of families in their children's education and to promote relationships among home, school, and community that can enhance the education of all children and youth. NCPIE represents parents, schools, communities, religious groups, and businesses.[7]

For more information about the National Coalition for Parent Involvement in Education, go to the Companion Website at http://www.prenhall.com/morrison, select chapter 16, then choose the Linking to Learning module to connect to the NCPIE site.

Web Site Connections

Many Web sites are available to help parents become more involved in their children's education. For example, the Family Education Network (http://www.familyeducation.com) and Parent Soup (http://www.parentsoup.com) offer resources and features on a wide array of educational topics. You may find other sites by entering the following keywords into one of the Internet's many available search engines:

parent involvement

community involvement

school partnerships

school/business relationships

school/community collaboration

For more information about the Family Education Network and Parent Soup, go to the Companion Website at http://www.prenhall.com/morrison, select chapter 16, then choose the Linking to Learning module to connect to the Family Education Network and Parent Soup sites.

Activities for Further Enrichment

Applications

1. List the various ways early childhood professionals communicate pupils' progress to families. Which methods do you think are the most and least effective? What specific methods do you plan to use?
2. Describe the methods and techniques you would use to publicize a parent meeting about how your school plans to involve families in their children's education.
3. You have just been appointed the program director for a family involvement program in first grade. Write objectives for the program. Develop specific activities for involving families and for providing services to them.
4. Develop specific guidelines that a child care center could use to facilitate the involvement of fathers, language-minority families, and families of children with disabilities.

Field Experiences

1. Arrange with a local school district to be present during a parent–teacher conference. Discuss with the teacher, prior to the visit, his or her objectives and procedures. After the conference, assess its success with the teacher.
2. As discussed in this chapter, there are many ways to involve parents, family members, and the community. Some things that you can do now to help you develop a program of family education and support are these:

   a. Identify your goals for family involvement and support.

   b. Develop a plan for implementing the goals that you identified.

c. Develop a plan for specifically involving fathers in your program.

Research

1. Visit social services agencies in your area, and list the services they offer.
   a. Describe how early childhood professionals can work with these agencies to meet the needs of children and families.
   b. Invite agency directors to meet with your class to discuss how they and early childhood professionals can work cooperatively to help families and children.
2. As families change, so, too, do the services they need. Interview families in as many settings as possible (e.g., urban, suburban, rural), from as many socioeconomic backgrounds as possible, and from as many kinds of families as possible. Determine what services they believe can help them most, then tell how you as a professional could help provide those services.

Readings for Further Enrichment

Carnegie Task Force on Meeting the Needs of Young Children. *Starting Points: Meeting the Needs of Our Youngest Children.* New York: Carnegie Corporation of New York, 2000.

This report focuses attention on the "quiet crisis" affecting millions of children under three and their families. It challenges professionals to create integrated programs for developing responsible parenthood, guaranteeing quality child care sources, ensuring basic health and protection, and mobilizing communities to support young children and their families.

Comer, J., Ben-Avie, M., Haynes, N., and Joyner, E. *Child by Child: The Comer Process for Change in Education.* New York: Teachers College Press, 1999.

Supports the notion that schools need to think and act beyond their safe boundaries by having caring adults reach out to children and their families. This can make schools work "when almost nothing else around them is working."

Quint, S. *Schooling Homeless Children: A Working Model for America's Public Schools.* New York: Teachers College Press, 1994.

This text makes the argument that teachers and other staff members need to make home visits for the sake of their students. It holds that children's basic needs—such as a place to take a nap or a clean set of underwear—always come first, and that there's no point in trying to teach these kids reading, math, or any other subject until these needs are met.

Smrekar, C., and Goldring, E. *School Choices in Urban America: Magnet Schools and the Pursuit of Equity.* New York: Teachers College Press, 1999.

This book offers a unique contribution to current policy debates by blending the often disconnected areas of school choice, equity, parental involvement, and desegregation to provide a current and intensive analysis of the social and political context of magnet schools.

Springate, K. W., and Stegelin, D. A. *Building School and Community Partnerships Through Parent Involvement.* Upper Saddle River, NJ: Prentice Hall, 1999.

This text focuses on the family as the "first teacher" of the child and provides the most effective strategies for involving parents in school settings. The authors examine the diversity of families in regard to culture, lifestyle, and specific issues, such as children with disabilities.

Linking to Learning

Alliance for Parental Involvement in Education

http://www.croton.com/allpie

A nonprofit organization that assists and encourages parental involvement in education, wherever that education takes place—in public schools, in private schools, at home.

Appalachia Education Laboratory

http://www.ael.org

Offers ways to keep abreast of what's happening with school–community partnerships to address the pressing needs of children and their families.

Communities in Schools of Washington, D.C. (CISDC)

http://www.cisdc.org/

CISDC works to improve the lives of children by building stronger bonds between local people and public schools. Includes information regarding communities and school partnerships, statistics, and links to other sources.

Early Childhood Educators' and Family Web Corner

http://users.sgi.net/~cokids/

Provides links to teacher pages, family pages, articles, and staff development resources.

Family Education Network

http://www.familyeducation.com

The Family Education Network is committed to strengthening and empowering families by providing communities with the counseling, education, resources, information, and training needed to

promote a positive and nurturing environment in which to raise children.

Institute for Responsive Education (IRE)

http://www.resp-ed.org

The IRE is a research-based assistance and advocacy agency promoting the partnership of schools, families, and communities with the ultimate goal of success for all children. While the primary focus of IRE is on urban educational reform in the United States, its mission is enriched and informed by also examining, communicating, and working with rural and urban schools throughout the world.

Making Lemonade

http://makinglemonade.com

In addition to chats, boards, and articles about forming support groups and helping children through divorce, this comprehensive site, run by a single mom with a sense of humor (check out the ever-changing department "and you thought you had it BAD . . . ?"), features links to a dating service and a newsletter, as well as sites for kids.

National Coalition for Parent Involvement in Education (NCPIE)

http://www.ncpie.org/

The National Coalition for Involvement in Education (NCPIE) is dedicated to developing family/school partnerships throughout America. Its mission is simple: involving parents and families in their children's lives and fostering relationships among home, school, and community, which all can enhance the education of our nation's young people.

National Network of Partnership-2000 Schools

http://www.csos.jhu.edu/p2000/

Supports the work of schools to involve families and the community and provides a research-based framework describing six types of involvement: parenting, communicating, volunteering, learning at home, decision making, and collaborating with the community.

National Parent Teacher Association (PTA)

http://www.pta.org/

Unveiling its voluntary National Standards for Parent/Family Involvement Programs, the PTA calls for schools to promote partnerships that will increase parent involvement and participation in promoting social, emotional, and academic growth of children.

NPIN (National Parent Information Network) Homepage

http://www.npin.org

Identifies specific Internet sources for parents and for those who work with parents.

nschool.com

http://www.nschool.com

For districts that want to use the Web to increase communication with parents—but are reluctant to spend thousands on software and hardware—the free nschool.com site is a good place to start.

Parent Soup

http://parentsoup.com

Offers resources and features on a wide array of educational topics.

ParentsPlace

http://parentsplace.com/family/singleparent

Covering a range of issues, including kids' self-esteem, dating, and handling household chores, this page of ParentsPlace offers a variety of informative, if earnest, articles. Livelier are its chat rooms and bulletin boards.

The Single & Custodial Father's Network

http://www.scfn.org/index.html

Created by a dad, the Single & Custodial Father's Network is a place for men who are primary caregivers to go. Here, you can hook up with others in the chat rooms and boards to explore everything from cooking to balancing work and family. This site also provides articles and links to more than twenty other sites.

ENDNOTES

[1] U.S. Department of Education, *Goals 2000* (Washington, DC: Author, 1994), n.p.

[2] Generations United, *Linking Youth and Old through Intergenerational Programs* (Washington, DC: Author, n.d.), n.p.

[3] Richard J. Stiggins, *Student-Centered Classroom Assessment*, 2nd ed. (Upper Saddle River, NJ: Merrill/Prentice Hall, 1997), p. 499.

[4] J. González-Mena, "Taking a Culturally Sensitive Approach in Infant-Toddler Programs," *Young Children* 1 (1992), pp. 8–9. Used with permission of the author.

[5] J. S. Cohen, *Parental Involvement in Education* ED 1.2:P75/6 (Washington, DC: U.S. Government Printing Office, 1991), 7.

[6] "Saving Our Schools," *Business Week* (September 14, 1992), 71.

[7] Family Involvement Partnership for Learning, *Community Update #23* (Washington, DC: Author, April 1995).

Appendix A

The NAEYC Code of Ethical Conduct

Preamble

NAEYC recognizes that many daily decisions required of those who work with young children are of a moral and ethical nature. The NAEYC Code of Ethical Conduct offers guidelines for responsible behavior and sets forth a common basis for resolving the principal ethical dilemmas encountered in early childhood education. The primary focus is on daily practice with children and their families in programs for children from birth to eight years of age: preschools, child care centers, family day care homes, kindergartens, and primary classrooms. Many of the provisions also apply to specialists who do not work directly with children, including program administrators, parent educators, college professors, and child care licensing specialists.

Standards of ethical behavior in early childhood education are based on commitment to core values that are deeply rooted in the history of our field. We have committed ourselves to:

Appreciating childhood as a unique and valuable stage of the human life cycle

Basing our work with children on knowledge of child development

Appreciating and supporting the close ties between the child and family

Recognizing that children are best understood in the context of family, culture, and society

Respecting the dignity, worth, and uniqueness of each individual (child, family member, and colleague)

Helping children and adults achieve their full potential in the context of relationships that are based on trust, respect, and positive regard

The Code sets forth a conception of our professional responsibilities in four sections, each addressing an arena of professional relationships: (1) children, (2) families, (3) colleagues, and (4) community and society. Each section includes an introduction to the pri-

---

Source: Code of Ethical Conduct and Statement of Commitment by S. Feeney and K. Kipnis. Copyright © 1992 by the National Association for the Education of Young Children. Reprinted by permission from the National Association for the Education of Young Children.

mary responsibilities of the early childhood practitioner in that arena, a set of ideals pointing in the direction of exemplary professional practice, and a set of principles defining practices that are required, prohibited, and permitted.

The ideals reflect the aspirations of practitioners. The principles are intended to guide conduct and assist practitioners in resolving ethical dilemmas encountered in the field. There is not necessarily a corresponding principle for each ideal. Both ideals and principles are intended to direct practitioners to those questions which, when responsibly answered, will provide the basis for conscientious decision making. While the Code provides specific direction for addressing some ethical dilemmas, many others will require the practitioner to combine the guidance of the Code with sound professional judgment.

The ideals and principles in this Code present a shared conception of professional responsibility that affirms our commitment to the core values of our field. The Code publicly acknowledges the responsibilities that we in the field have assumed and in so doing supports ethical behavior in our work. Practitioners who face ethical dilemmas are urged to seek guidance in the applicable parts of this Code and in the spirit that informs the whole.

Section I: Ethical Responsibilities to Children

Childhood is a unique and valuable stage in the life cycle. Our paramount responsibility is to provide safe, healthy, nurturing, and responsive settings for children. We are committed to supporting children's development by cherishing individual differences, by helping them learn to live and work cooperatively, and by promoting their self-esteem.

IDEALS

I–1.1 To be familiar with the knowledge base of early childhood education and to keep current through continuing education and in-service training.

I–1.2 To base program practices upon current knowledge in the field of child development and related disciplines and upon particular knowledge of each child.

I–1.3 To recognize and respect the uniqueness and the potential of each child.

I–1.4 To appreciate the special vulnerability of children.

I–1.5 To create and maintain safe and healthy settings that foster children's social, emotional, intellectual, and physical development and that respect their dignity and their contributions.

I–1.6 To support the right of children with special needs to participate, consistent with their ability, in regular childhood programs.

PRINCIPLES

P–1.1 Above all, we shall not harm children. We shall not participate in practices that are disrespectful, degrading, dangerous, exploitative, intimidating, psychologically damaging, or physically harmful to children. *This principle has precedence over all others in this Code.*

P–1.2 We shall not participate in practices that discriminate against children by denying benefits, giving special advantages, or excluding them from programs or activities on the basis of their race, religion, sex, national origin, or the status, behavior, or beliefs of their parents. (This principle does not apply to programs that have a lawful mandate to provide services to a particular population of children.)

P–1.3 We shall involve all of those with relevant knowledge (including staff and parents) in decisions concerning a child.

P–1.4 When, after appropriate efforts have been made with a child and the family, the child still does not appear to be benefitting from a program, we shall communicate our concern to the family in a positive way and offer them assistance in finding a more suitable setting.

P–1.5 We shall be familiar with the symptoms of child abuse and neglect and know and follow community procedures and state laws that protect children against abuse and neglect.

P–1.6 When we have evidence of child abuse or neglect, we shall report the evidence to the appropriate community agency and follow up to ensure that appropriate action has been taken. When possible, parents will be informed that the referral has been made.

P–1.7 When another person tells us of their suspicion that a child is being abused or neglected but we lack evidence, we shall assist that person in taking appropriate action to protect the child.

P–1.8 When a child protective agency fails to provide adequate protection for abused or neglected children, we acknowledge a collective ethical responsibility to work toward improvement of these services.

P–1.9 When we become aware of a practice or situation that endangers the health or safety of children, but has not been previously known to do so, we have an ethical responsibility to inform those who can remedy the situation and who can keep other children from being similarly endangered.

Section II: Ethical Responsibilities to Families

Families are of primary importance in children's development. (The term *family* may include others, besides parents, who are responsibly involved with the child.) Because the family and the early childhood educator have a common interest in the child's welfare, we acknowledge a primary responsibility to bring about collaboration between the home and school in ways that enhance the child's development.

IDEALS

I–2.1 To develop relationships of mutual trust with the families we serve.

I–2.2 To acknowledge and build upon strengths and competencies as we support families in their task of nurturing children.

I–2.3 To respect the dignity of each family and its culture, customs, and beliefs.

I–2.4 To respect families' childrearing values and their right to make decisions for their children.

I–2.5 To interpret each child's progress to parents within the framework of a developmental perspective and to help families understand and appreciate the value of developmentally appropriate early childhood programs.

I–2.6 To help family members improve their understanding of their children and to enhance their skills as parents.

I–2.7 To participate in building support networks for families by providing them with opportunities to interact with program staff and families.

PRINCIPLES

P–2.1 We shall not deny family members access to their child's classroom or program setting.

P–2.2 We shall inform families of program philosophy, policies, and personnel qualifications, and explain why we teach as we do.

P–2.3 We shall inform families of and, when appropriate, involve them in policy decisions.

P–2.4 We shall inform families of and, when appropriate, involve them in significant decisions affecting their child.

P–2.5 We shall inform the family of accidents involving their child, of risks such as exposures to contagious disease that may result in infection, and of events that might result in psychological damage.

P–2.6 We shall not permit or participate in research that could in any way hinder the education or development of the children in our programs. Families shall be fully informed of any proposed research projects involving their children and shall have the opportunity to give or withhold consent.

P–2.7 We shall not engage in or support exploitation of families. We shall not use our relationship with a family for private advantage or personal gain, or enter into relationships with family members that might impair our effectiveness in working with children.

P–2.8 We shall develop written policies for the protection of confidentiality and the disclosure of children's records. The policy documents shall be made available to all program personnel and families. Disclosure of children's records beyond family members, program personnel, and consultants having an obligation of confidentiality shall require familial consent (except in cases of abuse or neglect).

P–2.9 We shall maintain confidentiality and shall respect the family's right to privacy, refraining from disclosure of confidential information and intrusion into family life. However, when we are concerned about a child's welfare, it is permissible to reveal confidential information to agencies and individuals who may be able to act in the child's interest.

P–2.10 In cases where family members are in conflict we shall work openly, sharing our observations of the child, to help all parties involved make informed decisions. We shall refrain from becoming an advocate for one party.

P–2.11 We shall be familiar with and appropriately use community resources and professional services that support families. After a referral has been made, we shall follow up to ensure that services have been adequately provided.

Section III: Ethical Responsibilities to Colleagues

In a caring, cooperative work place human dignity is respected, professional satisfaction is promoted, and positive relationships are modeled. Our primary responsibility in this arena is to establish and maintain settings and relationships that support productive work and meet professional needs.

A—RESPONSIBILITIES TO CO-WORKERS: IDEALS

I–3A.1 To establish and maintain relationships of trust and cooperation with co-workers.

I–3A.2 To share resources and information with co-workers.

I–3A.3 To support co-workers in meeting their professional needs and in their professional development.

I–3A.4 To accord co-workers due recognition of professional achievement.

PRINCIPLES

P–3A.1 When we have concern about the professional behavior of a co-worker, we shall first let that person know of our concern and attempt to resolve the matter collegially.

P–3A.2 We shall exercise care in expressing views regarding the personal attributes or professional conduct of co-workers. Statements should be based on firsthand knowledge and relevant to the interests of children and programs.

B—RESPONSIBILITIES TO EMPLOYERS: IDEALS

I–3B.1 To assist the program in providing the highest quality of service.

I–3B.2 To maintain loyalty to the program and uphold its reputation.

PRINCIPLES

P–3B.1 When we do not agree with program policies, we shall first attempt to effect change through constructive action within the organization.

P–3B.2 We shall speak or act on behalf of an organization only when authorized. We shall take care to note when we are speaking for the organization and when we are expressing a personal judgment.

C—RESPONSIBILITIES TO EMPLOYEES: IDEALS

I–3C.1 To promote policies and working conditions that foster competence, well-being, and self-esteem in staff members.

I–3C.2 To create a climate of trust and candor that will enable staff to speak and act in the best interests of children, families, and the field of early childhood education.

I–3C.3 To strive to secure an adequate livelihood for those who work with or on behalf of young children.

PRINCIPLES

P–3C.1 In decisions concerning children and programs, we shall appropriately utilize the training, experience, and expertise of staff members.

P–3C.2 We shall provide staff members with working conditions that permit them to carry out their responsibilities, timely and nonthreatening evaluation procedures, written grievance procedures, constructive feedback, and opportunities for continuing professional development and advancement.

P–3C.3 We shall develop and maintain comprehensive written personnel policies that define program standards and, when applicable, that specify the extent to which employees are accountable for their conduct outside the work place. These policies shall be given to new staff members and shall be available for review by all staff members.

P–3C.4 Employees who do not meet program standards shall be informed of areas of concern and, when possible, assisted in improving their performance.

P–3C.5 Employees who are dismissed shall be informed of the reasons for the termination. When a dismissal is for cause, justification must be based on evidence of inadequate or inappropriate behavior that is accurately documented, current, and available for the employee to review.

P–3C.6 In making evaluations and recommendations, judgments shall be based on fact and relevant to the interests of children and programs.

P–3C.7 Hiring and promotion shall be based solely on a person's record of accomplishment and ability to carry out the responsibilities of the position.

P–3C.8 In hiring, promotion, and provision of training, we shall not participate in any form of discrimination based on race, religion, sex, national origin, handicap, age, or sexual preference. We shall be familiar with laws and regulations that pertain to employment discrimination.

Section IV: Ethical Responsibilities to Community and Society

Early childhood programs operate within a context of an immediate community made up of families and other institutions concerned with children's welfare. Our responsibilities to the community are to provide programs that meet its needs and to cooperate with agencies and professions that share responsibility for children. Because the larger society has a measure of responsibility for the welfare and protection of children, and because of our specialized expertise in child development, we acknowledge an obligation to serve as a voice for children everywhere.

IDEALS

I–4.1 To provide the community with high-quality, culturally sensitive programs and services.

I–4.2 To promote cooperation among agencies and professions concerned with the welfare of young children, their families, and their teachers.

I–4.3 To work, through education, research, and advocacy, toward an environmentally safe world in which all children are adequately fed, sheltered, and nurtured.

I–4.4 To work, through education, research, and advocacy, toward a society in which all young children have access to quality programs.

I–4.5 To promote knowledge and understanding of young children and their needs. To work toward greater social acknowledgement of children's rights and greater social acceptance of responsibility for their well-being.

I–4.6 To support policies and laws that promote the well-being of children and families. To oppose those that impair their well-being. To cooperate with other individuals and groups in these efforts.

I–4.7 To further the professional development of the field of early childhood education and to strengthen its commitment to realizing its core values as reflected in this Code.

PRINCIPLES

P–4.1 We shall communicate openly and truthfully about the nature and extent of services that we provide.

P–4.2 We shall not accept or continue to work in positions for which we are personally unsuited or professionally unqualified. We shall not offer services that we do not have the competence, qualifications, or resources to provide.

P–4.3 We shall be objective and accurate in reporting the knowledge upon which we base our program practices.

P–4.4 We shall cooperate with other professionals who work with children and their families.

P–4.5 We shall not hire or recommend for employment any person who is unsuited for a position with respect to competence, qualifications, or character.

P–4.6 We shall report the unethical or incompetent behavior of a colleague to a supervisor when informal resolution is not effective.

P–4.7 We shall be familiar with laws and regulations that serve to protect the children in our programs.

P–4.8 We shall not participate in practices which are in violation of laws and regulations that protect the children in our programs.

P–4.9 When we have evidence that an early childhood program is violating laws or regulations protecting children, we shall report it to persons responsible for the program. If compliance is not accomplished within a reasonable time, we will report the violation to appropriate authorities who can be expected to remedy the situation.

P-4.10 When we have evidence that an agency or a professional charged with providing services to children, families, or teachers is failing to meet its obligations, we acknowledge a collective ethical responsibility to report the problem to appropriate authorities or to the public.

P–4.11 When a program violates or requires its employees to violate this Code, it is permissible, after fair assessment of the evidence, to disclose the identity of that program.

Appendix B

NAEYC Guidelines for Developmentally Appropriate Practice in Early Childhood Programs

This statement defines and describes principles of developmentally appropriate practice in early childhood programs for administrators, teachers, parents, policymakers, and others who make decisions about the care and education of young children. An early childhood program is any group program in a center, school, or other facility that serves children from birth through age 8. Early childhood programs include child care centers, family child care homes, private and public preschools, kindergartens, and primary-grade schools.

The early childhood profession is responsible for establishing and promoting standards of high-quality, professional practice in early childhood programs. These standards must reflect current knowledge and shared beliefs about what constitutes high-quality, developmentally appropriate early childhood education in the context within which services are delivered.

This position paper is organized into several components, which include the following:

1. a description of the current context in which early childhood programs operate;
2. a description of the rationale and need for NAEYC's position statement;
3. a statement of NAEYC's commitment to children;
4. the statement of the position and definition of developmentally appropriate practice;
5. a summary of the principles of child development and learning and the theoretical perspectives that inform decisions about early childhood practice;
6. guidelines for making decisions about developmentally appropriate practices that address the following integrated components of early childhood practice: creating a caring community of learners, teaching to enhance children's learning and development, constructing appropriate

---

Source: From "NAEYC Position Statement: Developmentally Appropriate Practice in Early Childhood Programs Serving Children from Birth through Age 8—Adopted July 1996," Developmentally Appropriate Practice in Early Childhood Programs, *rev. ed., eds. S. Bredekamp & C. Copple (Washington, D.C.: National Association for the Education of Young Children, 1997), pp. 3–30.*

curriculum, assessing children's learning and development, and establishing reciprocal relationships with families;

7. a challenge to the field to move from either/or to both/and thinking; and
8. recommendations for policies necessary to ensure developmentally appropriate practices for all children.

This statement is designed to be used in conjunction with NAEYC's "Criteria for High Quality Early Childhood Programs," the standards for accreditation by the National Academy of Early Childhood Programs (NAEYC 1991), and with "Guidelines for Appropriate Curriculum Content and Assessment in Programs Serving Children Ages 3 through 8" (NAEYC & NAECS/SDE 1992; Bredekamp & Rosegrant 1992, 1995).

THE CURRENT CONTEXT OF EARLY CHILDHOOD PROGRAMS

The early childhood knowledge base has expanded considerably in recent years, affirming some of the profession's cherished beliefs about good practice and challenging others. In addition to gaining new knowledge, early childhood programs have experienced several important changes in recent years. The number of programs continues to increase not only in response to the growing demand for out-of-home child care but also in recognition of the critical importance of educational experiences during early years (Willer et al. 1991; NCES 1993). For example, in the late 1980s Head Start embarked on the largest expansion in its history, continuing this expansion into the 1990s with significant new services for families with infants and toddlers. The National Education Goals Panel established as an objective of Goal 1 that by the year 2000 all children will have access to high-quality, developmentally appropriate preschool programs (NEGP 1991). Welfare reform portends a greatly increased demand for child care services for even the youngest children from very-low-income families.

Some characteristics of early childhood programs have also changed in recent years. Increasingly, programs serve children and families from diverse cultural and linguistic backgrounds, requiring that all programs demonstrate understanding of and responsiveness to cultural and linguistic diversity. Because culture and language are critical components of children's development, practices cannot be developmentally appropriate unless they are responsive to cultural and linguistic diversity.

The Americans with Disabilities Act and the Individuals with Disabilities Education Act now require that all early childhood programs make reasonable accommodations to provide access for children with disabilities or developmental delays (DEC/CEC & NAEYC 1993). This legal right reflects the growing consensus that young children with disabilities are best served in the same community settings where their typically developing peers are found (DEC/CEC 1994).

The trend toward full inclusion of children with disabilities must be reflected in descriptions of recommended practices, and considerable work has been done toward converging the perspectives of early childhood and early childhood special education (Carta et al. 1991; Mallory 1992, 1994; Wolery, Strain, & Bailey 1992; Bredekamp 1993b; DEC Task Force 1993; Mallory & New 1994b; Wolery & Wilbers 1994).

Other important program characteristics include age of children and length of program day. Children are now enrolled in programs at younger ages, many from infancy. The length of the program day for all ages of children has been extended in response to the need for extended hours of care for employed families. Similarly, program sponsorship has become more diverse. The public schools in the majority of states now provide prekindergarten programs, some for children as young as 3, and many offer before- and after-school child care (Mitchell, Seligson, & Marx 1989; Seppanen, Kaplan deVries, & Seligson 1993; Adams & Sandfort 1994).

Corporate America has become a more visible sponsor of child care programs, with several key corporations leading the way in promoting high quality (for example, IBM, AT&T, and the American Business Collaboration). Family child care homes have become an increasingly visible sector of the child care community, with greater emphasis on professional development and the National Association for Family Child Care taking the lead in establishing an accreditation system for high-quality family child care (Hollestelle 1993; Cohen & Modigliani 1994; Galinsky et al. 1994). Many different settings in this country provide services to young children, and it is legitimate—even beneficial—for these settings to vary in certain ways. However, since it is vital to meet children's learning and developmental needs wherever they are served, high standards of quality should apply to all settings.

The context in which early childhood programs operate today is also characterized by ongoing debates about how best to teach young children and discussions about what sort of practice is most likely to contribute to their development and learning. Perhaps the most important contribution of NAEYC's 1987 position statement on developmentally appropriate practice (Bredekamp 1987) was that it created an opportunity for increased conversation within and outside the early childhood field about practices. In revising the position statement, NAEYC's goal is not only to improve the quality of current early childhood practice but also to continue to encourage the kind of questioning and debate among early childhood professionals that are necessary for the continued growth of professional knowledge in the field. A related goal is to express NAEYC's position more clearly so that energy is not wasted in unproductive debate about apparent rather that real differences of opinion.

RATIONALE FOR THE POSITION STATEMENT

The increased demand for early childhood education services is partly due to the increased recognition of the crucial importance of experiences during the earliest years of life. Children's experiences during early childhood not only influence their later functioning in school but can have effects throughout life. For example, current research demonstrates the early and lasting effects of children's environments and experiences on brain development and cognition (Chugani, Phelps, & Mazziotta 1987; Caine & Caine 1991; Kuhl 1994). Studies show that, "From infancy through about age 10, brain cells not only form most of the connections they will maintain throughout life but during this time they retain their greatest malleability" (Dana Alliance for Brain Initiatives 1996, 7).

Positive, supportive relationships, important during the earliest years of life, appear essential not only for cognitive development but also for healthy emotional development and social attachment (Bowlby 1969; Stern 1985). The preschool years are an optimum time for development of fundamental motor skills (Gallahue 1993), language development (Dyson & Genishi 1993), and other key foundational aspects of development that have lifelong implications.

Recognition of the importance of the early years has heightened interest and support for early childhood education programs. A number of studies demonstrating long-term, positive consequences of participation in high-quality early childhood programs for children from low-income families influenced the expansion of Head Start and public school prekindergarten (Lazar & Darlington 1982; Lee, Brooks-Gunn. & Schuur 1988; Schweinhart, Barnes, & Weikart 1993; Campbell & Ramey 1995). Several decades of research clearly demonstrate that high-quality, developmentally appropriate early childhood programs produce short- and long-term positive effects on children's cognitive and social development (Barnett 1995).

From a thorough review of the research on the long-term effects of early childhood education programs, Barnett concludes that "across all studies, the findings were relatively uniform and constitute overwhelming evidence that early childhood care and education can produce sizeable improvements in school success" (1995, 40). Children from low-income families who participated in high-quality preschool programs were significantly less likely to

have been assigned to special education, retained in grade, engaged in crime, or to have dropped out of school. The longitudinal studies, in general, suggest positive consequences for programs that used an approach consistent with principles of developmentally appropriate practice (Lazar & Darlington 1982; Berreuta-Clement et al. 1984; Miller & Bizzell 1984; Schweinhart, Weikart, & Larner 1986; Schweinhart, Barnes, & Weikart 1993; Frede 1995; Schweinhart & Weikart 1996).

Research on the long-term effects of early childhood programs indicates that children who attend good-quality child care programs, even at very young ages, demonstrate positive outcomes, and children who attend poor-quality programs show negative effects (Vandell & Powers 1983; Phillips, McCartney, & Scarr 1987; Fields et al. 1988; Vandell, Henderson, &Wilson 1988; Arnett 1989; Vandell & Corasanti 1990; Burchinal et al. 1996). Specifically, children who experience high-quality, stable child care engage in more complex play, demonstrate more secure attachments to adults and other children, and score higher on measures of thinking ability and language development. High-quality child care can predict academic success, adjustment to school, and reduced behavioral problems for children in first grade (Howes 1988).

While the potential positive effects of high-quality child care are well documented, several large-scale evaluations of child care find that high-quality experiences are not the norm (Whitebook, Howes, & Phillips 1989; Howes, Phillips, & Whitebook 1992; Layzer, Goodson, & Moss 1993; Galinsky et al. 1994; Cost, Quality, & Child Outcomes Study Team 1995). Each of these studies, which included observations of child care and preschool quality in several states, found that good quality that supports children's health and social and cognitive development is being provided in only about 15% of programs.

Of even greater concern was the large percentage of classrooms and family child care homes that were rated "barely adequate" or "inadequate" for quality. From 12 to 20% of the children were in settings that were considered dangerous to their health and safety and harmful to their social and cognitive development. An alarming number of infants and toddlers (35 to 40%) were found to be in unsafe settings (Cost, Quality, & Child Outcomes Study Team 1995).

Experiences during the earliest years of formal schooling are also formative. Studies demonstrate that children's success or failure during the first years of school often predicts the course of later schooling (Alexander & Entwisle 1988; Slavin, Karweit, & Madden 1989). A growing body of research indicates that more developmentally appropriate teaching in preschool and kindergarten predicts greater success in the early grades (Frede & Barnett 1992; Marcon 1992; Charlesworth et al. 1993).

As with preschool and child care, the observed quality of children's early schooling is uneven (Durkin 1987, 1990; Hiebert & Papierz 1990; Bryant, Clifford, & Peisner 1991; Carnegie Task Force 1996). For instance, in a statewide observational study of kindergarten classrooms, Durkin (1987) found that despite assessment results indicating considerable individual variation in children's literacy skills, which would call for various teaching strategies as well as individual and small-group work, teachers relied on one instructional strategy—whole-group, phonics instruction—and judged children who did not learn well with this one method as unready for first grade. Currently, too many children—especially children from low-income families and some minority groups—experience school failure, are retained in grade, get assigned to special education, and eventually drop out of school (Natriello, McDill, & Pallas 1990; Legters & Slavin 1992).

Results such as these indicate that while early childhood programs have the potential for producing positive and lasting effects on children, this potential will not be achieved unless more attention is paid to ensuring that all programs meet the highest standards of quality. As the number and type of early childhood programs increase, the need increases for a shared vision and agreed-upon standards of professional practice.

NAEYC'S COMMITMENT TO CHILDREN

It is important to acknowledge at the outset the core values that undergird all of NAEYC's work. As stated in NAEYC's Code of Ethical Conduct, standards of professional practice in early childhood programs are based on commitment to certain fundamental values that are deeply rooted in the history of the early childhood field:

- appreciating childhood as a unique and valuable stage of the human life cycle [and valuing the quality of children's lives in the present, not just as preparation for the future];
- basing our work with children on knowledge of child development [and learning];
- appreciating and supporting the close ties between the child and family;
- recognizing that children are best understood in the context of family, culture, and society;
- respecting the dignity, worth, and uniqueness of each individual (child, family member, and colleague); and
- helping children and adults achieve their full potential in the context of relationships that are based on trust, respect, and positive regard. (Feeney & Kipnis 1992, 3)

Taken together, these core values define NAEYC's basic commitment to children and underlie its position on developmentally appropriate practice.

Statement of the Position

Based on an enduring commitment to act on behalf of children, NAEYC's mission is to promote high-quality, developmentally appropriate programs for all children and their families. Because we define developmentally appropriate programs as programs that contribute to children's development, we must articulate our goals for children's development. The principles of practice advocated in this position statement are based on a set of goals for children: what we want for them, both in their present lives and as they develop to adulthood, and what personal characteristics should be fostered because these contribute to a peaceful, prosperous, and democratic society.

As we enter the 21st century, enormous changes are taking place in daily life and work. At the same time, certain human capacities will undoubtedly remain important elements in individual and societal well-being—no matter what economic or technological changes take place. With a recognition of both the continuities in human existence and the rapid changes in our world, broad agreement is emerging (e.g., Resnick 1996) that when today's children become adults they will need the ability to

- communicate well, respect others and engage with them to work through differences of opinion, and function well as members of a team;
- analyze situations, make reasoned judgments, and solve new problems as they emerge;
- access information through various modes, including spoken and written language, and intelligently employ complex tools and technologies as they are developed; and
- continue to learn new approaches, skills, and knowledge as conditions and needs change.

Clearly, people in the decades ahead will need, more than ever, fully developed literacy and numeracy skills, and these abilities are key goals of the educational process. In science, social studies (which includes history and geography), music and the visual arts, physical education and health, children need to acquire a body of knowledge and skills, as identified by those in the various disciplines (e.g., Bredekamp & Rosegrant 1995).

Besides acquiring a body of knowledge and skills, children must develop positive dispositions and attitudes. They need to understand that effort is necessary for achievement, for

example, and they need to have curiosity and confidence in themselves as learners. Moreover, to live in a highly pluralistic society and world, young people need to develop a positive self-identity and a tolerance for others whose perspective and experience may be different from their own.

Beyond the shared goals of the early childhood field, every program for young children should establish its own goals in collaboration with families. All early childhood programs will not have identical goals; priorities may vary in some respects because programs serve a diversity of children and families. Such differences notwithstanding, NAEYC believes that all high-quality, developmentally appropriate programs will have certain attributes in common. A high-quality early childhood program is one that provides a safe and nurturing environment that promotes the physical, social, emotional, aesthetic, intellectual, and language development of each child while being sensitive to the needs and preferences of families.

Many factors influence the quality of an early childhood program, including (but not limited to) the extent to which knowledge about how children develop and learn is applied in program practices. Developmentally appropriate programs are based on what is known about how children develop and learn; such programs promote the development and enhance the learning of each individual child served.

Developmentally appropriate practices result from the process of professionals making decisions about the well-being and education of children based on at least three important kinds of information or knowledge:

1. what is known about child development and learning—knowledge of age-related human characteristics that permits general predictions within an age range about what activities, materials, interactions, or experiences will be safe, healthy, interesting, achievable, and also challenging to children;
2. what is known about the strengths, interests, and needs of each individual child in the group to be able to adapt for and be responsive to inevitable individual variation; and
3. knowledge of the social and cultural contexts in which children live to ensure that learning experiences are meaningful, relevant, and respectful for the participating children and their families.

Furthermore, each of these dimensions of knowledge—human development and learning, individual characteristics and experiences, and social and cultural contexts—is dynamic and changing, requiring that early childhood teachers remain learners throughout their careers.

An example illustrates the interrelatedness of these three dimensions of the decision-making process. Children all over the world acquire language at approximately the same period of the life span and in similar ways (Fernald 1992). But tremendous individual variation exists in the rate and pattern of language acquisition (Fenson et al. 1994). Also, children acquire the language or languages of the culture in which they live (Kuhl 1994). Thus, to adequately support a developmental task such as language acquisition, the teacher must draw on at least all three interrelated dimensions of knowledge to determine a developmentally appropriate strategy or intervention.

Principles of Child Development and Learning That Inform Developmentally Appropriate Practice

Developmentally appropriate practice is based on knowledge about how children develop and learn. As Katz states, "In a developmental approach to curriculum design, . . . [decisions] about what should be learned and how it would best be learned depend on what we know of the learner's developmental status and our understanding of the relationships

between early experience and subsequent development" (1995, 109). To guide their decisions about practice, all early childhood teachers need to understand the developmental changes that typically occur in the years from birth through age 8 and beyond, variations in development that may occur, and how best to support children's learning and development during these years.

A complete discussion of the knowledge base that informs early childhood practice is beyond the scope of this document (see, for example, Seefeldt 1992; Sroufe, Cooper, & DeHart 1992; Kostelnik, Soderman, & Whiren 1993; Spodek 1993; Berk 1996). Because development and learning are so complex, no one theory is sufficient to explain these phenomena. However, a broad-based review of the literature on early childhood education generates a set of principles to inform early childhood practice. Principles are generalizations that are sufficiently reliable that they should be taken into account when making decisions (Katz & Chard 1989; Katz 1995). Following is a list of empirically based principles of child development and learning that inform and guide decisions about developmentally appropriate practice.

1. **Domains of children's development—physical, social, emotional, and cognitive—are closely related. Development in one domain influences and is influenced by development in other domains.**

Development in one domain can limit or facilitate development in others (Sroufe, Cooper, & DeHart 1992; Kostelnik, Soderman, & Whiren 1993). For example, when babies begin to crawl or walk, their ability to explore the world expands, and their mobility, in turn, affects their cognitive development. Likewise, children's language skill affects their ability to establish social relationships with adults and other children, just as their skill in social interaction can support or impede their language development.

Because developmental domains are interrelated, educators should be aware of and use these interrelationships to organize children's learning experiences in ways that help children develop optimally in all areas and that make meaningful connections across domains.

Recognition of the connections across developmental domains is also useful for curriculum planning with the various age groups represented in the early childhood period. Curriculum with infants and toddlers is almost solely driven by the need to support their healthy development in all domains. During the primary grades, curriculum planning attempts to help children develop conceptual understandings that apply across related subject-matter disciplines.

2. **Development occurs in a relatively orderly sequence, with later abilities, skills, and knowledge building on those already acquired.**

Human development research indicates that relatively stable, predictable sequences of growth and change occur in children during the first nine years of life (Piaget 1952; Erikson 1963; Dyson & Genishi 1993; Gallahue 1993; Case & Okamoto 1996). Predictable changes occur in all domains of development—physical, emotional, social, language, and cognitive—although the ways that these changes are manifested and the meaning attached to them vary in different cultural contexts. Knowledge of typical development of children within the age span served by the program provides a general framework to guide how teachers prepare the learning environment and plan realistic curriculum goals and objectives and appropriate experiences.

3. **Development proceeds at varying rates from child to child as well as unevenly within different areas of each child's functioning.**

Individual variation has at least two dimensions: the inevitable variability around the average or normative course of development and the uniqueness of each person as an indi-

vidual (Sroufe, Cooper, & DeHart 1992). Each child is a unique person with an individual pattern and timing of growth, as well as individual personality, temperament, learning style, and experiential and family background. All children have their own strengths, needs, and interests; for some children, special learning and developmental needs or abilities are identified. Given the enormous variation among children of the same chronological age, a child's age must be recognized as only a crude index of developmental maturity.

Recognition that individual variation is not only to be expected but also valued requires that decisions about curriculum and adults' interactions with children be as individualized as possible. Emphasis on individual appropriateness is not the same as "individualism." Rather, this recognition requires that children be considered not solely as members of an age group, expected to perform to a predetermined norm and without adaptation to individual variation of any kind. Having high expectations for all children is important, but rigid expectations of group norms do not reflect what is known about real differences in individual development and learning during the early years. Group-norm expectancy can be especially harmful for children with special learning and developmental needs (NEGP 1991; Mallory 1992; Wolery, Strain, & Bailey 1992).

4. **Early experiences have both cumulative and delayed effects on individual children's development; optimal periods exist for certain types of development and learning.**

Children's early experiences, either positive or negative, are cumulative in the sense that if an experience occurs occasionally, it may have minimal effects. If positive or negative experiences occur frequently, however, they can have powerful, lasting, even "snowballing," effects (Katz & Chard 1989; Kostelnik, Soderman, & Whiren 1993; Wieder & Greenspan 1993). For example, a child's social experiences with other children in the preschool years help him develop social skills and confidence that enable him to make friends in the early school years, and these experiences further enhance the child's social competence. Conversely, children who fail to develop minimal social competence and are neglected or rejected by peers are at significant risk to drop out of school, become delinquent, and experience mental health problems in adulthood (Asher, Hymel, & Renshaw 1984; Parker & Asher 1987).

Similar patterns can be observed in babies whose cries and other attempts at communication are regularly responded to, thus enhancing their own sense of efficacy and increasing communicative competence. Likewise, when children have or do not have early literacy experiences, such as being read to regularly, their later success in learning to read is affected accordingly. Perhaps most convincing is the growing body of research demonstrating that social and sensorimotor experiences during the first three years directly affect neurological development of the brain, with important and lasting implications for children's capacity to learn (Dana Alliance for Brain Initiatives 1996).

Early experiences can also have delayed effects, either positive or negative, on subsequent development. For instance, some evidence suggests that reliance on extrinsic rewards (such as candy or money) to shape children's behavior, a strategy that can be very effective in the short term, under certain circumstances lessens children's intrinsic motivation to engage in the rewarded behavior in the long term (Dweck 1986; Kohn 1993). For example, paying children to read books may over time undermine their desire to read for their own enjoyment and edification.

At certain points in the life span, some kinds of learning and development occur most efficiently. For example, the first three years of life appear to be an optimal period for verbal language development (Kuhl 1994). Although delays in language development due to physical or environmental deficits can be ameliorated later on, such intervention usually requires considerable effort. Similarly, the preschool years appear to be optimum for fundamental motor development (that is, fundamental motor skills are more easily and efficiently acquired

at this age) (Gallahue 1995). Children who have many opportunities and adult support to practice large-motor skills (running, jumping, hopping, skipping) during this period have the cumulative benefit of being better able to acquire more sophisticated, complex motor skills (balancing on a beam or riding a two-wheel bike) in subsequent years. On the other hand, children whose early motor experiences are severely limited may struggle to acquire physical competence and may also experience delayed effects when attempting to participate in sports or personal fitness activities later in life.

5. Development proceeds in predictable directions toward greater complexity, organization, and internalization.

Learning during early childhood proceeds from behavioral knowledge to symbolic or representational knowledge (Bruner 1983). For example, children learn to navigate their homes and other familiar settings long before they can understand the words left and right or read a map of the house. Developmentally appropriate programs provide opportunities for children to broaden and deepen their behavioral knowledge by providing a variety of first-hand experiences and by helping children acquire symbolic knowledge through representing their experiences in a variety of media, such as drawing, painting, construction of models, dramatic play, verbal and written descriptions (Katz 1995).

Even very young children are able to use various media to represent their understanding of concepts. Furthermore, through representation of their knowledge, the knowledge itself is enhanced (Edwards, Gandini, & Forman 1993; Malaguzzi 1993; Forman 1994). Representational modes and media also vary with the age of the child. For instance, most learning for infants and toddlers is sensory and motoric, but by age 2 children use one object to stand for another in play (a block for a phone or a spoon for a guitar).

6. Development and learning occur in and are influenced by multiple social and cultural contexts.

Bronfenbrenner (1979, 1989, 1993) provides an ecological model for understanding human development. He explains that children's development is best understood within the sociocultural context of the family, educational setting, community, and broader society. These various contexts are interrelated, and all have an impact on the developing child. For example, even a child in a loving, supportive family within a strong, healthy community is affected by the biases of the larger society, such as racism or sexism, and may show the effects of negative stereotyping and discrimination.

We define culture as the customary beliefs and patterns of and for behavior, both explicit and implicit, that are passed on to future generations by the society they live in and/or by a social, religious, or ethnic group within it. Because culture is often discussed in the context of diversity or multiculturalism, people fail to recognize the powerful role that culture plays in influencing the development of all children. Every culture structures and interprets children's behavior and development (Edwards & Gandini 1989; Tobin, Wu, & Davidson 1989; Rogoff et al. 1993). As Bowman states, "Rules of development are the same for all children, but social contexts shape children's development into different configurations" (1994, 220). Early childhood teachers need to understand the influence of sociocultural contexts on learning, recognize children's developing competence, and accept a variety of ways for children to express their developmental achievements (Vygotsky 1978; Wertsch 1985; Forman, Minick, & Stone 1993; New 1993, 1994; Bowman & Stott 1994; Mallory & New 1994a; Phillips 1994; Bruner 1996; Wardle 1996).

Teachers should learn about the culture of the majority of the children they serve if that culture differs from their own. However, recognizing that development and learning are influenced by social and cultural contexts does not require teachers to understand all the nuances of every cultural group they may encounter in their practice; this would be an

impossible task. Rather, this fundamental recognition sensitizes teachers to the need to acknowledge how their own cultural experiences shape their perspective and to realize that multiple perspectives, in addition to their own, must be considered in decisions about children's development and learning.

Children are capable of learning to function in more than one cultural context simultaneously. However, if teachers set low expectations for children based on their home culture and language, children cannot develop and learn optimally. Education should be an additive process. For example, children whose primary language is not English should be able to learn English without being forced to give up their home language (NAEYC 1996a). Likewise, children who speak only English benefit from learning another language. The goal is that all children learn to function well in the society as a whole and move comfortably among groups of people who come from both similar and dissimilar backgrounds.

7. **Children are active learners, drawing on direct physical and social experience as well as culturally transmitted knowledge to construct their own understandings of the world around them.**

Children contribute to their own development and learning as they strive to make meaning out of their daily experiences in the home, the early childhood program, and the community. Principles of developmentally appropriate practice are based on several prominent theories that view intellectual development from a constructivist, interactive perspective (Dewey 1916; Piaget 1952; Vygotsky 1978; DeVries & Kohlberg 1990; Rogoff 1990; Gardner 1991; Kamii & Ewing 1996).

From birth, children are actively engaged in constructing their own understandings from their experiences, and these understandings are mediated by and clearly linked to the sociocultural context. Young children actively learn from observing and participating with other children and adults, including parents and teachers. Children need to form their own hypotheses and keep trying them out through social interaction, physical manipulation, and their own thought processes—observing what happens, reflecting on their findings, asking questions, and formulating answers. When objects, events, and other people challenge the working model that the child has mentally constructed, the child is forced to adjust the model or alter the mental structures to account for the new information. Throughout early childhood, the child in processing new experiences continually reshapes, expands, and reorganizes mental structures (Piaget 1952; Vygotsky 1978; Case & Okamoto 1996). When teachers and other adults use various strategies to encourage children to reflect on their experiences by planning beforehand and "revisiting" afterward, the knowledge and understanding gained from the experience is deepened (Copple, Sigel, & Saunders 1984; Edwards, Gandini, & Forman 1993; Stremmel & Fu 1993; Hohmann & Weikart 1995).

In the statement of this principle, the term "physical and social experience" is used in the broadest sense to include children's exposure to physical knowledge, learned through firsthand experience of using objects (observing that a ball thrown in the air falls down), and social knowledge, including the vast body of culturally acquired and transmitted knowledge that children need to function in the world. For example, children progressively construct their own understanding of various symbols, but the symbols they use (such as the alphabet or numerical system) are the ones used within their culture and transmitted to them by adults.

In recent years, discussions of cognitive development have at times become polarized (see Seifert 1993). Piaget's theory stressed that development of certain cognitive structures was a necessary prerequisite to learning (i.e., development precedes learning), while other research has demonstrated that instruction in specific concepts or strategies can facilitate development of more mature cognitive structures (learning precedes development) (Vygotsky 1978; Gelman & Baillargheon 1983). Current attempts to resolve this apparent

dichotomy (Seifert 1993; Sameroff & McDonough 1994; Case & Okamoto 1996) acknowledge that essentially both theoretical perspectives are correct in explaining aspects of cognitive development during early childhood. Strategic teaching, of course, can enhance children's learning. Yet, direct instruction may be totally ineffective; it fails when it is not attuned to the cognitive capacities and knowledge of the child at that point in development.

8. **Development and learning result from interaction of biological maturation and the environment, which includes both the physical and social worlds that children live in.**

The simplest way to express this principle is that human beings are products of both heredity and environment and these forces are interrelated. Behaviorists focus on the environmental influences that determine learning, while maturationists emphasize the unfolding of predetermined, hereditary characteristics. Each perspective is true to some extent, and yet neither perspective is sufficient to explain learning or development. More often today, development is viewed as the result of an interactive, transactional process between the growing, changing individual and his or her experiences in the social and physical worlds (Scarr & McCartney 1983; Plomin 1994a, b). For example, a child's genetic makeup may predict healthy growth, but inadequate nutrition in the early years of life may keep this potential from being fulfilled. Or a severe disability, whether inherited or environmentally caused, may be ameliorated through systematic, appropriate intervention. Likewise, a child's inherited temperament—whether a predisposition to be wary or outgoing—shapes and is shaped by how other children and adults communicate with that child.

9. **Play is an important vehicle for children's social, emotional, and cognitive development, as well as a reflection of their development.**

Understanding that children are active constructors of knowledge and that development and learning are the result of interactive processes, early childhood teachers recognize that children's play is a highly supportive context for these developing processes (Piaget 1952; Fein 1981; Bergen 1988; Smilansky & Shefatya 1990; Fromberg 1992; Berk & Winsler 1995). Play gives children opportunities to understand the world, interact with others in social ways, express and control emotions, and develop their symbolic capabilities. Children's play gives adults insights into children's development and opportunities to support the development of new strategies. Vygotsky (1978) believed that play leads development, with written language growing out of oral language through the vehicle of symbolic play that promotes the development of symbolic representation abilities. Play provides a context for children to practice newly acquired skills and also to function on the edge of their developing capacities to take on new social roles, attempt novel or challenging tasks, and solve complex problems that they would not (or could not)otherwise do (Mallory & New 1994b).

Research demonstrates the importance of sociodramatic play as a tool for learning curriculum content with 3- through 6-year-old children. When teachers provide a thematic organization for play; offer appropriate props, space, and time; and become involved in the play by extending and elaborating on children's ideas, children's language and literacy skills can be enhanced (Levy, Schaefer, & Phelps 1986; Schrader 1989, 1990; Morrow 1990; Pramling 1991; Levy, Wolfgang, & Koorland 1992).

In addition to supporting cognitive development, play serves important functions in children's physical, emotional, and social development (Herron & Sutton-Smith 1971). Children express and represent their ideas, thoughts, and feelings when engaged in symbolic play. During play a child can learn to deal with emotions, to interact with others, to resolve conflicts, and to gain a sense of competence—all in the safety that only play affords. Through play, children also can develop their imaginations and creativity. Therefore, child-initiated, teacher-supported play is an essential component of developmentally appropriate practice (Fein & Rivkin 1986).

10. Development advances when children have opportunities to practice newly acquired skills as well as when they experience a challenge just beyond the level of their present mastery.

Research demonstrates that children need to be able to successfully negotiate learning tasks most of the time if they are to maintain motivation and persistence (Lary 1990; Brophy 1992). Confronted by repeated failure, most children will simply stop trying. So most of the time, teachers should give young children tasks that with effort they can accomplish and present them with content that is accessible at their level of understanding. At the same time, children continually gravitate to situations and stimuli that give them the chance to work at their "growing edge" (Berk & Winsler 1995; Bodrova & Leong 1996). Moreover, in a task just beyond the child's independent reach, the adult and more-competent peers contribute significantly to development by providing the supportive "scaffolding" that allows the child to take the next step.

Development and learning are dynamic processes requiring that adults understand the continuum, observe children closely to match curriculum and teaching to children's emerging competencies, needs, and interests, and then help children move forward by targeting educational experiences to the edge of children's changing capacities so as to challenge but not frustrate them. Human beings, especially children, are highly motivated to understand what they almost, but not quite, comprehend and to master what they can almost, but not quite, do (White 1965; Vygotsky 1978). The principle of learning is that children can do things first in a supportive context and then later independently and in a variety of contexts. Rogoff (1990) describes the process of adult-assisted learning as "guided participation" to emphasize that children actively collaborate with others to move to more complex levels of understanding and skill.

11. Children demonstrate different modes of knowing and learning and different ways of representing what they know.

For some time, learning theorists and developmental psychologists have recognized that human beings come to understand the world in many ways and that individuals tend to have preferred or stronger modes of learning. Studies of differences in learning modalities have contrasted visual, auditory, or tactile learners. Other work has identified learners as field-dependent or independent (Witkin 1962). Gardner (1983) expanded on this concept by theorizing that human beings possess at least seven "intelligences." In addition to having the ones traditionally emphasized in schools, linguistic and logical-mathematical, individuals are more or less proficient in at least these other areas: musical, spatial, bodily-kinesthetic, intrapersonal, and interpersonal.

Malaguzzi (1993) used the metaphor of "100 languages" to describe the diverse modalities through which children come to understand the world and represent their knowledge. The processes of representing their understanding can with the assistance of teachers help children deepen, improve, and expand their understanding (Copple, Sigel, & Saunders 1984; Forman 1994; Katz 1995). The principle of diverse modalities implies that teachers should provide not only opportunities for individual children to use their preferred modes of learning to capitalize on their strengths (Hale-Benson 1986) but also opportunities to help children develop in the modes or intelligences in which they may not be as strong.

12. Children develop and learn best in the context of a community where they are safe and valued, their physical needs are met, and they feel psychologically secure.

Maslow (1954) conceptualized a hierarchy of needs in which learning was not considered possible unless physical and psychological needs for safety and security were first met. Because children's physical health and safety too often are threatened today, programs for young children must not only provide adequate health, safety, and nutrition but may also need to ensure more comprehensives services, such as physical, dental, and mental health

and social services (NASBE 1991; U.S. Department of Health & Human Services 1996). In addition, children's development in all areas is influenced by their ability to establish and maintain a limited number of positive, consistent primary relationships with adults and other children (Bowlby 1969; Stern 1985; Garbarino et al. 1992). These primary relationships begin in the family but extend over time to include children's teachers and members of the community; therefore, practices that are developmentally appropriate address children's physical, social, and emotional needs as well as their intellectual development.

A linear listing of principles of child development and learning, such as the above, cannot do justice to the complexity of the phenomena that it attempts to describe and explain. Just as all domains of development and learning are interrelated, so, too, there are relationships among the principles. Similarly, the following guidelines for practice do not match up one-to-one with the principles. Instead, early childhood professionals draw on all these fundamental ideas (as well as many others)when making decisions about their practice.

Guidelines for Decisions About Developmentally Appropriate Practice

An understanding of the nature of development and learning during the early childhood years, from birth through age 8, generates guidelines that inform the practices of early childhood educators. Developmentally appropriate practice requires that teachers integrate the many dimensions of their knowledge base. They must know about child development and the implications of this knowledge for how to teach, the content of the curriculum—what to teach and when—how to assess what children have learned, and how to adapt curriculum and instruction to children's individual strengths, needs, and interest. Further, they must know the particular children they teach and their families and be knowledgeable as well about the social and cultural context.

The following guidelines address five interrelated dimensions of early childhood professional practice: creating a caring community of learners, teaching to enhance development and learning, constructing appropriate curriculum, assessing children's development and learning, and establishing reciprocal relationships with families. (The word teacher is used to refer to any adult responsible for a group of children in any early childhood program, including infant/ toddler caregivers, family child care providers, and specialists in other disciplines who fulfill the role of teacher.)

Examples of appropriate and inappropriate practice in relation to each of these dimensions are given for infants and toddlers (Part 3, pp. 72–90), children 3 through 5 (Part 4, pp. 123–35), and children 6 through 8 (Part 5, pp. 161–78). In the references at the end of each part, readers will be able to find fuller discussion of the points summarized here and strategies for implementation.

1. CREATING A CARING COMMUNITY OF LEARNERS

Developmentally appropriate practices occur within a context that supports the development of relationships between adults and children, among children, among teachers, and between teachers and families. Such a community reflects what is known about the social construction of knowledge and the importance of establishing a caring, inclusive community in which all children can develop and learn.

A. The early childhood setting functions as a community of learners in which all participants consider and contribute to each other's well-being and learning.

B. Consistent, positive relationships with a limited number of adults and other children are a fundamental determinant of healthy human development and provide the context for children to learn about themselves and their world and also how to develop positive, constructive

relationships with other people. The early childhood classroom is a community in which each child is valued. Children learn to respect and acknowledge differences in abilities and talents and to value each person for his or her strengths.

C. Social relationships are an important context for learning. Each child has strengths or interests that contribute to the overall functioning of the group. When children have opportunities to play together, work on projects in small groups, and talk with other children and adults, their own development and learning are enhanced. Interacting with other children in small groups provides a context for children to operate on the edge of their developing capacities. The learning environment enables children to construct understanding through interactions with adults and other children.

D. The learning environment is designed to protect children's health and safety and is supportive of children's physiological needs for activity, sensory stimulation, fresh air, rest, and nourishment. The program provides a balance of rest and active movement for children throughout the program day. Outdoor experiences are provided for children of all ages. The program protects children's psychological safety; that is, children feel secure, relaxed, and comfortable rather than disengaged, frightened, worried, or stressed.

E. Children experience an organized environment and an orderly routine that provides an overall structure in which learning takes place; the environment is dynamic and changing but predictable and comprehensible from a child's point of view. The learning environment provides a variety of materials and opportunities for children to have firsthand, meaningful experiences.

2. TEACHING TO ENHANCE DEVELOPMENT AND LEARNING

Adults are responsible for ensuring children's healthy development and learning. From birth, relationships with adults are critical determinants of children's healthy social and emotional development and serve as well as mediators of language and intellectual development. At the same time, children are active constructors of their own understanding, who benefit from initiating and regulating their own learning activities and interacting with peers. Therefore, early childhood teachers strive to achieve an optimal balance between children's self-initiated learning and adult guidance or support.

Teachers accept responsibility for actively supporting children's development and provide occasions for children to acquire important knowledge and skills. Teachers use their knowledge of child development and learning to identify the range of activities, materials, and learning experiences that are appropriate for a group or individual child. This knowledge is used in conjunction with knowledge of the context and understanding about individual children's growth patterns, strengths, needs, interests, and experiences to design the curriculum and learning environment and guide teachers' interactions with children. The following guidelines describe aspects of the teachers' role in making decisions about practice:

A. Teachers respect, value, and accept children and treat them with dignity at all times.

B. Teachers make it a priority to know each child well.

(1) Teachers establish positive, personal relationships with children to foster the child's development and keep informed about the child's needs and potentials. Teachers listen to children and adapt their responses to children's differing needs, interests, styles, and abilities.

(2) Teachers continually observe children's spontaneous play and interaction with the physical environment and with other children to learn about their interests, abilities, and developmental progress. On the basis of this information, teachers plan experiences that enhance children's learning and development.

(3) Understanding that children develop and learn in the context of their families and communities, teachers establish relationships with families that increase their knowledge of children's lives outside the classroom and their awareness of the perspectives and priorities of those individuals most significant in the child's life.

(4) Teachers are alert to signs of undue stress and traumatic events in children's lives and aware of effective strategies to reduce stress and support the development of resilience.

(5) Teachers are responsible at all times for all children under their supervision and plan for children's increasing development of self-regulation abilities.

C. Teachers create an intellectually engaging, responsive environment to promote each child's learning and development.

(1) Teachers use their knowledge about children in general and the particular children in the group as well as their familiarity with what children need to learn and develop in each curriculum area to organize the environment and plan curriculum and teaching strategies.

(2) Teachers provide children with a rich variety of experiences, projects, materials, problems, and ideas to explore and investigate, ensuring that these are worthy of children's attention.

(3) Teachers provide children with opportunities to make meaningful choices and time to explore through active involvement. Teachers offer children the choice to participate in a small-group or a solitary activity, assist and guide children who are not yet able to use and enjoy child-choice activity periods, and provide opportunities for practice of skills as a self-chosen activity.

(4) Teachers organize the daily and weekly schedule and allocate time so as to provide children with extended blocks of time in which to engage in play, projects, and/or study in integrated curriculum.

D. Teachers make plans to enable children to attain key curriculum goals across various disciplines, such as language arts, mathematics, social studies, science, art, music, physical education, and health (see "Constructing Appropriate Curriculum," pp. 547–548).

(1) Teachers incorporate a wide variety of experiences, materials and equipment, and teaching strategies in constructing curriculum to accommodate a broad range of children's individual differences in prior experiences, maturation rates, styles of learning, needs, and interests.

(2) Teachers bring each child's home culture and language into the shared culture of the school so that the unique contributions of each group are recognized and valued by others.

(3) Teachers are prepared to meet identified special needs of individual children, including children with disabilities and those who exhibit unusual interests and skills. Teachers use all the strategies identified here, consult with appropriate specialists, and see that the child gets the specialized services he or she requires.

E. Teachers foster children's collaboration with peers on interesting, important enterprises.

(1) Teachers promote children's productive collaboration without taking over to the extent that children lose interest.

(2) Teachers use a variety of ways of flexibly grouping children for the purposes of instruction, supporting collaboration among children, and building a sense of community. At various times, children have opportunities to work individually, in small groups, and with the whole group.

F. Teachers develop, refine, and use a wide repertoire of teaching strategies to enhance children's learning and development.

(1) To help children develop their initiative, teachers encourage them to choose and plan their own learning activities.

(2) Teachers pose problems, ask questions, and make comments and suggestions that stimulate children's thinking and extend their learning.

(3) Teachers extend the range of children's interests and the scope of their thought through presenting novel experiences and introducing stimulating ideas, problems, experiences, or hypotheses.

(4) To sustain an individual child's effort or engagement in purposeful activities, teachers select from a range of strategies, including but not limited to modeling, demonstrating specific skills, and providing information, focused attention, physical proximity, verbal

encouragement, reinforcement and other behavioral procedures, as well as additional structure and modification of equipment or schedules as needed.

(5) Teachers coach and/or directly guide children in the acquisition of specific skills as needed.

(6) Teachers calibrate the complexity and challenge of activities to suit children's level of skill and knowledge, increasing the challenge as children gain competence and understanding.

(7) Teachers provide cues and other forms of "scaffolding" that enable the child to succeed in a task that is just beyond his or her ability to complete alone.

(8) To strengthen children's sense of competence and confidence as learners, motivation to persist, and willingness to take risks, teachers provide experiences for children to be genuinely successful and to be challenged.

(9) To enhance children's conceptual understanding, teachers use various strategies that encourage children to reflect on and "revisit" their learning experiences.

G. Teachers facilitate the development of responsibility and self-regulation in children.

(1) Teachers set clear, consistent, and fair limits for children's behavior and hold children accountable to standards of acceptable behavior. To the extent that children are able, teachers engage them in developing rules and procedures for behavior of class members.

(2) Teachers redirect children to more acceptable behavior or activity or use children's mistakes as learning opportunities, patiently reminding children of rules and their rationale as needed.

(3) Teachers listen and acknowledge children's feelings and frustrations, respond with respect, guide children to resolve conflicts, and model skills that help children to solve their own problems.

3. CONSTRUCTING APPROPRIATE CURRICULUM

The content of the early childhood curriculum is determined by many factors, including the subject matter of the disciplines, social or cultural values, and parental input. In developmentally appropriate programs, decisions about curriculum content also take into consideration the age and experience of the learners. Achieving success for all children depends, among other essentials, on providing a challenging, interesting, developmentally appropriate curriculum. NAEYC does not endorse specific curricula. However, one purpose of these guidelines is as a framework for making decisions about developing curriculum or selecting a curriculum model. Teachers who use a validated curriculum model benefit from the evidence of its effectiveness and the accumulated wisdom and experience of others.

In some respects, the curriculum strategies of many teachers today do not demand enough of children and in other ways demand too much of the wrong thing. On the one hand, narrowing the curriculum to those basic skills that can be easily measured on multiple-choice tests diminishes the intellectual challenge for many children. Such intellectually impoverished curriculum underestimates the true competence of children, which has been demonstrated to be much higher than is often assumed (Gelman & Baillargeon 1983; Gelman & Meck 1983; Edwards, Gandini, & Forman 1993; Resnick 1996). Watered-down, oversimplified curriculum leaves many children unchallenged, bored, uninterested, or unmotivated. In such situations, children's experiences are marked by a great many missed opportunities for learning.

On the other hand, curriculum expectations in the early years of schooling sometimes are not appropriate for the age groups served. When next-grade expectations of mastery of basic skills are routinely pushed down to the previous grade and whole group and teacher-led instruction is the dominant teaching strategy, children who cannot sit still and attend to teacher lectures or who are bored and unchallenged or frustrated by doing workbook pages for long periods of time are mislabeled as immature, disruptive, or unready for school (Shepard & Smith 1988). Constructing appropriate curriculum requires attention to at least the following guidelines for practice:

A. Developmentally appropriate curriculum provides for all areas of a child's development: physical, emotional, social, linguistic, aesthetic, and cognitive.

B. Curriculum includes a broad range of content across disciplines that is socially relevant, intellectually engaging, and personally meaningful to children.

C. Curriculum builds upon what children already know and are able to do (activating prior knowledge) to consolidate their learning and to foster their acquisition of new concepts and skills.

D. Effective curriculum plans frequently integrate across traditional subject-matter divisions to help children make meaningful connections and provide opportunities for rich conceptual development; focusing on one subject is also a valid strategy at times.

E. Curriculum promotes the development of knowledge and understanding, processes and skills, as well as the dispositions to use and apply skills and to go on learning.

F. Curriculum content has intellectual integrity, reflecting the key concepts and tools of inquiry of recognized disciplines in ways that are accessible and achievable for young children, ages 3 through 8 (e.g., Bredekamp & Rosegrant 1992, 1995). Children directly participate in study of the disciplines, for instance by conducting scientific experiments, writing, performing, solving mathematical problems, collecting and analyzing data, collecting oral history, and performing other roles of experts in the disciplines.

G. Curriculum provides opportunities to support children's home culture and language while also developing all children's abilities to participate in the shared culture of the program and the community.

H. Curriculum goals are realistic and attainable for most children in the designated age range for which they are designed.

I. When used, technology is physically and philosophically integrated in the classroom curriculum and teaching. (See "NAEYC Position Statement: Technology and Young Children—Ages Three through Eight" [NAEYC 1996b].)

4. ASSESSING CHILDREN'S LEARNING AND DEVELOPMENT

Assessment of individual children's development and learning is essential for planning and implementing appropriate curriculum. In developmentally appropriate programs, assessment and curriculum are integrated, with teachers continually engaging in observational assessment for the purpose of improving teaching and learning.

Accurate assessment of young children is difficult because their development and learning are rapid, uneven, episodic, and embedded within specific cultural and linguistic contexts. Too often, inaccurate and inappropriate assessment measures have been used to label, track, or otherwise harm young children. Developmentally appropriate assessment practices are based on the following guidelines:

A. Assessment of young children's progress and achievements is ongoing, strategic, and purposeful. The results of assessment are used to benefit children—in adapting curriculum and teaching to meet the developmental and learning needs of children, communicating with the child's family, and evaluating the program's effectiveness for the purpose of improving the program.

B. The content of assessments reflects progress toward important learning and developmental goals. The program has a systematic plan for collecting and using assessment information that is integrated with curriculum planning.

C. The methods of assessment are appropriate to the age and experiences of young children. Therefore, assessment of young children relies heavily on the results of observations of children's development, descriptive data, collections of representative work by children, and demonstrated performance during authentic, not contrived, activities. Input from families as well as children's evaluations of their own work are part of the overall assessment strategy.

D. Assessments are tailored to a specific purpose and used only for the purpose for which they have been demonstrated to produce reliable, valid information.

E. Decisions that have a major impact on children, such as enrollment or placement, are never made on the basis of a single developmental assessment or screening device but are based on multiple sources of relevant information, particularly observations by teachers and parents.

F. To identify children who have special learning or developmental needs and to plan appropriate curriculum and teaching for them, developmental assessments and observations are used.

G. Assessment recognizes individual variation in learners and allows for differences in styles and rates of learning. Assessment takes into consideration such factors as the child's facility in English, stage of language acquisition, and whether the child has had the time and opportunity to develop proficiency in his or her home language as well as in English.

H. Assessment legitimately addresses not only what children can do independently but what they can do with assistance from other children or adults. Teachers study children as individuals as well as in relationship to groups by documenting group projects and other collaborative work.

(For a more complete discussion of principles of appropriate assessment, see the position statement Guidelines for Appropriate Curriculum Content and Assessment for Children Ages 3 through 8 [NAEYC & NAECS/SDE 1992]; see also Shepard 1994.)

5. ESTABLISHING RECIPROCAL RELATIONSHIPS WITH FAMILIES

Developmentally appropriate practices derive from deep knowledge of individual children and the context within which they develop and learn. The younger the child, the more necessary it is for professionals to acquire this knowledge through relationships with children's families. The traditional approach to families has been a parent education orientation in which the professionals see themselves as knowing what is best for children and view parents as needing to be educated. There is also the limited view of parent involvement that sees PTA membership as the primary goal. These approaches do not adequately convey the complexity of the partnership between teachers and parents that is a fundamental element of good practice (Powell 1994).

When the parent education approach is criticized in favor of a more family-centered approach, this shift may be misunderstood to mean that parents dictate all program content and professionals abdicate responsibility, doing whatever parents want regardless of whether professionals agree that it is in children's best interest. Either of these extremes oversimplifies the importance of relationships with families and fails to provide the kind of environment in which parents and professionals work together to achieve shared goals for children; such programs with this focus are characterized by at least the following guidelines for practice:

A. Reciprocal relationships between teachers and families require mutual respect, cooperation, shared responsibility, and negotiation of conflicts toward achievement of shared goals.

B. Early childhood teachers work in collaborative partnerships with families, establishing and maintaining regular, frequent two-way communication with children's parents.

C. Parents are welcome in the program and participate in decisions about their children's care and education. Parents observe and participate and serve in decision-making roles in the program.

D. Teachers acknowledge parents' choices and goals for children and respond with sensitivity and respect to parents' preferences and concerns without abdicating professional responsibility to children.

E. Teachers and parents share their knowledge of the child and understanding of children's development and learning as part of day-to-day communication and planned conferences. Teachers support families in ways that maximally promote family decision-making capabilities and competence.

F. To ensure more accurate and complete information, the program involves families in assessing and planning for individual children.

G. The program links families with a range of services, based on identified resources, priorities, and concerns.

H. Teachers, parents, programs, social service and health agencies, and consultants who may have educational responsibility for the child at different times should, with family participation, share developmental information about children as they pass from one level or program to another.

Moving from Either/Or to Both/And Thinking in Early Childhood Practice

Some critical reactions to NAEYC's (1987) position statement on developmentally appropriate practice reflect a recurring tendency in the American discourse on education: the polarizing into *either/or* choices of many questions that are more fruitfully seen as *both/ands*. For example, heated debates have broken out about whether children in the early grades should receive whole-language or phonics instruction, when, in fact, the two approaches are quite compatible and most effective in combination.

It is true that there are practices that are clearly inappropriate for early childhood professionals—use of physical punishment or disparaging verbal comments about children, discriminating against children or their families, and many other examples that could be cited (see Parts 3, 4, and 5 for examples relevant to different age groups). However, most questions about practice require more complex responses. It is not that children need food **or** water; they need both.

To illustrate the many ways that early childhood practice draws on both/and thinking and to convey some of the complexity and interrelationship among the principles that guide our practice, we offer the following statements as **examples**:

- Children construct their own understanding of concepts, **and** they benefit from instruction by more competent peers and adults.
- Children benefit from opportunities to see connections across disciplines through integration of curriculum **and** from opportunities to engage in in-depth study within a content area.
- Children benefit from predictable structure and orderly routine in the learning environment **and** from the teachers' flexibility and spontaneity in responding to their emerging ideas, needs, and interests.
- Children benefit from opportunities to make meaningful choices about what they will do and learn **and** from having a clear understanding of the boundaries within which choices are permissible.
- Children benefit from situations that challenge them to work at the edge of their developing capacities **and** from ample opportunities to practice newly acquired skills and to acquire the disposition to persist.
- Children benefit from opportunities to collaborate with their peers and acquire a sense of being part of a community **and** from being treated as individuals with their own strengths, interests, and needs.
- Children need to develop a positive sense of their own self-identity **and** respect for other people whose perspectives and experiences may be different from their own.
- Children have enormous capacities to learn and almost boundless curiosity about the world, **and** they have recognized, age-related limits on their cognitive and linguistic capacities.
- Children benefit from engaging in self-initiated, spontaneous play, **and** from teacher-planned and -structured activities, projects, and experiences.

The above list is not exhaustive. Many more examples could be cited to convey the interrelationships among the principles of child development and learning or among the guidelines for early childhood practice.

Policies Essential for Achieving Developmentally Appropriate Early Childhood Programs

Early childhood professionals working in diverse situations with varying levels of funding and resources are responsible for implementing practices that are developmentally appropriate for the children they serve. Regardless of the resources available, professionals have an ethical responsibility to practice, to the best of their ability, according to the standards of their profession. Nevertheless, the kinds of practices advocated in this position statement are more likely to be implemented within an infrastructure of supportive policies and resources. NAEYC strongly recommends that policymaking groups at the state and local levels consider the following when implementing early childhood programs:

1. A comprehensive professional preparation and development system is in place to ensure that early childhood programs are staffed with qualified personnel (NAEYC 1994).
    - A system exists for early childhood professionals to acquire the knowledge and practical skills needed to practice through college-level specialized preparation in early childhood education/child development.
    - Teachers in early childhood programs are encouraged and supported to obtain and maintain, through study and participation in inservice training, current knowledge of child development and learning and its application to early childhood practice.
    - Specialists in early childhood special education are available to provide assistance and consultation in meeting the individual needs of children in the program.
    - In addition to management and supervision skills, administrators of early childhood programs have appropriate professional qualifications, including training specific to the education and development of young children, and they provide teachers time and opportunities to work collaboratively with colleagues and parents.
2. Funding is provided to ensure adequate staffing of early childhood programs and fair staff compensation that promotes continuity of relationships among adults and children (Willer 1990).
    - Funding is adequate to limit the size of the groups and provide sufficient numbers of adults to ensure individualized and appropriate care and education. Even the most well-qualified teacher cannot individualize instruction and adequately supervise too large a group of young children. An acceptable adult-child ratio for 4- and 5-year-olds is two adults with no more than 20 children. (Ruopp et al. 1979; Francis & Self 1982; Howes 1983; Taylor & Taylor 1989; Howes, Philips, & Whitebook 1992; Cost, Quality, & Child Outcomes Study Team 1995; Howes, Smith & Galinsky 1995). Younger children require much smaller groups. Group size and ratio of children to adults should increase gradually through the primary grades, but one teacher with no more than 18 children or two adults with no more than 25 children is optimum (Nye et al. 1992; Nye, Boyd-Zaharias, & Fulton 1994). Inclusion of children with disabilities may necessitate additional adults or smaller group size to ensure that all children's needs are met.
    - Programs offer staff salaries and benefits commensurate with the skills and qualifications required for specific roles to ensure the provision of quality services and the effective recruitment and retention of qualified, competent staff. (See Compensation Guidelines for Early Childhood Professionals [NAEYC 1993]).
    - Decisions related to how programs are staffed and how children are grouped result in increased opportunities for children to experience continuity of relationships with teachers and other children. Such strategies include but are not limited to multiage grouping and multiyear teacher-child relationships (Katz, Evangelou, & Hartman 1990; Zero to Three 1995; Burke 1996).

3. Resources and expertise are available to provide safe, stimulating learning environments with a sufficient number and variety of appropriate materials and equipment for the age group served (Bronson 1995; Kendrick, Kaufmann, & Messenger 1995).

4. Adequate systems for regulating and monitoring the quality of early childhood programs are in place (see position on licensing [NAEYC 1987]; accreditation criteria and procedures [NAEYC 1991]).

5. Community resources are available and used to support the comprehensive needs of children and families (Kagan 1991; NASBE 1991; Kagan et al. 1995; NCSL 1995).

6. When individual children do not make expected learning progress, neither grade retention nor social promotion are used; instead, initiatives such as more focused time, individualized instruction, tutoring, or other individual strategies are used to accelerate children's learning (Shepard & Smith 1989; Ross et al. 1995).

7. Early childhood programs use multiple indicators of progress in all development domains to evaluate the effect of the program on children's development and learning and regularly report children's progress to parents. Group-administered, standardized, multiple-choice achievement tests are not used before third grade, preferably before fourth grade. When such tests are used to demonstrate public accountability, a sampling method is used (see Shepard 1994).

References

Adams, G., & J. Sandfort. 1994. *First steps, promising futures: State prekindergarten initiatives in the early 1990s.* Washington. DC: Children's Defense Fund.

Alexander, K.L., & D.R. Entwisle. 1988. *Achievement in the first 2 years of school: Patterns and processes.* Monographs of the Society for Research in Child Development, vol. 53, no. 2, serial no. 218. Ann Arbor: University of Michigan.

Arnett, J. 1989. Caregivers in day-care centers: Does training matter? *Journal of Applied Developmental Psychology* 10 (4): 541–52.

Asher, S., S. Hymel, & P. Renshaw. 1984. Loneliness in children. *Child Development* 55: 1456–64.

Barnett, W.S. 1995. Long-term effects of early childhood programs on cognitive and school outcomes. *The Future of Children* 5 (3): 25–50.

Bergen, D. 1988. *Play as a medium for learning and development.* Portsmouth, NH: Heinemann.

Berk, L.E. 1996. *Infants and children: Prenatal through middle childhood.* 2d ed. Needham Heights, MA: Allyn & Bacon.

Berk, L., & A. Winsler. 1995. *Scaffolding children's learning: Vygotsky and early childhood education.* Washington, DC: NAEYC.

Berruetta-Clement, J.R., L.J. Schweinhart, W.S. Barnett, A.S. Epstein, & D.P. Weikart. 1984. *Changed lives: The effects of the Perry Preschool Program on youths through age 19.* Monographs of the High/Scope Educational Research Foundation, no. 8. Ypsilanti, MI: High/Scope Press.

Bodrova, E., & D. Leong. 1996. *Tools of the mind: The Vygotskian approach to early childhood education.* Englewood Cliffs, NJ: Merrill/Prentice Hall.

Bowlby, J. 1969. *Attachment and loss: Vol.1. Attachment.* New York: Basic.

Bowman, B. 1994. The challenge of diversity. *Phi Delta Kappan* 76 (3): 218–25.

Bowman, B., & F. Stott. 1994. Understanding development in a cultural context: The challenge for teachers. In *Diversity and developmentally appropriate practices: Challenges for early childhood education,* eds. B. Mallory & R. New, 119–34. New York: Teachers College Press.

Bredekamp, S., ed. 1987. *Developmentally appropriate practice in early childhood programs serving children from birth through age 8.* Exp. ed. Washington, DC: NAEYC.

Bredekamp, S. 1993a. Reflections on Reggio Emilia. *Young Children* 49 (1): 13–17.

Bredekamp, S. 1993b. The relationship between early childhood education and early childhood special education: Healthy marriage or family feud? *Topics in Early Childhood Special Education* 13 (3): 258–73.

Bredekamp, S., & T. Rosegrant, eds. 1992. *Reaching potentials: Appropriate curriculum and assessment for young children, volume 1.* Washington, DC: NAEYC.

Bredekamp, S., & T. Rosegrant, eds. 1995. *Reaching potentials: Transforming early childhood curriculum and assessment, volume 2.* Washington, DC: NAEYC.

Bronfenbrenner, U. 1979. *The ecology of human development: Experiments by nature and design.* Cambridge, MA: Harvard University Press.

Bronfenbrenner, U. 1989. Ecological systems theory. In *Annals of child development,* Vol. 6, ed. R. Vasta, 187–251. Greenwich, CT: JAI Press.

Bronfenbrenner, U. 1993. The ecology of cognitive development: Research models and fugitive findings. In *Development in context,* eds. R.H. Wozniak & K.W. Fischer, 3–44. Hillsdale, NJ: Erlbaum.

Bronson, M.B. 1995. *The right stuff for children birth to 8: Selecting play materials to support development.* Washington, DC: NAEYC.

Brophy, J. 1992. Probing the subtleties of subject matter teaching. *Educational Leadership* 49 (7): 4–8.

Bruner, J.S. 1993. *Child's talk: Learning to use language.* New York: Norton.

Bruner, J.S. 1996. *The culture of education.* Cambridge, MA: Harvard University Press.

Bryant, D.M., R. Clifford, & E.S. Peisner. 1991. Best practices for beginners: Developmental appropriateness in kindergarten. *American Educational Research Journal* 28 (4): 783–803.

Burchinal, M., J. Robert, L. Nabo, & D. Bryant. 1996. Quality of center child care and infant cognitive and language development. *Child Development* 67 (2): 606–20.

Burke, D. 1966. Multi-year teacher/student relationships are a long-overdue arrangement. *Phi Delta Kappan* 77 (5): 360–61.

Caine, R., & G. Caine. 1991. *Making connections: Teaching and the human brain.* New York: Addison-Wesley.

Campbell, F., & C. Ramey. 1995. Cognitive and school outcomes for high-risk African-American students at middle adolescence: Positive effects of early intervention. *American Educational Research Journal* 32 (4): 743–72.

Carnegie Task Force on Learning in the Primary Grades. 1996. *Years of promise: A comprehensive learning strategy for America's children.* New York: Carnegie Corporation of New York.

Carta, J., I. Schwartz, J. Atwater, & S. McConnell. 1991. Developmentally appropriate practice: Appraising its usefulness for young children with disabilities. *Topics in Early Childhood Special Education* 11 (1): 1–20.

Case, R., & Y. Okamoto. 1996. *The role of central conceptual structures in the development of children's thought.* Monographs of the Society of Research in Child Development, vol. 61, no. 2, serial no. 246. Chicago: University of Chicago Press.

Charlesworth, R., C.H. Hart, D.C. Burts, & M. DeWolf. 1993. The LSU studies: Building a research base for developmentally appropriate practice. In *Perspectives on developmentally appropriate practice,* vol. 5 of *Advances in early education and day care,* ed. S. Reifel, 3–28. Greenwich, CT: JAI Press.

Chugani, H., M.E. Phelps, & J.C. Mazziotta. 1987. Positron emission tomography study of human brain functional development. *Annals of Neurology* 22 (4): 495.

Cohen, N., & K. Modigliani. 1994. The family-to-family project: Developing family child care providers. In *The early childhood career lattice: Perspectives on professional development,* eds. J. Johnson & J.B. McCracken, 106–10. Washington, DC: NAEYC.

Copple, C., I.E. Sigel, & R. Saunders. 1984. *Educating the young thinker: Classroom strategies for cognitive growth.* Hillsdale, NJ: Erlbaum.

Cost, Quality, & Child Outcomes Study Team. 1995. *Cost, quality, and child outcomes in child care centers, public report.* 2d ed. Denver: Economics Department, University of Colorado at Denver.

Dana Alliance for Brain Initiatives. 1996. *Delivering results: A progress report on brain research.* Washington, DC: Author.

DEC/CEC (Division for Early Childhood of the Council for Exceptional Children). 1994. Position on inclusion. *Young Children* 49 (5): 78.

DEC (Division for Early Childhood) Task Force on Recommended Practices. 1993. *DEC recommended practices: Indicators of quality in programs for infants and young children with special needs and their families*. Reston, VA: Council for Exceptional Children.

DEC/CEC & NAEYC (Division for Early Childhood of the Council for Exceptional Children & the National Association for the Education of Young Children). 1993. *Understanding the ADA—The Americans with Disability Act: Information for early childhood programs*. Pittsburgh, PA, & Washington, DC: Authors.

DeVries, R., & W. Kohlberg. 1990. *Constructivist early education: Overview and comparison with other programs*. Washington, DC: NAEYC.

Dewey, J. 1916. *Democracy and education: An introduction to the philosophy of education*. New York: Macmillan.

Durkin, D. 1987. A classroom-observation study of reading instruction in kindergarten. *Early Childhood Research Quarterly* 2 (3): 275–300.

Durkin, D. 1990. Reading instruction in kindergarten: A look at some issues through the lens of new basal reader materials. *Early Children Research Quarterly* 5 (3): 299–316.

Dweck, C. 1986. Motivational processes affecting learning. *American Psychologist* 41: 1030–48.

Dyson, A.H., & C. Genishi. 1993. Visions of children as language users: Language and language education in early childhood. In *Handbook of research on the education of young children*, ed. B. Spodek, 122–36. New York: Macmillan.

Edwards, C.P., & L. Gandini. 1989. Teachers' expectations about the timing of developmental skills: A cross-cultural study. *Young Children* 44 (4): 15–19.

Edwards, C., L. Gandini, & G. Forman, eds. 1993. *The hundred languages of children: The Reggio Emilia approach to early childhood education*. Norwood, NJ: Ablex.

Erikson, E. 1963. *Childhood and society*. New York: Norton.

Feeney, S., & K. Kipnis. 1992. *Code of ethnical conduct & statement of commitment*. Washington, DC: NAEYC.

Fein, G. 1981. Pretend play: An integrative review. *Child Development* 52: 1095–118.

Fein, G., & M. Rivkin, eds. *The young child at play: Reviews of research*. Washington, DC: NAEYC.

Fenson, L., P. Dale, J.S. Reznick, E. Bates, D. Thal, & S. Pethick. 1994. *Variability in early communicative development*. Monographs of the Society for Research in Child Development, vol. 59, no. 2, serial no. 242. Chicago: University of Chicago Press.

Fernald, A. 1992. Human maternal vocalizations in infants as biologically relevant signals: An evolutionary perspective. In *The adapted mind: Evolutionary psychology and the generation of culture*, eds. J.H. Barkow, L. Cosmides, & J. Tooby, 391–428. New York: Oxford University Press.

Fields, T., W. Masi, S. Goldstein, S. Perry, & S. Parl. 1988. Infant day care facilities preschool social behavior. *Early Childhood Research Quarterly* 3 (4): 341–59.

Forman, G. 1994. Different media, different languages. In *Reflections on the Reggio Emilia approach*, eds. L. Katz & B. Cesarone, 37–46. Urbana, IL: ERIC Clearinghouse on EECE.

Forman, E.A., N. Minick, & C.A. Stone. 1993. *Contexts for learning: Sociocultural dynamics in children's development*. New York: Oxford University Press.

Francis, P., & P. Self. 1982. Imitative responsiveness of young children in day care and home settings: The importance of the child to caregiver ratio. *Child Study Journal* 12: 119–26.

Frede, E. 1995. The role of program quality in producing early childhood program benefits. *The Future of Children*, 5 (3): 115–132.

Frede, E., & W.S. Barnett. 1992. Developmentally appropriate public school preschool: A study of implementation of the High/Scope curriculum and its effects on disadvantaged children's skills at first grade. *Early Childhood Research Quarterly* 7 (4): 483–99.

Fromberg, D. 1992. Play. In *The early childhood curriculum: A review of current research*, 2d ed., ed. C. Seefeldt, 35–74. New York: Teachers College Press.

Galinsky, E., C. Howes, S. Kontos, & M. Shinn. 1994. *The study of children in family child care and relative care: Highlights of findings*. New York: Families and Work Institute.

Gallahue, D. 1993. Motor development and movement skill acquisition in early childhood education. In *Handbook of research on the education of young children*, ed. B. Spodek, 24–41. New York: Macmillan.

Gallahue, D. 1995. Transforming physical education curriculum. In *Reaching potentials: Transforming early childhood curriculum and assessment, volume 2*, eds. S. Bredekamp & T. Rosegrant, 125–44. Washington, DC: NAEYC.

Garbarino, J., N. Dubrow, K. Kostelny, & C. Pardo. 1992. *Children in danger: Coping with the consequences of community violence*. San Francisco: Jossey-Bass.

Gardner, H. 1983. *Frames of mind: The theory of multiple intelligences*. New York: Basic.

Gardner, H. 1991. *The unschooled mind: How children think and how schools should teach*. New York: Basic.

Gelman, R., & R. Baillargeon. 1983. A review of some Piagetian concepts. In *Handbook of Child Psychology*, vol. 3, ed. P.H. Mussen, 167–230. New York: Wiley.

Gelman, R., & E. Meck. 1983. Preschoolers' counting: Principles before skill. *Cognition* 13: 343–59.

Hale-Benson, J. 1986. *Black children: Their roots, cultures, and learning styles*. Rev. ed. Baltimore: Johns Hopkins University Press.

Herron, R., & B. Sutton-Smith. 1971. *Child's play*. New York: Wiley.

Hiebert, E.H., & J.M. Papierz. 1990. The emergent literacy construct and kindergarten and readiness books of basal reading series. *Early Childhood Research Quarterly* 5 (3): 317–34.

Hohmann, M., & D. Weikart. 1995. *Educating young children: Active learning practices for preschool and child care programs*. Ypsilanti, MI: High/Scope Educational Research Foundation.

Hollestelle, K. 1993. At the core: Entrepreneurial skills for family child care providers. In *The early childhood career lattice: Perspectives on professional development*, eds. J. Johnson & J.B. McCracken, 63–65. Washington, DC: NAEYC.

Howes, C. 1983. Caregiver behavior in center and family day care. *Journal of Applied Developmental Psychology* 4: 96–107.

Howes, C. 1988. Relations between early child care and schooling. *Developmental Psychology* 24 (1): 53–57.

Howes, C., D.A. Phillips, M. Whitebook. 1992. Thresholds of quality: Implications for the social development of children in center-based child care. *Child Development* 63 (2): 449–60.

Howes, C., E. Smith, & E. Galinsky. 1995. *The Florida child care quality improvement study*. New York: Families and Work Institute.

Kagan, S.L. 1991. *United we stand: Collaboration for child care and early education services*. New York: Teachers College Press.

Kagan, S., S. Goffin, S. Golub, & E. Pritchard. 1995. *Toward systematic reform: Service integration for young children and their families*. Falls Church, VA: National Center for Service Integration.

Kamil, C., & J.K. Ewing. 1996. Basing teaching on Piaget's constructivism. *Childhood Education* 72 (5): 260–64.

Katz, L. 1995. *Talks with teachers of young children: A collection*. Norwood, NJ: Ablex.

Katz, L., & S. Chard. 1989. *Engaging children minds: The project approach*. Norwood, NJ: Ablex.

Katz, L., D. Evangelou, & J. Hartman. 1990. *The case for mixed-age grouping in early education*. Washington, DC: NAEYC.

Kendrick, A., R. Kaufmann, & K. Messenger, eds. 1995. *Healthy young children: A manual for programs*. Washington, DC: NAEYC.

Kohn, A. 1993. *Punished by rewards*. Boston: Houghton Mifflin.

Kostelnik, M., A Soderman, & A. Whiren. 1993. *Developmentally appropriate programs in early childhood education*. New York: Macmillan.

Kuhl, P. 1994. Learning and representation in speech and language. *Current Opinion in Neurobiology* 4: 812–22.

Lary, R.T. 1990. Successful students. *Education Issues* 3 (2): 11–17.

Layzer, J.I., B.D. Goodson, & M. Moss. 1993. *Life in preschool: Volume one of an observational study of early childhood programs for disadvantaged four-year-olds*. Cambridge, MA: Abt Association.

Lazar, I., & R. Darlington. 1982. *Lasting effects of early education: A report from the consortium for longitudinal studies*. Monographs of the Society for Research in Child Development, vol. 47, nos. 2-3, serial no. 195. Chicago: University of Chicago Press.

Lee, V.E., J. Brooks-Gunn, & E. Schuur. 1988. Does Head Start work? A 1-year follow-up comparison of disadvantaged children attending Head Start, no preschool, and other preschool programs. *Developmental Psychology* 24 (2): 210–22.

Legters, N., & R.E. Slavin. 1992. Elementary students at risk: A status report. Paper commissioned by the Carnegie Corporation of New York for meeting on elementary-school reform. 1–2 June.

Levy, A.K., L. Schaefer, & P.C. Phelps. 1986. Increasing preschool effectiveness: Enhancing the language abilities of 3- and 4-year-old children through planned sociodramatic play. *Early Childhood Research Quarterly* 1 (2): 133–40.

Levy, A.K., C.H. Wolfgang, & M.A. Koorland. 1992. Sociodramatic play as a method for enhancing the language performance of kindergarten age students. *Early Childhood Research Quarterly* 7 (2): 245–62.

Malaguzzi, L. 1993. History, ideas, and basic philosophy. In *The hundred languages of children: The Reggio Emilia approach to early childhood education*, eds. C. Edwards, L. Gandini, & G. Forman, 41–89.Norwood, NJ: Ablex.

Mallory, B. 1992. Is it always appropriate to be developmental? Convergent models for early intervention practice. *Topics in Early Childhood Special Education* 11 (4): 1–12.

Mallory, B. 1994. Inclusive policy, practice, and theory for young children with developmental differences. In *Diversity and developmentally appropriate practices: Challenges for early childhood education*, eds. B. Mallory & R. New, 44–61. New York: Teachers College Press.

Mallory, B.L., & R.S. New. 1994a. *Diversity and developmentally appropriate practices: Challenges for early childhood education*. New York: Teachers College Press.

Mallory, B.L., & R.S. New. 1994b. Social constructivist theory and principles of inclusions: Challenges for early childhood special education. *Journal of Special Education* 28 (3): 322–37.

Marcon, R.A. 1992. Differential effects of three preschool models on inner-city 4-year-olds. *Early Childhood Research Quarterly* 7 (4): 517–30.

Maslow, A. 1954. *Motivation and personality*. New York: Harper & Row.

Miller, L.B., & R.P. Bizzell. 1984. Long-term effects of four preschool programs: Ninth and tenth-grade results. *Child Development* 55 (4): 1570–87.

Mitchell, A., M. Seligson, & F. Marx. 1989. *Early childhood programs and the public schools*. Dover, MA: Auburn House.

Morrow, L.M. 1990. Preparing the classroom environment to promote literacy during play. *Early Childhood Research Quarterly* 5 (4): 537–54.

NAEYC. 1987. *NAEYC position statement on licensing and other forms of regulation of early childhood programs in centers and family day care*. Washington, DC: Author.

NAEYC. 1991. *Accreditation criteria and procedures of the National Academy of Early Childhood Programs*. Rev. ed. Washington, DC: Author.

NAEYC. 1993. *Compensation guidelines for early childhood professionals*. Washington, DC: Author.

NAEYC. 1994. NAEYC position statement: A conceptual framework for early childhood professional development, adopted November 1993. *Young Children* 49 (3): 68–77.

NAEYC. 1996a NAEYC position statement: Responding to linguistic and cultural diversity—Recommendations for effective early childhood education. *Young Children* 51 (2): 4–12.

NAEYC. 1996b. NAEYC position statement: Technology and young children—Ages three through eight. *Young Children* 51 (6): 11–16.

NAEYC & NAECS/SDE (National Association of Early Childhood Specialists in State Departments of Education). 1992. Guidelines for appropriate curriculum content and assessment in programs serving children ages 3 through 8. In *Reaching potentials: Appropriate curriculum and assessment for young children, volume 1*, eds. S. Bredekamp & T. Rosegrant, 9–27. Washington, DC: NAEYC.

NASBE (National Association of State Boards of Education). 1991. *Caring communities: Supporting young children and families.* Alexandria, VA: Author.

Natriello, G., E. McDill, & A. Pallas. 1990. *Schooling disadvantaged children: Racing against catastrophe.* New York: Teachers College Press.

NCES (National Center for Education Statistics). 1993. *The condition of education, 1993.* Washington, DC: U.S. Department of Education.

NCSL (National Conference of State Legislatures). 1995. *Early childhood care and education: An investment that works.* Denver: Author.

NEGP (National Education Goals Panel). 1991. *National education goals report: Building a nation of learners.* Washington, DC: Author.

New, R. 1993. Cultural variations on developmentally appropriate practice: Challenges to theory and practice. In *The hundred languages of children: The Reggio Emilia approach to early childhood education,* eds. C. Edwards, L. Gandini, & G. Forman, 215–32. Norwood, NJ: Ablex.

New, R. 1994. Culture, child development, and developmentally appropriate practices: Teachers as collaborative researchers. In *Diversity and developmentally appropriate practices: Challenges for early childhood education,* eds. B. Mallory & R. New, 65–83. New York: Teachers College Press.

Nye, B.A., J. Boyd-Zaharias, & B.D. Fulton. 1994. *The lasting benefits study: A continuing analysis of the effect of small class size in kindergarten through third grade on student achievement test scores in subsequent grade levels—seventh grade (1992–93),* technical report. Nashville: Center of Excellence for Research in Basic Skills, Tennessee State University.

Nye, B.A., J. Boyd-Zaharias, B.D. Fulton, & M.P. Wallenhorst. 1992. Smaller classes really are better. *The American School Board Journal* 179 (5): 31–33.

Parker, J.G., & S.R. Asher. 1987. Peer relations and later personal adjustment: Are low-accepted children at risk? *Psychology Bulletin* 102 (3): 357–89.

Phillips, C.B. 1994. The movement of African-American children through sociocultural contexts: A case of conflict resolution. In *Diversity and developmentally appropriate practices: Challenges for early childhood education,* eds. B. Mallory & R. New, 137–54. New York: Teachers College Press.

Phillips, D.A., K. McCartney, & S. Scarr. 1987. Child care quality and children's social development. *Developmental Psychology* 23 (4): 537–43.

Piaget, J. 1952. *The origins of intelligence in children.* New York: International Universities Press.

Plomin, R. 1994a. *Genetics and experience: The interplay between nature and nurture.* Thousand Oaks, CA: Sage.

Plomin, R. 1994b. Nature, nurture, and social development. *Social Development* 3: 37–53.

Powell, D. 1994. Parents, pluralism, and the NAEYC statement on developmentally appropriate practice. In *Diversity and developmentally appropriate practices: Challenges for early childhood education,* eds. B. Mallory & R. New, 166–82. New York: Teachers College Press.

Pramling, I. 1991. Learning about "the shop": An approach to learning in preschool. *Early Children Research Quarterly* 6 (2): 151–66.

Resnick, L. 1996. Schooling and the workplace: What relationship? In *Preparing youth for the 21st century,* 21–27. Washington, DC: Aspen Institute.

Rogoff, B. 1990. *Apprenticeship in thinking: Cognitive development in social context.* New York: Oxford University Press.

Rogoff, B., J. Mistry, A. Goncu, & C. Mosier. 1993. *Guided participation in cultural activity by toddlers and caregivers.* Monographs of the Society for Research in Child Development, vol. 58, no. 8, serial no. 236. Chicago: University of Chicago Press.

Ross, S.M., L.J. Smith, J. Casey, & R.E. Slavin. 1995. Increasing the academic success of disadvantaged children: An examination of alternative early intervention programs. *American Educational Research Journal* 32 (4): 773–800.

Ruopp, R., J. Travers, F. Glantz, & C. Coelen. 1979. *Children at the center: Final report of the National Day Care Study.* Cambridge, MA: Abt Associates.

Sameroff, A., & S. McDonough. 1994. Educational implications of developmental transition: Revisiting the 5- to 7-year shift. *Phi Delta Kappan* 76 (3): 188–93.

Scarr, S., & K. McCartney. 1983. How people make their own environments: A theory of genotype–environment effects. *Child Development* 54: 425–35.

Schrader, C.T. 1989. Written language use within the context of young children's symbolic play. *Early Childhood Research Quarterly* 4 (2): 225–44.

Schrader, C.T. 1990. Symbolic play as a curricular tool for early literacy development. *Early Childhood Research Quarterly* 5 (1): 79–103.

Schweinhart, L.J., & D.P. Weikart. 1996. *Lasting differences: The High/Scope preschool curriculum comparison study through age 23.* Monographs of the High/Scope Educational Research Foundation, no 12. Ypsilanti, MI: High/Scope Press.

Schweinhart, L.J., H.V. Barnes, & D.P. Weikart. 1993. *Significant benefits: The High/Scope Perry Preschool Study through age 27.* Monographs of the High/Scope Educational Research Foundation, no. 10, Ypsilanti, MI: High/Scope Press.

Schweinhart, L.J., D.P. Weikart, & M.B. Larner. 1986. Child-initiated activities in early childhood programs may help prevent delinquency. *Early Childhood Research Quarterly* 1 (3): 303–12.

Seefeldt, C., ed. 1992. *The early childhood curriculum: A review of current research.* 2d ed. New York: Teachers College Press.

Seifert, K. 1993. Cognitive development and early childhood education. In *Handbook of research on the education of young children,* ed. B. Spodek, 9–23. New York: Macmillan.

Seppanen, P.S., D. Kaplan deVries, & M. Seligson. 1993. *National study of before and after school programs.* Portsmouth, NH: RMC Research Corp.

Shepard, L. 1994. The challenges of assessing young children appropriately. *Phi Delta Kappan* 76 (3): 206–13.

Shepard, L.A., & M.L. Smith. 1988. Escalating academic demand in kindergarten: Some nonsolutions. *Elementary School Journal* 89 (2): 135–46.

Shepard, L.A., & M.L. Smith. 1989. *Flunking grades: Research and policies on retention.* Bristol, PA: Taylor & Francis.

Slavin, R., N. Karweit, & N. Madden, eds. 1989. *Effective programs for students at-risk.* Boston: Allyn & Bacon.

Smilansky, S., & L. Shefatya. 1990. *Facilitating play: A medium for promoting cognitive, socioemotional, and academic development in young children.* Gaithersburg, MD: Psychosocial & Educational Publications.

Spodek, B., ed. 1993. *Handbook of research on the education of young children.* New York: Macmillan.

Sroufe, L.A., R.G. Cooper, & G.B. DeHart. 1992. *Child development: Its nature and course.* 2d ed. New York: Knopf.

Stern, D. 1985. *The psychological world of the human infant.* New York: Basic.

Stremmel, A.J., & V.R. Fu. 1993. Teaching in the zone of proximal development: Implications for responsive teaching practice. *Child and Youth Care Forum* 22 (5): 337–50.

Taylor, J.M., & W.S. Taylor. 1989. *Communicable diseases and young children in group settings.* Boston: Little, Brown.

Tobin, J., D. Wu, & D. Davidson. 1989. *Preschool in three cultures.* New Haven, CT: Yale University Press.

U.S. Department of Health & Human Services. 1996. *Head Start performance standards.* Washington, DC: Author.

Vandell, D.L., & M.A. Corasanti. 1990. Variations in early child care: Do they predict subsequent social, emotional, and cognitive differences? *Early Childhood Research Quarterly* 5 (4): 555–72.

Vandell, D.L., & C.D. Powers. 1983. Day care quality and children's freeplay activities. *American Journal of Orthopsychiatry* 53 (4): 493–500.

Vandell, D.L., V.K. Henderson, & K.S. Wilson. 1988. A longitudinal study of children with day-care experiences of varying quality. *Child Development* 59 (5): 1286–92.

Vygotsky, L. 1978. *Mind in society: The development of higher psychological processes.* Cambridge, MA: Harvard University Press.

Wardle, F. 1996. Proposal: An anti-bias and ecological model for multicultural education. *Childhood Education* 72 (3): 152–56.

Wertsch, J. 1985. *Culture, communication, and cognition: Vygotskian perspectives*. New York: Cambridge University Press.

White, S.H. 1965. Evidence for a hierarchical arrangement of learning processes. In *Advances in child development and behavior*, eds. L.P. Lipsitt & C.C. Spiker, 187–220. New York: Academic Press.

Whitebook, M., C. Howes, & D. Philips. 1989. *The national child care staffing study: Who cares? Child care teachers and the quality of care in America.* Final report. Oakland, CA: Child Care Employee Project.

Wieder, S., & S.I. Greenspan. 1993. The emotional basis of learning. In *Handbook of research on the education of young children*, ed. B. Spodek, 77–104. New York: Macmillan.

Willer, B. 1990. *Reaching the full cost of quality in early childhood programs.* Washington, DC: NAEYC.

Willer, B., S.L. Hofferth, E.E. Kisker, P. Divine-Hawkins, E. Farquhar, & F.B. Glantz. 1991. *The demand and supply of child care in 1990.* Washington, DC.: NAEYC.

Witkin, H. 1962. *Psychological differentiation: Studies of development.* New York: Wiley.

Wolery, M., & J. Wilbers, eds. 1994. *Including children with special needs in early childhood programs.* Washington, DC: NAEYC.

Wolery, M., P. Strain, & D. Bailey. 1992. Reaching potentials of children with special needs. In *Reaching Potentials: Appropriate curriculum and assessment for young children, volume 1*, eds. S. Bredekamp & T. Rosegrant, 92–111. Washington, DC: NAEYC.

Zero to Three: The National Center, 1995. *Caring for infants and toddlers in groups: Developmentally appropriate practice*. Arlington, VA: Author.

Index